SOLIDWORKS 2026

A Power Guide for Beginners and Intermediate Users

CADArtifex

The premium provider of learning products and solutions

www.cadartifex.com

SOLIDWORKS 2026: A Power Guide for Beginners and Intermediate Users

Author: Sandeep Dogra
Email: info@cadartifex.com

Published by
CADArtifex
www.cadartifex.com

ISBN: 978-9394074941

NOTICE TO THE READER

The publisher and the author make no representations or warranties with respect to the accuracy or completeness of the contents of this work and specifically disclaim all warranties, including without limitation warranties of fitness for a particular purpose. Publisher does not guarantee any of the products described in the text or perform any independent analysis in connection with any of the product information contained in the text. No warranty may be created or extended by sales or promotional materials. This work is sold with the understanding that the publisher is not engaged in rendering legal, accounting, or other professional services. Neither the publisher nor the author shall be liable for damages arising herefrom. Further, readers should be aware that Internet Websites listed in this work may have changed or disappeared between when this work was written and when it is read.

Examination Copies

Textbooks received as examination copies in any form such as paperback and eBook are for review only and may not be made available for the use of the student. These files may not be transferred to any other party. Resale of examination copies is prohibited.

Electronic Files

The electronic file/eBook in any form of this textbook is licensed to the original user only and may not be transferred to any other party.

Disclaimer

The author has made sincere efforts to ensure the accuracy of the material described herein, however the author makes no warranty, expressed or implied, with respect to the quality, correctness, accuracy, or freedom from error of this document or the products it describes.

www.cadartifex.com

Dedication

First and foremost, I would like to thank my parents for being a great support throughout my career and while writing this book.

Heartfelt gratitude goes to my wife and my sisters for their patience and support in fulfilling this challenge.

I would also like to acknowledge the efforts of the employees at CADArtifex for their dedication in editing the contents of this textbook.

Video Courses by CADArtifex

Contents at a Glance

Table of Contents

Part 2. Creating 3D Models/Components

Preface

SOLIDWORKS, developed by Dassault Systèmes SOLIDWORKS Corp., a global leader in engineering software, delivers a comprehensive suite of 3D design tools for creating, simulating, publishing, and managing engineering data. By leveraging advanced solid modeling methodologies, SOLIDWORKS empowers engineers to enhance design performance, reduce the reliance on expensive physical prototypes, and minimize rework and project delays, ultimately saving both time and development costs.

SOLIDWORKS is a parametric, feature-driven solid modeling software designed for mechanical design and automation. It enables users to transform 2D sketches into detailed 3D solid models using intuitive yet powerful modeling tools. The 3D components and assemblies created within SOLIDWORKS can be seamlessly converted into 2D drawings with minimal effort. Furthermore, the software allows for design validation by simulating real-world operating conditions and evaluating the environmental impact of the products.

SOLIDWORKS 2026: A Power Guide for Beginners and Intermediate Users textbook is tailored for both instructor-led training and self-paced learning. It serves as an essential resource for engineers and designers seeking to master SOLIDWORKS for 3D mechanical design. Designed for new users and ideal for classroom instruction, this comprehensive guide spans 14 chapters across 780 pages, thoroughly covering core SOLIDWORKS environments, including Sketching, Part Modeling, Assembly, and Drawing. The book provides step-by-step instructions for creating parametric 3D solid components, assemblies, and 2D drawings using SOLIDWORKS. Additionally, it includes a dedicated chapter focused on creating multiple design configurations, making it a well-rounded resource for mastering the software.

This textbook goes beyond simply teaching the tools and commands of SOLIDWORKS, emphasizing the principles of design as well. Each chapter features detailed tutorials with step-by-step guidance for creating mechanical designs and drawings efficiently. Furthermore, every chapter concludes with practical hands-on test drives, enabling users to explore and experience the robust and intuitive technical capabilities of SOLIDWORKS.

Who Should Read This Book

This book is crafted to cater to a diverse audience, including beginners, advanced users, and SOLIDWORKS instructors. Its well-structured, easy-to-navigate chapters provide a clear understanding of various design methodologies, SOLIDWORKS tools, and fundamental design principles.

What Is Covered in This Textbook

SOLIDWORKS 2026: A Power Guide for Beginners and Intermediate Users textbook is designed to help you understand everything you need to know to start using SOLIDWORKS with clear step-by-step tutorials. This textbook covers the following:

*Chapter 1, "**Introduction to SOLIDWORKS**,"* introduces the SOLIDWORKS interface, different SOLIDWORKS environments, various components of SOLIDWORKS, and methods for invoking and customizing the shortcut menu, saving documents, and opening documents in SOLIDWORKS.

*Chapter 2, "**Drawing Sketches with SOLIDWORKS**,"* discusses how to invoke the Sketching environment, and methods for specifying unit systems, grids, and snap settings. It also introduces the various sketching tools such as Line, Arc, Circle, Rectangle, and Spline for creating sketches.

*Chapter 3, "**Editing and Modifying Sketches**,"* introduces various editing and modifying operations such as trimming unwanted sketched entities, extending sketch entities, mirroring, patterning, moving, and rotating sketch entities by using various editing/modifying tools of the Sketching environment.

*Chapter 4, "**Applying Geometric Relations and Dimensions**,"* introduces the concept of fully defined sketches, and creating fully defined sketches by applying geometric relations and dimensions. It also introduces different methods for applying geometric relations and dimensions. Methods for modification of the already applied dimensions and dimension properties such as dimension style, tolerance, and precision have also been discussed in addition to the introduction to different sketch states.

*Chapter 5, "**Creating Base Features of Solid Models**,"* discusses how to create extruded and revolved base features by using the Extruded Boss/Base and Revolved Boss/Base tools. This chapter also introduces you to various navigating tools such as Zoom In/Out and Zoom To Fit. Moreover, it explains how to manipulate the orientation of a model. Additionally, this chapter also elaborates on changing the display style and view of the model.

*Chapter 6, "**Creating Reference Geometries**,"* introduces three default planes: Front, Top, and Right. As these may not be enough for creating models having multiple features, therefore, the chapter discusses how to create additional reference planes. Additionally, this chapter also elaborates on creating reference axes, coordinates systems, and points.

*Chapter 7, "**Advanced Modeling - I**,"* introduces advanced options for creating extruded and revolved features. In addition, this chapter discusses how to create cut features and, how to work with different types of sketches, along with creating multiple features by using a single sketch having multiple contours, projecting edges of the features, editing individual features of a model, and importing 2D DXF and DWG files into current file as reference sketches. Moreover, this chapter also elaborates on measuring distance and angle between lines, points, faces, planes, and so on by using the Measure tool, as well as assigning appearance and material properties to a model. Additionally, the calculation of the mass properties of a model is also discussed.

*Chapter 8, "**Advanced Modeling - II**,"* discusses how to create sweep features, sweep cut features, lofted features, lofted cut features, boundary features, boundary cut features, curves, split faces, and 3D Sketches.

*Chapter 9, "**Patterning and Mirroring**,"* introduces various patterning and mirroring tools. After completing this chapter, you can create different types of patterns such as linear patterns, circular patterns, and curve driven patterns. Also, you can mirror features, faces, or bodies.

*Chapter 10, "**Advanced Modeling - III**,"* discusses how to create standard and customized holes such as counterbore and countersink. Creating cosmetic threads, real threads on holes, fasteners, and cylindrical features have also been discussed. Additionally, this chapter explains how to create stud features, constant and variable radius fillets, chamfer, rib features, and shell features.

Chapter 11, "***Working with Configurations***," discusses how to create multiple variations of a model within a single file by using the configurations. Creating configurations by using the Manual method and the Design Table method have been explained. This chapter also teaches how to save configurations as a separate file and how to suppress and unsuppress features of a model.

Chapter 12, "***Working with Assemblies - I***," discusses how to create assemblies by using the bottom-up assembly approach and how to work with standard, advanced, and mechanical mates. It also explains how to move and rotate the individual components within the Assembly environment, detect collisions between the components of an assembly, and work with SmartMates.

Chapter 13, "***Working with Assemblies - II***," discusses how to create assemblies using the top-down assembly approach. Methods for editing the individual components of an assembly as well as editing the existing mates applied between the components have been discussed along with methods for creating different types of patterns. The chapter also introduces you to mirroring components, creating assembly features, suppressing or unsuppressing the components, and inserting components in the Assembly environment having multiple configurations. It also discusses how to create and dissolve sub-assemblies, and include components as envelopes into sub-assemblies. This chapter also discusses creating, editing, or collapsing the exploded view of an assembly. Animating the exploded view, adding exploded lines, detecting interference, and creating BOM are also explained.

Chapter 14, "***Working with Drawings***," discusses how to create 2D drawings from parts and assemblies. This chapter introduces the concept of angle of projection, defining the angle of projection, and editing sheet format. In addition, this chapter discusses the application of reference and driving dimensions, adding notes, surface finish symbols, weld symbols, hole callouts, and so on in drawing views. In this chapter, adding Bill of Material (BOM) and balloons have also been introduced.

Some of the Icons/Terms used in this Textbook

Some of the icons and terms used in this textbook are as follows:

Note

Note: Notes highlight information requiring special attention.

Tip

Tip: Tips provide additional advice, which increases the efficiency of the users.

Flyout

A Flyout is a list in which a set of tools are grouped, see Figure 1.

Drop-down List

A drop-down list is a list in which a set of options is grouped, see Figure 2.

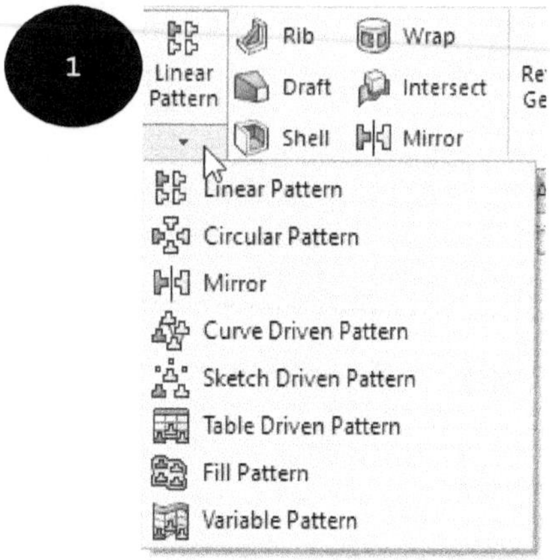

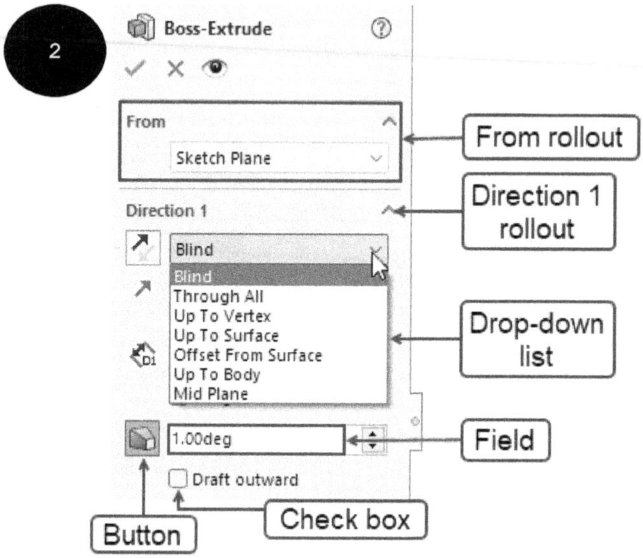

Rollout

A rollout is an area in which drop-down lists, fields, buttons, and check boxes are available to specify various parameters, see Figure 2. A rollout can either be in expanded or collapsed form. You can expand/collapse a rollout by clicking on the arrow available on the right of its title bar.

How to Download Online Resources

Students and faculty members can **download all parts/models** used in the illustrations, Tutorials and Hands-on Test Drives (exercises) of the textbook. In addition, faculty can also download PowerPoint Presentations (PPTs) of each chapter of the textbook.

To download the free online teaching and learning resources of the textbook, log on to our website (*cadartifex.com/login*). If you are a new user, you need to first sign up (*cadartifex.com/register*) for downloading the online resources of the textbook.

Interactive Support for Your Learning

In the book, you'll find **QR codes** next to key tutorial steps for certain tutorials. Scan these codes to access video demonstrations, designed to help you through any challenging parts of the process.

How to Contact the Author

We truly value your feedback and suggestions. Please feel free to reach out to us at *info@cadartifex.com* or visit *www.cadartifex.com* to share your feedback and download additional learning resources.

Thank you for choosing SOLIDWORKS 2026: A Power Guide for Beginners and Intermediate Users. We hope the knowledge and concepts presented in this textbook support you in achieving your professional objectives.

CHAPTER

1

Introduction to SOLIDWORKS

This chapter discusses the following topics:

- Installing SOLIDWORKS
- Getting Started with SOLIDWORKS
- Invoking the Part Modeling Environment
- Invoking the Assembly Environment
- Invoking the Drawing Environment
- Identifying SOLIDWORKS Documents
- Invoking a Shortcut Menu
- Customizing the Context Toolbar
- Customizing the CommandManager
- Working with Mouse Gestures
- Saving Documents
- Opening Existing Documents

Welcome to the world of Computer-Aided Design (CAD) with SOLIDWORKS. Developed by Dassault Systèmes SOLIDWORKS Corp., a global leader in engineering software, SOLIDWORKS provides a complete suite of 3D tools for creating, simulating, publishing, and managing design data. With its advanced solid modeling techniques, SOLIDWORKS empowers engineers to optimize design performance, reduce the need for costly prototypes, and eliminate rework and delays, saving both time and development costs.

SOLIDWORKS is a feature-based, parametric solid-modeling software designed for mechanical design and automation. It enables users to transform 2D sketches into detailed solid models using intuitive yet powerful modeling tools. The software offers an extensive array of features to create highly accurate components and assemblies, which can subsequently be converted into 2D engineering drawings for manufacturing purposes. Additionally, SOLIDWORKS allows for the validation of designs by simulating real-world conditions and evaluating the environmental impact of the products, ensuring robust and sustainable design solutions.

SOLIDWORKS employs a parametric, feature-based methodology for model creation, enabling precise and efficient design workflows. It facilitates seamless collaboration by allowing users to share designs with partners, subcontractors, and team members through innovative and intelligent methods. This enhances knowledge sharing, streamlines communication, and significantly reduces the design cycle duration.

Installing SOLIDWORKS

If you do not have SOLIDWORKS installed on your system, you first need to get it installed. However, before you start installing SOLIDWORKS, you need to evaluate the system requirements and ensure that you have a system capable of running SOLIDWORKS adequately. Below are the system requirements for installing SOLIDWORKS 2026.

1. Operating Systems: Windows 10 - 64-bit, Windows 11 - 64-bit
2. RAM: 8 GB or more (16 GB or more recommended)
3. Disk Space: 10 GB or more
4. Processor: x86_64 (Intel 64 or AMD64)
5. Graphics Card: SOLIDWORKS certified graphics cards and drivers

For more information about the system requirements for SOLIDWORKS, visit the SOLIDWORKS website at *solidworks.com/support/system-requirements*

Once the system is ready, install SOLIDWORKS by using the downloaded SOLIDWORKS setup files.

Getting Started with SOLIDWORKS

Once SOLIDWORKS 2026 is installed on your system, start SOLIDWORKS 2026 by double-clicking on the **SOLIDWORKS 2026** icon on the desktop of your system. The system prepares for starting SOLIDWORKS by loading all required files. Once all the required files have been loaded, the startup user interface of SOLIDWORKS 2026 appears along with the **Welcome** dialog box, see Figure 1.1.

1.1

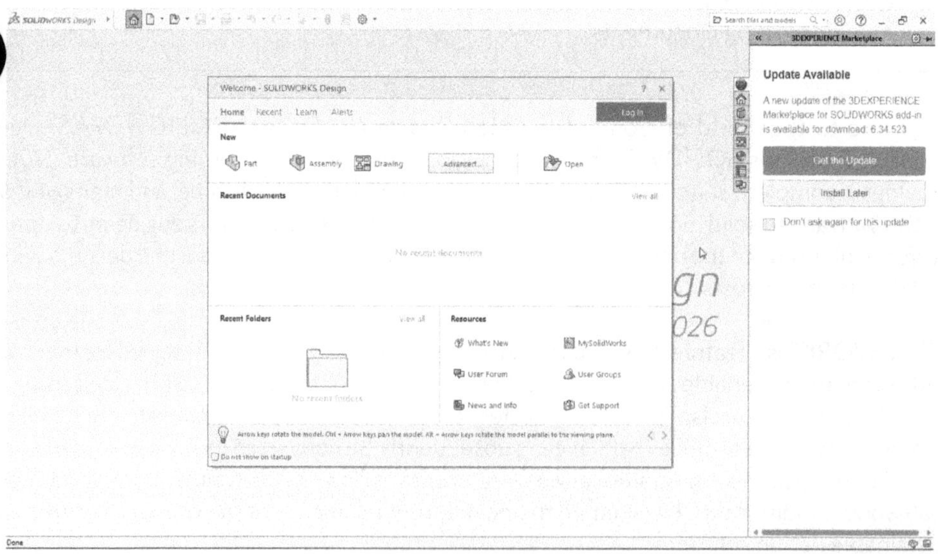

If you are starting SOLIDWORKS for the first time after installing the software, the **SOLIDWORKS License Agreement** window appears, see Figure 1.2. Click on the **Accept** button in the **SOLIDWORKS License Agreement** window to accept the license agreement and start SOLIDWORKS Desgin 2026.

1.2

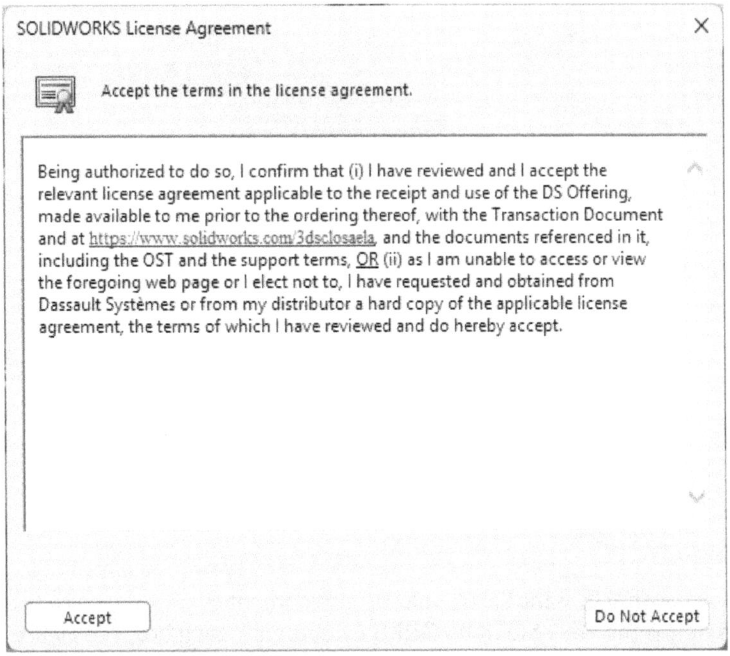

In SOLIDWORKS, the **Welcome** dialog box appears every time you start SOLIDWORKS and provides a convenient way to invoke new SOLIDWORKS documents, open existing documents, view recent documents and folders, access SOLIDWORKS resources, and stay updated on SOLIDWORKS news.

The **Welcome** dialog box has four tabs: **Home**, **Recent**, **Learn**, and **Alerts**. The options in the **Home** tab are used for invoking new SOLIDWORKS documents, opening existing documents, viewing recent documents and folders, and accessing SOLIDWORKS resources. The **Recent** tab displays a list of recent documents and folders. The **Learn** tab is used for accessing instructional resources such as tutorials, sample models, access to the 3D Content Center, certification program, and so on to help you learn more about SOLIDWORKS. The **Alerts** tab is used for updating you with SOLIDWORKS news and provides different types of alerts in different sections including **Troubleshooting** and **Technical Alerts**.

Tip: If the **Welcome** dialog box does not appear automatically, you can open it manually by clicking the **Welcome to SOLIDWORKS** tool on the **Standard** toolbar. Alternatively, click **Help > Welcome to SOLIDWORKS Design** located next to the SOLIDWORKS Search box to display the **Welcome** dialog box. The **Standard** toolbar and SOLIDWORKS Search will be discussed in detail later in this chapter.

In SOLIDWORKS, you can access various environments, including the Part modeling environment, Assembly environment, and Drawing environment, to create parts, assemblies, and 2D drawings. These environments can be activated using the respective buttons (**Part**, **Assembly**, and **Drawing**) available in the **Welcome** dialog box. The following sections discuss the methods for accessing these environments in detail.

Invoking the Part Modeling Environment

To access the Part modeling environment, click the **Part** button in the **Welcome** dialog box. The startup user interface of the Part modeling environment appears, as shown in Figure 1.3.

1.3

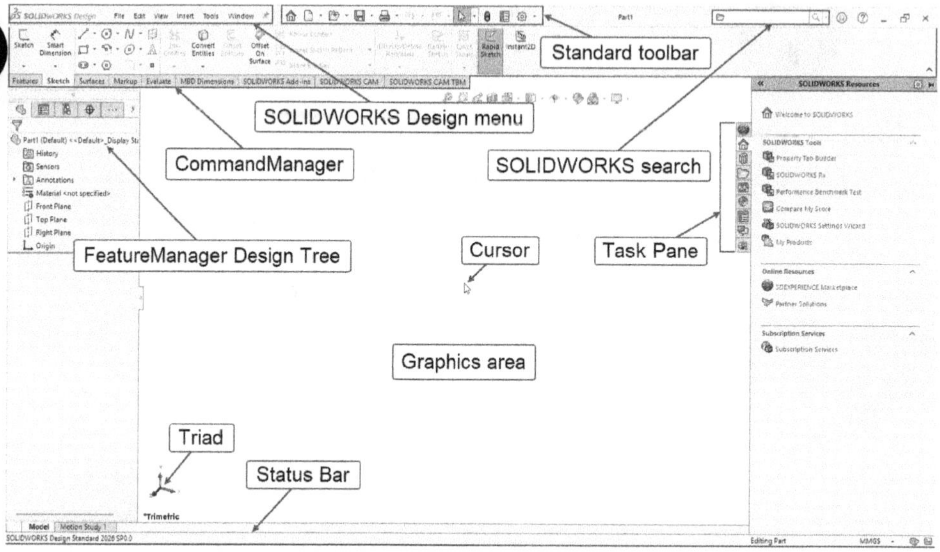

Alternatively, you can access the Part modeling environment by clicking the **New** tool in the **Standard** toolbar. This opens the **New SOLIDWORKS Document** dialog box, see Figure 1.4. In this dialog box, ensure the **Part** option is selected, and then click **OK** to proceed.

1.4

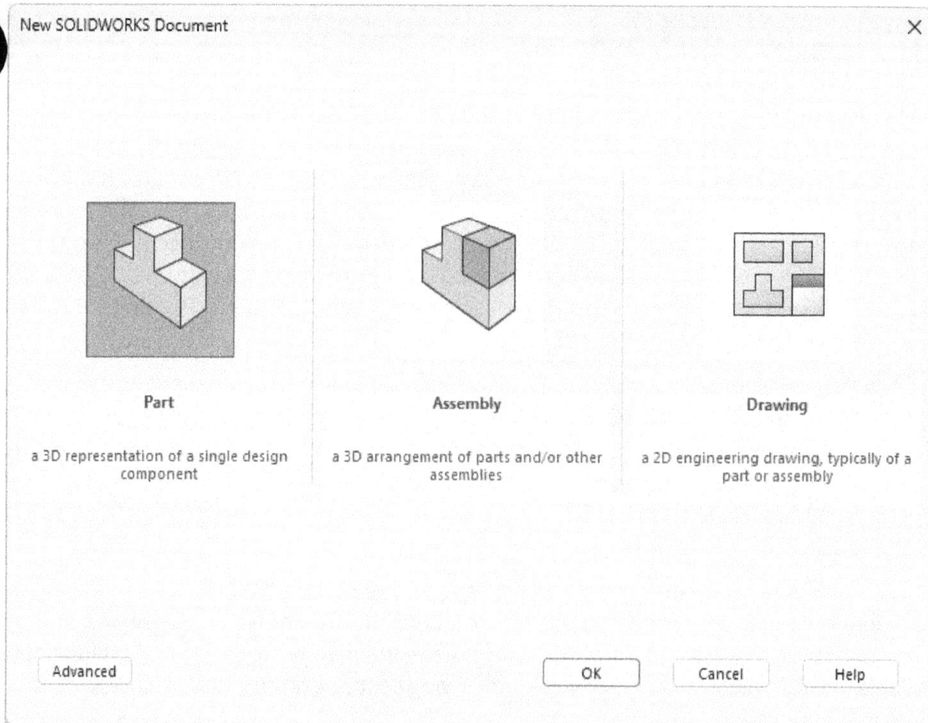

Note: If you invoke the Part modeling environment for the first time after installing the software, the **Units and Dimension Standard** dialog box appears, see Figure 1.5. In this dialog box, you specify the unit system to set as the default for SOLIDWORKS. In this textbook, the metric unit system and ANSI standard are used as the default settings.

1.5

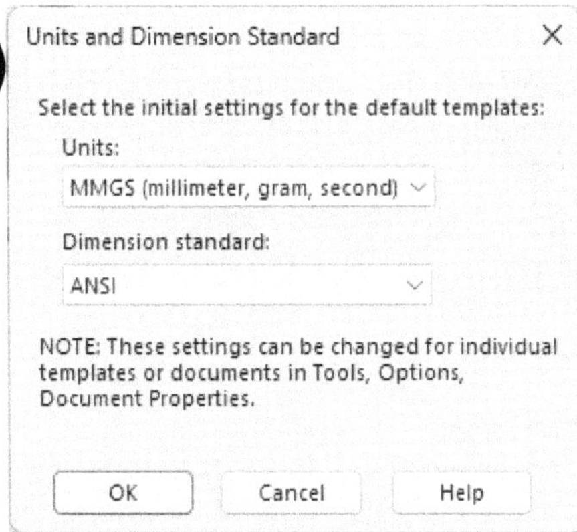

It is evident from the startup user interface of the Part modeling environment that SOLIDWORKS is very user-friendly. Some of the components of the startup user interface are discussed next.

Standard Toolbar

The **Standard** toolbar contains a set of the most frequently used tools such as **New**, **Open**, and **Save**, see Figure 1.6.

1.6

SOLIDWORKS Design Menus

The SOLIDWORKS Design Menus contains different menus such as **File**, **View**, and **Tools** for accessing different tools of SOLIDWORKS, see Figure 1.7.

1.7

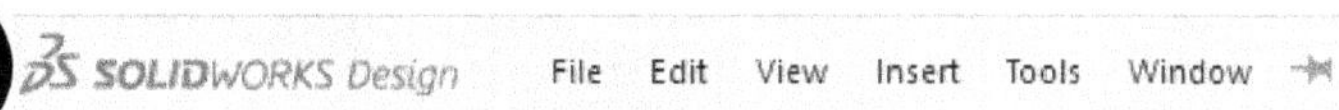

Note that the SOLIDWORKS Design Menus appears when you move the cursor on the SOLIDWORKS Design logo, which is available at the top left corner of the screen. You can keep the SOLIDWORKS Design Menus visible all the time by clicking on the push-pin button available at the end of the SOLIDWORKS Design Menus. Note that the tools in the different menus are dependent upon the type of environment invoked.

SOLIDWORKS Search

The SOLIDWORKS Search is a search tool for searching commands/tools, knowledge base (help topic), community forums, files, models, and so on, see Figure 1.8.

1.8

CommandManager

The CommandManager is located at the top of the graphics area and provides access to various SOLIDWORKS tools. Several CommandManagers are available in the Part modeling environment, including the **Features CommandManager**, **Sketch CommandManager**, **Evaluate CommandManager**, and more.

When you activate the **Features** tab in the CommandManager (see Figure 1.9), the **Features CommandManager** appears, offering tools for creating 3D solid models. By clicking the **Sketch** tab, the **Sketch CommandManager** appears, providing tools for creating sketches. The following sections discuss some of the CommandManagers of the Part modeling environment.

Note: The different environments in SOLIDWORKS (Part, Assembly, and Drawing) come with their own sets of CommandManagers, each tailored to the specific tools and functionalities required for that environment.

Features CommandManager

The **Features CommandManager** provides a variety of tools used for creating 3D models. To access these tools, click the **Features** tab in the CommandManager. Initially, most of the tools in the **Features CommandManager** are not activated. These tools become available once you create a base or the first feature of a model. Figure 1.9 shows the **Features CommandManager** and Figure 1.10 provides a 3D model for reference.

1.9

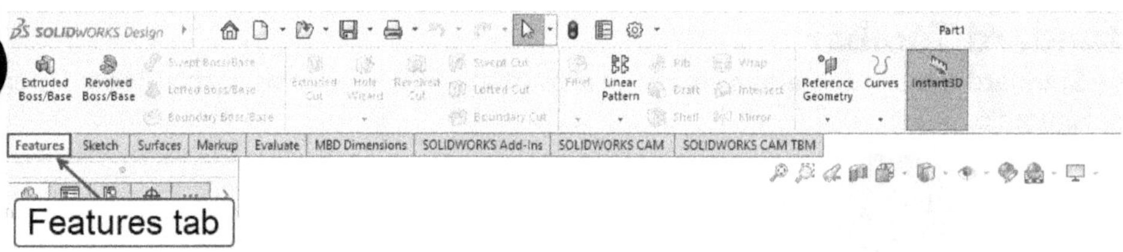

1.10

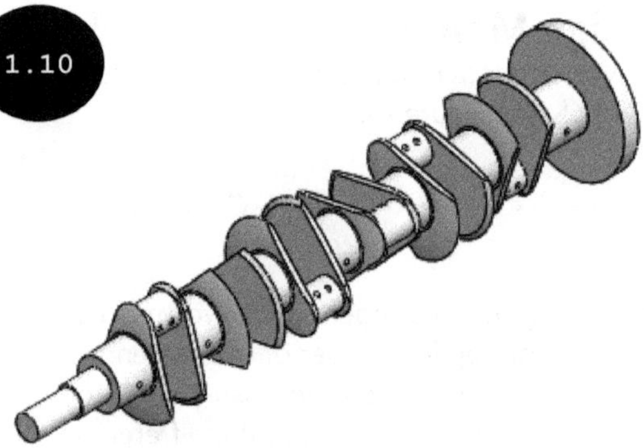

Sketch CommandManager

The **Sketch CommandManager** provides a variety of tools used for creating both 2D and 3D sketches. To access these tools, click the **Sketch** tab in the CommandManager. Figure 1.11 shows the **Sketch CommandManager** and Figure 1.12 displays a 2D sketch for reference.

1.11

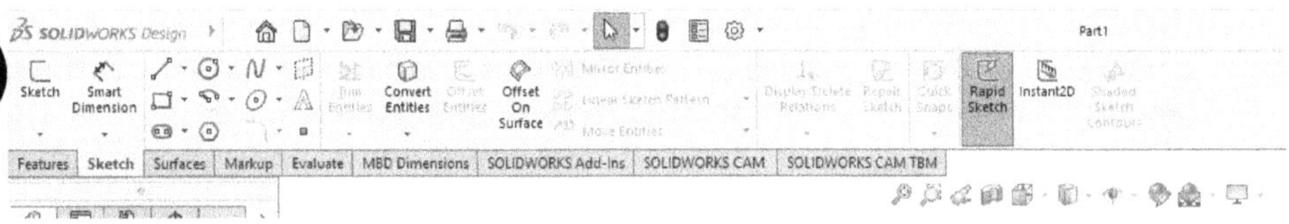

1.12

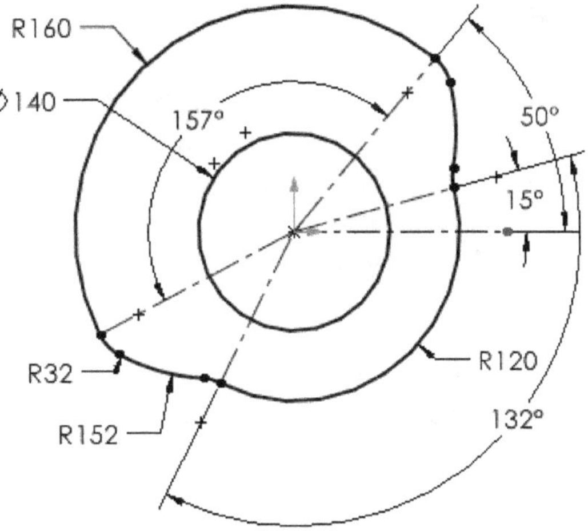

Evaluate CommandManager

The tools in the **Evaluate CommandManager** are used to evaluate a model by measuring entities, calculating mass properties, checking tangent or curvature continuity, performing draft analysis, calculating section properties, conducting geometry analysis, and more. To access these tools, click the **Evaluate** tab in the CommandManager, see Figure 1.13.

1.13

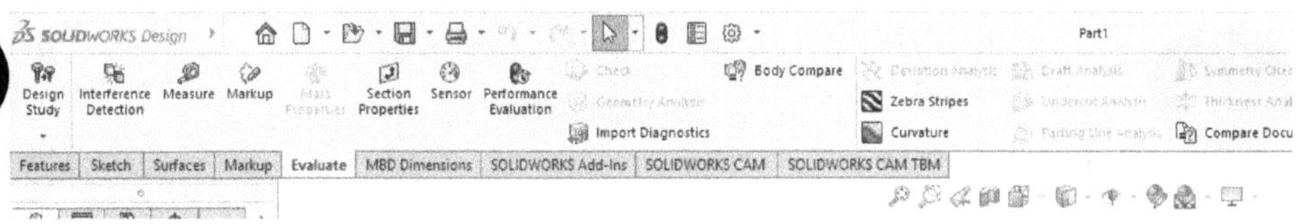

Note: Both the Surface modeling environment and the Sheet Metal environment in SOLIDWORKS can be accessed within the Part modeling environment.

Surfaces CommandManager

The **Surfaces CommandManager** provides a variety of tools for creating surface models. To access these tools, click on the **Surfaces** tab in the CommandManager, see Figure 1.14. Initially, most tools in the **Surfaces CommandManager** are not activated, but they become available once you create the base or first feature of a surface model.

1.14

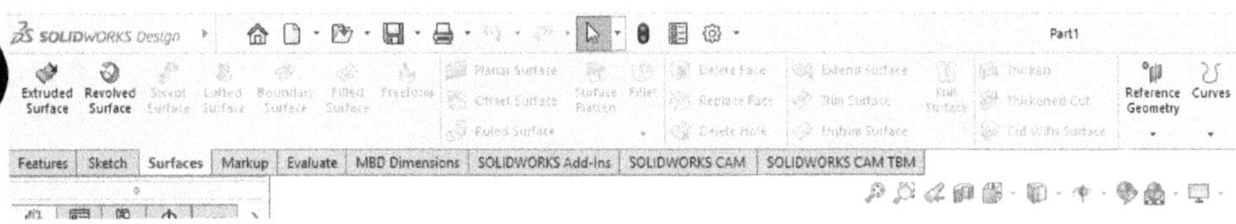

If the **Surfaces** tab is not available in the CommandManager, right-click on any of the CommandManager tabs. A shortcut menu appears, where you can click **Tabs > Surfaces** to make the **Surfaces** tab visible in the CommandManager. Figure 1.15 displays a surface model for reference.

1.15

Note: In addition to the default CommandManagers, such as the **Features CommandManager** and **Sketch CommandManager**, you can also add other CommandManagers that are not available by default.

To add a CommandManager, right-click on any of the available CommandManager tabs. A shortcut menu appears. Move the cursor over the **Tabs** option in the menu to display a cascading menu, see Figure 1.16. This menu lists the available CommandManagers. A tick mark next to a CommandManager indicates that it is already added. Click on the desired CommandManager in the menu to add the respective tab to the CommandManager.

1.16

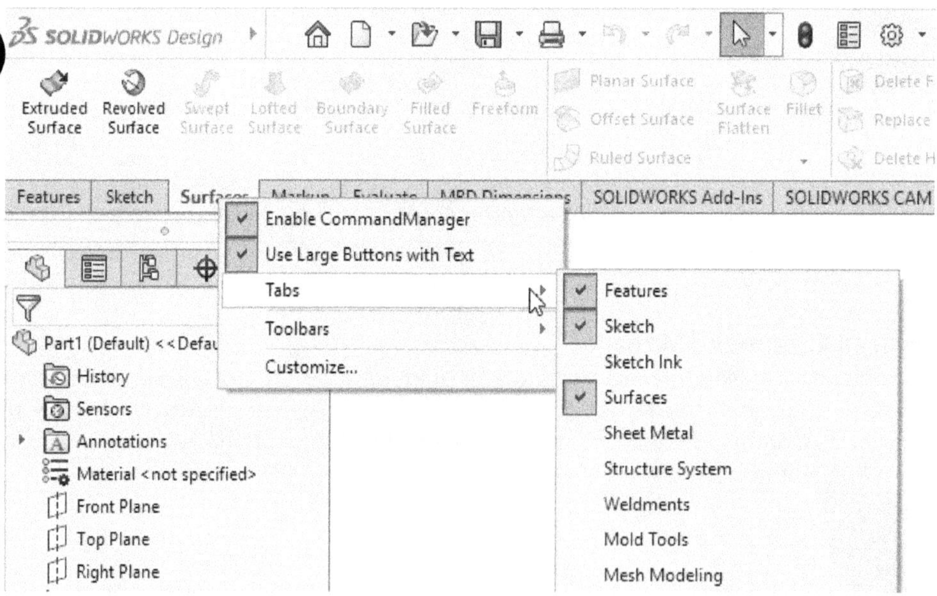

Sheet Metal CommandManager

The **Sheet Metal CommandManager** provides a variety of tools for creating sheet metal components. If the **Sheet Metal** tab is not visible in the CommandManager, right-click on any CommandManager tab to display a shortcut menu. Then, click **Tabs > Sheet Metal** in the shortcut menu. Figure 1.17 shows the **Sheet Metal CommandManager** and Figure 1.18 displays a sheet metal component for reference.

1.17

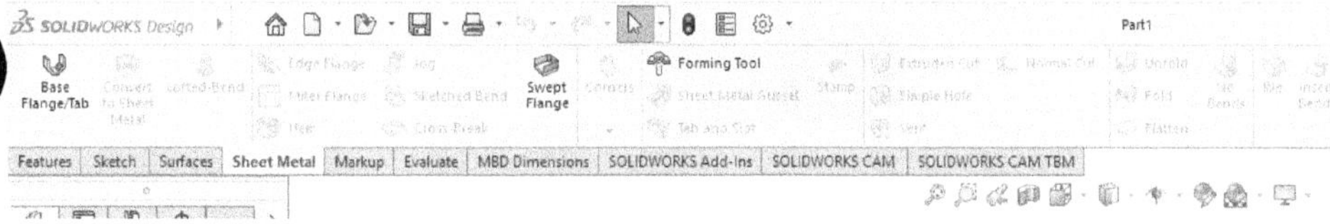

1.18

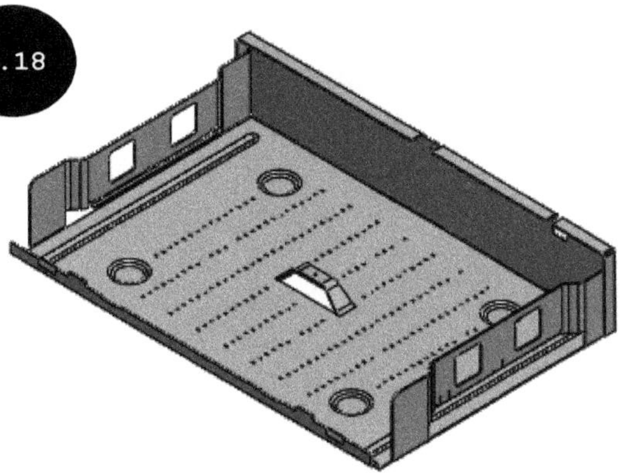

Weldments CommandManager

The **Weldments CommandManager** provides a variety of tools for creating weldment structures. Figure 1.19 shows the **Weldments CommandManager** and Figure 1.20 displays a weldment component for reference.

1.19

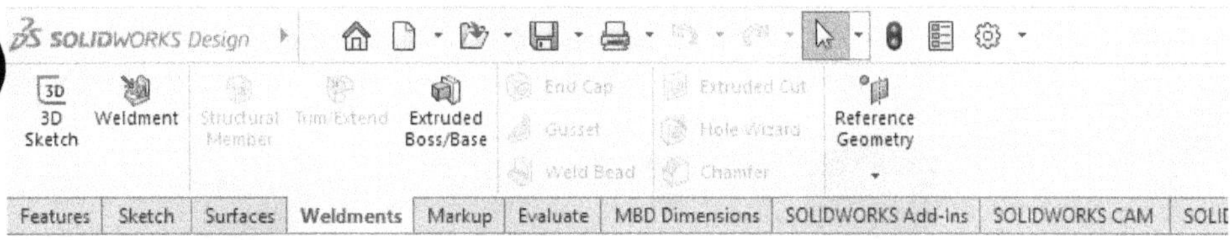

1.20

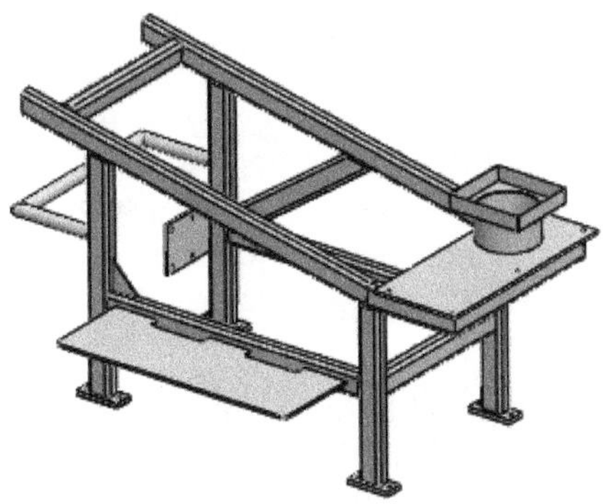

FeatureManager Design Tree

FeatureManager Design Tree appears on the left of the graphics area and keeps a record of all operations or features used for creating a model, see Figure 1.21. Note that the first created feature appears at the top and the next created features appear one after the other in the FeatureManager Design Tree. Also, in the FeatureManager Design Tree, three default planes and an origin appear, by default.

1.21

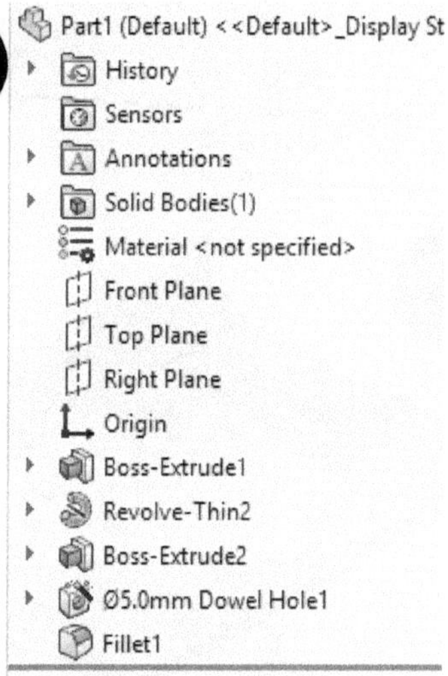

Tip: The features are logical operations that are performed to create a component. In other words, a component can be designed by creating a number of features such as extrude, sweep, hole, fillet, draft, and so on.

View (Heads-Up) Toolbar

The **View (Heads-Up)** toolbar is located at the top center of the graphics area, see Figure 1.22. It contains a variety of tools used to manipulate the view and display of the model in the graphics area.

1.22

Status Bar

The Status Bar is located at the bottom of the graphics area and provides information about the action to be taken based on the currently active tool. It also displays details such as the current state of the sketch being created, the coordinate system, and more.

Task Pane

The Task Pane appears on the right side of the screen and contains various tabs, including **3DEXPERIENCE Marketplace, SOLIDWORKS Resources, Design Library, File Explorer, View Palette, Custom Properties,** and **SOLIDWORKS User Forum**. These tabs provide access to various SOLIDWORKS online resources, applications, subscription services, libraries, and more, see Figure 1.23. Some of the tabs in the Task Pane are discussed next.

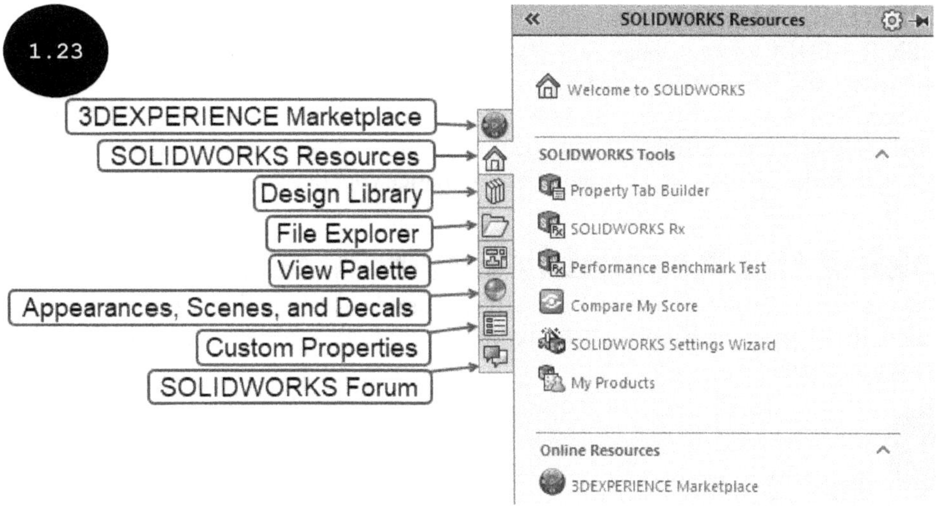

SOLIDWORKS Resources

The **SOLIDWORKS Resources Task Pane** provides tools to invoke the **Welcome** dialog box and links to access various SOLIDWORKS applications, online resources, and subscription services. To display the **SOLIDWORKS Resources Task Pane**, click on the **SOLIDWORKS Resources** tab in the Task Pane, as shown in Figure 1.23. Some of the options available in the **SOLIDWORKS Resources Task Pane** are discussed next.

Welcome to SOLIDWORKS

The **Welcome to SOLIDWORKS** tool in the **SOLIDWORKS Resources Task Pane** is used to invoke the **Welcome** dialog box, allowing you to start a new document or open an existing SOLIDWORKS document.

SOLIDWORKS Tools

The **SOLIDWORKS Tools** rollout is used to access various applications, including **Property Tab Builder**, **SOLIDWORKS Rx**, **Performance Benchmark Test**, and more.

Online Resources

The **Online Resources** rollout is used to access SOLIDWORKS partner solutions and the 3DExperience marketplace network, providing a range of external resources and services.

Design Library

The **Design Library Task Pane** is used to access the SOLIDWORKS design library, toolbox components, 3D Content Central, and SOLIDWORKS Content, providing easy access to various pre-existing designs and components for your projects.

Appearances, Scenes, and Decals

The **Appearances, Scenes, and Decals Task Pane** is used to change or modify the appearance of the model and the graphics display area, allowing you to adjust materials, lighting, and visual effects for your design.

3DEXPERIENCE Marketplace

The **3DEXPERIENCE Marketplace Task Pane** is used to collaborate and access the online 3D components catalog, which is managed by over 600 trusted suppliers and individual SOLIDWORKS users. It allows you to download parts and assemblies directly into your active SOLIDWORKS model. Additionally, it offers the capability to get your parts made, collaborate with leading manufacturers globally, and provides a variety of other benefits to enhance your design and manufacturing processes.

Invoking the Assembly Environment

To invoke the Assembly environment, click on the **Assembly** button in the **Welcome** dialog box. This action opens the Assembly environment, displaying the **Open** dialog box along with the **Begin Assembly PropertyManager**, see Figure 1.24.

1.24

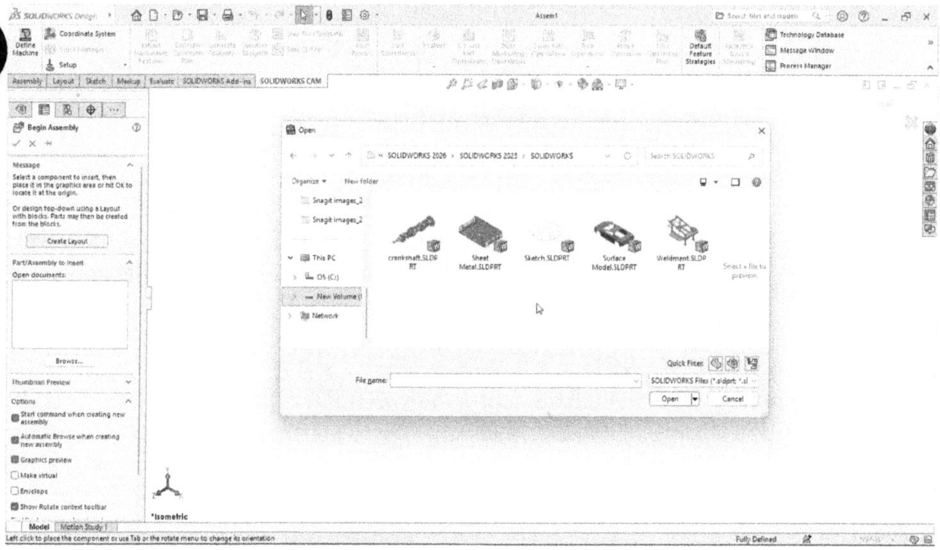

Alternatively, to invoke the Assembly environment, click on the **New** tool in the **Standard** toolbar. The **New SOLIDWORKS Document** dialog box appears. In this dialog box, click on the **Assembly** button and then click on the **OK** button.

The **Open** dialog box is used to insert a component into the Assembly environment. It appears automatically when you invoke the Assembly environment, provided no components are open in the current session of SOLIDWORKS. You will learn about inserting components into the Assembly environment and explore different methods for creating assemblies in later chapters.

Some of the components of the Assembly environment are the same as in the Part modeling environment. The **Assembly CommandManager** of the Assembly environment is discussed next.

Assembly CommandManager

The **Assembly CommandManager** provides different sets of tools that are used for inserting components into the assembly environment, applying mates between the inserted components, creating exploded views, creating patterns, and more. Figure 1.25 shows the **Assembly CommandManager** and Figure 1.26 shows an assembly for reference.

1.25

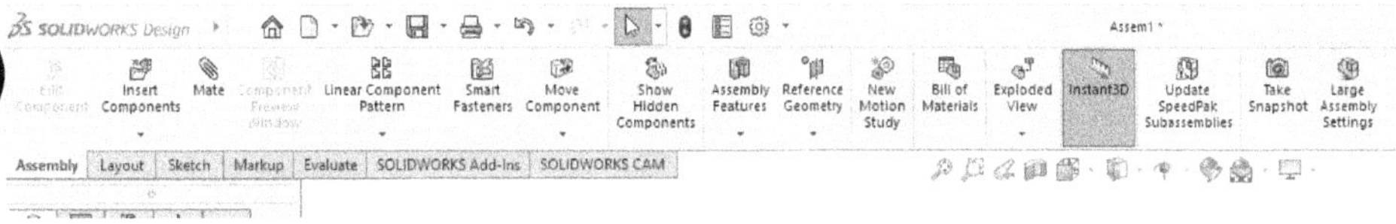

1.26

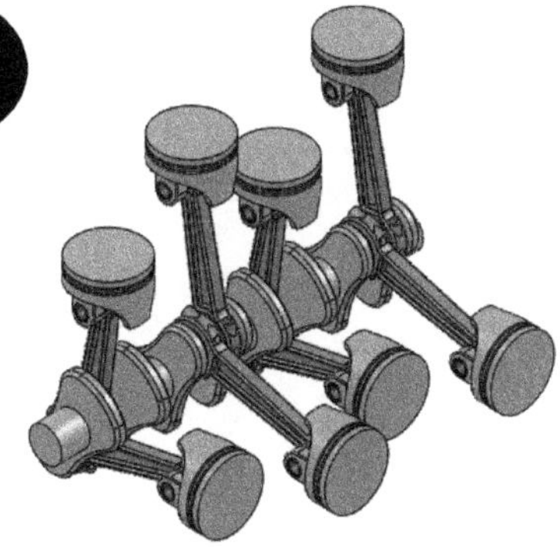

Invoking the Drawing Environment

To invoke the Drawing environment, click on the **New** tool in the **Standard** toolbar. The **New SOLIDWORKS Document** dialog box appears. In this dialog box, click on the **Drawing** button and then click **OK** button. This action opens the **Sheet Format/Size** dialog box (see Figure 1.27), where you can select the sheet size/format for your drawing. Alternatively, you can invoke the **Sheet Format/Size** dialog box by clicking the **Drawing** button in the **Welcome** dialog box.

1.27

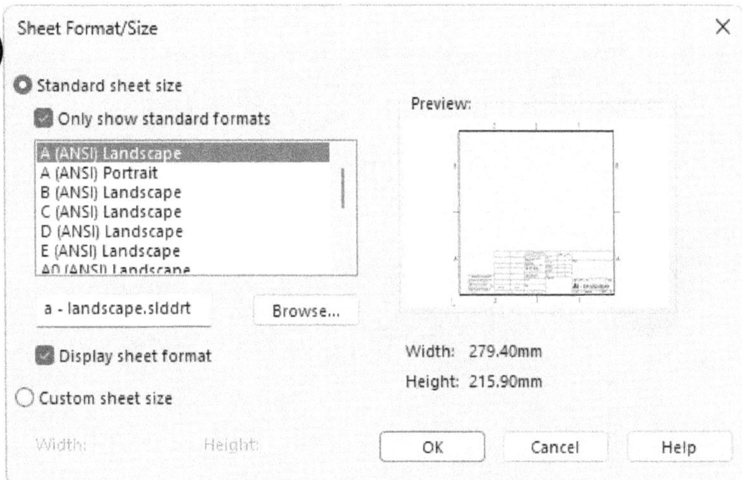

Once you have selected the sheet size and format in the **Sheet Format/Size** dialog box, click **OK** button. The Drawing environment startup interface appears, displaying the **Model View PropertyManager** on the left side of the drawing sheet, see Figure 1.28. The **Model View PropertyManager** is used to insert a component or an assembly into the Drawing environment to create its drawing views. You will learn more about creating drawing views in later chapters.

1.28

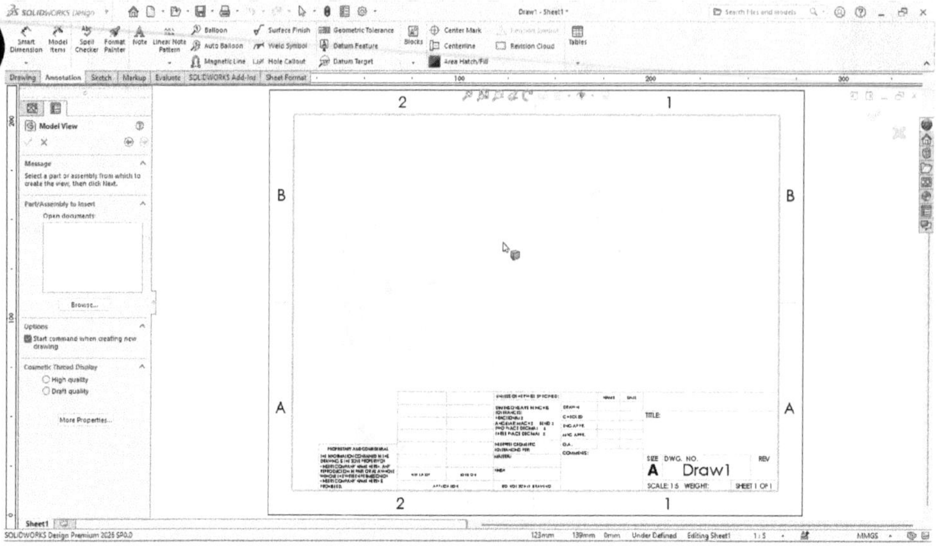

Most of the components of the Drawing environment are the same as the Part modeling environment. The **Drawing CommandManager** and **Annotation CommandManager** of the Drawing environment are discussed next.

Drawing CommandManager

The **Drawing CommandManager** offers various tools for creating different drawing views, including orthogonal views, section views, and detail views. Figure 1.29 shows the **Drawing CommandManager** and Figure 1.30 illustrates different drawing views of a component.

1.29

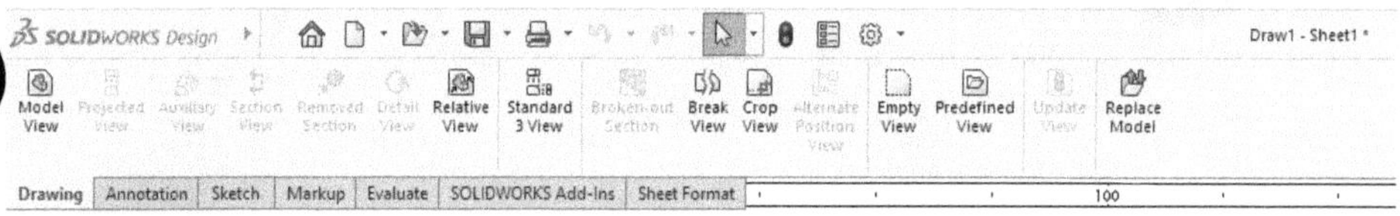

1.30

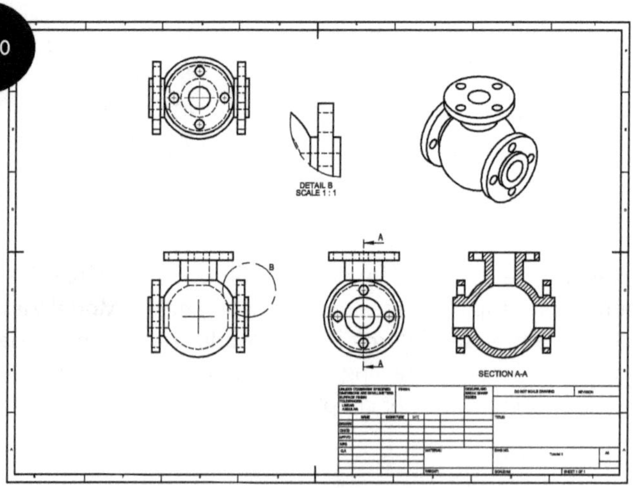

Annotation CommandManager

The **Annotation CommandManager** offers various tools for applying dimensions, notes, surface/welding symbols, creating BOM, and more. Figure 1.31 shows the **Annotation CommandManager** in the Drawing environment, while Figure 1.32 displays a drawing with dimensions for reference.

1.31

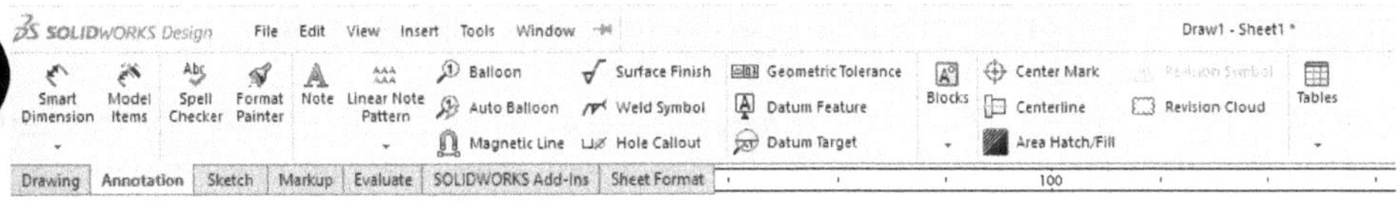

1.32

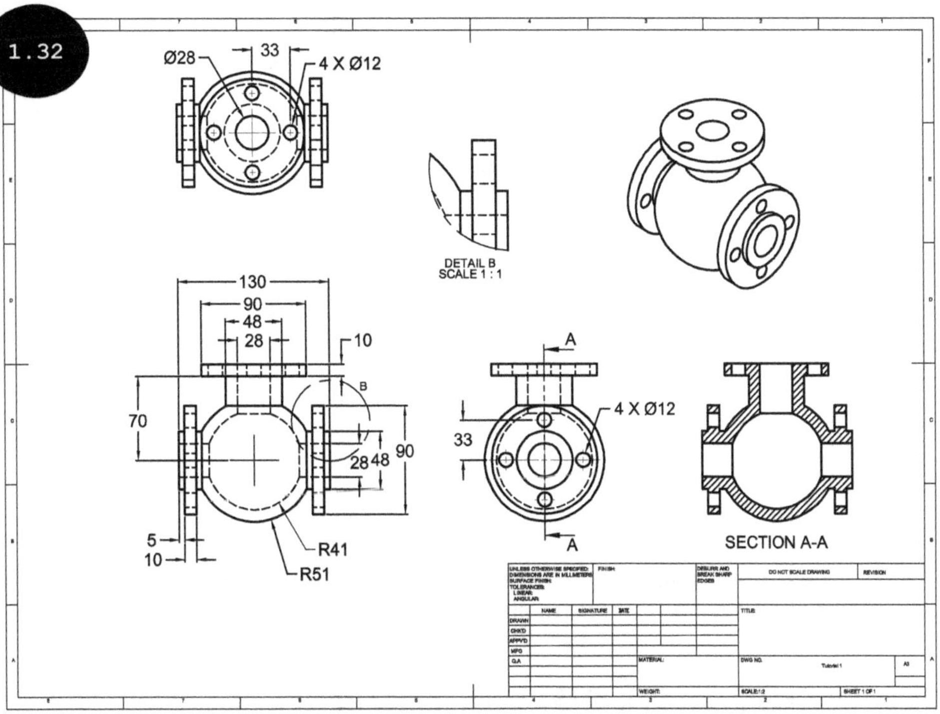

Identifying SOLIDWORKS Documents

The documents created in different environments (Part, Assembly, and Drawing) of SOLIDWORKS have different file extensions, see the table given below:

Documents	File Extension
Part	*.sldprt
Assembly	*.sldasm
Drawing	*.slddrw

Invoking a Shortcut Menu

A shortcut menu is displayed when you right-click in the graphics area, providing quick access to frequently used tools like **Zoom to Fit**, **Zoom In/Out**, and **Pan**, as shown in Figure 1.33. The shortcut menu also includes the **Context** toolbar, shown in the same figure. The tools available in both the **Context** toolbar and shortcut menu vary depending on the selected entity.

Figure 1.33 shows the shortcut menu when right-clicking in the empty area of the Part modeling environment, while Figure 1.34 shows the shortcut menu after selecting a face of a model.

1.33

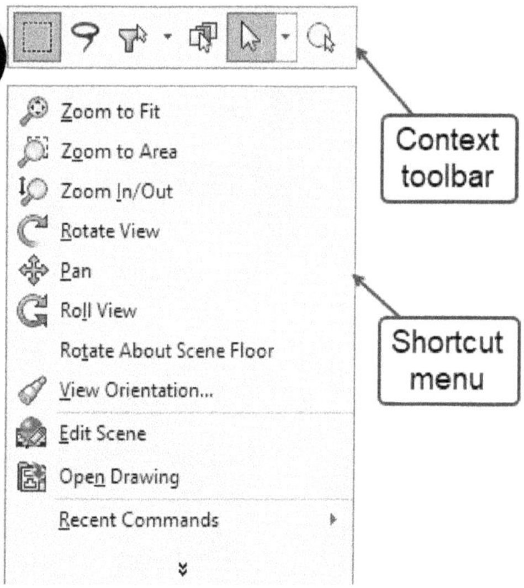

1.34

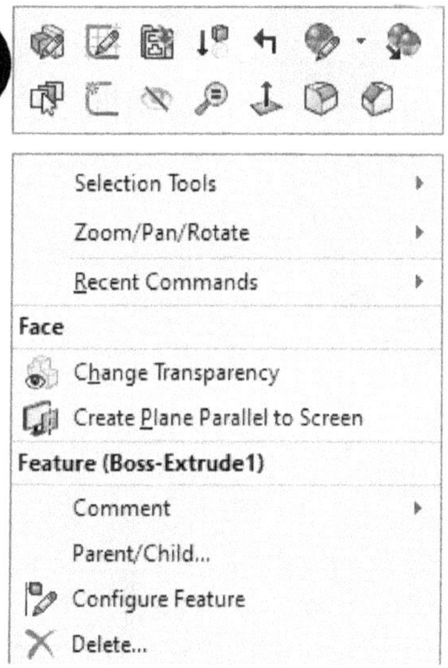

You can also customize the **Context** toolbar of a shortcut menu to add frequently used tools, as required. The method for customizing the **Context** toolbar is discussed next.

Customizing the Context Toolbar

In addition to the default tools displayed in the **Context** toolbar of a shortcut menu, you can customize it by adding frequently used tools, as required. To customize the **Context** toolbar, move your cursor over the **Context** toolbar in the shortcut menu and right-click. The **Customize** option appears, see Figure 1.35. Click on the **Customize** option. The **Customize** dialog box opens along with the **Graphics Area** toolbar, see Figure 1.36.

1.35

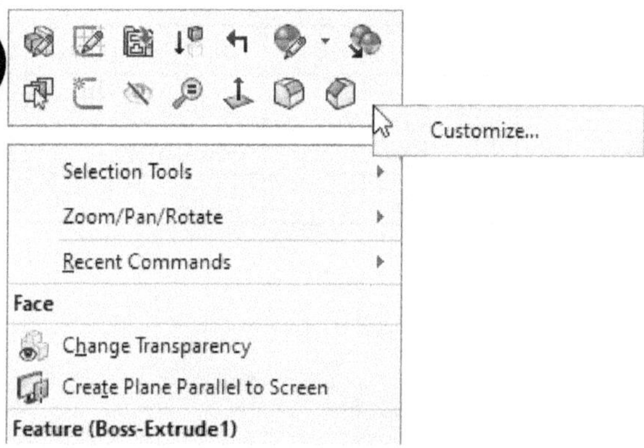

1.36

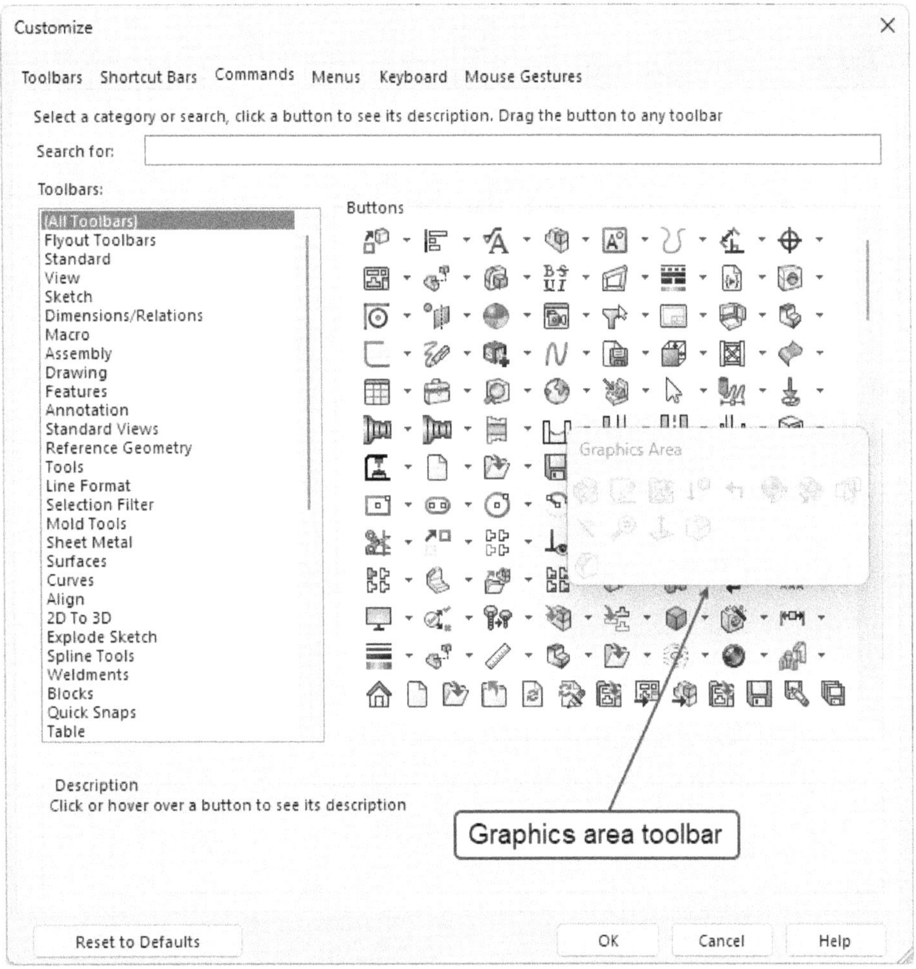

In the **Categories** area of the **Customize** dialog box, select the required category. The tools of the selected category appear on the right side of the dialog box in the **Buttons** area. You can drag and drop the tools from the **Buttons** area of the dialog box to the **Graphics Area** toolbar. Note that the tools added to the **Graphics Area** toolbar appear in the **Context** toolbar of the shortcut menu. Once you have added the required tools in the **Graphics Area** toolbar, click on the **OK** button in the dialog box.

Customizing the CommandManager

In addition to the default set of tools in a CommandManager, you can customize it to add more tools as needed. To customize a CommandManager, right-click on a tool within the CommandManager that you want to customize. A shortcut menu appears, see Figure 1.37. Click on the **Customize** option in the shortcut menu. The **Customize** dialog box opens, see Figure 1.38. Then, click on the **Commands** tab in the **Customize** dialog box, see Figure 1.38.

1.37

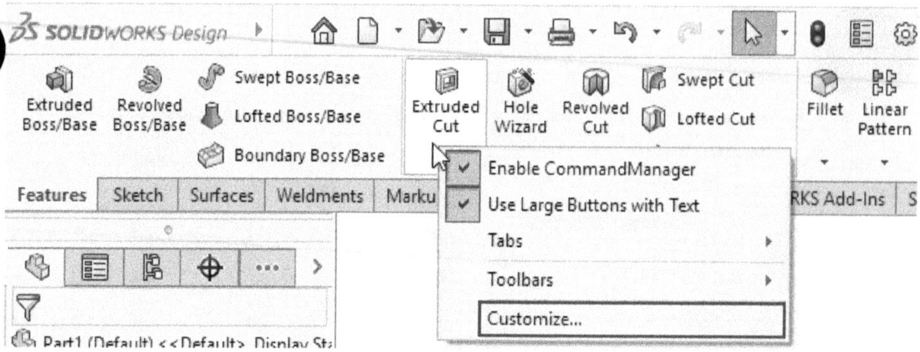

1.38

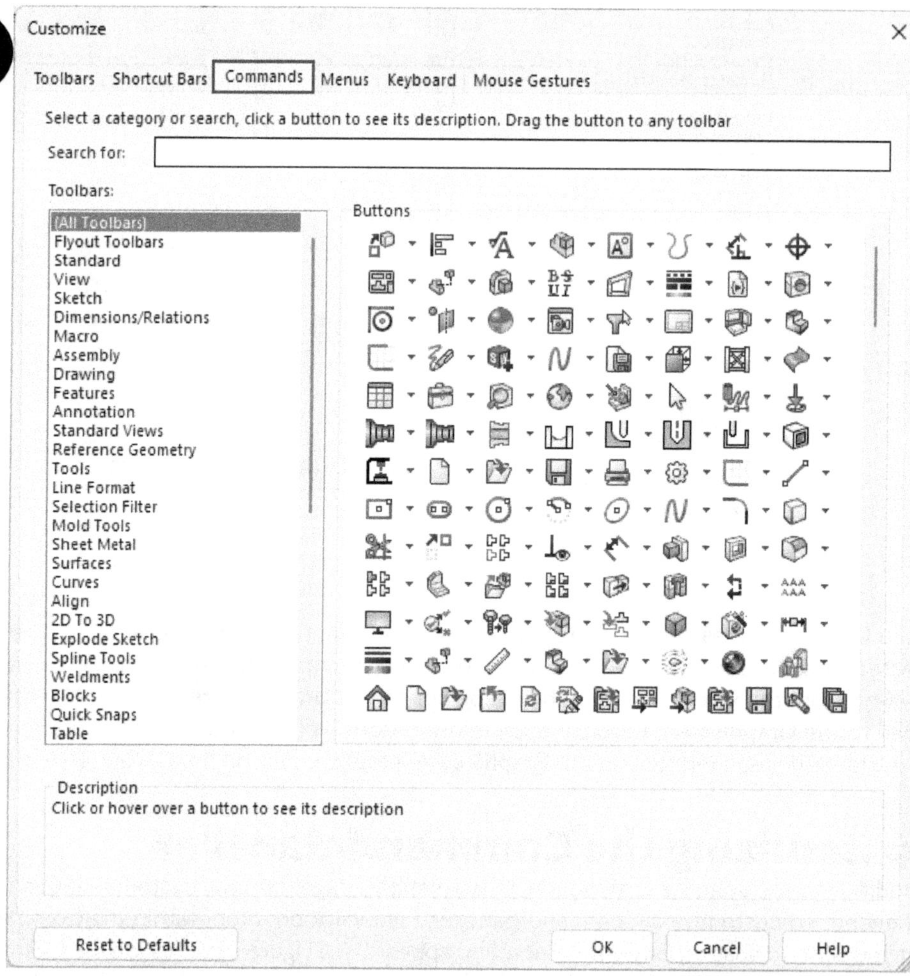

Next, select the required category of tools in the **Categories** area of the dialog box. The tools in the selected category appear on the right side of the dialog box in the **Buttons** area. Now, you can drag and drop the tools from the **Buttons** area of the dialog box to the CommandManager. You can also drag and drop the tools back to the **Buttons** area of the dialog box from the CommandManager. Once you have added the required tools in the CommandManager, click on the **OK** button in the dialog box.

Working with Mouse Gestures

Mouse Gestures provide a quick shortcut to access frequently used tools, see Figure 1.39. To display the Mouse Gestures, press and hold the right mouse button, then drag the cursor a short distance. The available default tools in the Mouse Gestures depend on the current SOLIDWORKS environment. By default, four tools are shown, but you can customize the number of tools to 2, 3, 4, 8, or 12.

To modify the number of tools displayed in the Mouse Gestures, go to **Tools > Customize** in the SOIDWORKS Design Menu. The **Customize** dialog box opens. Click on the **Mouse Gestures** tab, then select your preferred option from the drop-down list [**2 Gestures (Vertical), 2 Gestures (Horizontal), 3 Gestures, 4 Gestures, 8 Gestures**, or **12 Gestures**], see Figure 1.40. A preview of the Mouse Gestures, including the default tools for various SOLIDWORKS environments, appears on the right panel of the **Customize** dialog box.

1.39

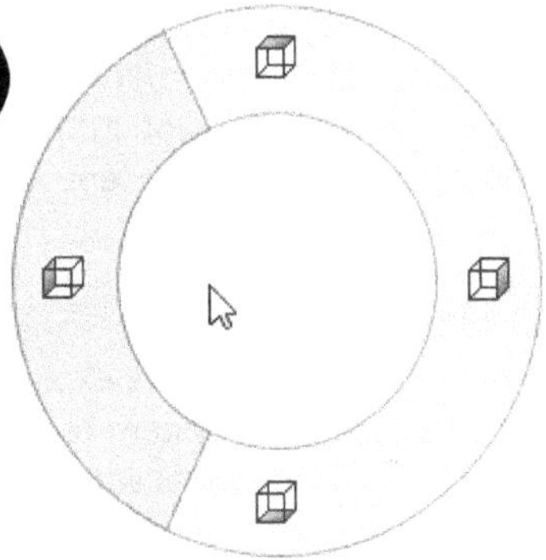

1.40

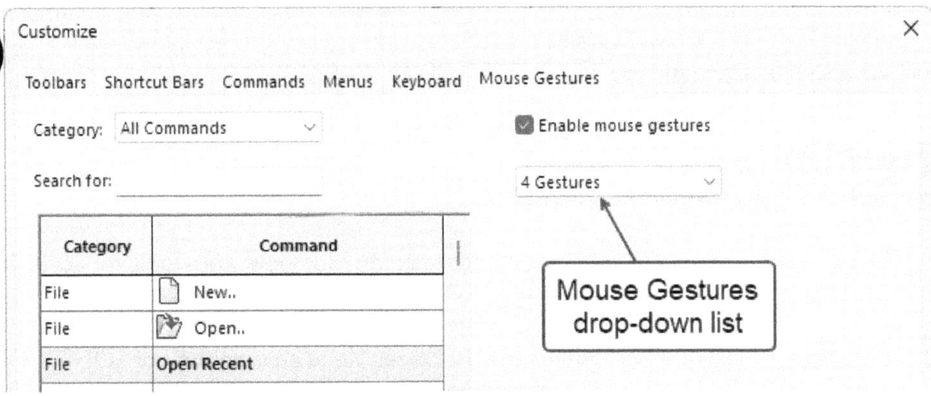

You can further customize the tools of Mouse Gestures for different SOLIDWORKS environments using the tools available in the **Mouse Gestures** tab of the **Customize** dialog box. To do this, drag and drop the tool you need from the list of available tools in the **Mouse Gestures** tab into the required Mouse Gesture position on the right side of the dialog box. Once you've customized the Mouse Gestures to your preference, close the **Customize** dialog box to apply the changes.

Saving Documents

To save a document created in any of the SOLIDWORKS environments, click on the **Save** tool in the **Standard** toolbar or go to **File > Save** in the SOLIDWORKS Design Menus. The **Save As** dialog box appears. Enter the desired name for the document in the **File name** field, then browse to the location where you want to save the document. Finally, click the **Save** button to save the document.

Opening Existing Documents

To open an existing SOLIDWORKS Document, click on the **Open** button in the **Welcome** dialog box. Alternatively, click on the **Open** tool in the **Standard** toolbar or click on **File > Open** in the SOLIDWORKS Design Menus. The **Open** dialog box appears. In this dialog box, select the **SOLIDWORKS Files (*.sldprt;**

*.sldasm; *.slddrw) file extension in the **File Type** drop-down list. Note that you can select the file extension depending on the type of document to be opened. After selecting the required file extension, browse to the location where the SOLIDWORKS document is saved and then click on the document to be opened. Next, click on the **Open** button in the dialog box. The selected document gets opened.

Similar to opening existing SOLIDWORKS documents, you can also open/import documents created in other CAD applications. SOLIDWORKS allows you to open documents created in CATIA V5, PTC Creo, Unigraphics/NX, Inventor, Solid Edge, CADKEY, Rhino, DWG, and so on by selecting the respective file extension in the **File Type** drop-down list of the **Open** dialog box. In addition to this, you can also open documents saved in universal CAD formats such as IGES, STEP, STL, and Parasolid.

Summary

In this chapter, you have explored the essential steps to get started with SOLIDWORKS. You have learned about the system requirements for installing SOLIDWORKS and how to navigate through different environments within the software. You've identified the different types of SOLIDWORKS documents and understood the components of the startup user interface. The chapter also covered how to invoke and customize the shortcut menu, along with saving and opening documents efficiently in SOLIDWORKS. This knowledge sets the groundwork for a smooth workflow as you progress through more advanced features and techniques in SOLIDWORKS.

Questions

Complete and verify the following sentences:

- The _________ contains different menus such as **File**, **View**, and **Tools** for accessing different tools of SOLIDWORKS.
- The surface modeling environment and the Sheet Metal environment of SOLIDWORKS can be invoked within the _________ environment.
- The file extension of the documents created in the Part modeling environment is _________, the Assembly environment is _________, and the Drawing environment is _________.
- The **Features CommandManager** is provided with different sets of tools that are used for creating _________.
- The _________ **CommandManager** is provided with different sets of tools that are used for inserting components in the assembly environment, applying mates, and so on.
- In SOLIDWORKS, you can open IGES and STEP files. (True/False)
- The FeatureManager Design Tree is used for keeping a record of all operations/features in an order. (True/False)
- In SOLIDWORKS, you cannot customize the tools in a CommandManager. (True/False)

CHAPTER

2

Drawing Sketches with SOLIDWORKS

This chapter discusses the following topics:

- Invoking the Part Modeling Environment
- Specifying Units
- Invoking the Sketching Environment
- Working with the Selection of Planes
- Specifying Grids and Snap Settings
- Drawing a Line Entity
- Drawing an Arc by using the Line tool
- Drawing a Centerline
- Drawing a Midpoint Line
- Drawing a Rectangle
- Drawing a Circle
- Drawing an Arc
- Drawing a Polygon
- Drawing a Slot
- Drawing an Ellipse
- Drawing an Elliptical Arc
- Drawing a Parabola
- Drawing Conic Curves
- Drawing a Spline
- Editing a Spline
- Modifying the Tangency Direction of Arc/Spline

SOLIDWORKS is a feature-based, parametric solid modeling software for mechanical design and automation. Before creating 3D models in SOLIDWORKS, it is important to understand that designing a 3D model requires building its features one at a time, see Figures 2.1 and 2.2. Features are divided into two main categories: sketch-based features and placed features. A feature created using a sketch is called a sketch-based feature, while a feature created on an existing feature without a sketch is known as a placed feature. Among these two categories, sketch-based features are typically the first to be created in any real-world component, making it important to focus initially on drawing accurate sketches.

Figure 2.1 illustrates a component that includes an extruded feature and a chamfer. The extruded feature is created using a sketch, making it a sketch-based feature. Conversely, the chamfer is a placed feature, as it does not require a sketch for its creation. Figure 2.2 depicts the process for creating this model.

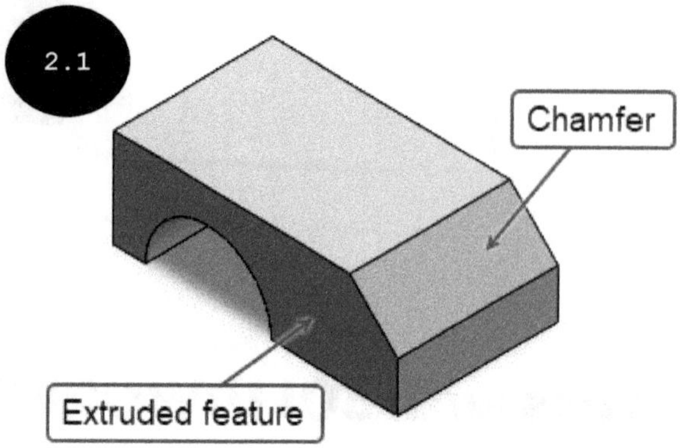

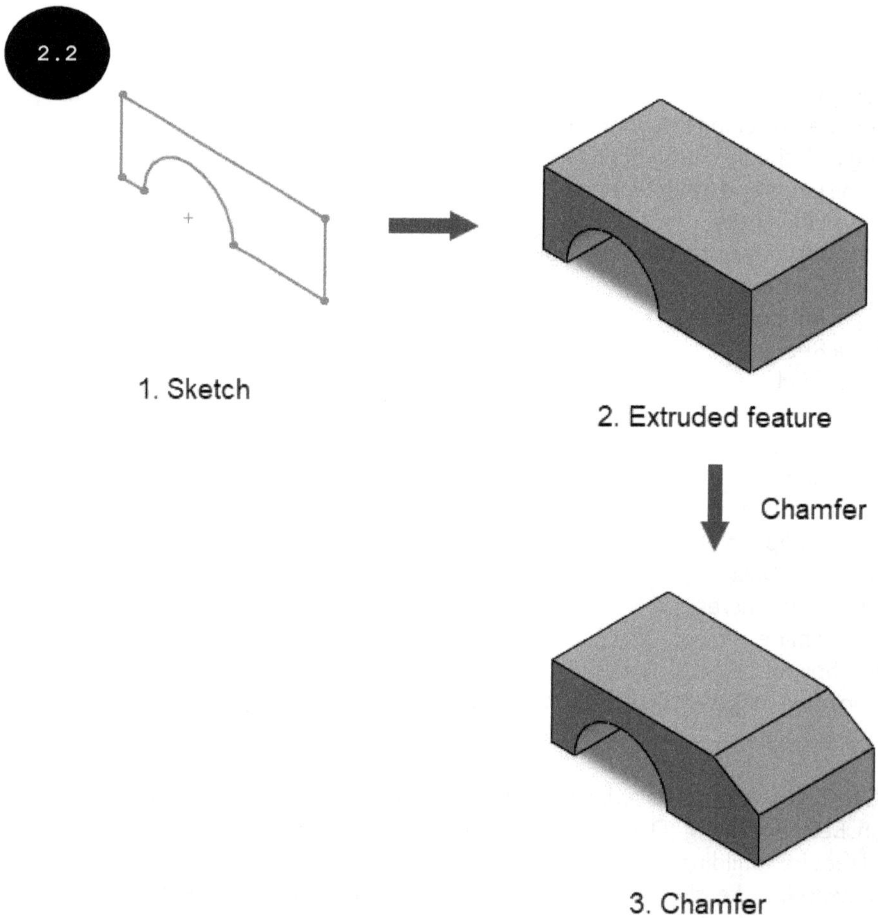

To start designing a component in SOLIDWORKS, mastering sketch creation is crucial since the base or first feature of any component is typically sketch-based. In SOLIDWORKS, you can create sketches using the various tools available in the Sketching environment, which is accessible within the Part modeling environment.

Invoking the Part Modeling Environment

To invoke the Part Modeling environment, start SOLIDWORKS by double-clicking the SOLIDWORKS 2026 icon on your desktop. After loading the necessary files, the startup user interface appears along with the **Welcome** dialog box, see Figure 2.3. This dialog box appears every time you start SOLIDWORKS and allows you to start a new document, open an existing one, or access SOLIDWORKS resources. In the **Welcome** dialog box, click the **Part** button. The startup user interface of the Part modeling environment appears, see Figure 2.4. Various components of this environment are discussed in Chapter 1.

2.3

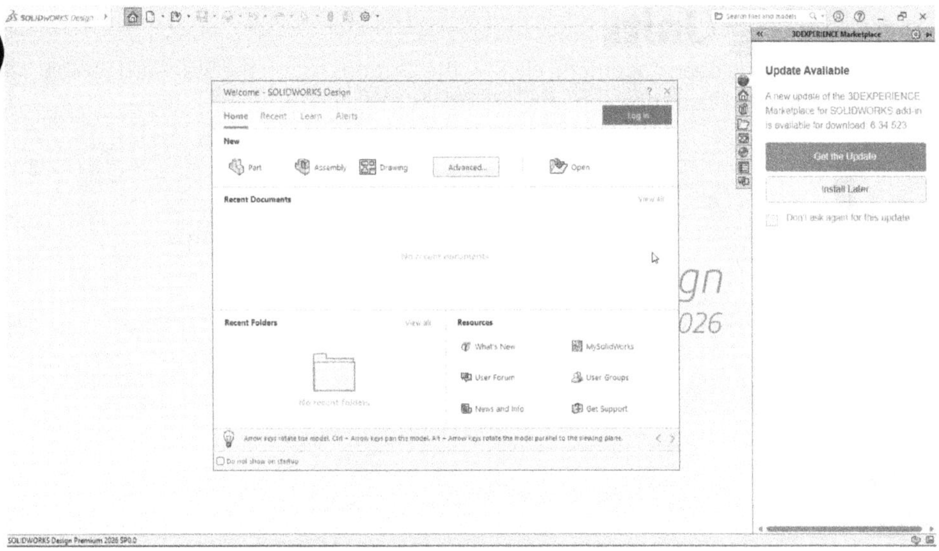

2.4

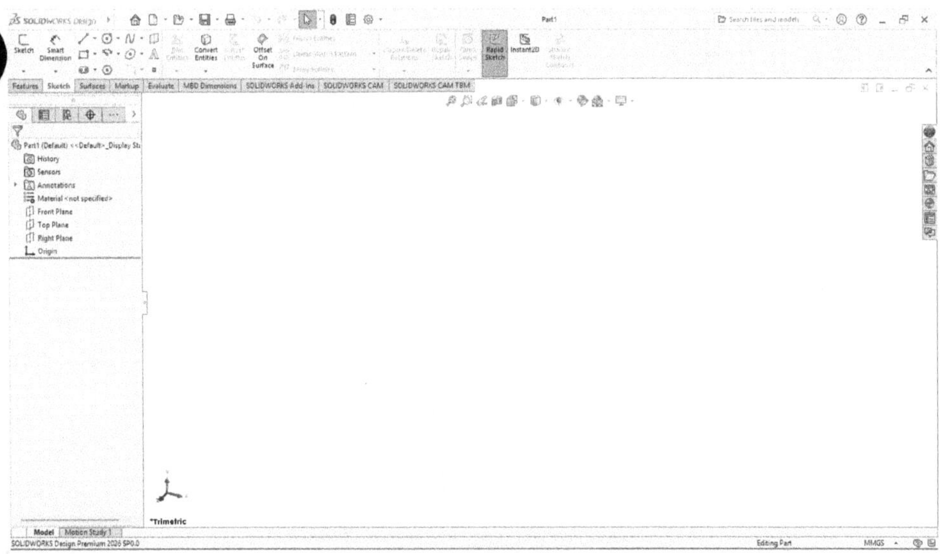

Once the Part modeling environment is invoked, you can access the Sketching environment to create a sketch. However, before accessing the Sketching environment, it is important to set up the units for the current open document.

Note: If you are invoking the Part modeling environment for the first time after installing SOLIDWORKS, the **Units and Dimension Standard** dialog box will appear. This dialog box allows you to specify the default units and measurement standards for your documents. The units and measurement settings you select in this dialog box will become the default for all new documents. However, SOLIDWORKS also allows you to modify these default unit settings at any point during your design process for any particular document, as discussed next.

Specifying Units

To specify units for an open document, click on the **Options** tool in the **Standard** toolbar, see Figure 2.5. The **System Options** dialog box appears, see Figure 2.6.

2.5

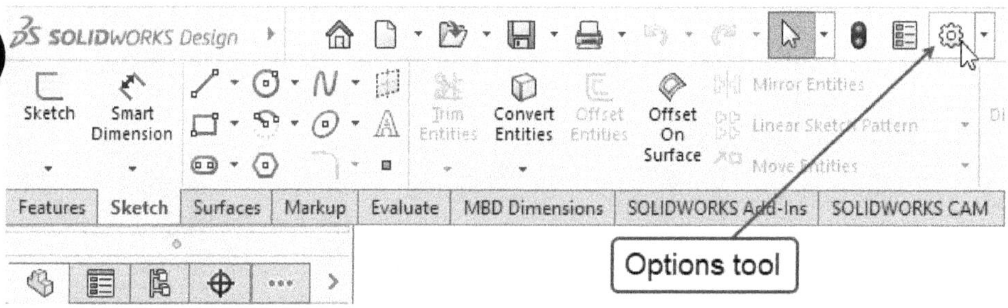

2.6

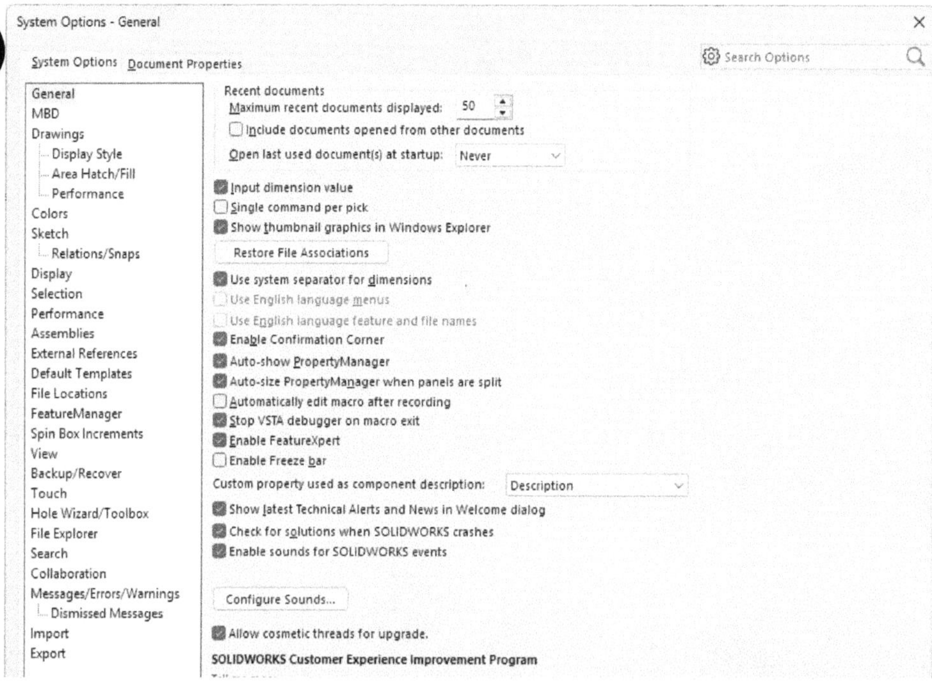

The **System Options** dialog box contains two tabs: **System Options** and **Document Properties**. By default, the **System Options** tab is activated. Click on the **Document Properties** tab in the dialog box. The name of the dialog box changes to **Document Properties,** and the options for setting document properties appear in the dialog box. Next, click on the **Units** option in the left panel of the dialog box. The options for setting the units appear in the right panel of the dialog box, see Figure 2.7.

2.7

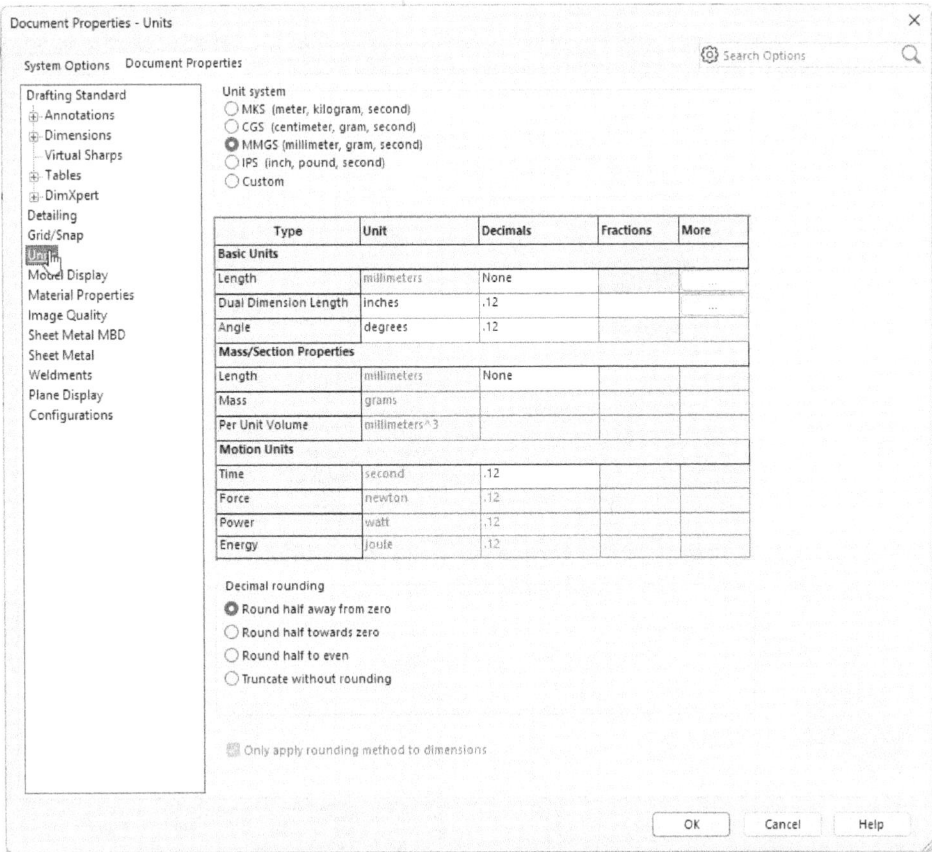

The **Unit system** area of the dialog box displays a list of predefined standard unit systems. In this area, you can select the required predefined unit system for the currently opened document. For example, to set the metric unit system for the currently opened document, click on the **MMGS (millimeter, gram, second)** radio button. Note that in the metric unit system, length is measured in millimeters, mass is calculated in grams, and time is represented in seconds.

You can also specify a unit system other than the default predefined standard unit systems by selecting the **Custom** radio button. When you select the **Custom** radio button, the fields in the table at the bottom of the dialog box become enabled. You can then change the unit of length measurement, angle measurement, mass calculation, and time as needed, beyond the standard combinations.

For example, to change the unit of length measurement, click on the field corresponding to the **Unit** column and the **Length** row in the table. A downward-facing arrow appears. Click on this arrow, and a drop-down list with various units for length measurement appears. You can then select the desired unit from this list. Similarly, you can change the units for other measurements in this table. Additionally, you can specify the number of decimal places for the measurements using the options in this table.

Once you set all the required units for the currently opened document, click the **OK** button to accept the changes and close the dialog box.

Note: Alternatively, to specify units for an open document, click on the **Unit System** area in the lower-right corner of the Status Bar, see Figure 2.8. The **Unit System** flyout appears. In this flyout, select the required predefined unit system for the currently opened document. Note that a tick-mark next to a unit system indicates that it is selected as the unit system for the current SOLIDWORKS document.

You can also open the **Document Properties - Units** dialog box to specify the unit system by clicking on the **Edit Document Units** option in the **Unit System** flyout.

2.8

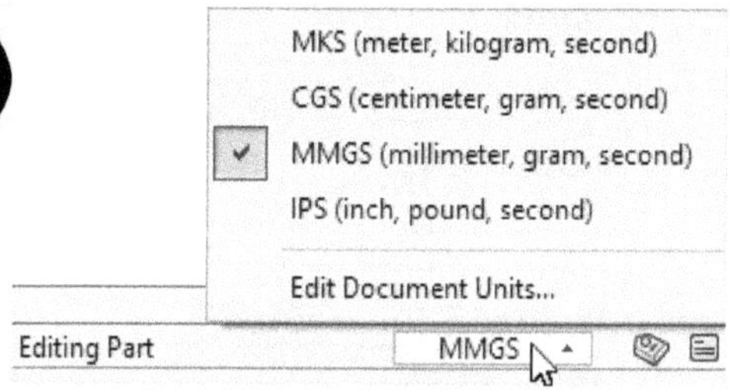

Invoking the Sketching Environment

After invoking the Part modeling environment and specifying units, you can access the Sketching environment to create the sketch for the first feature of a model. To do this, click on the **Sketch** tab in the CommandManager. The tools of the **Sketch CommandManager** appear, see Figure 2.9.

2.9

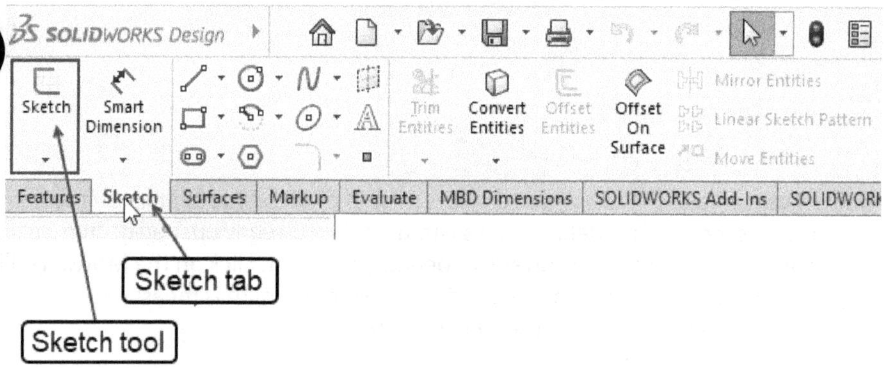

In the **Sketch CommandManager**, click on the **Sketch** tool, refer to Figure 2.9. The three default planes: Front, Top, and Right, which are mutually perpendicular to each other, appear in the graphics area, see Figure 2.10. Additionally, the **Edit Sketch PropertyManager** appears on the left side of the graphics area.

You can now select any of the three default planes as the sketching plane for creating the sketch. To select a plane, move the cursor over the desired plane. Click the left mouse button when the boundary of the plane is highlighted in the graphics area. Upon selecting a plane, the Sketching environment is invoked, and the Confirmation Corner appears at the top right of the graphics area, see Figure 2.11. The selected plane becomes the sketching plane and is oriented normal to the viewing direction for easier sketch creation.

Note that the Confirmation Corner consists of two icons: **Exit Sketch** and **Cancel Sketch**. The **Exit Sketch** icon is used to confirm the successful creation of the sketch and exit the Sketching environment. In contrast, the **Cancel Sketch** icon is used to discard the sketch and exit the environment without saving any changes.

2.10

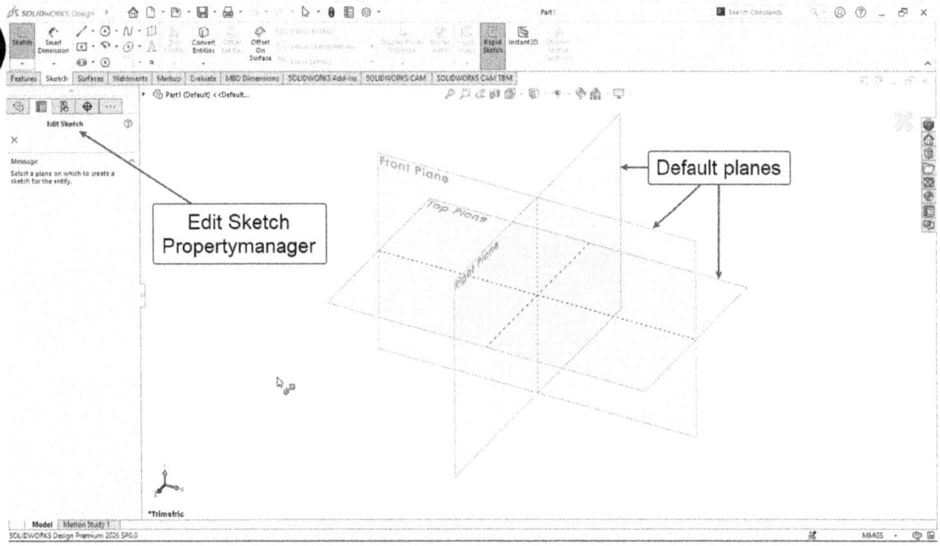

2.11

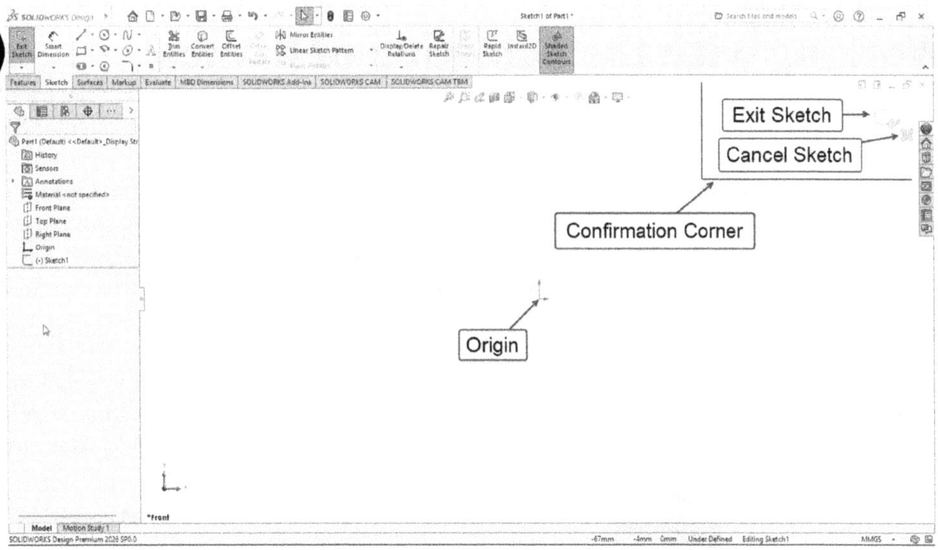

The Sketching environment also displays a red-colored point with two perpendicular arrows at the center of the graphics area. The red point represents the origin (0,0) of the Sketching environment, and the perpendicular arrows indicate the X-axis and Y-axis of the sketching plane.

If the red point does not appear by default in the graphics area, you can enable its visibility by clicking **Hide/Show Items > View Origins** in the **View (Heads-Up)** toolbar, see Figure 2.12. The **View Origins** tool is a toggle button, allowing you to turn the origin display on or off.

2.12

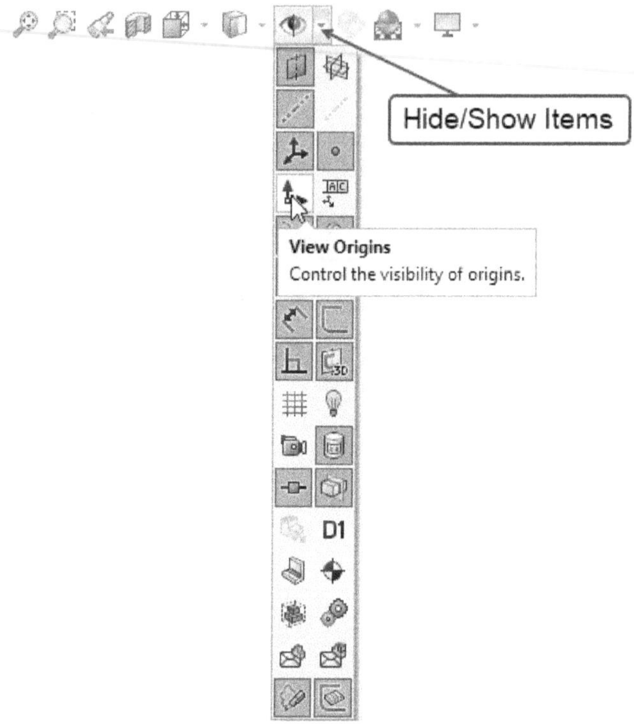

Working with the Selection of Planes

As previously mentioned, to invoke the Sketching environment, you need to select a plane as the sketching plane. Choosing the appropriate plane is crucial for defining the correct orientation of a model.

For example, consider the isometric view of a model with dimensions of 200 mm in length, 100 mm in width, and 40 mm in height, as shown in Figure 2.13. To create this model with the same orientation, you can select the Top plane as the sketching plane. Then, draw a rectangular sketch with dimensions 200 mm × 100 mm. Later, in the Part modeling environment, you can extrude this sketch to a depth of 40 mm to generate a 3D solid model.

If you choose the Front plane as the sketching plane instead, you will need to draw a rectangular sketch of 200 mm × 40 mm. Similarly, if you select the Right plane, you must create a rectangular sketch of 100 mm × 40 mm. You will learn about creating 3D solid models and extruding sketches in detail in later chapters.

2.13

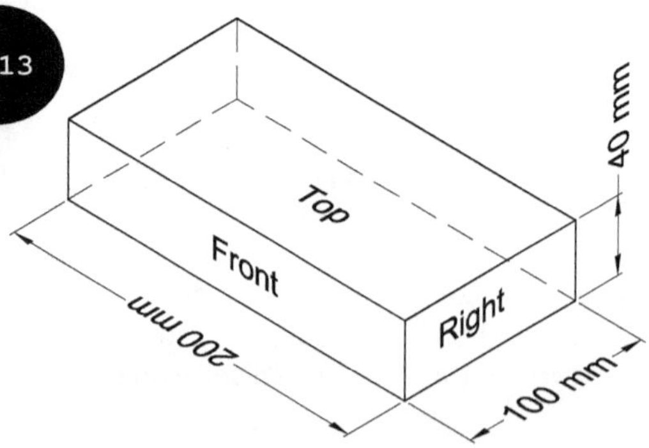

Once the Sketching environment is invoked, you can begin creating sketches using the various sketching tools available in the **Sketch CommandManager**. However, before starting the sketch, it is essential to understand how to configure grid and snap settings to ensure precision and control while sketching. These settings help you align and position sketch entities effectively, making the sketching process smoother and more accurate.

Specifying Grids and Snap Settings

Grids help you specify points in the drawing area for creating sketch entities and act as reference lines. By default, grids are not displayed in the drawing area. However, you can enable grid display and adjust snap settings to restrict cursor movement to specific intervals, improving accuracy and efficiency in your design process.

To turn on the display of grids and configure snap settings, click on the **Options** tool in the **Standard** toolbar. The **System Options - General** dialog box appears. In this dialog box, click on the **Document Properties** tab. The options related to document properties appear and the name of the dialog box changes to **Document Properties - Drafting Standard**. Next, click on the **Grid/Snap** option in the left panel of the dialog box. The options related to grids and snap settings appear on the right panel of the dialog box. Also, the name of the dialog box changes to **Document Properties - Grid/Snap**, see Figure 2.14.

2.14

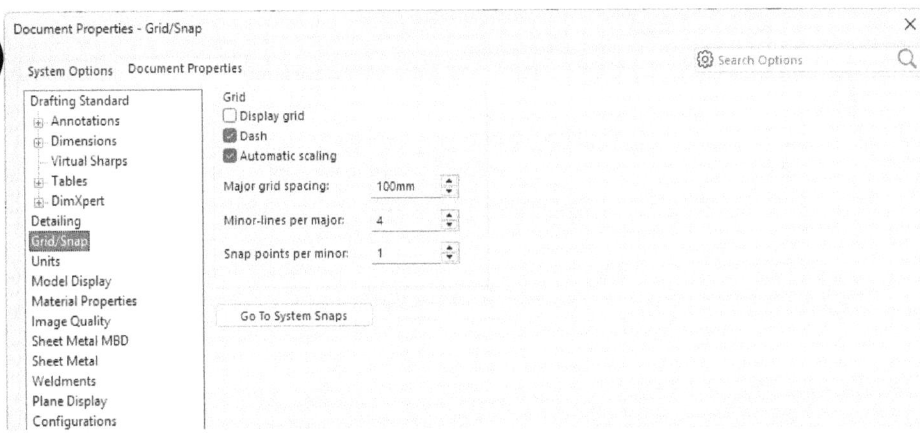

In the **Grid** area of the dialog box, you can customize the grid settings for better precision. The **Major grid spacing** field lets you specify the distance between two major grid lines, determining the primary intervals on the grid. The **Minor-lines per major** field defines the number of minor lines between two major grid lines. For example, entering a value of **5** in this field divides the space between two major grid lines into five equal parts both horizontally and vertically.

Additionally, the **Snap points per minor** field allows you to set the number of points the cursor can snap to between two minor grid lines, ensuring greater accuracy and control during sketching.

To enable the display of grids in the drawing area, select the **Display grid** check box in the **Grid** area of the dialog box. To activate the snap mode, which restricts the cursor to specific intervals based on the defined snap settings, click the **Go To System Snaps** button. This action opens the **System Options - Relations/Snaps** dialog box. In this dialog box, you can select the **Grid** check box to turn on the snap mode. If you enable the **Snap only when grid is displayed** check box, the cursor will only snap when the grids are visible in the drawing area. Snapping is particularly useful for defining precise points when creating sketch entities. Once you have set your grid and snap preferences, click **OK** to confirm the changes and exit the dialog box. Figure 2.15 illustrates the drawing area with the grids displayed.

2.15

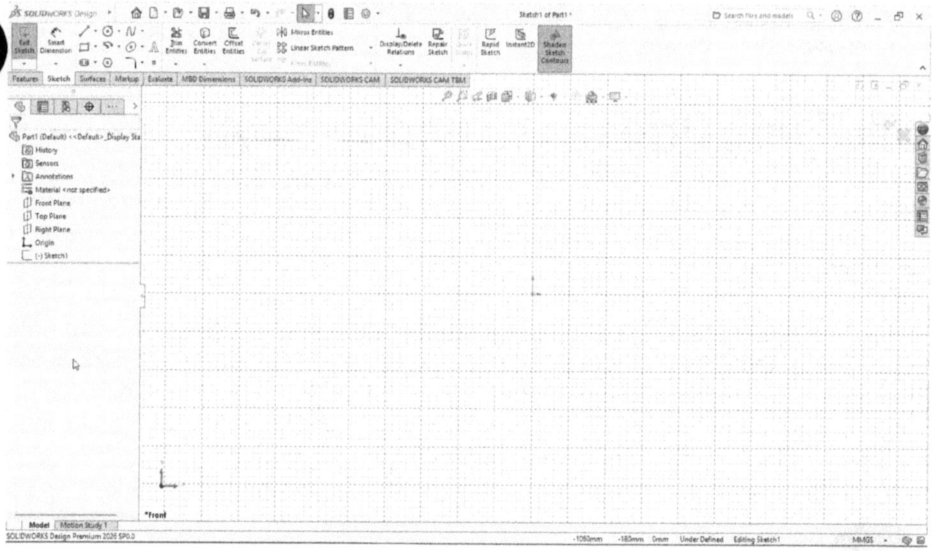

Note: In this textbook, the background color of the graphics area has been set to white for improved clarity of images. To change the background color, click the **Options** tool on the **Standard** toolbar and select the **Colors** option in the left panel of the **System Options - General** dialog box that opens. This action displays the color scheme settings in the right panel.

In the **Background appearance** area, choose the **Plain (Viewport Background color above)** radio button. Then, ensure the **Viewport Background** option is selected in the **Color scheme settings** area. Next, click the **Edit** button next to the **Color scheme settings** area, which opens the **Color** window. In this window, select white as the desired color and click **OK**. Finally, click **OK** again in the **System Options - Colors** dialog box to apply the changes and exit the dialog box. The background color of the drawing area is now set to white.

Drawing a Line Entity

A line is defined as the shortest distance between two points. To draw a line, click the **Line** tool in the **Sketch CommandManager**. The **Insert Line PropertyManager** appears on the left side of the drawing area (see Figure 2.16), and the cursor changes to the line cursor, which displays a pencil symbol along with a line.

2.16

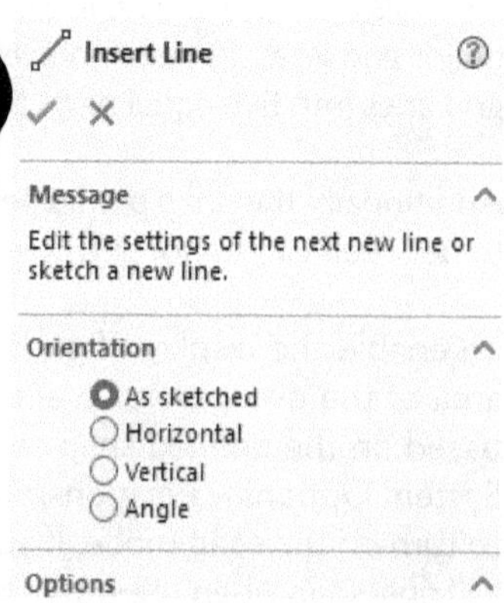

After activating the **Line** tool, click in the drawing area to specify the start point of the line, then click again to specify the end point. A line is drawn between the two specified points, see Figure 2.17. Additionally, a rubber band line appears, with one end fixed to the last specified point and the other end attached to the cursor. This indicates that you can continue drawing a chain of connected lines by clicking the left mouse button in the drawing area.

2.17

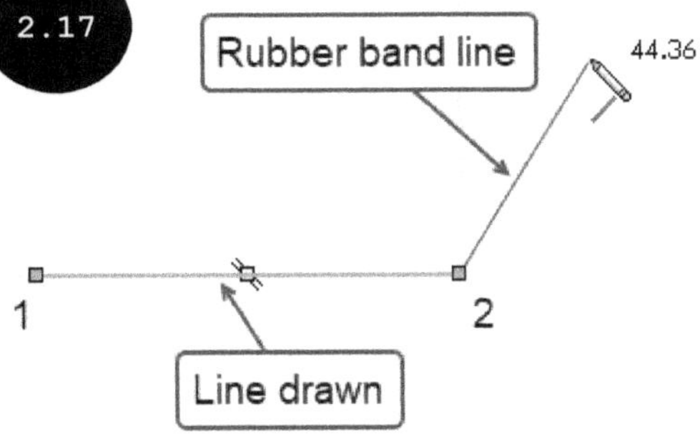

To end the creation of a line or a continuous chain of lines, press the ESC key or right-click in the drawing area and select the **Select** option from the shortcut menu that appears.

Note: While creating a line, when you move the cursor horizontally — or vertically | after specifying the start point, a symbol of horizontal or vertical relation appears near the cursor, see Figure 2.18. This symbol indicates that if you click the left mouse button to specify the endpoint, the corresponding relation will be applied to the line. You will learn more about relations in later chapters.

2.18

As mentioned earlier, when you activate the **Line** tool, the **Insert Line PropertyManager** appears on the left side of the drawing area, see Figure 2.19. This PropertyManager provides options to control the settings for drawing lines. These options are discussed below.

Message

The **Message** rollout of the **Insert Line PropertyManager** displays appropriate information about the required action to be performed for creating a line entity.

Orientation

The **Orientation** rollout is used for controlling the orientation of a line. The options in the **Orientation** rollout are discussed next.

2.19

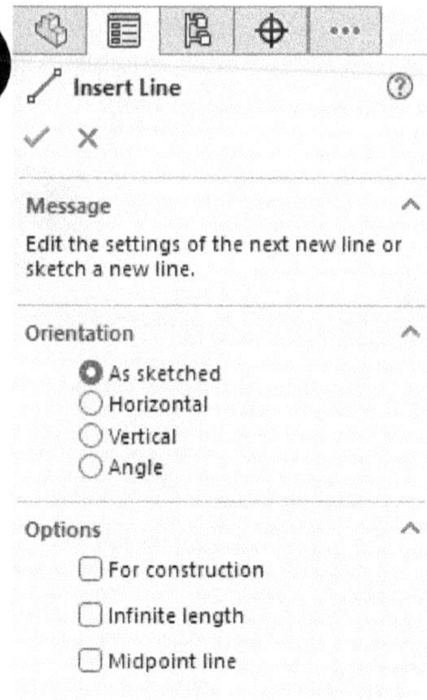

As sketched

By default, the **As sketched** radio button is activated in the **Orientation** rollout. As a result, you can draw a line with the desired orientation by clicking the left mouse button in the drawing area. In this case, the orientation of the line depends on the points you specify by clicking in the drawing area.

Horizontal

On selecting the **Horizontal** radio button in the **Orientation** rollout, you can draw horizontal lines by clicking the left mouse button in the drawing area. Notice that when you select this radio button, the **Parameters** rollout appears below the **Options** rollout in the PropertyManager, see Figure 2.20. In this rollout, the **Length** field is activated by default. You can specify the desired length for the horizontal line in this field. By default, the value **0** is entered in the field, allowing you to draw a horizontal line of any length by specifying two points in the drawing area.

2.20

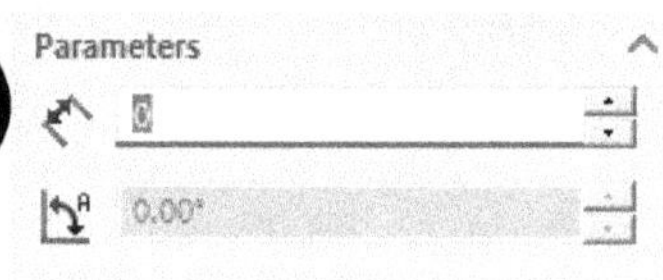

Vertical

Similar to drawing horizontal lines by selecting the **Horizontal** radio button, you can draw vertical lines by selecting the **Vertical** radio button in the **Orientation** rollout of the PropertyManager.

Angle

The **Angle** radio button is used to draw a line at a specified angle. When you select this radio button, the **Parameters** rollout appears in the PropertyManager, displaying the **Length** and **Angle** fields. You can specify the desired length and angle values for the line in the respective fields. By default, the value **0** is entered in both fields, allowing you to draw a line of any length and angle by specifying two points in the drawing area.

Note: The angle value of a line, entered in the **Angle** field of the **Parameters** rollout, is measured from the X axis.

Options

The options in the **Options** rollout of the **PropertyManager** are discussed next.

For construction

The **For construction** check box of the **Options** rollout is used to draw a construction or reference line.

Infinite length

The **Infinite length** check box is used to draw a line of infinite length. When selected, you can draw a line that extends infinitely in both directions by specifying two points in the drawing area.

Midpoint line

The **Midpoint line** check box is used to draw a line that is symmetric about a point. On selecting the **Midpoint line** check box, you need to first specify the midpoint of the line and then an endpoint by clicking the left mouse button in the drawing area. A line symmetric about the midpoint is drawn.

Tip: As SOLIDWORKS is a parametric, 3D solid modeling software, you can draw a sketch by specifying points arbitrarily in the drawing area. Once the sketch is drawn, you need to apply dimensions. You will learn about dimensioning sketch entities in later chapters.

However, in SOLIDWORKS, you can enter the required dimension value for a sketch entity while drawing it using the **Numeric Input** field, see Figure 2.21. This field appears during sketch creation if the **Enable on-screen numeric input on entity creation** check box is selected in the **System Options** dialog box. To configure this setting, click the **Options** tool in the **Standard** toolbar, select **Sketch** from the left panel of the **System Options** dialog box that appears, and then select or clear the **Enable on-screen numeric input on entity creation** option in the right panel to enable or disable the **Numeric Input** field.

In this chapter, the **Numeric Input** field is disabled, as the focus is on creating different types of sketch entities. Methods for applying dimensions and other parameters will be discussed in later chapters.

2.21

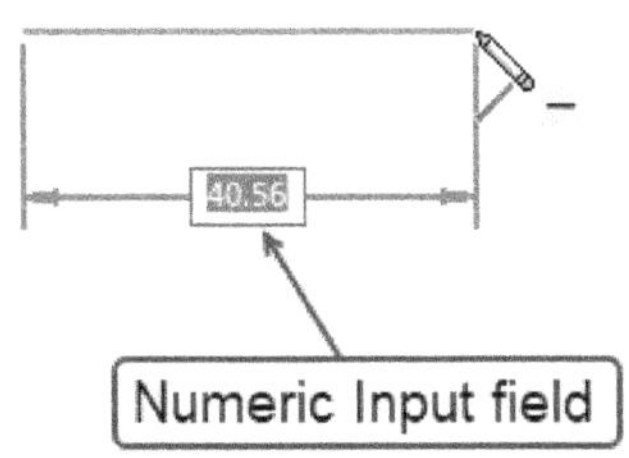

Tutorial 1

Draw a sketch of the model shown in Figure 2.22. The dimensions and the 3D model shown in the figure are for your reference only. You will learn about applying dimensions and creating 3D models in later chapters. All dimensions are in mm.

2.22

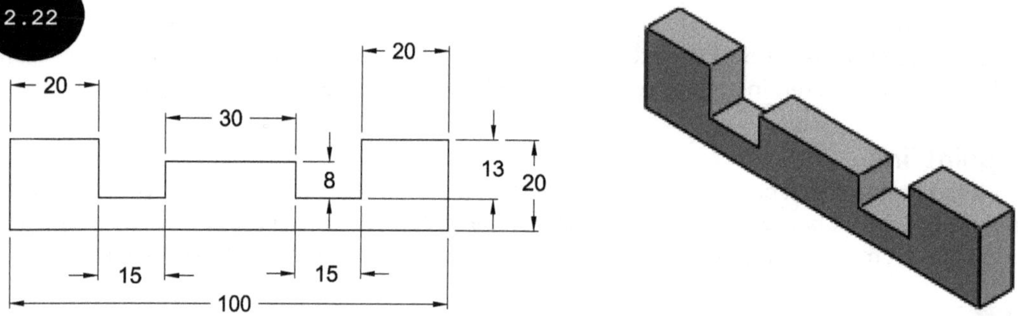

Section 1: Invoking the Part Modeling Environment

1. Start SOLIDWORKS by double-clicking on the SOLIDWORKS icon on your desktop. The startup user interface of SOLIDWORKS appears along with the **Welcome** dialog box, see Figure 2.23.

2.23

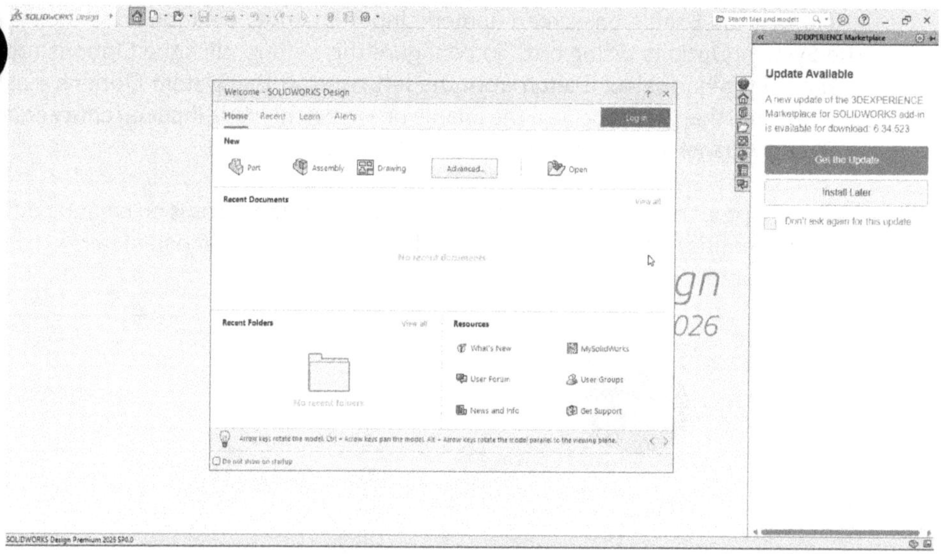

Note: If SOLIDWORKS is already open and the **Welcome** dialog box does not appear on the screen, you can invoke it by clicking on the **Welcome to SOLIDWORKS** tool in the **Standard** toolbar.

2. Click on the **Part** button in the **Welcome** dialog box. The Part modeling environment is invoked.

Section 2: Specifying Unit Settings

1. Move the cursor toward the lower right corner of the screen over the Status Bar and then click on the **Unit System** area in the Status Bar. The **Unit System** flyout appears, see Figure 2.24.

2. Ensure that the **MMGS (millimeter, gram, second)** option is tick-marked in this flyout.

Section 3: Invoking the Sketching Environment

1. Click on the **Sketch** tab in the CommandManager, see Figure 2.25. The tools of the **Sketch CommandManager** appear.

2. Click on the Sketch tool in the Sketch CommandManager, see Figure 2.25. Three default planes, mutually perpendicular to each other, appear in the graphics area.

2.24

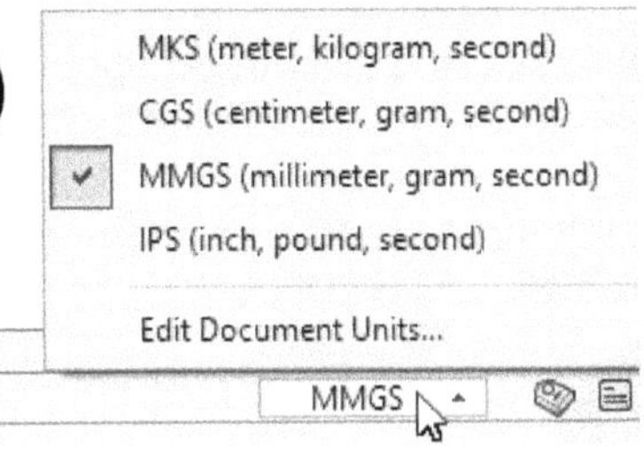

2.25

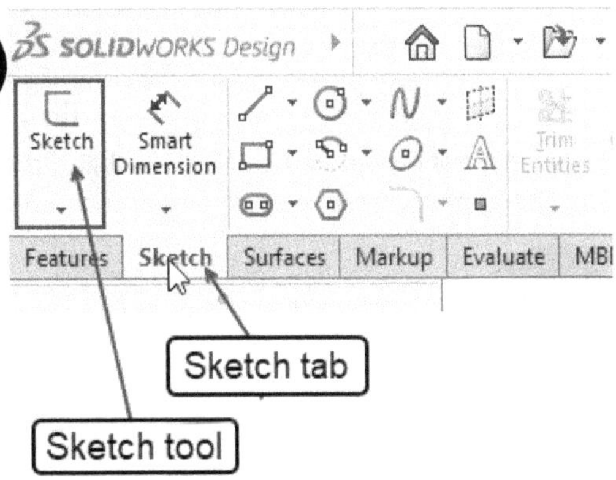

3. Move the cursor over the Front plane and then click the left mouse button, when the boundary of the plane is highlighted. The Sketching environment is invoked. Also, the Front plane is orientated normal to the viewing direction and the Confirmation corner appears at the upper right corner of the drawing area, see Figure 2.26.

2.26

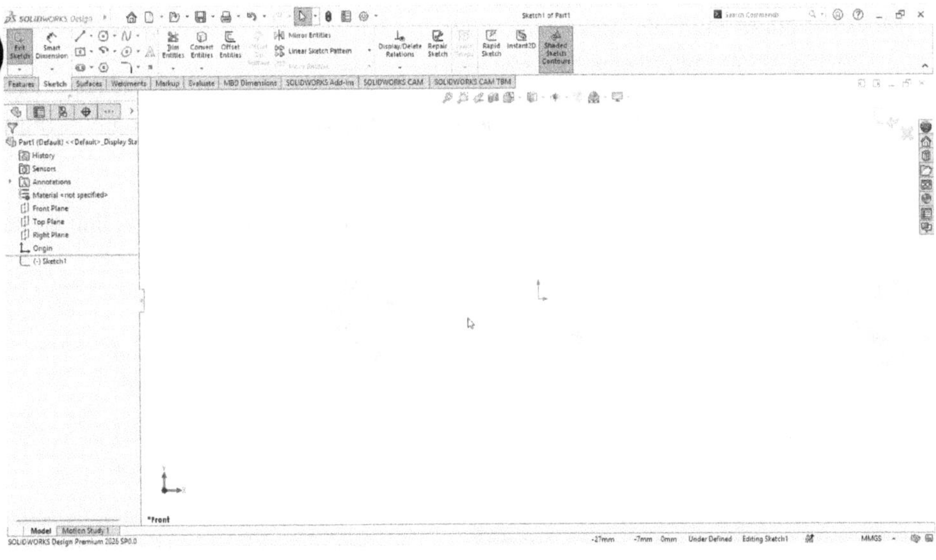

Note: In this tutorial, the display of grids and snap settings is turned off for creating the sketch by specifying points arbitrarily in the drawing area.

Section 4: Drawing the Sketch

1. Click on the **Line** tool in the **Sketch CommandManager**. The **Line** tool gets activated and the **Insert Line PropertyManager** appears on the left of the drawing area. Also, the appearance of the cursor changes to the line cursor.

2. Move the cursor to the origin and then click to specify the start point of the line when the cursor snaps to the origin.

3. Move the cursor horizontally toward the right and then click to specify the endpoint of the line when the length of the line appears close to 100 mm near the cursor, see Figure 2.27.

4. Move the cursor vertically upward and then click the left mouse button when the length of the line appears close to 20 mm near the cursor, see Figure 2.28.

2.27

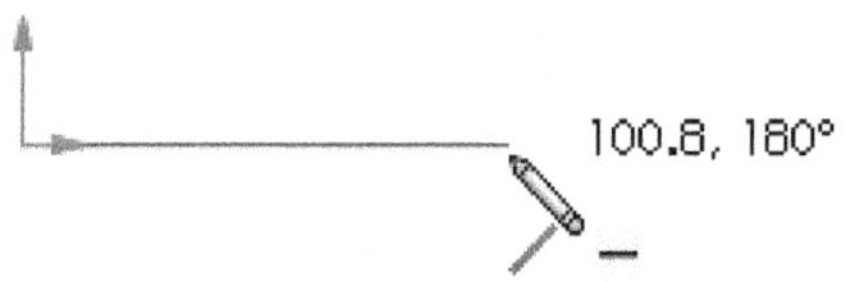

2.28

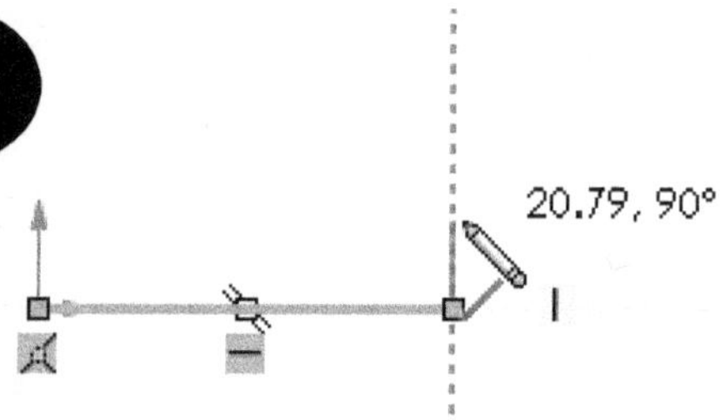

5. Move the cursor horizontally toward the left and then click when the length of the line appears close to 20 mm.

6. Move the cursor vertically downward and then click when the length of the line appears close to 13 mm near the cursor, see Figure 2.29.

7. Move the cursor horizontally toward the left and then click when the length of the line appears close to 15 mm.

8. Move the cursor vertically upward and then click when the length of the line appears close to 8 mm, see Figure 2.30.

2.29

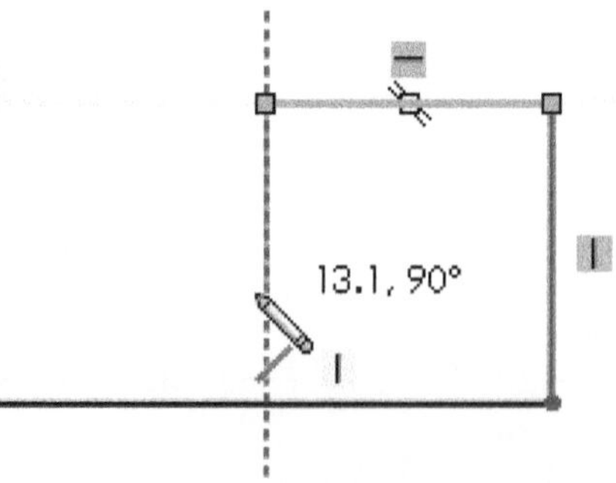

2.30

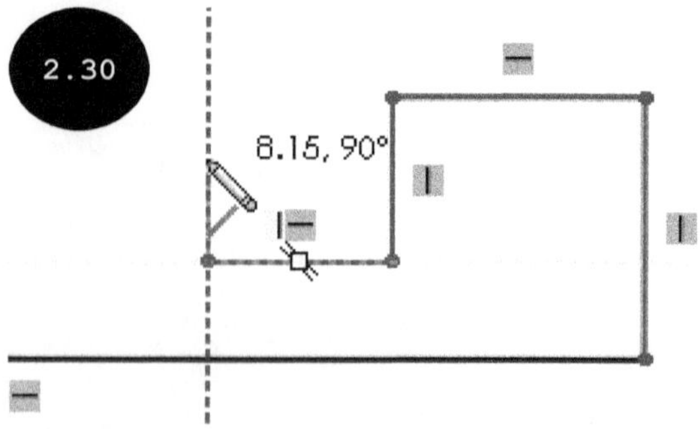

9. Move the cursor horizontally toward the left and then click when the length of the line appears close to 30 mm.

10. Move the cursor vertically downward and then click when the length of the line appears close to 8 mm, see Figure 2.31.

2.31

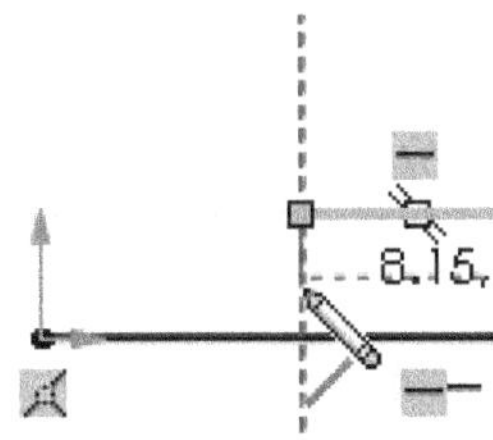

11. Similarly, draw the remaining sketch entities. Figure 2.32 shows the sketch after all the sketch entities have been drawn.

12. Right-click in the drawing area. A shortcut menu appears. In this shortcut menu, click on the **Select** option to exit the **Line** tool.

Tip: In Figure 2.32, the display of automatically applied relations such as horizontal and vertical is turned off. To turn on or off the display of relations in the drawing area, click on **Hide/Show Items > View Sketch Relations** in the **View (Heads-Up)** toolbar, see Figure 2.33.

2.32

2.33

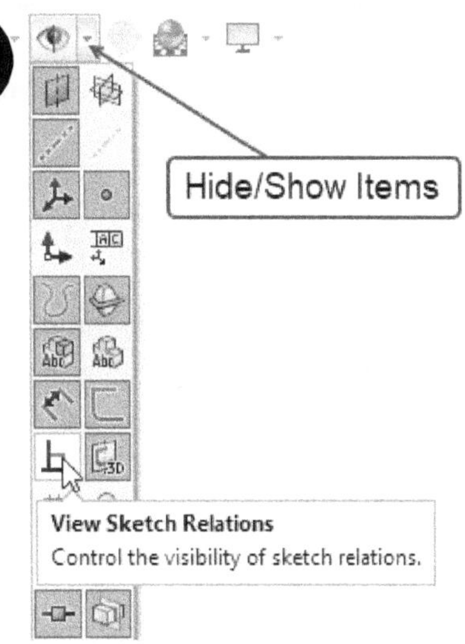

13. Click on the **Save** tool in the **Standard** toolbar. The **Save As** dialog box appears. Next, browse to the local drive of your system and create a folder with the name **SOLIDWORKS**. Next, create another folder with the name **Chapter 2** in the SOLIDWORKS folder.

14. Enter **Tutorial 1** in the **File name** field of the dialog box and then click on the **Save** button. The sketch is saved in the specified location.

Hands-on Test Drive 1

Draw a sketch of the model shown in Figure 2.34. The dimensions and the 3D model shown in the figure are for your reference only. You will learn about applying dimensions and creating 3D models in later chapters. All dimensions are in mm.

2.34

Drawing an Arc by using the Line Tool

In SOLIDWORKS, you can draw a tangent arc using the **Tangent Arc** tool, which is covered later in this chapter. In addition to this tool, it is also possible to draw a tangent arc using the **Line** tool. However, for this method to work, at least one line or arc entity must already be drawn in the drawing area. The method for drawing a tangent arc using the **Line** tool is discussed below:

1. Invoke the **Line** tool and then draw a line by specifying two points in the drawing area. Once the line is drawn, do not exit the **Line** tool. 

2. Move the cursor to a distance and then move it back to the last specified point. An orange-colored dot appears in the drawing area, see Figure 2.35.

3. Move the cursor away from the point. The arc mode is activated and a preview of a tangent arc appears in the drawing area, see Figure 2.36.

2.35

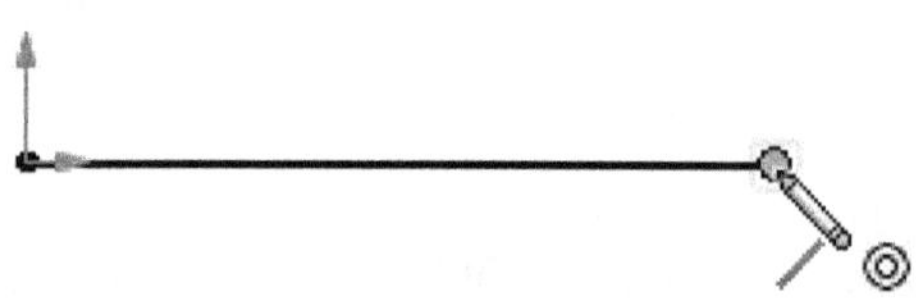

2.36

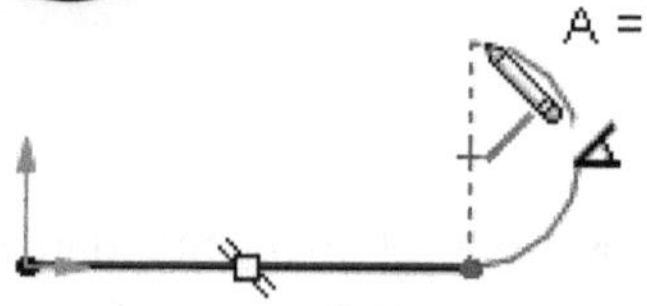

Note: The tangency of arc depends upon how you move the cursor from the last specified point in the drawing area. Figure 2.37 shows the possible movements of the cursor and the creation of arcs in the respective movements.

2.37

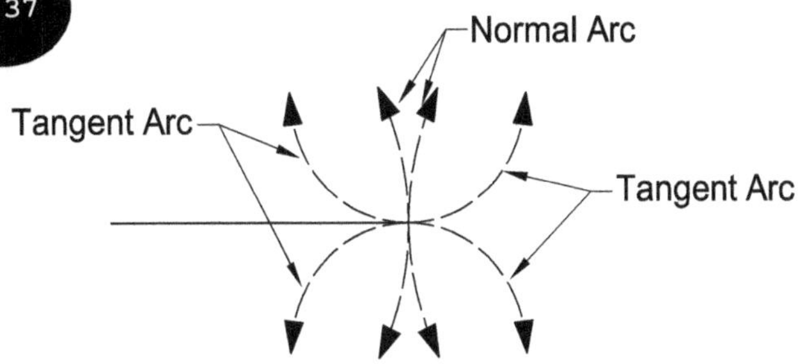

4. Click the left mouse button to specify the endpoint of the arc when the angle and radius values appear close to the required values. An arc is drawn, and the line mode is activated again. You can continue with the creation of line entities or move the cursor back to the last specified point to invoke the arc mode for drawing an arc.

5. Once you have created all entities, right-click in the drawing area and then click on the **Select** option in the shortcut menu that appears to exit the **Line** tool.

Tutorial 2

Draw a sketch of the model shown in Figure 2.38 using the **Line** tool. The dimensions and the 3D model shown in this figure are for your reference only. All dimensions are in mm. You will learn about applying dimensions and creating 3D models in later chapters.

2.38

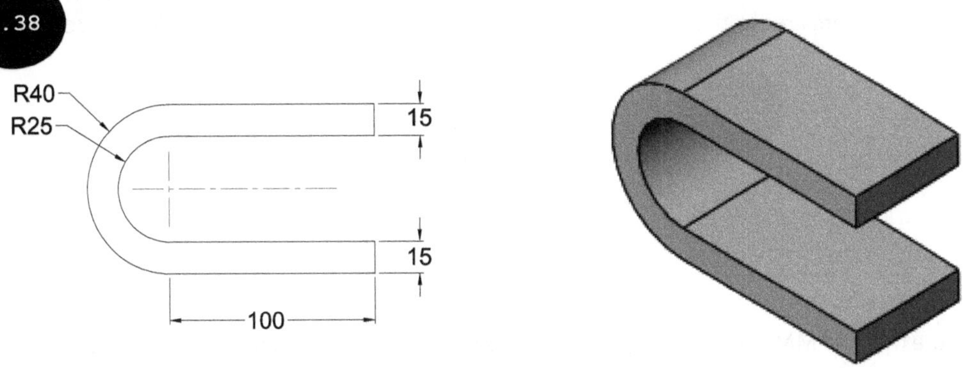

Section 1: Invoking the Part Modeling Environment

1. Start SOLIDWORKS by double-clicking on the SOLIDWORKS icon on your desktop, if not started already. The startup user interface of SOLIDWORKS appears along with the **Welcome** dialog box, see Figure 2.39.

2.39

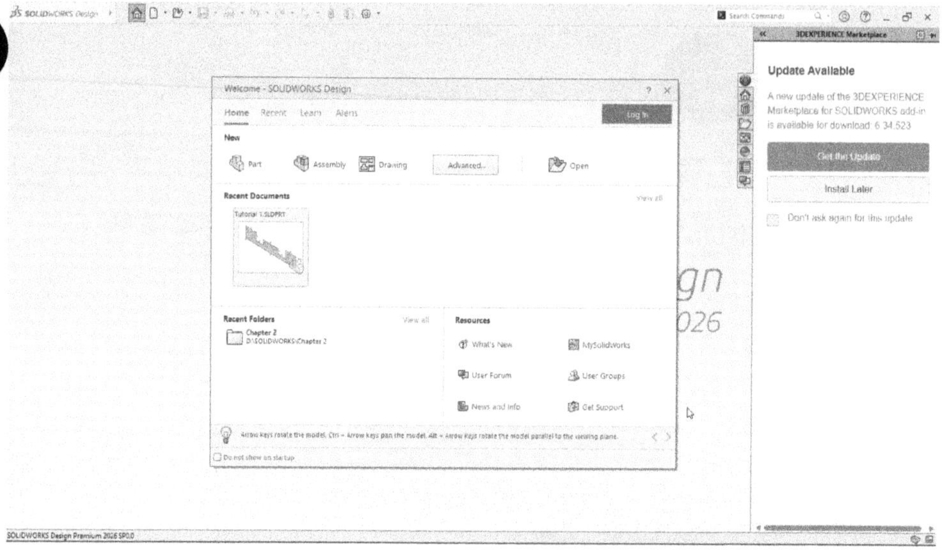

Note: If SOLIDWORKS is already open and the **Welcome** dialog box does not appear on the screen, you can invoke it by clicking the **Welcome to SOLIDWORKS** tool in the **Standard** toolbar.

2. Click on the **Part** button in the **Welcome** dialog box. The Part modeling environment is invoked.

Section 2: Specifying Unit Settings

1. Move the cursor toward the lower right corner of the screen over the Status Bar and then click on the **Unit System** area in the Status Bar. The **Unit System** flyout appears, see Figure 2.40.

2.40

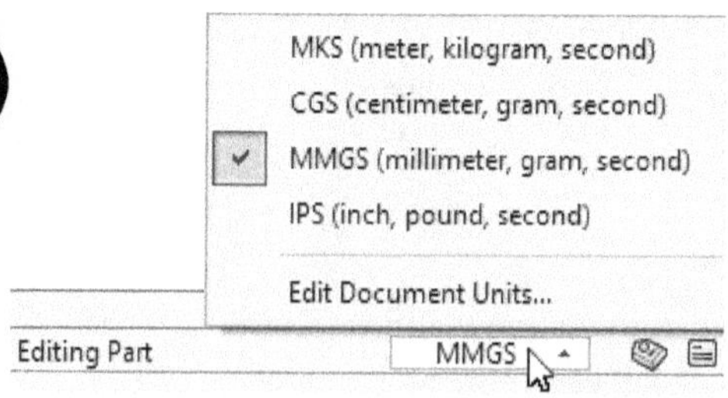

2. Ensure that the **MMGS (millimeter, gram, second)** option is tick-marked in this flyout.

Section 3: Invoking the Sketching Environment

1. Click on the **Sketch** tab in the CommandManager, see Figure 2.41. The tools of the **Sketch CommandManager** appear.

2. Click on the **Sketch** tool in the **Sketch CommandManager**, see Figure 2.41. Three default planes that are mutually perpendicular to each other appear in the graphics area.

2.41

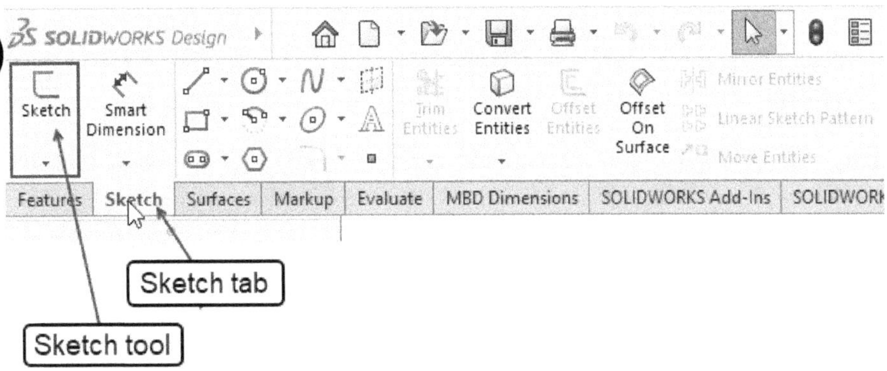

3. Move the cursor over the Front plane and then click when the boundary of the plane is highlighted. The Sketching environment is invoked and the Front plane is orientated normal to the viewing direction, see Figure 2.42.

2.42

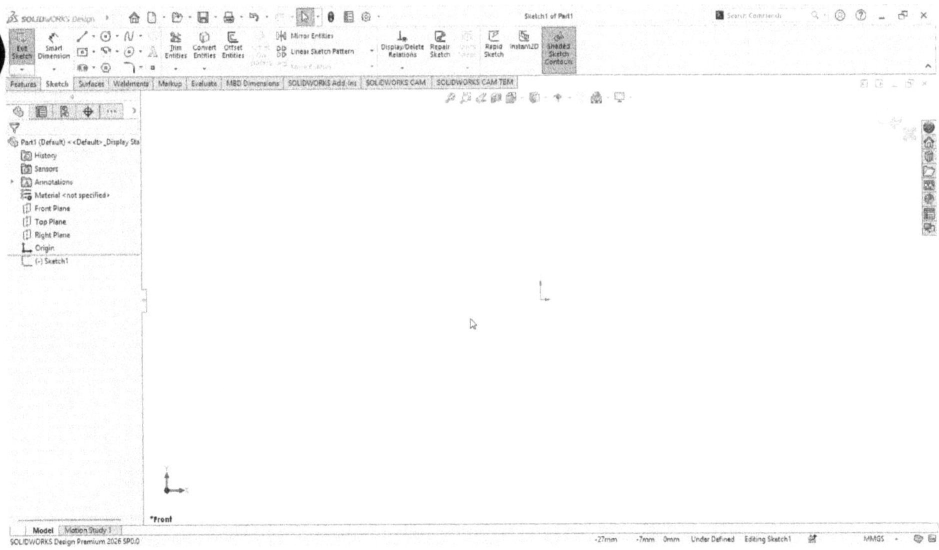

Note: It is evident from Figure 2.38 that all the sketch entities are multiples of 5 mm. Therefore, you can set the snap settings to ensure that the cursor snaps to increments of 5 mm only.

Section 4: Specifying Grids and Snap Settings

1. Click on the **Options** tool in the **Standard** toolbar. The **System Options - General** dialog box appears.

2. Click on the **Document Properties** tab in the dialog box. The name of the dialog box changes to **Document Properties - Drafting Standard.**

3. Click on the **Grid/Snap** option in the left panel of the dialog box. The options for grids and snap settings appear on the right panel of the dialog box. Also, the name of the dialog box changes to **Document Properties - Grid/Snap.**

4. Enter **20** in the **Major grid spacing** field, **4** in the **Minor -lines per major** field, and **1** in the **Snap points per minor** field of the **Grid** area in the dialog box.

5. Select the **Display grid** check box in the **Grid** area of the dialog box to turn on the display of grids in the drawing area based on the grid settings specified in the above step.

6. Click on the **Go To System Snaps** button in the **Document Properties - Grid/Snap** dialog box. The name of the dialog box changes to **System Options - Relations/Snaps.**

7. Select the **Grid** check box in the **Sketch snaps** area of the dialog box to turn on the snap mode.

8. Click on the **OK** button in the dialog box. The grids and snap settings have been specified and the dialog box is closed. Also, the drawing area appears similar to the one shown in Figure 2.43.

2.43

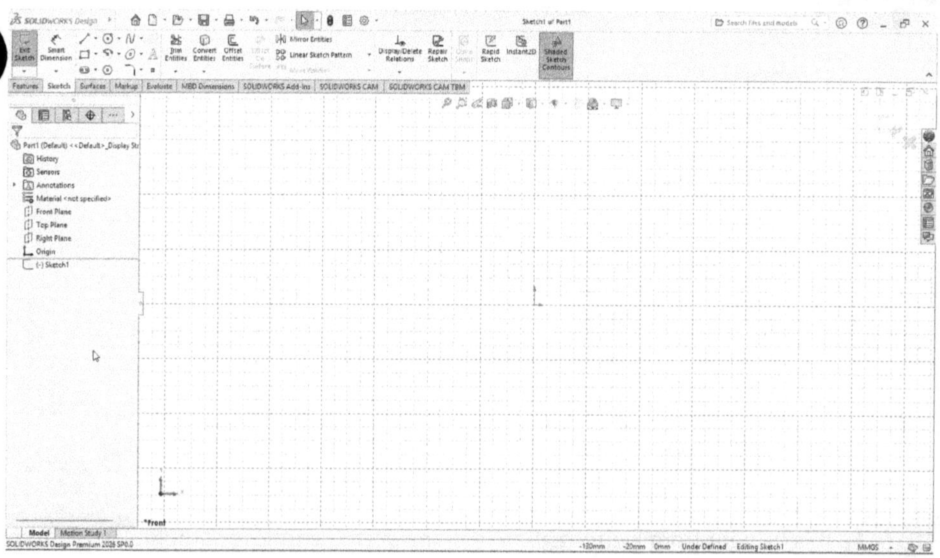

Once the units, grids, and snap settings have been specified, you can start creating the sketch by using the **Line** tool.

Section 5: Drawing the Sketch

1. Click on the **Line** tool in the **Sketch CommandManager**. The **Line** tool gets activated and the **Insert Line PropertyManager** appears on the left of the drawing area. Also, the appearance of the cursor changes to the line cursor.

2. Move the cursor to the origin and click to specify the start point of the line when the cursor snaps to the origin.

3. Move the cursor horizontally toward the left and then click to specify the second point of the line when the length of the line appears as 100 mm near the cursor, see Figure 2.44. Notice that when you move the cursor in the drawing area, it snaps gradually to an incremental distance of 5 mm.

4. Move the cursor to a distance and then move it back to the last specified point. An orange-colored dot appears in the drawing area, see Figure 2.45.

2.44
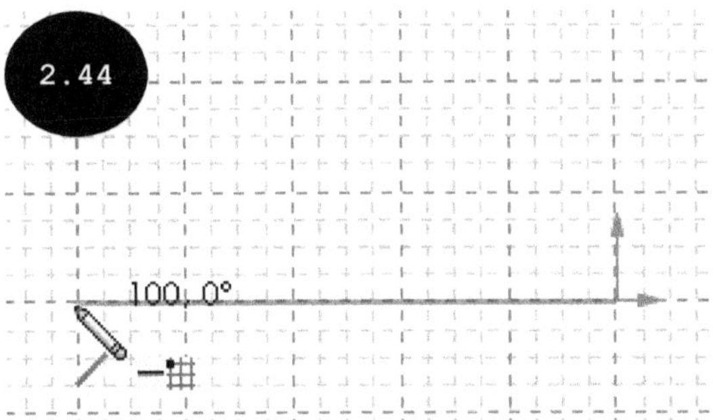

2.45
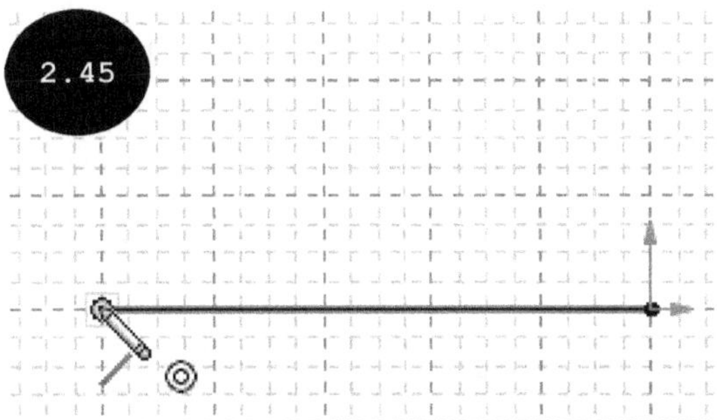

5. Move the cursor horizontally toward the left to a distance and then move it vertically upward. The arc mode is activated and the preview of the tangent arc appears in the drawing area, see Figure 2.46.

6. Click to specify the endpoint of the tangent arc when the angle and radius values of the arc appear as 180 degrees and 40 mm, respectively near the cursor, see Figure 2.47. The tangent arc is created, and the preview of a line appears attached to the cursor.

2.46
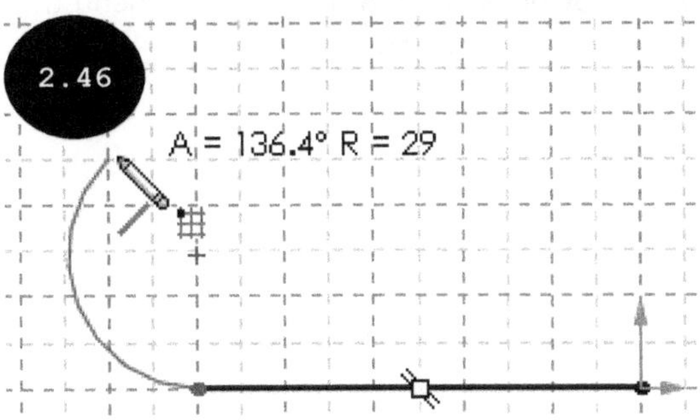

2.47
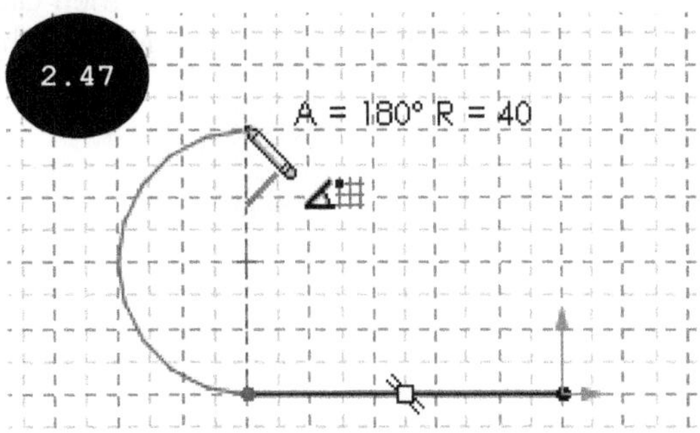

7. Move the cursor horizontally toward the right and click when the length of the line appears as 100 mm near the cursor.

8. Move the cursor vertically downward and click when the length of the line appears as 15 mm.

9. Move the cursor horizontally toward the left and click when the length of the line appears as 100 mm.

10. Move the cursor to a distance and then move it back to the last specified point. An orange-colored dot appears in the drawing area, see Figure 2.48.

11. Move the cursor horizontally toward the left to a distance and then move it vertically downward. The arc mode is activated, and the preview of the tangent arc appears in the drawing area, see Figure 2.49.

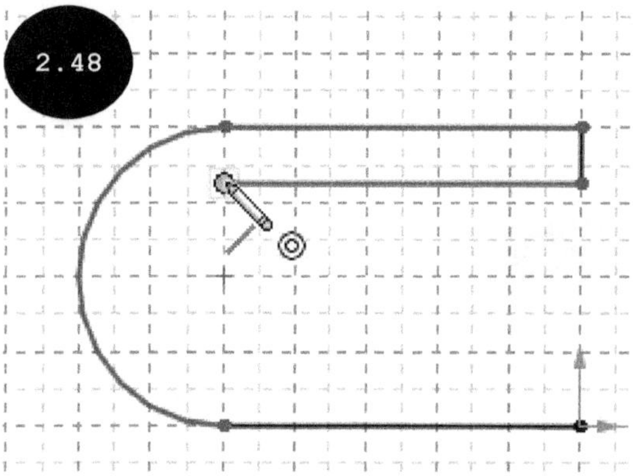

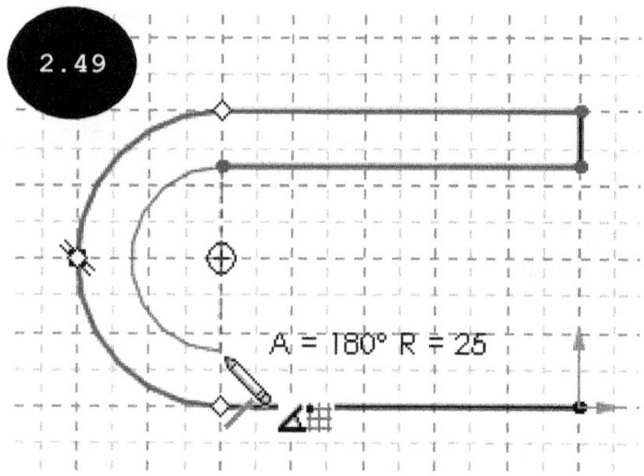

12. Click to specify the endpoint of the tangent arc when the angle and radius values of the arc appear as 180 degrees and 25 mm, respectively, refer to Figure 2.49. The tangent arc is created and the line mode is activated.

13. Move the cursor horizontally toward the right and then click when the length of the line appears as 100 mm near the cursor.

14. Move the cursor vertically downward and then click when the cursor snaps to the start point of the first sketch entity.

15. Right-click in the drawing area and then click on the **Select** option in the shortcut menu that appears to exit the **Line** tool. The final sketch is drawn, see Figure 2.50.

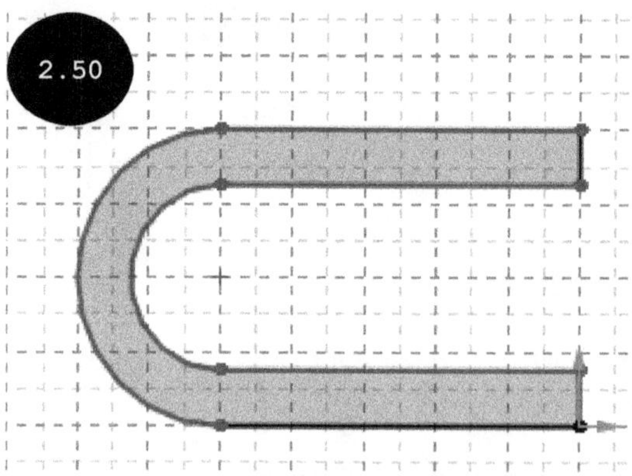

16. Click on the **Save** tool in the **Standard** toolbar. The **Save As** dialog box appears. Next, browse to the Chapter 2 folder of the SOLIDWORKS folder. You need to create these folders in the local drive of your system, if not created earlier.

17. Enter **Tutorial 2** in the **File name** field of the dialog box and then click on the **Save** button. The sketch is saved in the specified location.

Hands-on Test Drive 2

Draw a sketch of the model shown in Figure 2.51. The dimensions and the 3D model shown in the figure are for your reference only. Draw all entities of the sketch by using the **Line** tool. As all the dimensions of the sketch are multiples of 5 mm, you can set the snap settings such that the cursor snaps to an increment of 5 mm only. All dimensions are in mm.

2.51

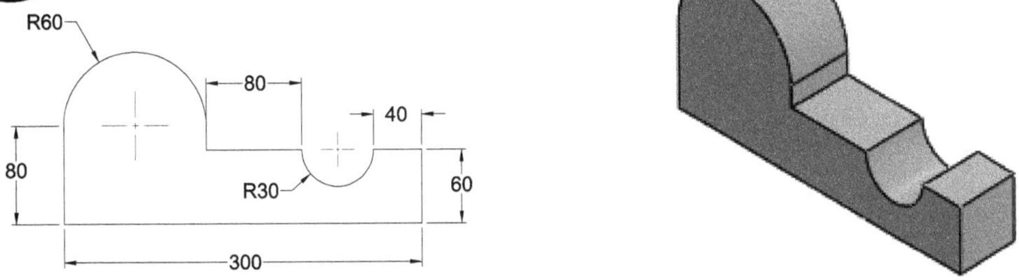

Drawing a Centerline

Centerlines are reference or construction lines used to aid in sketches. In SOLIDWORKS, you can draw a centerline using the **Centerline** tool. To do this, click the down arrow next to the **Line** tool in the **Sketch CommandManager**. The **Line** flyout appears, see Figure 2.52. In this flyout, click on the **Centerline** tool to activate it.

2.52

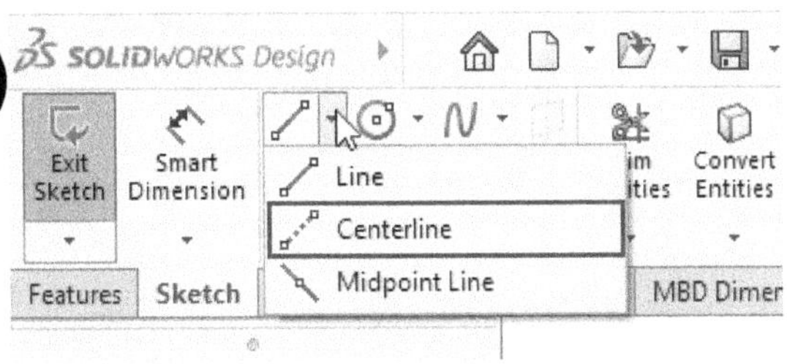

When the **Centerline** tool is activated, the **Insert Line PropertyManager** appears to the left of the drawing area, see Figure 2.53. By default, the **For construction** check box is selected, allowing you to draw construction lines by specifying points in the drawing area. The options in the PropertyManager are the same as those discussed when drawing standard line entities. The method for drawing centerlines is also the same as for drawing regular lines. Figure 2.54 illustrates a horizontal centerline drawn by specifying two points in the drawing area.

2.53

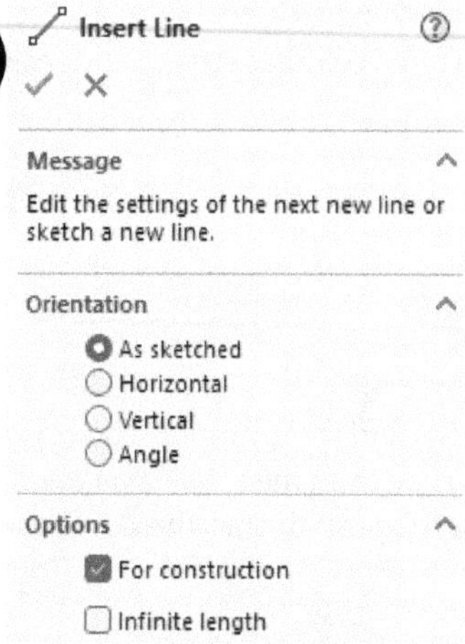

2.54

Drawing a Midpoint Line

A midpoint line is created symmetrically about its midpoint. In SOLIDWORKS, you draw midpoint lines using the **Midpoint Line** tool. To activate the **Midpoint Line** tool, click the arrow next to the **Line** tool in the **Sketch CommandManager**, then click on the **Midpoint Line** tool in the flyout that appears, see Figure 2.55. The **Midpoint Line** tool activates, and the **Insert Line PropertyManager** appears to the left of the drawing area, see Figure 2.56. In this PropertyManager, the **Midpoint Line** check box is selected by default, enabling you to create a midpoint line by specifying points in the drawing area.

2.55

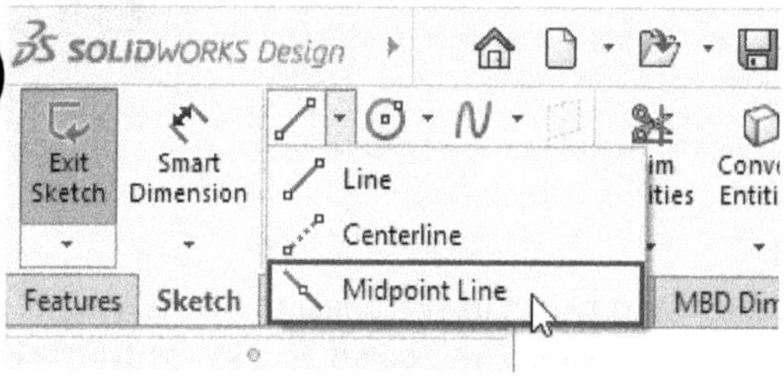

2.56

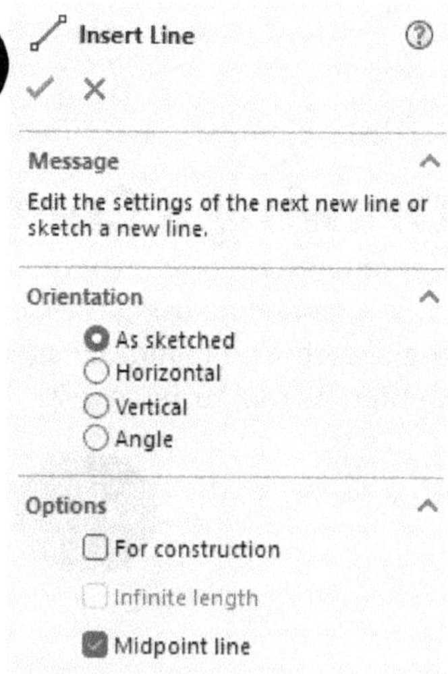

After activating the **Midpoint Line** tool, click to specify the midpoint of the line in the drawing area. Then, move the cursor to the required location to define the endpoint of the line. As you move the cursor, a preview of a line, symmetrical about the specified midpoint, appears, see Figure 2.57. Finally, click to specify the endpoint of the line. The midpoint line is created.

2.57

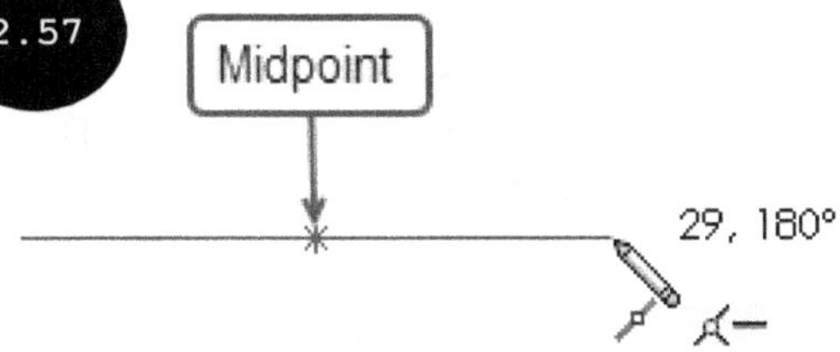

Drawing a Rectangle

In SOLIDWORKS, you can draw a rectangle using different methods with the tools in the **Rectangle** flyout of the **Sketch CommandManager**, see Figure 2.58. To access the **Rectangle** flyout, click on the arrow next to the active rectangle tool in the **Sketch CommandManager**, see Figure 2.58. The tools for drawing a rectangle are discussed next.

2.58

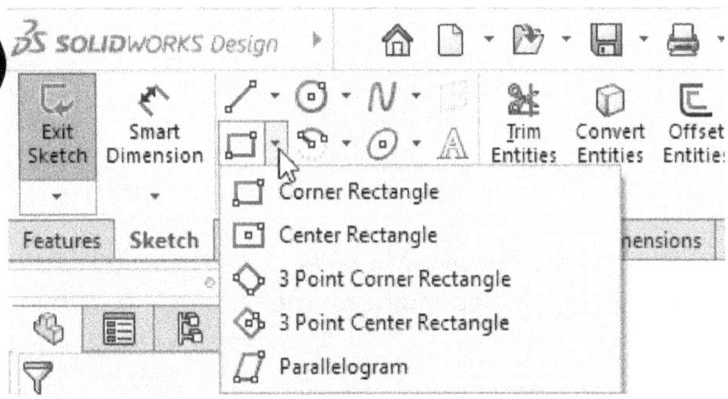

Corner Rectangle Tool

The **Corner Rectangle** tool is used to draw a rectangle by specifying its two diagonally opposite corners. The first corner defines the position of the rectangle, while the second corner defines the length and width of the rectangle, see Figure 2.59.

2.59

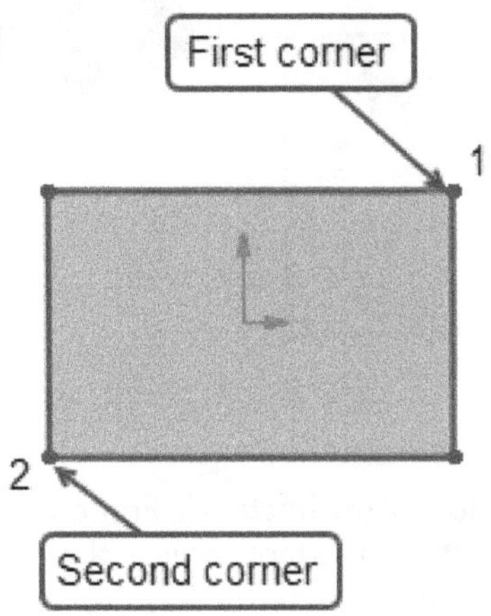

To create a rectangle using the **Corner Rectangle** tool, click on the **Corner Rectangle** tool in the **Sketch CommandManager**, see Figure 2.60. The **Corner Rectangle** tool gets activated and the **Rectangle PropertyManager** appears to the left of the drawing area, see Figure 2.61. Next, click to specify two diagonally opposite corners one by one in the drawing area, refer to Figure 2.59. A rectangle is created. The options in the **Rectangle PropertyManager** are discussed next.

2.60

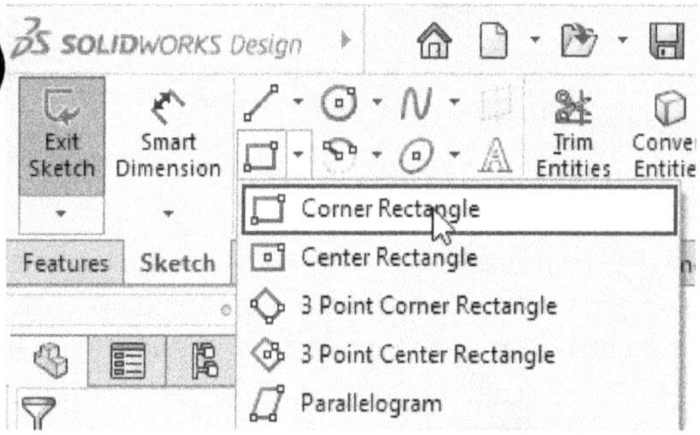

2.61

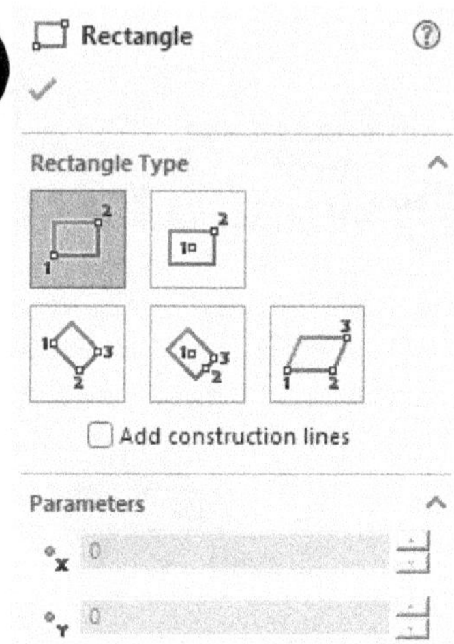

Rectangle Type

The **Rectangle Type** rollout of the PropertyManager is used to switch between different rectangle tools for drawing a rectangle. By default, depending on the rectangle tool invoked, the respective button is activated in this rollout.

The **Add Construction Lines** check box in the **Rectangle Type** rollout is used to add construction lines to the rectangle. When you select this check box, two radio buttons, **From Corners** and **From Midpoints**, become available, refer to Figure 2.61. By selecting the **From Corners** radio button, construction lines will be added to connect the diagonally opposite corners of the rectangle, see Figure 2.62. On the other hand, by selecting the **From Midpoints** radio button, construction lines will be added to connect the midpoints of the rectangle's line segments, see Figure 2.63.

2.62

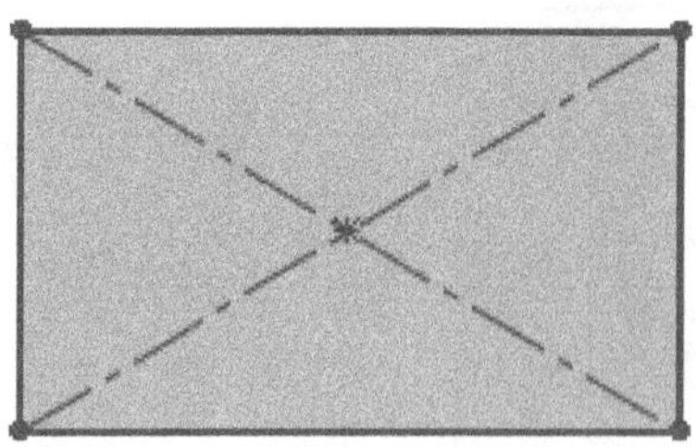

2.63

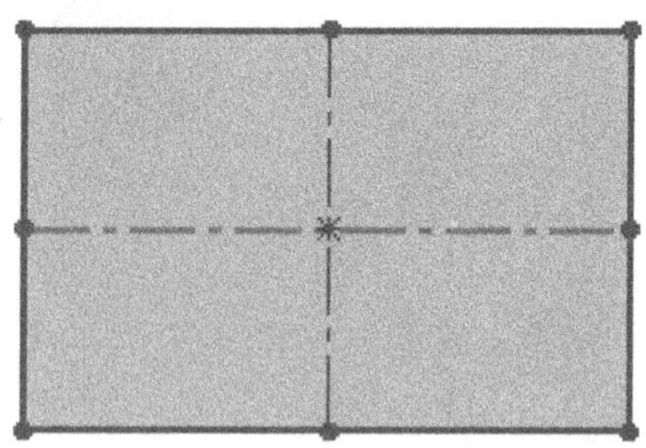

Parameters

The options in the **Parameters** rollout of the **Rectangle PropertyManager** are used to display or control the parameters of the rectangle. It is important to note that all the options in this rollout become enabled once the rectangle is drawn and selected in the drawing area. This allows you to modify various dimensions and other properties of the rectangle after it has been created.

Center Rectangle Tool

The **Center Rectangle** tool is used to draw a rectangle by specifying its center point and a corner point, see Figure 2.64. To do this, invoke the **Rectangle** flyout and then click on the **Center Rectangle** tool. Next, click to specify the center point and a corner point of the rectangle in the drawing area. The rectangle gets created.

2.64

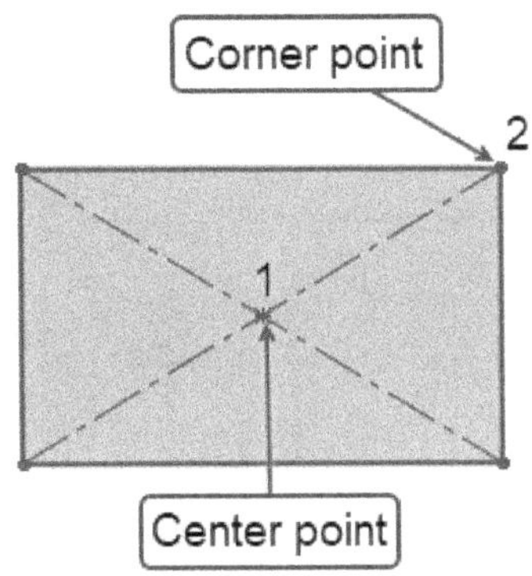

3 Point Corner Rectangle Tool

The **3 Point Corner Rectangle** tool is used to draw a rectangle by specifying three corners. To do this, invoke the **Rectangle** flyout and then click on the **3 Point Corner Rectangle** tool. Next, click to specify three corner points of the rectangle in the drawing area one by one, see Figure 2.65. The rectangle gets created. The first two corners define the width and orientation of the rectangle, and the third corner defines the length of the rectangle.

3 Point Center Rectangle Tool

The **3 Point Center Rectangle** tool of the **Rectangle** flyout is used to draw a rectangle by specifying three points, see Figure 2.66. The first point defines the center of the rectangle, the second point defines the width and orientation of the rectangle, and the third point defines the length of the rectangle.

2.65

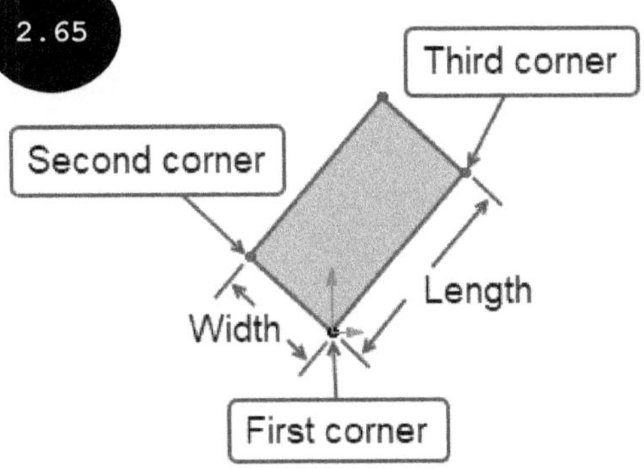

2.66

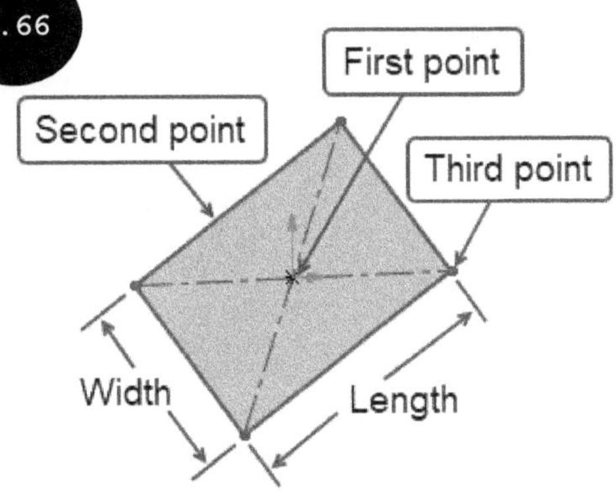

Parallelogram Tool

The **Parallelogram** tool is used to draw a parallelogram, where the adjacent sides are not perpendicular to each other. To do this, invoke the **Rectangle** flyout and then click on the **Parallelogram** tool. Then, click to specify three points in the drawing area one by one, refer to Figure 2.67. The first two points define the width and orientation of the parallelogram, while the third point defines the length and the angle between the sides of the parallelogram.

2.67

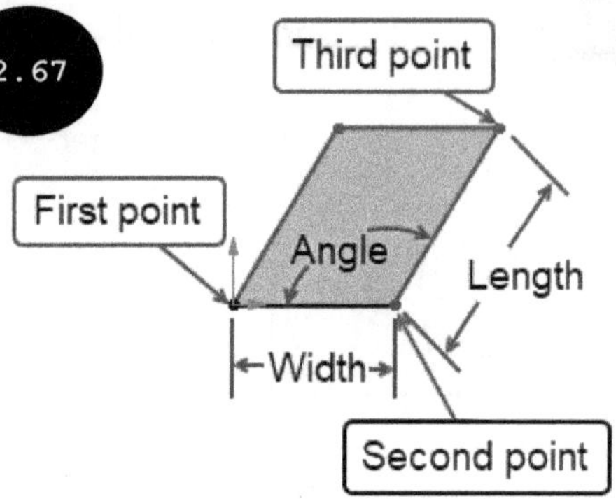

Drawing a Circle

In SOLIDWORKS, you can draw a circle using the **Circle** and **Perimeter Circle** tools available in the **Circle** flyout of the **Sketch CommandManager**, see Figure 2.68. To access the **Circle** flyout, click on the arrow next to an active circle tool in the **Sketch CommandManager**, see Figure 2.68. The tools for drawing a circle are discussed next.

2.68

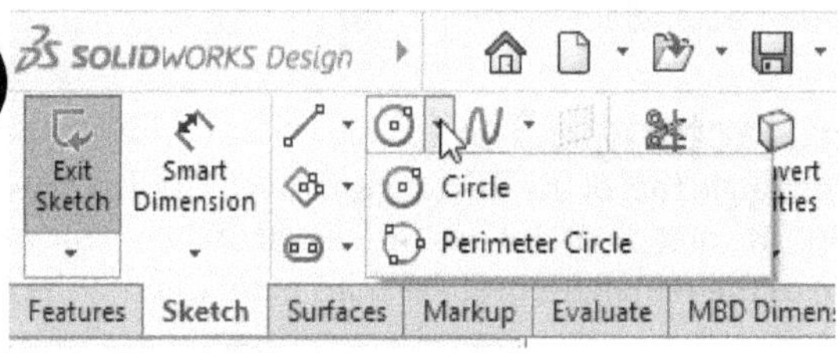

Circle Tool

The **Circle** tool is used to draw a circle by specifying its center point and a point on its circumference, see Figure 2.69.

2.69

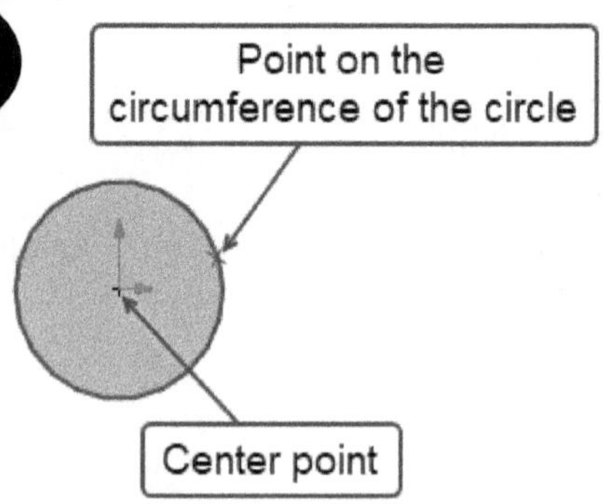

Perimeter Circle Tool

The **Perimeter Circle** tool is used to draw a circle by specifying three points on its circumference, see Figure 2.70.

2.70

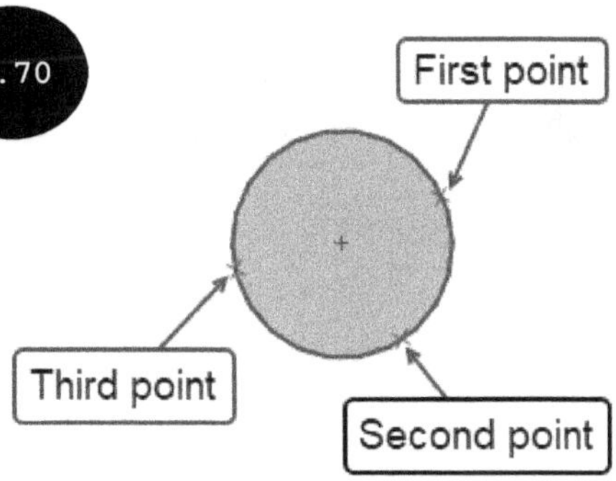

Tip: You can also convert a circle into a construction circle. To do this, select the circle in the drawing area. The **Circle PropertyManager** and a Pop-up toolbar appear. Select the **For construction** check box in the **Options** rollout of the **Circle PropertyManager.** The selected circle converts into a construction circle. Alternatively, click on the **Construction Geometry** tool in the Pop-up toolbar to convert the circle into a construction circle.

Drawing an Arc

In SOLIDWORKS, you can draw an arc using different methods with the tools in the **Arc** flyout of the **Sketch CommandManager**, see Figure 2.71. To access the **Arc** flyout, click on the arrow next to the active arc tool in the **Sketch CommandManager**, see Figure 2.71. The tools for drawing an arc are discussed next.

Centerpoint Arc Tool

The **Centerpoint Arc** tool of the **Arc** flyout is used to draw an arc by defining its center point, start point, and endpoint one by one in the drawing area, see Figure 2.72.

2.71

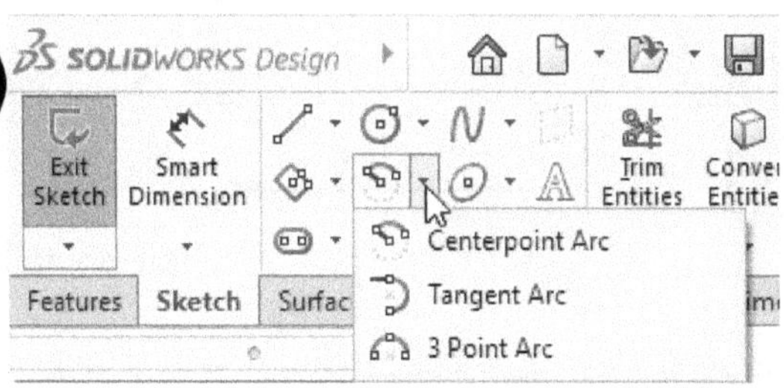

2.72

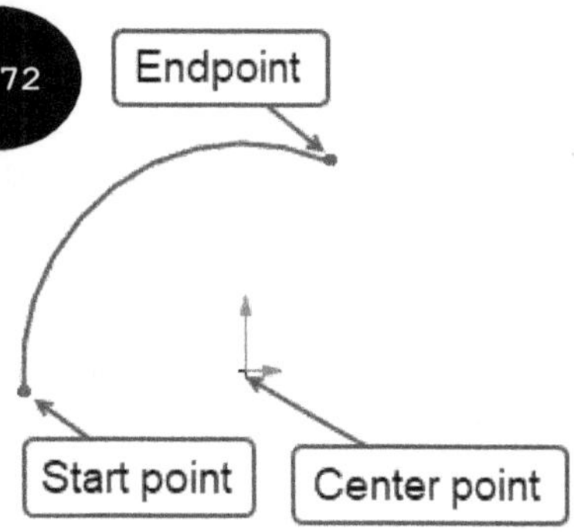

3 Point Arc Tool

The **3 Point Arc** tool of the **Arc** flyout is used to draw an arc by defining three points on its arc length one by one in the drawing area, see Figure 2.73.

2.73

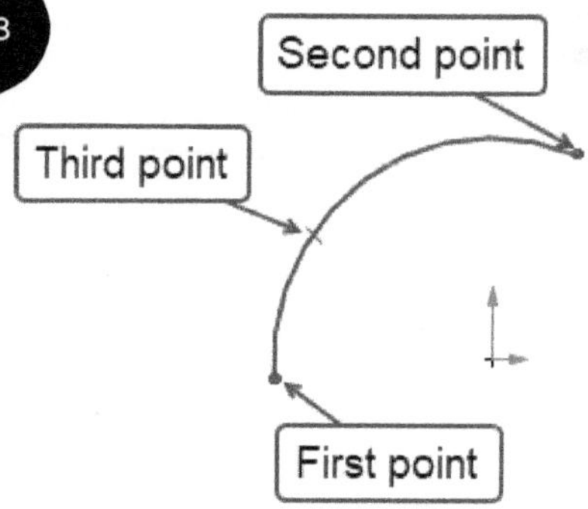

Tangent Arc Tool

The **Tangent Arc** tool is used to draw an arc tangent to an existing entity, see Figure 2.74. You can draw an arc tangent to a line, an arc, or a spline entity using this tool.

To draw a tangent arc, invoke the **Arc** flyout and click on the **Tangent Arc** tool. Then, move the cursor to the endpoint of an existing entity (such as a line, arc, or spline) in the drawing area. Click to specify the start point of the tangent arc when the cursor snaps to it. A preview of a tangent arc appears in the drawing area, with its endpoint attached to the cursor. Move the cursor in the desired direction and click to specify the endpoint of the tangent arc in the drawing area, see Figure 2.75. An arc tangent to the existing entity is drawn.

2.74

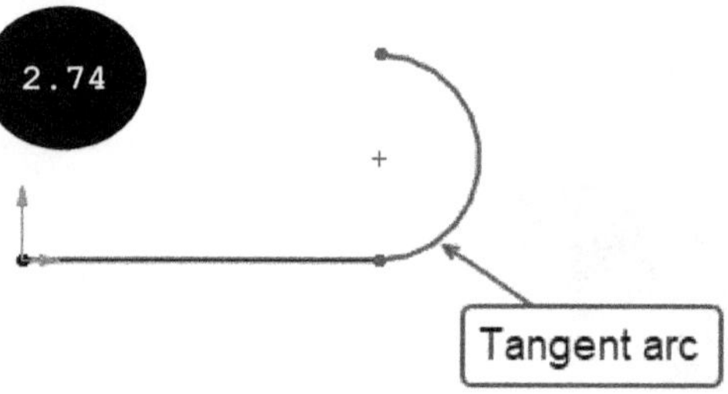

2.75

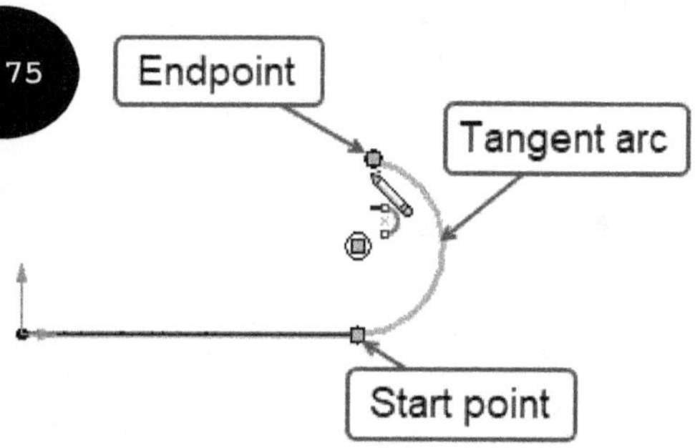

Note that the **Tangent Arc** tool remains activated, allowing you to continue creating tangent arcs one after another by clicking the left mouse button. Once you have finished drawing the tangent arcs, right-click in the drawing area and select the **Select** option from the shortcut menu to exit the tool.

Note: The tangency of arc depends upon how you move the cursor from the specified start point in the drawing area. Figure 2.76 shows the possible movements of the cursor and the creation of arcs in the respective movements.

2.76

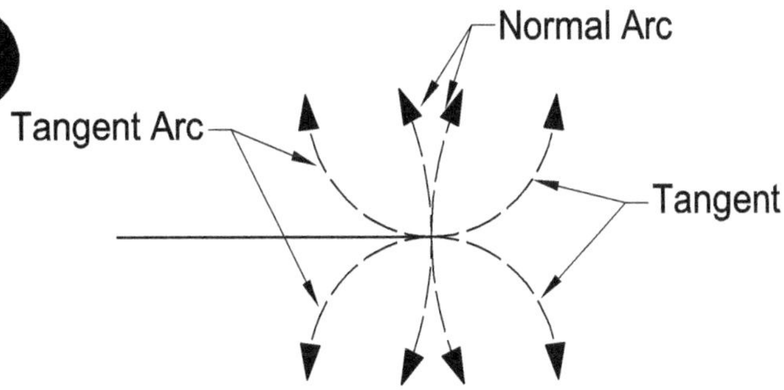

Drawing a Polygon

A polygon is a multi-sided geometry where all sides have equal length and all angles are equal, see Figure 2.77. In SOLIDWORKS, you can draw a polygon of sides ranging from 3 to 40.

To draw a polygon, click on the **Polygon** tool in the **Sketch CommandManager**. The **Polygon PropertyManager** appears, see Figure 2.78. The options in this PropertyManager are discussed next.

2.77

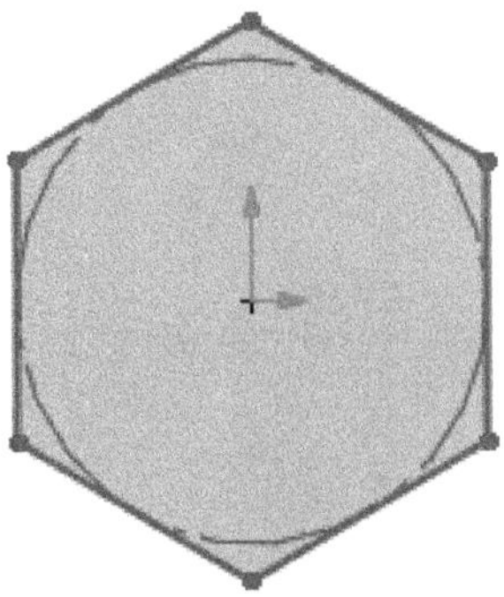

2.78

Options

By default, the **For construction** check box is cleared in the **Options** rollout of the PropertyManager, refer to Figure 2.78. As a result, the polygon created will consist of solid sketch entities, see Figure 2.79. If you select the **For construction** check box, the resultant polygon will be created as a construction entities, see Figure 2.80.

2.79

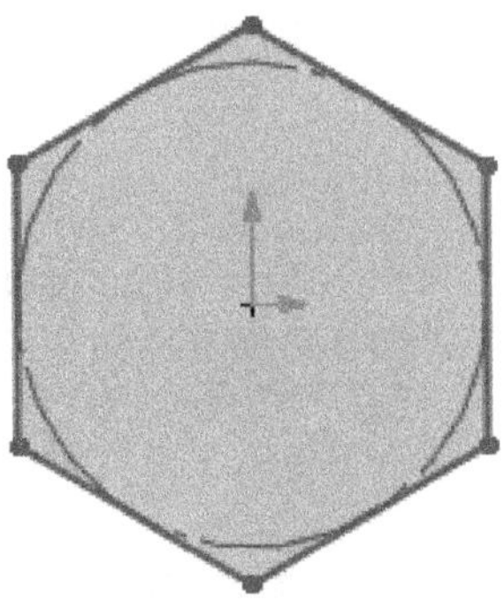

2.80

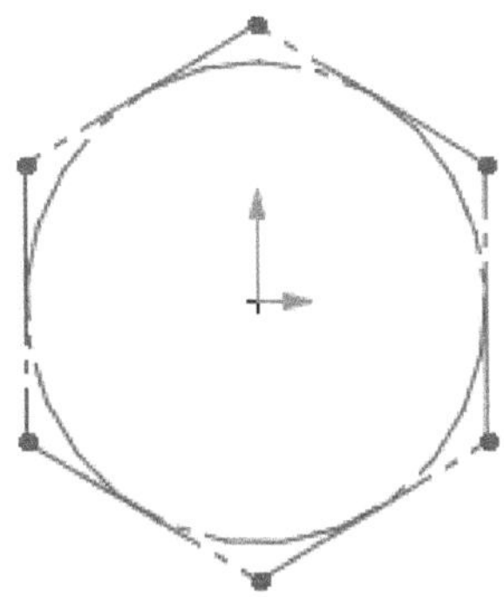

Parameters

The options in the **Parameters** rollout are used to specify parameters for creating a polygon. The options are discussed next.

Number of Sides

The **Number of Sides** field is used to specify the number of sides of the polygon. You can specify the number of sides of the polygon in the range between 3 to 40.

Inscribed circle

The **Inscribed circle** radio button is used to create a polygon by drawing an imaginary construction circle inside the polygon. In this method, the midpoints of all sides of the polygon will touch the circumference of the imaginary construction circle, see Figure 2.81.

Circumscribed circle

The **Circumscribed circle** radio button is used to create a polygon by drawing an imaginary construction circle outside the polygon. In this method, all vertices of the polygon will touch the circumference of the imaginary construction circle, see Figure 2.82.

2.81

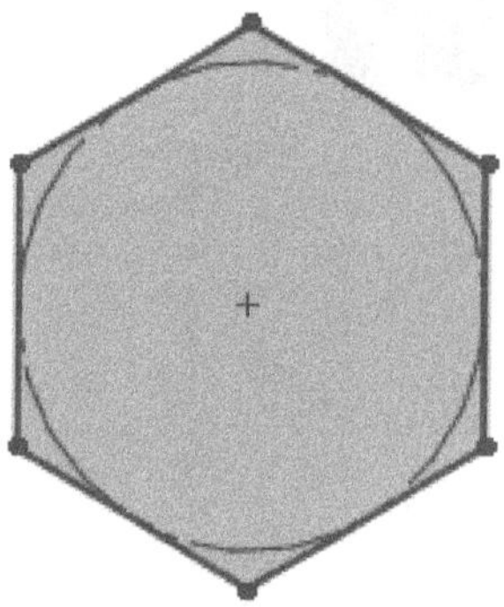

2.82

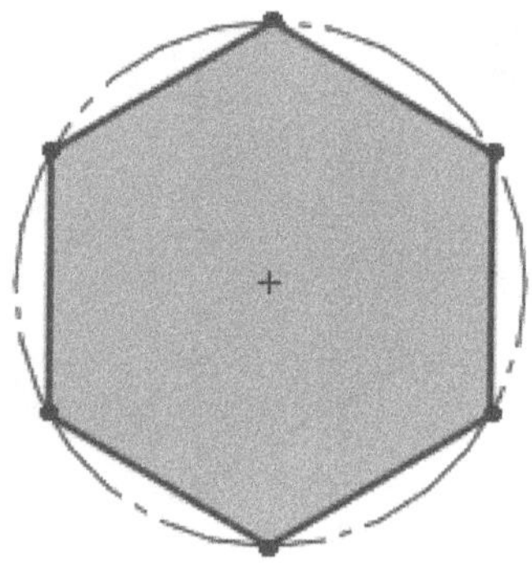

New Polygon

The **New Polygon** button is used to draw a new polygon.

When the **Polygon PropertyManager** is invoked, enter the number of sides of the polygon in the **Number of Sides** field of the PropertyManager. Then, select the required radio button, either **Inscribed circle** or **Circumscribed circle**, to create a polygon with an inscribed or circumscribed circle, as discussed above. Next, click to specify the center point of the polygon. A preview of the polygon appears. Finally, click to specify a point anywhere in the drawing area to complete the creation of the polygon with the specified number of sides.

Note: After creating a polygon, it is selected in the drawing area. Also, the current parameters of the polygon appear in the respective fields of the PropertyManager. You can modify the current parameters such as X and Y coordinate values of the center of the polygon, diameter of the imaginary construction circle, and the angle of rotation of the polygon by using the **Center X Coordinate**, **Center Y Coordinate**, **Circle Diameter**, and **Angle** fields of the PropertyManager, respectively.

Drawing a Slot

In SOLIDWORKS, you can draw both straight and arc slots by using the tools in the **Slot** flyout, see Figure 2.83. To access the **Slot** flyout, click on the arrow next to the active slot tool in the **Sketch CommandManager**, see Figure 2.83. The tools for drawing slots are discussed next.

2.83

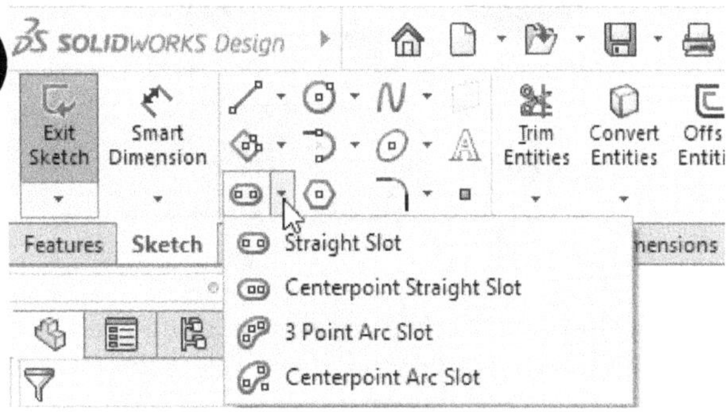

Straight Slot Tool

The **Straight Slot** tool is used to create a straight slot by specifying its start point, endpoint, and a point to define its width, see Figure 2.84. To draw a straight slot, click on the **Straight Slot** tool in the **Slot** flyout. The **Slot PropertyManager** appears, see Figure 2.85. Next, click to specify the start point, endpoint, and a point to define the width of the slot in the drawing area one by one. A straight slot gets created. The options in the **Slot PropertyManager** are discussed next.

2.84

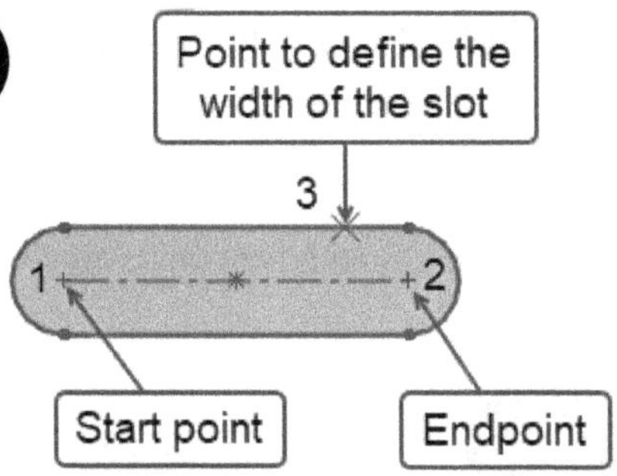

2.85

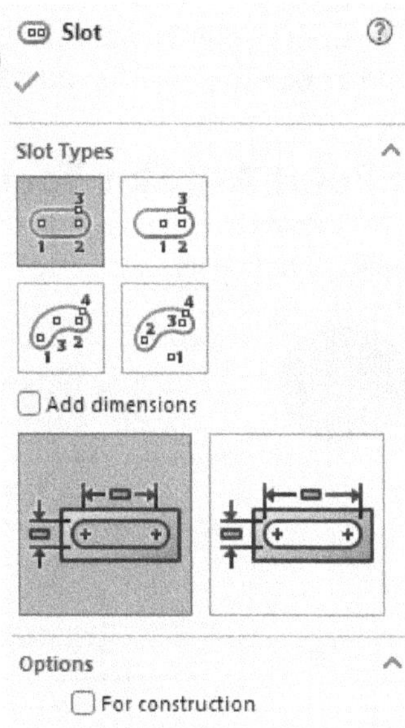

Slot Types

The **Slot Types** rollout allows you to switch between different slot tools. By default, the slot tool initially selected is activated in the **Slot Types** rollout.

The **Add dimensions** check box in the **Slot Types** rollout is cleared by default, meaning no dimensions are applied to the resultant slot. If you select this check box, dimensions will be applied to the slot when it is drawn, see Figure 2.86.

2.86

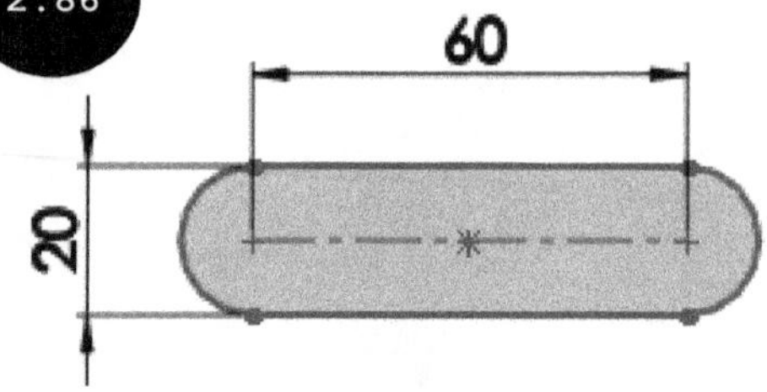

The **Center-to-Center** button in the **Slot Types** rollout is activated by default, meaning the straight slot measures the length from center to center. If you select the **Overall Length** button, the straight slot measures the overall (end-to-end) length.

Parameters

The options in the **Parameters** rollout of the PropertyManager are used to display or control the parameters of the slot. Note that the options of this rollout get enabled once the slot is drawn and is selected in the drawing area. You can modify the X and Y coordinate values of the center point of the slot, the width of the slot, and the length of the slot using the respective fields of this rollout.

Centerpoint Straight Slot Tool

The **Centerpoint Straight Slot** tool is used to draw a straight slot by specifying its center point, endpoint, and a point to define its width, see Figure 2.87.

3 Point Arc Slot Tool

The **3 Point Arc Slot** tool is used to draw an arc slot by specifying three points on its arc length and a point to define its width, see Figure 2.88.

2.87

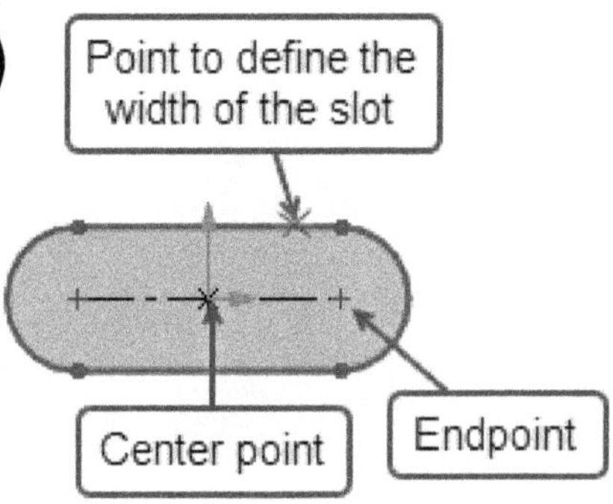

2.88

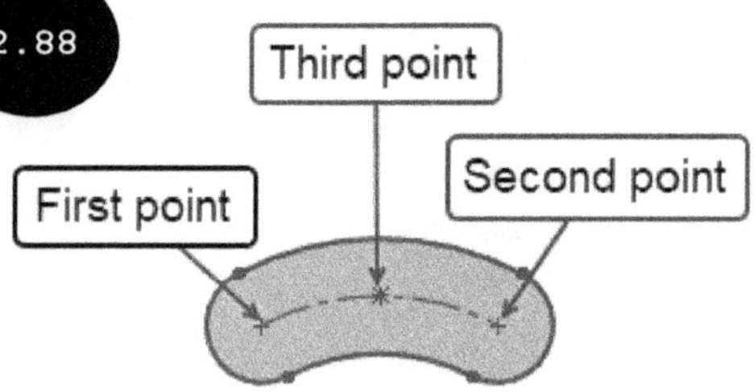

Centerpoint Arc Slot Tool

The **Centerpoint Arc Slot** tool is used to draw an arc slot by specifying its center point, start point, endpoint, and a point to define its width, see Figure 2.89.

2.89

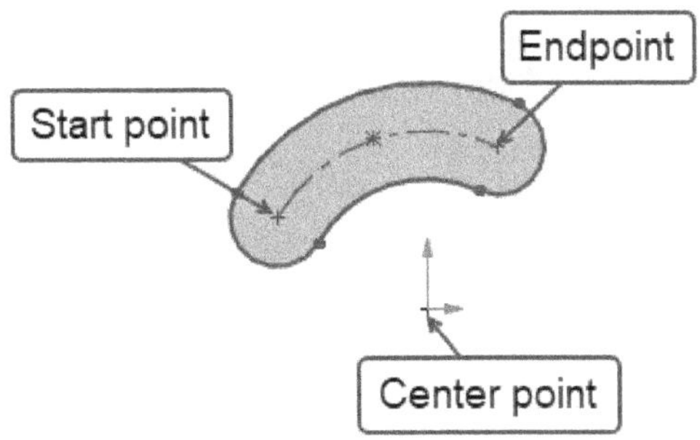

Drawing an Ellipse

An ellipse is drawn by defining its major and minor axes, see Figure 2.90. You can draw an ellipse using the **Ellipse** tool of the **Sketch CommandManager**. The method for drawing an ellipse is discussed below:

1. Click on the **Ellipse** tool in the **Sketch CommandManager**. The **Ellipse** tool gets activated and the **Ellipse PropertyManager** appears.

2.90

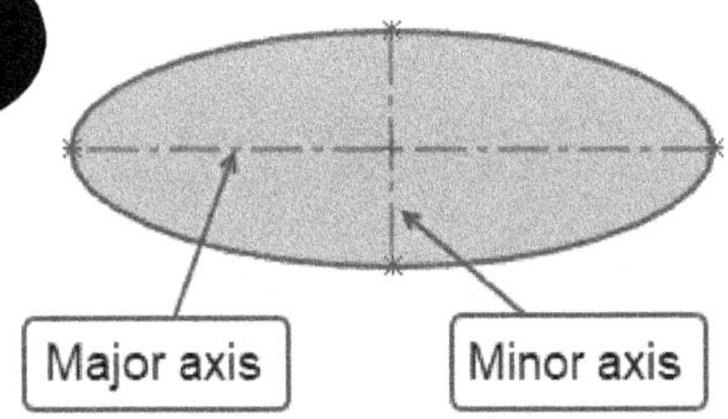

2. Select the **Add construction** check box in the **Options** rollout of the PropertyManager for adding construction lines representing major and minor axes of the ellipse if needed, refer to Figure 2.90.
3. Click to specify the center point of the ellipse (see Figure 2.91), and then move the cursor to a distance. A construction circle appears in the drawing area.
4. Click to define the major axis of the ellipse (see Figure 2.91), and then move the cursor to a distance. A preview of the ellipse appears, see Figure 2.91.

2.91

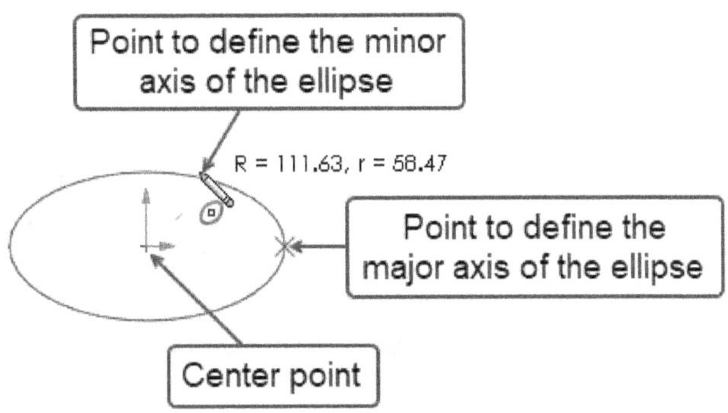

5. Click to specify the minor axis of the ellipse. The ellipse is drawn.

6. Right-click in the drawing area and then click on the **Select** option in the shortcut menu that appears to exit the **Ellipse** tool.

Drawing an Elliptical Arc

You can draw an elliptical arc using the **Partial Ellipse** tool of the **Ellipse** flyout, see Figures 2.92 and 2.93. Figure 2.92 highlights the **Partial Ellipse** tool within the **Ellipse** flyout, and Figure 2.93 illustrates an example of an elliptical arc. The method for drawing an elliptical arc is discussed below:

2.92

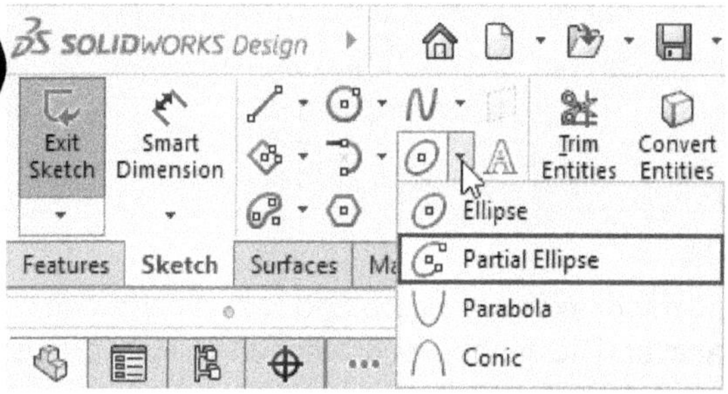

2.93

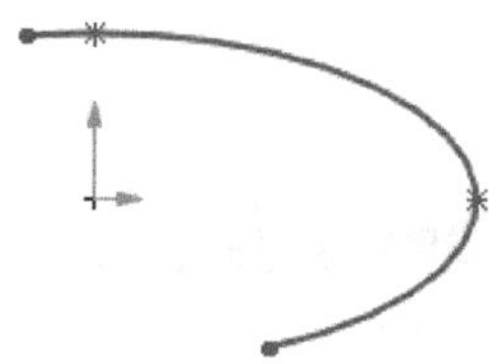

1. Invoke the **Ellipse** flyout by clicking on the arrow next to the **Ellipse** tool in the **Sketch CommandManager** and then click on the **Partial Ellipse** tool, refer to Figure 2.92.

2. Click to specify the center point of the elliptical arc in the drawing area. A reference circle appears.

3. Click to define the major axis of the elliptical arc in the drawing area and then move the cursor to a distance. The preview of an imaginary ellipse appears, see Figure 2.94.

4. Click to specify the start point of the elliptical arc in the drawing area and then move the cursor to a distance. The preview of an elliptical arc appears, see Figure 2.95.

2.94

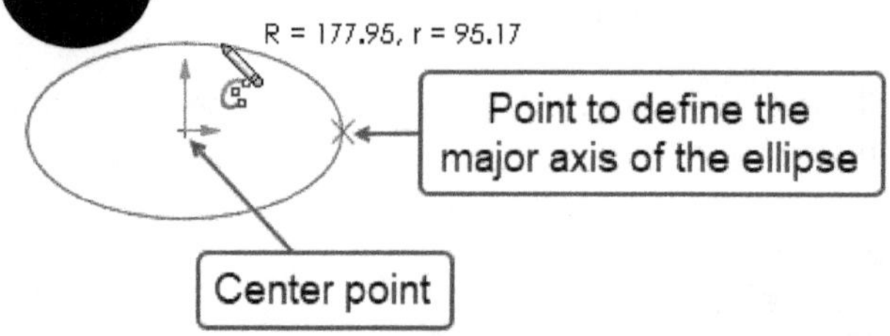

2.95

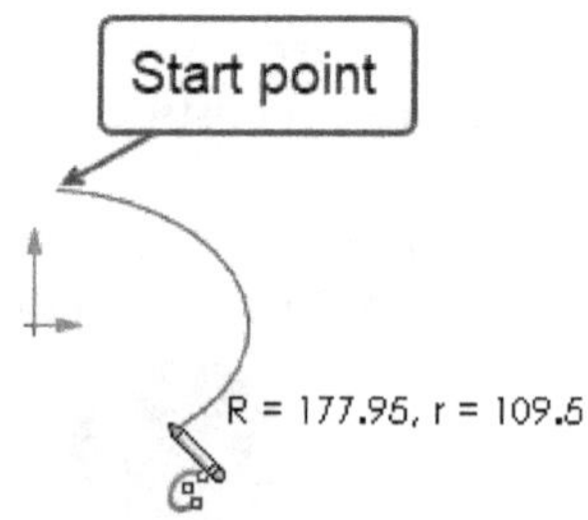

5. Click to specify the endpoint of the elliptical arc. The elliptical arc is created, see Figure 2.96.

6. Right-click in the drawing area and then click on the **Select** option in the shortcut menu that appears to exit the **Partial Ellipse** tool.

2.96

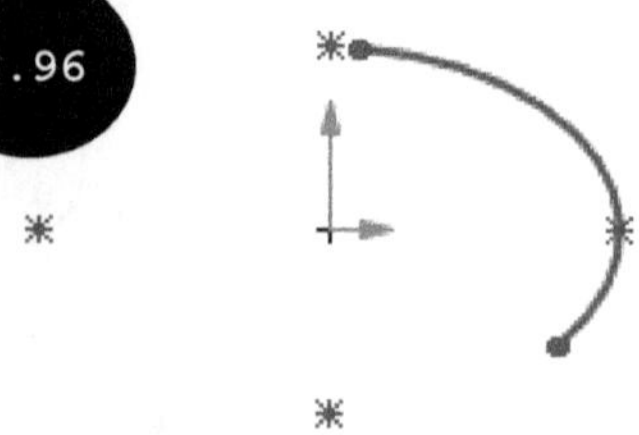

Drawing a Parabola

A Parabola is a symmetrical plane curve formed by the intersection of a cone and a plane parallel to its side. You can draw a parabola by defining its focus point, apex point, and two points (start point and endpoint) on the parabolic curve, see Figure 2.97. You can draw a parabola using the **Parabola** tool available in the **Ellipse** flyout. The method for drawing a parabola is discussed below:

2.97

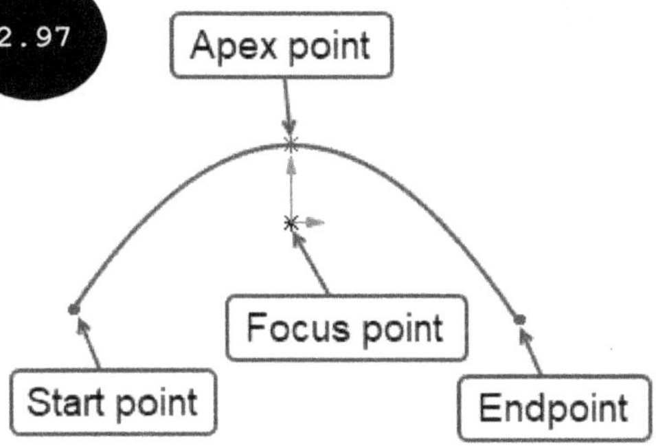

1. Invoke the **Ellipse** flyout and then click on the **Parabola** tool. The **Parabola** tool gets activated.
2. Click to specify the focus point of the parabola in the drawing area and then move the cursor to a distance. A construction parabola appears, and the cursor is attached at its apex, see Figure 2.98.
3. Click to specify the apex of the parabola. The preview of an imaginary parabola appears.
4. Move the cursor over the imaginary parabola and then click to specify the start point of the parabola, see Figure 2.99.
5. Move the cursor clockwise or counterclockwise and then click to specify the endpoint of the parabola. The parabola is drawn, see Figure 2.99.
6. Right-click in the drawing area and then click on the **Select** option in the shortcut menu that appears to exit the tool.

2.98

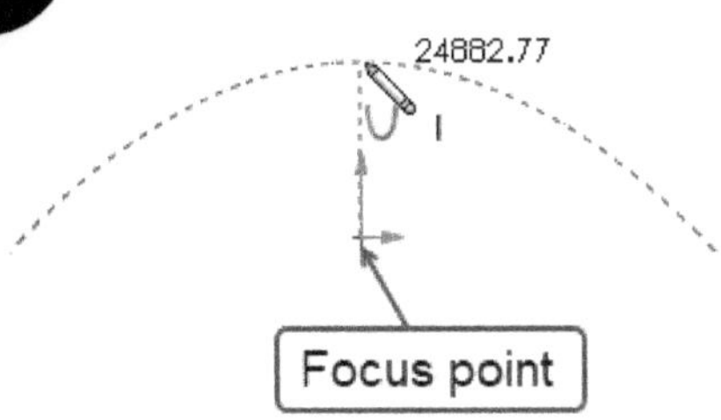

2.99

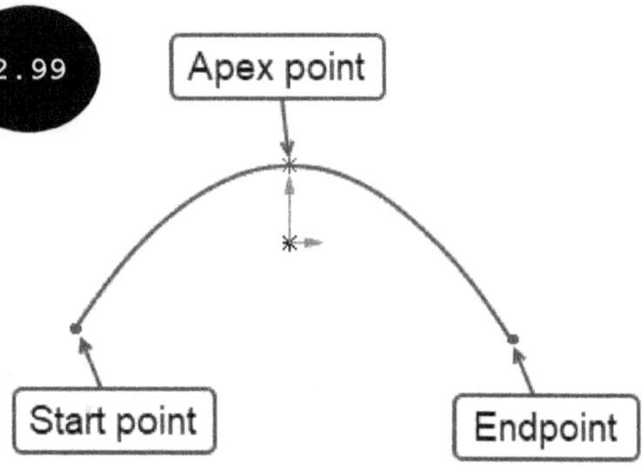

Drawing Conic Curves

SOLIDWORKS allows you to draw conic curves by specifying the start point, endpoint, top vertex, and Rho value, see Figure 2.100. You can draw conic curves using the **Conic** tool available in the **Ellipse** flyout. The method for drawing conic curves is discussed below:

2.100

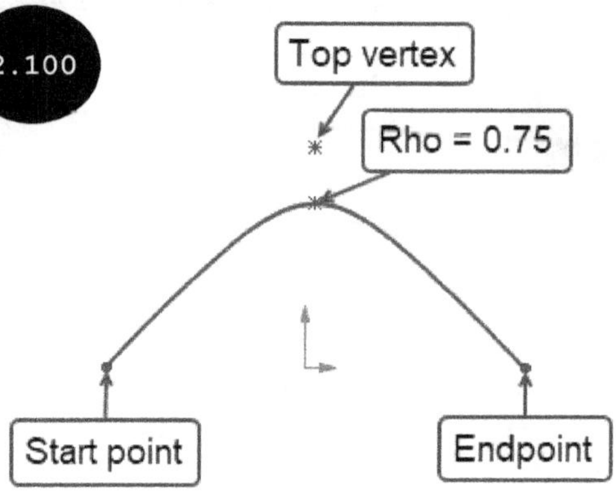

1. Click on the **Conic** tool in the **Ellipse** flyout. The **Conic** tool gets activated.

2. Click to specify the start point of the curve in the drawing area and then move the cursor to a distance. A construction line appears.

3. Click to specify the endpoint of the curve and then move the cursor to a distance. A preview of the conic curve appears, see Figure 2.101.

4. Click to specify the top vertex of the conic curve and then move the cursor upward or downward to a distance. A preview of the conic curve appears. Also, the current Rho value of the curve appears near the cursor, see Figure 2.102.

2.101

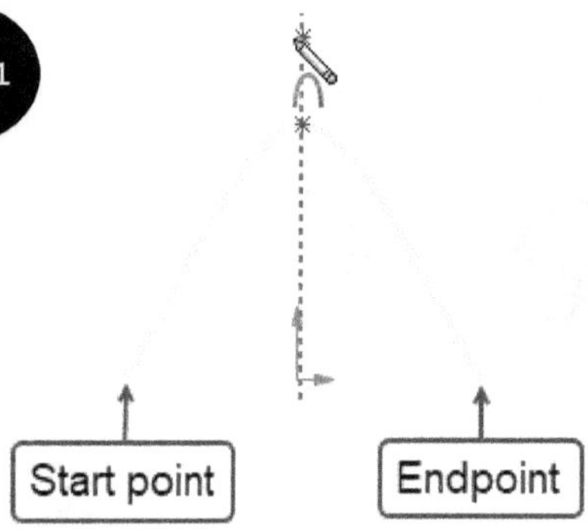

2.102

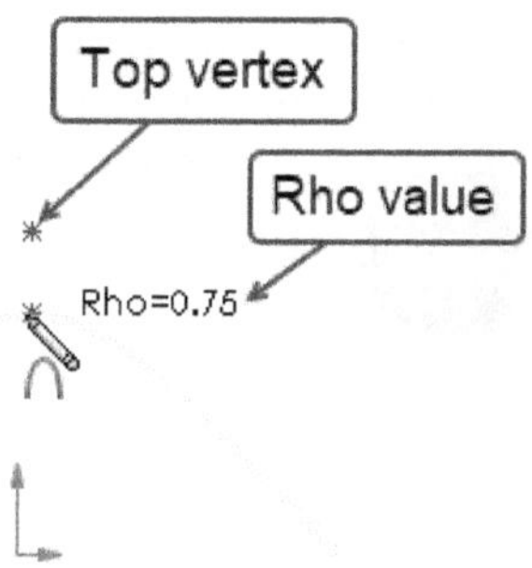

5. Move the cursor to the location where the Rho value appears closer to the required one and then click to specify the apex of the conic curve, see Figure 2.103.

2.103

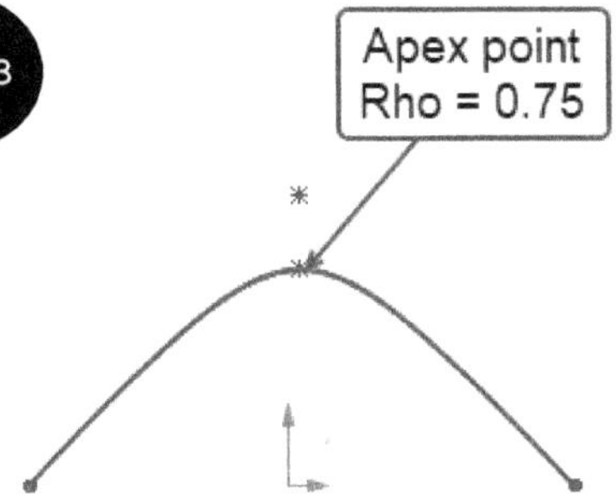

Note: The Rho value of the conic curve defines the type of curve. If the Rho value is less than 0.5 then the conic curve will be an ellipse. If the Rho value is equal to 0.5 then the conic curve will be a parabola. If the Rho value is greater than 0.5 then the conic curve will be a hyperbola.

6. Right-click in the drawing area and then click on the **Select** option in the shortcut menu that appears to exit the **Conic** tool.

Drawing a Spline

A Spline is defined as a curve having a high degree of smoothness and is used for creating free-form features. You can draw a spline by specifying two or more control points in the drawing area. In SOLIDWORKS, you can also draw a spline by defining mathematical equations. The different tools for drawing splines are discussed next.

Spline Tool

The **Spline** tool is used to create a spline by defining two or more control points in the drawing area, see Figure 2.104. The resulting spline will pass through the specified control points. The method for drawing a spline using the **Spline** tool is discussed below:

2.104

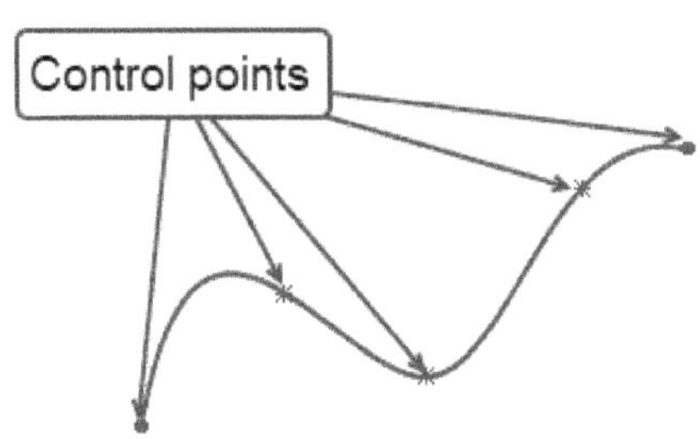

1. Click on the **Spline** tool in the **Sketch CommandManager**. The **Spline** tool gets activated and the cursor changes to the spline cursor .

2. Click to specify the first control point and then the second point of the spline in the drawing area. A preview of the spline curve appears in the drawing area such that it passes through the specified control points, see Figure 2.105.

3. Click to specify the third control point of the spline. A preview of the curve, passing through the three control points, appears in the drawing area. You can continue specifying control points for similarly drawing the spline.

4. Once all control points have been specified for drawing the spline, right-click and then click on the **Select** option in the shortcut menu that appears to exit the tool. Figure 2.106 shows a spline drawn by specifying five control points in the drawing area.

2.105

2.106

Equation Driven Curve Tool

The **Equation Driven Curve** tool is used to create an equation-driven spline. To do this, click on the arrow next to the **Spline** tool in the **Sketch CommandManager**. The **Spline** flyout appears, see Figure 2.107. Next, click on the **Equation Driven Curve** tool in the **Spline** flyout. The **Equation Driven Curve PropertyManager** appears on the left of the drawing area, see Figure 2.108. By using this PropertyManager, you can create two types of equation-driven splines: **Explicit** and **Parametric**. The methods for creating both these types of equation-driven splines are discussed next.

2.107

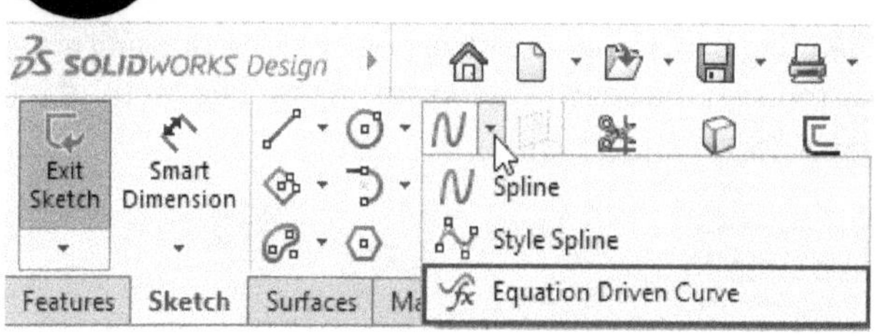

2.108

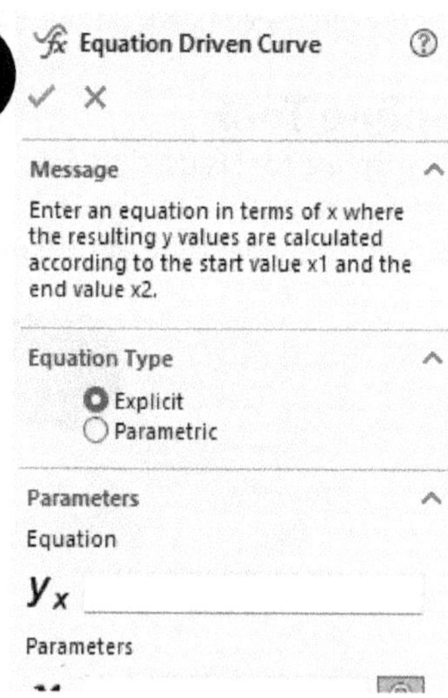

Creating an Explicit Equation Driven Spline

1. Invoke the **Spline** flyout and then click on the **Equation Driven Curve** tool. The **Equation Driven Curve PropertyManager** appears.

2. Ensure that the **Explicit** radio button is selected in the **Equation Type** rollout for creating an explicit equation-driven spline.

Explicit: The **Explicit** radio button is used to create a spline by defining an equation that calculates the 'Y' values of the control points as a function of 'X'. When this radio button is selected, you can define an equation for 'Y' as a function of 'X' in the **Yx** field of the **Parameters** rollout. Also, you can define the start and end values for the function 'X' in the **x1** and **x2** fields of the **Parameters** rollout, refer to Figure 2.109.

3. Enter the equation for 'Y' as the function of 'X' in the **Yx** field of the **Parameters** rollout. For example, enter the equation '**2* sin(x)^12**' in the **Yx** field, refer to Figure 2.109.

Parameters: The **Parameters** rollout is used for defining the driving equation and its start and end function values in their respective fields.

Note: The availability of options in the **Parameters** rollout depends on the type of radio button (**Explicit** or **Parametric**) selected in the **Equation Type** rollout of the PropertyManager.

4. Enter the start and end values of the function 'X' in the **x1** and **x2** fields. For example, enter '**0**' in the **X1** field and '**38**' in the **X2** field as the start and end function values, respectively, refer to Figure 2.109.

5. After defining the driving equation and its function values, press ENTER. A preview of the equation-driven spline appears in the drawing area.

6. Click on the green tick-mark ✓ button in the PropertyManager. The equation-driven spline is drawn, see Figure 2.110.

2.109

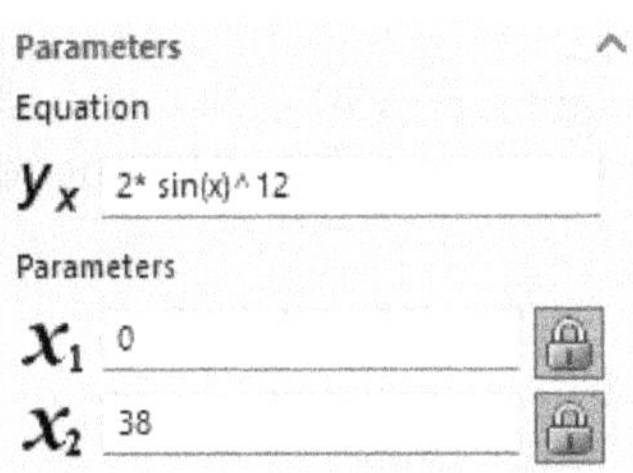

2.110

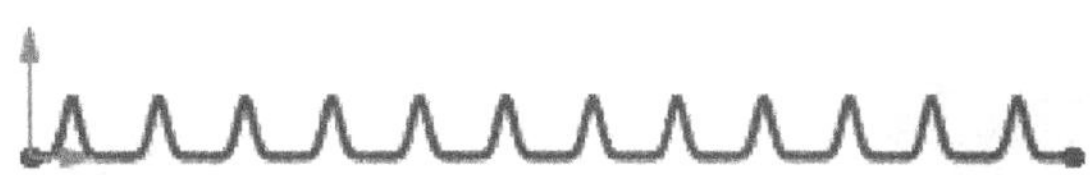

Creating a Parametric Equation Driven Spline

1. Invoke the **Spline** flyout and then click on the **Equation Driven Curve** tool. The **Equation Driven Curve PropertyManager** appears.

2. Select the **Parametric** radio button in the **Equation Type** rollout for creating a parametric equation-driven spline.

Parametric: The **Parametric** radio button is used to create a spline by defining two equations. The first equation calculates the 'X' values and the second equation calculates the 'Y' values of the control points as the function of 't'. When this radio button is selected, you can define equations for 'X' and 'Y' as the functions of 't' in the **Xt** and **Yt** fields of the **Parameters** rollout. Also, you can define the start and end values for the function 't' in the **t1** and **t2** fields of the **Parameters** rollout, refer to Figure 2.111.

3. Enter equations for 'X' and 'Y' as the functions of 't' in the **Xt** and **Yt** fields of the **Parameters** rollout, respectively. For example, enter **'t + sin(t)^2'** in the **Xt** field and **'2* sin(t)'** in the **Yt** field of the PropertyManager, refer to Figure 2.111.

4. Enter the start and end values of the function 't' in the **t1** and **t2** fields of the **Parameters** area. For example, enter **'0'** in the **t1** field and **'38'** in the **t2** field as the start and end values, respectively, refer to Figure 2.111.

5. After defining equations and the required function values, press ENTER. A preview of an equation-driven spline appears in the drawing area.

6. Click on the green tick-mark ✓ button in the PropertyManager. The equation-driven spline is drawn, see Figure 2.112.

2.111

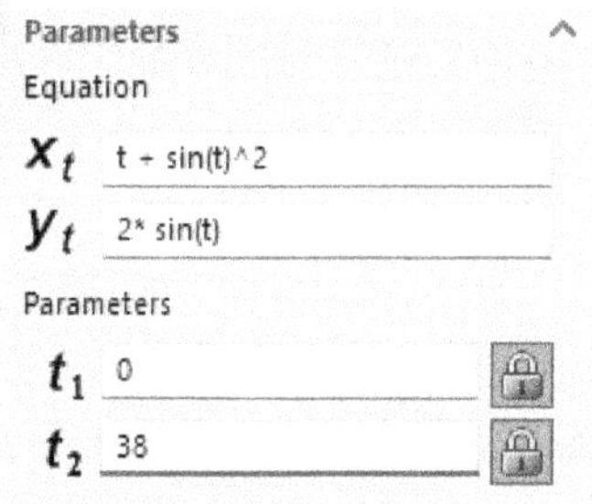

2.112

Style Spline Tool

The **Style Spline** tool is used to create bezier splines of 3 degrees, 5 degrees, and 7 degrees by defining control points in the drawing area, see Figure 2.113. A bezier spline is created such that it passes near the control points specified in the drawing area and is used for creating smooth and complex shaped features. Note that the minimum number of control points required to create bezier splines of 3 degrees, 5 degrees, and 7 degrees are 4, 6, and 8, respectively. The method for drawing a style or bezier spline is discussed below:

2.113

1. Click on the **Style Spline** tool in the **Spline** flyout. The **Insert Style Spline PropertyManager** appears, see Figure 2.114.

2. Select the **Bezier**, **B-Spline: Degree 3**, **B-Spline: Degree 5**, or **B-Spline: Degree 7** radio button in the PropertyManager, see Figure 2.114.

3. Click to specify the first control point of the spline in the drawing area.

2.114

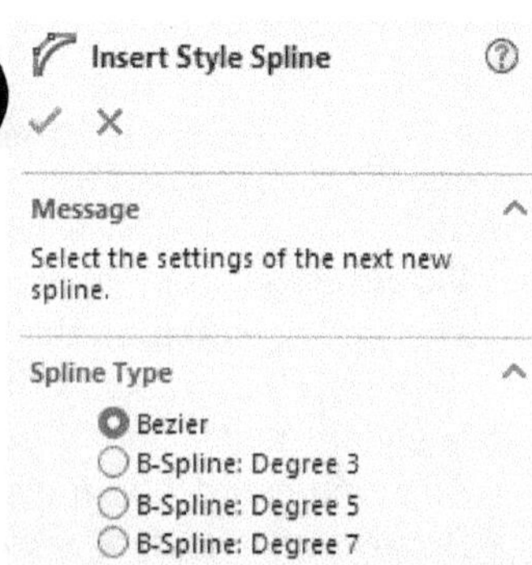

4. Move the cursor to a distance and then click to specify the second control point of the spline.

5. Click to specify the third control point of the spline. A preview of the spline appears in the drawing area such that it passes near the specified control points, see Figure 2.115. You can continue specifying control points for drawing the spline in the drawing area in a similar manner.

2.115

6. Once all control points have been specified for drawing the spline, right-click and then click on the **Select** option in the shortcut menu that appears to exit the tool.

Fit Spline Tool

The **Fit Spline** tool is used for converting multiple sketch entities into a single spline curve. To convert the sketch entities into a spline, click on **Tools > Spline Tools > Fit Spline** in the SOLIDWORKS Design Menus. The **Fit Spline PropertyManager** appears, see Figure 2.116. Next, select sketch entities to be converted into a spline, see Figure 2.117. The preview of a fit spline appears in the drawing area. Now, you can specify parameters for creating the fit spline, as required by using the options in the **Fit Spline PropertyManager**. The options in this PropertyManager are discussed next.

2.116

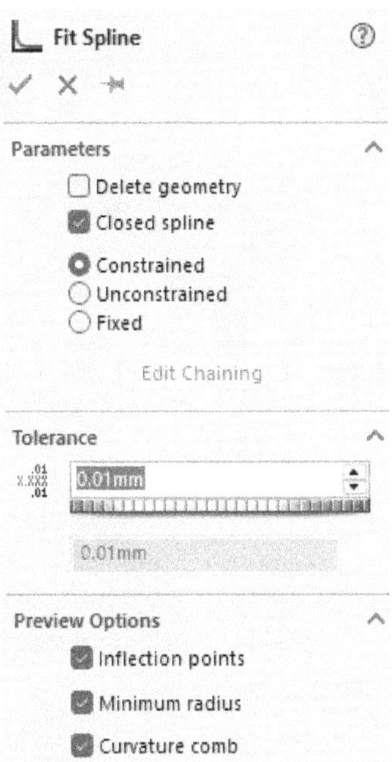

2.117

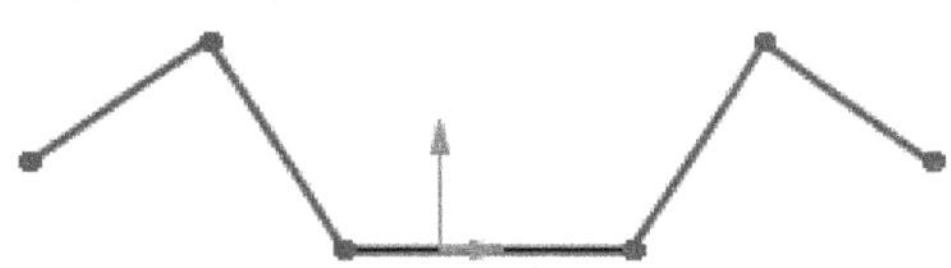

Parameters

The options in the **Parameters** rollout of the PropertyManager are used to specify different parameters for converting sketch entities into a spline curve. The options are discussed next.

Delete geometry

On selecting the **Delete geometry** check box, the original/parent-selected entities will be deleted from the drawing area and the resultant spline will be created.

Constrained

By default, the **Constrained** radio button is selected. As a result, the parametric links are applied between the original sketch entities and the resultant spline curve. Therefore, any change made in the original entities will also reflect in the spline and vice-versa.

Unconstrained

On selecting the **Unconstrained** radio button, the parametric links between the original sketch entities and the resultant spline curve will be broken. As a result, a change made in the original entities will not reflect in the spline and vice-versa.

Fixed

On selecting the **Fixed** radio button, the fixed relation will be applied to the resultant spline. As a result, changes such as position, dimensions, and so on cannot be made to the resultant spline. However, the original entities that are unconstrained with the resultant spline curve will be free to change.

Closed spline

By default, the **Closed spline** check box is selected. As a result, a closed spline will be created by closing the open ends of the selected entities. Figures 2.118 and 2.119 show a preview of the resultant spline with the **Closed spline** check box cleared and selected, respectively.

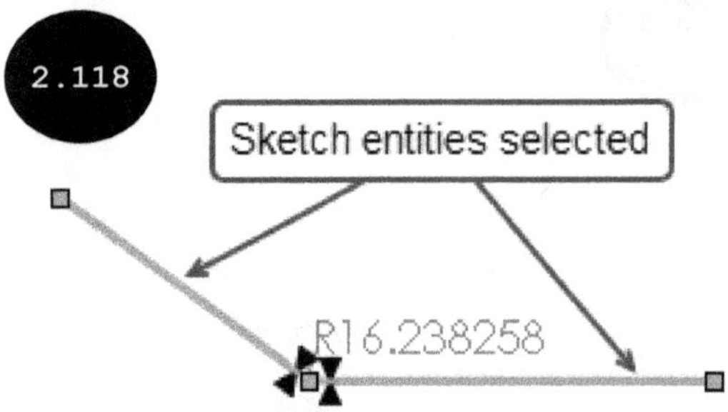

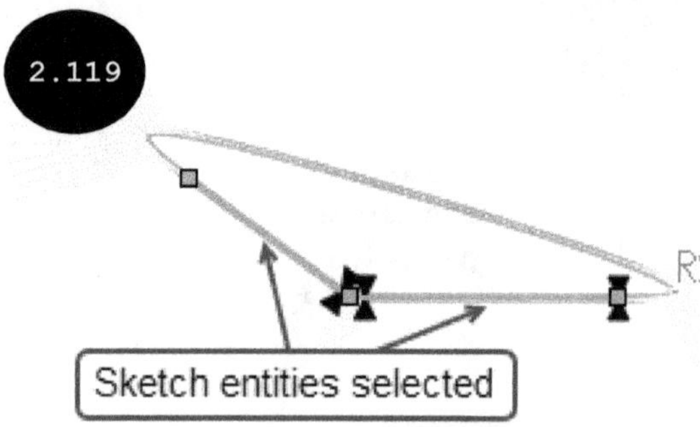

Edit Chaining

The **Edit Chaining** button is used to alter the creation of a chain of contiguous splines. Note that this button is activated only on selecting non-contiguous entities. Figure 2.120 shows non-contiguous entities (entities that are not in contact with each other). Figure 2.121 shows a preview of the default resultant contiguous spline and Figure 2.122 shows a preview of the resulting contiguous spline that appears on clicking the **Edit Chaining** button.

2.120

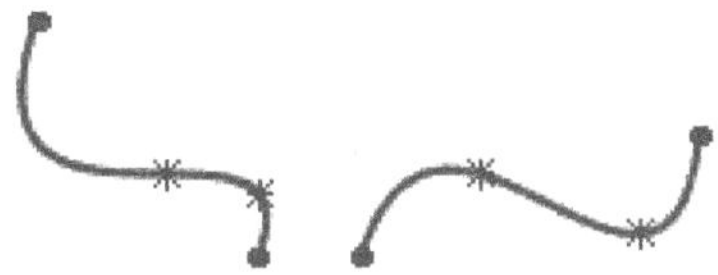

2.121

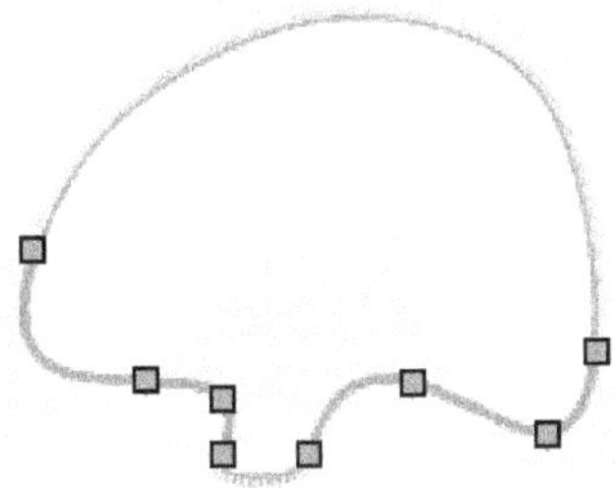

2.122

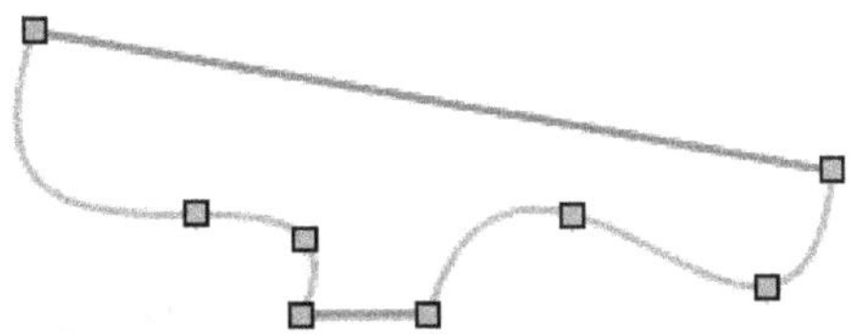

Tolerance

The **Tolerance** rollout is used to specify the maximum deviation allowed for the original sketch entities. You can enter the tolerance value in the **Tolerance** field of this rollout. You can also drag the thumbwheel on the bottom of the **Tolerance** field to set the tolerance value.

Preview Options

The options in this rollout are used to control the preview of the resultant spline and are discussed next.

Inflection points

By default, the **Inflection points** check box is selected. As a result, a preview of the spline appears with inflection points where the concavity of the spline changes. You can click on an inflection point to check for an alternative solution.

Minimum radius

By default, the **Minimum radius** check box is selected. As a result, a preview of the spline appears with minimum radius measurement on the spline.

Curvature comb

By default, the **Curvature comb** check box is selected. As a result, the visual enhancement of the slope as well as the curvature appears in the drawing area.

After specifying the required parameters for creating the fit spline, click on the green tick-mark ✓ button in the PropertyManager. The fit spline is created. Figure 2.123 shows an open-fit spline created with its original sketched entities deleted.

2.123

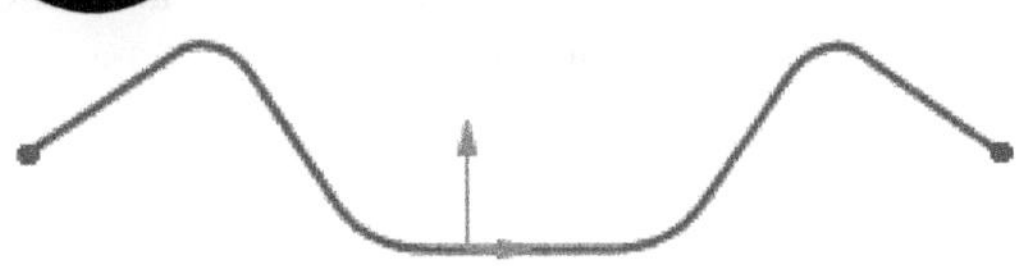

Editing a Spline

Editing a spline is essential for achieving complex shapes and maintaining smoothness and curvature. You can edit a spline using its control points and spline handles. Control points are specified in the drawing area when creating the spline. To modify a spline using control points, click on the control point of the spline you wish to edit. The selected control point highlights and displays the corresponding spline handle in the drawing area, see Figure 2.124. Additionally, the **Point PropertyManager** appears to the left of the drawing area.

You can drag the selected control point by pressing and holding the left mouse button to adjust its location in the drawing area. Alternatively, you can enter new X and Y coordinate values for the selected control point in the respective fields of the **Control Vertex Parameters** rollout of the **Point PropertyManager**.

You can use the spline handle to edit the curvature of a spline. Figure 2.125 shows the spline handle components. The different components of a spline handle are discussed next.

2.124

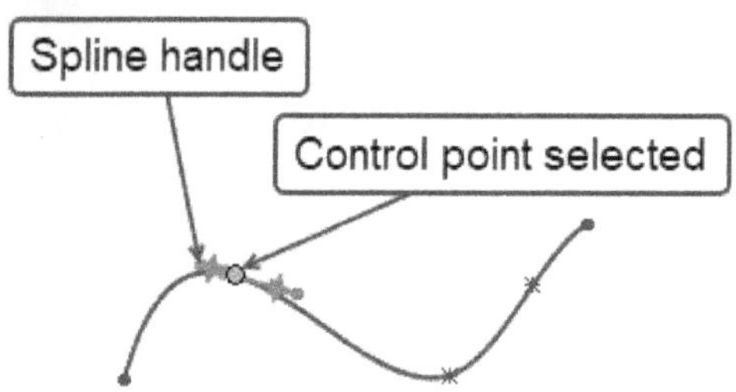

2.125

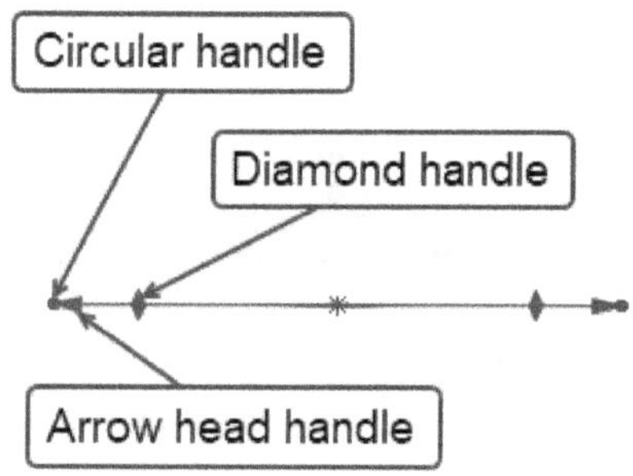

Circular handle

The circular handles of a spline handle are used to control the tangency, curvature, and angle of inclination of the spline, asymmetrically about the control point by dragging the spline handle. If you drag a circular handle by pressing the ALT key, the tangency, curvature, and the angle of inclination of the spline are controlled, symmetrically about the control point.

Arrow head handle

The arrow head handles of a spline handle are used to control the tangency of the spline, asymmetrically about the control point by dragging it. If you drag the arrow head handle by pressing the ALT key, the tangency is controlled, symmetrically about the control point.

Diamond handle

The diamond handles of a spline handle are used to control the tangent vector or the tangency angle of the spline by dragging it.

Modifying the Tangency Direction of Arc/Spline

In SOLIDWORKS, you can reverse or flip the tangency direction of an arc or a spline, see Figure 2.126. To do this, right-click on the tangent arc or spline whose tangency direction you want to flip. Then, click on the **Reverse Endpoint Tangent** tool in the shortcut menu that appears.

2.126

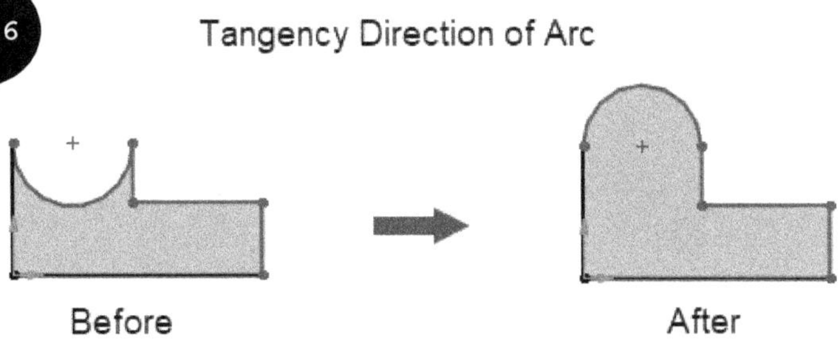

Tutorial 3

Draw a sketch of the model shown in Figure 2.127. The dimensions and the 3D model shown in the figure are for your reference only. All dimensions are in mm. You will learn about applying dimensions and creating the 3D model in later chapters.

2.127

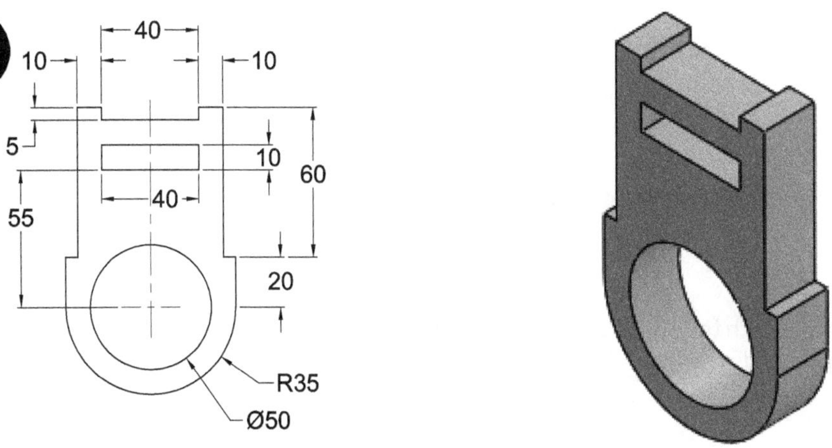

Section 1: Invoking the Part Modeling Environment

1. Start SOLIDWORKS by double-clicking on the SOLIDWORKS icon on your desktop. The startup user interface of SOLIDWORKS appears along with the **Welcome** dialog box, see Figure 2.128.

2. Click on the **Part** button in the **Welcome** dialog box. The Part modeling environment is invoked.

2.128

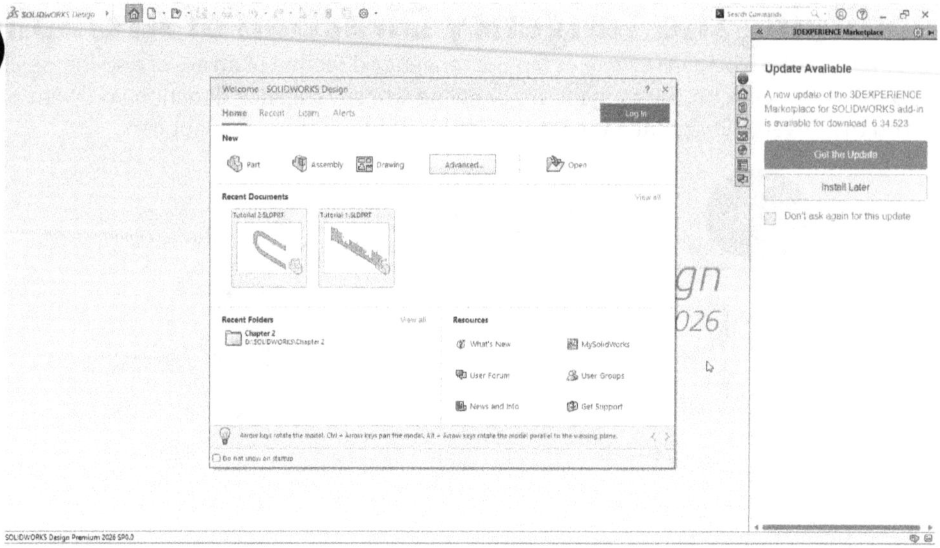

Section 2: Specifying Unit Settings

1. Move the cursor toward the lower right corner of the screen over the Status Bar and click on the **Unit System** area in the Status Bar. The **Unit System** flyout appears, see Figure 2.129.

2. Ensure that the **MMGS (millimeter, gram, second)** option is tick-marked in this flyout.

2.129

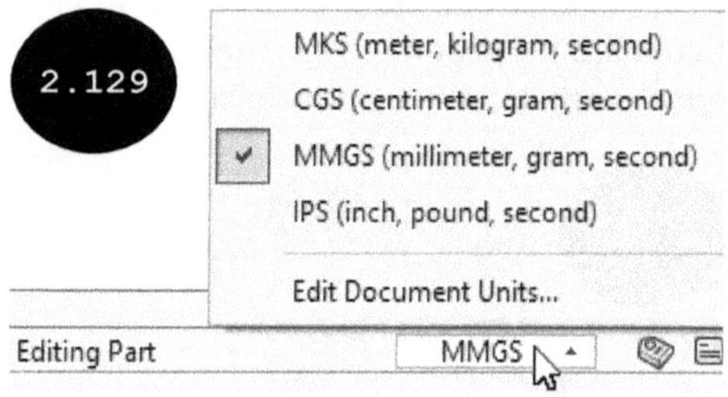

Section 3: Invoking the Sketching Environment

1. Click on the **Sketch** tab in the CommandManager, see Figure 2.130. The tools of the **Sketch CommandManager** appear.

2. Click on the **Sketch** tool in the **Sketch CommandManager**, see Figure 2.130. Three default planes mutually perpendicular to each other appear in the graphics area.

2.130

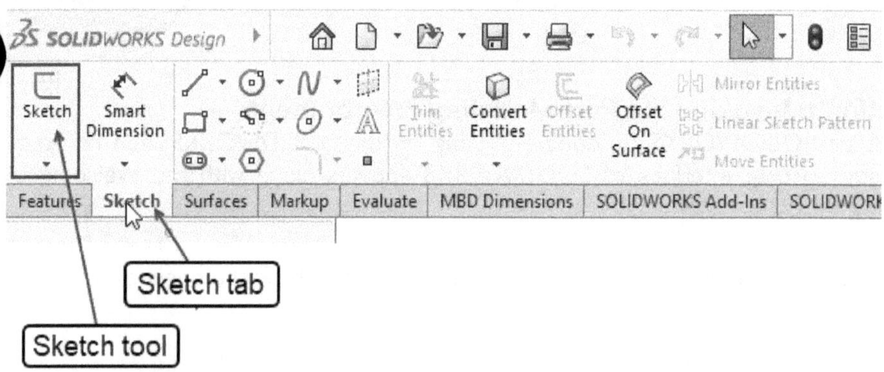

3. Move the cursor over the Front plane and then click the left mouse button when the boundary of the plane gets highlighted. The Sketching environment is invoked. Also, the Front plane is orientated normal to the viewing direction.

   As all the sketch entities are multiples of 5 mm, you need to set the snap settings such that the cursor snaps to an increment of 5 mm only.

Section 4: Specifying Grids and Snap Settings

1. Click on the **Options** tool in the **Standard** toolbar. The **System Options - General** dialog box appears.

2. Click on the **Document Properties** tab in the **System Options - General** dialog box. The name of the dialog box changes to **Document Properties - Drafting Standard**.

3. Click on the **Grid/Snap** option in the left panel of the dialog box. The options for specifying the grids and snap settings appear on the right panel of the dialog box. Also, the name of the dialog box changes to **Document Properties - Grid/Snap**.

4. Enter **20** in the **Major grid spacing** field, **4** in the **Minor-lines per major** field, and **1** in the **Snap points per minor** field of the **Grid** area in the dialog box.

5. Select the **Display grid** check box in the **Grid** area of the dialog box to turn on the display of grids in the drawing area.

6. Click on the **Go To System Snaps** button in the **Document Properties - Grid/Snap** dialog box. The name of the dialog box changes to **System Options - Relations/Snaps**.

7. Ensure that the **Grid** check box and the **Angle** check box are selected in the **Sketch snaps** area of the dialog box.

8. Ensure that the snap angle value is specified as 45 degrees in the **Snap angle** field of the dialog box.

9. Click on the **OK** button in the dialog box. The grids and snap settings are specified and the dialog box is closed. Also, grids appear in the drawing area, see Figure 2.131.

2.131

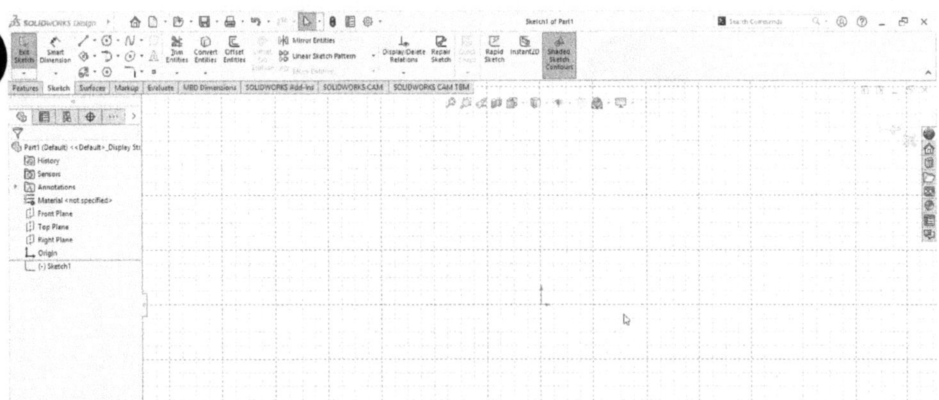

Section 5: Drawing the Sketch

Once the units, grids, and snap settings have been specified, you need to start drawing the sketch.

1. Click on the **Circle** tool in the **Sketch CommandManager**. The **Circle** tool gets activated and the **Circle PropertyManager** appears on the left of the drawing area. Also, the appearance of the cursor changes to the circle cursor.

2. Move the cursor to the origin and then click to specify the center point of the circle when the cursor snaps to the origin.

3. Move the cursor horizontally toward the right and then click to specify a point when the radius of the circle appears as 25 mm near the cursor, see Figure 2.132. A circle of radius 25 mm is drawn. Next, press the **ESC** key to exit the **Circle** tool.

4. Invoke the **Arc** flyout by clicking on the arrow next to the active arc tool in the **Sketch CommandManager**, see Figure 2.133.

2.132

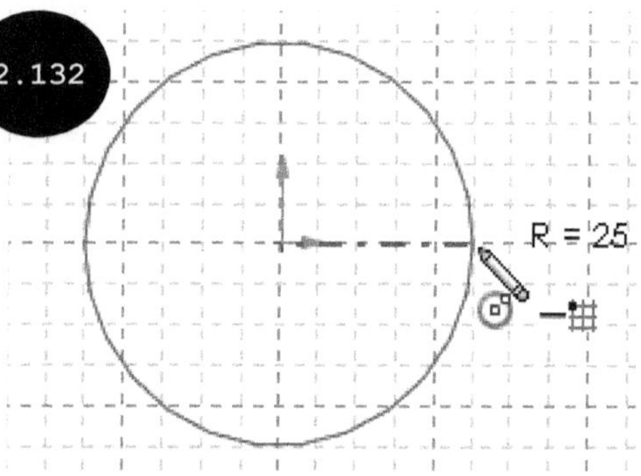

2.133

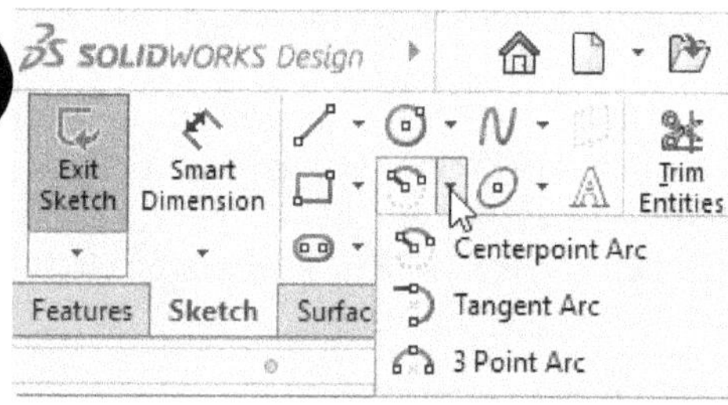

5. Click on the **Centerpoint Arc** tool in the **Arc** flyout. The **Centerpoint Arc** tool gets activated.

6. Move the cursor to the origin and then click to specify the center point of the arc when the cursor snaps to the origin.

7. Move the cursor horizontally toward the right. A preview of an imaginary circle appears in the drawing area, see Figure 2.134. Next, click to specify the start point of the arc when the radius of the imaginary circle appears as 35 mm near the cursor, see Figure 2.134.

2.134

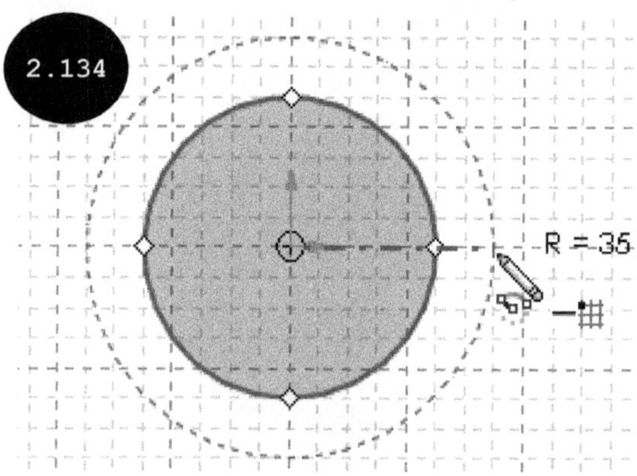

8. Move the cursor in the clockwise direction. A preview of the arc appears in the drawing area. Next, click to specify the endpoint of the arc when the angle value appears as 180 degrees near the cursor, see Figure 2.135. The arc is drawn. Next, press the ESC key to exit the tool.

2.135

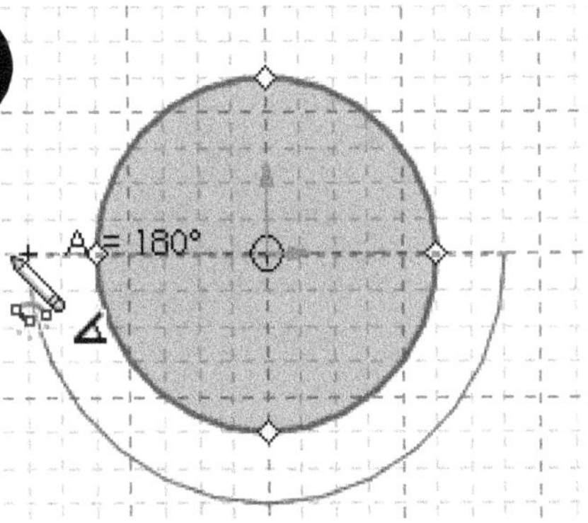

9. Click on the **Line** tool in the **Sketch CommandManager**. The **Line** tool gets activated.

10. Move the cursor to the start point of the previously drawn arc and then click the left mouse button when the cursor snaps to it, see Figure 2.136.

11. Move the cursor vertically upward and click when the length of the line appears as 20 mm near the cursor. A line of length 20 mm is drawn.

12. Move the cursor horizontally toward the left and click when the length of the line appears as 5 mm.

13. Move the cursor vertically upward and click when the length of the line appears as 60 mm, see Figure 2.137.

2.136

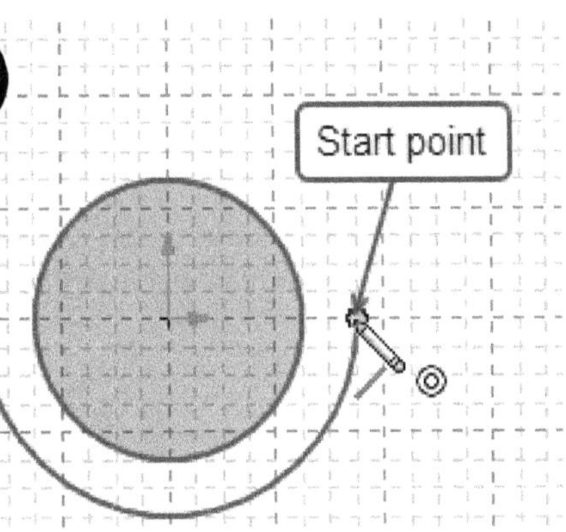

2.137

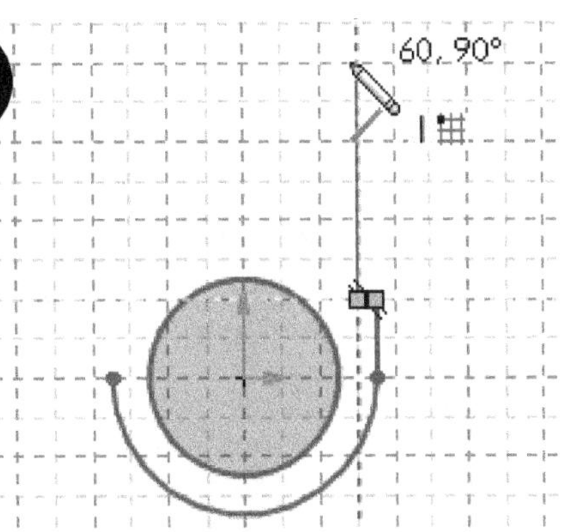

14. Move the cursor horizontally toward the left and click when the length of the line appears as 10 mm.

15. Move the cursor vertically downward and click when the length of the line appears as 5 mm.

16. Move the cursor horizontally toward the left and click when the length of the line appears as 40 mm.

17. Move the cursor vertically upward and click when the length of the line appears as 5 mm.

18. Move the cursor horizontally toward the left and click when the length appears as 10 mm.

19. Move the cursor vertically downward and click when the length of the line appears as 60 mm.

20. Move the cursor horizontally toward the left and click when the length appears as 5 mm.

21. Move the cursor vertically downward and click when the cursor snaps to the endpoint of the arc. The sketch appears similar to the one shown in Figure 2.138. Next, press **ESC**to exit the **Line** tool.

22. Invoke the **Rectangle** flyout (see Figure 2.139), and then click on the **Corner Rectangle** tool.

2.138

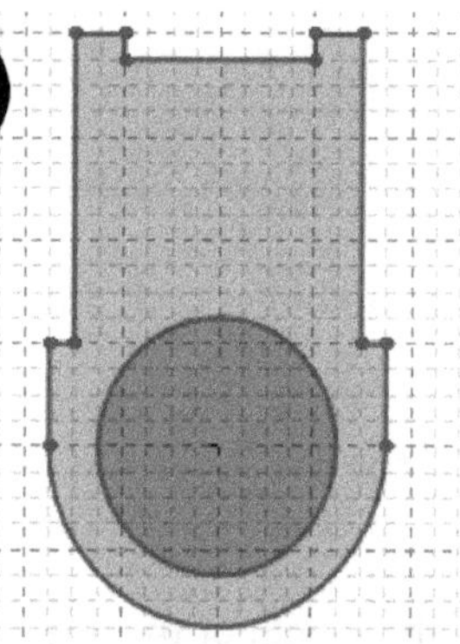

2.139

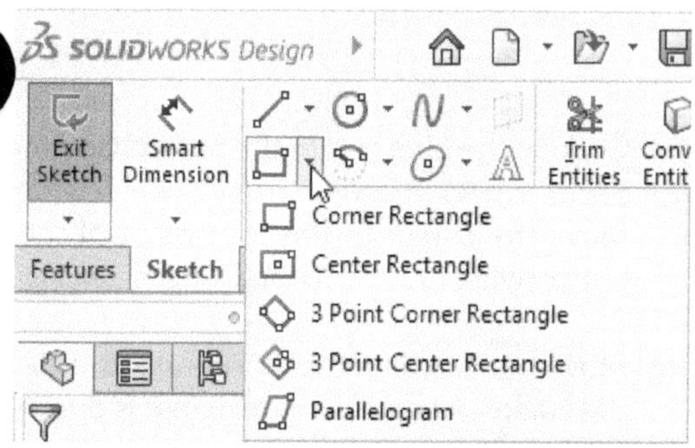

23. Move the cursor in the drawing area and then click the left mouse button when the coordinates (X, Y, Z) appear as "**20, 65, 0**" respectively in the Status Bar, which is available at the bottom of the screen, see Figure 2.140.

2.140

24. Move the cursor toward the left and click to specify the second corner point of the rectangle when "X = **40**" and "Y = **10**" values appear near the cursor, see Figure 2.141. Next, press the **ESC** key to exit the tool. Figure 2.142 shows the final sketch of Tutorial 3.

2.141

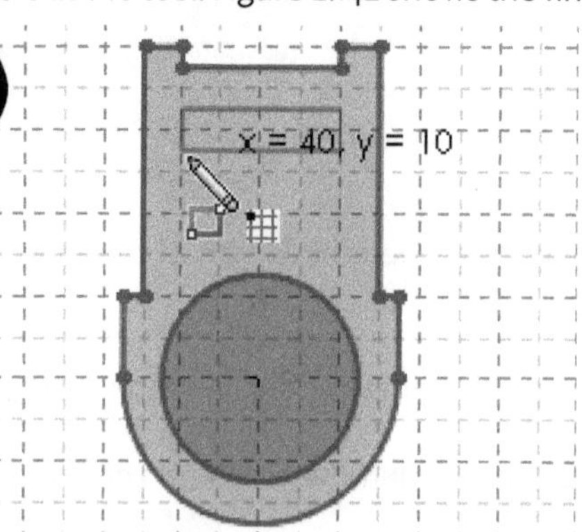

2.142

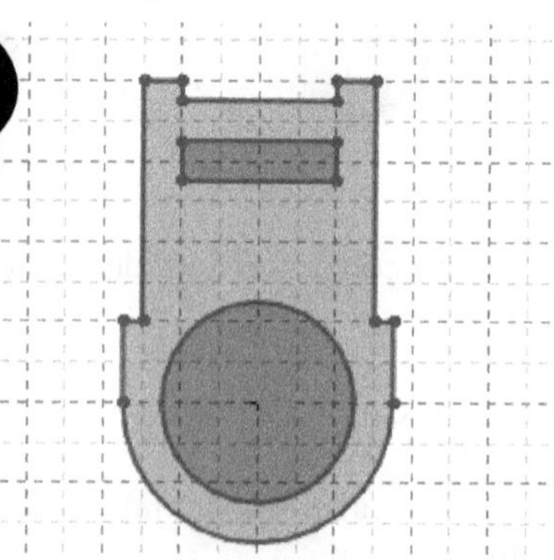

Section 6: Saving the Sketch

1. Click on the **Save** tool in the **Standard** toolbar. The **Save As** dialog box appears.
2. Browse to **SOLIDWORKS > Chapter 2** folder in the local drive of your system. Note that you need to create these folders, if not created earlier.
3. Enter **Tutorial 3** in the **File name** field of the dialog box.
4. Click on the **Save** button in the dialog box. The sketch is saved with the name Tutorial 3.

Tutorial 4

Draw a sketch of the model shown in Figure 2.143. The dimensions and the model shown in the figure are for your reference only. All dimensions are in mm. You will learn about applying dimensions and creating the 3D model in later chapters.

2.143

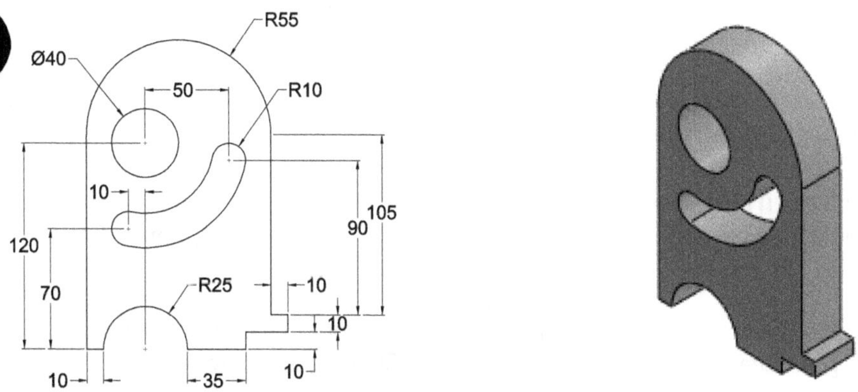

Section 1: Invoking the Part Modeling Environment

1. Start SOLIDWORKS by double-clicking on the SOLIDWORKS icon on your desktop. The startup user interface of SOLIDWORKS appears along with the **Welcome** dialog box.

Note: If SOLIDWORKS is already open and the **Welcome** dialog box does not appear on the screen, you can invoke the **Welcome** dialog box by clicking on the **Welcome to SOLIDWORKS** tool in the **Standard** toolbar.

---

2. Click on the **Part** button in the **Welcome** dialog box. The Part modeling environment is invoked.

Section 2: Specifying Unit Settings

1. Move the cursor toward the lower right corner of the screen over the Status Bar and then click on the **Unit System** area in the Status Bar. The **Unit System** flyout appears, see Figure 2.144.
2. Ensure that the **MMGS (millimeter, gram, second)** option is tick-marked in this flyout.

2.144

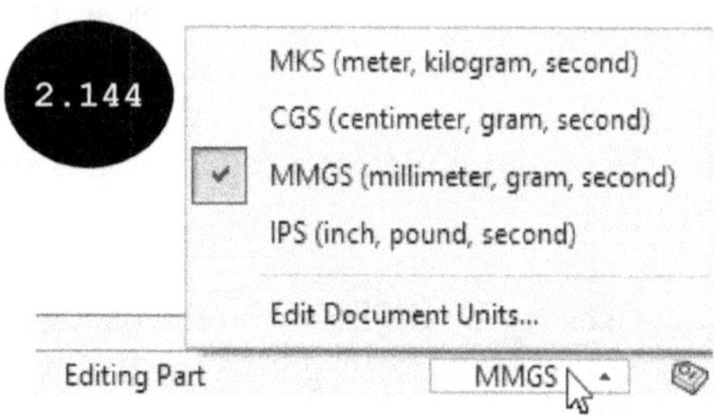

Section 3: Invoking the Sketching Environment

1. Click on the **Sketch** tab in the CommandManager, see Figure 2.145. The tools of the **Sketch CommandManager** appear.

2.145

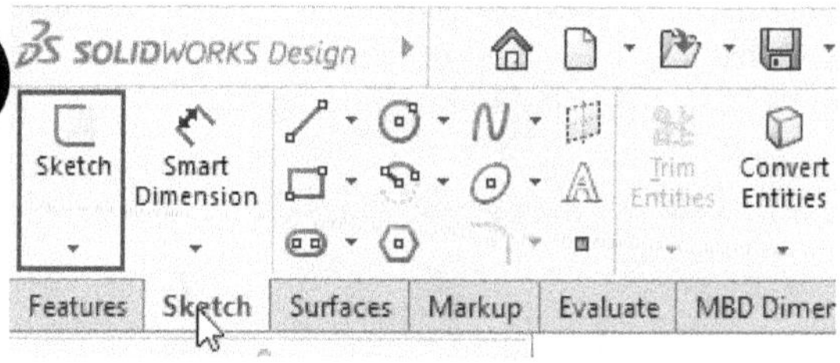

2. Click on the **Sketch** tool in the **Sketch CommandManager**. Three default planes mutually perpendicular to each other, appear in the graphics area.

3. Move the cursor over the Front plane and then click the left mouse button when the boundary of the plane gets highlighted. The Sketching environment is invoked. Also, the Front plane is orientated normal to the viewing direction.

   As all the sketch entities are multiples of 5 mm, you need to set the snap settings such that the cursor snaps to an increment of 5 mm.

Section 4: Specifying Grid and Snap Settings

1. Click on the **Options** tool in the **Standard** toolbar. The **System Options - General** dialog box appears.

2. Click on the **Document Properties** tab in the **System Options - General** dialog box. The name of the dialog box changes to **Document Properties - Drafting Standard.**

3. Click on the **Grid/Snap** option in the left panel of the dialog box. The options for specifying the grids and snap settings appear on the right panel of the dialog box.

4. Enter **20** in the **Major grid spacing** field, **4** in the **Minor-lines per major** field, and **1** in the **Snap points per minor** field of the **Grid** area in the dialog box.

5. Select the **Display grid** check box in the **Grid** area of the dialog box to turn on the display of grids in the drawing area.

6. Click on the **Go To System Snaps** button in the dialog box.

7. Ensure that the **Grid** check box and the **Angle** check box are selected in the **Sketch snaps** area of the dialog box.

8. Ensure that the snap angle value is specified as 45 degrees in the **Snap angle** field of the dialog box.

9. Click on the **OK** button in the dialog box. The grids and snap settings are specified, and the dialog box is closed. Also, grids appear in the drawing area.

Once the units, grids, and snap settings have been specified, you can start drawing the sketch. First, you need to draw the outer loop of the sketch and then the inner slot and the circle.

Section 5: Drawing the Outer Loop of the Sketch

1. Invoke the **Arc** flyout in the **Sketch CommandManager**, see Figure 2.146.
2. Click on the **Centerpoint Arc** tool in the **Arc** flyout. The **Centerpoint Arc** tool gets activated.
3. Move the cursor to the origin and then click when the cursor snaps to the origin.
4. Move the cursor horizontally toward the right. A preview of an imaginary circle appears in the drawing area. Next, click the left mouse button when the radius of the imaginary circle appears as 25 mm near the cursor.
5. Move the cursor in the anti-clockwise direction. A preview of an arc appears in the drawing area. Next, click the left mouse button when the angle value appears as 180 degrees near the cursor, see Figure 2.147. Next, press the ESC key to exit the **Centerpoint Arc** tool.

2.146

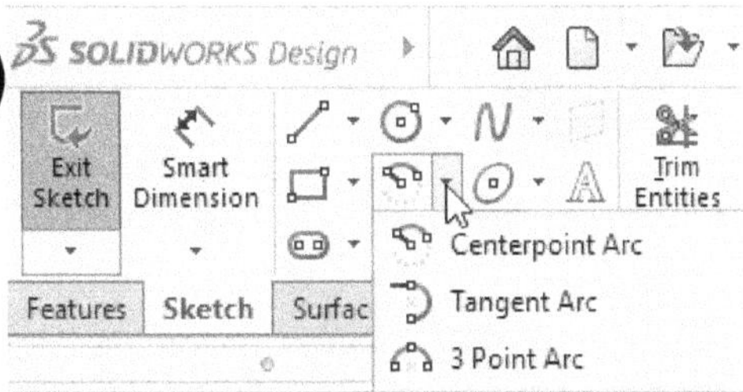

2.147

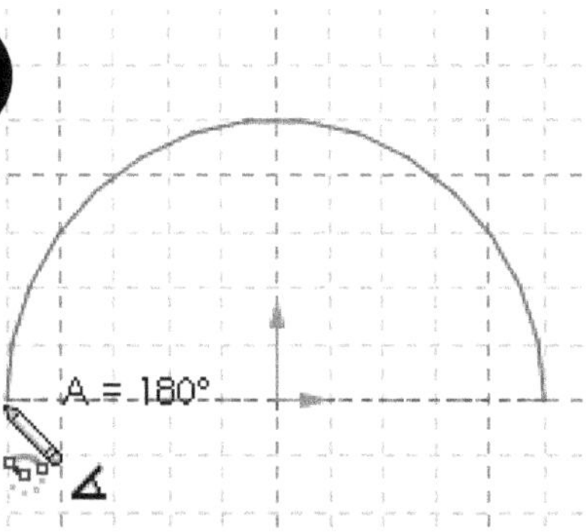

6. Click on the **Line** tool in the **Sketch CommandManager**. The **Line** tool gets activated.
7. Move the cursor to the start point of the previously drawn arc and then click the left mouse button when the cursor snaps to it, see Figure 2.148.
8. Move the cursor horizontally toward the right and click when the length of the line appears as 35 mm near the cursor, see Figure 2.149.

2.148

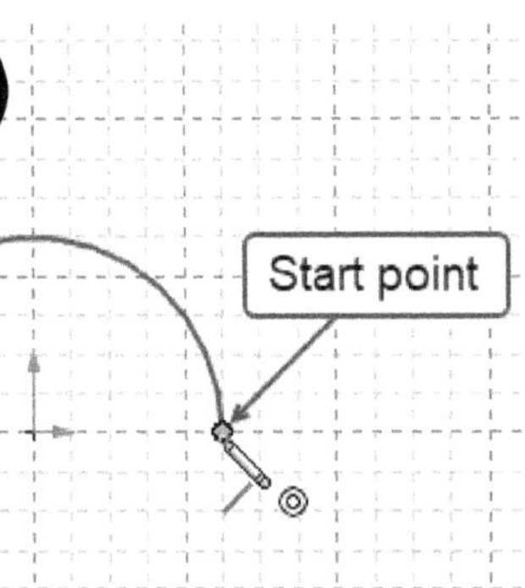

2.149

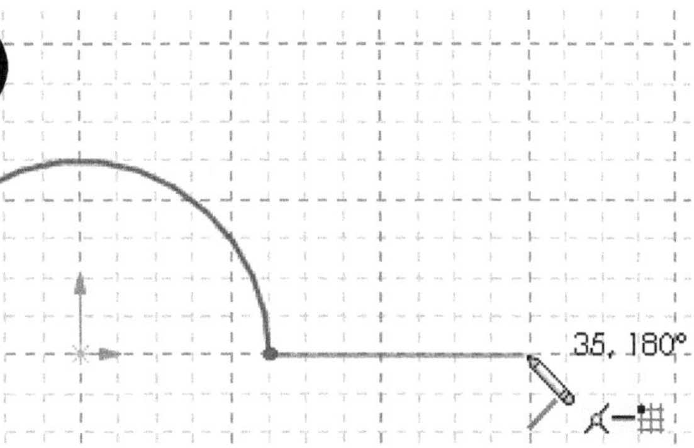

9. Move the cursor vertically upward and click when the length of the line appears as 10 mm.
10. Move the cursor horizontally toward the right and click when the length of the line appears as 25 mm.
11. Move the cursor vertically upward and click when the length of the line appears as 10 mm.
12. Move the cursor horizontally toward the left and click when the length of the line appears as 10 mm.
13. Move the cursor vertically upward and click when the length of the line appears as 105 mm.
14. Move the cursor to a distance and then move it back to the last specified point. An orange-colored dot appears in the drawing area, see Figure 2.150.
15. Move the cursor vertically upward to a distance and then move it horizontally toward the left. The arc mode gets activated, and a preview of the tangent arc appears, see Figure 2.151.

2.150

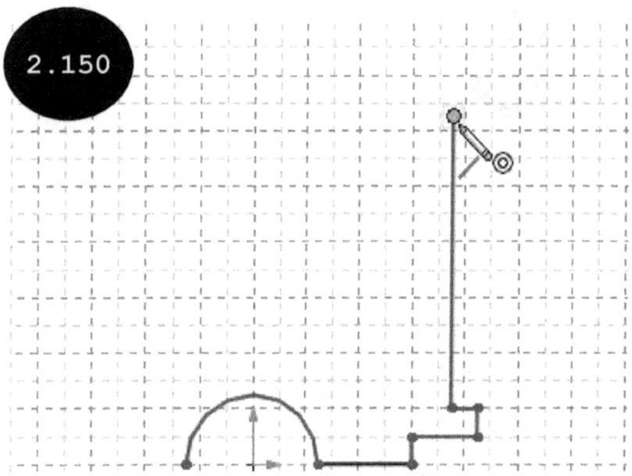

2.151

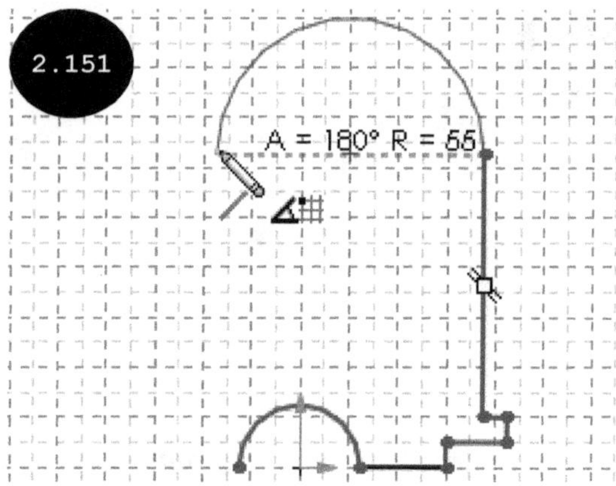

16. Click to specify the endpoint of the arc when the angle and radius values of the arc appear as 180 degrees and 55 mm, respectively near the cursor, see Figure 2.151.
17. Move the cursor vertically downward and click when the length of the line appears as 125 mm.
18. Move the cursor horizontally toward the right and click when the cursor snaps to the endpoint of the arc. The outer loop of the sketch is drawn, see Figure 2.152. Next, press the **ESC** key.

2.152

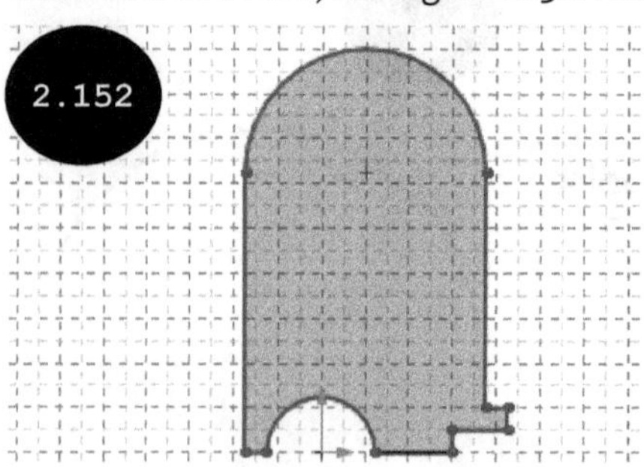

Section 6: Drawing the Slot and the Circle of the Sketch

1. Click on the **Circle** tool in the **Sketch CommandManager**. The **Circle** tool gets activated and the **Circle PropertyManager** appears on the left of the drawing area.

2. Move the cursor in the drawing area and then click the left mouse button when the coordinates (X, Y, Z) appear as "**0, 120, 0**" respectively in the Status Bar, which is available at the bottom of the screen, see Figure 2.153.

2.153

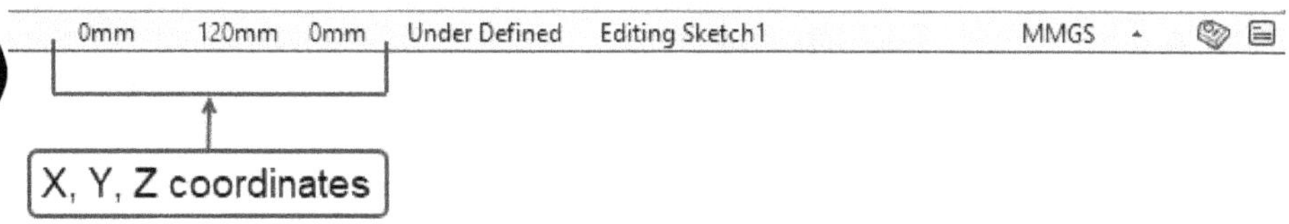

3. Move the cursor horizontally toward the right and click when the radius of the circle appears as 20 mm, see Figure 2.154. A circle of radius 20 mm is drawn. Next, press the ESC key to exit the **Circle** tool.

2.154

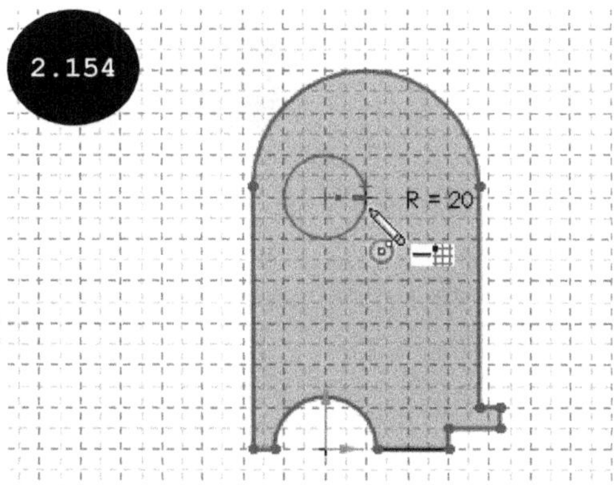

After creating the circle, you need to create the slot.

4. Invoke the **Slot** flyout in the **Sketch CommandManager** and then click on the **Centerpoint Arc Slot** tool, see Figure 2.155. The **Centerpoint Arc Slot** tool gets activated.

2.155

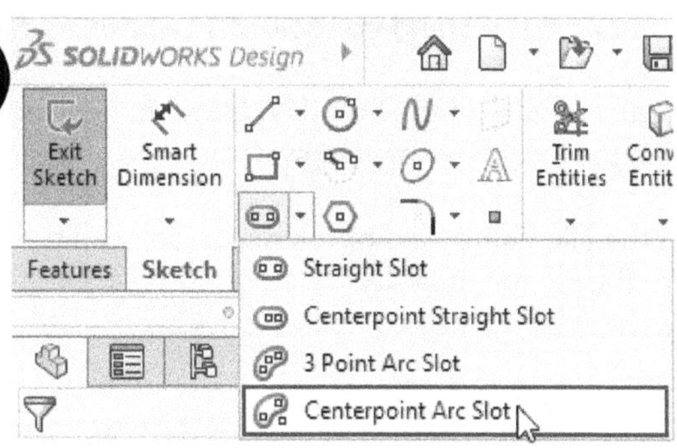

5. Move the cursor to the center point of the previously drawn circle and then click the left mouse button when the cursor snaps to it.

6. Move the cursor to the location where the coordinates "-10, 70, and 0" appear in the Status Bar, and then click the left mouse button at that location in the drawing area.

7. Move the cursor to a distance in the anti-clockwise direction. A preview of the arc appears. Next, click the left mouse button when coordinates "50, 110, 0" appear in the Status Bar.

8. Move the cursor to a distance in the drawing area. A preview of the slot arc appears in the drawing area. Next, click the left mouse button when the width of the slot appears close to 20 mm in the **Slot Width** field of the **Slot PropertyManager**. A slot gets drawn and is selected in the drawing area, by default. As a result, all its parameters appear in the **Parameters** rollout of the PropertyManager.

9. Enter **20** in the **Slot Width** field of the **Slot PropertyManager**, see Figure 2.156. A slot of width 20 mm is drawn, see Figure 2.157.

10. Click on the green tick-mark ✓ button in the PropertyManager. The final sketch of Tutorial 4 is shown in Figure 2.157.

2.156

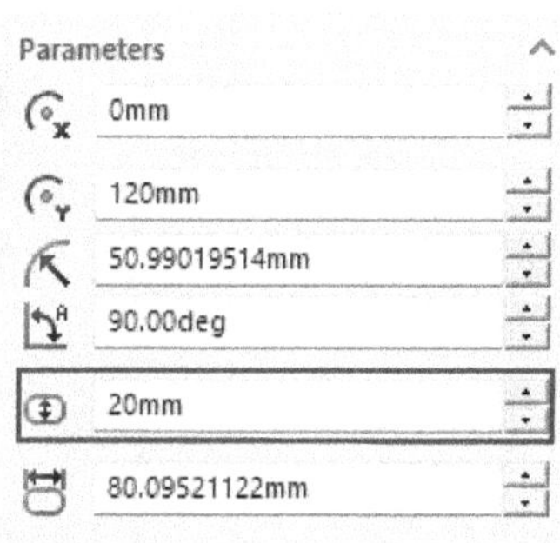

2.157

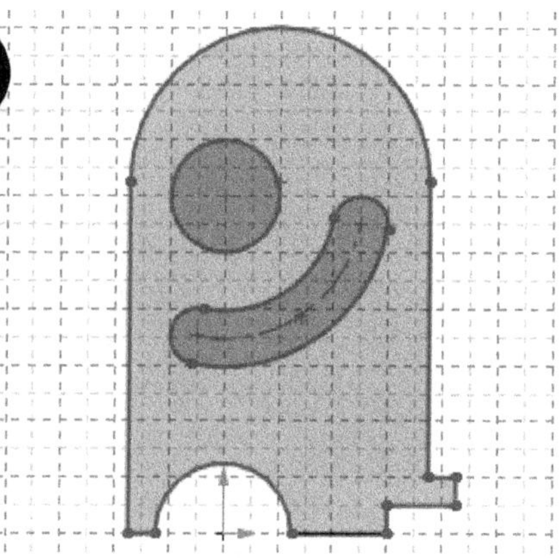

Section 7: Saving the Sketch

After creating the sketch, you need to save it.

1. Click on the **Save** tool in the **Standard** toolbar. The **Save As** dialog box appears.

2. Browse to the Chapter 2 folder of the SOLIDWORKS folder. You need to create these folders, if not created earlier in the local drive of your system.

3. Enter **Tutorial 4** in the **File name** field of the dialog box and then click on the **Save** button. The sketch is saved with the name Tutorial 4.

Hands-on Test Drive 3

Draw a sketch of the model shown in Figure 2.158. The dimensions and the 3D model shown in the figure are for your reference only. All dimensions are in mm.

2.158

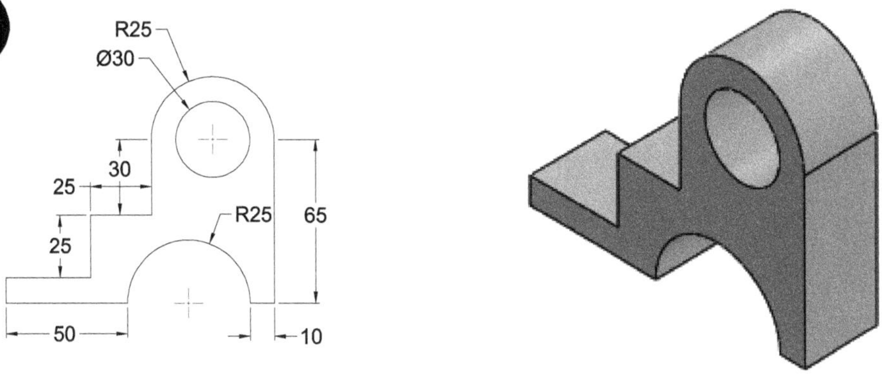

Hands-on Test Drive 4

Draw a sketch of the model shown in Figure 2.159. The dimensions and the 3D model shown in the figure are for your reference only. All dimensions are in mm.

2.159

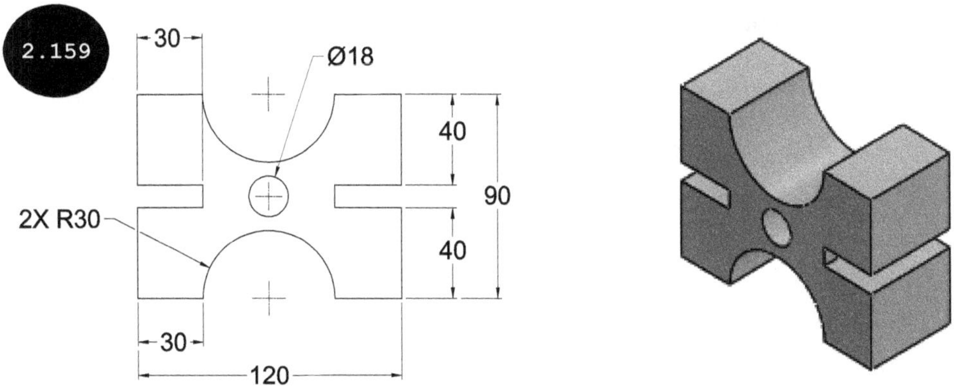

Summary

In this chapter, you have learned how to navigate the **Sketching environment** within the **Part modeling** environment in SOLIDWORKS. You explored how to specify unit systems, grids, and snap settings to ensure precise sketching. The chapter also covered various sketching tools, including **Line**, **Arc**, **Circle**, **Rectangle**, and **Spline**, to help you create accurate sketches. Additionally, you learned how to edit a spline and reverse the tangency direction of an arc or spline for greater control over your designs.

Questions

Complete and verify the following sentences:

- Features are divided into two main categories: _________ and _________.
- The _________ feature of any real-world component is sketch-based.
- A polygon has several sides ranging from _________ to _________.
- To draw an ellipse, you need to define its _________ axis and _________ axis.
- If the Rho value of a conic curve is less than 0.5 then the conic is an _______.
- A _________ line is created symmetrically about its midpoint.
- The _________ tool is used for creating an elliptical arc.
- The _________ tool is used for creating an equation-driven spline.
- A parabola is a symmetrical plane curve that is formed by the intersection of a cone with a plane parallel to its side. (True/False)
- You cannot draw a tangent arc by using the **Line** tool. (True/False)
- You can edit a spline by using its control points and spline handle. (True/False)
- A fillet feature is known as a placed feature. (True/False)

CHAPTER 3

Editing and Modifying Sketches

This chapter discusses the following topics:

- Trimming Sketch Entities
- Extending Sketch Entities
- Offsetting Sketch Entities
- Mirroring Sketch Entities
- Patterning Sketch Entities
- Creating a Sketch Fillet
- Creating a Sketch Chamfer
- Adding Text
- Moving a Sketch Entity
- Creating a Copy of Sketch Entities
- Rotating an Entity
- Scaling Sketch Entities
- Stretching an Entity

Editing and modifying a sketch is essential to achieving the desired shape. In SOLIDWORKS, the Sketching environment offers several editing operations, such as trimming unwanted sketch entities, extending entities, mirroring, patterning, moving, and rotating sketch entities, among others. These operations are discussed next.

Trimming Sketch Entities

You can trim unwanted sketch entities using the **Trim Entities** tool in the **Sketch CommandManager**. To do this, click on the **Trim Entities** tool in the **Sketch CommandManager**, see Figure 3.1. The **Trim PropertyManager** appears, see Figure 3.2. The options in this PropertyManager are discussed next.

3.1

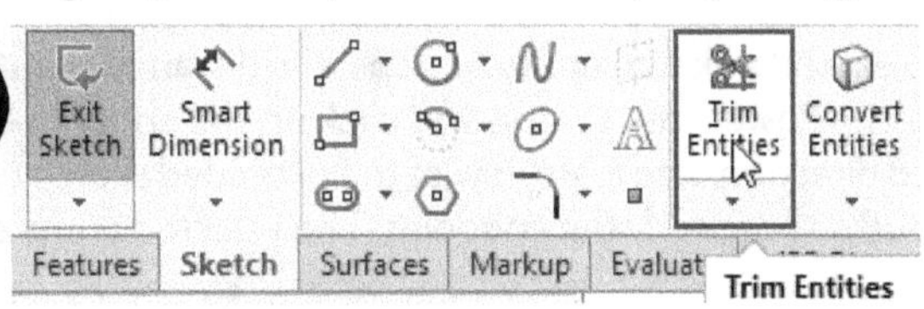

Message

The **Message** rollout of the PropertyManager displays the information about the action to be taken. The display of information in the **Message** rollout depends on the options selected in the **Options** rollout of the PropertyManager.

3.2

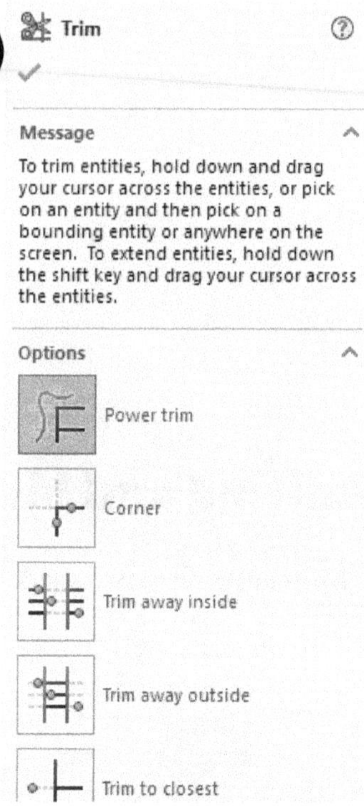

Options

The **Options** rollout provides various options for trimming sketch entities. The method for trimming sketch entities using each of these options is discussed next.

Power trim

Thme **Power trim** button in the **Options** rollout trims sketch entities by dragging the cursor across the entities to be trimmed. When you hold the left mouse button and drag the cursor after activating this button, a light-colored tracing line follows the cursor, and the sketch entities intersected by this line are trimmed at their nearest intersection. Figure 3.3 shows the sketch before trimming, while Figure 3.4 displays the same sketch after trimming the entities that intersected the tracing line.

3.3

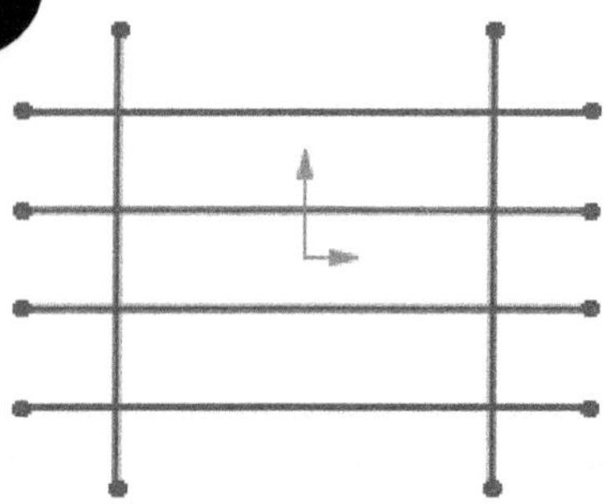

3.4

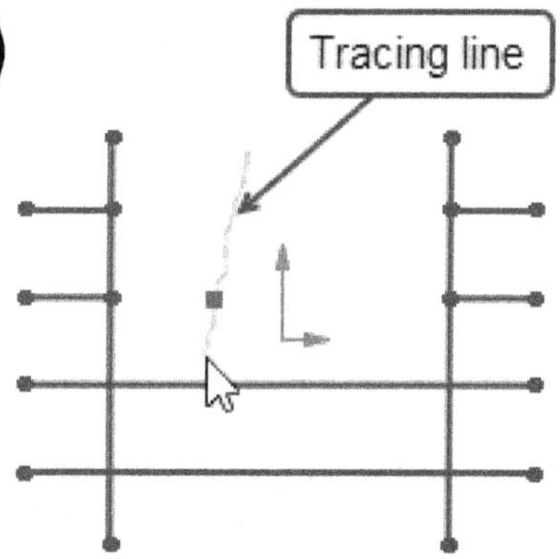

Note: In addition to trimming sketch entities with the **Power trim** button, you also extend sketch entities to their nearest intersection. To do this, after activating the **Power trim** button, press and hold the **SHIFT** key, and drag the cursor while holding the left mouse button. A light-colored tracing line follows the cursor, and the entities intersected by this line are extended to their nearest intersection. Figure 3.5 shows the sketch before extending a sketch entity, while Figure 3.6 displays the same sketch after extending the intersected entity.

You can also extend a sketch entity to a specific distance using the **Power trim** button. To do this, activate the **Power trim** button and click on the entity to extend. Next, move the cursor in the desired direction, and a preview of the extended sketch entity appears. Finally, click the left mouse button to specify the endpoint. The selected entity extends to the specified point.

3.5

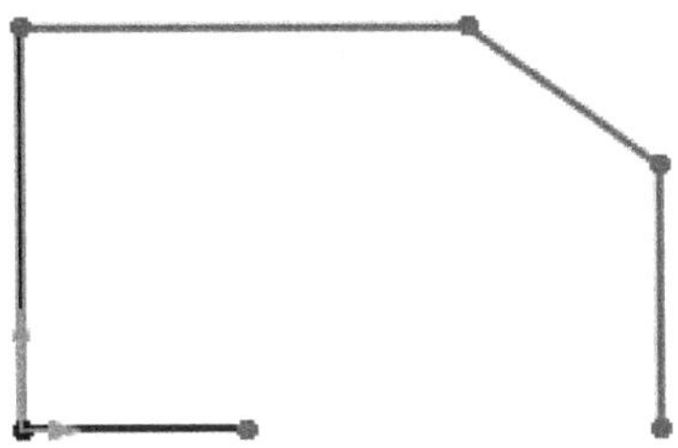

3.6

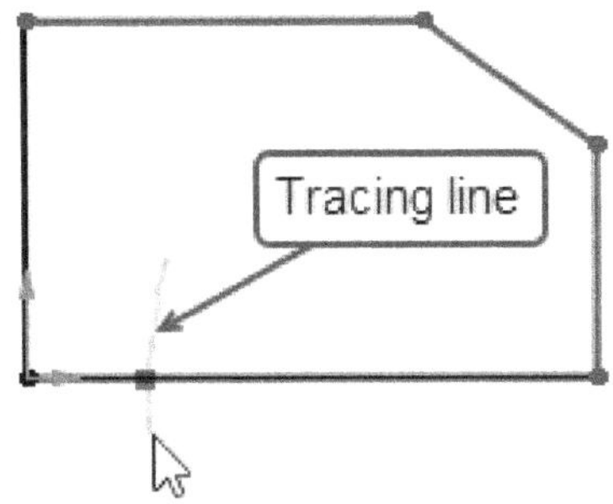

Corner

The **Corner** button is used to create a corner between two entities by trimming or extending them. To do this, click the **Corner** button in the **Trim PropertyManager**, and then select two sketch entities one at a time. A corner is created between the selected entities either by trimming or extending them, see Figures 3.7 and 3.8.

3.7

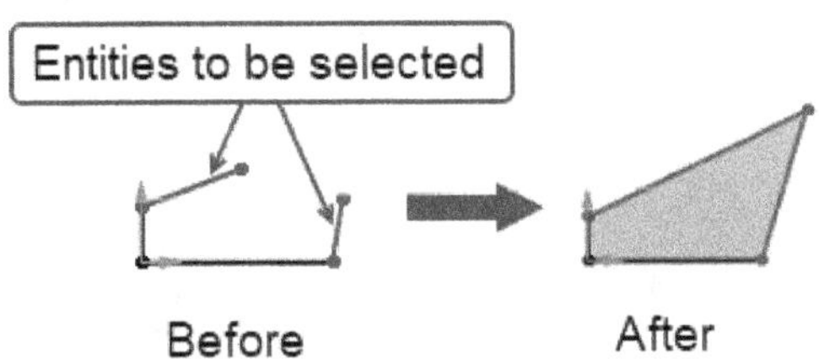

3.8

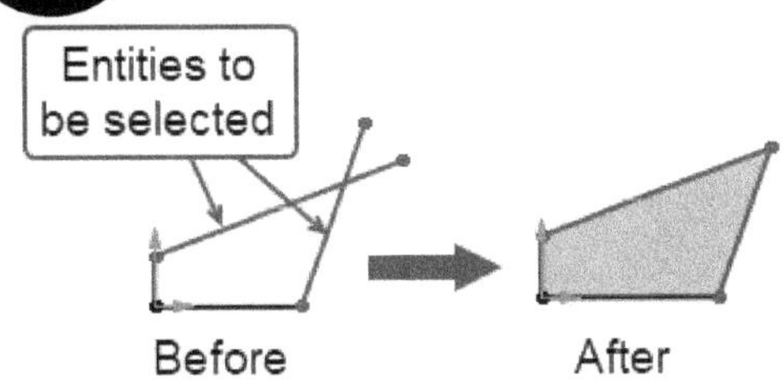

Trim away inside

The **Trim away inside** button is used to trim entities that lie within a defined boundary. To do this, click the **Trim away inside** button, and then select two entities one by one to define the boundary. Next, select the entities to be trimmed. The portions of the entities lying inside the boundary are trimmed. Figure 3.9 illustrates the boundary entities and the entities to be trimmed, while Figure 3.10 shows the resultant sketch after trimming the portions of the entities within the boundary.

3.9

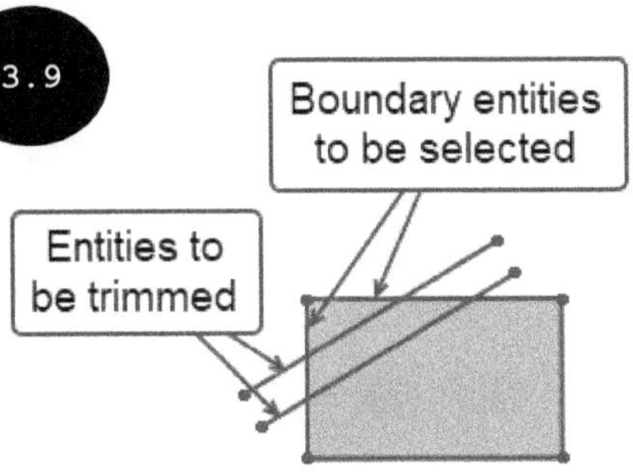

3.10

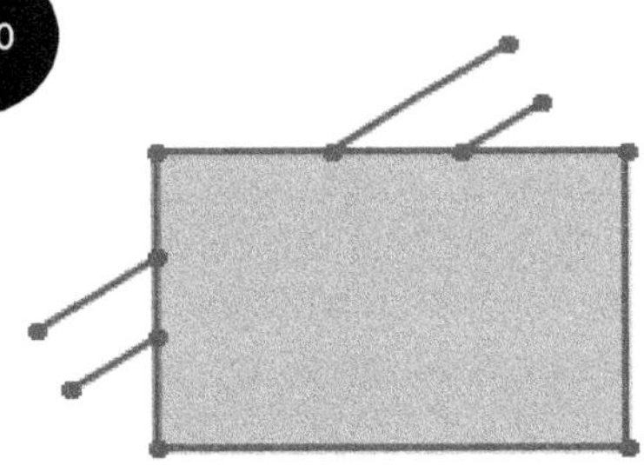

Trim away outside

The **Trim away outside** button is used to trim entities that lie outside a defined boundary. To do this, click the **Trim away outside** button, and then select two entities one at a time to define the boundary. Next, select the entities to be trimmed. The portions of the entities lying outside the boundary are trimmed. Figure 3.11 illustrates the boundary entities and the entities to be trimmed, while Figure 3.12 shows the resultant sketch after trimming the portions of the entities outside the boundary.

3.11

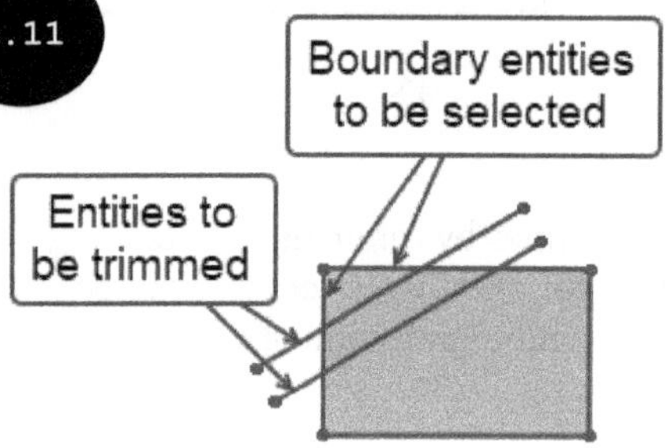

3.12

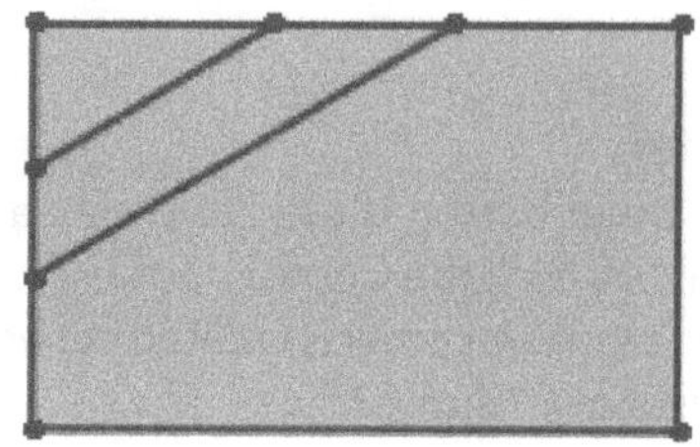

Trim to closest

The **Trim to closest** button is used to trim sketch entities at their nearest intersection by clicking the left mouse button. To do this, click the **Trim to closest** button, and then click the entity to be trimmed. The selected entity is trimmed at its nearest intersection, see Figures 3.13 and 3.14.

3.13

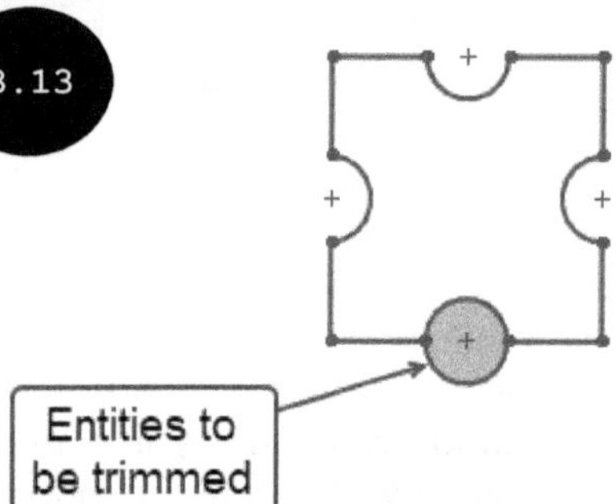

Before

3.14

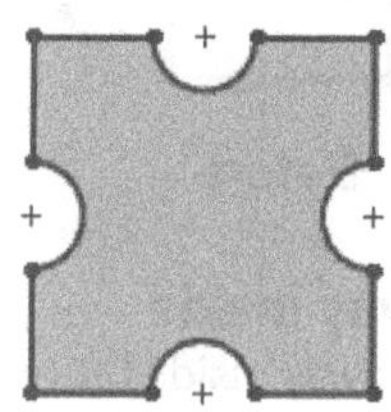

After

Keep trimmed entities as construction geometry

In SOLIDWORKS, you can convert trimmed entities into construction geometry by selecting the **Keep trimmed entities as construction geometry** check box of the PropertyManager.

Ignore trimming of construction geometry

In SOLIDWORKS, you can exclude construction geometries from being trimmed by selecting the **Ignore trimming of construction geometry** check box in the PropertyManager.

After trimming the sketch entities using the desired option as discussed above, press the ESC key to exit the **Trim PropertyManager**.

Extending Sketch Entities

You can extend sketch entities up to their nearest intersection using the **Extend Entities** tool. This tool is available in the **Trim** flyout of the **Sketch CommandManager**, see Figure 3.15. Figure 3.16 displays a sketch entity to be extended and Figure 3.17 shows the resultant sketch after extending the entity. The method for extending entities is discussed below:

3.15

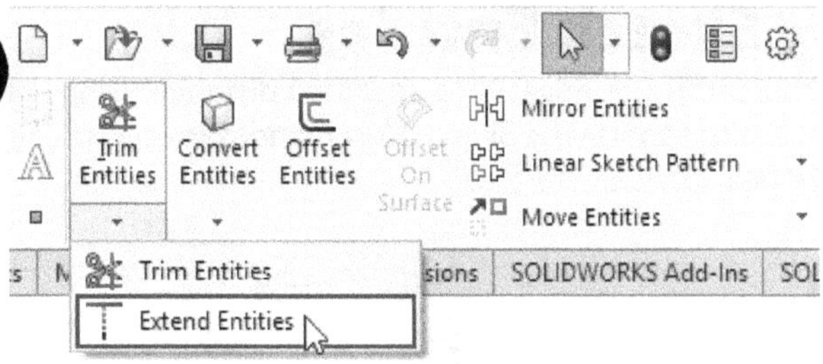

3.16

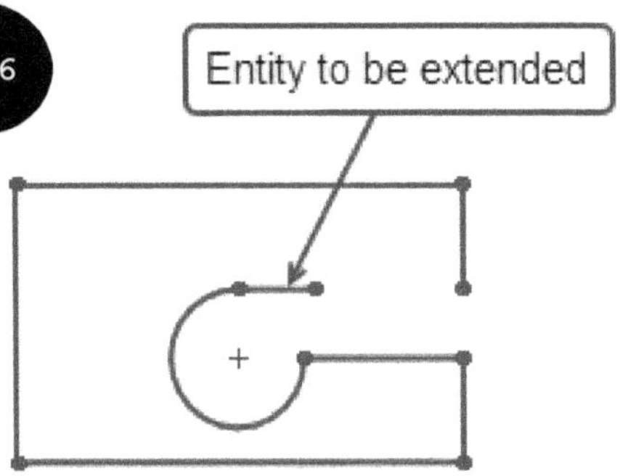

3.17

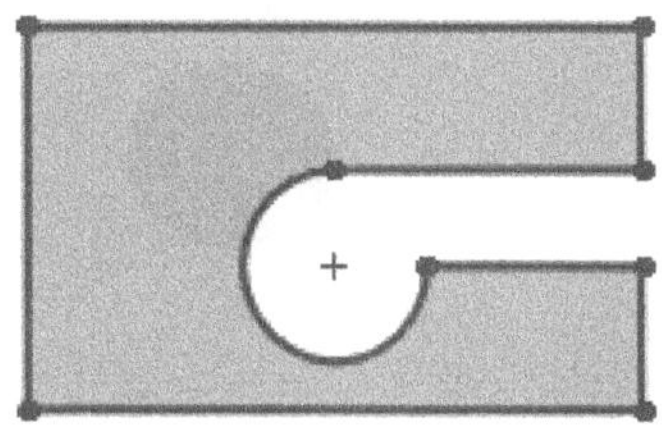

1. Click the arrow at the bottom of the **Trim Entities** tool in the **Sketch CommandManager**, and then select the **Extend Entities** tool in the flyout that appears, refer to Figure 3.15.

2. Move the cursor over the entity to be extended. A preview of the extended entity appears up to its next intersection in the drawing area, see Figure 3.18.

3.18

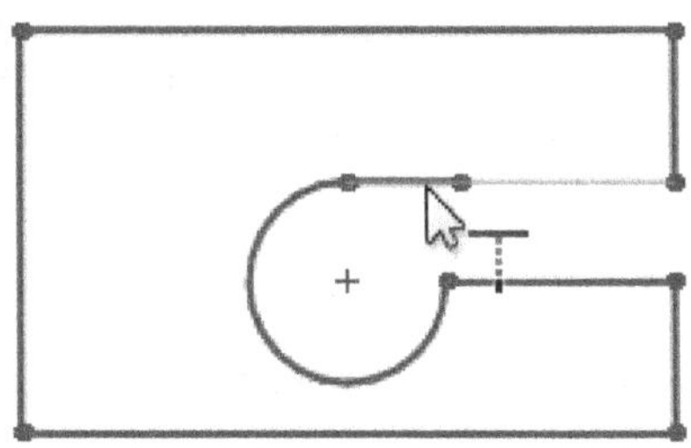

3. Click the left mouse button when the preview of the extended entity appears. The selected entity is extended up to the next intersection.

4. Similarly, you can extend other sketch entities. Once you have extended all the sketch entities, press the ESC key to exit the **Extend Entities** tool.

Note: The direction of the extended entity depends upon the position of the cursor over the entity. The endpoint of the entity, which is closer to the position of the cursor will be extended. To change the direction of extension, move the cursor to the other side of the sketch entity.

Offsetting Sketch Entities

You can offset sketch entities or edges by a specified distance using the **Offset Entities** tool. To do this, click the **Offset Entities** tool in the **Sketch CommandManager**, see Figure 3.19. The **Offset Entities PropertyManager** appears, see Figure 3.20.

3.19

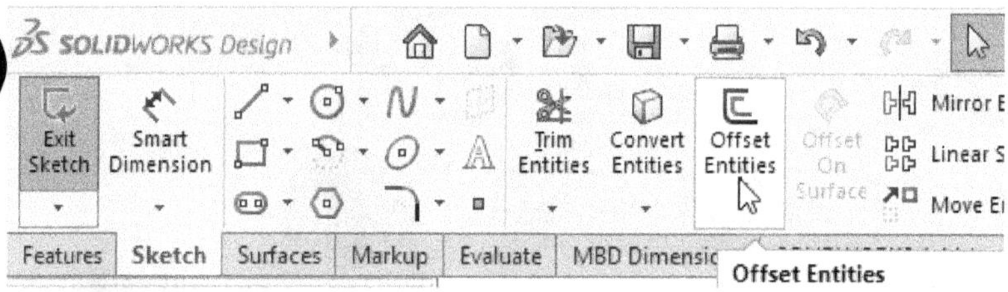

3.20

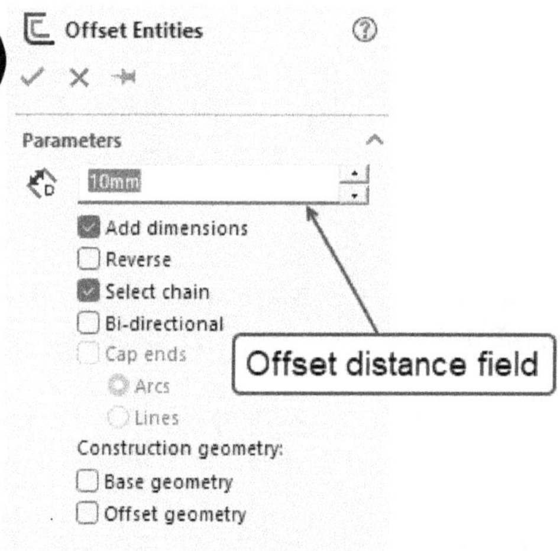

After invoking the **Offset Entities PropertyManager**, select the entity to offset in the drawing area. A preview of the offset entity appears with default parameters. You can adjust these default parameters using the options available in the PropertyManager. These options are discussed next.

Offset Distance

The **Offset Distance** field allows you to specify the desired offset distance for the selected sketch entity.

Tip: Besides controlling the offset distance using the **Offset Distance** field, you can also dynamically adjust the offset distance in the drawing area. To do this, press and hold the left mouse button in the drawing area and drag the cursor. As you drag, the offset distance updates dynamically, reflecting the changes in real time. Once the desired offset distance is reached, release the left mouse button to create the offset entity at the specified distance.

Add dimensions

Selecting the **Add dimensions** check box applies the offset dimension to the resultant sketch, see Figure 3.21.

3.21

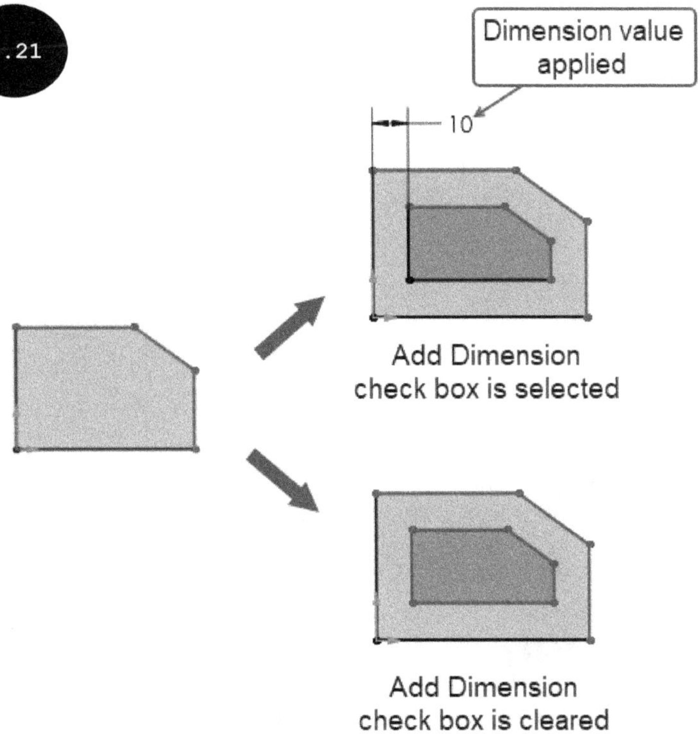

Reverse

Selecting the **Reverse** check box reverses the direction of the offset entities.

Select chain

Selecting the **Select Chain** check box automatically selects all the contiguous entities of the chosen entity in the drawing area.

Bi-directional

Selecting the **Bi-directional** check box offsets entities on both sides, see Figure 3.22.

3.22

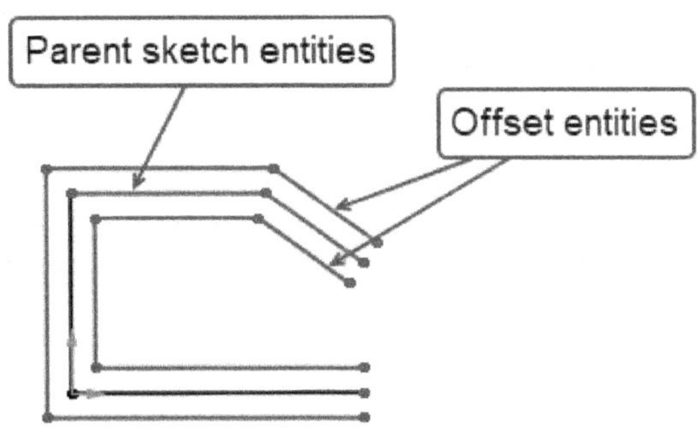

Cap ends

Selecting the **Cap ends** check box closes the open ends of the offset entities with either arcs or lines, based on the selection of the **Arcs** or **Lines** radio button in the PropertyManager, refer to Figures 3.23 and 3.24.

3.23

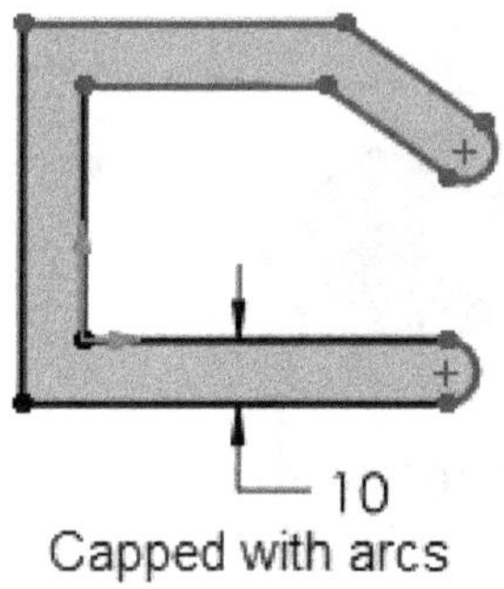

3.24

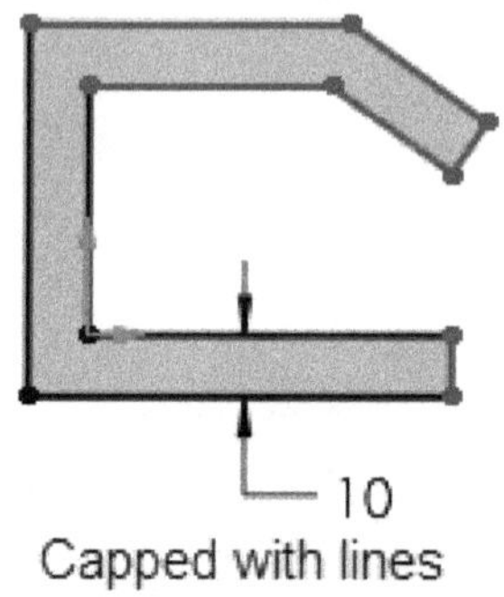

Note that when the **Cap ends** check box is selected, the **Arcs** and **Lines** radio buttons become enabled in the PropertyManager. By selecting the **Arcs** radio button, the offset entities are capped with arcs, see Figure 3.23. On the other hand, by selecting the **Lines** radio button, the offset entities are capped with lines, see Figure 3.24.

Construction geometry

Selecting the **Base geometry** check box converts the original or base sketch entities into construction entities, as shown in Figure 3.25 (a). On the other hand, selecting the **Offset geometry** check box converts the resultant offset entities into construction entities, as shown in Figure 3.25 (b).

3.25

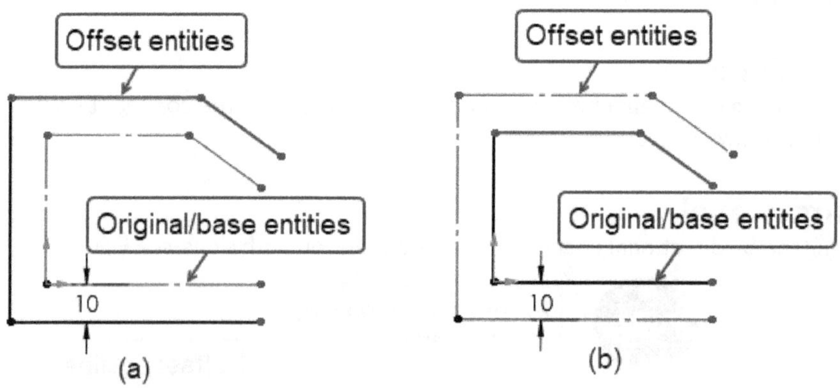

After specifying the required parameters, click on the green tick-mark ✓ button in the PropertyManager. The offset entities are created.

Mirroring Sketch Entities

In SOLIDWORKS, you can mirror sketch entities about a mirroring line using the **Mirror Entities** and **Dynamic Mirror** tools. You can select a line, a centerline, a linear edge, a reference plane, or a planar face as the mirroring line. The tools for mirroring sketch entities are discussed next.

Mirroring Entities using the Mirror Entities Tool

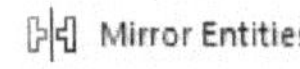

To mirror the sketch entities about a mirroring line using the **Mirror Entities** tool, click on the **Mirror Entities** tool in the **Sketch CommandManager**. The **Mirror PropertyManager** appears, see Figure 3.26. The options in this PropertyManager are discussed next.

3.26

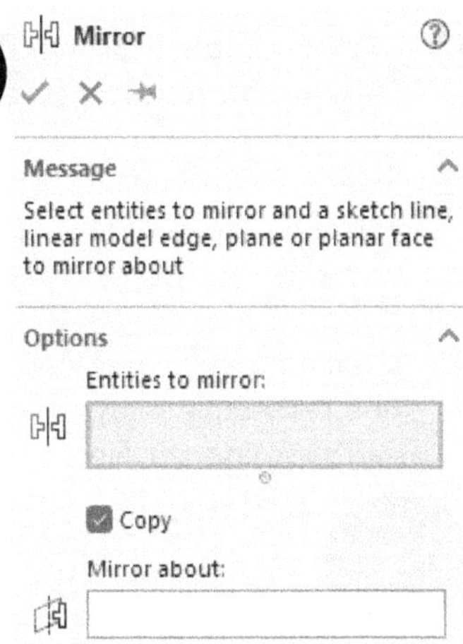

Entities to mirror

The **Entities to mirror** field of the PropertyManager is used to select entities to be mirrored. By default, this field is activated, allowing you to select entities by either clicking on them with the left mouse button or dragging the cursor over the entities to be mirrored. Note that as soon as you select entities, the names of the selected entities appear in this field. You can select entities to be mirrored before or after invoking the PropertyManager.

Copy

By default, the **Copy** check box is selected. As a result, the original/parent sketch entities are retained, and the mirror image of the selected entities is created. If you clear this check box, then the original sketch entities are removed from the sketch.

Mirror about

The **Mirror about** field is used to select a mirroring line about which the selected entities will be mirrored. To do this, click on the **Mirror about** field in the PropertyManager, then select a line, centerline, linear edge, reference plane, or planar face as the mirroring line. A preview of the mirrored entities appears in the drawing area. Finally, click the green tick-mark button in the PropertyManager to create the mirror image.

Figure 3.27 shows the entities to be mirrored and the mirroring line, while Figure 3.28 displays the resultant sketch after mirroring the entities about the selected mirroring line.

3.27

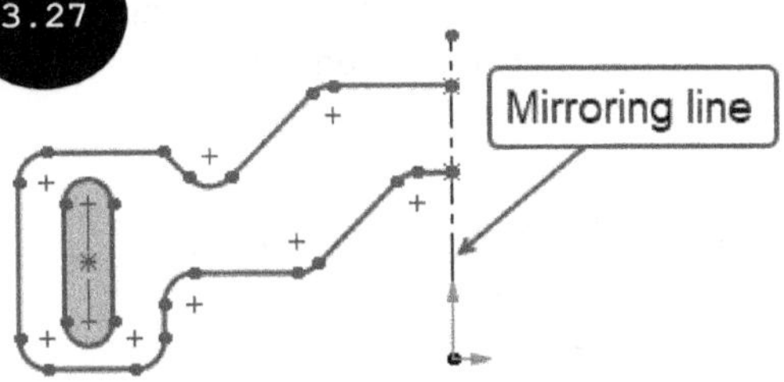

3.28

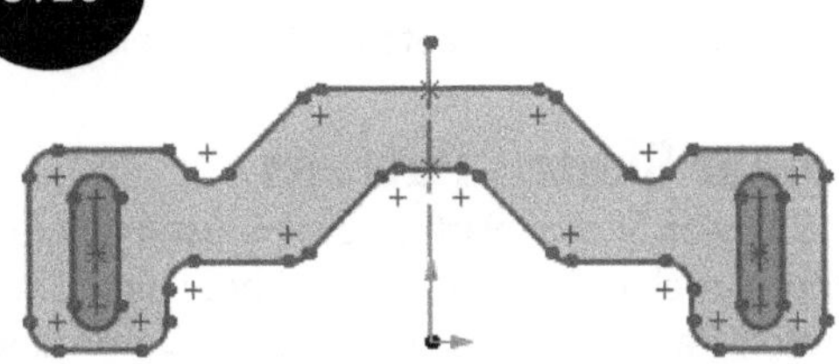

Note: When you mirror entities, a symmetric relation is applied between the original entities and the mirrored entities with respect to the mirroring line. As a result, on modifying the original entities, the mirrored entities get automatically modified and vice-versa. You will learn more about relations in later chapters.

Mirroring Entities by using the Dynamic Mirror Tool

The **Dynamic Mirror** tool is used to mirror entities about a mirroring line similar to mirroring entities using the **Mirror Entities** tool with the only difference that this tool dynamically mirrors entities while drawing them. The method for mirroring entities by using the **Dynamic Mirror** tool is discussed below:

1. Click on **Tools > Sketch Tools > Dynamic Mirror** in the SOLIDWORKS Design Menus. The **Dynamic Mirror** tool gets activated, and the **Mirror PropertyManager** appears.

2. Select a mirroring line. The symbol of a dynamic mirror appears on both ends of the selected mirroring line, see Figure 3.29. This symbol indicates that if you draw a sketch entity on either side of the mirroring line, the respective mirror image will automatically be created on the other side.

3. Draw entities on one side of the mirroring line by using sketching tools such as **Line** and **Circle**. The respective mirror images of the entities are created dynamically on the other side of the mirroring line, see Figure 3.30.

3.29

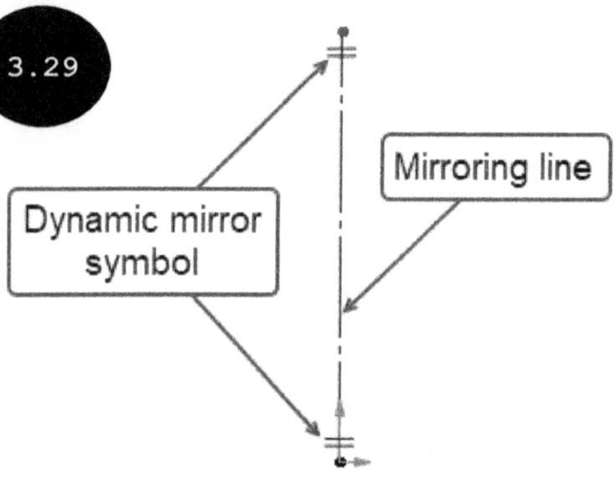

3.30

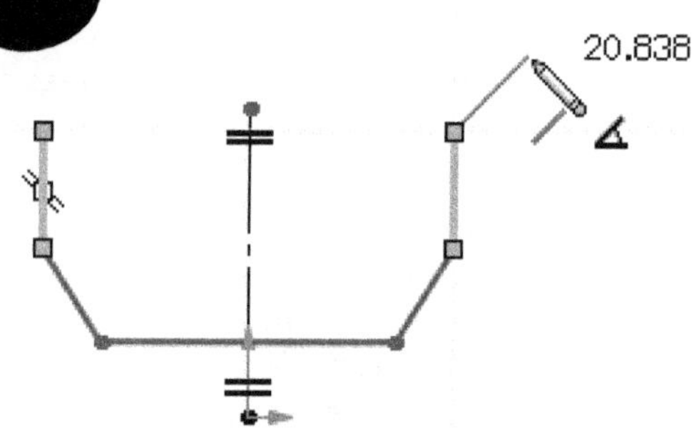

4. Once you have created the sketch, click on **Tools > Sketch Tools > Dynamic Mirror** in the SOLIDWORKS Design Menus to exit the **Dynamic Mirror** tool.

Patterning Sketch Entities

In SOLIDWORKS, you can create linear and circular patterns of sketch entities using the **Linear Sketch Pattern** and **Circular Sketch Pattern** tools, respectively. Both tools are discussed next.

Linear Sketch Pattern

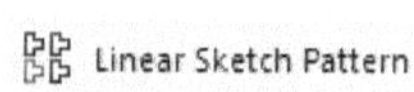

The **Linear Sketch Pattern** tool is used to create multiple instances of one or more sketch entities along two linear directions. To do this, click on the **Linear Sketch Pattern** tool in the **Sketch CommandManager**. The **Linear Pattern PropertyManager** appears, refer to Figure 3.31.

3.31

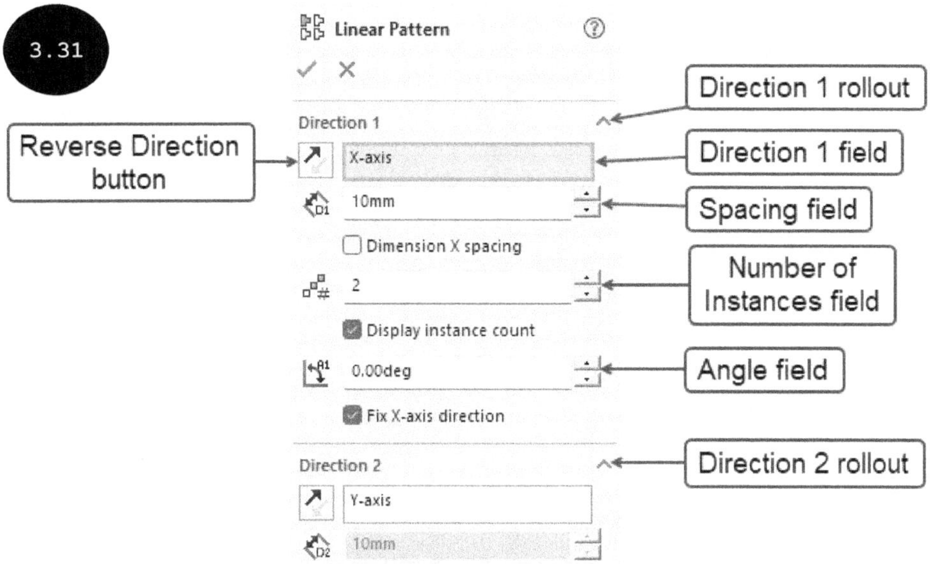

Once the **Linear Pattern PropertyManager** is invoked, click in the **Entities to Pattern** field and select one or more sketch entities in the drawing area. A preview of the linear pattern with default parameters appears in the drawing area. You can select the sketch entity to be patterned either before or after invoking the PropertyManager. The options in the **Linear Pattern PropertyManager** are used to define the parameters for creating the linear sketch pattern, which are discussed next.

Tip: In SOLIDWORKS, you can also select text as an entity to pattern. You will learn about adding text later in this chapter.

Direction 1

The options in the **Direction 1** rollout of the PropertyManager are used to specify the parameters for patterning sketch entities in Direction 1. The options of this rollout are discussed next.

Direction 1

By default, the **X-axis** is selected in the **Direction 1** field of the **Direction 1** rollout. As a result, the selected entities get patterned along the X-axis. You can also select a linear edge or a linear sketch entity as direction 1 of the pattern.

Reverse Direction

The **Reverse Direction** button is used to reverse direction 1 of the pattern.

Spacing

The **Spacing** field is used to specify the spacing between two pattern instances.

Number of Instances

The **Number of Instances** field is used to specify the number of instances to be created in direction 1.

Note: The number of pattern instances specified in the **Number of Instances** field is counted along with the parent or original instance. For example, if 6 is specified in the **Number of Instances** field, then 6 pattern instances will be created including the parent instance.

Angle

The **Angle** field is used to specify an angle for direction 1 concerning the X-axis. By default, a 0-degree angle is specified in this field. As a result, a linear pattern is created along direction 1 at a 0-degree angle, see Figure 3.32. Figure 3.33 shows the preview of the linear pattern along direction 1 (X-axis) at a 12-degree angle.

3.32

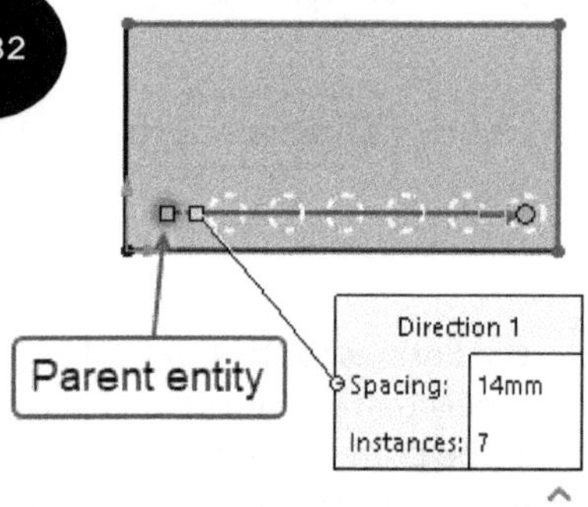

3.33

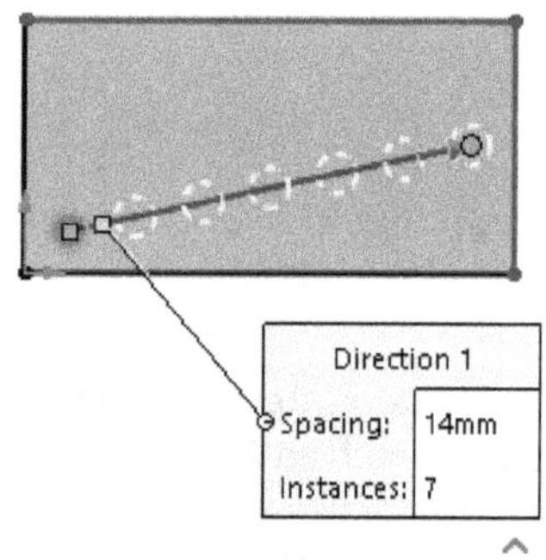

Note: In the preview of the linear pattern, an arrow appears with a dot at its tip, refer to Figures 3.32 and 3.33. You can also change the orientation or the angle of the pattern direction by dragging this dot in the drawing area.

Dimension X spacing

On selecting the **Dimension X spacing** check box, the distance specified between two pattern instances is applied in the resulting pattern sketch, see Figure 3.34.

Display Instance count

On selecting the **Display instance count** check box, the number of pattern instances specified in direction 1 is displayed in the resultant pattern sketch, see Figure 3.34.

3.34

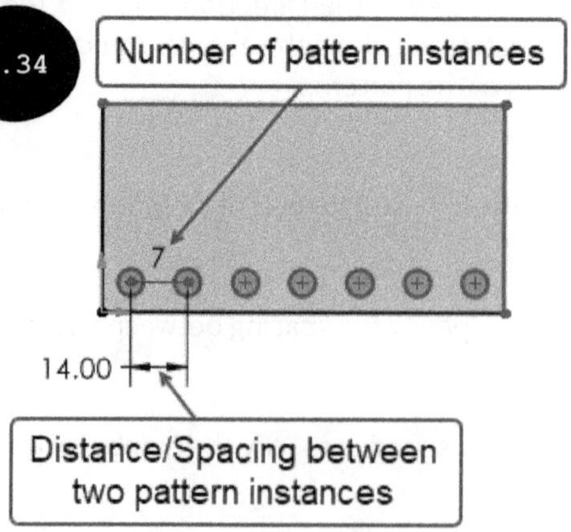

Fix X-axis direction

By default, the **Fix X-axis direction** check box is selected in the **Direction 1** rollout. As a result, a constraint is applied to fix the rotation of instances along the X-axis.

Direction 2

The options in the **Direction 2** rollout are the same as the options in the **Direction 1** rollout with the only difference that the options of the **Direction 2** rollout are used to specify parameters for the linear pattern in the second direction (direction 2), which is Y axis, by default, see Figure 3.35.

3.35

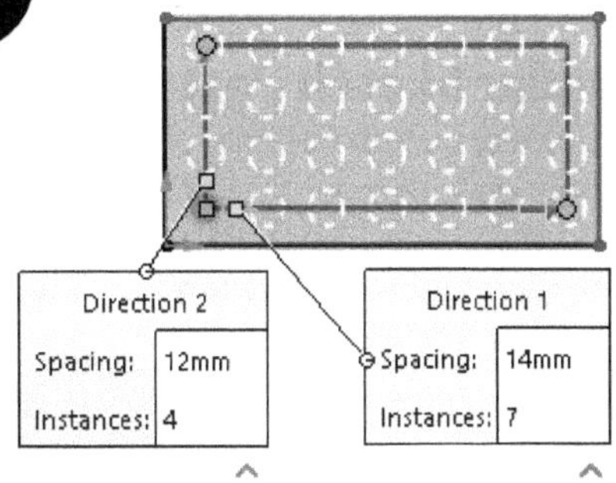

Note: By default, none of the options of the **Direction 2** rollout are enabled except the **Number of Instances** field. This is because **1** is specified in the **Number of Instances** field of the **Direction 2** rollout as the number of pattern instances. On specifying the number of pattern instances as two or more than two, the other options of the **Direction 2** rollout get enabled.

Entities to Pattern

The **Entities to Pattern** field in the **Entities to Pattern** rollout lists the sketch entities selected for patterning. You can select entities either before or after invoking the PropertyManager.

Instances to Skip

The **Instances to Skip** rollout in the PropertyManager allows you to skip or remove unwanted instances from the pattern. To skip instances, expand the **Instances to Skip** rollout by clicking the arrow in its title bar. Then, activate the field in the expanded rollout by clicking on it. Pink dots appear over all pattern instances in the drawing area, see Figure 3.36. Hover the cursor over the pink dot of the instance you want to skip, and click the left mouse button. The preview of the selected instance is disabled, removing it from the resultant pattern, as illustrated in Figure 3.37. Note that the skipped instance is listed in the **Instances to Skip** field of the PropertyManager. Repeat this process to skip multiple instances by clicking on their corresponding pink dots.

3.36

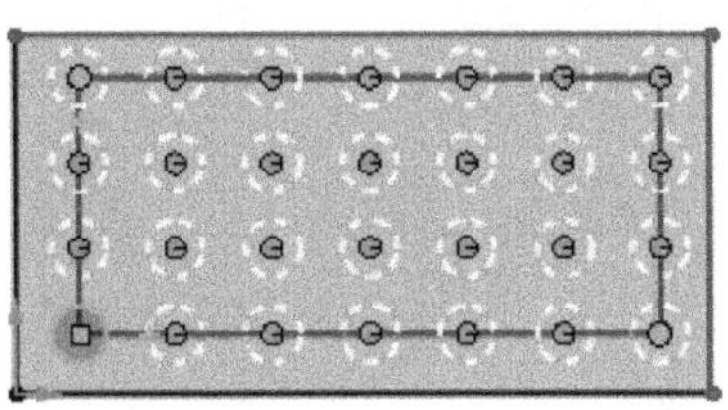

3.37

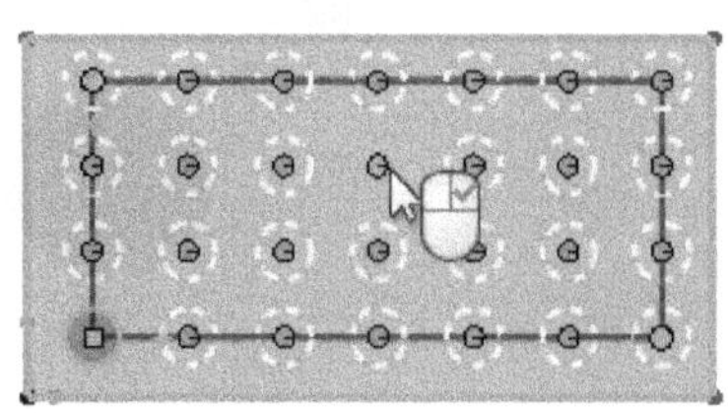

Note: To recall skipped instances of the pattern, click on the dots of the skipped instances in the pattern preview. Alternatively, select an instance listed in the **Instances to Skip** rollout, right-click to open the shortcut menu, and choose the **Delete** option. This removes the selected instance from the list of skipped instances, restoring it to the pattern.

After defining parameters for patterning the sketch entities in the **Linear Pattern PropertyManager**, click on the green tick-mark ✓ button in the PropertyManager to create the linear pattern.

Circular Sketch Pattern

The **Circular Sketch Pattern** tool is used to create multiple instances of one or more sketch entities in a circular pattern around a center point. To do this, invoke the **Pattern** flyout by clicking on the arrow next to the **Linear Sketch Pattern** tool in the **Sketch CommandManager**, see Figure 3.38. Next, click on the **Circular Sketch Pattern** tool. The **Circular Pattern PropertyManager** appears, see Figure 3.39.

3.38

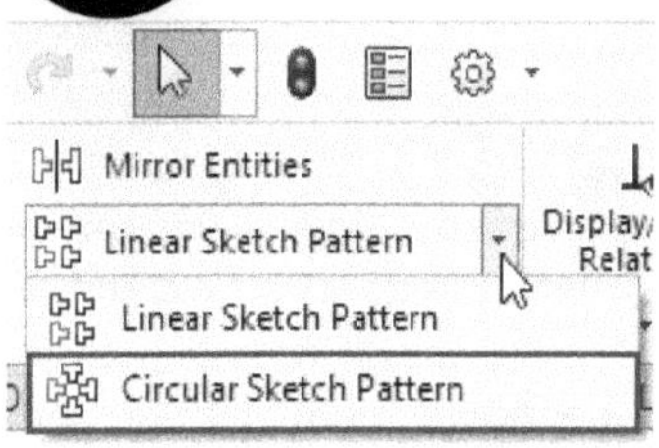

3.39

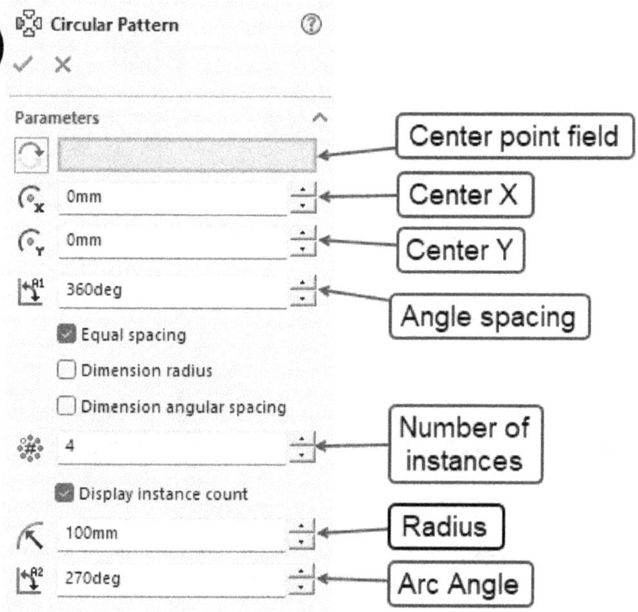

Once the **Circular Pattern PropertyManager** is invoked, click in the **Entities to Pattern** field and select one or more sketch entities in the drawing area. A preview of the circular pattern with default parameters appears, see Figure 3.40. Also, the names of the selected entities appear in the **Entities to Pattern** field of the PropertyManager. You can select entities to be patterned either before or after invoking the PropertyManager. The options in the **Circular Pattern PropertyManager** are used for defining parameters for creating the circular sketch pattern. The options are discussed next.

3.40

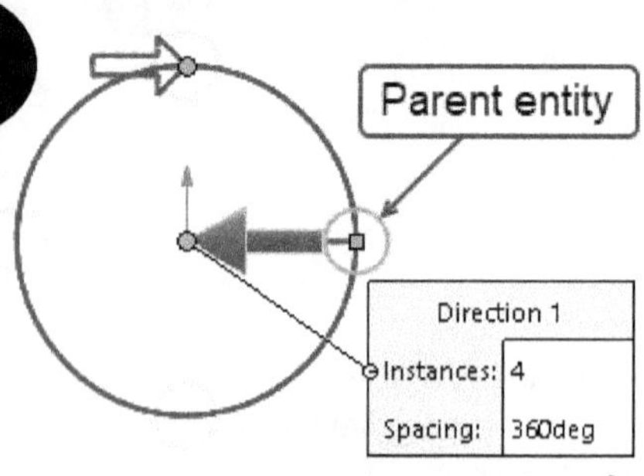

Parameters

The options in the **Parameters** rollout are used to specify parameters for patterning sketch entities circularly. The options of this rollout are discussed next.

Center Point

The **Center Point** field is used to specify a center point for patterning the instances, circularly. Note that as soon as you select entities to be patterned, the origin point (0,0) is selected as the center point of the circular pattern, see Figure 3.40. You can also select any sketch point as the center point of the circular pattern by activating this field.

Center X / Center Y

The **Center X** and **Center Y** fields are used to specify the X and Y coordinates of the center point, respectively.

Tip: You can also define the center point of the pattern by dragging the dot that appears at the tip of the arrow in the preview of the pattern. As you change the location of the dot by dragging it, the coordinates of the center point update accordingly in the **Center X** and **Center Y** fields.

Angle spacing

The **Angle Spacing** field is used to specify the total angle value for the pattern. By default, this value is set to 360 degrees, creating a circular pattern that spans 360 degrees with instances evenly distributed. This occurs because the **Equal Spacing** check box is selected by default in the rollout.

Equal spacing

By default, the **Equal spacing** check box is selected. As a result, all the pattern instances are adjusted within the total angle value specified in the **Angle spacing** field, equally. However, on clearing this check box, the angle value entered in the **Angle spacing** field is used as the angle between two instances of the pattern.

Dimension radius

On selecting the **Dimension radius** check box, the radius dimension of the circular pattern is applied in the resultant pattern, see Figure 3.41.

Dimension angular spacing

On selecting the **Dimension angular spacing** check box, the angular spacing between two instances is applied in the resultant pattern, see Figure 3.41.

3.41

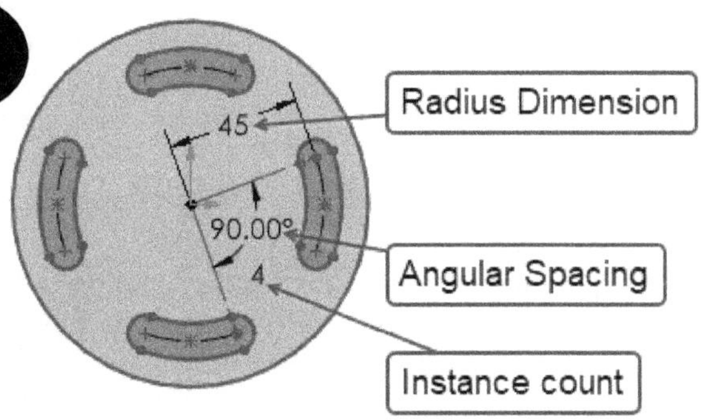

Number of Instances

The **Number of Instances** field is used to specify the total number of instances in the pattern. Note that the number of instances specified in this field is counted along with the parent instance. In SOLIDWORKS, you can specify the number of instances without any limit.

Display instance count

On selecting the **Display instance count** check box, the pattern instances count appears in the resultant pattern, refer to Figure 3.41.

Radius

The **Radius** field is used to specify the pattern radius. By default, the **Radius** field displays the pattern radius by keeping the origin as the center point. You can change the default radius value by entering a new radius value in this field.

Arc Angle

The **Arc Angle** field is used to specify the angle value from the center of the selected entities to the center point of the pattern.

Instances to Skip

The **Instances to Skip** rollout in the PropertyManager is used to exclude specific instances from the circular pattern. To do this, expand the rollout by clicking the arrow in its title bar. Then, click on the field in the expanded rollout to activate it. Pink dots appear on all pattern instances in the drawing area, see Figure 3.42. Hover over the pink dot of the instance you want to skip and click the left mouse button. The preview of the selected instance is disabled (refer to Figure 3.43), removing it from the final pattern. Also, the pink dot changes to an orange dot, and the corresponding instance number is displayed in the field of the **Instances to Skip** rollout.

3.42

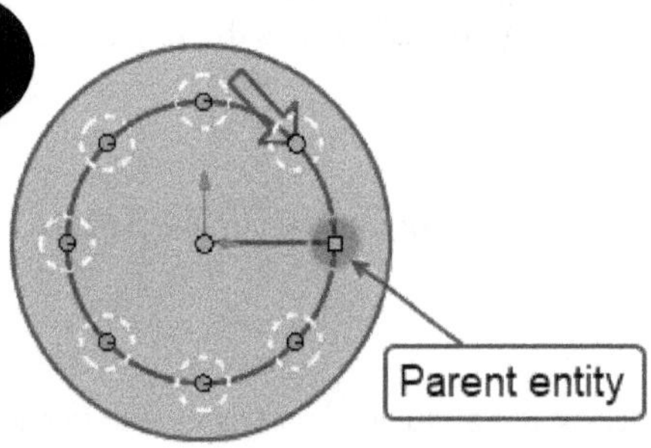

3.43

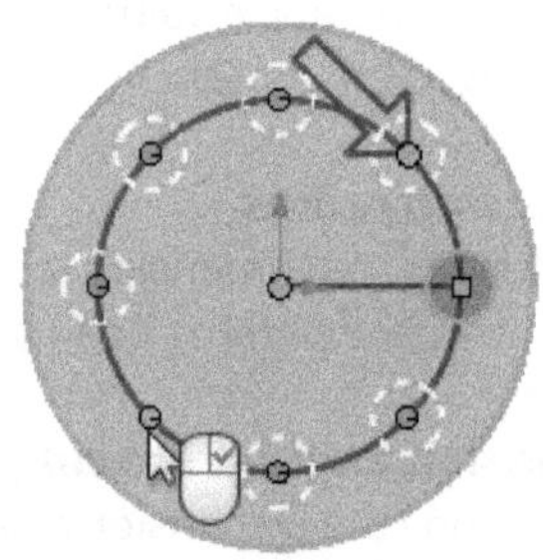

Note: To recall skipped instances of the pattern, click on the dots of the skipped instances in the pattern preview. Alternatively, select an instance listed in the **Instances to Skip** rollout, right-click to open the shortcut menu, and choose the **Delete** option. This removes the selected instance from the list of skipped instances, restoring it to the pattern.

After defining the required parameters for patterning the sketch entities in the **Circular Pattern PropertyManager**, click on the green tick-mark button to create the circular pattern.

Creating a Sketch Fillet

A sketch fillet is used to remove the corner at the intersection of two sketch entities by creating a tangent arc of constant radii, see Figure 3.44. In the Sketching environment, you can create sketch fillets using the **Sketch Fillet** tool.

3.44

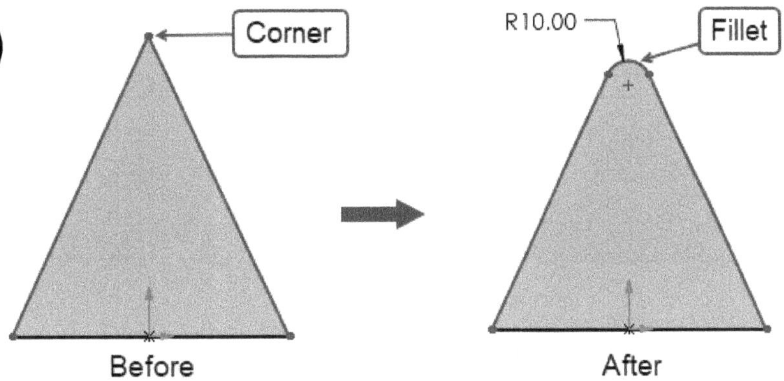

To create sketch fillets, click on the **Sketch Fillet** tool in the **Sketch CommandManager**, see Figure 3.45. The **Sketch Fillet PropertyManager** appears, see Figure 3.46.

3.45

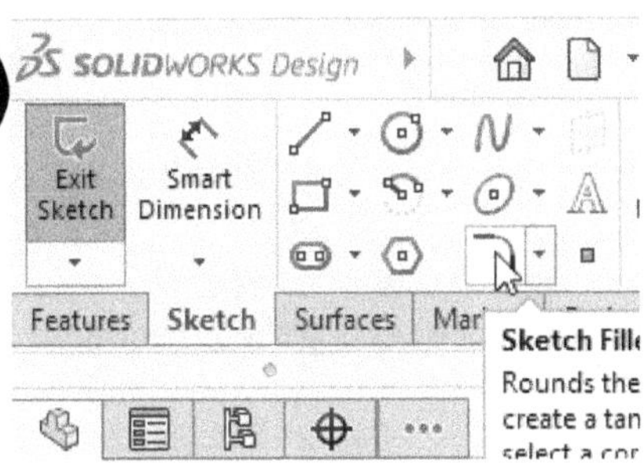

3.46

Next, enter the fillet radius in the **Fillet Radius** field of the **Fillet Parameters** rollout in the PropertyManager. By default, the **Keep constrained corners** check box is selected in the **Fillet Parameters** rollout. As a result, if the corner/vertex to be filleted has dimensions, then a virtual intersection point is created at the corner to maintain dimensions, whereas if the corner/vertex has relations, then the **SOLIDWORKS** message window appears which informs that if the fillet is created, the applied relation will be deleted. The **Dimension each fillet** check box of the PropertyManager is used for applying radius dimension to all the fillets created in the drawing area.

After specifying the fillet radius, move the cursor over the corner/vertex of the sketch to be filleted. A preview of the fillet appears in the drawing area, see Figure 3.47. Next, click the left mouse button to accept the fillet preview. Similarly, click on the other corners of the sketch to create fillets of a specified radius, see Figure 3.48. Next, click on the green tick-mark button in the PropertyManager. The fillets of specified radius are created at the selected corners of the sketch, see Figure 3.49. By default, the fillet radius is applied to one of the fillets and an equal relation is applied among all the fillets. However, if the **Dimension each fillet** check box is selected in the **Fillet Parameters** rollout of the PropertyManager, then the fillet radius is applied to all the fillets created in the drawing area.

3.47

3.48

3.49

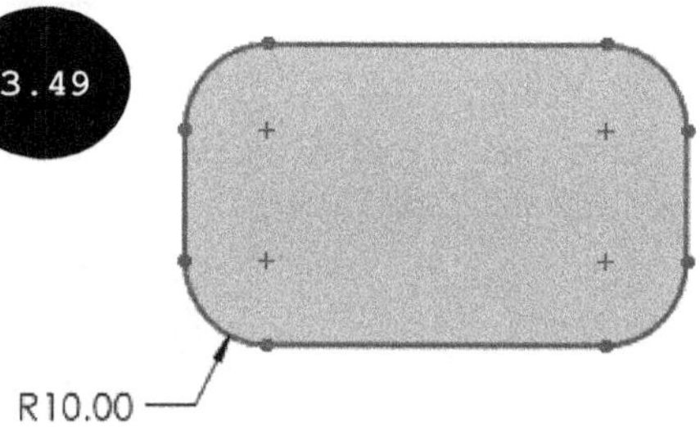

Tip: Instead of selecting a corner, you can also select two intersecting sketch entities for creating the fillet of specified radius at their intersection.

Creating a Sketch Chamfer

A chamfer is a bevel edge that is non-perpendicular to its adjacent sketch entities. You can create a sketch chamfer to the adjacent entities of the sketch using the **Sketch Chamfer** tool, see Figure 3.50.

3.50

To create a sketch chamfer, click on the arrow next to the **Sketch Fillet** tool in the **Sketch CommandManager**. A flyout appears, see Figure 3.51. In this flyout, click on the **Sketch Chamfer** tool. The **Sketch Chamfer PropertyManager** appears with options to create a chamfer, see Figure 3.52. The options are discussed next.

3.51

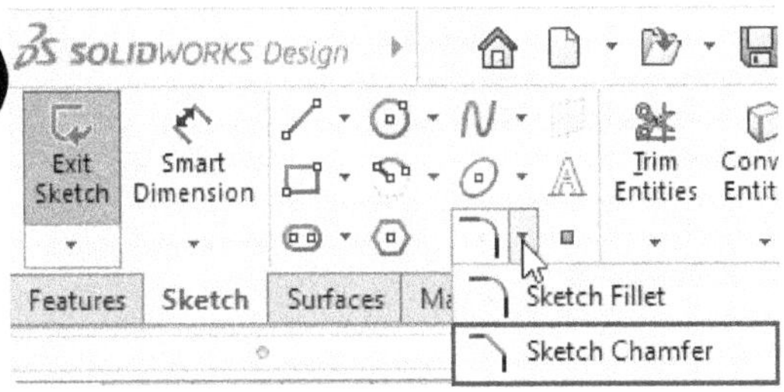

3.52

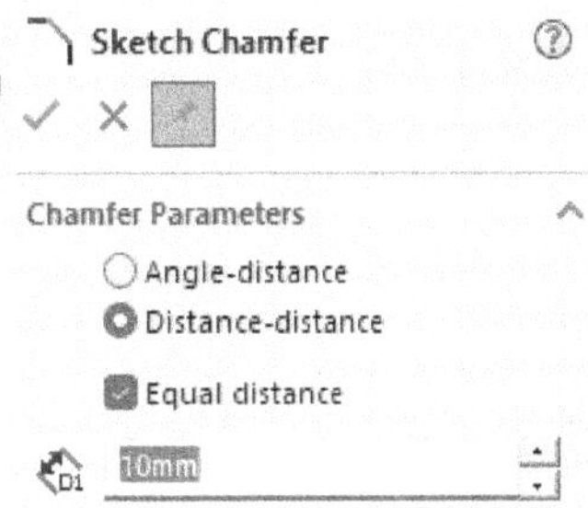

Distance-Distance

The **Distance-distance** radio button of the PropertyManager is used to create a chamfer by specifying distance values from both the adjacent sketch entities in the **Distance 1** and **Distance 2** fields of the PropertyManager, see Figure 3.53. Note that if the **Equal distance** check box is selected in the PropertyManager then the **Distance 2** field is not available in the PropertyManager and the distance value specified in the **Distance 1** field is applied on both sides of the sketch entities, see Figure 3.54.

3.53

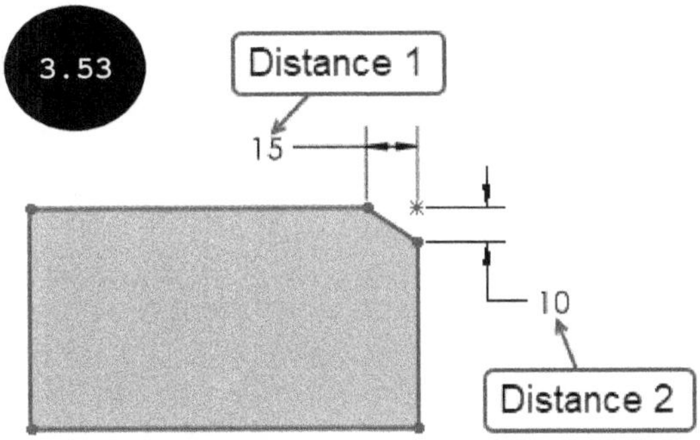

3.54

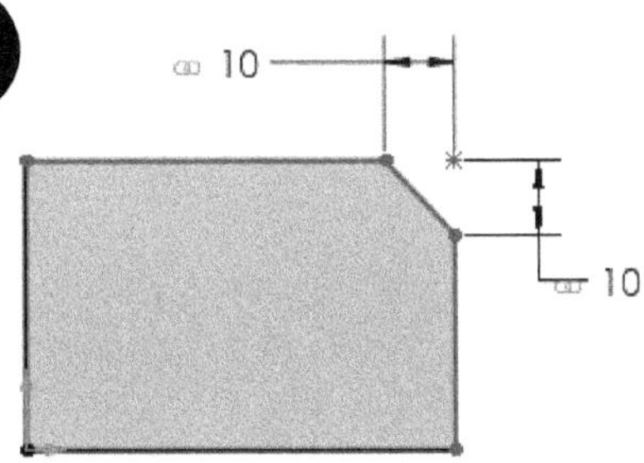

Angle-Distance

The **Angle-distance** radio button of the PropertyManager is used to create a chamfer by specifying the angle and distance values in the **Direction 1 Angle** and **Distance 1** fields of the PropertyManager, respectively, see Figure 3.55.

3.55

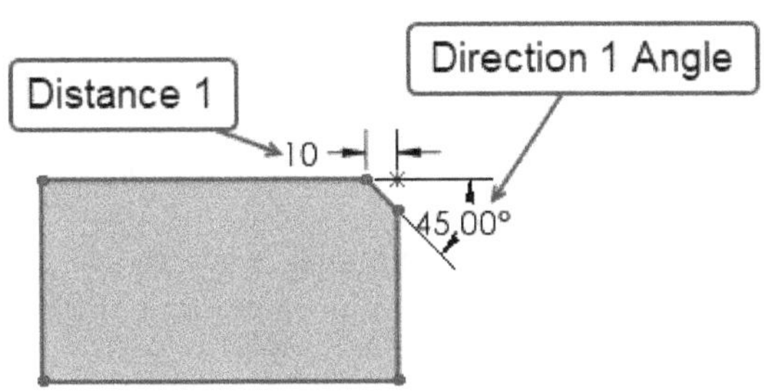

After selecting the required radio button (**Distance-distance** or **Angle-distance**) and specifying the required parameters in the PropertyManager, select the adjacent entities of the sketch one by one. The chamfer is created between the selected entities. Note that instead of selecting adjacent entities of the sketch, you can also select a vertex that is created at the intersection of two sketch entities for creating the chamfer. After creating the chamfer, press the ESC key to exit the **Sketch Chamfer** tool.

Adding Text

To add text in the sketching environment, click on the **Text** tool in the **Sketch CommandManager**. The **Sketch Text PropertyManager** appears, see Figure 3.56. The options in this PropertyManager are discussed next.

3.56

Curves

By default, the **Curves** field is activated in the **Curves** rollout. This allows you to select edges, curves, sketches, and sketch segments along which the text will be added. You can select a single or multiple connected sketch entities by clicking the left mouse button on each entity one by one.

Text

In the **Text** field of the **Text** rollout, you can enter the required text. Note that as you enter the text, it appears in the drawing area along the selected curve. If a curve is not selected in the **Curves** field of the PropertyManager, then the entered text appears horizontally starting from the origin.

You can use the default document font for the text by selecting the **Use document font** check box. You can also define a font other than the default document font. To do this, clear the **Use document font** check box and then click on the **Font** button. The **Choose Font** dialog box appears. In this dialog box, select the required font, font style, font height, and so on.

You can also define the width of each text character and the spacing between two text characters by using the **Width Factor** and **Spacing** fields respectively, see Figure 3.57. Note that these fields are enabled when the **Use document font** check box is cleared.

3.57

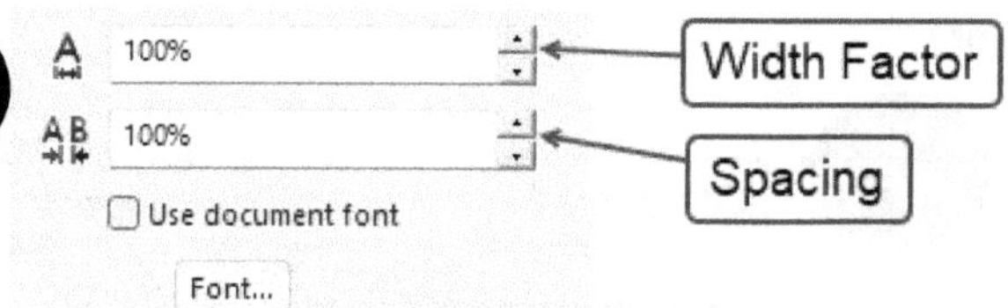

The other options in the **Sketch Text PropertyManager** are used to specify the text style, text alignment, and flipping the text horizontally or vertically. Note that some of these options are activated only if an entity is selected in the **Curves** field.

After writing the required text and specifying the required settings, click on the green tick-mark in the PropertyManager. The text gets added in the drawing area.

Moving a Sketch Entity

You can move a sketch entity from one position to another in the drawing area using the **Move Entities** tool. To do this, click on the **Move Entities** tool in the **Sketch CommandManager**. The **Move PropertyManager** appears, see Figure 3.58. The options in this PropertyManager are discussed next.

3.58

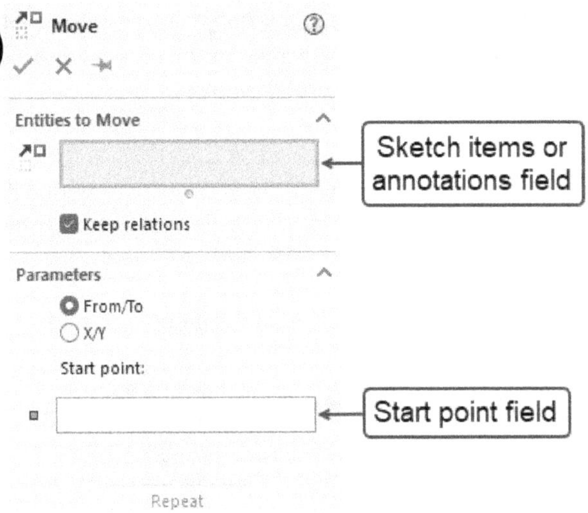

Entities to Move

The options in the **Entities to Move** rollout are used to select entities to be moved. These options are discussed next.

Sketch items or annotations

The **Sketch items or annotations** field of the **Entities to Move** rollout is used to select entities to be moved. By default, this field is activated. As a result, you can select entities to be moved in the drawing area. You can select entities to be moved before or after invoking the PropertyManager. The names of the selected entities are displayed in this field.

Keep relations

The **Keep relations** check box is used to maintain existing relations between the entities. If the **Keep relations** check box is selected, the existing relations between the sketch entities to be moved and the other entities of the sketch are maintained. However, on clearing this check box, the relations between the sketch entities to be moved and the other entities of the sketch will be broken.

Parameters

The **Parameters** rollout allows you to select an option for moving the entities, which are discussed next.

From/To

By default, the **From/To** radio button is selected in the **Parameters** rollout. As a result, you can move the selected entities from one location to the other concerning a base point. To move entities, when this radio button is selected, click on the **Start point** field and then specify a point in the drawing area as the base point for moving the selected entities. As soon as you specify a base point, the selected entities get attached to the cursor and as you move the cursor, the entities move dynamically in the drawing area. Next, click to specify a new position for the selected entities in the drawing area.

X/Y

The **X/Y** radio button is used to move sketch entities by specifying translation distances along the X and Y axes from the original location of the entities. When you select the **X/Y** radio button, the **ΔX** and **ΔY** fields get enabled in the rollout. In these fields, you can specify the translation distance along the X and Y axes. Note that the distance specified in the **ΔX** and **ΔY** fields is measured from the center point of the original location of the sketch entities.

Repeat

The **Repeat** button is used to move sketch entities with an incremental distance specified in the **ΔX** and **ΔY** fields. Note that every time you click on the **Repeat** button, the selected entities move to the incremental distance that is specified in the **ΔX** and **ΔY** fields.

After specifying the required parameters, click on the green tick mark ✓ in the PropertyManager.

Creating a Copy of Sketch Entities

You can create a copy of a set of sketch entities using the **Copy Entities** tool. To copy sketch entities, click on the arrow next to the **Move Entities** tool and then click on the **Copy Entities** tool in the flyout that appears, see Figure 3.59. The **Copy PropertyManager** appears, see Figure 3.60. Next, select the sketch entities to be copied and then select the required radio button (**From/To** or **X/Y**) in the **Parameters** rollout. Depending upon the radio button selected, you can specify a new location for the entities in the drawing area. The copy of selected entities is created at the specified location.

3.59

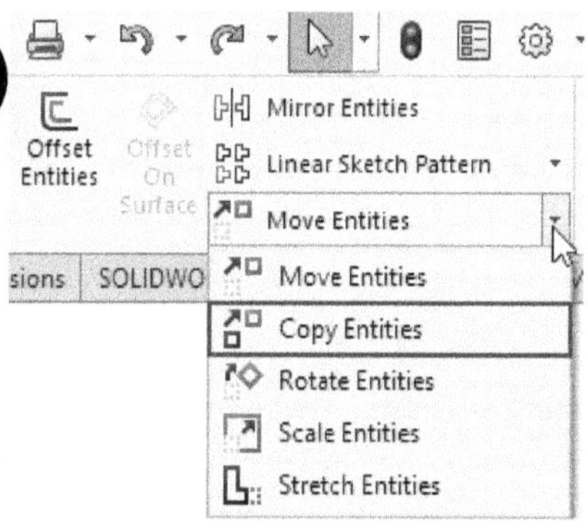

3.60

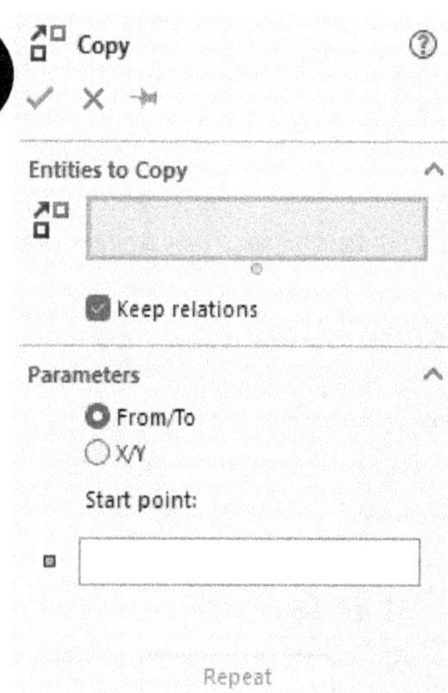

Note: The options in the **Copy PropertyManager** are the same as those of the **Move PropertyManager** with the only difference that the options in this PropertyManager are used for copying selected entities in the new location.

Tip: In SOLIDWORKS, you can also select text as an entity to be copied.

Rotating an Entity

You can rotate one or more sketch entities by an angle using the **Rotate Entities** tool. To do this, click on the arrow next to the **Move Entities** tool. A flyout appears, refer to Figure 3.59. In the flyout, click on the **Rotate Entities** tool. The **Rotate PropertyManager** appears, see Figure 3.61. The options in this PropertyManager are discussed next.

3.61

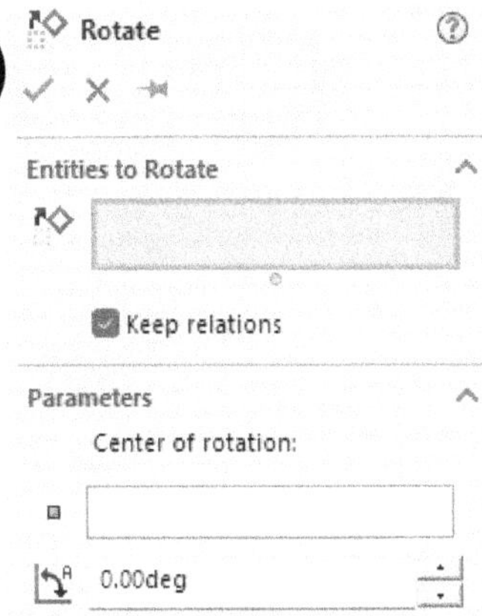

Entities to Rotate

The options of the **Entities to Rotate** rollout are used to select entities to be rotated. The options are discussed next.

Sketch items or annotations

The **Sketch items or annotations** field is used to select entities to be rotated. By default, this field is activated. As a result, you can select entities to be rotated in the drawing area. You can select entities to be rotated before or after invoking the PropertyManager. The names of the selected entities are displayed in this field.

Keep relations

The **Keep relations** check box is used to maintain existing relations between sketch entities. If this check box is selected, the existing relations between sketch entities are to be rotated and the other entities of the sketch are maintained. However, on clearing this check box, the relations between the sketch entities to be rotated and the other entities of the sketch will be broken.

Parameters

The **Parameters** rollout of the PropertyManager is used to specify parameters for rotating sketch entities. The options in this rollout are discussed next.

Center of rotation

The **Center of rotation** field is used to specify a base point or a center point of rotation. To do this, click on the **Center of rotation** field and then specify a point in the drawing area by clicking the left mouse button. A triad appears in the drawing area, see Figure 3.62. Also, the **Angle** field gets activated below this field in the PropertyManager. Now, you can specify the angle of rotation in the **Angle** field and then press ENTER. A preview of the rotated sketch entities appears in the drawing area. You can also use the spinner arrows in the **Angle** field to specify the angle of rotation. Next, click on the green tick-mark button in the PropertyManager. The selected entities get rotated at the specified angle of rotation. Figure 3.62 shows a sketch before and after rotating its slot at an angle of 30 degrees around its center point.

Tip: When you specify a positive angle value, the direction of rotation will be anti-clockwise, whereas, on specifying a negative angle value, the direction of rotation will be clockwise.

3.62

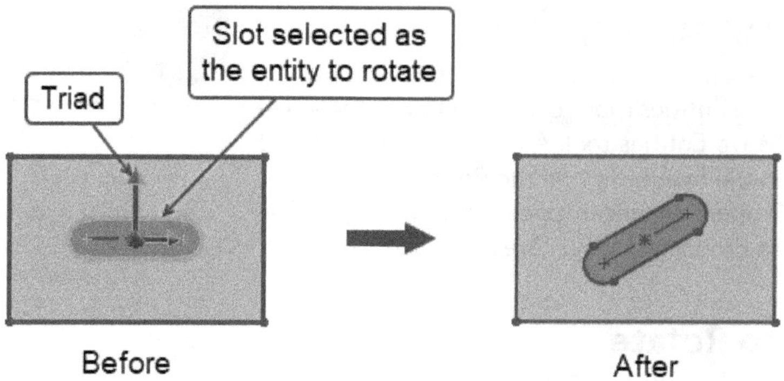

Scaling Sketch Entities

In SOLIDWORKS, you adjust the size of sketch entities by increasing or decreasing their scale using the **Scale Entities** tool. To do this, click on the arrow next to the **Move Entities** tool and then click on the **Scale Entities** tool in the flyout that appears, see Figure 3.63. The **Scale PropertyManager** appears, see Figure 3.64. The options in this PropertyManager are discussed next.

3.63

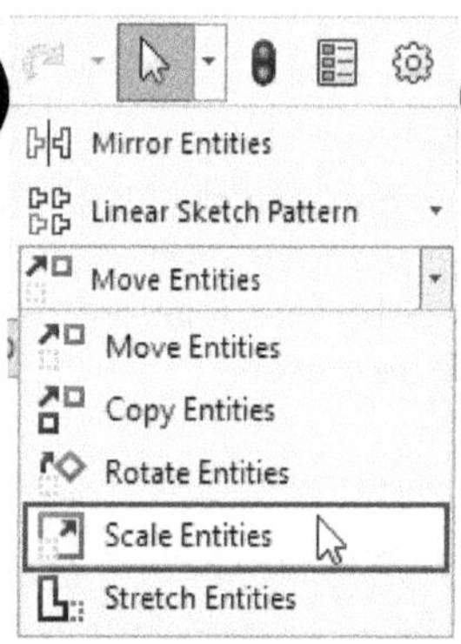

3.64

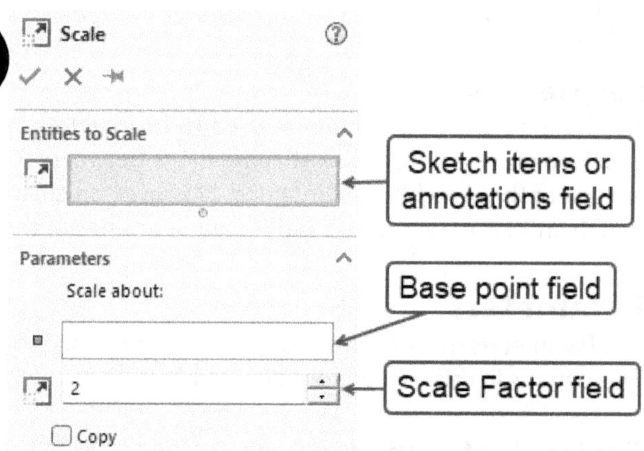

Entities to Scale

The **Sketch items or annotations** field of the **Entities to Scale** rollout is used to select entities to be scaled. You can select entities before or after invoking the PropertyManager.

Parameters

The options in the **Parameters** rollout are used to specify parameters for scaling the selected sketch entities. The options are discussed next.

Base point / Scale Factor

The **Base point** field of the **Parameters** rollout is used to specify a base point or a center point for scaling the selected entities. To do this, click on the **Base point** field and then click in the drawing area to specify a base point. A yellow colored dot appears in the drawing area, which represents the base point for scaling the entities, see Figure 3.65. Next, specify the scale factor in the **Scale Factor** field. You can also use the spinner arrows of the **Scale Factor** field to specify the scale factor. A preview of the scaled sketch of the specified scale factor appears in the drawing area, see Figure 3.65. Next, click on the green tick-mark button in the PropertyManager. The selected entities are scaled.

3.65

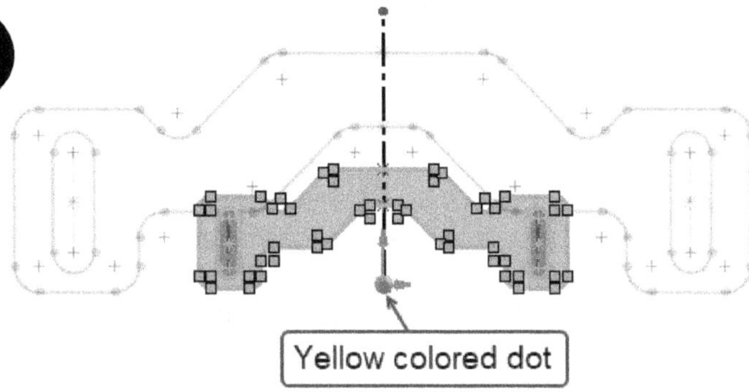

Copy

By default, the **Copy** check box is cleared in the PropertyManager. As a result, the selected entities are scaled to the new scale factor without retaining a copy of the original entities in the drawing area. However, if you select the **Copy** check box, the original entities are retained, and a copy of scaled entities is created in the drawing area. Note that on selecting the **Copy** check box, the **Number of Copies** field gets enabled in the rollout. In this field, you can specify the number of copies of the scaled entities to be created.

After specifying all the parameters, click on the green tick-mark button in the PropertyManager. The selected entities are scaled accordingly in the drawing area.

Note: The original sketch entities are not included in the count specified in the **Number of Copies** field. For instance, if you set this field to 2, two scaled copies of the sketch entities will be created in addition to the original. Note that each copy will be created using the incremental scale factor.

Stretching an Entity

You can stretch entities of a sketch using the **Stretch Entities** tool. To do this, click on the arrow next to the **Move Entities** tool. A flyout appears. In this flyout, click on the **Stretch Entities** tool. The **Stretch PropertyManager** appears, see Figure 3.66. The options in this PropertyManager are discussed next.

3.66

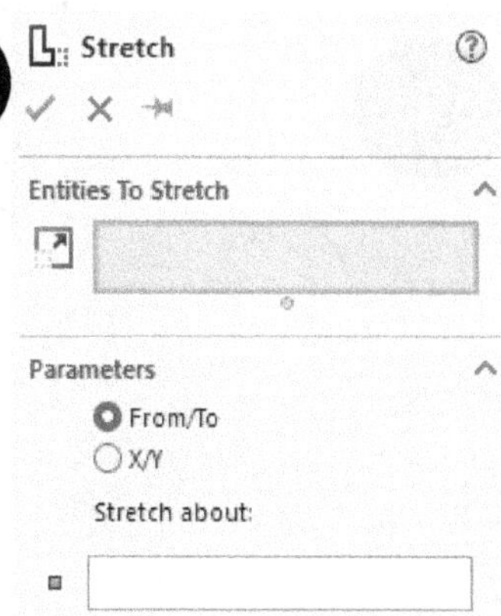

Entities to Stretch

The **Sketch items or annotations** field of the **Entities to Stretch** rollout is used for selecting entities to be stretched. By default, this field is activated. As a result, you can select entities to be stretched.

Tip: It is recommended to select entities by drawing a cross window such that it partially encloses the entities to be stretched. You can draw a cross window by dragging the cursor from right to left, diagonally.

Parameters

The options in the **Parameters** rollout are used to choose an option for stretching the entities. The options are discussed next.

From/To

The **From/To** radio button is used to stretch entities from a base point. On selecting this radio button, the **Base point** field gets enabled in the **Parameters** rollout. Click on this field to activate it and then select a base point for stretching the entities. After specifying a base point, move the cursor. A preview of the stretched entities appears in the drawing area. Next, click to specify a new position for the stretched entities in the drawing area.

X/Y

The **X/Y** radio button is used to stretch entities by specifying a translation distance along the X and Y axes from the original location of the entities. When you select the **X/Y** radio button, the **ΔX** and **ΔY** fields get enabled in the **Parameters** rollout. In these fields, you can specify translation distances along the X and Y axes.

Repeat

The **Repeat** button is used to stretch entities to an incremental distance specified in the **ΔX** and **ΔY** fields.

After selecting the entities to be stretched and the required radio button (**From/To** or **X/Y**), specify a new position for the stretched entities in the drawing area.

Tutorial 1

Draw a sketch of the model, as shown in Figure 3.67. The dimensions and the 3D model shown in this figure are for your reference only. You will learn about applying dimensions and creating the 3D model in later chapters. All dimensions are in mm.

3.67

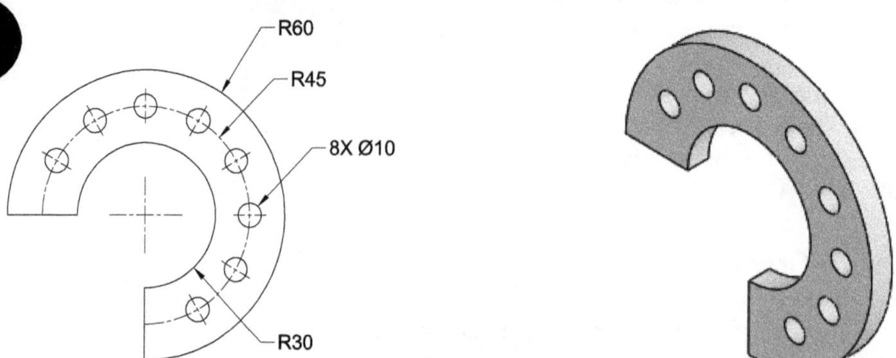

Section 1: Invoke the Part Modeling Environment

1. Start SOLIDWORKS by double-clicking on the SOLIDWORKS icon on your desktop. The startup user interface of SOLIDWORKS appears along with the **Welcome** dialog box.

Note: If SOLIDWORKS is already open and the **Welcome** dialog box does not appear on the screen, you can invoke it by clicking on the **Welcome to SOLIDWORKS** tool in the **Standard** toolbar.

2. Click on the **Part** button in the **Welcome** dialog box. The Part modeling environment is invoked.

Section 2: Specifying Unit Settings

1. Move the cursor toward the lower right corner of the screen over the Status Bar and then click on the **Unit System** area in the Status Bar. The **Unit System** flyout appears, see Figure 3.68.

3.68

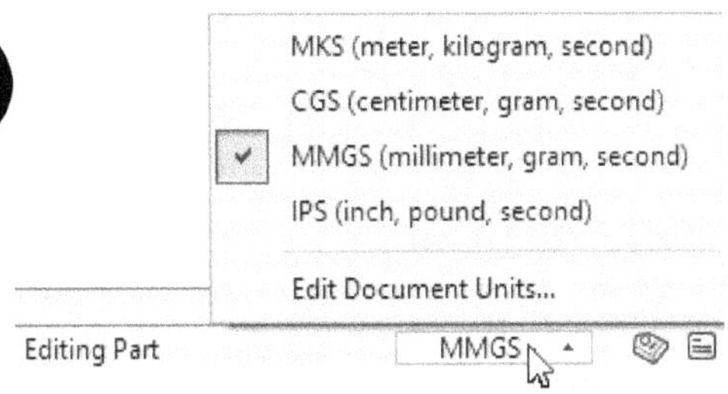

2. Ensure that the **MMGS (millimeter, gram, second)** option is tick-marked in this flyout.

Section 3: Invoking the Sketching Environment

1. Click on the **Sketch** tab in the CommandManager. The tools of the **Sketch CommandManager** appear.

2. Click on the **Sketch** tool in the **Sketch CommandManager**. Three default planes mutually perpendicular to each other appear in the graphics area.

3. Move the cursor over the Front plane and click when the boundary of the plane gets highlighted. The Sketching environment is invoked. Also, the Front plane is orientated normal to the viewing direction and the Confirmation corner appears at the upper right corner of the drawing area.

Section 4: Specifying the Snap Settings

Now, you need to set the snap settings such that the cursor snaps to an increment of 5 mm.

1. Click on the **Options** tool in the **Standard** toolbar. The **System Options - General** dialog box appears.

2. In this dialog box, click on the **Document Properties** tab. The name of the dialog box changes to **Document Properties - Drafting Standard**.

3. Click on the **Grid/Snap** option in the left panel of the dialog box. The options for specifying the grids and snap settings are displayed on the right panel of the dialog box.

4. Enter **20** in the **Major grid spacing** field, **4** in the **Minor-lines per major** field, and **1** in the **Snap points per minor** field of the **Grid** area in the dialog box.

5. Ensure that the **Display grid** check box of the **Grid** area in the dialog box is cleared to turn off the display of grids in the drawing area. If you want to turn on the display of grids in the drawing area, then you can select this check box.

6. Click on the **Go To System Snaps** button in the dialog box. The name of the dialog box changes to **System Options - Relations/Snaps**.

7. Ensure that the **Grid** and **Angle** check boxes are selected in the **Sketch snaps** area of the dialog box to turn on the snap mode.

8. Ensure that the **Snap only when grid is displayed** check box, available below the **Grid** check box is cleared.

9. Click on the **OK** button in the dialog box. The snap settings are specified, and the dialog box is closed.

Section 5: Drawing Sketch Entities

Once the units and snap settings have been specified, you need to start drawing the sketch.

1. Click on the **Circle** tool in the **Sketch CommandManager**. The **Circle** tool gets activated and the **Circle PropertyManager** appears on the left of the drawing area.

2. Move the cursor to the origin and then click to specify the center point of the circle when the cursor snaps to the origin.

3. Move the cursor horizontally to the right to define the radius. A preview of the circle appears, and the radius value is displayed near the cursor. When the radius reads 60 mm, click in the drawing area to specify the point, see Figure 3.69. A circle of radius 60 mm is created. Note that the **Circle** tool is remains active.

3.69

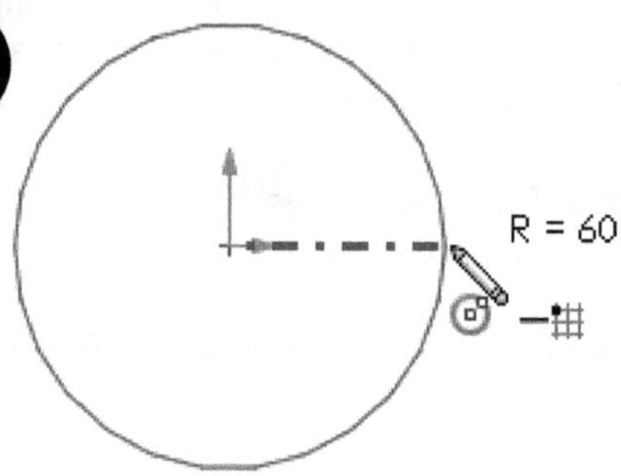

4. Move the cursor to the origin and then click to specify the center point of another circle when the cursor snaps to the origin.

5. Move the cursor horizontally to the right and click when the radius of the circle appears as 30 mm, see Figure 3.70.

   After creating circles of radii 60 mm and 30 mm, you need to create a construction circle of radius 45 mm that will define the PCD of holes.

6. Create a circle of radius 45 mm whose center point is at the origin, refer to Figure 3.71. After creating a circle of radius 45 mm, right-click in the drawing area and click on the **Select** option in the shortcut menu to terminate the creation of the circle and exit the **Circle** tool.

3.70

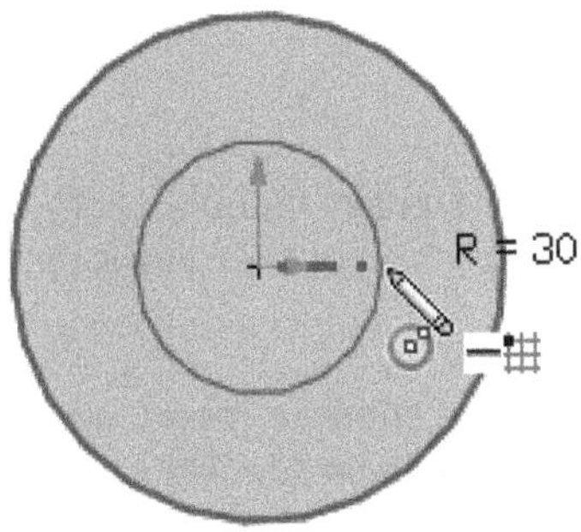

3.71

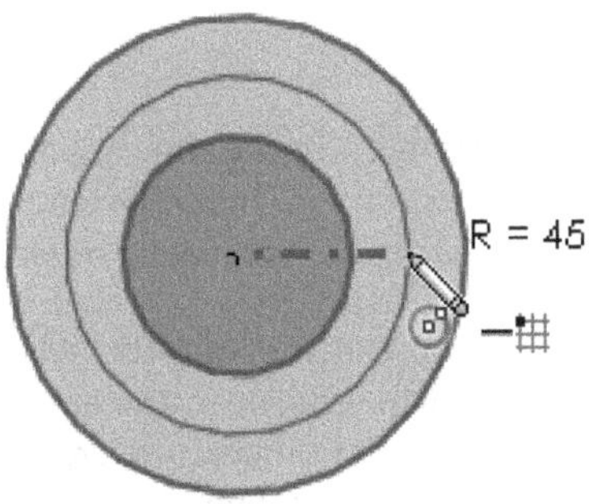

Once you have created a circle of radius 45 mm, you need to convert it into a construction circle.

7. Click on the circle of radius 45 mm in the drawing area. The **Circle PropertyManager** appears on the left of the drawing area. Also, a Pop-up toolbar appears near the cursor, see Figure 3.72.

8. Click on the **Construction Geometry** tool in the Pop-up toolbar, see Figure 3.72. The selected circle of radius 45 mm is converted into a construction circle, see Figure 3.73. Alternatively, select the **For construction** check box in the **Options** rollout of the PropertyManager to convert the circle into a construction circle.

3.72

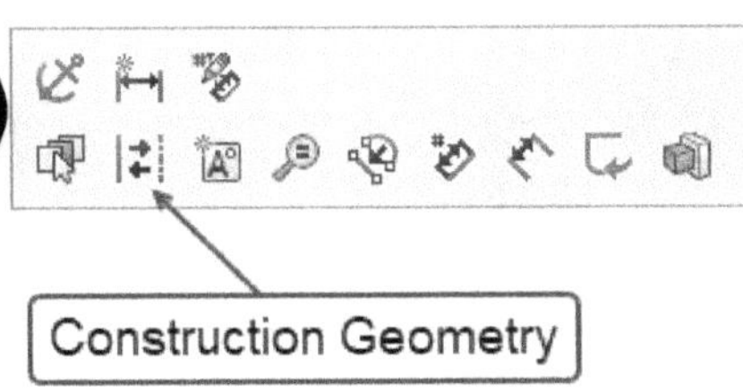

3.73

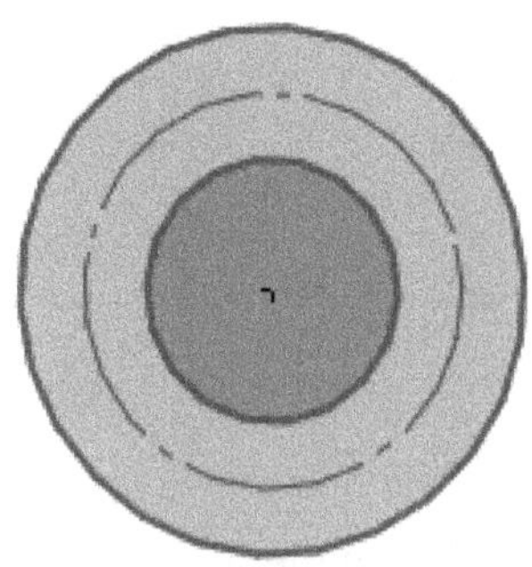

9. Click on the **Line** tool in the **Sketch CommandManager**. The **Insert Line PropertyManager** appears.

10. Specify the start point of the line at the origin and then move the cursor horizontally toward the left.

11. Click to specify the endpoint of the line when the length of the line appears as 60 mm and the cursor snaps to the outer circle, see Figure 3.74.

3.74

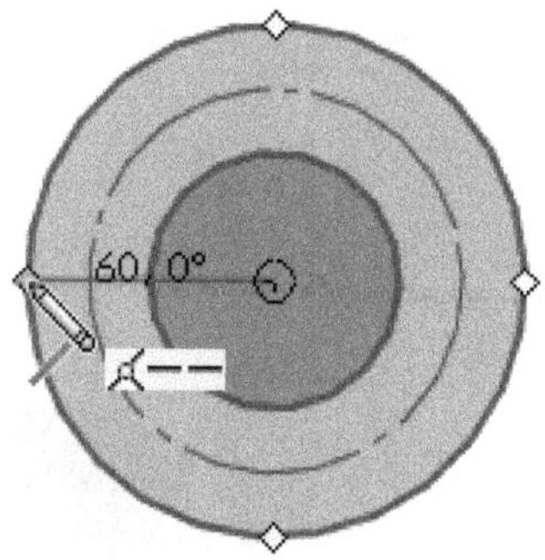

12. Right-click in the drawing area and then click on the **End chain (double-click)** option in the shortcut menu to terminate the creation of the continuous chain of lines. However, the **Line** tool is still active for creating other line entities.

Tip: To exit the **Line** tool, click on the **Select** option in the shortcut menu, which appears on right-clicking in the drawing area. If you select the **End chain (double-click)** option in the shortcut menu, the creation of continuous chain of lines gets terminated but the **Line** tool remains active.

13. Move the cursor to the origin and click to specify the start point of the line when the cursor snaps to the origin.

14. Move the cursor vertically downward and click to specify the endpoint of the line when the length of the line appears as 60 mm and the cursor snaps to the outer circle, see Figure 3.75.

3.75

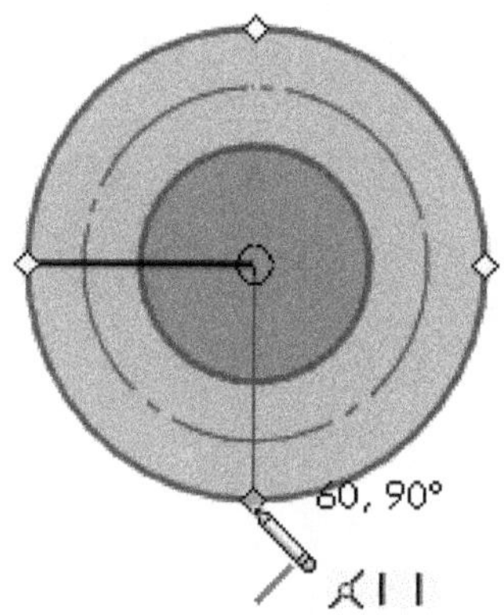

15. Right-click in the drawing area and then click on the **Select** option in the shortcut menu that appears to exit the **Line** tool.

Now, you need to create a circle of diameter 10 mm. It is evident from Figure 3.67 that the circles of diameter 10 mm are 10 in count. As the diameter of all the circles is the same and the circles are on the same PCD (Pitch Circle Diameter), you can create one circle and then create a circular pattern to create the remaining circles.

16. Click on the **Circle** tool in the **Sketch CommandManager**. The **Circle PropertyManager** appears.

17. Click to specify the center point of the circle when the cursor snaps to the right quadrant of the construction circle, see Figure 3.76. Also, the coordinates (X, Y, Z) appear as "45, 0, 0" in the Status Bar, see Figure 3.77.

3.76

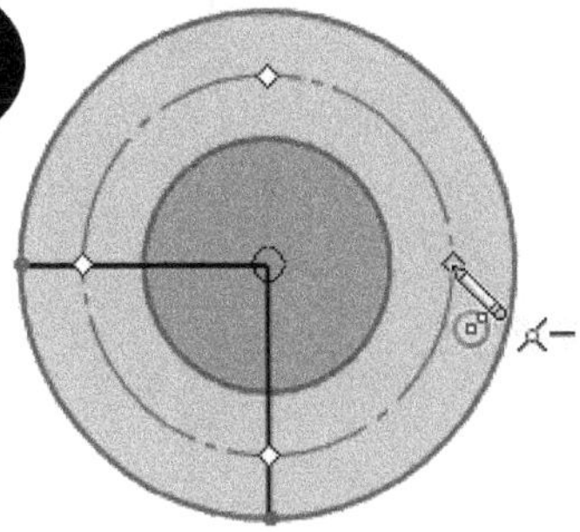

3.77

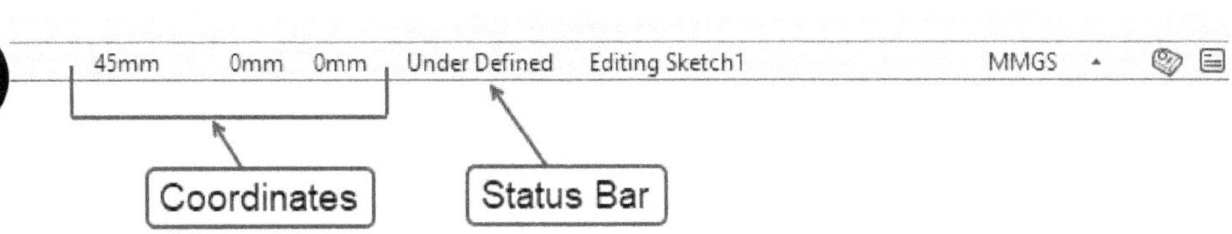

18. Move the cursor horizontally toward the right and then click when the radius of the circle appears 5 mm near the cursor, see Figure 3.78.

3.78

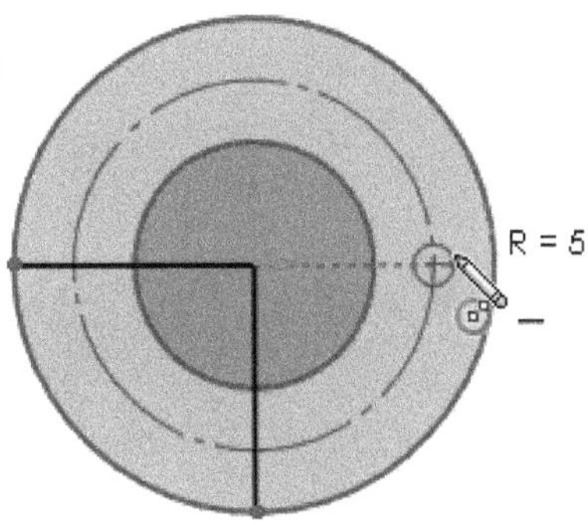

19. Right-click in the drawing area and then click on the **Select** option in the shortcut menu that appears to exit the **Circle** tool.

Section 6: Trimming Sketch Entities

Now, you need to trim the unwanted sketch entities of the sketch.

1. Click on the **Trim Entities** tool in the **Sketch CommandManager**. The **Trim PropertyManager** appears on the left of the drawing area. Trim Entities

2. Click on the **Trim to closest** button in the **Options** rollout of the PropertyManager.

3. Ensure that the **Keep trimmed entities as construction geometry** and **Ignore trimming of construction geometry** check boxes are cleared in the PropertyManager.

4. Move the cursor over the portion of the entity to be trimmed (see Figure 3.79) and click when it is highlighted. The selected portion of the entity is then trimmed, see Figure 3.80.

3.79

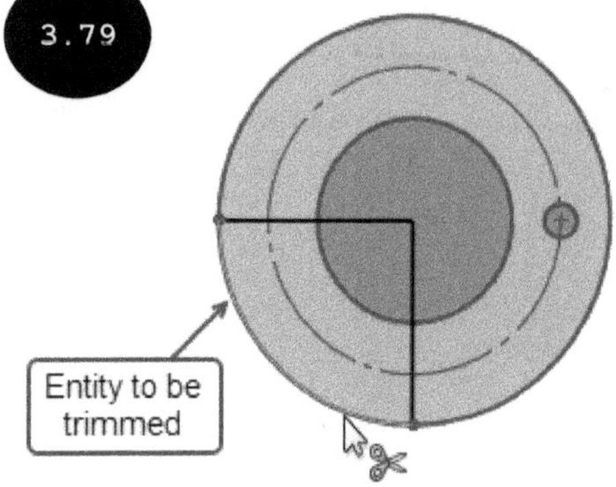

3.80

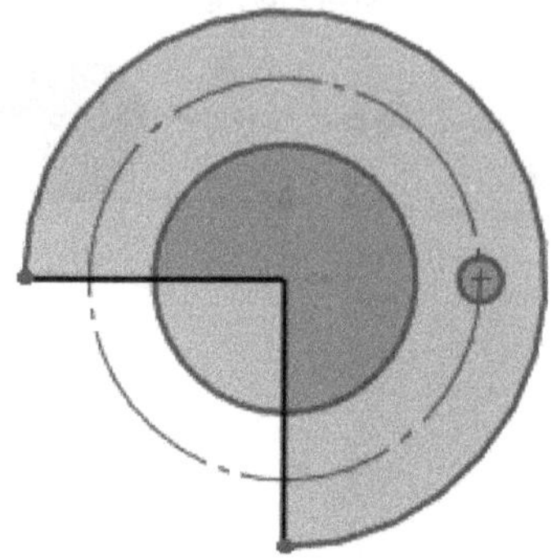

5. Similarly, trim the other unwanted portions of the entities of the sketch. Figure 3.81 shows entities to be trimmed and Figure 3.82 shows the sketch after trimming all the unwanted entities.

3.81

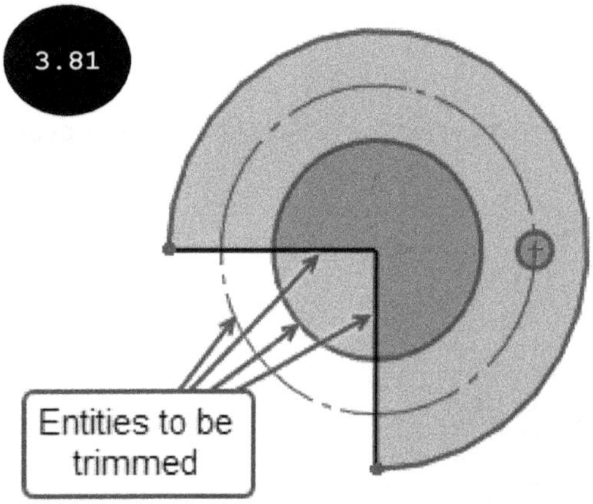

3.82

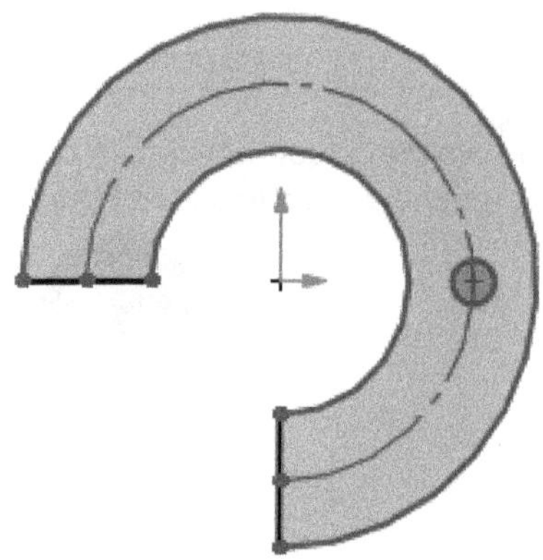

6. Click on the green tick-mark button in the PropertyManager to exit the **Trim Entities** tool.

Section 7: Creating the Circular Pattern

Now, you need to create a circular pattern.

1. Select the previously created circle of radius 5 mm in the drawing area.

2. Click on the arrow next to the **Linear Sketch Pattern** tool. The **Pattern** flyout appears, see Figure 3.83.

3.83

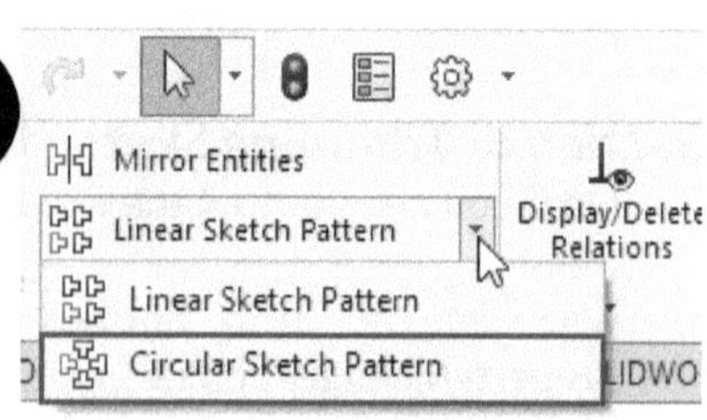

3. Click on the **Circular Sketch Pattern** tool in the **Pattern** flyout. A preview of the circular pattern appears along with the display of the **Circular Pattern PropertyManager**.

4. Ensure that the **Equal spacing** check box is selected in the **Parameters** rollout to apply equal spacing among all pattern instances.

5. Ensure that the **360** degree is entered in the **Angle spacing** field of the **Parameter** rollout.

6. Enter **12** in the **Number of Instances** field as the total number of pattern instances to be created.

7. Expand the **Instances to Skip** rollout by clicking the arrow in its title bar, see Figure 3.84. Then, click inside the field in the expanded rollout to activate it. Pink dots appear on all pattern instances in the drawing area, see Figure 3.85.

   Now, you need to skip the four lower-left instances of the pattern.

3.84

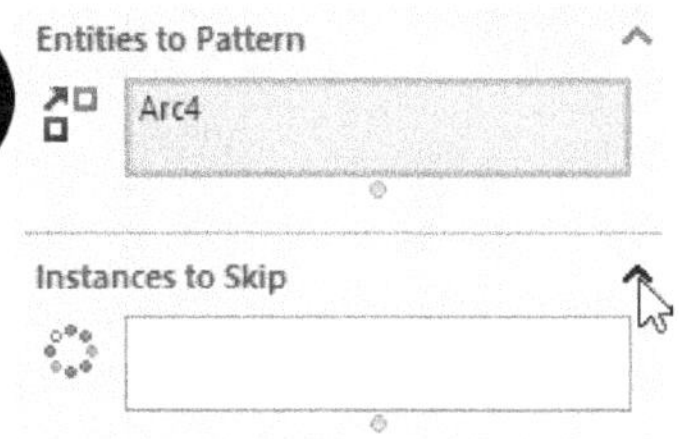

8. Click on the pink dots of the instances to be skipped (total 4 instances), see Figure 3.85.

9. Click on the green tick-mark button in the PropertyManager. The resultant circular pattern is created after removing the four selected instances, see Figure 3.86.

3.85

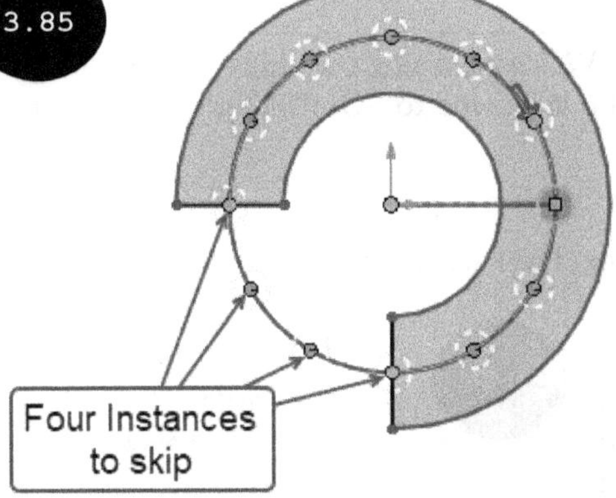

3.86

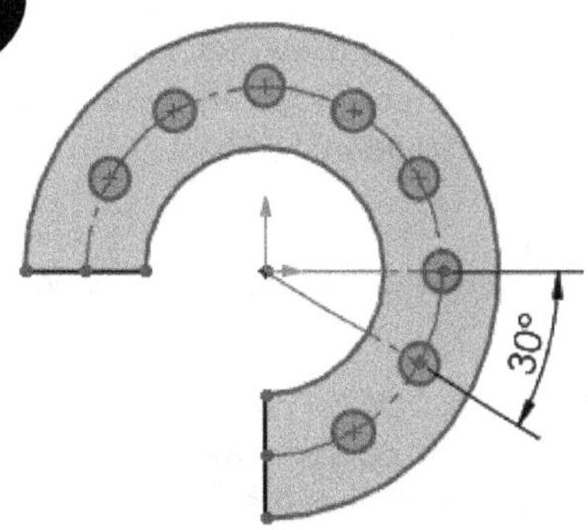

Note: The circular pattern shown in Figure 3.86 has been created with the **Dimension angular spacing** check box selected in the PropertyManager.

Section 8: Saving the Sketch

1. Click on the **Save** tool in the **Standard** toolbar. The **Save As** dialog box appears.

2. Browse to the SOLIDWORKS folder and then create a folder with the name **Chapter 3** in the SOLIDWORKS folder.

3. Enter **Tutorial 1** in the **File name** field of the dialog box. Next, click on the **Save** button. The sketch is saved with the name Tutorial 1.

Tutorial 2

Draw a sketch of the model, as shown in Figure 3.87. The dimensions and the 3D model shown in the figure are for your reference only. You will learn about applying dimensions and creating the 3D model in later chapters. All dimensions are in mm.

3.87

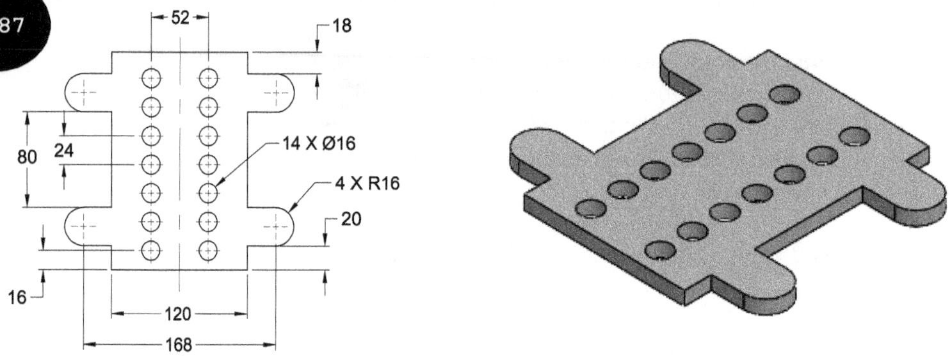

Section 1: Invoke the Part Modeling Environment

1. Start SOLIDWORKS by double-clicking on the SOLIDWORKS icon on your desktop. The startup user interface of SOLIDWORKS appears along with the **Welcome** dialog box.

Note: If SOLIDWORKS is already open and the **Welcome** dialog box does not appear on the screen, you can invoke it by clicking on the **Welcome to SOLIDWORKS** tool in the **Standard** toolbar.

2. Click on the **Part** button in the **Welcome** dialog box. The Part modeling environment is invoked.

Section 2: Specifying Unit Settings

1. Move the cursor toward the lower right corner of the screen over the Status Bar and then click on the **Unit System** area in the Status Bar. The **Unit System** flyout appears, see Figure 3.88.

3.88

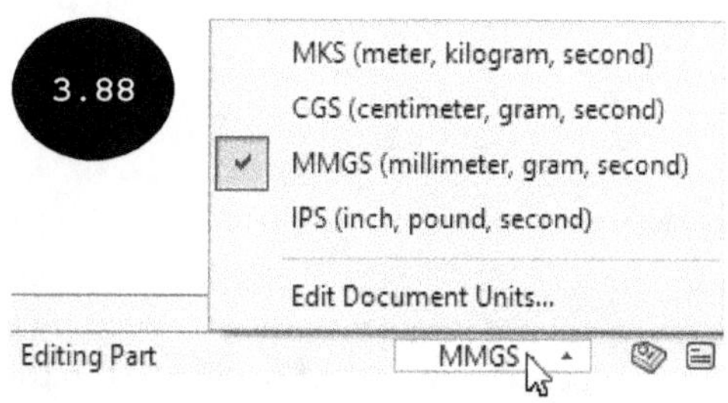

2. Ensure that the **MMGS (millimeter, gram, second)** option is tick-marked in this flyout.

Section 3: Invoking the Sketching Environment

1. Click on the **Sketch** tab in the CommandManager. The tools of the **Sketch CommandManager** appear.

2. Click on the **Sketch** tool in the **Sketch CommandManager**. Three default planes mutually perpendicular to each other appear in the graphics area.

3. Move the cursor over the Top plane and then click the left mouse button when the boundary of the plane gets highlighted. The Sketching environment is invoked. Also, the Top plane is orientated normal to the viewing direction.

Section 4: Specifying the Snap Settings

Once the Sketching environment has been invoked, you can set the snap settings such that the cursor snaps to an increment of 2 mm, since all dimensions of the sketch are multiples of 2 mm.

1. Click on the **Options** tool in the **Standard** toolbar. The **System Options - General** dialog box appears.
2. Click on the **Document Properties** tab in this dialog box. The name of the dialog box changes to **Document Properties - Drafting Standard**.
3. Click on the **Grid/Snap** option in the left panel of the dialog box. The options for specifying the grids and snap settings are displayed on the right panel of the dialog box.
4. Enter **10** in the **Major grid spacing** field, **5** in the **Minor-lines per major** field, and **1** in the **Snap points per minor** field of the **Grid** area in the dialog box.
5. Ensure that the **Display grid** check box is cleared in the **Grid** area of the dialog box to turn off the display of grids in the drawing area. If you want to turn on the display of grids in the drawing area, you can select this check box.
6. Click on the **Go To System Snaps** button in the dialog box. The name of the dialog box changes to **System Options - Relations/Snaps**.
7. Select the **Grid** and **Angle** check boxes in the **Sketch snaps** area of the dialog box to turn on the snap mode. Also, ensure that the **Snap only when grid is displayed** check box, below the **Grid** check box is cleared in the dialog box.
8. Click on the **OK** button. The snap settings have been specified and the dialog box is closed.

Section 5: Drawing the Sketch

It is evident from Figure 3.87 that the sketch is symmetric about its center line, therefore, you can draw the right half of the outer loop of the sketch and then mirror it to create its left half.

1. Click on the **Line** tool in the **Sketch CommandManager**. The **Line** tool gets invoked.
2. Move the cursor to the origin and then click to specify the start point of the line when the cursor snaps to the origin.
3. Move the cursor horizontally toward the right and then click to specify the endpoint of the first line when the length of the line appears as 60 mm near the cursor, see Figure 3.89.
4. Move the cursor vertically upward and then click to specify the endpoint of the second line entity when the length of the line appears as 20 mm, see Figure 3.90.

3.89

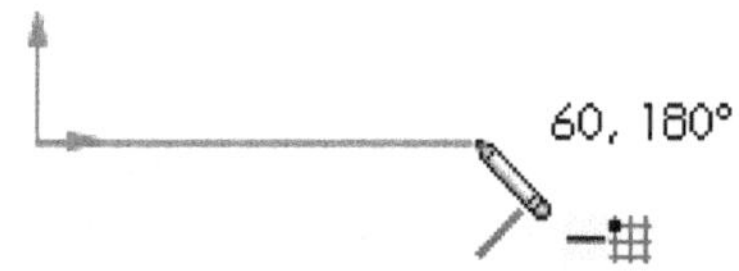

3.90

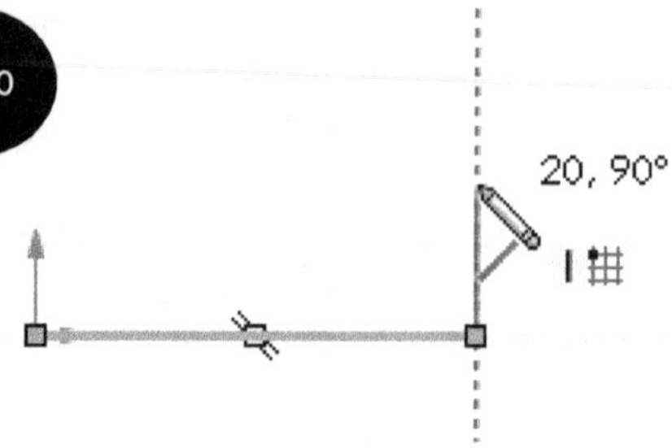

5. Move the cursor horizontally toward the right and click to specify the endpoint of the line when the length of the line appears as 24 mm, see Figure 3.91.

   Now, you need to create an arc of radius 16 mm. To create an arc, you can use the arc tools. However, in this tutorial, you will create arcs by using the **Line** tool.

6. Move the cursor to a distance and then move it back to the last specified endpoint. An orange-colored dot appears, see Figure 3.92.

3.91

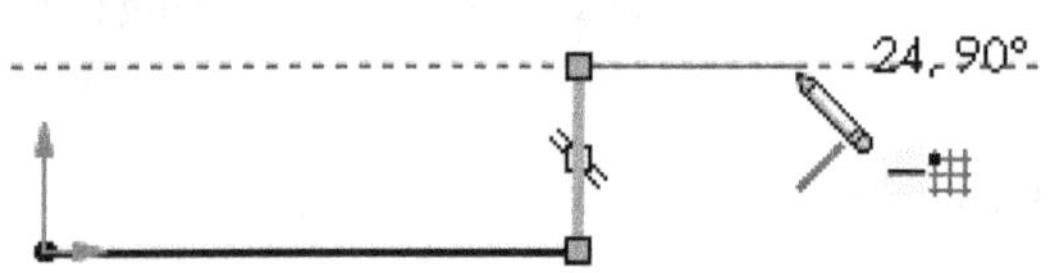

3.92

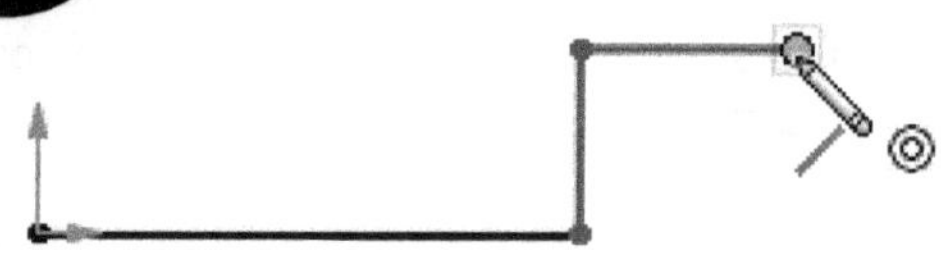

7. Move the cursor horizontally toward the right to a distance and then vertically upward. The arc mode is invoked, and the preview of an arc appears in the drawing area, see Figure 3.93.

8. Click to specify the endpoint of the arc when the radius and angle values of the arc appear as 16 mm and 180 degrees, respectively, near the cursor, see Figure 3.93. The arc is created, and the line mode is invoked again.

9. Move the cursor horizontally toward the left and click when the length of the line appears as 24 mm, see Figure 3.94.

3.93

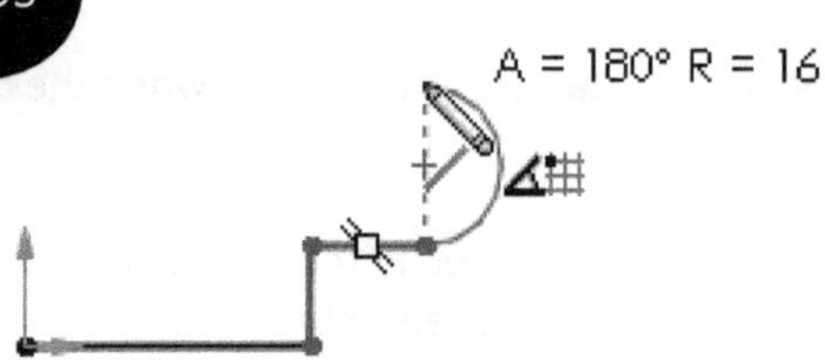

3.94

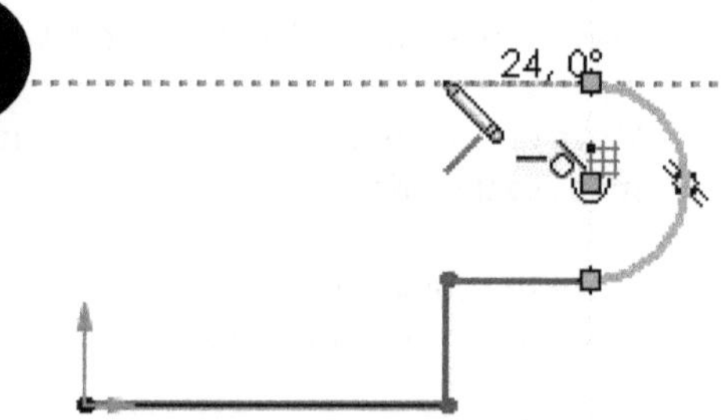

10. Move the cursor vertically upward and click when the length of the line appears as 80 mm.

11. Move the cursor horizontally toward the right and then click when the length of the line appears as 24 mm.

    Now, you need to create an arc of radius 16 mm.

12. Move the cursor to a distance and then move it back to the last specified endpoint. An orange-colored dot appears, see Figure 3.95.

13. Move the cursor horizontally toward the right to a distance and then vertically upward. The arc mode is invoked and the preview of an arc appears in the drawing area, see Figure 3.96.

14. Click to specify the endpoint of the arc when the radius and angle values of the arc appear as 16 mm and 180 degrees, respectively, see Figure 3.96. The arc is created and the line mode is invoked again.

3.95

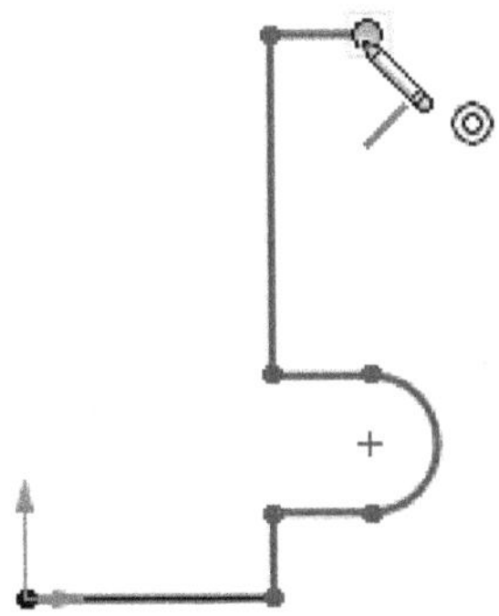

3.96

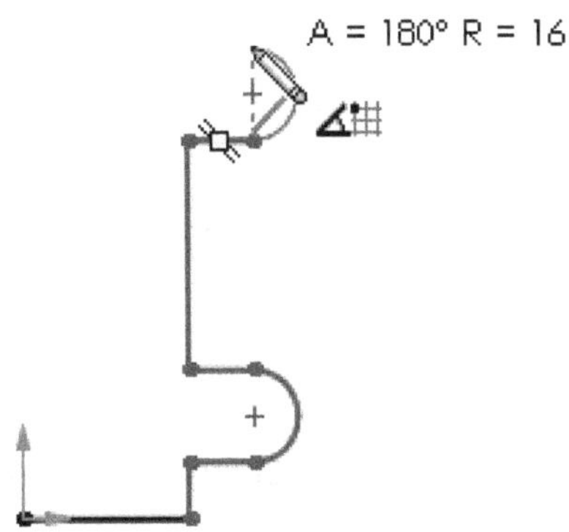

15. Move the cursor horizontally toward the left and click when the length of the line appears as 24 mm.

16. Move the cursor vertically upward and click when the length of the line appears as 18 mm.

17. Move the cursor horizontally toward the left and then click when the length of the line appears as 60 mm. The outer right half of the sketch is created, see Figure 3.97. Next, right-click in the drawing area and then click on the **Select** option in the shortcut menu that appears, to exit the **Line** tool.

3.97

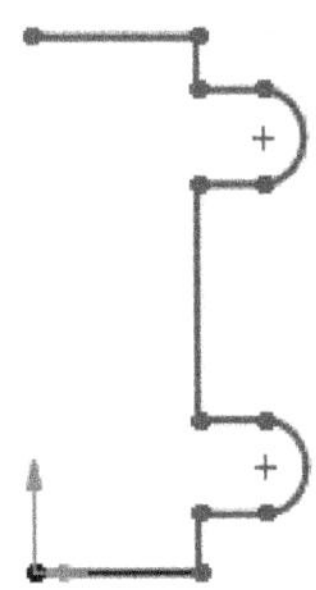

Section 6: Drawing the Centerline

After creating the right half of the sketch, you can mirror it about a centerline to create the left half of the sketch.

1. Click on the arrow next to the **Line** tool. The **Line** flyout appears, see Figure 3.98.

3.98

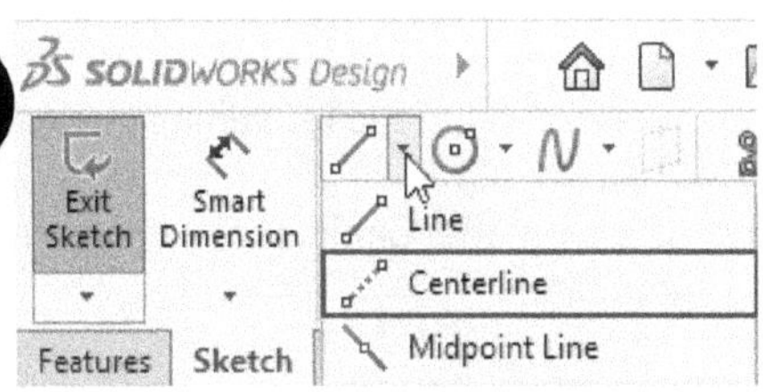

2. Click on the **Centerline** tool in the **Line** flyout. The **Insert Line PropertyManager** appears with the **For construction** check box selected in it.

3. Move the cursor to the origin and then click to specify the start point of the centerline when the cursor snaps to the origin.

4. Move the cursor vertically upward and then click to specify the endpoint of the vertical centerline of any length, see Figure 3.99. Next, right-click and then click on the **Select** option in the shortcut menu that appears to exit the **Centerline** tool.

Section 7: Mirroring Sketch Entities

After creating the centerline, you need to mirror the sketch about the centerline.

1. Click on the **Mirror Entities** tool in the **Sketch CommandManager**. The **Mirror PropertyManager** appears.

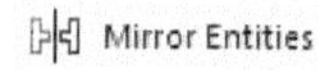

2. Select all the sketch entities except the centerline. The names of the selected entities appear in the **Entities to mirror** field of the PropertyManager.

3. Click on the **Mirror about** field in the PropertyManager to activate it.

4. Click on the centerline as the mirroring line in the drawing area. A preview of the mirror entities appears.

5. Ensure that the **Copy** check box is selected in the PropertyManager.

6. Click on the green tick-mark ✓ button in the PropertyManager. The selected entities get mirrored about the centerline, see Figure 3.100.

3.99

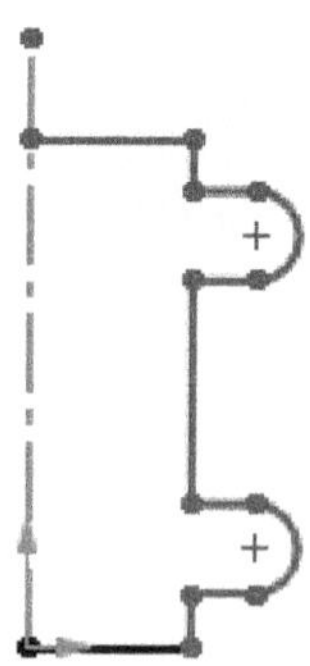

3.100

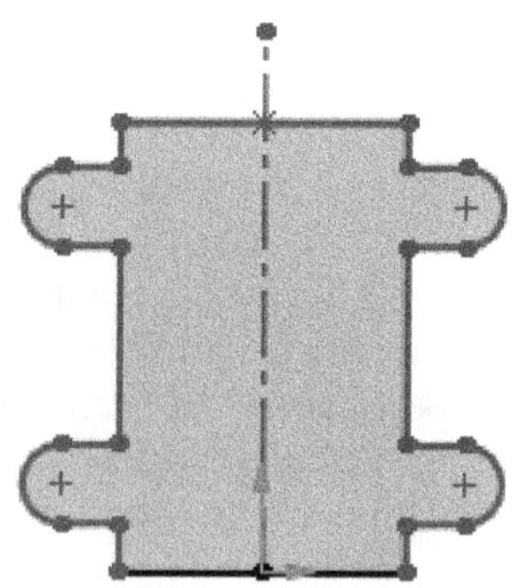

Section 8: Creating the Circle

Now, you need to create a circle of diameter 16 mm and then its linear pattern along the X and Y axes to create the remaining circles.

1. Click on the **Circle** tool in the **Sketch CommandManager**. The **Circle PropertyManager** appears.

2. Click to specify the center point of the circle in the drawing area when the coordinates (X, Y, Z) appear "**-26, 16, 0**" in the Status Bar, see Figure 3.101.

3.101

3. Move the cursor horizontally toward the right and then click when the radius of the circle appears as 8 mm, see Figure 3.102. The circle of radius 8 mm is created.

3.102

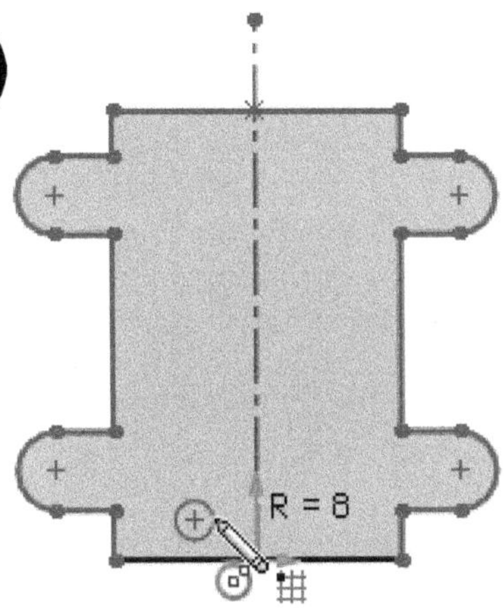

4. Right-click in the drawing area and then click on the **Select** option in the shortcut menu that appears to exit the **Circle** tool.

Section 9: Creating the Linear Pattern

Now, you need to create the linear pattern of the circle to create the remaining circles of the sketch.

1. Ensure that the previously created circle of radius 8 mm is selected in the drawing area.

2. Click on the **Linear Sketch Pattern** tool in the **Sketch CommandManager**. The **Linear Pattern PropertyManager** appears. Also, a preview of the linear pattern along the X-axis appears with the default parameters.

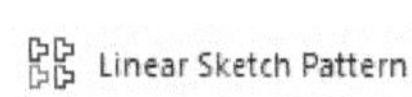

3. Enter **2** in the **Number of Instances** field of the **Direction 1** rollout in the PropertyManager.

4. Enter **52** in the **Spacing** field of the **Direction 1** rollout as the distance between two instances.

5. Enter **7** in the **Number of Instances** field of the **Direction 2** rollout as the number of instances to be created along the Y-axis. Next, click anywhere in the drawing area. A preview of the linear pattern appears along the Y-axis.

6. Enter **24** in the **Spacing** field of the **Direction 2** rollout as the distance between two instances along the Y-axis.

7. Click on the green tick-mark ✓ button in the PropertyManager. The linear pattern is created, see Figure 3.103.

3.103

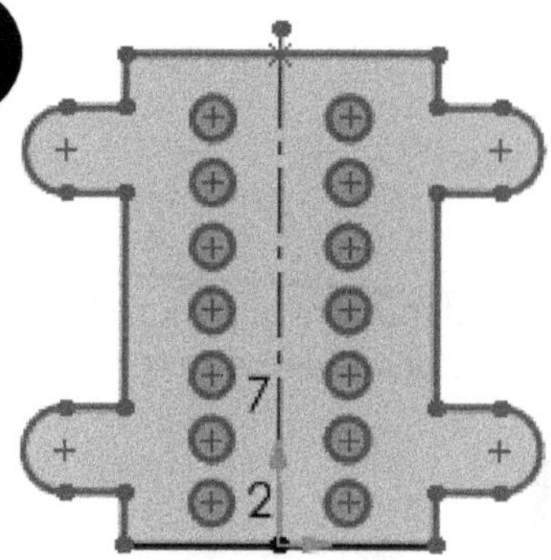

Note: Figure 3.103 shows the display of instance counts (7 and 2) in direction 1 and direction 2 of the linear pattern, respectively, as the **Display instance count** check box was selected in the **Direction 1** and **Direction 2** rollouts of the **Linear Pattern PropertyManager** while creating the linear pattern.

Section 10: Saving the Sketch

1. Click on the **Save** tool in the **Standard** toolbar. The **Save As** dialog box appears.
2. Browse to the Chapter 3 folder in the SOLIDWORKS folder.
3. Enter **Tutorial 2** in the **File name** field of the dialog box. Next, click on the **Save** button. The sketch is saved with the name Tutorial 2.

Tutorial 3

Draw a sketch of the model, as shown in Figure 3.104. The dimensions and the 3D model shown in the figure are for your reference only. You will learn about applying dimensions and creating the 3D model in later chapters. All dimensions are in mm.

3.104

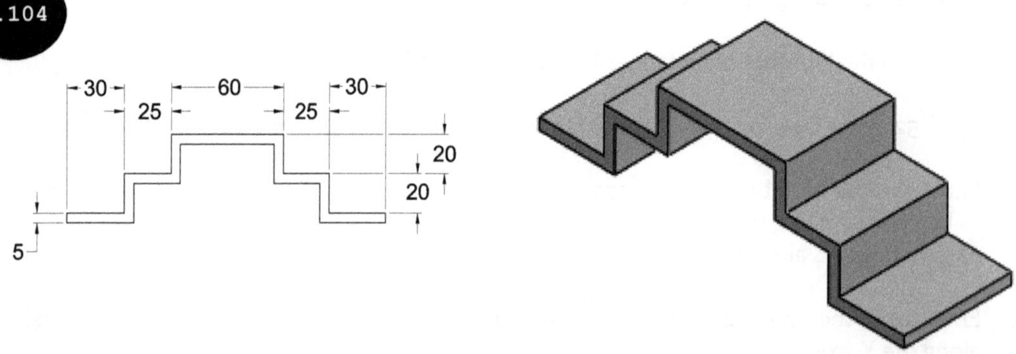

Section 1: Invoke the Part Modeling Environment

1. Start SOLIDWORKS by double-clicking on the SOLIDWORKS icon on your desktop. The startup user interface of SOLIDWORKS appears along with the **Welcome** dialog box.

Note: If SOLIDWORKS is already open and the **Welcome** dialog box does not appear on the screen, you can invoke it by clicking on the **Welcome to SOLIDWORKS** tool in the **Standard** toolbar.

2. Click on the **Part** button in the **Welcome** dialog box. The Part modeling environment is invoked.

Section 2: Specifying Unit Settings

1. Move the cursor toward the lower right corner of the screen over the Status Bar and then click on the **Unit System** area in the Status Bar. The **Unit System** flyout appears, see Figure 3.105.

2. Ensure that the **MMGS (millimeter, gram, second)** option is tick-marked in this flyout.

3.105

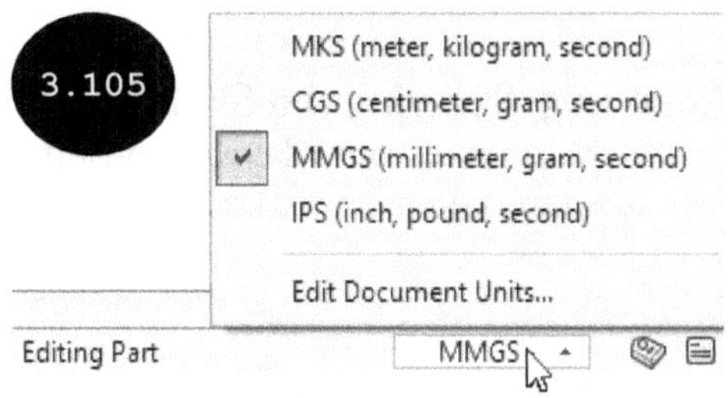

Section 3: Invoking the Sketching Environment

1. Click on the **Sketch** tab in the CommandManager. The tools of the **Sketch CommandManager** appear.

2. Click on the **Sketch** tool in the **Sketch CommandManager**. Three default planes mutually perpendicular to each other appear in the graphics area.

3. Select the Front plane as the sketching plane. The Sketching environment is invoked and the Front plane gets orientated normal to the viewing direction.

Section 4: Specifying the Snap Settings

Now, you need to set the snap settings such that the cursor snaps to an increment of 5 mm, as the dimensions of all the sketch entities are multiples of 5 mm.

1. Click on the **Options** tool in the **Standard** toolbar. The **System Options - General** dialog box appears.

2. Click on the **Document Properties** tab in this dialog box. The name of the dialog box changes to **Document Properties - Drafting Standard**.

3. Click on the **Grid/Snap** option in the left panel of the dialog box.

4. Enter **50** in the **Major grid spacing** field, **10** in the **Minor-lines per major** field, and **1** in the **Snap points per minor** field in the **Grid** area of the dialog box.

5. Ensure that the **Display grid** check box is cleared in the **Grid** area of the dialog box to turn off the display of grids in the drawing area. If you want to turn on the display of grids in the drawing area, you can select this check box.

6. Click on the **Go To System Snaps** button in the dialog box.

7. Select the **Grid** and **Angle** check boxes in the **Sketch snaps** area of the dialog box to turn on the snap mode. Also, ensure that the **Snap only when grid is displayed** check box, below the **Grid** check box is cleared.

8. Click on the **OK** button in the dialog box. The snap settings are specified, and the dialog box is closed.

Section 5: Drawing the Sketch

In this tutorial, you will create the left half of the upper sketch entities and mirror it dynamically about the center line to create the right half of the upper entities of the sketch.

1. Click on the arrow next to the **Line** tool. The **Line** flyout appears, see Figure 3.106.

3.106

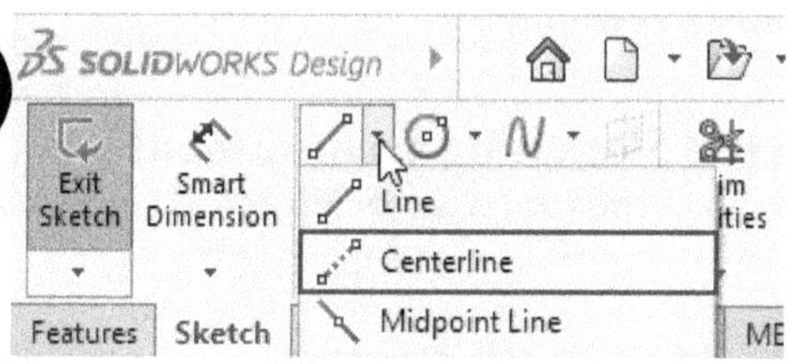

2. Click on the **Centerline** tool in the flyout. The **Insert Line PropertyManager** appears with the **For construction** check box selected.

3. Move the cursor to the origin and then click to specify the start point of the centerline when the cursor snaps to the origin.

4. Move the cursor vertically upward and then click to specify the endpoint of the vertical centerline of any length in the drawing area. Next, press the ESC key.

   After creating a vertical centerline, you need to invoke the **Dynamic Mirror** tool so that while creating entities on one side of the centerline, the respective mirror entities are created dynamically on the other side of the centerline.

5. Click on **Tools > Sketch Tools > Dynamic Mirror** in the SOLIDWORKS Design Menus. The **Mirror PropertyManager** appears. 

6. Move the cursor over the centerline in the drawing area and then click on it. The symbol of the dynamic mirror, which is represented by two small horizontal lines appears on both sides of the centerline, see Figure 3.107.

7. Click on the **Line** tool in the **Sketch CommandManager**. The **Insert Line PropertyManager** appears.

8. Move the cursor in the drawing area, where the coordinates (X, Y, Z) appear as "**-85, 0, 0**" respectively in the Status Bar, and then click the left mouse button at that location to specify the start point of the line.

9. Move the cursor horizontally toward the right and then click to specify the endpoint of the first line when the length of the line appears as 30 mm near the cursor. A horizontal line of length 30 mm is created. Also, its mirror image is created on the other side of the centerline, automatically, see Figure 3.108.

3.107

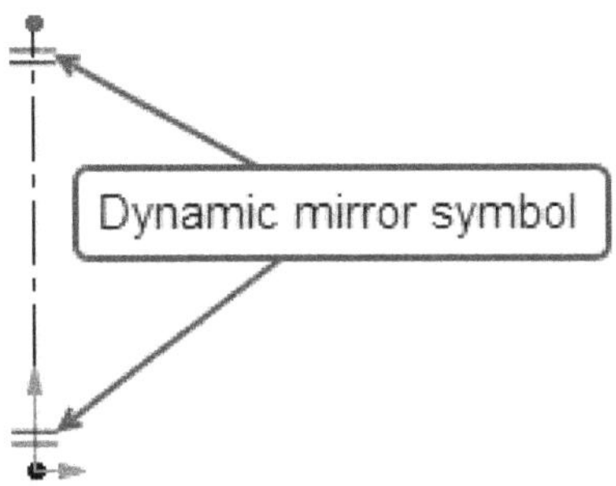

3.108

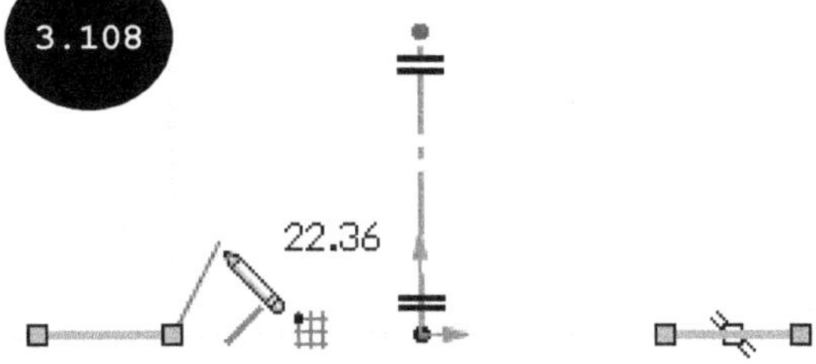

10. Move the cursor vertically upward and then click to create a line of length 20 mm. A line of length 20 mm is also created on the other side of the centerline, see Figure 3.109. Note that as you are creating entities on the left of the centerline, the respective mirror images are being created on the right of the centerline since the **Dynamic Mirror** tool is invoked.

11. Move the cursor horizontally toward the right and then click to create a line of length 25 mm.

12. Move the cursor vertically upward and then click to create a line of length 20 mm.

13. Move the cursor horizontally toward the right and click when the cursor snaps to the centerline. The upper loop of the sketch is created, see Figure 3.110.

3.109

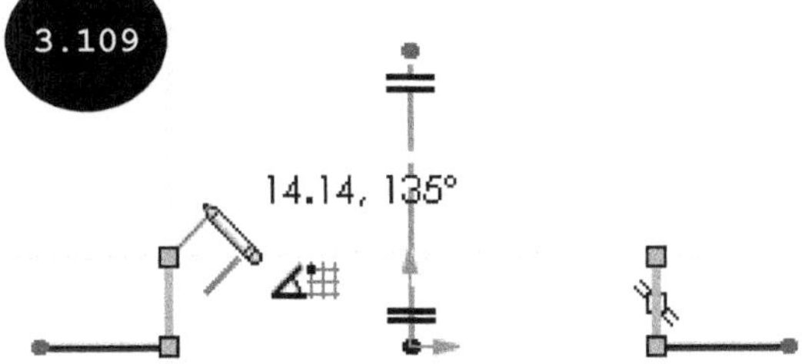

3.110

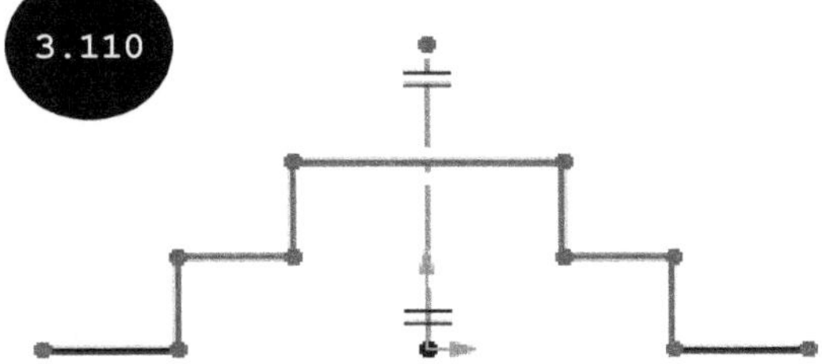

14. Right-click in the drawing area and then click on the **Select** option in the shortcut menu that appears to exit the **Line** tool.

Now, you need to exit the **Dynamic Mirror** tool.

15. Click on **Tools** > **Sketch Tools** > **Dynamic Mirror** in the SOLIDWORKS Design Menus to exit the **Dynamic Mirror** tool.

Section 6: Offsetting the Sketch Entities

After creating the upper loop of the sketch, you need to offset it to a distance of 5 mm.

1. Click on the **Offset Entities** tool. The **Offset Entities PropertyManager** appears.

2. Ensure that the **Select chain** check box is selected in the PropertyManager.
3. Select an entity of the upper loop of the sketch. All contiguous entities of the selected entity get selected and a preview of offset entities appears in the drawing area, see Figure 3.111.
4. Ensure that the direction of offset entities is on the lower side of the sketch, see Figure 3.111. If not, click on the **Reverse** check box to reverse the direction of offset entities to downward.
5. Enter **5** in the **Offset Distance** field of the PropertyManager and then press ENTER.
6. Select the **Cap ends** check box. The **Arcs** and **Lines** radio buttons are enabled.
7. Select the **Lines** radio button to cap the open ends of offset entities with lines.
8. Ensure that the **Base geometry** and **Offset geometry** check boxes are cleared.
9. Click on the green tick-mark ✓ button. The sketch is created, see Figure 3.112.

3.111

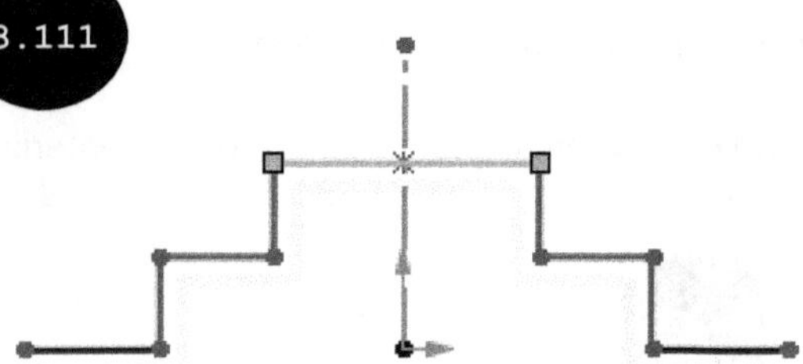

3.112

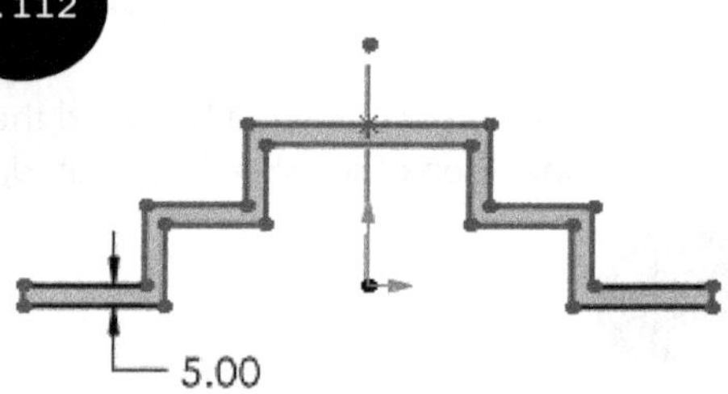

Section 7: Saving the Sketch

1. Click on the **Save** tool in the **Standard** toolbar. The **Save As** dialog box appears.
2. Browse to the Chapter 3 folder in the SOLIDWORKS folder.
3. Enter **Tutorial 3** in the **File name** field of the dialog box. Next, click on the **Save** button. The model is saved with the name Tutorial 3.

Hands-on Test Drive 1

Draw a sketch of the model, as shown in Figure 3.113. The dimensions and the 3D model are for your reference only. All dimensions are in mm.

3.113

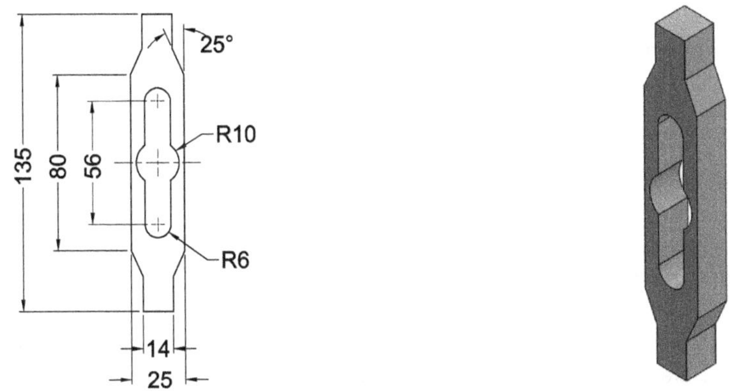

Hands-on Test Drive 2

Draw a sketch of the model, as shown in Figure 3.114. The dimensions and the 3D model are for your reference only. All dimensions are in mm.

3.114

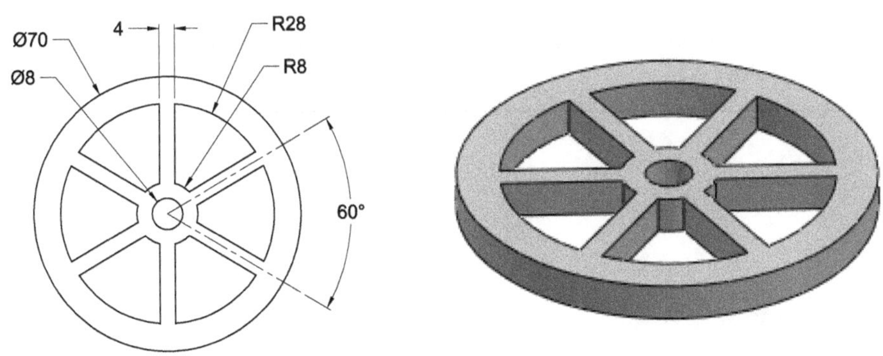

Summary

In this chapter, you have learned how to edit and modify sketch entities using various tools, such as **Trim Entities, Extend Entities, Offset Entities, Mirror Entities,** and **Linear Sketch Pattern**. You explored how pattern tools enable the creation of linear and circular patterns, while the mirror tool helps create mirrored images of selected entities. Additionally, you have learned how to move, copy, rotate, scale, and stretch sketch entities using their respective tools. These skills will help you efficiently create and modify sketches in SOLIDWORKS.

Questions

Complete and verify the following sentences:

- The _________ tool is used for offsetting sketch entities at a specified offset distance.
- You can rotate sketch entities at an angle by using the _________ tool.
- You can stretch the sketch entities of a sketch by using the _________ tool.
- To rotate sketch entities anti-clockwise, you need to define a _______ angle value.
- While offsetting sketch entities, if you select the _______ check box, all the contiguous entities of the selected entity get selected.
- The number of pattern instances specified in the **Number of Instances** field includes the parent or original instance selected for the pattern. (True/False)
- The original set of sketch entities is not counted in the number of copies specified in the **Number of Copies** field while scaling sketch entities. (True/False)
- You cannot recall the skipped pattern instances. (True/False)
- In addition to trimming sketch entities, you can extend sketch entities by using the **Trim Entities** tool. (True/False)

CHAPTER

4

Applying Geometric Relations and Dimensions

This chapter discusses the following topics:

- Working with Geometric Relations
- Applying Geometric Relations
- Controlling the Display of Geometric Relations
- Applying Dimensions
- Modifying/Editing Dimensions
- Working with Different States of a Sketch

Once you have created a sketch using the sketching tools, the next step is to make it fully defined by applying the appropriate geometric relations and dimensions. A fully defined sketch is one where all degrees of freedom are fixed, meaning its shape and position cannot be altered by simply dragging its entities. You will learn more about fully defined sketches later in this chapter. Before that, it is important to first understand geometric relations and dimensions.

Working with Geometric Relations

Geometric relations are used to restrict certain degrees of freedom in a sketch. You can apply geometric relations to sketch entities, between sketch entities, and between sketch entities and planes, axes, edges, or vertices. Some geometric relations, such as horizontal, vertical, and coincident, are automatically applied while drawing sketch entities. For example, when drawing a line, if you move the cursor horizontally to the left or right, a symbol indicating the horizontal relation will appear near the cursor, see Figure 4.1. This means that if you specify the endpoint of the line, the horizontal relation will be applied to it.

4.1

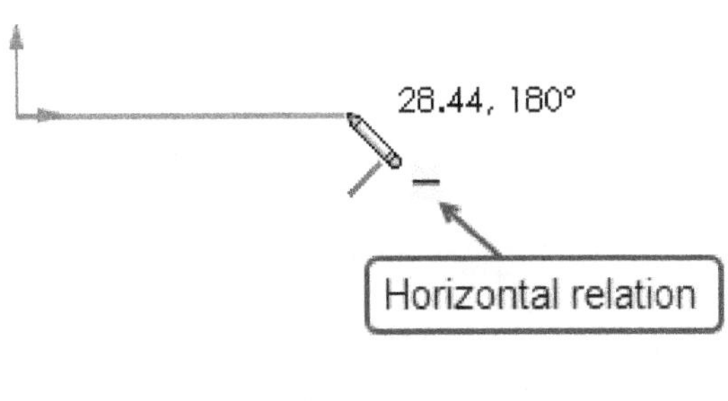

Similarly, if you move the cursor vertically upward or downward, a symbol indicating the vertical relation will appear near the cursor, see Figure 4.2. This indicates that the vertical relation will be applied when you specify the endpoint of the line. Various geometric relations are discussed next.

4.2

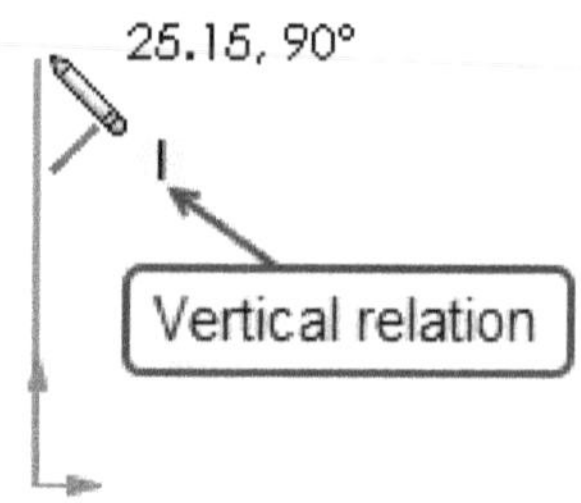

Horizontal Relation

The Horizontal relation is used to set the orientation of an entity to horizontal. This relation can be applied to a line, centerline, or between two points or vertices, ensuring that the selected entity or entities align horizontally.

Vertical Relation

The Vertical relation is used to set the orientation of an entity to vertical. This relation can be applied to a line, centerline, or between two points or vertices, ensuring that the selected entity or entities align vertically.

Coincident Relation

The Coincident relation is used to coincide two points or vertices. This relation can be applied between a point and a line, arc, or ellipse. Additionally, you can apply a coincident relation between a sketch point and the origin, ensuring that the two entities share the same location.

Collinear Relation

The Collinear relation is used to make two or more lines collinear with each other. This relation can also be applied to align line entities with a linear edge or a reference plane, ensuring they share the same straight path.

Perpendicular Relation

The Perpendicular relation is used to make two line entities perpendicular to each other. This relation can also be applied to make a line perpendicular to a linear edge or a plane, ensuring a 90-degree angle between the selected entities.

Parallel Relation

The Parallel relation is used to make two or more line entities parallel to each other. This relation can also be applied to make line entities parallel to a linear edge or a plane, ensuring that the selected entities maintain the same orientation and direction.

Tangent Relation

The Tangent relation is used to make two sketch entities, such as a circle and a line, tangent to each other. This relation can also be applied to make two circles, two arcs, two ellipses, two splines, or a combination of these entities tangent to each other. Additionally, you can make sketch entities tangent to a linear or a circular edge of a model, ensuring they touch at exactly one point without intersecting.

Concentric Relation

The Concentric relation is used to make two or more arcs or circles, a point and an arc, or a point and a circle concentric to each other. In this relation, the selected entities share the same center point. Additionally, you can make sketch entities, such as arcs or circles, concentric with a vertex or cylindrical edge of a model, ensuring they have the same center.

Coradial Relation

The Coradial relation is used to make two or more arcs or circles coradial to each other. In this relation, the selected entities share both the same center point and radius. Additionally, you can make sketch entities, such as arcs or circles, coradial to a circular edge of a model, ensuring they have the same center and radius.

Equal Relation

The Equal relation is used to make two or more arcs, circles, or lines equal to each other. In this relation, the length of line entities and the radii of arc entities become equal, ensuring that the selected entities are identical in size.

Equal Curve Length Relation

The Equal Curve Length relation is used to make curved segments equal in length. This relation can be applied between a circle and an arc, two circles, two arcs, a line and a circle, a circle and a spline, or a spline and a line, ensuring that the selected curved entities have the same length.

Midpoint Relation

The Midpoint relation is used to make a point coincident at the middle of a line entity. You can apply this relation between a sketch point and a line, a vertex and a line, or a sketch point and a linear edge, ensuring that the point is positioned at the midpoint of the selected entity.

Symmetric Relation

The Symmetric relation is used to make two points, two lines, two arcs, two circles, or two ellipses symmetric about a centerline. This ensures that the selected entities are positioned equally on either side of the centerline, maintaining symmetry.

Merge Relation

The Merge relation is used to merge two points so that they share a single point. This relation can be applied to the endpoints of two lines, ensuring that the endpoints coincide at the same location.

Pierce Relation

The Pierce relation is used to coincide a sketch point with an axis, an edge, or a curve of another sketch. This ensures that the sketch point lies exactly on the selected entity of the other sketch.

Fix Relation

The Fix relation is used to fix the current position and size of a sketch entity, preventing it from being modified. However, for a fixed line or arc entity, its endpoints remain free to move, while the overall position and size of the entity remain fixed.

Torsion Continuity Relation

The Torsion Continuity relation is used to create smooth continuity with equal curvature between a spline and another sketch entity (such as a line, an arc, or another spline) that share a common endpoint, see Figure 4.3. This relation ensures that the transition between the entities is smooth and continuous. You can also apply this relation between a spline and an edge of a model that shares a common endpoint.

4.3

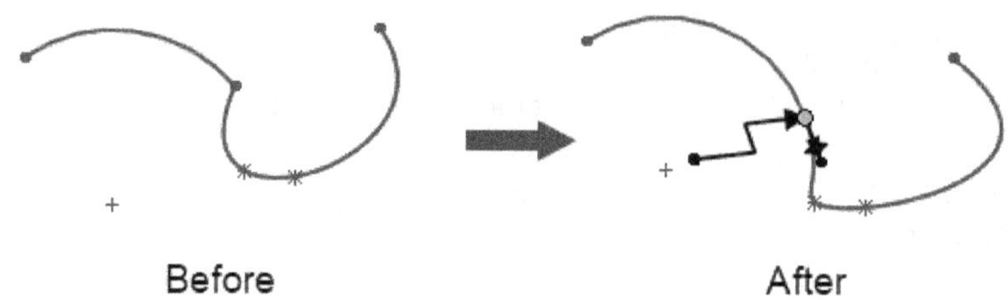

Applying Geometric Relations

In SOLIDWORKS, you can apply geometric relations either by using the **Add Relation** tool or the Pop-up toolbar. Both methods for applying geometric relations are discussed next.

Applying Geometric Relation by Using the Add Relation Tool

To apply a geometric relation using the **Add Relation** tool, click on the arrow at the bottom of the **Display/Delete Relations** tool in the **Sketch CommandManager**. A flyout appears, see Figure 4.4. In this flyout, click on the **Add Relation** tool. The **Add Relations PropertyManager** appears. The **Selected Entities** rollout of the PropertyManager is used for selecting entities for applying relation in the drawing area.

After selecting the entities for applying a relation in the drawing area, the **Add Relations PropertyManager** gets modified, and the names of selected entities appear in the **Selected Entities** rollout. Figure 4.5 shows the modified PropertyManager after selecting two circles. The options in the modified PropertyManager are discussed next.

4.4

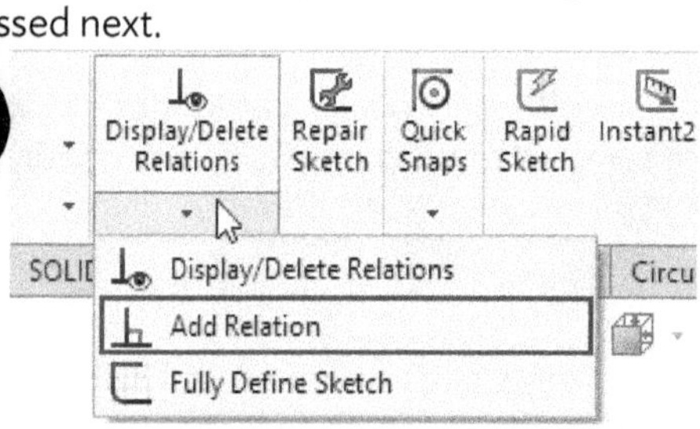

4.5

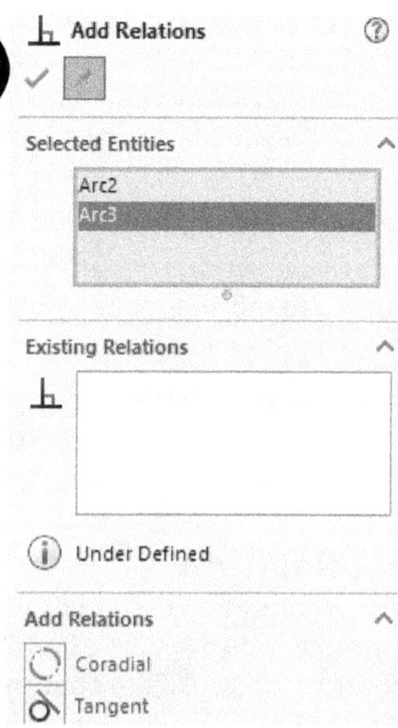

Selected Entities

The **Selected Entities** rollout displays the list of entities selected for applying a relation. You can select entities by clicking the left mouse button in the drawing area. You can also remove an entity from the selection list. To do this, select the entity in the **Selected Entities** field and then right-click. A shortcut menu appears. In this shortcut menu, click on the **Delete** option. The selected entity gets removed from the selection list. If you click on the **Clear Selections** option in the shortcut menu, all the selected entities will be removed from the selection list.

Existing Relations

The **Existing Relations** rollout displays a list of already applied relations between the selected entities.

Tip: You can delete relations that are already applied between the selected entities. To do this, select the relations in the **Existing Relations** field of the rollout and then right-click. A shortcut menu appears. In this shortcut menu, click on the **Delete** option. The selected relations get deleted and removed from the list. If you click on the **Delete All** option in the shortcut menu, all the existing relations that were applied between the selected entities will be deleted.

Add Relations

The **Add Relations** rollout displays a list of all the possible relations that can be applied between the selected entities. Also, the most suitable relation gets highlighted by default, refer to Figure 4.5.

You can click on the required relation to be applied between the selected entities in the **Add Relations** rollout. The selected relation gets applied. Next, click on the green tick-mark button in the PropertyManager.

Tip: You can also delete an already applied relation by selecting it in the drawing area and pressing the DELETE key.

Applying Geometric Relation by using the Pop-up Toolbar

In addition to applying geometric relations using the **Add Relations PropertyManager**, you can apply relations using the Pop-up toolbar, which is a more time-saving method. This method is discussed below:

1. Select sketch entities in the drawing area by pressing the CTRL key without invoking any tool.

2. Release the CTRL key and do not move the cursor. A Pop-up toolbar appears, refer to Figure 4.6.

4.6

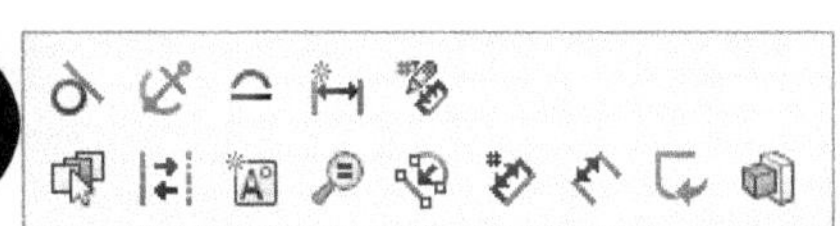

Note: The availability of relations in the Pop-up toolbar depends upon the type of entities selected. Figure 4.6 shows the Pop-up toolbar that appears on selecting two circles.

3. Click on the required relation in the Pop-up toolbar. The selected relation is applied between the selected entities.

Controlling the Display of Geometric Relations

You can control the display or visibility of the applied geometric relations in the drawing area using the **View Sketch Relations** tool of the **View (Heads-Up)** toolbar. To do this, click on the **Hide/Show Items** arrow in the **View (Heads-Up)** toolbar. A flyout appears, see Figure 4.7. In this flyout, click on the **View Sketch Relations** tool. The display of all the applied geometric relations is either turned on or off. Note that this is a toggle tool.

4.7

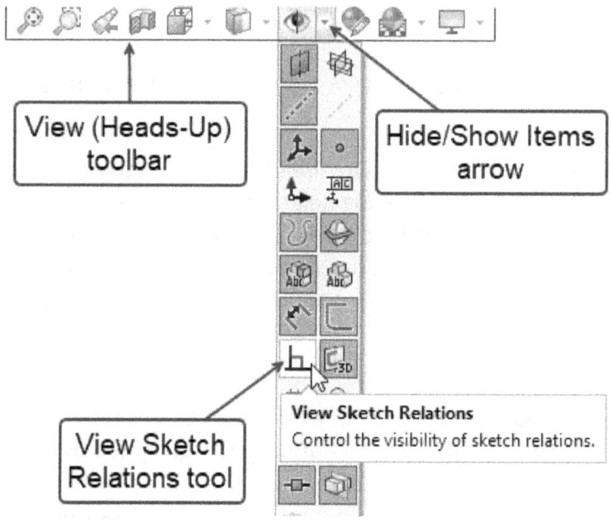

Applying Dimensions

Once a sketch is drawn and the required geometric relations are applied, the next step is to apply dimensions using the dimension tools. As SOLIDWORKS is a parametric software, the parameters of sketch entities, such as length and angle, are controlled or driven by dimension values. Modifying a dimension value will automatically adjust the respective sketch entity accordingly. The tools for applying dimensions are grouped in the **Dimensions** flyout. To invoke this flyout, click on the arrow at the bottom of the **Smart Dimension** tool in the **Sketch CommandManager**, see Figure 4.8. The methods for applying dimensions using various dimension tools are discussed next.

4.8

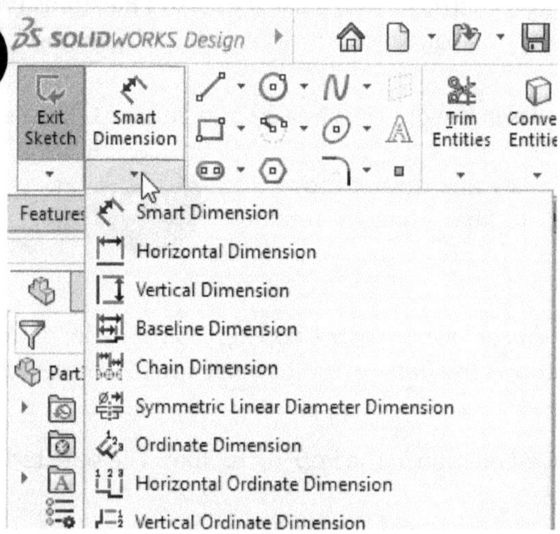

Working with Smart Dimension Tool

The **Smart Dimension** tool is used to apply dimensions based on the type of entity selected. For example, if you select a circle, the diameter dimension will be applied, and if you select a line, a linear dimension will be applied.

To apply dimensions using the **Smart Dimension** tool, click on it in the **Sketch CommandManager**. The cursor changes to a dimension cursor, prompting you to select the entity to be dimensioned. Once you select an entity in the drawing area, a dimension with the current value appears attached to the cursor, depending on the entity selected, see Figure 4.9.

4.9

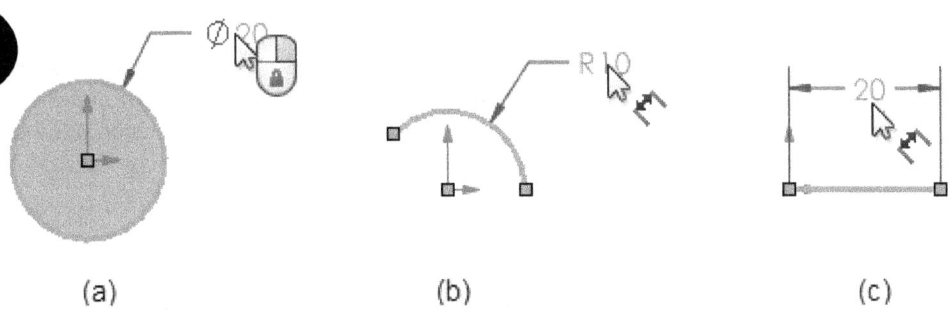

After selecting the entity, move the cursor to the desired location in the drawing area, and click the left mouse button. The **Modify** dialog box appears (see Figure 4.10), displaying the current dimension value of the selected entity by default. Enter the required dimension value and click the green checkmark button to apply the dimension to the selected entity. Figure 4.10 shows the various components of the **Modify** dialog box, which are discussed next for a closer understanding of the dialog box.

4.10

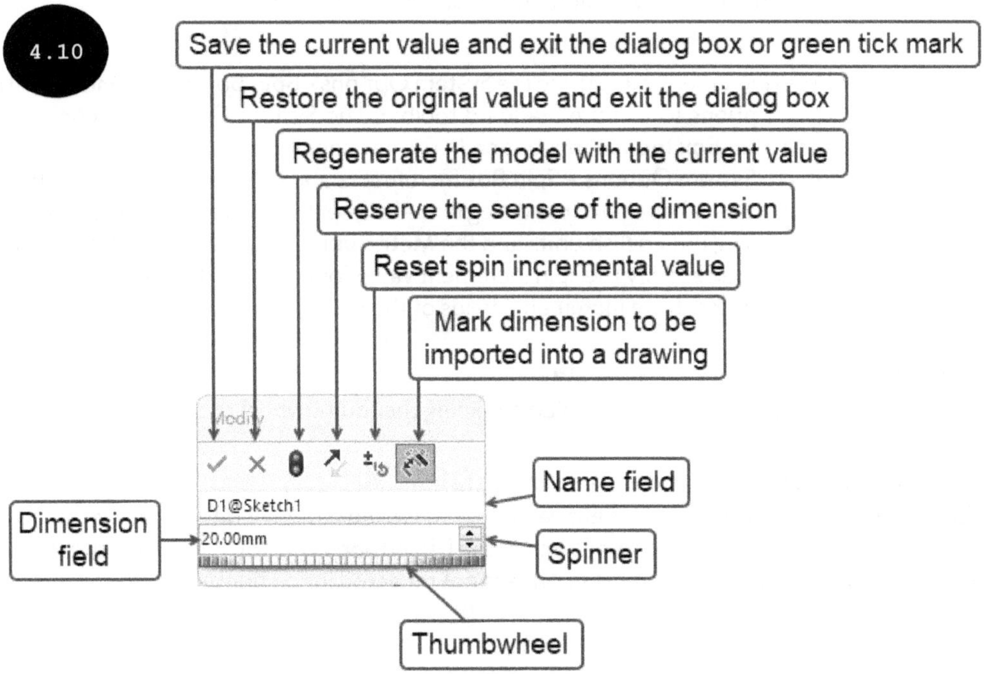

Name Field

The **Name** field of the **Modify** dialog box displays the name of the dimension. By default, the name of a dimension is assigned as D1, D2, D3 ..., or Dn. You can specify a name other than the default one in this field.

Dimension field

The **Dimension** field is used to specify the dimension value for the sketch entity. By default, this field displays the current dimension value of the sketch entity. You can enter a new dimension value in this field.

Spinner

You can also set or control the dimension value using the Spinner. On clicking the up arrow of the Spinner, the dimension value increases. Similarly, on clicking the down arrow of the Spinner, the dimension value decreases. Note that the increment or decrement of the dimension value is based on the predefined spin increment value set. You can control the predefined spin increment value by using the **Reset spin increment value** button of the dialog box, which is discussed next.

Reset spin increment value

The **Reset spin increment value** button is used to set the spin increment value for dimension. To do this, click on the **Reset spin increment value** button in the **Modify** dialog box. The **Increment** window appears with the default spin increment value. Enter the required spin increment value in the field of this window and then press the **ENTER** key. The newly entered value is set as the current spin increment value for the dimension and the window is closed.

Note: On selecting the **Make Default** check box in the **Increment** window, the specified spin increment value is set as default for other dimensions as well.

You can also set the spin increment value using the **System Options - Spin Box Increments** dialog box. To do this, click on the **Options** tool in the **Standard** toolbar. The **System Options - General** dialog box appears. Select the **Spin Box Increments** option in the left panel of the dialog box. The name of the dialog box changes to **System Options - Spin Box Increments** and the options for setting the spin increment value appear in the right panel of the dialog box. Next, set the required spin increment value for linear dimensions by using the **English units** and the **Metric units** fields of the **Length increments** area of the dialog box. You can specify the spin increment value for angle and time measurements by using the **Angle increments** and **Time increments** fields of the dialog box, respectively.

Thumbwheel

You can also set or control the dimension value by sliding the thumbwheel of the **Modify** dialog box.

Regenerate the model with the current value

The **Regenerate the model with the current value** button is used to regenerate or refresh the drawing with the current dimension value that is entered in the **Dimension** field. You can regenerate or refresh your drawing if the change in the dimension value is not reflected in the drawing area.

Reverse the sense of the dimension

The **Reverse the sense of the dimension** button is used to flip or reverse the dimension value from a positive dimension value to a negative dimension value and vice versa. Note that this button is enabled only when the selected dimension is a linear dimension.

Save the current value and exit the dialog

The **Save the current value and exit the dialog** button (green tick-mark) of the dialog box is used to accept the change made in the dimension value in the **Dimension** field and to exit the dialog box.

Restore the original value and exit the dialog

The **Restore the original value and exit the dialog** button (red cross mark) is used to discard any changes made to the dimension value. Clicking this button restores the original dimension value and closes the **Modify** dialog box.

As discussed earlier, the **Smart Dimension** tool is used for applying dimensions depending upon the type of sketch entity or entities selected. You can apply horizontal, vertical, aligned, angular, diameter, radius, and linear diameter dimensions by using this tool. The methods for applying various types of dimensions using the **Smart Dimension** tool are discussed next.

Applying Horizontal Dimension by using the Smart Dimension Tool

To apply horizontal dimension using the **Smart Dimension** tool, click on the **Smart Dimension** tool and then select the required sketch entity or entities. You can select a horizontal sketch entity, an inclined sketch entity, two points, or two vertical sketch entities for applying the horizontal dimension, see Figure 4.11. After selecting one or more entities, the current dimension value of the selected entity or entities is attached to the cursor. Next, move the cursor vertically up or down and then click the left mouse button in the drawing area to specify the placement point for the horizontal dimension. The **Modify** dialog box appears. Next, enter the required dimension value in the **Dimension** field of the **Modify** dialog box and then click on the green tick-mark button. The horizontal dimension is applied, see Figure 4.11.

4.11

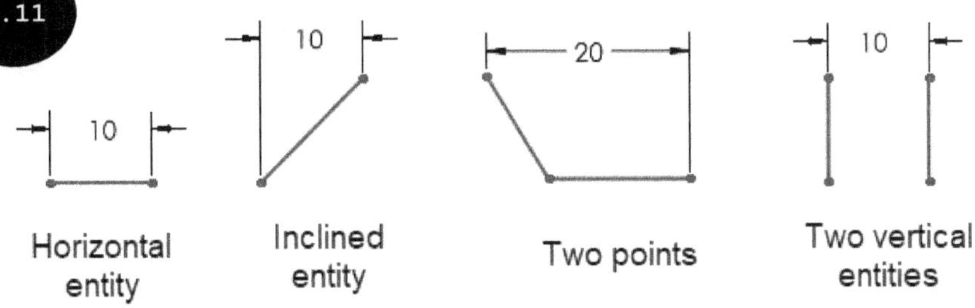

Tip: After selecting an inclined entity or two sketch points, if you move the cursor in a direction other than vertically up or down, then the vertical or aligned dimension gets attached to the cursor.

Applying Vertical Dimension by using the Smart Dimension Tool

Similar to applying horizontal dimension using the **Smart Dimension** tool, you can apply vertical dimension to a vertical sketch entity, an inclined sketch entity, between two points, or between two horizontal sketch entities, see Figure 4.12. Note that to apply a vertical dimension, you need to move the cursor horizontally toward the right or left after selecting the desired entity.

4.12

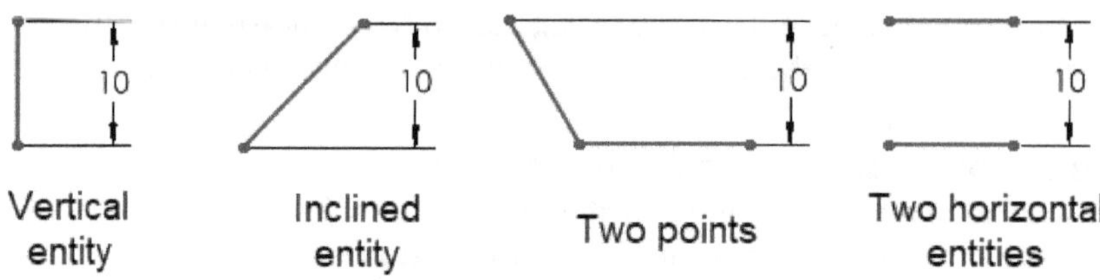

Applying Aligned Dimension by using the Smart Dimension Tool

Similar to applying horizontal and vertical dimensions using the **Smart Dimension** tool, you can apply an aligned dimension to an inclined sketch entity or between two points, see Figure 4.13. The aligned dimension is generally used for measuring the aligned length of an inclined line. Note that after selecting one or more entities for applying aligned dimension, you need to move the cursor in a direction perpendicular to the selected entity to specify the placement point.

4.13

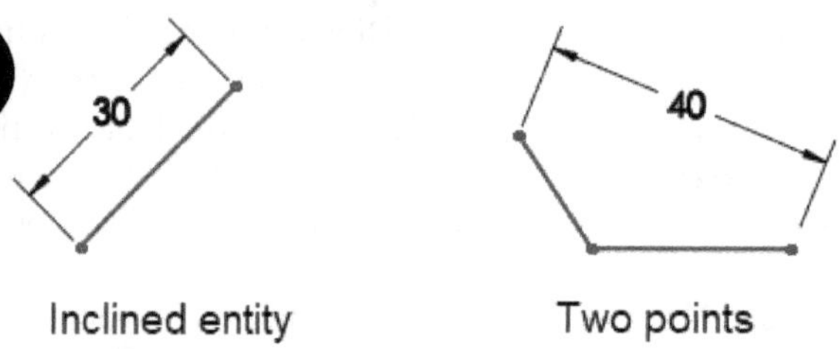

Applying Angular Dimension by using the Smart Dimension Tool

You can apply angular dimension between two non-parallel line entities or three points by using the **Smart Dimension** tool. To do this, activate the **Smart Dimension** tool and then select two non-parallel line entities in the drawing area. The angular dimension between the selected entities gets attached to the cursor, see Figure 4.14. Next, move the cursor to a location where you want to place the dimension and then click to specify the placement point. The **Modify** dialog box appears. Enter the required angular value in this dialog box and then press ENTER or click on the green tick-mark button. The angular dimension is applied between the two selected line entities depending upon the location of the placement point in the drawing area, see Figure 4.14.

4.14

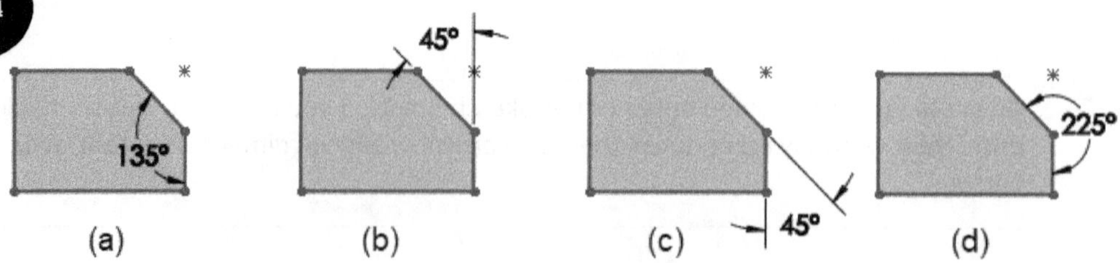

To apply angular dimension between three points, activate the **Smart Dimension** tool and then select three points in the drawing area, see Figure 4.15. An angular dimension between the selected points is attached to the cursor. Next, move the cursor to a location where you want to place the attached angular dimension and then click to specify the placement point. The **Modify** dialog box appears. Enter the required angular value in this dialog box and then press ENTER. The angular dimension is applied between the three selected points, see Figure 4.15.

4.15

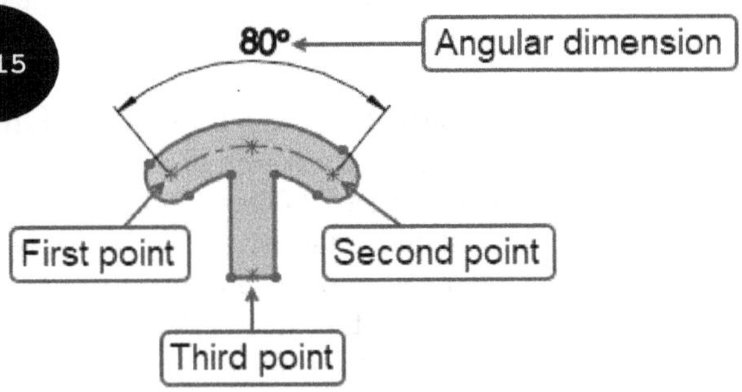

Applying Diameter Dimension by using the Smart Dimension Tool

The diameter dimension can be applied to a circle using the **Smart Dimension** tool. To do this, click on the **Smart Dimension** tool and then select a circle. The diameter dimension gets attached to the cursor. Next, move the cursor to the required location and then click to specify a placement point in the drawing area. The **Modify** dialog box appears. Enter the diameter value in this dialog box and then press ENTER. The diameter dimension is applied, see Figure 4.16.

4.16

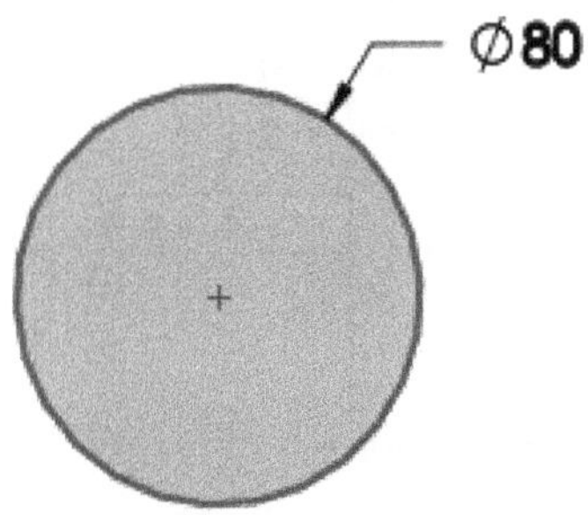

Applying Radius Dimension by using the Smart Dimension Tool

The radius dimension can be applied to an arc using the **Smart Dimension** tool. To do this, click on the **Smart Dimension** tool and then select an arc. The radius dimension gets attached to the cursor. Move the cursor to the required location and click to specify a placement point in the drawing area. The **Modify** dialog box appears. Enter the radius value in this dialog box and then press ENTER. The radius dimension is applied, see Figure 4.17.

4.17

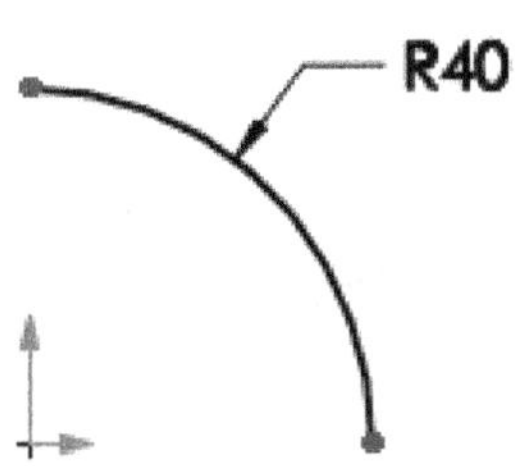

Note: As discussed, you can apply a radius dimension to an arc and a diameter dimension to a circle. However, you can also convert an already applied radius dimension to a diameter dimension or vice versa. To do this, ensure that the **Smart Dimension** tool is activated, then right-click on the applied radius or diameter dimension to display a shortcut menu. Next, select the **Display As Diameter** option or **Display As Radius** option, respectively, from the shortcut menu. The selected dimension is converted accordingly.

Applying Linear Diameter Dimension by using the Smart Dimension Tool

The Linear diameter dimension can be applied to a sketch of a revolved feature, see Figure 4.18. To apply a linear diameter dimension, click on the **Smart Dimension** tool and then select a linear sketch entity of the sketch. The linear dimension gets attached to the cursor. Next, select a centerline or revolving axis of the sketch. The linear dimension between the selected line and the centerline gets attached to the cursor. Move the cursor to the other side of the centerline or the revolving axis. The linear diameter dimension appears. Next, click to specify a placement point in the drawing area. The **Modify** dialog box appears. Enter the linear diameter value in the dialog box and then press ENTER. The linear diameter dimension is applied.

4.18

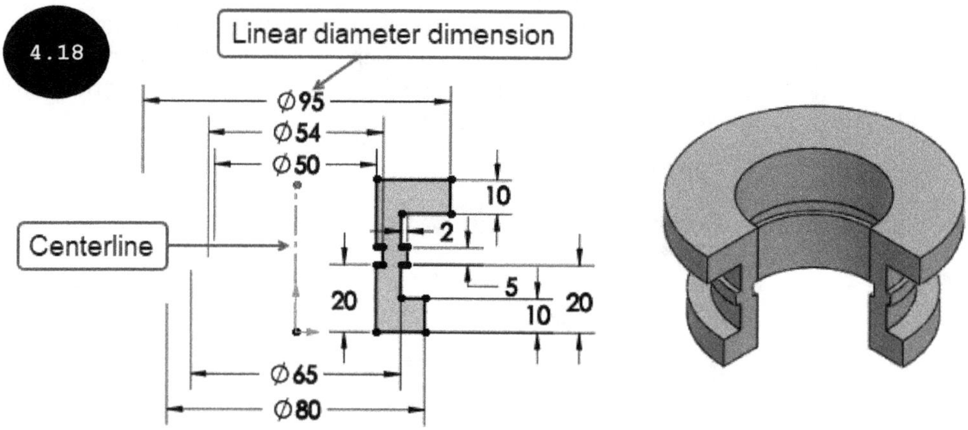

Note: In SOLIDWORKS, when you select a sketch entity, the preview of its dimension appears in the graphics area. To enable this feature, invoke the **System Options** dialog box by clicking on the **Options** tool in the **Standard** toolbar, see Figure 4.19. In the **System Options** dialog box, select the **Sketch** option in the left panel, and then check the **Preview sketch dimension when selected** check box, see Figure 4.20. Finally, click on the **OK** button to confirm the display of the sketch dimension preview and exit the dialog box.

4.19

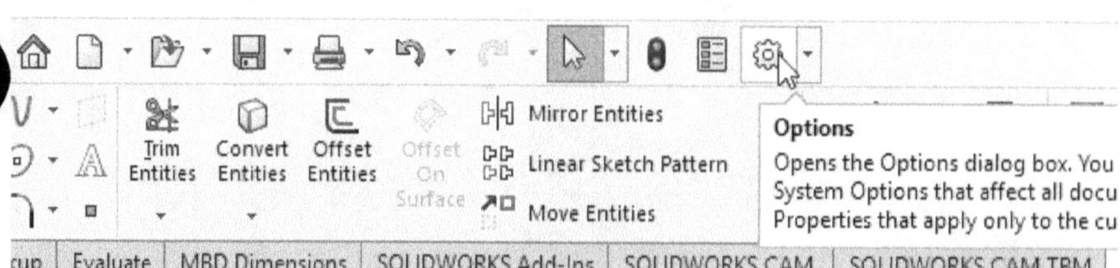

4.20

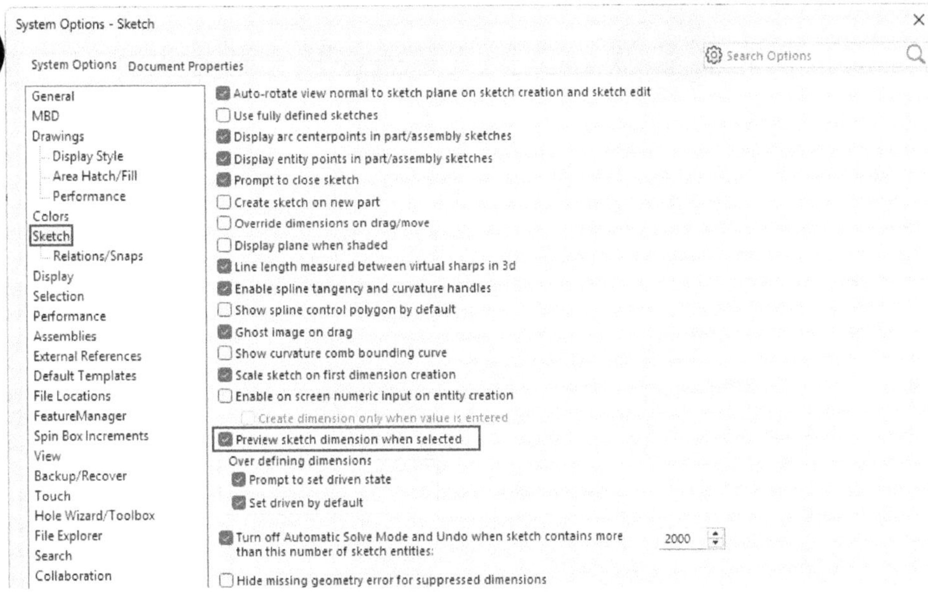

Working with Horizontal Dimension and Vertical Dimension Tools

In addition to applying horizontal and vertical dimensions using the **Smart Dimension** tool, you can also apply these dimensions by using the **Horizontal Dimension** and **Vertical Dimension** tools in the **Dimension** flyout, see Figure 4.21.

To apply a horizontal dimension using the **Horizontal Dimension** tool, click on the arrow below the **Smart Dimension** tool to display the **Dimension** flyout, refer to Figure 4.21. Next, click on the **Horizontal Dimension** tool and then select the sketch entity to be dimensioned. The horizontal dimension attaches to the cursor. Move the cursor to the desired location for placing the dimension and click to specify the placement point in the drawing area. The **Modify** dialog box appears. Enter the required dimension value in the **Modify** dialog box and press ENTER. The horizontal dimension is then applied.

4.21

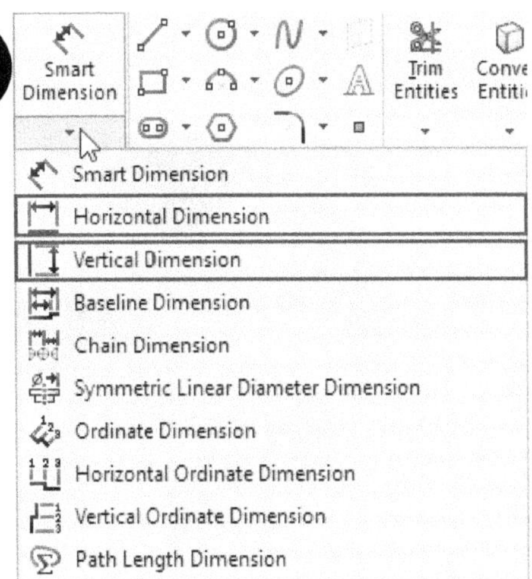

Similarly, you can apply a vertical dimension using the **Vertical Dimension** tool.

Working with Baseline Dimension Tool

The **Baseline Dimension** tool is used to apply baseline dimensions to a sketch. Baseline dimensions are a series of parallel linear dimensions measured from the same base entity, see Figure 4.22. The baseline dimensions are used for eliminating cumulative errors that can occur due to the rounded dimension values between consecutive adjacent dimensions or due to the upper and lower dimension limits.

4.22

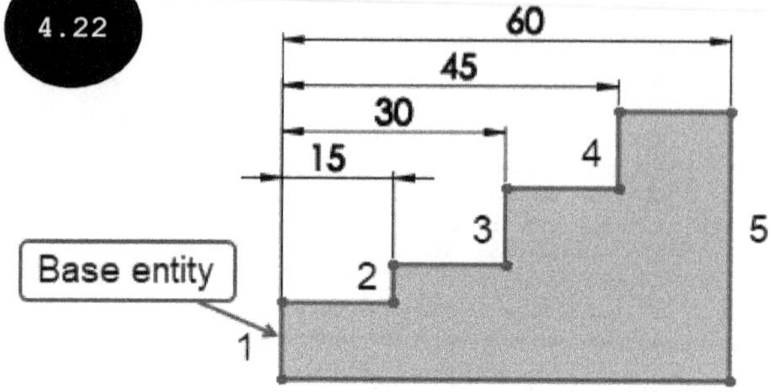

To apply baseline dimensions, click on the arrow below the **Smart Dimension** tool and then click on the **Baseline Dimension** tool in the **Dimension** flyout that appears. You are prompted to select a base entity. Click to select a linear sketch entity (1) as the base entity, refer to Figure 4.22. You can select a line or a vertex as the base entity. Next, click to select the second entity (2) to be dimensioned from the base entity. A dimension is applied between the base entity (1) and the second entity (2). Next, select the third entity. A linear dimension is applied between the base entity and the third entity, refer to Figure 4.22. Similarly, you can select other entities one by one for applying baseline dimensions measuring from the base entity, refer to Figure 4.22.

Working with Chain Dimension Tool

The **Chain Dimension** tool is used to apply a series of connected linear dimensions to a sketch. These chain dimensions are placed end to end, where the second extension line of one dimension serves as the first extension line for the next, creating a continuous sequence. Refer to Figure 4.23 for an illustration of this concept.

4.23

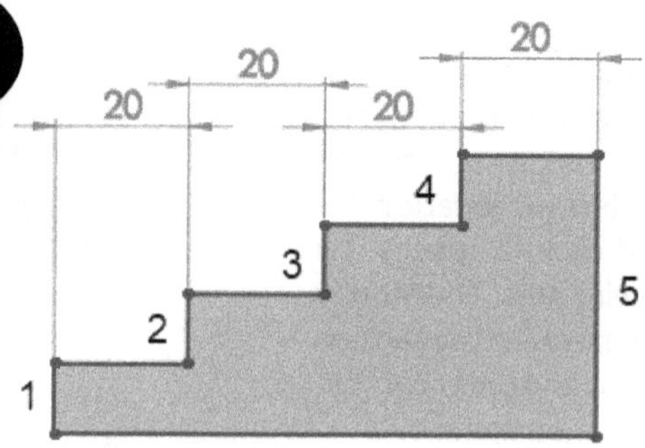

To apply chain dimensions, invoke the **Dimension** flyout and then click on the **Chain Dimension** tool. You are prompted to select a line entity or a vertex. Click to select the first line entity (1) and then the second line entity (2) in the drawing area. A linear dimension is applied between the selected entities, refer to Figure 4.23. Next, select the third line entity (3). A linear dimension is applied between the second and the third line entities. Similarly, you can select other line entities one by one in the drawing area to continue applying chain dimensions, refer to Figure 4.23. Note that the chain dimensions are driven dimensions and cannot be edited.

Working with Symmetric Linear Diameter Dimension Tool

The **Symmetric Linear Diameter Dimension** tool is used to apply symmetric linear diameter dimensions to a sketch of a revolve feature. A symmetric linear diameter dimension is represented using a single dimension leader, see Figure 4.24.

4.24

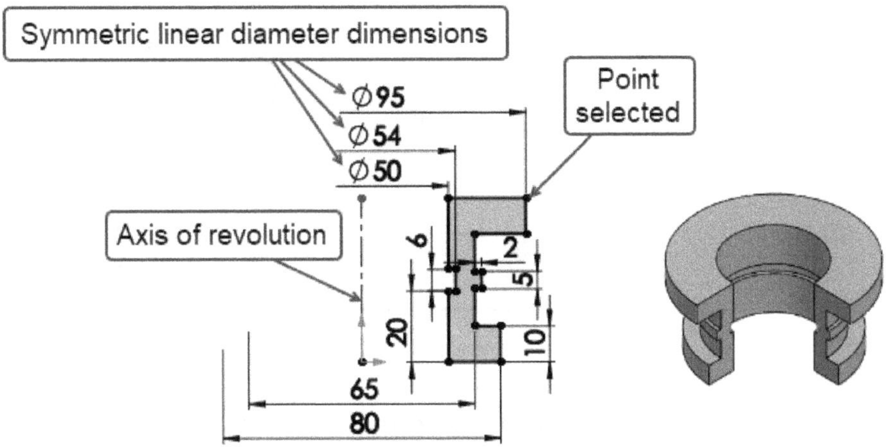

To apply symmetric linear diameter dimensions, invoke the **Dimension** flyout and then click on the **Symmetric Linear Diameter Dimension** tool. The **Symmetric Linear Diameter Dimension PropertyManager** appears, see Figure 4.25. Next, select a line or a centerline as the axis of revolution and then select a linear sketch entity or a point, refer to Figure 4.24. The symmetric linear diameter dimension gets attached to the cursor. Next, click to specify its placement point in the drawing area. The symmetric linear diameter dimension is applied. Similarly, you can apply other symmetric linear diameter dimensions individually.

4.25

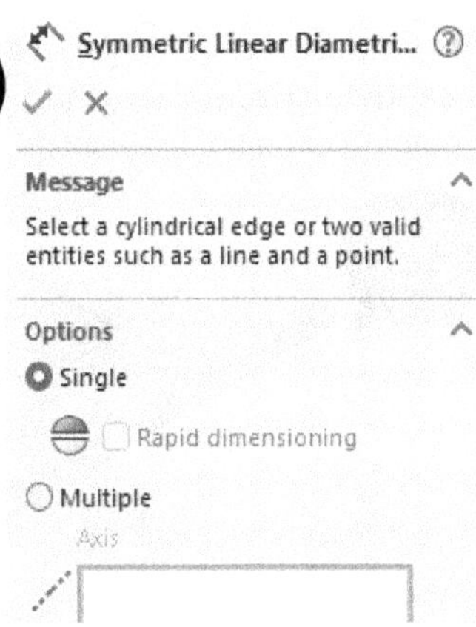

Note: By default, the **Single** radio button is activated in the **Options** rollout of the PropertyManager. As a result, you can apply a single symmetric linear diameter dimension between a centerline and a linear sketch entity at a time. To apply multiple symmetric linear diameter dimensions, select the **Multiple** radio button in the PropertyManager. The **Axis** field gets enabled for selecting a line or a centerline as an axis of revolution. After defining an axis of revolution, select multiple linear sketch entities or points one by one for applying multiple symmetric linear diameter dimensions with respect to the selected axis of revolution.

After applying all the symmetric linear diameter dimensions, exit the PropertyManager.

Working with Ordinate Dimension Tool

The **Ordinate Dimension** tool is used to apply dimensions measured from a base entity within a sketch. The base entity serves as the starting point for all measurements, ensuring consistent and accurate dimensions, refer to Figure 4.26. Ordinate dimensions are commonly used for components manufactured using CNC machines.

4.26

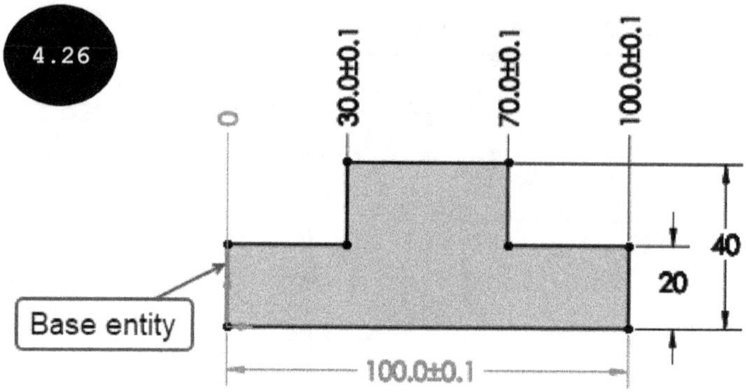

In Figure 4.27, a component is displayed, and Figure 4.28 shows the sketch used to create this model. In the sketch, horizontal dimensions have a symmetric tolerance of 0.1 mm. For entities measuring 100 mm, 30 mm, and 40 mm, the maximum accepted lengths become 100.1 mm, 30.1 mm, and 40.1 mm, respectively. Adding these values results in 100.3 mm (30.1 + 40.1 + 30.1), but the actual maximum accepted horizontal length of the component is 100.1 mm. This 0.2 mm discrepancy highlights the limitation of chain dimensions.

4.27

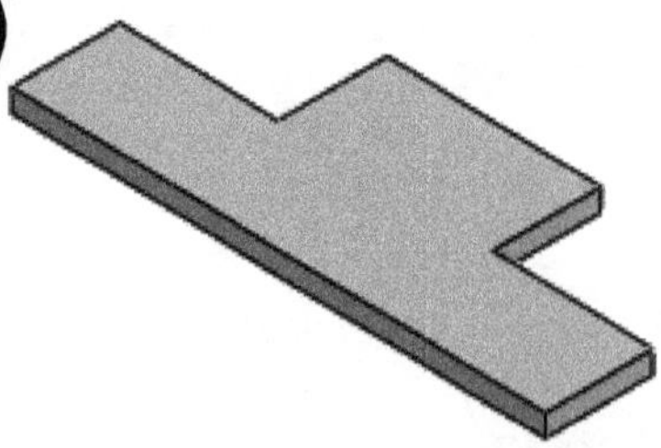

4.28

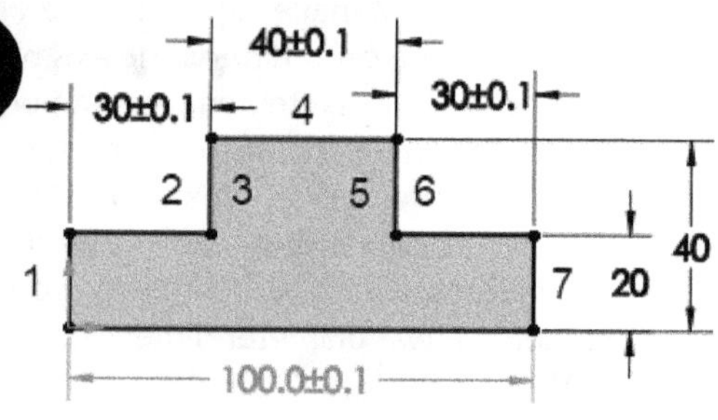

To address this issue, ordinate dimensions are applied, ensuring accurate measurement by referencing a single base entity. Figure 4.26 demonstrates a sketch with ordinate dimensions applied, showing 100.1 mm as the correct maximum accepted horizontal length of the component.

You can apply horizontal and vertical ordinate dimensions by using the **Ordinate Dimension** tool. The methods for applying horizontal and vertical ordinate dimensions are discussed next.

Applying Horizontal Ordinate Dimensions

To apply a horizontal ordinate dimension, click the arrow below the **Smart Dimension** tool to access the **Dimension** flyout. Next, select the **Ordinate Dimension** tool in the flyout. You are prompted to choose a base entity for measuring all dimensions. Select a vertical entity (1 in Figure 4.29) as the base entity. The dimension value 0 attaches to the cursor. Click in the drawing area to place the 0 dimension value, then select a second vertical entity (2 in Figure 4.29) to apply the horizontal distance measured from the 0 value. Continue selecting other vertical entities in the sketch to measure their horizontal distances from the base entity, see Figure 4.29.

Applying Vertical Ordinate Dimensions

To apply a vertical ordinate dimension, you use the **Ordinate Dimension** tool in a similar manner to applying a horizontal ordinate dimension. Begin by invoking the **Ordinate Dimension** tool and selecting a horizontal entity as the base entity. The **0** dimension value immediately attaches to the cursor. Click in the drawing area to place the **0** value (see Figure 4.30). Then, select the second horizontal entity to apply the vertical distance measured from the **0** value. Continue selecting other horizontal entities in the sketch to measure their vertical distances from the base entity, see Figure 4.30.

4.29

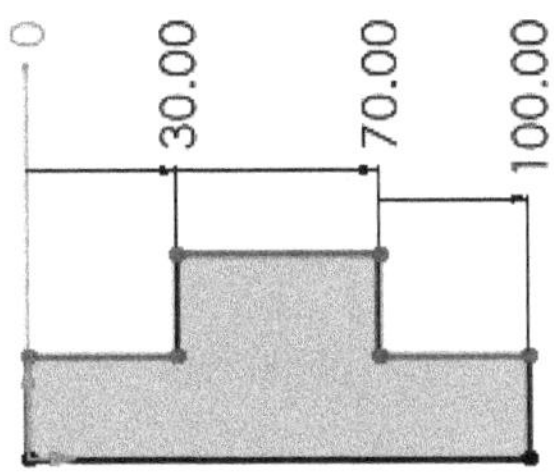

4.30

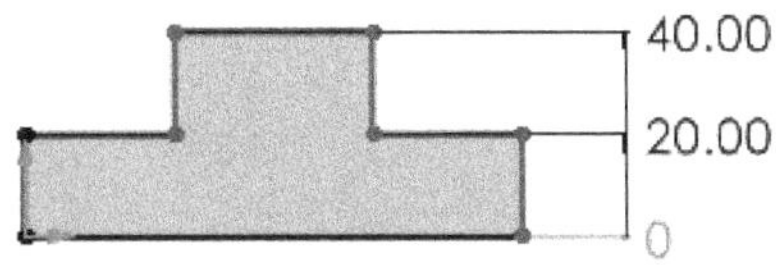

Tip: Similar to applying horizontal and vertical ordinate dimensions using the **Ordinate Dimension** tool, you can also apply them using the **Horizontal Ordinate Dimension** and **Vertical Ordinate Dimension** tools, respectively.

Working with Path Length Dimension Tool

The **Path Length Dimension** tool is used to apply path length dimensions to a series of end-to-end connected sketch entities forming a chain, see Figure 4.31. Note that the path length dimensions are driving dimensions. As a result, on modifying or editing the path length dimension value, the sketch entities of the path get modified or driven accordingly in the drawing area.

4.31

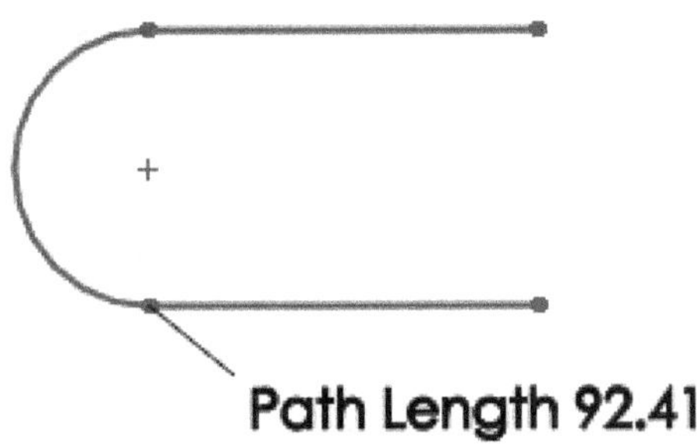

To apply a path length dimension, invoke the **Dimension** flyout and then click on the **Path Length Dimension** tool. The **Path Length PropertyManager** appears, and you are prompted to select entities that are connected end to end and form a chain of entities. Select two or more sketch entities in the drawing area. All the selected entities are listed in the **Selected Entities** field of the PropertyManager. Next, click on the green tick-mark button in the PropertyManager or press ENTER. The selected entities become a single chain of entities and the path length dimension gets applied, refer to Figure 4.31.

Tip: You can also remove an entity from the selection list in the **Selected Entities** field of the **Path Length PropertyManager**. To do this, select the entity in the **Selected Entities** field and then right-click. A shortcut menu appears. In this shortcut menu, click on the **Delete** option. The selected entity gets removed from the selection list. If you click on the **Clear Selections** option in the shortcut menu that appears, all the selected entities get removed from the selection list.

Working with Auto Insert Dimension Tool

In SOLIDWORKS, you can automatically apply the most appropriate dimension to one or more selected sketch entities using the **Auto Insert Dimension** tool.

To access this tool, select one or more sketch entities in the drawing area, such as a line, arc, or circle. You can select combinations of entities by holding down the CTRL key, for example, two lines at an angle, two parallel lines, two arcs, two circles, an arc and a line, or a circle and a line.

After selecting the entities, release the CTRL key to display the Pop-up toolbar in the drawing area, see Figure 4.32. In this toolbar, click the **Auto Insert Dimension** tool. The **Modify** toolbar appears, where you can enter the required dimension value. After entering the value, click the green tick-mark button in the dialog box. The most appropriate dimension type, such as linear, radial, diameter, or angular is applied based on the selected entities. For example, a linear dimension applies to a line, a radial dimension to an arc, a diameter dimension to a circle, and an angular dimension between two non-parallel lines.

4.32

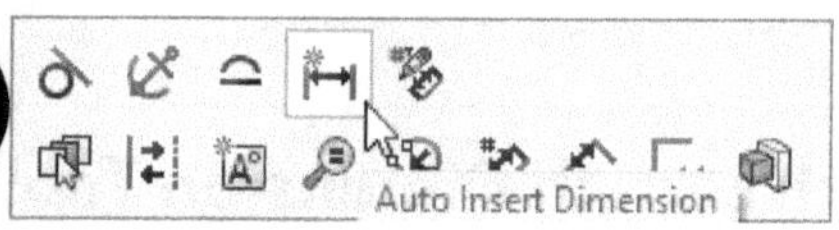

Modifying/Editing Dimensions

After applying dimensions, you may need to modify them due to changes or revisions in the design. To modify an already applied dimension, click on the dimension value you wish to change. The **Dimension Input Value** box appears, displaying the current dimension value in the drawing area, see Figure 4.33.

4.33

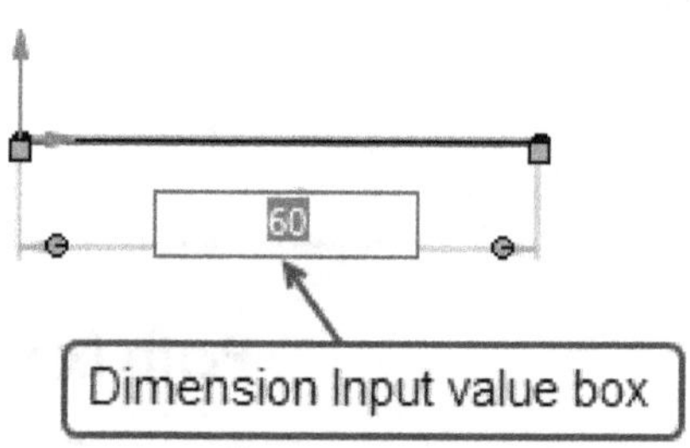

Note: The **Dimension Input Value** box appears only when the **Instant2D** tool is activated in the **Sketch CommandManager**.

In the **Dimension Input Value** box, enter the new dimension value and press ENTER to modify the selected dimension.

Alternatively, you can double-click on a dimension value in the drawing area. The **Modify** dialog box appears, where you can enter the new dimension value. Press ENTER or click the green tick-mark ✓ button to apply the changes.

Working with Different States of a Sketch

In SOLIDWORKS, a sketch can be either under-defined, fully-defined, or over-defined. All these states of the sketch are discussed next.

Under Defined Sketch

An under-defined sketch is a sketch, in which all degrees of freedom are not fixed, which means that the entities of the sketch can change their shape, size, and position when dragged. Figure 4.34 shows a rectangular sketch in which the length of the rectangle is defined as 50 mm. However, the width and position of the rectangle concerning the origin are not defined. This means that the width and position of the rectangle can be changed by dragging the respective entities of the rectangle. Note that the current status of the sketch appears on the right in the Status Bar, which is available on the lower side of the drawing area. By default, the entities of an under-defined sketch appear in blue color in the drawing area.

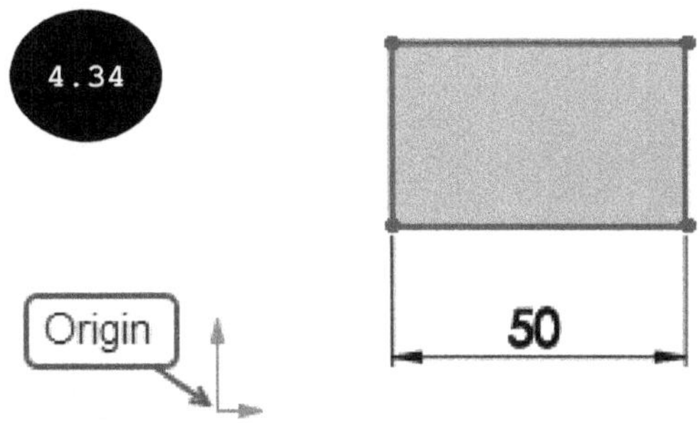

Fully Defined Sketch

A fully defined sketch is a sketch, in which all degrees of freedom are fixed. This means that the entities of the sketch cannot change their shape, size, and position when dragged. Figure 4.35 shows a rectangular sketch in which the length, width, and position of the sketch are defined. Note that the entities of a fully defined sketch appear in black.

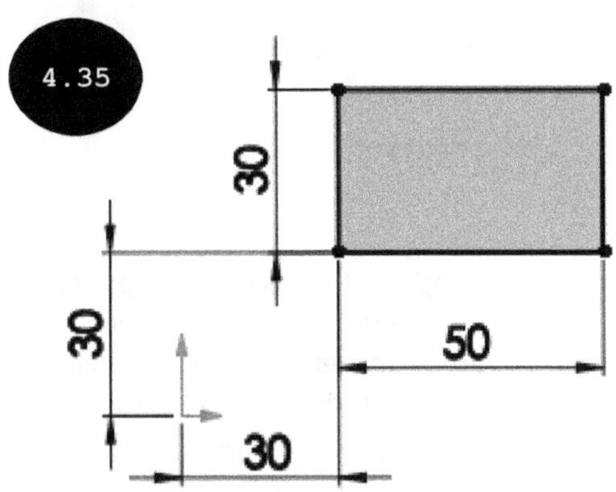

Tip: The sketch shown in Figure 4.35 is a fully defined sketch as all its entities are dimensioned and the required geometrical relations have been applied, that is horizontal relations applied to the horizontal entities and vertical relations applied to the vertical entities. Note that horizontal and vertical relations are applied automatically to the entities while they are being drawn.

Over Defined Sketch

An over-defined sketch is a sketch that is over-defined by dimensions or geometric relations. Figure 4.36 shows an over-defined rectangular sketch in which applying dimensions to both sides of the rectangle makes it over-defined. Note that the entities of an over-defined sketch appear in yellow color.

4.36

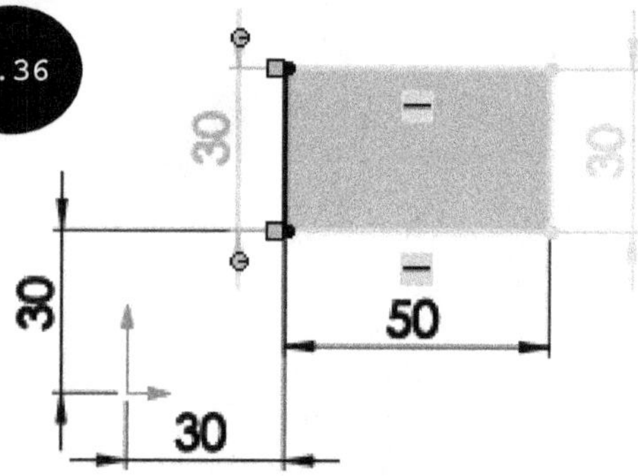

Note that when you apply an over-defined dimension to an entity, the **Make Dimension Driven?** dialog box appears, see Figure 4.37. In this dialog box, if you select the **Make this dimension driven** radio button and click on the **OK** button, then the newly applied dimension becomes a driven dimension and acts as a reference dimension only. As a result, the sketch cannot become an over-defined sketch. However, if you select the **Leave this dimension driving** radio button and click on the **OK** button, then the newly applied dimension becomes a driving dimension. As a result, the sketch becomes over-defined.

4.37

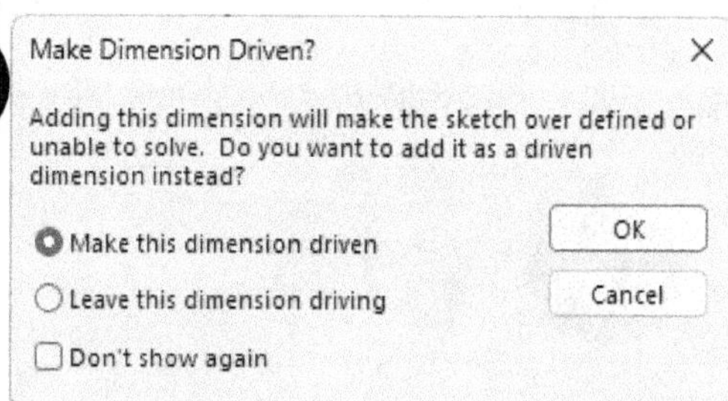

Note: In SOLIDWORKS, when you apply a dimension, it is applied with default properties. You can modify default dimension properties such as dimension style, tolerance, and precision by using the **Dimension PropertyManager** that appears when a dimension is selected in the drawing area. You will learn about modifying dimension properties in Chapter 14, while creating 2D drawings in the Drawing environment. The options for modifying dimension properties of a dimension in the Sketching environment are same as in the Drawing environment.

Tip: In SOLIDWORKS, you can choose to apply dimensions to entities as they are being drawn. To do this, click on the **Options** tool in the **Standard** toolbar. The **System Options - General** dialog box appears. Select the **Sketch** option in the left panel of the dialog box. The name of the dialog box changes to **System Options - Sketch**. Next, select the **Enable on screen numeric input on entity creation** check box in the right panel of the dialog box. This check box displays the **Numeric Input** field for entering the dimension value while drawing a sketch entity, see Figure 4.38. Also, the **Add dimensions** check box appears in the respective PropertyManager of the sketch entity being drawn. On selecting this check box, the dimensions get applied to sketch entities drawn in the drawing area, automatically.

4.38

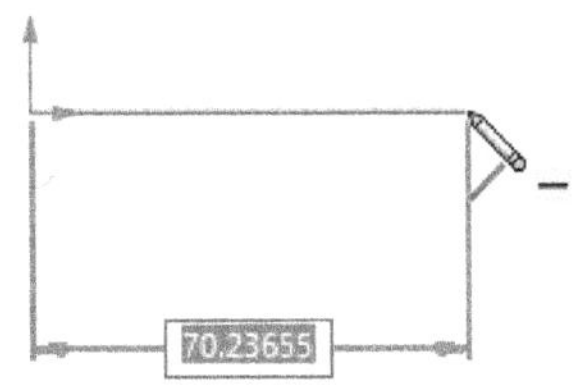

However, if you select the **Create dimension only when the value is entered** check box along with the **Enable on screen numeric input on entity creation** check box in the **System Options - Sketch** dialog box, then the dimensions get applied to the sketch entities only if you enter the dimension values in the **Numeric Input** field that appears while drawing them.

Tutorial 1

Draw the sketch shown in Figure 4.39 and make it fully defined by applying all dimensions and relations. The 3D model shown in this figure is for your reference only. You will learn about creating the 3D model in the later chapters. All dimensions are in mm.

4.39

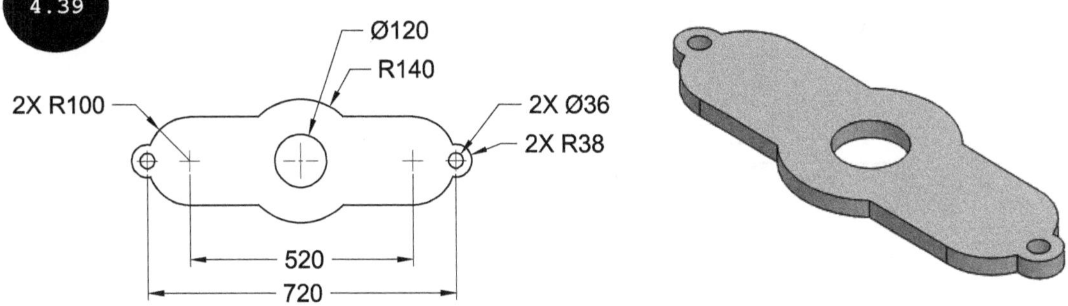

Section 1: Invoking the Part Modeling Environment

1. Start SOLIDWORKS by double-clicking on the SOLIDWORKS icon on your desktop. The startup user interface of SOLIDWORKS appears along with the **Welcome** dialog box.

Note: If SOLIDWORKS is already open and the **Welcome** dialog box does not appear on the screen, you can invoke it by clicking on the **Welcome to SOLIDWORKS** tool in the **Standard** toolbar.

2. Click on the **Part** button in the **Welcome** dialog box. The Part modeling environment is invoked.

Section 2: Specifying Unit Settings

1. Move the cursor toward the lower right corner of the screen over the Status Bar and then click on the **Unit System** area in the Status Bar. The **Unit System** flyout appears, see Figure 4.40.

4.40

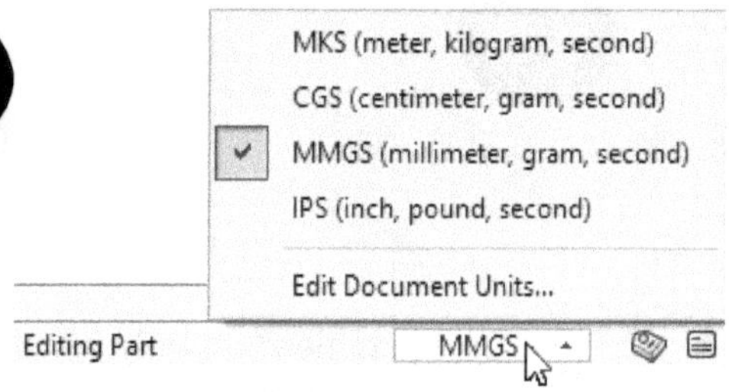

2. Ensure that the **MMGS (millimeter, gram, second)** option is tick-marked in this flyout.

Section 3: Invoking the Sketching Environment

1. Click on the **Sketch** tab in the CommandManager. The tools of the **Sketch CommandManager** appear, see Figure 4.41.

4.41

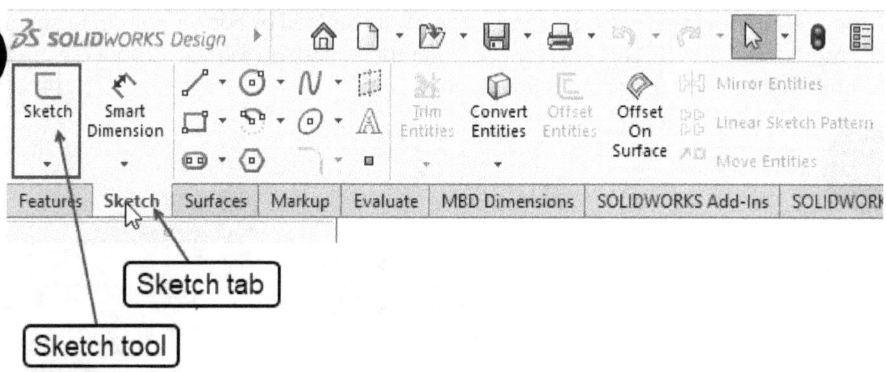

2. Click on the **Sketch** tool in the **Sketch CommandManager**. Three default planes mutually perpendicular to each other appear in the graphics area.

3. Move the cursor over the Top plane and then click on it when the boundary of the plane gets highlighted. The Sketching environment is invoked. Also, the Top plane is orientated normal to the viewing direction.

Section 4: Specifying Grid and Snap Settings

Now, you need to ensure that the snap mode is turned off. As SOLIDWORKS is a parametric software, you can turn off the snap mode and create the sketch entities by specifying points arbitrarily in the drawing area and then applying the required dimensions.

1. Click on the **Options** tool in the **Standard** toolbar. The **System Options - General** dialog box appears.
2. Click on the **Document Properties** tab in the dialog box. The name of the dialog box changes to **Document Properties - Drafting Standard**.
3. Click on the **Grid/Snap** option in the left panel of the dialog box. The options related to grid and snap settings appear.
4. Ensure that the **Display grid** check box is cleared in the **Grid** area.
5. Click on the **Go To System Snaps** button in the dialog box. The name of the dialog box changes to **System Options - Relations/Snaps**.
6. Ensure that the **Grid** check box in the **Sketch snaps** area of the dialog box is cleared.
7. Click on the **OK** button to accept the changes made and close the dialog box.

Section 5: Creating the Sketch

Now, you need to create the sketch by using the sketching tools.

1. Click on the **Circle** tool in the **Sketch CommandManager**. The **Circle** tool is invoked and the **Circle PropertyManager** appears.
2. Move the cursor to the origin and then click to specify the center point of the circle when the cursor snaps to the origin.
3. Move the cursor horizontally toward the right and click when the radius of the circle appears close to 60 mm near the cursor, see Figure 4.42. A circle of radius close to 60 mm is created and the **Circle** tool is still active.

4.42

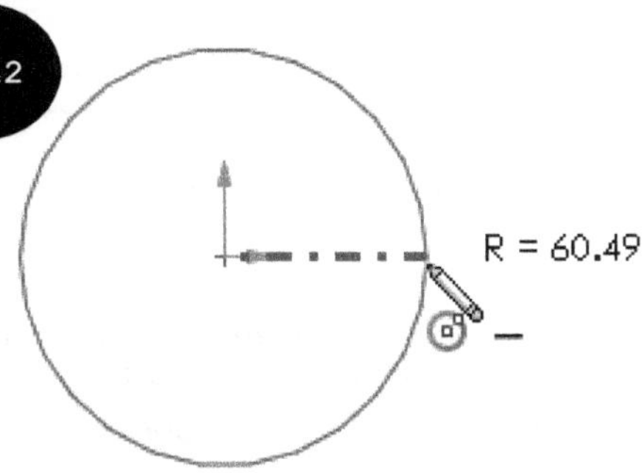

4. Move the cursor to the origin again and click to specify the center point of another circle when the cursor snaps to it.

5. Move the cursor horizontally toward the right and click when the radius of the circle appears close to 140 mm near the cursor, see Figure 4.43. A circle of radius close to 140 mm is created and the **Circle** tool is still active.

4.43

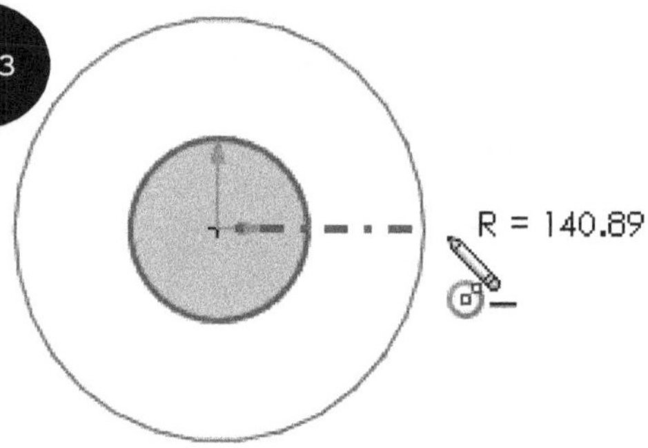

Tip: While drawing sketch entities, you may need to zoom in or zoom out of the drawing display area. To do this, scroll the middle mouse button. Alternatively, you can click on the **View > Modify > Zoom In/Out** in the SOLIDWORKS Design Menus and then drag the cursor upward or downward. Next, to exit the tool, press the ESC key.

6. Right-click in the drawing area and then click on the **Select** option in the shortcut menu that appears to exit the **Circle** tool.

7. Invoke the **Slot** flyout (see Figure 4.44), and then click on the **Centerpoint Straight Slot** tool.

4.44

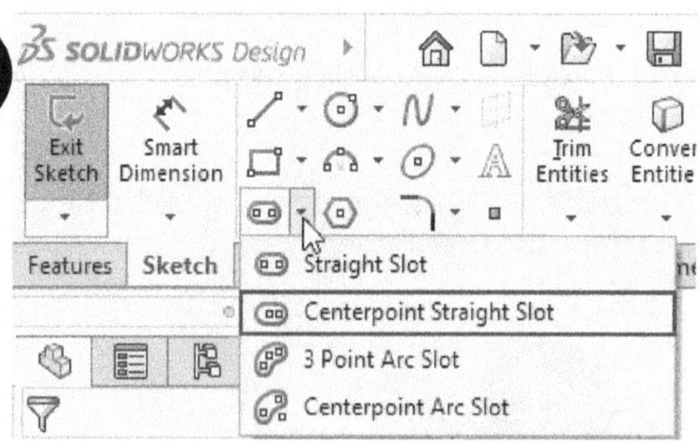

8. Move the cursor to the origin and then click to specify the center point of the slot when the cursor snaps to the origin.

9. Move the cursor horizontally toward the right and click when the half length of the slot appears close to 260 mm (520/2 = 260) near the cursor, see Figure 4.45. Next, move the cursor to a distance in the drawing area. A preview of the slot appears.

4.45

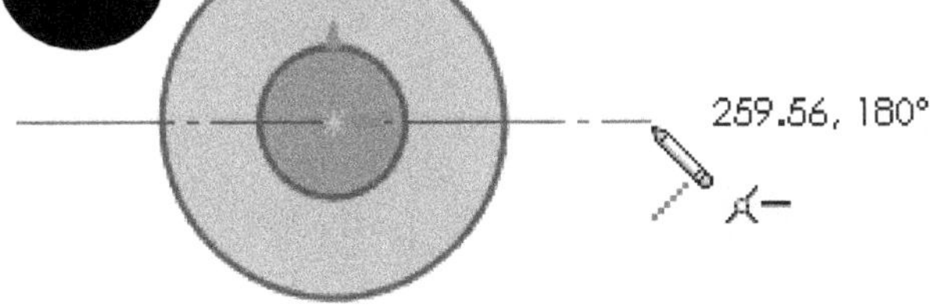

10. Click the left mouse button when the width of the slot appears close to 200 mm in the **Parameters** rollout of the **Slot PropertyManager**, see Figure 4.46. The slot is created, see Figure 4.47. Next, press the ESC key to exit the **Centerpoint Straight Slot** tool.

4.46

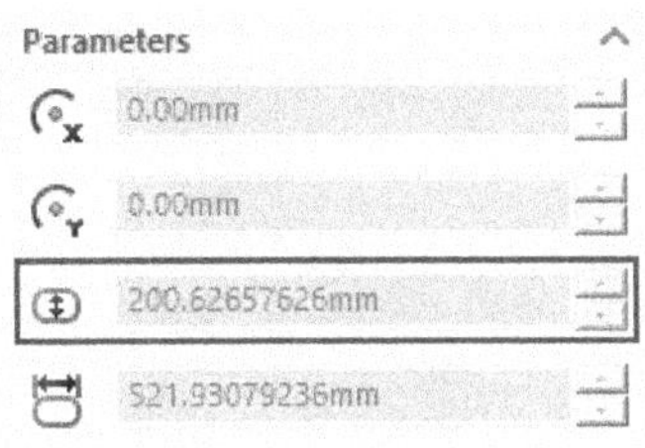

4.47

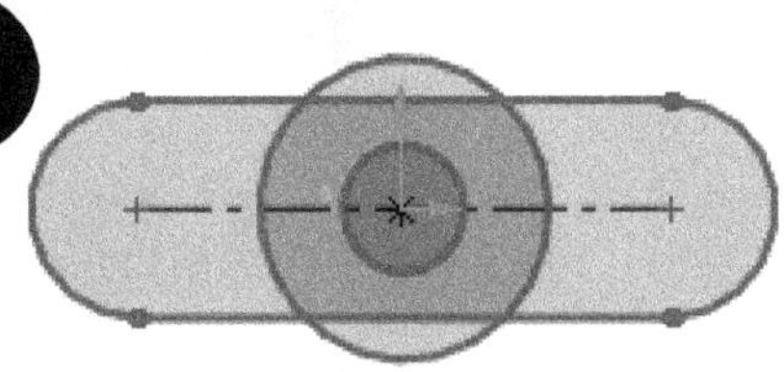

11. Click on the **Zoom to Fit** tool in the **View (Heads-Up)** toolbar to fit the sketch completely inside the screen.

12. Click on the **Circle** tool in the **Sketch CommandManager** and then move the cursor toward the midpoint of the right slot arc, see Figure 4.48.

4.48

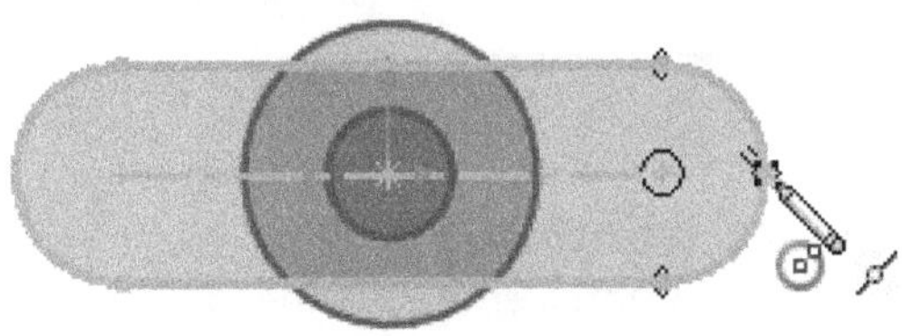

13. Click to specify the center point of the circle when the circle snaps to the midpoint of the slot arc, see Figure 4.49.

14. Move the cursor horizontally toward the right and click when the radius of the circle appears close to 18 mm near the cursor, see Figure 4.49. A circle of radius close to 18 mm is created and the **Circle** tool is still active.

4.49

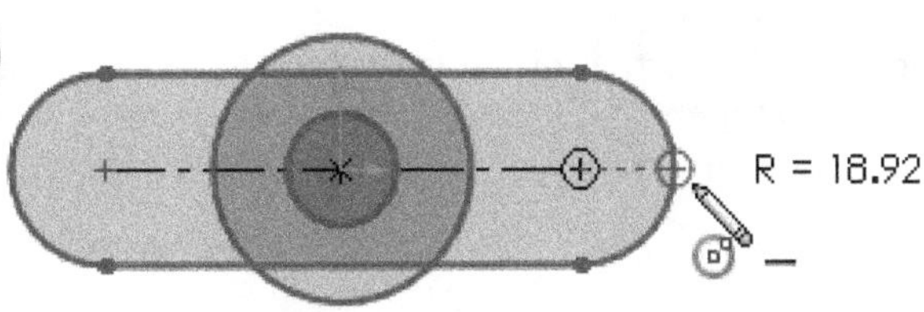

15. Move the cursor to the center point of the previously created circle of radius close to 18 mm and then click to specify the center point of another circle when the cursor snaps to it.

16. Move the cursor horizontally toward the right and click when the radius of the circle appears close to 38 mm near the cursor, see Figure 4.50. The circle is created.

17. Similarly, create two circles of the same diameter on the left side of the slot, see Figure 4.51. Next, press the ESC key to exit the **Circle** tool.

4.50

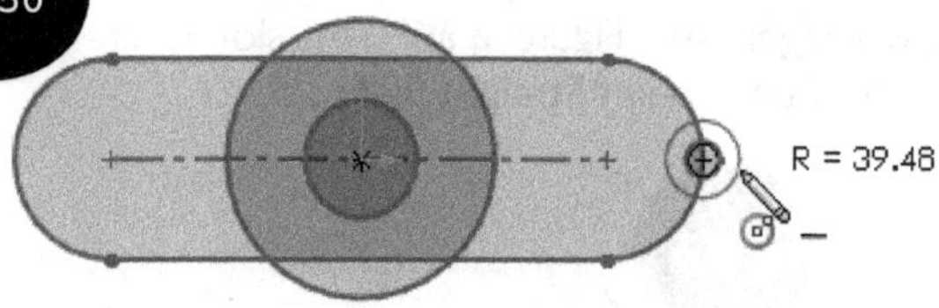

4.51

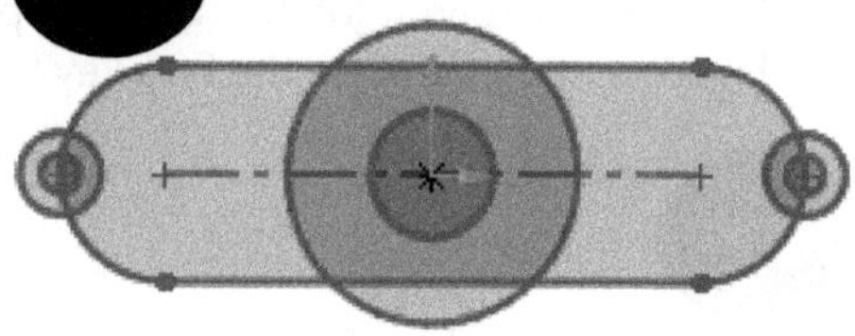

18. Click on the arrow next to the **Line** tool. The **Line** flyout appears, see Figure 4.52.

19. Click on the **Centerline** tool in the **Line** flyout and then create a vertical centerline of any length starting from the origin, see Figure 4.53. Next, press the ESC key to exit the **Centerline** tool.

4.52

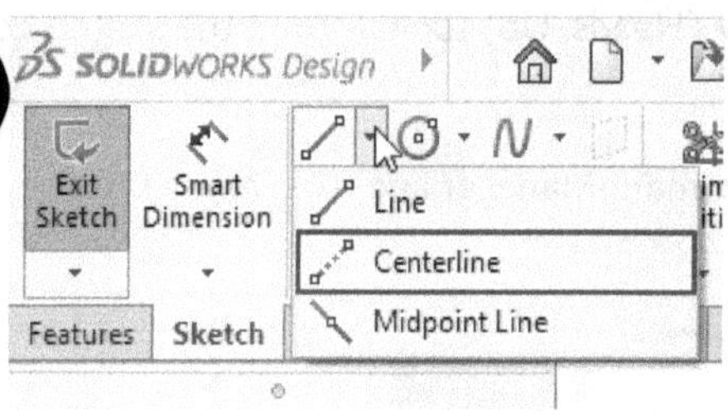

4.53

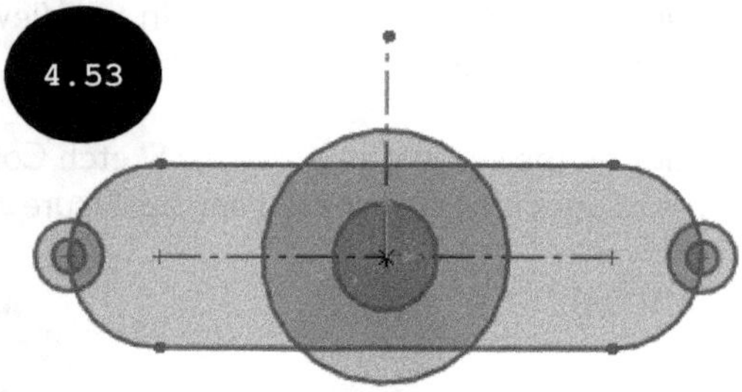

Section 6: Trimming Sketch Entities

Now, you need to trim the unwanted entities of the sketch.

1. Click on the **Trim Entities** tool in the **Sketch CommandManager**. The **Trim PropertyManager** appears on the left of the drawing area.

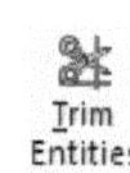

2. Click on the **Trim to closest** button in the **Options** rollout of the PropertyManager. The appearance of the cursor changes to trim cursor.

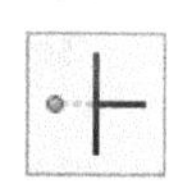

3. Ensure that the **Keep trimmed entities as construction geometry** and **Ignore trimming of construction geometry** check boxes are cleared in the PropertyManager.

4. Move the cursor over the portion of the lower horizontal slot entity that lies inside the circle, see Figure 4.54. Next, click the left mouse button when it gets highlighted. The **SOLIDWORKS** message window appears informing you that the trim operation will destroy the slot entity.

4.54

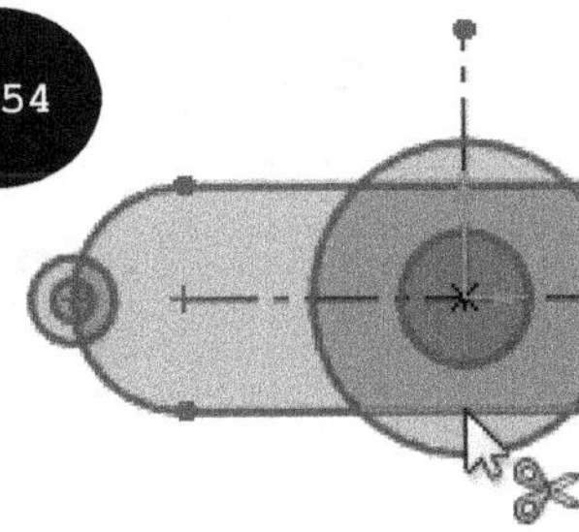

5. Click on the **OK** button in the **SOLIDWORKS** message window. The selected portion of the entity is trimmed, see Figure 4.55. Also, the **Trim Entities** tool is still active.

4.55

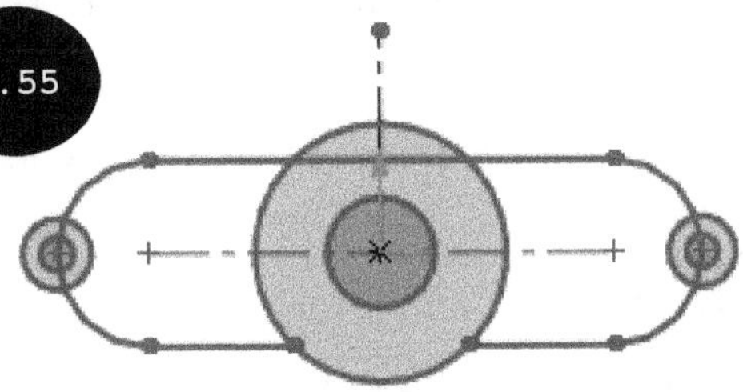

6. Similarly, click on the other unwanted entities of the sketch one by one to trim them. Figure 4.56 shows the sketch after trimming all the unwanted entities. Note that while trimming the sketch entities, if the **SOLIDWORKS** message window appears, then click on the **Yes** button to continue the process of trimming sketch entities.

4.56

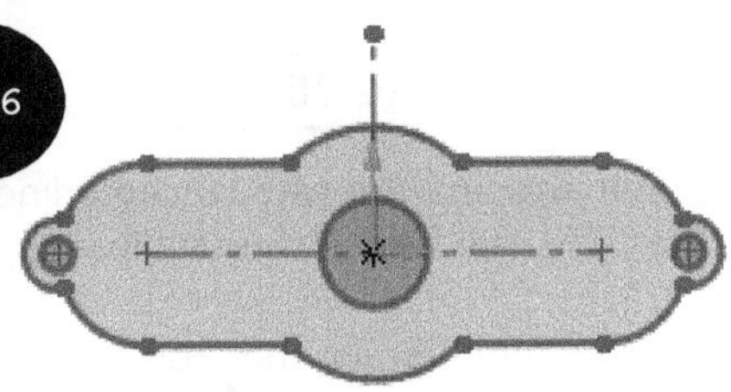

Tip: While trimming sketch entities, you may need to zoom in or zoom out of the drawing display area. To do this, scroll the middle mouse button. Alternatively, you can click on the **View > Modify > Zoom In/Out** in the SOLIDWORKS Design Menus and then drag the cursor upward or downward. Next, to exit the tool, press the ESC key.

7. Once you have completed the trimming operation, press the ESC key to exit the tool.

Section 7: Applying Relations

After creating the sketch, you need to make it fully defined by applying proper relations and dimensions to the sketch entities.

1. Select two smaller circles of diameter 36 mm (radius 18 mm) by pressing the CTRL key to apply an equal relation between them, see Figure 4.57. Next, release the CTRL key and do not move the cursor. The Pop-up toolbar appears, see Figure 4.58. Also, the **Properties PropertyManager** appears on the left of the drawing area.

4.57

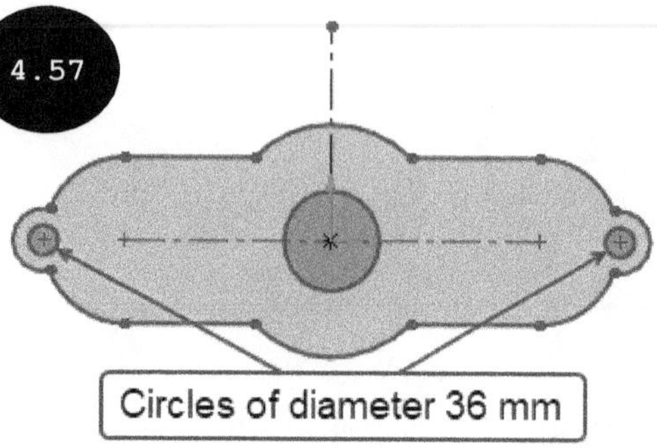

4.58

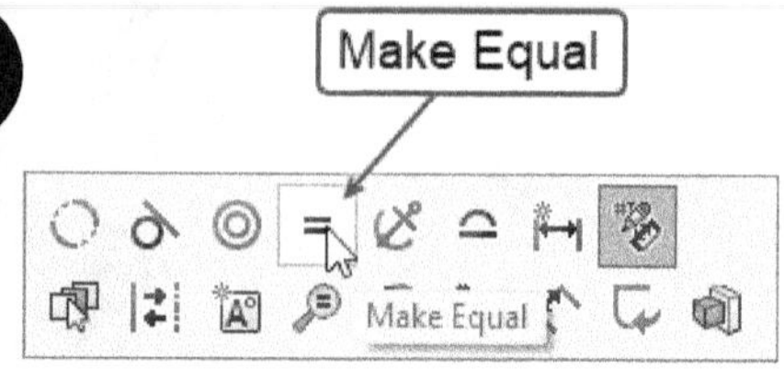

2. Click on the **Make Equal** tool in the Pop-up toolbar, see Figure 4.58. An equal relation is applied between the selected circles.

3. Similarly, select arcs of radius 38 mm by pressing the CTRL key and then apply an equal relation between them, see Figure 4.59.

4.59

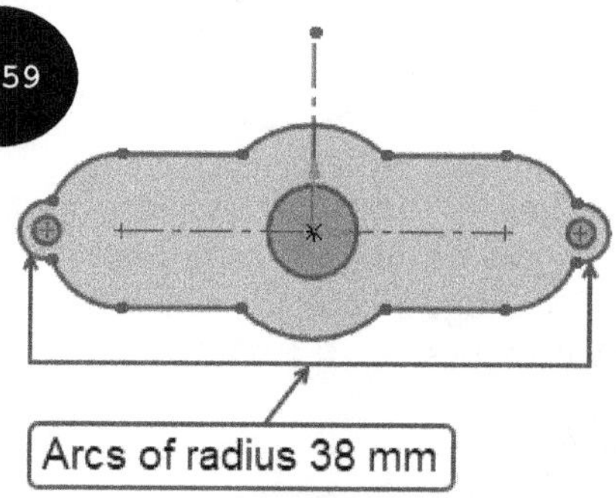

4. Select the center points of slot arcs and the vertical centerline by pressing the CTRL key, see Figure 4.60. Next, release the CTRL key. The Pop-up toolbar appears.

5. Click on the **Make Symmetric** tool in the Pop-up toolbar. A symmetric relation is applied between the center points of slot arcs and the vertical centerline.

6. Similarly, select the center points of two circles of diameter 36 mm and the vertical centerline by pressing the CTRL key (see Figure 4.61), and then apply a symmetric relation between them.

4.60

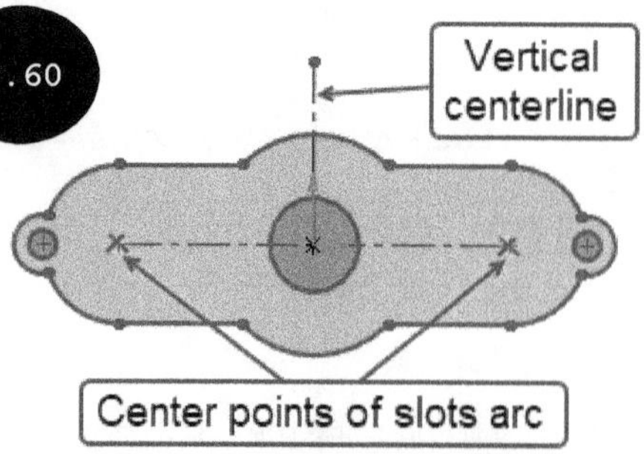

4.61

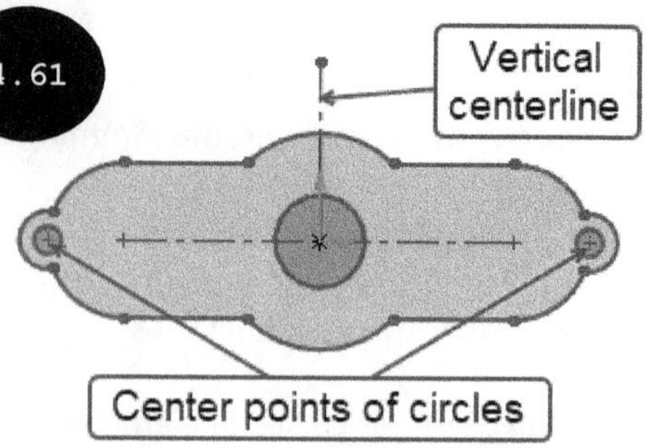

7. Similarly, apply tangent relations between four sets of tangent line and arc entities one by one, see Figure 4.62.

4.62

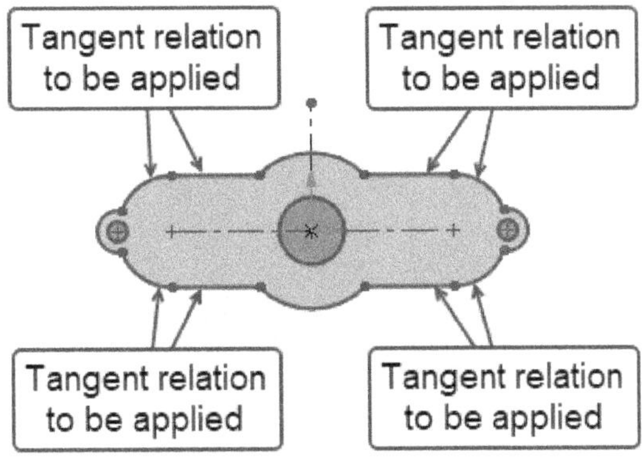

8. Select the horizontal centerline and the origin by pressing the CTRL key (see Figure 4.63), and then release the CTRL key. The Pop-up toolbar appears.

4.63

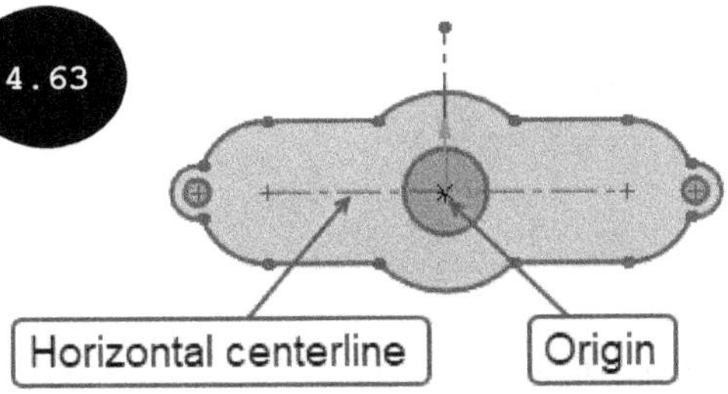

9. Click on the **Make Coincident** tool in the Pop-up toolbar. A coincident relation is applied between the horizontal centerline and the origin.

10. Apply horizontal relation to all horizontal lines (four) of the sketch one by one.

11. Select the center points of two circles of diameter 36 mm and the origin by pressing the CTRL key (see Figure 4.64), and then release the CTRL key. The Pop-up toolbar appears. In this Pop-up toolbar, click on the **Make Horizontal** tool to apply the horizontal relation between them.

4.64

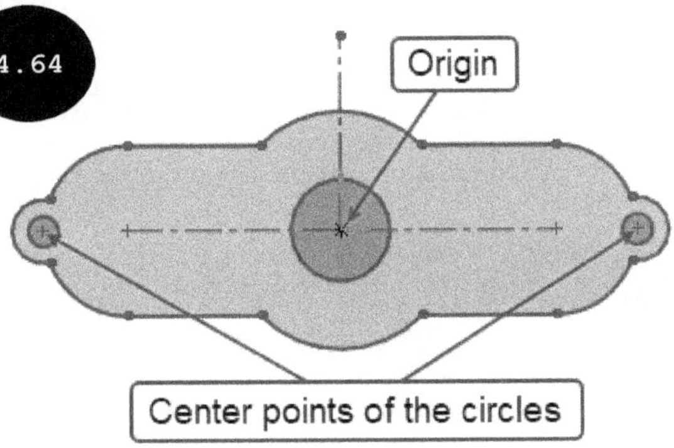

Note: You can turn on or off the display of the applied relations in the drawing area by clicking on the **View Sketch Relations** tool in the **Hide/Show Items** flyout of the **View (Heads-Up)** toolbar, see Figure 4.65.

4.65

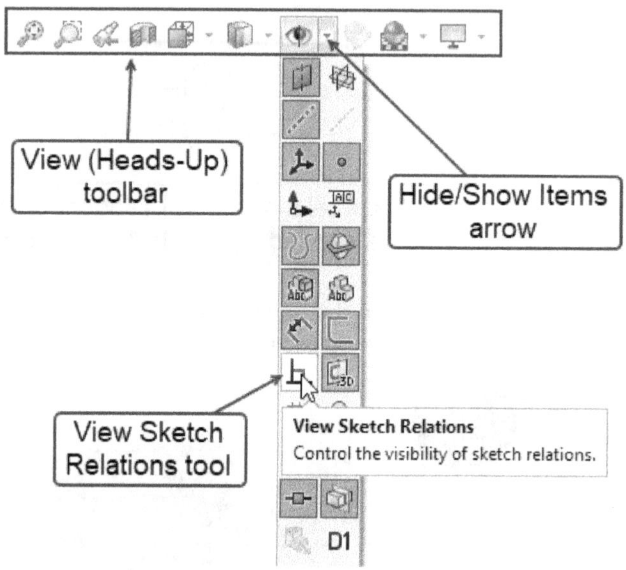

Section 8: Applying Dimensions

After applying the required relations, you need to apply dimensions to make the sketch fully defined.

1. Click on the **Smart Dimension** tool in the **Sketch CommandManager**.

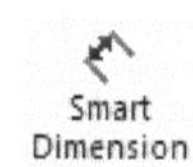

2. Select a circle whose center point is at the origin. The diameter dimension of the selected circle gets attached to the cursor, see Figure 4.66.

3. Move the cursor to the location where you want to place the dimension in the drawing area and then click to specify the placement point. The **Modify** dialog box appears, see Figure 4.67.

4.66

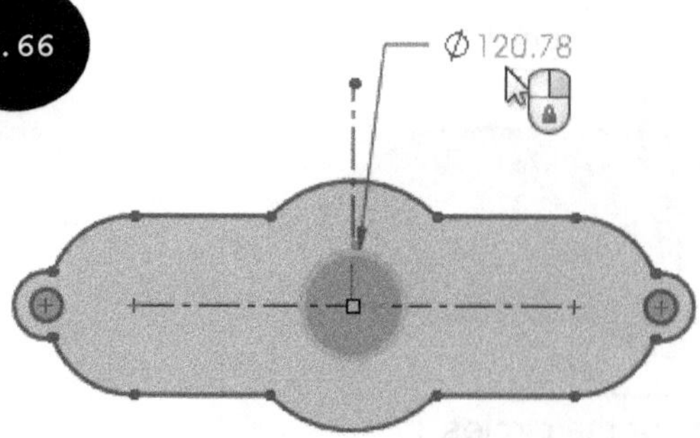

4.67

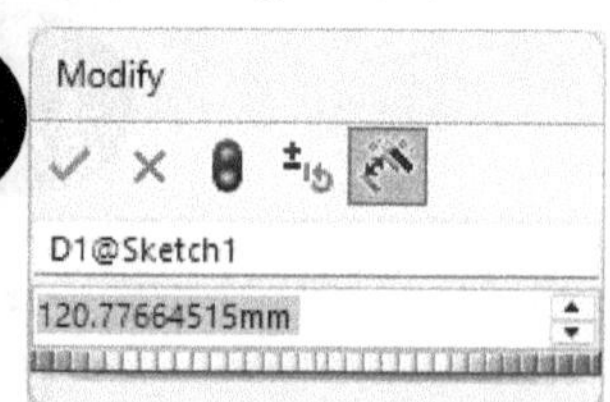

4. Enter **120** in the **Modify** dialog box and then click on the green tick-mark button. The diameter of the circle is modified to 120 mm and the diameter dimension is applied, see Figure 4.68.

5. Similarly, apply the remaining dimensions to the sketch. Figure 4.69 shows the fully defined sketch after applying all dimensions.

4.68

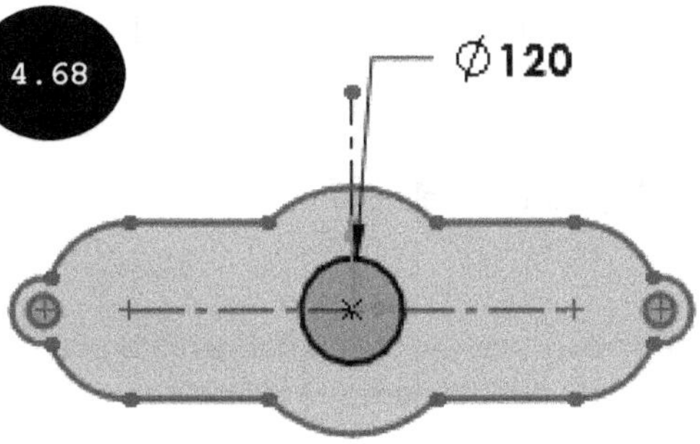

4.69

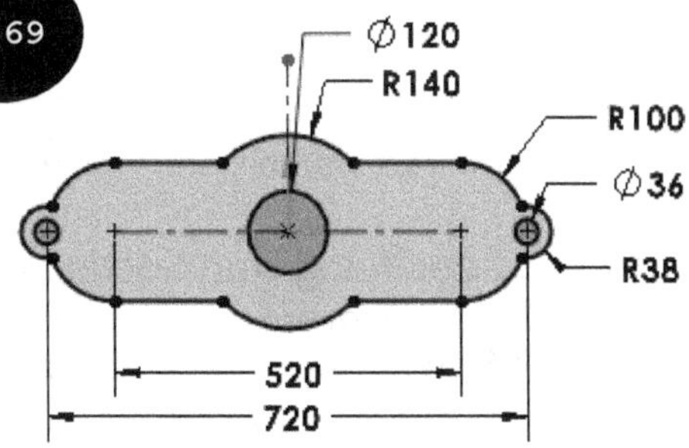

Section 9: Saving the Sketch

1. Click on the **Save** tool in the **Standard** toolbar. The **Save As** dialog box appears.

2. Browse to the SOLIDWORKS folder and then create a folder with the name **Chapter 4** in the SOLIDWORKS folder. Next, save the sketch with the name Tutorial 1 in the Chapter 4 folder.

Tutorial 2

Draw the sketch shown in Figure 4.70 and make it fully defined by applying all the required dimensions and relations. The 3D model shown in the figure is for your reference only. You will learn about creating the 3D model in later chapters. All dimensions are in mm.

4.70

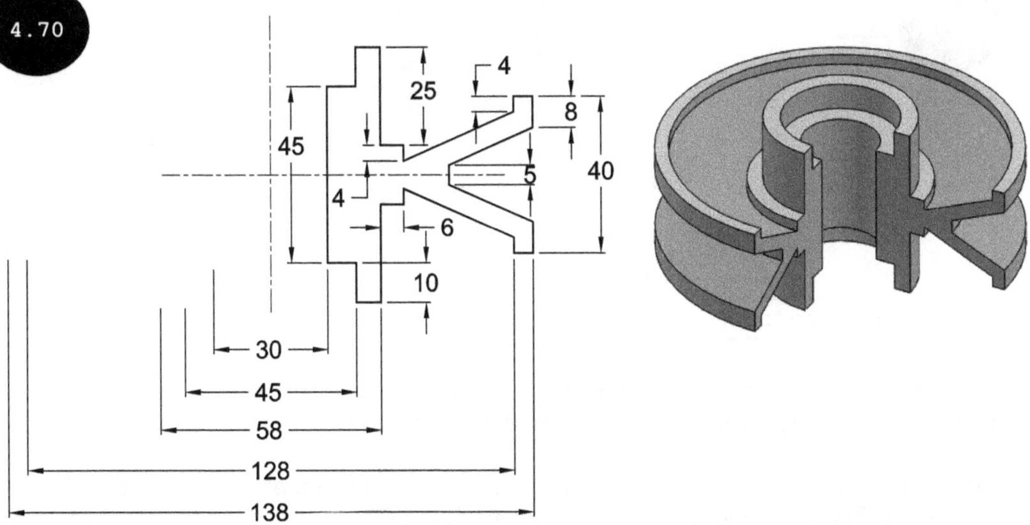

Section 1: Invoking the Part Modeling Environment

1. Start SOLIDWORKS by double-clicking on the SOLIDWORKS icon on your desktop. The startup user interface of SOLIDWORKS appears along with the **Welcome** dialog box.

Note: If SOLIDWORKS is already open and the **Welcome** dialog box does not appear on the screen, you can invoke it by clicking on the **Welcome to SOLIDWORKS tool** in the **Standard** toolbar.

2. Click on the **Part** button in the **Welcome** dialog box. The Part modeling environment is invoked.

Section 2: Specifying Unit Settings

1. Move the cursor toward the lower right corner of the screen over the Status Bar and then click on the **Unit System** area in the Status Bar. The **Unit System** flyout appears, see Figure 4.71.

4.71

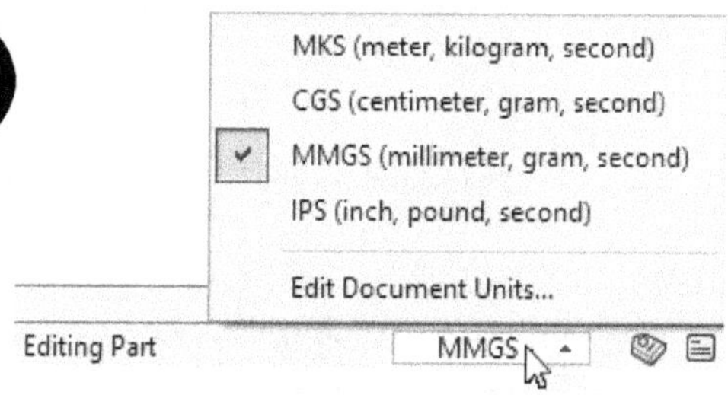

2. Ensure that the **MMGS (millimeter, gram, second)** option is tick-marked in this flyout.

Section 3: Invoking the Sketching Environment

1. Click on the **Sketch** tab in the CommandManager. The tools of the **Sketch CommandManager** appear, see Figure 4.72.

4.72

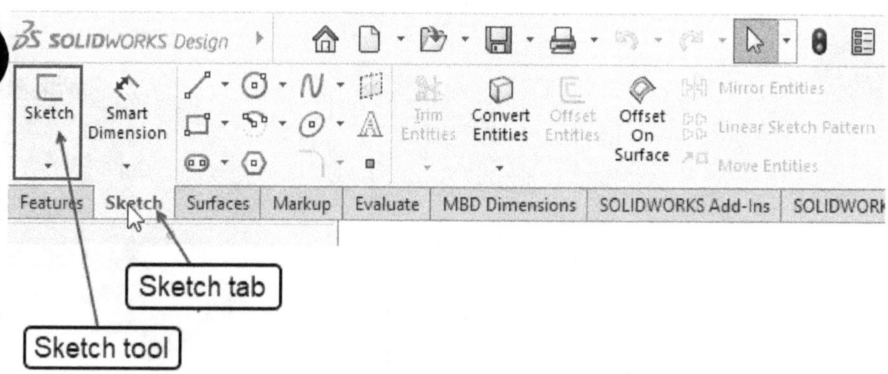

2. Click on the **Sketch** tool in the **Sketch CommandManager**. Three default planes mutually perpendicular to each other appear in the graphics area.

3. Move the cursor over the Front plane and then click on it when the boundary of the plane gets highlighted. The Sketching environment is invoked, and the Front plane is orientated normal to the viewing direction.

Section 4: Specifying Grid and Snap Settings

Now, you need to ensure that the snap mode is turned off. As SOLIDWORKS is a parametric software, you can turn off the snap mode and create a sketch by specifying points arbitrarily in the drawing area and then applying the required dimensions.

1. Click on the **Options** tool in the **Standard** toolbar. The **System Options - General** dialog box appears.

2. Click on the **Document Properties** tab in the dialog box. The name of the dialog box changes to **Document Properties - Drafting Standard.**

3. Click on the **Grid/Snap** option in the left panel of the dialog box and then ensure that the **Display grid** check box in the **Grid** area is cleared.

4. Click on the **Go To System Snaps** button and then ensure that the **Grid** check box in the **Sketch snaps** area of the dialog box is cleared.

5. Click on the **OK** button to accept the changes and close the dialog box.

Section 5: Drawing the Upper Half of the Sketch

In this section, you need to draw the upper half of the sketch.

1. Click on the arrow next to the **Line** tool. The **Line** flyout appears, see Figure 4.73.

4.73

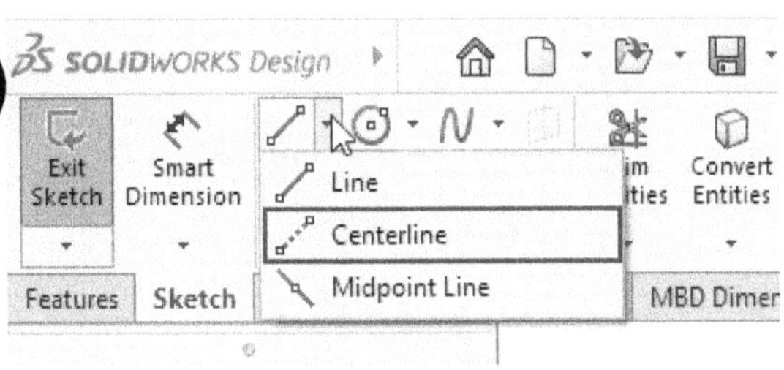

2. Click on the **Centerline** tool in the flyout. The **Centerline** tool is invoked.

3. Create vertical and horizontal centerlines of any length starting from the origin one by one, see Figure 4.74. Next, exit the **Centerline** tool.

4.74

4. Press and hold the right mouse button and then drag the cursor toward the left. The **Mouse Gestures** appears in the drawing area, see Figure 4.75.

4.75

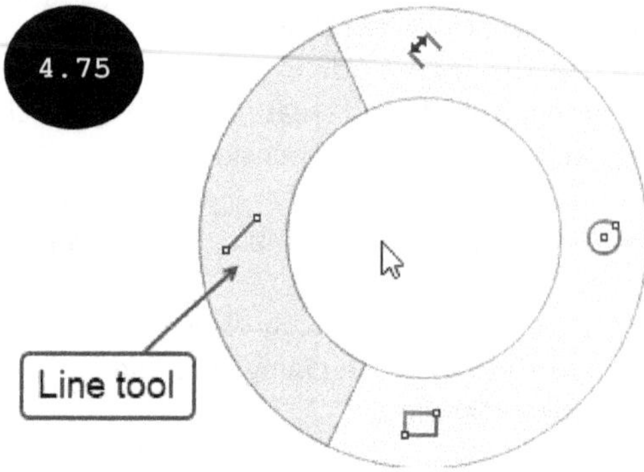

5. Drag the cursor over the **Line** tool in the **Mouse Gestures** by pressing and holding the right mouse button, see Figure 4.75. The **Line** tool gets activated and the **Mouse Gestures** is disabled. Also, the **Insert Line PropertyManager** appears on the left of the drawing area. Next, release the right mouse button.

6. Move the cursor over the horizontal centerline in the drawing area (see Figure 4.76), and then click to specify the start point of the line when the coordinates (X, Y, Z) appear close to "**15, 0, 0**" in the Status Bar, see Figure 4.77.

4.76

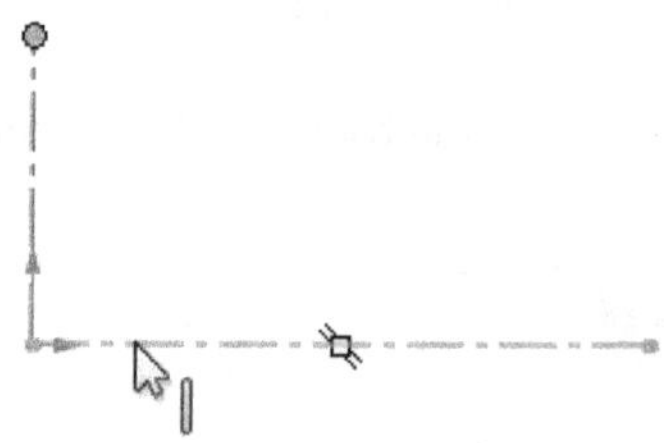

4.77

7. Move the cursor vertically upward and then click to specify the endpoint of the line when the length of the line appears close to 22.5 mm near the cursor, see Figure 4.78. A vertical line of length close to 22.5 mm is created.

4.78

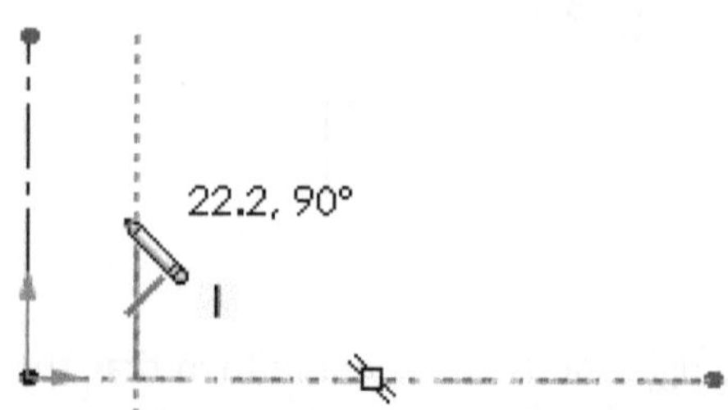

8. Move the cursor horizontally toward the right and click to specify the endpoint of the second line when the length of the line appears close to 7.5 mm. A horizontal line of length close to 7.5 mm is created.

9. Move the cursor vertically upward and click to specify the endpoint of the line when the length of the line appears close to 10 mm. A vertical line of length close to 10 mm is created.

10. Move the cursor horizontally toward the right and click when the length of the line appears close to 6.5 mm. A horizontal line of length close to 6.5 mm is created.

11. Move the cursor vertically downward and click when the length of the line appears close to 25 mm.

12. Move the cursor horizontally toward the right and click when the length of the line appears close to 6 mm.

13. Move the cursor vertically downward and click when the length of the line appears close to 4 mm.

14. Move the cursor toward the right at an angle (see Figure 4.79), and then click to specify the endpoint of the inclined line when a line appears similar to the one shown in Figure 4.79.

4.79

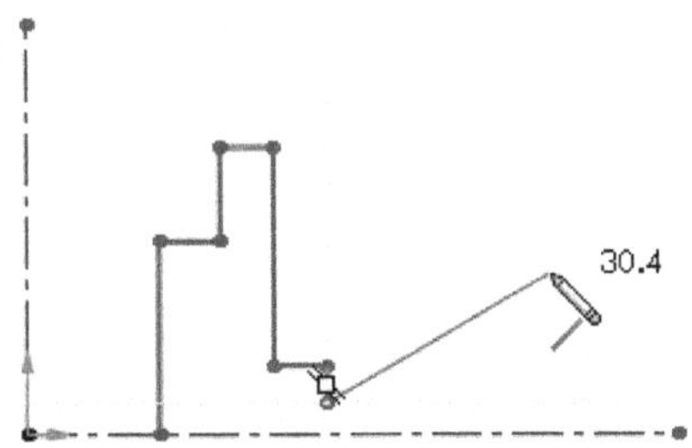

15. Move the cursor vertically upward and click when the length of the line appears close to 4 mm, see Figure 4.80.

4.80

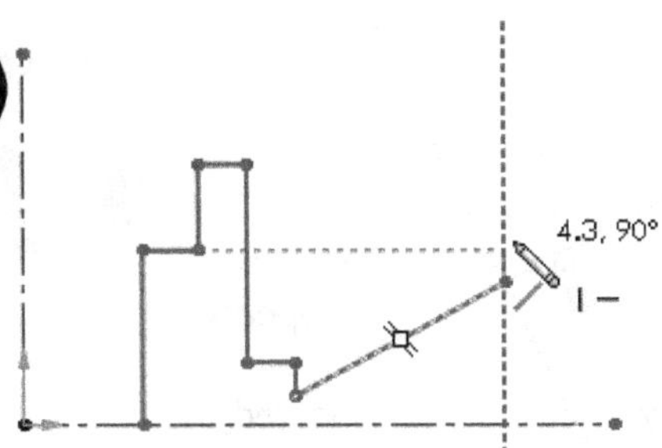

16. Move the cursor horizontally toward the right and click when the length of the line appears close to 5 mm.

17. Move the cursor vertically downward and click when the length of the line appears close to 8 mm.

18. Move the cursor parallel to the inclined line toward the left (see Figure 4.81), and then click the left mouse button just above the horizontal centerline, see Figure 4.81.

4.81

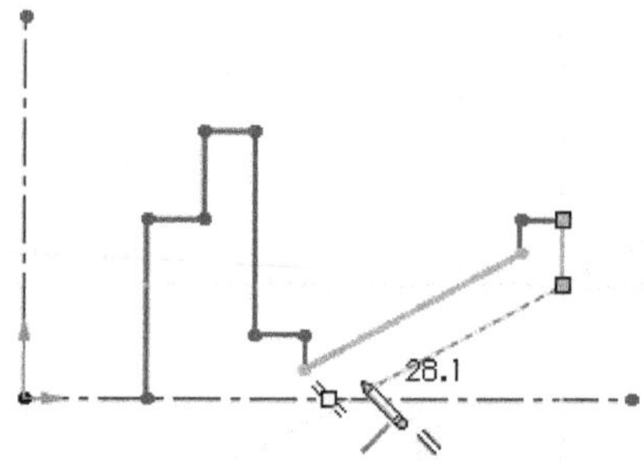

19. Move the cursor vertically downward and then click the left mouse button when the cursor snaps to the horizontal centerline. Next, press the ESC key to exit the **Line** tool. Figure 4.82 shows the sketch after creating the upper half.

4.82

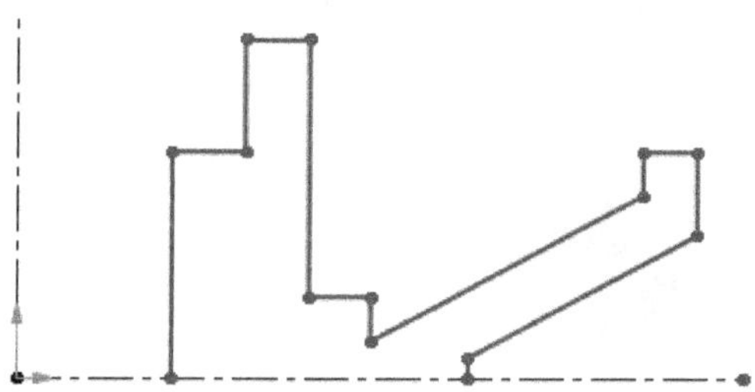

Section 6: Mirroring Sketch Entities

After creating the upper half of the sketch, you need to mirror it to create the lower half.

1. Click on the **Mirror Entities** tool in the **Sketch CommandManager**. The **Mirror PropertyManager** appears on the left of the drawing area. Mirror Entities

2. Select all the sketch entities to be mirrored except the vertical and horizontal centerlines.

3. Click on the **Mirror about** field in the PropertyManager and then click on the horizontal centerline as the mirroring line in the drawing area. A preview of the lower half of the sketch appears.

4. Ensure that the **Copy** check box is selected in the PropertyManager. Next, click on the green tick-mark ✓ button in the PropertyManager. The lower half of the sketch is created, see Figure 4.83.

4.83

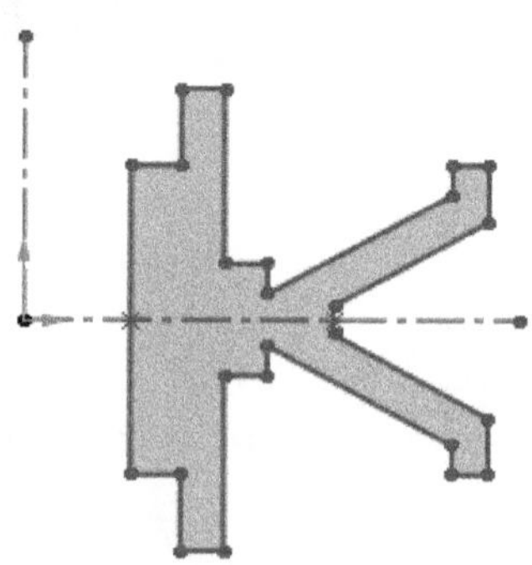

Section 7: Applying Dimensions

Now, you need to apply dimensions to make the sketch fully defined.

1. Press and hold the right mouse button and then drag the cursor vertically upward to a distance. The **Mouse Gestures** appears in the drawing area, see Figure 4.84.

2. Drag the cursor over the **Smart Dimension** tool in the **Mouse Gestures** by pressing and holding the right mouse button, see Figure 4.84. The **Smart Dimension** tool gets activated, and you are prompted to select the entities to be dimensioned. Now, release the right mouse button.

4.84

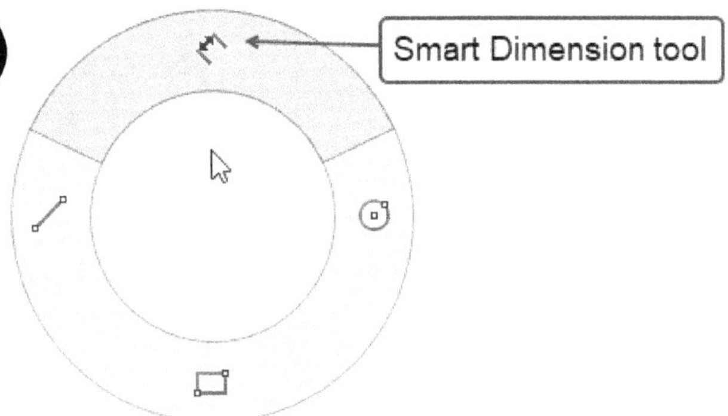

3. Click the left mouse button on the leftmost vertical line of the sketch, see Figure 4.85. The linear dimension of the selected line gets attached to the cursor.

4.85

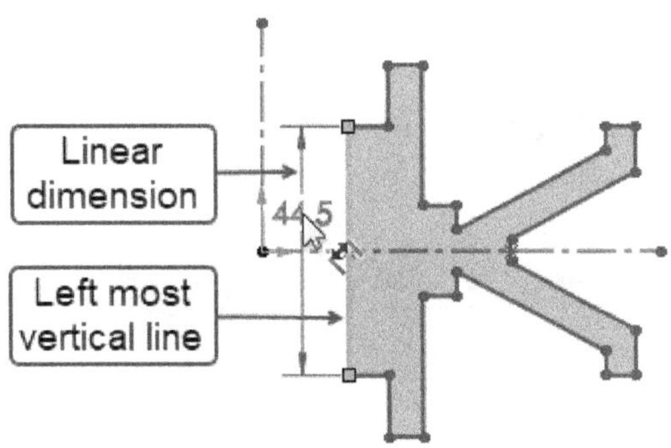

4. Move the cursor toward the left to a distance and then click to specify the placement point. The **Modify** dialog box appears, see Figure 4.86.

4.86

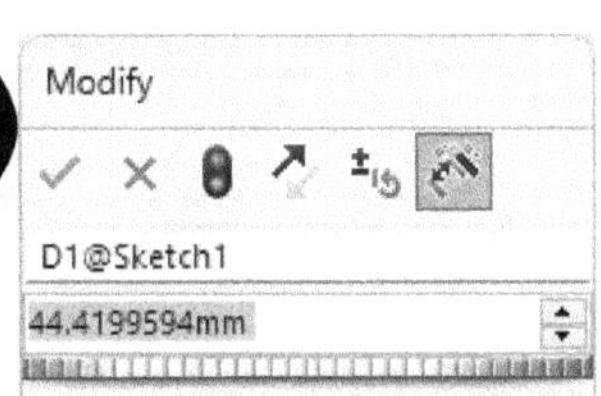

5. Enter **45** in the **Modify** dialog box and then click on the green tick-mark ✓ button. The length of the line is modified to 45 mm and the linear dimension is applied, see Figure 4.87.

6. Similarly, apply the remaining linear dimensions, see Figure 4.88.

4.87

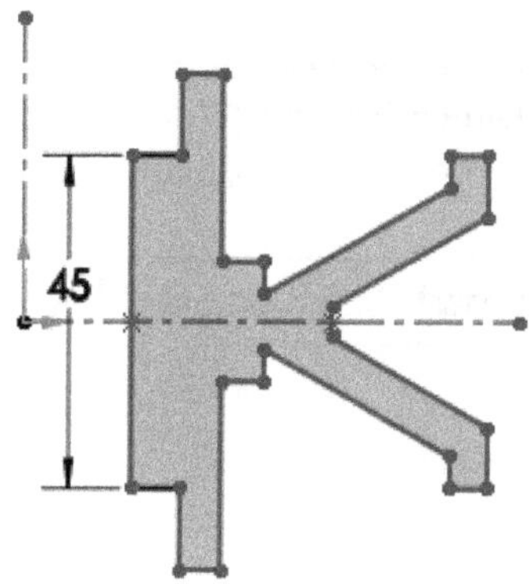

4.88

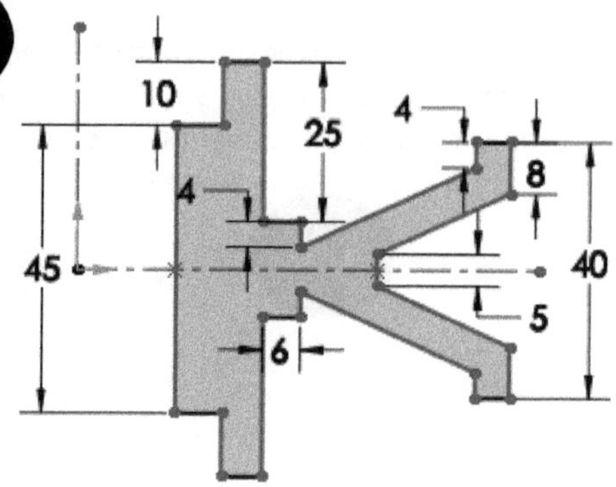

Now, you need to apply linear diameter dimensions to the sketch.

7. Ensure that the **Smart Dimension** tool is activated, and then select the leftmost vertical line of length 45 mm. The linear dimension gets attached to the cursor. Next, select the vertical centerline and then move the cursor to the left of the vertical centerline. The linear diameter dimension is attached to the cursor, see Figure 4.89.

8. Click the left mouse button to specify the placement point for the linear diameter dimension. The **Modify** dialog box appears.

9. Enter **30** in the **Modify** dialog box and then click on the green tick-mark ✓ button. The linear diameter dimension is applied, see Figure 4.90.

4.89

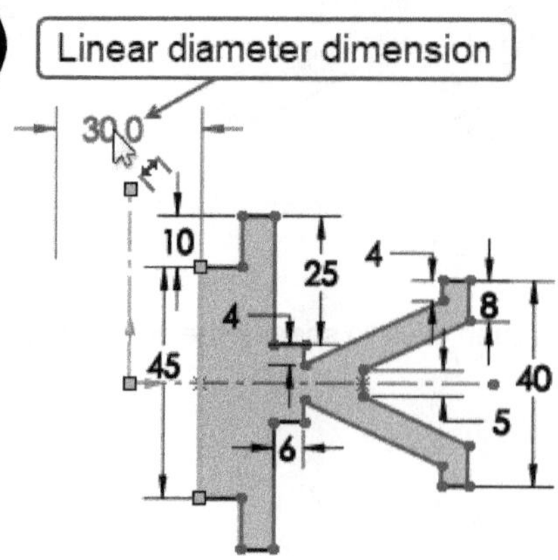

4.90

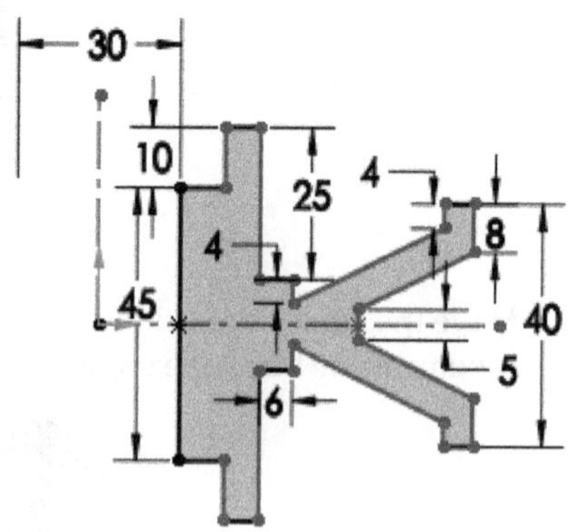

10. Select the vertical line of length 10 mm (see Figure 4.91), and then move the cursor above the previously applied dimension. A linear diameter dimension appears, see Figure 4.91.

11. Click to specify the placement point for the dimension. The **Modify** dialog box appears.

12. Enter **45** in the **Modify** dialog box and then click on the green tick-mark button. The linear diameter dimension gets applied, see Figure 4.92.

4.91

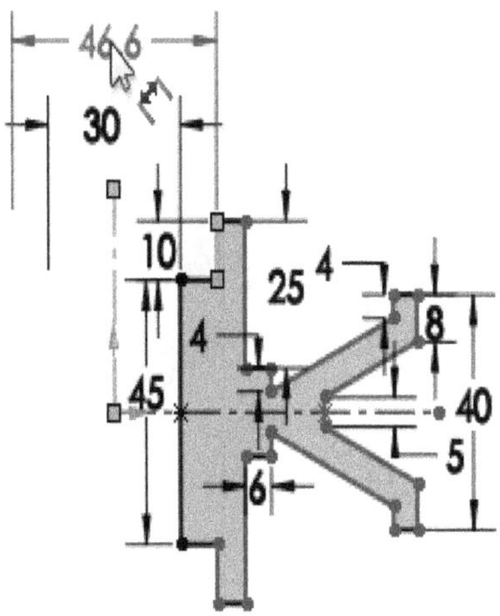

4.92

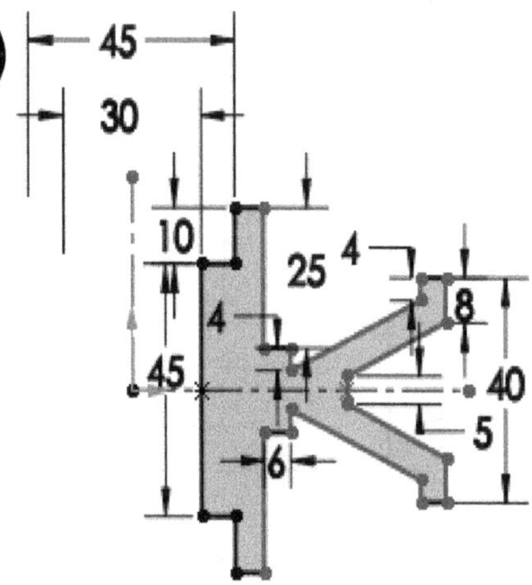

13. Similarly, apply the remaining linear diameter dimensions to the sketch, see Figure 4.93. Next, press the ESC key to exit the **Smart Dimensions** tool. Figure 4.93 shows the fully defined sketch.

4.93

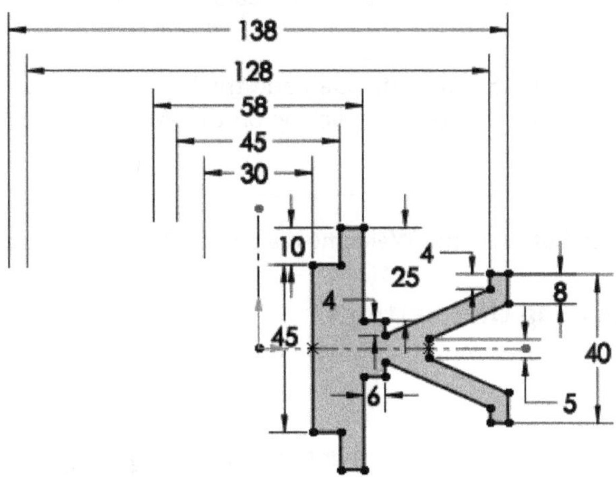

Section 8: Saving the Sketch

After creating the sketch, you need to save it.

1. Click on the **Save** tool of the **Standard** toolbar. The **Save As** window appears.

2. Browse to the Chapter 4 folder and then save the sketch with the name Tutorial 2. If the folder is not created, create a folder with the name **Chapter 4** in the SOLIDWORKS folder.

Tutorial 3

Draw the sketch shown in Figure 4.94 and make it fully defined by applying all the required dimensions and relations. The 3D model shown in the figure is for your reference only. You will learn about creating the 3D model in later chapters. All dimensions are in mm.

4.94

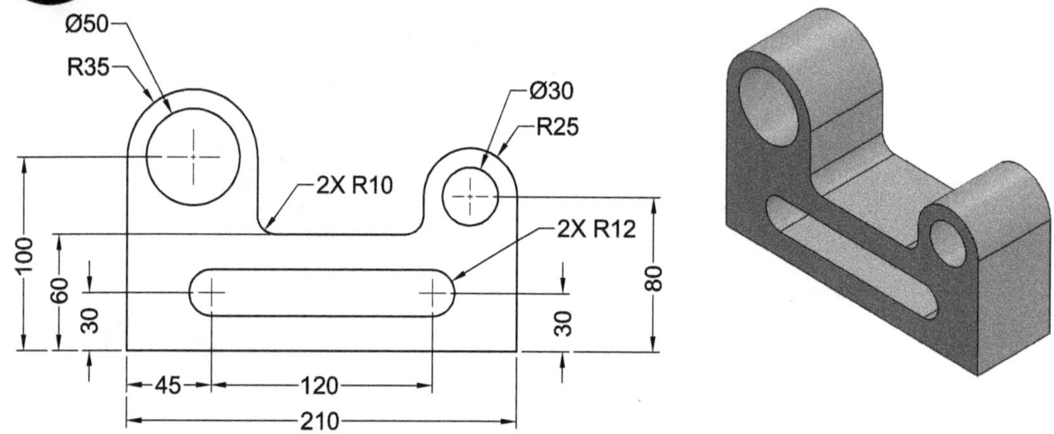

Section 1: Invoking the Part Modeling Environment

1. Start SOLIDWORKS by double-clicking on the SOLIDWORKS icon on your desktop. The startup user interface of SOLIDWORKS appears along with the **Welcome** dialog box.

Note: If SOLIDWORKS is already open and the **Welcome** dialog box does not appear on the screen, you can invoke it by clicking on the **Welcome to SOLIDWORKS** tool in the **Standard** toolbar.

2. Click on the **Part** button in the **Welcome** dialog box. The Part modeling environment is invoked.

Section 2: Specifying Unit Settings

Once the Sketching environment has been invoked, specify the metric unit system for measurement.

1. Move the cursor toward the lower right corner of the screen over the Status Bar and then click on the **Unit System** area in the Status Bar. The **Unit System** flyout appears, see Figure 4.95.

2. Ensure that the **MMGS (millimeter, gram, second)** option is tick-marked in this flyout.

4.95

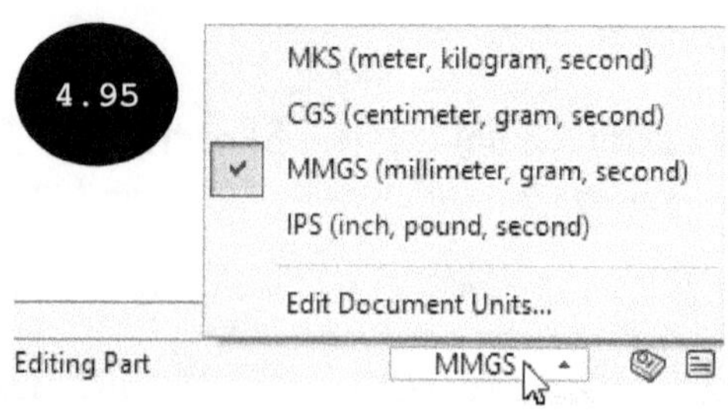

Section 3: Invoking the Sketching Environment

1. Click on the **Sketch** tab in the CommandManager. The tools of the **Sketch CommandManager** appear.

2. Click on the **Sketch** tool in the **Sketch CommandManager**. Three default planes mutually perpendicular to each other appear in the graphics area.

3. Move the cursor over the Front plane and then click the left mouse button when the boundary of the Front plane gets highlighted. The Sketching environment is invoked, and the Front plane is orientated normal to the viewing direction.

Section 4: Drawing Sketch Entities

Now, you need to create the sketch by using the sketching tools.

1. Ensure that the snap mode is turned off. Press and hold the right mouse button and then drag the cursor toward the left. The **Mouse Gestures** appears in the drawing area, see Figure 4.96.

4.96

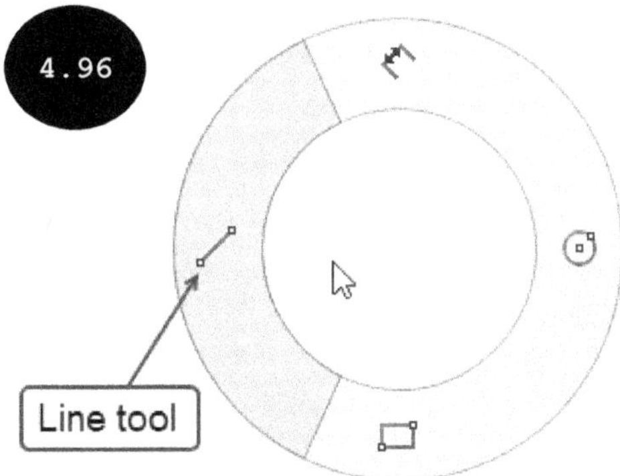

2. Drag the cursor over the **Line** tool in the **Mouse Gestures** by pressing and holding the right mouse button. The **Line** tool gets activated, and the **Mouse Gestures** is disabled. Next, release the right mouse button.

3. Move the cursor to the origin and then click to specify the start point of the line when the cursor snaps to the origin and the coincident symbol appears, see Figure 4.97.

4.97

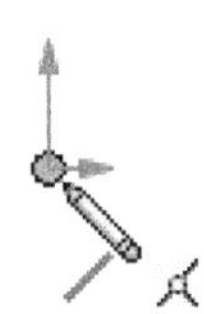

Note: If you specify a point when a relation symbol appears such as coincident, horizontal, or vertical near the cursor, the respective relation will be applied between entities.

4. Move the cursor horizontally toward the right and click to specify the endpoint of the line when the length of a line appears close to 210 mm along with the symbol of a horizontal relation near the cursor, see Figure 4.98. A horizontal line of length close to 210 mm is created. Also, the horizontal relation is applied to the line.

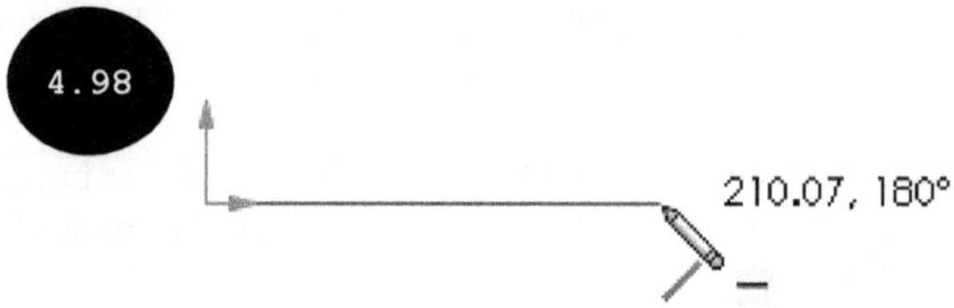

Tip: While drawing sketch entities, you may need to increase or decrease the drawing display area. You can zoom into or zoom out of the drawing display area by scrolling the middle mouse button. Alternatively, click on the **View > Modify > Zoom In/Out** in the SOLIDWORKS Design Menus and then drag the cursor upward or downward by pressing the left mouse button.

5. Move the cursor vertically upward and create a vertical line of length close to 80 mm.

   Now, you need to create a tangent arc.

6. Move the cursor to a distance and then move it back to the last specified point. An orange-colored dot appears, see Figure 4.99.

7. Move the cursor vertically upward to a distance and then move it horizontally toward the left. The arc mode is activated, and the preview of a tangent arc appears, see Figure 4.100.

8. Click to specify the endpoint of the tangent arc when the angle and radius of the arc appear close to 180 degrees and 25 mm, respectively, see Figure 4.100. A tangent arc of radius close to 25 mm is created and the line mode is activated again.

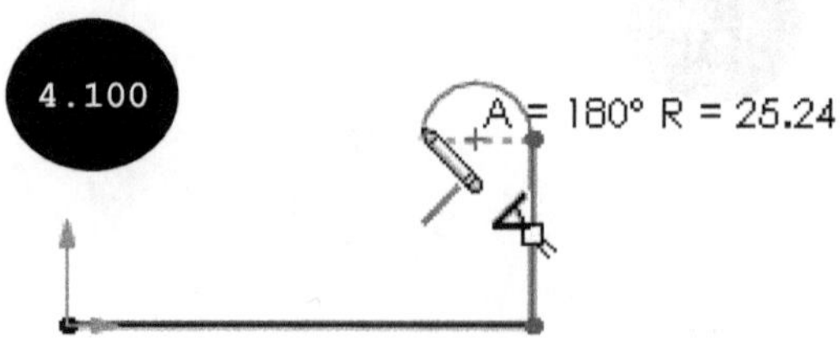

9. Move the cursor vertically downward and create a vertical line of length close to 20 mm.

10. Move the cursor horizontally toward the left and create a horizontal line close to 90 mm.

11. Move the cursor vertically upward and create a vertical line of length close to 40 mm.

12. Create a tangent arc of a radius close to 35 mm and an angle close to 180 degrees, see Figure 4101. Also, ensure that the endpoint of the tangent arc is aligned with the start point of the first line entity, see Figure 4.101.

13. Move the cursor vertically downward and click to specify the endpoint of the line when the cursor snaps to the start point of the first line entity, see Figure 4.102. Press the ESC key to exit the tool.

4.101

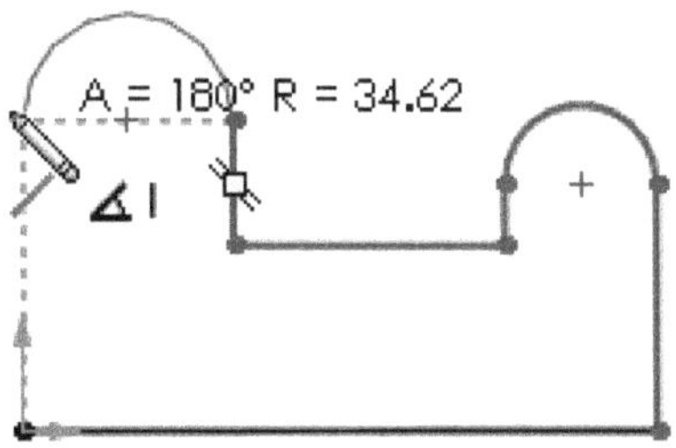

4.102

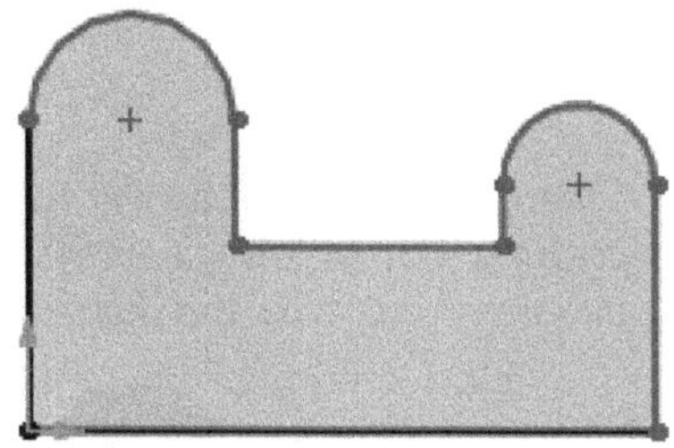

Now, you need to create circles of the sketch.

14. Press and hold the right mouse button and then drag the cursor toward the right. The **Mouse Gestures** appears in the drawing area, see Figure 4.103.

4.103

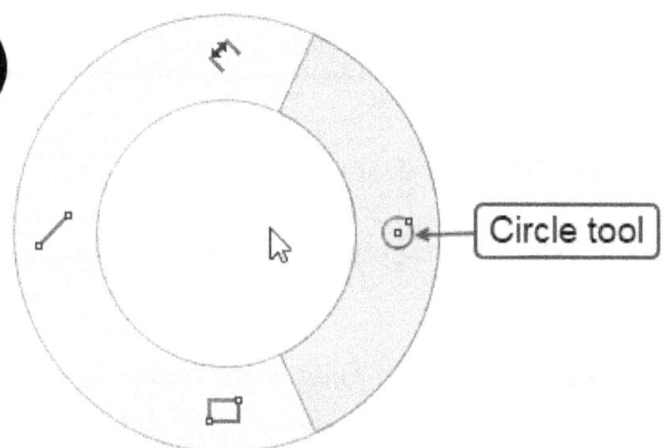

15. Drag the cursor over the **Circle** tool in the **Mouse Gestures**. The **Circle** tool gets activated, and the **Mouse Gestures** is disabled. Next, release the right mouse button.

16. Create two circles of diameter close to 50 mm and 30 mm, respectively, see Figure 4.104. Next, exit the **Circle** tool.

4.104

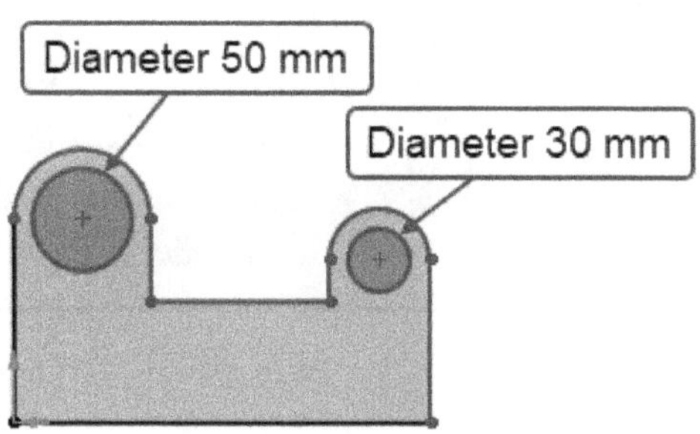

17. Invoke the **Slot** flyout (see Figure 4.105), and then click on the **Straight Slot** tool in the flyout.

4.105

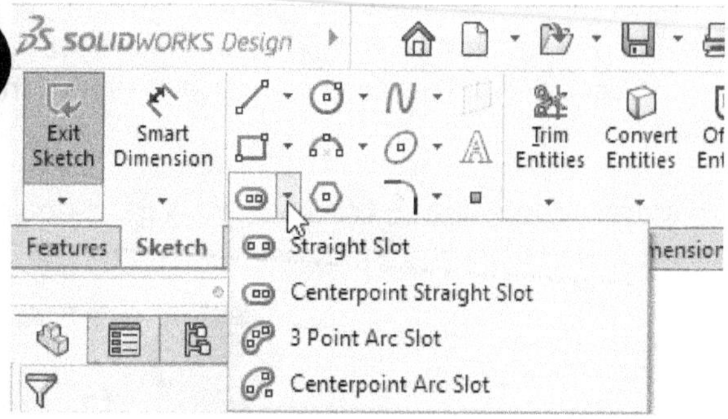

18. Create a straight slot similar to the one shown in Figure 4.106 and then exit the tool. You can create a slot of any parameters because later in this tutorial, you will be required to apply dimensions to make the sketch fully defined.

4.106

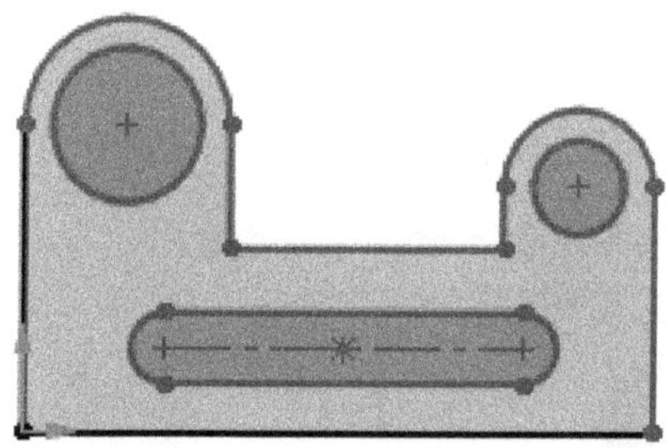

Now, you need to create fillets in the sketch.

19. Click on the **Sketch Fillet** tool in the **Sketch CommandManager**. The **Sketch Fillet PropertyManager** appears.

20. Enter **10** in the **Fillet Radius** field of the **Fillet Parameters** rollout in the PropertyManager.

21. Move the cursor over the upper right vertex of the sketch, see Figure 4.107. A preview of the fillet appears. Next, click the left mouse button to accept the fillet preview.

4.107

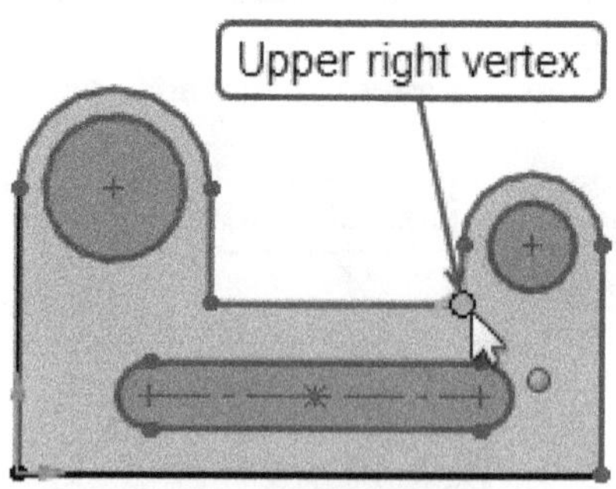

22. Similarly, move the cursor over the upper left vertex of the sketch, see Figure 4.108. A preview of the fillet appears. Next, click the left mouse button to accept the fillet preview.

4.108

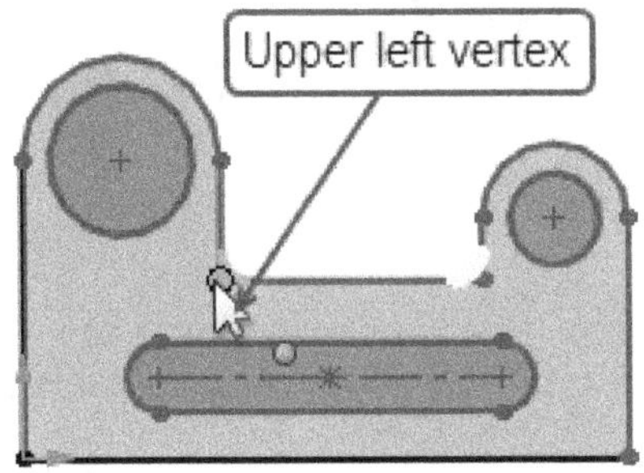

23. After selecting the vertices to create fillets, click on the green tick-mark button in the PropertyManager. Fillets of radius 10 mm are created, see Figure 4.109. Also, the radius dimension is applied to one of the fillets and an equal relation is applied between both the fillets.

4.109

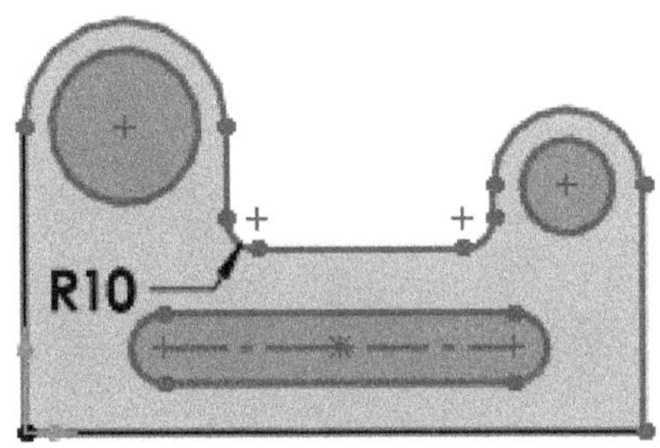

Section 5: Applying Dimensions

After creating the sketch, you need to apply the required relations and dimensions to make the sketch fully defined. In this sketch, all the required relations have been applied automatically while creating the entities. Therefore, you need to apply dimensions only.

1. Click on the **Smart Dimension** tool in the **Sketch CommandManager**.

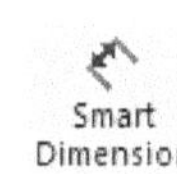

2. Click on the lower horizontal line of the sketch and then move the cursor downward. The linear dimension gets attached to the cursor, see Figure 4.110.

4.110

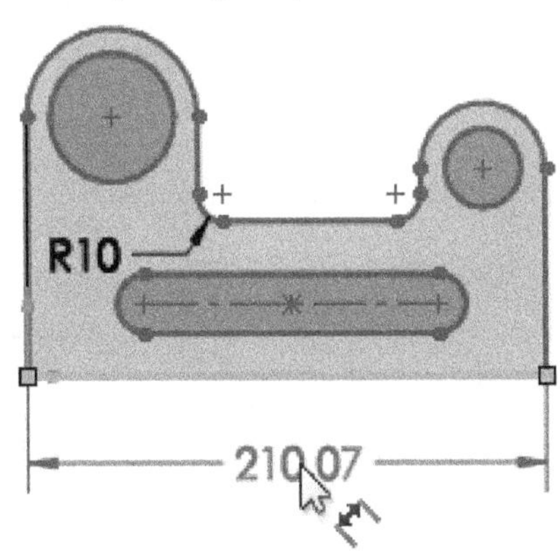

3. Click to specify the placement point for the attached linear dimension in the drawing area. The **Modify** dialog box appears, see Figure 4.111.

4.111

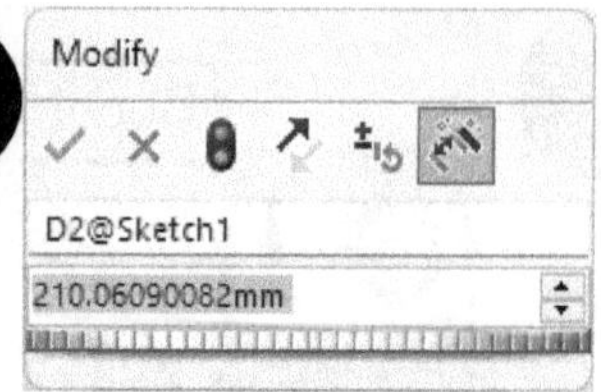

4. Enter **210** in the **Modify** dialog box and then click on the green tick-mark ✓ button. The length of the line is modified to 210 mm and the linear dimension is applied.

5. Similarly, apply the remaining dimensions to the sketch by using the **Smart Dimension** tool, see Figure 4.112.

6. Press the ESC key to exit the tool. Figure 4.112 shows the final sketch.

4.112

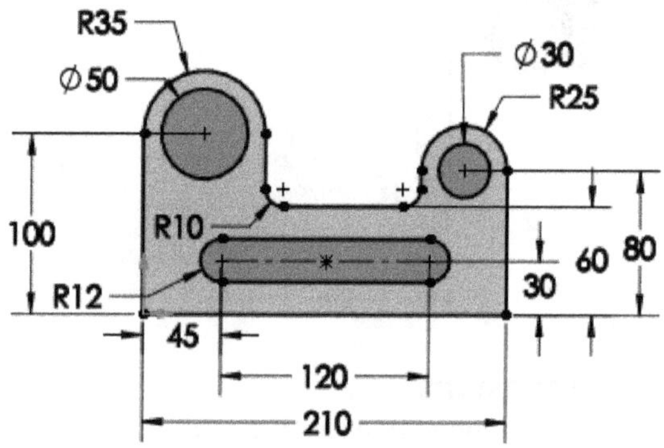

Tip: After placing a dimension in the required location, you may need to further change its location in order to place other dimensions. To change the location of an existing dimension, press and hold the left mouse button over the dimension and then drag it to a new location. Next, release the left mouse button.

Section 6: Saving the Sketch

After creating the sketch, you need to save it.

1. Click on the **Save** tool in the **Standard** toolbar. The **Save As** dialog box appears.

2. Browse to the Chapter 4 folder and then save the sketch with the name Tutorial 3.

Hands-on Test Drive 1

Draw a sketch of the model shown in Figure 4.113 and apply the required dimensions to make it fully defined. The 3D model shown in the figure is for your reference only. You will learn about creating the 3D models in later chapters. All dimensions are in mm.

4.113

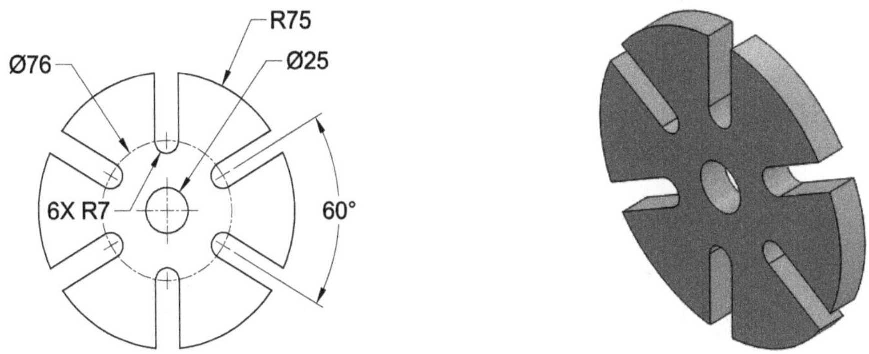

Hands-on Test Drive 2

Draw a sketch of the model shown in Figure 4.114. The 3D model shown in the figure is for your reference only. You will learn about creating the 3D models in later chapters. All dimensions are in mm.

4.114

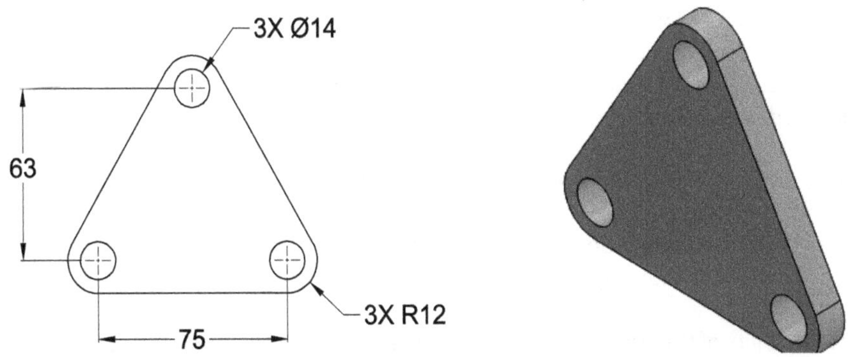

Hands-on Test Drive 3

Draw a sketch of the model shown in Figure 4.115 and apply the required dimensions. The 3D model is shown for your reference. All dimensions are in mm.

4.115

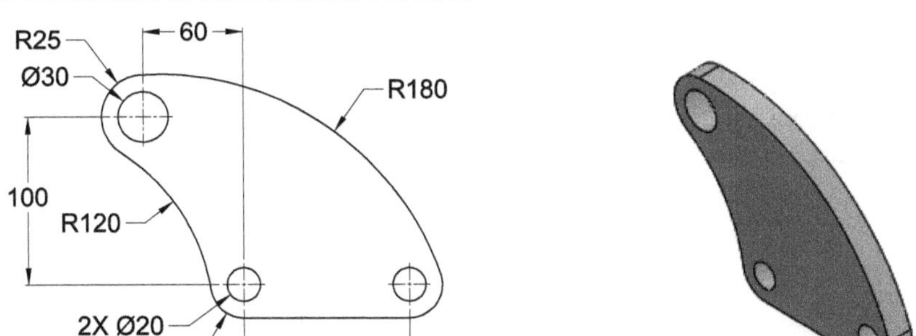

Summary

In this chapter, you explored the process of creating fully defined sketches by applying geometric relations and dimensions. You learned how to control the display of geometric relations, edit dimensions, and identify the different states of a sketch: under-defined, fully defined, and over-defined. These concepts are essential for ensuring precision and stability in your designs.

Questions

Complete and verify the following sentences:

- The _________ relation is used for coinciding a sketch point onto a line, an arc, or an elliptical entity.
- You can control the display or visibility of the applied geometric relations by using the _________ tool.
- The _________ dimension is applied to a sketch representing revolve features.
- The _______ dimensions are measured from a base entity.
- All degrees of freedom of a _______ sketch are fixed.
- The _______ tool is used for applying path length dimensions to a series of end-to-end connected sketch entities forming a chain.
- The _______ tool is used for applying a dimension, depending upon the type of entity selected.
- On selecting the **Enable on screen numeric input on entity creation** check box, the _______ field appears while drawing a sketch entity in the drawing area for entering the dimension value.
- The availability of the suggested relations in the Pop-up toolbar depends upon the type of entities selected. (True/False)
- You cannot modify dimensions once they have been applied. (True/False)
- You cannot delete relations that have already been applied between the selected entities. (True/False)
- Geometric relations are used for restricting some degrees of freedom of a sketch. (True/False)

CHAPTER

5

Creating Base Features of Solid Models

This chapter discusses the following topics:

- Creating an Extruded Feature
- Creating a Revolved Feature
- Navigating a 3D Model in the Graphics Area
- Manipulating View Orientation of a Model
- Changing the Display Style of a Model
- Changing the View of a Model

Once a sketch has been created and fully defined, you can convert it into a solid feature by using the feature modeling tools, see Figure 5.1.

5.1

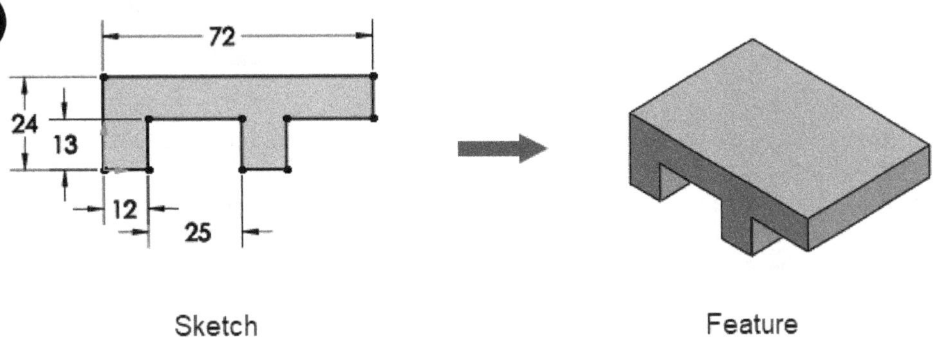

All the feature modeling tools are available in the **Features CommandManager** in the Part modeling environment, see Figure 5.2. To create a 3D solid model, you need to create all its features one by one using the feature modeling tools, see Figure 5.3. The first created feature of a model is known as the base feature or the parent feature of the model.

5.2

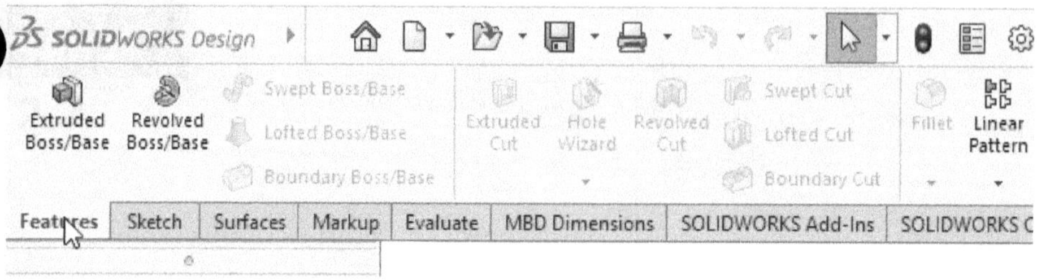

5.3

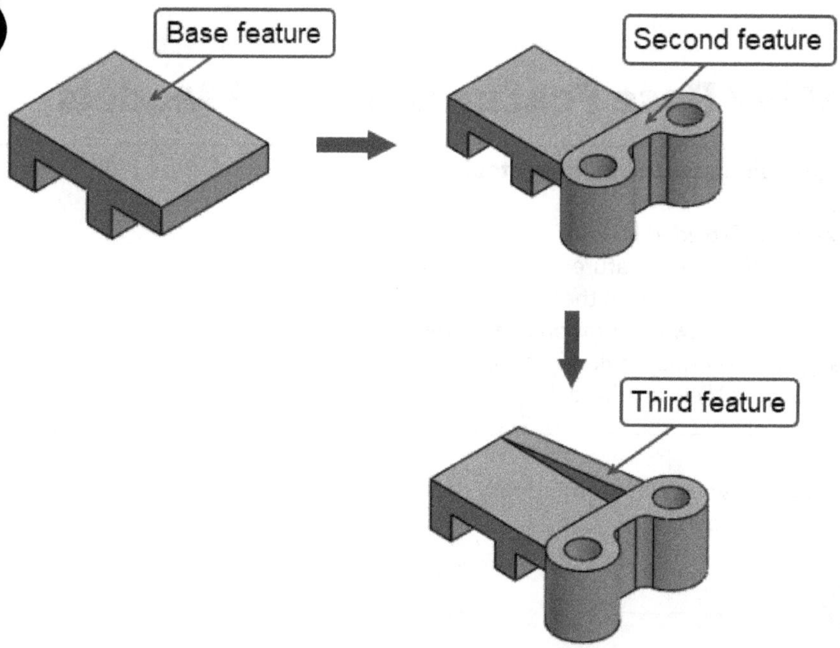

Note that most of the tools in the **Features CommandManager** are initially inactive. These tools become active after the base feature of a model is created. In SOLIDWORKS, you can create the base feature of a model by using the **Extruded Boss/Base**, **Revolved Boss/Base**, **Swept Boss/Base**, **Lofted Boss/Base**, or **Boundary Boss/Base** tool. However, the **Swept Boss/Base**, **Lofted Boss/Base**, and **Boundary Boss/Base** tools will only become active once the necessary profiles or sketches for these features are created. You will explore these tools in later chapters. In this chapter, the focus is on creating a base feature using the **Extruded Boss/Base** and **Revolved Boss/Base** tools.

Creating an Extruded Feature

An extruded feature is created by adding material normal to or at an angle to the sketching plane. In SOLIDWORKS, you can create an extruded feature using the **Extruded Boss/Base** tool. Note that the sketch of the extruded feature defines its geometry. Figure 5.4 shows different extruded features created from the respective sketches.

5.4

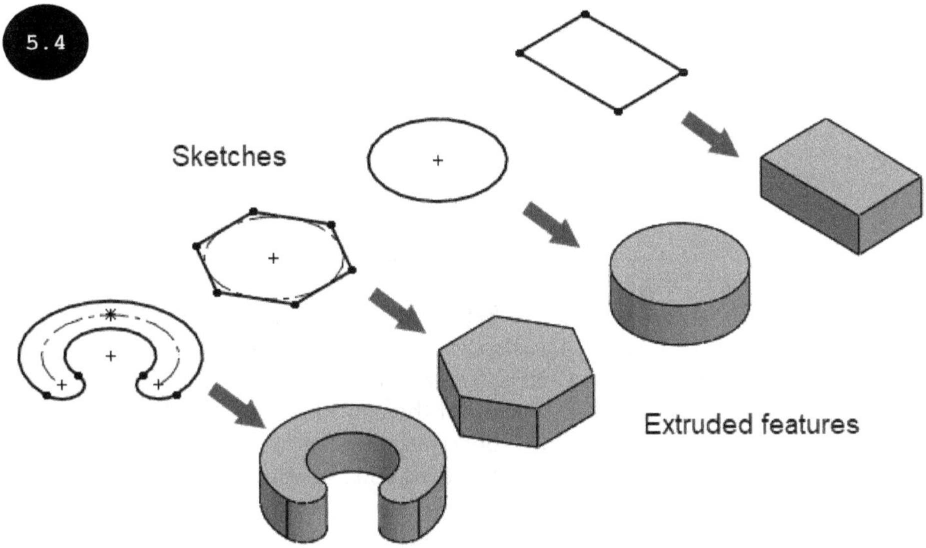

After creating the sketch using the sketching tools, do not exit the Sketching environment. Click on the **Features** tab in the CommandManager to display the tools of the **Features CommandManager**, see Figure 5.5. Next, click on the **Extruded Boss/Base** tool. A preview of the extruded feature appears in the graphics area with the default extrusion parameters. Also, the orientation of the model changes to trimetric, and the **Boss-Extrude PropertyManager** appears on the left side of the graphics area, see Figure 5.6.

5.5

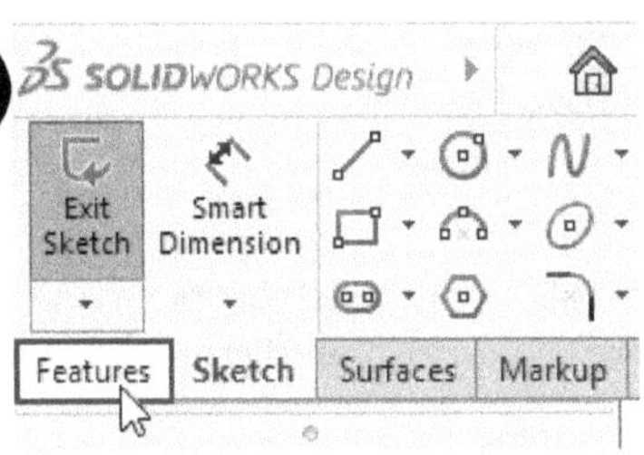

5.6

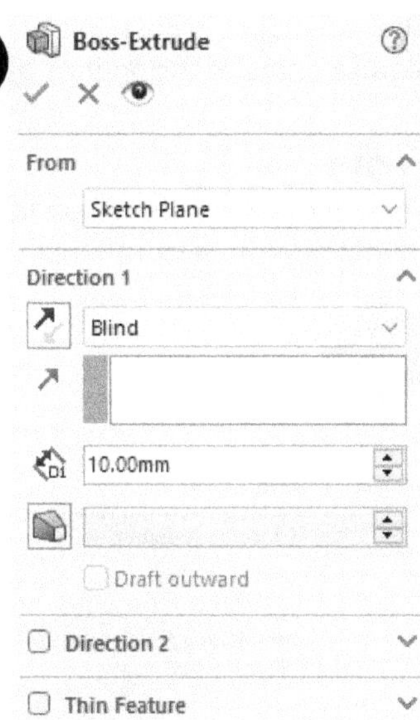

Figure 5.7 shows a rectangular sketch created on the Top plane in the Sketching environment, while Figure 5.8 displays a preview of the resulting extruded feature in trimetric orientation.

5.7

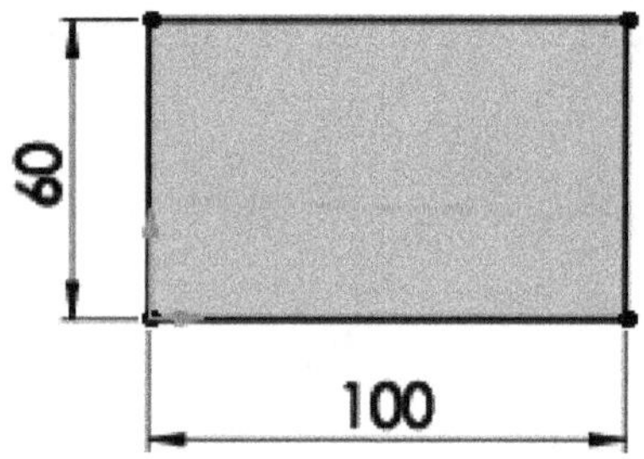

5.8

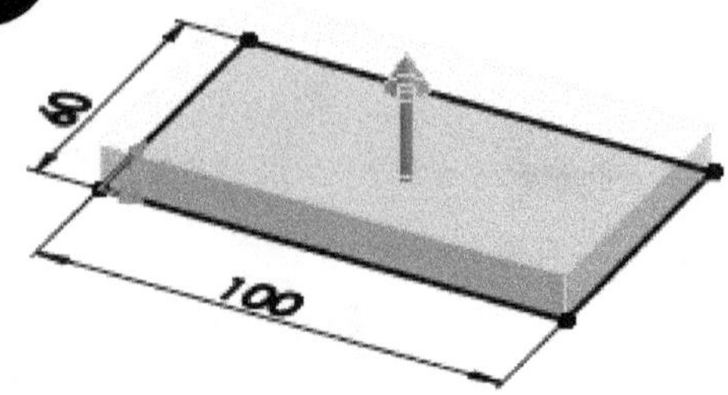

Note: If you exit the Sketching environment after creating the sketch and the sketch is not selected in the graphics area, invoking the **Extruded Boss/Base** tool will display the **Extrude PropertyManager**, see Figure 5.9. Also, you will be prompted to either select a sketch to extrude or choose a sketching plane to create the sketch. When you select the sketch to extrude in the graphics area, a preview of the extruded feature will appear with default parameters, and the **Boss-Extrude PropertyManager** will appear on the left of the graphics area. If the sketch to be extruded is not created, you can select the sketching plane to create the sketch in the Sketching environment. After creating the sketch, exit the Sketching environment.

You can exit the Sketching environment by clicking the **Exit Sketch** tool in the **Sketch CommandManager**. Alternatively, click the **Exit Sketch** icon in the Confirmation Corner, located at the top right corner of the graphics area, to exit the Sketching environment.

The options in the **Boss-Extrude PropertyManager** are used for specifying parameters for the extruded feature. Some of the options of this PropertyManager are discussed next.

From

The options in the **Start Condition** drop-down list of the **From** rollout are used for specifying the start condition for the extruded feature, see Figure 5.10. The options of this drop-down list are discussed next.

5.9

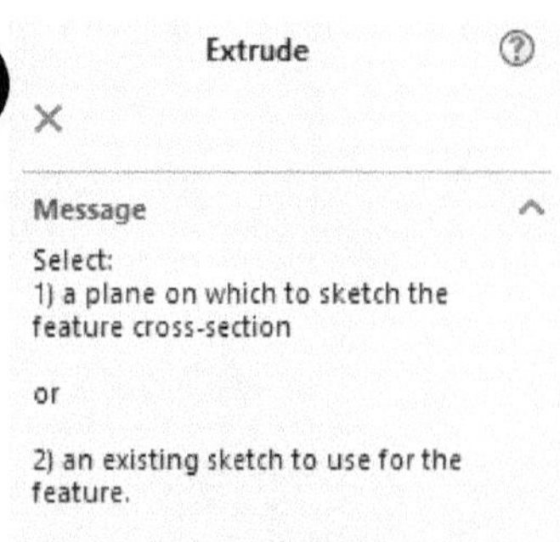

5.10

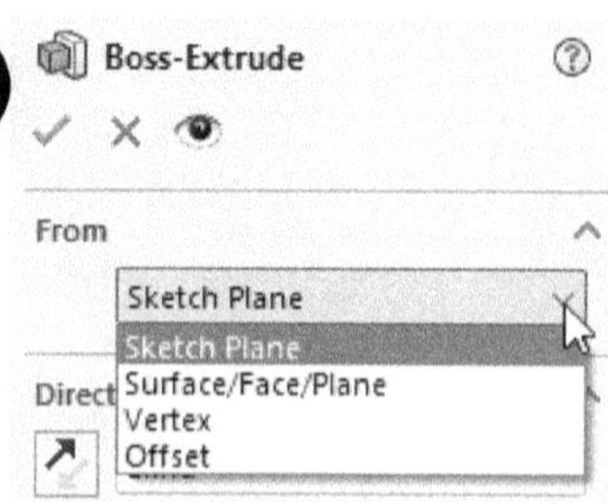

Sketch Plane

By default, the **Sketch Plane** option is selected in the **Start Condition** drop-down list of the **From** rollout. As a result, extrusion starts exactly from the sketching plane of the sketch. Figure 5.11 shows a preview of the extruded feature from its front view when the **Sketch Plane** option is selected.

5.11

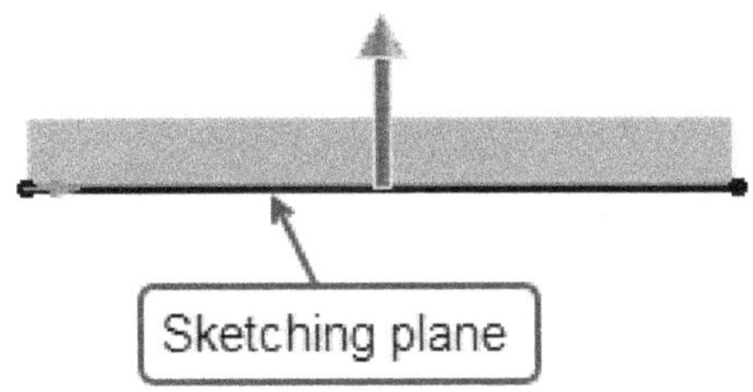

Offset

The **Offset** option is used to create an extruded feature at an offset distance from the sketching plane. On selecting this option, the **Enter Offset Value** field and the **Reverse Direction** button appear in the **From** rollout, see Figure 5.12. By default, a **0** value is entered in the **Enter Offset Value** field. You can enter the required offset value in this field. You can also use the up and down arrows of the Spinner available to the right of this field to set the offset value. Figure 5.13 shows a preview of the extruded feature from its front view after specifying an offset distance. To reverse the offset direction, click on the **Reverse Direction** button in the **From** rollout.

5.12

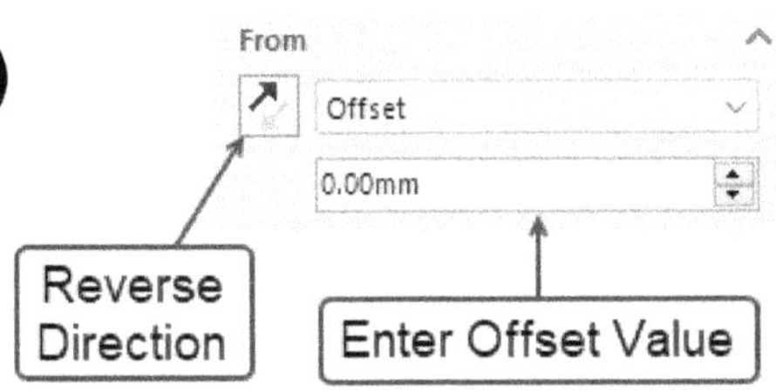

5.13

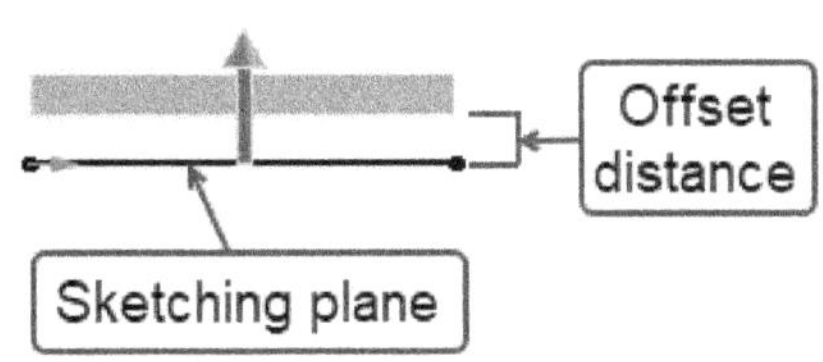

Note: The **Surface/Face/Plane** and **Vertex** options of the **Start Condition** drop-down list are used while creating the second and further features of the model and are discussed in later chapters.

Direction 1

The options in the **Direction 1** rollout of the PropertyManager are used to specify the end condition for the extruded feature in Direction 1. The options are discussed next.

End Condition

The options in the **End Condition** drop-down list are used to define the end condition for the extruded feature, see Figure 5.14. The options of this drop-down list are discussed next.

5.14

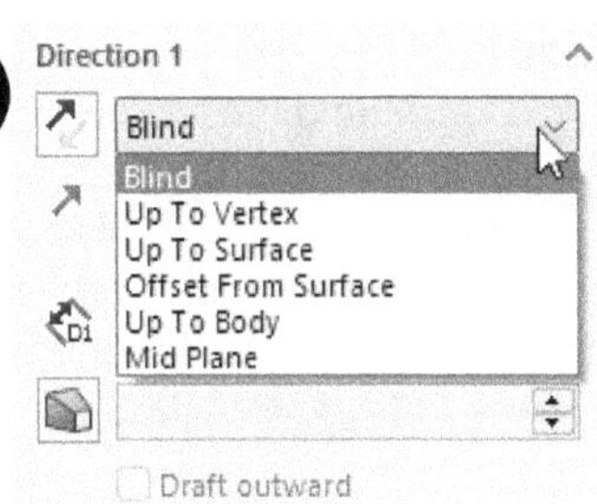

Blind

The **Blind** option of the **End Condition** drop-down list is used to specify the end condition of the extrusion by specifying the depth value in the **Depth** field of the **Direction 1** rollout, see Figure 5.15.

5.15

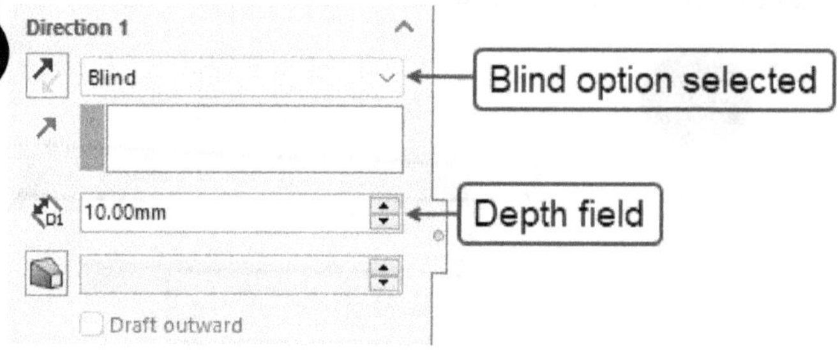

Mid Plane

The **Mid Plane** option of the **End Condition** drop-down list is used to extrude the feature symmetrically about the sketching plane, see Figure 5.16. After selecting this option, you can enter the depth value of extrusion in the **Depth** field of the rollout. The depth value specified in this field is divided equally into both sides of the sketching plane and creates a symmetrically extruded feature. For example, if the depth value specified in the **Depth** field is 100 mm then the resultant feature is created by adding 50 mm of material to each side of the sketching plane.

5.16

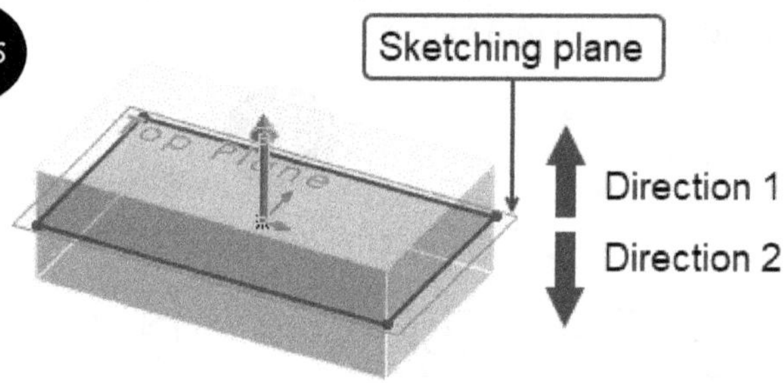

Note: The other options in the **End Condition** drop-down list, such as **Up To Vertex, Up To Surface, Up To Body**, and **Offset From Surface**, are used when creating the second and subsequent features of the model. These options are discussed in later chapters.

Reverse Direction

The **Reverse Direction** button of the **Direction 1** rollout is used to reverse the direction of extrusion from one side of the sketching plane to the other.

Depth

The **Depth** field of the **Direction 1** rollout is used to specify the depth of extrusion. You can enter a value for the depth of extrusion in this field or use the up and down arrows of the Spinner that are available to the right of this field to set the depth value. Note that on clicking the down arrow of the Spinner, the depth value decreases, whereas on clicking the up arrow of the Spinner, the depth value increases. Also, note that the **Depth** field appears only when the **Blind** or **Mid Plane** option is selected in the **End Condition** drop-down list.

Direction of Extrusion

The **Direction of Extrusion** field allows you to define an extrusion direction other than the default, which is normal to the sketching plane. By default, the extrusion direction is set to be normal to the sketching plane. To specify an alternate direction, click the **Direction of Extrusion** field, and then select a linear sketch entity, linear edge, or axis to define the direction. Figure 5.17 illustrates the sketch to be extruded, with a linear sketch line defining the direction of extrusion, while Figure 5.18 shows a preview of the resulting extruded feature.

5.17

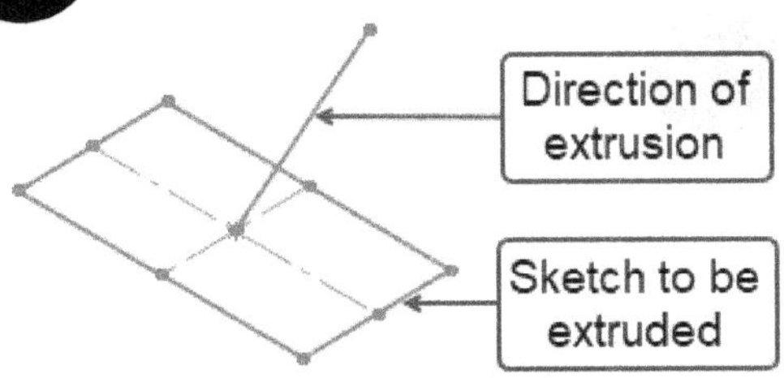

5.18

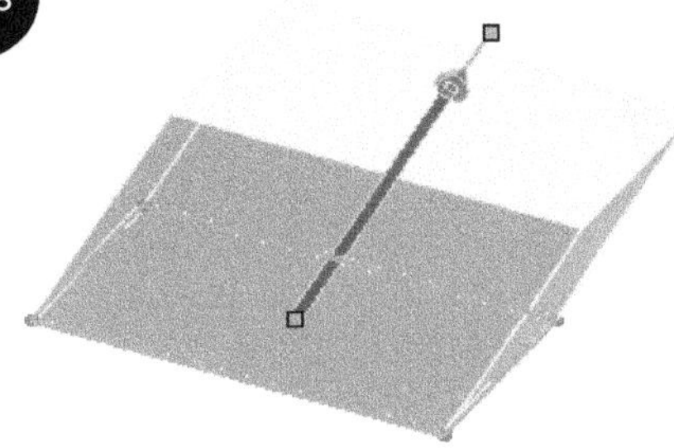

Tip: In Figure 5.16, the sketch to be extruded is created on the Top plane, while the sketch used to define the direction of extrusion is created on the Front plane at an angle of 60 degrees from the X-axis.

Draft On/Off

The **Draft On/Off** button is used to apply a draft or taper to the extruded feature. By default, this button is not activated, so the resulting extruded feature is created with straight faces, without any draft angle. To add a draft angle or taper, click the **Draft On/Off** button. A preview of the feature with the default draft angle appears in the graphics area. Additionally, the **Draft Angle** field and the **Draft Outward** check box become available in the rollout.

You can enter a draft angle in the **Draft Angle** field. By default, the **Draft outward** check box is cleared in the rollout. As a result, the draft is added in the inward direction of the sketch, see Figure 5.19. If you select this check box, the draft will be added in the outward direction of the sketch, see Figure 5.20.

5.19

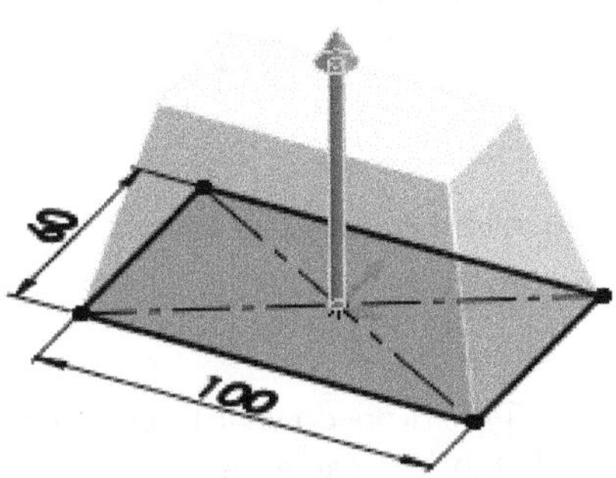

5.20

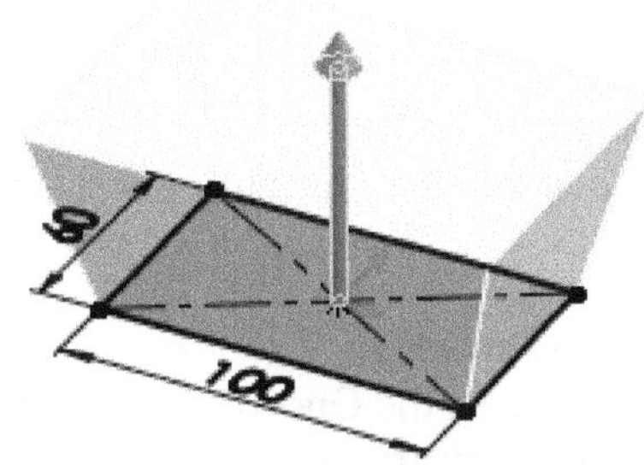

Direction 2

The options in the **Direction 2** rollout are the same as those in the **Direction 1** rollout of the PropertyManager with the only difference that the options of the **Direction 2** rollout are used for specifying the end condition in the second direction of the sketching plane. Note that by default, this rollout is collapsed. As a result, extrusion takes place only in one direction of the sketching plane. To add material in the second direction of the sketching plane, expand this rollout by selecting the check box in its title bar, see Figure 5.21. Figure 5.22 shows the preview of a feature, extruded on both sides of the sketching plane with different extrusion depths. Note that the **Direction 2** rollout will not be available if the **Mid Plane** option is selected in the **End Condition** drop-down list of the **Direction 1** rollout.

5.21

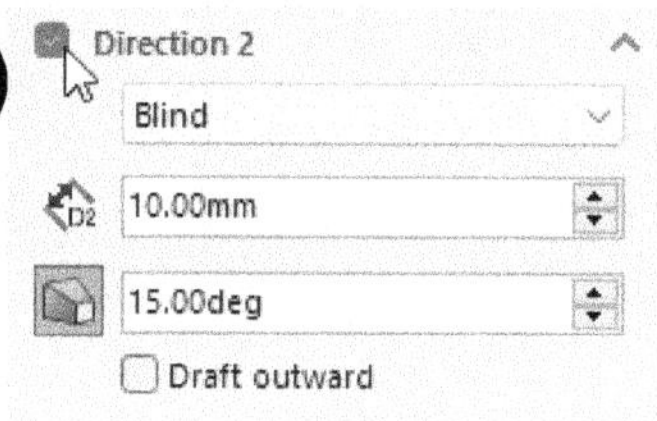

5.22

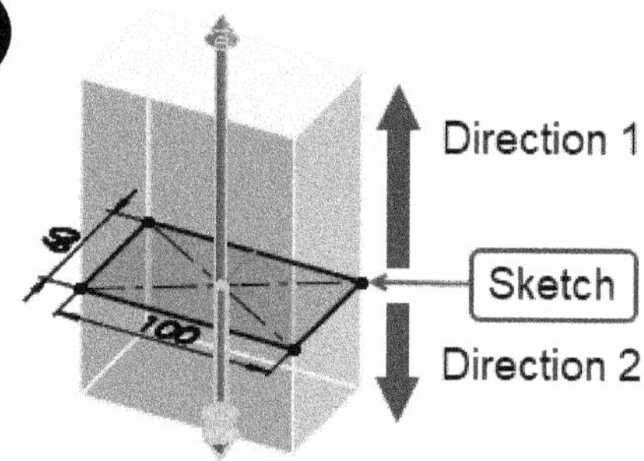

Thin Feature

The options in the **Thin Feature** rollout of the PropertyManager are used to create a thin solid feature of specified wall thickness, see Figure 5.23. By default, this rollout is collapsed. To expand it, select the check box in the title bar of this rollout, see Figure 5.24. Once expanded, a preview of the thin feature with the default wall thickness appears in the graphics area. The options in this rollout are discussed next.

5.23

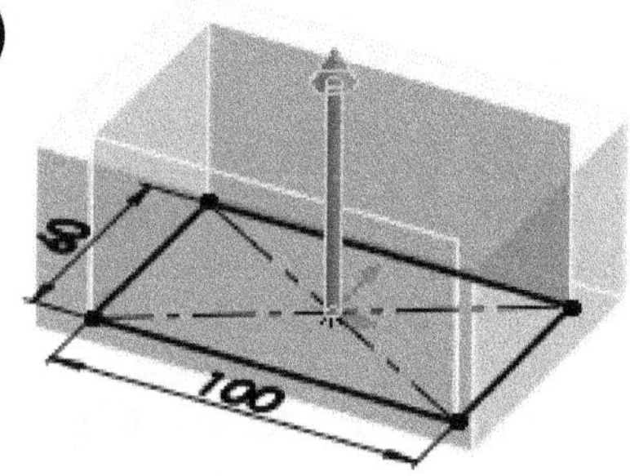

5.24

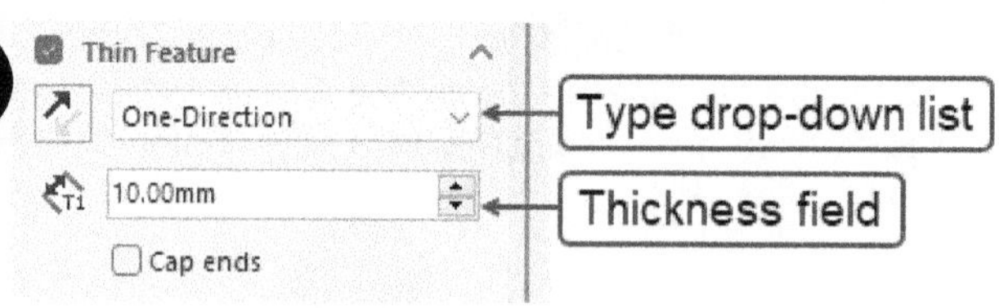

Type

The options in the **Type** drop-down list of the **Thin Feature** rollout are used for selecting a method to add thickness and are discussed next.

One-Direction

By default, the **One-Direction** option is selected in the **Type** drop-down list, see Figure 5.24. As a result, the thickness is added in one direction of the sketch. You can enter a thickness value for the thin feature in the **Thickness** field of this rollout. To reverse the direction of thickness to the other side of the sketch, click on the **Reverse Direction** button of this rollout. Figures 5.25 and 5.26

show the previews of a thin feature with material added in the outward and inward directions of the sketch, respectively.

5.25

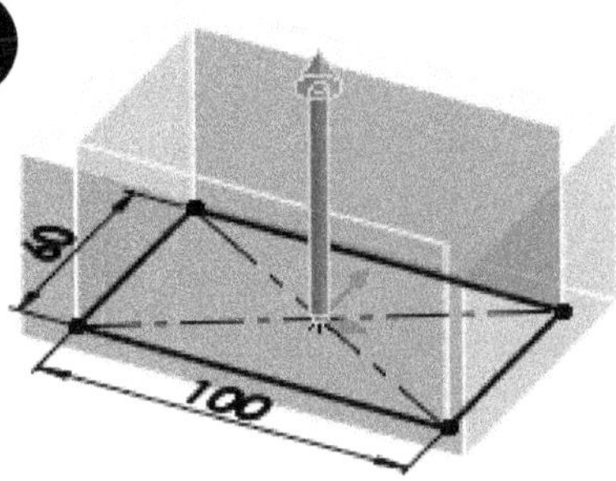

5.26

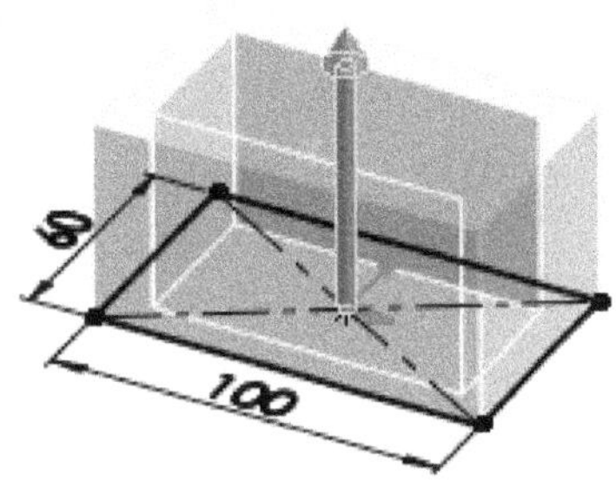

Mid-Plane

The **Mid-Plane** option of the **Type** drop-down list is used to add thickness symmetrically on both sides of the sketch. You can enter a thickness value in the **Thickness** field of the rollout. Note that the thickness value entered in the **Thickness** field is divided equally on both sides of the sketch and creates a thin feature.

Two-Direction

The **Two-Direction** option is used to add different thickness values to both sides of the sketch. As soon as you select this option, the **Direction 1 Thickness** and **Direction 2 Thickness** fields become available in the rollout. You can enter different thickness values in direction 1 and direction 2 of the sketch in the respective fields.

Note: You can create a thin feature from a closed or an open sketch. Figure 5.27 shows the preview of a thin feature by using an open sketch. Note that if the sketch is an open sketch, then the **Thin Feature** rollout of the PropertyManager expands automatically for creating the thin extruded feature.

5.27

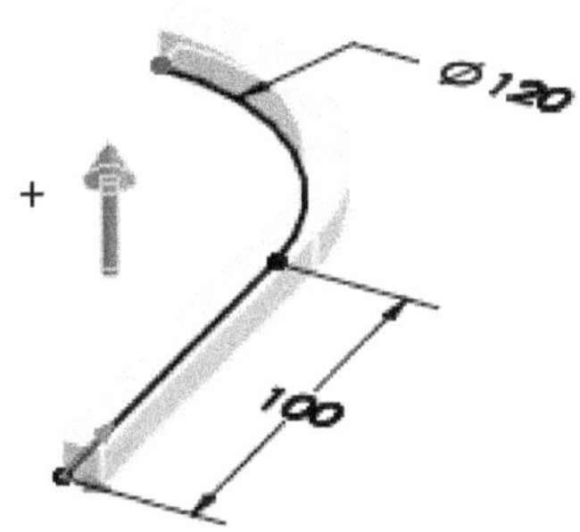

Cap ends

The **Cap ends** check box is used to close the thin feature by adding caps on both its open ends. When you select this check box, , the open ends of the thin feature are capped, and a hollow thin feature is created. You can also specify the required thickness for cap ends of the hollow thin feature in the **Cap Thickness** field. Note that the **Cap ends** check box is available only when you create a thin feature by using a closed sketch.

Auto-fillet corners

The **Auto-fillet corners** check box is available while creating a thin feature using an open sketch. This check box is used for removing sharp corners from the resultant thin feature by adding rounds of specified radius value, refer to Figure 5.28. You can specify the radius value of the rounds in the **Fillet Radius** field that appears in the rollout when the **Auto-fillet corners** check box is selected.

5.28

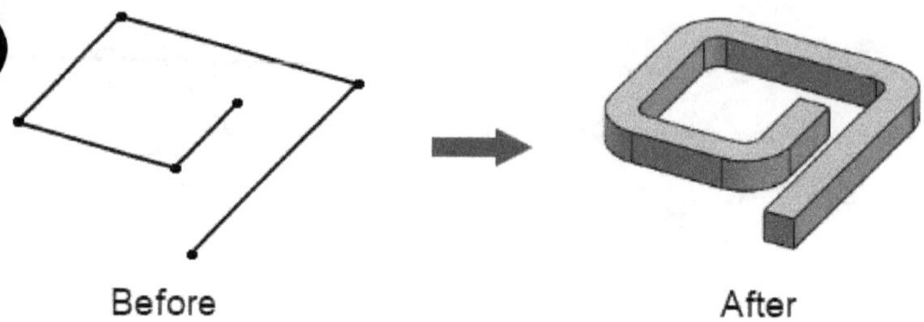

Selected Contours

The **Selected Contours** rollout of the PropertyManager is used to select contours or closed regions of a sketch for extrusion. Figure 5.29 shows a sketch with multiple contours/ closed regions (3 contours). Note that by default, when you extrude a sketch having multiple contours, the most suitable contour gets extruded, see Figure 5.30. In this figure, contour 1 of the sketch shown in Figure 5.29 has been extruded by default and the remaining contours are left unextruded.

5.29

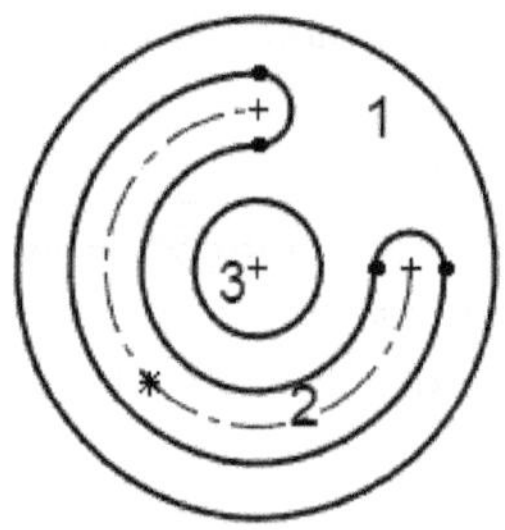

5.30

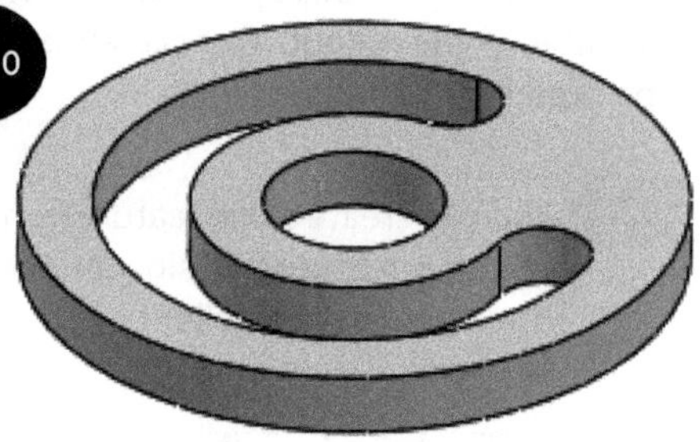

In addition to the default extrusion of the most suitable closed region of a multi-contour sketch, SOLIDWORKS allows you to select a required contour of a sketch to be extruded using the **Selected Contours** rollout. To do this, expand the **Selected Contours** rollout of the PropertyManager and then move the cursor over a closed contour of the sketch to be extruded in the graphics area. Next, click the left mouse button when it gets highlighted, see Figure 5.31. As soon as you select a contour, the preview of the extruded feature appears such that the material is added to the selected closed contour of the sketch. Similarly, you can select multiple contours of a sketch to be extruded.

5.31

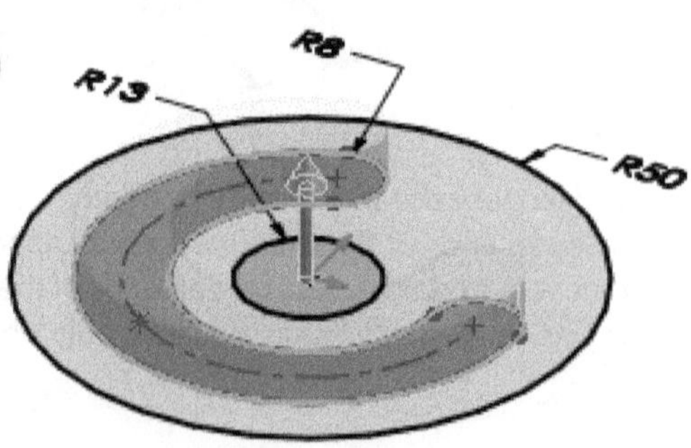

After specifying the required parameters for extruding the sketch, click on the green tick-mark button in the PropertyManager to accept the defined parameters and create the extruded feature.

Creating a Revolved Feature

A revolved feature is created by adding material through the revolution of a sketch around an axis. The sketch to be revolved must be positioned on one side of the axis of revolution. To create a revolved feature, you can use the **Revolved Boss/Base** tool. Figure 5.32 shows the sketches and their corresponding revolved features, which are created by revolving the sketches around their respective axes of revolution.

5.32

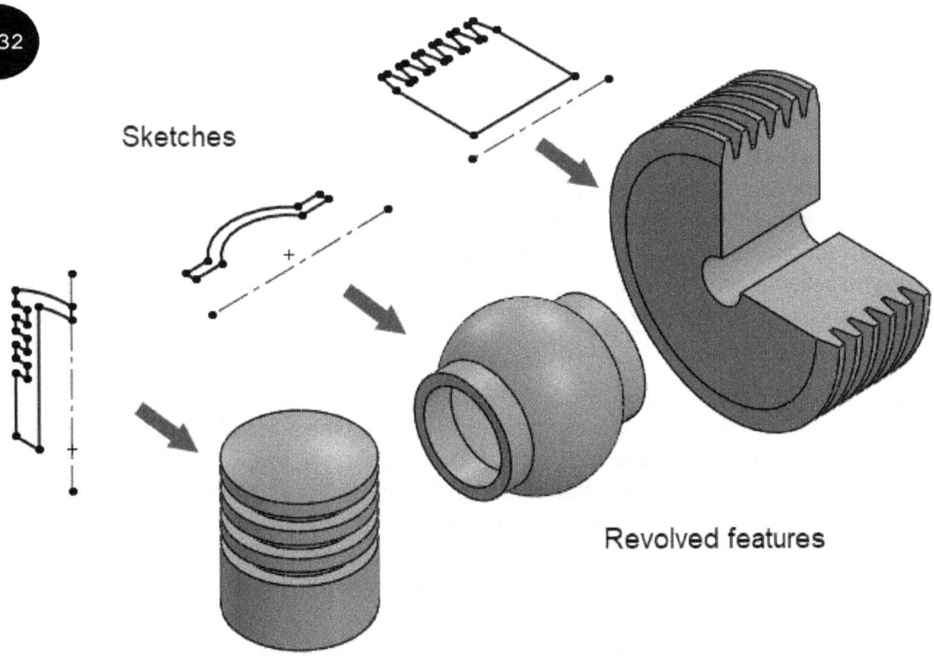

After drawing the sketch and a centerline as the axis of revolution for a revolved feature in the Sketching environment, do not exit the Sketching environment. Click on the **Features** tab in the CommandManager, and then click on the **Revolved Boss/Base** tool, see Figure 5.33. A preview of the revolved feature appears with default parameters. Additionally, the **Revolve PropertyManager** appears on the left side of the graphics area, see Figure 5.34. If the preview does not appear in the graphics area, you need to manually define the axis of revolution.

5.33

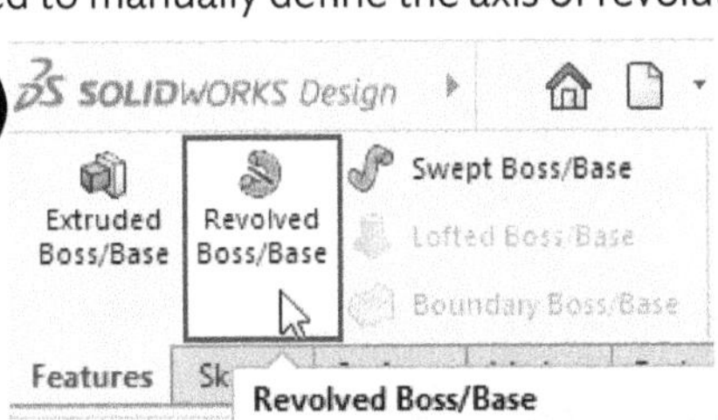

5.34

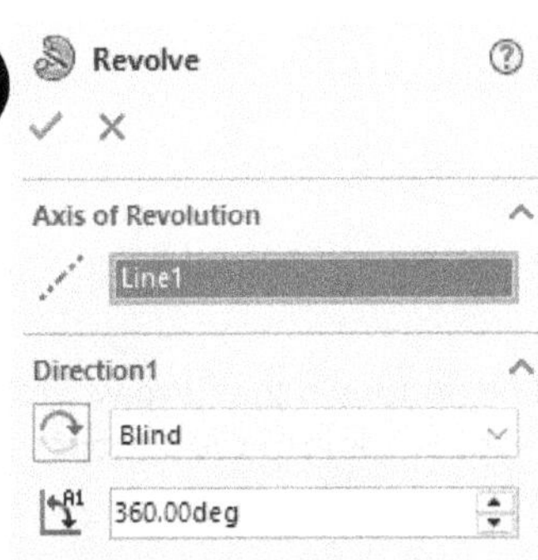

Figure 5.35 shows a sketch with a centerline created on the Front plane, while Figure 5.36 displays the preview of the resulting revolved feature.

5.35

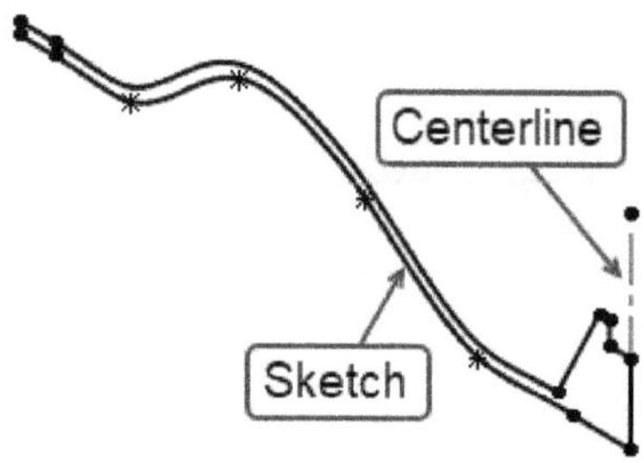

5.36

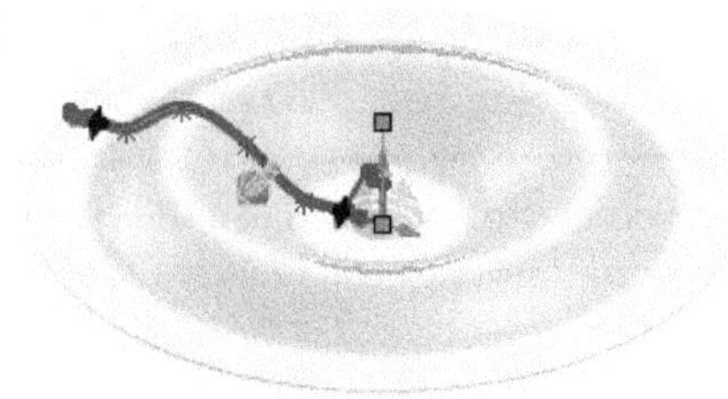

Tip: If the sketch to be revolved has only one centerline, then the centerline drawn will automatically be selected as the axis of revolution and the preview of the resultant revolved feature appears in the graphics area. However, if the sketch has two or more centerlines or does not have any centerline, then on invoking the **Revolved Boss/Base** tool, the preview of the revolved feature does not appear, and you are prompted to select a centerline as the axis of revolution. As soon as you select a centerline, the preview of the revolved feature appears in the graphics area. You can select a linear sketch entity, a centerline, an axis, or an edge as the axis of revolution.

Note: If you exit the Sketching environment after creating the sketch for the revolved feature and the sketch is not selected in the graphics area, clicking the **Revolved Boss/Base** tool will display the **Revolve PropertyManager**, similar to the one shown in Figure 5.37. Also, you will be prompted to either select the sketch to be revolved or a sketching plane to create the sketch. Once you select the sketch to revolve, a preview of the revolved feature will appear in the graphics area. The **Revolve PropertyManager** will then update and appear as shown in Figure 5.34. Note that if the sketch for the revolved feature is not created, you can select the sketching plane to create the sketch.

5.37

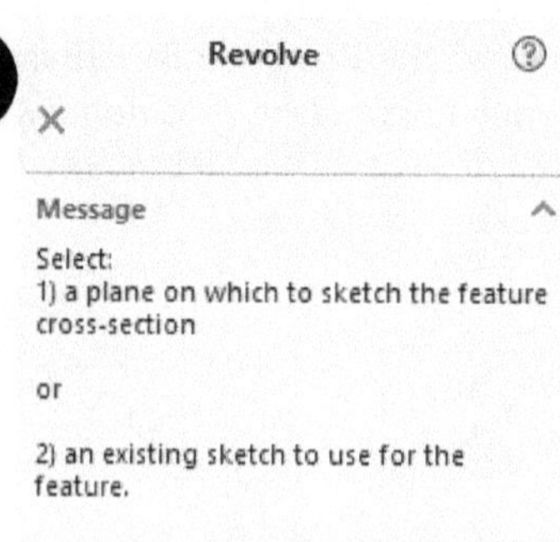

The options in the **Revolve PropertyManager** are used to specify parameters for creating the revolved feature. Some of the options of the **Revolve PropertyManager** are discussed next.

Axis of Revolution

The **Axis of Revolution** field lets you define the axis for revolving the feature. You can choose a linear sketch entity, a centerline, an axis, or a linear edge as the axis of revolution. Note that if the sketch has only one centerline, it will automatically be selected as the axis of revolution when the **Revolve PropertyManager** is invoked. However, if the sketch contains two or more centerlines, you will be prompted to select the axis of revolution.

Direction 1

The options in the **Direction 1** rollout of the PropertyManager are used to define the end condition of the revolved feature on one side of the Sketching plane. The options are discussed next.

Revolve Type

The **Revolve Type** drop-down list of the **Direction 1** rollout is used for selecting a method for revolving the sketch, see Figure 5.38. The options of this drop-down list are discussed next.

5.38

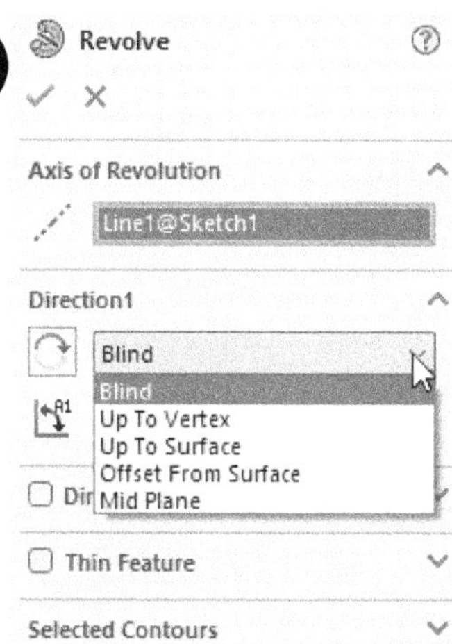

Blind

The **Blind** option of the **Revolve Type** drop-down list is used to define the end condition or termination of the revolved feature by specifying the angle of revolution. By default, this option is selected in this drop-down list. As a result, the **Direction 1 Angle** field is available in the **Direction 1** rollout. You can enter a required angle value in this field.

Mid Plane

The **Mid Plane** option is used to revolve a sketch about a centerline symmetrically on both sides of the sketching plane, see Figure 5.39. After selecting this option, you can enter the angle of revolution in the **Direction 1 Angle** field of the rollout. Depending upon the angle value entered in this field, the material is added symmetrically on both sides of the sketching plane by revolving the sketch about the axis of revolution.

5.39

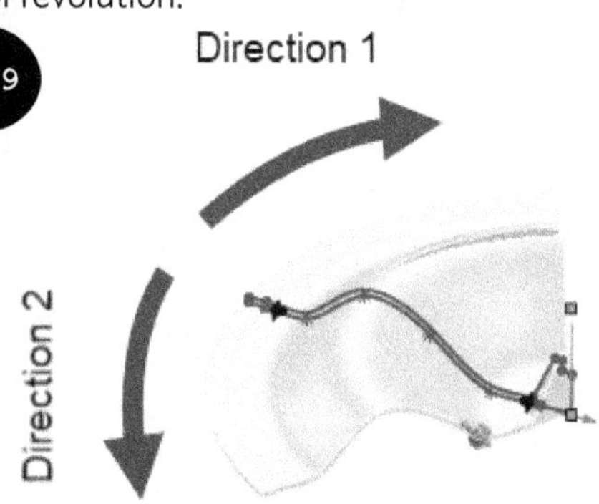

Note: The **Up To Vertex**, **Up To Surface**, and **Offset From Surface** options in the **Revolve Type** drop-down list are used when creating the second and subsequent features of the model. These options will be discussed in later chapters.

Reverse Direction

The **Reverse Direction** button of the rollout is used to reverse the direction of revolution from one side of the sketching plane to the other side. This option is not available if the **Mid Plane** option is selected in the **Revolve Type** drop-down list of the PropertyManager.

Direction 2

The options in the **Direction 2** rollout are the same as those in the **Direction 1** rollout of the PropertyManager with the only difference that the options of the **Direction 2** rollout are used for specifying the end condition of the revolved feature in the second direction of the sketching plane. Note that by default, this rollout is collapsed. As a result, the material is added only in one direction of the sketching plane by revolving the sketch. To add material in the second direction of the sketching plane, expand this rollout by selecting the check box in its title bar, see Figure 5.40. Figure 5.41 shows the preview of a revolved feature with different revolving angles in direction 1 and direction 2 of the sketching plane. Note that the **Direction 2** rollout is not available in the PropertyManager if the **Mid Plane** option is selected in the **Revolve Type** drop-down list of the **Direction 1** rollout.

5.40

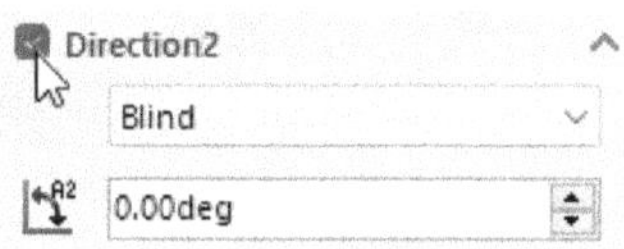

5.41

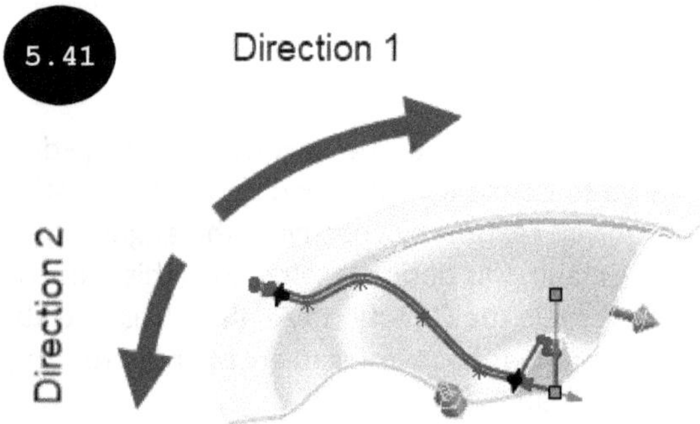

Thin Feature

The options in the **Thin Feature** rollout are used to create a thin revolved feature with a uniform wall thickness, see Figure 5.42. By default, this rollout is collapsed and the options in this rollout are not activated. To expand the **Thin Feature** rollout, click on the check box in its title bar. As soon as the **Thin Feature** rollout expands, a preview of the thin feature with default parameters appears in the graphics area. The options in this rollout are the same as discussed earlier while creating the thin extruded feature.

5.42

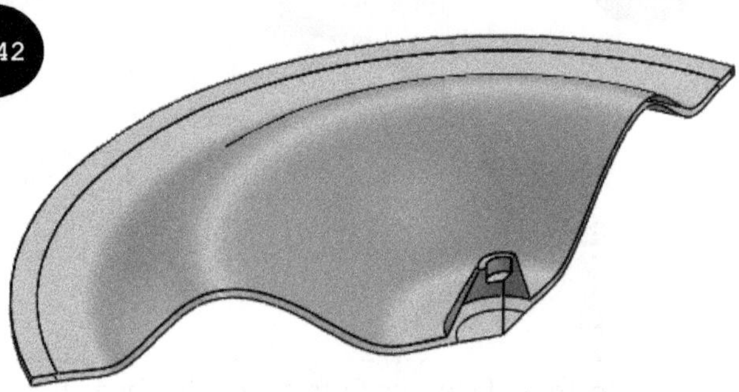

Selected Contours

The **Selected Contours** rollout is used to select one or more contours or closed regions of a multi-contour sketch to revolve them. To revolve a contour of a multi-contour sketch, expand the **Selected Contours** rollout of the PropertyManager and then move the cursor over a closed contour of the sketch to be revolved. Next, click on the closed contour when it gets highlighted in the graphics area. The preview of the revolved feature appears such that material has been added by revolving the selected contour about the centerline.

After specifying the required parameters for revolving the sketch, click on the green tick-mark ✓ button in the **Revolve PropertyManager** to accept the defined parameters and create the revolved feature.

Navigating a 3D Model in the Graphics Area

In SOLIDWORKS, you can navigate a model using the mouse buttons and the navigating tools. You can access the navigating tools in the **View (Heads-Up)** toolbar, see Figure 5.43. Alternatively, you can also access the navigating tools in the SOLIDWORKS Design Menus or in the shortcut menu that appears by right-clicking in the graphics area. The different navigating tools are discussed next.

5.43

Zoom In/Out

You can zoom in or out of the graphics area dynamically using the **Zoom In/Out** tool. In other words, you can enlarge or reduce the view of the model, dynamically by using the **Zoom In/Out** tool.

To zoom in or out a model in the graphics area using the **Zoom In/Out** tool, click on **View > Modify > Zoom In/Out** in the SOLIDWORKS Design Menus, see Figure 5.44. The **Zoom In/Out** tool gets activated. Next, drag the cursor upward or downward in the graphics area by pressing and holding the left mouse button. On dragging the cursor upward, the view gets enlarged, whereas on dragging the cursor downward, the view gets reduced. Note that in the process of zooming in or zooming out the view, the scale of the model remains the same. However, the viewing distance gets modified to enlarge or reduce the view of the model.

5.44

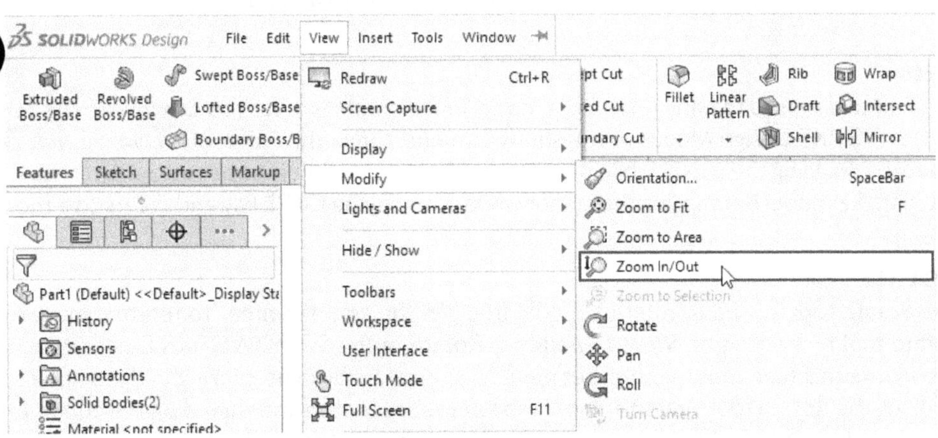

Alternatively, you can invoke the **Zoom In/Out** tool from the shortcut menu. To do this, right-click in the graphics area and then click on the **Zoom In/Out** tool in the shortcut menu that appears, see Figure 5.45. Next, drag the cursor upward or downward in the graphics area.

5.45

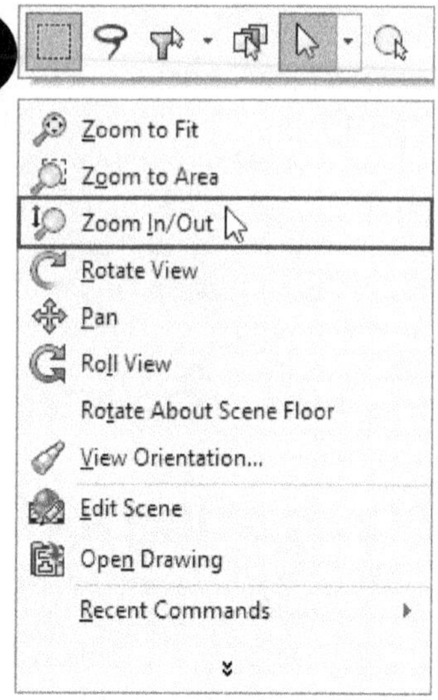

You can also zoom in to or zoom out of the graphics area by scrolling up or down the middle mouse button. Besides, you can press and hold the SHIFT key plus the middle mouse button and then drag the cursor in the graphics area upward or downward to zoom in or zoom out, respectively.

Zoom To Fit

The **Zoom To Fit** tool is used to fit a model completely inside the graphics area. To do this, click on the **Zoom To Fit** tool in the **View (Heads-Up)** toolbar. Alternatively, click on **View > Modify > Zoom to Fit** in the SOLIDWORKS Design Menus. You can also invoke this tool from the shortcut menu that appears by right-clicking in the graphics area. Besides, you can also press the F key to fit the model completely inside the graphics area.

Zoom to Area

The **Zoom to Area** tool is used to zoom in a particular portion or an area of a model by defining a boundary box. To do this, click on the **Zoom to Area** tool in the **View (Heads-Up)** toolbar and then define a boundary box by dragging the cursor around the portion of a model to be zoomed. The area inside the boundary box gets enlarged. You can also access the **Zoom to Area** tool from the SOLIDWORKS Design Menus or the shortcut menu.

Zoom to Selection

The **Zoom to Selection** tool is used to fit a selected object or geometry completely in the graphics area. To fit a selected object or geometry in the graphics area, invoke the **Zoom to Selection** tool by clicking on **View > Modify > Zoom to Selection** in the SOLIDWORKS Design Menus. Note that this tool gets enabled only if the object to be fit is selected in the graphics area.

Pan

The **Pan** tool is used to pan and move a model in the graphics area. You can invoke this tool from the SOLIDWORKS Design Menus or the shortcut menu. Once the **Pan** tool is invoked, you can pan the model by dragging the cursor while pressing and holding the left mouse button. Alternatively, you can also pan the model by dragging the cursor while pressing the CTRL key and the middle mouse button.

Rotate

The **Rotate** tool is used to rotate a model freely in the graphics area. To rotate a model, invoke the **Rotate** tool by clicking on **View > Modify > Rotate** in the SOLIDWORKS Design Menus. You can also invoke this tool from the shortcut menu that appears by right-clicking in the graphics area. After invoking the **Rotate** tool, press and hold the left mouse button and then drag the cursor to rotate the model freely in the graphics area. Alternatively, you can drag the cursor by pressing the middle mouse button to rotate the model.

Manipulating View Orientation of a Model

Manipulating the view orientation of a 3D model is essential for reviewing it from different perspectives and angles. In SOLIDWORKS, you can adjust the orientation of a 3D model to predefined standard views, including front, back, top, right, left, bottom, and isometric, using the navigation tools available in the **View Orientation** flyout and **Orientation** dialog box, refer to Figure 5.46. Additionally, you can manipulate the view orientation using the **Reference Triad** and **View Selector Cube**, refer to Figure 5.47. Besides these predefined views, you also have the option to create custom views. Various methods for manipulating the orientation of a model are discussed below.

5.46

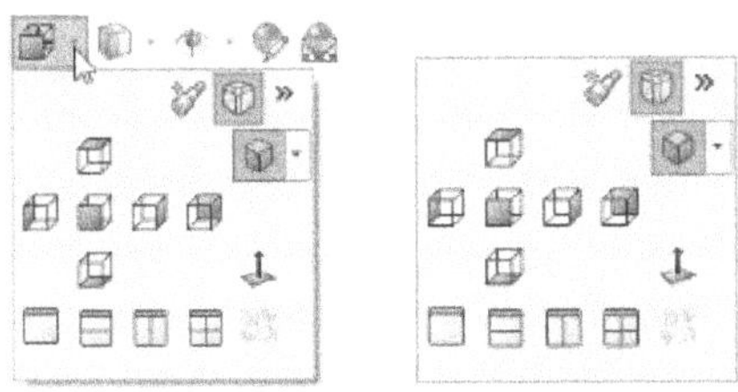

View orientation flyout   Orientation dialog box

5.47

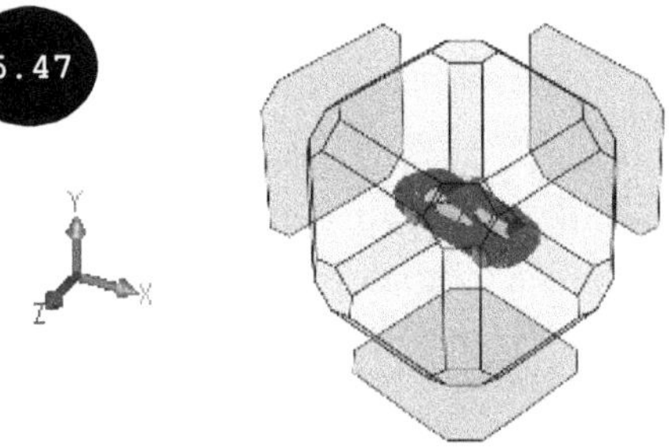

Reference Triad   View Selector Cube

Manipulating View Orientation Using the View Orientation Flyout

To manipulate the orientation of a model using the tools available in the **View Orientation** flyout, click the arrow next to the **View Orientation** tool in the **View (Heads-Up)** toolbar to display the **View Orientation** flyout, see Figure 5.48. The various tools in the flyout are discussed next.

5.48

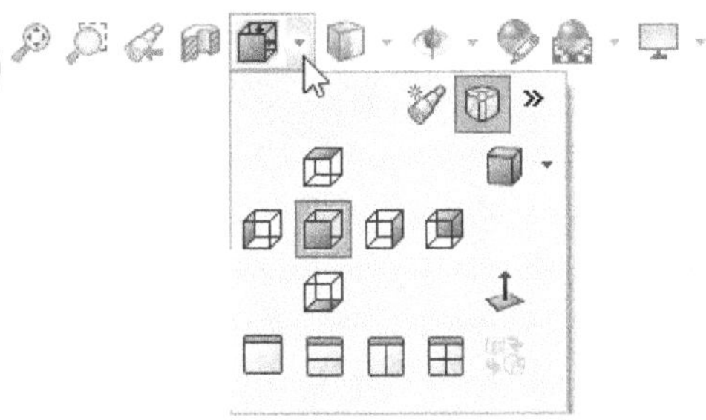

Top, Front, Right, Left, Bottom, Back, Isometric Tools

The **Top**, **Front**, **Right**, **Left**, **Bottom**, **Back**, and **Isometric** tools of the **View Orientation** flyout are used to display the respective predefined standard views of a model in the graphics area.

Normal To Tool

The **Normal To** tool of the **View Orientation** flyout is used to display a selected face of a model normal to the viewing direction. If you are in the Sketching environment, then you can use this tool to make the current sketching plane normal to the viewing direction.

View Drop-down List

The tools in the **View** drop-down list of the **View Orientation** flyout are used to display the isometric, dimetric, or trimetric views of a model. Figure 5.49 shows the **View** drop-down list of the **View Orientation** flyout. By default, the **Trimetric** tool is activated in this drop-down list. As a result, on invoking the **View Orientation** flyout, the trimetric view of the model is displayed in the graphics area. You can activate the required tool to display the respective view of the model.

5.49

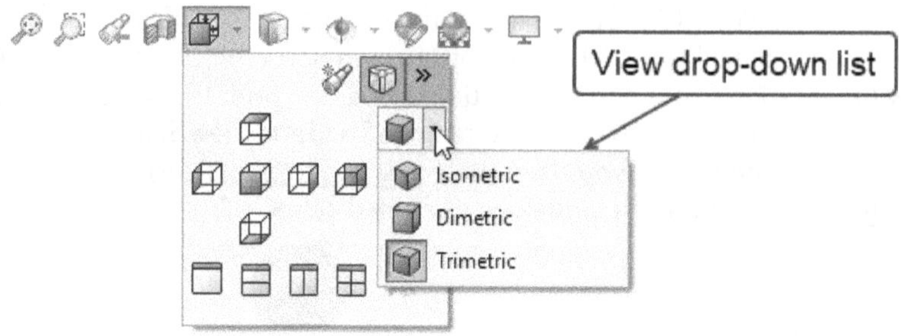

View Selector Tool

The **View Selector** tool of the **View Orientation** flyout is used to display the **View Selector Cube** around the 3D model available in the graphics area, see Figure 5.50. Note that the orientation of the model inside the **View Selector Cube** depends upon the tool activated in the **View** drop-down list of the flyout.

5.50

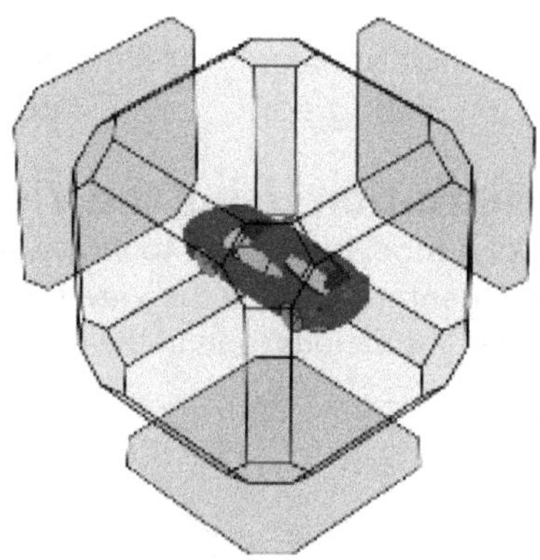

You can also use the faces of the **View Selector Cube** to manipulate the orientation of the model which is discussed later in this chapter.

New View

The **New View** tool is used for creating a custom or user-defined view of a model. To do this, first set the orientation of the model as required, by using different navigating tools. Next, click on the **New View** tool. The **Named View** dialog box appears. In the **View name** field of this dialog box, enter the name of the custom view and then click on the **OK** button. The view is created, and the name of the view created is added in the **View Orientation** flyout. You can display the model as per the custom view at any time by clicking on its name in the **View Orientation** flyout. Similarly, you can create multiple custom views of a model.

Manipulating View Orientation Using the Orientation Dialog box

To manipulate the view orientation of a model using the **Orientation** dialog box, press the SPACEBAR key. The **Orientation** dialog box appears in the graphics area. Most of the tools available in the **Orientation** dialog box are the same as discussed earlier and the remaining tools are discussed next.

Pin/Unpin the dialog

The **Pin/Unpin the dialog** tool is used to pin the dialog box in the graphics area. By default, this tool is not activated. As a result, when you invoke a view such as front, top, or right of a model by clicking on the respective tool in the **Orientation** dialog box, the view of the model is displayed, and the dialog box disappears. If you do not want to exit the dialog box, click to activate the **Pin/Unpin the dialog** tool in the dialog box.

Previous View

The **Previous View** tool is used to revert the model to its previous orientation. Note that you can undo the last ten views of the model by using this tool.

Update Standard Views Tool

The **Update Standard Views** tool is used to update or change the predefined standard views such as the top, front, and right of a model, as required. To do this, first, orient the 3D model in the graphics area according to your requirements and then click on the **Update Standard Views** tool. Next, click on the required standard tool such as **Top** or **Front** in the **Orientation** dialog box. The **SOLIDWORKS** message window appears. The message window informs that changing the standard view will change the orientation of the standard orthogonal views of this model. Click on the **Yes** button to make this change. The selected standard view gets updated to the current display of the model in the graphics area.

Reset Standard Views Tool

The **Reset Standard Views** tool is used to reset all the standard views back to the default settings. If you have updated any of the standard views as per your requirement and you want to restore the default standard orientations, click on the **Reset Standard Views** tool. The **SOLIDWORKS** message window appears. The message window asks you whether you want to reset all the standard views to the default settings. Click on the **Yes** button to reset all the views to the default settings.

Up Axis Flyout

By default, the **Apply Y-up views** option is selected in the **Up Axis Flyout** of the **Orientation** dialog box. As a result, the Y-axis is set as the default up axis for the orientation of all the standard orthogonal, named, and child views in the graphics area. On selecting the **Apply Z-up views** option in the flyout, the Z-axis becomes the default up axis for the orientation of all views. Note that when you select the **Apply Z-up views** option, the SOLIDWORKS message window appears which informs you that switching to Z-up views will change the orientation of all standard orthogonal, named, and child views. Click on the **Yes** button in this message window if you wish to make this change. Figure 5.51 shows the isometric view of a model when **Apply Y-up views** option is selected and Figure 5.52 shows the isometric view of a model when **Apply Z-up views** option is selected.

5.51

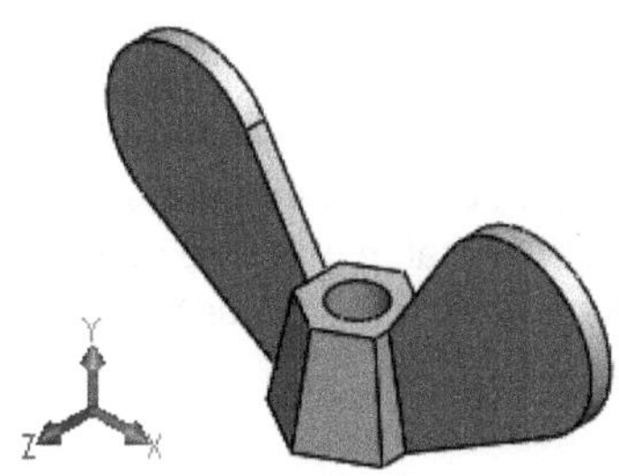

5.52

Manipulating View Orientation Using the View Selector Cube

You can also manipulate the view orientation of a model using the **View Selector Cube**. It is one of the easiest ways to achieve different views such as right, left, front, back, top, bottom, or isometric of a 3D model.

To manipulate the orientation of a 3D model by using the **View Selector Cube**, move the cursor over the face of the **View Selector Cube**. The face gets highlighted, and the **Preview** window appears at the upper right corner of the graphics area. Next, click on the face, see Figure 5.53. The orientation of the model depends upon the face of the **View Selector Cube** selected.

5.53

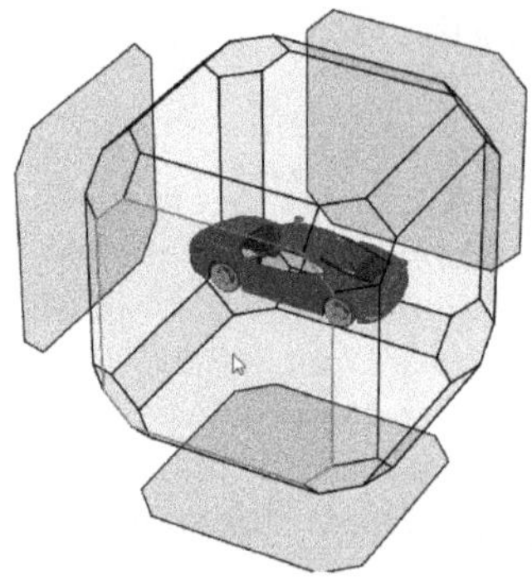

Note: The default orientation of a model inside the **View Selector Cube** depends upon the tool activated in the **View** drop-down list of the **View Orientation** flyout as well as in the **Orientation** dialog box.

Manipulating View Orientation Using the Reference Triad

The reference triad appears at the lower left corner of the graphics area and guides you while changing the view orientation of a model. You can also use the reference triad to manipulate the view orientation of a model normal to the screen, 180 degrees, or 90 degrees about an axis.

To orient the model normal to the screen, click on an axis of the triad. The model gets oriented normal to the screen concerning the selected axis of the triad. Note that the direction of the axis selected becomes normal to the screen. To orient the model by 180 degrees, click on the axis that is normal to the screen. To orient the model by 90 degrees about an axis, press the SHIFT key and then click on an axis as the axis of rotation.

You can also rotate the model at a predefined angle that is specified in the **System Options - View** dialog box. To do this, press the ALT key and then click on an axis of the triad. To specify the predefined angle, click on the **Options** tool in the **Standard** toolbar. The **System Options - General** dialog box appears. In this dialog box, click on the **View** option in the left panel of the dialog box. The name of the dialog box changes to **System Options - View**. By using the **Arrow keys** field of this dialog box, you can specify the predefined angle for rotation by using the triad.

Changing the Display Style of a Model

You can change the display style of a 3D model to wireframe, hidden lines visible, hidden lines removed, shaded, and shaded with edges display styles. The tools used for changing the display style of the model are available in the **Display Style** flyout of the **View (Heads-Up)** toolbar, see Figure 5.54. The tools are discussed next.

5.54

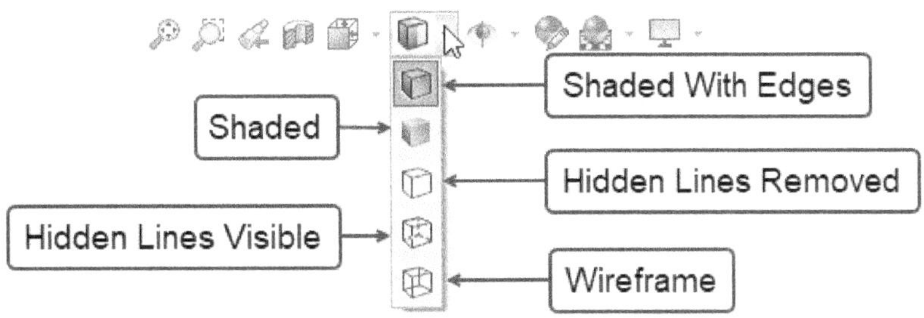

Shaded With Edges

The **Shaded With Edges** tool is used to display a model in the 'shaded with edges' display style. In this style, the model is displayed in shaded mode with the display of outer edges turned on, see Figure 5.55. This tool is activated by default. As a result, the model is displayed in the 'shaded with edges' display style in the graphics area, by default.

Shaded

The **Shaded** tool is used to display a model in the 'shaded' display style. In this style, the model is displayed in shaded mode with the display of edges turned off, see Figure 5.56.

5.55

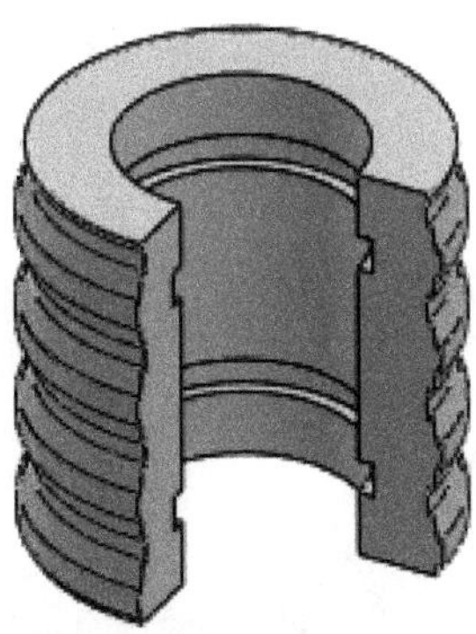

5.56

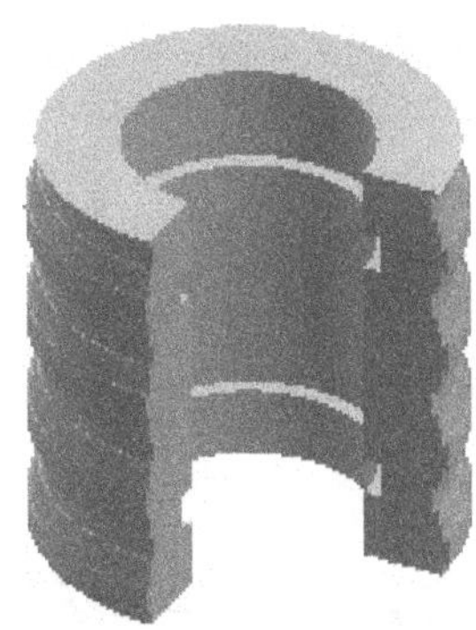

Hidden Lines Removed

The **Hidden Lines Removed** tool is used to display a model in the 'hidden lines removed' display style. In this style, the hidden lines of the model are not visible in the display of the model, see Figure 5.57.

Hidden Lines Visible

The **Hidden Lines Visible** tool is used to display a model in the 'hidden lines visible' display style. In this style, the visibility of the hidden lines of the model is turned on and hidden lines appear as dotted lines, see Figure 5.58.

5.57

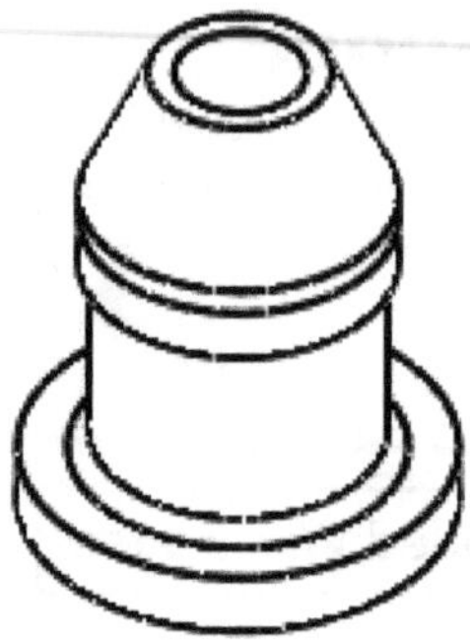

5.58

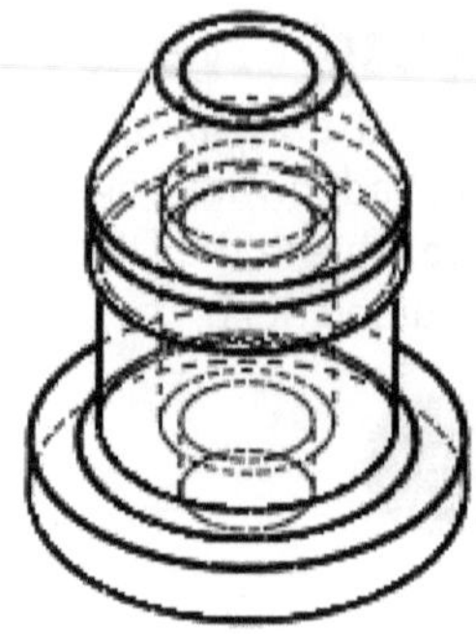

Wireframe

The **Wireframe** tool is used to display a model in the 'wireframe' display style. In this style, the hidden lines of the model are displayed as solid lines, see Figure 5.59.

5.59

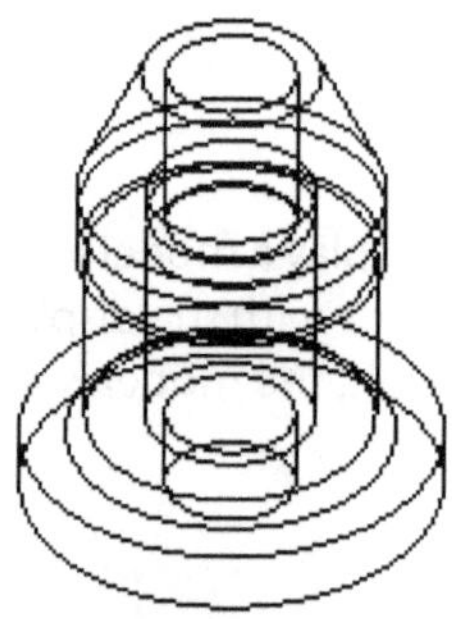

Changing the View of a Model

In SOLIDWORKS, you can change the view of a model to perspective, shadows, ambient occlusion, and cartoon effect using the tools available in in the **View Settings** flyout of the **View (Heads-Up)** toolbar, see Figure 5.60. The tools are discussed next.

5.60

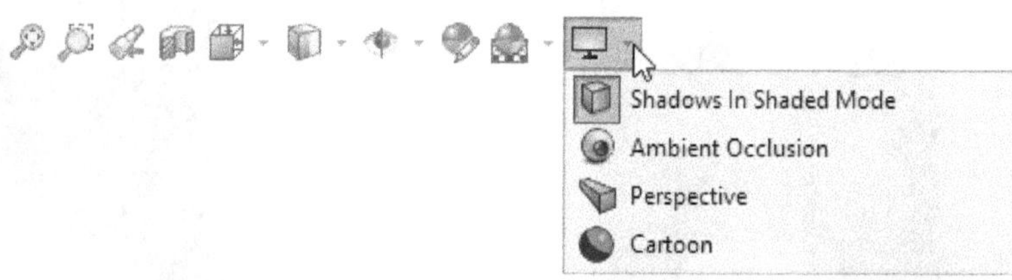

Shadows In Shaded Mode

The **Shadows In Shaded Mode** tool is used to display a model with its shadow, see Figure 5.61. In this view of the model, the shadow appears at the bottom of the model as the light appears from the top. Note that the shadow of the model rotates following the rotation of the model.

5.61

Perspective

The **Perspective** tool is used to display the perspective view of a model, see Figure 5.62. A perspective view appears as it is viewed normally from the eyes. Note that the perspective view depends upon the size of the model and the distance between the model and the viewer.

5.62

Ambient Occlusion

The **Ambient Occlusion** tool is used to display the ambient view of a model. The ambient view is displayed due to the attenuation of the ambient light.

Cartoon

The **Cartoon** tool is used for displaying the cartoon rendering view of a model. The cartoon rendering view is displayed by adding a non-photorealistic cartoon effect to a model.

Tutorial 1

Create the sketch of the model shown in Figure 5.63 and then extrude it to a depth of 15 mm. All dimensions are in mm.

5.63

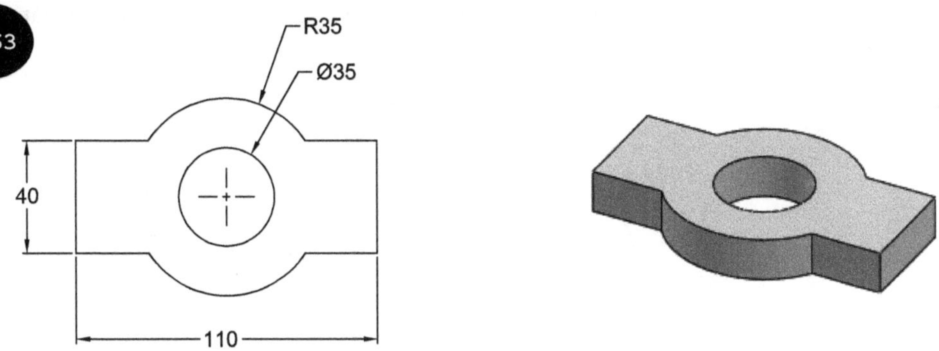

Section 1: Starting SOLIDWORKS

1. Start SOLIDWORKS by double-clicking on the SOLIDWORKS icon on your desktop. The startup user interface of SOLIDWORKS appears along with the **Welcome** dialog box.

Note: If SOLIDWORKS is already open and the **Welcome** dialog box does not appear on the screen, you can invoke it by clicking on the **Welcome to SOLIDWORKS** tool in the **Standard** toolbar.

2. Click on the **Part** button in the **Welcome** dialog box. The Part modeling environment is invoked.

3. Ensure that the **MMGS (millimeter, gram, second)** unit system is set as the current unit system for the opened part document.

Section 2: Creating the Sketch

Now, you need to create a sketch of the model.

1. Click on the **Sketch** tab in the CommandManager and then click on the **Sketch** tool in the **Sketch CommandManager**, see Figure 5.64. Three default planes mutually perpendicular to each other appear in the graphics area.

2. Move the cursor over the Top plane and click when the boundary of the plane gets highlighted. The Sketching environment is invoked. Also, the Top plane is orientated normal to the viewing direction.

5.64

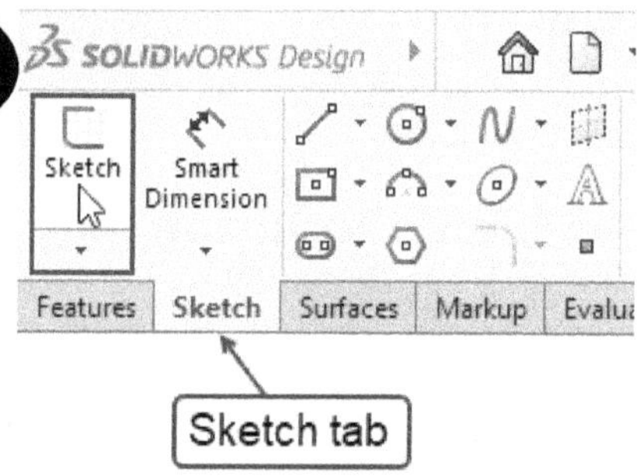

3. Click on the **Circle** tool in the **Sketch CommandManager**. The **Circle** tool is invoked and the **Circle PropertyManager** appears.

4. Create a circle of diameter close to 35 mm, see Figure 5.65. Note that the center point of the circle is at the origin. Also, the **Circle** tool remains activated.

5. Create another circle of diameter close to 70 mm at the origin, see Figure 5.66. After creating the circles, press the ESC key to exit the **Circle** tool.

5.65

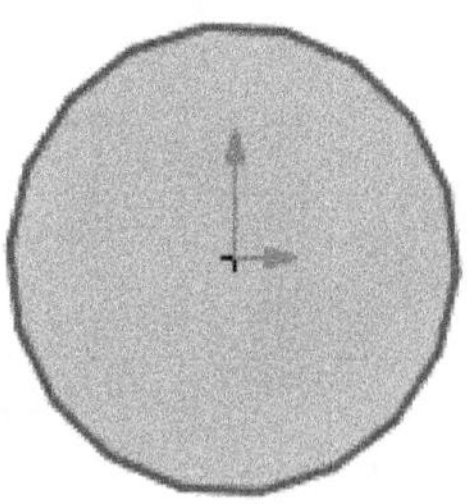

5.66

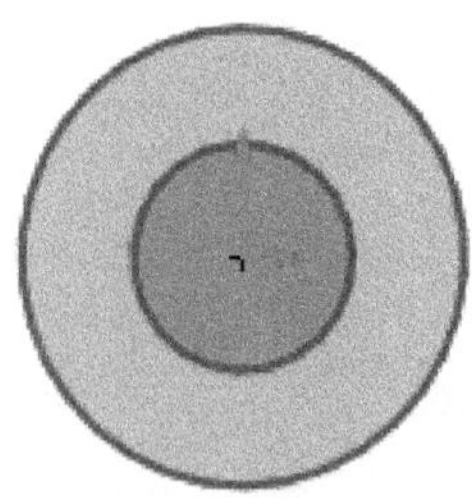

Now, you need to create a center-point rectangle.

6. Create a center point rectangle similar to the one shown in Figure 5.67 by using the **Center Rectangle** tool. Note that the center of the rectangle is at the origin. Also, the smallest circle of the sketch lies completely inside the rectangle drawn.

5.67

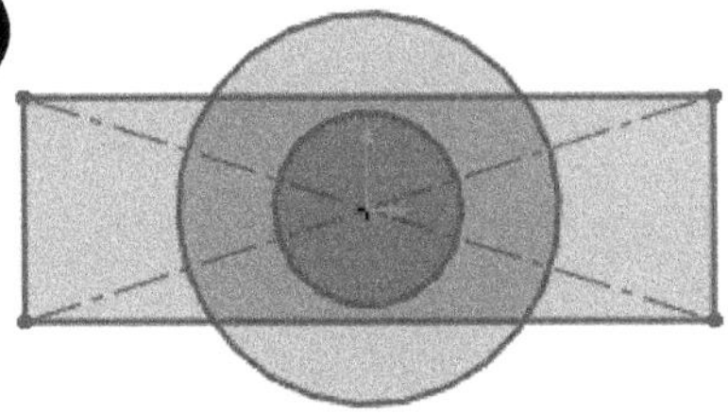

Now, you need to trim the unwanted entities of the sketch.

7. Click on the **Trim Entities** tool in the **Sketch CommandManager**. The **Trim PropertyManager** appears on the left of the drawing area.

8. Click on the **Trim to closest** button in the **Options** rollout of the PropertyManager for trimming the entities of the sketch to their nearest intersection. The appearance of the cursor changes to trim cursor.

9. Ensure that the **Keep trimmed entities as construction geometry** and **Ignore trimming of construction geometry** check boxes are cleared in the PropertyManager.

10. Move the cursor over the portion of the lower horizontal rectangle entity that lies inside the outer circle, see Figure 5.68. Next, click the left mouse button when it gets highlighted. The selected portion of the entity is trimmed, see Figure 5.69. Also, the **Trim Entities** tool is still active.

5.68

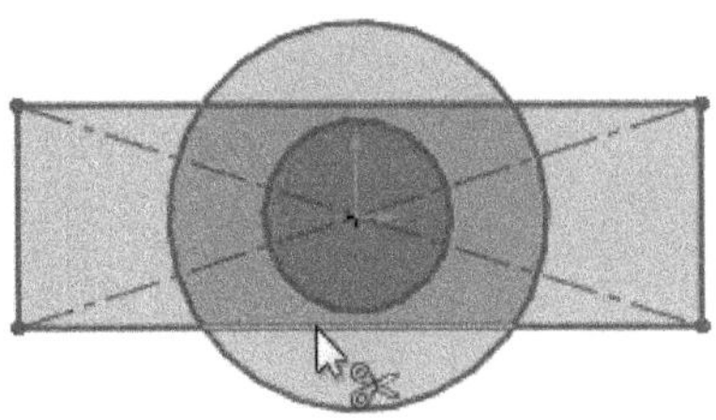

5.69

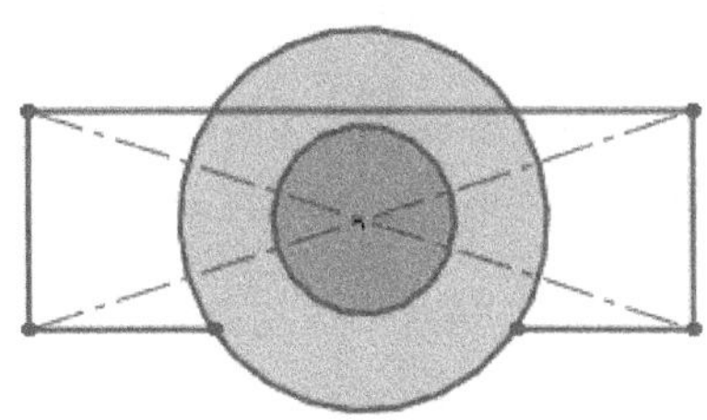

11. Similarly, click on the other unwanted entities of the sketch one by one to trim them. Figure 5.70 shows the sketch after trimming all the unwanted sketch entities. Note that while trimming the sketch entities, if the **SOLIDWORKS** message window appears, then click on the **Yes** button in the **SOLIDWORKS** message window to continue the process of trimming sketch entities.

5.70

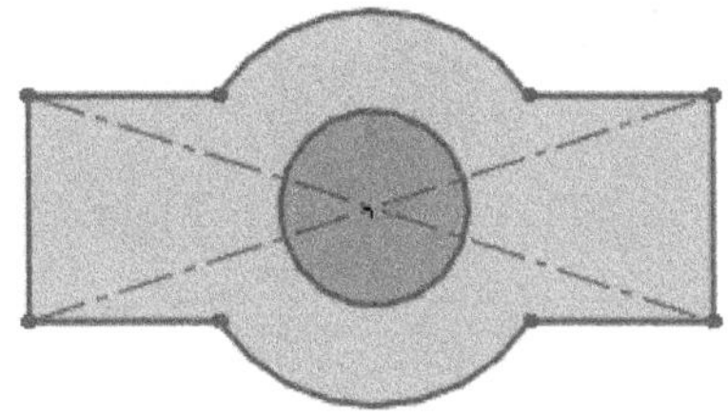

Tip: While trimming sketch entities, you may need to zoom in or zoom out of the drawing display area. To do this, scroll the middle mouse button up or down, respectively.

12. Once you have completed the trimming operation, press the ESC key to exit the tool.

Now, you need to apply the required dimensions to the sketch entities.

13. Apply all the required dimensions to the sketch by using the **Smart Dimension** tool, see Figure 5.71.

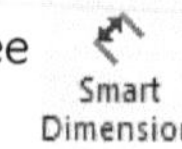

Section 3: Creating an Extruded Feature

After creating the sketch, you can extrude it.

1. Click on the **Features** tab in the CommandManager. The tools of the **Features CommandManager** appear, see Figure 5.72.

5.71

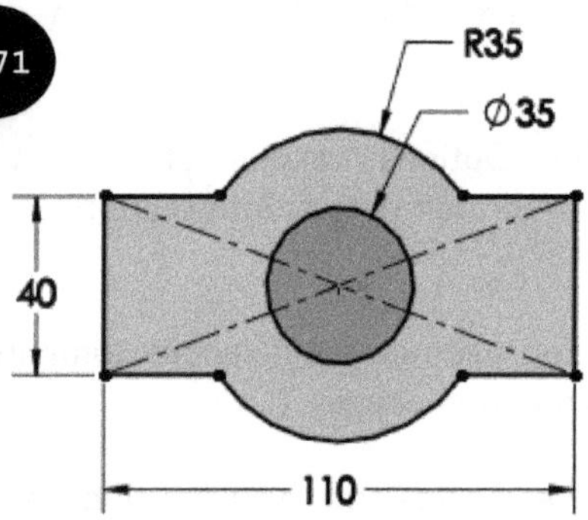

5.72

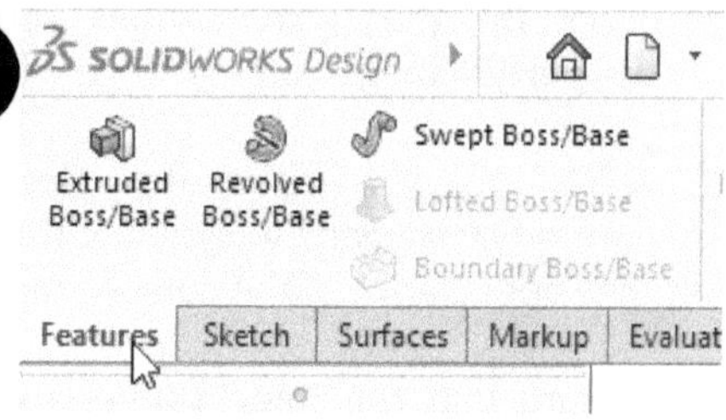

2. Click on the **Extruded Boss/Base** tool in the **Features Command Manager**. The **Boss-Extrude PropertyManager** and the preview of the extruded feature appear, see Figure 5.73. Also, the orientation of the model changes to Trimetric.

3. Enter **15** in the **Depth** field of the **Direction 1** rollout in the PropertyManager and then press ENTER. The default depth of the extruded feature changes to 15 mm.

4. Click on the green tick-mark ✓ in the PropertyManager. The extruded feature is created, see Figure 5.74.

5.73

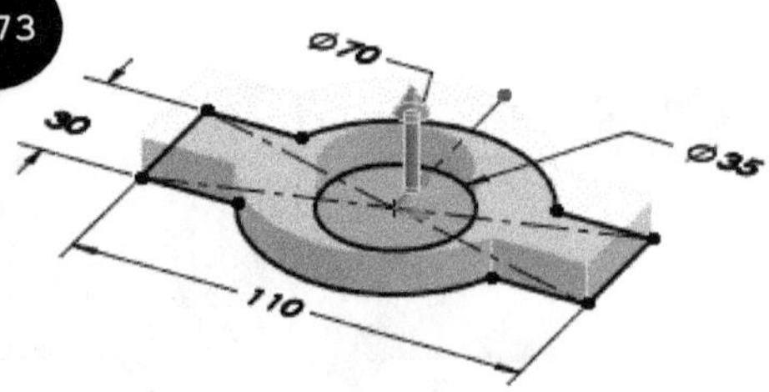

5.74

Section 4: Saving the Model

Now, you need to save the model.

1. Click on the **Save** tool in the **Standard** toolbar. The model is saved with the name **Tutorial 1** in the the Chapter 5 folder.

Tutorial 2

Open the sketch created in Tutorial 1 of Chapter 4 (see Figure 5.75), and then create the 3D model by extruding it to a depth of 40 mm, see Figure 5.76. All dimensions are in mm.

5.75

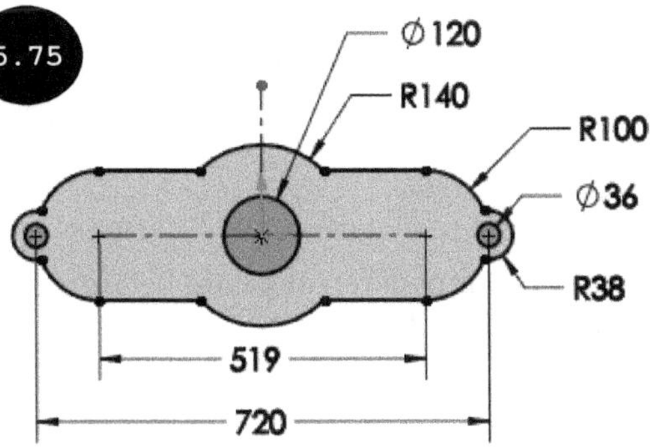

5.76

Section 1: Starting SOLIDWORKS

1. Start SOLIDWORKS by double-clicking on the SOLIDWORKS icon on your desktop. The startup user interface of SOLIDWORKS appears along with the **Welcome** dialog box.

Note: If SOLIDWORKS is already open and the **Welcome** dialog box does not appear on the screen, you can invoke it by clicking on the **Welcome to SOLIDWORKS** tool in the **Standard** toolbar.

Section 2: Opening the Sketch of Tutorial 1, Chapter 4

Now, you need to open the sketch of Tutorial 1 that is created in the Chapter 4.

1. Click on the **Open** button in the **Welcome** dialog box. The **Open** dialog box appears. Alternatively, you can invoke the **Open** dialog box by clicking on the **Open** tool in the **Standard** toolbar.

2. Browse to the Chapter 4 folder of the SOLIDWORKS folder and then select the **Tutorial 1** file.

3. Click on the **Open** button in the dialog box. The sketch of Tutorial 1 created in Chapter 4 is opened in the current session of SOLIDWORKS, see Figure 5.77.

5.77

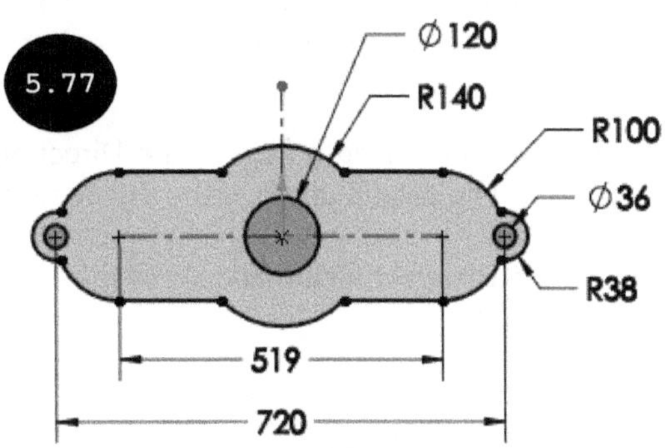

Note: If you have not created the Tutorial 1 of the Chapter 4 then you need to first create it, as discussed in the Chapter 4.

Section 3: Saving the Sketch

Now, you need to save the sketch with the name "Tutorial 2" in the Chapter 5 folder.

1. Click on **File** > **Save As** in the SOLIDWORKS Design Menus. The **Save As** dialog box appears.

2. Browse to the SOLIDWORKS folder and then create a folder with the name **Chapter 5** in it with the name Tutorial 2.

3. Click on the **Save** button to save the sketch in the Chapter 5 folder.

Note: It is important to save the sketch in different locations or different names before making any modification, so that the original file does not get modified.

Section 4: Extruding the Sketch

Now, you can extrude the sketch and convert it into a feature.

1. Click on the **Features** tab in the CommandManager. The tools of the **Features CommandManager** appear, see Figure 5.78.

5.78

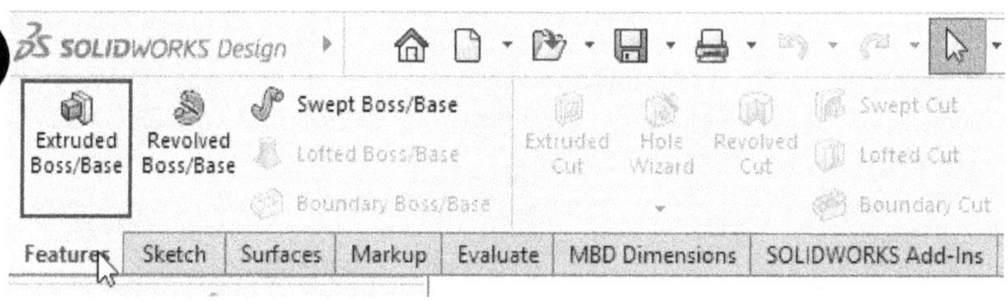

2. Click on the **Extruded Boss/Base** tool in the **Features Command Manager**. The **Boss-Extrude PropertyManager** and the preview of the extruded feature appear, see Figure 5.79. Also, the orientation of the model changes to Trimetric.

Note: If you exit the Sketching environment after creating the sketch, then you need to select the sketch to be extruded before or after invoking the **Extruded Boss/Base** tool.

3. Enter **40** in the **Depth** field of the **Direction 1** rollout in the PropertyManager and then press ENTER. The default depth of the extruded feature changes to 40 mm.

4. Click on the green tick-mark in the PropertyManager. The extruded feature is created, see Figure 5.80.

5.79

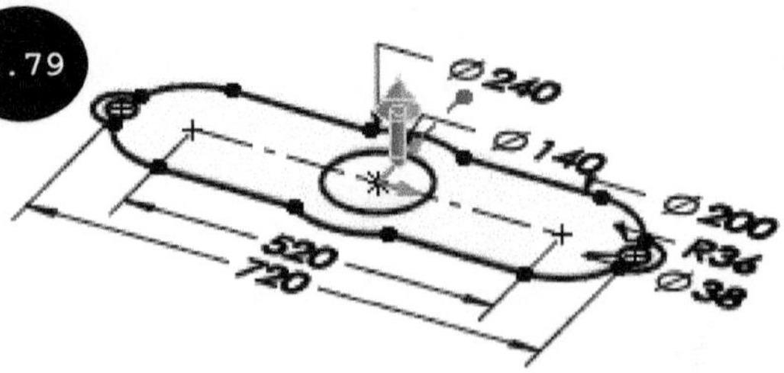

5.80

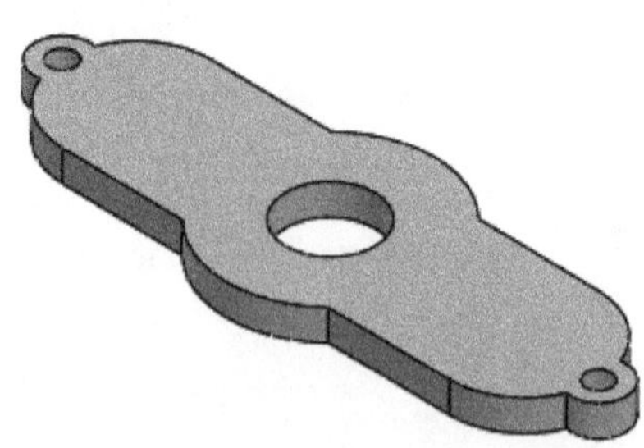

Section 5: Saving the Model

Now, you need to save the model.

1. Click on the **Save** tool in the **Standard** toolbar. The model is saved with the name **Tutorial 2** in the Chapter 5 folder.

Tutorial 3

Open the sketch created in Tutorial 2 of Chapter 4 (see Figure 5.81), and then revolve it around the vertical centerline at an angle of 270 degrees, see Figure 5.82. Also, change the display style of the model to the 'hidden lines removed' display style. All dimensions are in mm.

5.81

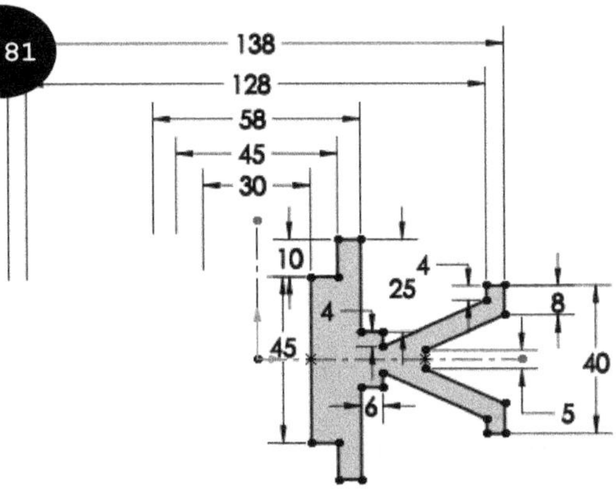

5.82

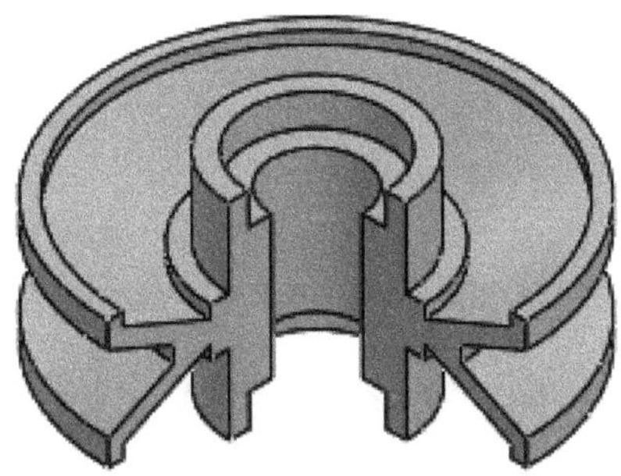

Section 1: Starting SOLIDWORKS

1. Start SOLIDWORKS by double-clicking on the SOLIDWORKS icon on your desktop. The startup user interface of SOLIDWORKS appears along with the **Welcome** dialog box.

Note: If SOLIDWORKS is already open and the **Welcome** dialog box does not appear on the screen, then you can invoke the same by clicking on the **Welcome to SOLIDWORKS** tool in the **Standard** toolbar.

Section 2: Opening the Sketch of Tutorial 2, Chapter 4

Now, you need to open the sketch of Tutorial 2 that is created in the Chapter 4.

1. Click on the **Open** button in the **Welcome** dialog box. The **Open** dialog box appears.

Tip: You can also invoke the **Open** dialog box by clicking on the **Open** tool in the **Standard** toolbar.

2. Browse to the Chapter 4 folder of the SOLIDWORKS folder and then select the **Tutorial 2** file.

3. Click on the **Open** button in the dialog box. The sketch of Tutorial 2 created in Chapter 4 is opened in the current session of SOLIDWORKS, see Figure 5.83.

5.83

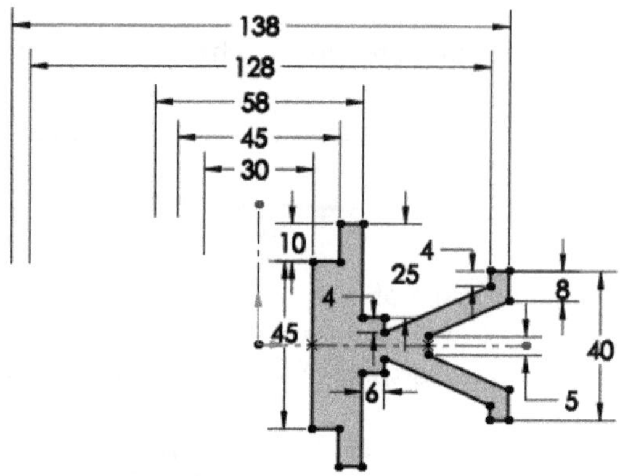

Note: If you have not created the Tutorial 2 of the Chapter 4 then you need to first create it, as discussed in the Chapter 4.

Section 3: Saving the Sketch

Now, you need to save the sketch with the name "Tutorial 3" in the Chapter 5 folder.

1. Click on **File > Save As** in the SOLIDWORKS Design Menus. The **Save As** dialog box appears.

2. Browse to the Chapter 5 folder of the SOLIDWORKS folder and then save the sketch in it with the name Tutorial 3. If the Chapter 5 folder is not created, then you need to first create this folder inside the SOLIDWORKS folder.

Section 4: Revolving the Sketch

1. Click on the **Features** tab in the CommandManager. The tools of the **Features CommandManager** appear, see Figure 5.84.

5.84

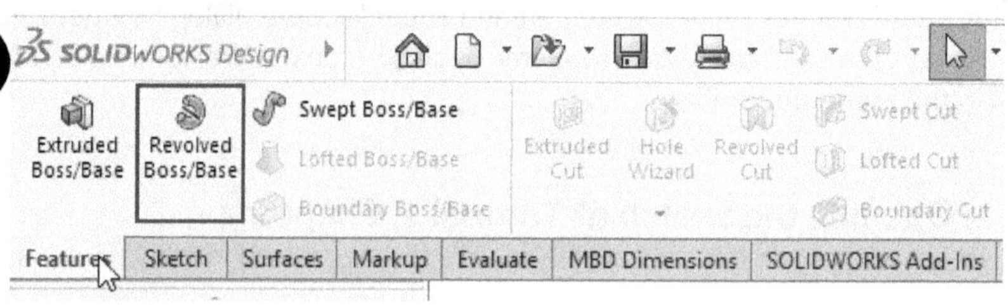

2. Click on the **Revolved Boss/Base** tool in the **Features Command Manager**. The **Revolve PropertyManager** appears and the orientation of the sketch changes to Trimetric. Also, you are prompted to select a centerline as the axis of revolution.

Tip: If the sketch to be revolved has only one centerline, then the centerline drawn will automatically be selected as the axis of revolution and the preview of the resultant revolved feature appears in the graphics area. However, if the sketch has two or more centerlines then on invoking the **Revolved Boss/Base** tool, you will be prompted to select a centerline as the axis of revolution.

3. Select the vertical centerline of the sketch as the axis of revolution. A preview of the revolved feature appears in the graphics area, see Figure 5.85.

4. Enter **270** degrees in the **Direction 1 Angle** field of the **Direction 1** rollout in the PropertyManager and then press the ENTER key.

5. Click on the **Reverse Direction** button in the **Direction 1** rollout to match the orientation of the feature to the one shown in Figure 5.86, if needed.

6. Click on the green tick-mark ✓ in the PropertyManager. The revolved feature is created, see Figure 5.86.

5.85

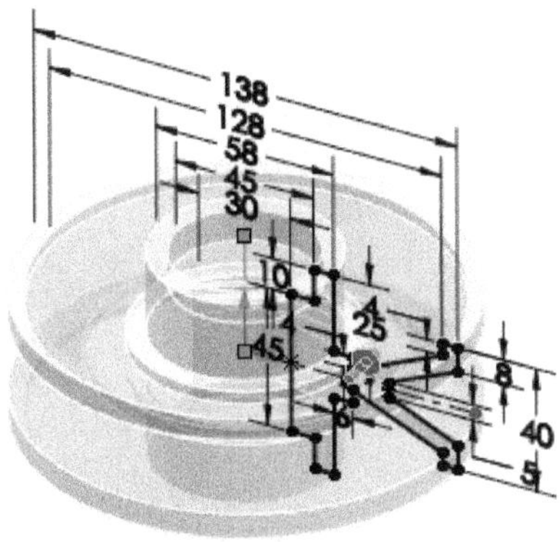

5.86

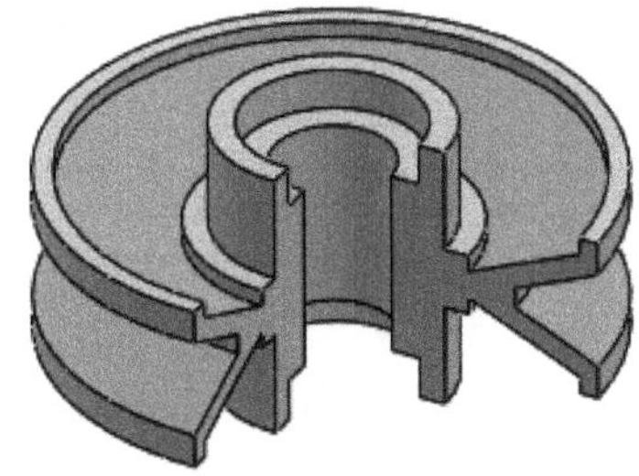

Section 5: Changing the Display Style

Now, you can change the display style of the model to the 'hidden lines removed' display style.

1. Invoke the **Display Style** flyout of the **View (Heads-Up)** toolbar, see Figure 5.87.

2. Click on the **Hidden Lines Removed** tool in the **Display Style** flyout. The display style of the model is changed to the 'hidden lines removed' display style, see Figure 5.88.

5.87

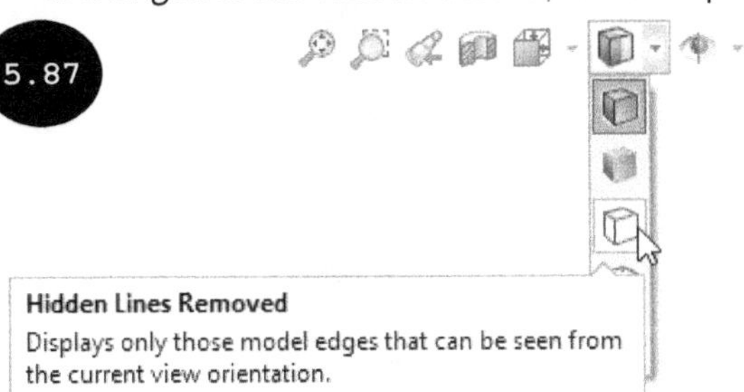

5.88

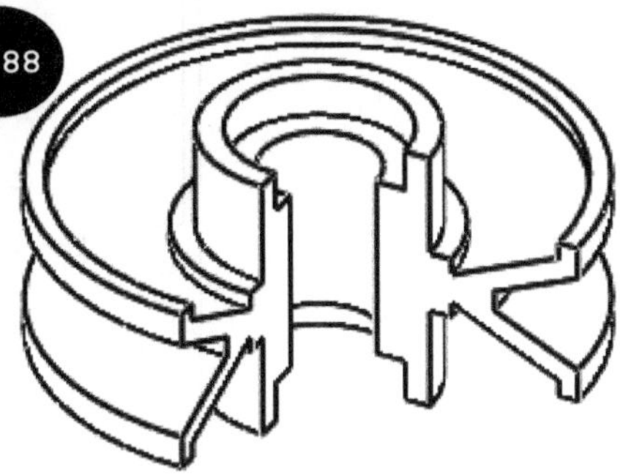

Section 6: Saving the Model

Now, you need to save the model.

1. Click on the **Save** tool in the **Standard** toolbar. The model is saved with the name **Tutorial 3** in the Chapter 5 folder.

Hands-on Test Drive 1

Open the sketch created in the Tutorial 1 of the Chapter 4 (see Figure 5.89), and then create the 3D model by extruding it to a depth of 60 mm, see Figure 5.89. All dimensions are in mm.

5.89

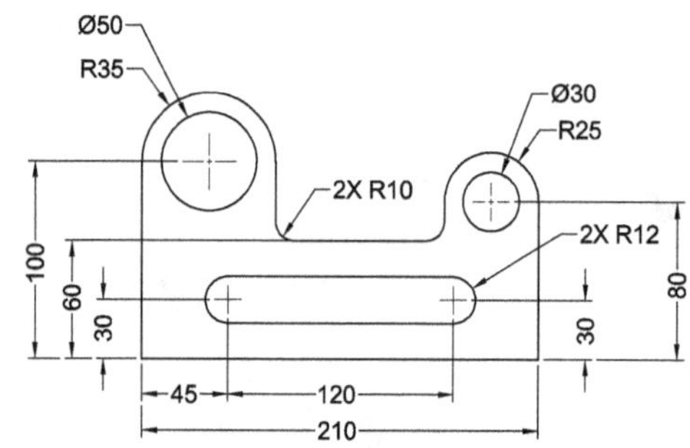

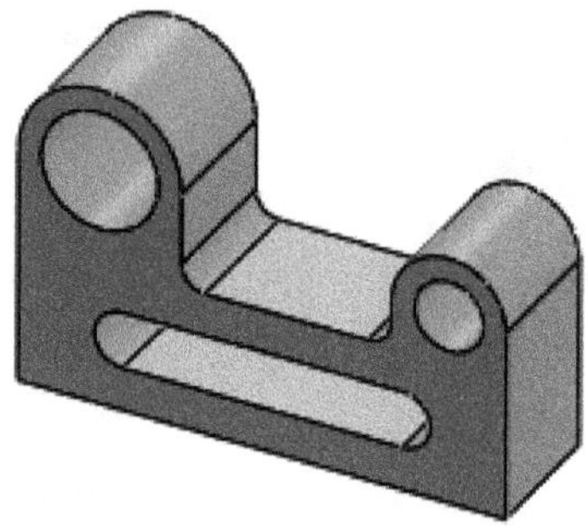

Hands-on Test Drive 2

Create a revolved model, as shown in Figure 5.90. All dimensions are in mm. Note that to create a revolved feature, you need to create its sketch on either side of the axis of revolution.

5.90

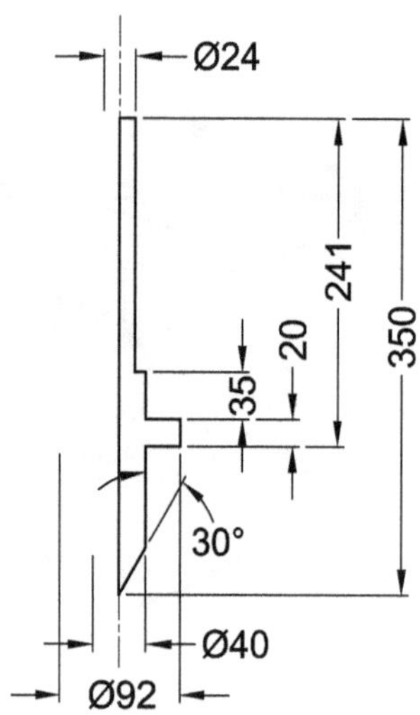

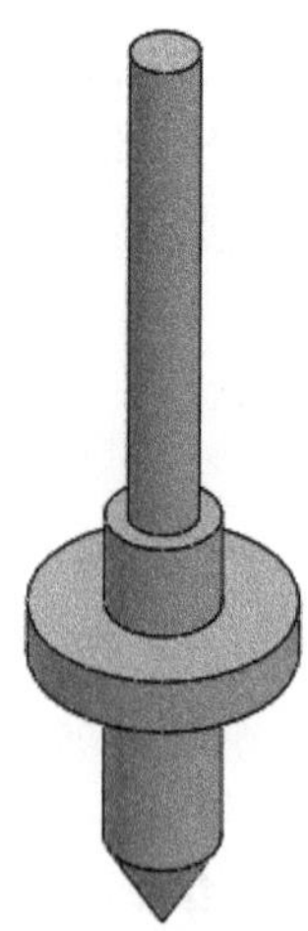

Hands-on Test Drive 3

Create an extruded model, as shown in Figure 5.91. All dimensions are in mm. The depth of extrusion is 2 mm.

5.91

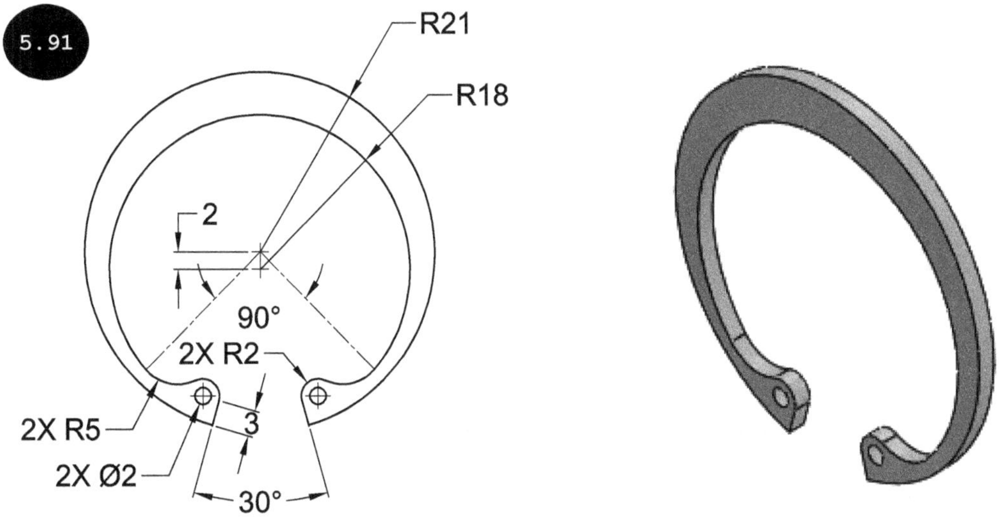

Hands-on Test Drive 4

Create a revolve model as shown in Figure 5.92. All dimensions are in mm. The angle of revolution is 360 degrees.

5.92

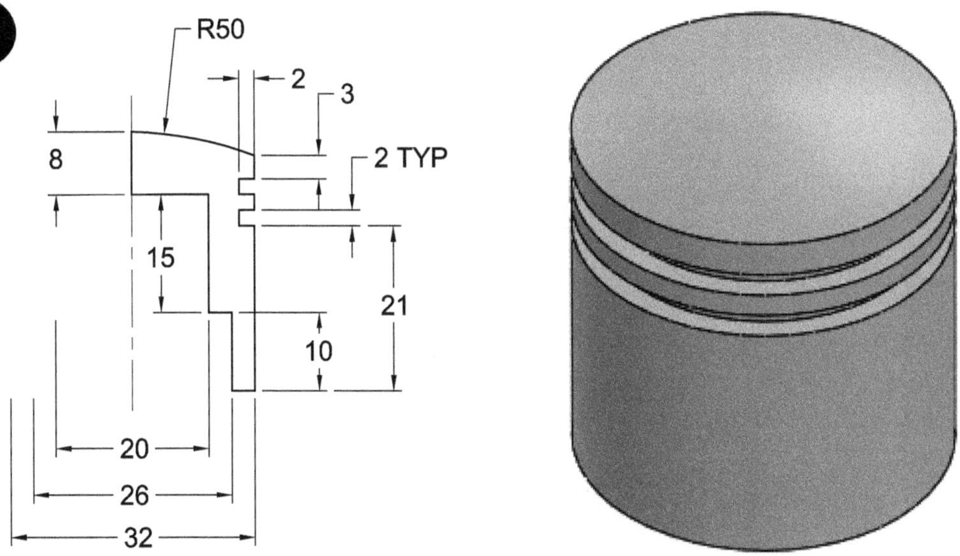

Summary

In this chapter, you have learned how to create extruded and revolved base features using the **Extruded Boss/Base** and **Revolved Boss/Base tools**. The chapter covered techniques for navigating a model using mouse buttons and tools like **Zoom In/Out** and **Zoom To Fit**. You also explored methods for adjusting the view orientation to predefined standard views (front, top, right, left) and custom views. Additionally, you learned how to modify the display style and adjust the overall view of a model to enhance your design experience. These skills are fundamental for efficiently creating, navigating, and manipulating 3D models in SOLIDWORKS.

Questions

Complete and verify the following sentences:

- The _________ tool is used for creating a feature by adding material normal to the sketching plane.
- The _________ tool is used for creating a feature by revolving the sketch around a centerline as the axis of revolution.
- The _________ tool is used for fitting a model completely inside the graphics area.
- The _________ tool of the **View Orientation** flyout is used for displaying the **View Selector Cube** around the 3D model available in the graphics area.
- The _______ button of the **Boss-Extrude PropertyManager** is used for tapering the extrude feature.
- The _______ option is used for extruding a feature symmetrically about the sketching plane.
- You can only create a thin feature from an open sketch. (True/False)
- In SOLIDWORKS, manipulating the view orientation of a model by using the **View Selector Cube** is one of the easiest ways to achieve different views such as right, left, and isometric. (True/False)
- In SOLIDWORKS, you cannot navigate a model by using the mouse buttons. (True/False)
- While creating a revolved feature, if the sketch to be revolved has only one centerline, then the drawn centerline is automatically selected as the axis of revolution. (True/False)

CHAPTER

6

Creating Reference Geometries

This chapter discusses the following topics:

- Creating Reference Planes
- Creating a Reference Axis
- Creating a Reference Coordinate System
- Creating a Reference Point
- Creating a Bounding Box

In SOLIDWORKS, the three default reference planes: **Front**, **Top**, and **Right** are typically sufficient for creating features such as extrudes and revolves, as discussed in previous chapters. However, for more complex real-world models with multiple features, these default planes may sometimes be inadequate. To address this, SOLIDWORKS provides the ability to create additional reference planes as needed, supporting the development of such models. Various types of reference planes can be created using the **Plane** tool, available in the **Reference Geometry** flyout of the **Features CommandManager**, see Figure 6.1.

6.1

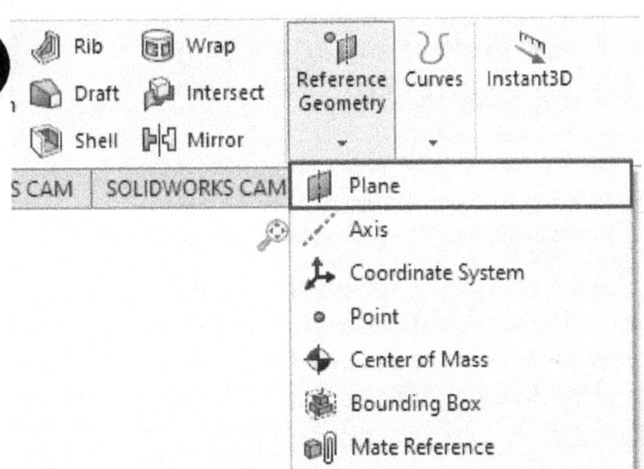

For instance, Figure 6.2 displays a model created by sequentially creating its features. This model consists of four features: the first is an extruded feature created on the Right plane; the second is an extruded cut feature made on the top planar face of the first feature; the third is a user-defined reference plane set at an angle; and the fourth is another extruded feature created on the previously defined reference plane.

6.2

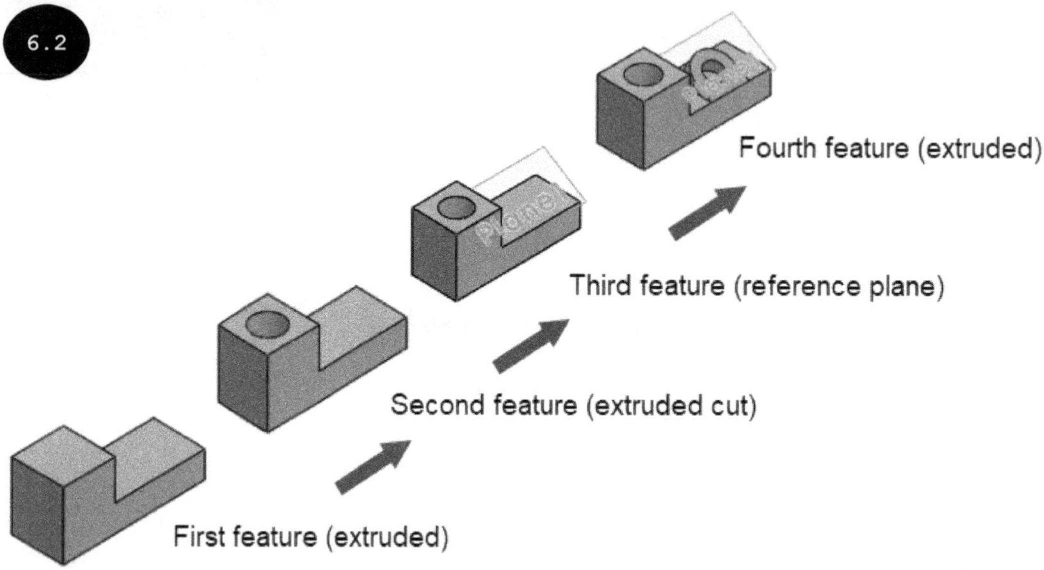

Note: The above figure clearly demonstrates that additional reference planes may be necessary for creating certain features of a model.

Creating Reference Planes

In SOLIDWORKS, you can create various types of reference planes using the **Plane** tool, such as a plane at an offset distance from a planar face, a plane at an angle, a plane tangent to a cylindrical face, a plane perpendicular to a planar face, and more.

To create a reference plane, click on the arrow at the bottom of the **Reference Geometry** tool in the **Features CommandManager**. The **Reference Geometry** flyout appears, refer to Figure 6.1. In this flyout, click on the **Plane** tool. The **Plane PropertyManager** appears, see Figure 6.3. The options in this PropertyManager are used for creating different types of reference planes and are discussed next.

6.3

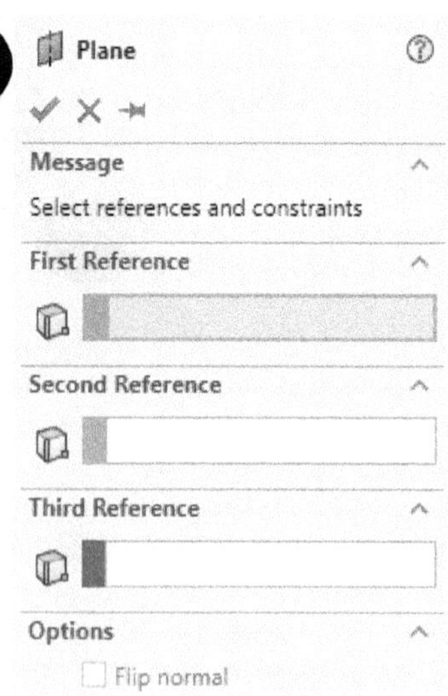

Message

The **Message** rollout of the PropertyManager displays appropriate information about the action to be taken for creating a reference plane as well as displays the current status of the reference plane. If the current status of the plane is displayed as fully defined, then it means that all the required references for creating the plane have been defined. Note that the background color of the rollout changes to green as soon as the status of the plane becomes fully defined. Also, note that for creating a fully defined reference plane, a maximum of three references are required.

First Reference

The **First Reference** rollout is used to define the first reference for creating a plane. You can select a face, plane, vertex, point, edge, or curve as the first reference, depending on the type of plane you want to create. For instance, to create a plane at an offset distance from a planar face of the model, you would select the planar face as the first reference. Once the first reference is selected, the **First Reference** rollout expands, displaying all possible relations and options that can be applied between the reference and the plane, see Figure 6.4. Also, the most suitable relation is selected by default in the expanded rollout. Figure 6.4 illustrates the expanded **First Reference** rollout when a planar face is selected as the first reference. As a result, the **Offset Distance** button is automatically activated, allowing you to specify the offset distance between the selected face and the plane, thereby creating a plane at the specified offset. The methods for creating various types of reference planes are discussed later in this chapter.

6.4

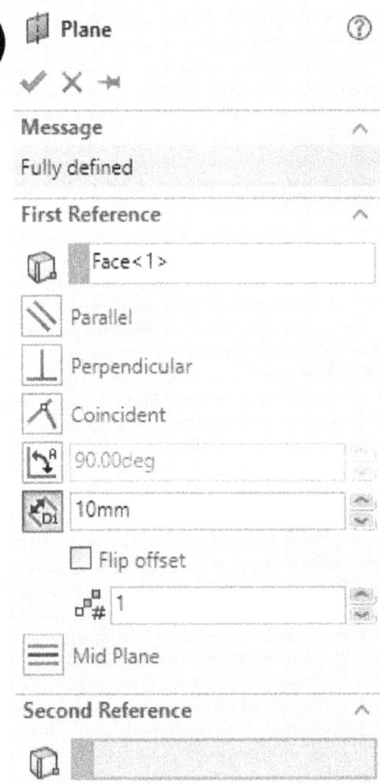

Second Reference

The **Second Reference** rollout is used for defining the second reference for creating a reference plane. You need to define the second reference while creating planes such as a plane at an angle, a plane tangent to a cylindrical face, a plane perpendicular to a planar face, and so on. You will learn more about creating different types of planes by specifying a second reference later in this chapter.

Third Reference

The **Third Reference** rollout is used for defining the third reference for creating a reference plane. You need to define the third reference while creating a reference plane, which passes through three points or vertices.

In SOLIDWORKS, you need to focus more on creating reference planes rather than selecting options in the **Plane PropertyManager**. This is because when you select a reference geometry for creating a plane, the most suitable option gets automatically selected in the PropertyManager. Also, the preview of the respective reference plane appears in the graphics area. The methods for creating different types of reference planes are discussed next.

Creating a Plane at an Offset Distance

1. Invoke the **Plane PropertyManager** by clicking on the **Plane** tool in the **Reference Geometry** flyout, as discussed earlier.

2. Click on a planar face or a plane in the graphics area as the first reference. A preview of the offset plane appears, see Figure 6.5.

3. Enter the required offset distance value in the **Offset distance** field, which is available in front of the **Offset distance** button.

4. Flip the direction of the plane by selecting the **Flip offset** check box (see Figure 6.6), if needed.

6.5

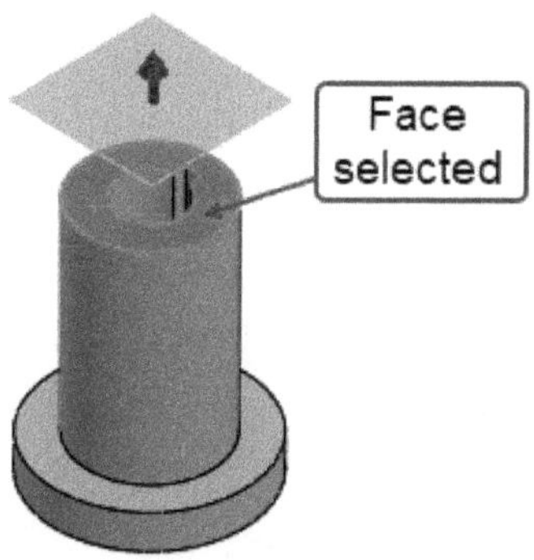

6.6

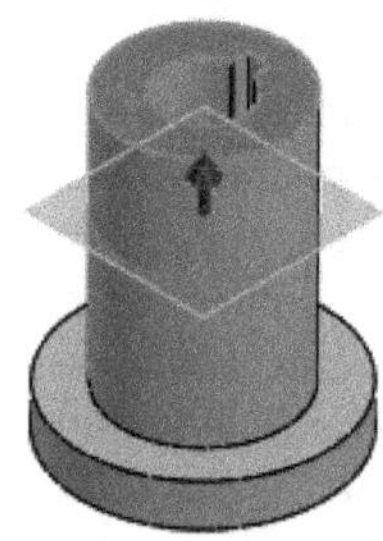

Tip: You can also specify the required number of planes to create in the **Number of planes to create** field of the PropertyManager. By default, the value is set to 1, which creates only one reference plane with the specified offset distance. This field is enabled only when the **Offset distance** or **At angle** button is selected in the PropertyManager.

5. Click on the green tick-mark ✓ in the PropertyManager. A reference plane at the specified offset distance is created.

Creating a Parallel Plane

1. Invoke the **Reference Geometry** flyout and then click on the **Plane** tool.

2. Select a planar face or a plane as the first reference in the graphics area.

3. Select a point, a vertex, or a linear edge as the second reference in the graphics area. A preview of the reference plane parallel to the selected face and passing through the selected vertex/point appears in the graphics area, see Figure 6.7.

Note: On selecting a linear edge as the second reference, you need to click on the **Parallel** button in the **First Reference** rollout of the PropertyManager to create a parallel plane.

4. Click on the green tick-mark ✓ in the PropertyManager. A parallel plane is created.

6.7

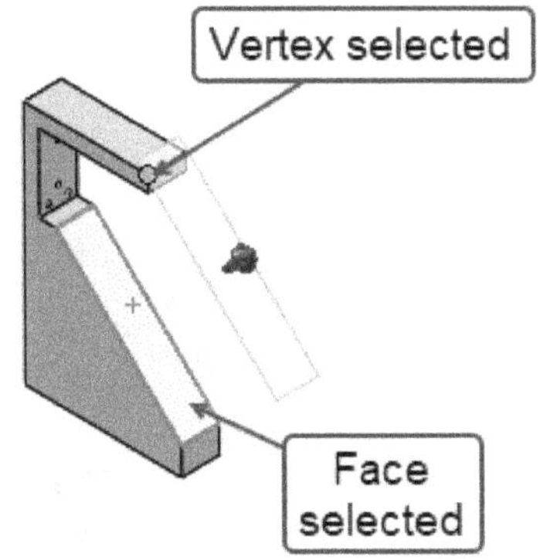

Creating a Plane at an Angle

1. Invoke the **Plane PropertyManager**.

2. Select a planar face or a plane as the first reference in the graphics area. Next, click on the **At angle** button in the **First Reference** rollout of the PropertyManager.

3. Enter the required angle value in the **Angle** field that appears in front of the **At angle** button.

4. Select an edge (linear), an axis, or a sketch line as the second reference. A preview of the reference plane appears, see Figure 6.8.

6.8

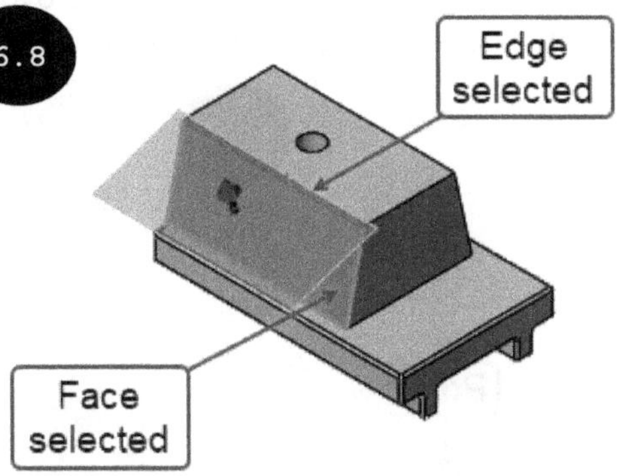

5. Flip the direction of the angle by selecting the **Flip offset** check box if needed.

6. Click on the green tick-mark ✓ in the PropertyManager. A reference plane at the specified angle is created.

Creating a Plane passing through Three Points/Vertices

1. Invoke the **Plane PropertyManager** and then select a point or a vertex as the first reference in the graphics area.

2. Select the second point or vertex as the second reference.

3. Select the third point or vertex as the third reference. A preview of the reference plane passing through three points/vertices appears in the graphics area, see Figure 6.9.

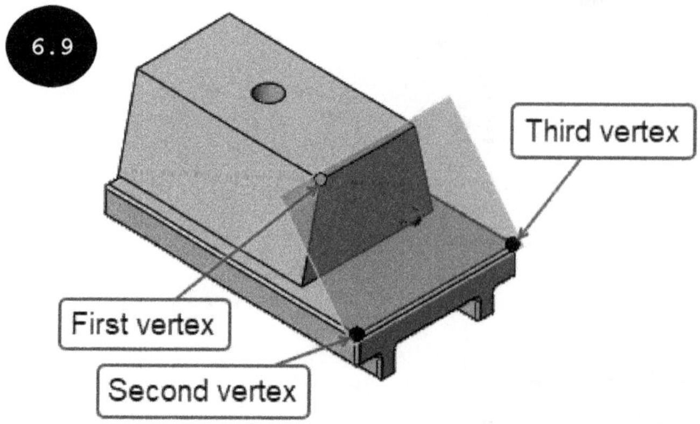

4. Click on the green tick-mark in the PropertyManager. A reference plane passing through three specified points/vertices is created.

Creating a Plane Normal to a Curve

1. Invoke the **Plane PropertyManager** and then select a curve as the first reference in the graphics area, see Figure 6.10.

2. Select a point of the curve as the second reference, see Figure 6.10. A preview of the reference plane normal to the curve and passing through the selected point appears, see Figure 6.11.

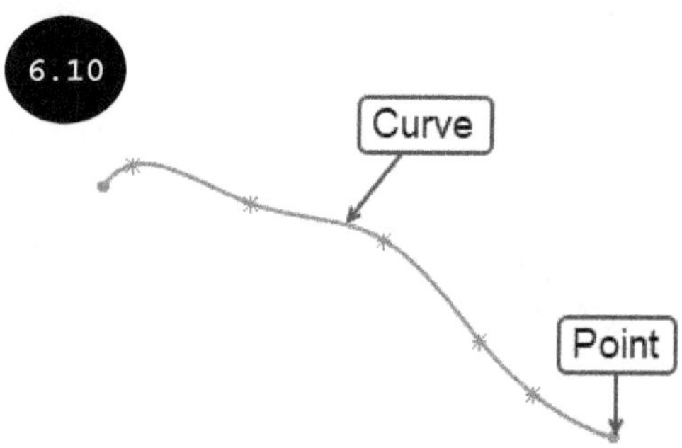

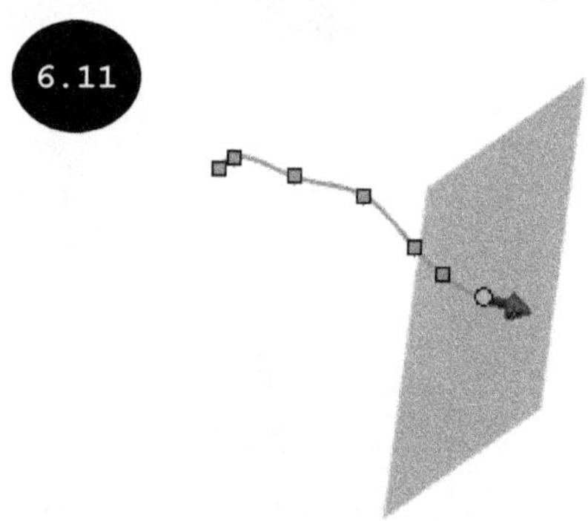

3. Click on the green tick-mark in the PropertyManager. A reference plane normal to the curve and passing through the point is created.

Creating a Plane in the middle of two Faces/Planes

1. Invoke the **Plane PropertyManager**.

2. Select a planar face of the model as the first reference, see Figure 6.12.

3. Select the second planar face of the model as the second reference, see Figure 6.12. A preview of the plane passing through the middle of the two selected faces appears in the graphics area, see Figure 6.12.

6.12

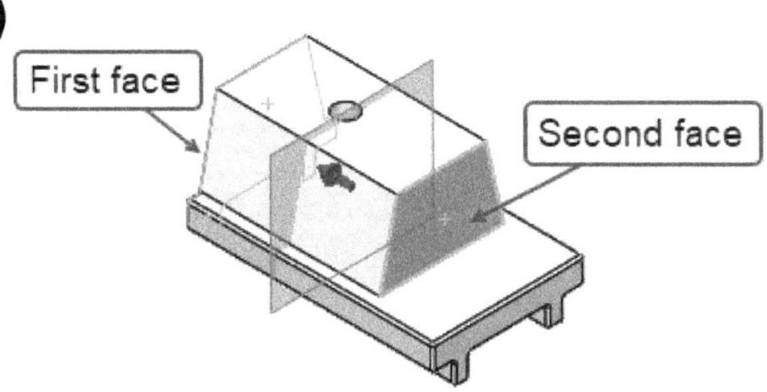

4. Click on the green tick-mark ✓ in the PropertyManager. A reference plane in the middle of the two selected faces is created.

Creating a Plane Tangent to a Cylindrical Face

1. Invoke the **Plane PropertyManager**.

2. Select a cylindrical face of the model as the first reference, see Figure 6.13. A preview of the plane tangent to the selected cylindrical face appears in the graphics area.

3. Select a planar face or a plane as the second reference, see Figure 6.13. A preview of the plane tangent to the cylindrical face and perpendicular to the planar face appears, see Figure 6.14.

6.13

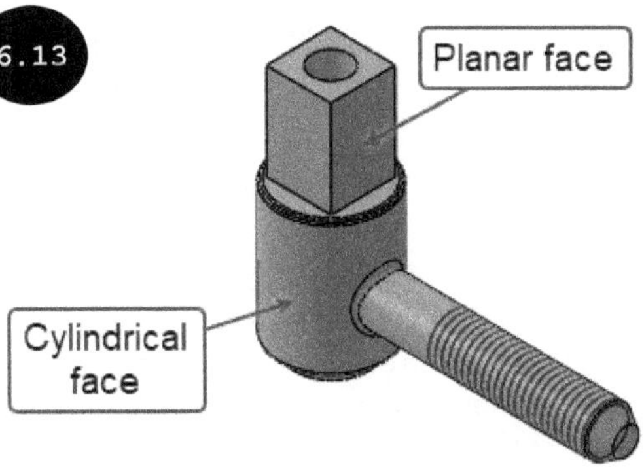

6.14

Note: As soon as you specify the second reference (a planar face), the **Perpendicular** button gets activated automatically in the **Second Reference** rollout. As a result, the preview of the reference plane appears tangent to the cylindrical face and perpendicular to the selected planar face. If you click on the **Parallel** button in the **Second Reference** rollout, the preview of the tangent plane gets modified and appears as tangent to the cylindrical face and parallel to the selected planar face. You can also flip the direction of the plane by selecting the **Flip offset** check box in the **First Reference** rollout.

4. Click on the green tick-mark ✓ in the PropertyManager. A reference plane tangent to the selected cylindrical face and perpendicular/parallel to the planar face is created.

Creating a Plane Parallel to the Screen

1. Invoke the **Plane PropertyManager**.

2. Select a vertex as the first reference, see Figure 6.15.

3. Click on the **Parallel to screen** button in the **First Reference** rollout. A preview of the plane normal to the viewing direction and passing through the vertex appears, see Figure 6.16.

6.15

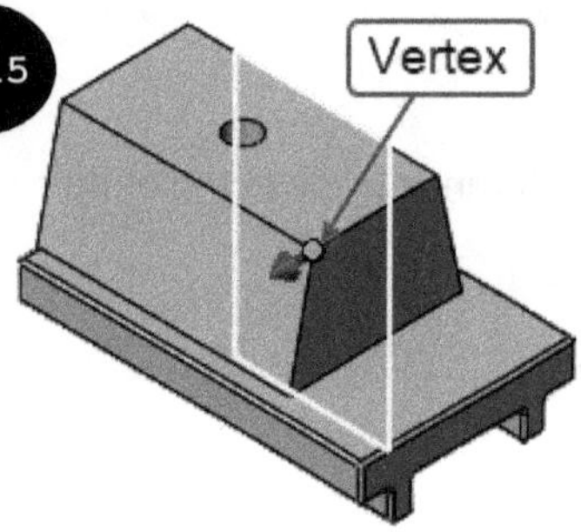

6.16

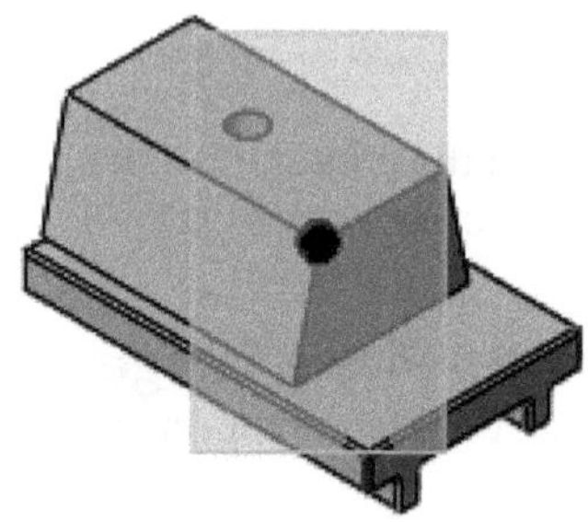

4. Enter the offset distance in the **Offset distance** field of the PropertyManager, if needed.

Note: If the value entered in the **Offset distance** field is 0 (zero) then the plane will be created normal to the viewing direction and passing through the selected vertex. To create a plane at an offset distance from the vertex and normal to the viewing direction, you need to enter the offset distance value in the **Offset distance** field of the PropertyManager.

5. Click on the green tick-mark in the PropertyManager. A reference plane normal to the viewing direction (parallel to the screen) and passing through the vertex is created.

Note: Alternatively, you can create a reference plane parallel to the screen without invoking the **Plane PropertyManager**. To do this, right-click on a face or an edge of a model in the graphics area and then click on the **Create Plane Parallel to Screen** option in the shortcut menu that appears. A 3D point is created where you right-click on the model and a reference plane parallel to the screen is created at that point.

Creating a Projected Plane onto a Non-Planar Face

1. Invoke the **Plane PropertyManager**.

2. Select a point to be projected onto a non-planar face as the first reference, see Figure 6.17.

3. Select the non-planar face of the model to create a projected plane, see Figure 6.17. A preview of the projected plane appears in the graphics area.

6.17

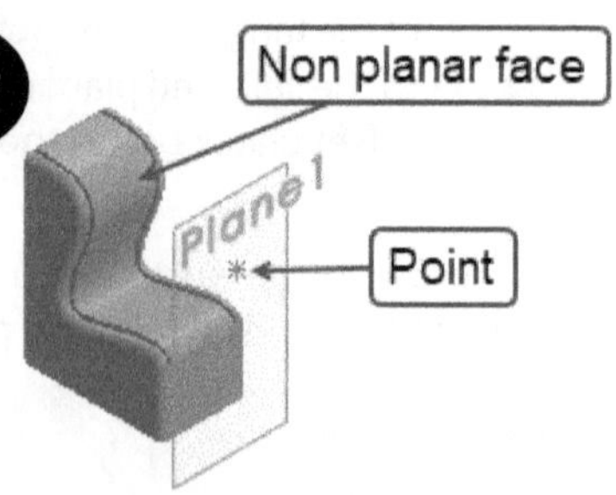

Note: By default, the preview of the projected plane appears by projecting the selected point to the nearest location on the non-planar face, see Figure 6.18. This is because the **Nearest location on surface** radio button is selected by default in the **First Reference** rollout. On selecting the **Along sketch normal** radio button, the preview of the plane appears by projecting the selected point normal to the non-planar face, see Figure 6.19. You can also flip the projection direction of the plane by selecting the **Flip offset** check box, if needed. Note that the **Flip offset** check box is enabled only when the **Along sketch normal** radio button is selected in the PropertyManager.

6.18

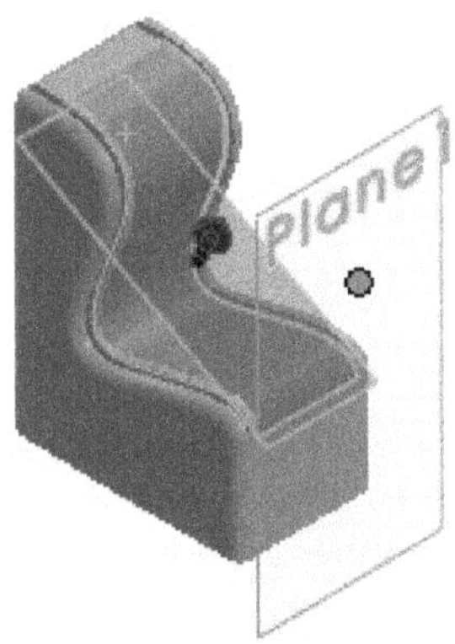

6.19

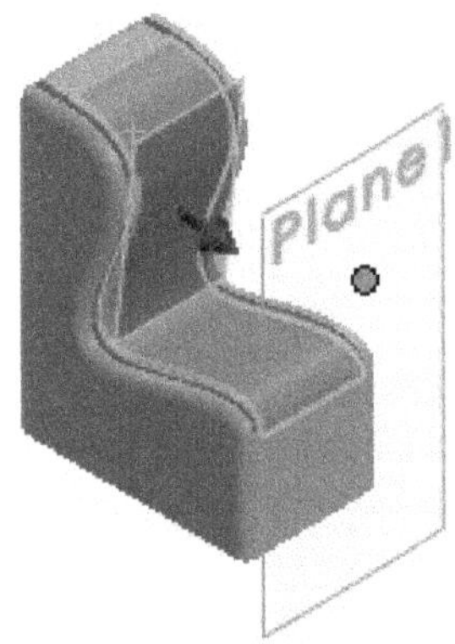

4. Select the required radio button in the **First Reference** rollout (**Nearest location on surface** or **Along sketch normal**). The preview of the projected plane appears.

5. Click on the green tick-mark ✓ in the PropertyManager. The projected plane is created.

Creating a Reference Axis

Similar to creating a reference plane, you can create a reference axis that can be used as the axis of revolution for creating features such as revolved and circular patterns. To create a reference axis, click on the **Axis** tool in the **Reference Geometry** flyout, see Figure 6.20. The **Axis PropertyManager** appears, see Figure 6.21. The options in the **Axis PropertyManager** are used for creating different types of axes and are discussed next.

6.20

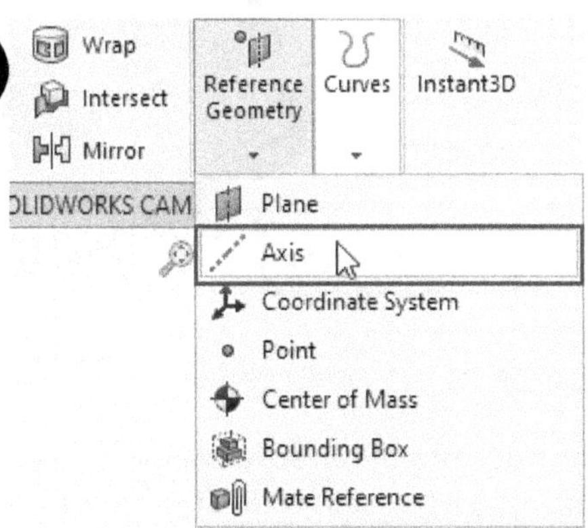

6.21

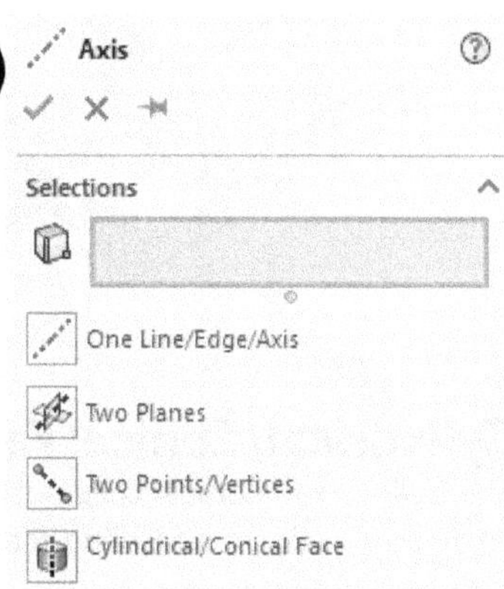

One Line/Edge/Axis

The **One Line/Edge/Axis** button of the PropertyManager is used to create an axis along an existing line, linear edge, or axis. To do this, click on the **One Line/Edge/Axis** button in the PropertyManager and then select a line, a linear edge, or an axis in the graphics area. The preview of the axis along the selected entity appears in the graphics area. Next, click on the green tick-mark ✓ in the PropertyManager. The reference axis is created. Figure 6.22 shows a reference axis created along the edge of a model.

6.22

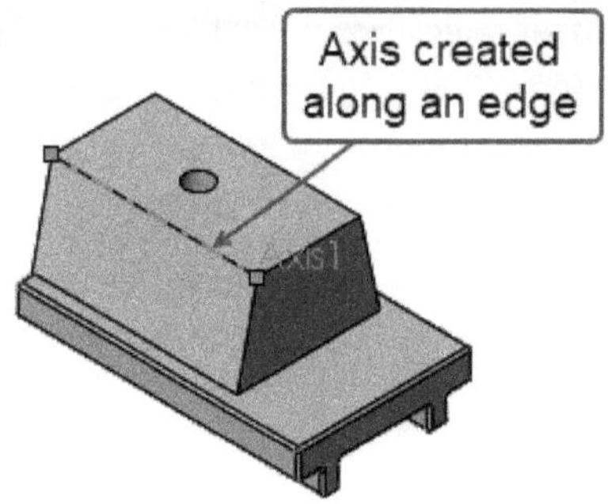

Two Planes

The **Two Planes** button is used to create an axis at the intersection of two planar faces or planes. To do this, click on the **Two Planes** button of the PropertyManager and then select two planar faces or planes. The preview of the axis at the intersection of the selected entities appears in the graphics area. Next, click on the green tick-mark ✓ in the PropertyManager. The reference axis is created. Note that the planes or the planar faces selected need to be non-parallel to each other. Figure 6.23 shows a reference axis created at the intersection of two selected faces.

Two Points/Vertices

The **Two Points/Vertices** button is used to create an axis that passes through two points or vertices. To do this, click on the **Two Points/Vertices** button and then select two points or vertices. A preview of the resultant axis appears in the graphics area, see Figure 6.24. Next, click on the green tick-mark ✓ in the PropertyManager. The reference axis is created such that it passes through the selected vertices.

6.23

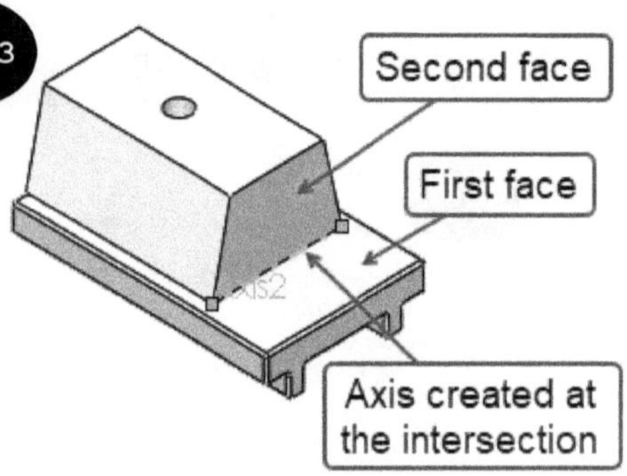

6.24

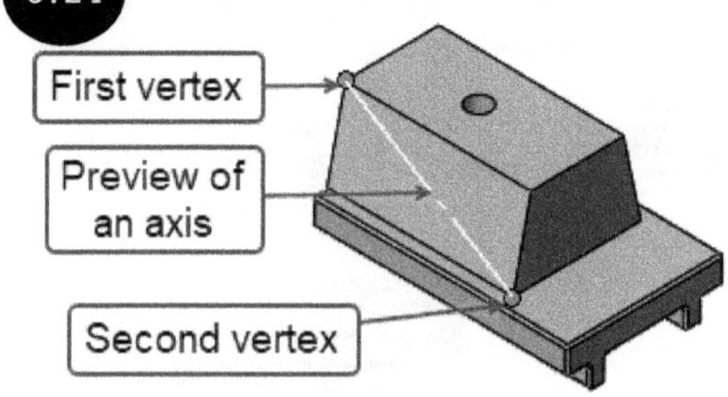

Cylindrical/Conical Face

The **Cylindrical/Conical Face** button is used to create an axis along the axis of a cylindrical/conical face. To do this, click on the **Cylindrical/Conical Face** button and then select a cylindrical or a conical face.

A preview of the resultant axis appears in the graphics area, see Figures 6.25 and 6.26. Next, click on the green tick-mark ✓ in the PropertyManager. A reference axis is created.

6.25

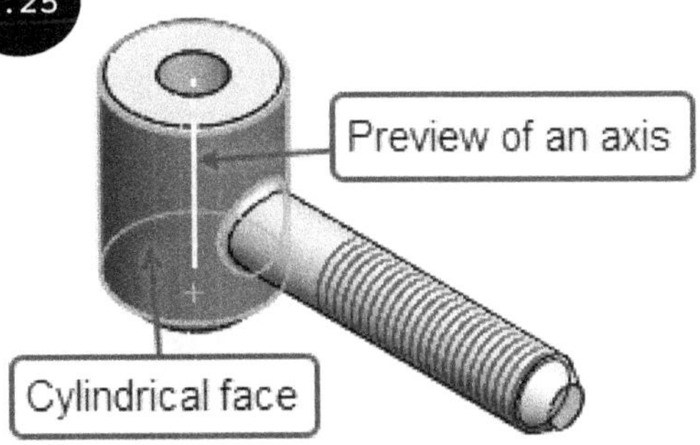

6.26

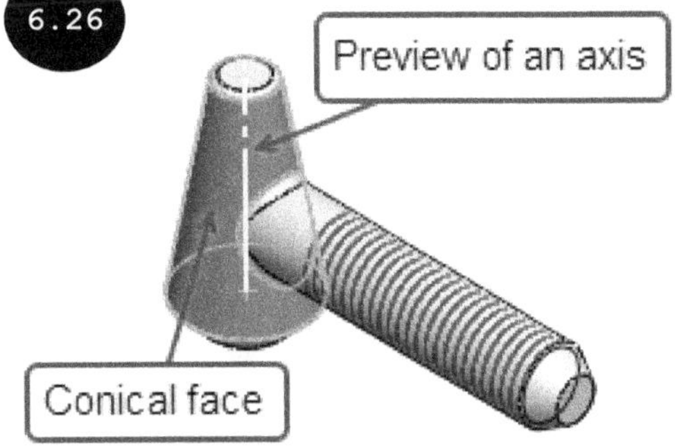

Point and Face/Plane

The **Point and Face/Plane** button is used to create an axis normal to a face or a plane and passing through a point or a vertex. To do this, click on the **Point and Face/Plane** button and then select a planar face or a plane and a point or a vertex, see Figure 6.27. A preview of an axis normal to the selected face and passing through the selected point appears in the graphics area, see Figure 6.28. Next, click on the green tick-mark ✓ in the PropertyManager. A reference axis is created.

6.27

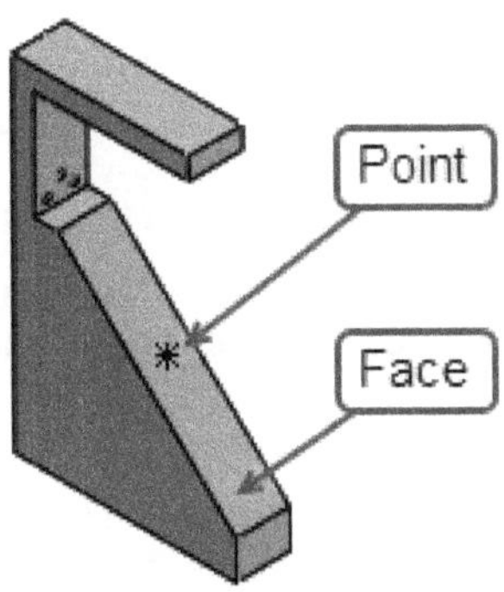

6.28

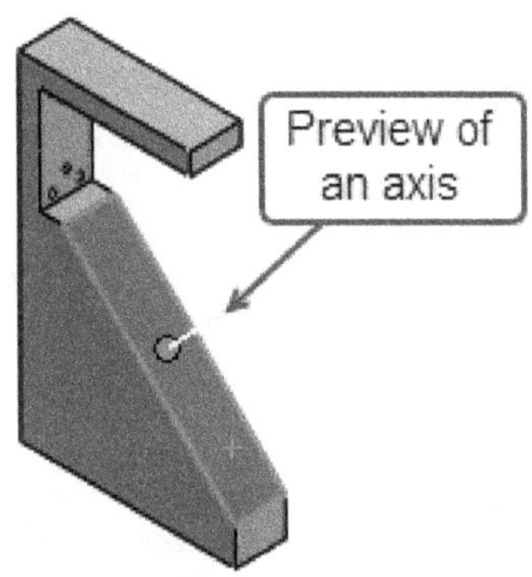

Creating a Reference Coordinate System

In addition to creating a reference plane and an axis, you can also create a reference coordinate system using the **Coordinate System** tool of the **Reference Geometry** flyout, see Figure 6.29. The coordinate system is mainly used for machining or analyzing a model by positioning the origin of the model relative to its features. You can also use a reference coordinate system for applying relations, calculating mass properties, measurements, and so on. The method for creating a reference coordinate system is discussed below:

1. Invoke the **Reference Geometry** flyout and then click on the **Coordinate System** tool, see Figure 6.29. The **Coordinate System PropertyManager** appears, see Figure 6.30. Also, a preview of the coordinate system appears at the origin of the graphics area.

6.29

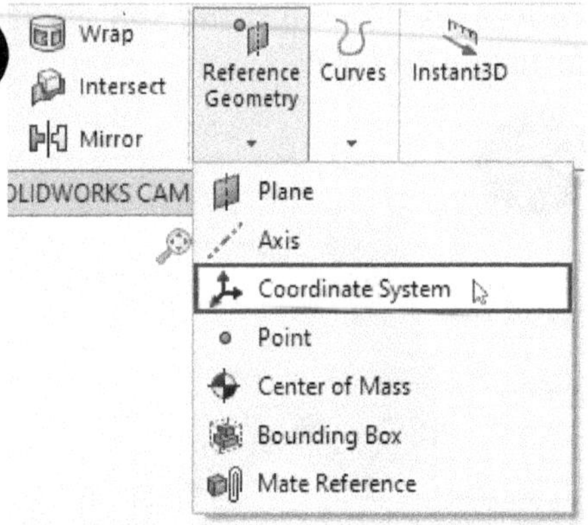

6.30

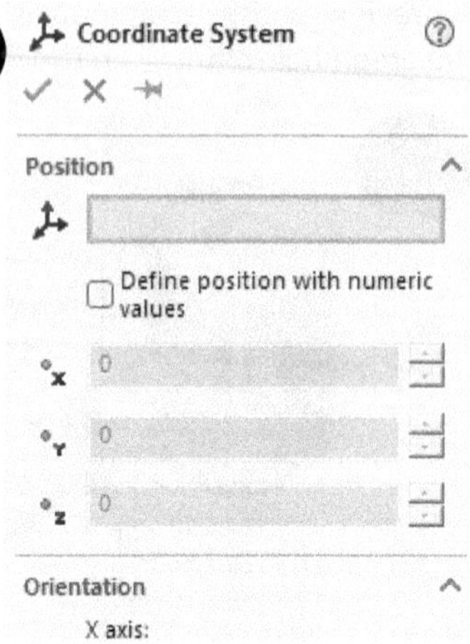

2. Select a point or a vertex as the origin of the coordinate system. You can also input numeric values to define the position of the coordinate system. To do this, select the **Define position with numeric values** check box in the **Position** rollout of the PropertyManager. The **X Coordinate**, **Y Coordinate**, and **Z Coordinate** fields get activated below the check box. Next, enter the coordinate values in the respective fields to define the position of the coordinate system.

3. Click on the **X Axis Direction Reference** field in the **Orientation** rollout of the PropertyManager and then select a linear edge of the model, refer to Figure 6.31. The X-axis of the coordinate system is aligned along with the selected linear edge. You can also reverse the direction of the axis by clicking on the **Reverse X Axis Direction** button to the left of the **X Axis Direction Reference** field.

4. Similarly, specify the direction of the Y-axis and the Z-axis of the coordinate system by using the **Y Axis Direction Reference** and the **Z Axis Direction Reference** fields of the **Orientation** rollout of the PropertyManager, respectively.

Note: You can also define the orientation of the coordinate system by rotating it about one or all of the defined axes. To do this, select the **Define rotation with numeric values** check box in the **Orientation** rollout of the PropertyManager. The **X Rotation Angle**, **Y Rotation Angle**, and **Z Rotation Angle** fields get activated below the check box. Next, enter the rotation angle values in the respective fields to define the orientation of the coordinate system.

5. Click on the green tick-mark ✓ in the PropertyManager. The resultant coordinate system is created, see Figure 6.31.

6.31

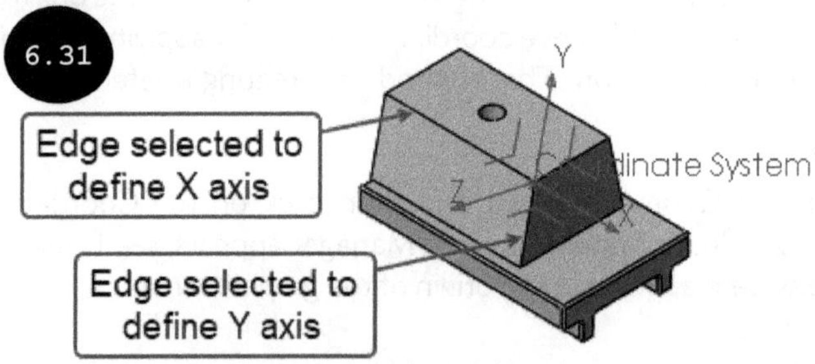

Creating a Reference Point

A reference point can be created anywhere in a 3D model or space and is used as a reference for measuring distance, creating planes, and so on. To create a reference point, invoke the **Reference Geometry** flyout and then click on the **Point** tool. The **Point PropertyManager** appears, see Figure 6.32. The options in this PropertyManager are discussed next.

6.32

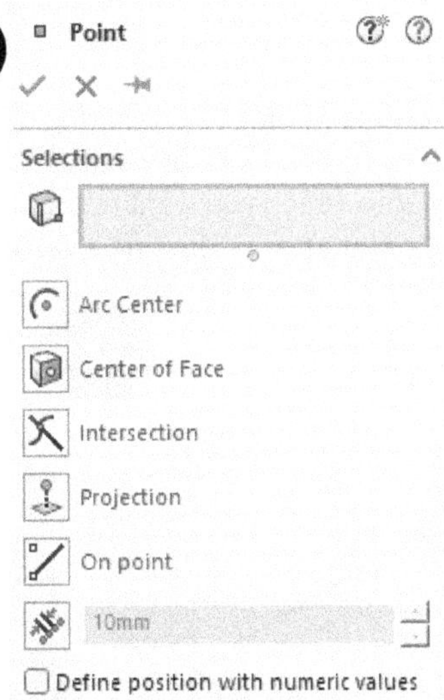

Reference Entities

The **Reference Entities** field is used to select reference entities for creating a point.

Arc Center

The **Arc Center** button is used to create a point at the center of a circular or semi-circular edge, see Figure 6.33. As soon as you select a circular edge or a semi-circular edge, the preview of the reference point at its center appears and the **Arc Center** button gets activated in the PropertyManager.

Center of Face

The **Center of Face** button is used to create a point at the center of a planar or a non-planar face, see Figure 6.34. As soon as you select a planar or a non-planar face, the preview of the reference point at the center of the selected face appears and the **Center of Face** button gets activated in the PropertyManager.

6.33

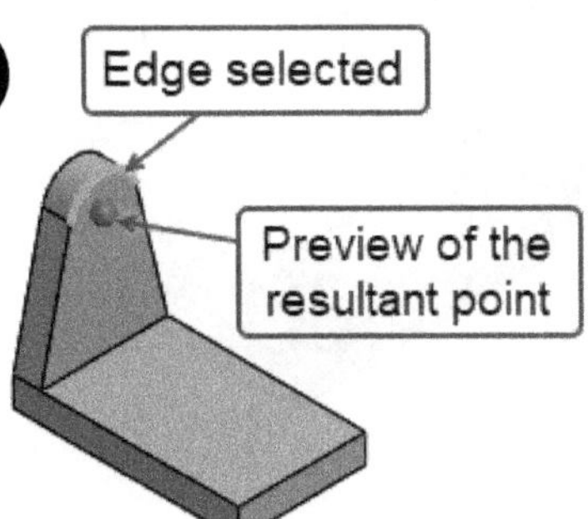

6.34

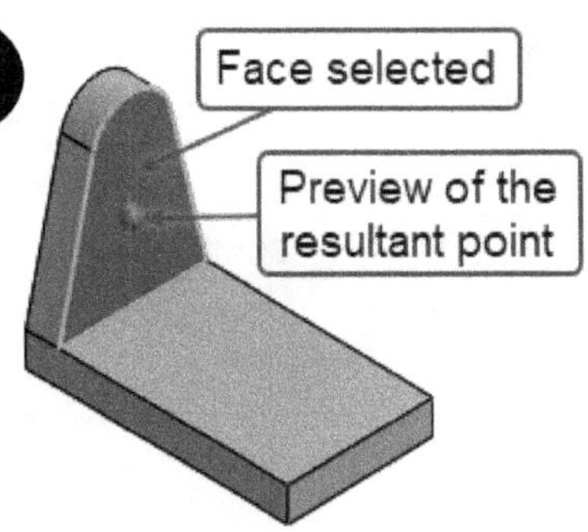

Intersection

The **Intersection** button is used to create a point at the intersection of two entities. You can select edges, curves, sketch segments, or a combination of these with a face or with each other as the entities to create a point. As soon as you select entities, the preview of a reference point appears at the intersection of the selected entities. Also, the **Intersection** button gets activated in the PropertyManager. Figure 6.35 shows the preview of a reference point at the intersection of two edges.

Projection

The **Projection** button is used to create a point by projecting one entity onto another entity of a model. You can select sketch points, end points of curves, or vertices as the entities to be projected and a planar or a non-planar face as the entity onto which you want to project the selected point/vertex. Figure 6.36 shows the preview of a reference point after projecting a vertex onto a planar face.

6.35

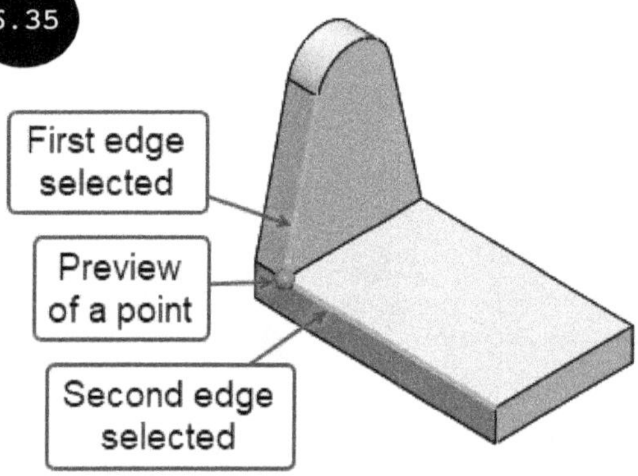

6.36

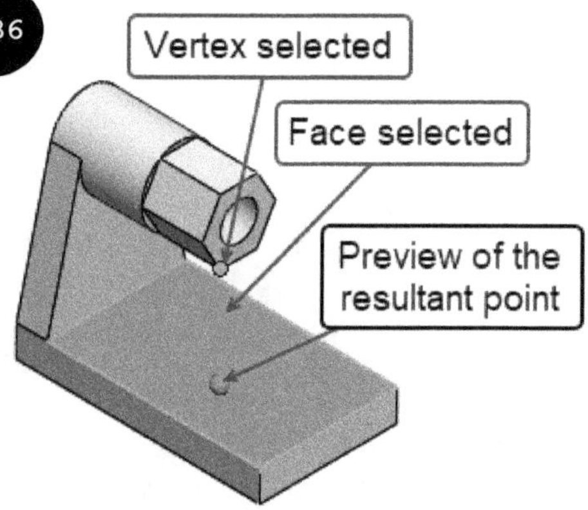

On point

The **On point** button is used to create a reference point onto a point of a sketch. On selecting a point of a sketch, the **On point** button gets activated in the PropertyManager and the preview of the resultant reference point appears in the graphics area. Figure 6.37 shows a sketch point and Figure 6.38 shows the preview of the resultant reference point that appears on the selected point of the sketch.

6.37

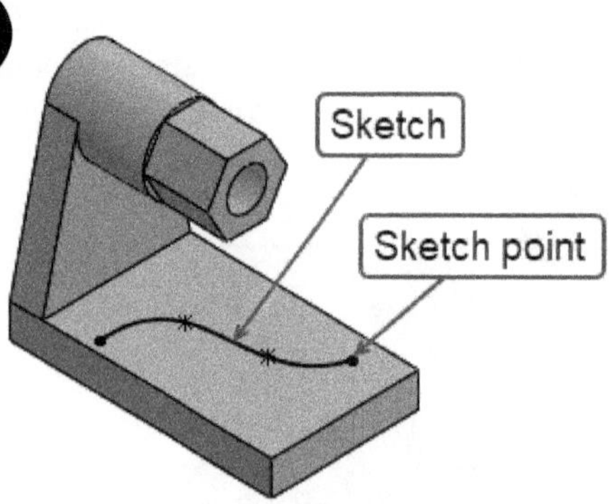

6.38

Along curve distance or multiple reference point

The **Along curve distance or multiple reference point** button is used to create a reference point on an edge, a curve, or a sketch entity. As soon as you select an edge, a curve, or a sketch entity, this button gets activated and the preview of a reference point appears in the graphics area with default settings, see Figure 6.39. Also, three radio buttons: **Distance**, **Percentage**, and **Evenly Distribute** appear in the PropertyManager, see Figure 6.40. These radio buttons are discussed next.

6.39

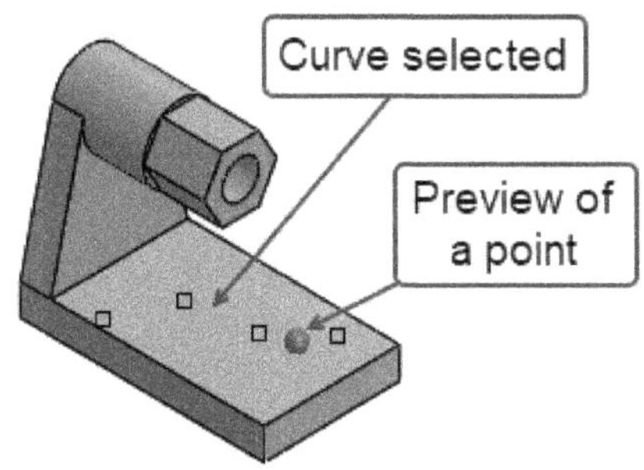

6.40

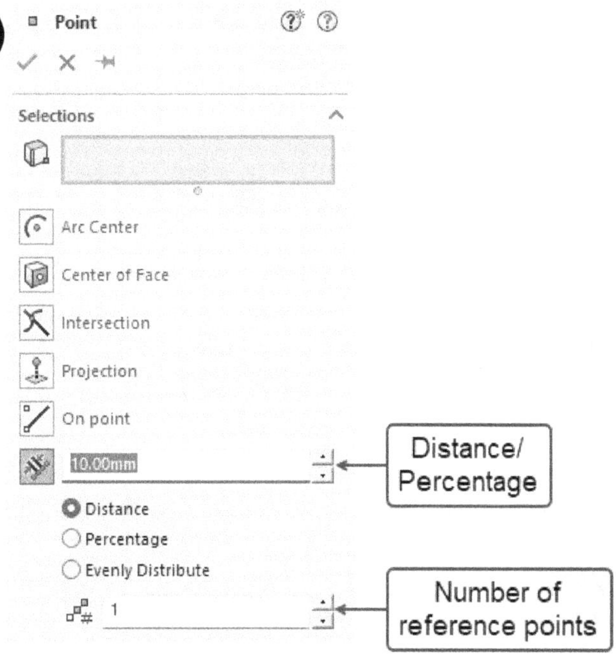

Distance

This radio button is used to specify the position of a reference point by specifying a distance value in the **Distance/Percentage** field of the PropertyManager.

Percentage

This radio button is used to specify the position of a reference point by specifying a percentage value in the **Distance/Percentage** field. Note that the percentage value is calculated in terms of the total length of the selected entity.

Evenly Distribute

This radio button is used to evenly distribute a specified number of reference points along the selected entity.

Number of reference points

This field is used to specify the number of reference points to be created on a selected entity. By default, **1** is displayed in this field. As a result, only one reference point is created on the selected entity. You can create multiple reference points on the selected entity by specifying the required number in this field.

Define position with numeric values

6.41

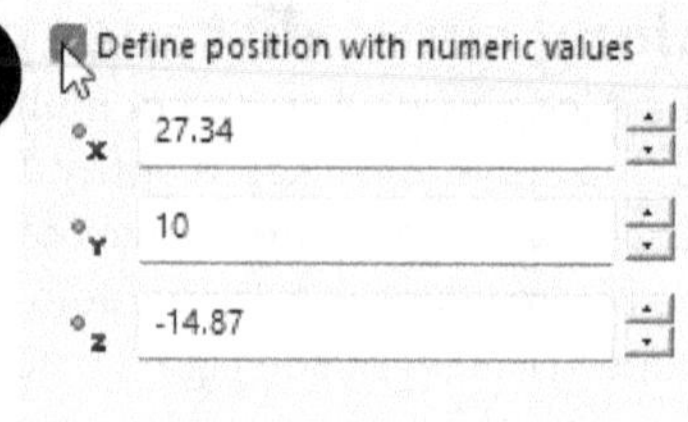

You can also define the position of the coordinate system by entering numeric X, Y, and Z values. To do this, select the **Define position with numeric values** check box in the **Position** rollout of the PropertyManager. This enables the **X Coordinate, Y Coordinate,** and **Z Coordinate** fields, see Figure 6.41. Next, enter the required X, Y, and Z values in the respective fields to specify the position of the coordinate system.

Once the preview of the reference point appears in the graphics area, click on the green tick-mark ✓ in the PropertyManager. The respective reference point is created.

Creating a Bounding Box

6.42

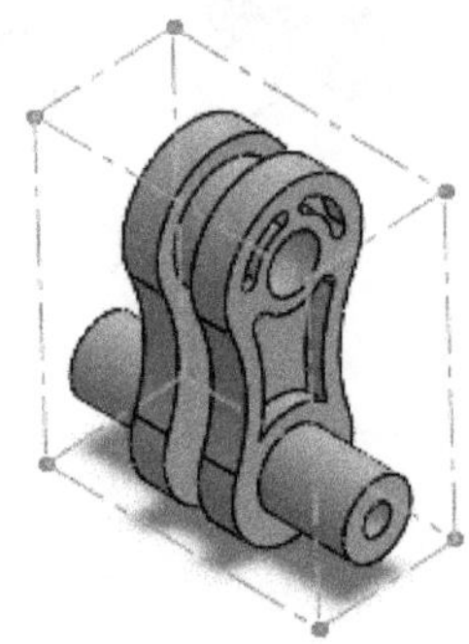

A Bounding Box is a box that completely encloses a model (multibody, single body, or sheet metal) within a minimum volume, see Figure 6.42. It is used for determining the overall size and space of the model which is required to pack and ship the product. The method for creating a bounding box is discussed below:

1. Invoke the **Reference Geometry** flyout and then click on the **Bounding Box** tool, see Figure 6.43. The **Bounding Box PropertyManager** appears, see Figure 6.44.

6.43

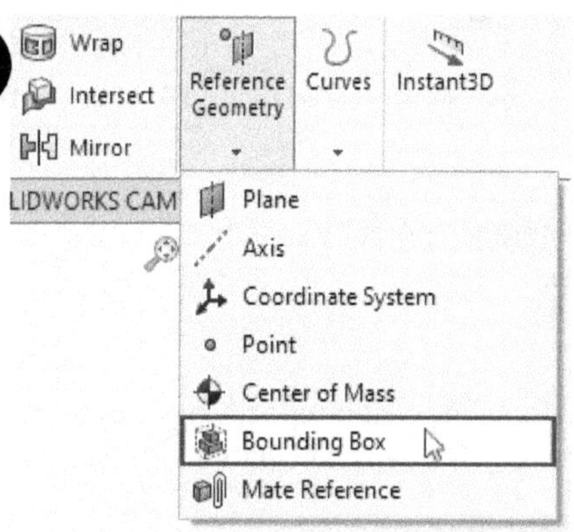

6.44

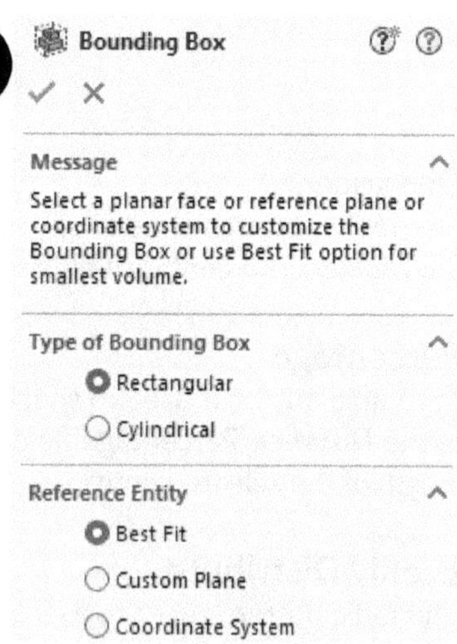

2. Select either the **Rectangular** or **Cylindrical** radio button in the **Type of Bounding Box** rollout (refer to Figure 6.44) to create a boundary box around the model with either a rectangular or cylindrical shape.

3. Ensure that the **Best Fit** radio button is selected in the PropertyManager to define the orientation of the bounding box based on the X-Y plane. Alternatively, you can define the orientation by selecting a custom reference plane or a coordinate system using the **Custom Plane** or **Coordinate System** radio button, respectively.

Note: You can also include the hidden bodies and surfaces of the model in the bounding box by selecting the **Include hidden bodies** and **Include surfaces** check boxes.

4. Click on the green tick-mark ✓ in the PropertyManager. The bounding box is created around the model in the graphics area. Also, it is added in the **FeatureManager Design Tree** after the origin.

Note: The bounding box updates automatically on adding or removing features in the model. Also, you can hide/show or suppress/unsuppress the bounding box. To do this, right-click on **Bounding Box** in the FeatureManager Design Tree and then click on the **Hide** /**Show** or **Suppress** /**Unsuppress** in the Pop-up menu.

In SOLIDWORKS, when you suppress or hide the bounding box feature, it does not rebuild, which improves the overall performance of the system.

Now, you can view the properties of the bounding box.

5. Click on **File > Properties** in the SOLIDWORKS Design menus. The **Properties** window appears. In this window, click on the **Configuration Properties** tab to view the properties such as length, width, and volume of the bounding box.

Tutorial 1

Create a multi-feature model, as shown in Figure 6.45. You need to create the model by creating all its features one by one. All dimensions are in mm.

6.45

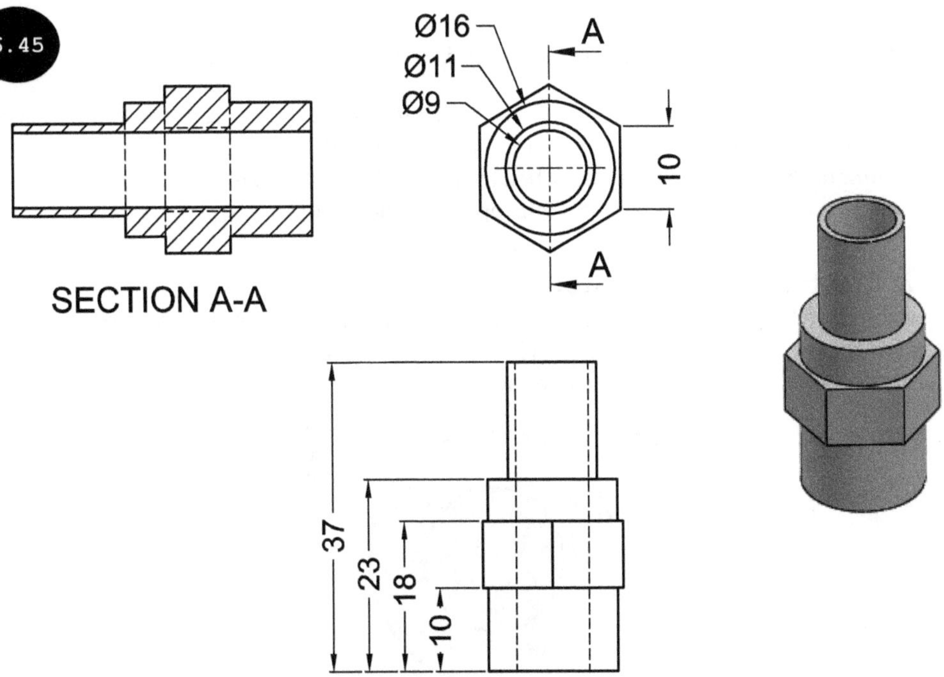

Section 1: Starting SOLIDWORKS

1. Start SOLIDWORKS by double-clicking on the SOLIDWORKS icon on your desktop. The startup user interface of SOLIDWORKS appears along with the **Welcome** dialog box.

Note: If SOLIDWORKS is already open and the **Welcome** dialog box does not appear on the screen, you can invoke it by clicking on the **Welcome to SOLIDWORKS** tool in the **Standard** toolbar.

Section 2: Invoking the Part Modeling Environment

1. Click on the **Part** button in the **Welcome** dialog box. The Part modeling environment is invoked.

   Now, you can set the unit system and create the base feature of the model.

Section 3: Specifying Unit Settings

1. Move the cursor toward the lower right corner of the screen over the Status Bar and then click on the **Unit System** area, see Figure 6.46. The **Unit System** flyout appears.

6.46

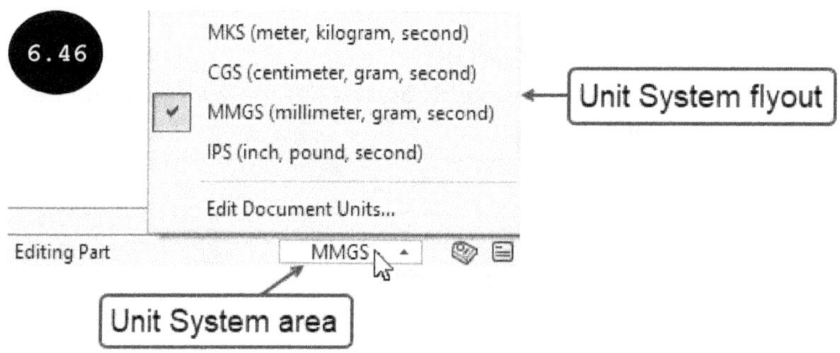

2. Ensure that the **MMGS (millimeter, gram, second)** option is tick-marked in the flyout.

Tip: A tick-mark in front of any unit system in the **Unit System** flyout indicates that it is selected as the unit system for the current document of SOLIDWORKS. You can also open the **Document Properties - Units** dialog box to specify the unit system for the current document by clicking on the **Edit Document Units** option in the flyout.

Section 4: Creating the Base Feature

1. Invoke the Sketching environment by selecting the Top plane as the sketching plane and then create two circles of diameters 9 mm and 16 mm as the sketch of the base feature, see Figure 6.47. Ensure that the center points of the circles are at the origin.

6.47

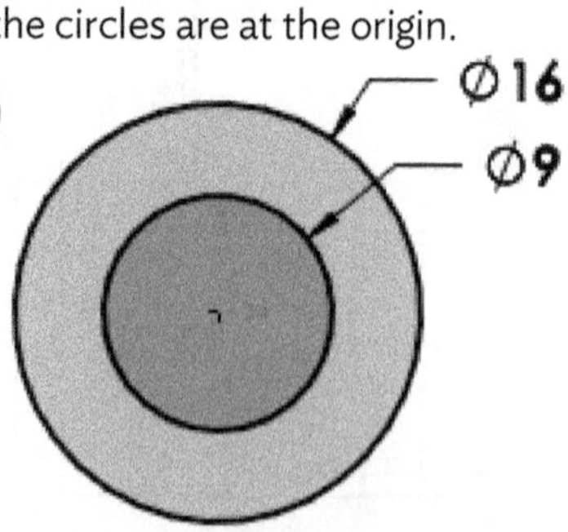

2. Click on the **Features** tab in the CommandManager, see Figure 6.48. The tools of the **Features CommandManager** appear.

6.48

3. Click on the **Extruded Boss/Base** tool in the **Features CommandManager**. The **Boss-Extrude PropertyManager** and the preview of the extruded feature appear, see Figure 6.49.

4. Enter **10** in the **Depth** field of the **Direction 1** rollout and then press ENTER. Next, click on the green tick-mark ✓ in the PropertyManager. The base feature is created, see Figure 6.50.

6.49

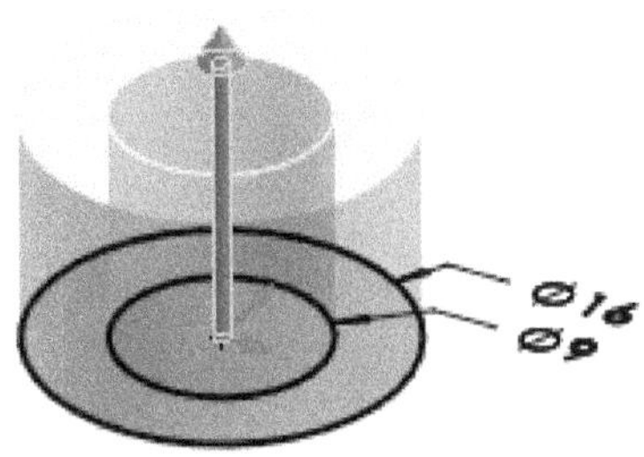

6.50

Section 5: Creating Second Feature

1. Click on the **Sketch** tab to invoke the **Sketch CommandManager**, (see Figure 6.51) and then click on the **Sketch** tool. The **Edit Sketch PropertyManager** appears and you are prompted to select a sketching plane for creating the sketch of the second feature.

2. Click on the top planar face of the base feature as the sketching plane, see Figure 6.52. The Sketching environment is invoked.

6.51

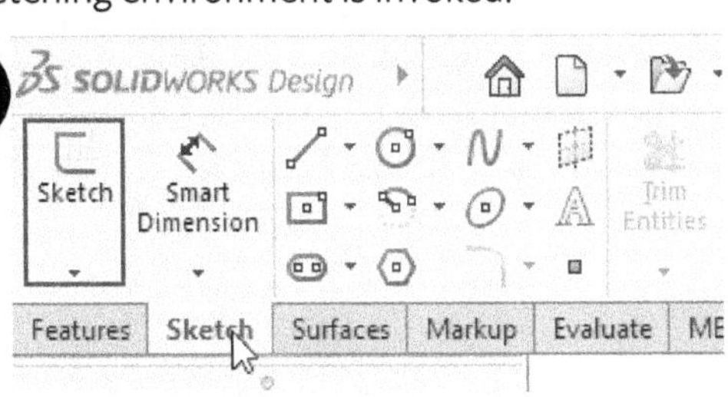

6.52

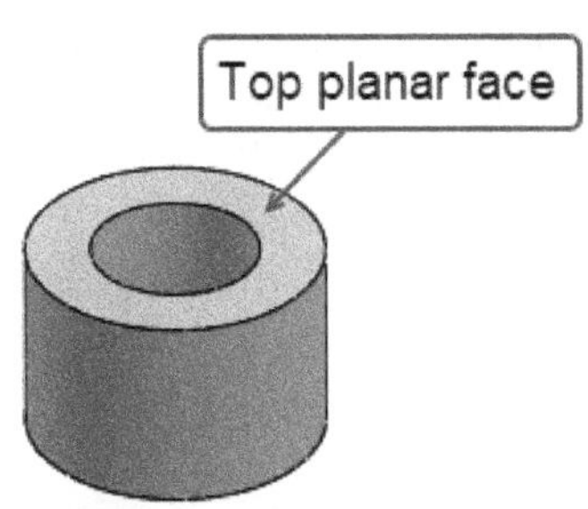

3. Invoke the **View Orientation** flyout by clicking on the **View Orientation** tool in the **View (Heads-Up)** toolbar, see Figure 6.53. Next, click on the **Normal To** tool in the flyout to change the orientation of the model as normal to the viewing direction, if not changed by default.

6.53

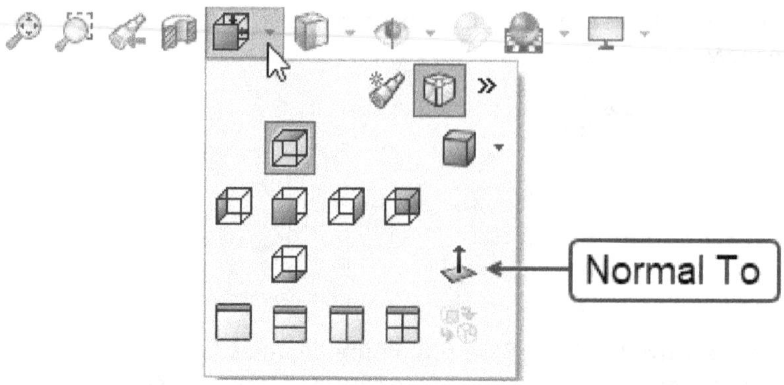

4. Create a polygon of 6 sides and a circle of diameter 9 mm by using the **Polygon** and **Circle** tools as the sketch of the second feature, see Figure 6.54. Also, apply the required dimensions and relations to make the sketch fully defined.

6.54

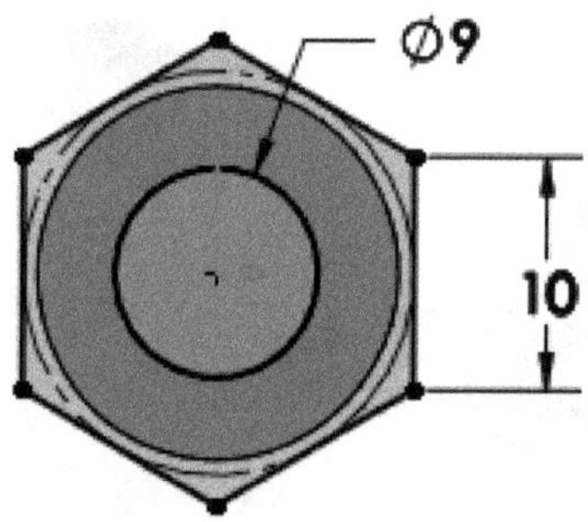

Tip: In addition to the required dimensions, you need to apply a vertical relation to a vertical line of the polygon to make the sketch fully defined.

5. Click on the **Features** tab in the CommandManager to display the tools of the **Features CommandManager**.

6. Click on the **Extruded Boss/Base** tool in the **Features CommandManager**. The **Boss-Extrude PropertyManager** and a preview of the extruded feature appear. Next, change the orientation of the model to isometric, see Figure 6.55. To do this, invoke the **View Orientation** flyout of the **View (Heads-Up)** toolbar and then click on the **Isometric** tool.

6.55

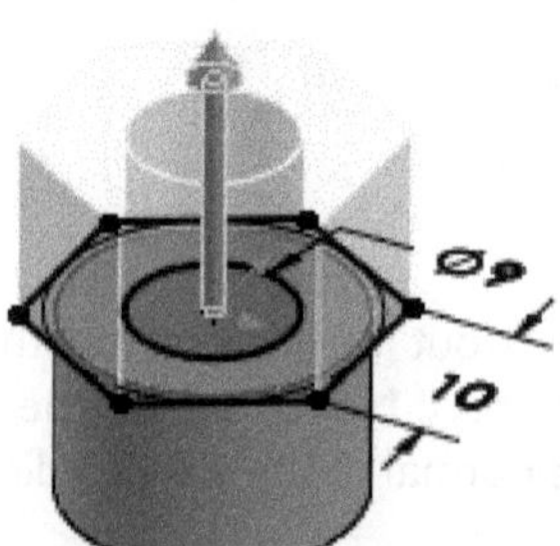

7. Enter **8** in the **Depth** field of the **Direction 1** rollout and then press ENTER.

8. Click on the green tick-mark in the PropertyManager. The extruded feature is created, see Figure 6.56.

6.56

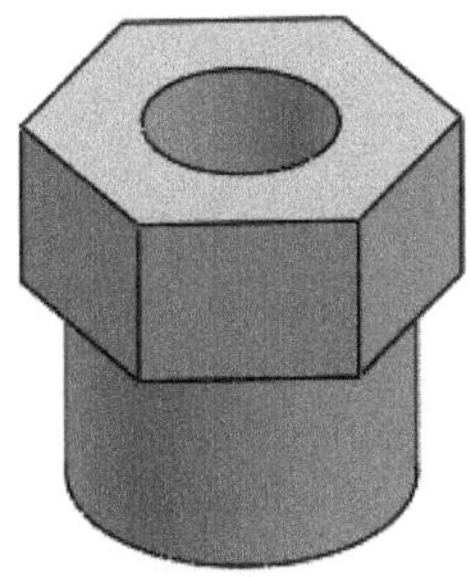

Section 6: Creating the Third Feature

1. Invoke the Sketching environment by selecting the top planar face of the second feature as the sketching plane.

2. Change the orientation of the model as normal to the viewing direction, if not changed by default. To do this, click on the **View Orientation** tool in the **View (Heads-Up)** toolbar and then click on the **Normal To** tool in the **View Orientation** flyout that appears, see Figure 6.57.

3. Create the sketch of the third feature by creating two circles of diameter 9 mm and 16 mm by using the **Circle** tool and then apply dimensions, see Figure 6.58.

6.57

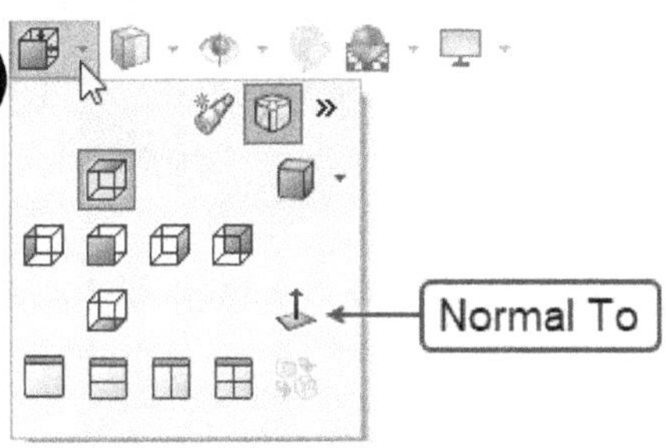

6.58

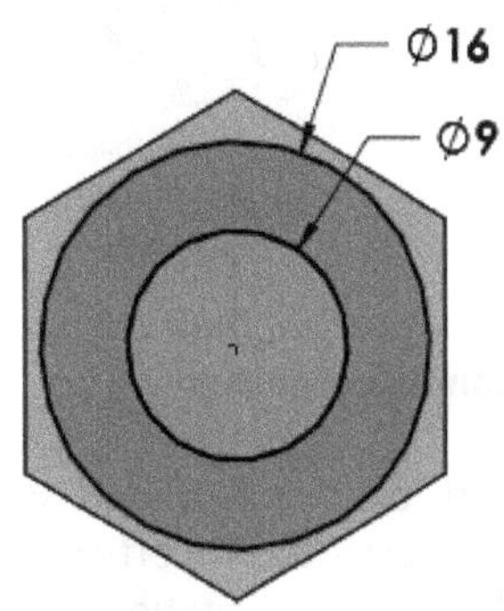

4. Click on the **Features** tab in the CommandManager to display the tools of the **Features CommandManager**.

5. Click on the **Extruded Boss/Base** tool in the **Features Command Manager**. A preview of the extruded feature appears. Next, change the orientation of the model to isometric, see Figure 6.59.

6. Enter **5** in the **Depth** field in the **Direction 1** rollout and then press ENTER.

7. Click on the green tick-mark in the PropertyManager. The extruded feature is created, see Figure 6.60.

6.59

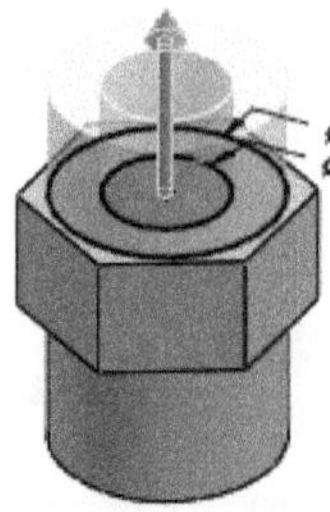

6.60

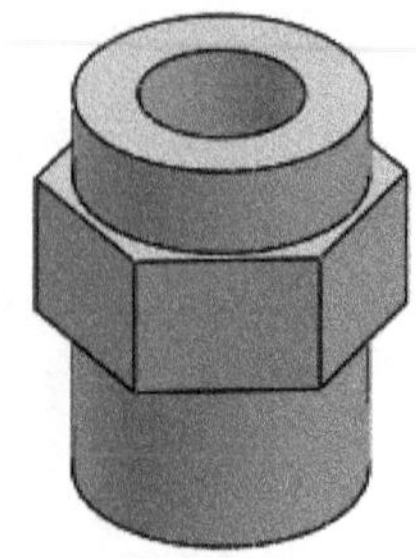

Section 7: Creating the Fourth Feature

1. Invoke the Sketching environment by selecting the top planar face of the third feature as the sketching plane, see Figure 6.61. The orientation of the model changes to normal to the viewing direction.

2. Create the sketch of the fourth feature by creating two circles of diameter 9 mm and 11 mm by using the **Circle** tool and then apply dimensions, see Figure 6.62.

6.61

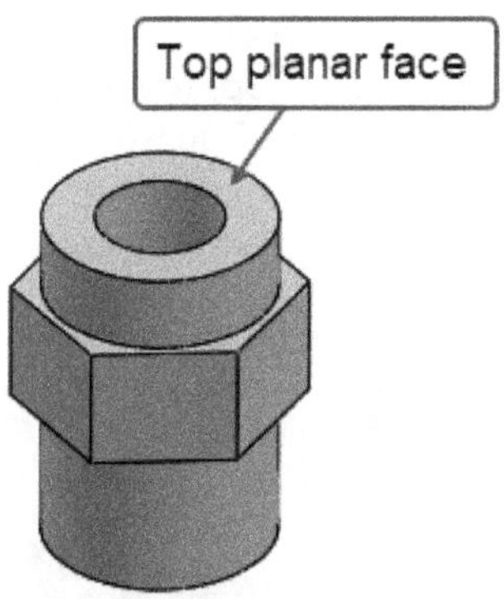

6.62

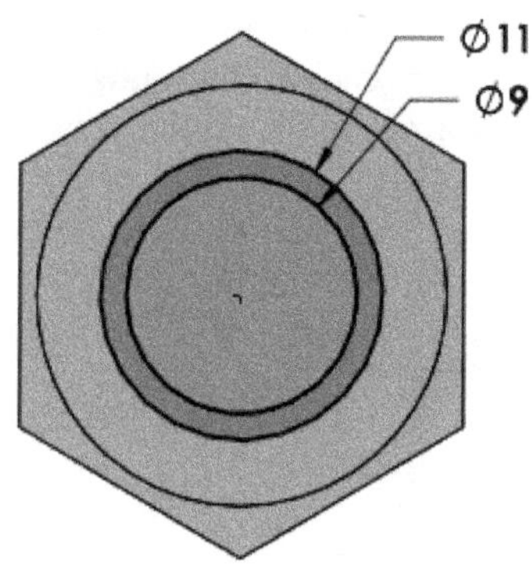

3. Click on the **Features** tab in the CommandManager to display the tools of the **Features CommandManager**.

4. Click on the **Extruded Boss/Base** tool in the **Features CommandManager**. The **Boss-Extrude PropertyManager** and the preview of the extruded feature appear. Next, change the orientation of the model to isometric, see Figure 6.63.

6.63

5. Enter **14** in the **Depth** field of the **Direction 1** rollout and then press ENTER.

6. Click on the green tick-mark ✓ in the PropertyManager. The extruded feature is created. Figure 6.64 shows the model after creating all its features.

6.64

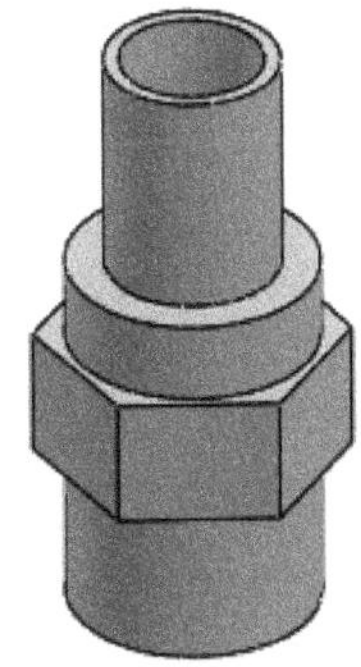

Section 8: Saving the Model

1. Click on the **Save** tool in the **Standard** toolbar. The **Save As** dialog box appears.

2. Browse to the SOLIDWORKS folder and then create a folder with the name Chapter 6.

3. Enter **Tutorial 1** in the **File name** field as the name of the file and then click on the **Save** button. The model is saved with the name Tutorial 1 in the Chapter 6 folder.

Tutorial 2

Create a model, as shown in Figure 6.65. All dimensions are in mm.

6.65

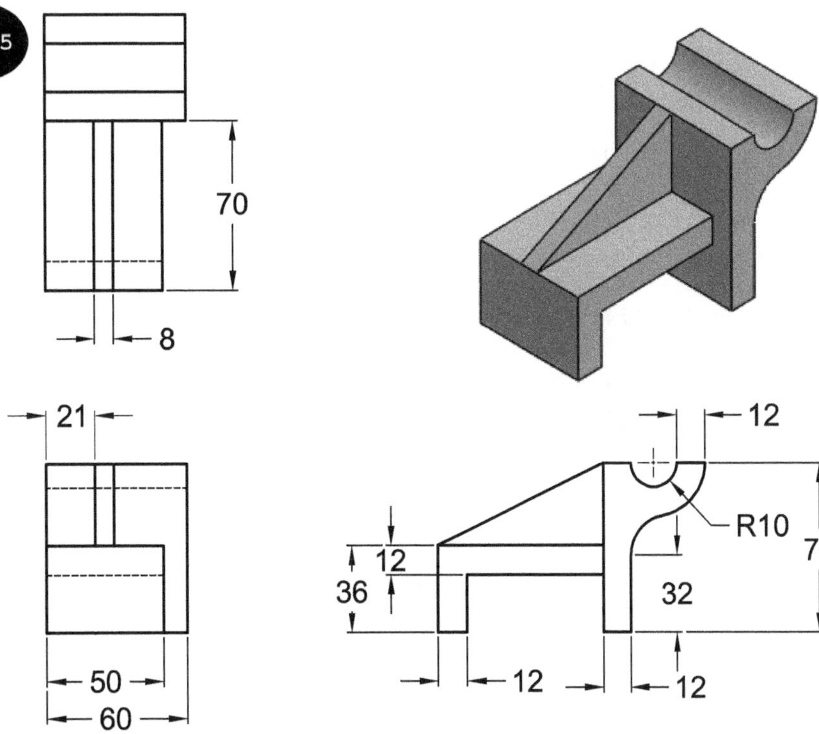

Section 1: Starting SOLIDWORKS

1. Start SOLIDWORKS by double-clicking on the SOLIDWORKS icon on your desktop. The startup user interface of SOLIDWORKS appears along with the **Welcome** dialog box.

Note: If SOLIDWORKS is already open and the **Welcome** dialog box does not appear on the screen, you can invoke it by clicking on the **Welcome to SOLIDWORKS** tool in the **Standard** toolbar.

Section 2: Invoking the Part Modeling Environment

1. Click on the **Part** button in the **Welcome** dialog box. The Part modeling environment is invoked.

Section 3: Specifying Unit Settings

1. Move the cursor toward the lower right corner of the screen over the Status Bar and then click on the **Unit System** area. The **Unit System** flyout appears, see Figure 6.66.

6.66

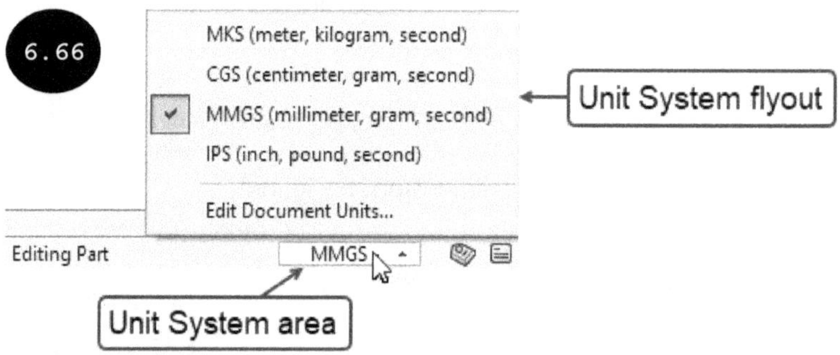

2. Ensure that the **MMGS (millimeter, gram, second)** option is tick-marked in the flyout.

Section 4: Creating the Base/First Feature

1. Invoke the Sketching environment by selecting the Right plane as the sketching plane.

2. Create the sketch of the base feature and then apply the required relations and dimensions to the sketch, see Figure 6.67.

6.67

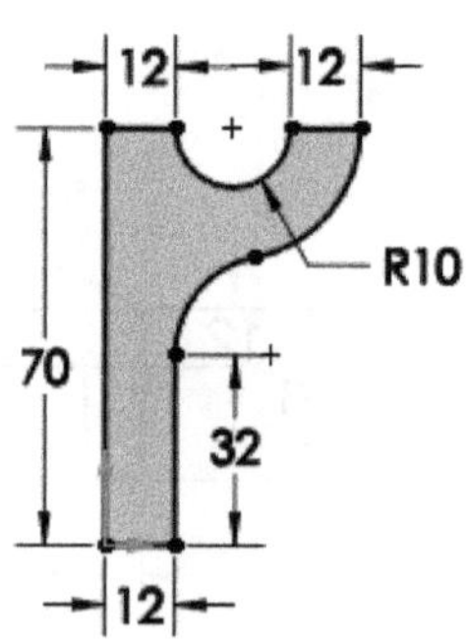

Tip: To make the sketch fully defined, you need to apply tangent relation between line 2 and arc 3, arc 3 and arc 4 of the sketch, refer to Figure 6.68. Also, apply concentric relation between arc 4 and arc 6, refer to Figure 6.68. If the sketch is still not fully defined, then you need to apply the horizontal relation between the center point of the arc 6 and an endpoint of the line 7. Also, it is assumed that the horizontal and vertical relations are applied automatically while drawing the respective lines of the sketch. The sketch shown in the Figure 6.68 has been numbered for your reference only.

3. Click on the **Features** tab in the CommandManager and then click on the **Extruded Boss/Base** tool. The **Boss-Extrude PropertyManager** and a preview of the extruded feature appear, see Figure 6.69.

6.68

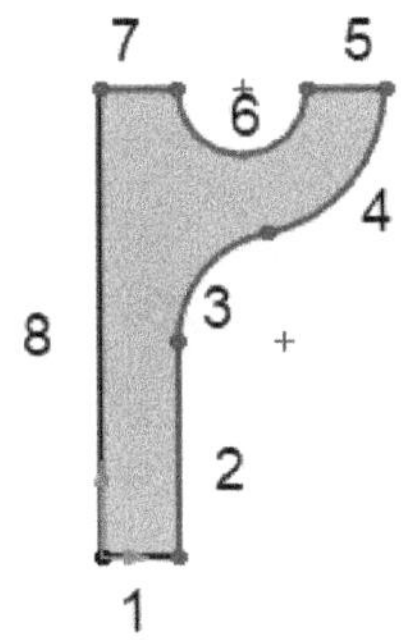

6.69

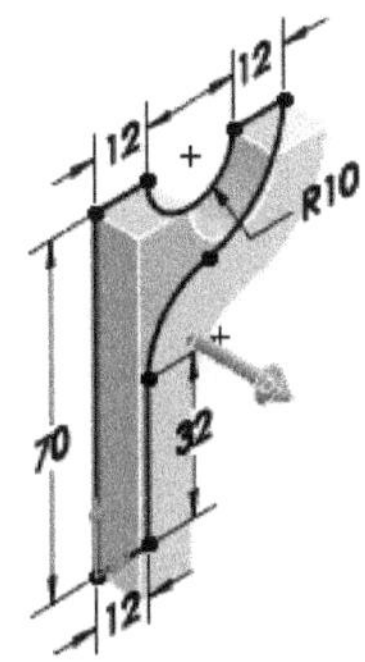

4. Invoke the **End Condition** drop-down list in the **Direction 1** rollout of the PropertyManager, see Figure 6.70.

5. Click on the **Mid Plane** option in the **End Condition** drop-down list.

6. Enter **60** in the **Depth** field of the **Direction 1** rollout and then press ENTER. The depth of extrusion is added symmetrically to both sides of the sketching plane, see Figure 6.71.

6.70

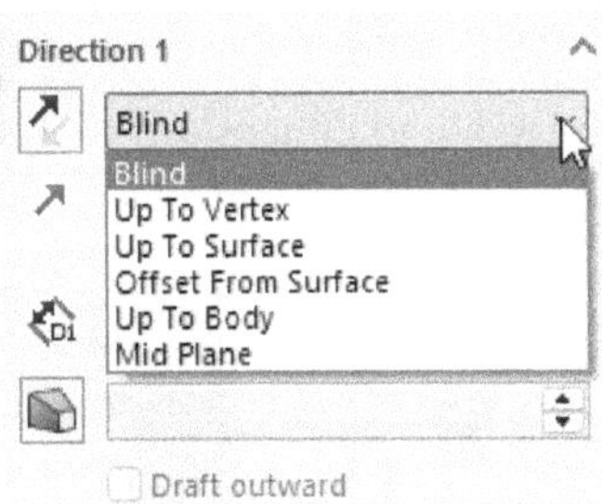

6.71

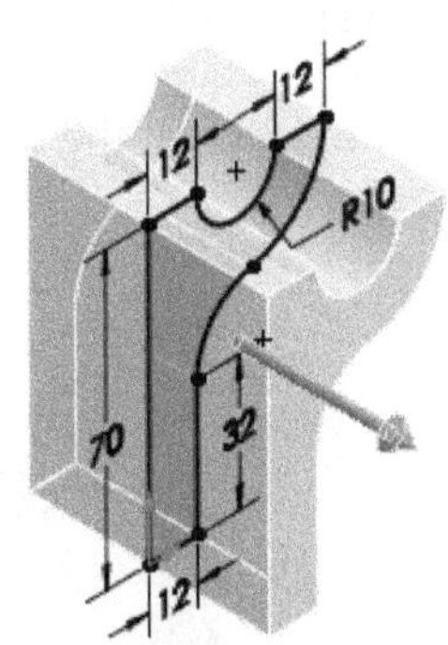

7. Click on the green tick-mark ✓ in the PropertyManager. The extruded feature is created symmetrically about the sketching plane.

Section 5: Creating the Second Feature

To create the second feature of the model, you first need to create a reference plane at an offset distance of 10 mm from the right planar face of the base feature.

1. Invoke the **Reference Geometry** flyout in the **Features CommandManager**, see Figure 6.72.

2. Click on the **Plane** tool of this flyout. The **Plane PropertyManager** appears.

3. Select the right planar face of the base feature as the first reference. The preview of an offset reference plane appears in the graphics area, see Figure 6.73.

6.72

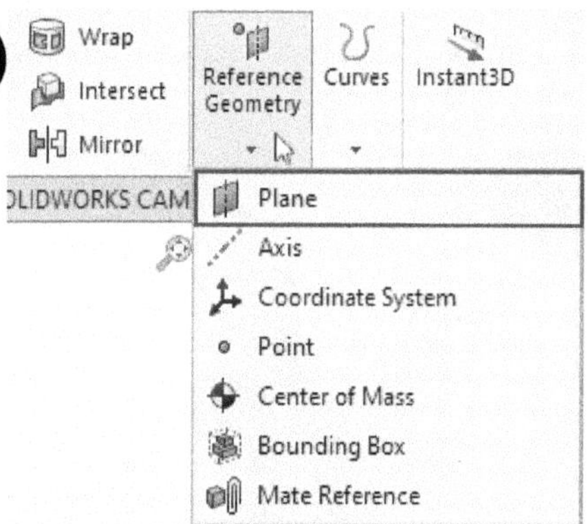

6.73

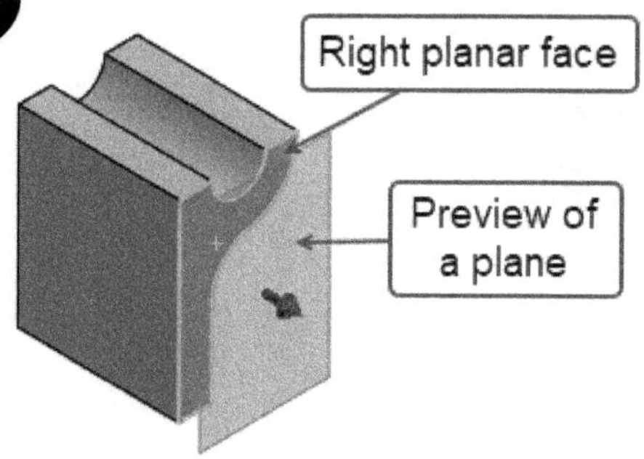

4. Enter **10** in the **Offset distance** field of the **First Reference** rollout in the PropertyManager and then select the **Flip offset** check box to flip the direction of the plane.

5. Click on the green tick-mark ✓ in the PropertyManager. The offset reference plane is created, see Figure 6.74.

   After creating the reference plane, create the second feature of the model.

6. Invoke the Sketching environment by selecting the newly created reference plane as the sketching plane. The model is oriented normal to the viewing direction.

7. Create the sketch of the second feature and then apply the required dimensions to the sketch, see Figure 6.75.

6.74

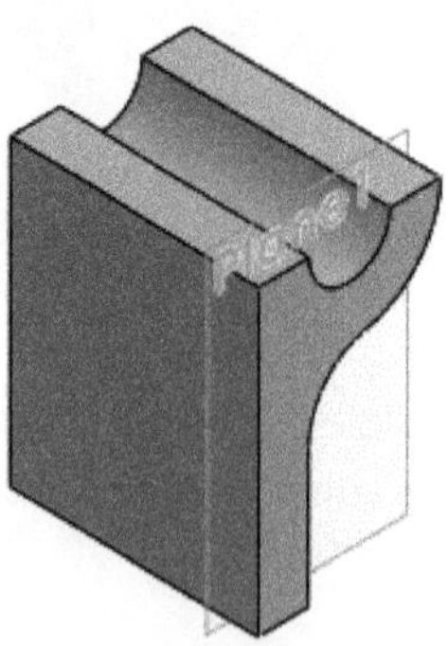

6.75

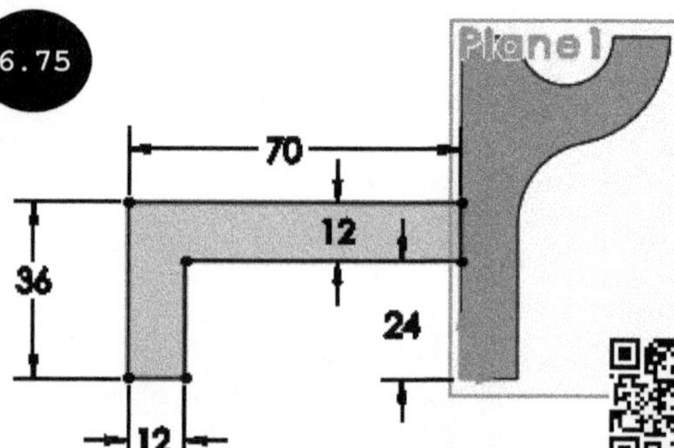

8. Click on the **Features** tab in the CommandManager to display the tools of the **Features CommandManager**.

9. Click on the **Extruded Boss/Base** tool in the **Features CommandManager**. The **Boss-Extrude PropertyManager** and the preview of the extruded feature appear. Next, change the orientation of the model to isometric.

10. Ensure that the **Blind** option is selected in the **End Condition** drop-down list in the **Direction 1** rollout of the PropertyManager

11. Click on the **Reverse Direction** button in the **Direction 1** rollout to reverse the direction of extrusion similar to the one shown in Figure 6.76.

12. Enter **50** in the **Depth** field of the **Direction 1** rollout and then press ENTER. Next, click on the green tick-mark in the PropertyManager. The extruded feature is created, see Figure 6.77.

6.76

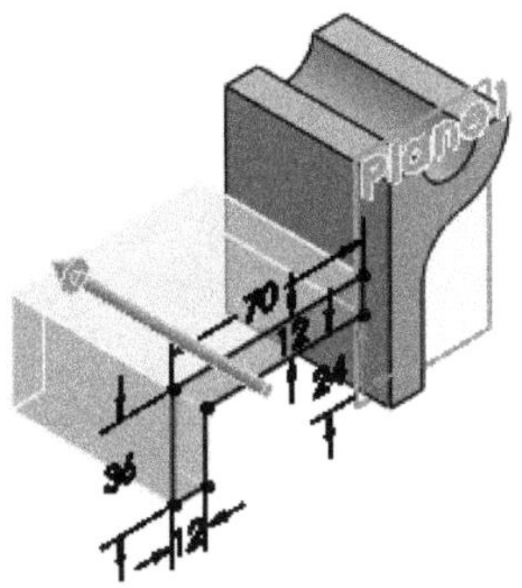

6.77

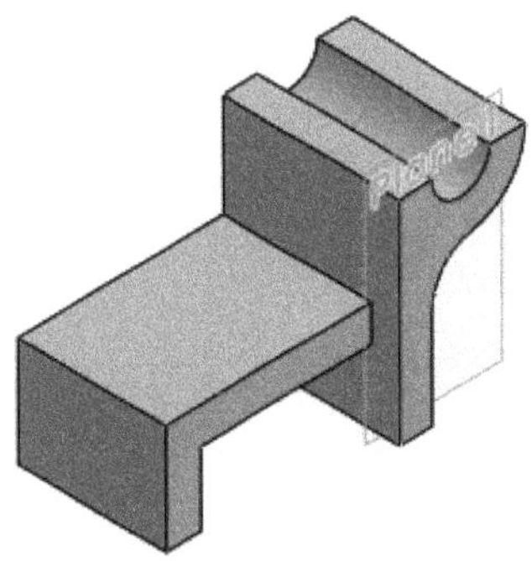

Section 6: Creating the Third Feature

To create the third feature of the model, you need to create a reference plane in the middle of the second feature.

1. Invoke the **Reference Geometry** flyout in the **Features CommandManager**, see Figure 6.78.

2. Click on the **Plane** tool in this flyout. The **Plane PropertyManager** appears.

3. Select the right planar face of the second feature as the first reference. The preview of an offset reference plane appears in the graphics area, see Figure 6.79.

6.78

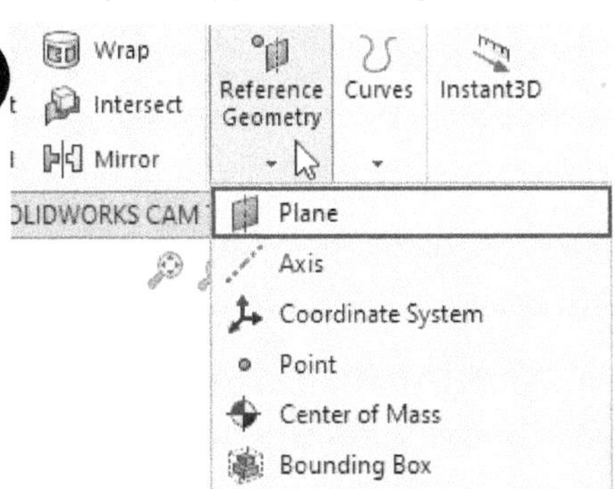

6.79

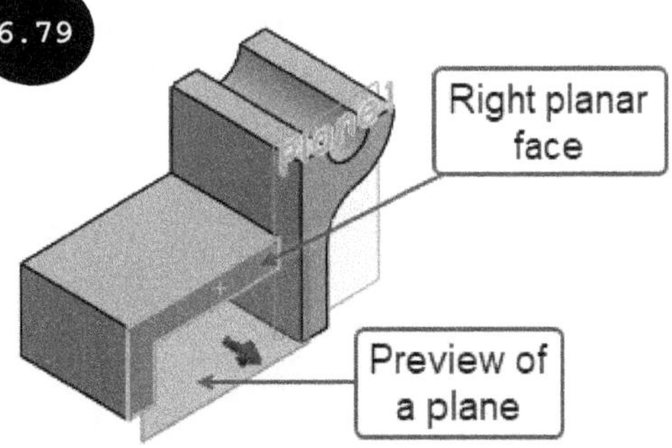

4. Rotate the model such that the left planar face of the second feature can be viewed in the graphics area, see Figure 6.80.

Tip: To rotate the model, right-click in the graphics area and then click on **Zoom/Pan/Rotate > Rotate View** in the shortcut menu that appears. Next, drag the cursor in the graphics area by pressing and holding the left mouse button. Once the required view of the model has been achieved, exit the **Rotate View** tool by pressing the ESC key. Alternatively, you can rotate the model by dragging the cursor while pressing the middle mouse button.

5. Click on the left planar face of the second feature as the second reference for creating the plane. A preview of the reference plane in the middle of the two selected faces appears in the graphics area, see Figure 6.81.

6.80

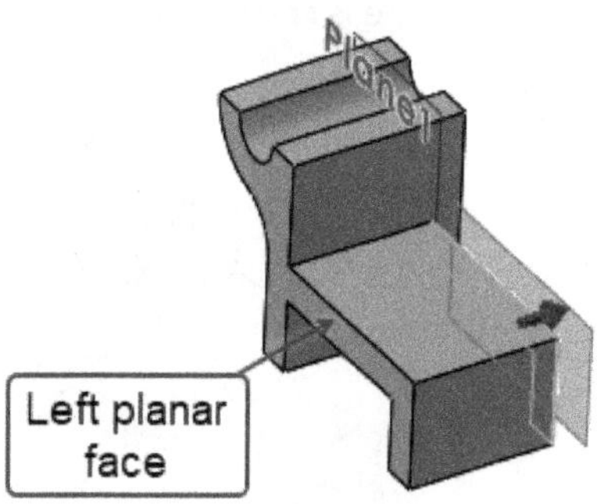

6.81

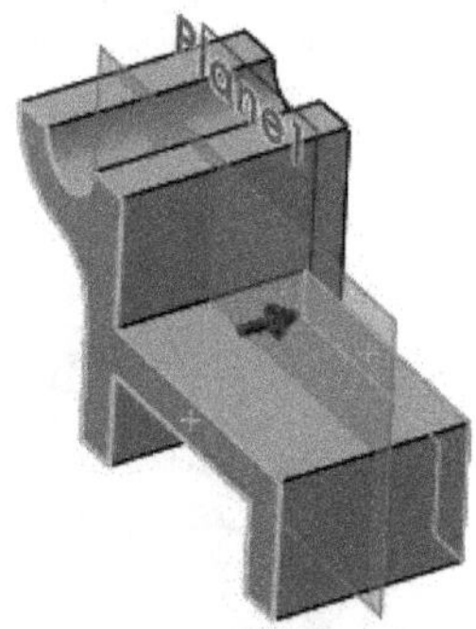

6. Change the view orientation of the model to isometric.

7. Click on the green-tick mark ✓ in the PropertyManager. The reference plane at the middle of the two selected faces is created.

   After creating the reference plane, you can create the third feature of the model. This feature can be created easily by using the **Rib** tool. You will learn about the **Rib** tool in later chapters. In this tutorial, you will create the feature by using the **Extruded Boss/Base** tool.

8. Invoke the Sketching environment by selecting the newly created reference plane as the sketching plane. The model is oriented normal to the viewing direction.

9. Create the closed sketch of the third feature (three line entities), see Figure 6.82. The entities of the sketch shown in Figure 6.82 have been created by taking reference to the vertices of the existing features of the model.

10. Click on the **Features** tab in the CommandManager to display the tools of the **Features CommandManager**.

11. Click on the **Extruded Boss/Base** tool in the **Features CommandManager**. The **Boss-Extrude PropertyManager** and a preview of the extruded feature appear. Next, change the orientation of the model to isometric.

12. Invoke the **End Condition** drop-down list in the **Direction 1** rollout, (see Figure 6.83) and then click on the **Mid Plane** option.

6.82

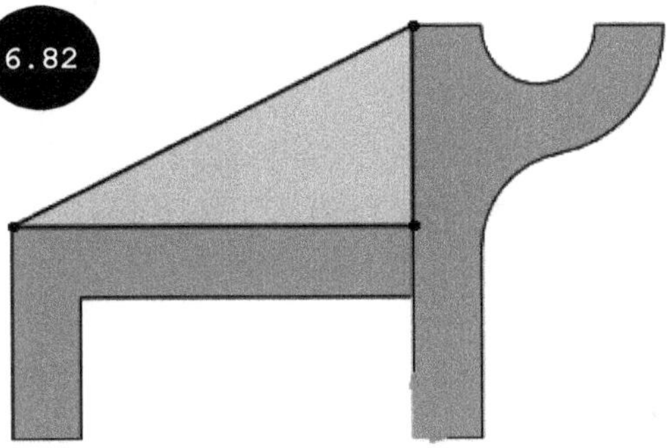

6.83

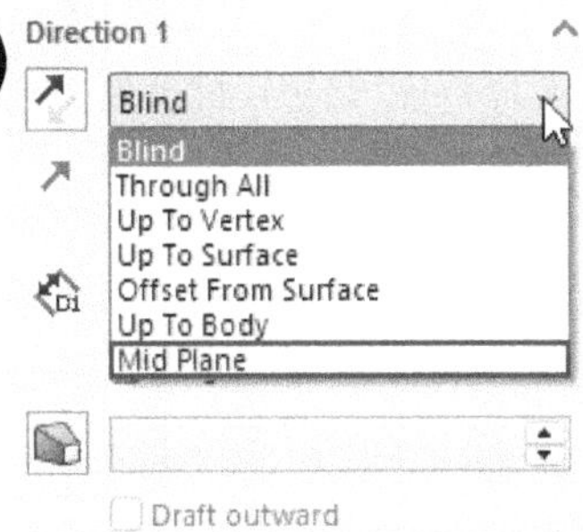

Note: In figure 6.82, the display of **Plane 1** and **Plane 2** is turned off for the clarity of image. To do this, click on the plane in the FeatureManager Design Tree. A pop-up toolbar appears. Next, click on the **Hide** tool in the pop-up toolbar.

13. Enter **8** in the **Depth** field of the **Direction 1** rollout and then press ENTER. The depth of extrusion is added symmetrically to both sides of the sketching plane, see Figure 6.84.

14. Click on the green tick-mark in the PropertyManager. The extruded feature is created. Figure 6.85 shows the final model after creating all its features.

6.84

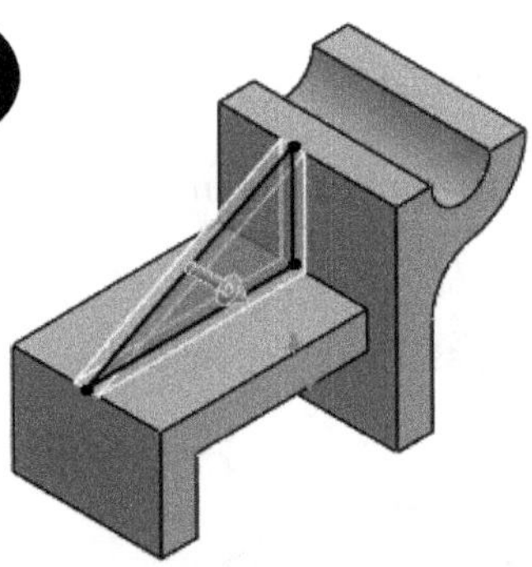

6.85

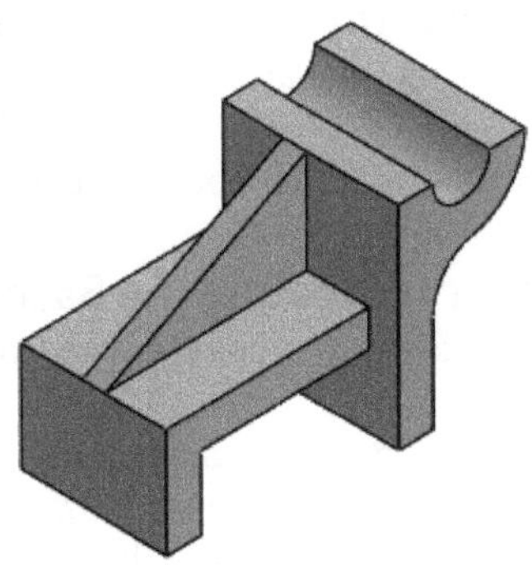

Section 7: Saving the Model

1. Click on the **Save** tool of the **Standard** toolbar. The **Save As** dialog box appears.

2. Browse to the Chapter 6 folder of SOLIDWORKS and then save the model with the name Tutorial 2. You need to create the Chapter 6 folder inside the SOLIDWORKS folder, if not created earlier.

Tutorial 3

Create a model, as shown in Figure 6.86. All dimensions are in mm.

6.86

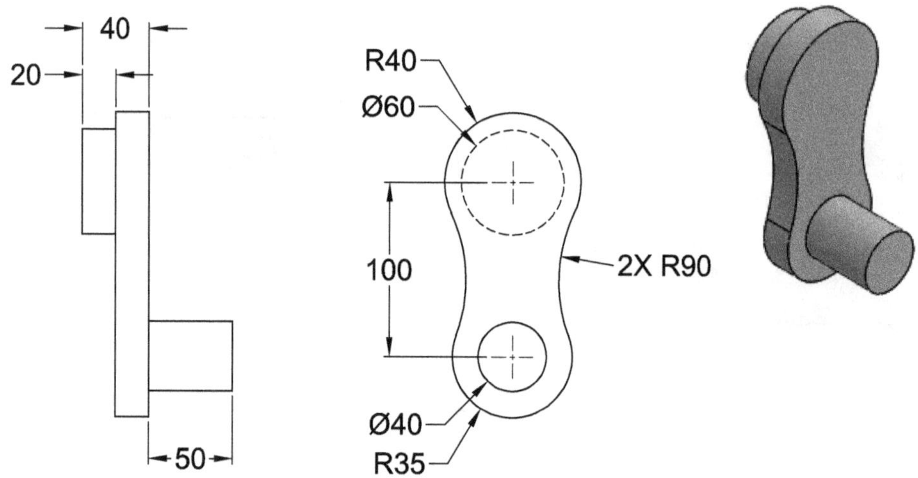

Section 1: Starting SOLIDWORKS

1. Start SOLIDWORKS by double-clicking on the SOLIDWORKS icon on your desktop. The initial screen of SOLIDWORKS appears along with the **Welcome** dialog box.

Note: If SOLIDWORKS is already open and the **Welcome** dialog box does not appear on the screen, you can invoke it by clicking on the **Welcome to SOLIDWORKS tool** in the **Standard** toolbar.

Section 2: Invoking the Part Modeling Environment

1. Click on the **Part** button in the **Welcome** dialog box. The Part modeling environment is invoked.

2. Ensure that the metric unit system is selected as the unit system for this document.

Section 3: Creating the Base/First Feature

1. Invoke the Sketching environment by selecting the Right plane as the sketching plane.

2. Create a circle and apply the diameter dimension, see Figure 6.87. Ensure that the center point of the circle is at the origin.

3. Click on the **Features** tab in the CommandManager and then click on the **Extruded Boss/Base** tool. A preview of the extruded feature appears in the graphics area.

6.87

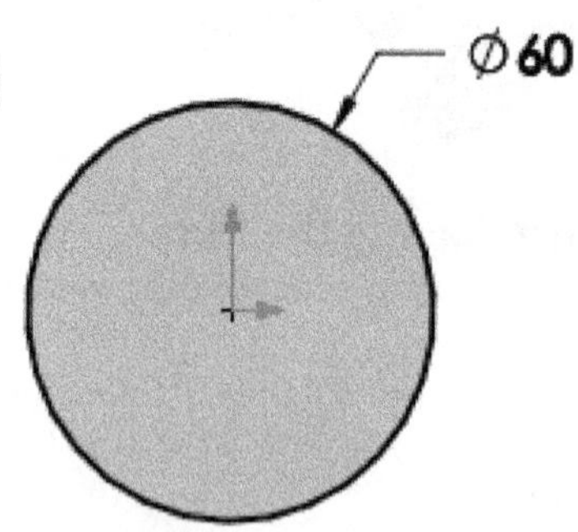

4. Enter **20** in the **Depth** field of the **Direction 1** rollout and then press ENTER.

5. Click on the green tick-mark ✓ in the PropertyManager. The extruded feature is created, see Figure 6.88.

6.88

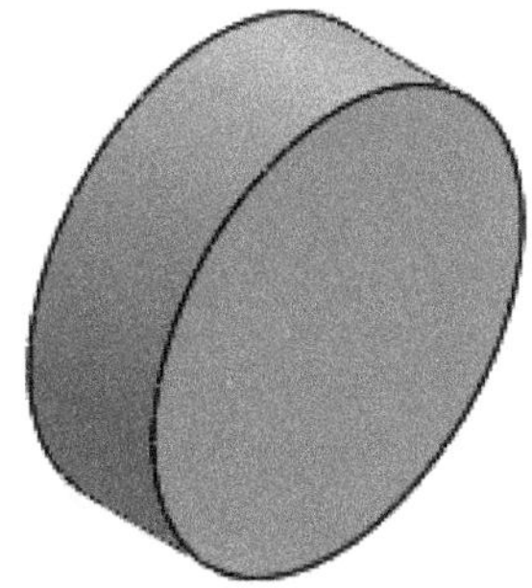

Section 4: Creating the Second Feature

1. Invoke the Sketching environment by selecting the right planar face of the base feature as the sketching plane, see Figure 6.89. The model is oriented normal to the viewing direction.

2. Create the sketch of the second feature and then apply the required relations and dimensions, see Figure 6.90.

6.89

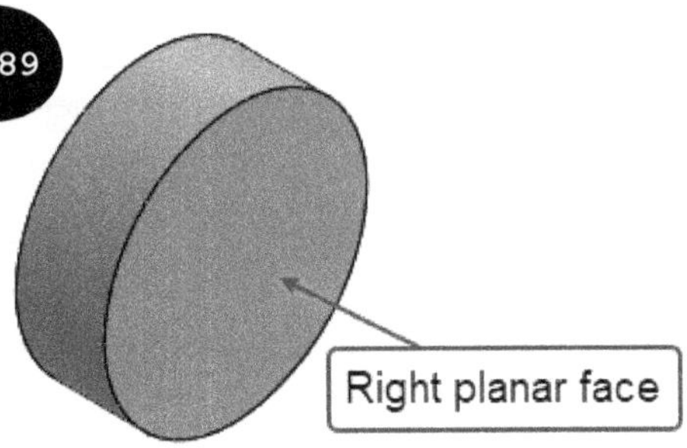

6.90

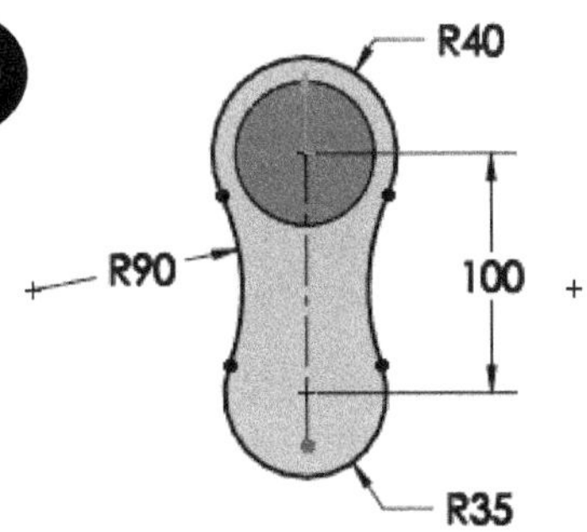

3. Click on the **Features** tab and then click on the **Extruded Boss/Base** tool. The **Boss-Extrude PropertyManager** and the preview of the extruded feature appear. Next, change the orientation of the model to isometric, see Figure 6.91.

6.91

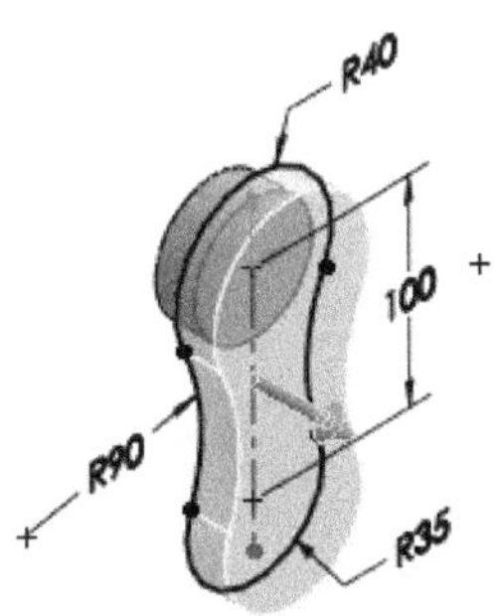

4. Enter **20** in the **Depth** field of the **Direction 1** rollout and then press ENTER.

5. Click on the green tick-mark ✓ in the PropertyManager. The extruded feature is created, see Figure 6.92.

6.92

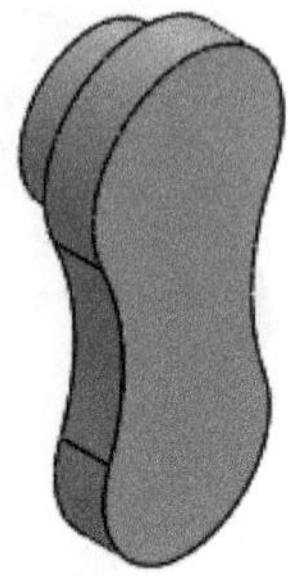

Section 5: Creating the Third Feature

1. Invoke the Sketching environment by selecting the right planar face of the second feature as the sketching plane. The model is oriented normal to the viewing direction.

2. Create a circle and apply the diameter dimension, see Figure 6.93. Ensure that a concentric relation is applied between the circle and the bottom semi-circular edge of the second feature.

3. Click on the **Features** tab and then click on the **Extruded Boss/Base** tool. The **Boss-Extrude PropertyManager** and the preview of the extruded feature appear. Next, change the orientation of the model to isometric.

4. Enter **50** in the **Depth** field of the **Direction 1** rollout and then press ENTER.

5. Click on the green tick-mark ✓ in the PropertyManager. The extruded feature is created. Figure 6.94 shows the final model after creating all its features.

6.93

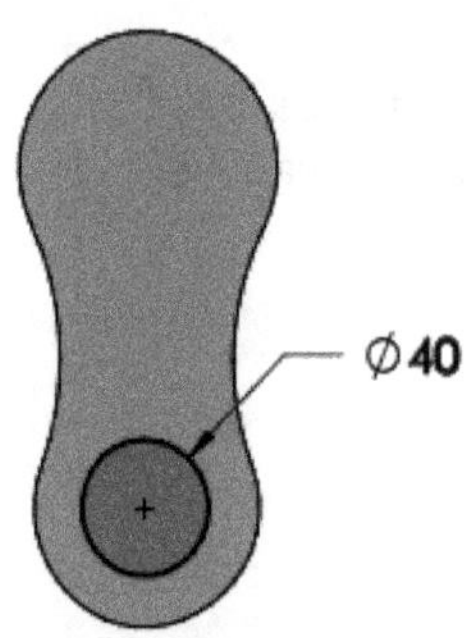

6.94

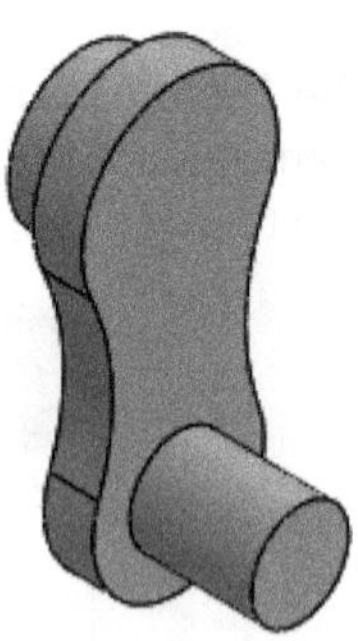

Section 6: Saving the Model

1. Click on the **Save** tool in the **Standard** toolbar. The **Save As** dialog box appears.

2. Browse to the Chapter 6 folder of the SOLIDWORKS folder and then save the model with the name Tutorial 3.

Hands-on Test Drive 1

Create the model, as shown in Figure 6.95. All dimensions are in mm.

6.95

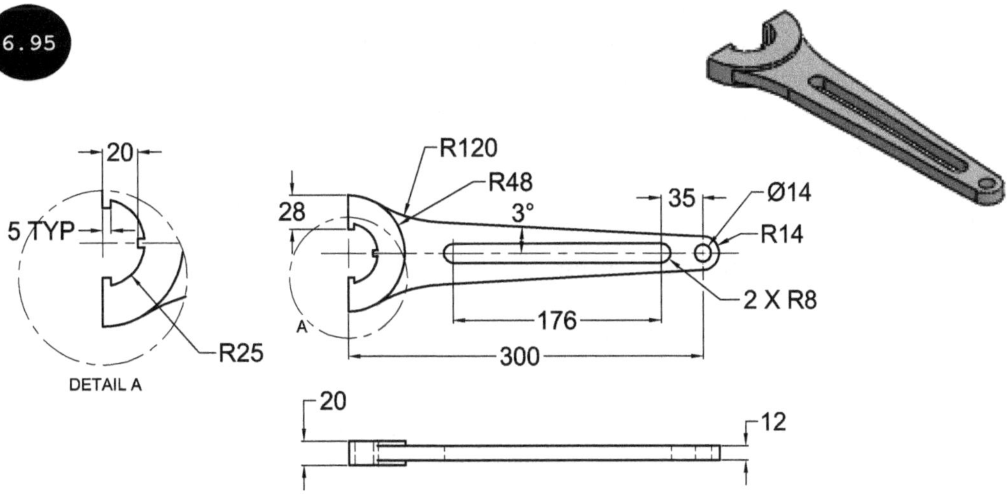

Hands-on Test Drive 2

Create the model, as shown in Figure 6.96. All dimensions are in mm.

6.96

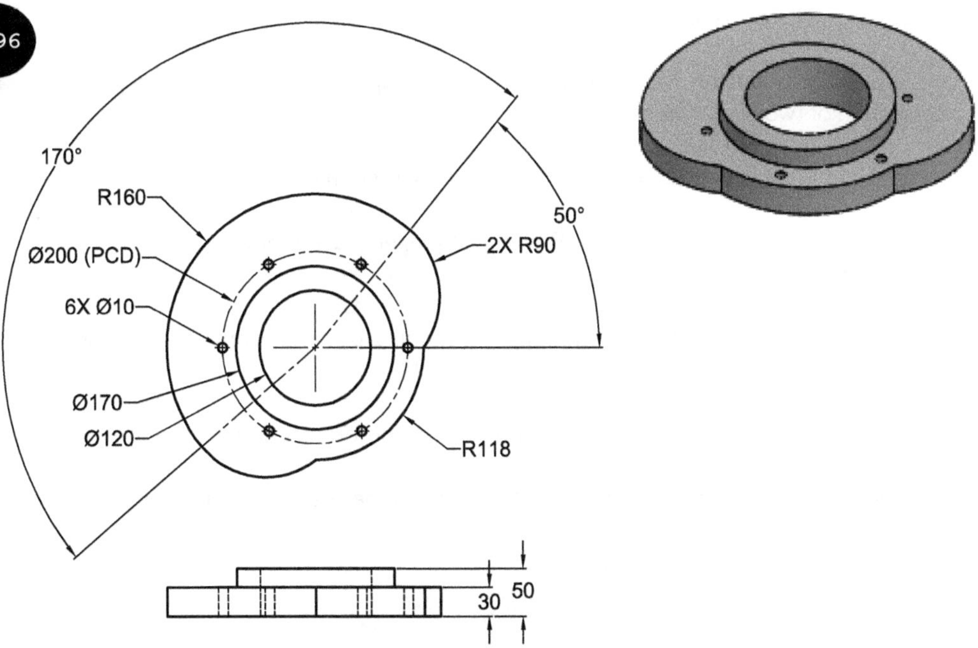

Summary

In this chapter, you learned that the three default planes may not always suffice for creating models with multiple features. To address this, methods for creating additional reference planes were explained. You also explored techniques for creating a reference axis, reference coordinate system, and reference point using their respective tools. Furthermore, the chapter discussed the method for creating a bounding box, which helps determine the overall size and space of the model, an essential consideration for packaging and shipping products. These skills are fundamental for managing complex designs and ensuring accuracy in the modeling process.

Questions

Complete and verify the following sentences:

- You can create reference planes by using the _________ tool.
- To create a reference plane parallel to a planar face of a model, you need to define two references: the first reference can be a planar face and the second reference can be a _________, _________, or _________.
- To create a reference plane at an angle to a planar face/plane, you need to define two references: the first reference can be a planar face/plane and the second reference can be a _________, _________, or _________.
- The _________ tool is used for creating a reference axis.
- The _________ button in the **Axis PropertyManager** is used for creating an axis at the intersection of two planar faces or planes.
- The _________ tool is used for creating coordinate systems.
- The _________ button in the **Point PropertyManager** is used for creating a point at the center of a planar or a non-planar face.
- The _________ tool is used for creating a bounding box that completely encloses a model within a minimum volume.
- In SOLIDWORKS, you can create a reference point at the intersection of two entities. (True/False)
- You cannot select a planar face of existing features as the sketching plane for creating a feature. (True/False)

CHAPTER

7

Advanced Modeling - I

This chapter discusses the following topics:

- Exploring Advanced Options of Extruded Boss/Base Tool
- Exploring Advanced Options of Revolved Boss/Base Tool
- Creating Cut Features
- Working with Different Types of Sketches
- Working with Contours of a Sketch
- Displaying Shaded Sketch Contours
- Projecting Edges onto the Sketching Plane
- Editing a Feature and its Sketch
- Importing 2D DXF or DWG Files
- Displaying the Earlier State of a Model
- Reordering Features of a Model
- Measuring the Distance between Entities
- Assigning an Appearance/Texture
- Applying a Material
- Calculating Mass Properties

In the previous chapters, you learned to create features using the **Extruded Boss/Base and Revolved Boss/Base** tools. This chapter delves into the advanced options of these tools to help you create more complex features. You will also learn how to create cut features using the **Extruded Cut and Revolved Cut** tools.

Additionally, this chapter covers how to work with different types of sketches, measure distances between model entities, assign appearances to models, apply material properties, calculate mass properties, and more. These techniques will equip you with the skills necessary to manage advanced design tasks and improve your modeling capabilities.

Exploring Advanced Options of Extruded Boss/Base Tool

As discussed earlier, when extruding a sketch using the **Extruded Boss/Base** tool, the **Boss-Extrude PropertyManager** appears to the left of the graphics area, see Figure 7.1. Some of the options of this PropertyManager are covered earlier while creating the base feature of a model. The remaining options are discussed next.

Start Condition Drop-down List

The options in the **Start Condition** drop-down list of the **From** rollout are used for defining the start condition of extrusion, see Figure 7.2. The **Sketch Plane** and **Offset** options of this drop-down list are covered earlier while creating base features and the remaining options are discussed next.

7.1

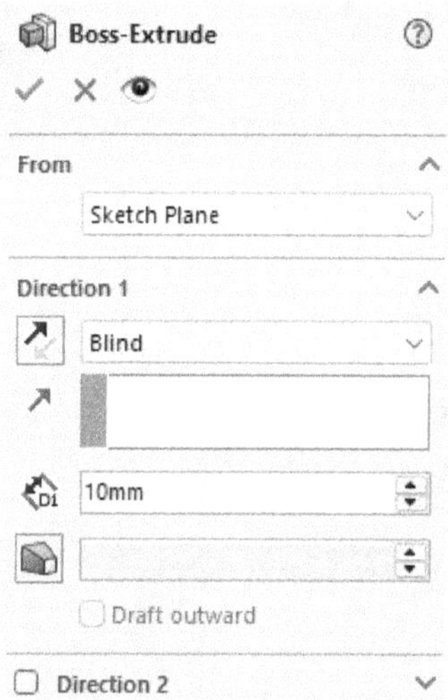

7.2

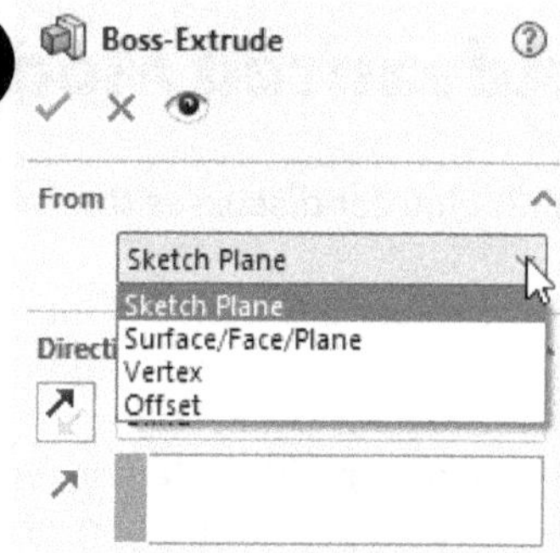

Surface/Face/Plane

The **Surface/Face/Plane** option of the **Start Condition** drop-down list is used to select a surface, a face, or a plane as the start condition of the extrusion. On selecting this option, the **Select A Surface/Face/Plane** field appears below the **Start Condition** drop-down list and is activated by default. As a result, you can select a surface, a face, or a plane as the start condition of the extrusion. Figure 7.3 shows a sketch to be extruded and a face to be selected as the start condition of extrusion. Figure 7.4 shows a preview of the resultant extruded feature after selecting the face as the start condition.

7.3

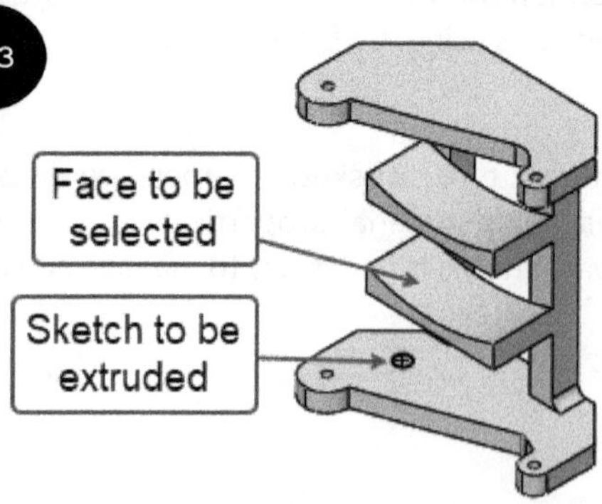

7.4

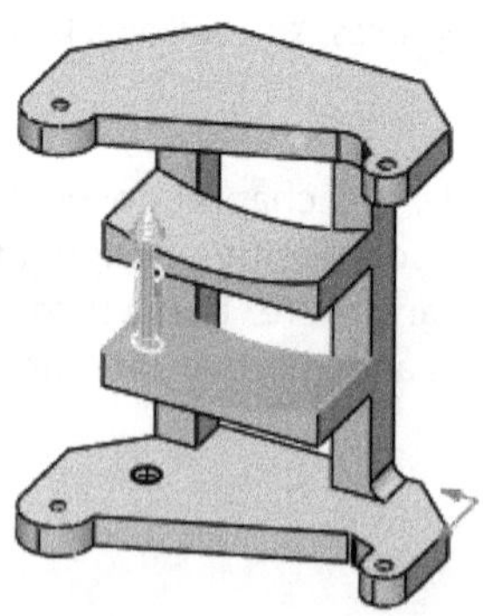

Note: You can select a planar face or a plane as the start condition of the extrusion, even if it does not completely enclose the entire sketch.

Vertex

The **Vertex** option is used to select a vertex of a model as the start condition of the extrusion. On selecting this option, the **Select A Vertex** field appears below the **Start Condition** drop-down list and is activated by default. As a result, you can select a vertex as the start condition of the extrusion, see Figure 7.5.

7.5

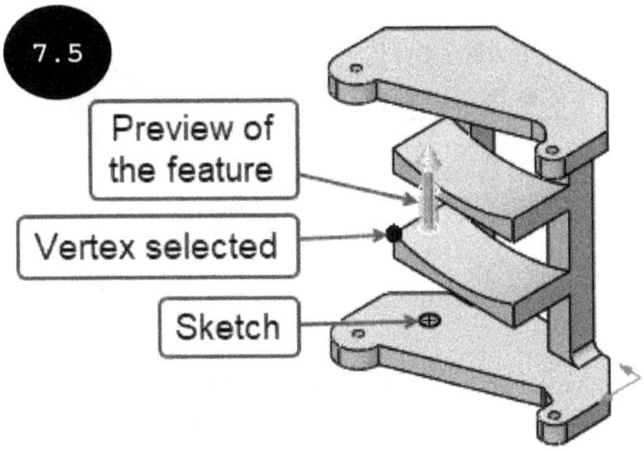

End Condition Drop-down List

The **End Condition** drop-down list of the **Direction 1** rollout is used to define the end condition of the extrusion, see Figure 7.6. The **Blind** and **Mid Plane** options of this drop-down list are discussed earlier while creating base features and the remaining options are discussed next.

Up To Vertex

The **Up To Vertex** option is used to define the end condition or termination of the extrusion by selecting a vertex. On selecting this option, the **Vertex** field becomes available in the rollout and is activated, by default. As a result, you can select a vertex of the model up to which you want to extrude the feature. Figure 7.7 shows a preview of a feature whose end condition is defined by selecting a vertex of the model.

7.6

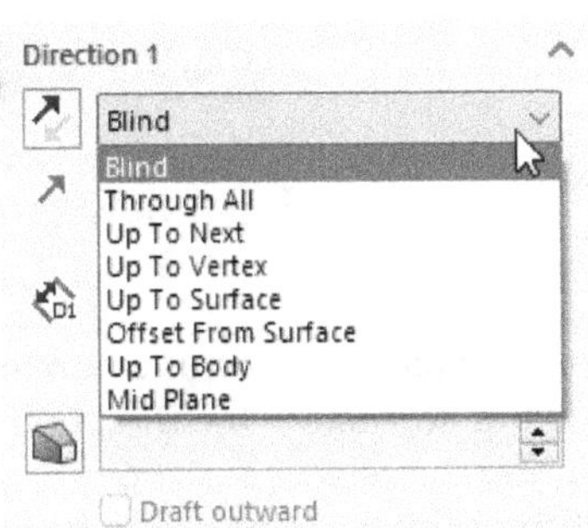

7.7

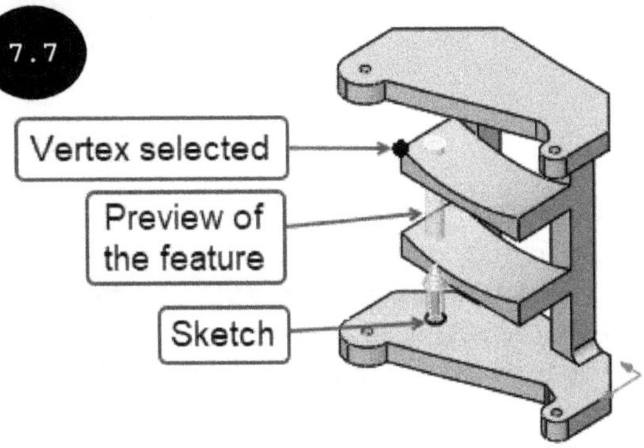

Up To Surface

The **Up To Surface** option is used to define the end condition or termination of the extrusion up to a surface. When you select the **Up To Surface** option, the **Face/Plane** field becomes available in the **Direction 1** rollout and is activated, by default. As a result, you can select a surface, a face, or a plane up to which you want to extrude the feature. Figure 7.8 shows a preview of a feature whose end condition is defined by selecting the face of the model.

7.8

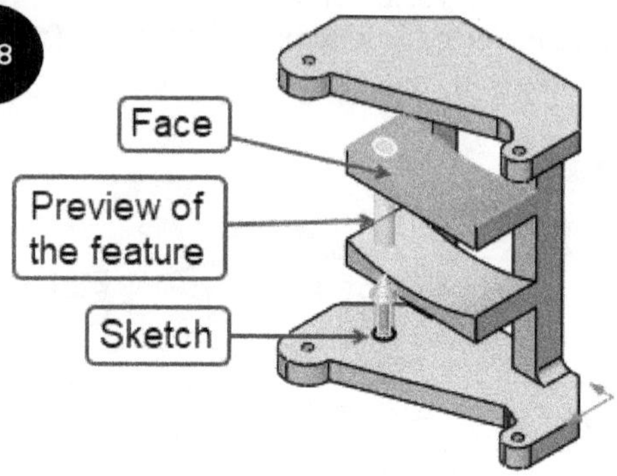

Offset From Surface

The **Offset From Surface** option is used to define the end condition or termination of the extrusion at an offset distance from a surface, see Figure 7.9. When you select the **Offset From Surface** option, the **Face/Plane** and **Offset Distance** fields become available in the **Direction 1** rollout. Select an existing surface, a face, or a plane of the model as the end condition of extrusion and enter the offset distance value in the **Offset Distance** field. Once you enter the offset distance value, the resultant feature is terminated at an offset distance from the selected face. Figure 7.9 shows a preview of a feature whose end condition is defined at an offset distance from the face of the model.

7.9

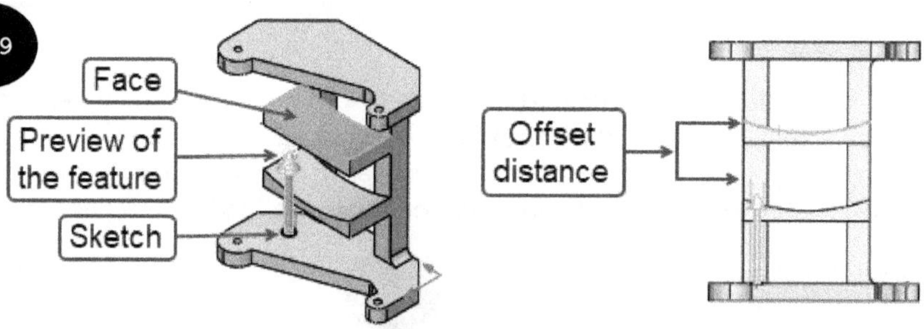

Isometric view Front view

Up To Body

The **Up To Body** option is used to define the end condition or termination of extrusion up to a body. When you select this option, the **Solid/Surface Body** field becomes available in the **Direction 1** rollout of the PropertyManager and is activated, by default. As a result, you can select a solid body or a surface body up to which you want to extrude the feature. Note that this option can be used when multiple bodies are available in the graphics area. You can create bodies in the Part environment by clearing the **Merge result** check box of the PropertyManager, which is discussed next.

Merge result
The **Merge result** check box of the **Direction 1** rollout is used to merge a feature with the existing features of the model. By default, this check box is selected. As a result, the feature of the model being created merges with the existing features of the model. If you clear this check box, the feature being created does not merge with the existing features and a separate body will be created. Note that this check box is not available while creating the base/first feature of a model.

Note: The options in the **Direction 2** rollout of the **Boss-Extrude PropertyManager** are same as those of the **Direction 1** rollout with the only difference that the options of the **Direction 2** rollout are used for specifying the end condition of extrusion in the second direction of the sketching plane.

Exploring Advanced Options of Revolved Boss/Base Tool
As discussed earlier, when revolving a sketch using the **Revolved Boss/Base** tool, the **Revolve PropertyManager** appears to the left of the graphics area, see Figure 7.10. Some of the options in the **Revolve Type** drop-down list of the PropertyManager are discussed earlier while creating the base revolved feature of a model. The remaining options such as **Up To Vertex** and **Up To Surface** of this drop-down list are the same as discussed earlier with the only difference being that these options are used for creating a revolved feature. Figure 7.10 shows the **Revolve PropertyManager** with the expanded **Revolve Type** drop-down list.

7.10

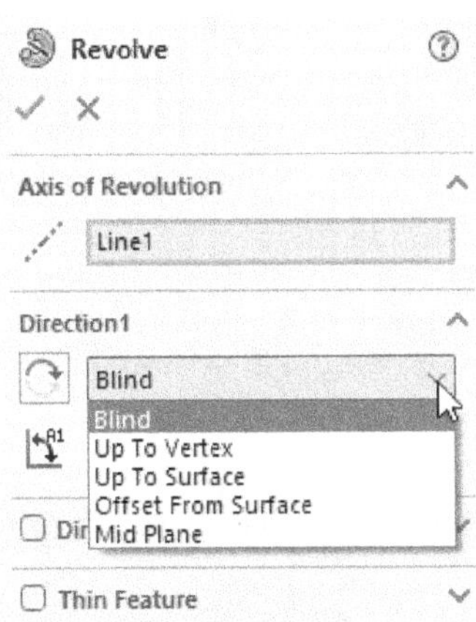

Creating Cut Features
Similar to adding material by extruding and revolving a sketch, you can remove material from a model using the **Extruded Cut** and **Revolved Cut** tools. By using these tools, you can create an extruded cut feature and a revolved cut feature. Both the features are discussed next.

Creating Extruded Cut Features

You can create an extruded cut feature using the **Extruded Cut** tool of the **Features CommandManager**. An extruded cut feature is created by removing material from a model. Note that the geometry of the material removed is defined by the sketch of the cut feature.
Figure 7.11 shows a sketch, which is created on the top planar face of the model and the resultant extruded cut feature.

7.11

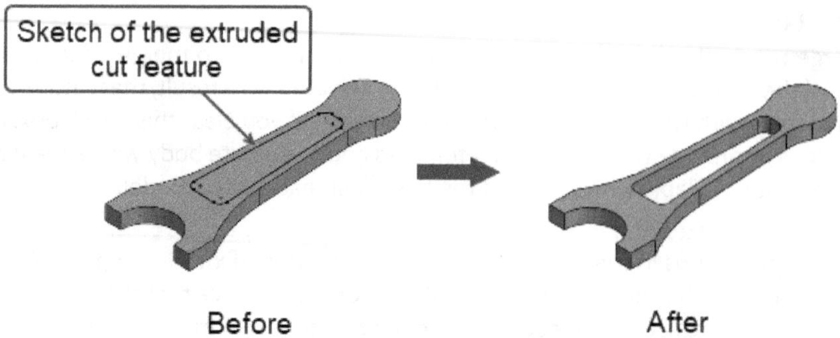

To create an extruded cut feature, click on the **Extruded Cut** tool in the **Features CommandManager**. The **Extrude PropertyManager** appears. Next, select the sketch in the graphics area. A preview of the extruded cut feature appears in the graphics area with default parameters. Also, the **Cut-Extrude PropertyManager** appears on the left of the graphics area, see Figure 7.12. Note that you can select the sketch before or after invoking the **Extruded Cut** tool. The options in the **Cut-Extrude PropertyManager** are used for defining the parameters of the extruded cut feature. These options are the same as those discussed earlier while creating the extruded feature, with the only difference being that these options are used for removing material from the model. You can also flip the side of the material to be removed by using the **Flip side to cut** check box of the PropertyManager, see Figure 7.13. After specifying parameters for creating the extruded cut feature, click on the green tick-mark ✓ in the PropertyManager. The extruded cut feature is created.

7.12

7.13

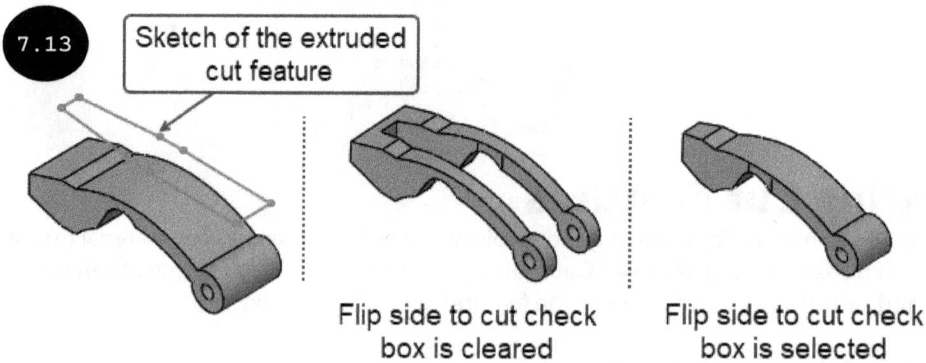

Note: In SOLIDWORKS, similar to creating a thin extruded feature with rounded corners, you can also create a thin extruded cut feature with rounded corners of specified radius value using the **Auto-fillet corners** check box. This check box is available in the **Thin Feature** rollout of the PropertyManager only while creating a thin extruded cut feature using an open sketch.

Creating Revolved Cut Features

You can create a revolved cut feature using the **Revolved Cut** tool. A revolved cut feature is created by removing material from a model by revolving the sketch around an axis of revolution. Note that the sketch to be revolved should be on either side of the axis of revolution. Figure 7.14 shows a sketch to be revolved and Figure 7.15 shows the resultant revolved cut feature. The method for creating a revolved cut feature is discussed below:

7.14

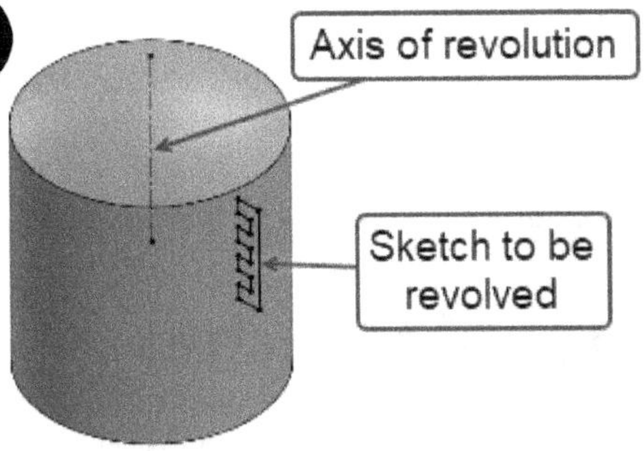

7.15

1. Create a sketch of the revolved cut feature with a centerline as the axis of revolution. After creating the sketch, do not exit the Sketching environment.

2. Click on the **Features** tab in the CommandManager and then click on the **Revolved Cut** tool. A preview of the revolved cut feature appears in the graphics area. Also, the **Cut-Revolve PropertyManager** appears to the left of the graphics area, see Figure 7.16.

7.16

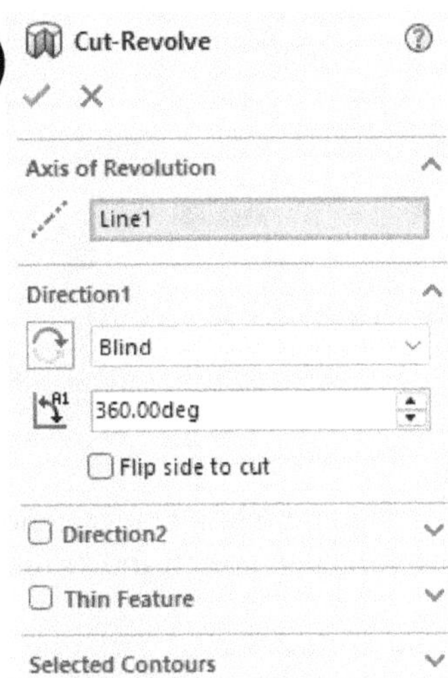

Note: If the sketch has two or more than two centerlines then on invoking the **Revolved Cut** tool, you are prompted to select a centerline as the axis of revolution. After selecting a centerline, a preview of the revolved cut feature appears. You can select a centerline, a linear sketch entity, a linear edge, or an axis as the axis of revolution.

Tip: If you exit the Sketching environment after creating the sketch and the sketch is not selected in the graphics area, then on clicking the **Revolved Cut** tool, the **Revolve PropertyManager** appears. Also, you are prompted to select a sketch to be revolved or a sketching plane to create a sketch of the revolved cut feature. Select a centerline of the sketch as the axis of revolution, a preview of the revolved cut feature appears in the graphics area. Also, the **Cut-Revolve PropertyManager** appears on the left of the graphics area.

3. Specify the required parameters of the revolved cut feature in the PropertyManager. The options in the **Cut-Revolve PropertyManager** are the same as those discussed earlier.

4. Click on the green tick-mark ✓ in the PropertyManager. The revolved cut feature is created.

Working with Different Types of Sketches

It is important to understand different types of sketches and their performance, some of the important types being Closed sketches, Open sketches, Nested sketches, and Intersecting sketches. All these sketches have been discussed next.

Closed Sketches

Closed sketches are those in which all entities are connected end to end without any gaps. On extruding a closed sketch, a solid extruded feature is created. Figure 7.17 shows a closed sketch having one closed contour and its resultant extruded feature.

7.17

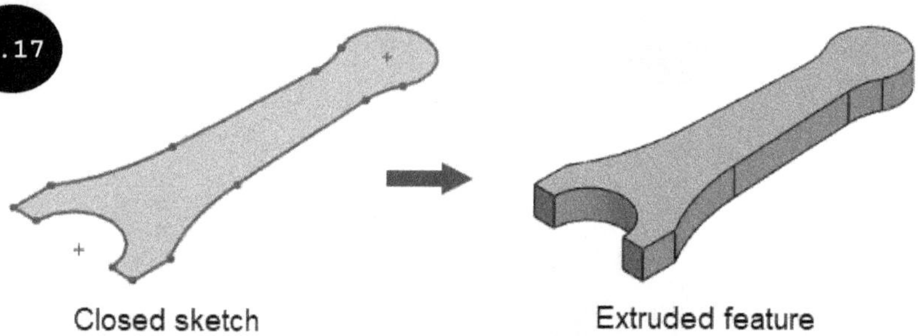

Open Sketches

Open Sketches are those that are open from one or more ends. On extruding an open sketch, a thin feature is created. Figure 7.18 shows an open sketch and its resultant thin extruded feature.

7.18

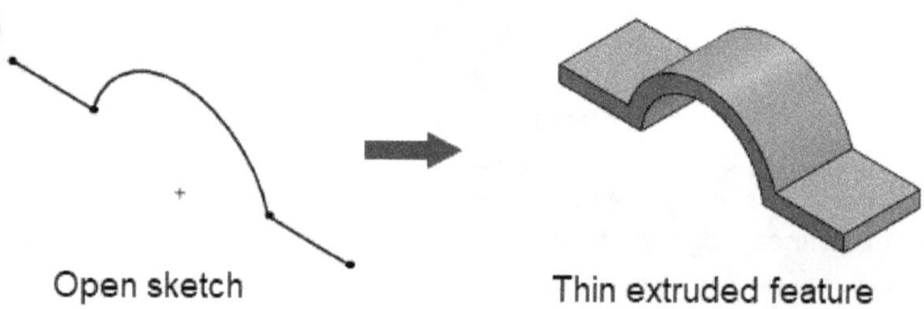

Nested Sketches

Nested sketches are similar to closed sketches with the only difference being that the nested sketches have more than one closed contour. On extruding a nested sketch having multiple closed contours, a solid feature is created by adding the material to the most suitable closed contour of the sketch. Figure 7.19 shows a nested sketch having two closed contours and its resultant extruded feature. Figure 7.20 shows a nested sketch having three closed contours and its resultant extruded feature.

7.19

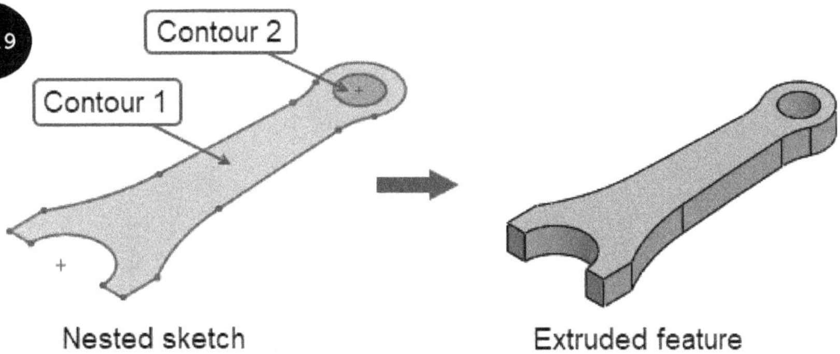

7.20

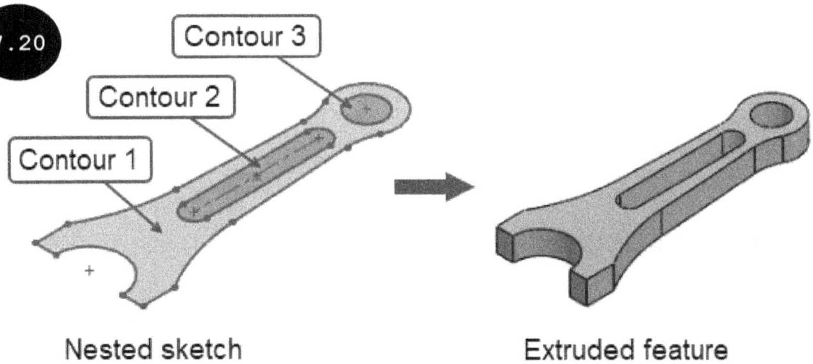

However, on extruding a nested sketch similar to the one shown in Figure 7.21, you will be prompted to select a contour of the sketch to be extruded. You can select the required closed contour of the sketch by using the **Selected Contours** rollout of the PropertyManager, as discussed in earlier chapters. Figure 7.22 shows the preview of an extruded feature that appears on selecting a contour of a nested sketch. You will learn more about extruding different contours or closed regions of a nested sketch later in this chapter.

7.21

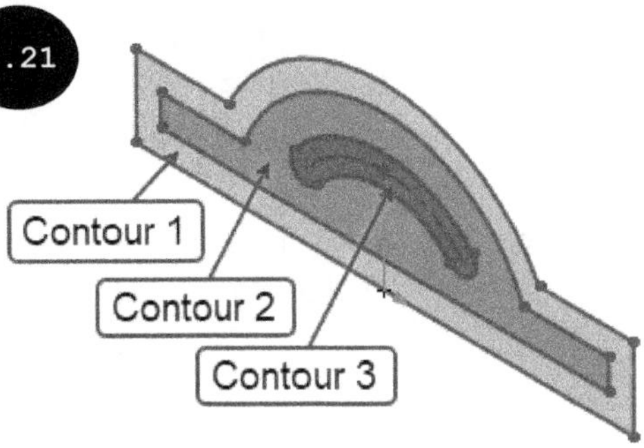

7.22

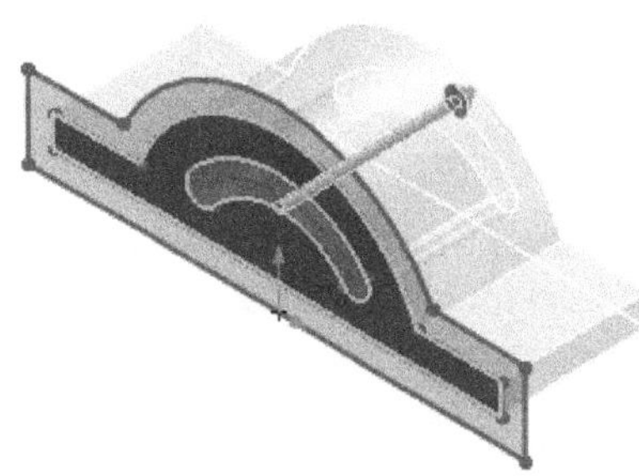

Intersecting Sketches

Intersecting sketches have intersections among the entities of the sketch, see Figure 7.23. On extruding an intersecting sketch, the automatic selection of a closed contour to add material does not take place and you are prompted to select a closed contour of the intersecting sketch to be extruded. You can select the required contour by using the **Selected Contours** rollout of the PropertyManager. Figure 7.23 shows an intersecting sketch and Figure 7.24 shows the preview of an extruded feature by extruding a closed contour of the intersecting sketch. You will learn more about extruding closed contours of a sketch later in this chapter.

7.23

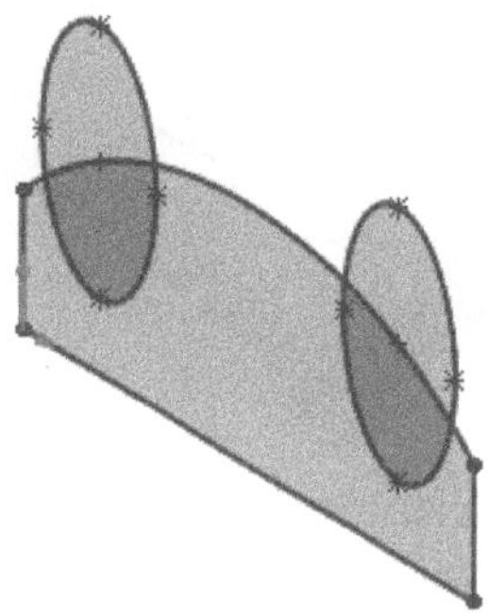

7.24

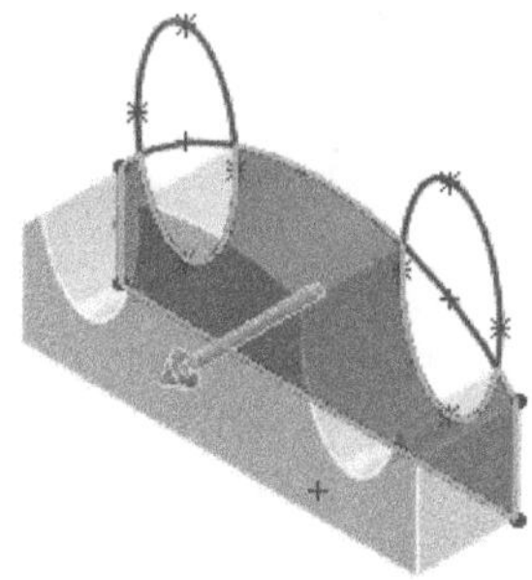

Note: Working with different types of sketches such as closed sketches, open sketches, nested sketches, and intersecting sketches is the same for all tools such as **Extruded Base/Boss** and **Revolved Base/Boss** tools.

Working with Contours of a Sketch

In SOLIDWORKS, you can also create multiple features by using a single sketch that has multiple contours. Figure 7.25 shows a sketch having multiple contours and Figure 7.26 shows the resultant multi-feature model created by using this sketch.

7.25

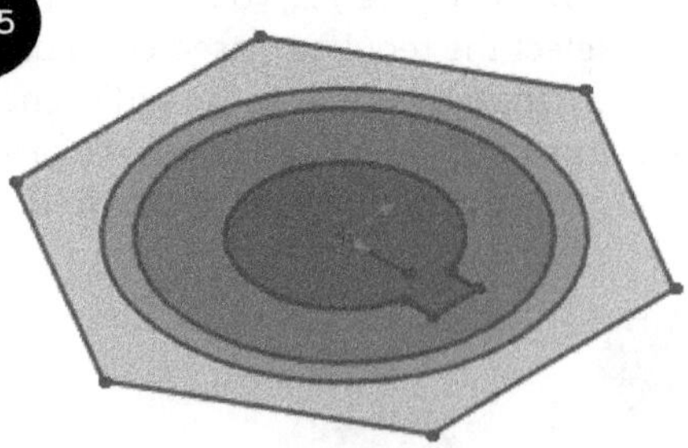

7.26

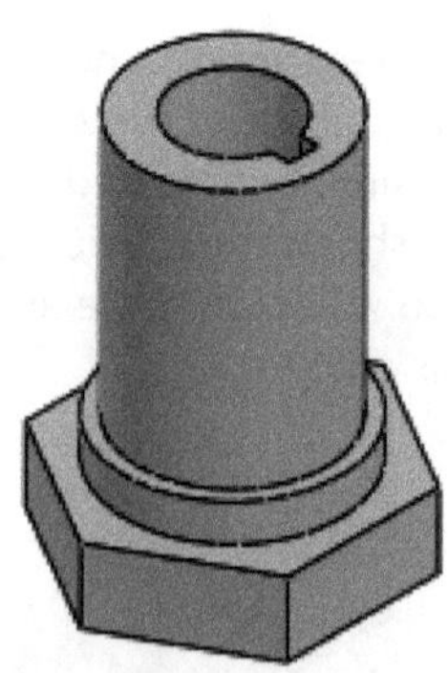

To extrude the contours of a sketch, you can use the **Selected Contours** rollout of the PropertyManager or the **Contour Select Tool**. The methods for creating features by extruding the contours of a sketch are discussed next.

Extruding Contours by using the Selected Contours Rollout

1. Create a sketch that has multiple contours in the Sketching environment, refer to Figure 7.27. Next, exit the Sketching environment.

7.27

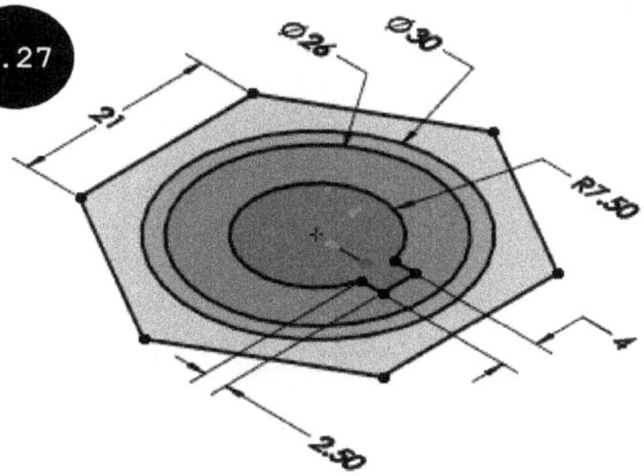

2. Ensure that the sketch is selected in the graphics area. If not selected, click on the sketch name in the FeatureManager Design Tree to select it.

3. Invoke the **Extruded Boss/Base** or **Revolved Boss/Base** tool, as required. Depending upon the tool invoked, the PropertyManager of the respective tool appears with the expanded **Selected Contours** rollout. Also, the cursor changes to a contour cursor.

4. Move the cursor over the contour of the sketch to be selected and then click when it gets highlighted in the graphics area. A preview of the feature appears, see Figure 7.28.

7.28

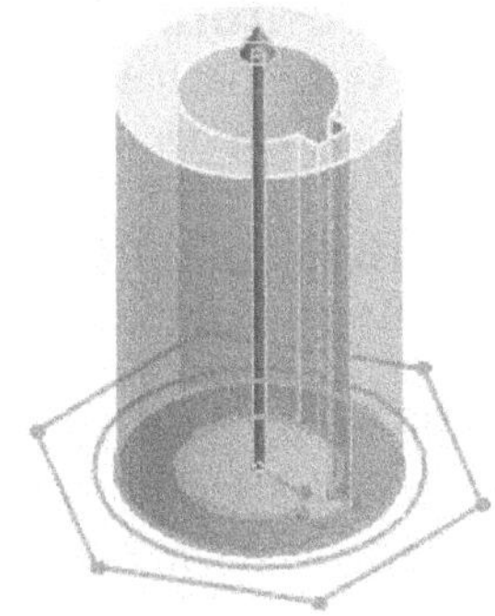

5. Specify parameters for creating the feature in the PropertyManager.

6. Click on the green tick-mark ✓ to confirm the creation of the feature. The feature is created, and its name is added to the FeatureManager Design Tree. Also, the sketch disappears from the graphics area.

   Now, you can use the sketch of the previously created feature to create the other features of the model.

7. Expand the node of the previously created feature in the FeatureManager Design Tree by clicking on the arrow in front of it, see Figure 7.29.

8. Click on the sketch of the previously created feature in the FeatureManager Design Tree. A Pop-up toolbar appears, click on the **Show** tool in it, see Figure 7.29.

7.29

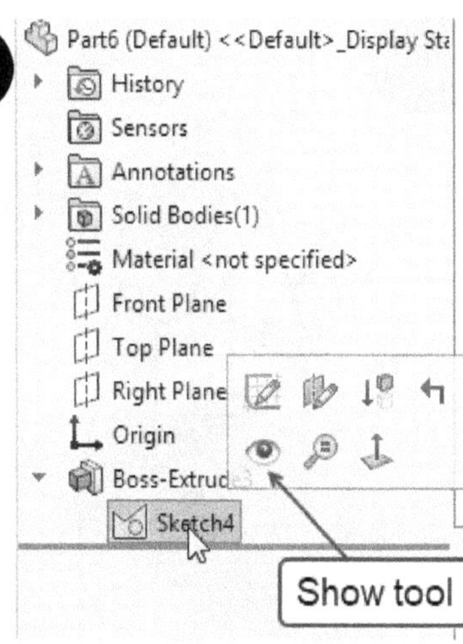

9. Repeat steps 2 to 6 to create the remaining features by using different contours of the same sketch. Figure 7.30 shows a model created by extruding multi-contours of a sketch.

7.30

Note: In Figure 7.30, the sketch has been hidden. To hide the sketch, click on the sketch in the graphics area. A Pop-up toolbar appears. Next, click on the **Hide** tool.

Extruding Contours by using the Contour Select Tool

1. Create a sketch that has multiple contours in the Sketching environment and then do not exit the Sketching environment. Next, change the orientation of the model to isometric.

2. Press and hold the ALT key in the graphics area. The **Contour Select Tool** gets activated and the cursor changes to the contour cursor.

3. Move the cursor over the contour to be extruded and then click the left mouse button when the contour gets highlighted in the graphics area. The **Extruded Boss/Base** tool appears near the cursor, see Figure 7.31.

4. Click on the **Extruded Boss/Base** tool that appears near the cursor in the graphics area. The preview of the feature appears in the graphics area with default parameters, see Figure 7.32. Also, the **Boss-Extrude PropertyManager** appears on the left of the graphics area.

7.31

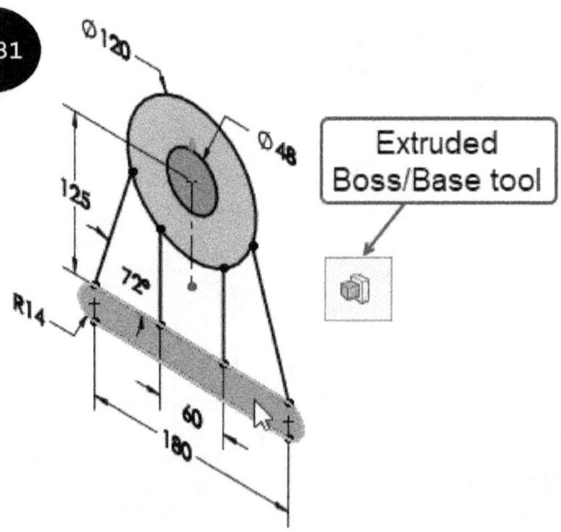

7.32

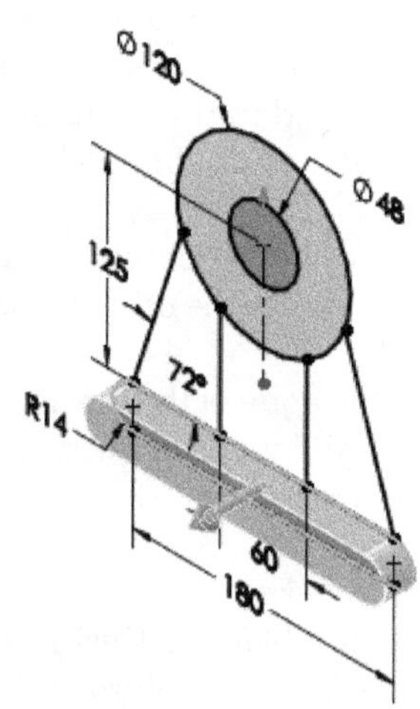

5. Specify parameters for creating the feature and then click on the green tick-mark ✓ in the PropertyManager. The feature is created and its name is added to the FeatureManager Design Tree. Also, the sketch disappears from the graphics area.

Note: Alternatively, to invoke the **Contour Select Tool**, right-click in the graphics area. A shortcut menu appears. Expand the shortcut menu by clicking on the double arrows available at its bottom. Next, click on **Contour Select Tool** in the expanded shortcut menu. You can invoke the **Contour Select Tool** from the shortcut menu in the Sketching environment as well as in the Part modeling environment.

Now, you can use the sketch of the previously created feature to create the other features of the model.

6. Expand the node of the previously created feature in the FeatureManager Design Tree. Next, click on the sketch of the feature and then click on the **Show** tool in the Pop-up toolbar that appears, see Figure 7.33. The display of the sketch gets turned on in the graphics area.

7.33

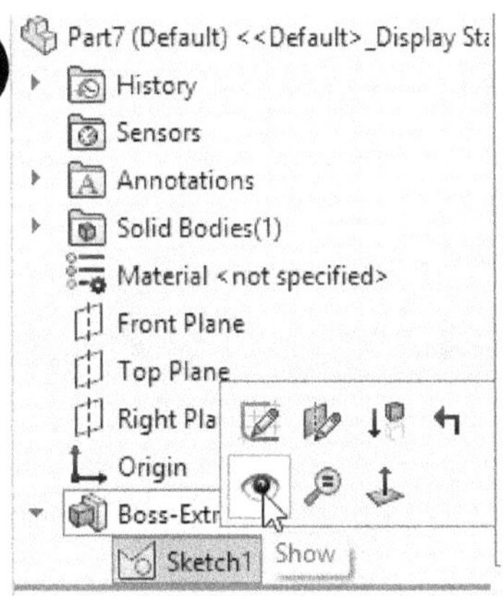

7. Right-click in the graphics area and then expand the shortcut menu that appears by clicking on the double arrows available below it.

8. Click on the **Contour Select Tool** in the expanded shortcut menu, see Figure 7.34. The **Contour Select Tool** gets activated and the cursor is changed to the contour cursor.

9. Move the cursor toward the sketch and then click on it. Next, move the cursor over the required contour of the sketch and then click on it when it gets highlighted in the graphics area.

10. Click on the **Extruded Boss/Base** tool in the **Features CommandManager**. A preview of the feature appears in the graphics area.

11. Specify parameters for creating the feature in the PropertyManager and then click on the green tick-mark ✓ in the PropertyManager. The feature is created and its name is added to the FeatureManager Design Tree.

12. Repeat steps 7 to 11 to create the remaining features by using different contours of the same sketch. Figure 7.35 shows a model created by using multi-contours of a sketch.

7.34

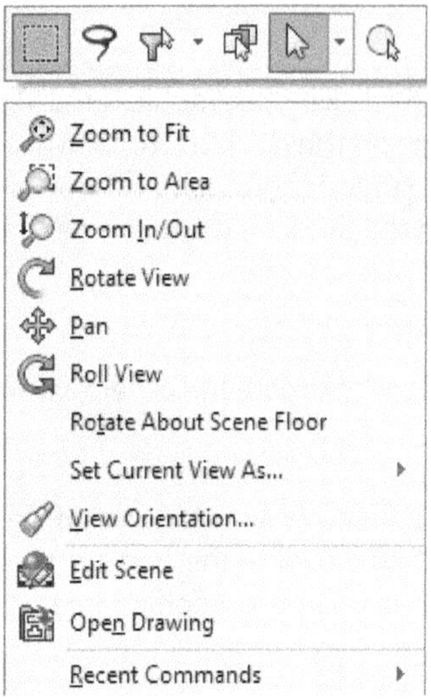

7.35

Note: In Figure 7.35, the sketch has been hidden. To hide the sketch, click on the sketch in the graphics area. A Pop-up toolbar appears. Next, click on the **Hide** tool in the toolbar.

Displaying Shaded Sketch Contours

In SOLIDWORKS, the closed contours of a sketch are displayed in different blue shades (lightest to darkest blue shades), see Figure 7.36. In this figure, the outermost circle has the lightest blue shade and the innermost circle has the darkest blue shade. It helps to easily identify whether the geometry is fully closed or not.

7.36

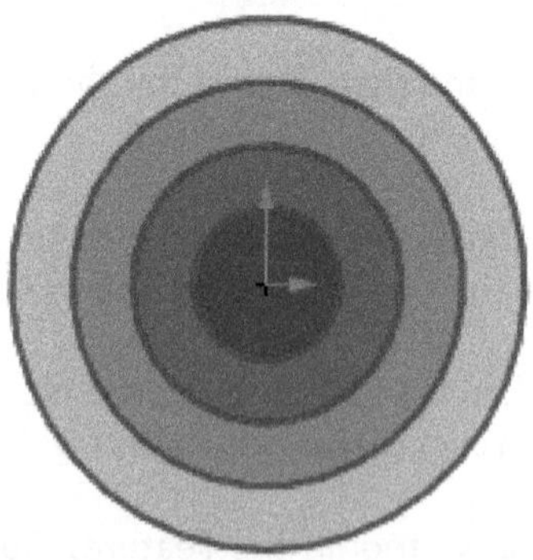

Note that if the geometry is not fully closed then it will not be displayed in a blue shade. You can turn on or off the display of shaded sketch contours in the Sketching environment by using the **Shaded Sketch Contours** tool, refer to Figure 7.37. By default, the **Shaded Sketch Contours** tool is activated in the **Sketch CommandManager**. As a result, the display of shaded sketch contours is turned on. To turn off the display of shaded sketch contours, click on the **Shaded Sketch Contours** tool in the **Sketch CommandManager**, see Figure 7.37.

7.37

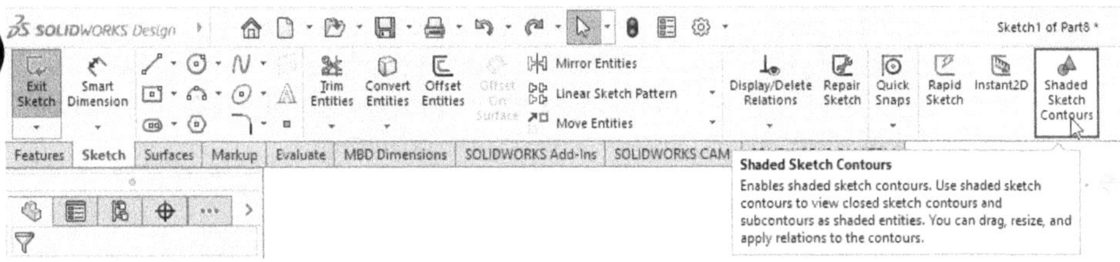

Projecting Edges onto the Sketching Plane

In SOLIDWORKS, while sketching, you can project edges of the existing features onto the current sketching plane by using the **Convert Entities** tool, see Figure 7.38. You can also project the edges of a body or a component onto the current sketching plane by using the **Silhouette Entities** tool. Besides, you can project the geometries of the existing features that intersect with the currently active sketching plane by using the **Intersection Curve** tool. All these tools are discussed next.

7.38

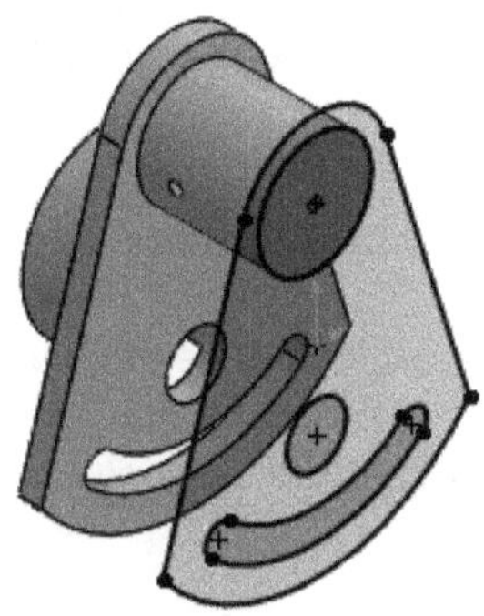

Projecting Edges of Existing Features

Convert Entities

To project the edges of the existing features onto the current sketching plane, click on the **Convert Entities** tool in the **Sketch CommandManager**. The **Convert Entities PropertyManager** appears, see Figure 7.39. The options in the PropertyManager are discussed next.

7.39

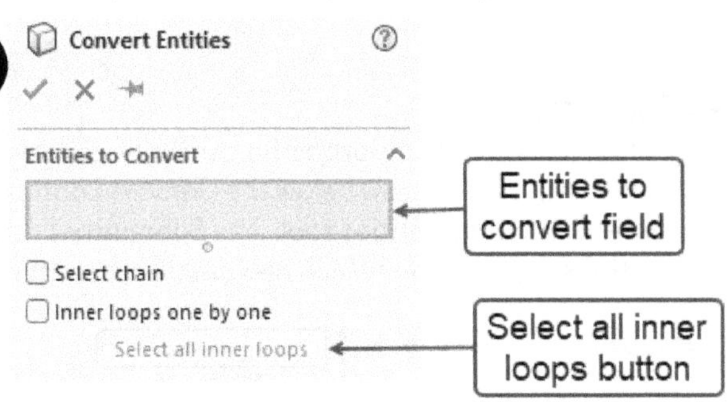

Entities to Convert

The **Entities to Convert** field is used to select edges, faces, or sketch entities to be projected onto the current sketching plane. By default, this field is activated. As a result, you can select edges, faces, or sketch entities by clicking the left mouse button.

Note: On selecting a face, you can project all its outer or inner loops onto the current sketching plane. By default, the edges of the outer loop of the face will be projected onto the current sketching plane. To project the edges of the inner loops of the face, you need to click on the **Select all inner loops** button in the PropertyManager.

Select chain
The **Select chain** check box is used to select all contiguous entities of a selected entity.

Inner loops one by one
The **Inner loops one by one** check box allows you to select the inner loops of the face one by one.

Select all inner loops
The **Select all inner loops** button is used to select all inner loops of the selected face. Note that this button is enabled only after selecting the face of a model. As soon as you click on the **Select all inner loops** button, the edges of all inner loops of the face get selected for projection.

For Construction
The **For Construction** check box allows you to converts the selected edges into construction geometry.

After selecting edges, faces, or sketch entities to be projected, click on the green tick-mark ✓ in the PropertyManager. The selected edges are projected onto the current sketching plane as sketch entities. Now, you can convert the sketch into a feature by using the feature modeling tools such as **Extruded Boss/Base** and **Revolved Boss/Base**.

Note: You can select edges, faces, or sketch entities of the existing features of a model before or after invoking the **Convert Entities** tool. However, if you select a face to be projected before invoking the **Convert Entities** tool, then only the edges of the outer loop of the selected face get projected onto the current sketching plane.

Projecting Edges of a Body
You can project the edges of an existing body onto the current sketching plane by using the **Silhouette Entities** tool. To do this, click on the arrow below the **Convert Entities** tool to invoke a flyout, see Figure 7.40. Next, click on the **Silhouette Entities** tool. The **Silhouette Entities PropertyManager** appears, see Figure 7.41. The options in the PropertyManager are discussed next.

7.40

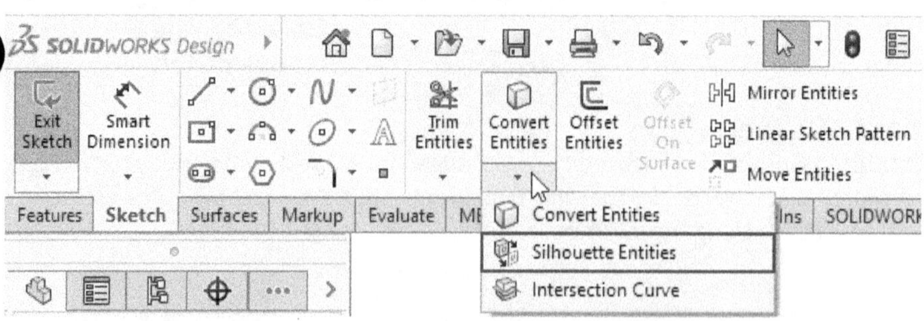

7.41

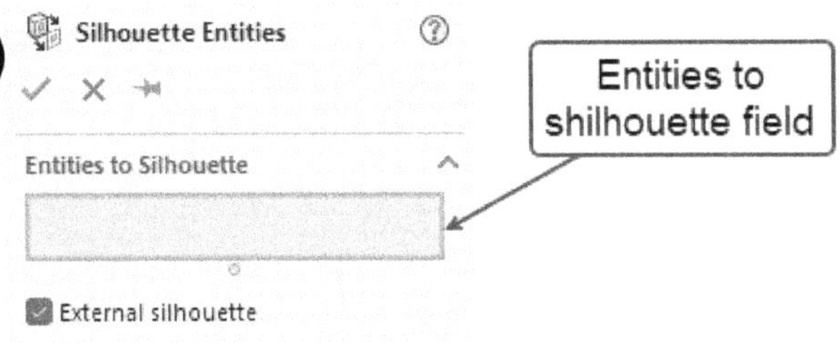

Entities to Silhouette

The **Entities to Silhouette** field is used to select bodies for projecting their edges onto the current sketching plane. By default, this field is activated. As a result, you can select bodies by clicking the left mouse button.

External Silhouette

When the **External Silhouette** check box is selected, then only the outer boundaries of the selected bodies get projected onto the current sketching plane as sketch entities. However, when this check box is cleared, then the inner loops of the bodies get projected as well.

After selecting the bodies, click on the green tick-mark ✓ in the PropertyManager. The edges of the selected body or bodies get projected as sketch entities onto the current sketching plane.

Projecting Intersecting Geometries of Existing Features

In SOLIDWORKS, you can project the geometries of the existing features that intersect with the currently active sketching plane using the **Intersection Curve** tool, see Figure 7.42. To do this, click on the arrow below the **Convert Entities** tool and then click on the **Intersection Curve** tool in the flyout that appears. The **Intersection Curves PropertyManager** appears, see Figure 7.43. Also, you are prompted to select intersecting geometries of the features to be projected. Select all the intersecting geometries of the model in the graphics area one by one and then click on the green tick-mark ✓ in the PropertyManager. The sketch curve is created at the intersection of the selected geometries and the sketching plane, see Figure 7.42.

7.42

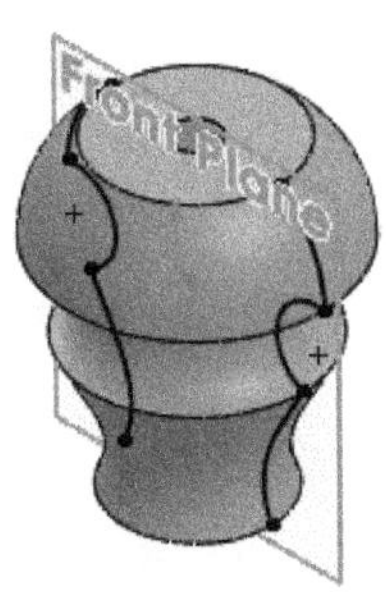

7.43

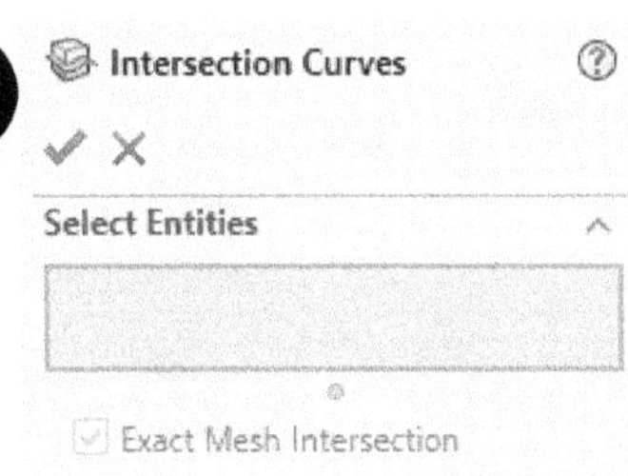

Editing a Feature and its Sketch

SOLIDWORKS allows you to edit features of a model as per the design change. As mentioned earlier, the FeatureManager Design Tree displays a list of all features created for a model, see Figure 7.44. In SOLIDWORKS, you can edit individual features and their sketches. The methods for editing a feature and its sketch are discussed next.

Editing a Feature

1. Click on the feature to be edited in the FeatureManager Design Tree and then click on the **Edit Feature** tool in the Pop-up toolbar that appears, see Figure 7.44. The respective PropertyManager appears.

2. Change the parameters as per your requirement by entering the new values in the PropertyManager.

3. After editing the feature parameters, click on the green tick-mark ✓ in the PropertyManager.

Editing the Sketch of a Feature

1. Click on a feature in the FeatureManager Design Tree and then click on the **Edit Sketch** tool in the Pop-up toolbar that appears, see Figure 7.45. The Sketching environment is invoked.

7.44

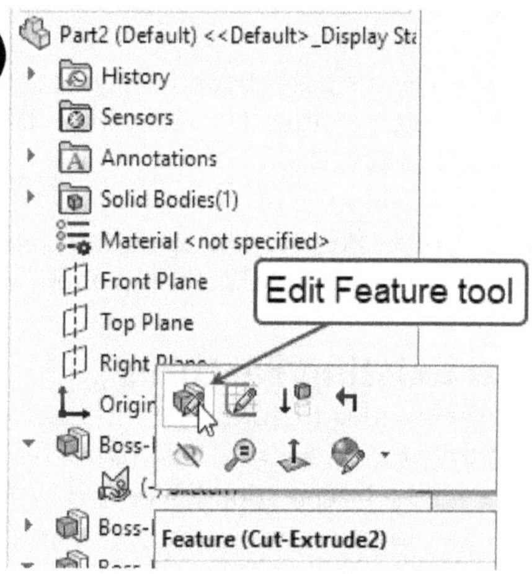

7.45

2. By using the sketching tools in the Sketching environment, you can modify the sketch of the feature as per your requirement.

3. After modifying the sketch of the feature, exit the Sketching environment.

Note: You can also select a sketch to be edited in the FeatureManager Design Tree and then click on the **Edit Sketch** tool in the Pop-up toolbar that appears to invoke the Sketching environment for editing it.

Importing 2D DXF or DWG Files

In SOLIDWORKS, you can import an existing 2D DXF or DWG file as a reference sketch. To do this, click on the **Open** button in the **Welcome** dialog box. Alternatively, click on the **Open** tool in the **Standard** toolbar or click on **File > Open** in the SOLIDWORKS Design menus. The **Open** dialog box appears. In this dialog box, select the **Autodesk AutoCAD Files (*.dwg; *.dxf)** file extension in the **File Type** drop-down list. Next, browse to the location where the required document (*.dxf* or *.dwg*) is saved, and then click on the document to be opened. Next, click on the **Open** button in the dialog box. The **DXF/DWG Import** dialog box appears. In this dialog box, select the **Import to a new part as** radio button. Next, select the **Import as reference** check box under **2D sketch** radio button and then click on the **Finish** button. The selected file is opened as a reference sketch.

By default, the imported reference sketch cannot be edited. To make the reference sketch editable, right-click on its name in the FeatureManager Design Tree and then select the **Make Edit Sketch** option in the shortcut menu that appears. The imported reference sketch becomes an editable sketch. Now, you can edit it similar to editing a sketch of a feature.

Displaying the Earlier State of a Model

In SOLIDWORKS, you can display the earlier state of a model by using the Rollback Bar. By default, the Rollback Bar is displayed at the end of the last feature of the model in the FeatureManager Design Tree, see Figure 7.46.

You can drag the Rollback Bar up in the FeatureManager Design Tree and place it above the features to be rolled back, see Figure 7.47. The earlier state of the model appears in the graphics area such that the features located below the Rollback Bar are not displayed in the graphics area. Additionally, their names are shown in grey within the FeatureManager Design Tree, indicating their inactive status. You can add new features or edit existing features while the model is in the rolled-back state. You can also drag the Rollback Bar down in the FeatureManager Design Tree.

7.46

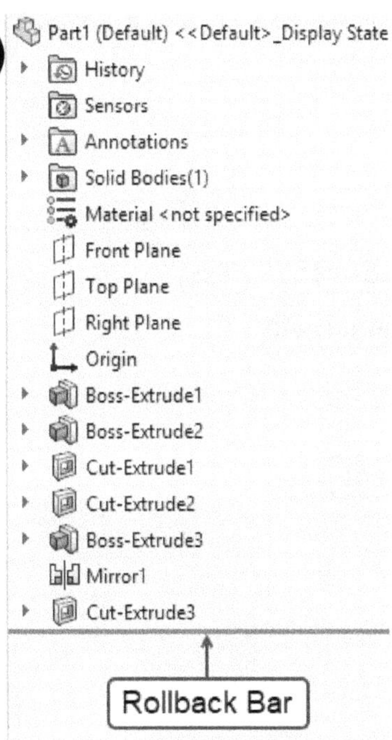

7.47

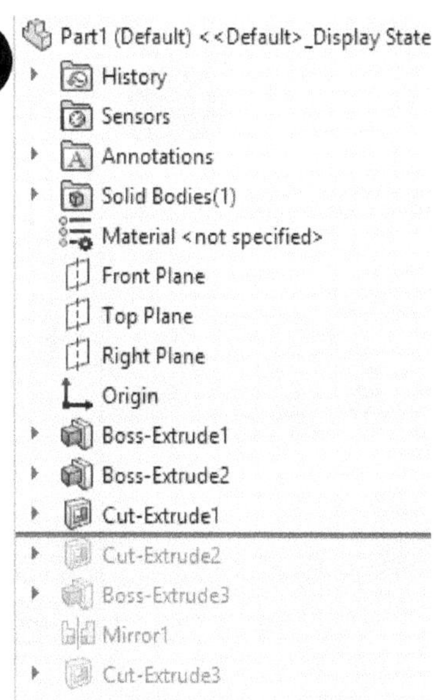

Reordering Features of a Model

By default, all the features of a model appear in a sequential order in the FeatureManager Design Tree. The first created feature appears at the top and the next created features appear one after the other in the FeatureManager Design Tree. In SOLIDWORKS, you can also change the order of a feature by dragging it to a new location in the FeatureManager Design Tree. Note that you cannot place a child feature above its parent feature in the FeatureManager Design Tree.

Measuring the Distance between Entities

In SOLIDWORKS, you can measure the distance and angle between lines, points, faces, planes, and so on using the **Measure** tool in the **Evaluate CommandManager**, see Figure 7.48. Also, you can measure the radius and other parameters of different geometrical entities.

7.48

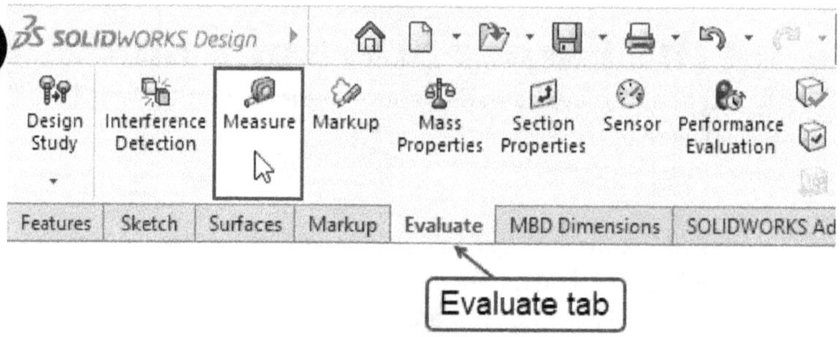

To measure the distance between entities, click on the **Evaluate** tab and then click on the **Measure** tool in the **Evaluate CommandManager**, see Figure 7.48. The **Measure** window appears, see Figure 7.49. You can expand the **Measure** window to display the Input box and Display area by clicking on the arrow available on its right, see Figure 7.50. Some of the options of this window are discussed next.

7.49

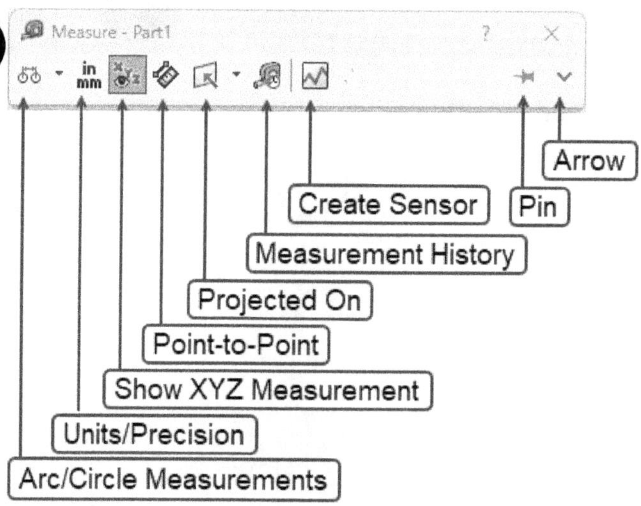

7.50

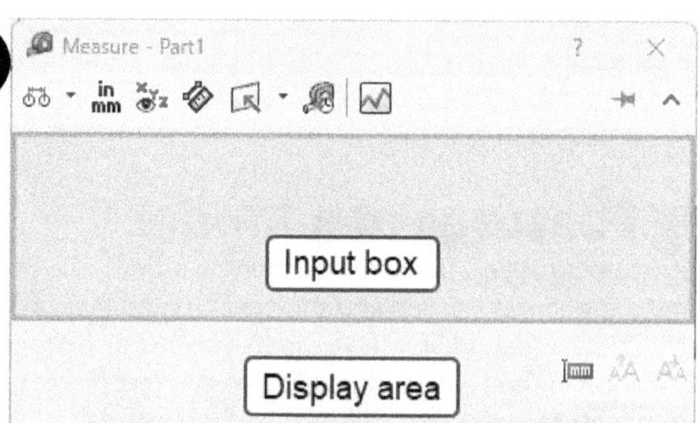

Arc/Circle Measurements

The options in the **Arc/Circle Measurements** drop-down list are used to specify the method of measuring distance between circular or semi-circular entities, see Figure 7.51. To invoke this drop-down list, click on the arrow next to the **Arc/Circle Measurements** button in the window. The options in the **Arc/Circle Measurements** drop-down list are discussed next.

7.51

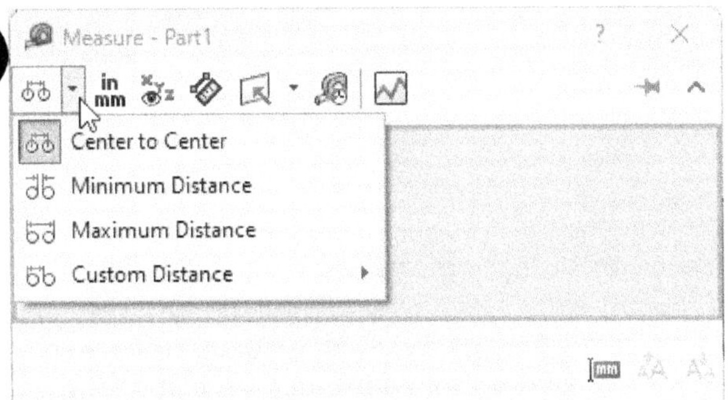

Center to Center

This option of the **Arc/Circle Measurements** drop-down list is used to measure the center-to-center distance between two arc entities, circular entities, or cylindrical faces. On selecting this option, the center-to-center distance between the selected entities is measured and appears in the graphics area as well as in the Display area of the expanded **Measure** window, see Figure 7.52.

7.52

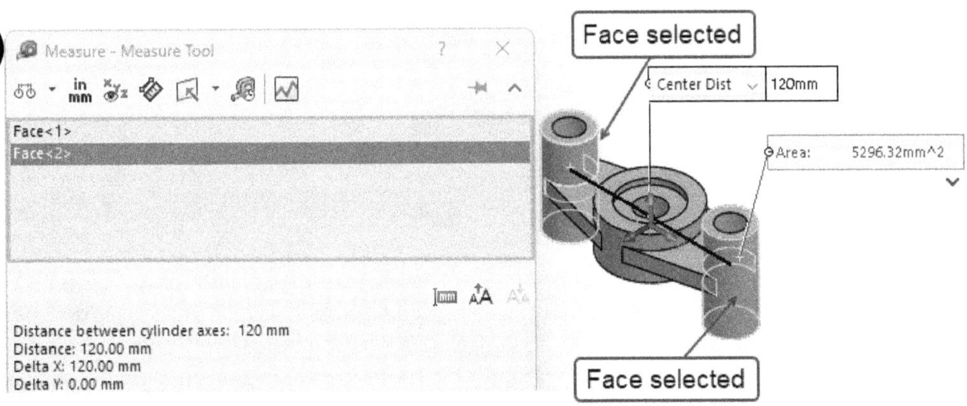

Note: You can increase or decrease the Display area of the **Measure** window by dragging its border.

Minimum Distance

This option is used to measure the minimum distance between two selected arcs or circular entities, see Figure 7.53.

Maximum Distance

This option is used to measure the maximum distance between two selected arcs or circular entities, see Figure 7.54.

7.53

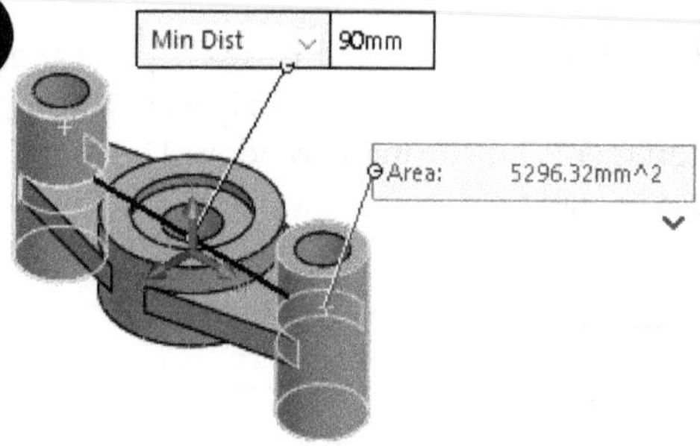

7.54

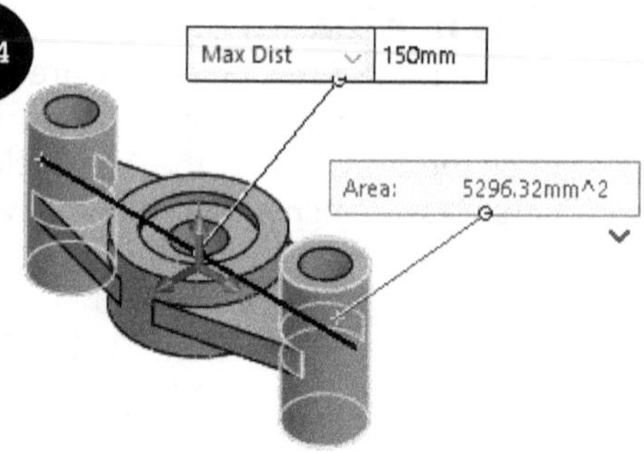

Custom Distance

The **Custom Distance** option is used to measure the distance between entities, as per a user-defined arrangement. When you move the cursor over the **Custom Distance** option in the drop-down list, a cascading menu appears, see Figure 7.55. By using this cascading menu, you can specify the start and end conditions of the measurement. Depending upon the start and end conditions specified, the respective distance between the selected entities is measured and appears in the graphics area as well as in the Display area of the **Measure** window.

7.55

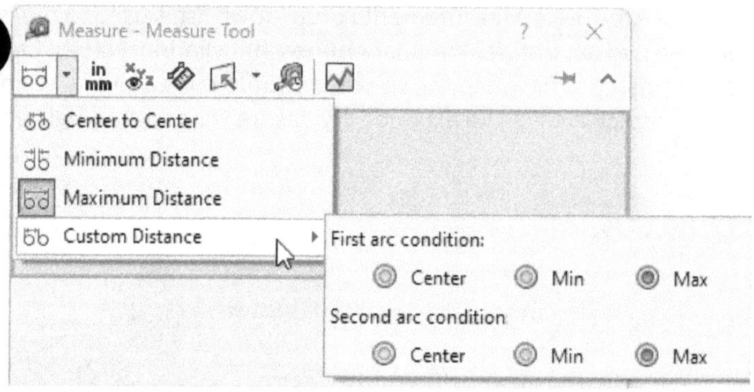

Note: As discussed, the results of measurement appear in the graphics area as well as in the **Display** area of the **Measure** window. You can copy the numerical value of the measurement results to the clipboard. To do this, move the cursor to the numerical value to be copied in the **Display** area of the **Measure** window, the numerical value gets highlighted, see Figure 7.56. Next, click the left mouse button to copy the highlighted value. Now, you can paste the copied value at the required location in any file.

You can choose to select the numerical value with or without units in the **Display** area of the **Measure** window. To do this, click on the **Quick Copy Setting** tool in the **Measure** window. The **Quick copy setting** window appears, see Figure 7.57. Select the required radio button (**Select number only** or **Select number and units**) and then click on the **OK** button in the **Quick copy setting** window to accept the changes made.

You can increase or decrease the font size of the text that appears in the **Display** area of the **Measure** window by using the **Increase Font Size** or **Decrease Font Size** buttons, respectively. These buttons appear in the **Display** area of the window. Note that you cannot decrease the font size below the default size.

7.56

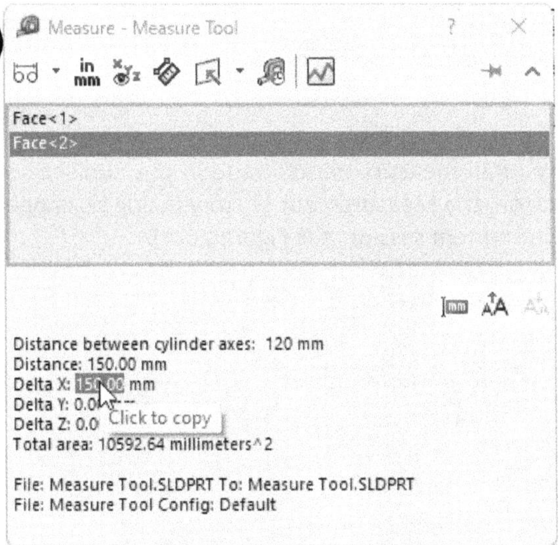

7.57

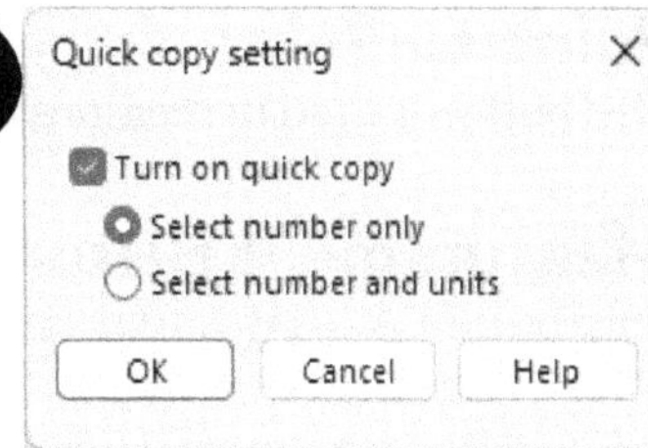

Tip: You can invoke the **Measure** tool for measuring distance between entities even if any other tool is active. You can also use this tool while working with a sketch, a part, an assembly, or a drawing file.

Units/Precision

This button is used to specify units and precision of measurement. When you click on the **Units/Precision** button, the **Measure Units/Precision** dialog box appears, see Figure 7.58. By default, the **Use document settings** radio button is selected in this dialog box. As a result, the units and precision specified in the current document of SOLIDWORKS are used for measurement. By selecting the **Use custom settings** radio button, you can customize the units and precision values for measurement.

Show XYZ Measurements

This button is used for measuring the dX, dY, and dZ measurements between the selected entities, see Figure 7.59.

7.58

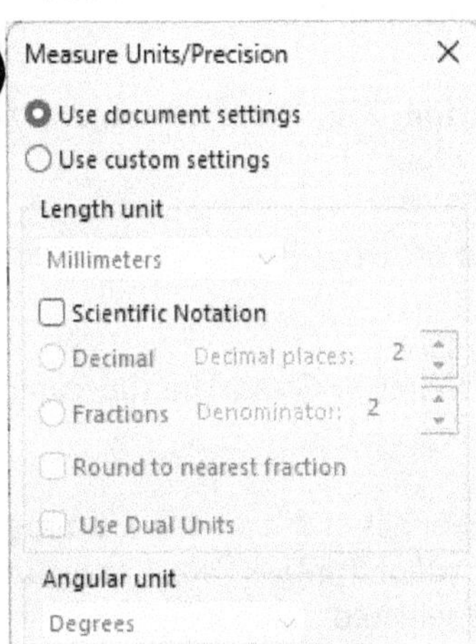

7.59

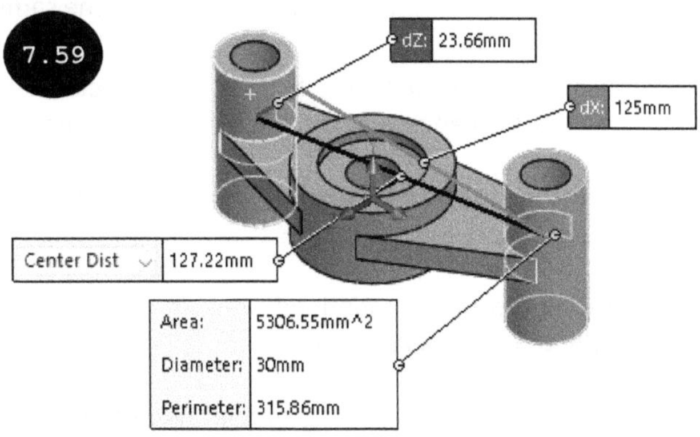

Point-to-Point

This button is used to measure the distance between two points or vertices.

Measurement History

This button is used to display the history of all measurements made in the current session of SOLIDWORKS. When you click on this button, the **Measurement History** dialog box appears with the details of measurement made so far in the current session, see Figure 7.60.

7.60

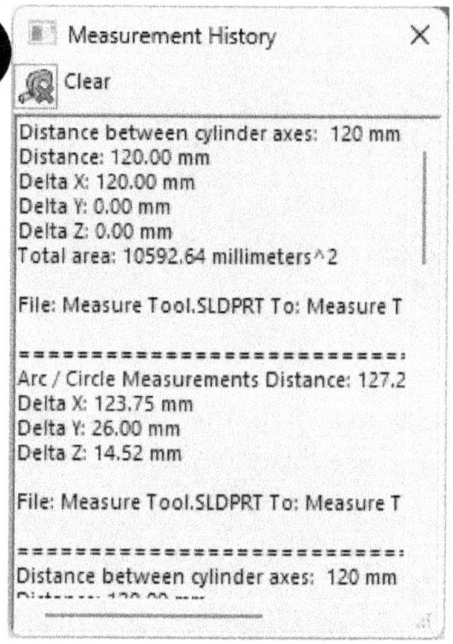

Assigning an Appearance/Texture

In SOLIDWORKS, you can change the default appearance or texture of a model by assigning a predefined or customized appearance to the model, its features, and faces. The methods for assigning a predefined and customized appearance are discussed next.

Assigning a Predefined Appearance/Texture

You can assign a predefined appearance or texture to a model by using the **Appearances, Scenes, and Decals Task Pane**, see Figure 7.61. The method for the same is discussed next.

1. Click on the **Appearances, Scenes, and Decals** tab in the Task Pane, see Figure 7.61. The **Appearances Scenes, and Decals Task Pane** appears.

2. Expand the **Appearances(color)** node by clicking on the arrow in front of it. The predefined appearance categories appear.

3. Expand the required predefined category such as **Plastic**, **Metal**, or **Glass**. The sub-categories of the selected category appear.

4. Select the required sub-category, see Figure 7.61. The thumbnails of the predefined appearances available in the selected sub-category appear in the lower half of the Task Pane, see Figure 7.61. In this figure, the **Steel** sub-category of the **Metal** category is selected.

7.61

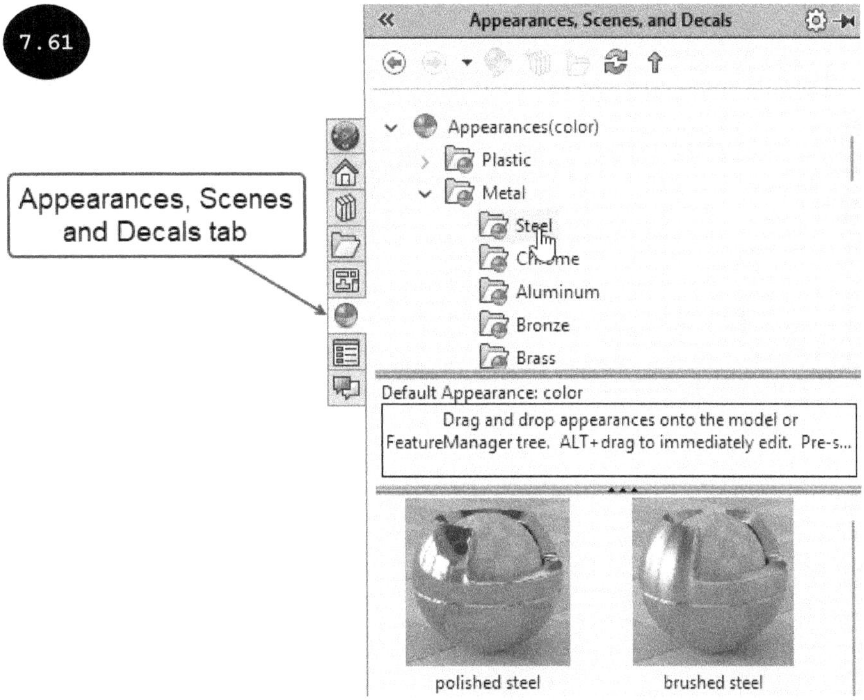

5. Drag and drop the required predefined appearance (thumbnail) from the lower half of the Task Pane over the face of the model by pressing and holding the left mouse button. A Pop-up toolbar appears, see Figure 7.62.

7.62

Note: The options in the Pop-up toolbar allow you to choose the required target for assigning the appearance. You can assign the appearance to a face, a feature, a body, or a part by clicking on the respective tool in the Pop-up toolbar.

6. Click on the required tool in the Pop-up toolbar. The appearance is assigned to the model depending on the tool selected in the Pop-up toolbar.

Note: If you drag and drop the appearance thumbnail in the empty area, the appearance will be assigned to the entire model.

Assigning a Customized Appearance

In addition to assigning a predefined appearance to faces, features, or bodies, you can also customize the appearance properties as required and then assign them. To do this, click on the **Edit Appearance** tool in the **View (Heads-up)** toolbar, see Figure 7.63. The **color PropertyManager** appears on the left side of the graphics area, see Figure 7.64. The **Appearances, Scenes, and Decals Task Pane** also appears to the right of the graphics area. The options in the **color PropertyManager** are used for assigning colors, material appearances, and transparency to faces, features, or bodies.

7.63

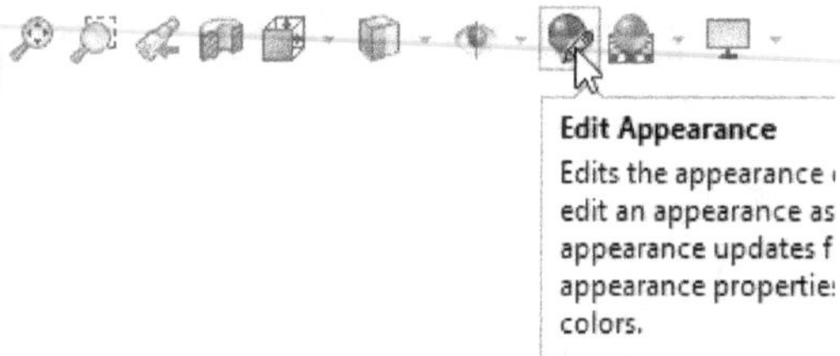

7.64

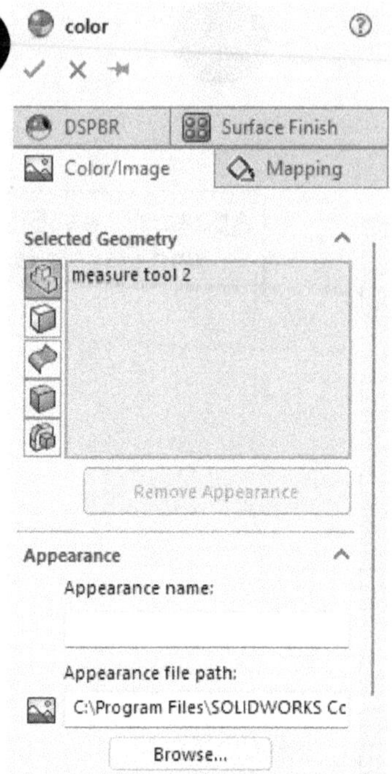

Note: If the model already has an appearance or texture assigned, then on clicking the **Edit Appearance** tool in the **View (Heads-up)** toolbar, the respective PropertyManager appears, which allows you to edit properties of the assigned appearance or texture.

You can also invoke the **color PropertyManager** by clicking on **Edit > Appearance > Appearance** in the SOLIDWORKS Design menus. Alternatively, select a face of the model. A Pop-up toolbar appears, see Figure 7.65. In this Pop-up toolbar, click on the arrow next to the **Appearances** tool and then click on the *face name, feature name, body name,* or *part name* in the flyout that appears to display the **color PropertyManager**.

7.65

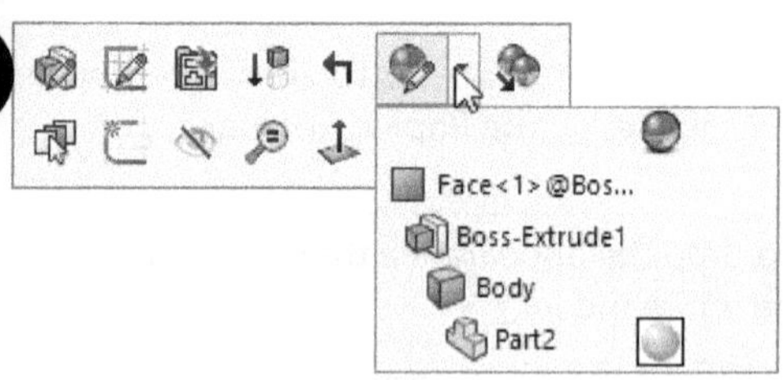

The options in the color PropertyManager are organized into four tabs: **Color/Image, Mapping, Surface Finish**, and **DSPBR**. Some of the options available in these tabs are discussed next. Note that the availability of the tabs in the PropertyManager depends on the installed graphics card.

Color/Image Tab

By default, the **Color/Image** tab is activated in the PropertyManager. As a result, the additional and advanced options for assigning an appearance (color or image file) appear in the PropertyManager, see Figure 7.66. Some of these options are discussed next.

Selected Geometry

The **Selected Geometry** rollout is used to select geometries for applying appearances. You can select a part, faces, surfaces, bodies, or features as geometries by clicking on the respective button (**Select Part**, **Select Faces**, **Select Surfaces**, **Select Bodies**, or **Select Features**) available to the left of this rollout, see Figure 7.66.

For example, to assign a color to specific faces of a model, click **Select Faces** and then select the required faces in the graphics area. The names of the selected faces are displayed in the **Selected Entities** field of this rollout.

7.66

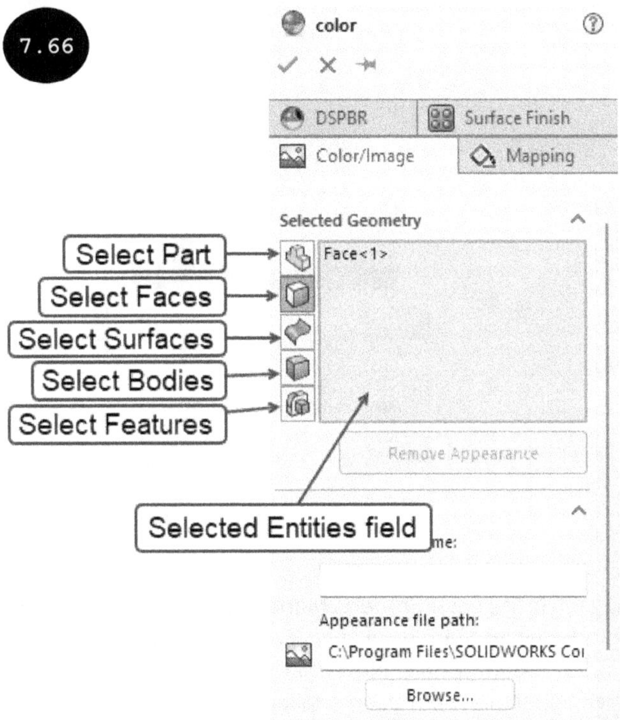

Note: To remove the already selected geometries from the **Selected Entities** field, right-click on the **Selected Entities** field and then select the **Clear Selection** option from the shortcut menu that appears. All the selected geometries get removed from the selection.

You can also remove individual geometries. To do this, select a geometry in the **Selected Entities** field of the rollout, right-click, and then select **Delete** from the shortcut menu that appears. The selected geometry gets removed from the selection.

Appearance: This rollout is used to select an image file as the appearance for the selected geometries. By default, the **color.p2m** file is selected. You can also select any other file such as JPG and TIFF as the image file to be assigned. To do this, click on the **Browse** button of this rollout. The **Open** dialog box appears. Select the required file type in the **File Type** drop-down list of the dialog box and then browse to the location where the image file has been saved. Next, select it and then click on the **Open** button in the dialog box. The **Save As** dialog box appears. Click on the **Save** button to save the file as *.p2m* for future use. The selected image file is assigned to the model. You can also save the current appearance file for future use by using the **Save Appearance** button of the rollout.

Color

The **Color** rollout is used to select the required color to be assigned to the selected geometries, see Figure 7.67.

7.67

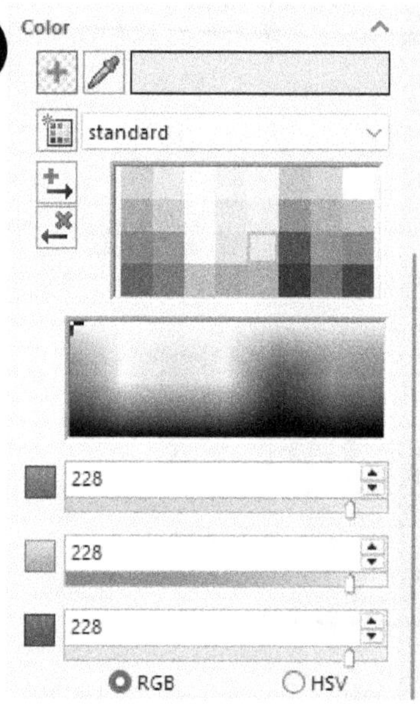

Mapping Tab

On clicking the **Mapping** tab in the **color PropertyManager**, the options used for mapping the selected image file on the selected geometry are displayed. By using these options, you can control the size, orientation, and location of the image file. Note that these options become available only when an image file or a predefined appearance has been applied to the geometry.

Surface Finish Tab

On clicking the **Surface Finish** tab in the **color PropertyManager**, the options that are used to specify the surface finishing for the appearance such as knurled, dimpled, or sandblasted are displayed.

DSPBR Tab

When you click the **DSPBR** tab in the **color PropertyManager** (see Figure 7.68), options for defining physically based rendering (PBR) properties for the selected appearance are displayed. DSPBR stands for Dassault Systèmes Physically Based Rendering. The options available in this tab allow you to control how the material behaves under lighting conditions and how it appears in both SOLIDWORKS and SOLIDWORKS Visualize.

7.68

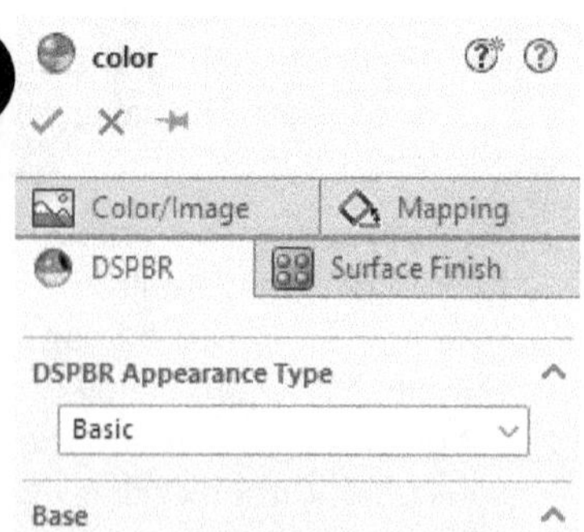

After customizing or editing the appearance properties and assigning them to a model or its geometries, exit the PropertyManager.

Applying a Material

In SOLIDWORKS, you can apply standard material properties such as density, elastic modulus, and tensile strength to a model. Note that assigning standard material properties to a model is important to calculate its mass properties as well as to perform static and dynamic analysis.

SOLIDWORKS contains almost all standard materials in its material library. You can directly apply the required standard material to a model from the material library. In addition to applying standard material, you can also customize the material properties and apply them to a model. The methods for applying a standard material and a custom material are discussed next.

Applying a Standard Material

1. Right-click on the **Material <not specified>** option in the FeatureManager Design Tree (see Figure 7.69), and then click on the **Edit Material** option in the shortcut menu that appears. The **Material** dialog box appears, refer to Figure 7.70.

7.69

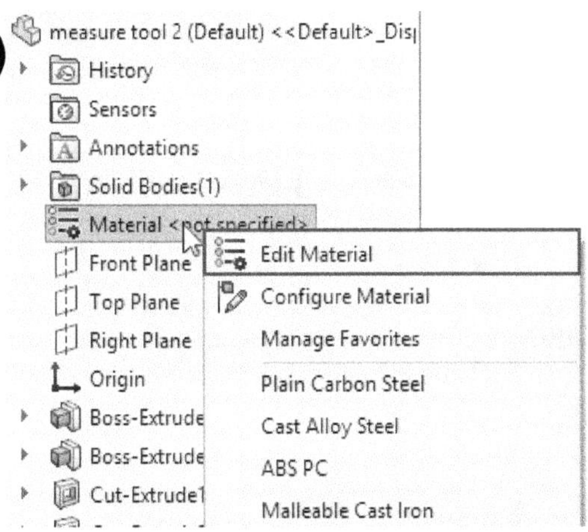

2. Expand the **SOLIDWORKS Materials** node, if not expanded by default. The different material categories such as Steel, Iron, and Aluminium Alloys appear in the dialog box.

3. Expand the required material category. The materials available in the expanded material category appear, see Figure 7.70.

4. Select the required material from the list of available materials. The properties of the selected material appear on the right half of the dialog box, see Figure 7.70.

5. Click on the **Apply** button in the dialog box. The material properties of the selected material get applied to the model. Next, click on the **Close** button to exit the dialog box.

7.70

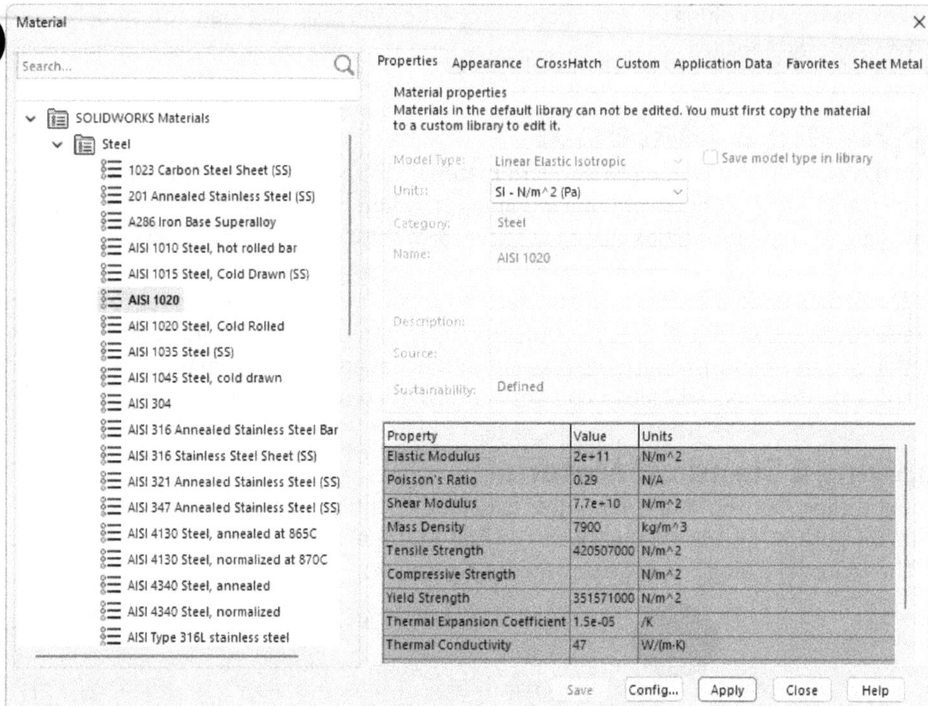

Applying Customized Material Properties

1. Invoke the **Material** dialog box and then right-click on the **Custom Materials** node in the dialog box. A shortcut menu appears, see Figure 7.71.

2. Click on the **New Category** option in the shortcut menu, see Figure 7.71. A new category is added. Also, its default name **New Category** appears in an edit field.

7.71

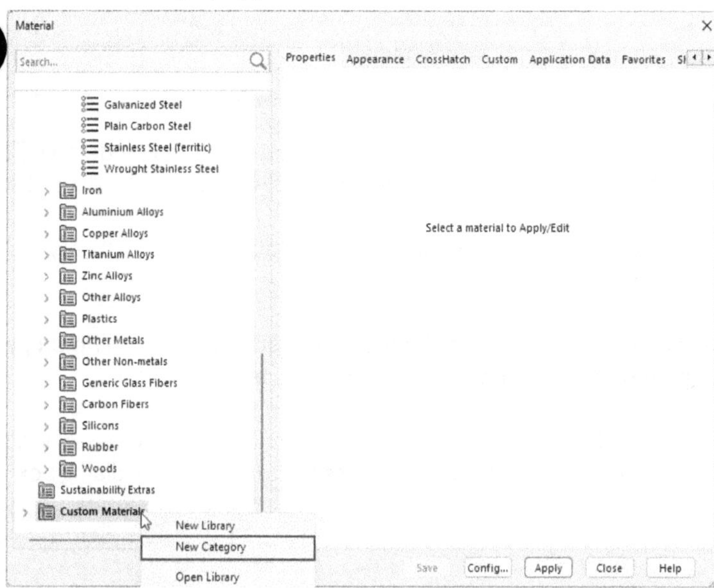

3. Enter a new name for the newly added category in the edit field and then click outside the edit field. Next, right-click on the newly added category in the dialog box and then click on the **New Material** option in the shortcut menu that appears. A new material is added under the selected category. Also, its default name **Default** appears in an edit field.

4. Enter a new name for the newly added material in the edit field and then click outside the edit field. Next, click on the newly added material. The default properties of the selected material appear on the right half of the dialog box, see Figure 7.72. In this figure, the **SW CAD** material category and the **SW 1001** material are added in the **Custom Material** node.

5. Specify new material properties such as Poisson's ratio, Density, and Yield Strength as required in the respective fields of the dialog box. Next, click on the **Save** button and then click on the **Apply** button. The newly added material properties are saved and applied to the model.

6. Click on the **Close** button to exit the dialog box.

Note: You can also copy material properties of a standard material and then edit them. To do this, select a standard material and then right-click to display a shortcut menu. Next, click on the **Copy** option in the shortcut menu. After copying a standard material, select a custom material category in the **Custom Material** node of the dialog box and then right-click to display a shortcut menu. In the shortcut menu, click on the **Paste** option. The copied standard material is added in the selected custom material category. Now, you can edit the material properties of the standard material as required and then click on the **Apply** button in the dialog box.

7.72

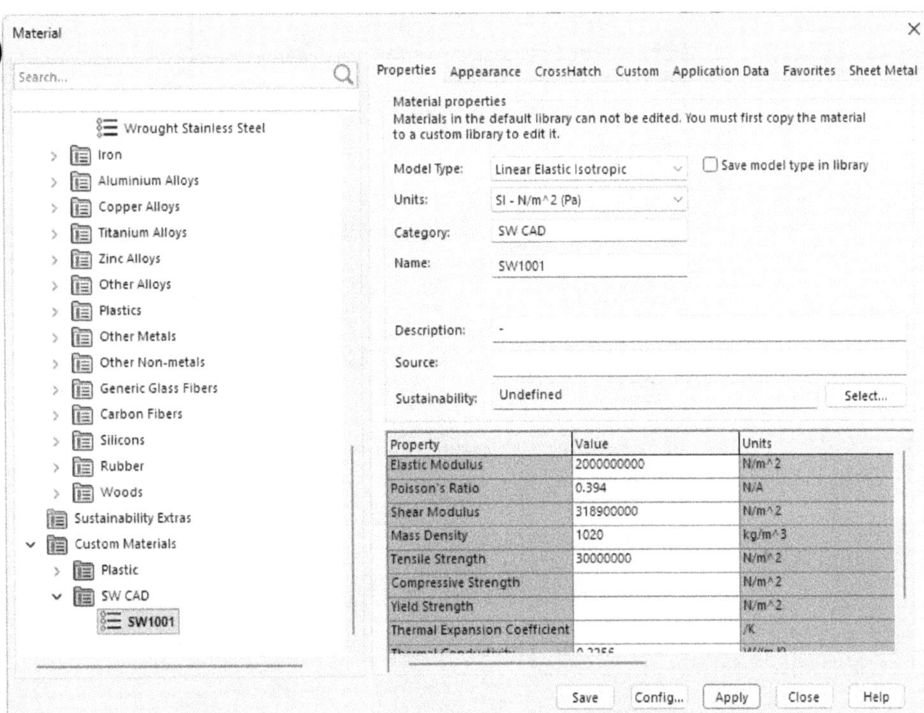

Calculating Mass Properties

In SOLIDWORKS, after assigning material properties to a model, you can calculate its mass properties such as mass and volume using the **Mass Properties** tool of the **Evaluate CommandManager**, see Figure 7.73. To calculate the mass properties of a model, click on the **Mass Properties** tool. The **Mass Properties** dialog box appears and displays the mass properties of the model, see Figure 7.74. The options of the dialog box are discussed next.

7.73

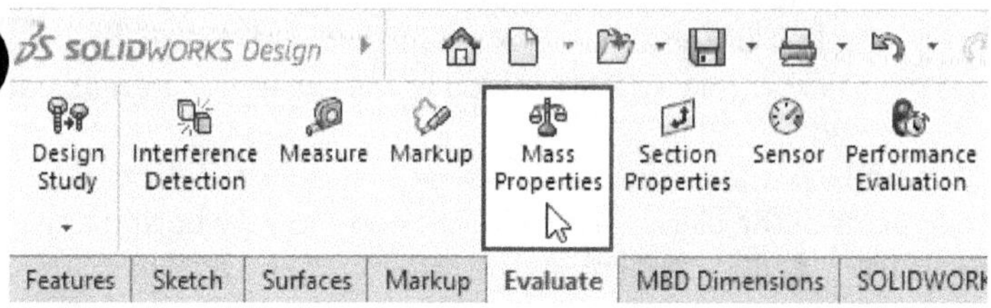

7.74

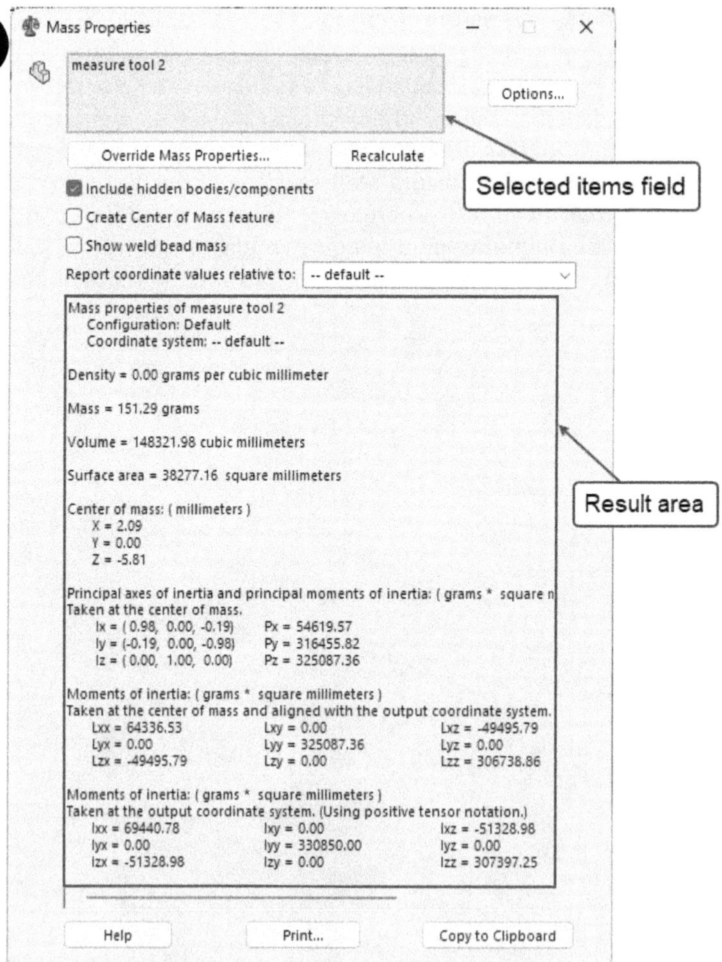

Selected Items

This field of the dialog box is used to select a model for calculating its mass properties. By default, on invoking the **Mass Properties** tool, the model available in the graphics area gets automatically selected and its name appears in this field, see Figure 7.74. Also, properties such as mass, volume, and center of mass of the selected model appear in the **Result** area of the dialog box, see Figure 7.74.

Options

This button is used to specify unit settings for calculating the mass properties. When you click on the **Options** button, the **Mass/Section Property Options** dialog box appears. By default, the **Use document settings** radio button is selected in this dialog box. As a result, the units and precision values specified for the current document of SOLIDWORKS are used for calculating mass properties. To specify the custom unit settings for calculating the mass properties, select the **Use custom settings** radio button, see Figure 7.75. All the edit fields of the dialog box get activated which allows you to specify custom unit settings, see Figure 7.75. After customizing the unit settings, click on the OK button.

7.75

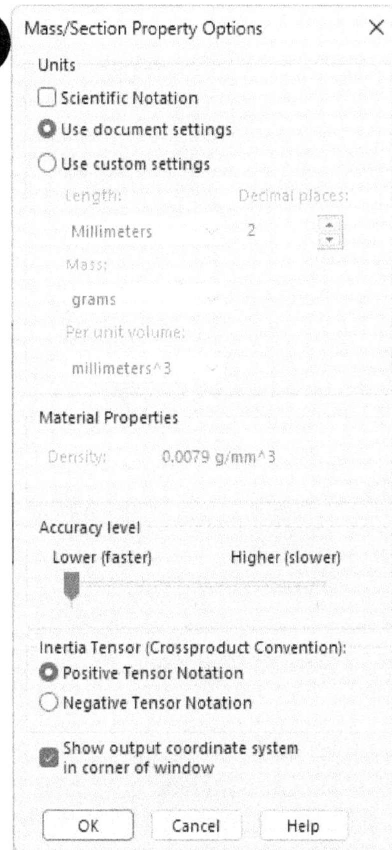

Recalculate

This button is used to recalculate the mass properties of the model in case you have made changes in the model or added/deleted any item in the selection set.

Override Mass Properties

This button is used to override the calculated mass properties of a model. On clicking this button, the **Override Mass Properties** dialog box appears. This dialog box is used for overriding the default calculated mass properties such as mass and center of mass of the model. Note that the edit fields of this dialog box are not enabled, by default. To enable these edit fields, you need to select the respective checkboxes: **Override mass**, **Override center of mass**, and **Override moments of inertia** of the dialog box, see Figure 7.76. In this figure, the **Override mass**, **Override center of mass**, and **Override moments of inertia** checkboxes of the dialog box are selected. As a result, all the respective edit fields of the dialog box are enabled. In these edit fields, you can specify override values for mass, center of mass, and moments of inertia. After defining the override mass properties, click on the OK button in the dialog box.

Note: The override properties specified for a model are not the actual properties of the model.

7.76

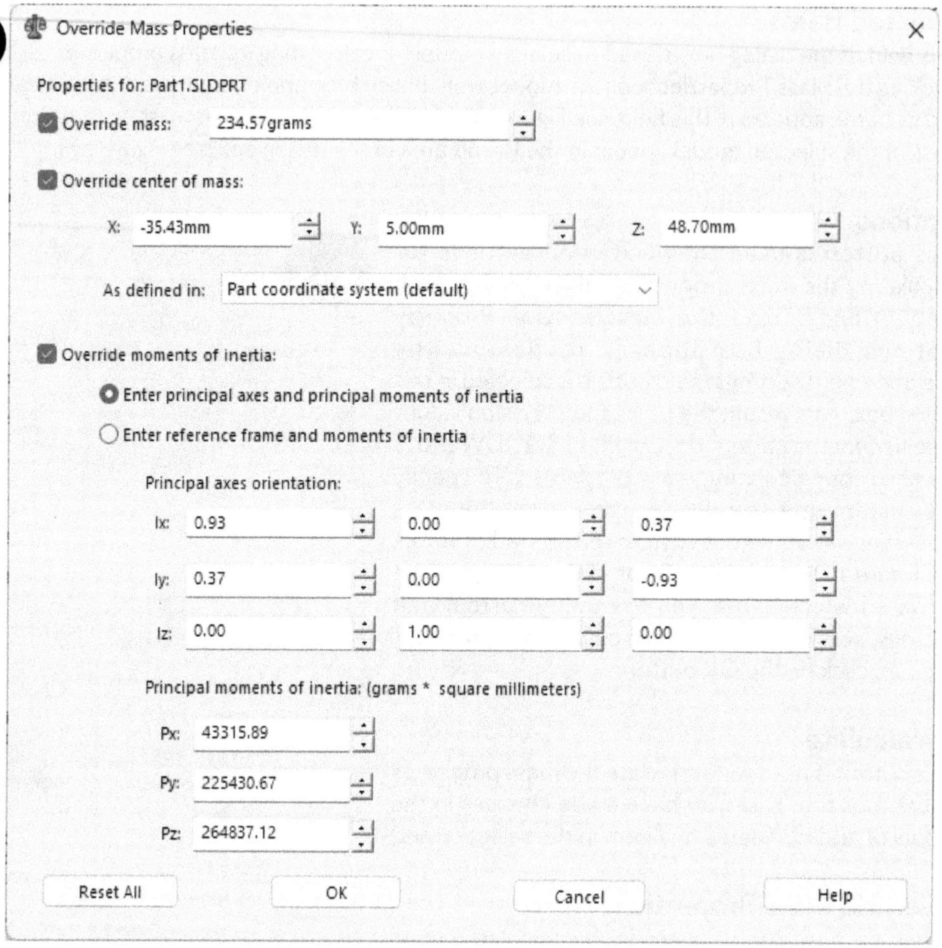

Include hidden bodies/components

By default, the **Include hidden bodies/components** check box of the **Mass Properties** dialog box is selected. As a result, all hidden bodies or components of the selected model are included while calculating the mass properties. However, on clearing this check box, the hidden bodies/components are not included in the calculation.

Create Center of Mass feature

On selecting the **Create Center of Mass feature** check box, the center of mass of the model appears in the graphics area and its symbol is added to the FeatureManager Design Tree as soon as you exit the **Mass Properties** dialog box.

Note: The center of mass of the model appears in the graphics area either when it is selected in the FeatureManager Design Tree, or its visibility is turned on in the graphics area. To turn on the visibility of the center of mass, invoke the **Hide/Show Items** flyout of the **View (Heads-Up)** toolbar and then click on the **View Center of Mass** tool, see Figure 7.77.

7.77

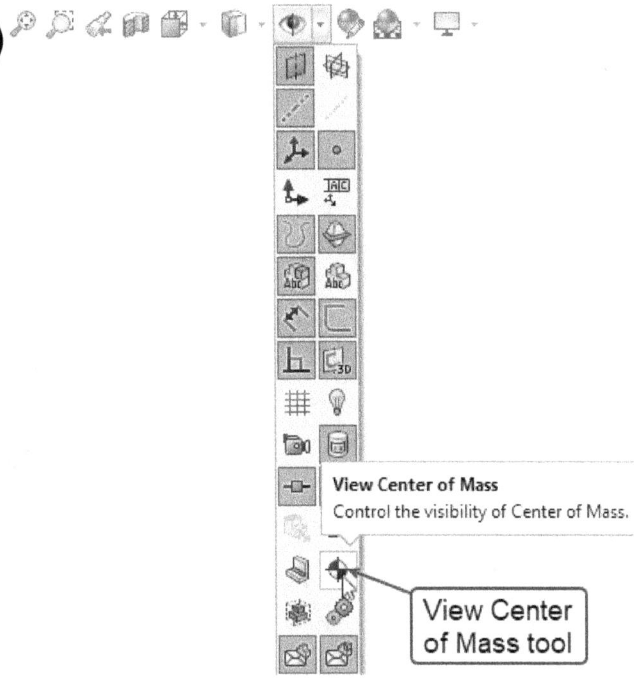

Show weld bead mass
On selecting the **Create Center of Mass feature** check box, the total weld mass of the model appears in the result area of the dialog box.

Report coordinate values relative to
This drop-down list of the **Mass Properties** dialog box is used for selecting a coordinate system concerning which the mass properties are to be calculated. By default, the **default** option is selected. As a result, the default coordinate system is used for calculating the mass properties of the model.

Note: The **Report coordinate values relative to** drop-down list displays coordinate systems that are created in the current document of SOLIDWORKS. In case you have not created any coordinate system, then only the **default** option is available in this drop-down list.

Result
This area of the dialog box is used to display the calculated results of the model.

Print
This button is used to print the calculated results.

Copy to Clipboard
This button is used to copy the results to the clipboard.

After reviewing the mass properties of the model in the **Mass Properties** dialog box, exit the dialog box.

Tutorial 1

Create a model, as shown in Figure 7.78. You need to create the model by creating all its features one by one. All dimensions are in mm.

7.78

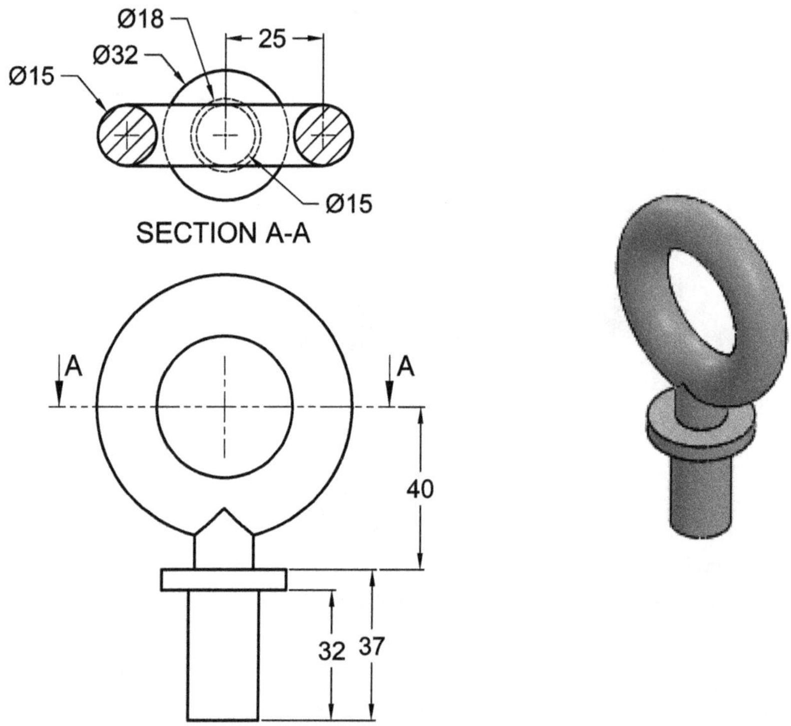

Section 1: Starting SOLIDWORKS

1. Start SOLIDWORKS by double-clicking on the SOLIDWORKS icon on your desktop. The initial screen of SOLIDWORKS appears along with the **Welcome** dialog box.

Section 2: Invoking the Part Modeling Environment

1. Click on the **Part** button in the **Welcome** dialog box. The Part modeling environment is invoked.

   Now, you can set the unit system and create the base/first feature of the model.

Section 3: Specifying Unit Settings

1. Move the cursor toward the lower right corner of the screen over the Status Bar and then click on the **Unit System** area. The **Unit System** flyout appears, see Figure 7.79.

7.79

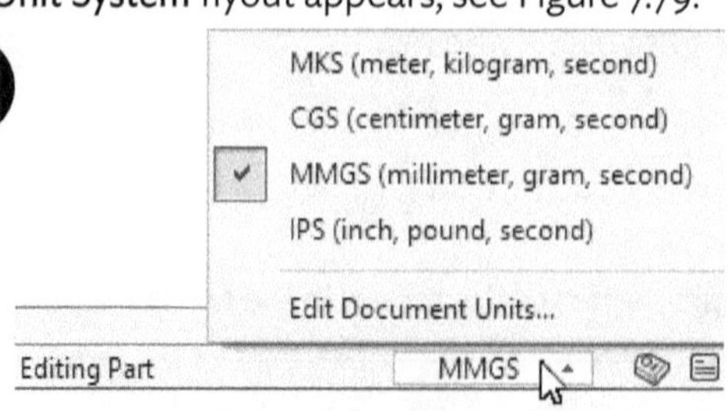

2. Ensure that the **MMGS (millimeter, gram, second)** option is tick-marked in this flyout as the unit system for the current document.

Section 4: Creating the Base Feature - Revolved Feature

1. Invoke the Sketching environment by selecting the Top plane as the sketching plane and then create the sketch of the base feature, see Figure 7.80. The base feature of the model is a revolved feature.

Tip: To make the sketch of the base feature fully defined as shown in Figure 7.80, you need to ensure that the centerpoint of the circle has coincident relation with the horizontal centerline. The vertical centerline in the figure will be used as the axis of revolution for creating the revolved feature.

2. Click on the **Features** tab in the CommandManager to display the tools of the **Features CommandManager**, see Figure 7.81.

7.80

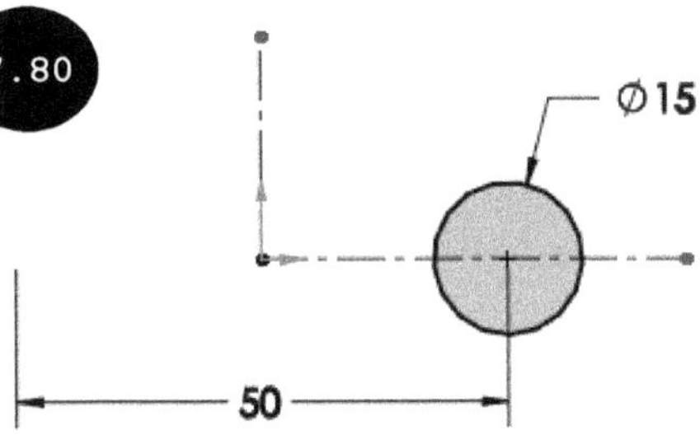

7.81

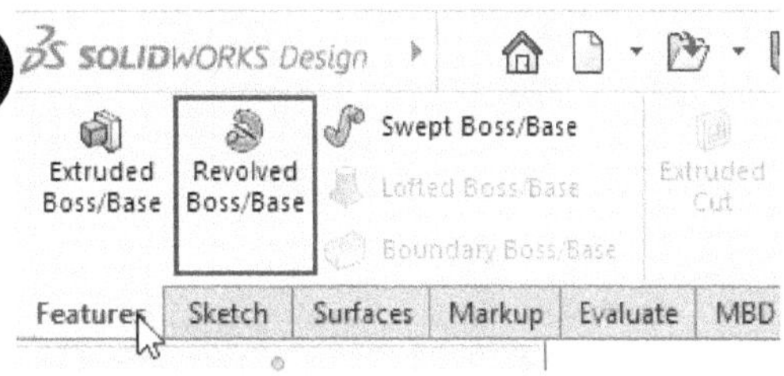

3. Click on the **Revolved Boss/Base** tool in the **Features CommandManager**. The **Revolve PropertyManager** appears. Also, the orientation of the sketch changes to trimetric orientation, see Figure 7.82.

Note: If the sketch to be revolved has only one centerline, then on invoking the **Revolved Boss/Base** tool, the available centerline will automatically be selected as the axis of revolution and a preview of the revolved feature appears in the graphics area.

4. Click on the vertical centerline of the sketch as the axis of revolution. A preview of the revolved feature appears in the graphics area, see Figure 7.83.

7.82

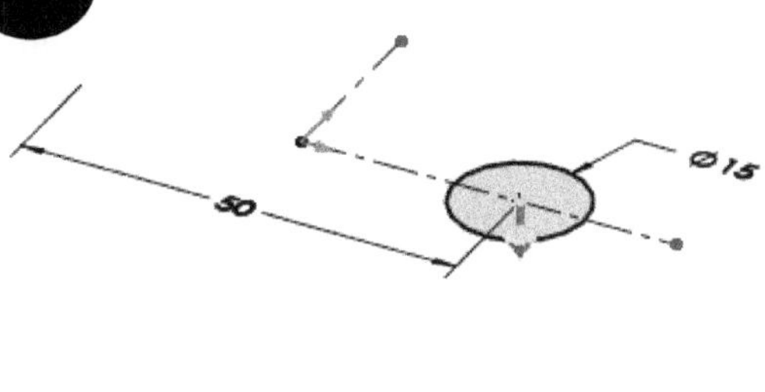

7.83

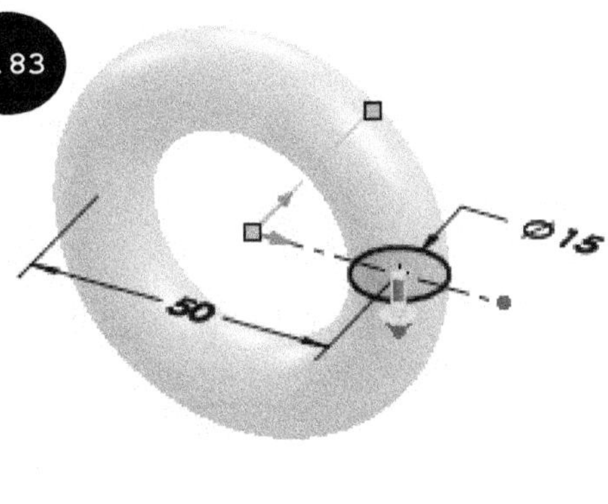

5. Ensure that a 360-degrees angle is specified in the **Direction 1 Angle** field of the PropertyManager.

6. Click on the green tick-mark ✓ in the PropertyManager. The base/first revolved feature is created, see Figure 7.84.

Section 5: Creating the Second Feature - Extruded Feature

To create the second feature of the model, you first need to create a reference plane at an offset distance of 40 mm from the Top plane.

1. Invoke the **Reference Geometry** flyout in the **Features CommandManager**, see Figure 7.85.

7.84

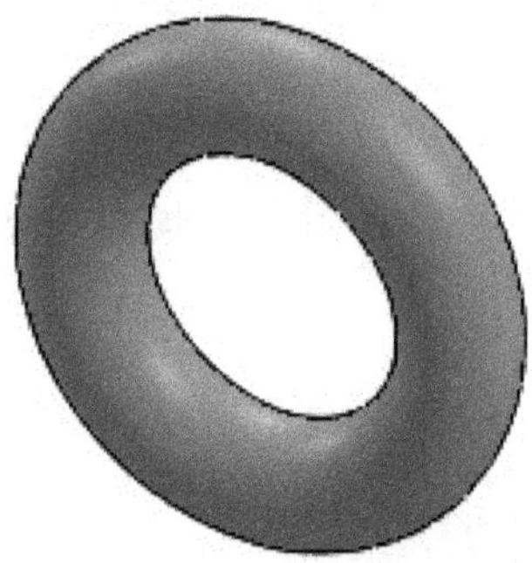

7.85

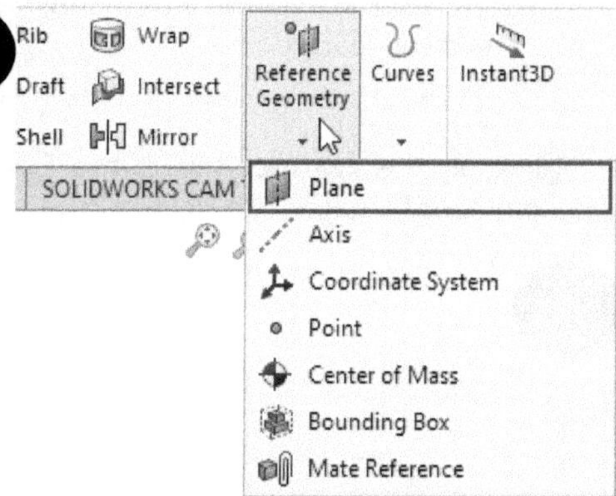

2. Click on the **Plane** tool in this flyout. The **Plane PropertyManager** appears.

3. Expand the FeatureManager Design Tree, which is now available at the top left corner of the graphics area by clicking on the arrow in front of it, see Figure 7.86.

7.86

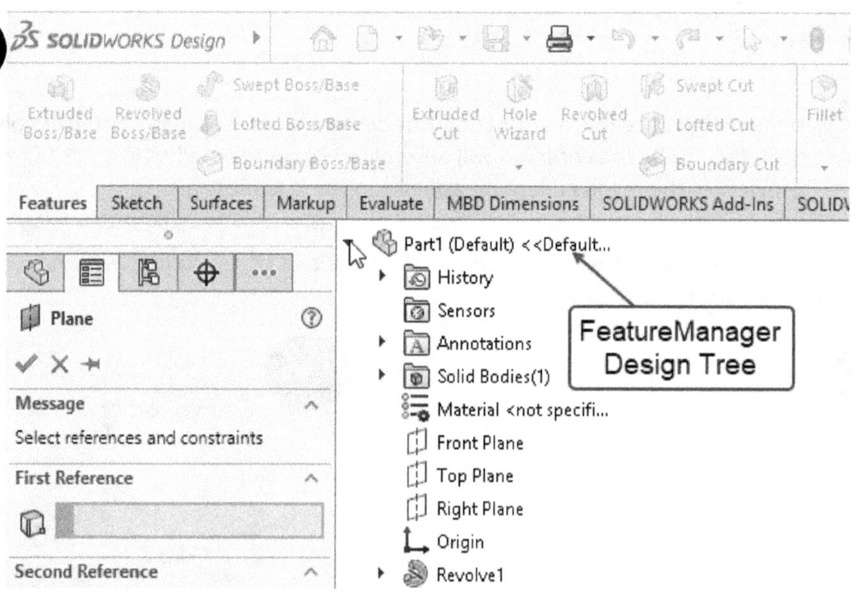

4. Click on the **Top Plane** in the FeatureManager Design Tree as the first reference. A preview of an offset plane appears in the graphics area, see Figure 7.87.

5. Select the **Flip offset** check box in the **First Reference** rollout of the PropertyManager to flip the direction of the plane downward.

6. Enter **40** in the **Offset distance** field in the **First Reference** rollout of the PropertyManager.

7. Click on the green tick-mark ✓ in the PropertyManager. The offset reference plane is created, see Figure 7.88.

7.87

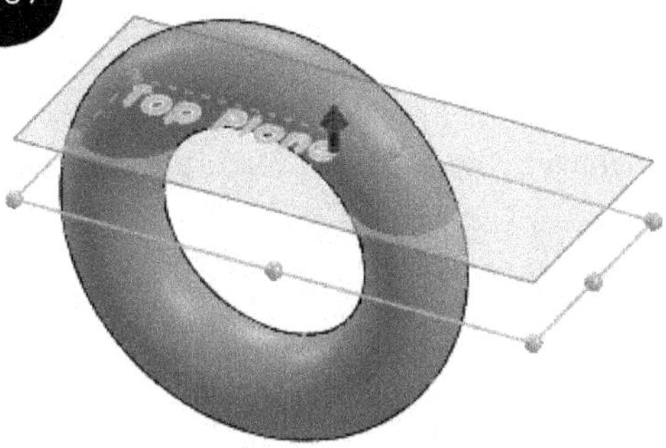

7.88

Now, you need to create the second feature of the model by selecting the newly created plane as the sketching plane.

8. Invoke the Sketching environment by selecting the newly created plane as the sketching plane. The orientation of the model changes as normal to the viewing direction.

9. Create the sketch of the second feature (a circle of diameter 15 mm) and then apply the diameter dimension, see Figure 7.89.

10. Click on the **Features** tab in the CommandManager, then click on the **Extruded Boss/Base** tool. The **Boss-Extrude PropertyManager** and the preview of the extruded feature appear. Next, change the orientation of the model to isometric, see Figure 7.90.

7.89

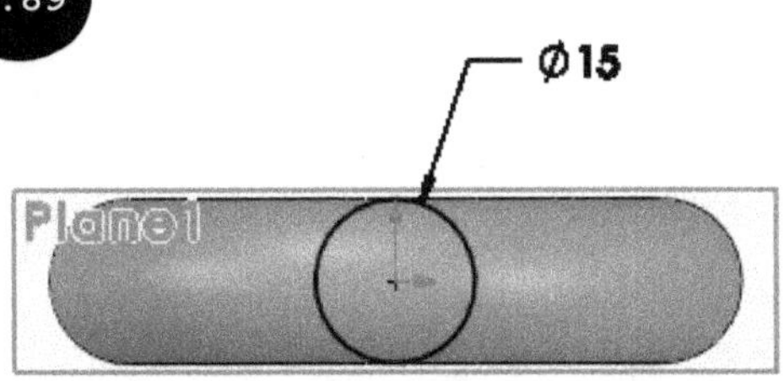

7.90

11. Invoke the **End Condition** drop-down list in the **Direction 1** rollout, see Figure 7.91.

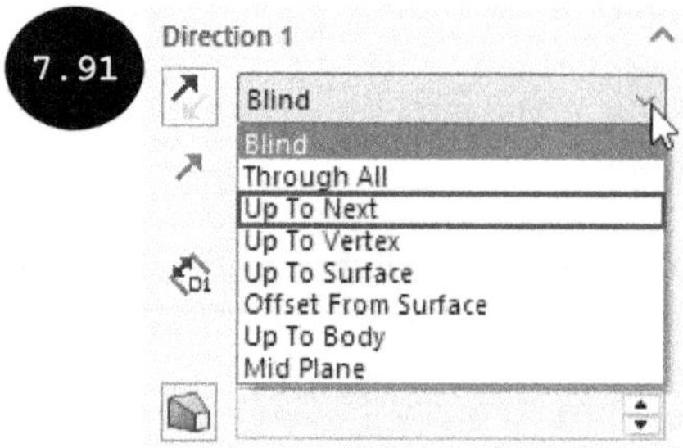

12. Click on the **Up To Next** option in the **End Condition** drop-down list. The preview of the feature gets modified in the graphics area such that it gets terminated at its next intersection, see Figure 7.92.

13. Click on the green tick-mark in the PropertyManager. The extruded feature is created, see Figure 7.93.

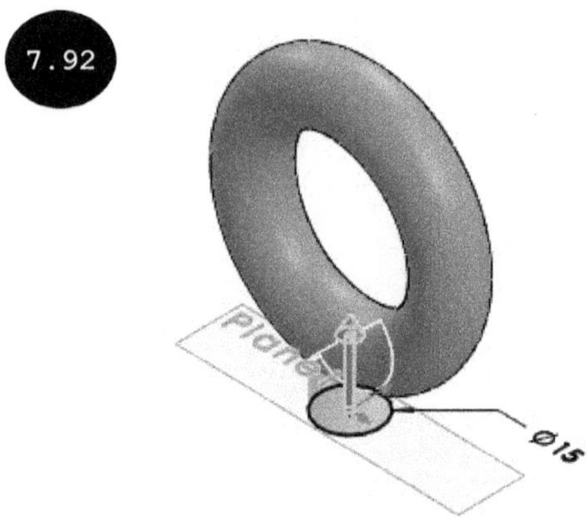

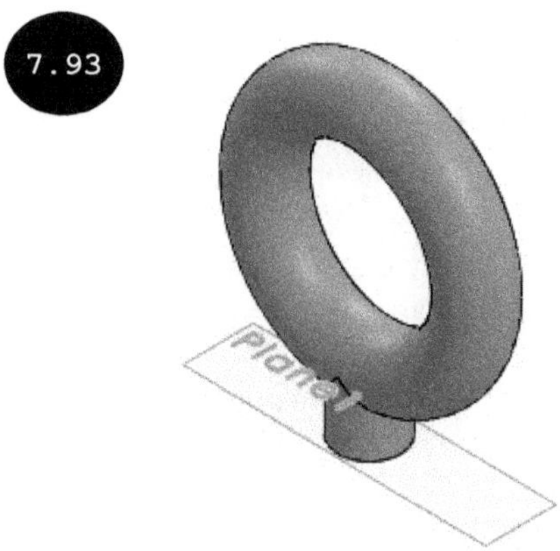

Section 6: Hiding the Reference Plane

1. Click on the reference plane in the graphics area. A Pop-up toolbar appears, see Figure 7.94.

2. Click on the **Hide** tool in the Pop-up toolbar, see Figure 7.94. The selected reference plane no longer appears in the graphics area.

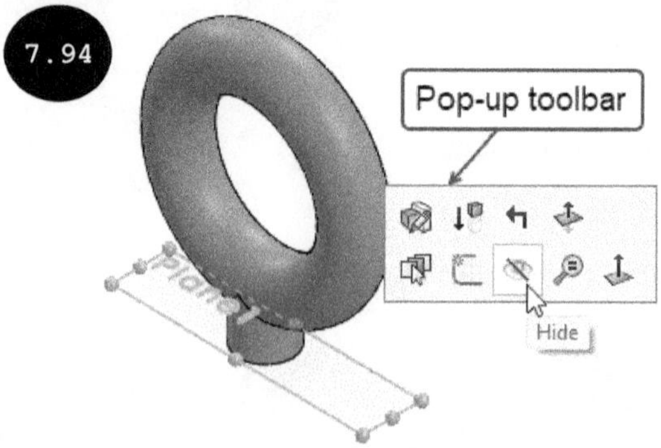

Section 7: Creating the Third Feature - Extruded Feature

1. Rotate the model such that the bottom planar face of the second feature can be viewed, see Figure 7.95.

7.95

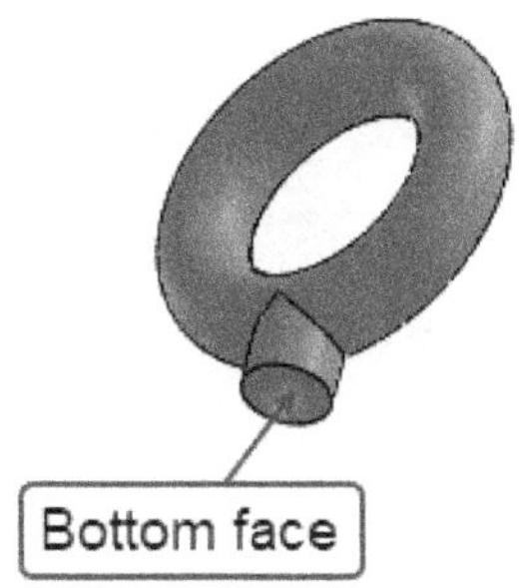

2. Invoke the Sketching environment by selecting the bottom planar face of the second feature as the sketching plane. The orientation of the model changes as normal to the viewing direction.

3. Create the sketch of the third feature (a circle of diameter 32 mm), see Figure 7.96.

4. Click on the **Features** tab and then click on the **Extruded Boss/Base** tool. The **Boss-Extrude PropertyManager** and a preview of the extruded feature appear. Next, change the orientation of the model to isometric.

5. Enter **5** in the **Depth** field of the **Direction 1** rollout and then press ENTER.

6. Click on the green tick-mark ✓ in the PropertyManager. The extruded feature is created, see Figure 7.97.

7.96

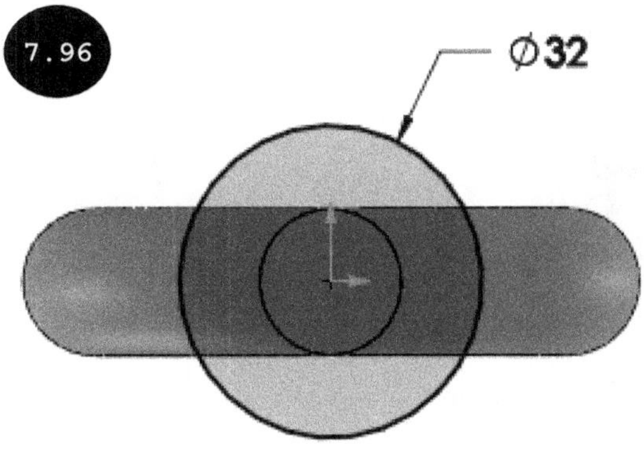

7.97

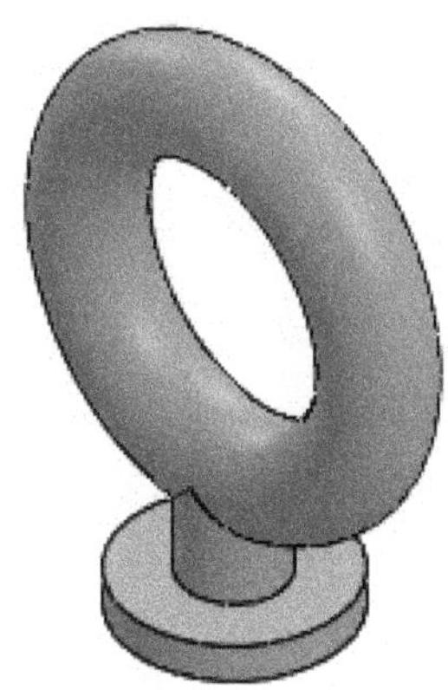

Section 8: Creating the Fourth Feature - Extruded Feature

1. Rotate the model such that the bottom planar face of the third feature can be viewed. Next, invoke the Sketching environment by selecting the bottom planar face of the third feature as the sketching plane. The orientation of the model changes as normal to the viewing direction.

2. Create the sketch of the fourth feature (a circle of diameter 18 mm), see Figure 7.98.

7.98

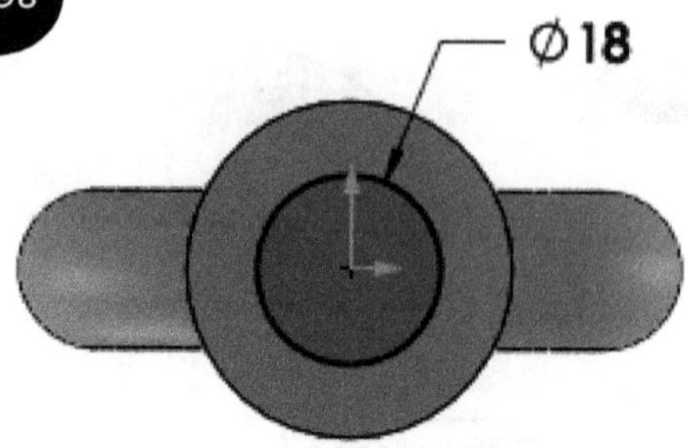

3. Click on the **Extruded Boss/Base** tool in the **Features CommandManager**. The **Boss-Extrude PropertyManager** and a preview of the extruded feature appear. Next, change the orientation of the model to isometric.

4. Enter **32** in the **Depth** field of the **Direction 1** rollout and then press ENTER.

5. Click on the green tick-mark ✓ in the PropertyManager. The extruded feature is created, see Figure 7.99.

7.99

Section 9: Saving the Model

1. Click on the **Save** tool in the **Standard** toolbar. The **Save As** window appears.

2. Browse to the SOLIDWORKS folder and then create a folder with the name **Chapter 7**.

3. Enter **Tutorial 1** in the **File name** field of the dialog box as the name of the file and then click on the **Save** button. The model is saved as Tutorial 1 in the Chapter 7 folder.

Tutorial 2

Create a model, as shown in Figure 7.100. After creating the model, assign the Alloy Steel material and calculate the mass properties of the model. All dimensions are in mm.

7.100

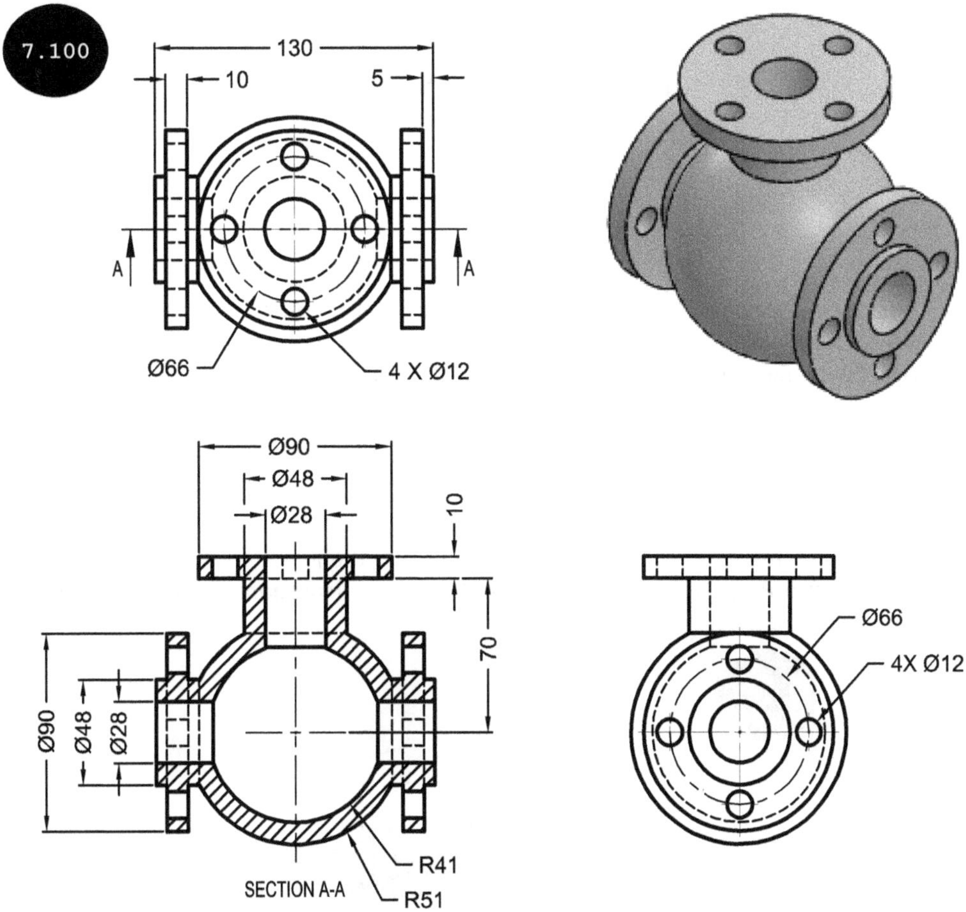

Section 1: Invoking the Part Modeling Environment

1. Start SOLIDWORKS and then invoke the Part modeling environment.

2. Ensure that MMGS (millimeter, gram, second) is selected as the unit system for the current part document.

Section 2: Creating the Base Feature - Revolved Feature

1. Invoke the Sketching environment by selecting the Front plane as the sketching plane and then create the sketch of the base feature, see Figure 7.101. Do not exit the Sketching environment. Note that the base feature of the model is a revolved feature.

7.101

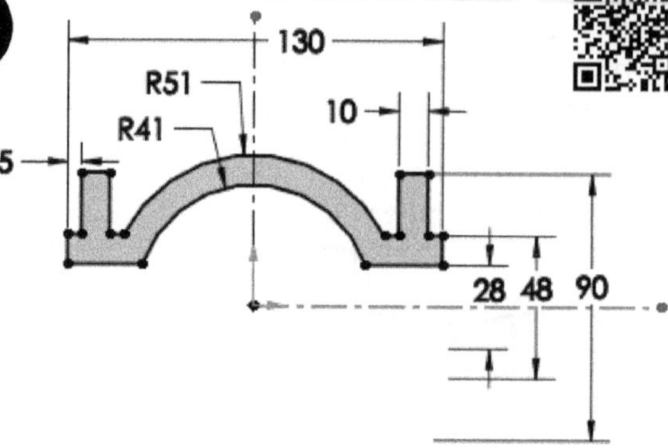

Tip: The sketch of the base feature shown in Figure 7.101 is symmetric about the vertical centerline. As a result, you need to apply symmetric relations to the sketch entities with respect to the vertical centerline. Also, you need to apply equal relations between the entities of equal length and collinear relations between the aligned entities of the sketch. You can also create line entities on one side of the vertical centerline and then mirror them to create entities on the other side of the vertical centerline.

2. Click on the **Features** tab in the CommandManager and then click on the **Revolved Boss/Base** tool. The **Revolve PropertyManager** appears. Also, the orientation of the sketch changes to trimetric, see Figure 7.102.

7.102

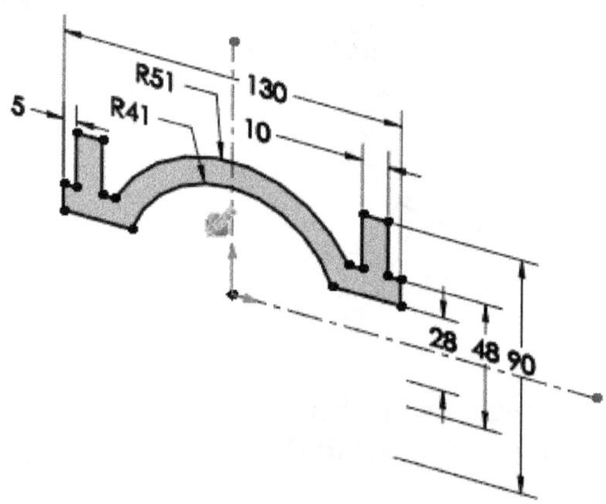

Note: If the sketch to be revolved has only one centerline, then on invoking the **Revolved Boss/Base** tool, the available centerline will automatically be selected as the axis of revolution and the preview of the revolved feature appears in the graphics area.

3. Click on the horizontal centerline of the sketch as the axis of revolution. A preview of the revolved feature appears in the graphics area.

4. Ensure that a 360-degrees angle is specified in the **Direction 1 Angle** field of the PropertyManager.

5. Click on the green tick-mark ✓ in the PropertyManager. The base/first revolved feature is created, see Figure 7.103.

Section 3: Creating the Second Feature - Extruded Feature

To create the second feature of the model, you first need to create a reference plane at an offset distance of 70 mm from the Top plane.

1. Invoke the **Reference Geometry** flyout of the **Features CommandManager**, see Figure 7.104.

7.103

7.104

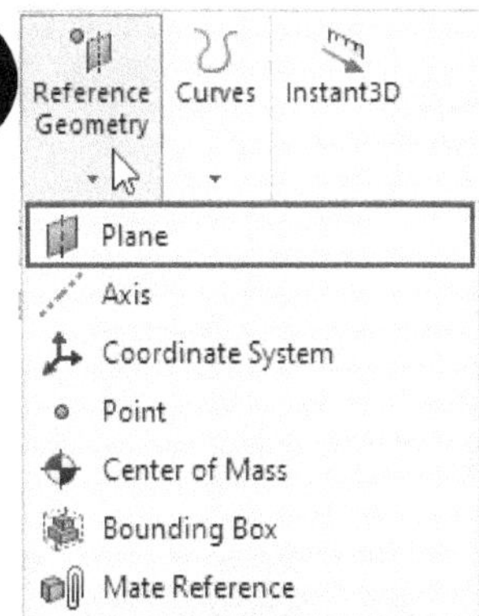

2. Click on the **Plane** tool of the **Reference Geometry** flyout. The **Plane PropertyManager** appears.

3. Expand the FeatureManager Design Tree, which is now available at the top left corner of the graphics area by clicking on the arrow in front of it.

4. Click on the **Top Plane** in the FeatureManager Design Tree as the first reference. A preview of an offset reference plane appears in the graphics area.

5. Enter **70** in the **Offset distance** field of the **First Reference** rollout in the PropertyManager.

6. Click on the green tick-mark ✓ in the PropertyManager. The reference plane is created at an offset distance of 70 mm, see Figure 7.105.

7.105

Now, you can create the second feature of the model by using the newly created plane.

7. Invoke the Sketching environment by selecting the newly created reference plane as the sketching plane. The orientation of the model changes as normal to the viewing direction.

8. Create the sketch of the second feature (a circle of diameter 48 mm), see Figure 7.106. Do not exit the Sketching environment.

7.106

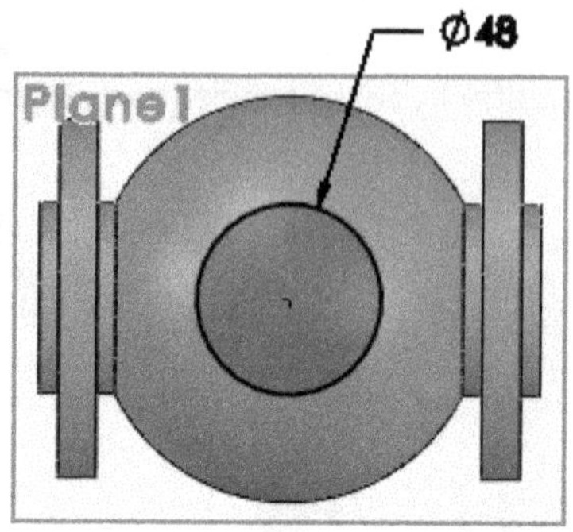

9. Click on the **Features** tab to display the tools of the **Features CommandManager**.

10. Click on the **Extruded Boss/Base** tool in the **Features CommandManager**. The **Boss-Extrude PropertyManager** and a preview of the extruded feature appear. Next, change the orientation of the model to isometric, see Figure 7.107.

11. Click on the **Reverse Direction** button in the **Direction 1** rollout of the PropertyManager to reverse the direction of extrusion downward.

12. Invoke the **End Condition** drop-down list in the **Direction 1** rollout, see Figure 7.108.

7.107

7.108

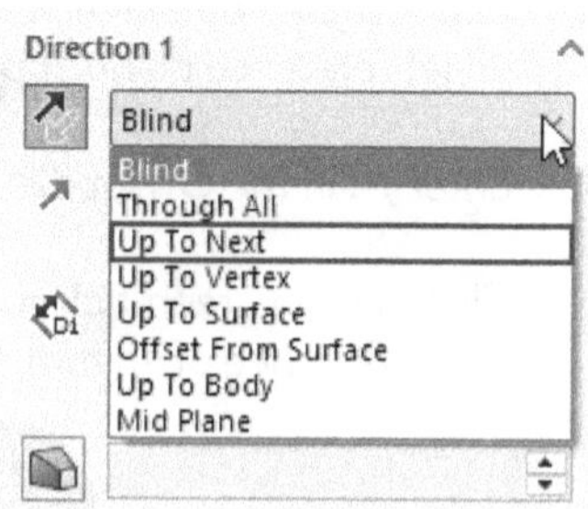

13. Click on the **Up To Next** option in the **End Condition** drop-down list. The preview of the feature gets modified in the graphics area such that it has been terminated at its next intersection.

14. Click on the green tick-mark in the PropertyManager. The extruded feature is created, see Figure 7.109.

7.109

Section 4: Hiding the Reference Plane

1. Click on the reference plane in the graphics area. A Pop-up toolbar appears, see Figure 7.110.

2. Click on the **Hide** tool in the Pop-up toolbar, see Figure 7.110. The selected reference plane gets hidden in the graphics area.

7.110

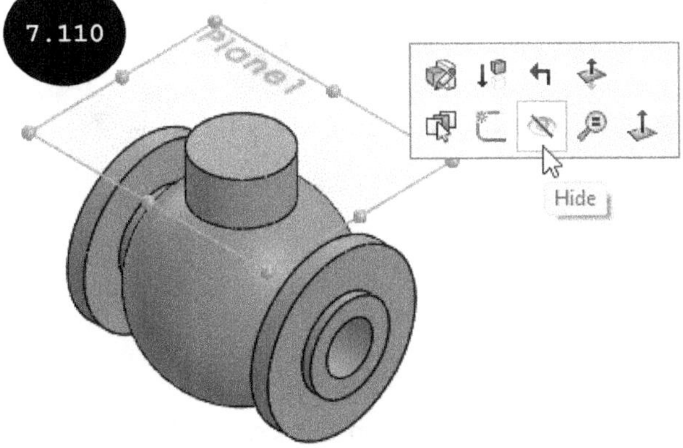

Section 5: Creating the Third Feature - Extruded Feature

1. Invoke the Sketching environment by selecting the top planar face of the second feature as the sketching plane. The orientation of the model changes as normal to the viewing direction.

2. Create the sketch of the third feature (a circle of diameter 90 mm), see Figure 7.111.

7.111

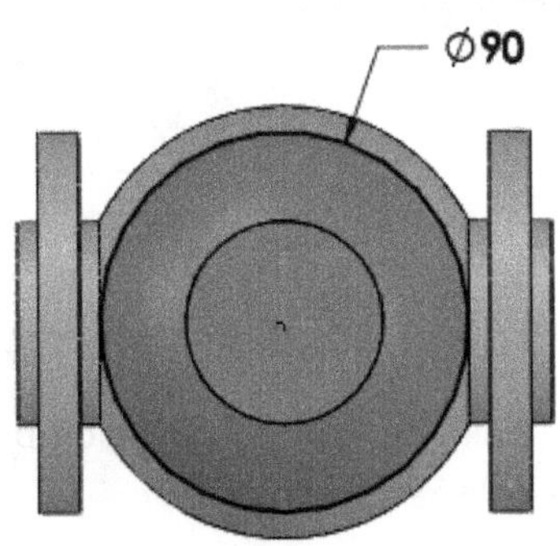

3. Click on the **Features** tab to display the tools of the **Features CommandManager**.

4. Click on the **Extruded Boss/Base** tool. The **Boss-Extrude PropertyManager** and the preview of the extruded feature appear. Next, change the orientation of the model to isometric.

Extruded Boss/Base

5. Enter **10** in the **Depth** field in the **Direction 1** rollout and then press ENTER.

6. Click on the green tick-mark ✓ in the PropertyManager. The extruded feature is created, see Figure 7.112.

Section 6: Creating the Fourth Feature - Extruded Cut Feature

1. Invoke the Sketching environment by selecting the top planar face of the third feature as the sketching plane. The orientation of the model changes as normal to the viewing direction.

2. Create the sketch of the fourth feature (a circle of diameter 28 mm), see Figure 7.113. Do not exit the Sketching environment.

7.112

7.113

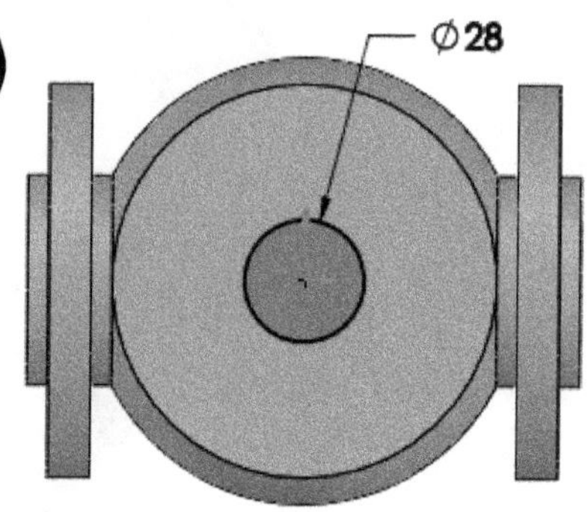

3. Click on the **Features** tab and then click on the **Extruded Cut** tool in the **Features CommandManager**. The **Cut-Extrude PropertyManager** and a preview of the extruded cut feature appear. Next, change the orientation of the model to isometric.

Extruded Cut

4. Invoke the **End Condition** drop-down list of the **Direction 1** rollout, see Figure 7.114.

7.114

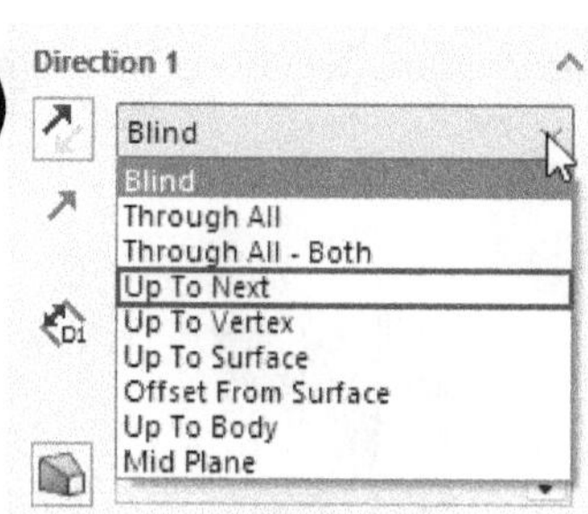

5. Click on the **Up To Next** option in the **End Condition** drop-down list. A preview of the extruded cut feature appears in the graphics area.

6. Click on the green tick-mark ✓ in the PropertyManager. The extruded cut feature is created, see Figure 7.115.

7.115

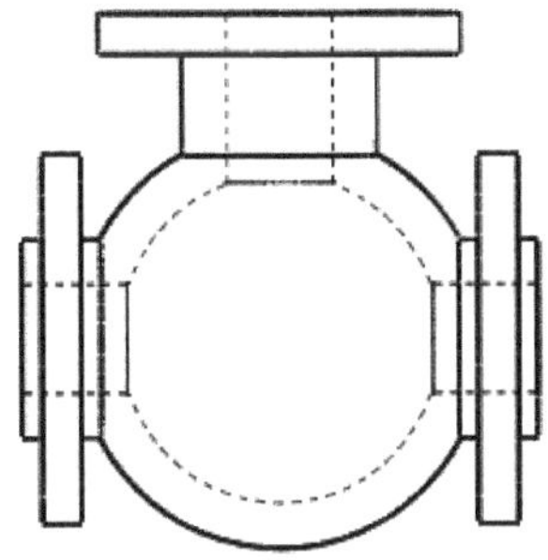

Note: In Figure 7.115, the display style of the model has been changed to the 'hidden lines visible' display style by clicking on the **Hidden Lines Visible** tool in the **Display Style** flyout of the **View (Heads-Up)** toolbar. Also, the orientation of the model has been changed to the Front view for better understanding of the cut feature.

Section 7: Creating the Fifth Feature - Extruded Cut Feature

1. Invoke the Sketching environment by selecting the right planar face of the model as the sketching plane, see Figure 7.116. The orientation of the model changes as normal to the viewing direction.

2. Create a circle of diameter 12 mm and apply the required dimensions, see Figure 7.117. Note that you need to apply a vertical relation between the origin and the center point of the circle to make it fully defined.

7.116

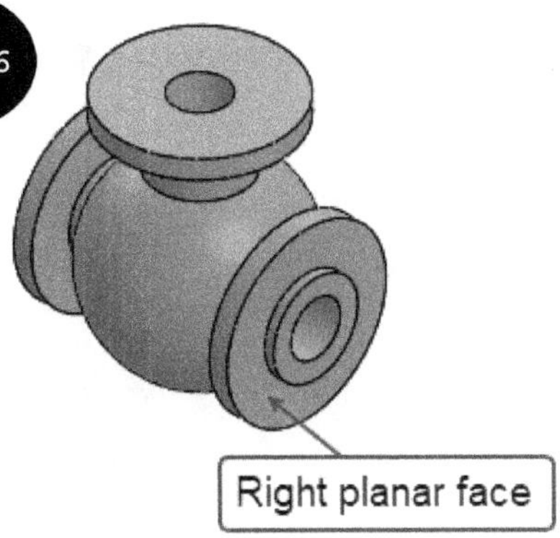

7.117

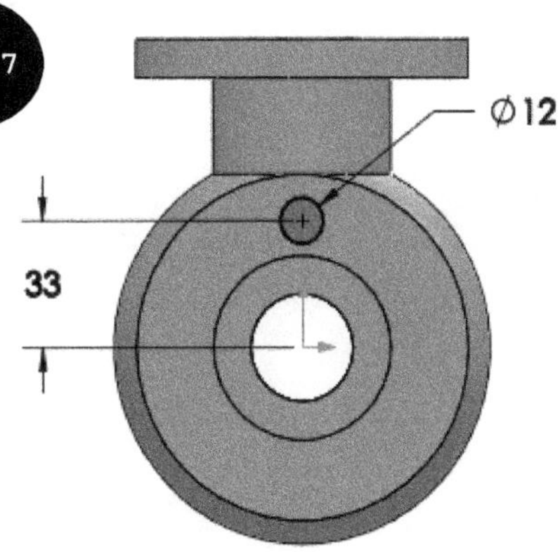

3. Click on the **Circular Sketch Pattern** tool in the **Pattern** flyout of the **Sketch CommandManager**, see Figure 7.118, and then create a circular pattern of the circle for creating remaining circles of the same diameter, see Figure 7.119. Ensure that the center point of the circular pattern is at the origin. Next, exit the tool.

7.118

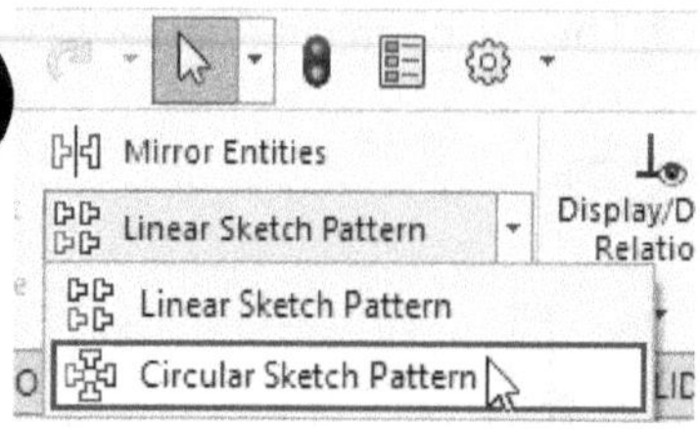

7.119

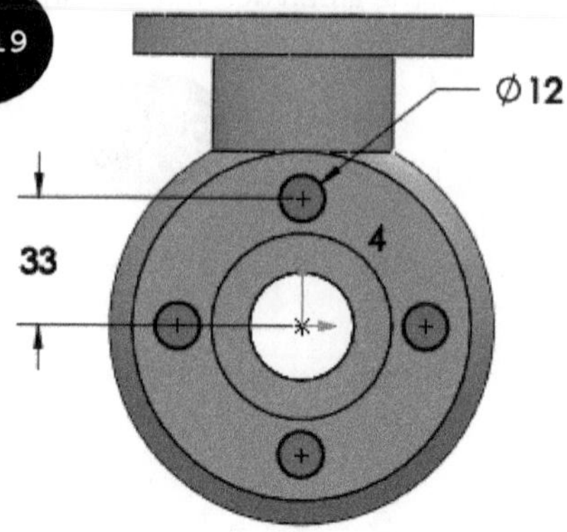

Note: Similar to patterning sketch entities in the Sketching environment, you can pattern features in the Part modeling environment. You will learn how to pattern features in the Part modeling environment in later chapters.

4. Click on the **Extruded Cut** tool in the **Features CommandManager**. The **Cut-Extrude PropertyManager** and a preview of the extruded cut feature appear. Next, change the orientation of the model to isometric, see Figure 7.120.

5. Invoke the **End Condition** drop-down list of the **Direction 1** rollout and then click on the **Up To Next** option.

6. Click on the green tick-mark ✓ in the PropertyManager. The extruded cut feature is created, see Figure 7.121.

7.120

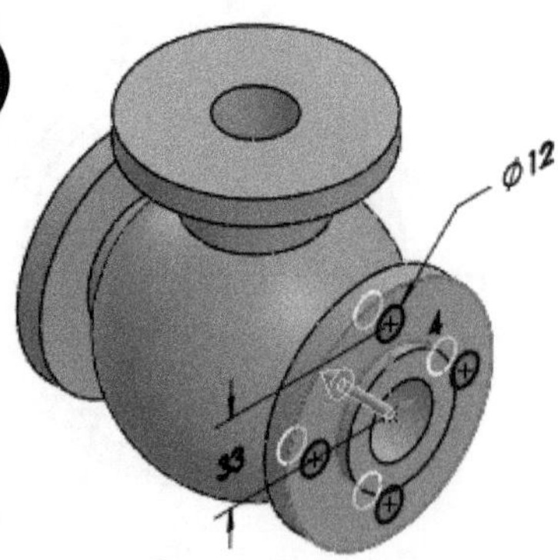

7.121

Section 8: Creating the Sixth Feature - Extruded Cut Feature

1. Similar to creating the extruded cut feature on the right planar face of the model, create the extruded cut feature on the left planar face of the model, see Figure 7.122. You can also mirror the extruded cut feature by selecting the Right plane as the mirroring plane to create the extruded cut feature on the left planar face. You will learn about mirroring features in later chapters.

7.122

Section 9: Creating the Seventh Feature - Extruded Cut Feature

1. Similar to creating the extruded cut feature on the right and left planar faces of the model, create the extruded cut feature on the top planar face of the model, see Figure 7.123.

Section 10: Assigning the Material

1. Right-click on the **Material <not specified>** option in the FeatureManager Design Tree. A shortcut menu appears, see Figure 7.124.

7.123

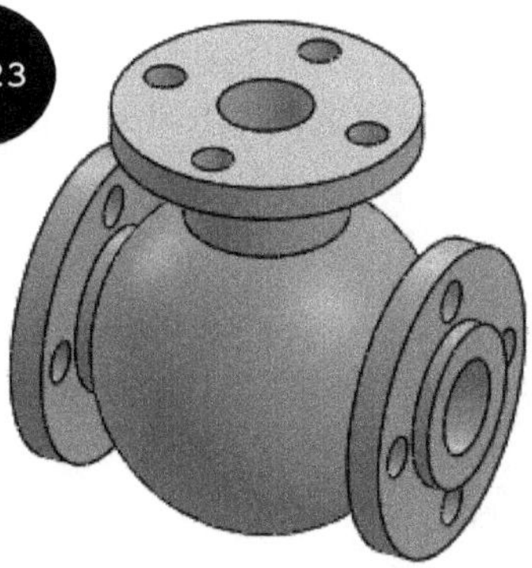

7.124

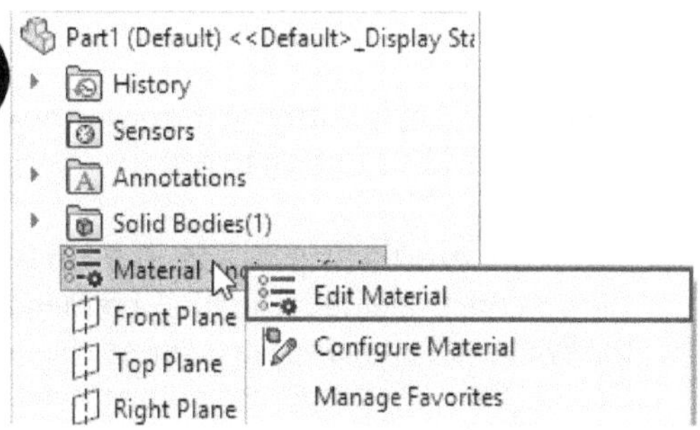

2. Click on the **Edit Material** option in the shortcut menu. The **Material** dialog box appears, see Figure 7.125.

3. Expand the **SOLIDWORKS Materials** node, if not expanded by default. The different material categories such as Steel, Iron, and Aluminium Alloys appear in the dialog box.

4. Expand the **Steel** material category and then click on the **Alloy Steel** material, see Figure 7.125. All material properties of the Alloy Steel material appear on the right side of the dialog box.

7.125

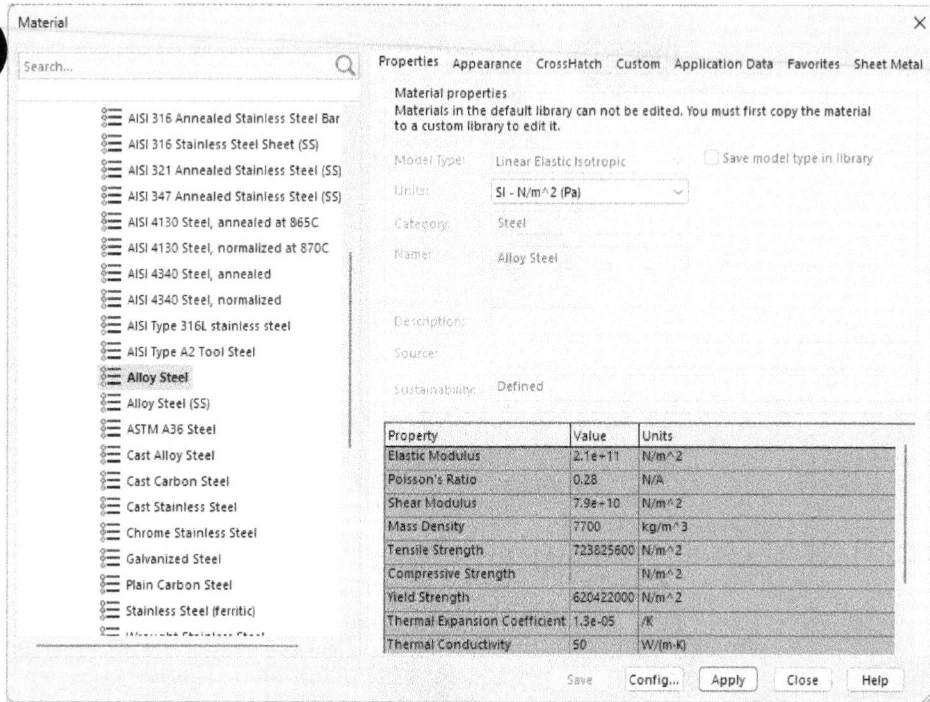

5. Click on the **Apply** button in the dialog box. The Alloy Steel material is applied to the model. Next, click on the **Close** button to exit the dialog box.

Section 11: Calculating Mass Properties

1. Click on the **Evaluate** tab in the CommandManager and then click on the **Mass Properties** tool in the **Evaluate CommandManager**, see Figure 7.126. The **Mass Properties** dialog box appears, which displays the mass properties of the model.

7.126

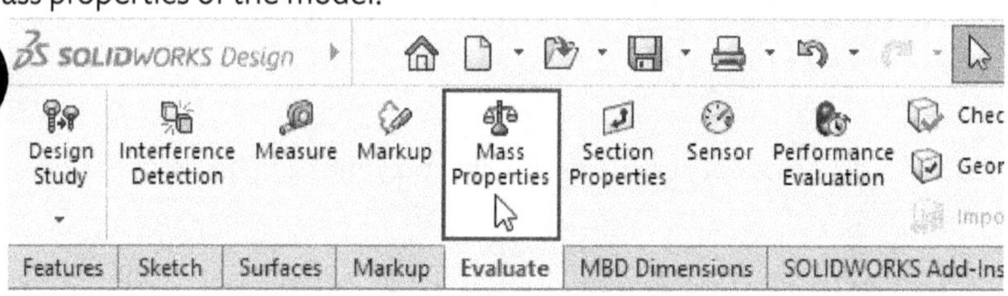

2. After reviewing the mass properties, exit the **Mass Properties** dialog box.

Section 12: Saving the Model

1. Click on the **Save** tool of the **Standard** toolbar. The **Save As** dialog box appears.

2. Browse to the Chapter 7 folder of the SOLIDWORKS folder and then save the file with the name Tutorial 2.

Tutorial 3

Create a model, as shown in Figure 7.127. After creating the model, assign the AISI 316 Stainless Steel Sheet (SS) material and calculate the mass properties of the model. All dimensions are in mm.

7.127

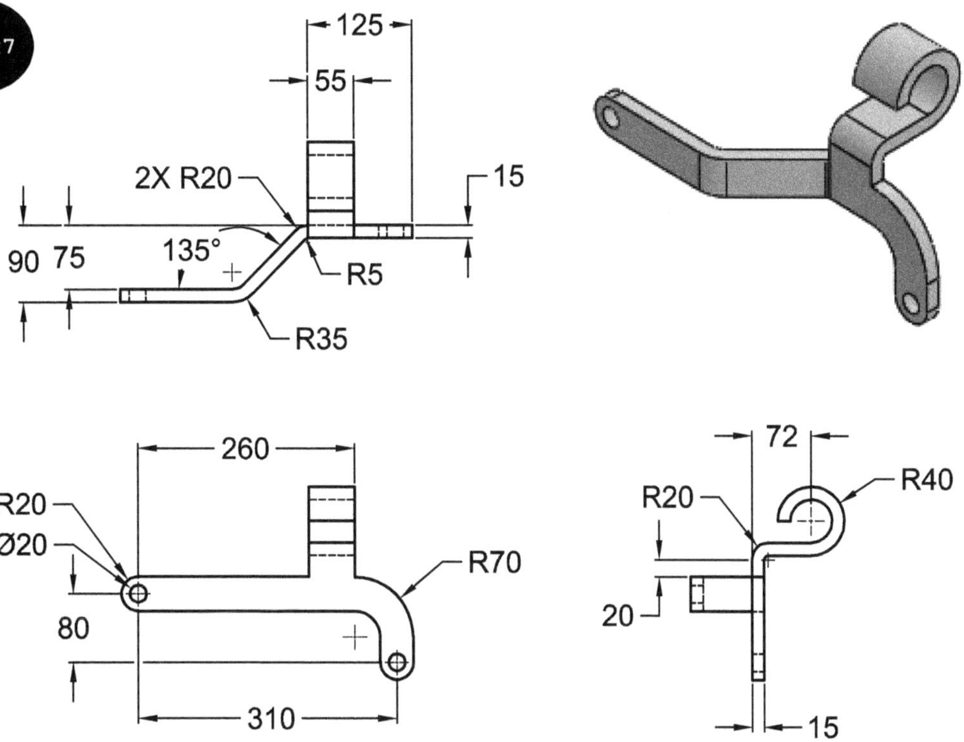

Section 1: Invoking the Part Modeling Environment

1. Start SOLIDWORKS and then invoke the Part modeling environment.

2. Ensure that MMGS (millimeter, gram, second) is selected as the unit system for the current part document.

Section 2: Creating the Base Feature - Extruded Feature

1. Invoke the Sketching environment by selecting the Front plane as the sketching plane and then create the sketch of the base feature, see Figure 7.128. After creating the sketch, do not exit the Sketching environment.

Tip: To make the sketch of the base feature fully defined as shown in Figure 7.128, you need to apply the required relations such as tangent relations between connecting lines and arcs, equal relations between the entities having equal radius and diameter, and concentric relation between the arcs sharing the same center point.

7.128

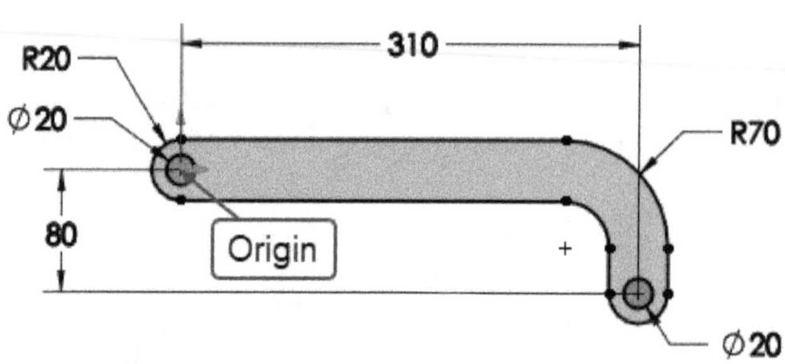

2. Click on the **Features** tab in the CommandManager and then click on the **Extruded Boss/Base** tool. The **Boss-Extrude PropertyManager** and the preview of the extruded feature appear, see Figure 7.129.

3. Invoke the **End Condition** drop-down list in the **Direction 1** rollout, see Figure 7.130.

7.129

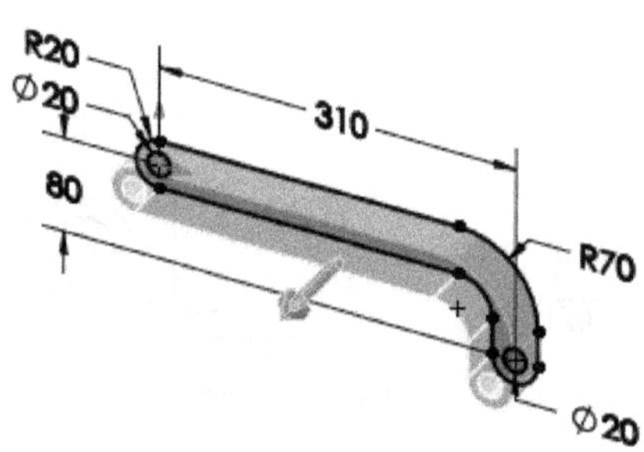

7.130

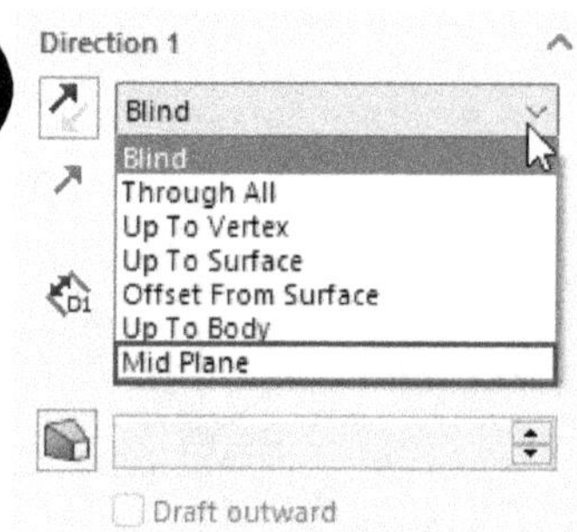

4. Click on the **Mid Plane** option in the **End Condition** drop-down list. A preview of the feature symmetric about the sketching plane appears in the graphics area.

5. Enter **90** in the **Depth** field in the **Direction 1** rollout of the PropertyManager.

6. Click on the green tick-mark ✓ in the PropertyManager. The extruded feature is created, see Figure 7.131.

7.131

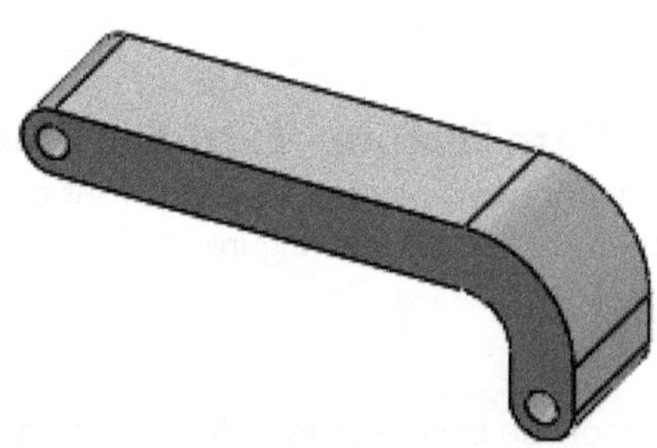

Section 3: Creating the Second Feature - Extruded Cut Feature

1. Invoke the Sketching environment by selecting the top planar face of the base feature as the sketching plane. The orientation of the model is changed as normal to the viewing direction.

2. Create a sketch of the second feature, see Figure 7.132. Do not exit the Sketching environment.

7.132

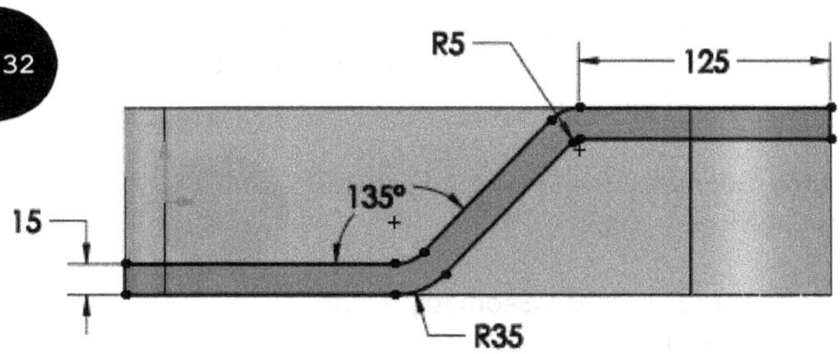

Tip: To create the sketch shown in Figure 7.132, you can use the **Line** tool to construct a closed sketch by creating all the line and arc segments one by one. Alternatively, you can first create an open loop of the sketch and then use the **Offset Entities** tool to offset it by 15 mm, adding lines to cap the ends and form a closed sketch.

3. Click on the **Extruded Cut** tool in the **Features CommandManager**. The **Cut-Extrude PropertyManager** and a preview of the extruded cut feature appear. Next, change the orientation of the model to isometric, see Figure 7.133.

4. Invoke the **End Condition** drop-down list in the **Direction 1** rollout, see Figure 7.134.

7.133

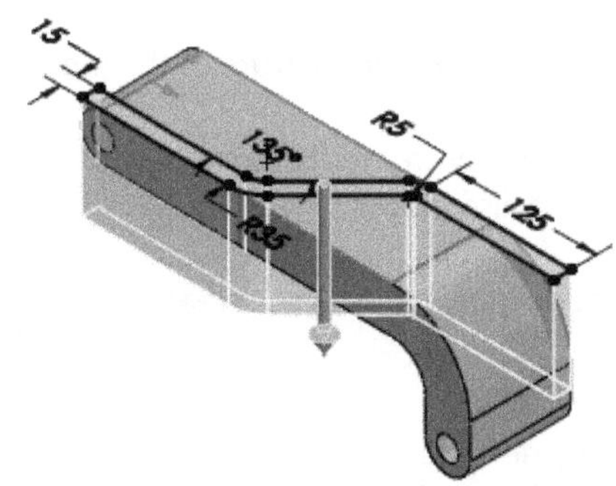

7.134

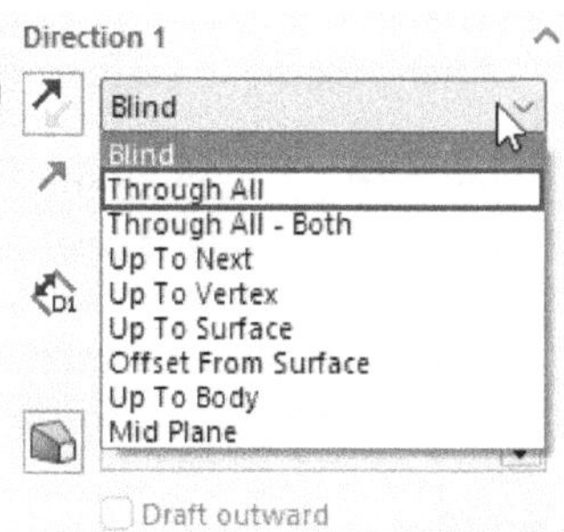

5. Click on the **Through All** option in the **End Condition** drop-down list.

6. Click on the **Flip side to cut** check box in the **Direction 1** rollout of the PropertyManager. The side of the cut material gets flipped.

7. Click on the green tick-mark ✓ in the PropertyManager. An extruded cut feature is created, see Figure 7.135.

7.135

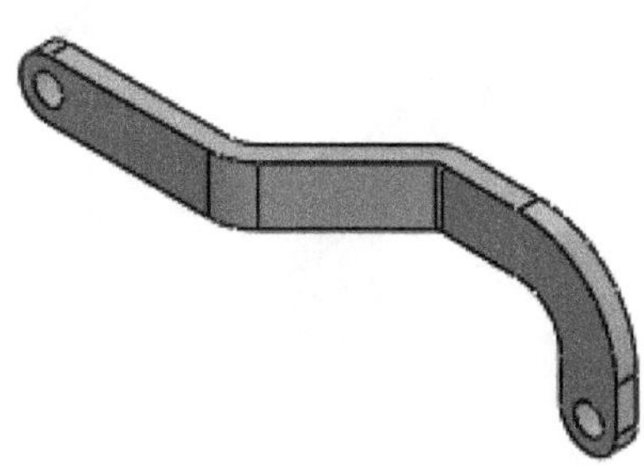

Section 4: Creating the Third Feature - Extruded Feature

To create the third feature of the model, you first need to create a reference plane at an offset distance of 205 mm from the Right plane.

1. Invoke the **Reference Geometry** flyout of the **Features CommandManager**, see Figure 7.136.

7.136

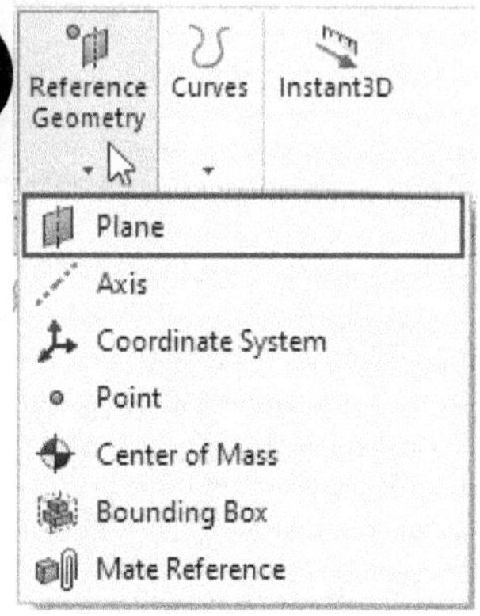

2. Click on the **Plane** tool in the **Reference Geometry** flyout. The **Plane PropertyManager** appears.

3. Expand the FeatureManager Design Tree, which is now available in the top left corner of the graphics area, by clicking on the arrow in front of it.

4. Click on the **Right Plane** as the first reference. A preview of an offset reference plane appears in the graphics area.

5. Enter **205** in the **Offset distance** field of the **First Reference** rollout in the PropertyManager.

6. Click on the green tick-mark ✓ in the PropertyManager. The reference plane is created, see Figure 7.137.

   After creating the reference plane, you need to create the third feature of the model.

7. Invoke the Sketching environment by selecting the newly created reference plane as the sketching plane. The model is oriented normal to the viewing direction.

8. Create the closed sketch of the third feature, see Figure 7.138. After creating the sketch, do not exit the Sketching environment.

Tip: To make the sketch of the third feature fully defined as shown in Figure 7.138, you need to apply the required relations such as tangent relations between connecting lines and arcs and concentric relation between the arcs sharing the same center point.

7.137

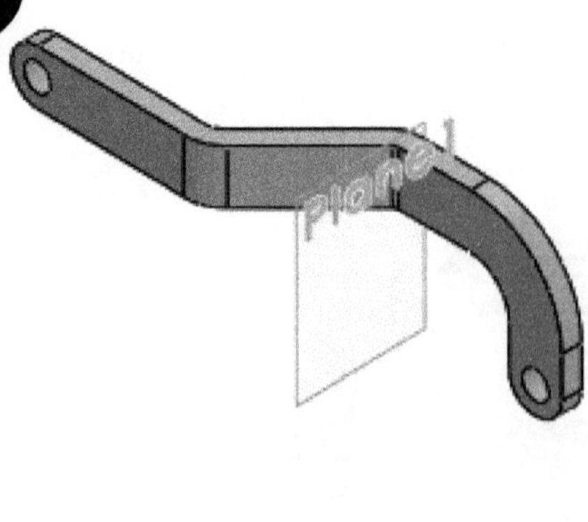

7.138

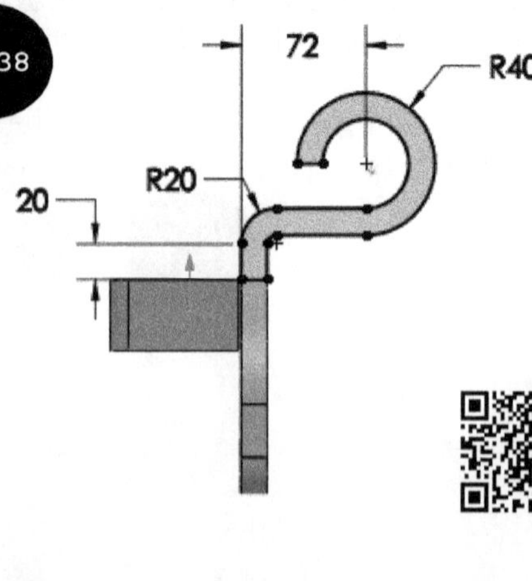

9. Click on the **Features** tab in the CommandManager to display the tools of the **Features CommandManager**.

10. Click on the **Extruded Boss/Base** tool in the **Features CommandManager**. The **Boss-Extrude PropertyManager** and a preview of the extruded feature appear. Next, change the orientation of the model to isometric, see Figure 7.139.

11. Ensure that the **Blind** option is selected in the **End Condition** drop-down list in the **Direction 1** rollout.

12. Enter **55** in the **Depth** field in the **Direction 1** rollout of the PropertyManager. Next, press ENTER.

13. Click on the green tick-mark ✓ in the PropertyManager. The extruded feature is created, see Figure 7.140. Next, hide the reference plane.

7.139

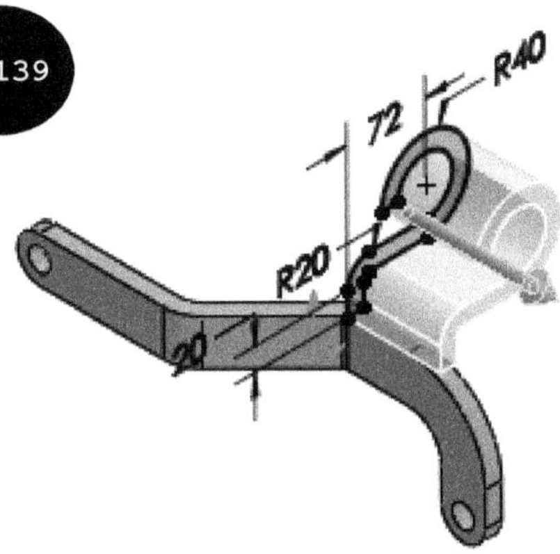

7.140

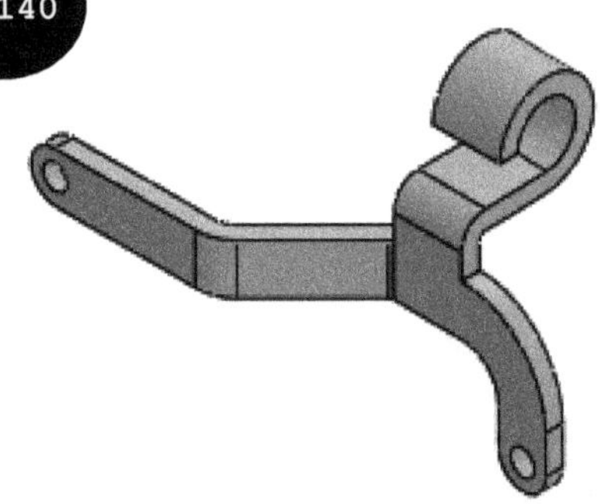

Section 5: Assigning the Material

1. Right-click on the **Material <not specified>** option in the FeatureManager Design Tree. A shortcut menu appears, see Figure 7.141.

7.141

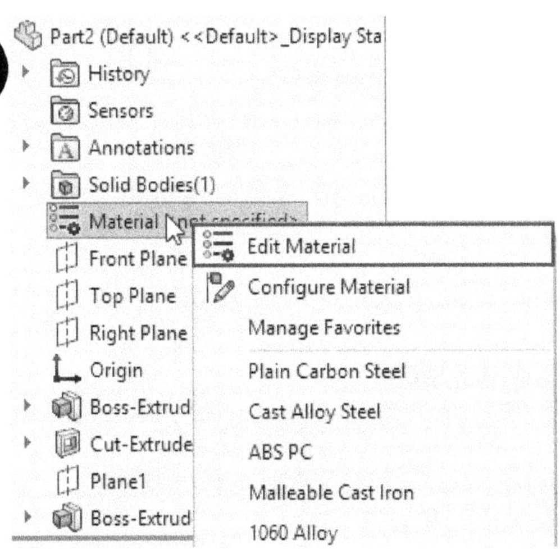

2. Click on the **Edit Material** option in the shortcut menu. The **Material** dialog box appears.

3. Expand the **SOLIDWORKS Materials** node, if not expanded by default. The different material categories such as Steel, Iron, and Aluminium Alloys appear in the dialog box.

4. Expand the **Steel** category. The materials in the **Steel** category appear, see Figure 7.142.

5. Click on the **AISI 316 Stainless Steel Sheet (SS)** material in the list of available materials, see Figure 7.142. The material properties of the selected material appear on the right panel of the dialog box.

7.142

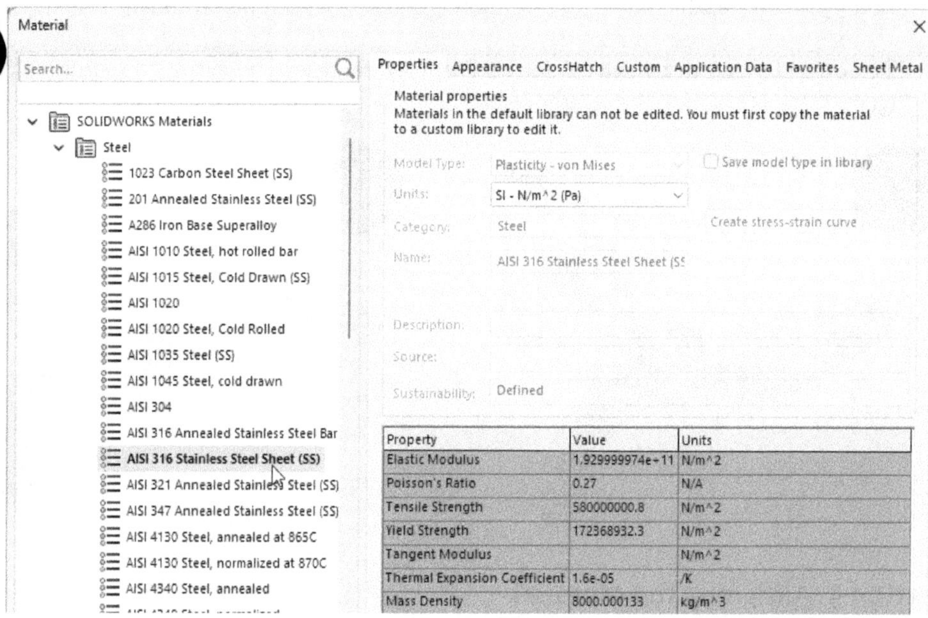

6. Click on the **Apply** button in the dialog box. The material is applied to the model. Next, click on the **Close** button to exit the dialog box.

Section 6: Calculating Mass Properties

1. Click on the **Evaluate** tab to display the tools of the **Evaluate CommandManager**.

2. Click on the **Mass Properties** tool in the **Evaluate CommandManager**. The **Mass Properties** dialog box appears and displays the mass properties of the model.

3. After reviewing the mass properties, exit the **Mass Properties** dialog box.

Section 7: Saving the Model

1. Click on the **Save** tool of the **Standard** toolbar. The **Save As** dialog box appears.

2. Browse to the Chapter 7 folder of the SOLIDWORKS folder and then save the model with the name Tutorial 3.

Hands-on Test Drive 1

Create a model, as shown in Figure 7.143. After creating the model, apply the Cast Alloy Steel material to the model and calculate its mass properties. All dimensions are in mm.

7.143

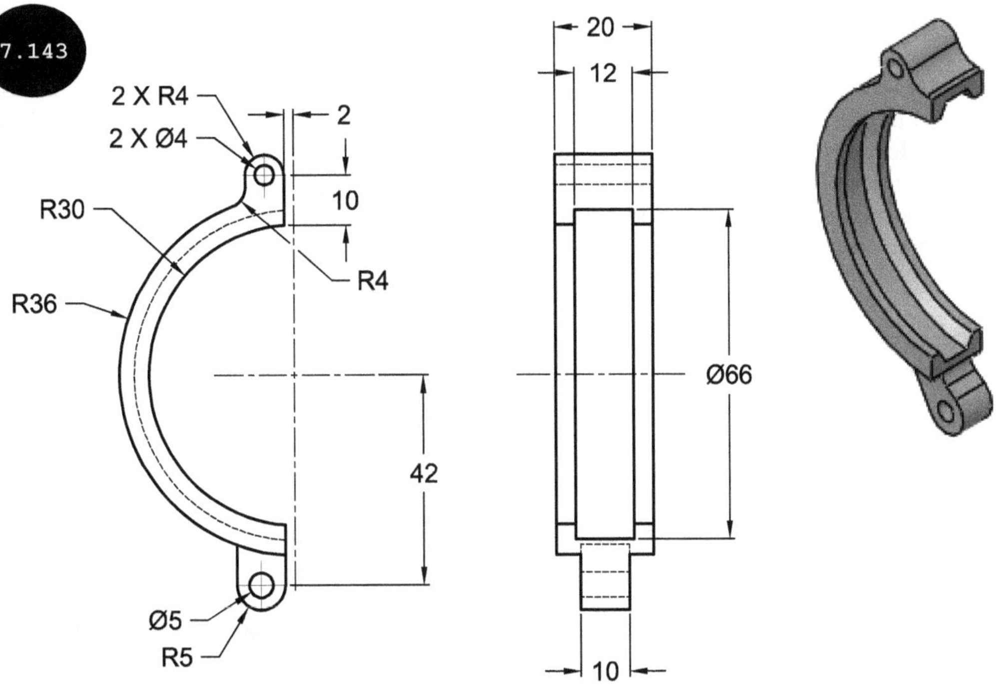

Hands-on Test Drive 2

Create a model, as shown in Figure 7.144. After creating the model, apply the Alloy Steel (SS) material to the model and calculate its mass properties. All dimensions are in mm.

7.144

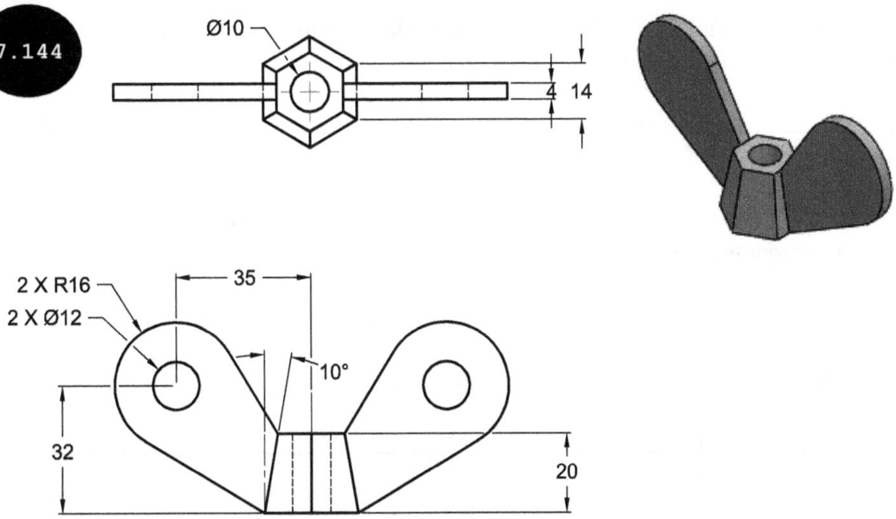

Summary

In this chapter, you explored advanced techniques for creating extruded and revolved features, as well as using the **Extruded Cut** and **Revolved Cut** tools to create cut features. You learned how to work with various types of sketches, such as closed, open, and nested sketches, and how to create multiple features from a single sketch containing multiple contours or regions.

The chapter also covered projecting edges of existing features onto the current sketch plane using the **Convert Entities** tool and editing features or sketches to reflect design changes. Additionally, you learned how to measure distances and angles between lines, points, faces, and planes using the **Measure** tool, assign appearances and textures to models, features, and faces, apply material properties, and calculate the mass properties of a model. These skills are essential for handling complex designs and ensuring accuracy in your modeling process.

Questions

Complete and verify the following sentences:

- The options in the _________ drop-down list are used for defining the start condition of extrusion.
- The _________ option is used for selecting a surface, a face, or a plane as the start condition of extrusion.
- The _________ option is used for defining the end condition or termination of extrusion by selecting a vertex.
- You can create extruded cut features by using the _________ tool.
- The _________ sketches have all the entities connected end to end with each other without any gaps.
- You can project the edges of existing features as sketch entities onto the current sketching plane by using the _________ tool.
- The _________ tool is used for calculating mass properties such as the mass and volume of a model.
- A revolved cut feature is created by removing material from the model by revolving a sketch around a centerline or an axis. (True/False)
- You can edit individual features and their sketches as per your requirements. (True/False)
- In SOLIDWORKS, you cannot customize material properties. (True/False)

CHAPTER
8

Advanced Modeling - II

This chapter discusses the following topics:

- Creating a Sweep Feature
- Creating a Sweep Cut Feature
- Creating a Lofted feature
- Creating a Lofted Cut Feature
- Creating a Boundary Feature
- Creating a Boundary Cut Feature
- Creating Curves
- Splitting Faces of a Model
- Creating 3D Sketches

In the previous chapters, you explored the fundamental modeling tools for creating features like extrude and revolve, both for adding and removing material. You also learned the essential workflow for building models, starting with a base feature and progressively adding subsequent features. Additionally, techniques such as navigating models, adjusting view orientations, changing display styles, assigning materials, and calculating mass properties were covered, along with other foundational tools and methods.

In this chapter, we will delve into advanced modeling tools, including **Swept Boss/Base**, **Lofted Boss/Base**, and **Boundary Boss/Base**. You will also discover how to split model faces and create various types of 3D curves and sketches.

Creating a Sweep Feature

A sweep feature is created by adding material by sweeping a profile along a defined path. Figure 8.1 shows a profile and a path. Figure 8.2 shows the resultant sweep feature created by sweeping the profile along the path.

8.1

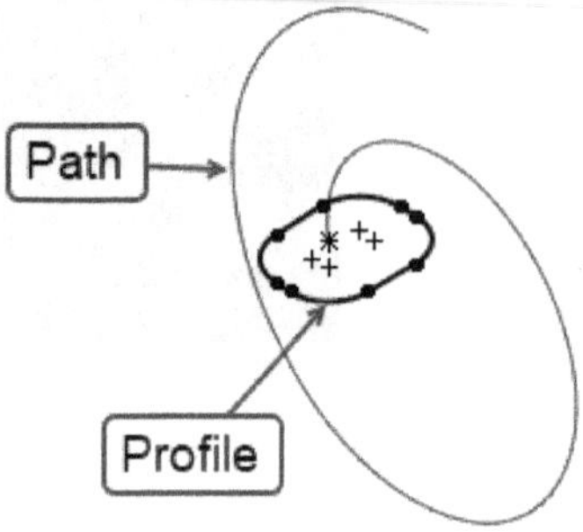

8.2

It is evident from the above figures that to create a sweep feature, you first need to create a path and a profile where the profile follows the path and creates a sweep feature. To create a profile, you need to identify the cross-section of the feature to be created. To create a path, you need to identify the route/path taken by the profile for creating the feature. In SOLIDWORKS, you can create a sweep feature by using the **Swept Boss/Base** tool of the **Features CommandManager**. Note that for creating a sweep feature, you need to take care of the following points:

1. The profile must be a closed sketch. You can also select the face of a model as a profile. Besides, you can also select an edge or a group of edges of a model that forms a closed loop as a profile.
2. The path can be an open or closed sketch, which is made up of a set of end-to-end connected sketched entities, a curve, or a set of model edges.
3. The starting point of the path must intersect the plane of the profile.
4. The profile and path as well as the resultant sweep feature must not self-intersect.

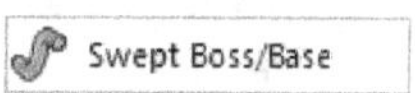

After creating the path and the profile, click on the **Swept Boss/Base** tool in the **Features CommandManager**. The **Sweep PropertyManager** appears, see Figure 8.3. The options in the PropertyManager are discussed next.

8.3

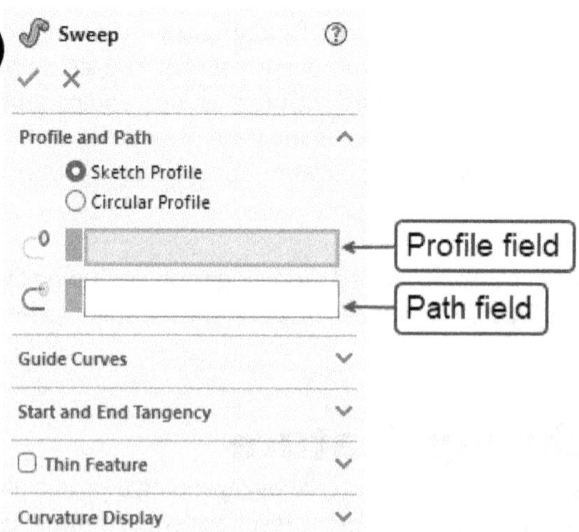

Profile and Path

The options in the **Profile and Path** rollout of the PropertyManager are used to select a profile and a path. The options are discussed next.

Sketch Profile

The **Sketch Profile** radio button of the **Profile and Path** rollout is selected, by default. As a result, the **Profile** and the **Path** fields are available in the PropertyManager, refer to Figure 8.3. The **Profile** field is used to select a profile of the sweep feature. You can select a closed sketch, a face, or an edge/group of edges that form a closed loop as a profile, see Figure 8.4. The **Path** field is used to select a path of the sweep feature, see Figure 8.4. You can select an open or a closed sketch, an edge, or a curve as the path of the sweep feature.

8.4

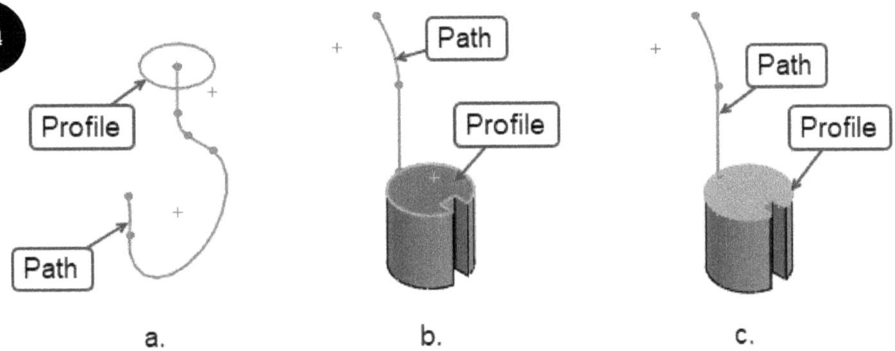

As soon as you select a profile and a path, a preview of the resultant sweep feature appears in the graphics area, see Figure 8.5.

8.5

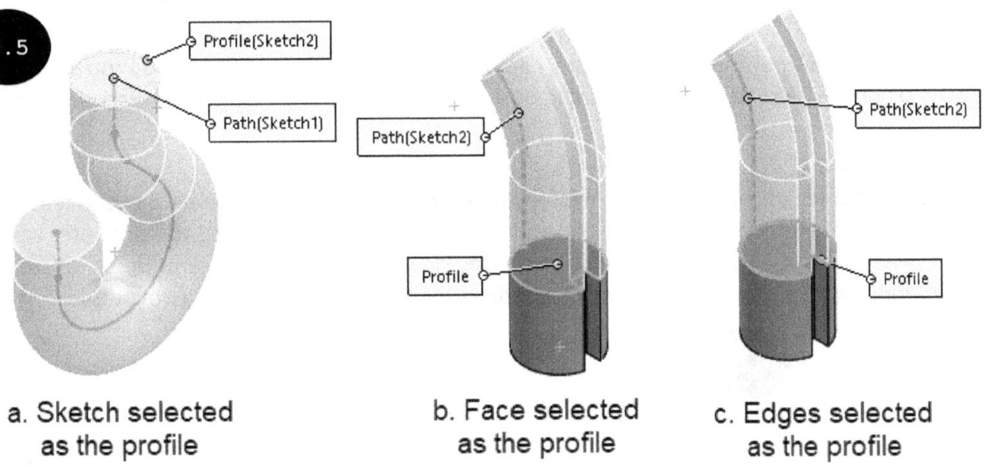

Note: If the profile is created between the endpoints of the path (see Figure 8.6), then the preview of the sweep feature appears on either side of the profile, see Figure 8.7. Also, three buttons: **Direction 1**, **Bidirectional**, and **Direction 2** become available in the **Profile and Path** rollout, (see Figure 8.8). The **Direction 1** and **Direction 2** buttons are used for sweeping the profile to either side, whereas the **Bidirectional** button is used for sweeping the profile to both its sides.

8.6

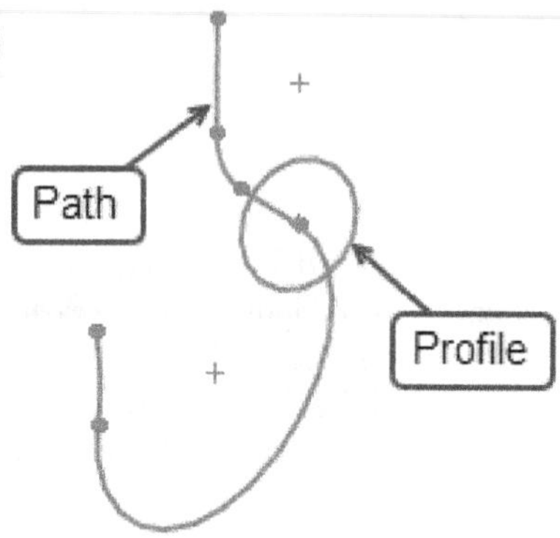

8.7

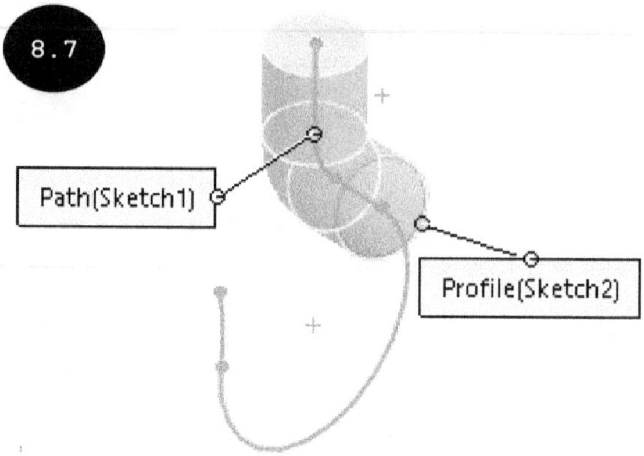

8.8

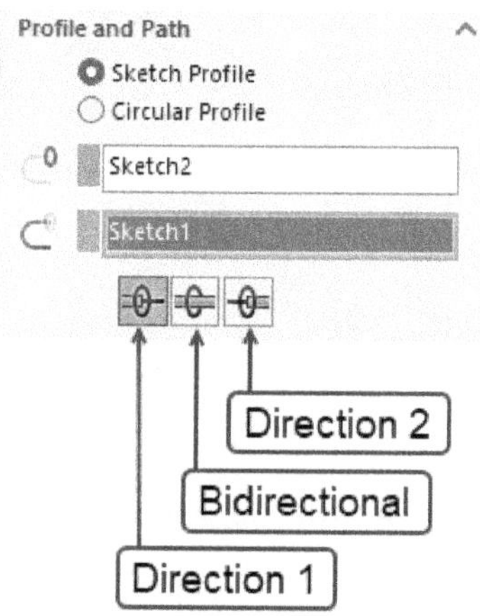

To accept the preview of the sweep feature, click on the green tick-mark ✓ in the PropertyManager. The sweep feature is created. The remaining options of the PropertyManager are discussed next.

Circular Profile

The **Circular Profile** radio button of the **Profile and Path** rollout is used to create a sweep feature that has a circular cross-section such as a solid rod or hollow tube by specifying the diameter value. To create a sweep feature by using this radio button, you do not need to select a profile. On selecting the **Circular Profile** radio button, the **Path** and **Diameter** fields become available in the rollout, see Figure 8.9.

8.9

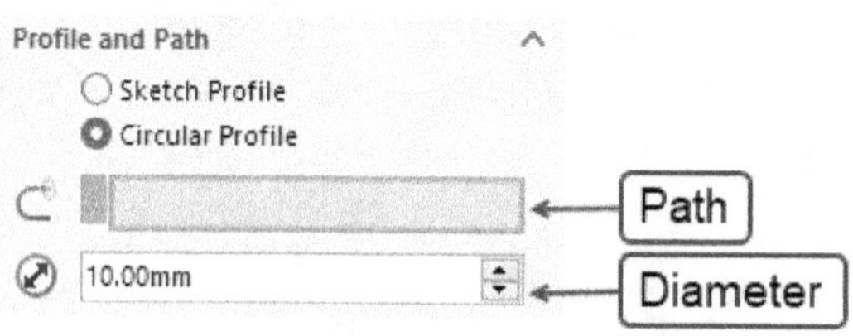

The **Path** field is used to select a path of the sweep feature. By default, this field is active. As a result, you can select an open or a closed sketch, an edge, or a curve as the path of the sweep feature. The **Diameter** field of the rollout is used for specifying the diameter value of the circular profile. After selecting the path, a preview of the sweep feature having a circular profile of a specified diameter appears in the graphics area, see Figure 8.10. In this figure, an edge is selected as the path of the sweep feature.

8.10

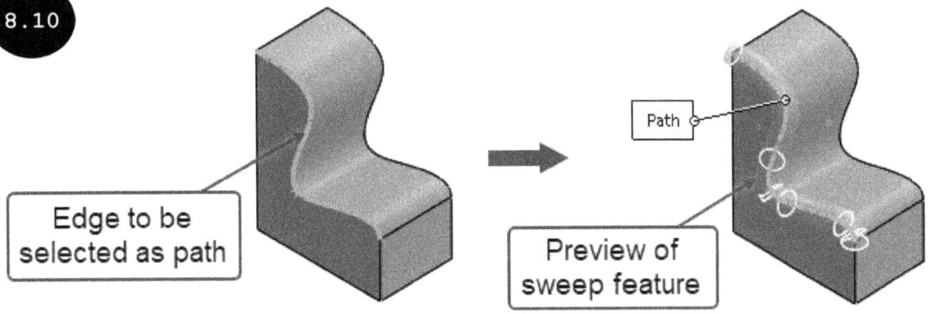

The options in the other rollouts of the **Sweep PropertyManager** are used to control the parameters of the sweep feature. These options are discussed next.

Options

By default, the **Options** rollout of the PropertyManager is collapsed. To expand this rollout, click on the arrow available on its right, see Figure 8.11. Note that some of the options of the **Options** rollout are not available while creating a base/first feature. Also, the availability of options in this rollout depends upon the selection of **Sketch Profile** or **Circular Profile** radio button in the **Profile and Path** rollout of the PropertyManager. The options of the **Options** rollout are discussed next.

8.11

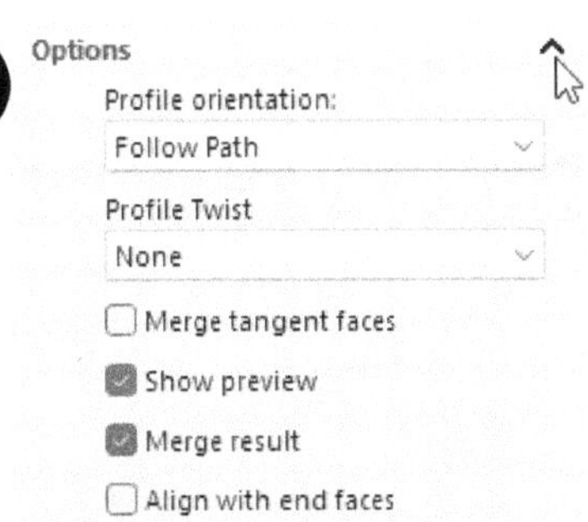

Profile orientation drop-down list

The options in the **Profile orientation** drop-down list are used to control the orientation of the profile along the path, see Figure 8.12. The options are discussed next.

8.12

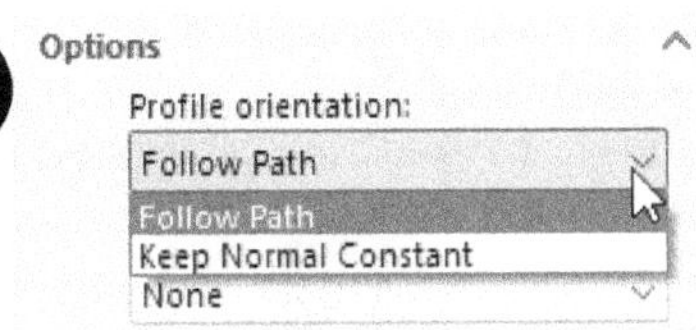

Follow Path

By default, the **Follow Path** option is selected in the drop-down list. As a result, the profile follows the path by maintaining the same angle of orientation from start to end by aligning itself normal to the path, see Figures 8.13 and 8.14.

8.13

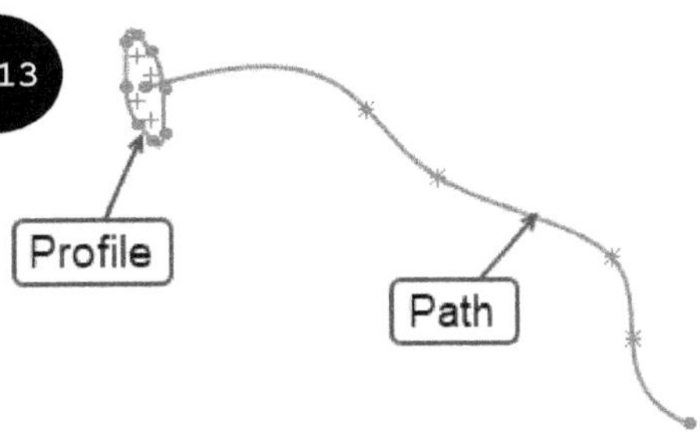

8.14

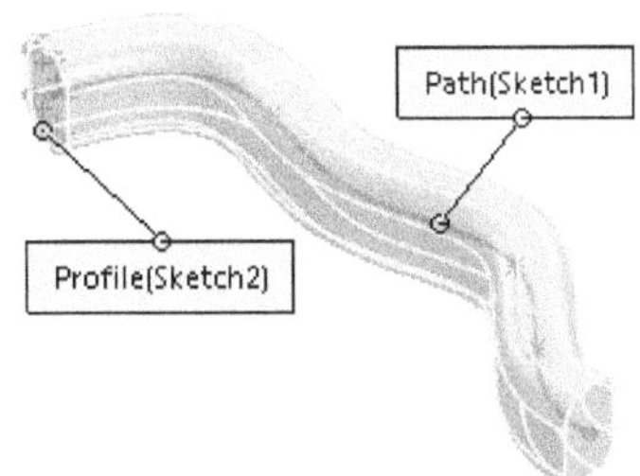

Keep Normal Constant

On selecting the **Keep Normal Constant** option, the profile follows a path such that it remains parallel throughout the path. In other words, the start and end sections of the resultant sweep feature are parallel to each other. Figure 8.15 shows the preview of a sweep feature when the **Follow Path** option is selected, and Figure 8.16 shows the preview of the sweep feature when the **Keep Normal Constant** option is selected.

8.15

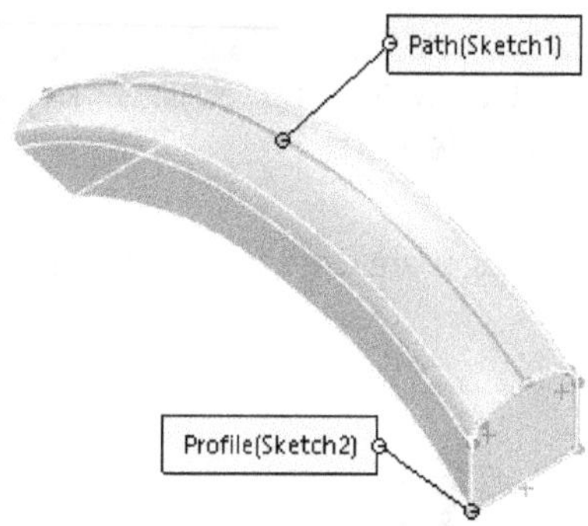

8.16

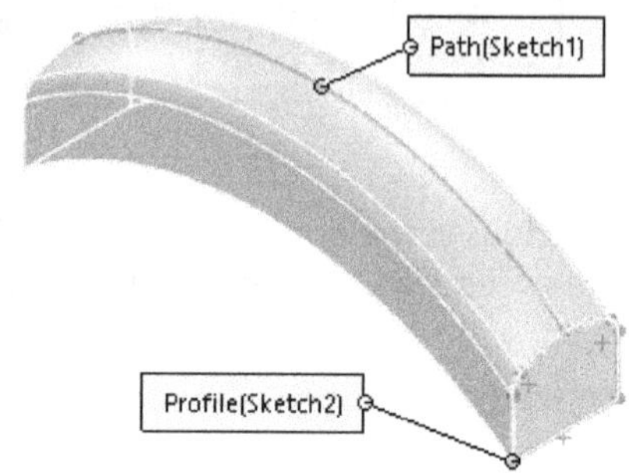

Profile Twist drop-down list

The options in the **Profile Twist** drop-down list are used to control the twisting or alignment of the profile along the path, see Figure 8.17. The options are discussed next.

8.17

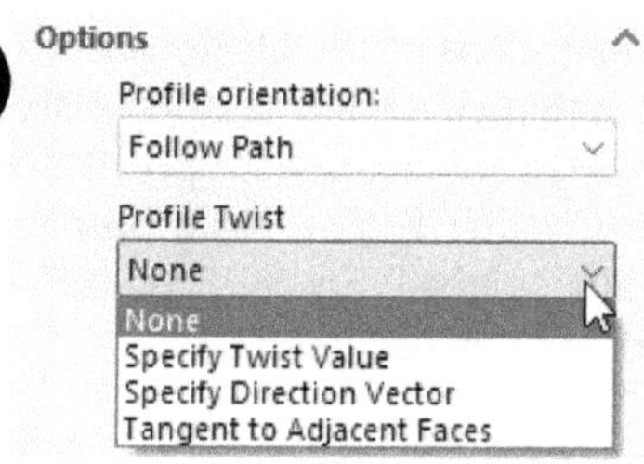

None

By default, the **None** option is selected in the **Profile Twist** drop-down list. As a result, the profile follows a path such that it maintains normal alignment.

Specify Twist Value

By selecting the **Specify Twist Value** option, you can twist the profile along the path, see Figures 8.18 through 8.21. Figures 8.18 and 8.20 show the path and profile, respectively and Figures 8.19 and 8.21 show the preview of the resultant twisted sweep feature.

8.18

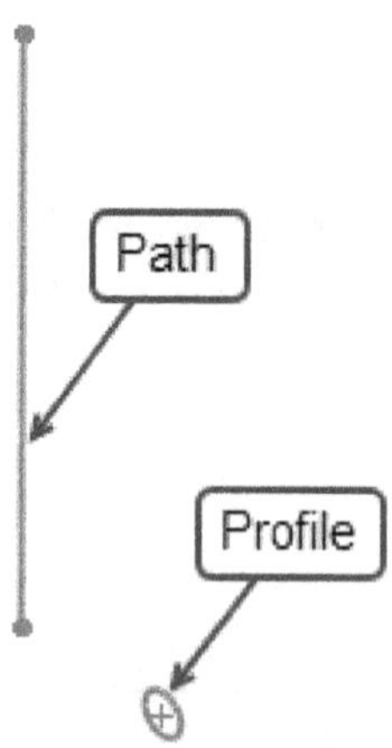

8.19

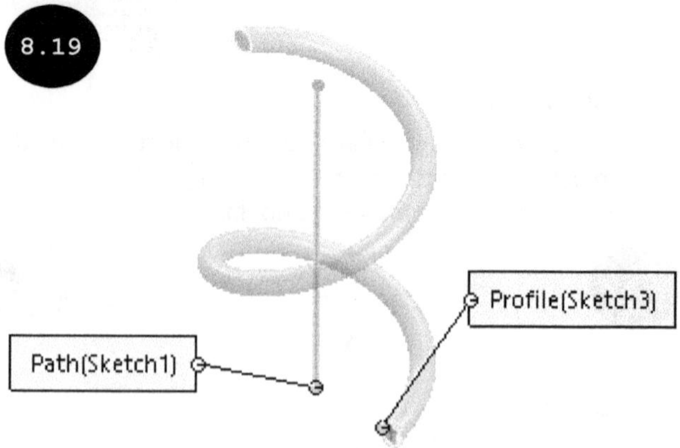

8.20

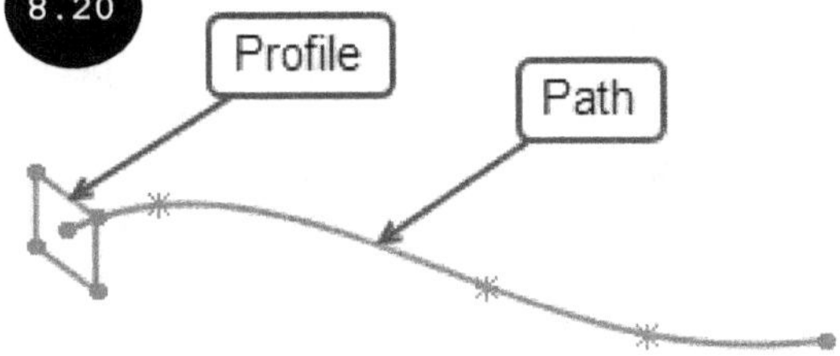

8.21

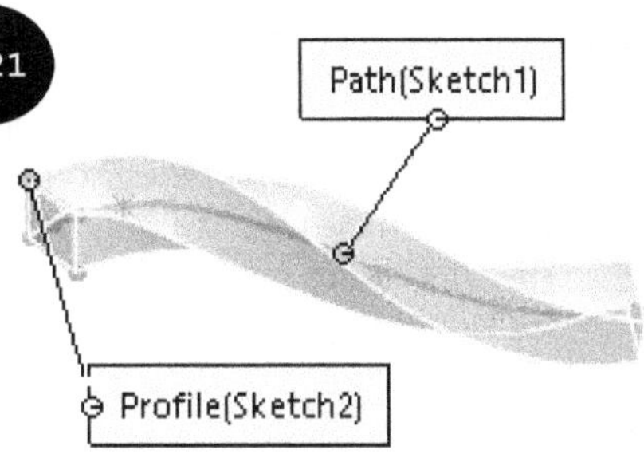

After selecting the **Specify Twist Value** option, the **Twist control** drop-down list and **Direction 1** field become available in the **Options** rollout, see Figure 8.22. The options in the **Twist control** drop-down list are used to control the twisting of the profile along the path. The options are discussed next.

8.22

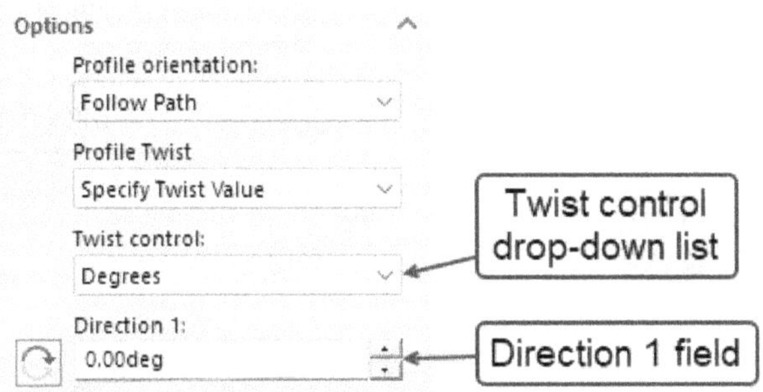

Degrees: By default, the **Degrees** option is selected in the **Twist control** drop-down list. As a result, you need to specify the twist angle in degrees in the **Direction 1** field of the rollout.

Radians: The **Radians** option is used to specify the twist angle in radians in the **Direction 1** field of the **Options** rollout.

Revolutions: By selecting the **Revolutions** option, you can specify the number of revolutions for the profile along the path in the **Direction 1** field. Figures 8.23 and 8.24 show the preview of a sweep feature after entering 3 in the **Direction 1** field as the number of revolutions.

8.23

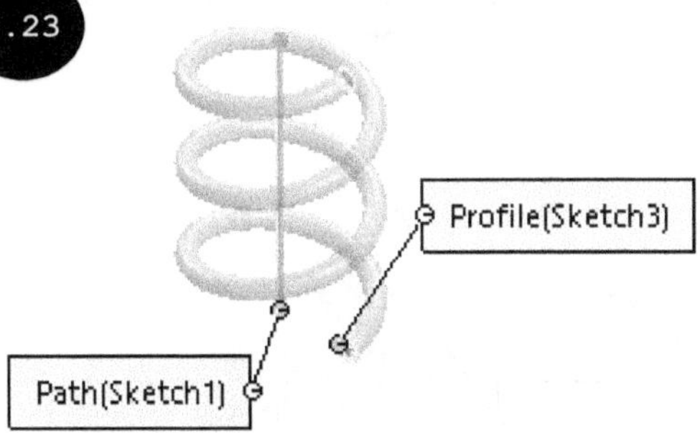

8.24

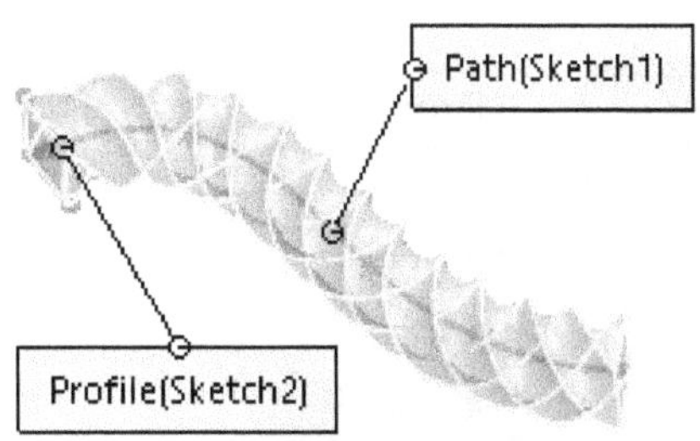

Note: If the profile is created between the endpoints of the path (refer to Figure 8.25), and you are creating a bidirectional sweep feature (see Figure 8.26), then on selecting the **Specify Twist Value** option in the **Profile Twist** drop-down list, the **Direction 2** field also becomes available in the rollout along with the **Twist control** drop-down list and the **Direction 1** field. The **Direction 2** field specifies the twist angle in the second direction of the sweep feature, see Figure 8.27.

8.25

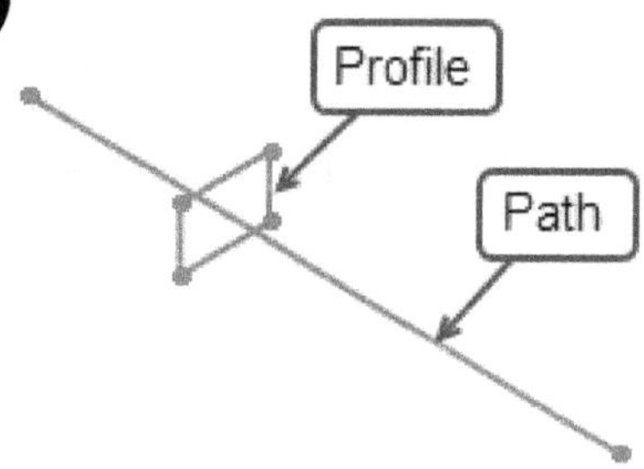

8.26

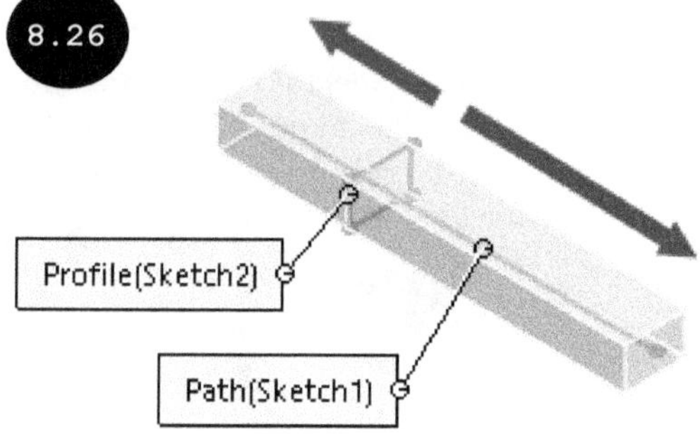

8.27

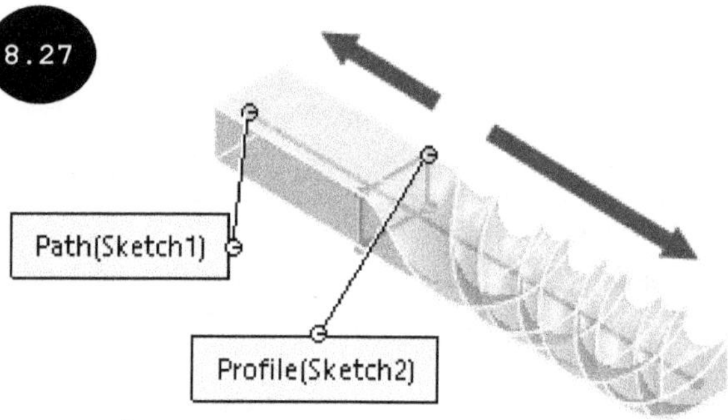

Specify Direction Vector

On selecting the **Specify Direction Vector** option in the **Profile Twist** drop-down list, the **Direction Vector** field becomes available. The **Direction Vector** field is used to select a direction vector for aligning the profile. You can select a plane, a planar face, a line, or a linear edge as the direction vector. Figure 8.28 shows a path, a profile, and a direction vector. Figure 8.29 shows the preview of the resultant sweep feature by selecting the Top plane as the direction vector.

8.28

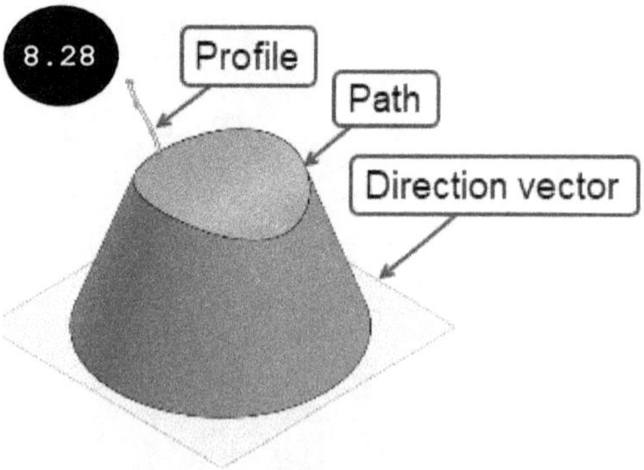

8.29

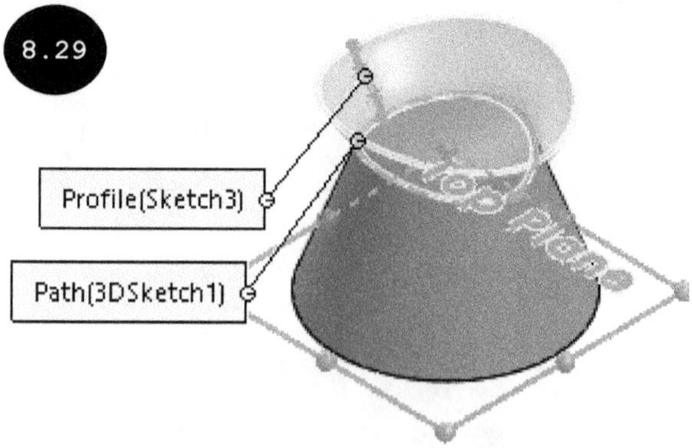

Tip: The path shown in the Figure 8.28 is a 3D closed edge of the model. You can select an open or a closed edge of a model as a path for creating the sweep feature.

Minimum Twist

On selecting the **Minimum Twist** option in the **Profile Twist** drop-down list, a minimum twist is applied to the profile while following the path to avoid self-intersection, see Figure 8.30. Note that this option works better with a 3D path and is available in the drop-down list only if a 3D sketch or a 3D edge is selected as the path of the sweep feature. You will learn more about creating 3D sketches later in this chapter. Figure 8.30 shows the preview of a sweep feature when the **Minimum Twist** option is selected.

8.30

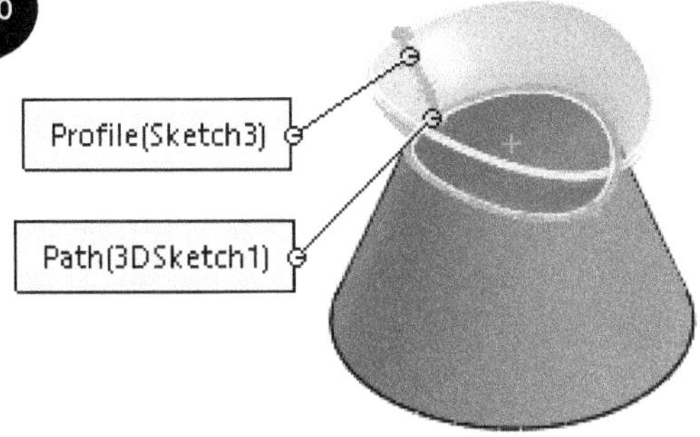

Tangent to Adjacent Faces

On selecting the **Tangent to Adjacent Faces** option, the profile maintains tangency with the adjacent face of the path, see Figure 8.31. This option works only if the path has an adjacent face.

Natural

On selecting the **Natural** option in the **Profile Twist** drop-down list, the profile follows a path such that it maintains a natural twist, see Figure 8.32. Note that this option works better with a 3D path and is available in the drop-down list only if a 3D sketch or a 3D edge is selected as the path of the sweep feature. You will learn more about creating 3D sketches later in this chapter.

8.31

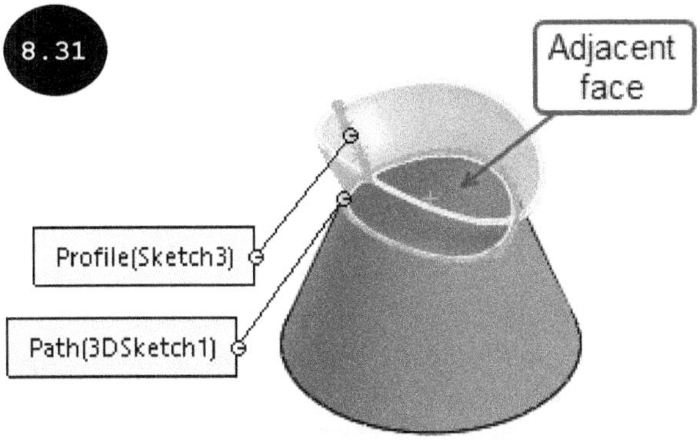

8.32

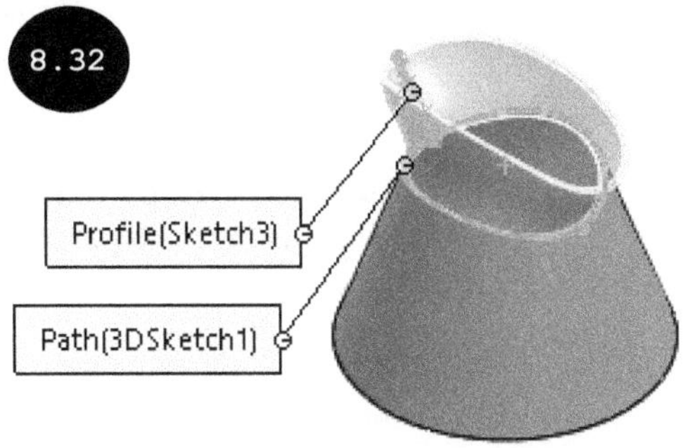

Follow Path and First Guide Curve

On selecting the **Follow Path and First Guide Curve** option, the profile follows the path as well as the first guide curve, see Figures 8.33 and 8.34. A guide curve is used to guide the profile (section) of the sweep feature. Note that this option is available in the drop-down list only after selecting a guide curve by using the **Guide Curves** rollout of the PropertyManager. To select a guide curve, expand the **Guide Curves** rollout by clicking on the arrow available in front of it, see Figure 8.35. The field in this rollout is activated by default and is used to select guide curves from the graphics area. Ensure that the guide curve you select has a pierce relation with the profile of the sweep feature. Figure 8.33 shows a path, a profile, and a guide curve. Figure 8.34 shows the preview of the resultant sweep feature.

8.33

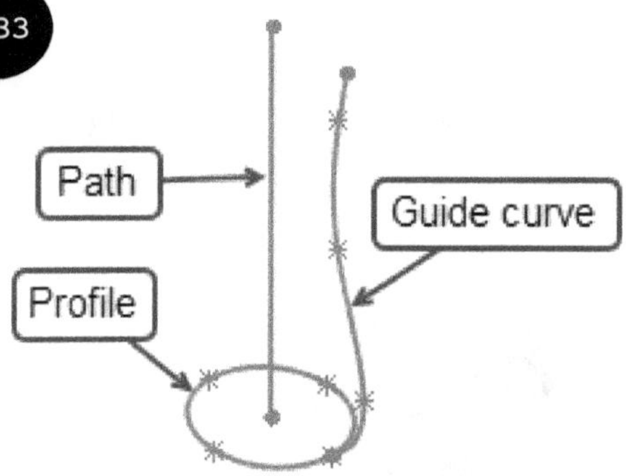

8.34

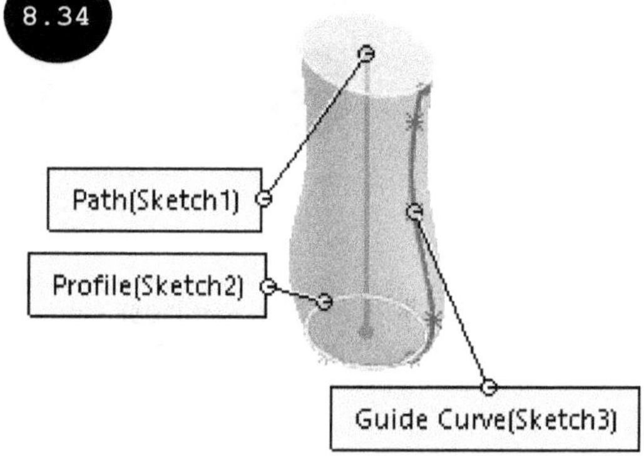

8.35

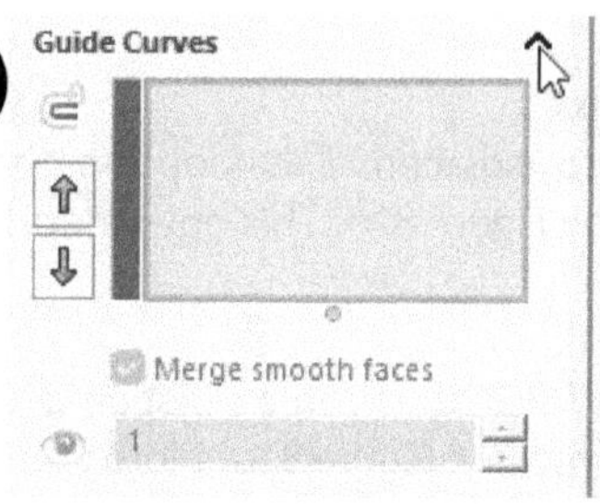

Note: In Figure 8.33, the path and the guide curve are created on the Front plane as individual sketches, and the profile is created on the Top plane. Also, the start point of the guide curve has a pierce relation with the profile of the sweep feature.

Follow First and Second Guide Curves

On selecting the **Follow First and Second Guide Curves** option, the profile follows the path, and the first and second guide curves, see Figures 8.36 and 8.37. By using this option, you can guide the profile (section) of a sweep feature by using two guide curves. Note that this option is available in the drop-down list only after selecting two guide curves by using the **Guide Curves** rollout of the PropertyManager. To select guide curves, expand the **Guide Curves** rollout, refer to Figure 8.35. Next, select two guide curves one by one in the graphics area. Figure 8.36 shows a path, a profile, and two guide curves. Figure 8.37 shows the preview of the resultant sweep feature.

8.36

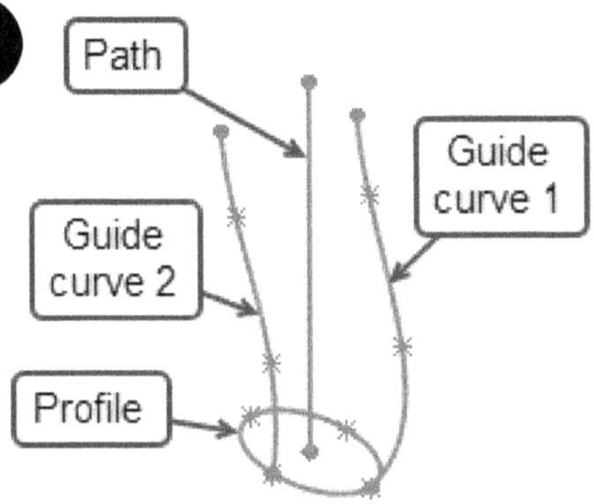

8.37

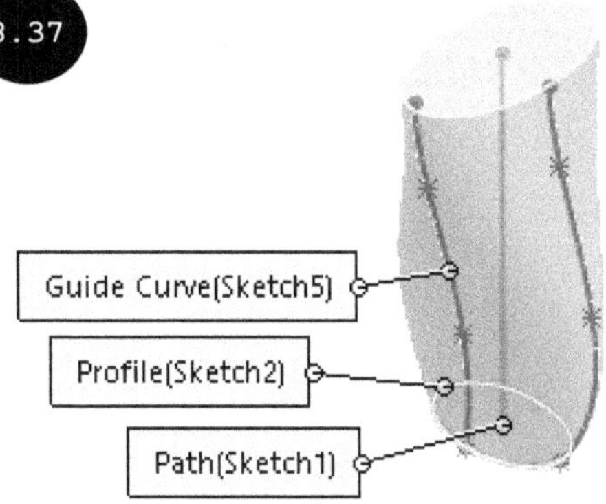

Note: In Figure 8.36, the path and the guide curve 1 are created on the Front plane as individual sketches, and the guide curve 2 is created on the Right plane. Also, a profile is created on the Top plane.

Tip: If the profile fails to follow both the guide curves, then you need to make sure that the resultant sweep feature does not self intersect. Also, the guide curves must have a pierce relation with the profile of the sweep feature.

Merge tangent faces

On selecting the **Merge tangent faces** check box in the **Options** rollout, the tangent faces of the resultant sweep feature get merged and appear as a single face. Figure 8.38 shows a sweep feature that is created by selecting the **Merge tangent faces** check box, whereas Figure 8.39 shows a sweep feature that is created by clearing the **Merge tangent faces** check box.

8.38

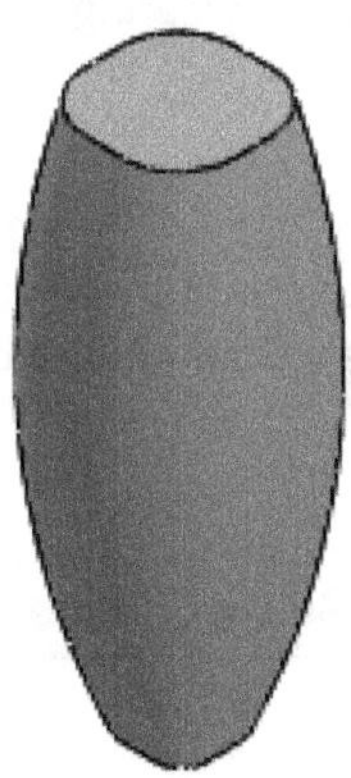

8.39

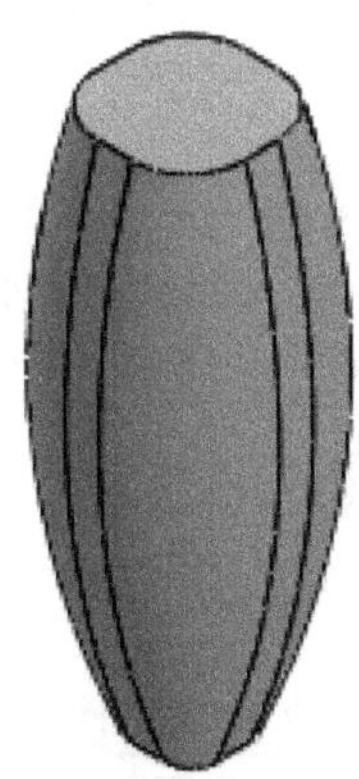

Merge result

By default, the **Merge result** check box is selected in the **Options** rollout, see Figure 8.40. As a result, the resultant sweep feature merges with the existing features of the model and forms a single body. On clearing this check box, the sweep feature will not merge with the existing features of the model and make a separate body. Note that this check box is not available while creating the base/first feature of a model.

8.40

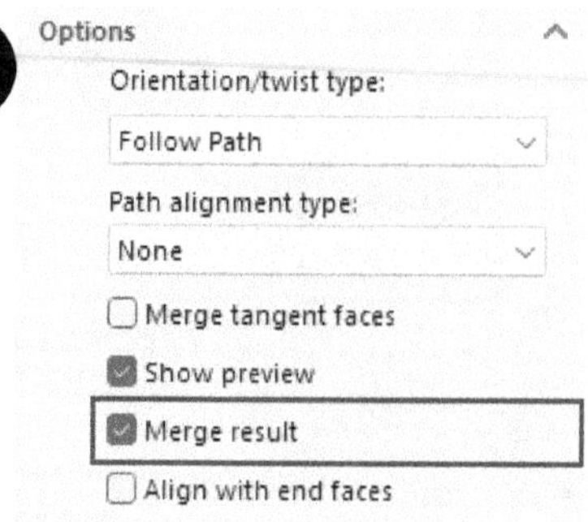

Align with end faces

On selecting the **Align with end faces** check box, the end section of the sweep feature gets aligned with the face of an existing feature, which is encountered by the path. Note that this check box is not available if the sweep feature being created is the base feature of a model. Figure 8.41 shows the preview of a sweep feature when the **Align with end faces** check box is selected and Figure 8.42 shows the preview of a sweep feature when the **Align with end faces** check box is cleared.

8.41

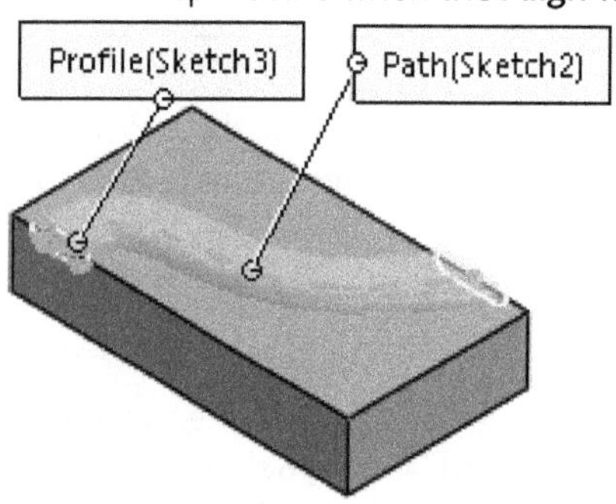

8.42

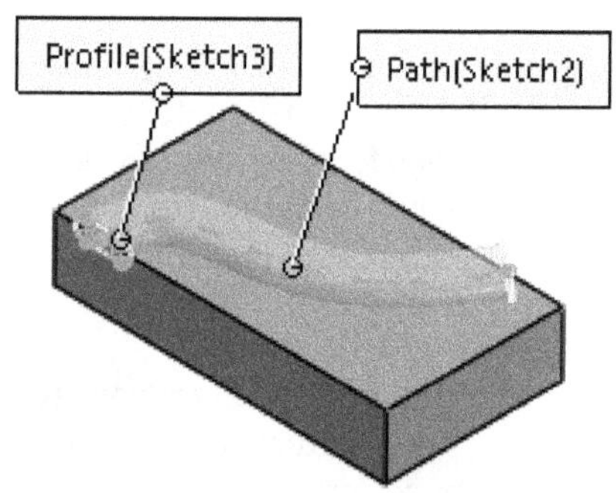

Show preview

By default, the **Show preview** check box is selected. As a result, while creating a sweep feature, its preview appears in the graphics area.

Guide Curves

The **Guide Curves** rollout of the **Sweep PropertyManager** is used to select guide curves for creating the sweep feature, see Figure 8.43. The options in the **Guide Curves** rollout are discussed next.

8.43

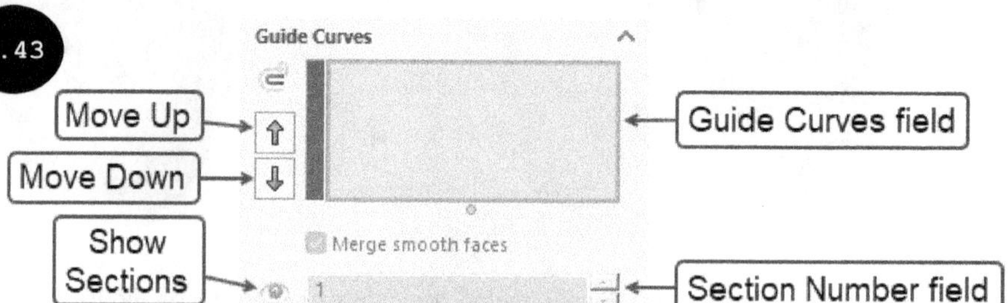

Guide Curves field

The **Guide Curves** field is used for selecting guide curves in the graphics area. Guide curves are used to guide the profile of the sweep feature along the path. On selecting guide curves, their names appear in this field in the sequence in which they are selected. You can select one or two guide curves for creating a sweep feature, as discussed earlier. Note that the guide curves should have a pierce relation with the profile of the sweep feature.

Move Up and Move Down

The **Move Up** and **Move Down** buttons are used to change the order or sequence of guide curves in the **Guide Curves** field. These buttons are available to the left of the **Guide Curves** field.

Merge smooth faces

By default, the **Merge smooth faces** check box is selected. As a result, the smooth or tangent segments of the sweep feature get merged. Figure 8.44 shows a sweep feature that is created by selecting the **Merge smooth faces** check box. Figure 8.45 shows a sweep feature that is created by clearing the **Merge smooth faces** check box.

8.44

8.45

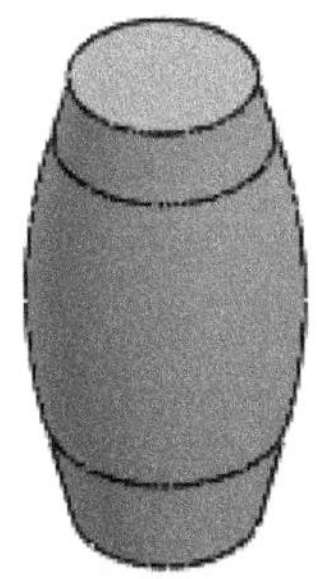

Show Sections

The **Show Sections** button of the rollout is used to view the intermediate sections of the sweep feature being created by using guide curves. By default, the **Show Sections** button is not activated. To activate this button, click on it. The **Section Number** field gets enabled in the rollout. On entering a section number in this field, the preview of the respective section appears in the graphics area, see Figure 8.46.

8.46

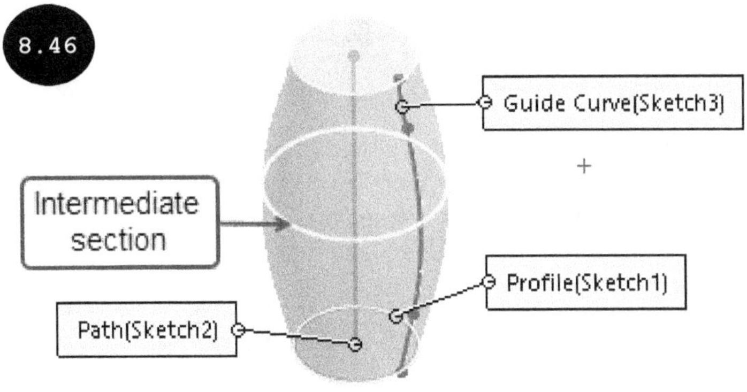

Start and End Tangency

The options in the **Start and End Tangency** rollout of the PropertyManager are used to specify the start and end tangency of the sweep feature. This rollout has two drop-down lists: **Start tangency type** and **End tangency type**, see Figure 8.47. The options in the drop-down lists are discussed next.

8.47

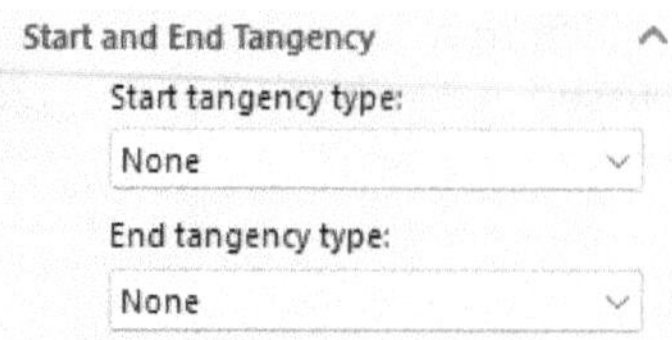

Start tangency type

The options in the **Start tangency type** drop-down list are used to specify the start tangency for a sweep feature. By default, the **None** option is selected in this drop-down list. As a result, tangency is not maintained at the start of the sweep feature. On selecting the **Path Tangent** option, the sweep feature maintains tangency with the path at its start. Figure 8.48 shows the preview of a sweep feature when the **None** option is selected, and Figure 8.49 shows the preview of a sweep feature when the **Path Tangent** option is selected as the start tangency type.

8.48

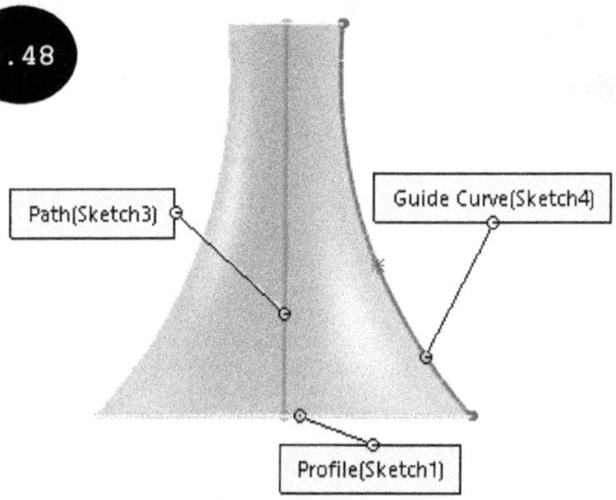

8.49

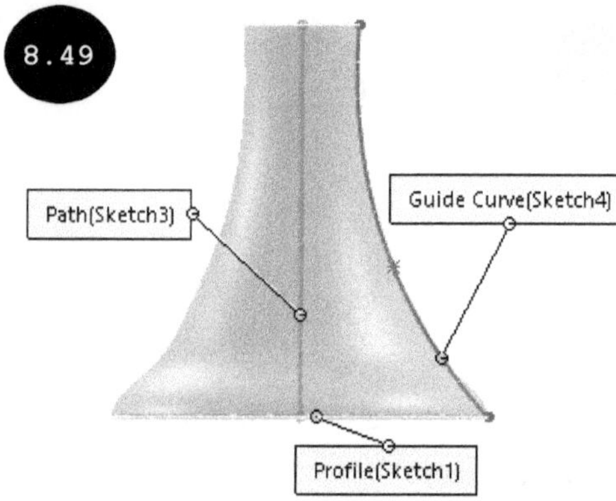

End tangency type

The options in the **End tangency type** drop-down list are used to specify the end tangency type for a sweep feature. By default, the **None** option is selected in this drop-down list. As a result, the tangency is not maintained at the end of the sweep feature. On selecting the **Path Tangent** option, the sweep feature maintains tangency with the path at its end.

Thin Feature

The **Thin Feature** rollout of the PropertyManager is used to create a thin sweep feature, see Figure 8.50. To create a thin sweep feature, expand this rollout by clicking on the check box on its title bar, see Figure 8.51. The options for creating the thin sweep feature are the same as those discussed earlier while creating the thin extruded and thin revolved features.

8.50

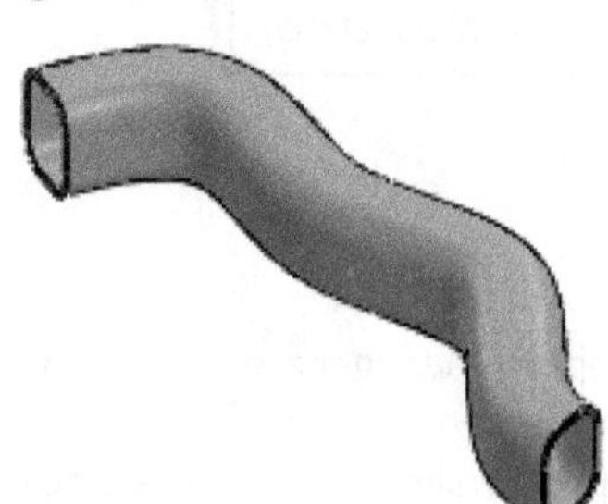

8.51

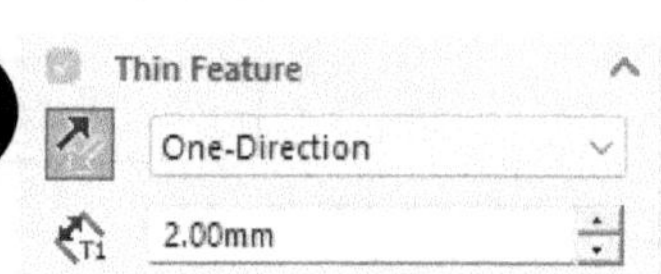

Curvature Display

The options in the **Curvature Display** rollout are used to control the display style of the preview that appears in the graphics area, see Figure 8.52. The options are discussed next.

8.52

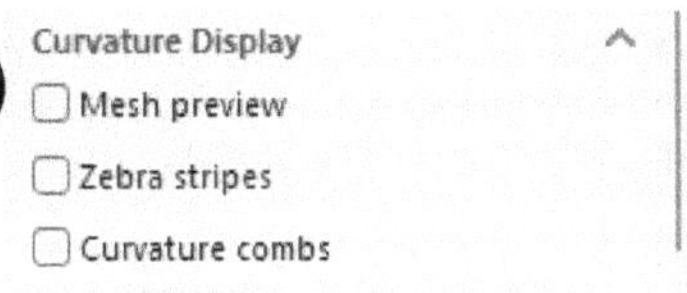

Mesh preview

This check box is used to display a mesh preview in the graphics area, see Figure 8.53. You can control the mesh density by using the **Mesh density** slider that appears below this check box.

8.53

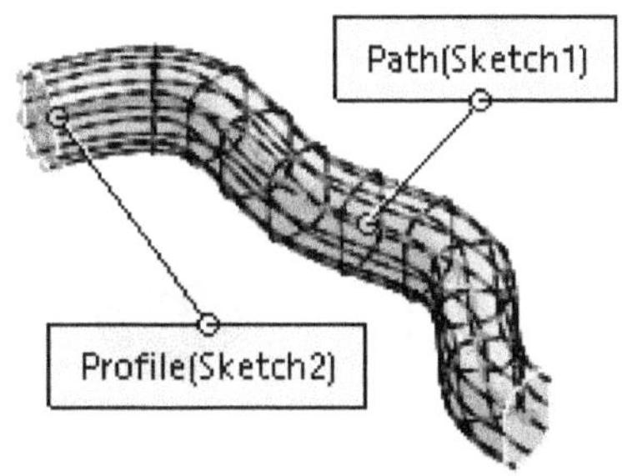

Zebra stripes

This check box is used to turn on the appearance of zebra stripes in the preview of the feature, see Figure 8.54. The zebra stripes help you find small changes made in the feature by making them visible, which are hard to see in the standard display style.

Curvature combs

This check box is used to turn on the appearance of curvature combs in the preview of the feature, see Figure 8.55. You can control the scale and density of the displayed curvature combs by using the **Scale** and the **Density** sliders of the rollout.

8.54

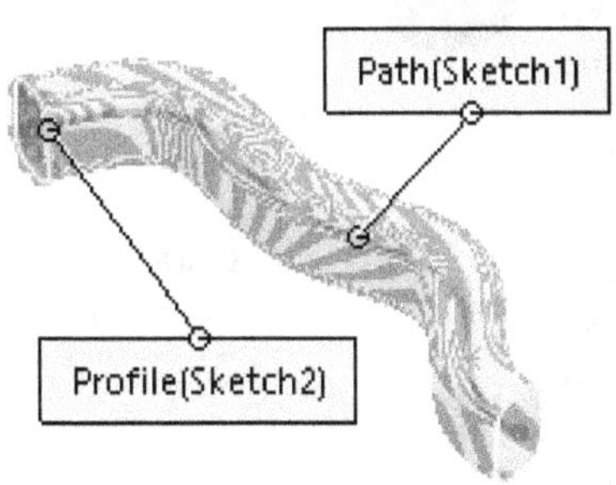

8.55

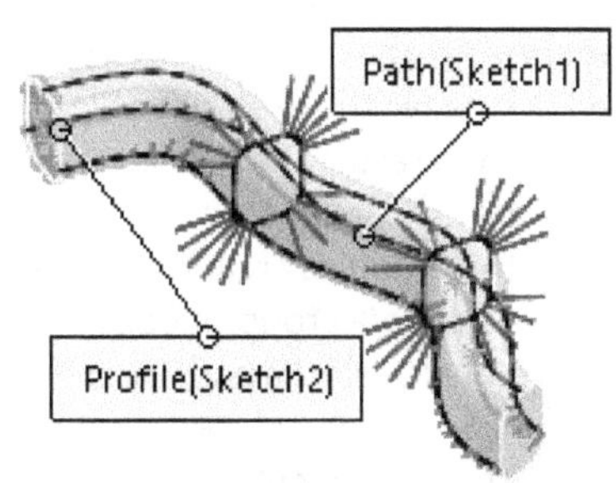

After specifying the required options and parameters for creating a sweep feature, click on the green tick-mark ✓ button in the PropertyManager. A sweep feature is created.

Creating a Sweep Cut Feature

Swept Cut

The method for creating a sweep cut feature is the same as that for creating a sweep feature with the only difference being that a sweep-cut feature is created by removing material from the model, see Figures 8.56 through 8.59. You can create sweep cut features by using the **Swept Cut** tool. Figures 8.56 and 8.58 show the profile and the path, respectively. Figures 8.57 and 8.59 show the resultant sweep cut features created such that the material is removed from the model by sweeping the profile along the path.

8.56

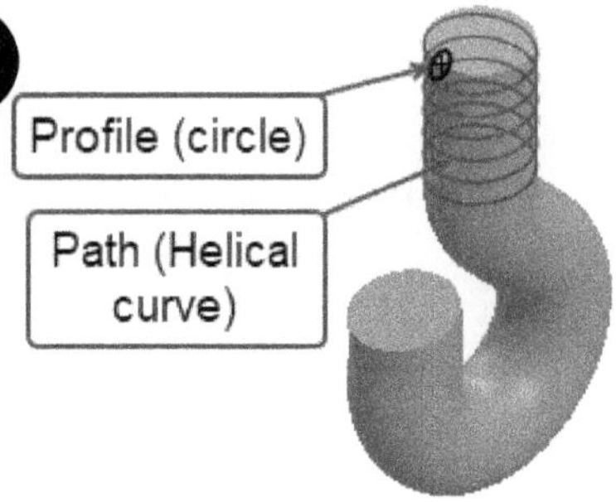

8.57

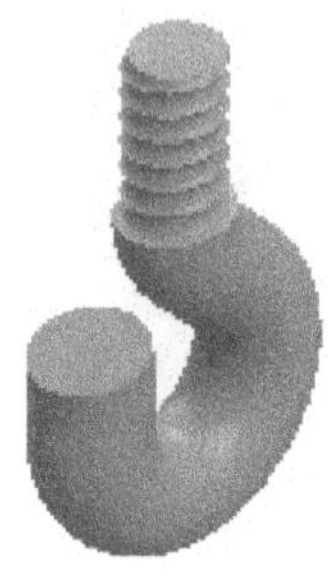

8.58

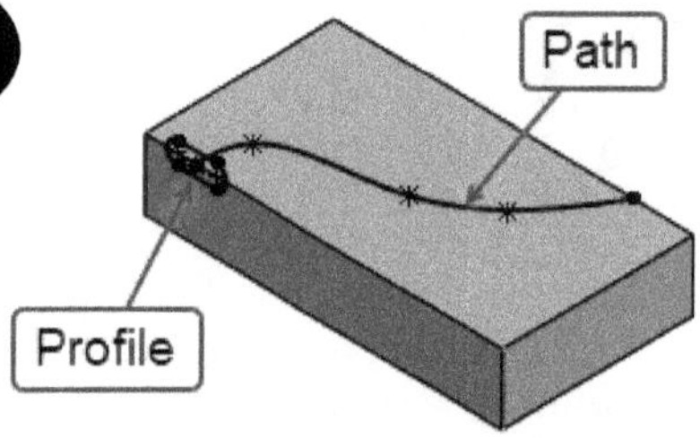

8.59

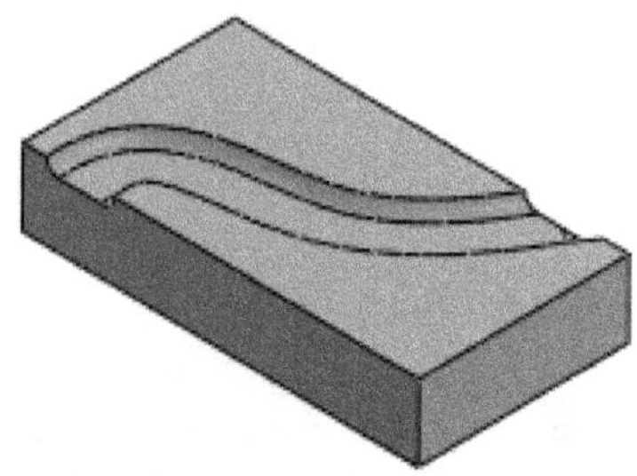

Note: In Figure 8.56, a helical curve has been created as the path and a circle has been created as the profile. You will learn about creating helical curves later in this chapter.

To create a sweep cut feature, click on the **Swept Cut** tool in the **Features CommandManager**. The **Cut-Sweep PropertyManager** appears, see Figure 8.60. In this PropertyManager, the **Sketch Profile** radio button is selected, by default. As a result, the **Profile** and **Path** fields are enabled in the PropertyManager. Select a profile of the sweep cut feature in the graphics area. You can select a closed sketch, a face, or an edge/a group of edges that form a closed loop as a profile. Next, select a path for the sweep cut feature. You can select an open or a closed sketch, an edge, or a curve as the path of the sweep cut feature. After selecting the profile and path, a preview of the sweep cut feature appears in the graphics area.

8.60

On selecting the **Circular Profile** radio button of the PropertyManager, you can create a circular sweep cut feature similar to creating a circular sweep feature without creating the sketch of the profile.

On selecting the **Solid Profile** radio button, the **Tool body** and **Path** fields get enabled in the **Profile and Path** rollout of the PropertyManager, see Figure 8.61. The **Tool body** field is activated by default and is used for selecting a tool body that follows the path to create a sweep cut feature. Figure 8.62 shows a tool body and a helical path, and Figure 8.63 shows the resultant sweep cut feature. Also, refer to Figures 8.64 and 8.65 for a tool body, a path, and the resultant sweep cut feature. Note that the options for creating a sweep cut feature are the same as those discussed earlier while creating the sweep feature.

8.61

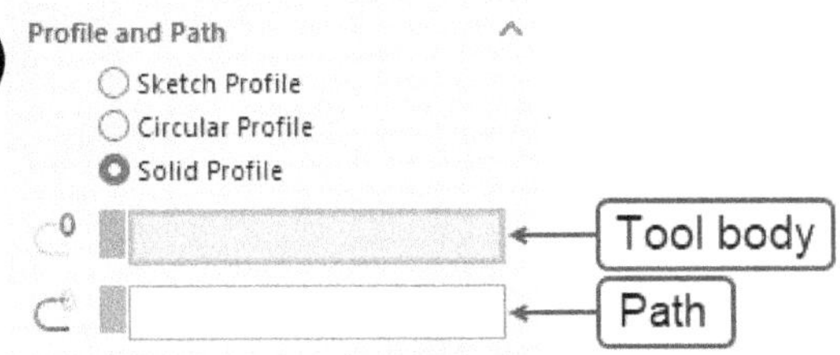

8.62

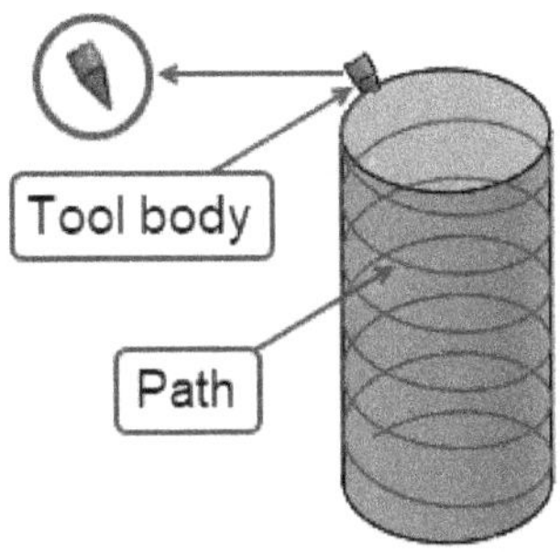

8.63

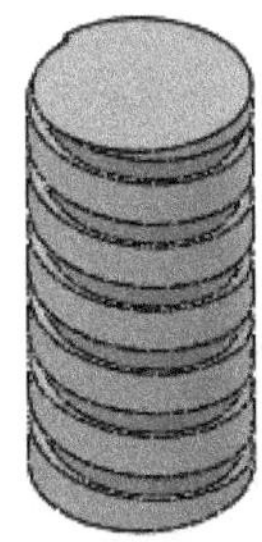

8.64

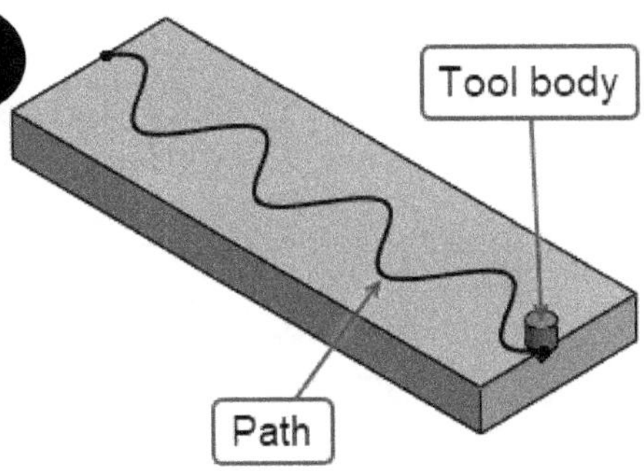

8.65

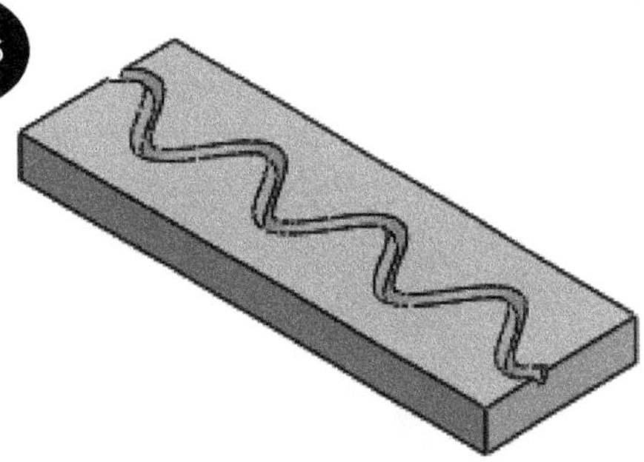

Note: In Figures 8.62 and 8.64, a solid body is used as a tool body to follow the path. The tool body should be created as a separate body. To achieve this, you need to clear the **Merge result** check box in the respective PropertyManager while creating the tool body. By clearing this check box, the resulting feature will be created as a separate body. Additionally, in Figure 8.62, a helical curve is used as the path. You will learn how to create a helical curve later in this chapter.

Creating a Lofted feature

A lofted feature is created by lofting two or more profiles (sections) such that the cross-sectional shape of the lofted feature transits from one profile to another. Figure 8.66 shows two dissimilar profiles/sections that are created on different planes having an offset distance between each other. Figure 8.67 shows the resultant lofted feature created.

8.66

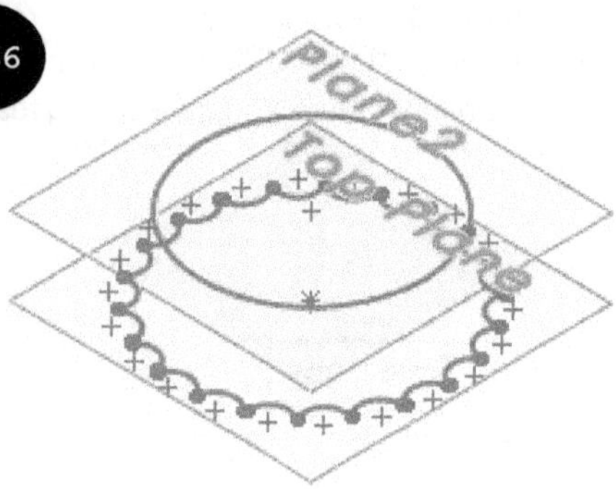

8.67

It is evident from the above figures that for creating a lofted feature, you first need to create all its sections that define the shape of the lofted feature. In SOLIDWORKS, you can create a lofted feature by using the **Lofted Boss/Base** tool of the **Features CommandManager**. Note that for creating a lofted feature, you need to take care of the following points:

1. Two or more profiles/sections (similar or dissimilar) must be available in the graphics area before invoking the **Lofted Boss/Base** tool.
2. Profiles must be closed. You can select closed sketches, faces, or edges as profiles.
3. All profiles must be created as different sketches.
4. The profiles and the resultant lofted feature must not be self-intersected.

To create a lofted feature, click on the **Lofted Boss/Base** tool in the **Features CommandManager**. The **Loft PropertyManager** appears, see Figure 8.68. The options in this PropertyManager are discussed next.

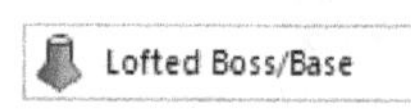

8.68

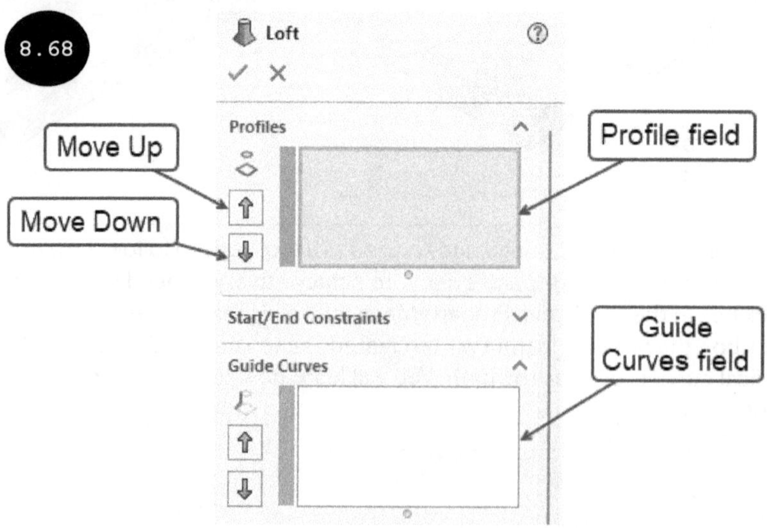

Profiles

The **Profiles** rollout of the PropertyManager is used to select profiles of the lofted feature. You can select two or more similar or dissimilar closed profiles to create a lofted feature. After selecting the profiles, a preview of the lofted feature appears in the graphics area with connectors, that connect the profiles, see Figure 8.69. Also, the names of the selected profiles appear in the **Profile** field of the rollout in the order in which they are selected. You can change the order of selection by using the **Move Up** and **Move Down** buttons of the **Profile** rollout, refer to Figure 8.68.

8.69

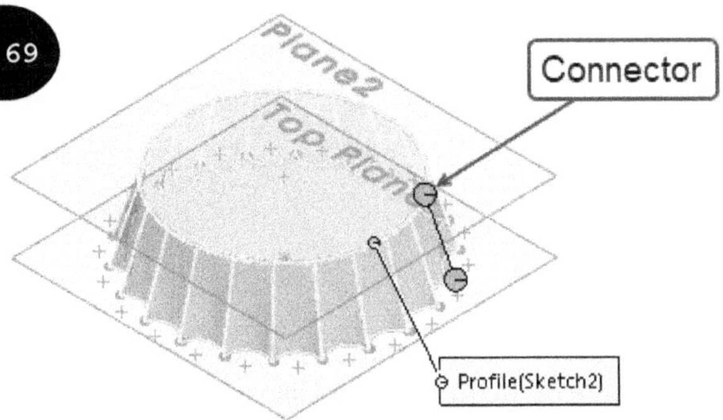

Note: You need to select profiles of a loft feature such that the connectors appear in one direction in its preview to avoid twisting in the feature, see Figure 8.69. If needed, you can change the position of the connectors by dragging them.

To create a twist in a lofted feature, you can drag the connectors that appear in its preview. By default, only one handle appears with its connectors in the preview of a lofted feature, refer to Figure 8.69. You can turn on the display of all handles in the preview of a lofted feature. To do this, right-click in the graphics area and then select the **Show All Connectors** option in the shortcut menu that appears.

Start/End Constraints

The options in the **Start/End Constraint** rollout are used to define normal, tangent, or curvature continuity as the start and end constraints of a lofted feature. By default, this rollout is collapsed. To expand the rollout, click on the arrow in its title bar, see Figure 8.70. The options in this rollout are discussed next.

Start constraint

The options in the **Start constraint** drop-down list are used to define the start constraint for a lofted feature, see Figure 8.71. The options in this drop-down list are discussed next.

8.70

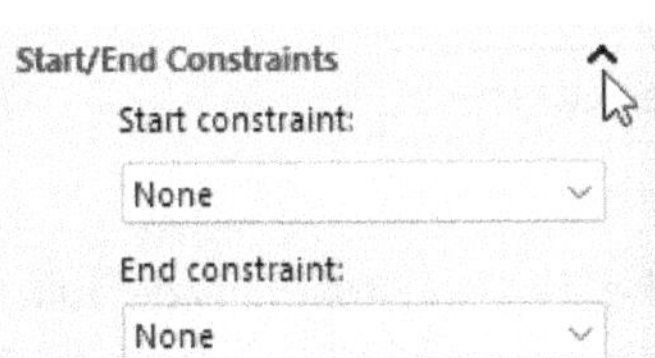

8.71

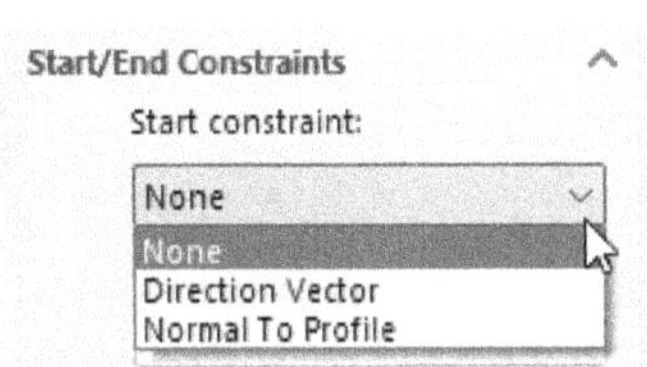

None

By default, the **None** option is selected in the **Start constraint** drop-down list. As a result, no constraint is applied and the cross-sectional shape transits from one profile to another, linearly, see Figures 8.72 and 8.73. Figure 8.72 shows profiles and Figure 8.73 shows the preview of the resultant lofted feature.

8.72

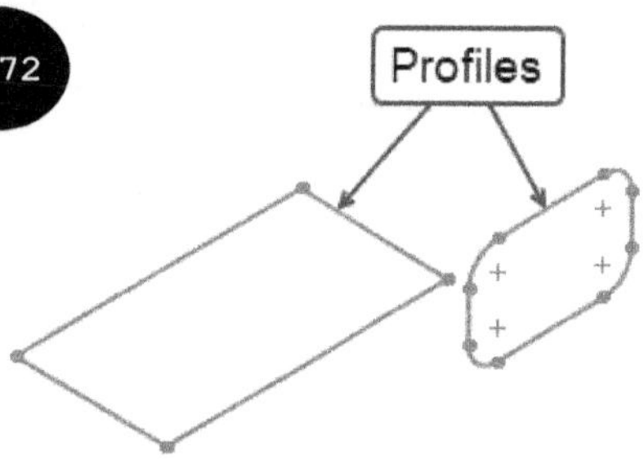

8.73

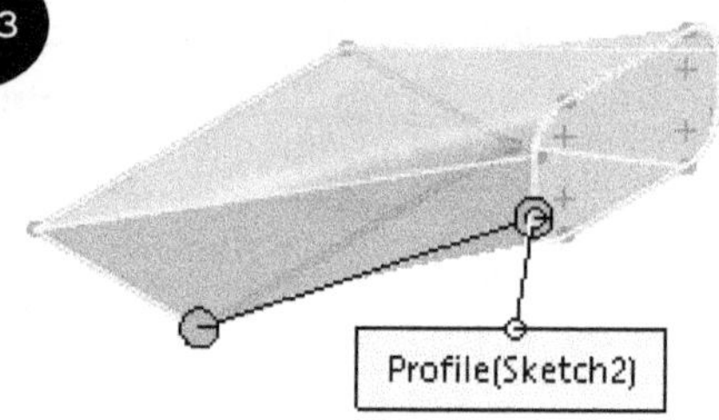

Direction Vector

On selecting the **Direction Vector** option, the **Direction Vector**, **Draft angle**, and **Start Tangent Length** fields become available in the rollout, see Figure 8.74.

8.74

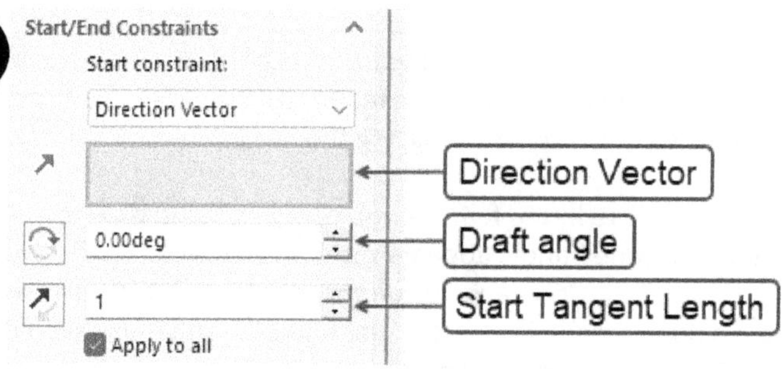

The **Direction Vector** field is used to select a direction vector that defines the start constraint for a lofted feature. You can select a plane, a linear edge, a linear sketch entity, or an axis as a direction vector. Figure 8.75 shows a preview of the lofted feature after selecting the Top plane as the direction vector.

8.75

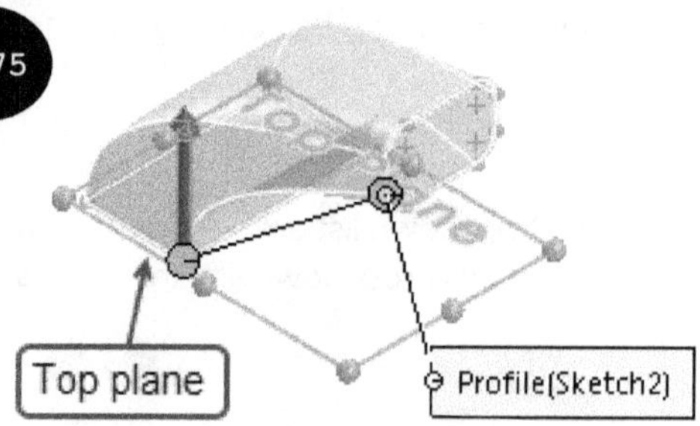

The **Draft angle** field is used to define the draft angle for the start constraint. By default, the draft angle is set to 0 degrees. You can specify the draft angle, as required. Figure 8.76 shows the front view of the preview of a lofted feature having the draft angle set to 0 degrees and Figure 8.77 shows the front view of the preview of a lofted feature having the draft angle set to 20 degrees.

8.76

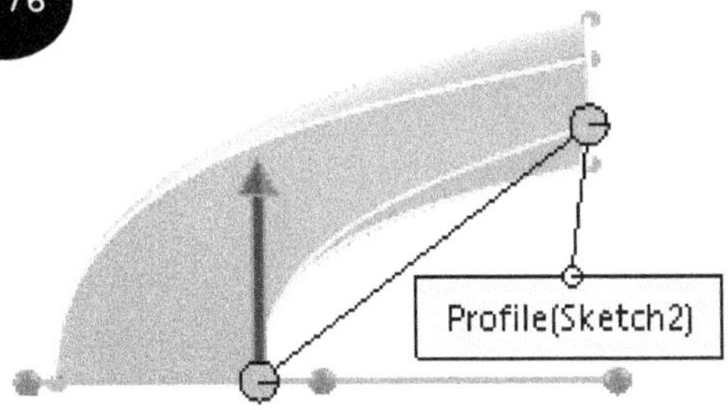

8.77

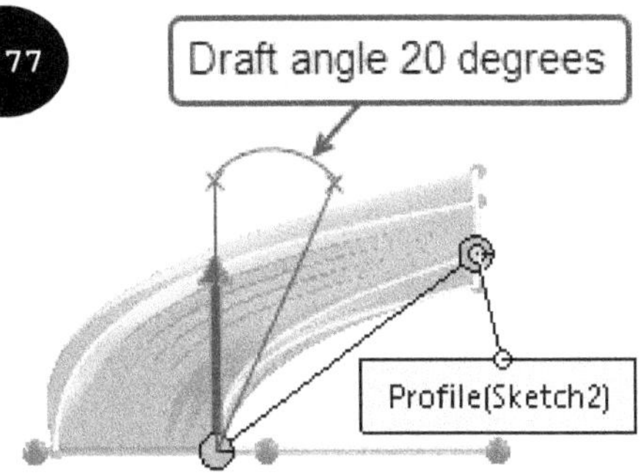

The **Start Tangent Length** field is used to define the start tangent length for the start constraint. By default, the start tangent length is specified as 1. Figure 8.78 shows a preview of the lofted feature with the draft angle set to 0 degrees and the start tangent length set to 2.

8.78

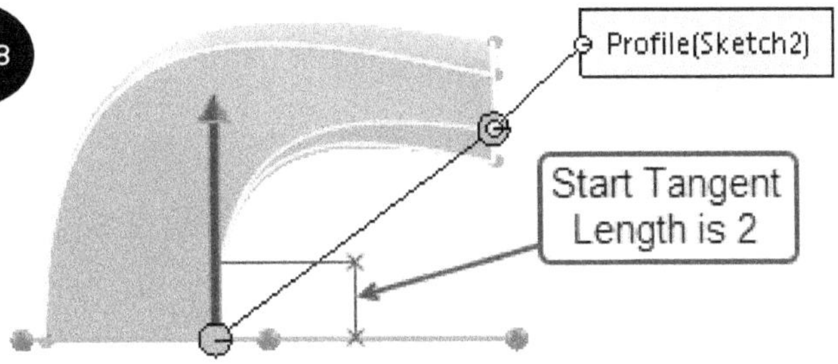

Normal To Profile

On selecting the **Normal To Profile** option in the **Start constraint** drop-down list, the tangency constraint is applied normal to the start section of the lofted feature. Also, the **Draft angle** and **Start Tangent Length** fields are enabled. The methods for specifying draft angle and start tangent length are the same as those discussed earlier.

Tangency To Face

On selecting the **Tangency To Face** option in the **Start constraint** drop-down list, the start section of the lofted feature maintains tangency with the adjacent face of the existing geometry, see Figure 8.79. You can define the start tangent length of the feature in the **Start Tangent Length** field of the rollout.

Note: The **Tangency To Face** option becomes available only when an adjacent face of an existing geometry is available in the graphics area. If the loft feature being created is the base/first feature, then this option will not be available in the drop-down list.

8.79

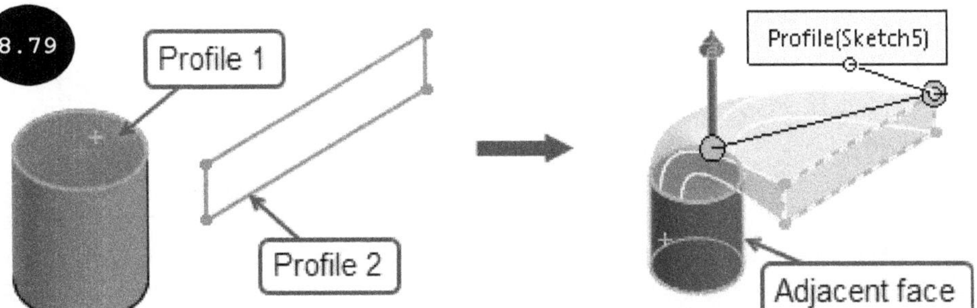

Curvature To Face

On selecting the **Curvature To Face** option, the start profile of a lofted feature maintains curvature continuity with the adjacent faces of the existing geometry.

Note: If the loft feature being created is the base/first feature, then the **Curvature To Face** option will not be available in the drop-down list.

Reverse Direction and Reverse Tangent Direction

The **Reverse Direction** and **Reverse Tangent Direction** buttons of the **Start/End Constraint** rollout are used for reversing the direction of the applied constraints, see Figure 8.80. Note that the **Reverse Direction** button is available after selecting the **Direction Vector** or **Normal To Profile** option in the **Start constraint** drop-down list. On the other hand, the **Reverse Tangent Direction** button is available if the **Direction Vector**, **Normal To Profile**, **Tangency To Face**, or **Curvature To Face** option is selected.

8.80

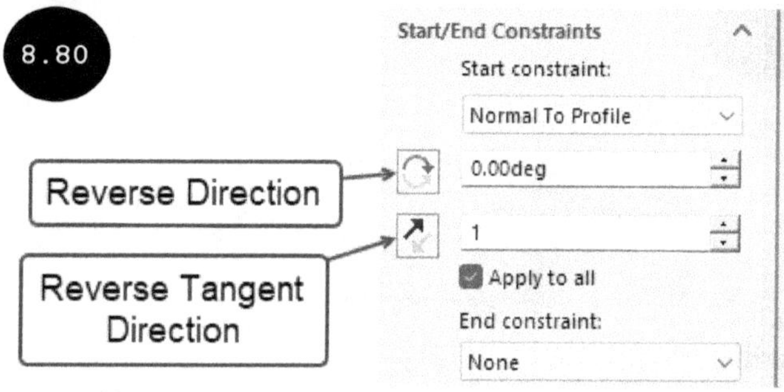

Apply to all

The **Apply to all** check box is selected in the rollout, by default. As a result, only one handle appears in the preview of the lofted feature (see Figure 8.81) and it is used for controlling the constraints of the entire profile. If you clear the **Apply to all** check box, multiple handles appear in the preview of the lofted feature, see Figure 8.82. These handles are used for controlling the constraints of individual segments for the profile. You can modify the constraints of a lofted feature by dragging the handles that appear in the preview of the lofted feature.

8.81

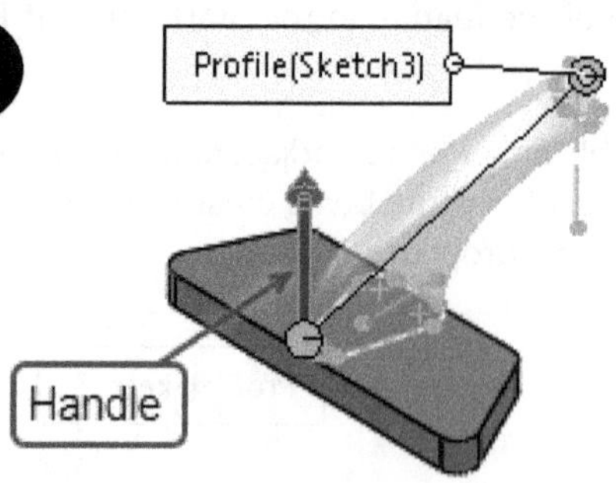

8.82

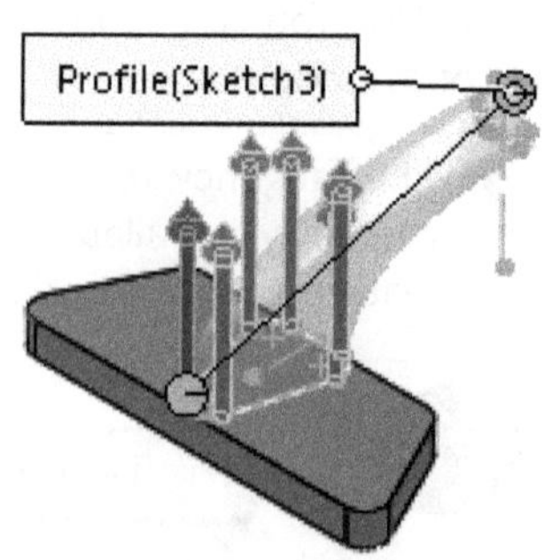

End constraint

The **End constraint** drop-down list is used to define the end constraint of a lofted feature. The options in this drop-down list are the same as those discussed earlier with the only difference that these options are used for defining the end constraint. Figure 8.83 shows the preview of a lofted feature when the start and end constraints are not defined, whereas Figure 8.84 shows the preview of a lofted feature when the end constraint is defined as normal to the profile.

8.83

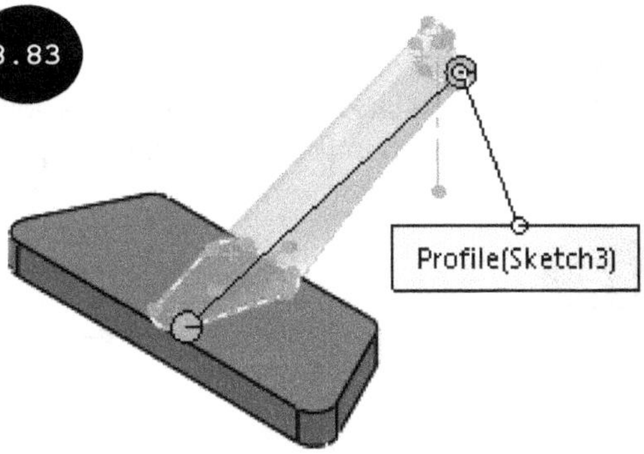

8.84

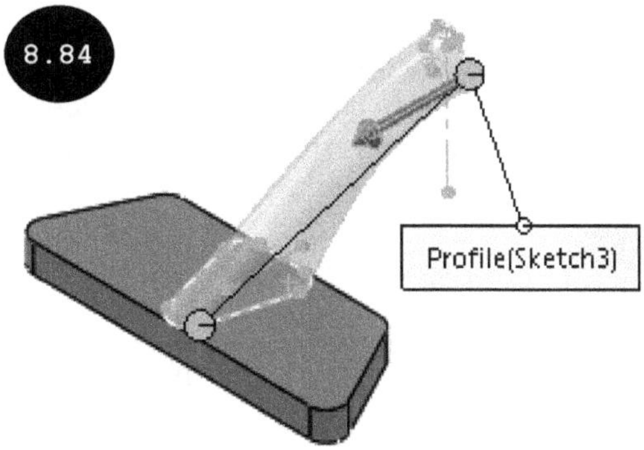

Guide Curves

Guide curves are used for guiding the cross-sectional shape of a lofted feature. You can create multiple guide curves for controlling the cross-sectional shape of a lofted feature. The **Guide Curves** rollout of the PropertyManager is used for selecting guide curves of the lofted feature. Figure 8.85 shows two profiles and two guide curves, and Figure 8.86 shows the resultant lofted feature. Note that guide curves must have pierce relations with the profiles of the feature.

8.85

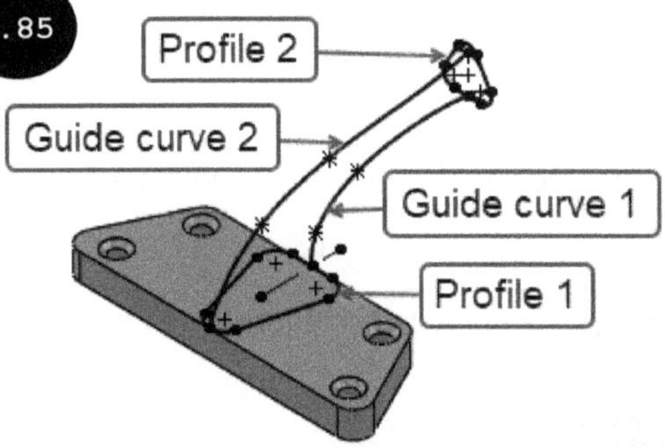

8.86

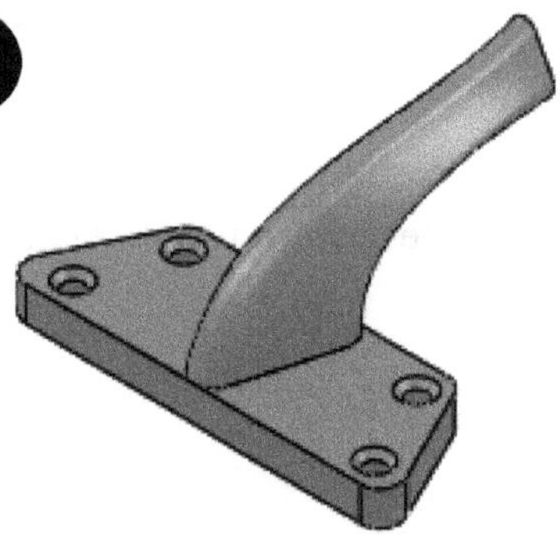

To select guide curves, click on the **Guide Curves** field in the **Guide Curves** rollout and then select the guide curves. A preview of the lofted feature appears such that its cross-sectional shape has been controlled by the guide curves. Also, the **Guide curves influence type** drop-down list appears, see Figure 8.87. The options in this drop-down list are used for controlling the influence of guide curves. The options are discussed next.

8.87

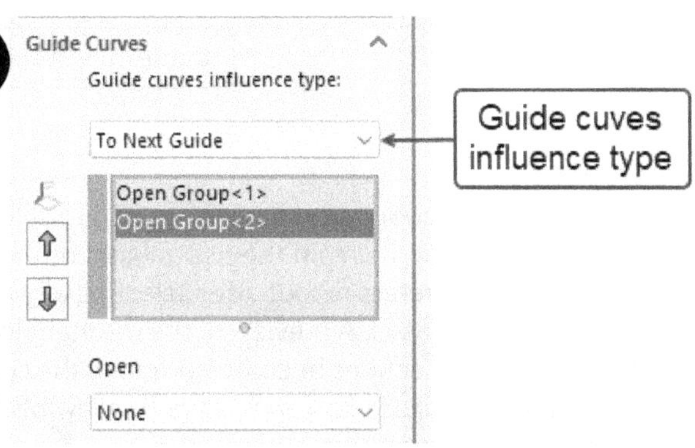

To Next Guide
The **To Next Guide** option in the **Guide curves influence type** drop-down list is used to extend the influence of the guide curve to the next guide curve only. Figure 8.88 shows two profiles and a guide curve. Figure 8.89 shows the preview of the resultant lofted feature when the **To Next Guide** option is selected.

8.88

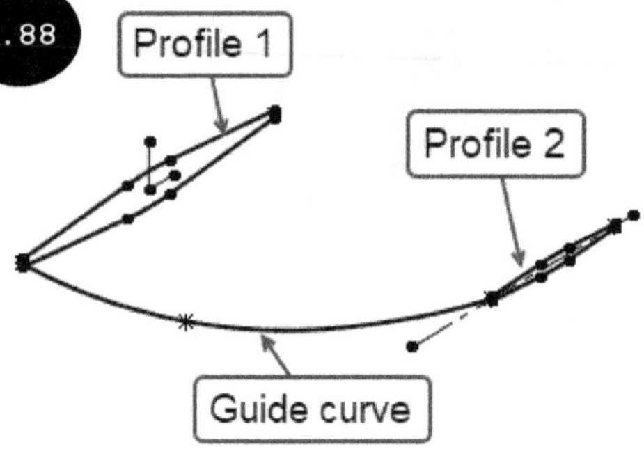

8.89

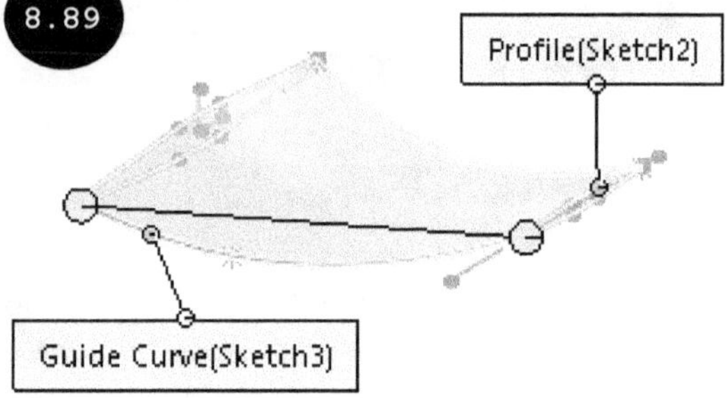

To Next Sharp
The **To Next Sharp** option is used to extend the influence of the guide curve to the next sharp, see Figure 8.90. A sharp is a hard corner of the profile.

To Next Edge
The **To Next Edge** option is used to extend the influence of the guide curve to the next edge.

Global
The **Global** option is used to extend the influence of the guide curve to the entire lofted feature, see Figure 8.91.

8.90

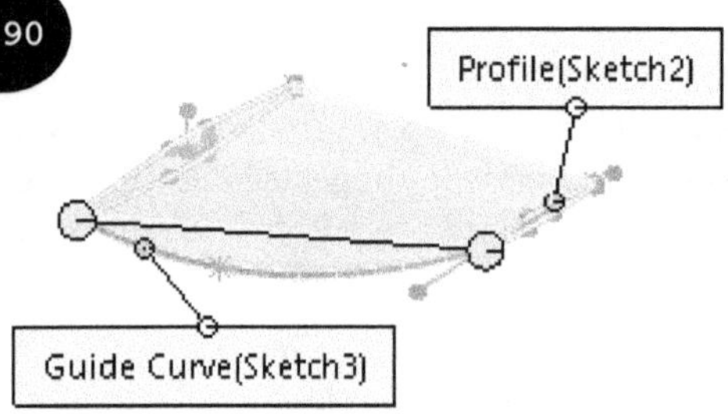

8.91

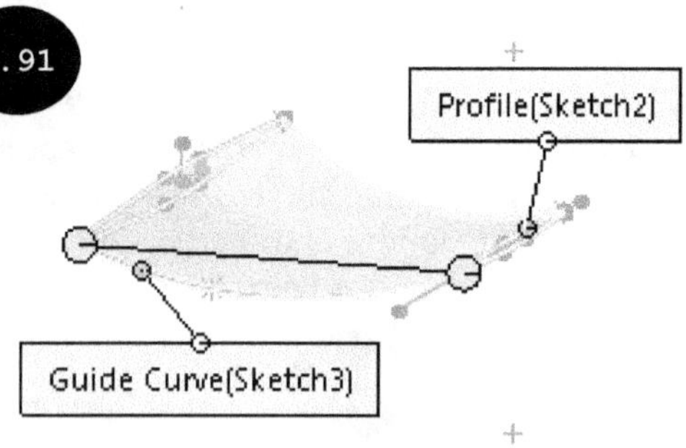

Centerline Parameters
The **Centerline Parameters** rollout of the PropertyManager is used to select a centerline for creating a lofted feature. The centerline is used to maintain the neutral axis of the lofted feature. To select a centerline, expand the **Centerline Parameters** rollout after selecting all profiles of the lofted feature. Next, select a centerline for the lofted feature. A preview of the resultant lofted feature appears in the graphics area such that its intermediate sections become normal to the centerline. Figure 8.92 shows different profiles and a centerline, and Figure 8.93 shows the preview of the resultant lofted feature after selecting the centerline.

8.92

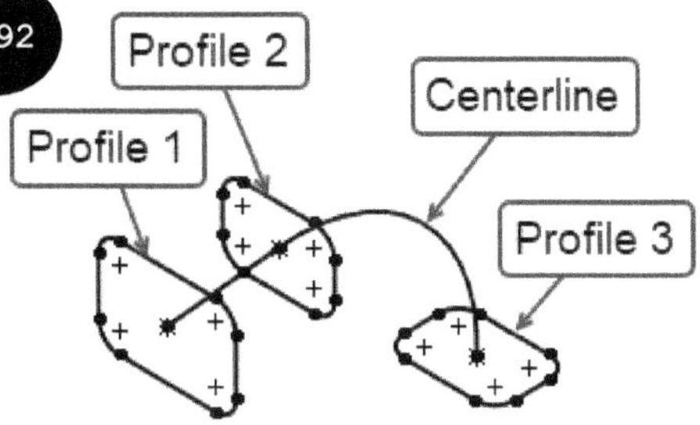

8.93

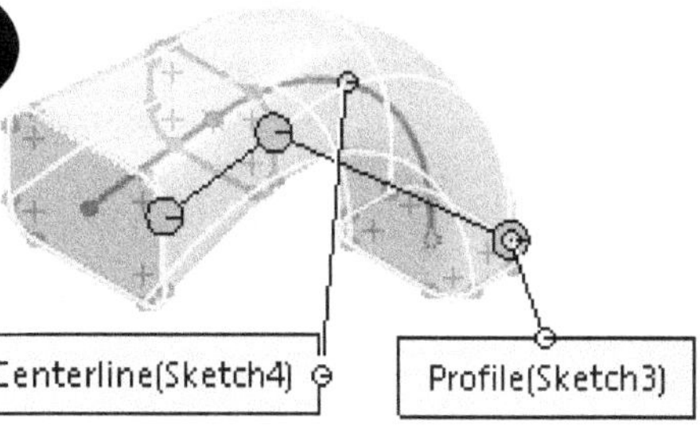

The **Show Sections** button of the **Centerline Parameters** rollout is used to show different sections of the lofted feature in the graphics area. On activating this button, the display of different sections is turned on. Also, the **Section Number** field is enabled. In this field, you can enter the section number to be displayed in the graphics area.

Sketch Tools

The **Sketch Tools** rollout is used to edit the 3D sketch sections/profiles of a lofted feature, see Figure 8.94. You can edit the 3D profiles of a lofted feature by dragging them in the graphics area using the **Drag Sketch** button of this rollout. Note that the **Drag Sketch** button is enabled only when the profiles of the lofted feature being edited are drawn as 3D sketches. You will learn about drawing 3D sketches later in this chapter.

Options

The options in the **Options** rollout of the PropertyManager are used for merging tangent faces of the feature, creating close lofted features, showing previews, and merging results, see Figure 8.95. The options of this rollout are discussed next.

8.94

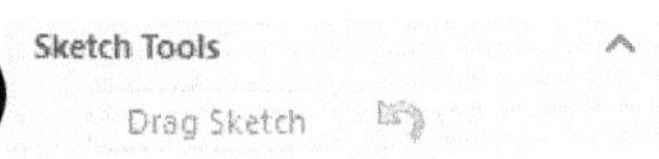

8.95

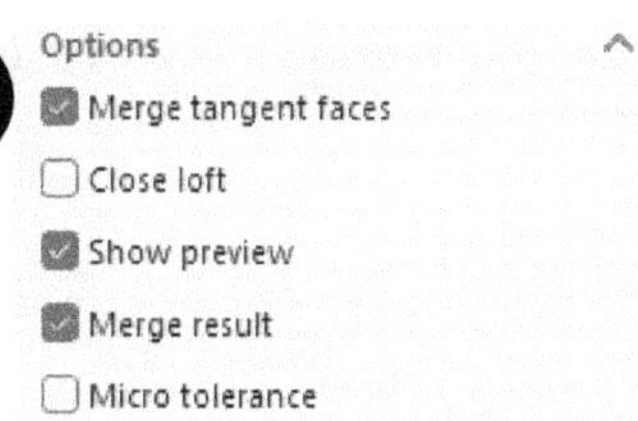

Merge tangent faces

On selecting the **Merge tangent faces** check box, the tangent faces of the feature merge with each other. Figure 8.96 shows a lofted feature that is created when the **Merge tangent faces** check box is selected and Figure 8.97 shows a lofted feature that is created when the **Merge tangent faces** check box is cleared.

8.96

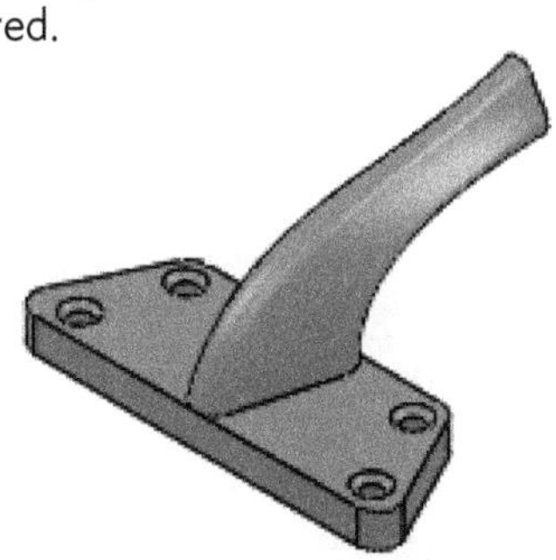

8.97

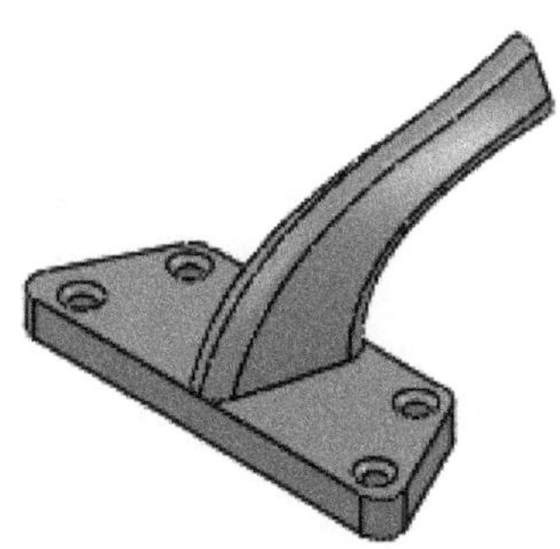

Close Loft

The **Close loft** check box is used for creating a lofted feature such that the start and end profiles of the lofted feature join automatically with each other and create a closed lofted feature. Figure 8.98 shows the preview of an open lofted feature when the **Close loft** check box is cleared, and Figure 8.99 shows the preview of a closed lofted feature when the **Close loft** check box is selected.

8.98

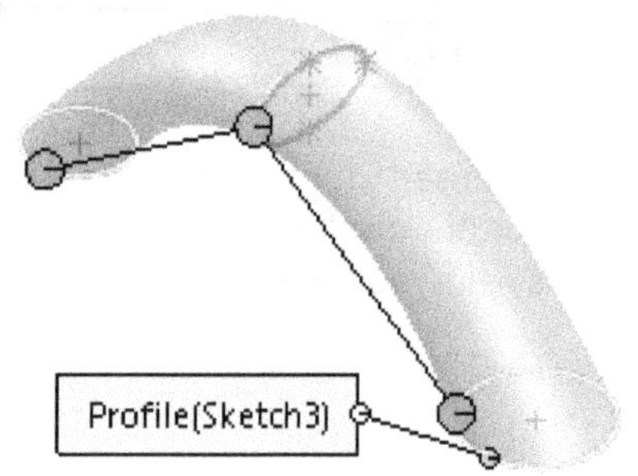

8.99

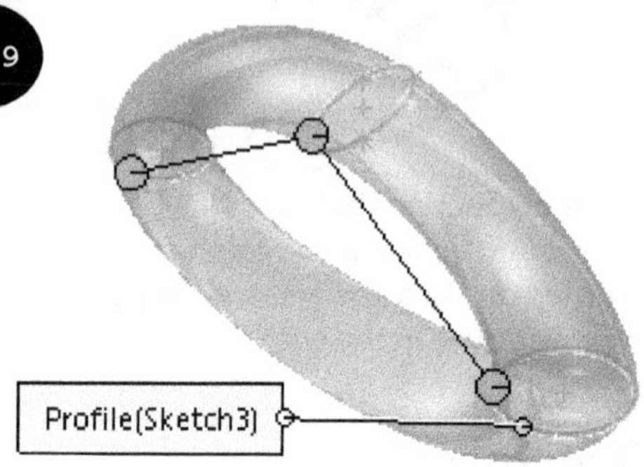

Note: To create a closed lofted feature, minimum three sections are required. Also, the total angle between the start and end sections should be more than 120 degrees.

Show preview

The **Show preview** check box is used to display the preview of the lofted feature in the graphics area. By default, this check box is selected. As a result, a preview of the lofted feature appears in the graphics area.

Thin Feature

The **Thin Feature** rollout is used to create a thin lofted feature, see Figure 8.100. The options in this rollout are the same as those discussed earlier while creating the thin extruded and revolved features.

8.100

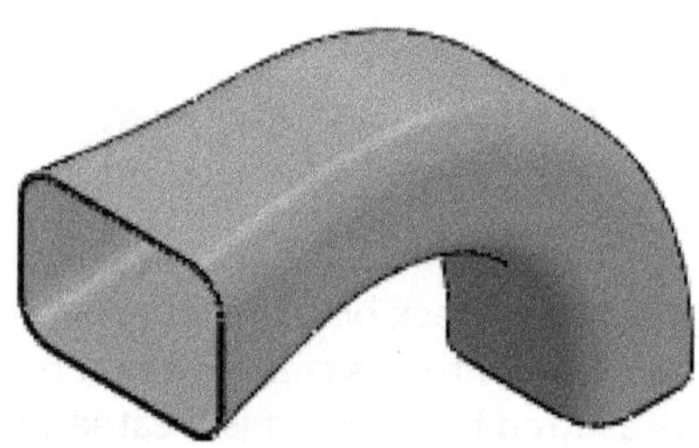

Curvature Display

The options in the **Curvature Display** rollout are used to control the display style of the preview that appears in the graphics area and are the same as discussed earlier.

After selecting the required options for creating a lofted feature, click on the green tick-mark ✓ button in the PropertyManager. A lofted feature is created.

Creating a Lofted Cut Feature

The method for creating a lofted cut feature is the same as that of creating a lofted feature with the only difference being that a lofted cut feature is created by removing material from the model. You can create a lofted cut feature by using the **Lofted Cut** tool in the **Features CommandManager**. Figure 8.101 shows profiles of a lofted cut feature. Figure 8.102 shows a preview of the resultant lofted cut feature and Figure 8.103 shows the resultant lofted cut feature created.

8.101

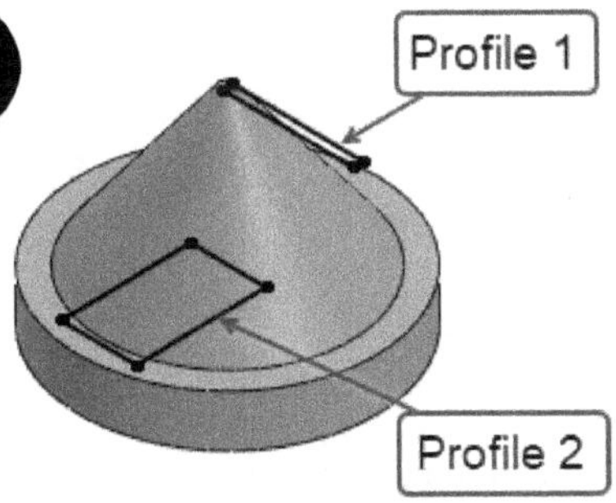

8.102

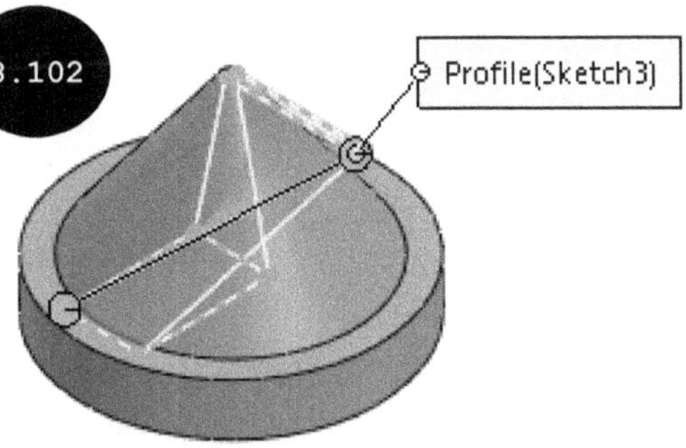

8.103

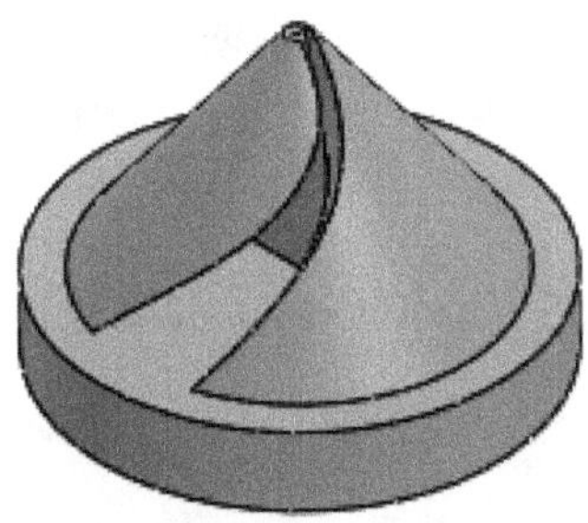

Creating a Boundary Feature

Boundary features are high-quality, complex-shaped, and accurate features. These are used for maintaining high curvature continuity as well as for creating complex shape features. You can create boundary features by using the **Boundary Boss/Base** tool, which is a powerful tool in the Part modeling environment. To create a boundary feature, you need to create all sections of a boundary feature as direction 1 guides and all curves as direction 2 guides. Figure 8.104 shows two sections as direction 1 guides and two curves as direction 2 guides of a boundary feature. Figure 8.105 shows the resultant boundary feature.

8.104

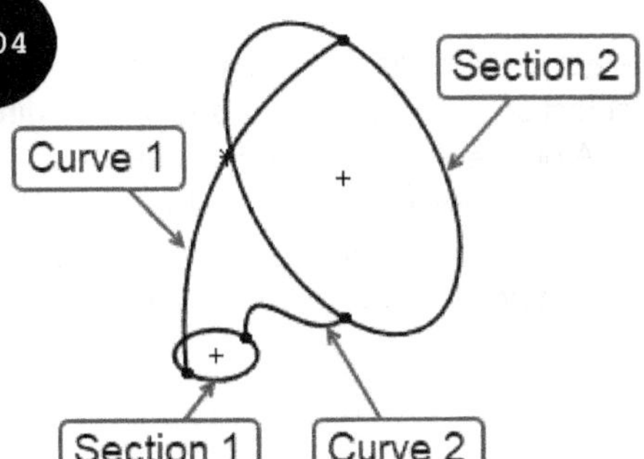

8.105

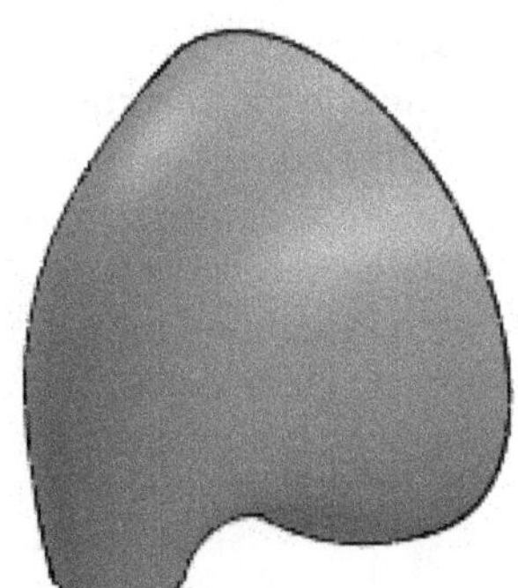

Figure 8.106 shows one section as direction 1 guide and three curves as direction 2 guides. Figure 8.107 shows the resultant boundary feature.

8.106

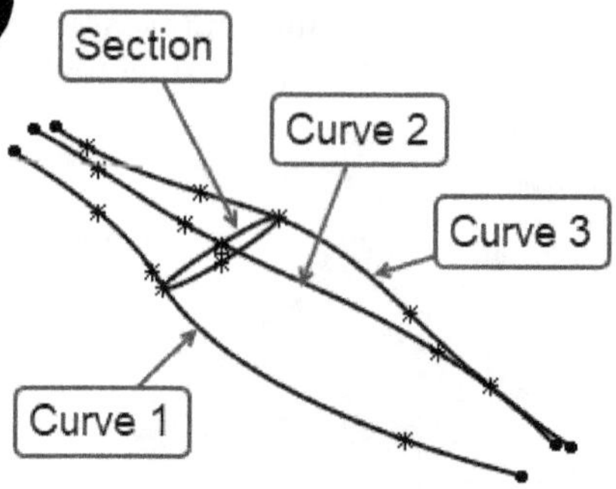

8.107

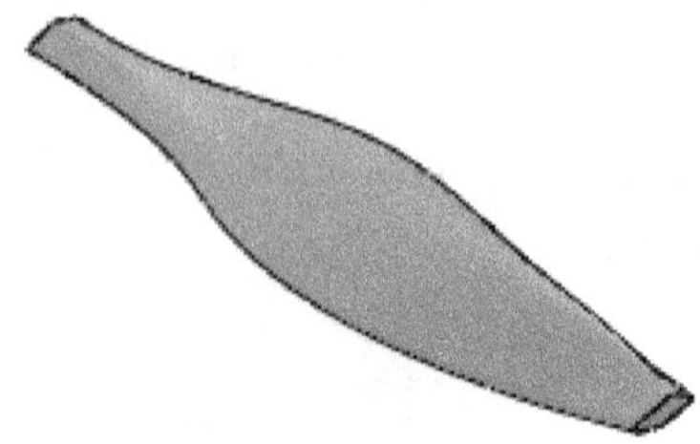

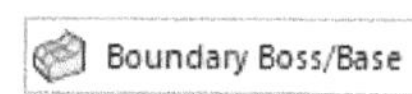

To create a boundary feature, create all sections and curves as direction 1 and direction 2 guides of the boundary feature, respectively, and then click on the **Boundary Boss/Base** tool in the **Features CommandManager**. The **Boundary PropertyManager** appears, see Figure 8.108. The options in this PropertyManager are discussed next.

8.108

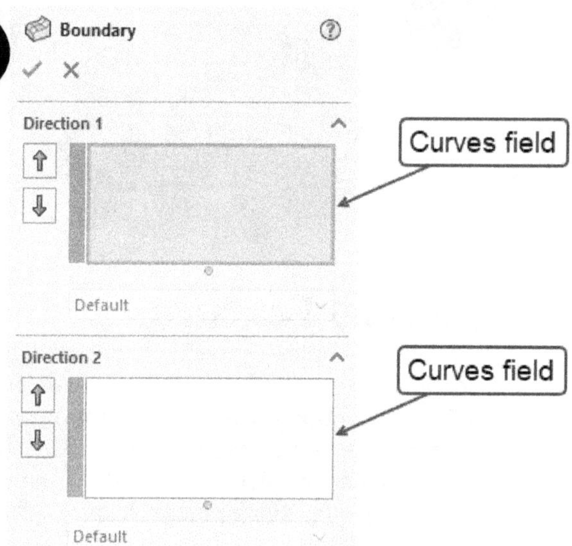

Direction 1

The **Curves** field in the **Direction 1** rollout is used to select sections as Direction 1 guides. By default, this field is activated. As a result, you are prompted to select sections. Select the sections as direction 1 guides in the graphics area one by one, see Figure 8.109. A preview of the boundary feature appears in the graphics area, see Figure 8.110. Also, the **Tangent Type** drop-down list and the **Draft angle** field are enabled in the **Direction 1** rollout, see Figure 8.111. You can select multiple sections or a single section as the direction 1 guide curve. The options in the **Tangent Type** drop-down list are the same as those discussed earlier while creating the lofted feature.

8.109

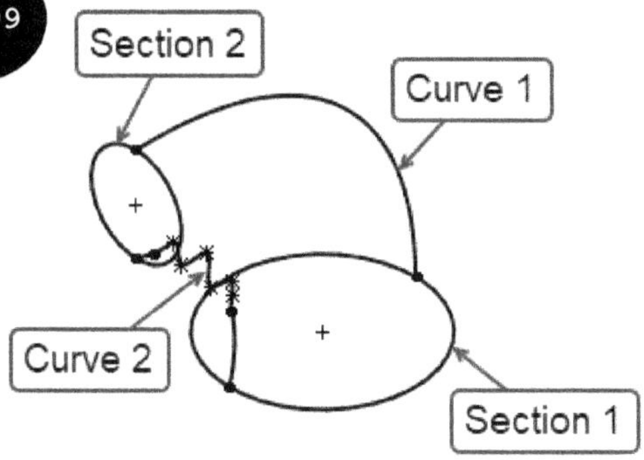

8.110

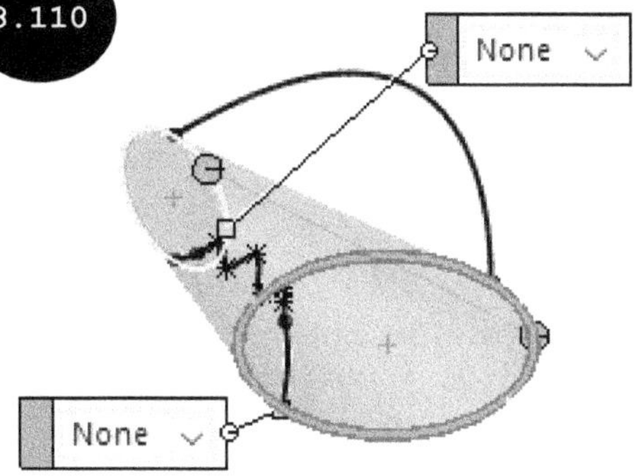

8.111

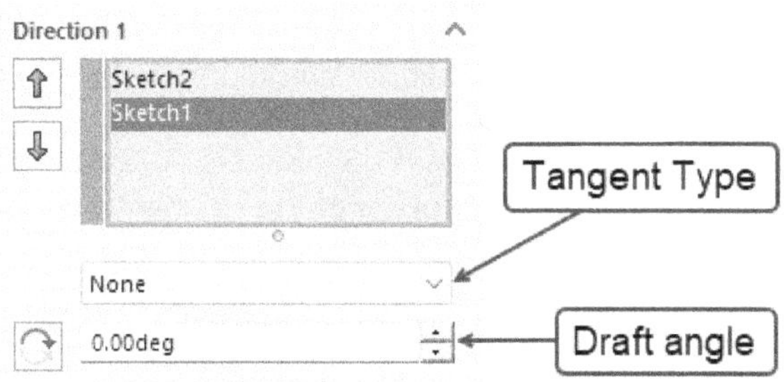

Tip: In the preview of the boundary feature, you can drag the connectors, which are connecting the sections to create a twist in the boundary feature, as required.

Direction 2

The **Curves** field in the **Direction 2** rollout is used to select the curves as Direction 2 guides. Click on this field and then select curves in the graphics area. The preview of the boundary feature is modified concerning the curves selected, see Figure 8.112. You can select multiple curves as direction 2 guide curves to control the shape of the boundary feature. Besides, you can specify the type of tangent continuity by using the options in the **Tangent Type** drop-down list of the **Direction 2** rollout. You can also control the influence of curves by using the options in the **Curve Influence Type** drop-down list of this rollout.

8.112

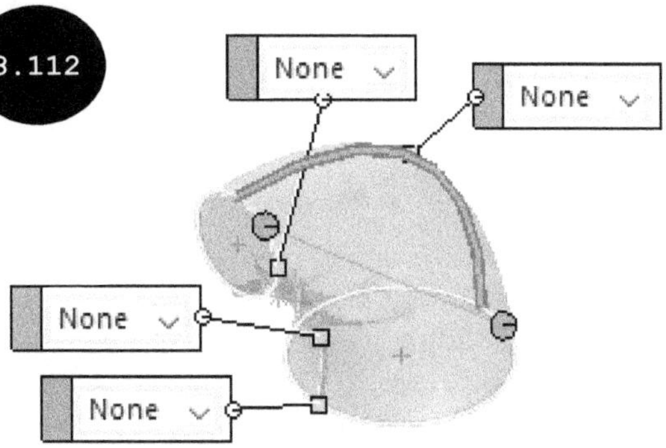

Tip: You can also flip the connectors to achieve the required shape. To flip the direction of connectors, select the curve/section whose connectors are to be flipped in the **Curves** field of the **Direction 1** or **Direction 2** rollout. Next, right-click to display a shortcut menu. In this shortcut menu, click on the **Flip Connectors** option. The direction of connectors gets flipped.

Options and Preview

The options in the **Options and Preview** rollout are the same as those discussed earlier while creating the lofted feature except the **Trim by direction 1** check box, which is discussed next.

Trim by direction 1

The **Trim by direction 1** check box is used to trim an extended portion of a feature, which is beyond the direction 1 guides. To trim the extended portion of the feature by direction 1 curves, select this check box. Figure 8.113 shows two sections as direction 1 guides and one curve as a direction 2 guide. Figure 8.114 shows a preview of the resultant boundary feature when the **Trim by direction 1** check box is cleared, and Figure 8.115 shows a preview of the resultant boundary feature when the **Trim by direction 1** check box is selected.

8.113

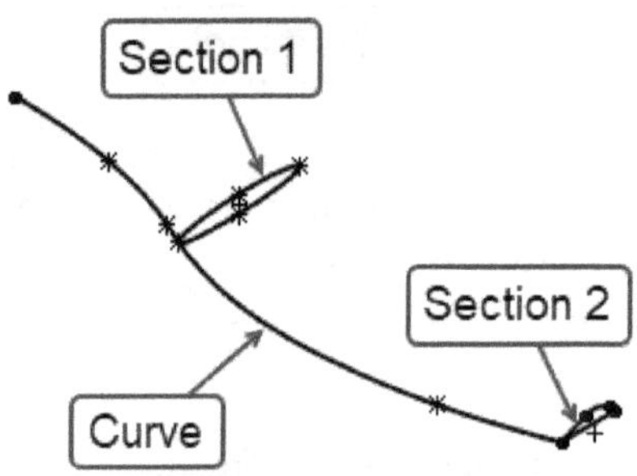

8.114

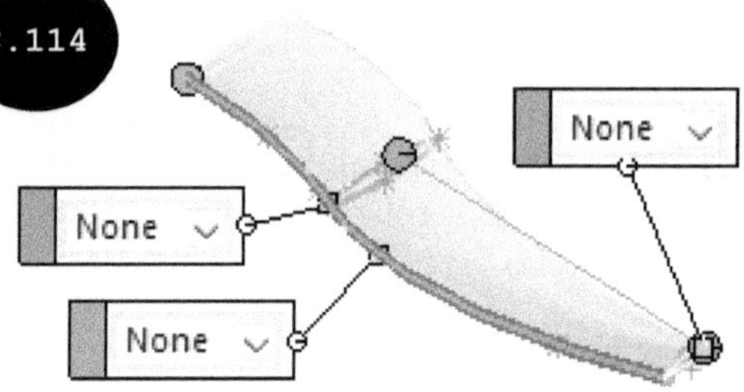

8.115

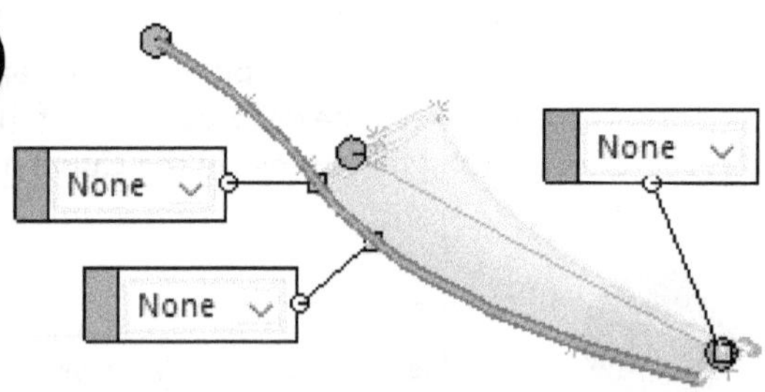

Thin Feature

The **Thin Feature** rollout is used to create a thin boundary feature, see Figure 8.116. The options in this rollout are the same as those discussed earlier while creating the thin extruded and revolved features.

8.116

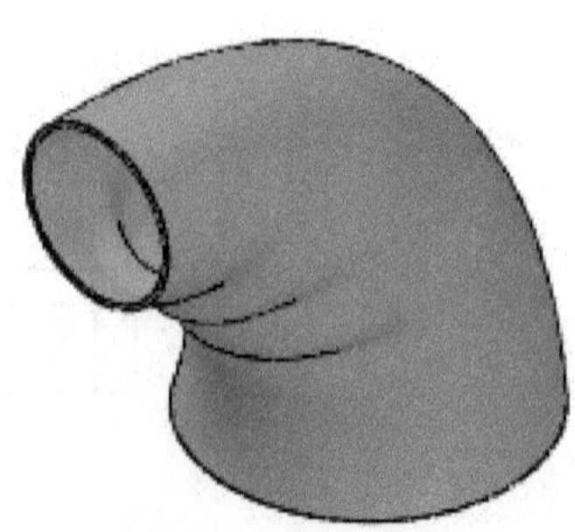

Curvature Display
The options in the **Curvature Display** rollout are the same as discussed earlier.

After selecting the required options, click on the green tick-mark ✓ button to accept the preview of the feature. A boundary feature is created.

Creating a Boundary Cut Feature

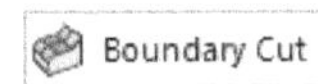

The method for creating a boundary cut feature is the same as creating a boundary feature with the only difference being that the boundary cut feature is created by removing material from the model. You can create a boundary cut feature by using the **Boundary Cut** tool in the **Features CommandManager**.

Creating Curves
In SOLIDWORKS, you can create different types of curves. Curves are mainly used as the path, guide curves, and so on for creating features such as sweep, lofted, and boundary. The tools for creating different types of curves are grouped in the **Curves** flyout, see Figure 8.117. The methods for creating different types of curves are discussed next.

8.117

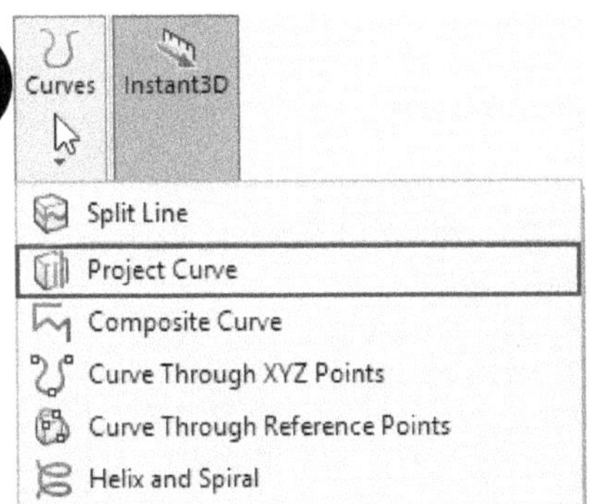

Creating Projected Curves
In SOLIDWORKS, you can create projected curves using the **Project Curve** tool. The **Project Curve** tool is used to create projected curves by using two methods: Sketch on Faces and Sketch on Sketch. In the Sketch on Faces method, the projected curve is created by projecting a sketch onto an existing face of a model, see Figure 8.118. You can select planar faces or curved faces to project a sketch.

8.118

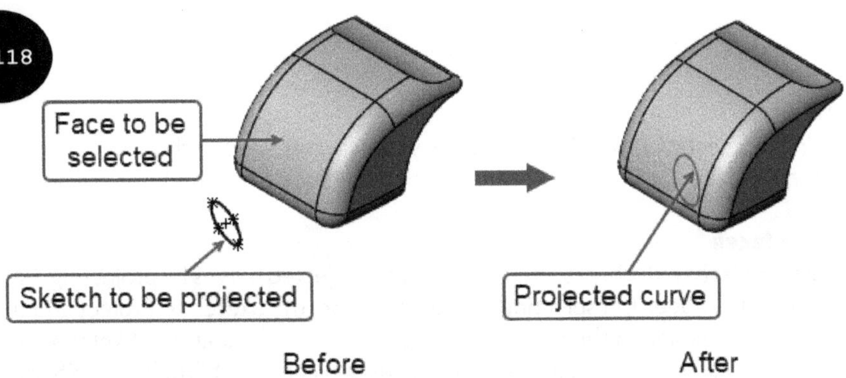

In the **Sketch on Sketch** method, the projected curve is created by projecting one sketch onto the other sketch such that the resultant projected curve represents the intersection of sketches, see Figure 8.119.

8.119

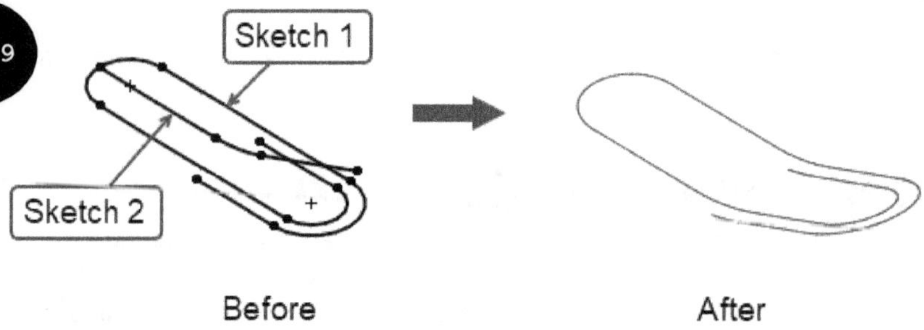

Tip: In Figure 8.119, Sketch 1 is created on the Top plane and Sketch 2 is created on the Front plane.

To create a projected curve, invoke the **Curves** flyout by clicking on the arrow at its bottom in the **Features CommandManager**, refer to Figure 8.117. Next, click on the **Project Curve** tool in the flyout. The **Projected Curve PropertyManager** appears, see Figure 8.120. The options in this PropertyManager are discussed next.

8.120

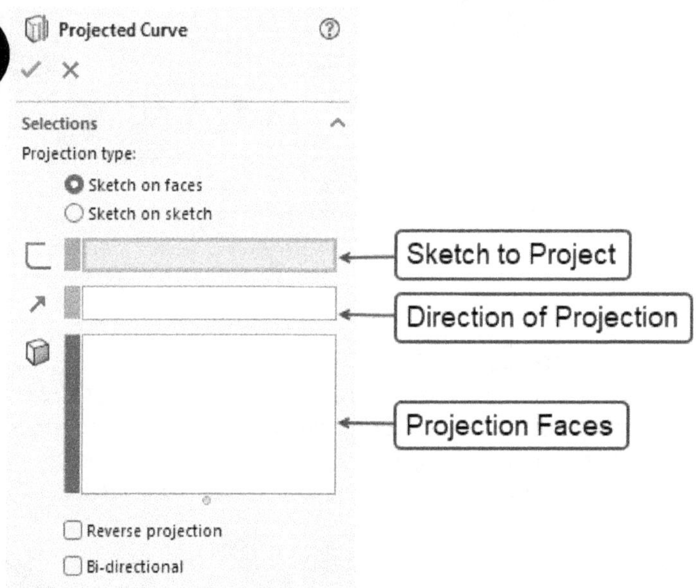

Selections

The options in the **Selections** rollout of the PropertyManager are used to choose the required projection method: **Sketch on faces** or **Sketch on sketch**. Both these projection methods are discussed next.

Sketch on faces

The **Sketch on faces** radio button is used to create projected curves by projecting a sketch onto an existing face of a model. On selecting this radio button, the **Sketch to Project** and the **Projection Faces** fields are enabled in the rollout, see Figure 8.120. By default, the **Sketch to Project** field is activated. As a result, you can select a sketch to be projected. In SOLIDWORKS, you can select a sketch that has multiple closed or open contours. Additionally, you can select a 3D sketch. Click on the sketch to be projected in the graphics area, see Figure 8.121. The name of the selected sketch appears in the **Sketch to Project** field. Also, the **Projection Faces** field gets activated and you are prompted to select projection faces.

Click on one or more faces in the graphics area, as the projection face, see Figure 8.121. A preview of the projected curve appears on the selected faces in the graphics area, see Figure 8.122. Ensure that the direction of the projection is toward the selected projection face. You can reverse the direction of projection using the **Reverse projection** check box. In SOLIDWORKS, you can also project the sketch on both sides of the sketching plane by selecting the **Bi-directional** check box in the PropertyManager, see Figure 8.123.

You can also define the direction of projection by activating the **Direction of Projection** field and selecting a plane, an edge, a sketch entity, or a face as the direction of the projected curve. Next, click on the green tick-mark ✓ in the PropertyManager. The projected curve is created.

8.121

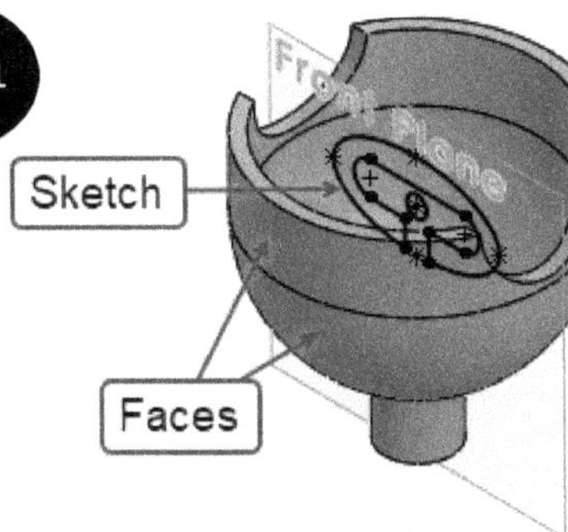

8.122

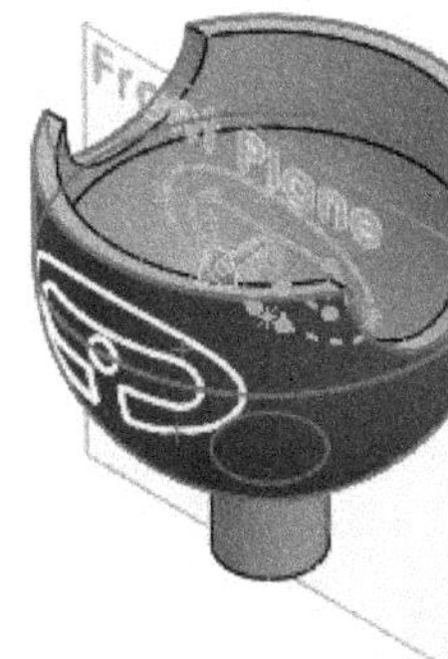

8.123

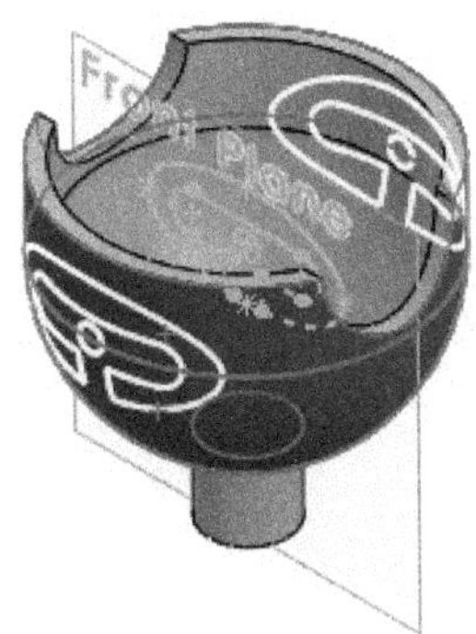

Note: By default, the direction of projection is normal to the sketching plane, refer to Figures 8.122 and 8.123. In SOLIDWORKS, you can also define the direction of projection by selecting an axis, a linear sketch entity, a linear edge, a plane, or a planar face. To do this, click on the **Direction of Projection** field in the PropertyManager and then select an entity as the direction of projection in the graphics area.

Sketch on sketch

The **Sketch on sketch** radio button is used to project one sketch onto another sketch such that the resultant projected curve represents the intersection of sketches. On selecting this radio button, the **Sketches to Project** field is enabled in the rollout. By default, this field is activated. As a result, you can select sketches to be projected. Select the sketches to be projected in the graphics area one by one by clicking the left mouse button, see Figure 8.124. A preview of the projected curve appears in the graphics area. Next, click on the green tick-mark ✓ in the PropertyManager. The projected curve is created, see Figure 8.125.

8.124

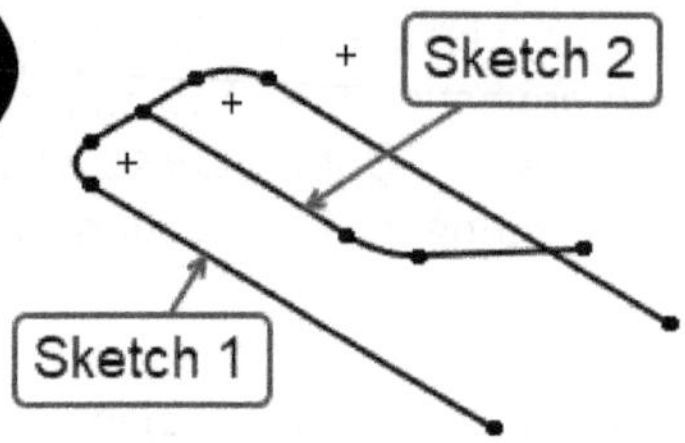

8.125

Tip: In Figure 8.124, Sketch 1 is created on the Top plane and Sketch 2 is created on the Front plane.

Creating Helical and Spiral Curves

You can create helical and spiral curves using the **Helix and Spiral** tool of the **Curves** flyout. You can use helical and spiral curves as paths, guide curves, and so on, to create sweep and lofted features. For example, Figure 8.126 shows a helical curve and the resultant sweep feature created by using it. To create a helical curve or a spiral curve in SOLIDWORKS, you first need to create a circle that defines the start diameter of the helical or spiral curve.

8.126

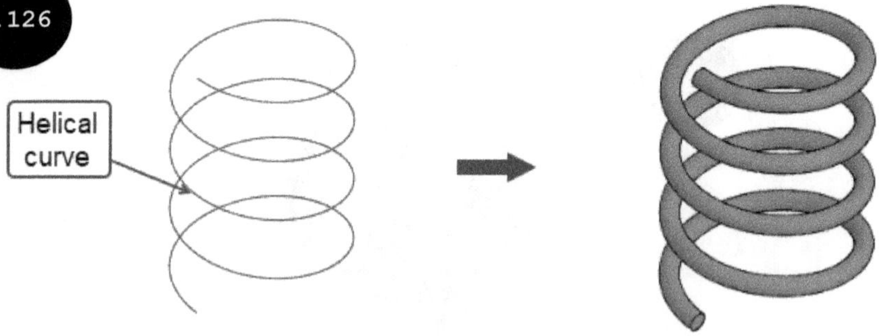

To create a helical or spiral curve, create a circle and then exit the Sketching environment. Next, invoke the **Curves** flyout in the **Features CommandManager** and then click on the **Helix and Spiral** tool, see Figure 8.127. The **Helix/Spiral PropertyManager** appears and you are prompted to select a circle or a sketching plane for creating a circle.

8.127

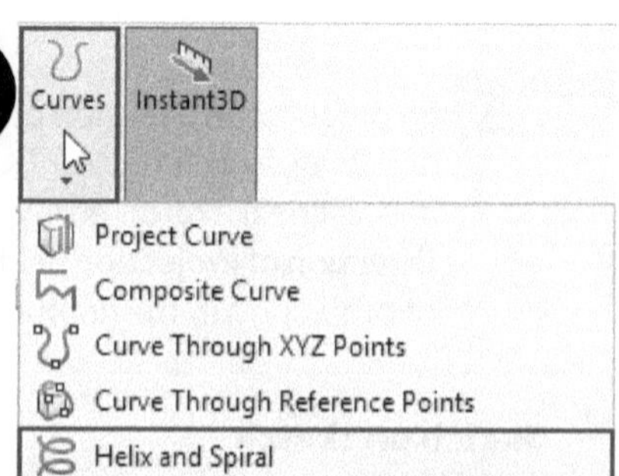

Note: You can select a circle before or after invoking the **Helix and Spiral** tool. If the circle is selected before invoking the tool, then the preview of a curve appears directly in the graphics area. Also, the **Helix/Spiral PropertyManager** appears with options for creating a helix/spiral curve, refer to Figure 8.128.

Tip: You can also access the **Helix and Spiral** tool in the **Curves** flyout of the **Features CommandManager** within the Sketching environment.

Select a circle in the graphics area that will define the start diameter of the curve. The **Helix/Spiral PropertyManager** appears similar to the one shown in Figure 8.128. Also, the preview of a curve appears in the graphics area with default parameters, see Figure 8.129.

8.128

8.129

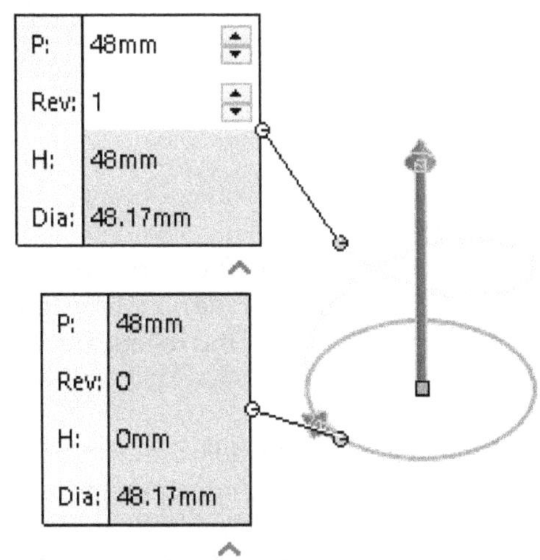

The options in the **Helix/Spiral PropertyManager** are used to create a constant pitch helical curve, a variable pitch helical curve, or a spiral curve. The options are discussed next.

Defined By

The **Defined By** rollout is used to define the type of curve (helical or spiral) to be created and the method to be adopted for creating it. The options in this rollout are available in a drop-down list, see Figure 8.130. The options are discussed next.

8.130

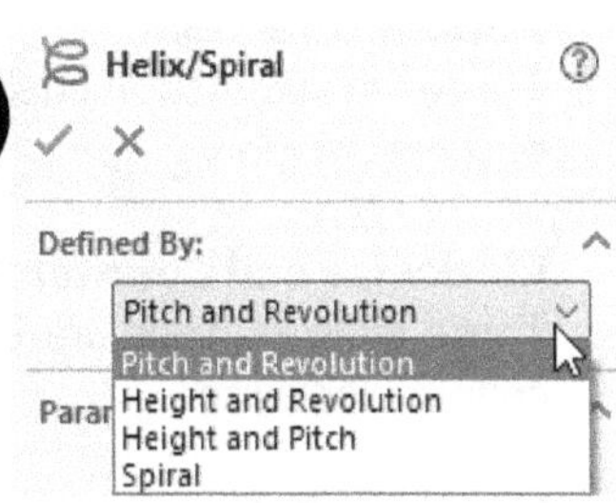

Pitch and Revolution

The **Pitch and Revolution** option is used to create a helical curve by defining its pitch and number of revolutions. On selecting this option, the options for creating a helical curve by defining its pitch and revolutions get enabled in the **Parameters** rollout of the PropertyManager.

Height and Revolution

The **Height and Revolution** option is used to create a helical curve by defining its total height and number of revolutions. On selecting this option, the options for creating a helical curve by defining its height and revolutions are enabled in the **Parameters** rollout of the PropertyManager.

Height and Pitch

The **Height and Pitch** option is used to create a helical curve by defining its total height and pitch. On selecting this option, the options for creating a helical curve by defining its height and pitch are enabled in the **Parameters** rollout of the PropertyManager.

Spiral

The **Spiral** option is used to create a spiral curve by defining its pitch and number of revolutions. On selecting this option, the options for creating a spiral curve by defining its pitch and revolutions are enabled in the **Parameters** rollout. Figure 8.131 shows a spiral curve.

8.131

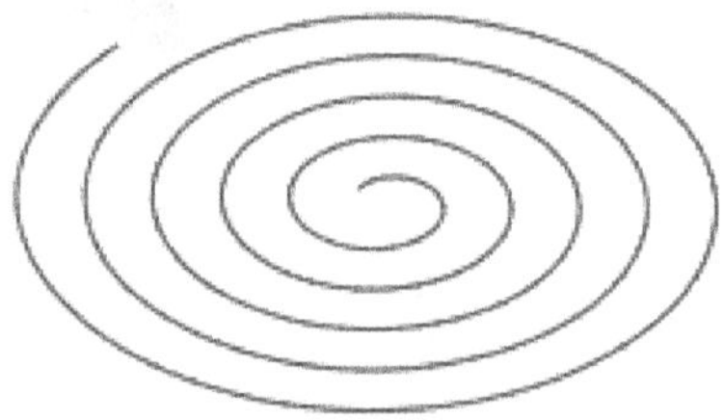

Parameters

The **Parameters** rollout of the PropertyManager is used to specify the parameters for creating a curve. The availability of most of the options in this rollout depends upon the option selected in the **Defined By** rollout. The options of this rollout are discussed next.

Constant pitch

The **Constant pitch** radio button is used to create a helical curve with constant pitch throughout the helix height, see Figure 8.132.

8.132

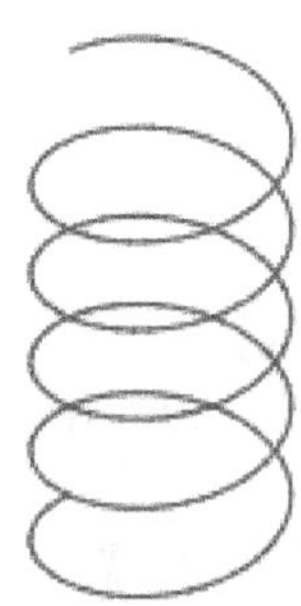

Pitch, Revolutions, Height, and Start angle

These fields are used to specify pitch, revolutions, height, and start angle for the curve, respectively.

Reverse direction

The **Reverse direction** check box is used to reverse the direction of curve creation.

Clockwise and Counterclockwise

These radio buttons are used to specify the direction of the revolution, either clockwise or counterclockwise.

Variable pitch

The **Variable pitch** radio button is used to create a helical curve with variable pitch and variable diameter, see Figures 8.133 and 8.134. On selecting this radio button, the **Region**

parameters table appears in the rollout, see Figure 8.135. In the **Region parameters** table, you can enter a variable pitch and diameter in the respective fields for creating a helical curve, see Figure 8.135. Note that the availability of options in this table depends upon the option selected in the **Defined By** rollout of the PropertyManager.

8.133

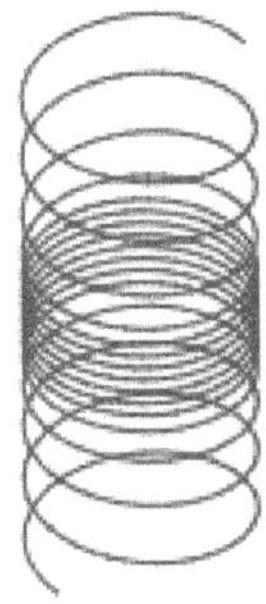

8.134

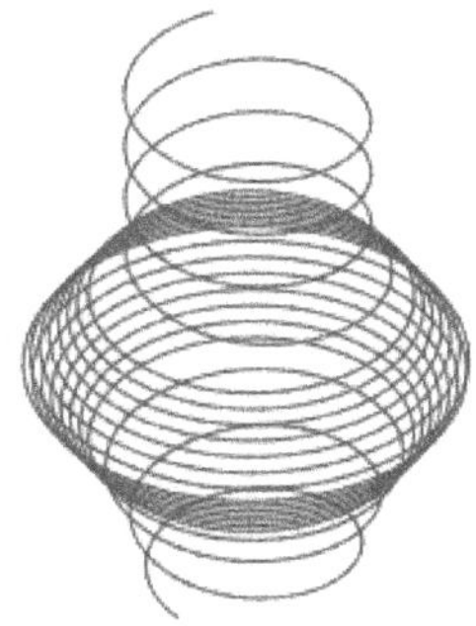

8.135

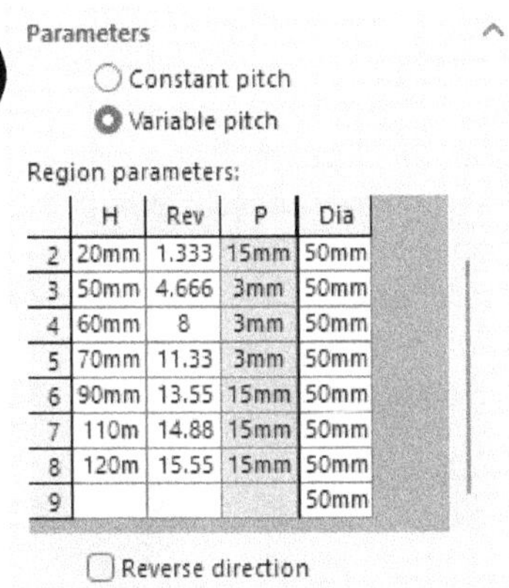

	H	Rev	P	Dia
2	20mm	1.333	15mm	50mm
3	50mm	4.666	3mm	50mm
4	60mm	8	3mm	50mm
5	70mm	11.33	3mm	50mm
6	90mm	13.55	15mm	50mm
7	110m	14.88	15mm	50mm
8	120m	15.55	15mm	50mm
9				50mm

Note: If the **Height and Pitch** option is selected in the **Defined By** rollout then in the **Region parameters** table, you can enter a variable pitch at different heights as well as variable diameter at different heights, see Figure 8.135. If you select the **Height and Revolution** option, then the **Region parameters** table allows you to specify revolutions and variable diameter at different heights. Also, a variable pitch of the curve will automatically be calculated based on the number of revolutions at different heights. To enter values in the table, click on the respective fields of the table.

Taper Helix

The **Taper Helix** rollout of the PropertyManager is used to create a tapered helical curve, see Figure 8.136. This rollout is available when the **Constant pitch** radio button is selected in the **Parameters** rollout. By default, the options of the **Taper Helix** rollout are not activated. To activate the options of this rollout, select the check box in its title bar. The **Taper Angle** field of this rollout is used for specifying the taper angle of the helical curve. Note that if the **Taper outward** check box is cleared in this rollout, then the helical curve tapers inward to the sketch. If you select the **Taper outward** check box, then the helical curve tapers outward to the sketch.

8.136

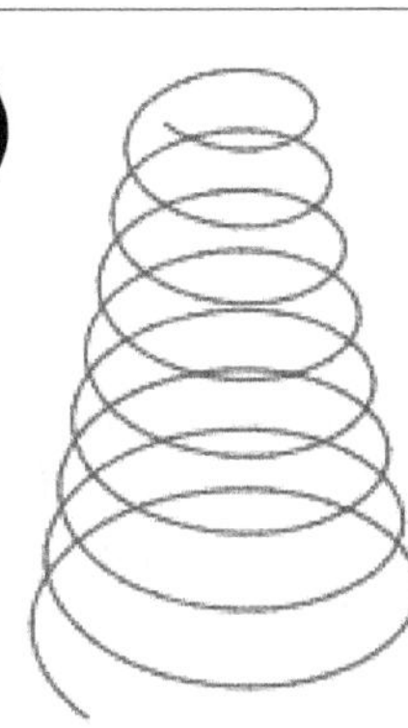

Creating Curves by Specifying XYZ Points

You can create a curve by specifying coordinates (X, Y, Z) that define its shape. To do this, open the **Curves** flyout and click the **Curve Through XYZ Points** tool. The **Curve Through XYZ Points PropertyManager**, see Figure 8.137.

In the **Curve Through XYZ Points PropertyManager**, you can specify the coordinates (X, Y, Z) of multiple points relative to the origin (0, 0, 0) to create a curve.

8.137

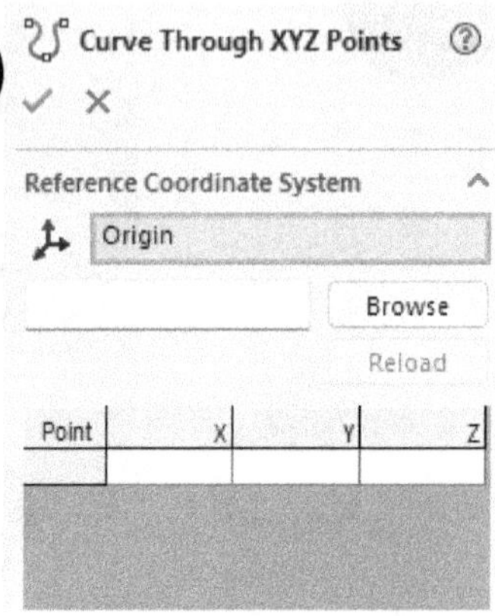

To specify coordinates in the PropertyManager, double-click on the field corresponding to the first row and the **X** column to activate it in the table. Once this field has been activated, you can enter the X coordinate of the first point concerning the origin. Similarly, you can activate the **Y** and **Z** fields and then enter the Y and Z coordinates of the first point. Note that, by default, only one row is available in this table of the PropertyManager. However, the moment you activate a field of the first row, the second or next row gets added automatically in the PropertyManager. Specify the coordinates of the second point in the second row. Similarly, you can specify the coordinates of the other points in the PropertyManager. Note that as you specify the coordinates in the table, a preview of the curve appears in the graphics area. Figure 8.138 shows the **Curve Through XYZ Points PropertyManager** with coordinates of multiple points specified and Figure 8.139 shows the resultant curve.

8.138

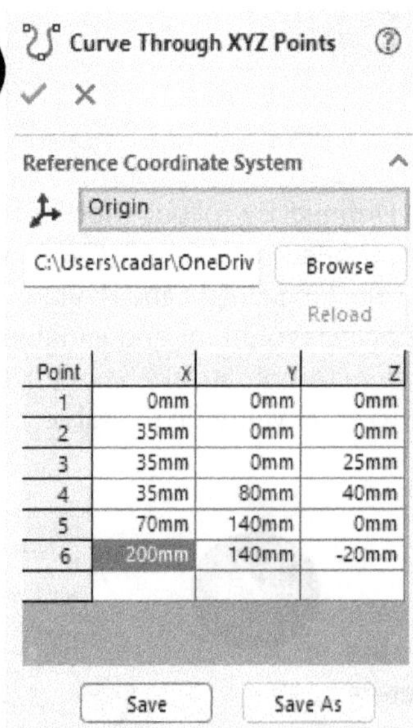

8.139

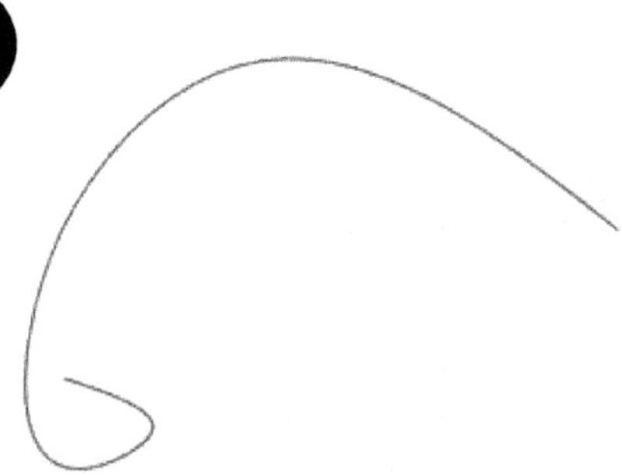

You can also save all coordinates of the points specified in the table as a *.sldcrv* file in the local drive of your computer for further use. To do this, click on the **Save** button in the PropertyManager. The **Save As** dialog box appears. In this dialog box, browse to the location where you want to save the file and then specify a name for the file in the **File name** edit box. Next, click on the **Save** button in the **Save As** dialog box. The file is saved as a *.sldcrv* file. Once you have specified the coordinates of the points in the PropertyManager, click on the green tick-mark ✓ button. The curve is created.

If you have a *.sldcrv* or *.txt* (notepad) file containing information about the coordinates of the points for creating a curve, click on the **Browse** button in the **Curve Through XYZ Points PropertyManager**. The **Open** dialog box appears. In this dialog box, browse to the location where the *.sldcrv* or *.txt* (notepad) file is saved. Note that by default, the **Curves (*.sldcrv)** option is selected in the **File Type** drop-down list of the dialog box. As a result, you can only import the *.sldcrv* file. To import a *.txt* (notepad) file, you need to select the **Text Files (*.txt)** option in the **File Type** drop-down list. After selecting the required file type in the drop-down list, select the file, and then click on the **Open** button. The coordinate points of the selected file get filled in the **Browse File Path** field. Also, a preview of the curve appears in the graphics area.

Tip: In *.txt* (notepad) file, the coordinates of all points should be written in separate lines. Also, the coordinates (X, Y, Z) of a point should be separated by a comma and a space (X, Y, Z).

Creating Curves by Selecting Reference Points

In SOLIDWORKS, you can create 3D curves by selecting reference points in the graphics area. The reference points can be located in the same or different planes. You can also select vertices of the model or sketch points as reference points for creating a curve. To create a curve by selecting reference points, invoke the **Curves** flyout and then click on the **Curve Through Reference Points** tool. The **Curve Through Reference Points PropertyManager** appears, see Figure 8.140. Next, select sketch points or vertices in the graphics area one by one by clicking the left mouse button. A preview of the respective curve appears, see Figure 8.141. Also, the names of the selected points/vertices get listed in the **Through Points** field of the PropertyManager. Next, click on the green tick-mark ✓ in the PropertyManager. The curve is created.

8.140

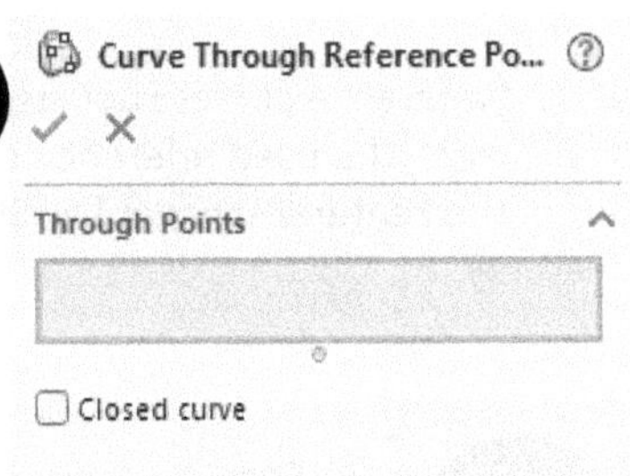

8.141

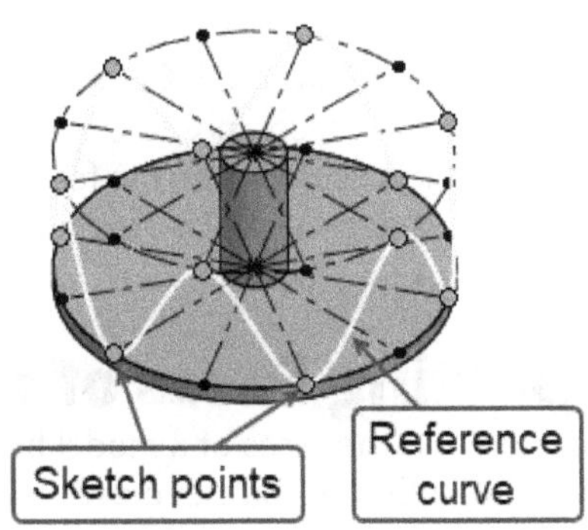

Note: On selecting the **Closed curve** check box in the PropertyManager, a closed curve is created by connecting the specified start point and end point of the curve.

Creating a Composite Curve

A composite curve is created by joining two or more than two curves together. You can join multiple curves or sketches together and create a single composite curve by using the **Composite Curve** tool of the **Curves** flyout.

To create a composite curve, click on the **Composite Curve** tool in the **Curves** flyout. The **Composite Curve PropertyManager** appears, see Figure 8.142. Next, select curves one by one in the graphics area by clicking the left mouse button and then click on the green tick-mark ✓ in the PropertyManager. A composite curve is created. You can select sketch entities, curves, and edges for creating a composite curve. Note that the curves to be joined must be connected end to end and have a pierce relation with each other. Figure 8.143 shows individual curves (five curves) and Figure 8.144 shows the resultant composite curve. Figure 8.145 shows a sweep feature created by sweeping a profile (circle) along the composite curve shown in Figure 8.144.

8.142

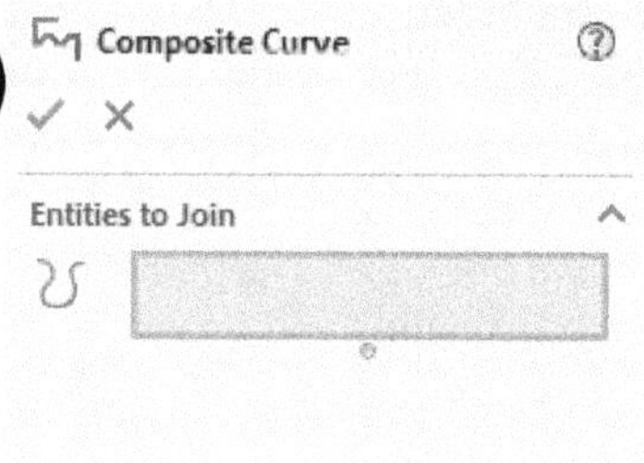

8.143

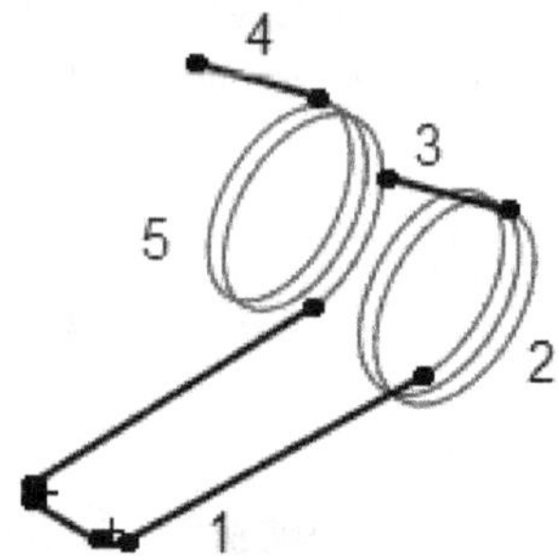

8.144

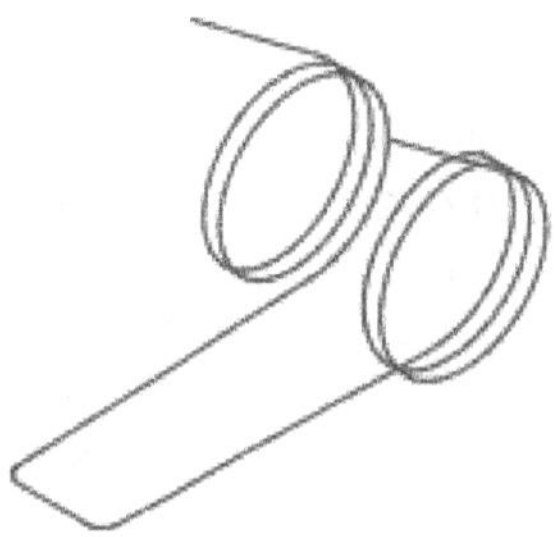

8.145

Note: In SOLIDWORKS, when you create a feature by using reference curves such as projected curves, composite curves, helical curves, and spiral curves; the used reference curves are not absorbed by the feature and appear separately in the FeatureManager Design Tree so that they can be used further for creating other features.

Splitting Faces of a Model

You can split the faces of a model by creating split lines. In SOLIDWORKS, you can create split lines by using the **Split Line** tool. To do this, click on the **Split Line** tool in the **Curves** flyout. The **Split Line PropertyManager** appears, see Figure 8.146. The options in this PropertyManager are discussed next.

8.146

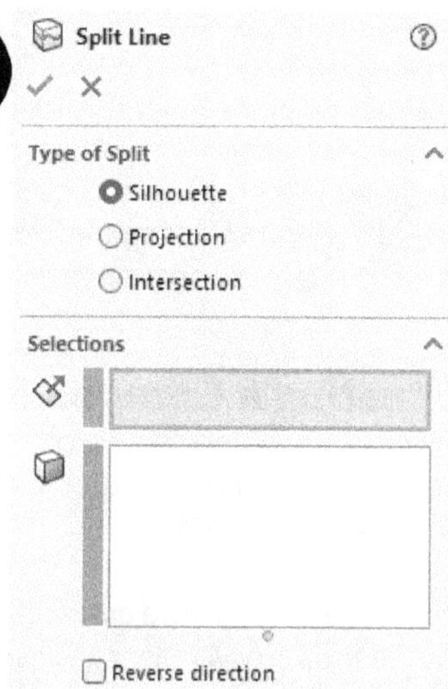

Type of Split

The options in the **Type of Split** rollout are used to select the type of split method to be used for splitting the faces of a model. The options are discussed next.

Projection

The **Projection** radio button is used to split faces by projecting a sketch. Figure 8.147 shows a sketch to be projected and the face of a model to be split. Figure 8.148 shows the resultant model after splitting the face by creating split lines. Note that split lines divide a face into different faces concerning the projected sketch. After splitting a face into multiple faces, you can apply different textures or appearances to them.

8.147

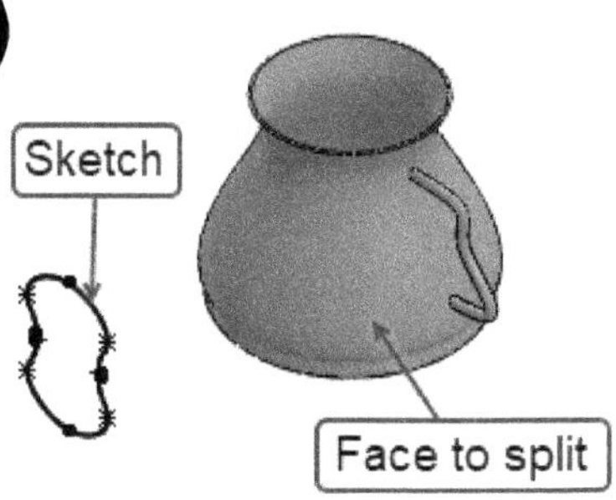

8.148

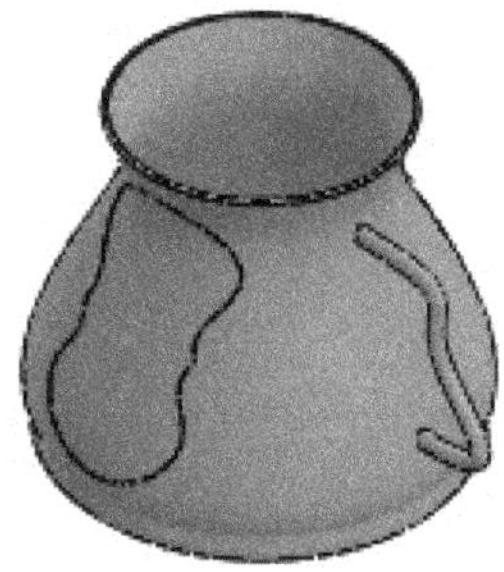

On selecting the **Projection** radio button, the **Sketch to Project** and **Faces to Split** fields are enabled in the **Selections** rollout of the PropertyManager, see Figure 8.149. By default, the **Sketch to Project** field is activated. As a result, you can select the sketch to be projected. After selecting the sketch to be projected, the **Faces to Split** field gets activated in the PropertyManager. Now, select the faces to be split. You can select curved faces or planar faces as the faces to be split. To project the split line in one direction, select the **Single direction** check box and to reverse the direction of projection, click on the **Reverse direction** check box in the PropertyManager. Next, click on the green tick-mark ✓ in the PropertyManager. The selected faces are split.

8.149

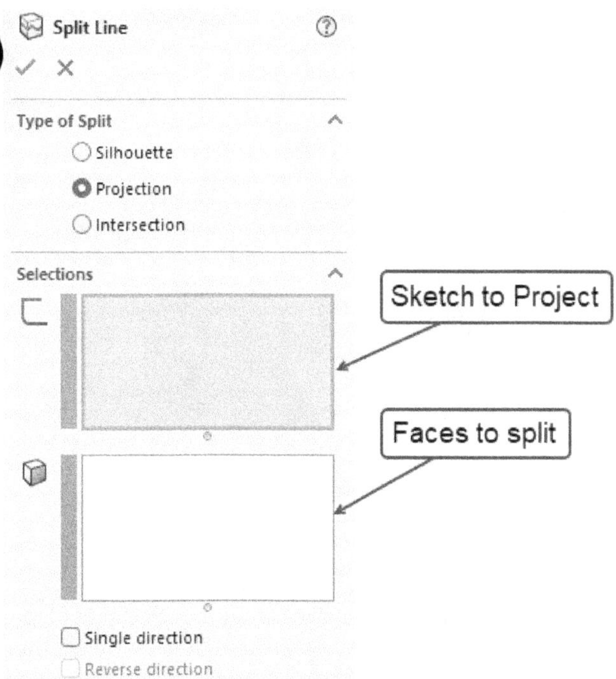

Intersection

The **Intersection** radio button is used to split faces by creating split lines at the intersection of two objects. The objects can be solid bodies, surfaces, faces, or in combination with a plane. Figure 8.150 shows the face of a model and a plane. Figure 8.151 shows the resultant model after splitting the face at the intersection with the plane.

8.150

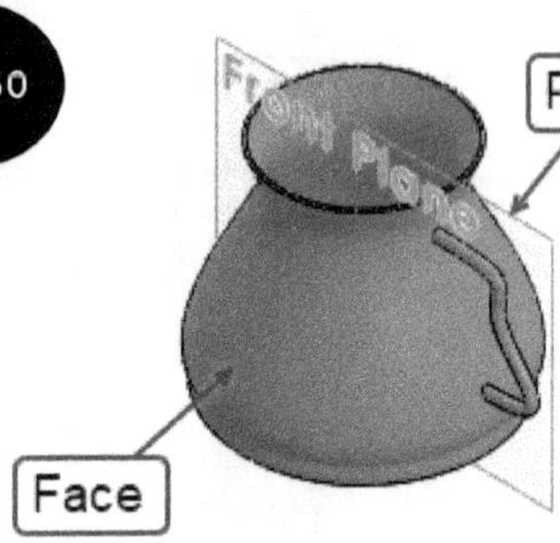

8.151

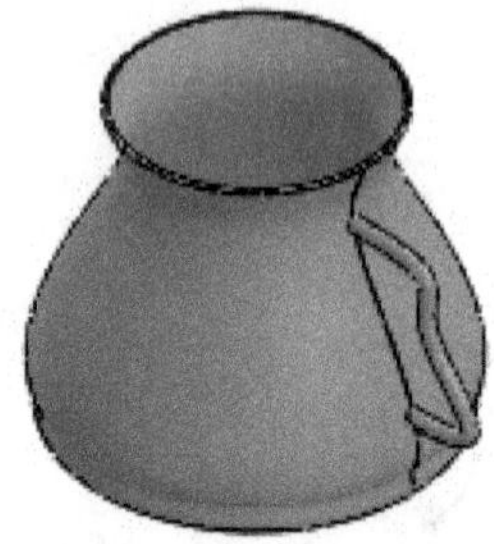

On selecting the **Intersection** radio button, the **Splitting Bodies/Faces/Planes** and **Faces/Bodies to Split** fields are enabled in the **Selections** rollout of the PropertyManager. By default, the **Splitting Bodies/Faces/Planes** field is activated. As a result, you can select bodies, faces, or planes as the splitting objects, see Figure 8.152. After selecting the splitting objects, click on the **Faces/Bodies to Split** field and then select faces or bodies to be split, see Figure 8.152. A preview of split lines appears in the graphics area, see Figure 8.153. Next, click on the green tick-mark ✓ in the PropertyManager. The selected face gets split, see Figure 8.154. Note that in Figure 8.154, the visibility of the splitting object is turned off.

8.152

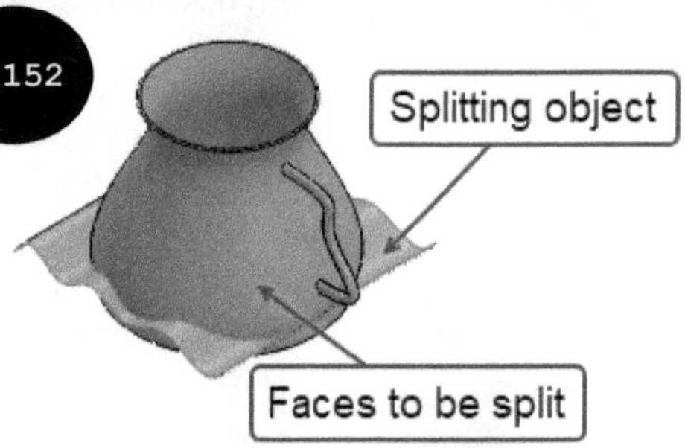

8.153

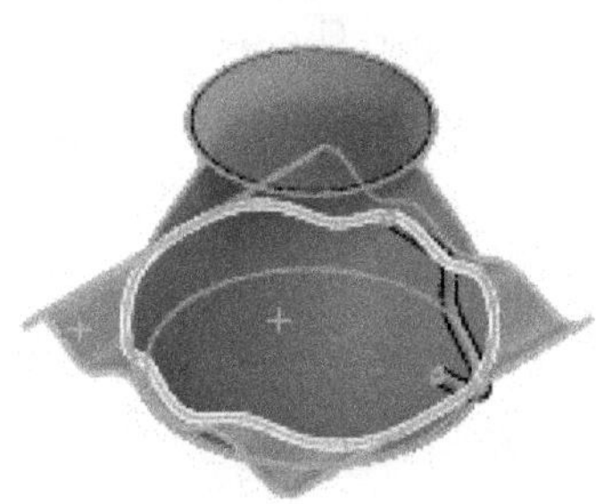

8.154

Note: The splitting object shown in Figure 8.152 is an extruded surface. An extruded surface is created by using the **Extruded Surface** tool in the **Surfaces CommandManager**. The options for creating an extruded surface are same as those discussed earlier, while creating an extruded solid feature with the only difference that the extruded surface has zero thickness.

Silhouette

The **Silhouette** radio button is used to split faces at the intersection between a direction of projection and a curved face. Figure 8.155 shows a direction of projection and a curved face to be split. Figure 8.156 shows the split line created at the intersection of the projection direction and the curve face selected.

8.155

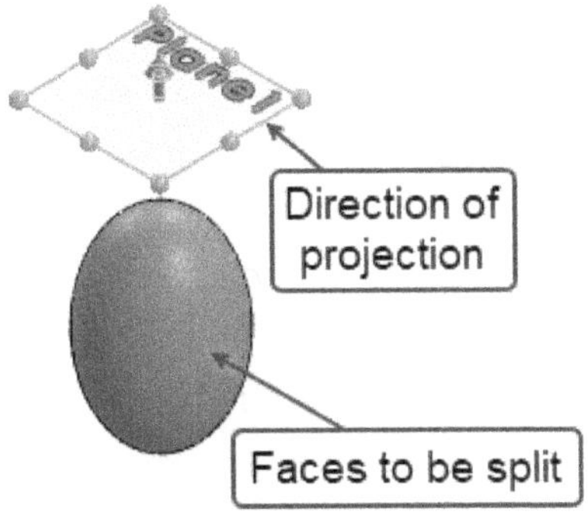

8.156

On selecting the **Silhouette** radio button, the **Direction of Pull** and **Faces to Split** fields are enabled in the **Selections** rollout of the PropertyManager. By default, the **Direction of Pull** field is activated. As a result, you can select a plane or a planar face as the direction of projection or pull. After selecting a plane or a planar face as the direction of projection (see Figure 8.155), the **Faces to Split** field gets activated. Now, you can select the curved faces to be split. Note that in the case of creating the silhouette split line, you can only select curved faces as the faces to be split. After selecting the curved faces, specify the draft angle value in the **Angle** field of the PropertyManager. Next, click on the green tick-mark ✓ in the PropertyManager. The split line is created. Figure 8.156 shows the split line created with the draft angle value set to 0 degrees in the **Angle** field. Figure 8.157 shows the split line created with the draft angle value set to 40 degrees.

8.157

Creating 3D Sketches

In SOLIDWORKS, in addition to creating 2D sketches and 3D curves, you can also create 3D sketches in the 3D Sketching environment. Most of the time, 3D sketches are used as a 3D path and a guide curve for creating sweep, lofted, and boundary features. To create 3D sketches, you need to invoke the 3D Sketching environment of SOLIDWORKS. To do this, click on the arrow at the bottom of the **Sketch** tool in the **Sketch CommandManager**, see Figure 8.158. The **Sketch** flyout appears. In this flyout, click on the **3D Sketch** tool, see Figure 8.158. The 3D Sketching environment is invoked, see Figure 8.159.

8.158

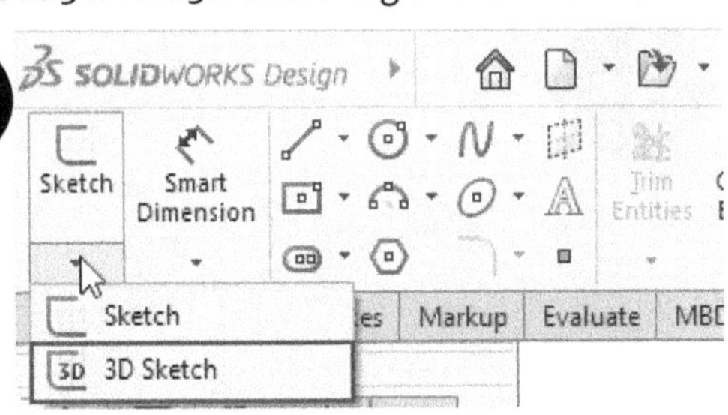

8.159

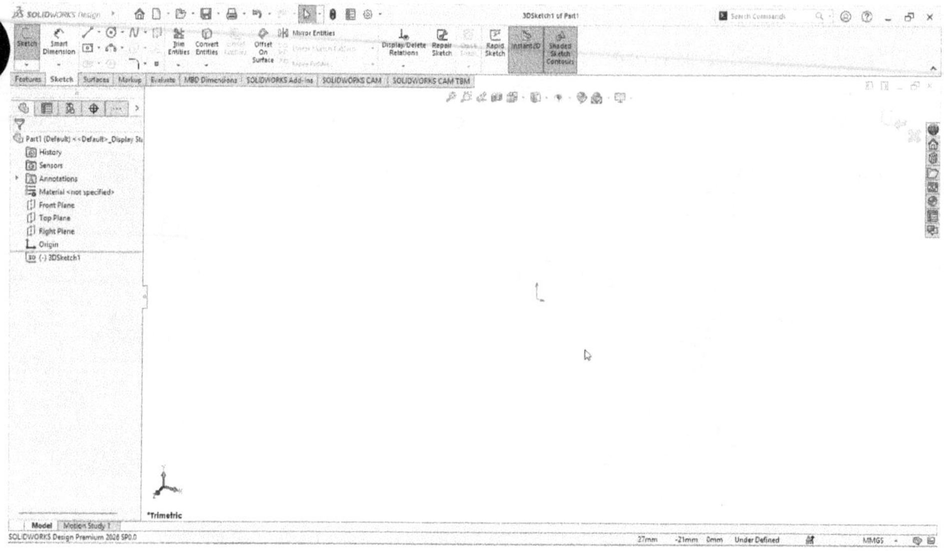

Now, in 3D Sketching environment, you can create 3D sketches using the tools available in the **Sketch CommandManager**. Some of the tools such as **Polygon**, **Ellipse**, **Offset Entities**, and **Move Entities** are not enabled. This is because these tools cannot be used for creating 3D sketches. Some of the tools of the 3D Sketching environment are discussed next.

Using the Line Tool in the 3D Sketching Environment

1. Invoke the 3D Sketching environment by clicking on the **3D Sketch** tool in the **Sketch** flyout that appears by clicking the arrow at the bottom of the **Sketch** tool in the **Sketch CommandManager**, refer to Figure 8.158.

2. Click on the **Line** tool in the **Sketch CommandManager**. The cursor changes to a line cursor with the display of **XY** at its bottom, see Figure 8.160. The display of XY indicates that the XY plane (Front plane) is activated as the current sketching plane. You can press the **TAB** key to switch.

8.160

3. Press the **TAB** key until the required sketching plane is activated.

4. Specify the start point of the line by clicking the left mouse button in the graphics area.

5. Move the cursor to a distance from the start point. A rubber band line appears whose one end is fixed at the specified start point and the other end is attached to the cursor, see Figure 8.161.

8.161

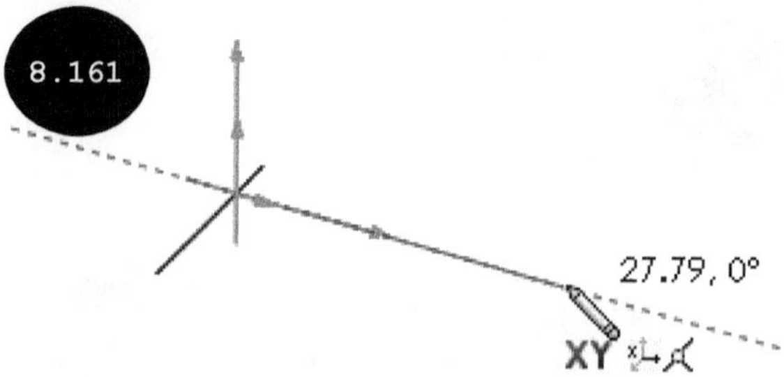

Tip: You can toggle the sketching plane even after specifying the start point of the line by using the **TAB** key.

6. Move the cursor to the required location in the drawing area and then click to specify the endpoint of the first line when the length of the line appears close to the required one, near the cursor. Next, move the cursor to a distance. A preview of the rubber band line appears.

7. Press the **TAB** key to switch the sketching plane, if required.

8. Move the cursor to the required location and then click to specify the endpoint of the next line, see Figure 8.162. In Figure 8.162, the sketching plane has been changed to YZ.

9. Similarly, create other line entities of the 3D sketch in different sketching planes, as required, see Figure 8.163.

8.162

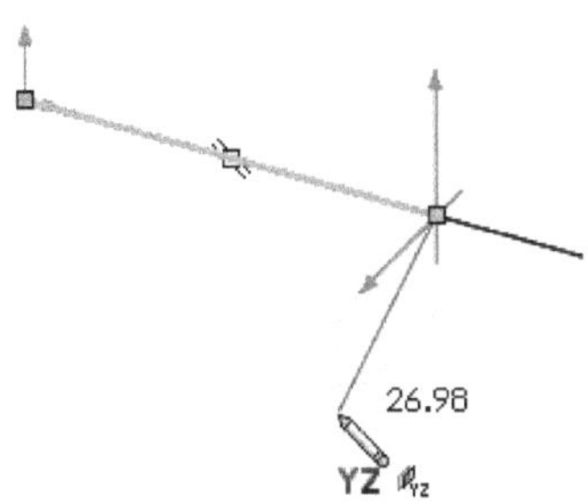

8.163

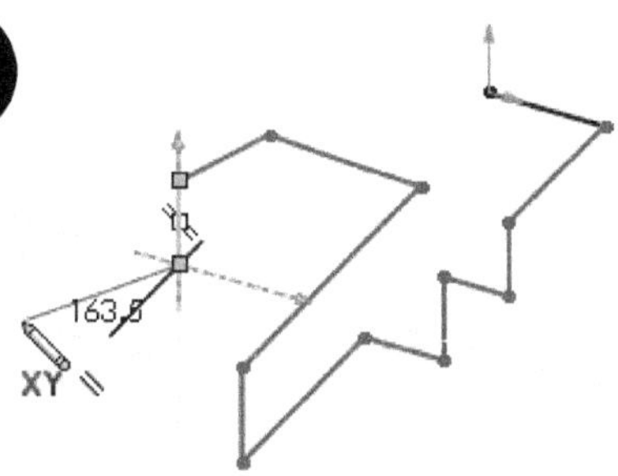

10. After creating all sketch entities of the 3D sketch, right-click in the graphics area, and then click on the **Select** option in the shortcut menu that appears to exit the **Line** tool.

Note: The procedure for applying dimensions to a 3D sketch in the 3D Sketching environment is same as applying dimensions to a 2D sketch by using the dimension tools.

11. Click on the 3D **Sketch** tool in the **Sketch CommandManager** to exit the 3D Sketching environment. Alternatively, click on the **Exit Sketch** icon in the Confirmation corner.

Figure 8.164 shows a 3D Sketch and Figure 8.165 shows a sweep feature created by sweeping a circular profile along the 3D sketch.

8.164

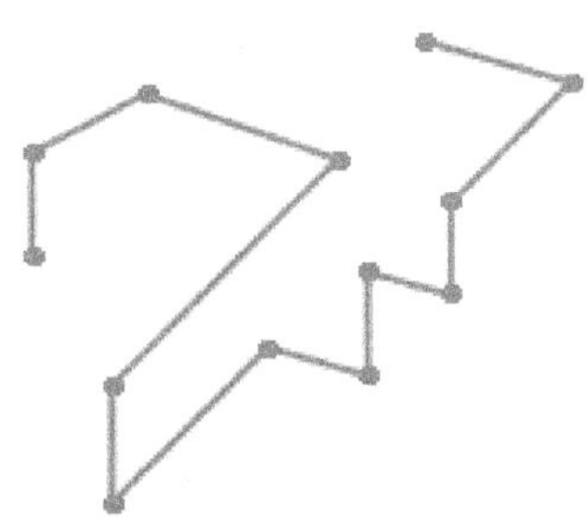

8.165

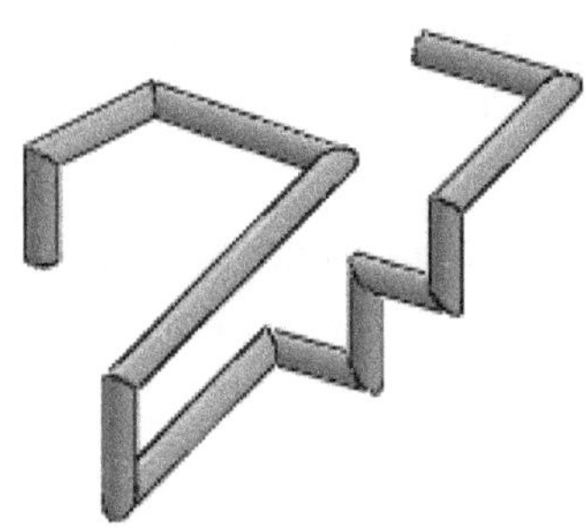

Using the Spline Tool in the 3D Sketching Environment

1. Invoke the 3D Sketching environment by clicking on the **3D Sketch** tool in the **Sketch** flyout that appears on clicking the arrow at the bottom of the **Sketch** tool in the **Sketch CommandManager**.

2. Press CTRL + 7 to change the current orientation of the sketch to isometric.

3. Click on the **Spline** tool in the **Sketch CommandManager**. The display of cursor changes such that **XY** appears at its bottom, see Figure 8.166. The display of XY indicates that the XY plane (Front plane) is activated as the current sketching plane. You can press the **TAB** key to switch from one sketching plane to another for creating a 3D sketch.

8.166

4. Press the **TAB** key until the required sketching plane has been activated and its name appears below the cursor.

5. Click to specify the first control point of the spline in the graphics area. Next, move the cursor to a distance from the specified control point. A rubber band spline appears whose one end is fixed at the first control point and the other end is attached to the cursor, see Figure 8.167.

6. Press the **TAB** key to switch the sketching plane, as required.

7. Move the cursor to the required location and then click to specify the second control point of the spline, see Figure 8.168. Next, move the cursor to a distance. A preview of another rubber band spline appears such that it passes through the specified control points.

8.167

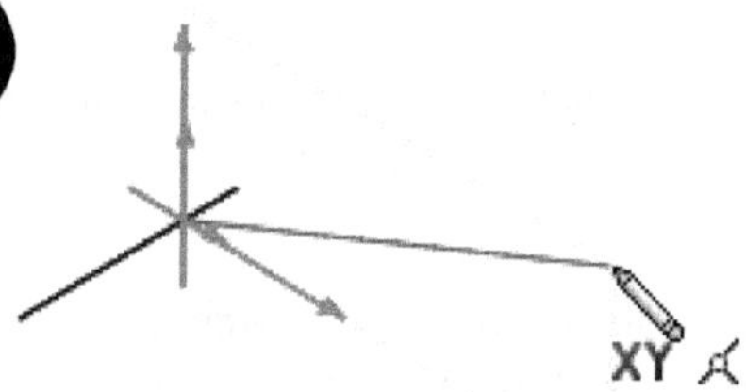

8.168

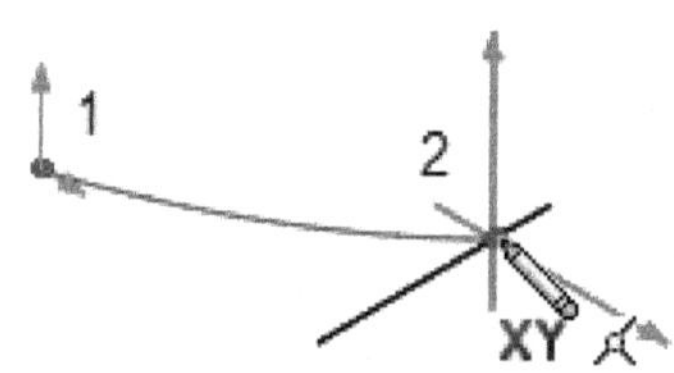

Tip: In Figure 8.168, the second control point of the spline is specified on the XY plane.

8. Press the **TAB** key to switch the sketching plane, if required. Next, move the cursor to the required location and then click to specify the third control point of the spline, see Figure 8.169.

Tip: In Figure 8.169, the third control point of the spline is specified on the XY plane.

8.169

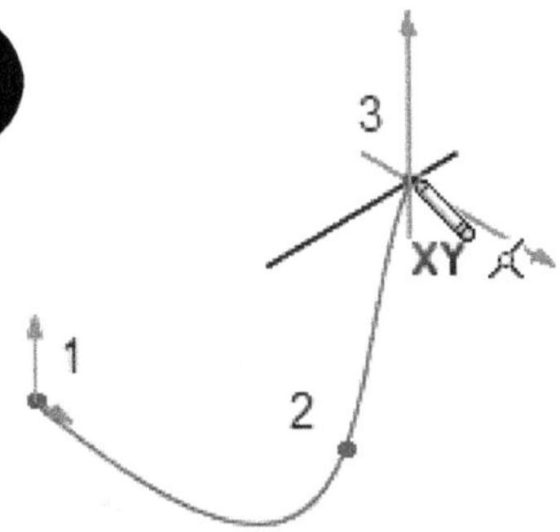

9. Press the **TAB** key to switch the sketching plane, as required. Next, move the cursor to the required location and then click to specify the fourth control point of the spline, see Figure 8.170. In Figure 8.170, the fourth control point of the spline is specified on the YZ plane.

10. Similarly, specify the remaining control points of the spline on different planes, as required. Once you have specified all control points of the spline, press the ESC key to exit the **Spline** tool. Figure 8.171 shows a spline created by specifying control points on different planes.

8.170

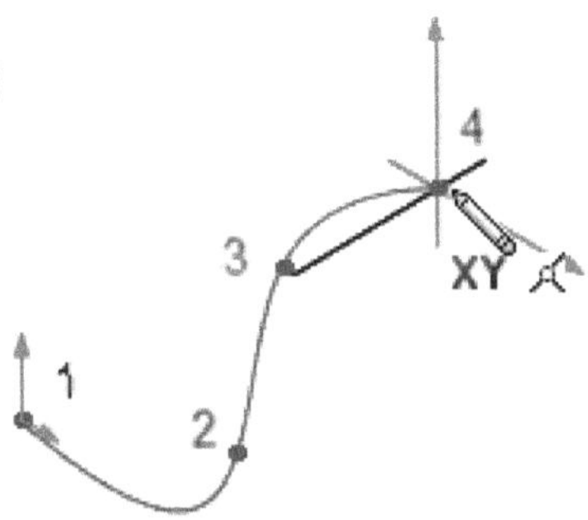

8.171

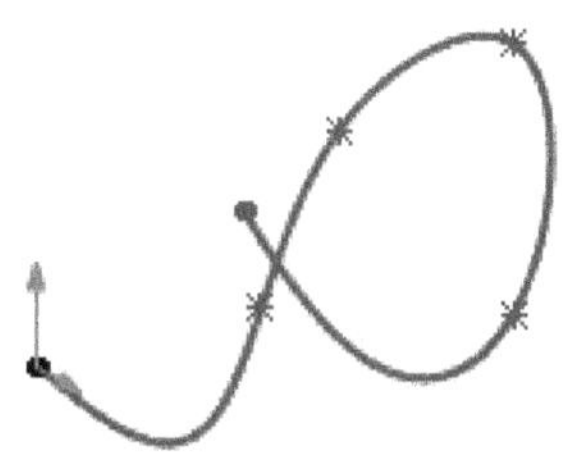

Tip: After creating the 3D spline, you can further control the shape of the spline by dragging its control points, as discussed while creating 2D spline. Once the 3D spline is created and the required modification has been made, exit the 3D Sketching environment. Figure 8.172 shows a 3D spline and Figure 8.173 shows the resultant sweep feature created by sweeping a rectangular profile along the 3D spline.

8.172

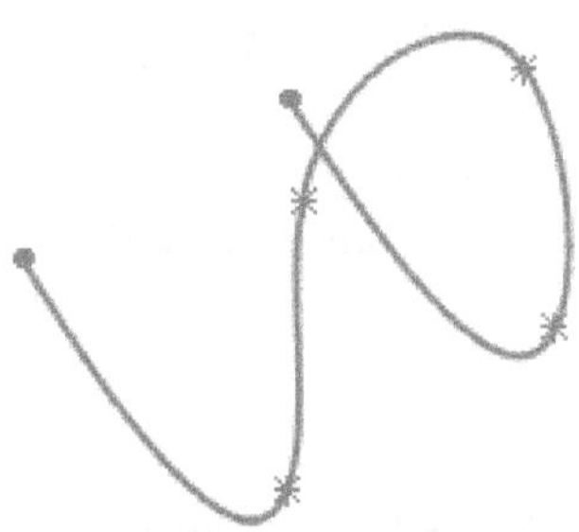

8.173

In the 3D sketching environment, the methods for creating rectangles, arcs, circles, points, and centerlines by using their respective tools are the same as discussed earlier while creating 2D sketches.

Tutorial 1

Create a model, as shown in Figure 8.174. The different views and dimensions are given in the same figure. All dimensions are in mm.

8.174

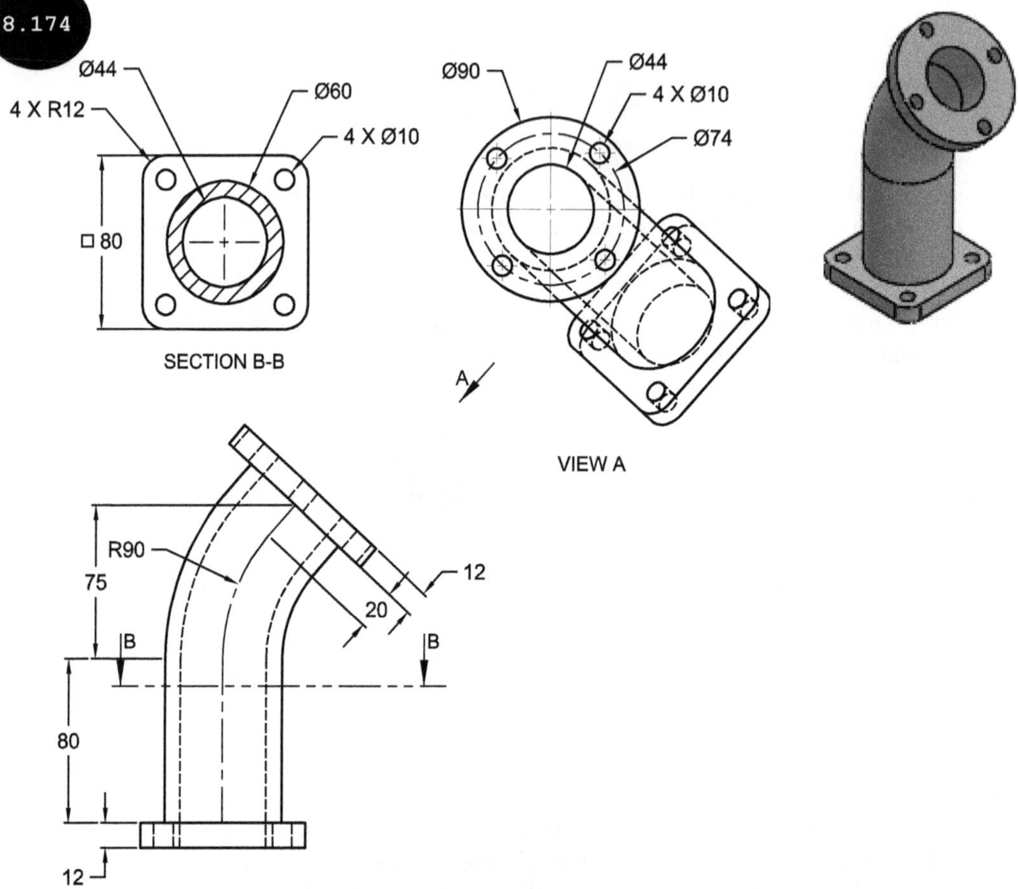

Section 1: Starting SOLIDWORKS

1. Start SOLIDWORKS by double-clicking on the SOLIDWORKS icon on your desktop. The startup user interface of SOLIDWORKS appears along with the **Welcome** dialog box.

Note: If SOLIDWORKS is already open and the **Welcome** dialog box does not appear on the screen, then you can invoke the same by clicking on the **Welcome to SOLIDWORKS** tool in the **Standard** toolbar.

Section 2: Invoking the Part Modeling Environment

1. Click on the **Part** button in the **Welcome** dialog box. The Part modeling environment is invoked.

Once the Part modeling environment has been invoked, you can set the unit system and create the base/first feature of the model.

Section 3: Specifying Unit Settings

1. Move the cursor toward the lower right corner of the screen over the Status Bar and then click on the **Unit System** area in the Status Bar. The **Unit System** flyout appears, see Figure 8.175.

2. Ensure that the **MMGS (millimeter, gram, second)** option is tick-marked in this flyout as the unit system for the current document.

8.175

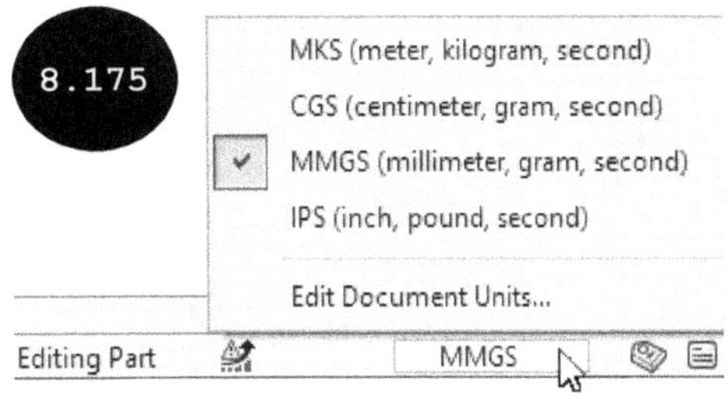

Section 4: Creating the Base Feature - Sweep Feature

1. Invoke the Sketching environment by selecting the Front plane as the sketching plane and then create a path of the sweep feature and apply dimensions, see Figure 8.176.

8.176

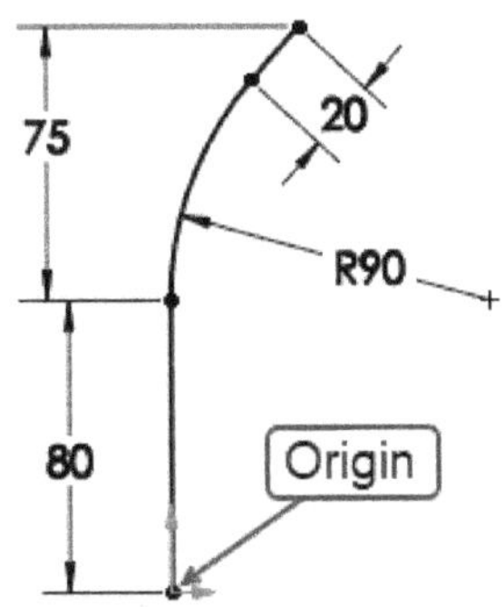

2. Exit the Sketching environment by clicking on the **Exit Sketch** tool in the **Sketch CommandManager**. Next, click anywhere in the graphics area to exit the current selection.

   After creating the path of the sweep feature, you need to create a sweep feature having a circular profile.

3. Click on the **Swept Boss/Base** tool in the **Features CommandManager**. The **Sweep PropertyManager** appears.

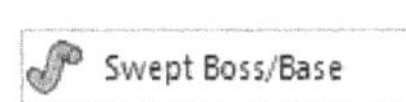

4. Click on the **Circular Profile** radio button in the **Profile and Path** rollout of the PropertyManager.

5. Click on the path of the sweep feature in the graphics area. A preview of the sweep feature appears with the default diameter of a circular profile.

6. Enter **60** in the **Diameter** field of the **Profile and Path** rollout and then press ENTER. A preview of the sweep feature appears, see Figure 8.177. Change the orientation of the model to isometric.

7. Expand the **Thin Feature** rollout of the PropertyManager by selecting the check box in its title bar, see Figure 8.178.

8.177

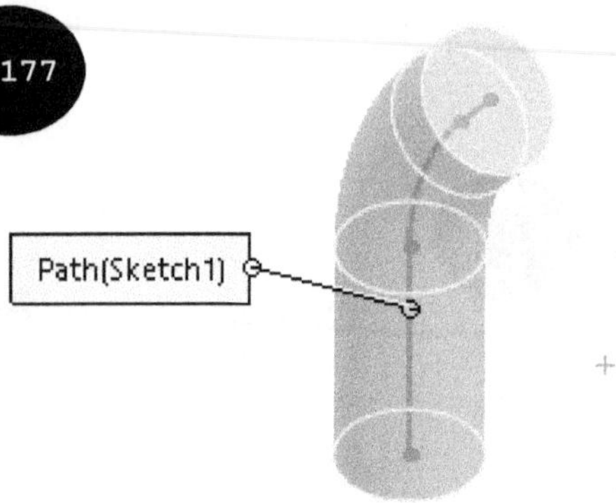

8.178

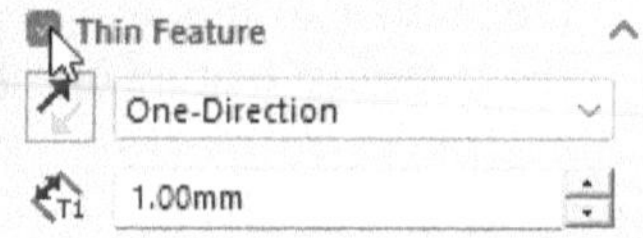

8. Enter **8** in the **Thickness** field of the **Thin Feature** rollout.

9. Click on the **Reverse Direction** button in the **Thin Feature** rollout to reverse the direction of material addition such that the material is added inward to the profile, see Figure 8.179.

10. Click on the green tick-mark in the PropertyManager. The thin sweep feature is created, see Figure 8.180.

8.179

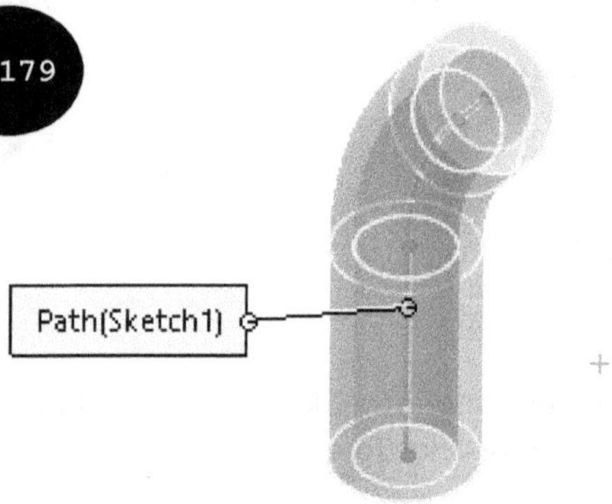

8.180

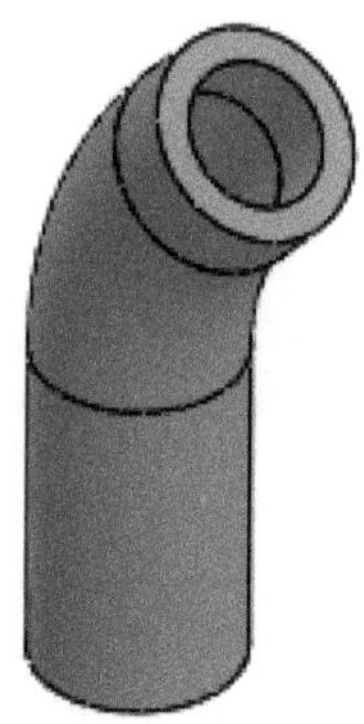

Section 5: Creating Second Feature - Extruded Feature

1. Rotate the model such that the bottom face of the base feature (sweep) can be viewed, see Figure 8.181. To rotate a model, right-click in the graphics area and then click on the **Rotate View** option in the shortcut menu that appears. Next, press and hold the left mouse button and then drag the cursor. Alternatively, press and hold the middle mouse button and then drag the cursor in the graphics area.

8.181

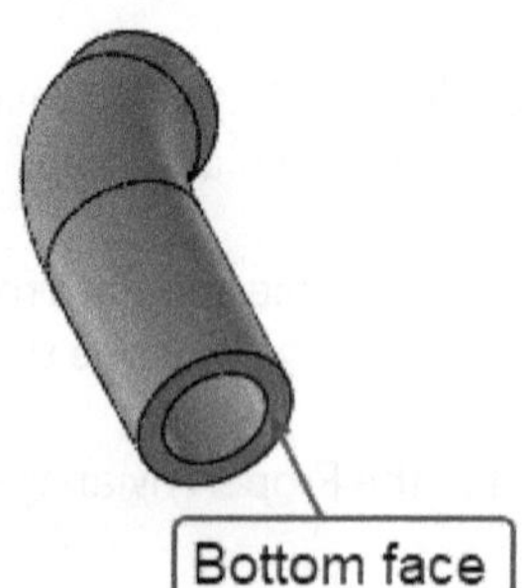

2. Invoke the Sketching environment by selecting the bottom face of the base feature (sweep) as the sketching plane. The model gets oriented normal to the viewing direction.

3. Create the sketch of the second feature, see Figure 8.182. After creating the sketch, do not exit the Sketching environment.

8.182

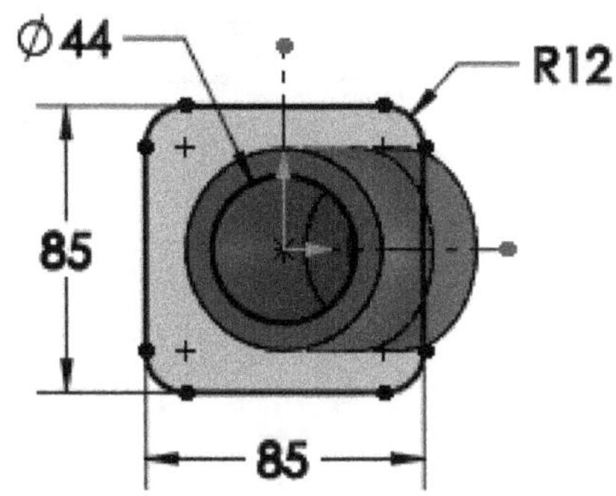

Tip: The sketch created in Figure 8.182 is symmetric about the vertical and horizontal centerlines. Also, the arcs of the sketch are of the same radius and are created by using the **Fillet** tool.

4. Click on the **Features** tab in the CommandManager to display the tools of the **Features CommandManager**.

5. Click on the **Extruded Boss/Base** tool in the **Features CommandManager**. The **Boss-Extrude PropertyManager** and a preview of the extruded feature appear. Next, change the orientation of the model to isometric, see Figure 8.183.

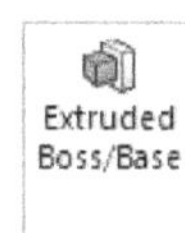

6. Enter **12** in the **Depth** field of the **Direction 1** rollout in the PropertyManager.

7. Click on the green tick-mark ✓ in the PropertyManager. The extruded feature is created, see Figure 8.184.

8.183

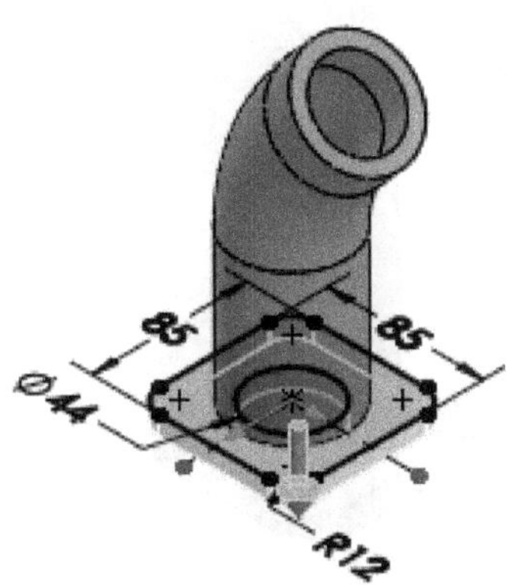

8.184

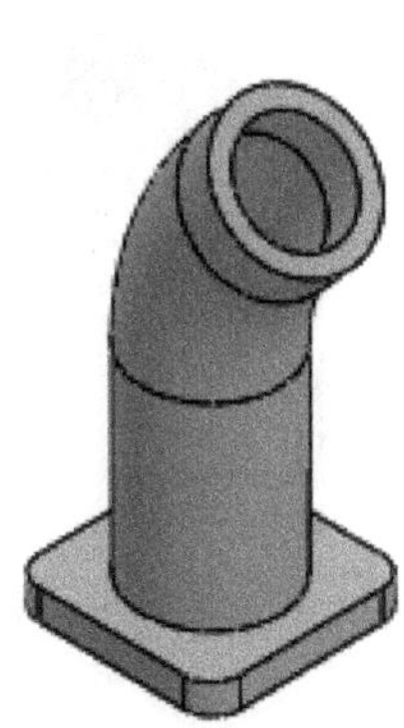

Section 6: Creating the Third Feature - Extruded Cut Feature

1. Invoke the Sketching environment by selecting the top planar face of the second feature as the sketching plane. The model gets oriented normal to the viewing direction.

2. Create a sketch (four circles of diameter 10 mm) of the third feature, see Figure 8.185.

8.185

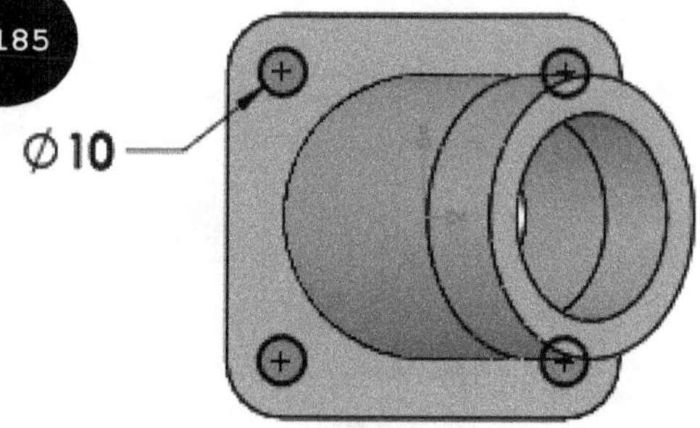

Tip: The sketch of the third feature shown in Figure 8.185 has four circles of the same diameter; therefore, an equal relation is applied among all the circles. Also, a concentric relation is applied between the center point of circles and the respective semi-circular edges of the second feature. You can also create one circle and then pattern it circularly to create the remaining circles.

3. Click on the **Features** tab in the CommandManager and then click on the **Extruded Cut** tool. The **Cut-Extrude PropertyManager** and a preview of the cut feature appear. Next, change the orientation of the model to isometric, see Figure 8.186.

4. Invoke the **End Condition** drop-down list in the **Direction 1** rollout of the PropertyManager and then select the **Through All** option.

5. Click on the green tick-mark ✓ in the PropertyManager. The extruded cut feature is created, see Figure 8.187.

8.186

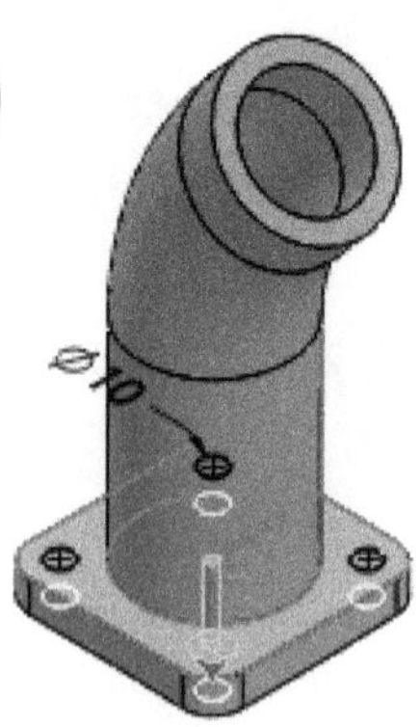

8.187

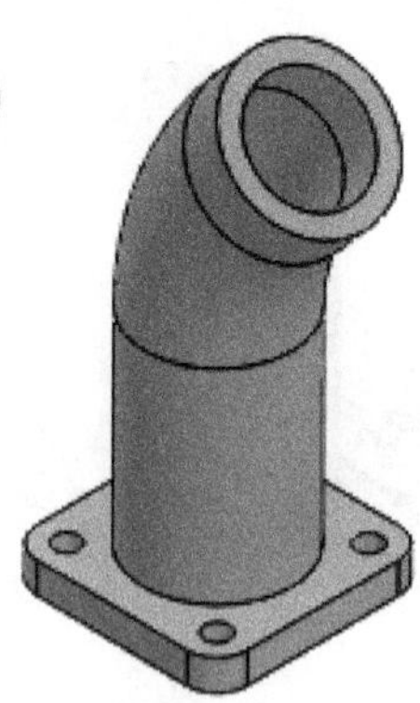

Section 7: Creating the Fourth Feature - Extruded Feature

1. Invoke the Sketching environment by selecting the top planar face of the sweep feature (first feature) as the sketching plane, see Figure 8.188. The model gets oriented normal to the viewing direction.

2. Create the sketch (two circles of diameter 90 mm and 44 mm) of the fourth feature, see Figure 8.189.

8.188

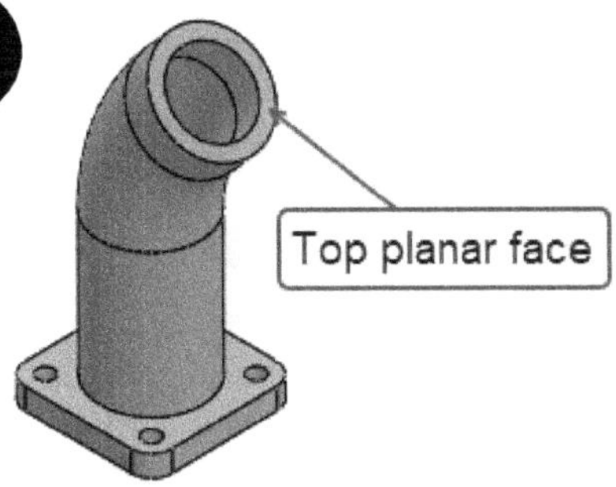

8.189

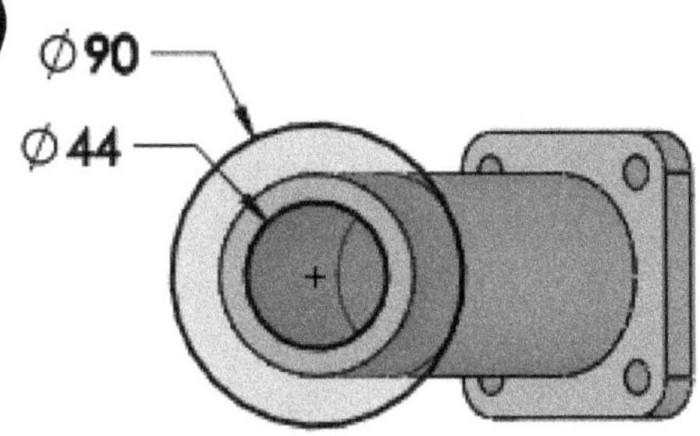

Tip: The sketch of the fourth feature shown in Figure 8.189 has two circles, which are concentric to the top circular edge of the sweep feature. You need to take the reference of the top circular edges of the sweep feature for specifying the center point of the circles.

3. Click on the **Features** tab in the CommandManager and then click on the **Extruded Boss/Base** tool. The **Boss-Extrude PropertyManager** and a preview of the extruded feature appear. Next, change the orientation of the model to isometric, see Figure 8.190.

4. Enter **12** in the **Depth** field of the **Direction 1** rollout in the PropertyManager.

5. Click on the green tick-mark ✓ in the PropertyManager. The extruded feature is created, see Figure 8.191.

8.190

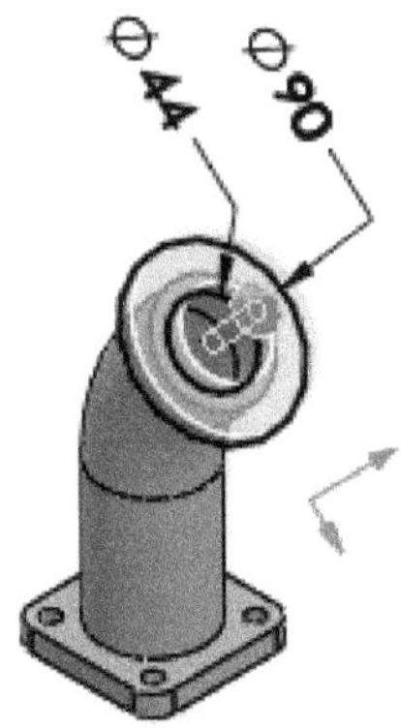

8.191

Section 8: Creating the Fifth Feature - Extruded Cut Feature

1. Invoke the Sketching environment by selecting the top planar face of the fourth feature as the sketching plane. The model gets oriented normal to the viewing direction.

2. Create a circle of diameter 10 mm, see Figure 8.192. Next, create its circular pattern to create the remaining circles of the same diameter by using the **Circular Sketch Pattern** tool, see Figure 8.193. Note that you need to change the position of the center point of the pattern to the center point of the circular edge of the fourth feature by dragging the dot that appears at the tip of the arrow in the pattern preview.

8.192

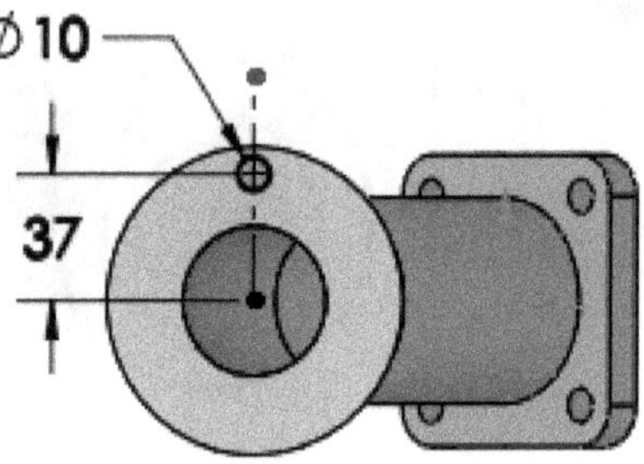

8.193

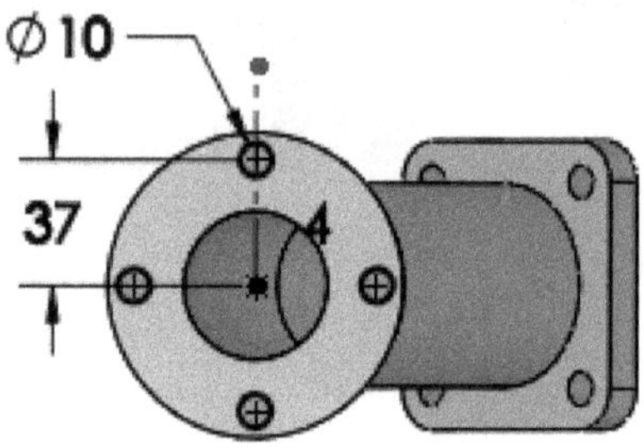

Tip: In Figure 8.192, the center point of the circle has coincident relation with the vertical centerline. Also, the start point of the vertical centerline is coincident with the center point of the circular edge of the fourth feature.

While specifying the start point of the vertical centerline shown in Figure 8.192, move the cursor over the outer circular edge of the fourth feature. The center point of the circular edge gets highlighted. Next, move the cursor to the highlighted center point and then click to specify the start point of the vertical centerline when the cursor snaps to it.

In Figure 8.193, the center point of the outer circular edge of the model and the center point of circular sketch pattern has coincident relation.

3. Click on the **Extruded Cut** tool in the **Features CommandManager**. The **Cut-Extrude PropertyManager** and a preview of the extruded cut feature appear. Next, change the orientation of the model to isometric, see Figure 8.194.

8.194

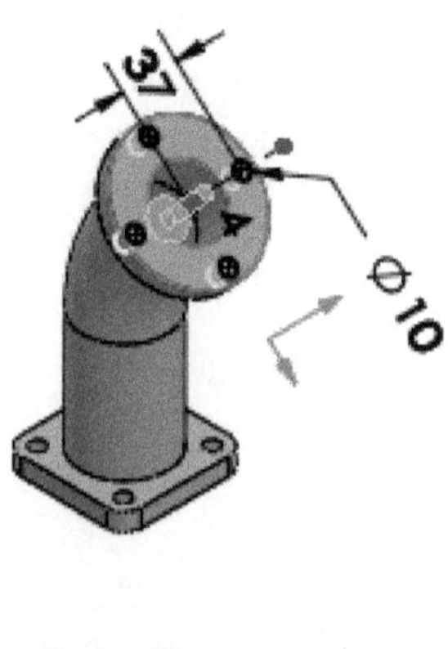

4. Invoke the **End Condition** drop-down list in the **Direction 1** rollout of the PropertyManager and then click on the **Up to Next** option.

5. Click on the green tick-mark ✓ in the PropertyManager. The extruded cut feature is created, see Figure 8.195.

8.195

Section 9: Saving the Model

1. Click on the **Save** tool of the **Standard** toolbar. The **Save As** window appears.

2. Browse to the SOLIDWORKS folder and then create a folder with the name **Chapter 8** in the SOLIDWORKS folder.

3. Enter **Tutorial 1** in the **File name** field of the dialog box as the name of the file and then click on the **Save** button. The model is saved with the name Tutorial 1 in the Chapter 8 folder.

Tutorial 2

Create a model, as shown in Figure 8.196. The different views and dimensions are given in the same figure. All dimensions are in mm.

8.196

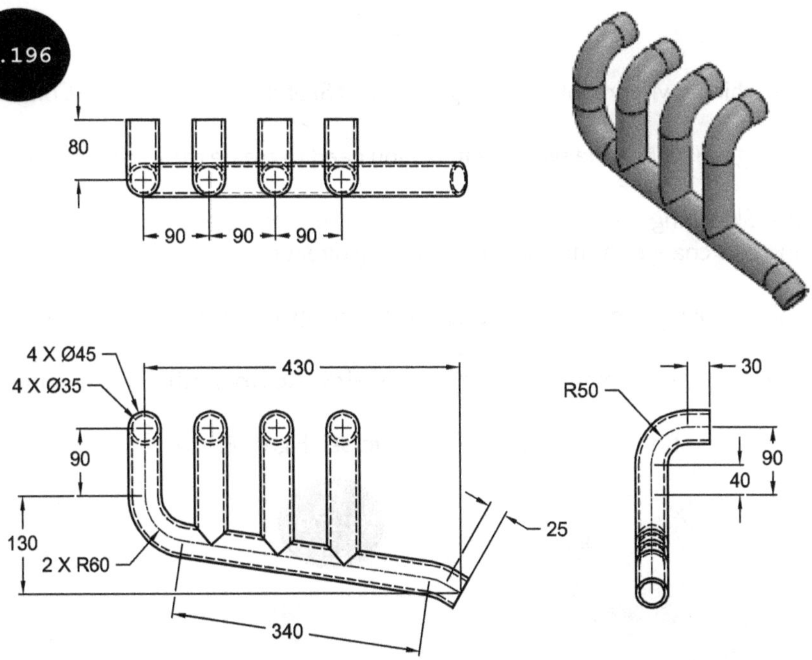

Section 1: Invoking the Part Modeling Environment

1. Start SOLIDWORKS and then invoke the Part modeling environment.

   Once the Part modeling environment has been invoked, you can set the unit system and create the base/first feature of the model.

Section 2: Specifying Unit Settings

1. Ensure that the **MMGS (millimeter, gram, second)** unit system is selected as the current unit system for the document, see Figure 8.197.

Section 3: Creating the Base Feature - Sweep Feature

1. Invoke the Sketching environment by selecting the Right plane as the sketching plane and then create the path of the sweep feature, see Figure 8.198.

8.197

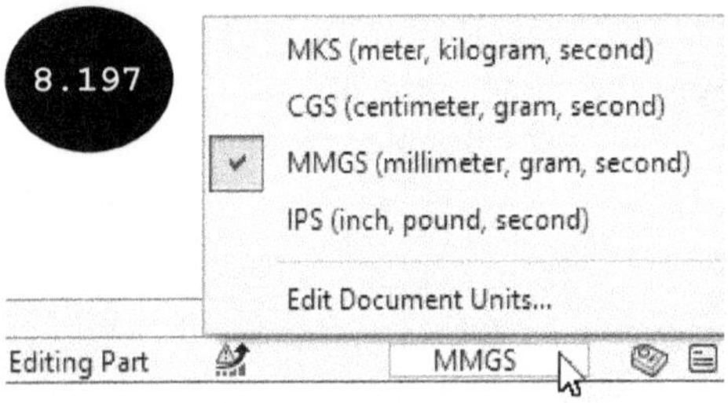

8.198

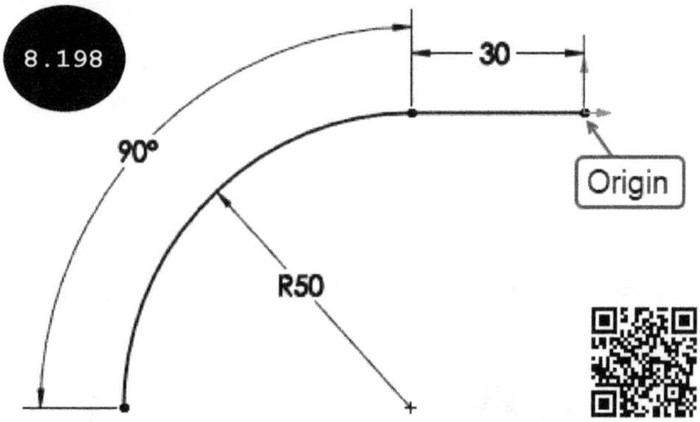

2. Exit the Sketching environment by clicking on the **Exit Sketch** tool in the **Sketch CommandManager**.

   After creating the path of the sweep feature, you need to create the profile for the sweep feature.

3. Invoke the Sketching environment by selecting the Front plane as the sketching plane. The orientation gets changed as normal to the viewing direction.

4. Create a sketch of the profile (two circles of diameter 45 mm and 35 mm), see Figure 8.199.

5. Exit the Sketching environment by clicking on the **Exit Sketch** tool in the **Sketch CommandManager**.

6. Change the orientation of the model to isometric, see Figure 8.200.

8.199

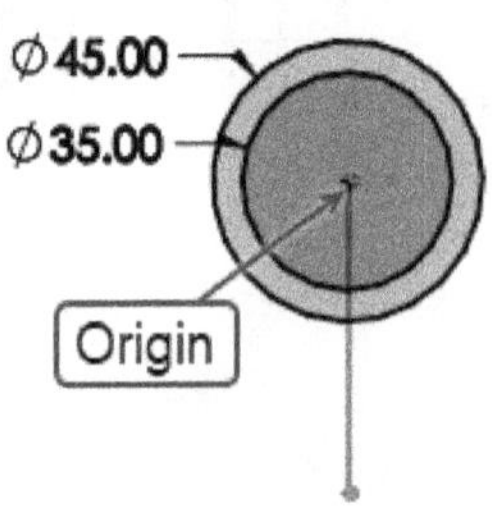

8.200

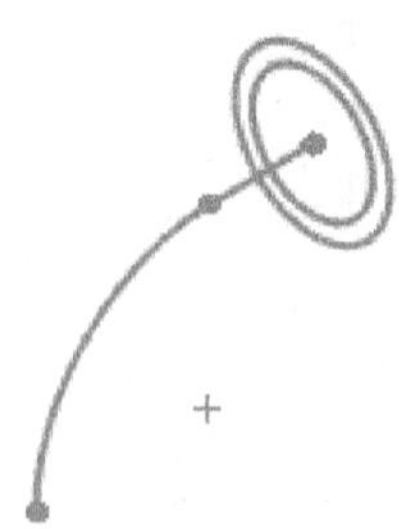

After creating the path and the profile, you need to create the sweep feature.

7. Click on the **Swept Boss/Base** tool. The **Sweep PropertyManager** appears. 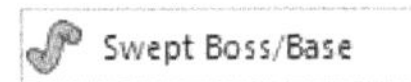

8. Ensure that the **Sketch Profile** radio button is selected in the **Profile and Path** rollout.

9. Click on the profile (two circles) of the sweep feature in the graphics area. The **Path** field in the **Sweep PropertyManager** gets activated.

10. Click on the path of the sweep feature in the graphics area. A preview of the sweep feature appears in the graphics area, see Figure 8.201.

Tip: Instead of creating a sketch of the profile (two circles) for creating the sweep feature, you can also select the **Circular Profile** radio button in the **Sweep PropertyManager** and then specify the diameter of circular profile in the **Diameter** field of the PropertyManager. This is because the profile of the sweep feature is a circular profile.

11. Click on the green tick-mark ✓ in the PropertyManager. The sweep feature is created, see Figure 8.202.

8.201

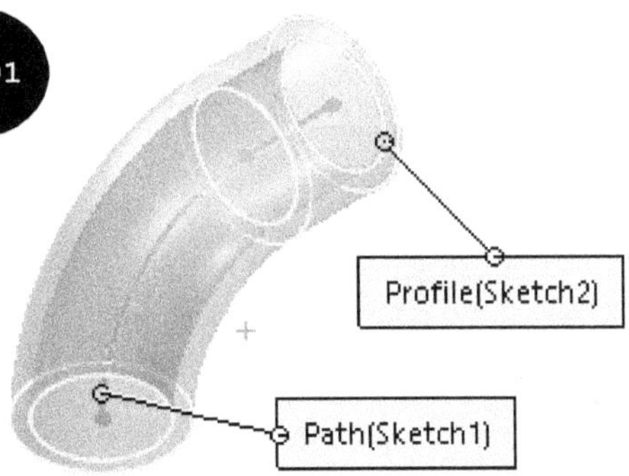

8.202

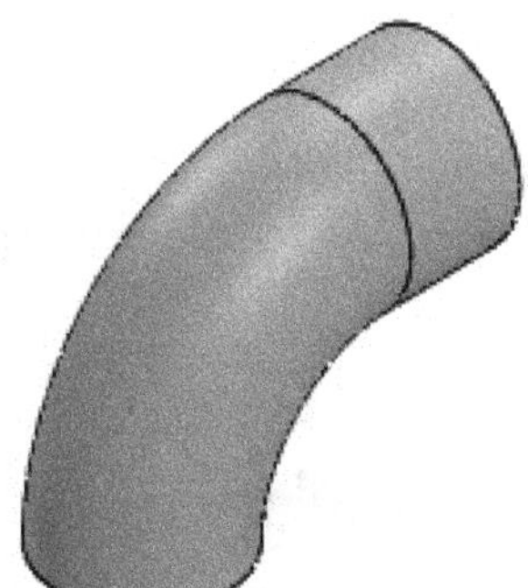

Section 4: Creating the Second Feature - Sweep Feature

To create the second feature of the model, you first need to create a reference plane at an offset distance of 80 mm from the Front plane.

1. Invoke the **Reference Geometry** flyout in the **Features CommandManager**, see Figure 8.203.

8.203

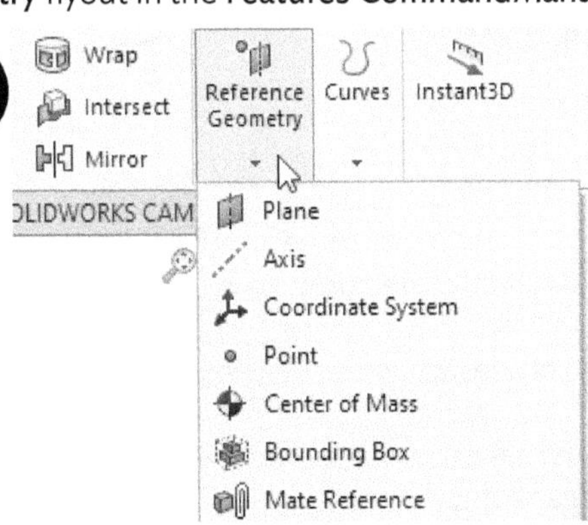

2. Click on the **Plane** tool in the flyout. The **Plane PropertyManager** appears.

3. Expand the FeatureManager Design Tree, which is now available in the top left corner of the graphics area by clicking on the arrow in front of it and then click on the **Front Plane** as the first reference. A preview of an offset reference plane appears in the graphics area.

4. Enter **80** in the **Offset distance** field of the **First Reference** rollout. Ensure that the direction of plane creation is the same as shown in Figure 8.204.

8.204

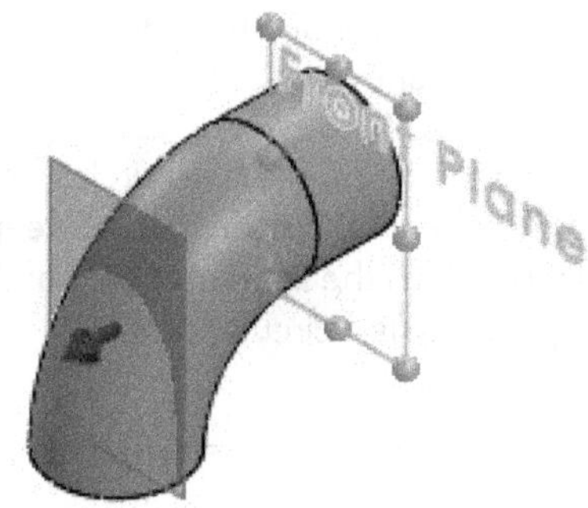

5. Click on the green tick-mark ✓ in the PropertyManager. The offset reference plane is created.

6. Invoke the Sketching environment by selecting the newly created reference plane as the sketching plane. The model gets oriented normal to the viewing direction.

7. Create the path of the second sweep feature, see Figure 8.205. Note that in this figure, an equal relation has been applied between both the arcs of the sketch having the same radius.

8.205

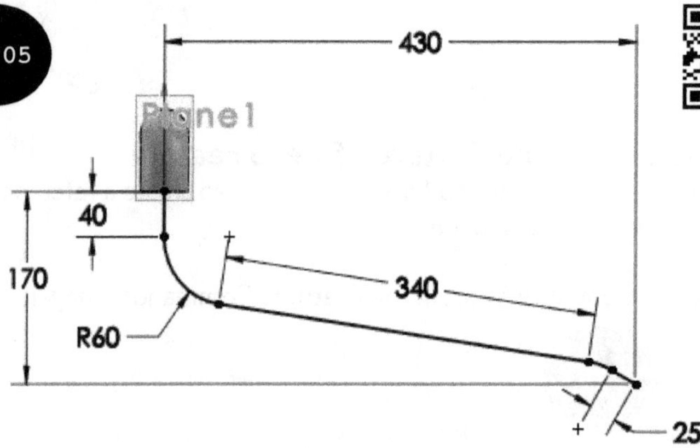

8. Exit the Sketching environment by clicking on the **Exit Sketch** tool in the **Sketch CommandManager**. Next, press CTRL + 7 to change the orientation to isometric. Next, hide the reference plane.

After creating the path of the sweep feature, you need to create the sweep feature.

9. Click on the **Swept Boss/Base** tool in the **Features CommandManager**. The **Sweep PropertyManager** appears.

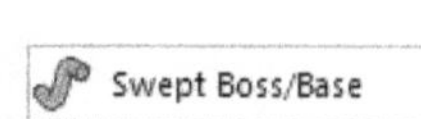

10. Ensure that the **Sketch Profile** radio button is selected in the **Profile and Path** rollout.

11. Rotate the model such that the bottom face of the first feature (sweep) can be viewed, see Figure 8.206. To rotate the model, right-click in the graphics area and then click on the **Zoom/Pan/Rotate > Rotate View** tool in the shortcut menu that appears. Next, press and hold the left mouse button and then drag the cursor. Once the required orientation of the model has been achieved, press the ESC key to exit the **Rotate View** tool.

12. Select the bottom face of the first feature (sweep) as the profile of the second sweep feature, see Figure 8.206.

13. Click on the path of the sweep feature in the graphics area. A preview of the sweep feature appears, see Figure 8.207. Next, press CTRL + 7 to change the orientation of the model to isometric.

8.206

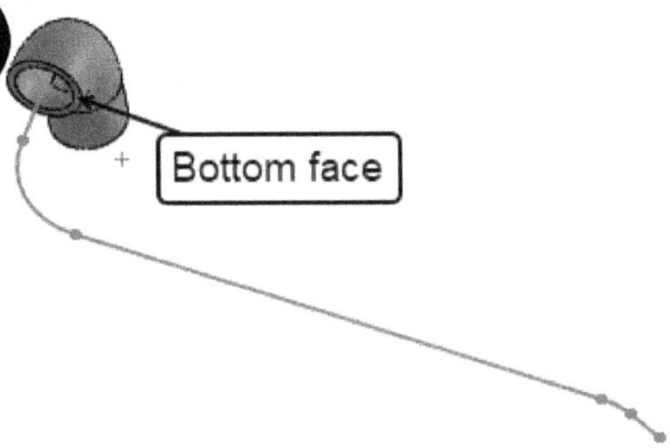

8.207

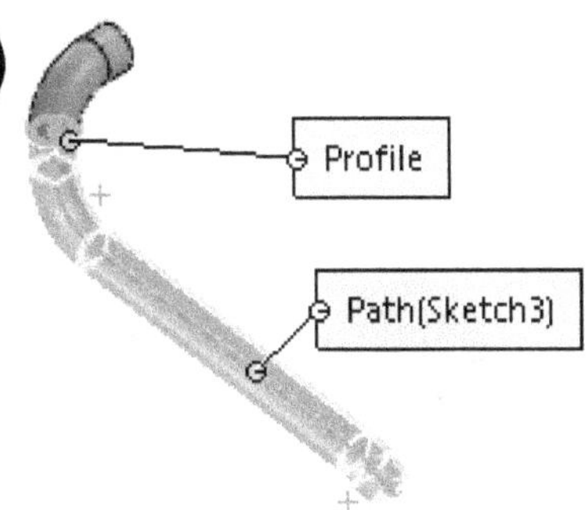

14. Click on the green tick-mark ✓ in the PropertyManager. The sweep feature is created, see Figure 8.208. Next, hide the reference plane.

8.208

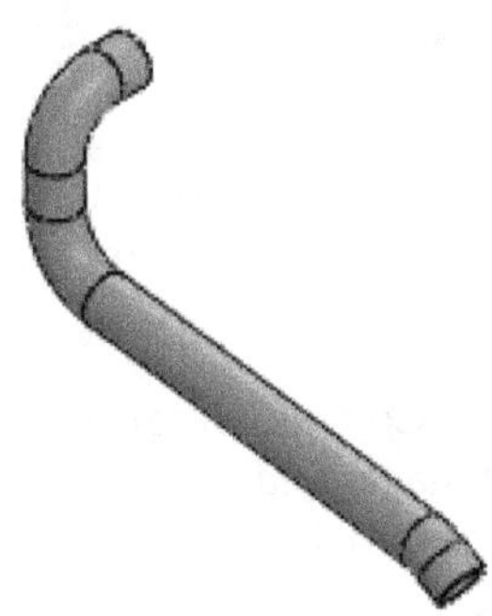

Section 5: Creating the Third Feature - Extruded Feature

To create the third feature of the model, you first need to create a reference plane at an offset distance of 50 mm from the Top plane.

1. Invoke the **Reference Geometry** flyout in the **Features CommandManager** and then click on the **Plane** tool to invoke the **Plane PropertyManager**.

2. Expand the FeatureManager Design Tree, which is now available in the top left corner of the graphics area, by clicking on the arrow in front of it.

3. Click on the **Top Plane** in the FeatureManager Design Tree as the first reference. The preview of an offset reference plane appears in the graphics area.

4. Enter **50** in the **Offset distance** field of the **First Reference** rollout of the PropertyManager.

5. Select the **Flip offset** check box in the **First Reference** rollout to reverse the direction of the plane downward.

6. Click on the green tick-mark ✓ in the PropertyManager. The offset reference plane is created, see Figure 8.209.

7. Invoke the Sketching environment by selecting the newly created reference plane as the sketching plane. The orientation of the model is changed as normal to the viewing direction.

8.209

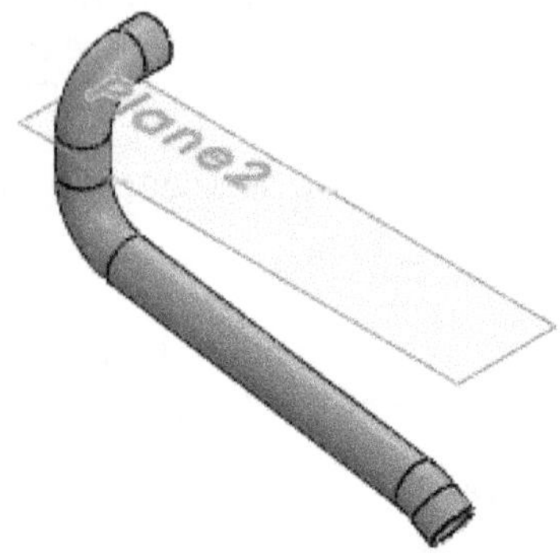

8. Create the sketch of the third feature (three circles of the same diameter), see Figure 8.210.

8.210

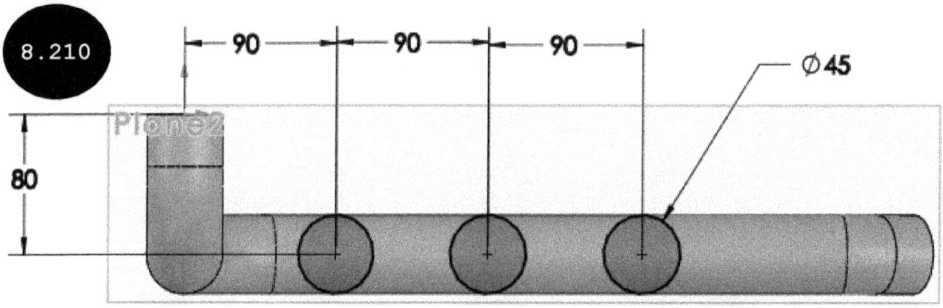

Tip: To fully define the sketch in Figure 8.210, you have to apply horizontal relation between the center points of the circles. Also, an equal relation has been applied between all the circles.

9. Click on the **Features** tab in the CommandManager, then click on the **Extruded Boss/Base** tool. The **Boss-Extrude PropertyManager** and a preview of the extruded feature appear. Next, change the orientation of the model to isometric, see Figure 8.211.

8.211

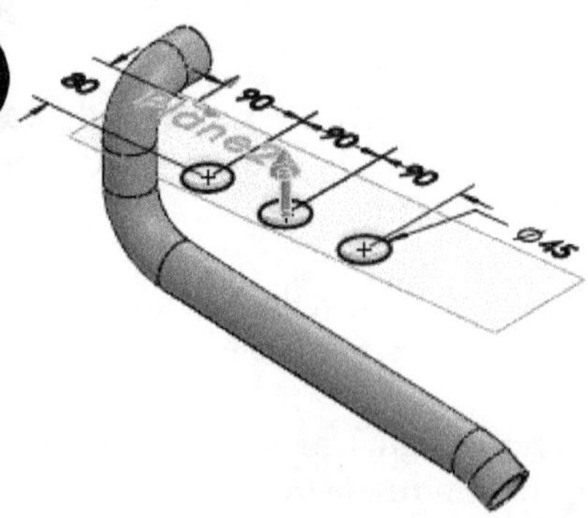

10. Click on the **Reverse Direction** button in the **Direction 1** rollout to reverse the direction of extrusion downward.

11. Invoke the **End Condition** drop-down list of the **Direction 1** rollout and then select the **Up To Next** option. A preview of the extruded feature appears in the graphics area such that it has been terminated at its next intersection.

12. Click on the green tick-mark ✓ in the PropertyManager. The extruded feature is created, see Figure 8.212.

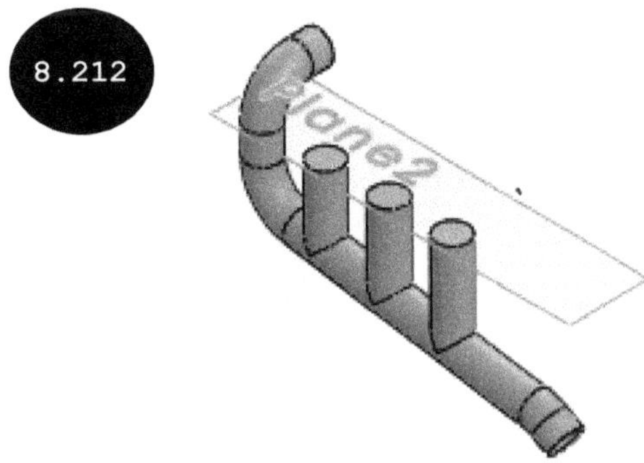

13. Hide the reference plane by clicking on the **Hide** option in the Pop-up toolbar that appears as soon as you select the plane to be hidden in the graphics area.

Section 6: Creating the Fourth Feature - Extruded Cut Feature

1. Invoke the Sketching environment by selecting the top planar face of the third feature as the sketching plane, see Figure 8.213. The orientation of the model is changed as normal to the viewing direction.

2. Create a sketch of the fourth feature (three circles of the same diameter), see Figure 8.214.

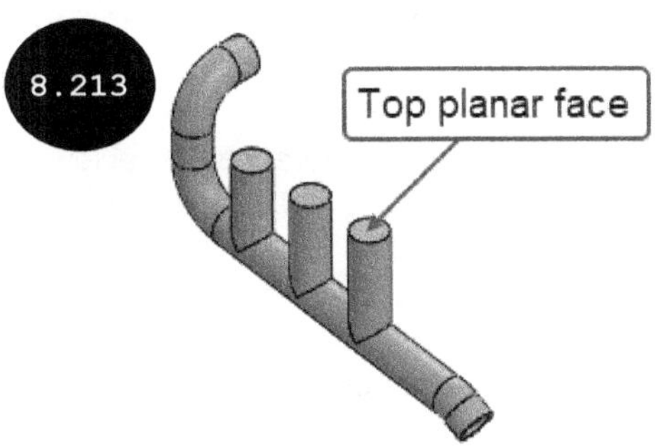

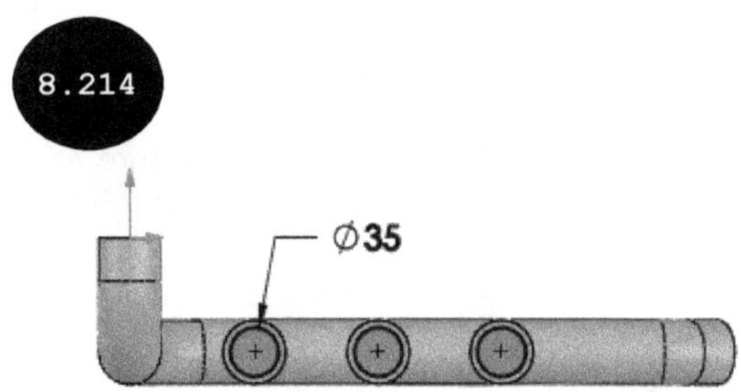

Tip: The sketch of the fourth feature shown in Figure 8.214 has three circles, which are concentric to the circular edges of the extruded feature. Also, an equal relation has been applied between all the circles.

3. Click on the **Extruded Cut** tool in the **Features CommandManager**. The **Cut-Extrude PropertyManager** and a preview of the extruded cut feature appear. Next, change the orientation of the model to isometric.

4. Invoke the **End Condition** drop-down list in the **Direction 1** rollout of the PropertyManager.

5. Click on the **Up To Next** option in the **End Condition** drop-down list. A preview of the extruded cut feature appears in the graphics area such that it has been terminated at its next intersection.

6. Click on the green tick-mark ✓ in the PropertyManager. The extruded cut feature is created, see Figure 8.215.

Section 7: Creating the Fifth Feature - Sweep Feature

To create the fifth feature of the model, you first need to create a reference plane at an offset distance of 90 mm from the Right plane.

1. Invoke the **Reference Geometry** flyout in the **Features CommandManager**, see Figure 8.216.

8.215

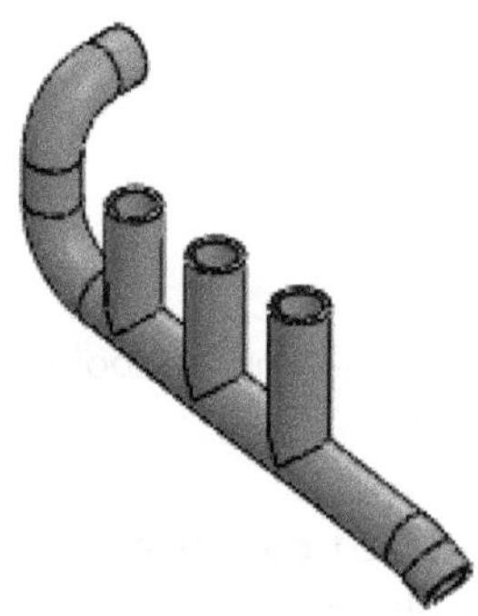

8.216

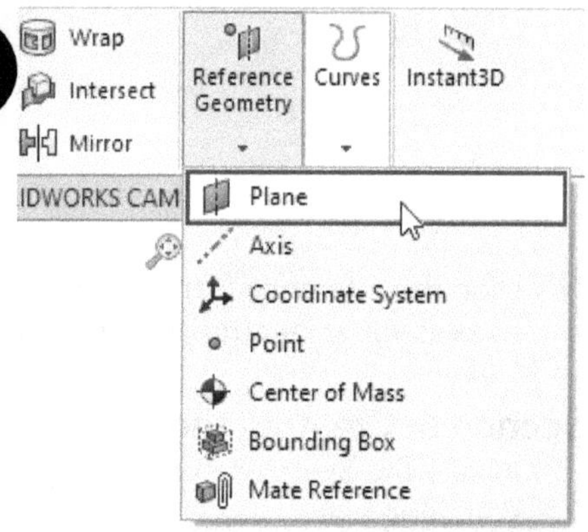

2. Click on the **Plane** tool in the flyout. The **Plane PropertyManager** appears.

3. Expand the FeatureManager Design Tree by clicking on the arrow in front of it, which is now available in the top left corner of the graphics area.

4. Click on the **Right Plane** in the FeatureManager Design Tree as the first reference. A preview of an offset reference plane appears in the graphics area.

5. Enter **90** in the **Offset distance** field of the **First Reference** rollout of the **Plane PropertyManager**.

6. Click on the green tick-mark ✓ in the PropertyManager. The offset reference plane is created, see Figure 8.217.

7. Invoke the Sketching environment by selecting the newly created reference plane as the sketching plane. The orientation of the model is changed as normal to the viewing direction.

8. Create the path of the sweep feature, see Figure 8.218.

8.217

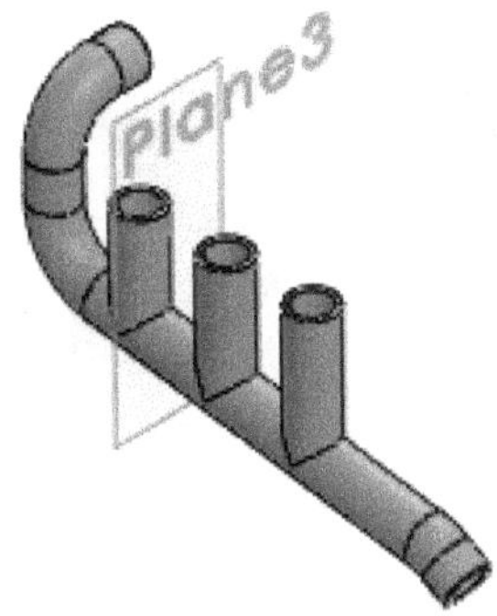

8.218

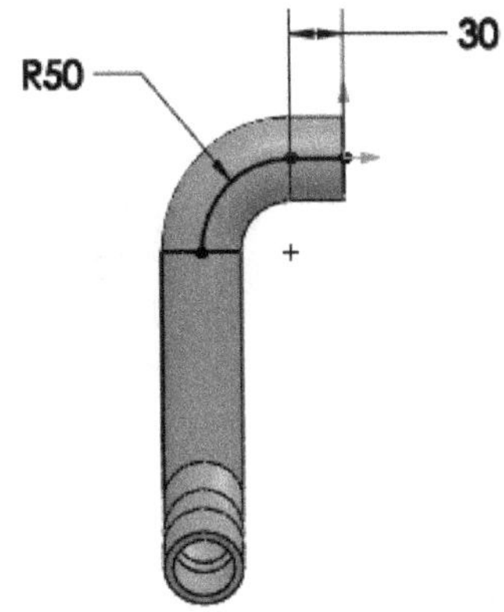

9. Exit the Sketching environment by clicking on the **Exit Sketch** tool in the **Sketch CommandManager**.

10. Change the current orientation of the model to isometric, see Figure 8.219. Next, hide the reference plane.

    After creating the path, you need to create the sweep feature.

11. Click on the **Swept Boss/Base** tool. The **Sweep PropertyManager** appears.

12. Ensure that the **Sketch Profile** radio button is selected in the **Profile and Path** rollout of the PropertyManager.

13. Select the top planar face of the extruded feature as the profile of the feature, see Figure 8.220.

8.219

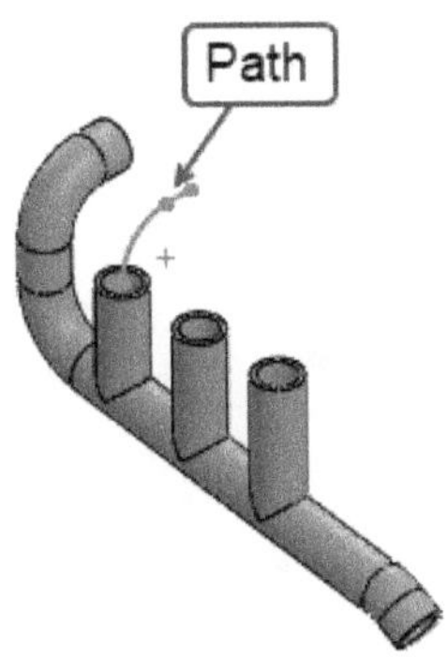

8.220

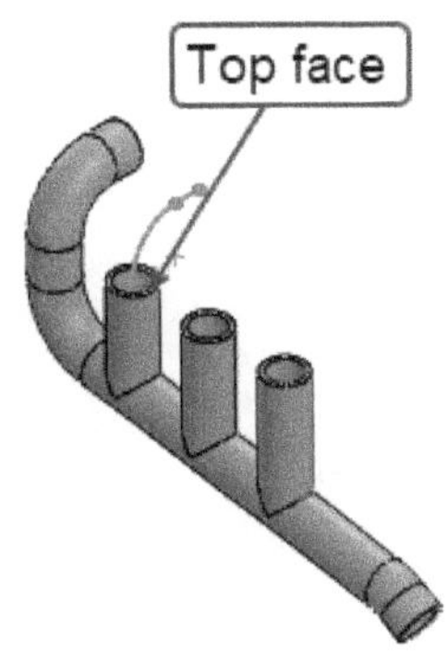

14. Select the path of the sweep feature in the graphics area. A preview of the sweep feature appears, see Figure 8.221.

15. Click on the green tick-mark ✓ in the PropertyManager. The sweep feature is created, see Figure 8.222.

8.221

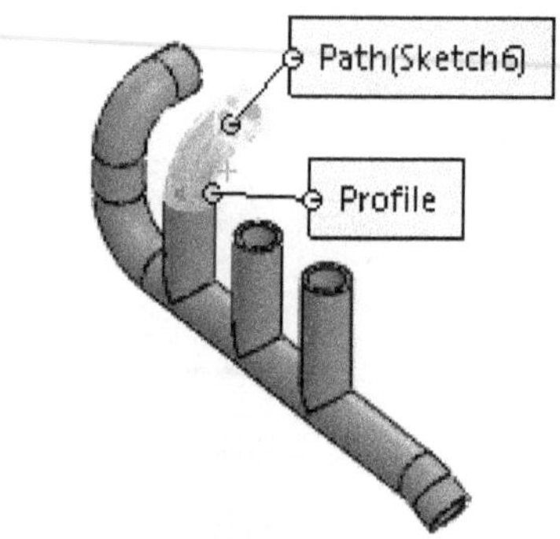

8.222

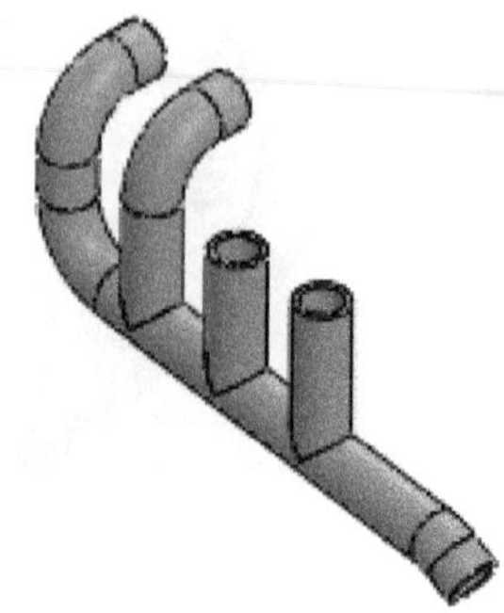

Section 8: Creating the Sixth and Seventh Features - Sweep Features

To create the sixth and seventh features (sweep), you can use the sketch of the fifth feature (sweep) of the model as the path.

1. Expand the node of the fifth feature (previously created sweep feature) in the FeatureManager Design Tree, see Figure 8.223.

2. Select the sketch (path) of the fifth feature (sweep feature) in the FeatureManager Design Tree, see Figure 8.223.

8.223

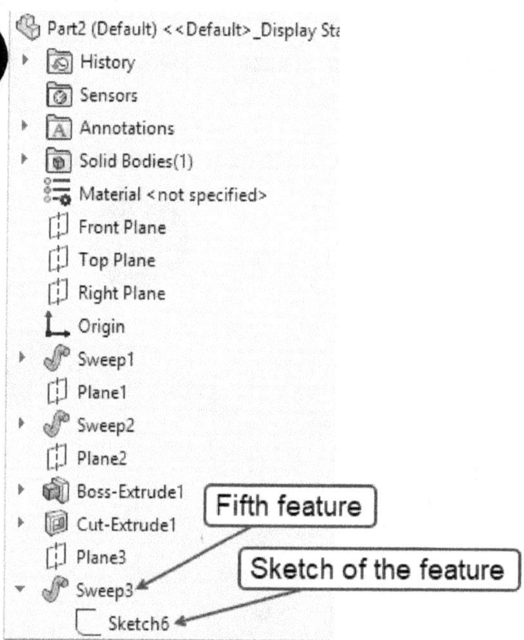

3. Click on the **Swept Boss/Base** tool in the **Features CommandManager**. The **Sweep PropertyManager** appears. Also, the selected sketch of the fifth feature is selected as the path of the sixth feature (sweep), see Figure 8.224.

4. Select the top planar face of the extruded feature as the profile of the sweep feature, see Figure 8.224. A preview of the sweep feature appears in the graphics area, see Figure 8.225.

8.224

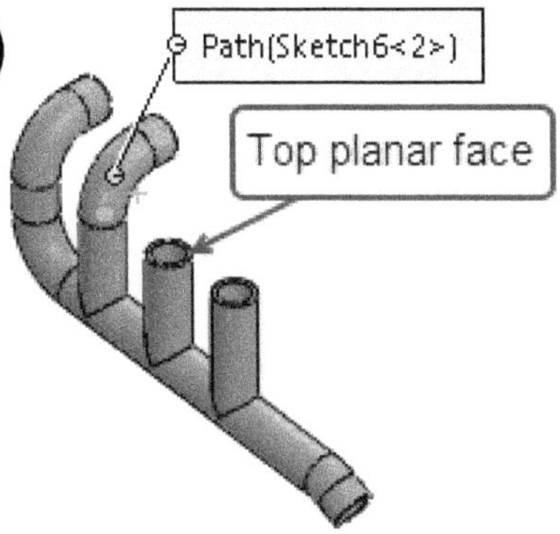

8.225

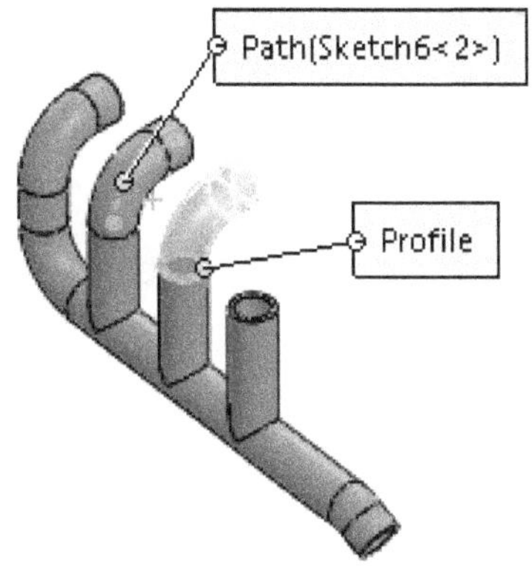

5. Click on the green tick-mark ✓ in the PropertyManager. The sweep feature is created, see Figure 8.226.

8.226

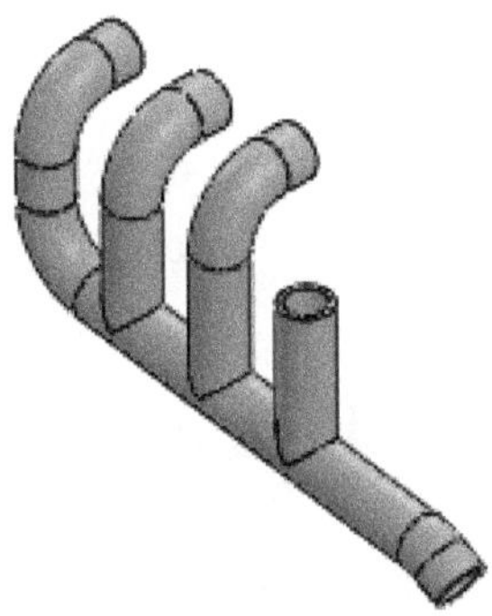

6. Similarly, create the seventh feature, which is a sweep feature, by using the sketch of the fifth feature as the path. Figure 8.227 shows the final model.

8.227

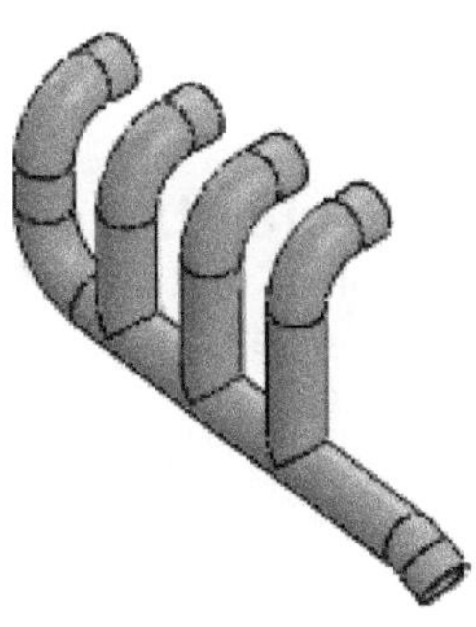

Section 9: Saving the Model

1. Click on the **Save** tool in the **Standard** toolbar. The **Save As** window appears.

2. Browse to the Chapter 8 folder of the SOLIDWORKS folder and then save the model with the name Tutorial 2.

Tutorial 3

Create a model, as shown in Figure 8.228. All dimensions are in mm.

8.228

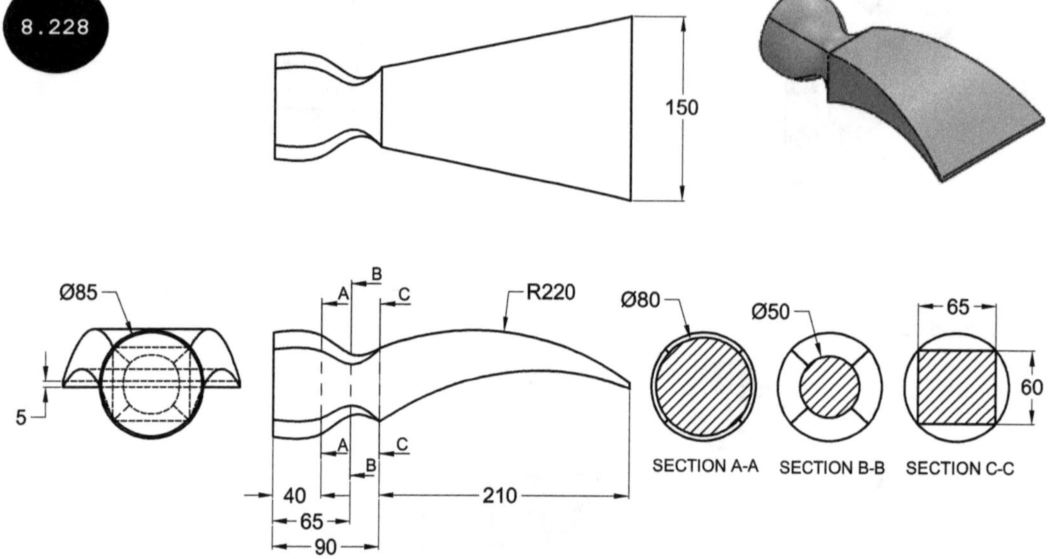

Section 1: Invoking the Part Modeling Environment

1. Start SOLIDWORKS and then invoke the Part modeling environment.

   Once the Part modeling environment is invoked, you need to set the unit system and create the base/first feature of the model.

Section 2: Specifying Unit Settings

1. Ensure that the **MMGS (millimeter, gram, second)** unit system is set as the current unit system for the opened part document.

Section 3: Creating the Base Feature - Lofted Feature

To create the base/first feature (lofted feature) of the model, you first need to create all its sections (profiles) on different planes.

1. Invoke the Sketching environment by selecting the Right plane as the sketching plane.

8.229

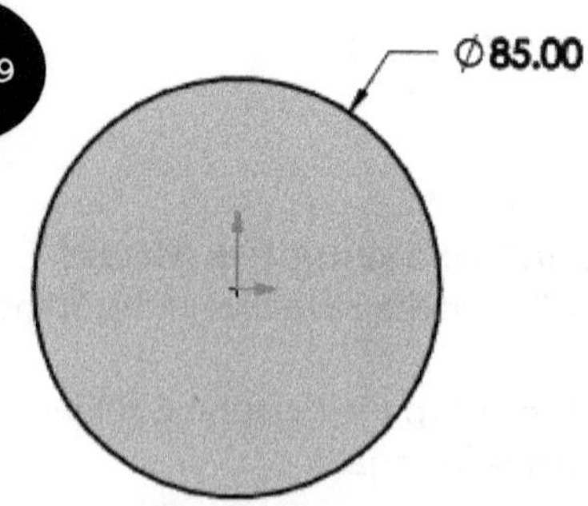

2. Create the first section (profile) of the lofted feature, which is a circle of diameter 85 mm, see Figure 8.229.

3. Exit the Sketching environment and then press CTRL + 7 to change the orientation of the model to isometric.

After creating the first section (profile) of the lofted feature, you need to create the second section at an offset distance of 40 mm from the Right plane.

4. Create a reference plane at an offset distance of 40 mm from the Right plane by using the **Plane** tool of the **Reference Geometry** flyout, see Figure 8.230.

8.230

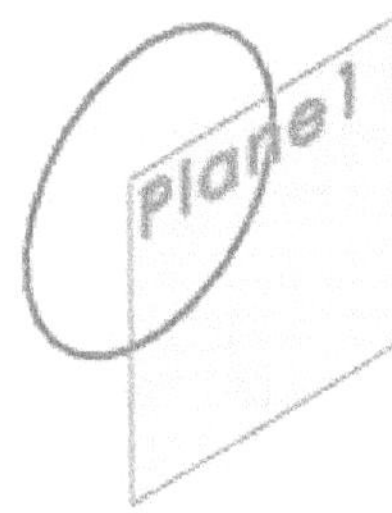

5. Invoke the Sketching environment by selecting the newly created reference plane as the sketching plane. The orientation of the model is changed as normal to the viewing direction.

6. Create the second section (a circle of diameter 80 mm) of the lofted feature, see Figure 8.231. Next, exit the Sketching environment.

7. Press CTRL + 7 to change the orientation of the model to isometric.

   After creating the second section (profile), you need to create the third section of the feature.

8. Create a reference plane at an offset distance of 65 mm from the Right plane by using the **Plane** tool in the **Reference Geometry** flyout, see Figure 8.232.

8.231

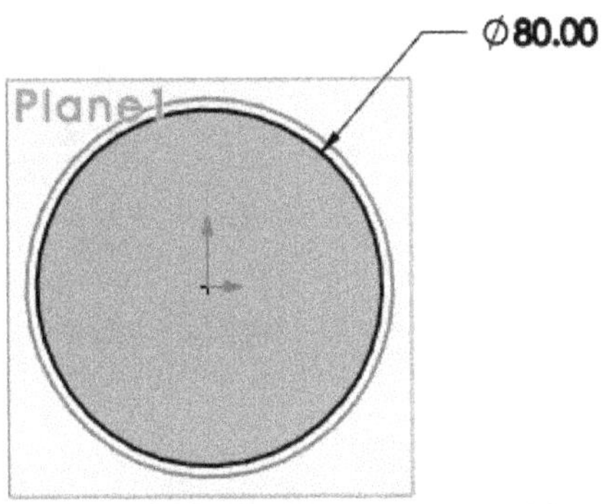

8.232

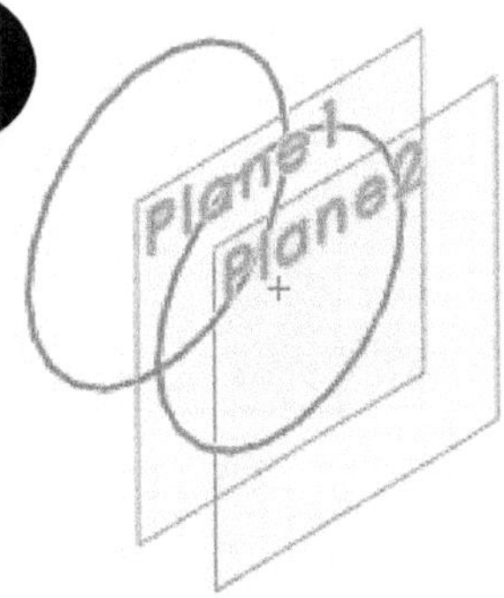

9. Invoke the Sketching environment by selecting the newly created reference plane as the sketching plane. The orientation of the model is changed as normal to the viewing direction.

10. Create the third section (a circle of diameter 50 mm) of the lofted feature, see Figure 8.233. Next, exit the Sketching environment.

8.233

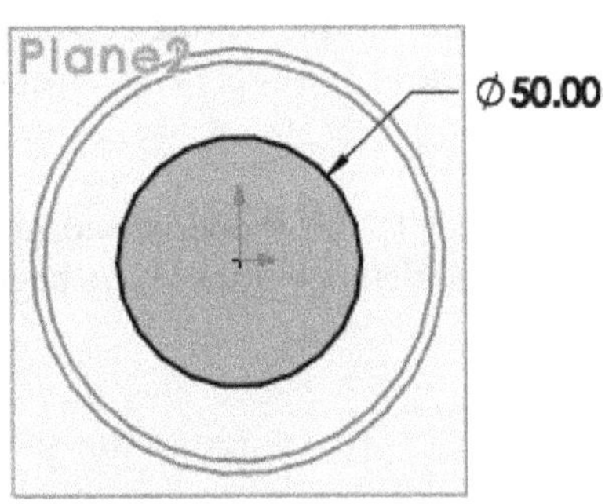

11. Press CTRL + 7 to change the current orientation of the model to isometric.

After creating the third section (profile), you need to create the fourth section of the feature.

12. Create a reference plane at an offset distance of 90 mm from the Right plane by using the **Plane** tool, see Figure 8.234.

8.234

13. Invoke the Sketching environment by selecting the newly created reference plane as the sketching plane. The orientation of the model is changed as normal to the viewing direction.

14. Create the fourth section (rectangle of 65 X 60) of the lofted feature, see Figure 8.235.

15. Exit the Sketching environment and then press CTRL + 7 to change the current orientation to isometric, see Figure 8.236.

8.235

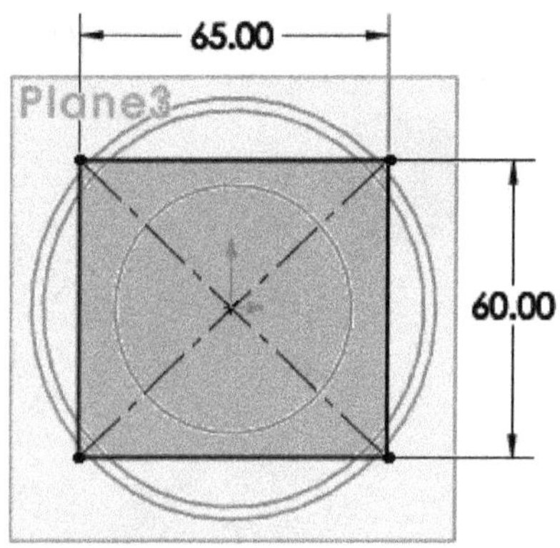

8.236

After creating all sections of the lofted feature, you can create the lofted feature.

16. Click on the **Lofted Boss/Base** tool in the **Features CommandManager**. The **Loft PropertyManager** appears.

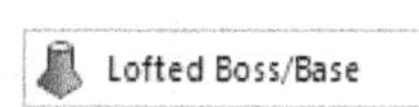

17. Select all the sections (profiles) of the lofted feature in the graphics area one by one by clicking the left mouse button. A preview of the lofted feature appears in the graphics area, see Figure 8.237. Ensure that the connectors appear in one direction in the preview to avoid twisting in the feature, see Figure 8.237.

18. Click on the green tick-mark ✓ in the PropertyManager. The lofted feature is created, see Figure 8.238. In Figure 8.238, the reference planes have been hidden.

8.237

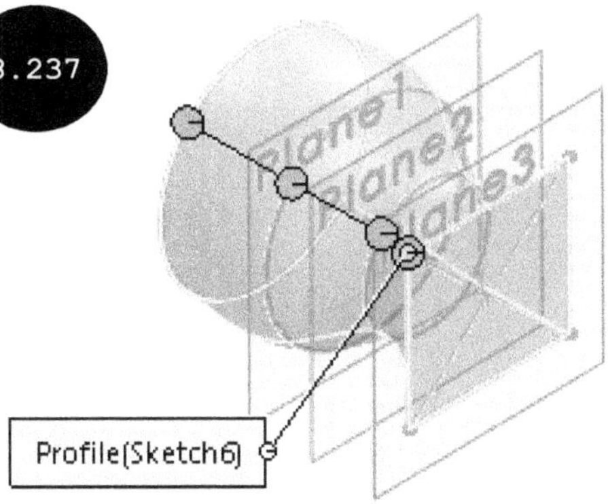

8.238

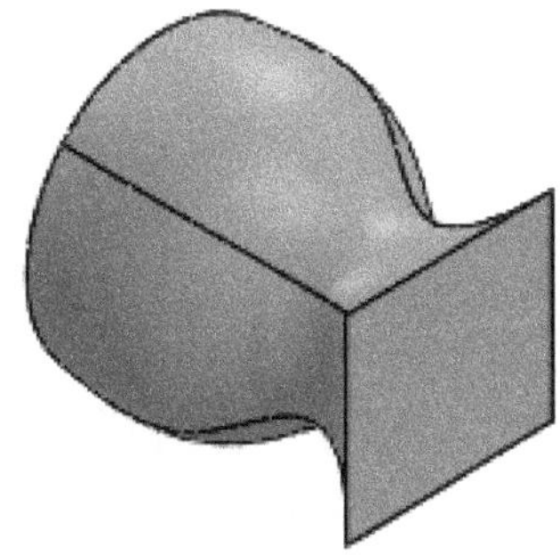

19. Hide the reference planes by clicking on the **Hide** tool in the Pop-up toolbar, which appears as soon as you select a plane to be hidden.

Section 4: Creating the Second Feature - Lofted Feature

Now, you need to create the second feature of the model, which is a lofted feature.

1. Create a reference plane at an offset distance of 210 mm from the right planar face of the base feature by using the **Plane** tool, see Figure 8.239.

2. Invoke the Sketching environment by selecting the newly created reference plane as the sketching plane. The orientation of the model is changed as normal to the viewing direction.

3. Create a section (rectangle of 150mm X 5mm) of the lofted feature, see Figure 8.240.

8.239

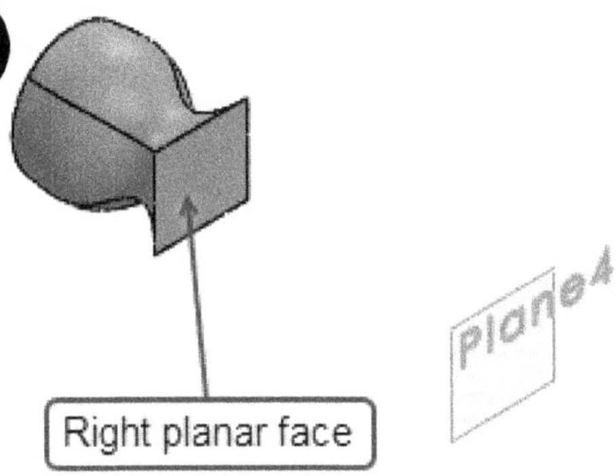

8.240

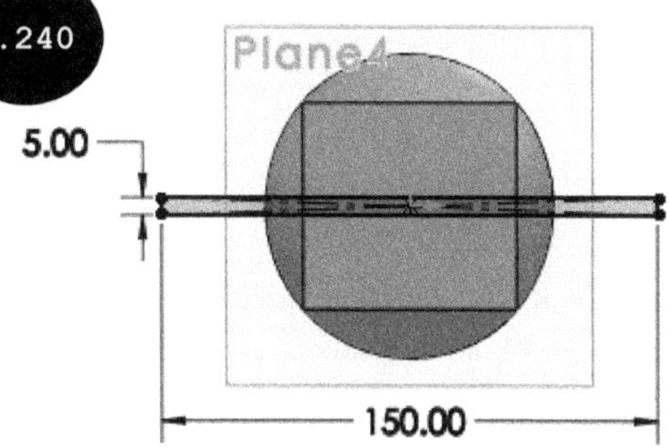

4. Exit the Sketching environment and then change the current orientation to isometric.

   Now, you need to create a guide curve for the lofted feature on the Front plane.

5. Invoke the Sketching environment by selecting the Front plane as the sketching plane. The orientation of the model is changed as normal to the viewing direction.

6. Create the guide curve (an arc of radius 220 mm) of the lofted feature, see Figure 8.241.

Note: The endpoints of the guide curve (arc) shown in the Figure 8.241 have Pierce relation with the top line segment of the rectangular section of the lofted feature and the top edge of the right planar face of the base feature, respectively.

7. Exit the Sketching environment and then change the current orientation to isometric.

   Now, you need to create the lofted feature.

8. Click on the **Lofted Boss/Base** tool in the **Features CommandManager**. The **Loft PropertyManager** appears.

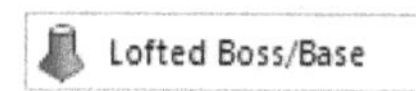

9. Select the right planar face of the base feature as the first section of the lofted feature and then select the rectangular section (rectangle of 150 X 5) as the second section of the lofted feature. A preview of the lofted feature appears in the graphics area, see Figure 8.242.

10. Ensure that the connectors appear in one direction in the preview to avoid twisting in the feature, see Figure 8.242. If needed, you can change the position of the connectors by dragging them.

8.241

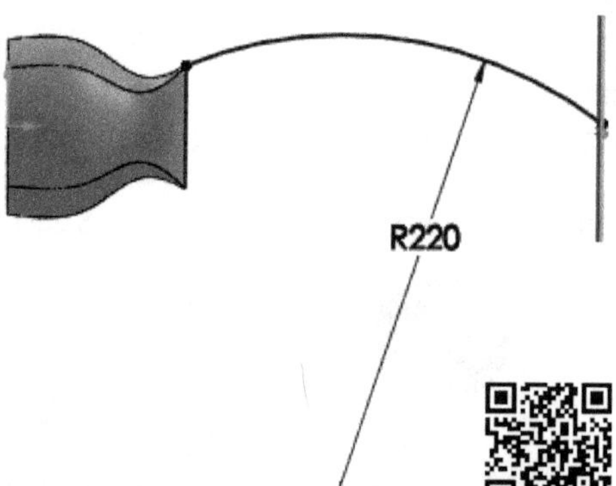

8.242

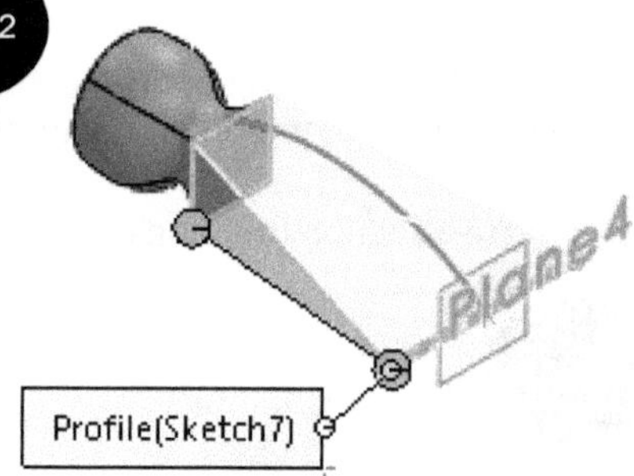

11. Click on the **Guide Curves** field in the **Guide Curves** rollout of the PropertyManager. The **Guide Curves** field is activated.

12. Click on the guide curve (arc of radius 220 mm) in the graphics area. A preview of the lofted feature appears such that it is guided by the guide curve, see Figure 8.243.

8.243

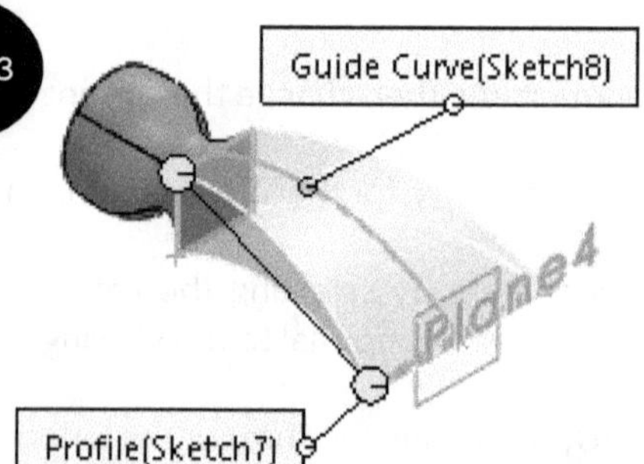

13. Click on the green tick-mark ✓ in the PropertyManager. The lofted feature is created, see Figure 8.244. Next, hide the reference plane.

8.244

Section 5: Saving the Model

1. Click on the **Save** tool of the **Standard** toolbar. The **Save As** window appears.

2. Browse to the Chapter 8 folder of the SOLIDWORKS folder and then save the model with the name Tutorial 3.

Tutorial 4

Create a model, as shown in Figure 8.245. All dimensions are in mm.

8.245

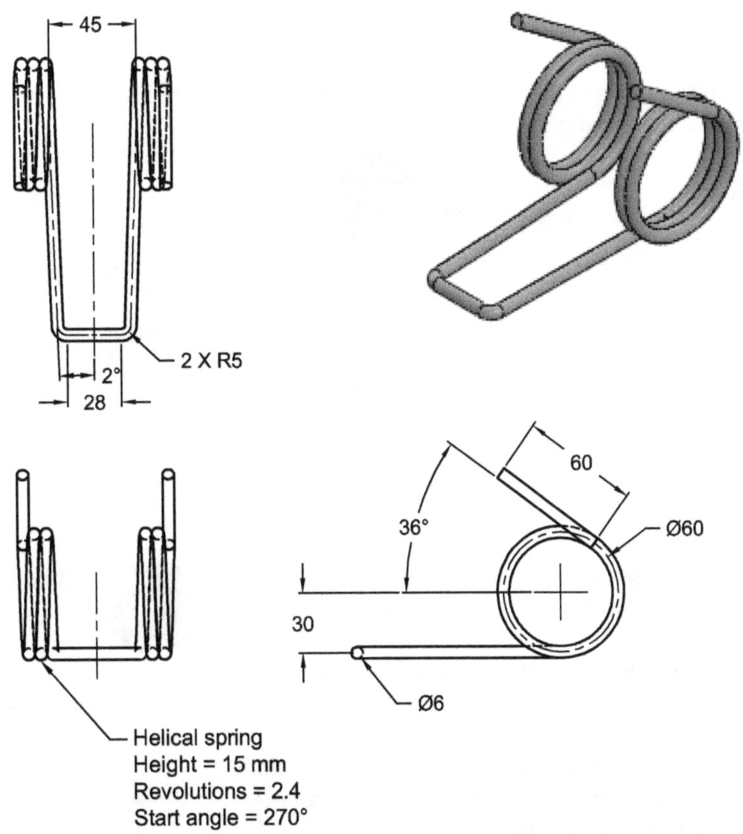

Section 1: Invoking the Part Modeling Environment

1. Start SOLIDWORKS and then invoke the Part modeling environment.

   Once the Part modeling environment is invoked, you can set the unit system and create the base/first feature of the model.

2. Ensure that the **MMGS (millimeter, gram, second)** unit system is set for the currently opened part document.

Section 2: Creating the First Curve - Helical Curve

1. Invoke the Sketching environment by selecting the Right plane as the sketching plane and then create a circle of diameter 60 mm, which will define the diameter of the helical curve, see Figure 8.246.

2. Exit the Sketching environment by clicking on the **Exit Sketch** button.

3. Invoke the **Curves** flyout in the **Features CommandManager** and then click on the **Helix and Spiral** tool. The **Helix/Spiral PropertyManager** appears.

Note: If the circle has been selected before invoking the **Helix and Spiral** tool, then the **Helix/Spiral PropertyManager** as well as the preview of the helical curve appear. You can select the circle to define the diameter of the helical curve before or after invoking the **Helix and Spiral** tool.

4. Click on the circle in the graphics area. A preview of the helical curve appears, see Figure 8.247. Change the orientation to isometric.

8.246

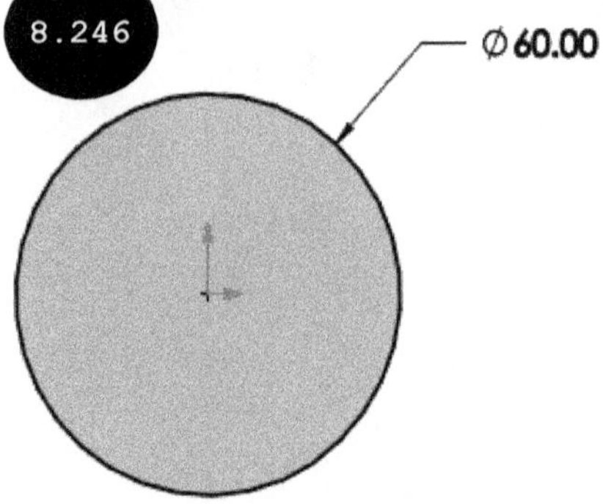

8.247

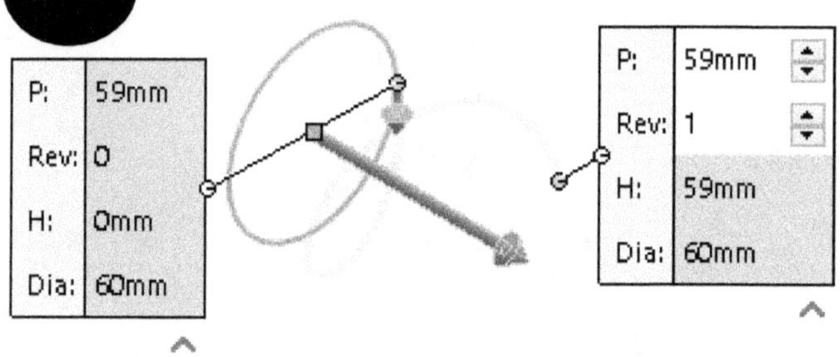

5. Invoke the **Type** drop-down list in the **Defined By** rollout of the PropertyManager, see Figure 8.248.

6. Select the **Height and Revolution** option in the **Type** drop-down list.

7. Enter **15** in the **Height** field, **2.4** in the **Revolutions** field, and **270** in the **Start angle** field of the **Parameters** rollout in the PropertyManager.

8.248

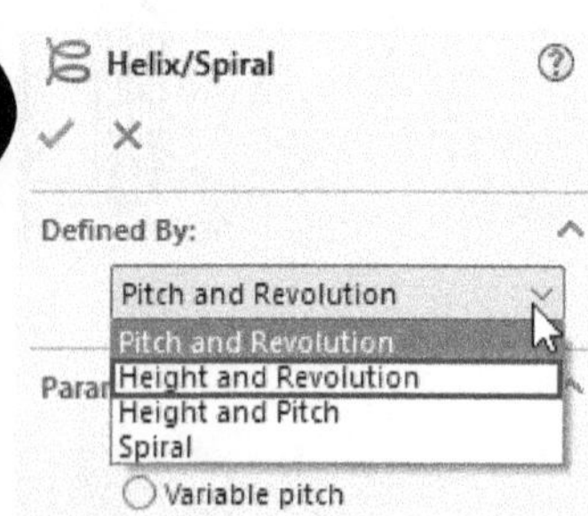

8. Select the **Reverse direction** check box in the **Parameters** rollout. The direction of the curve creation gets reversed, see Figure 8.249.

9. Ensure that the **Counterclockwise** radio button is selected in the rollout.

10. Click on the green tick-mark ✓ in the PropertyManager. The helical curve is created, see Figure 8.250.

8.249

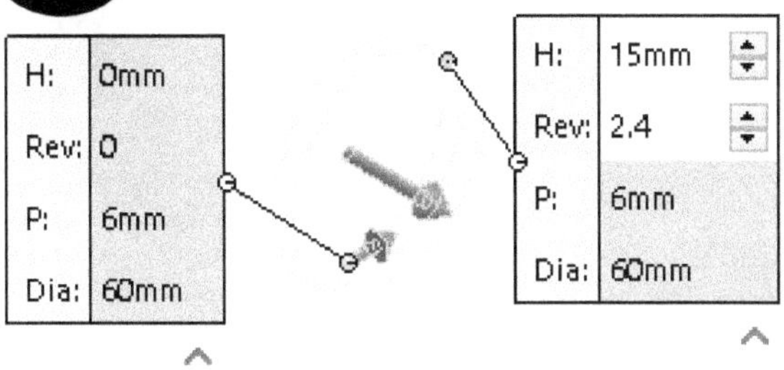

8.250

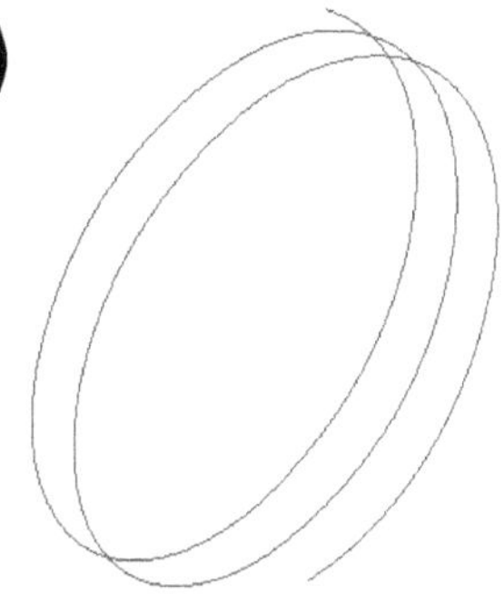

Section 3: Creating the Second Curve - Helical Curve

After creating the first helical curve, you need to create the second helical curve at an offset distance of 45 mm from the Right Plane.

1. Create a reference plane at an offset distance of 45 mm from the Right plane by using the **Plane** tool, see Figure 8.251.

2. Invoke the Sketching environment by selecting the newly created reference plane as the sketching plane. The orientation of the model is changed as normal to the viewing direction.

3. Create a circle of diameter 60 mm to define the diameter of the second helical curve, see Figure 8.252.

8.251

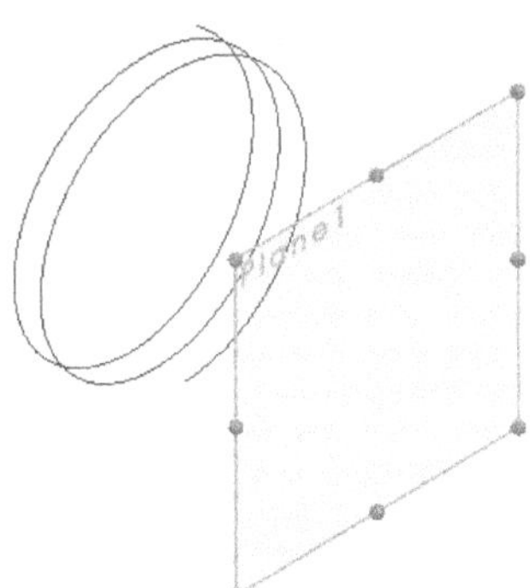

8.252

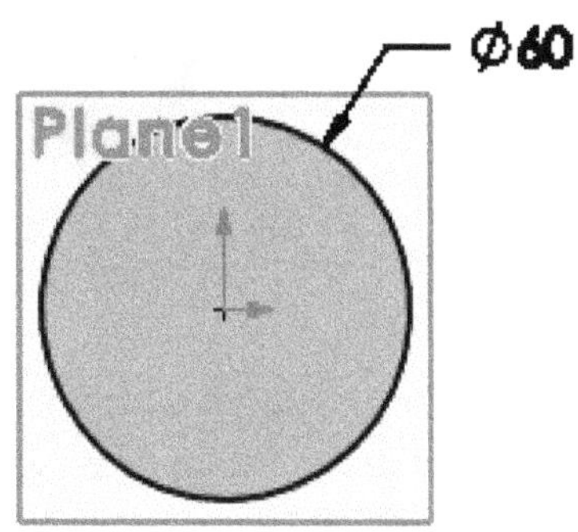

4. Invoke the **Curves** flyout in the **Features CommandManager** and then click on the **Helix and Spiral** tool. A preview of the helical curve as well as the **Helix/Spiral PropertyManager** appear.

5. Press CTRL + 7 to change the current orientation of the model to isometric.

6. Select the **Height and Revolution** option in the **Type** drop-down list of the **Defined By** rollout.

7. Enter **15** in the **Height** field, **2.4** in the **Revolutions** field, and **270** in the **Start angle** field of the **Parameters** rollout of the PropertyManager.

8. Ensure that the **Reverse direction** check box is cleared in the rollout.

9. Ensure that the **Counterclockwise** radio button is selected in the rollout.

10. Click on the green tick-mark ✓ in the PropertyManager. The second helical curve is created, see Figure 8.253.

11. Hide the reference plane by selecting the **Hide** option in the Pop-up toolbar that appears on selecting the plane.

8.253

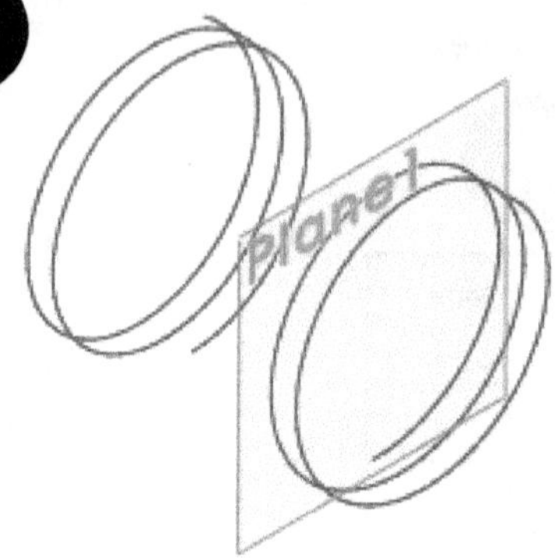

Section 4: Creating the Third Curve - Sketch

After creating the helical curves, you need to create a sketch on a reference plane, which is parallel to the Top Plane and passes through the start point of the first helical curve.

1. Create a reference plane parallel to the Top Plane and pass through the start point of the first helical curve, see Figures 8.254 and 8.255. Figure 8.254 shows the preview of the plane.

8.254

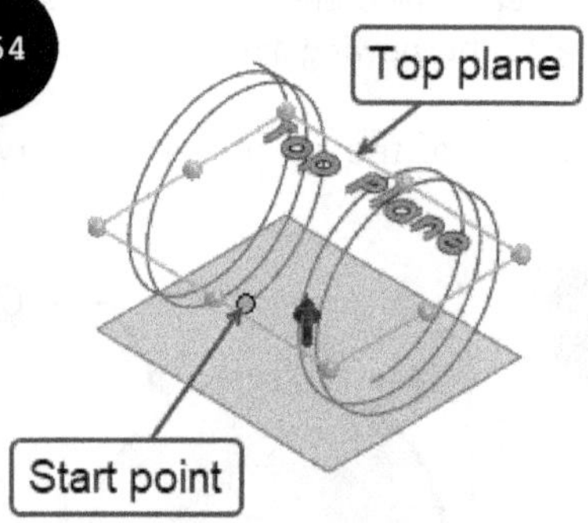

8.255

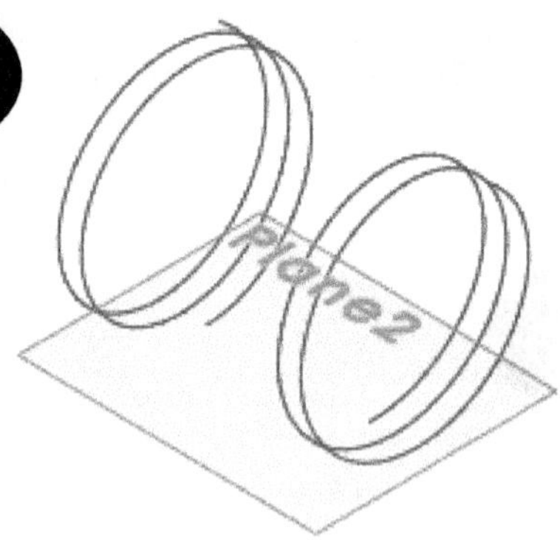

Note: To create a reference plane parallel to the Top plane and passing through the start point of the first helical curve, you need to select the Top plane as the first reference and the start point of the first helical curve as the second reference.

2. Invoke the Sketching environment by selecting the newly created reference plane as the sketching plane. The orientation of the model is changed as normal to the viewing direction.

3. Create a sketch as the third curve in the drawing area, see Figure 8.256. Note that both the endpoints of the sketch shown in Figure 8.256 have a pierce relation with the respective helical curves.

4. Exit the Sketching environment by clicking on the **Exit Sketch** tool and then hide the reference plane.

5. Press CTRL + 7 to change the orientation of the model to isometric, see Figure 8.257.

8.256

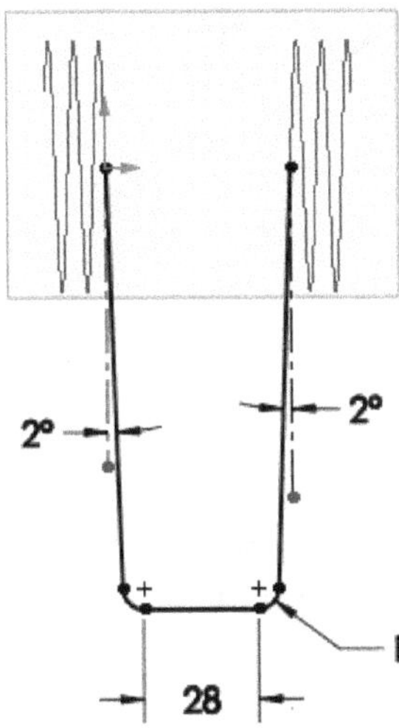

8.257

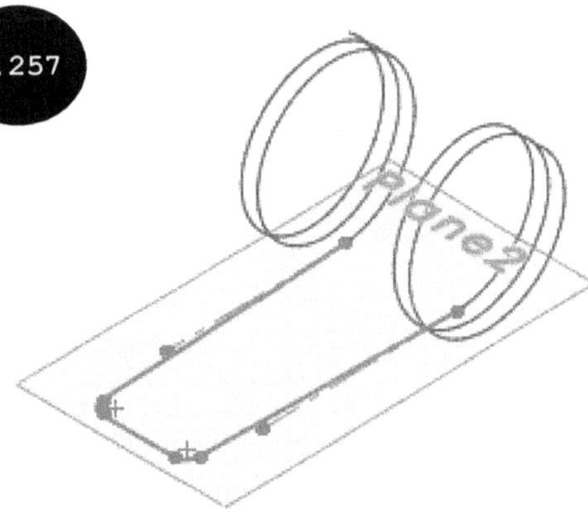

Section 5: Creating the Fourth Curve - Sketch

You need to create the fourth curve on a reference plane, which is parallel to the Right plane and passes through the endpoint of the first helical curve.

1. Create a reference plane parallel to the Right plane and pass through the endpoint of the first helical curve, see Figures 8.258 and 8.259. Figure 8.258 shows a preview of the reference plane.

8.258

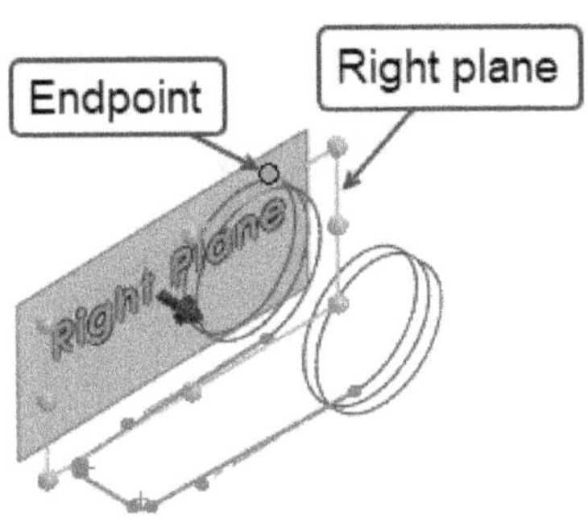

8.259

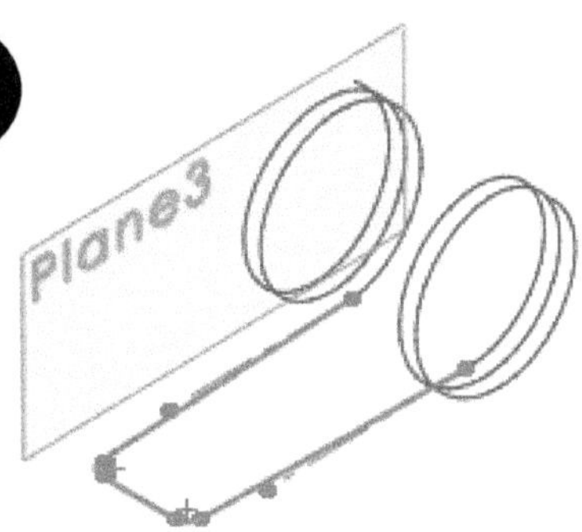

Note: To create a reference plane parallel to the Right plane and passing through the endpoint of the first helical curve, you need to select the Right plane as the first reference and the endpoint of the first helical curve as the second reference for creating the plane.

2. Invoke the Sketching environment by selecting the newly created reference plane as the sketching plane. The orientation of the model is changed as normal to the viewing direction.

3. Create the fourth sketch (an inclined line of length 60 mm), see Figure 8.260.

8.260

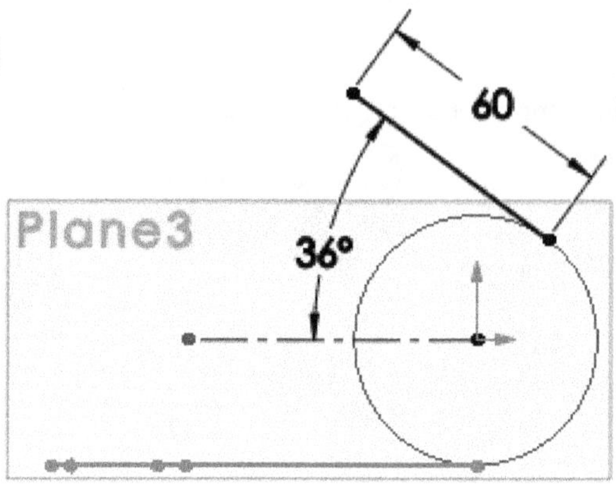

Note: The start point of the inclined line shown in Figure 8.260 has a Pierce relation with the first helical curve. To apply the Pierce relation, select the start point of the line and then select the first helical curve. A Pop-up toolbar appears. In this Pop-up toolbar, click on the **Pierce** tool. You may need to rotate the model to select the first helical curve.

4. Exit the Sketching environment by clicking on the **Exit Sketch** button and then hide the reference plane.

5. Press CTRL + 7 to change the current orientation of the model to isometric, see Figure 8.261.

8.261

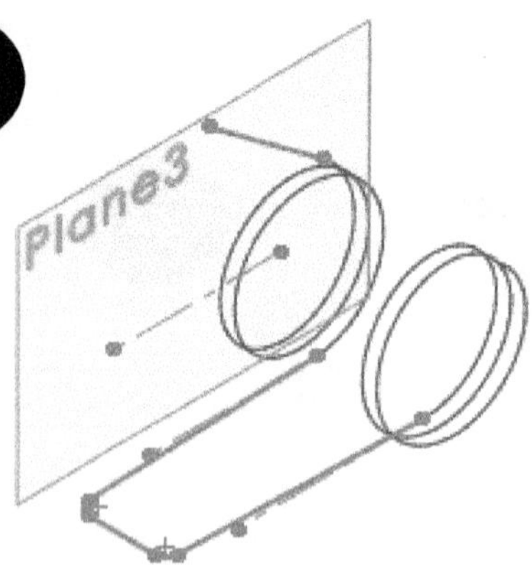

Section 6: Creating the Fifth Curve - Sketch

You need to create the fifth curve on a reference plane, which is parallel to the Right plane and passes through the endpoint of the second helical curve.

1. Create a reference plane parallel to the Right plane and pass through the endpoint of the second helical curve, see Figures 8.262 and 8.263. Figure 8.262 shows a preview of the reference plane.

8.262

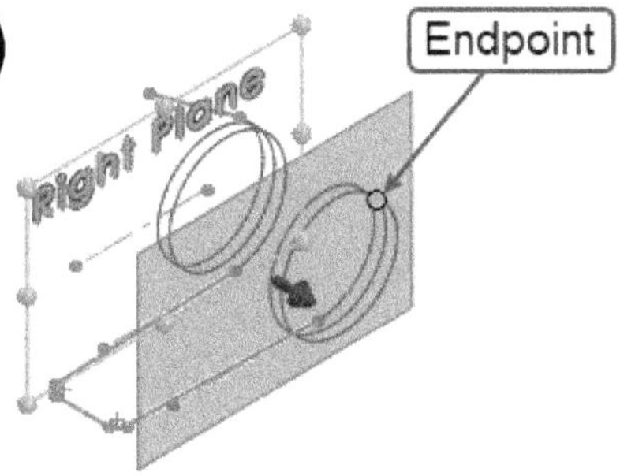

8.263

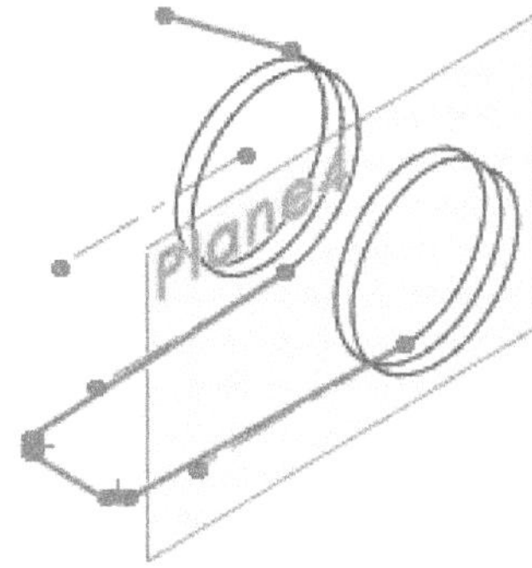

2. Invoke the Sketching environment by selecting the newly created reference plane as the sketching plane. The orientation of the model is changed as normal to the viewing direction.

3. Create the sketch (an inclined line of length 60 mm), see Figure 8.264. Note that the inclined line shown in Figure 8.264 has been created by specifying its start point and endpoint on the start point and endpoint of the existing inclined line, respectively.

4. Exit the Sketching environment by clicking on the **Exit Sketch** tool and then hide the reference plane.

5. Press CTRL + 7 to change the current orientation of the model to isometric, see Figure 8.265.

8.264

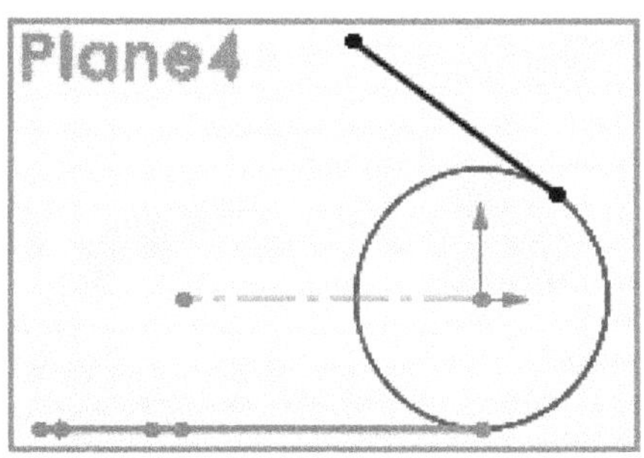

8.265

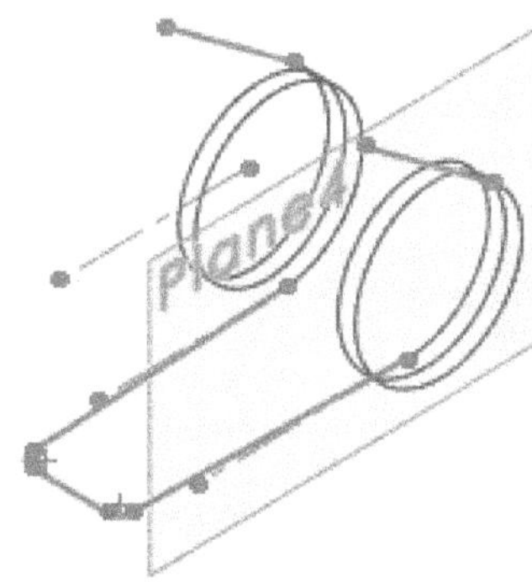

Section 7: Creating the Composite Curve - Sweep Path

After creating all curves (helical curve and sketches), you need to create a composite curve as the path of the sweep feature by combining all the curves.

1. Invoke the **Curves** flyout in the **Features CommandManager** and then click on the **Composite Curve** tool. The **Composite Curve PropertyManager** appears.

2. Select all the curves (two helical curves and three sketches), one by one in the graphics area by clicking the left mouse button.

3. Click on the green tick-mark ✓ in the PropertyManager. The composite curve is created, see Figure 8.266.

8.266

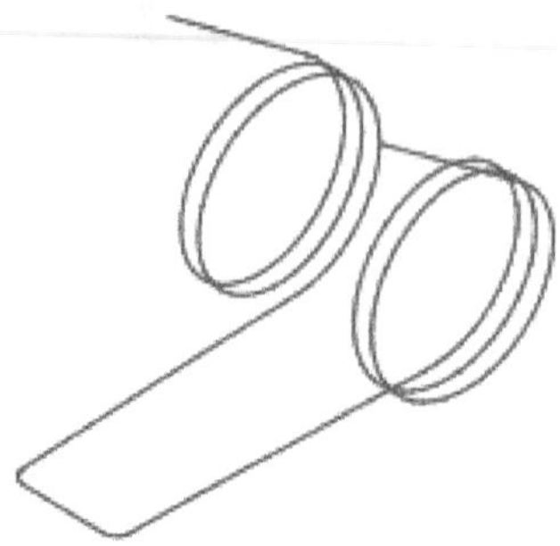

Section 8: Creating the Sweep Feature

After creating the path, you need to create a sweep feature with a circular profile.

1. Click on the **Swept Boss/Base** tool in the **Features CommandManager**. The **Sweep PropertyManager** appears.

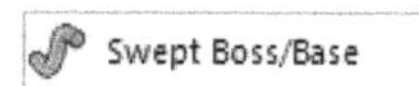

2. Click on the **Circular Profile** radio button in the **Profile and Path** rollout of the PropertyManager.

3. Click on the path (composite curve) of the sweep feature in the graphics area.

4. Enter **6** in the **Diameter** field of the **Profile and Path** rollout and then press ENTER. A preview of the sweep feature appears, see Figure 8.267.

5. Click on the green tick-mark ✓ in the PropertyManager. The sweep feature is created, see Figure 8.268.

8.267

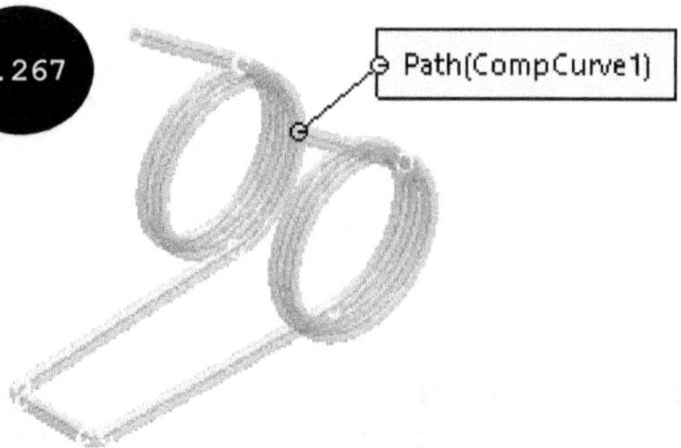

8.268

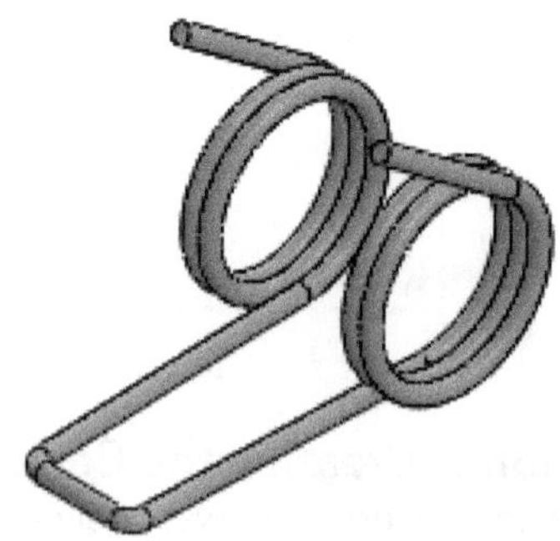

Note: In Figure 8.268, the composite curve (path) has been hidden. To hide the composite curve, click on the composite curve in the FeatureManager Design Tree and then click on the **Hide** tool in the Pop-up toolbar that appears.

Section 9: Saving the Model

1. Click on the **Save** tool of the **Standard** toolbar. The **Save As** window appears.
2. Browse to the Chapter 8 folder of the SOLIDWORKS folder and then save the model with the name Tutorial 4.

Hands-on Test Drive 1

Create a model as shown in Figure 8.269. After creating the model, apply the Cast Alloy Steel material and then calculate its mass properties. All dimensions are in mm.

8.269

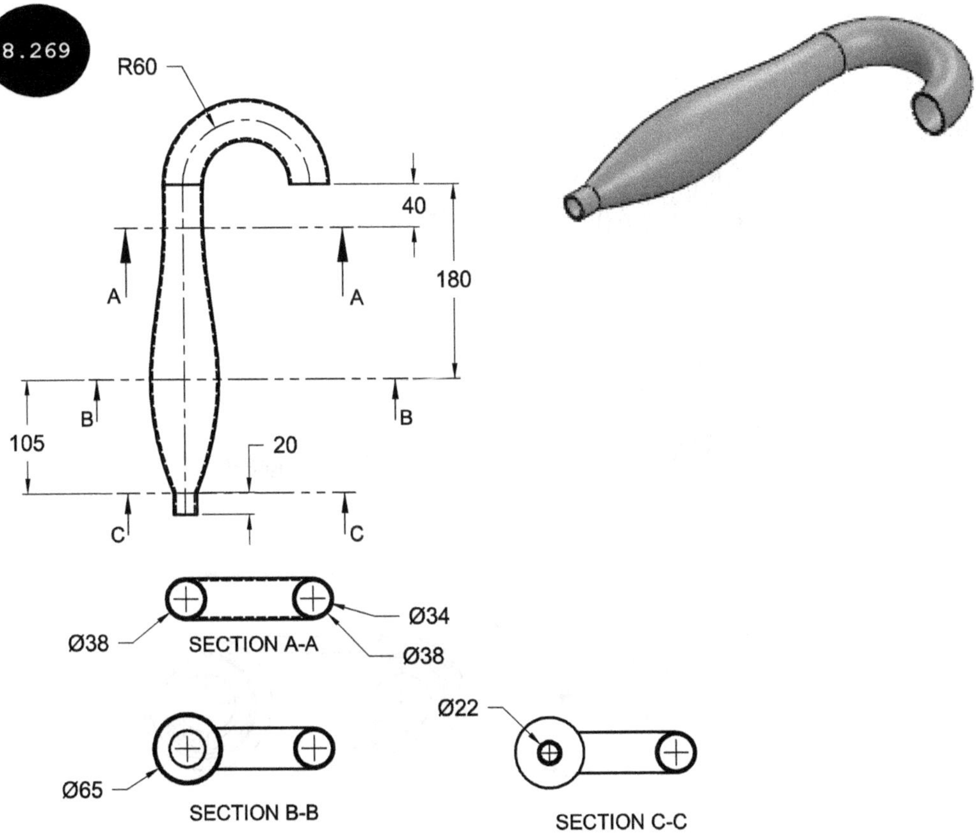

Hands-on Test Drive 2

Create a model as shown in Figure 8.270 and then apply the Alloy Steel material. Also, calculate the mass properties of the model. All dimensions are in mm and the start angle is 90 degrees.

8.270

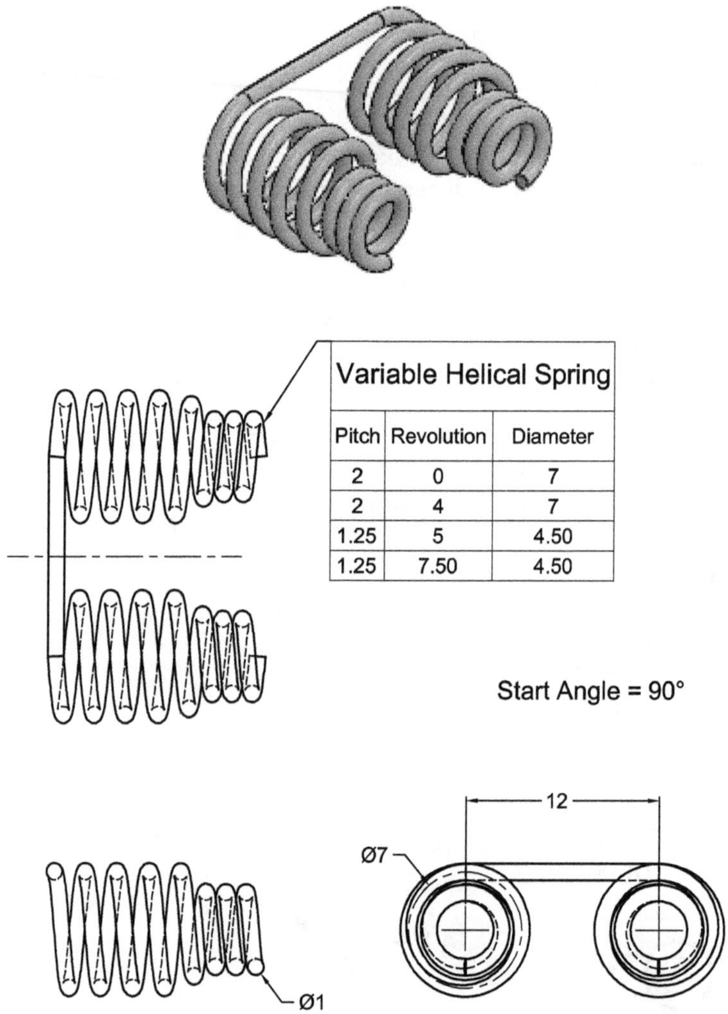

Variable Helical Spring		
Pitch	Revolution	Diameter
2	0	7
2	4	7
1.25	5	4.50
1.25	7.50	4.50

Hands-on Test Drive 3

Create a model as shown in Figure 8.271 and then apply the Alloy Steel material. Also, calculate the mass properties of the model. All dimensions are in mm and the start angle is 90 degrees.

8.271

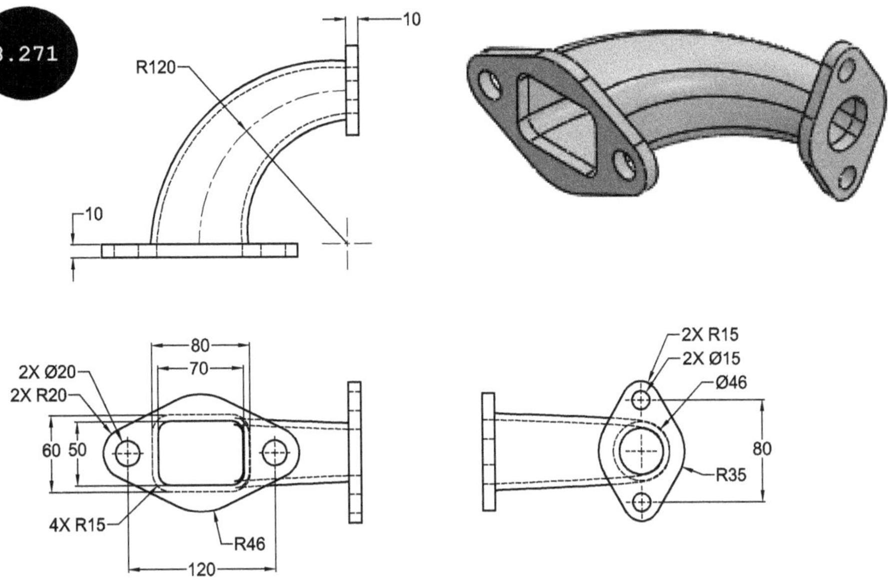

Summary

In this chapter, you learned how to create advanced features such as sweep features, sweep cut features, lofted features, lofted cut features, boundary features, and boundary cut features, enabling you to design complex models effectively.

You also explored various methods for creating curves, including projected curves, helical and spiral curves, curves through XYZ points, curves from reference points, and composite curves. Techniques for splitting model faces and constructing 3D sketches were covered to enhance your modeling skills.

Questions

Complete and verify the following sentences:

- The _________ tool is used for creating sweep features.
- While creating a sweep feature, the _________ option is selected by default. As a result, the profile follows the path.

- Selecting the _________ option creates a sweep feature such that the profile twists along a path.
- By selecting the _________ option, you can select a tool body following the path to create a sweep cut feature.
- You can create projected curves by using two methods: _________ and _________.
- The _________ radio button is used for creating a helical curve with a variable pitch.
- By selecting the _________ option, you can create a helical curve by defining its pitch and number of revolutions.
- The _________ tool is used for creating a curve by specifying coordinate points.
- The profiles/sections of a lofted feature must be closed. (True/False)
- In SOLIDWORKS, you cannot create tapered helical curves. (True/False)
- For creating a sweep feature, the start point of the path must lie on the plane of the profile created. (True/False)

CHAPTER

9

Patterning and Mirroring

This chapter discusses the following topics:

- Patterning Features/Faces/Bodies
- Creating a Linear Pattern
- Creating a Circular Pattern
- Creating a Curve Driven Pattern
- Creating a Sketch Driven Pattern
- Creating a Table Driven Pattern
- Creating a Fill Pattern
- Creating a Variable Pattern
- Mirroring Features/Faces/Bodies

Patterning and mirroring are advanced design techniques that significantly enhance the efficiency and speed of the design process. These tools enable designers to replicate features systematically, reducing manual effort and saving valuable time. For instance, when designing a plate with 1,000 identical holes, instead of creating all the holes one by one, you can create one hole and then pattern it to create the remaining holes. Similarly, if the geometry is symmetric, you can create one of its sides and mirror it to create the other side. The various methods used for patterning and mirroring features, faces, or bodies are discussed next.

Patterning Features/Faces/Bodies

In SOLIDWORKS, you can create different types of patterns, such as linear patterns, circular patterns, curve driven patterns, sketch driven patterns, table driven patterns, fill patterns, and variable patterns. The tools used for creating different types of patterns are grouped in the **Pattern** flyout of the **Features CommandManager**, see Figure 9.1.

9.1

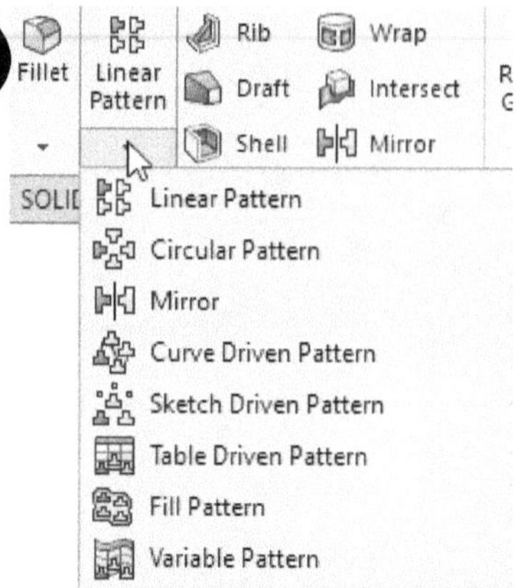

Different types of patterns that can be created by using the pattern tools are discussed next.

Creating a Linear Pattern

Creating multiple instances of features, faces, or bodies in one or two linear directions is known as a linear pattern, see Figure 9.2.

9.2

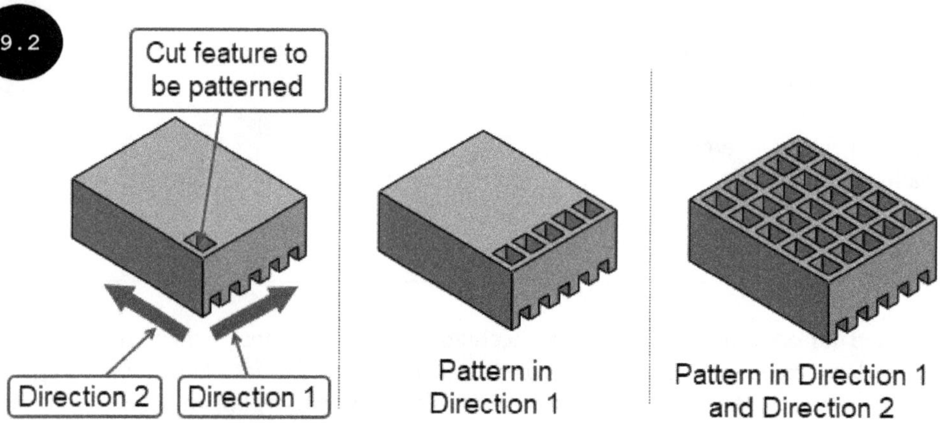

To create a linear pattern, click on the **Linear Pattern** tool in the **Features CommandManager**. The **Linear Pattern PropertyManager** appears, see Figure 9.3. The options in this PropertyManager are discussed next.

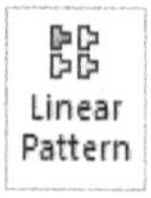

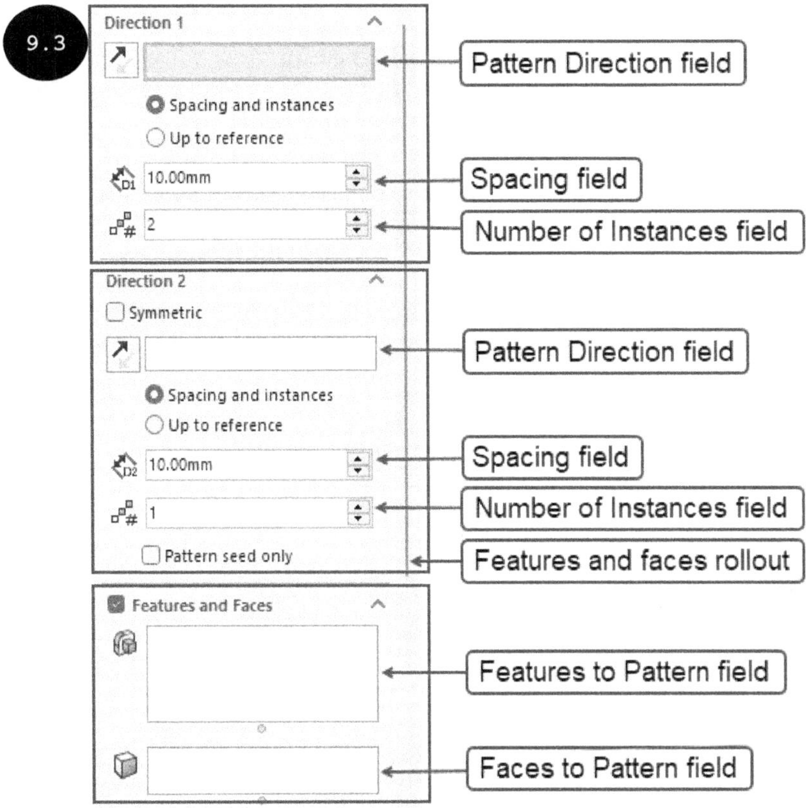

Features and Faces

The **Features and Faces** rollout of the PropertyManager is used to select features and faces to be patterned, see Figure 9.4. To select features to be patterned, click on the **Features to Pattern** field in this rollout and then select features from the graphics area or the FeatureManager Design Tree. On selecting the features to be patterned, the names of the selected features appear in the **Features to Pattern** field. The features selected to be patterned are known as seed or parent features.

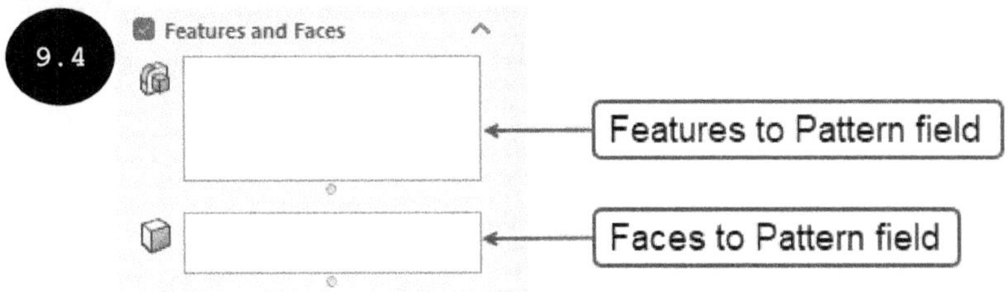

You can also pattern the faces of a model that forms a closed volume. To do this, click on the **Faces to Pattern** field in the rollout and then select faces to be patterned in the graphics area. Note that faces to be patterned should form a closed volume and make up a feature.

Bodies

The **Bodies** rollout is used to select bodies to be patterned. To select bodies, you need to expand the **Bodies** rollout by clicking on the check box in the title bar of this rollout and then select the bodies to be patterned from the graphics area or the FeatureManager Design Tree.

Tip: You can select features, faces, or bodies to be patterned before or after invoking the **Linear Pattern PropertyManager**.

After selecting features, faces, or bodies to be patterned, you need to define the directions of the pattern using the **Direction 1** and **Direction 2** rollouts of the PropertyManager, which are discussed next.

Direction 1

The options in the **Direction 1** rollout of the PropertyManager are used to create multiple instances or copies of selected features, faces, or bodies in Direction 1, see Figure 9.5. The options are discussed next.

9.5

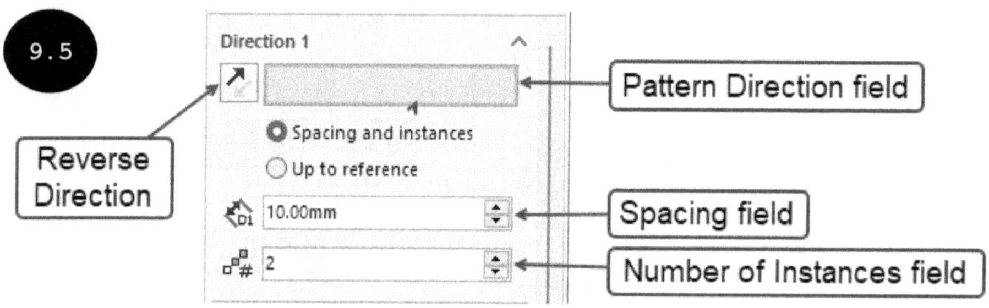

Pattern Direction

The **Pattern Direction** field is used to specify the direction of the pattern. To do this, click on the **Pattern Direction** field and then specify the direction of the pattern. You can select a linear edge, a linear sketch entity, an axis, a planar face, a conical/circular face, a circular edge, a reference plane, or a dimension as the direction of the pattern. After specifying the direction of the pattern, a preview of the linear pattern appears in the graphics area with a callout attached to the specified direction and an arrow appears pointing toward the direction of the pattern, see Figures 9.6 and 9.7. In Figure 9.6, a linear edge is selected as the pattern direction and in Figure 9.7, a circular face is selected as the pattern direction.

9.6

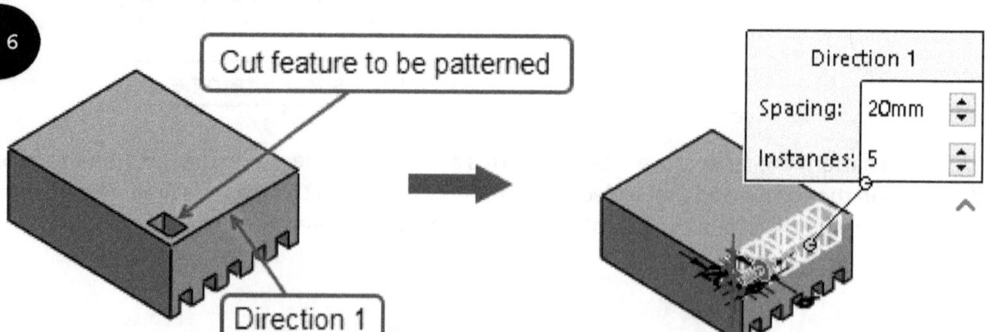

9.7

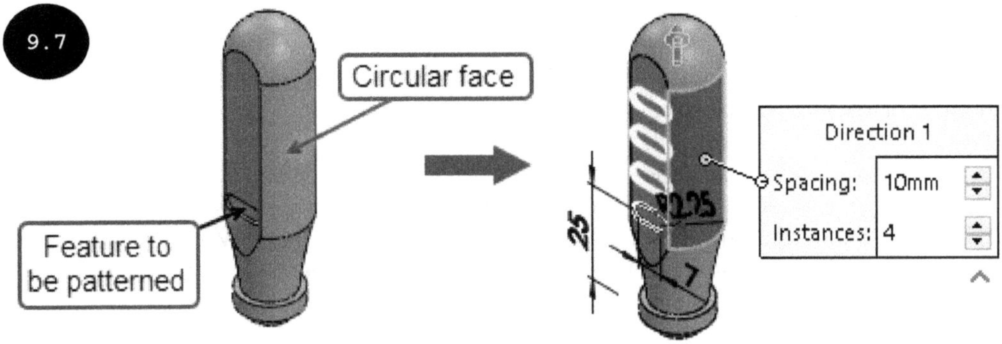

Spacing and instances

The **Spacing and instances** radio button is selected, by default. As a result, the **Spacing** and **Number of Instances** fields become available in the rollout. These fields are discussed next.

Spacing: The **Spacing** field is used to specify the spacing between two pattern instances. You can also specify the spacing between pattern instances by using the callout, which appears in the preview of the linear pattern in the graphics area. To do this, click on the **Spacing** field in the callout and then enter the required value as the spacing between the pattern instances in it.

Number of Instances: The **Number of Instances** field is used to specify the number of instances to be created in the pattern direction. Note that the number of instances specified in the **Number of Instances** field also includes the parent feature. You can also specify the number of instances in the callout, which appears in the preview of the linear pattern in the graphics area.

Reverse Direction

The **Reverse Direction** button is used to reverse the direction of the pattern.

Up to reference

On selecting the **Up to reference** radio button, the options of the **Direction 1** rollout appear, as shown in Figure 9.8. These options are used to create a linear pattern by specifying a reference geometry up to which the linear pattern is to be created based on the number of instances or spacing between the instances that are specified in the respective fields. The options are discussed next.

9.8

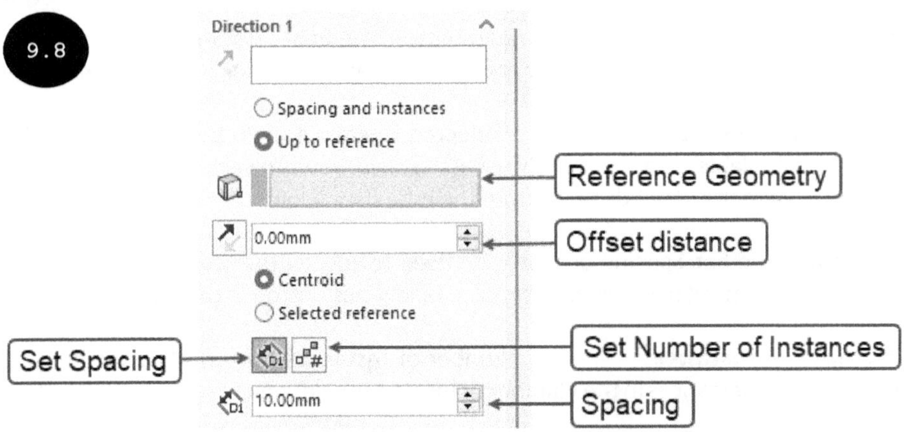

Reference Geometry: The **Reference Geometry** field is used to select a reference geometry that controls the pattern based on the specified number of instances or spacing. When the reference geometry is modified, the associated pattern updates automatically by adjusting the number of instances or the spacing between them.

In Figure 9.9, a preview and the resultant linear pattern are shown, with a vertex selected as the reference geometry and a spacing of 15 mm between instances. Figure 9.10 demonstrates the linear pattern after increasing the length of the model. Note that when the model's length is modified, the linear pattern automatically adjusts the number of instances to maintain the specified spacing between them.

9.9

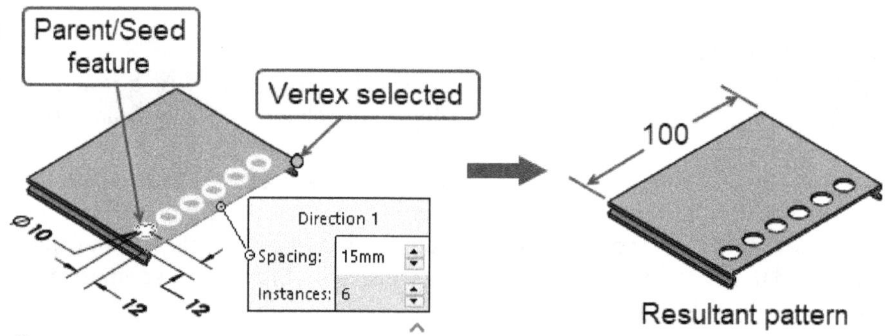

9.10

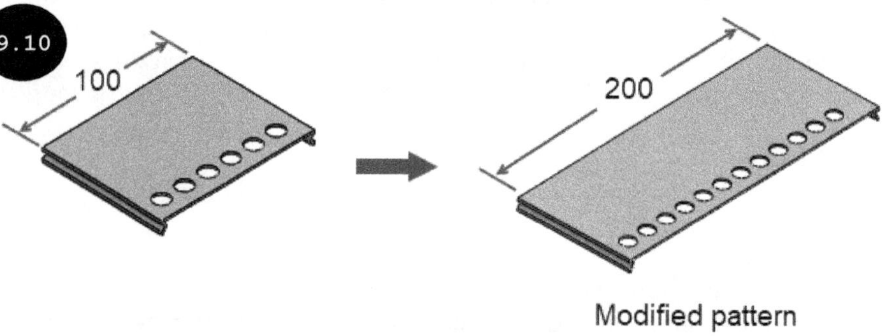

Offset distance: The **Offset distance** field is used to specify the offset distance between the last pattern instance and the reference geometry.

Centroid: On selecting the **Centroid** radio button, the offset distance specified in the **Offset distance** field is measured from the center of the last pattern instance to the reference geometry.

Selected reference: On selecting the **Selected reference** radio button, the **Seed Reference** field becomes available in the rollout. By using this field, you can select a reference of the parent feature to measure the offset distance from the reference geometry.

Set Spacing: The **Set Spacing** button is used to specify the spacing between the pattern instances in the **Spacing** field, which is enabled below this button in the rollout.

Set Number of Instances: The **Set Number of Instances** button is used to specify the number of pattern instances in the **Number of Instances** field, which is enabled below this button.

Direction 2

The options in the **Direction 2** rollout are used to create multiple instances of the selected feature in Direction 2. Figure 9.11 shows the preview of a linear pattern with 9 instances in Direction 1 and 4 instances in Direction 2.

9.11

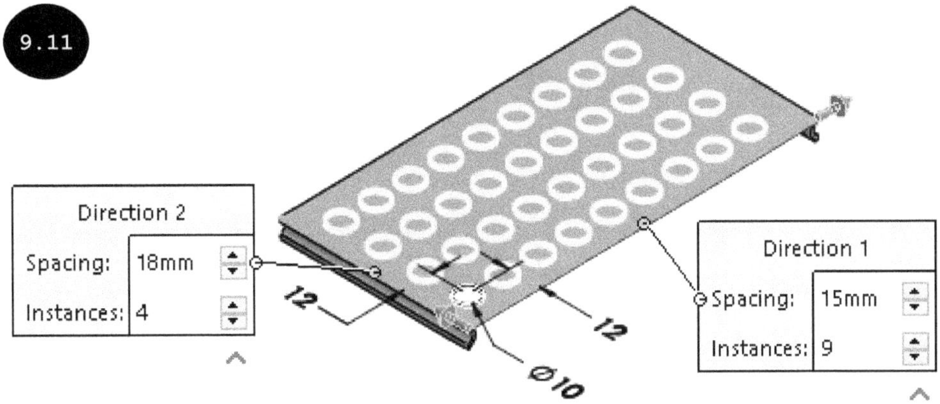

The options in the **Direction 2** rollout are the same as those in the **Direction 1** rollout, except the **Pattern seed only** and **Symmetric** check boxes, which are discussed next.

Pattern seed only

On selecting the **Pattern seed only** check box, the pattern is created such that only the seed/parent feature gets patterned, and the pattern instances of Direction 1 are not replicated in Direction 2, see Figure 9.12.

9.12

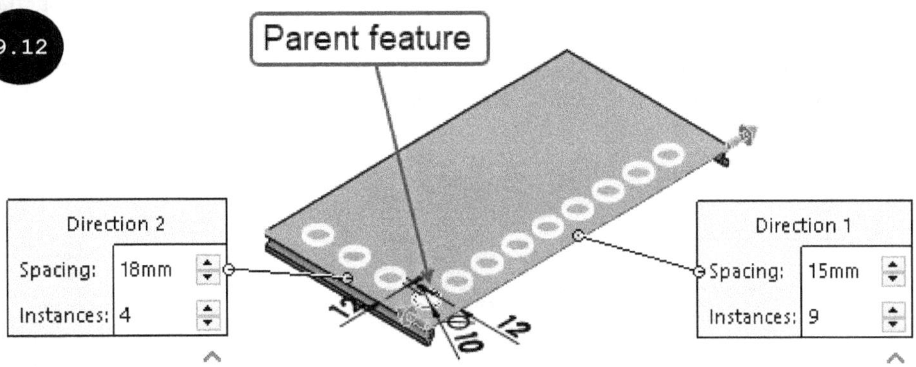

Symmetric

On selecting the **Symmetric** check box, the pattern instances are created symmetrically on both sides of the seed/parent feature, see Figure 9.13.

Note: When the **Symmetric** check box is selected, the options in the **Direction 2** rollout are disabled. Subsequently, a preview of a symmetric linear pattern appears, with identical parameters on both sides of the seed/parent feature, as specified in the **Direction 1** rollout.

9.13

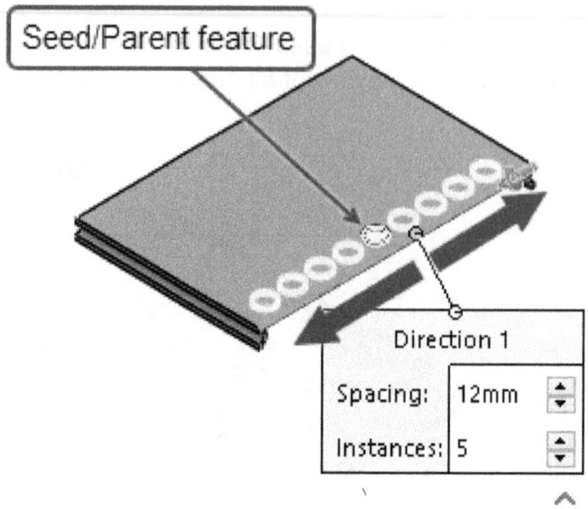

Instances to Skip

The **Instances to Skip** rollout is used to skip some of the instances of the pattern. To skip pattern instances, expand the **Instances to Skip** rollout by clicking on the arrow in the title bar of this rollout, see Figure 9.14.

9.14

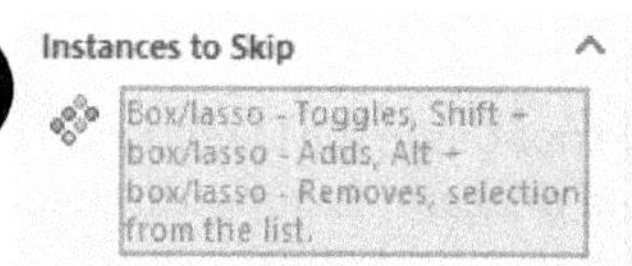

On expanding the **Instances to Skip** rollout, pink dots are displayed at the center of all pattern instances in the graphics area, see Figure 9.15. Move the cursor over the pink dot of a pattern instance to be skipped and then click the left mouse button when the appearance of the cursor changes to the hand cursor, see Figure 9.15. The selected pattern instance disappears or skips and the pink dot changes to white, see Figure 9.16. Also, the pattern instance number appears in the **Instances to Skip** field of the rollout. Similarly, you can skip multiple instances of the pattern, as required. You can also use Window selection and Lasso selection methods to skip pattern instances.

9.15

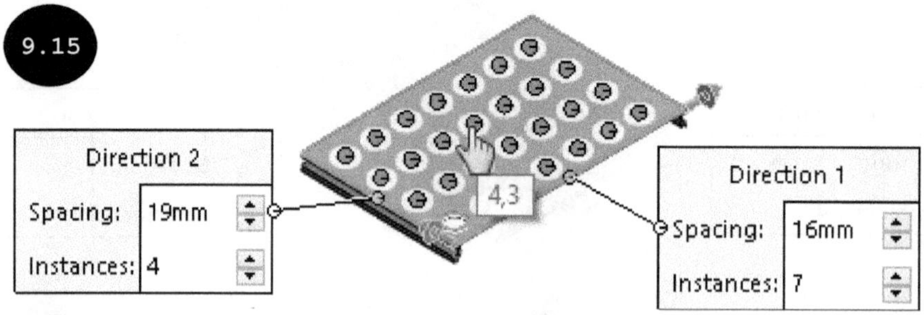

9.16

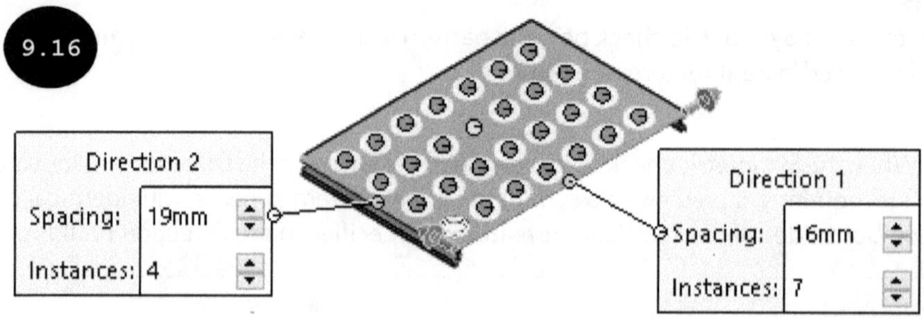

Tip: To skip pattern instances by using the Window selection method, draw a window around the instances by dragging the cursor after pressing and holding the left mouse button. Similarly, to skip pattern instances by using the Lasso selection method, right-click in the graphics area and then click on the **Lasso Selection** option in the shortcut menu that appears. Next, drag the cursor by pressing and holding the left mouse button around the pattern instances to be skipped.

You can also restore the skipped instances by clicking on the white dot of the instance to be restored in the graphics area or by using the Window and Lasso selection methods.

Options

The options in the **Options** rollout are discussed next.

Vary sketch

The **Vary sketch** check box is used to vary the instances of a pattern relative to a specified path. Figure 9.17 shows a feature to be patterned and Figure 9.18 shows the resultant variable linear pattern created by selecting the **Vary sketch** check box.

9.17

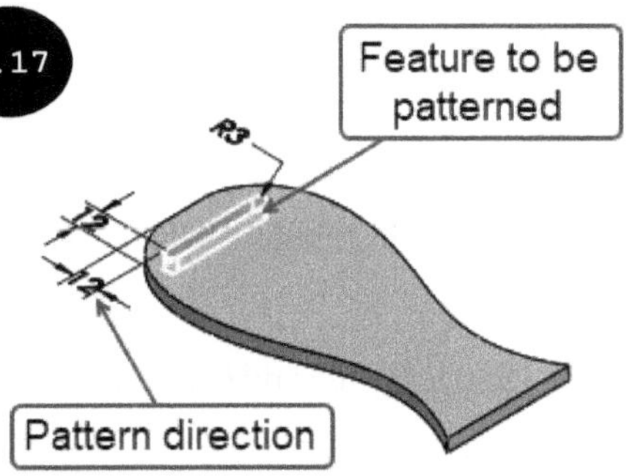

9.18

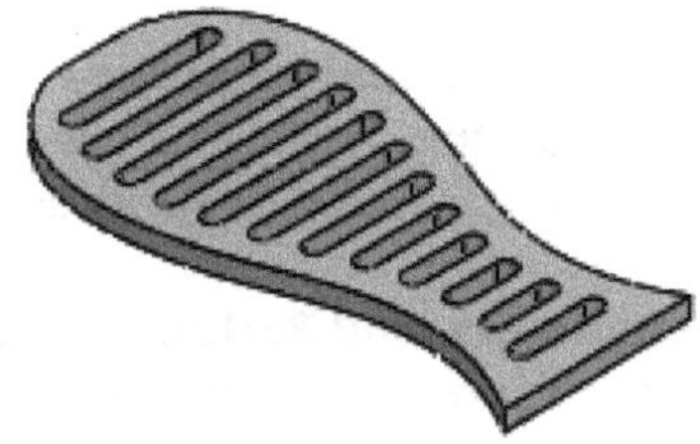

Note: The sketch of the feature to be varied must include a reference sketch or curve, which will act as the path for the feature to follow, as shown in Figure 9.19. In this figure, the side edges of the model are projected as reference curves to vary the feature. Additionally, the varying length of the sketch should not be constrained by dimensions, as seen in Figure 9.17. In this case, the sketch of the cut feature to be varied is fully defined by applying dimensions relative to the reference curve (path), while the length of the feature remains un-dimensioned.

9.19

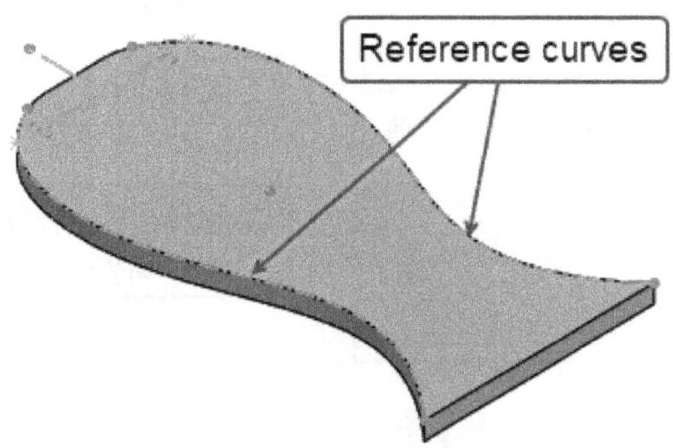

Geometry pattern

By default, the **Geometry pattern** check box is cleared. As a result, all the pattern instances maintain the same geometrical relations as those of the parent feature. For example, Figure 9.20 shows the front view of a model in the 'hidden lines visible' display style, in which the cut feature is created by defining the end condition as 4 mm offset from the bottom face of the model. Figure 9.21 shows the resultant pattern of the cut feature that is created by clearing the **Geometry pattern** check box, whereas Figure 9.22 shows the resultant pattern of the cut feature when the **Geometry pattern** check box is selected.

9.20

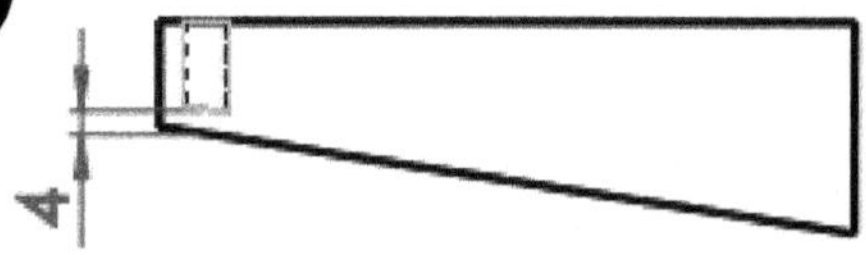

9.21

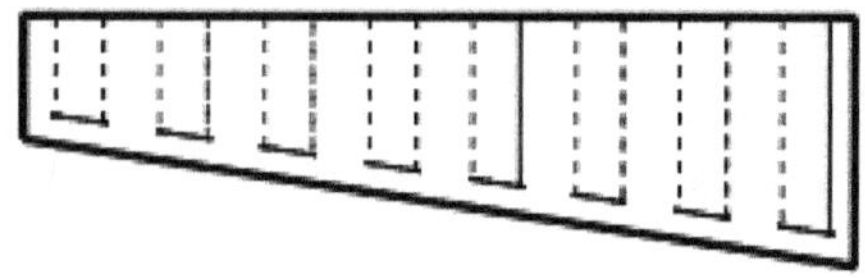

9.22

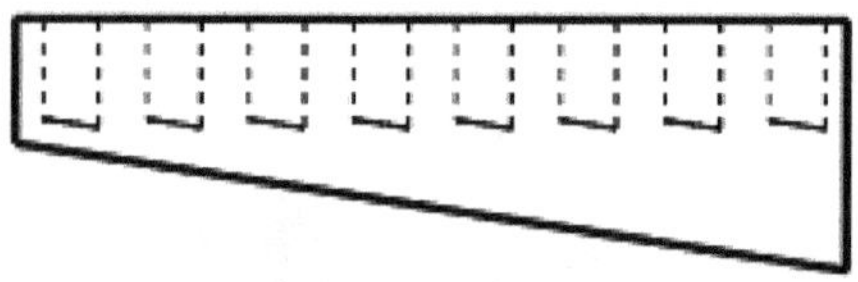

Propagate visual properties

By default, this check box is selected. As a result, all the visual properties such as colors, textures, and cosmetic thread of the parent feature are propagated to all the instances of the pattern.

Full preview and Partial preview

The **Full preview** and **Partial preview** radio buttons are used to display full and partial previews of the pattern in the graphics area, respectively.

Instances to Vary

The **Instances to Vary** rollout is used to create a pattern with incremental spacing between pattern instances in Direction 1 and Direction 2. Besides creating a pattern with incremental spacing between instances, you can also vary the geometry of instances. Note that this rollout is enabled only after selecting a feature to be patterned and a direction of the pattern. Once this rollout is enabled, you need to expand it by selecting the check box in its title bar, see Figure 9.23. The options in this rollout are discussed next.

9.23

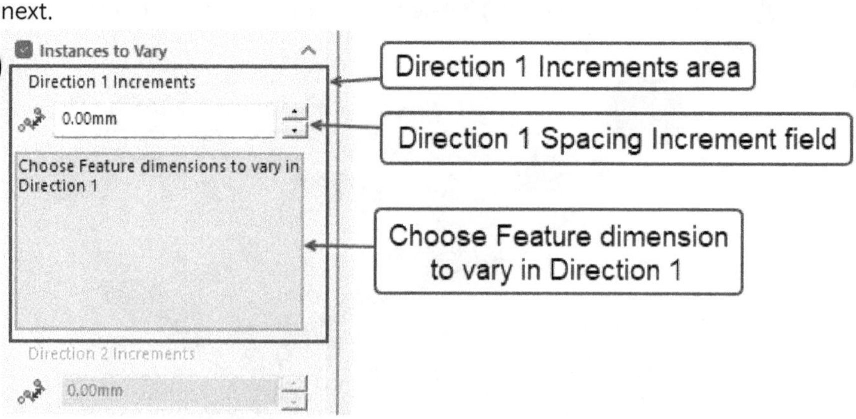

Direction 1 Increments

The **Direction 1 Increments** area of this rollout is used to specify incremental values for the pattern instances in Direction 1. The options in this area are discussed below:

Direction 1 Spacing Increment: This field is used to specify the incremental spacing between pattern instances. Figure 9.24 shows the preview of a pattern with an incremental spacing of 5 mm specified in this field.

9.24

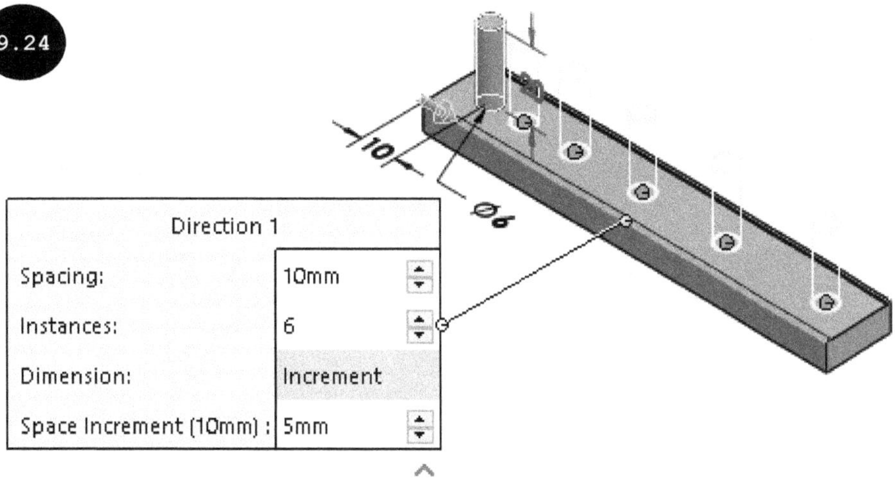

Choose Feature dimensions to vary in Direction 1: This field is used to select the dimensions of the parent feature such as diameter and height to be varied in the pattern instances. Click on the dimensions in the graphics area to be varied. A table with dimension name, dimension value, and increment value columns appears in this field, see Figure 9.25. Now, you can double-click on the field corresponding to the increment value column to activate its editing mode and then enter the increment value for the selected dimension. Figure 9.26 shows a linear pattern created with an incremental spacing of 5 mm, incremental diameter of 2 mm, and incremental height of 4 mm.

9.25

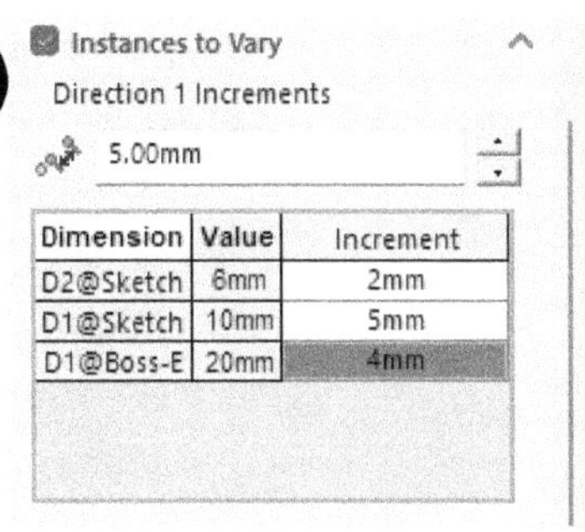

9.26

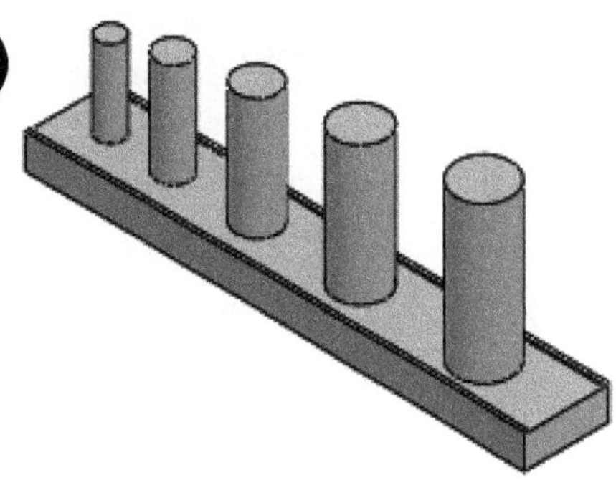

Direction 2 Increments

The **Direction 2 Increments** area is used to specify the incremental spacing between pattern instances and the incremental dimensions in Direction 2. The options in this area are the same as those discussed in the **Direction 1 Increments** area. Note that the options in this area are enabled only when you pattern features in Direction 2.

Creating a Circular Pattern

Creating multiple instances of features, faces, or bodies, circularly around an axis results in a circular pattern, see Figure 9.27. To create a circular pattern, click on the arrow at the bottom of the **Linear Pattern** tool. The **Pattern** flyout appears, see Figure 9.28. In this flyout, click on the **Circular Pattern** tool. The **CirPattern PropertyManager** appears, see Figure 9.29. The options in the **CirPattern PropertyManager** are discussed next.

9.27

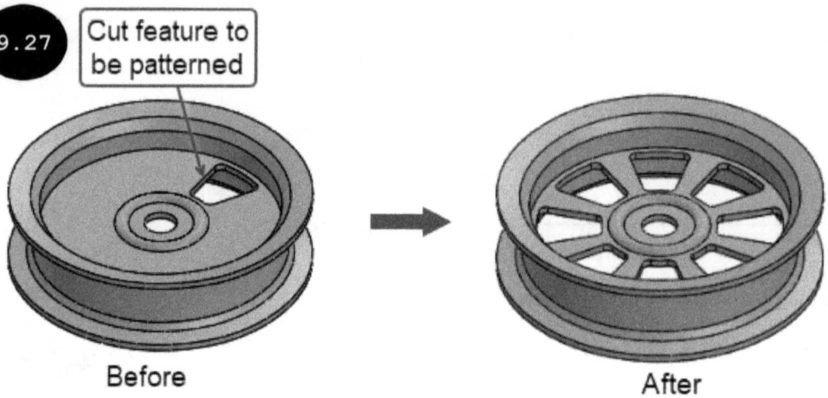

9.28

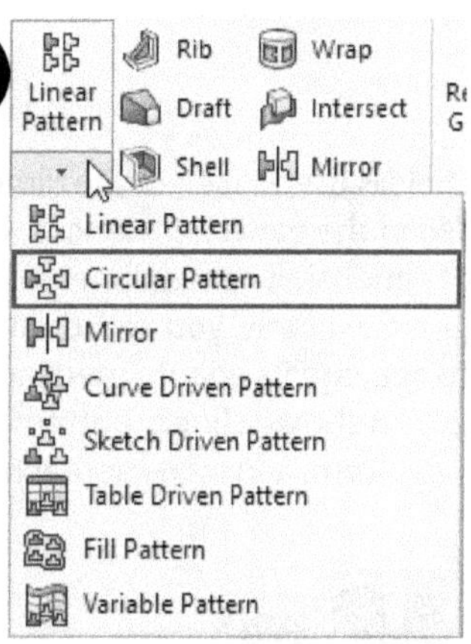

9.29

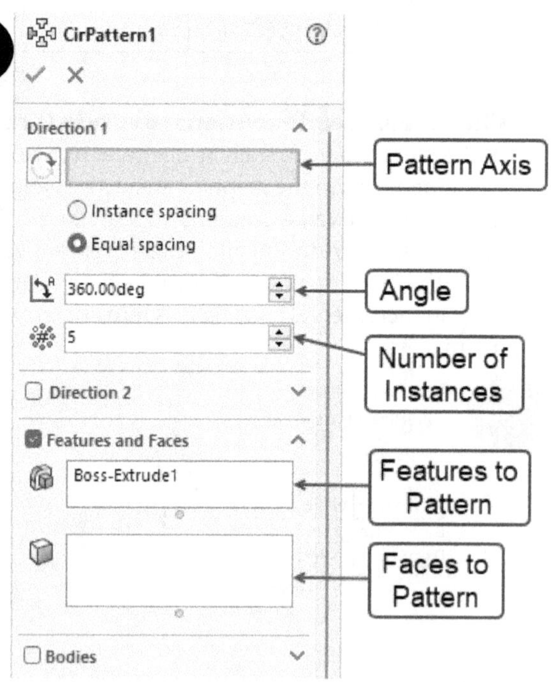

Features and Faces

The **Features and Faces** rollout is used to select features or faces to be patterned, circularly around an axis. By default, the **Features to Pattern** field is activated in this rollout. As a result, you can select features to be patterned from the graphics area or the FeatureManager Design Tree. After selecting the features to be patterned, the names of the selected features are listed in the **Features to Pattern** field. You can select features to be patterned before and after invoking the PropertyManager.

To select the faces to be patterned, click on the **Faces to Pattern** field in the rollout (see Figure 9.29), and then select the faces of the model to be patterned. Note that the faces to be patterned should form a closed volume.

Direction 1

The options in the **Direction 1** rollout are used to specify parameters for creating a circular pattern in Direction 1 around a pattern axis. The options are discussed next.

Pattern Axis

The **Pattern Axis** field is used to select an axis around which you want to create a circular pattern. To do this, click on the **Pattern Axis** field, and then select an axis, a circular face, a circular edge, a linear edge, a linear sketch, or an angular dimension as the pattern axis, see Figure 9.30. This figure shows a preview of a circular pattern when a circular face is selected as the pattern axis. Note that in the case of selecting a circular face, a circular edge, or an angular dimension as the pattern axis, the respective center axis gets automatically determined and is used as the axis of the circular pattern. After selecting a pattern axis, a preview of the circular feature appears in the graphics area with a callout attached to the pattern axis, see Figure 9.30.

9.30

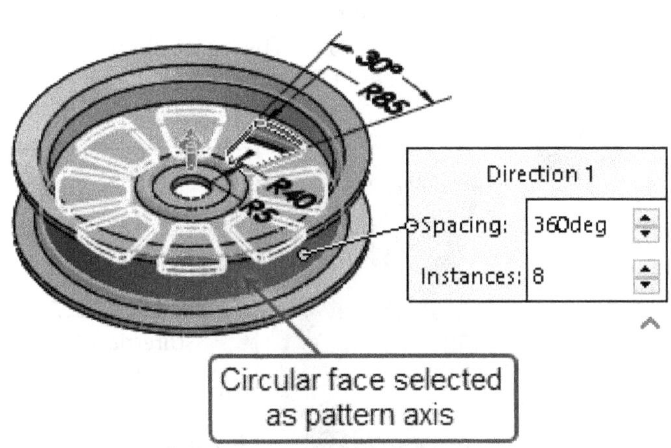

Angle

The **Angle** field is used to specify the angle value between pattern instances. You can also specify the angle between pattern instances by using the callout that appears in the graphics area. Note that if the **Equal spacing** radio button is selected in the rollout, then the angle value specified in the **Angle** field is considered as the total angle of the pattern and all pattern instances are arranged within the specified angle value with equal angular spacing among all instances. If the **Instance spacing** radio button is selected in the rollout, then the angle value specified in the **Angle** field is used as the angle between two pattern instances.

Number of Instances

The **Number of Instances** field is used to specify the number of instances to be created in the pattern. Figure 9.31 shows a preview of a circular pattern with 5 pattern instances. Note that the number of instances specified in this field also includes the parent or seed feature. You can also specify the number of instances in the callout that appears in the graphics area.

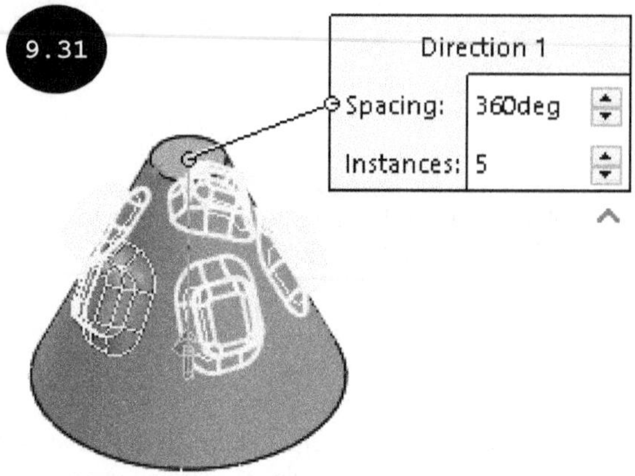

Reverse Direction

The **Reverse Direction** button is used to reverse the angle of rotation.

Direction 2

The options in the **Direction 2** rollout are used to specify parameters for creating a circular pattern in Direction 2 around the pattern axis, see Figure 9.32. This figure shows a preview of a circular pattern with 5 instances in Direction 1 and 2 instances in Direction 2.

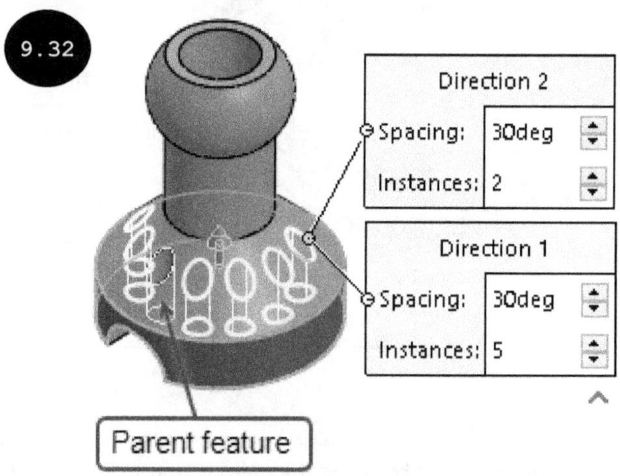

The options in the **Direction 2** rollout are the same as the options discussed in the **Direction 1** rollout of the PropertyManager except for the **Symmetric** check box, which is used for creating a circular pattern symmetrically, in both directions of the parent or seed feature.

The options in the remaining rollouts of the PropertyManager such as **Instances to Skip** and **Instances to Vary** are the same as those discussed while creating the linear pattern.

Creating a Curve Driven Pattern

Creating multiple instances of features, faces, or bodies along a curve is known as a curve driven pattern, see Figure 9.33. This figure shows a feature to be patterned, a closed sketch as the curve, and the resultant curve driven pattern. You can select a 2D/3D open or closed sketch, or an edge as the curve to drive the pattern instances.

9.33

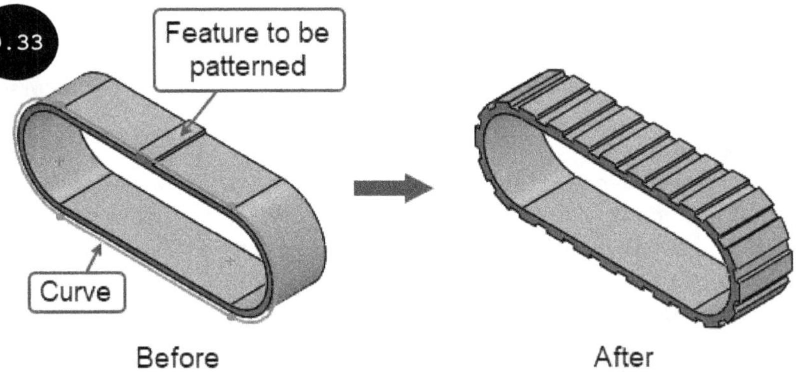

To create a curve driven pattern, click on the arrow at the bottom of the **Linear Pattern** tool. The **Pattern** flyout appears, see Figure 9.34. In this flyout, click on the **Curve Driven Pattern** tool. The **Curve Driven Pattern PropertyManager** appears, see Figure 9.35. The options in this PropertyManager are discussed next.

9.34

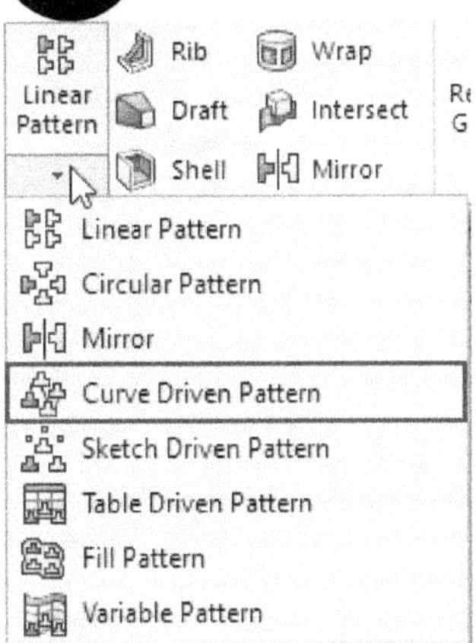

9.35

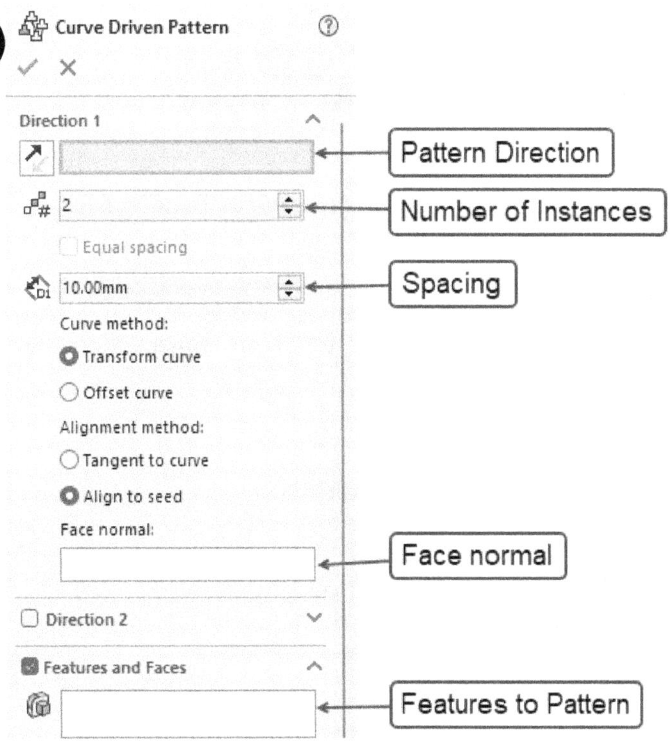

Features and Faces

The **Features and Faces** rollout of the PropertyManager is used to select features or faces to be patterned. To select the features to be patterned, click on the **Features to Pattern** field in this rollout and then select the features either from the graphics area or from the FeatureManager Design Tree. You can select features to be patterned before or after invoking the PropertyManager.

To select faces to be patterned, click on the **Faces to Pattern** field in the rollout and then select the faces in the graphics area. Note that faces to be patterned should form a closed volume.

Direction 1

The options in the **Direction 1** rollout are used to select a driving curve and for specifying parameters for creating a curve driven pattern in Direction 1. The options of this rollout are discussed below:

Pattern Direction

The **Pattern Direction** field is used to select a curve as the path for driving pattern instances. You can select a 2D/3D open or closed sketch, or an edge as the path for driving pattern instances. To do this, click on the **Pattern Direction** field and then select a curve from the graphics area. After selecting a curve, a preview of the curve-driven pattern appears in the graphics area with default parameters, see Figures 9.36 and 9.37. Figure 9.36 shows the preview of a curve-driven pattern in which a closed sketch is selected as the path for driving pattern instances and in Figure 9.37, an open sketch is selected as the path for driving pattern instances.

9.36

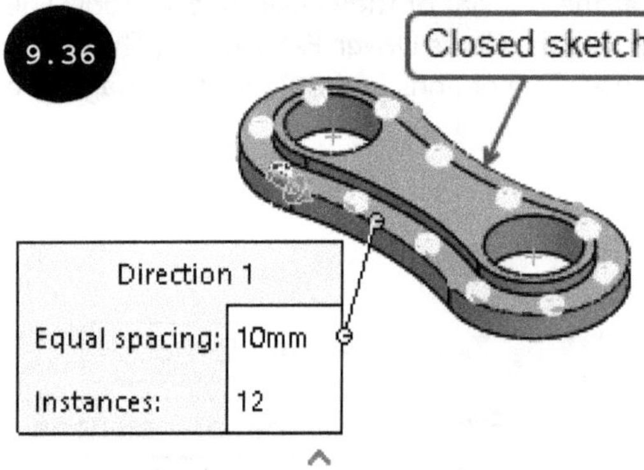

9.37

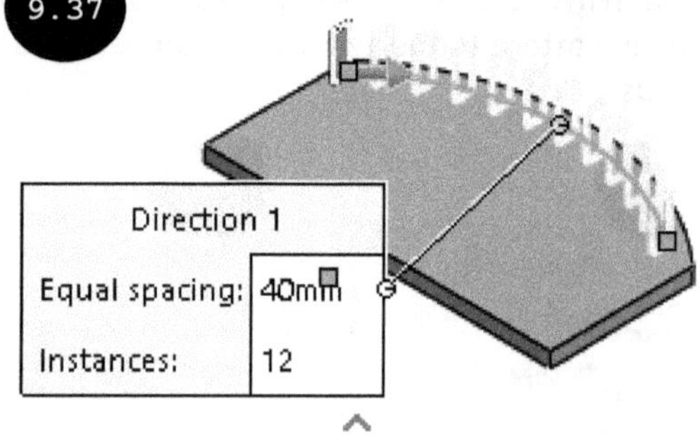

Note: If the sketch to be selected as the curve to drive pattern instances has multiple entities/segments, then it is recommended to select the sketch from the FeatureManager Design Tree.

Number of Instances

The **Number of Instances** field is used to specify the number of instances in a pattern.

Equal spacing

When the **Equal spacing** check box is selected, the spacing among all pattern instances is equally arranged in accordance with the total length of the curve selected. If you clear this check box, the **Spacing** field gets enabled, which is used for specifying the spacing between two pattern instances.

Reverse Direction

The **Reverse Direction** button is used to reverse the direction of the pattern.

Curve method

This area is used to select a method for transforming pattern instances along the curve, see Figure 9.38. The options in this area are discussed next.

9.38

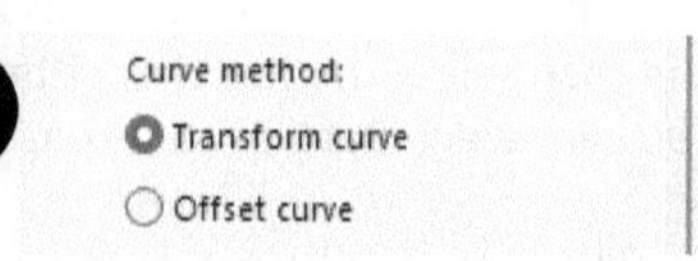

Transform curve: When the **Transform curve** radio button is selected, the delta X and delta Y distances between the parent feature and the origin of the curve are maintained by pattern instances, see Figure 9.39.

Offset curve: When the **Offset curve** radio button is selected, the normal distance between the parent feature and the origin of the curve is maintained by pattern instances, see Figure 9.40.

9.39

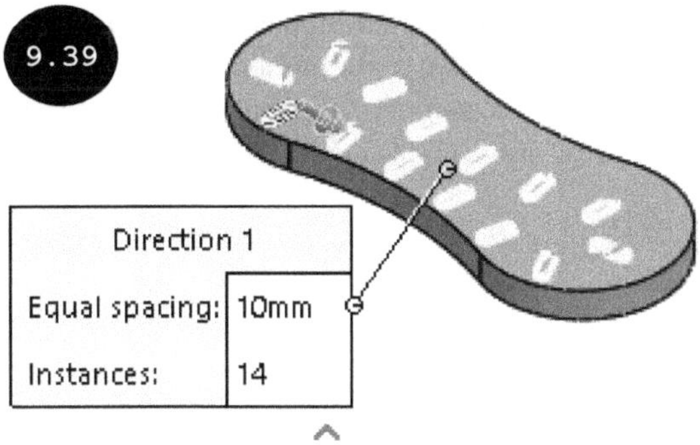

9.40

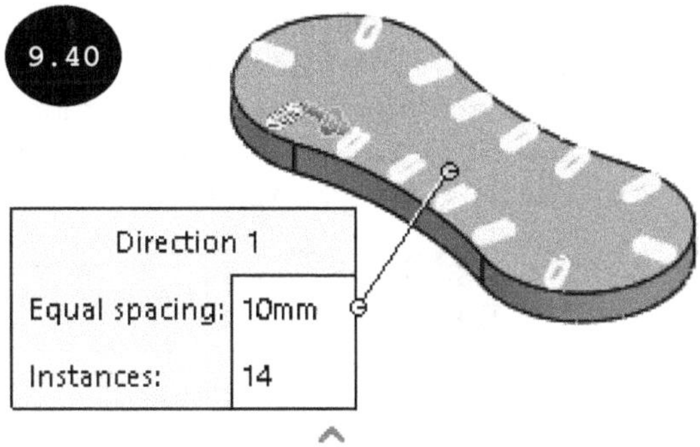

Note: The Transform curve method and the Offset curve method discussed above work in combination with the Alignment method (**Tangent to curve** or **Align to seed**), which is discussed next. In Figures 9.39 and 9.40, the **Tangent to curve** alignment method is selected.

Alignment method

This area is used to specify an alignment method for aligning instances along the curve, see Figure 9.41. The options in this area are discussed next.

9.41

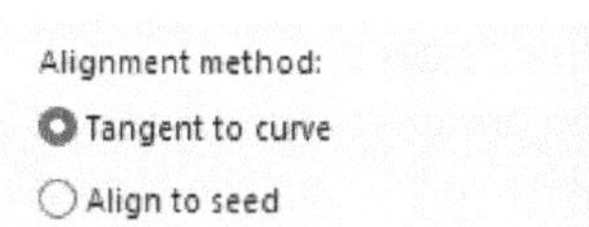

Tangent to curve: On selecting the **Tangent to curve** radio button, each pattern instance is aligned tangentially to the selected curve, see Figures 9.39 and 9.40.

Note: Figure 9.39 shows the preview of a curve driven pattern when the **Transform curve** and **Tangent to curve** radio buttons are selected and in Figure 9.40, the **Offset curve** and **Tangent to curve** radio buttons are selected.

Align to seed: On selecting the **Align to seed** radio button, each pattern instance is aligned to match the parent feature, see Figures 9.42 and 9.43.

9.42

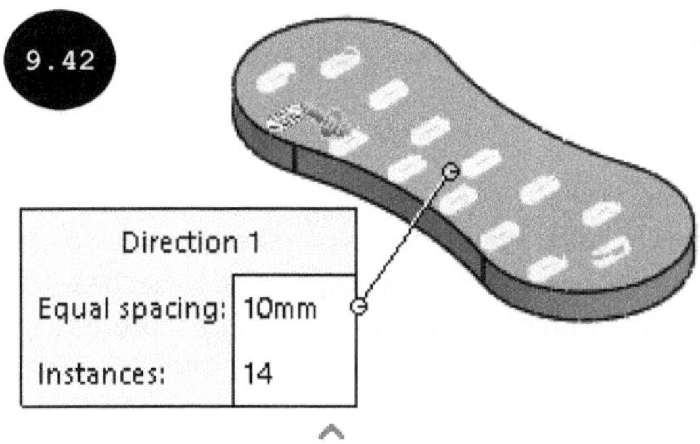

9.43

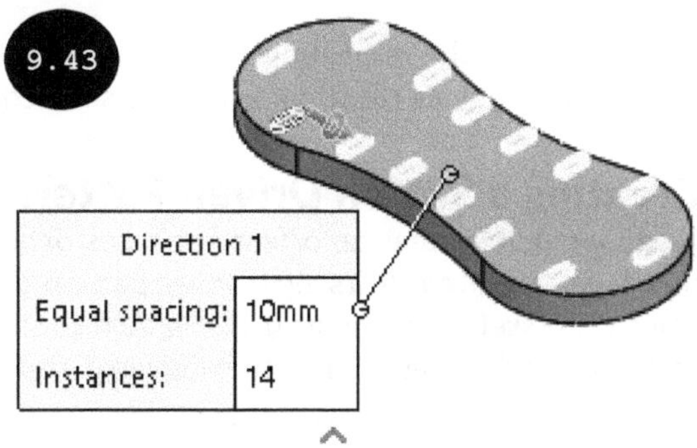

Note: Figure 9.42 shows the preview of a curve driven pattern when the **Transform curve** and **Align to seed** radio buttons are selected and in Figure 9.43, the **Offset curve** and **Align to seed** radio buttons are selected.

Face normal

The **Face normal** field of the **Direction 1** rollout is used to select a face, which is normal to the 3D curve selected as the path for driving instances, see Figure 9.44. Note that when you select a 3D curve as the path for driving pattern instances, you may need to select a face that is normal to the 3D curve. Figure 9.44 shows a feature to be patterned, a 3D curve (helix curve), a face normal, and the resultant curve-driven pattern.

9.44

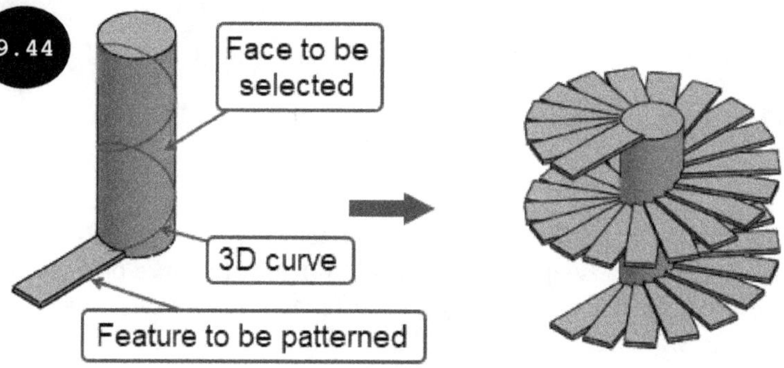

Direction 2

The options in the **Direction 2** rollout are used to create pattern instances in Direction 2. The options in this rollout are the same as those in the **Direction 1** rollout. Figure 9.45 shows a preview of a curve driven pattern in Direction 1 and Direction 2.

9.45

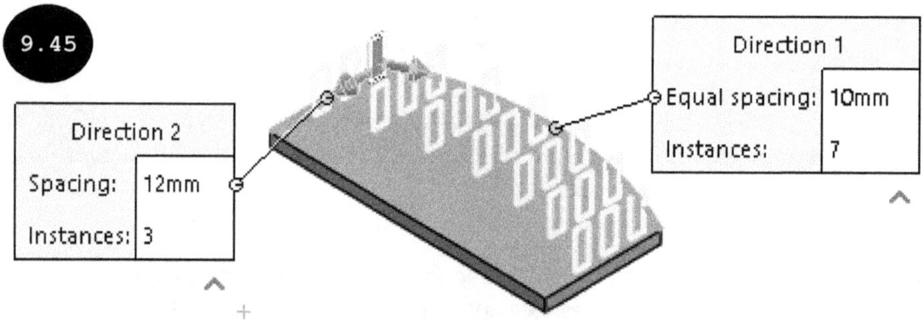

The options in the remaining rollouts such as **Bodies**, **Instances to Skip**, and **Options** of the PropertyManager are the same as those discussed earlier.

Creating a Sketch Driven Pattern

Creating multiple instances of features, faces, or bodies by using sketch points of a sketch is known as a sketch driven pattern. In a sketch driven pattern, the parent/seed feature is propagated to each sketch point of the sketch, see Figure 9.46. Figure 9.46 shows a sketch having multiple points, a feature to be patterned, and the resultant sketch-driven pattern.

9.46

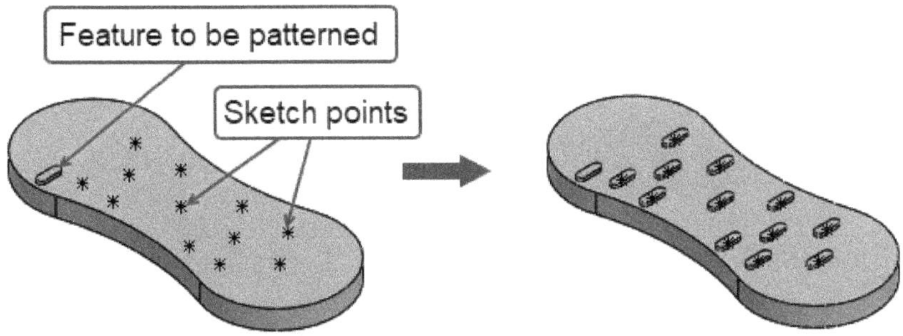

To create a sketch driven pattern, invoke the **Pattern** flyout and then click on the **Sketch Driven Pattern** tool. The **Sketch Driven Pattern PropertyManager** appears, see Figure 9.47. The options in the PropertyManager are discussed next.

9.47

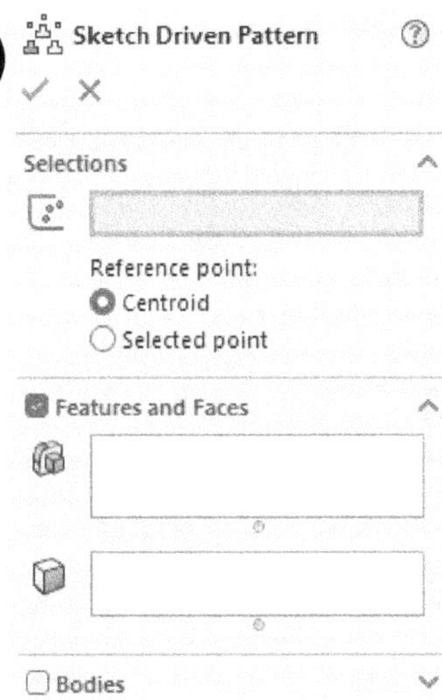

Features and Faces

The **Features and Faces** rollout of the PropertyManager is used to select the features or faces to be patterned. To select features to be patterned, click on the **Features to Pattern** field in this rollout and then select features either from the graphics area or the FeatureManager Design Tree. You can select features to be patterned before or after invoking the PropertyManager. To select the faces to be patterned, click on the **Faces to Pattern** field in the rollout and then select faces of a model that form a closed volume.

Selections

The options in the **Selections** rollout are used to select sketch points. The options are discussed below:

Reference Sketch

The **Reference Sketch** field is used to select a sketch having multiple points for driving the pattern instances. To do this, click on the **Reference Sketch** field to activate it and then select a sketch in the graphics area.

Centroid

By default, the **Centroid** radio button is selected. As a result, the centroid of the parent feature can be used as the base point for creating pattern instances and the center point of each pattern instance is coincident with the sketch point, see Figure 9.48.

9.48

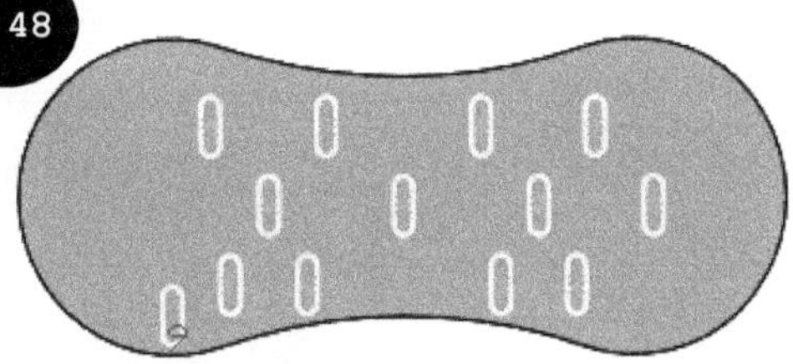

Selected point

On selecting the **Selected point** radio button, the **Reference Vertex** field appears in the rollout, which allows you to select a reference point as the base point for the pattern, see Figure 9.49.

9.49

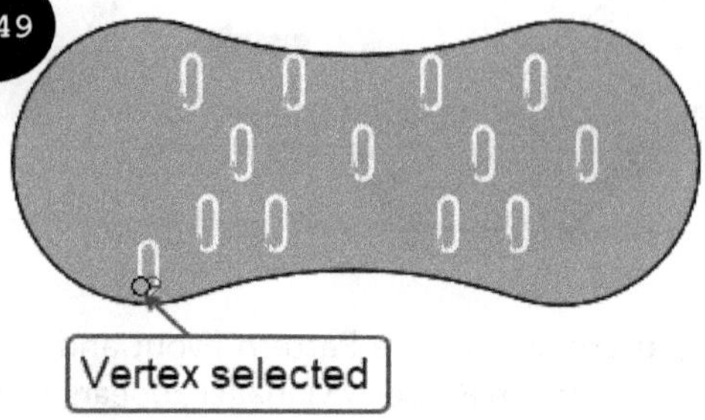

The options in the remaining rollouts such as **Bodies** and **Options** of the PropertyManager are the same as those discussed earlier.

Creating a Table Driven Pattern

A table-driven pattern is created by specifying coordinates (X, Y) for each pattern instance concerning a coordinate system. To create a table-driven pattern, you need to have a coordinate system created in the graphics area. You can create a coordinate system using the **Coordinate System** tool available in the **Reference Geometry** flyout, as discussed in Chapter 6. After creating a coordinate system, click on the **Table Driven Pattern** tool in the **Pattern** flyout. The **Table Driven Pattern** dialog box appears, see Figure 9.50. Most of the options in this dialog box are the same as those discussed earlier and the remaining options are discussed next.

9.50

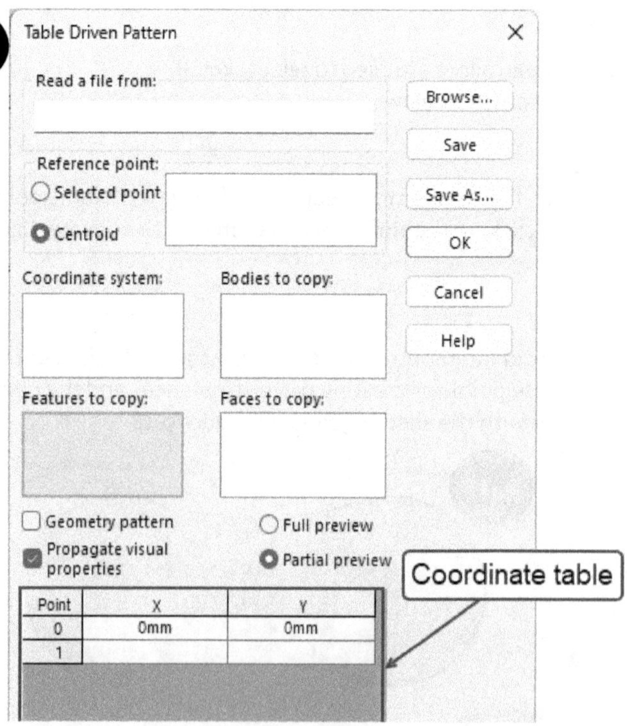

Features to copy

The **Features to copy** field is used to select features to be patterned. To do this, click on this field in the dialog box and then select features either from the graphics area or from the FeatureManager Design Tree.

Coordinate system

The **Coordinate system** field of the dialog box is used to select a coordinate system from the graphics area. Note that the origin of the selected coordinate system is used as the origin for the table-driven pattern. Figure 9.51 shows a feature to be patterned and a coordinate system.

9.51

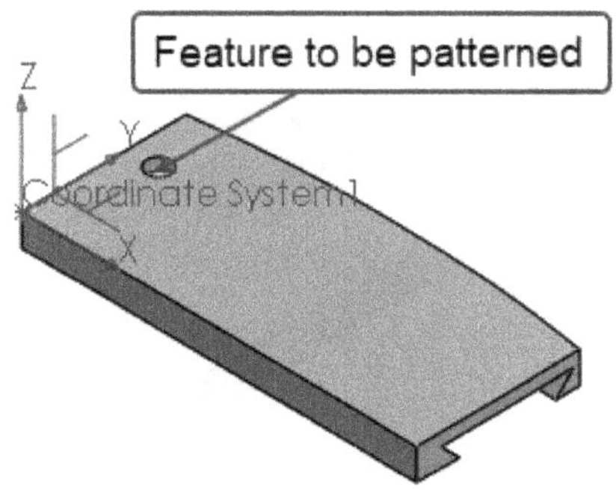

Coordinate table

The **Coordinate table** is available at the bottom of the **Table Driven Pattern** dialog box and is used to specify X and Y coordinates for each pattern instance concerning the selected coordinate system, see Figure 9.52. To specify the X coordinate of point 1 (first pattern instance), double-click on the **X** field corresponding to the **Point 1** field in the table. Similarly, specify the Y coordinate of point 1 (first pattern instance). Note that each row of this table represents a pattern instance, and its X and Y fields represent the coordinates of the pattern instance. You can add multiple rows in the table to specify the coordinates of multiple pattern instances. Note that a new row is added automatically in the table as soon as you double-click on a field of the last row in the table. Figure 9.52 shows the **Coordinate table** of the dialog box, in which the coordinates of 5 pattern instances, including the coordinates of the parent feature, are specified.

9.52

Point	X	Y
0	10mm	20mm
1	30mm	25mm
2	60mm	30mm
3	90mm	25mm
4	120mm	20mm
5		

Note: To delete a row in the table, select the row to be deleted and then press DELETE.

Save/Save As

The **Save/Save As** button is used to save the coordinates of the pattern instances specified in the table as an external *Pattern Table* file *(*.sldptab)* for later use.

Read a file from
The **Read a file from** field is used to import an existing *Pattern Table (*.sldptab)* or *Text Files (*.txt)* file containing coordinate points for creating a pattern. To create a pattern using an existing file, click on the **Browse** button. The **Open** dialog box appears. Select the *Pattern Table (*.sldptab)* or *Text Files (*.txt)* file and then click on the **Open** button. The coordinate points specified in the imported file get filled automatically in the **Coordinate table** of the dialog box.

OK
After specifying the parameters for creating the table-driven pattern, click on the **OK** button in the dialog box. Figure 9.53 shows the table-driven pattern created by specifying coordinates shown in Figure 9.52.

9.53

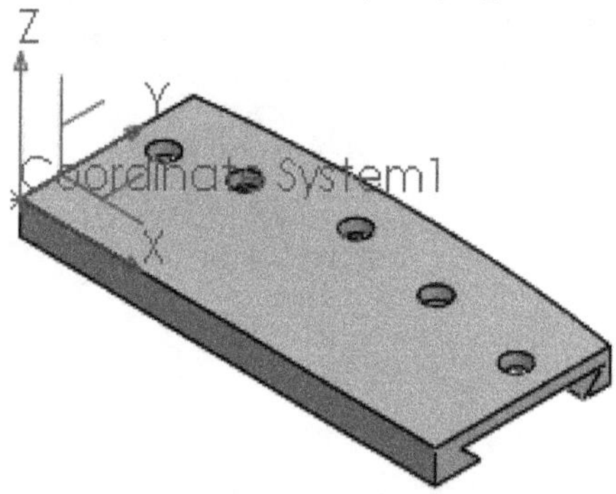

Creating a Fill Pattern
A fill pattern is created by populating an area with pattern instances. In the fill pattern, you can create multiple instances of features, faces, bodies, or a predefined cut shape by filling in a particular area of a model. To define an area to be filled in with pattern instances, you can select the face of a model or a closed sketch, see Figures 9.54 and 9.55. Figure 9.54 shows a feature to be patterned, a face to be filled, and the resultant fill pattern. Figure 9.55 shows the feature to be patterned, a closed sketch to be filled, and the resultant fill pattern.

9.54

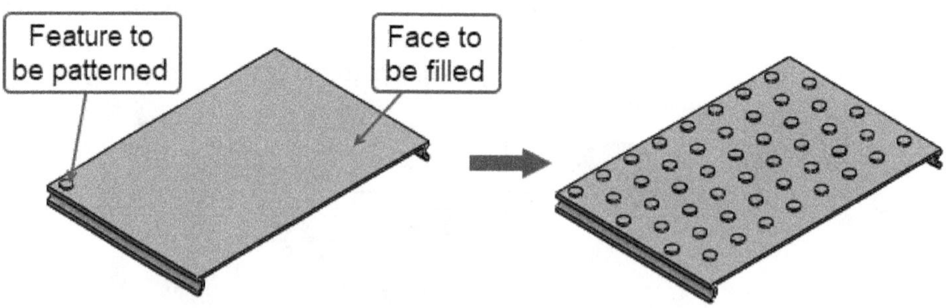

9.55

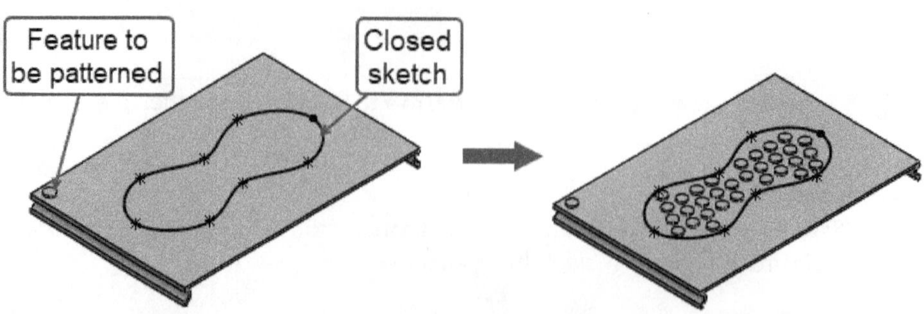

To create a fill pattern, invoke the **Pattern** flyout and then click on the **Fill Pattern** tool. The **Fill Pattern PropertyManager** appears, see Figure 9.56. The options in the PropertyManager are discussed next.

9.56

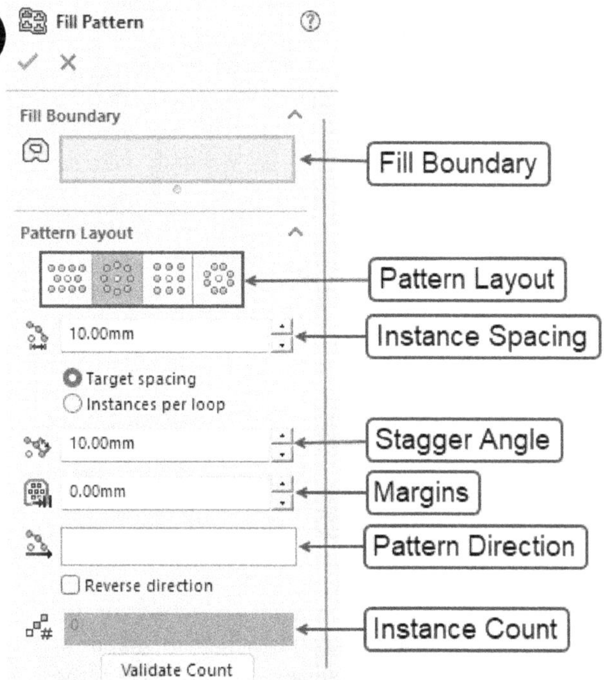

Fill Boundary

By default, the **Fill Boundary** field is activated in the **Fill Boundary** rollout of the PropertyManager. As a result, you are prompted to select a boundary to be filled in with pattern instances. You can select a face or a closed sketch as the boundary to be filled.

Features and Faces

The **Features and Faces** rollout of the PropertyManager is used to select features, faces, or a predefined cut shape to be patterned. By default, the **Selected features** radio button is selected in the rollout, see Figure 9.57. As a result, the **Features to Pattern** field is enabled. Click on this field to activate it and then select features to be patterned. After specifying a boundary to be filled and a feature to be patterned, a preview of the filled pattern appears in the graphics area, see Figure 9.58. In this figure, a face is selected as the boundary.

9.57

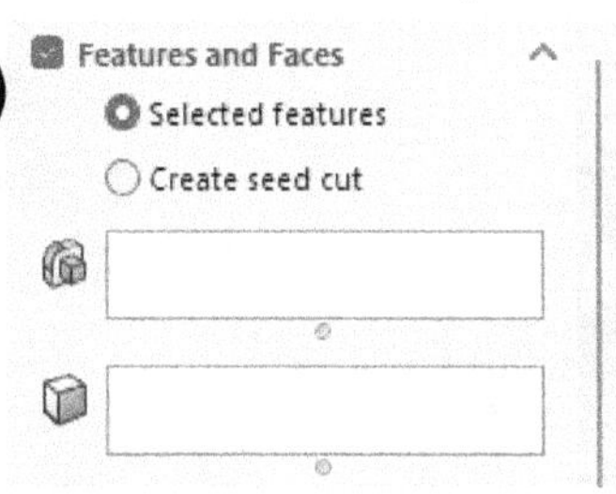

9.58

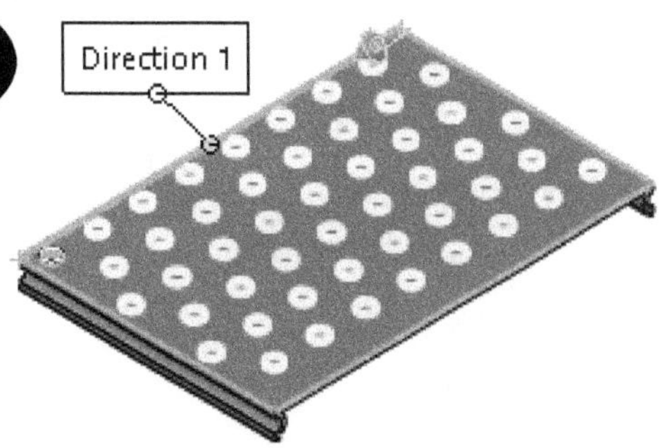

To select the faces to be patterned, click on the **Faces to Pattern** field of the rollout and then select faces to be patterned. Note that the faces to be patterned should form a closed volume.

On selecting the **Create seed cut** radio button in the **Features and Faces** rollout, different types of predefined cut shape buttons appear in the rollout, see Figure 9.59. By default, the **Circle** button is selected. As a result, the selected boundary is filled in with predefined circular cut features, see Figure 9.60. You can specify the required diameter for the predefined circular cut feature by using the **Diameter** field of the rollout. The **Vertex or Sketch Point** field is used for defining the center of the parent or seed feature. You can select a vertex or a sketch point to define the center of the parent feature. On doing so, the pattern starts from the defined center of the parent feature. Note that if you do not define the center of the parent feature, then the pattern will start from the center of the boundary face that is selected to be filled.

9.59

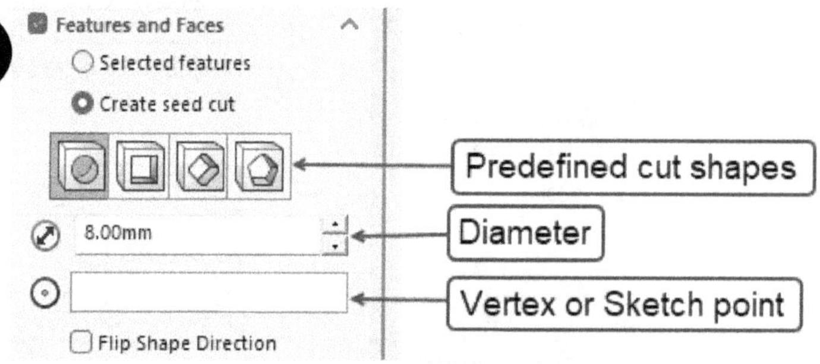

You can select circular, square, diamond, or polygon predefined cut shape by clicking on the respective buttons in the rollout, see Figures 9.60 through 9.63. The **Flip Shape Direction** check box in this rollout is used to reverse the direction of the seed feature on either side of the face selected as the boundary to be filled in the **Fill Boundary** field of the PropertyManager.

9.60

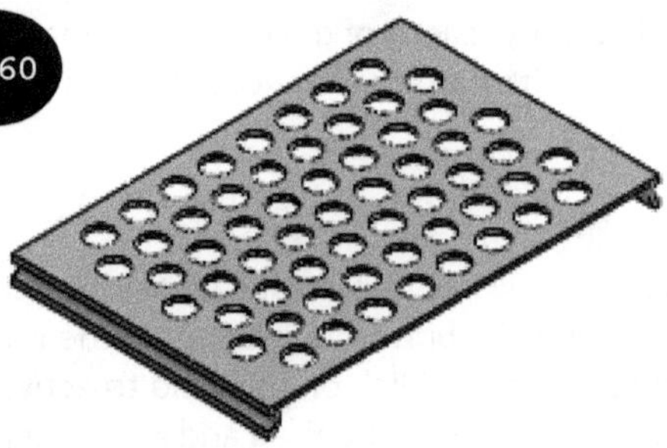

9.61

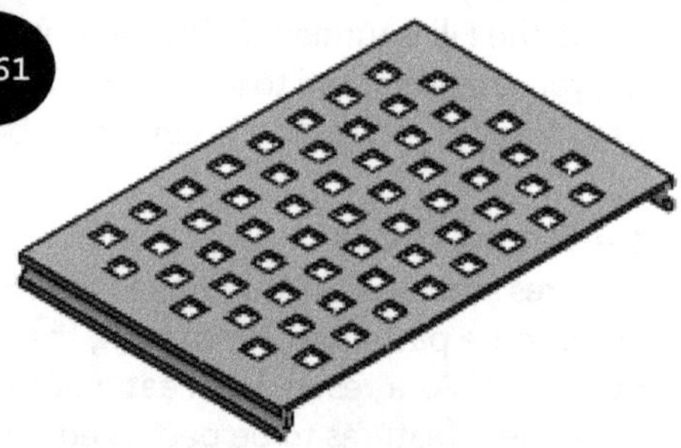

9.62

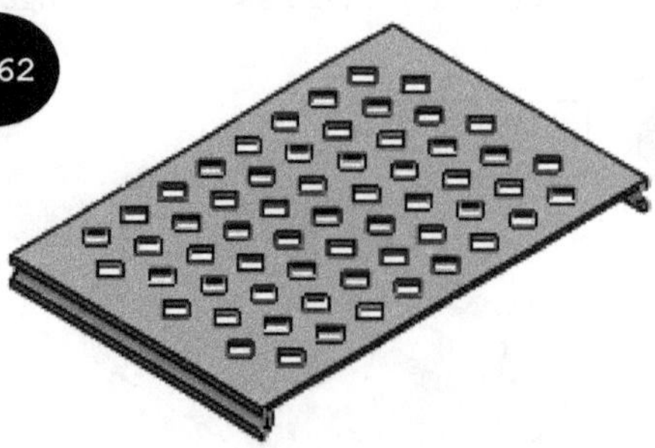

9.63

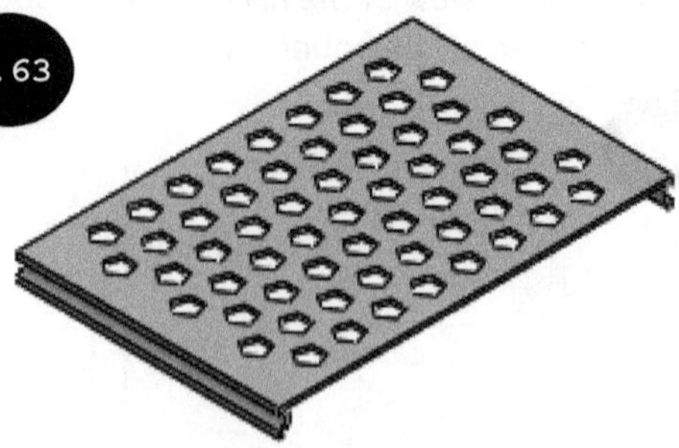

Pattern Layout

The options in the **Pattern Layout** rollout are used to select the type of layout for the fill pattern. You can select the **Perforation**, **Circular**, **Square**, or **Polygon** button to define the type of layout to be used for the fill pattern, see Figures 9.64 through 9.67.

9.64

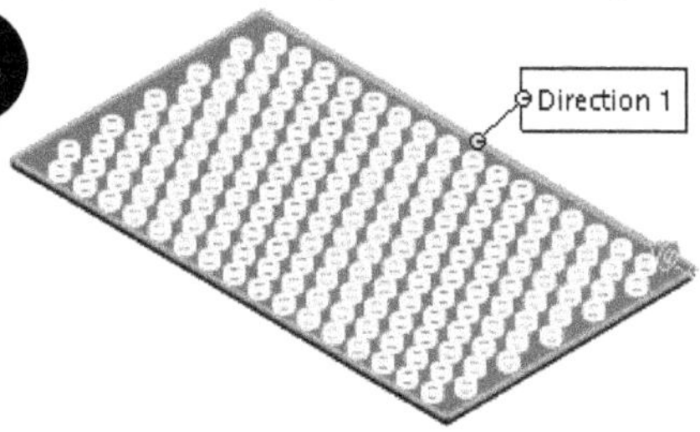

Perforation layout

9.65

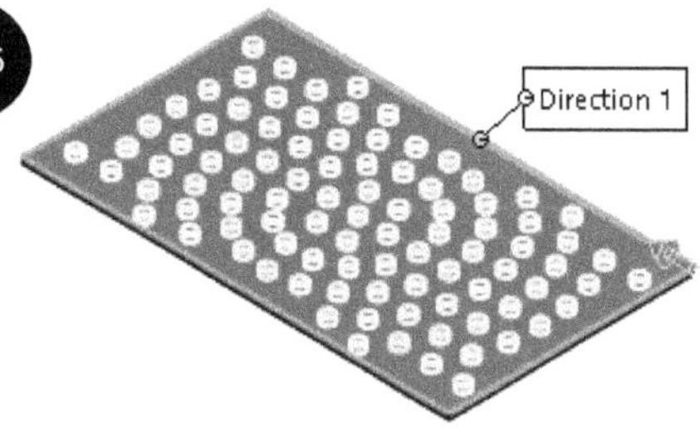

Circular layout

9.66

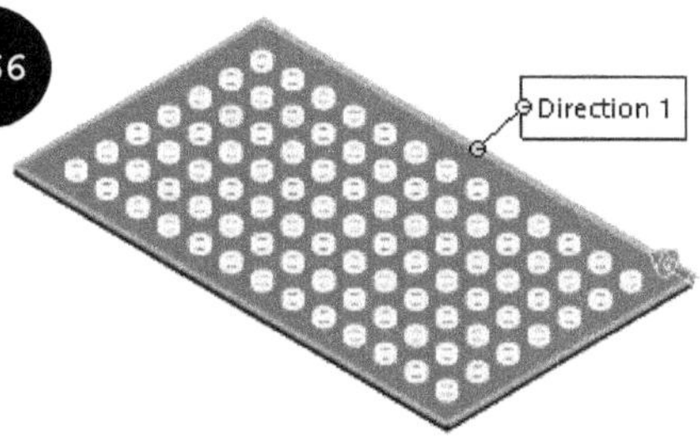

Square layout

9.67

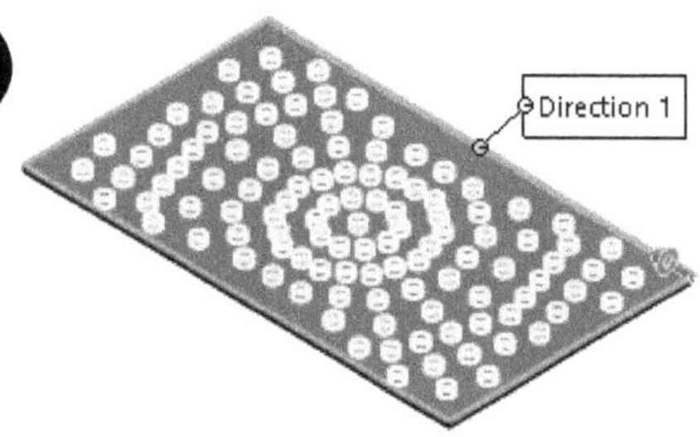

Polygon layout

You can use the remaining options of the **Pattern Layout** rollout to control the parameters of the pattern layout such as spacing between pattern instances, margin between the fill boundary and the outermost instance, and pattern direction.

Note: On selecting a face as the boundary of the fill pattern, the pattern direction is automatically selected and a preview of the pattern appears in the graphics area. However, on selecting a closed sketch as the boundary of the fill pattern, you may need to select a pattern direction. You can select a linear edge or a sketch entity as the pattern direction.

Creating a Variable Pattern

In SOLIDWORKS, you can create a variable pattern using the **Variable Pattern** tool of the **Pattern** flyout. This tool is used for creating a variable pattern such that you can vary dimensions and reference geometries of a feature, see Figure 9.68. In this figure, a variable pattern has been created by varying the length and angle of the slot feature.

9.68

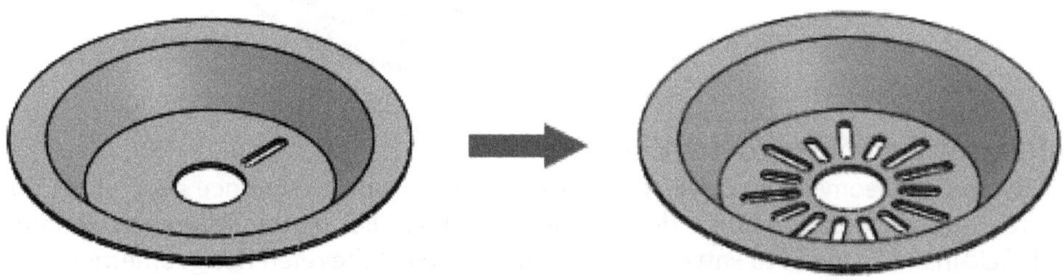

To create a variable pattern, invoke the **Pattern** flyout and then click on the **Variable Pattern** tool. The **Variable Pattern PropertyManager** appears, see Figure 9.69. The options in this PropertyManager are discussed next.

9.69

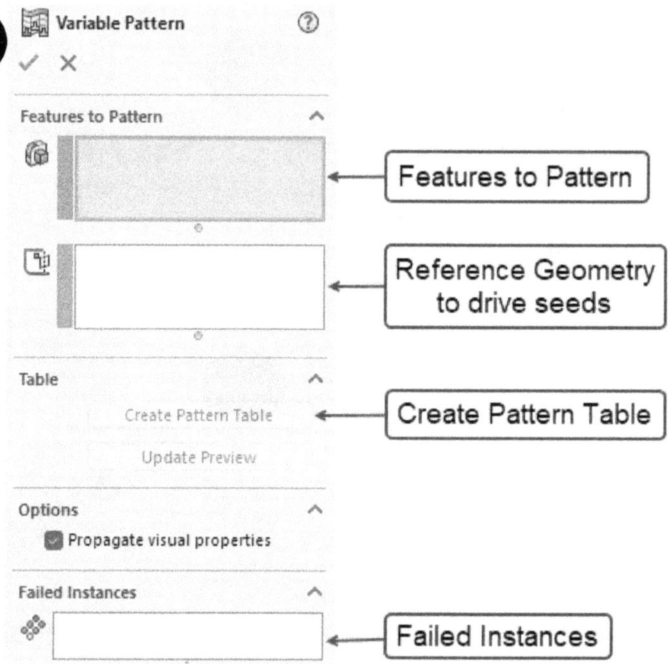

Features to Pattern

The **Features to Pattern** field is used to select features to be patterned. By default, this field is activated. As a result, you can select features to be patterned either from the graphics area or from the FeatureManager Design Tree. You can select extruded, cut extruded, revolved, cut revolved, sweep, cut sweep, lofted, cut lofted, fillet, chamfer, dome, and draft features as the features to be patterned for creating a variable pattern. Once you select a feature to be patterned, the respective dimensions appear in the graphics area so that you can select the dimensions to be varied in the pattern, see Figure 9.70.

9.70

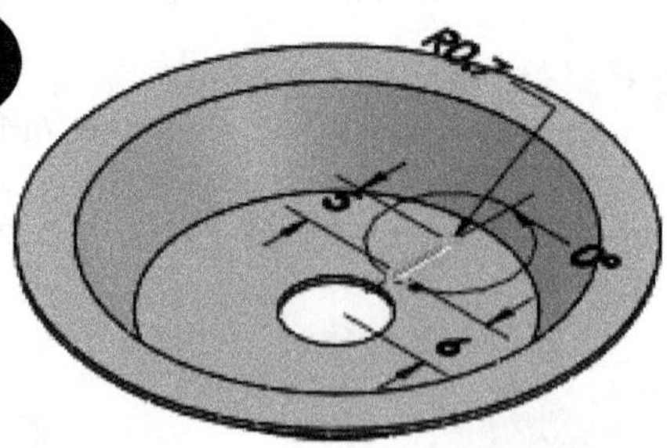

Reference Geometry to drive seeds

The **Reference Geometry to drive seeds** field is used to select reference geometries on which the selected seed or parent feature is dependent. To do this, click on the **Reference Geometry to drive seeds** field in the **Features to Pattern** rollout and then select the reference geometries. After selecting reference geometries, the respective dimensions of the selected geometries appear in the graphics area so that you can select them as the dimensions to be varied. You can select the axis, plane, point, curve, 2D sketch, or 3D sketch as reference geometries. Figure 9.71 shows an extruded feature that is selected as the feature to be patterned as well as the respective reference geometries (a plane and a 3D point) selected on which the extruded feature is dependent. Note that the extruded feature shown in the figure has been created on a non-planar face of the model with the help of a reference plane and a 3D point.

9.71

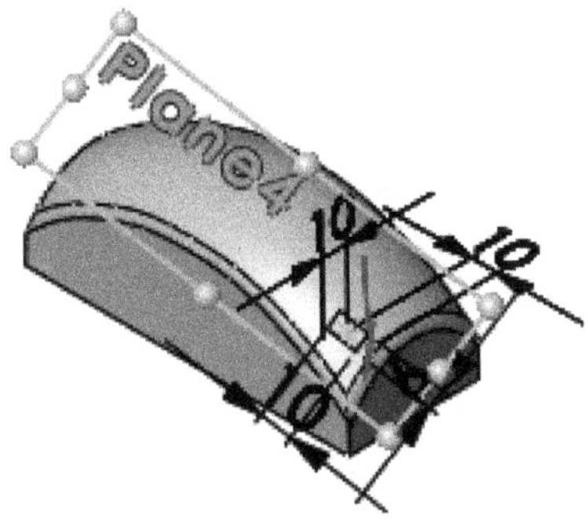

Create Pattern Table

The **Create Pattern Table** button of the PropertyManager is used to invoke the **Pattern Table** dialog box. The **Pattern Table** dialog box is used to select the dimensions of the features and reference geometries to be varied. Once the **Pattern Table** dialog box has been invoked, you can select the dimensions to be varied. Once you select the dimensions to be varied, the selected dimensions get listed in the **Pattern Table** dialog box, see Figure 9.72. In this figure, the angle and length dimensions of the slot feature of the model shown in Figure 9.70 are selected as the dimensions to be varied.

9.72

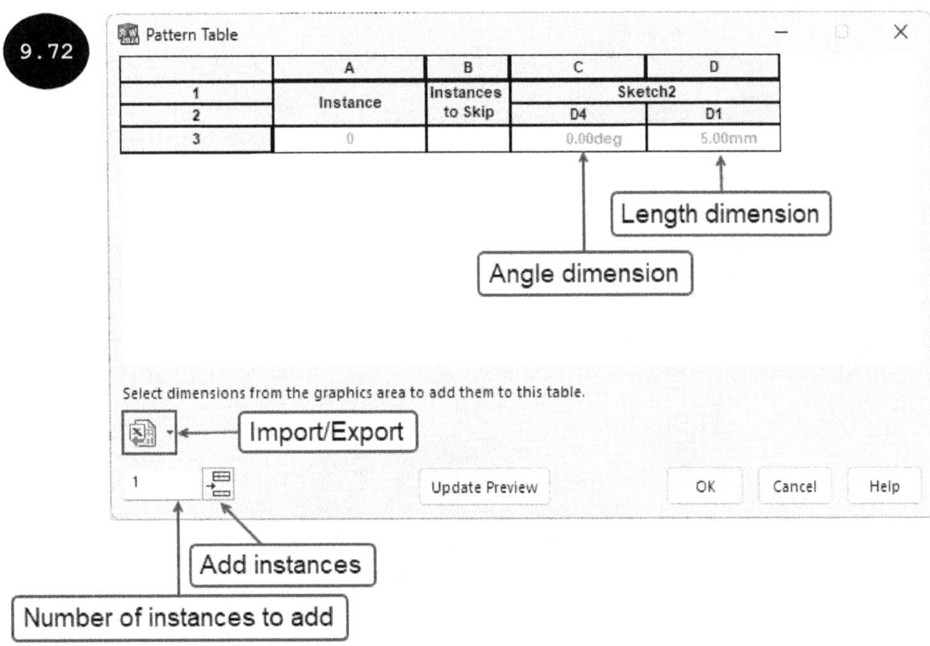

The **Number of instances to add** field of the **Pattern Table** dialog box is used to enter the number of instances to be created. After specifying the number of instances in this field, click on the **Add instances**

button in the dialog box. Multiple rows equivalent to the number of instances specified are added in the **Pattern Table** dialog box, see Figure 9.73. Note that each row of this dialog box represents a pattern instance. You can modify the dimensions for each pattern instance by entering the required dimension values in the respective fields of the dialog box, see Figure 9.73. This dialog box works in the same way as that of *Microsoft Office Excel*.

9.73

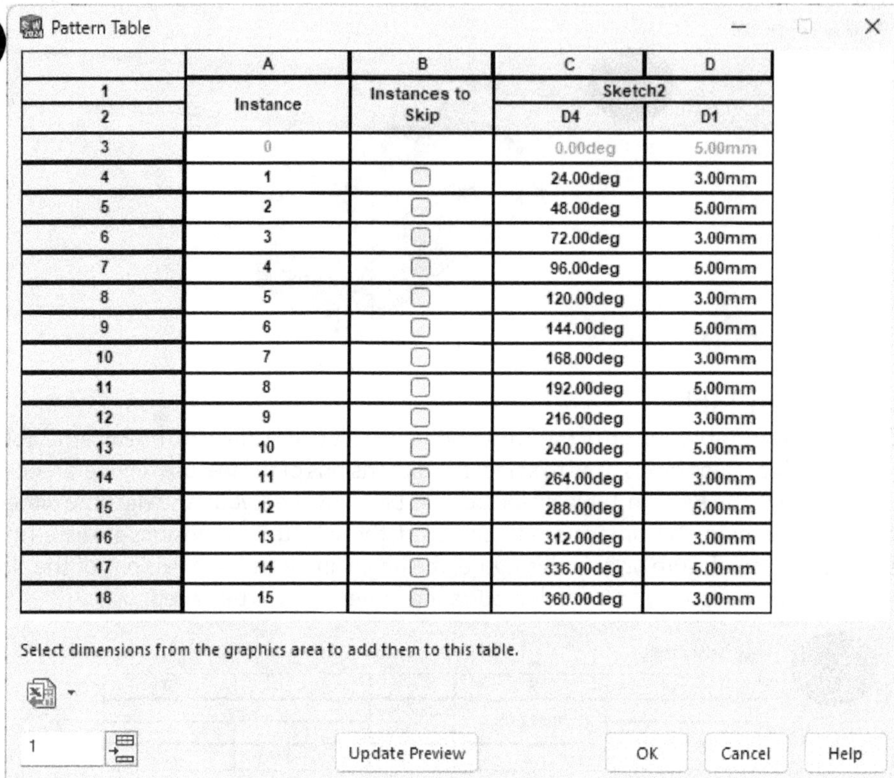

	A	B	C	D
1	Instance	Instances to Skip	Sketch2	
2			D4	D1
3	0		0.00deg	5.00mm
4	1	☐	24.00deg	3.00mm
5	2	☐	48.00deg	5.00mm
6	3	☐	72.00deg	3.00mm
7	4	☐	96.00deg	5.00mm
8	5	☐	120.00deg	3.00mm
9	6	☐	144.00deg	5.00mm
10	7	☐	168.00deg	3.00mm
11	8	☐	192.00deg	5.00mm
12	9	☐	216.00deg	3.00mm
13	10	☐	240.00deg	5.00mm
14	11	☐	264.00deg	3.00mm
15	12	☐	288.00deg	5.00mm
16	13	☐	312.00deg	3.00mm
17	14	☐	336.00deg	5.00mm
18	15	☐	360.00deg	3.00mm

After modifying the dimension values in the dialog box for each pattern instance, click on the **Update Preview** button. This button is used for updating the preview of pattern instances in the graphics area. You can also import an Excel file (**.xlsx*) containing variable dimensions of pattern instances by using the **Import from Excel** option in the dialog box. The **Export to Excel** option of the dialog box is used for saving the variable dimensions as an external Excel file for later use. After specifying variable dimensions for all pattern instances, click on the **OK** button. A variable pattern is created, see Figure 9.74.

9.74

Mirroring Features/Faces/Bodies

In SOLIDWORKS, you can mirror features, faces, or bodies about mirroring plane(s) by using the **Mirror** tool. You can select a plane or a planar face of the model as the mirroring plane. Figure 9.75 shows features to be mirrored, mirroring plane, and the resultant mirror feature created.

9.75

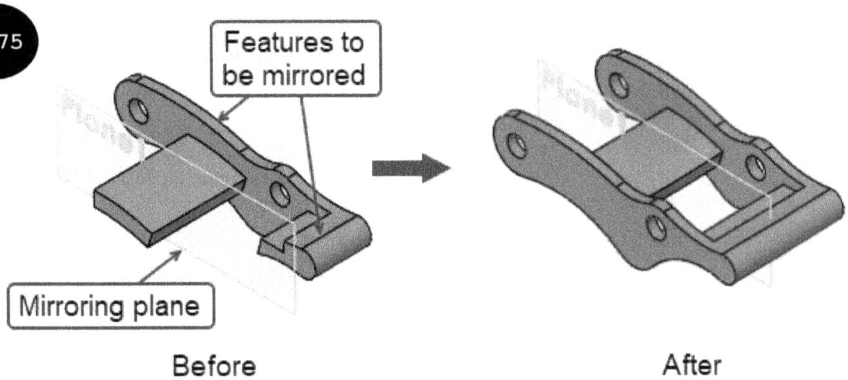

To create a mirror feature, click on the **Mirror** tool in the **Features CommandManager**. The **Mirror PropertyManager** appears, see Figure 9.76. You can also invoke the **Mirror** tool from the **Pattern** flyout. The options in the **Mirror PropertyManager** are discussed next.

9.76

Mirror Face/Plane

The **Mirror Face/Plane** field is used to select a mirroring plane. By default, this field is activated. As a result, you can select a plane or a planar face of the model in the graphics area as the mirroring plane for mirroring the selected features, refer to Figure 9.77.

Secondary Mirror Face/Plane

In SOLIDWORKS, you can also select a secondary mirroring plane to mirror selected features. This secondary plane is optional and works in addition to the primary mirroring plane selected earlier in the **Mirror Face/Plane** field. To select a secondary mirroring plane, ensure that the **Secondary Mirror Face/Plane** field is activated and then select a plane or a planar face as the secondary mirroring plane, refer to Figure 9.77.

Mirror seed only

On selecting the **Mirror seed only** check box, the mirror feature is created such that only the selected seed or parent feature gets mirrored about the secondary mirroring plane. Note that this check box is enabled only if the secondary mirroring plane is selected and is perpendicular to the mirroring plane selected in the **Mirror Face/Plane** field, refer to Figure 9.77.

Features to Mirror

The **Features to Mirror** field is used to select one or more features to be mirrored. To do this, click on this field and then select one or more features either from the graphics area or from the FeatureManager Design Tree. After selecting the mirroring plane(s) and the features to be mirrored, the preview of the mirror feature appears in the graphics area, see Figure 9.77. In this figure, the preview of a mirror feature appears after selecting both the mirroring planes. Also, the **Mirror seed only** check box is cleared. As discussed earlier, the selection of a secondary mirroring plane is optional for creating a mirror feature.

9.77

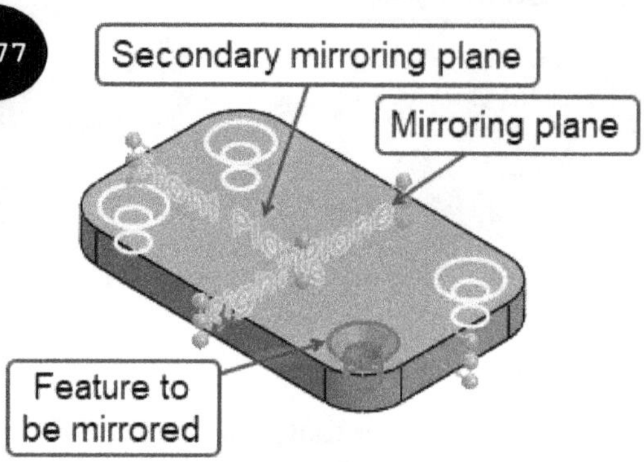

Faces to Mirror and Bodies to Mirror

The **Faces to Mirror** and **Bodies to Mirror** rollouts of the PropertyManager are used to select faces and bodies to be mirrored, respectively. Note that faces to be mirrored should form a closed volume and make up a feature.

Options

The options in the **Options** rollout are the same as those discussed earlier while creating patterns. By default, the **Geometry Pattern** check box is cleared in this rollout. The resultant mirror feature maintains the same geometrical relations as the parent feature. Figure 9.78 shows the front view of a model having a cut feature in the 'hidden lines visible' display style. This cut feature is created by defining its end condition as 4 mm offset from the bottom face of the model by using the **Offset from Surface** option. Figure 9.79 shows the resultant mirror feature created by clearing the **Geometry Pattern** check box and Figure 9.80 shows the resultant mirror feature created by selecting the **Geometry Pattern** check box.

9.78

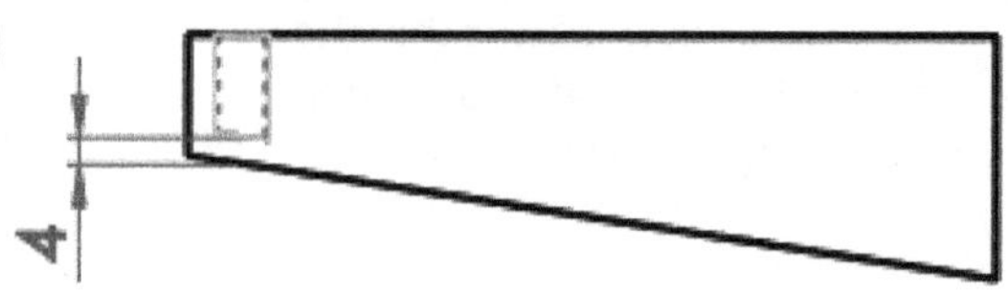

9.79

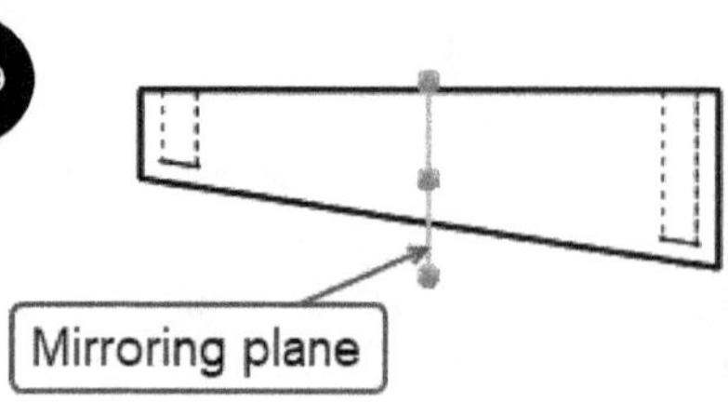

9.80

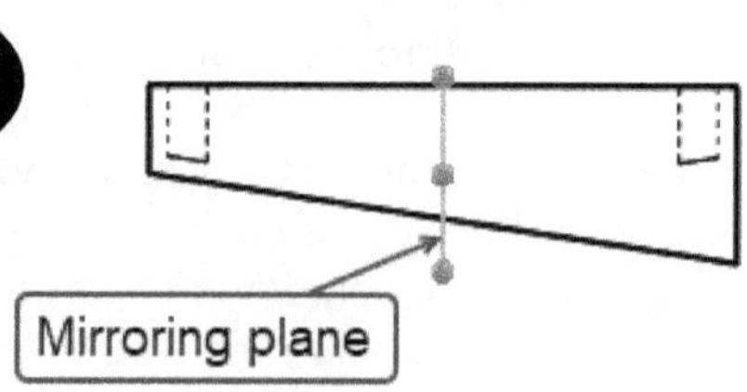

By default, the **Propagate visual properties** check box is selected in the **Options** rollout. As a result, all the visual properties such as colors, textures, and cosmetic thread of the parent feature are propagated to the resultant mirror feature.

Tutorial 1

Create a model, as shown in Figure 9.81. All dimensions are in mm.

9.81

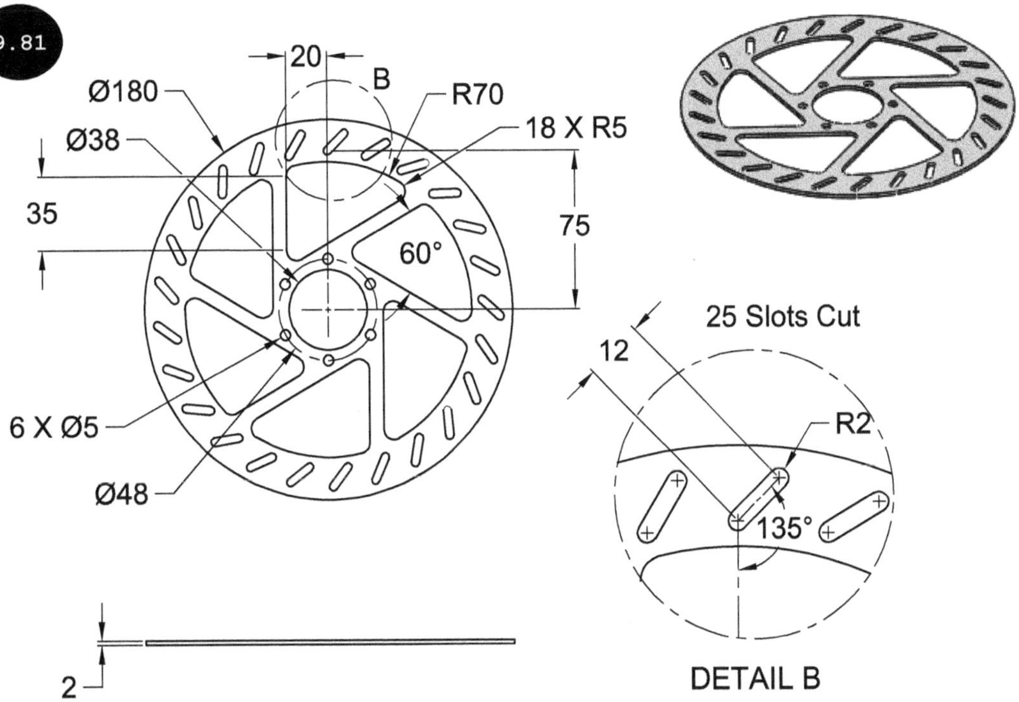

Section 1: Invoking the Part Modeling Environment

1. Start SOLIDWORKS and then click on the **Part** button in the **Welcome** dialog box. The Part modeling environment gets invoked.

Note: If SOLIDWORKS is already open and the **Welcome** dialog box does not appear on the screen, then you can invoke the same by clicking on the **Welcome to SOLIDWORKS** tool in the **Standard** toolbar.

Section 2: Specifying Unit Settings

1. Ensure that the **MMGS (millimeter, gram, second)** unit system is selected as the current unit system for the opened part document, see Figure 9.82.

Section 3: Creating the Base Feature - Extruded Feature

1. Invoke the Sketching environment by selecting the Top plane as the sketching plane.

2. Create the sketch of the base feature of the model, see Figure 9.83. After creating the sketch, do not exit the Sketching environment.

9.82

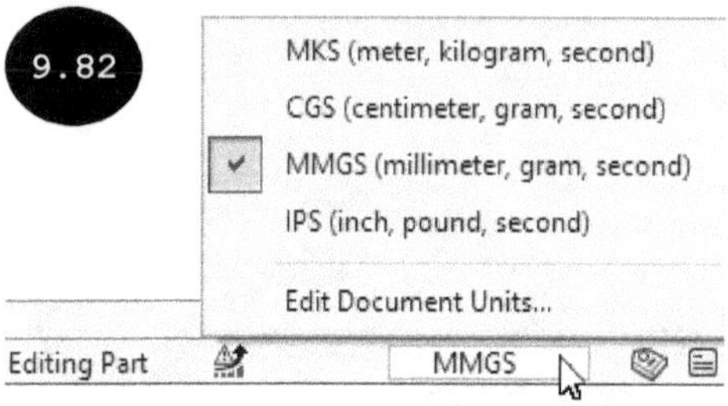

9.83

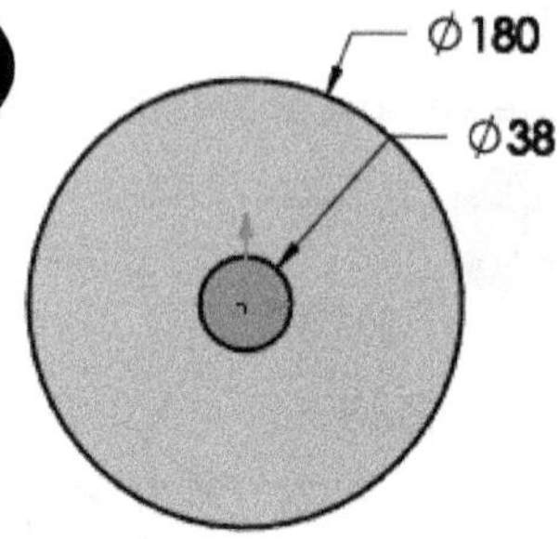

3. Click on the **Features** tab in the CommandManager to display the tools of the **Features CommandManager**.

4. Click on the **Extruded Boss/Base** tool. The **Boss-Extrude PropertyManager** and a preview of the extruded feature appear.

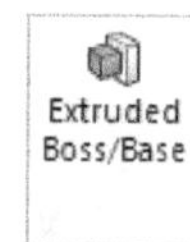

5. Enter **2** in the **Depth** field of the **Direction 1** rollout and then press ENTER.

6. Click on the green tick-mark ✓ in the PropertyManager. The extruded feature is created, see Figure 9.84.

Section 4: Creating the Second Feature - Extruded Cut Feature

1. Invoke the Sketching environment by selecting the top planar face of the base feature as the sketching plane. The model gets oriented normal to the viewing direction.

2. Create a sketch of the second feature, see Figure 9.85. After creating the sketch, do not exit the Sketching environment.

9.84

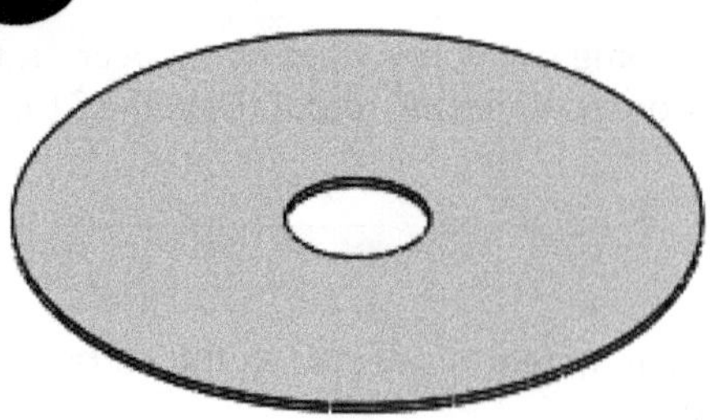

9.85

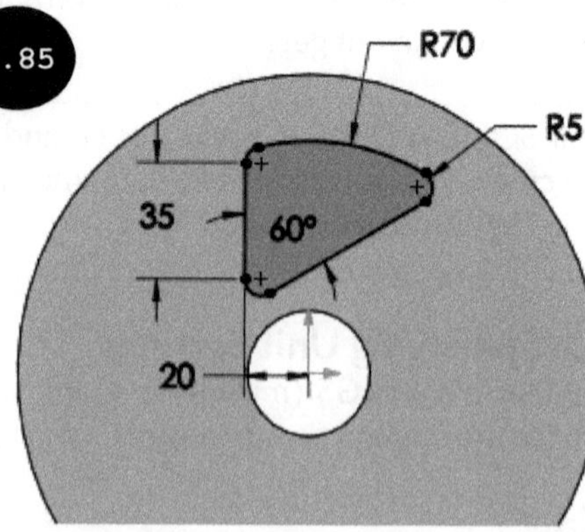

Tip: To fully define the sketch shown in Figure 9.85, you need to apply coincident relation between the center point of the arc of radius 70 mm and the origin.

3. Click on the **Features** tab in the CommandManager to display the tools of the **Features CommandManager**.

4. Click on the **Extruded Cut** tool in the **Features CommandManager**. The **Cut-Extrude PropertyManager** and a preview of the extruded cut feature appear. Next, change the orientation of the model to isometric.

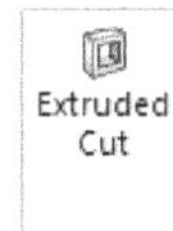

5. Invoke the **End Condition** drop-down list in the **Direction 1** rollout and then select the **Through All** option in it.

6. Click on the green tick-mark ✓ in the PropertyManager. The extruded cut feature is created, see Figure 9.86.

9.86

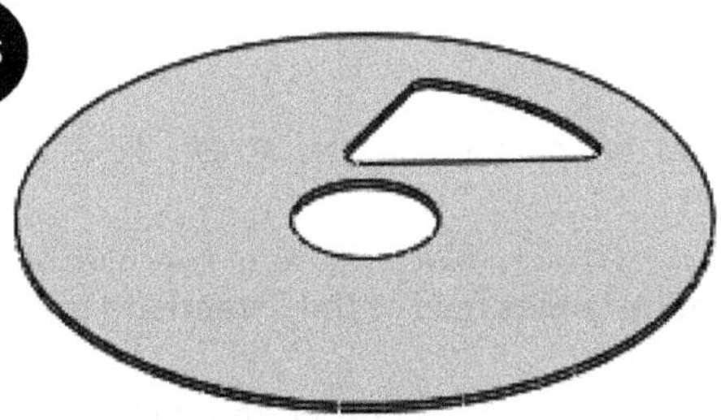

Section 5: Creating the Third Feature - Circular Pattern

1. Click on the arrow at the bottom of the **Linear Pattern** tool. The **Pattern** flyout appears, see Figure 9.87.

2. Click on the **Circular Pattern** tool in the **Pattern** flyout, see Figure 9.87. The **CirPattern PropertyManager** appears.

9.87

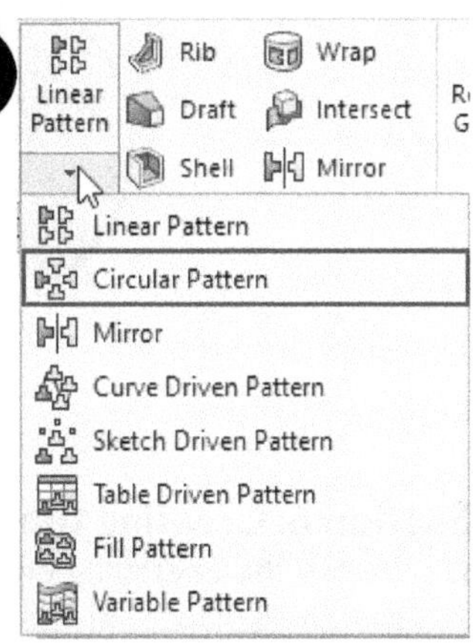

3. Expand the FeatureManager Design Tree, which is now available in the top left corner of the graphics area, by clicking on the arrow in front of it.

4. Click on the second feature (extruded cut) in the FeatureManager Design Tree as the feature to be patterned.

5. Click on the **Pattern Axis** field in the **Direction 1** rollout of the PropertyManager to activate it.

6. Click on the circular edge of the base feature to define the pattern axis, see Figure 9.88. A preview of the circular pattern appears, see Figure 9.88.

9.88

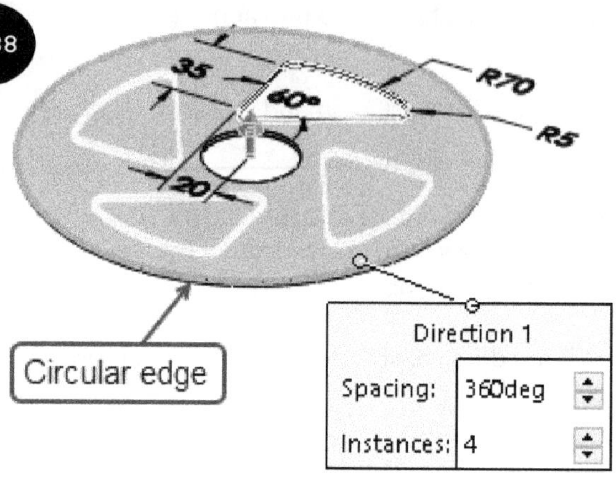

7. Ensure that the **Equal spacing** radio button is selected in the **Direction 1** rollout of the PropertyManager.

8. Ensure that **360** degrees is specified in the **Angle** field of the **Direction 1** rollout in the PropertyManager.

9. Enter **6** in the **Number of Instances** field of the **Direction 1** rollout.

10. Click on the green tick-mark ✓ in the PropertyManager. The circular pattern is created, see Figure 9.89.

9.89

Section 6: Creating the Fourth Feature - Extruded Cut Feature

1. Invoke the Sketching environment by selecting the top planar face of the base feature as the sketching plane. The model gets oriented normal to the viewing direction.

2. Create a sketch of the fourth feature of the model, see Figure 9.90. Do not exit the Sketching environment.

9.90

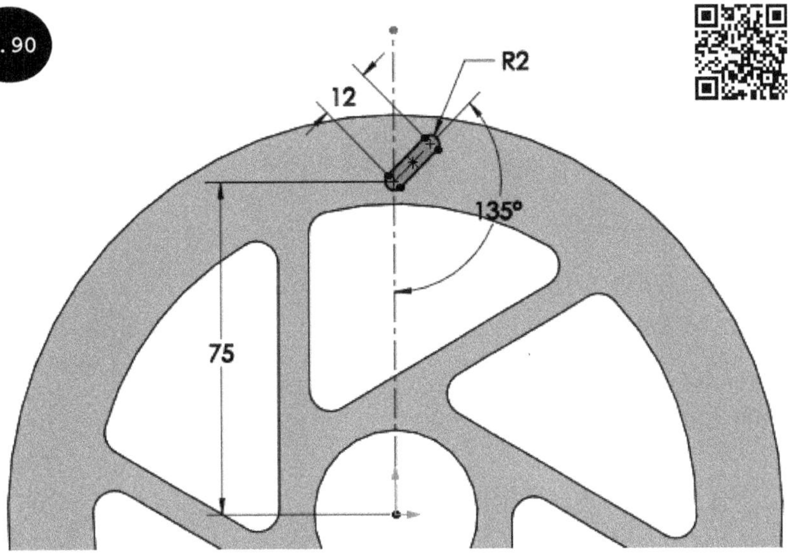

3. Click on the **Features** tab in the CommandManager and then click on the **Extruded Cut** tool. The **Cut-Extrude PropertyManager** and a preview of the extruded cut feature appear. Next, change the orientation of the model to isometric.

4. Invoke the **End Condition** drop-down list in the **Direction 1** rollout of the PropertyManager and then select the **Through All** option in it.

5. Click on the green tick-mark in the PropertyManager. The extruded cut feature is created, see Figure 9.91.

9.91

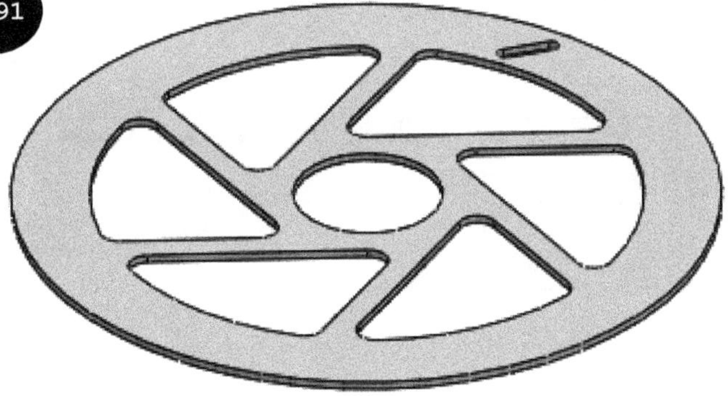

Section 7: Creating the Fifth Feature - Circular Pattern

1. Click on the arrow at the bottom of the **Linear Pattern** tool. The **Pattern** flyout appears, see Figure 9.92.

2. Click on the **Circular Pattern** tool in the **Pattern** flyout. The **CirPattern PropertyManager** appears.

3. Expand the FeatureManager Design Tree, which is now available in the top left corner of the graphics area, by clicking on the arrow in front of it.

4. Click on the fourth feature (previously created extruded cut feature) in the FeatureManager Design Tree as the feature to be patterned.

5. Click on the **Pattern Axis** field in the **Direction 1** rollout of the PropertyManager to activate it.

6. Click on the circular edge of the base feature to define the pattern axis. A preview of the circular pattern appears, see Figure 9.93.

9.92

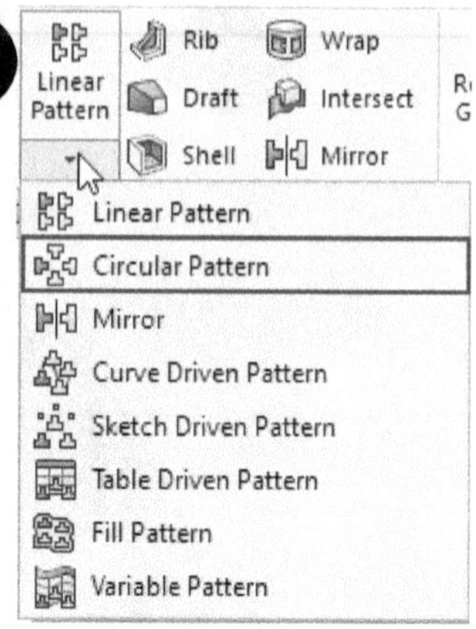

7. Ensure that the **Equal spacing** radio button is selected in the **Direction 1** rollout of the PropertyManager. Also, ensure that **360** degrees is specified in the **Angle** field of the **Direction 1** rollout.

8. Enter **25** in the **Number of Instances** field of the **Direction 1** rollout.

9. Click on the green tick-mark ✓ in the PropertyManager. The circular pattern is created, see Figure 9.94.

9.93

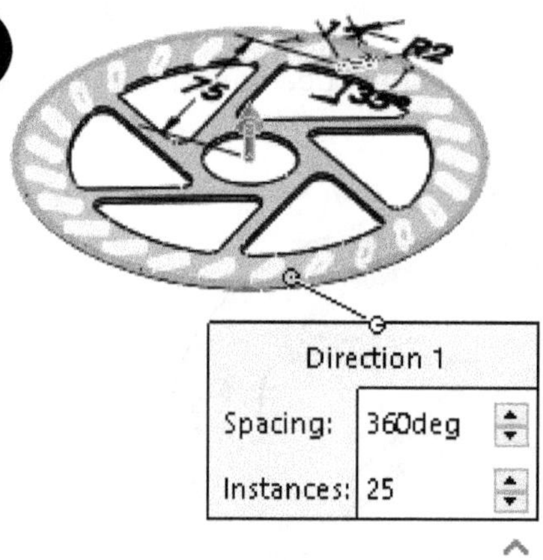

9.94

Section 8: Creating the Sixth Feature - Extruded Cut Feature

1. Invoke the Sketching environment by selecting the top planar face of the base feature as the sketching plane. The model gets oriented normal to the viewing direction.

2. Create a sketch of the sixth feature (circle of diameter 5 mm), see Figure 9.95. Do not exit the Sketching environment.

9.95

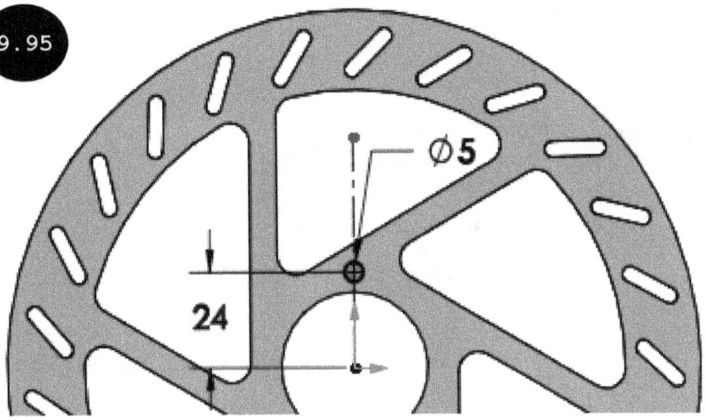

3. Click on the **Features** tab in the CommandManager and then click on the **Extruded Cut** tool. The **Cut-Extrude PropertyManager** and a preview of the extruded cut feature appear. Next, change the orientation of the model to isometric.

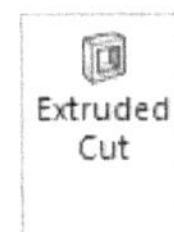

4. Select the **Through All** option in the **End Condition** drop-down list of the **Direction 1** rollout.

5. Click on the green tick-mark ✓ in the PropertyManager. The extruded cut feature is created, see Figure 9.96.

9.96

Section 9: Creating the Seventh Feature - Circular Pattern

1. Invoke the **Pattern** flyout and then click on the **Circular Pattern** tool. The **CirPattern PropertyManager** appears.

2. Expand the FeatureManager Design Tree, which is now available in the top left corner of the graphics area, by clicking on the arrow in front of it.

3. Click on the sixth feature (previously created extruded cut feature) from the FeatureManager Design Tree as the feature to be patterned.

4. Click on the **Pattern Axis** field in the **Direction 1** rollout of the PropertyManager.

5. Click on the circular edge of the base feature to define the pattern axis. A preview of the circular pattern appears, see Figure 9.97.

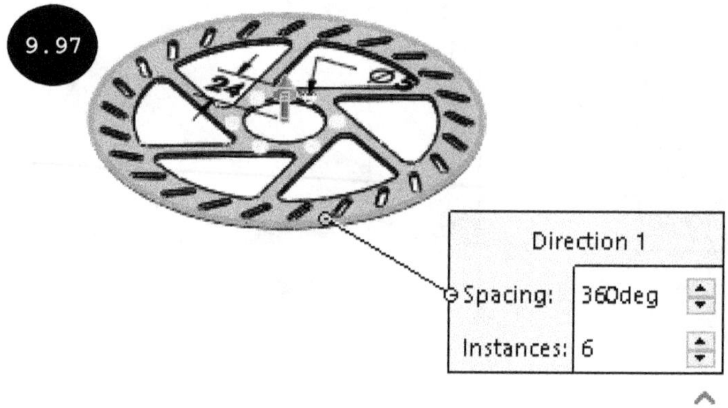

6. Ensure that the **Equal spacing** radio button is selected in the **Direction 1** rollout.

7. Ensure that **360** degrees is specified in the **Angle** field of the **Direction 1** rollout in the PropertyManager.

8. Enter **6** in the **Number of Instances** field of the **Direction 1** rollout.

9. Click on the green tick-mark in the PropertyManager. A circular pattern is created, see Figure 9.98.

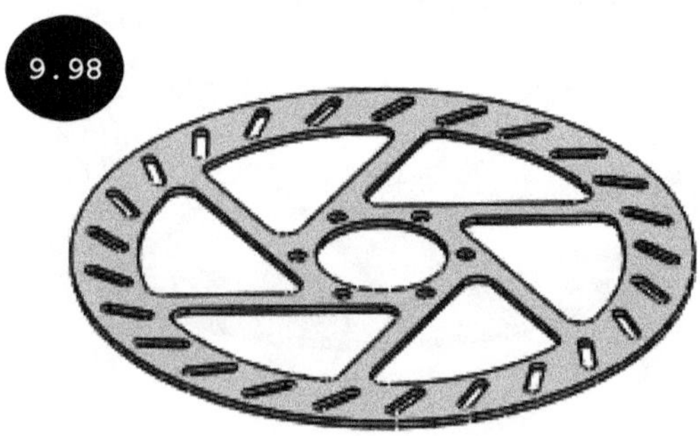

Section 10: Saving the Model

1. Click on the **Save** tool in the **Standard** toolbar. The **Save As** window appears.

2. Browse to the SOLIDWORKS folder and then create a folder with the name Chapter 9.

3. Enter **Tutorial 1** in the **File name** field of the dialog box and then click on the **Save** button. The model is saved with the name Tutorial 1 in the Chapter 9 folder.

Tutorial 2

Create a model, as shown in Figure 9.99. The different views and dimensions are given in the same figure. All dimensions are in mm.

9.99

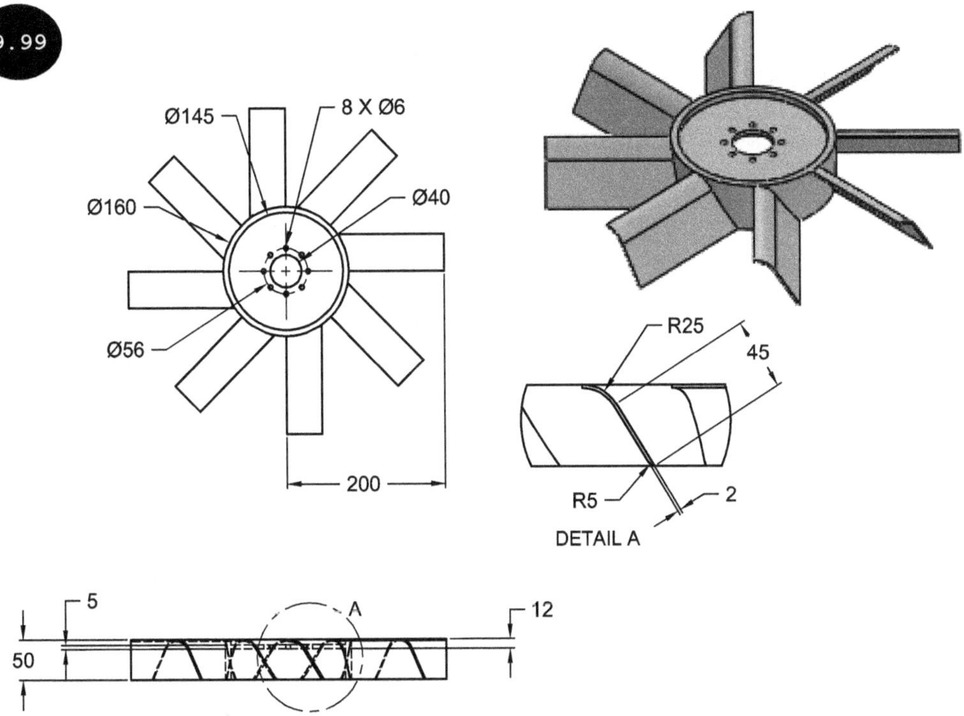

Section 1: Invoking the Part Modeling Environment

1. Start SOLIDWORKS and then invoke the Part modeling environment.

   Once the Part modeling environment is invoked, you need to set the unit system and create the base/first feature of the model.

Section 2: Specifying Unit Settings

1. Ensure that the **MMGS (millimeter, gram, second)** unit system is set for the currently opened part document.

Section 3: Creating the Base Feature - Extruded Feature

1. Invoke the Sketching environment by selecting the Top plane as the sketching plane.

2. Create a sketch of the base feature of the model, see Figure 9.100. After creating the sketch, do not exit the Sketching environment.

3. Click on the **Features** tab in the CommandManager. The tools of the **Features CommandManager** are displayed.

4. Click on the **Extruded Boss/Base** tool. The **Boss-Extrude PropertyManager** and a preview of the extruded feature appear.

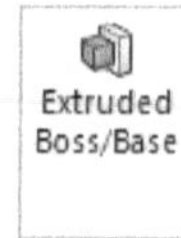

5. Invoke the **End Condition** drop-down list in the **Direction 1** rollout of the PropertyManager.

6. Select the **Mid Plane** option in the **End Condition** drop-down list.

7. Enter **50** in the **Depth** field of the **Direction 1** rollout and then press ENTER.

8. Click on the green tick-mark ✓ in the PropertyManager. The extruded feature is created, see Figure 9.101.

9.100

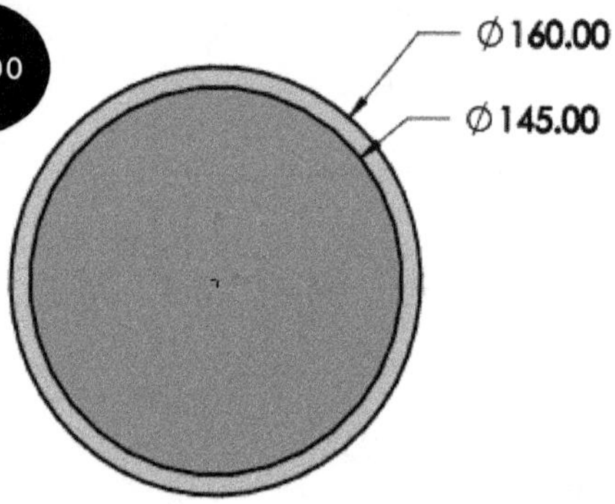

9.101

Section 4: Creating the Second Feature - Extruded Feature

1. Invoke the Sketching environment by selecting the top planar face of the base feature as the sketching plane. The model gets oriented normal to the viewing direction.

2. Create a sketch (two circles of diameter 145 mm and 40 mm) of the second feature, see Figure 9.102. After creating the sketch, do not exit the Sketching environment.

3. Click on the **Extruded Boss/Base** tool in the **Features CommandManager**. The **Boss-Extrude PropertyManager** and a preview of the extruded feature appear. Next, change the orientation of the model to isometric.

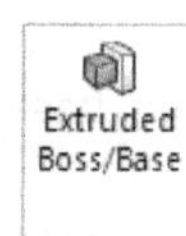

4. Invoke the **Start Condition** drop-down list in the **From** rollout of the PropertyManager, see Figure 9.103.

9.102

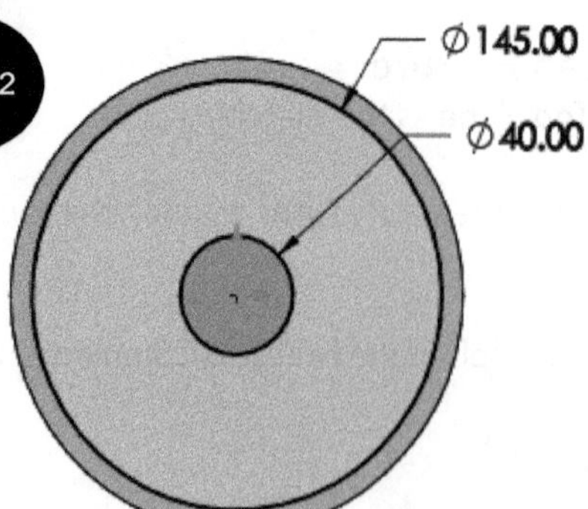

9.103

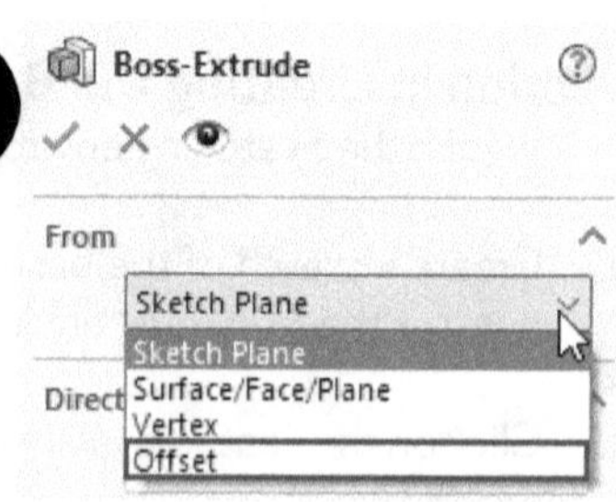

5. Select the **Offset** option in the **Start Condition** drop-down list of the **From** rollout.

6. Enter **12** in the **Enter Offset Value** field of the **From** rollout in the PropertyManager.

7. Click on the **Reverse Direction** button in the **From** rollout to reverse the direction of material addition downward.

8. Ensure that the **Blind** option is selected in the **End Condition** drop-down list of the **Direction 1** rollout.

9. Enter **5** in the **Depth** field of the **Direction 1** rollout in the PropertyManager.

10. Click on the green tick-mark in the PropertyManager. The extruded feature is created, see Figure 9.104.

9.104

Section 5: Creating the Third Feature - Extruded Cut Feature

1. Invoke the Sketching environment by selecting the top planar face of the second feature (previously created extruded feature) as the sketching plane. The model gets oriented normal to the viewing direction.

2. Create a circle of diameter 6 mm as the sketch of the third feature, see Figure 9.105. Do not exit the Sketching environment.

9.105

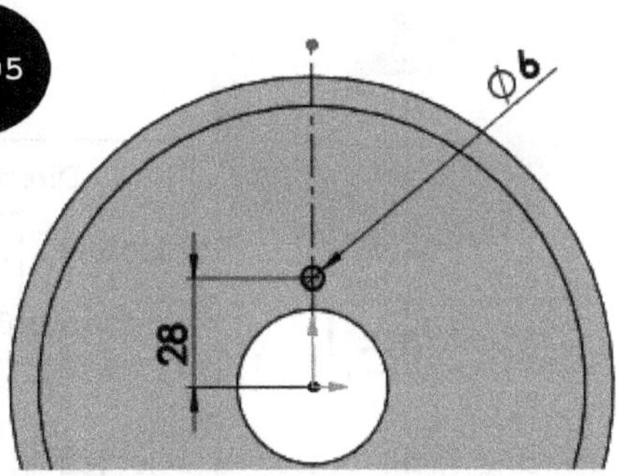

3. Click on the **Features** tab in the CommandManager and then click on the **Extruded Cut** tool. The **Cut-Extrude PropertyManager** and a preview of the extruded cut feature appear. Next, change the orientation of the model to isometric.

4. Invoke the **End Condition** drop-down list of the **Direction 1** rollout and then select the **Through All** option.

5. Click on the green tick-mark ✓ in the PropertyManager. The extruded cut feature is created, see Figure 9.106.

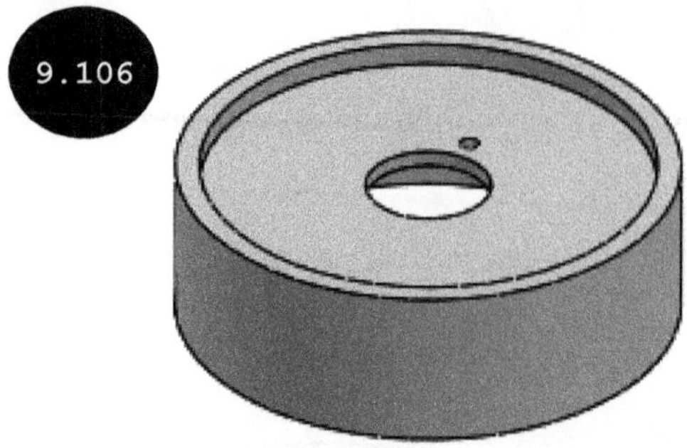

Section 6: Creating the Fourth Feature - Circular Pattern

1. Invoke the **Pattern** flyout by clicking on the arrow at the bottom of the **Linear Pattern** tool.

2. Click on the **Circular Pattern** tool in the **Pattern** flyout. The **CirPattern PropertyManager** appears.

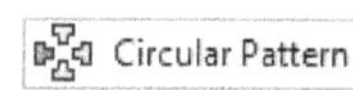

3. Expand the FeatureManager Design Tree, which is now available in the top left corner of the graphics area, by clicking on the arrow in front of it.

4. Click on the third feature (previously created extruded cut) in the FeatureManager Design Tree as the feature to be patterned.

5. Click on the **Pattern Axis** field in the **Direction 1** rollout of the PropertyManager to activate it.

6. Click on the outer circular face of the base feature in the graphics area to define the pattern axis, see Figure 9.107. A preview of the circular pattern appears, see Figure 9.107.

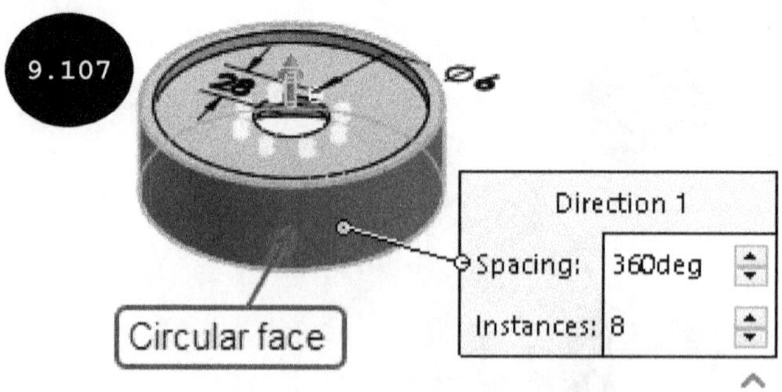

7. Ensure that the **Equal spacing** radio button is selected in the **Direction 1** rollout of the PropertyManager.

8. Ensure that **360** degrees is specified in the **Angle** field of the **Direction 1** rollout in the PropertyManager.

9. Enter **8** in the **Number of Instances** field of the **Direction 1** rollout.

10. Click on the green tick-mark ✓ in the PropertyManager. A circular pattern is created, see Figure 9.108.

Section 7: Creating the Fifth Feature - Extruded Feature

The fifth feature of the model is an extruded feature and its sketch is to be created on a reference plane, which is at an offset distance of 200 mm from the Right plane.

1. Invoke the **Plane PropertyManager** by clicking on the **Plane** tool in the **Reference Geometry** flyout and then create a reference plane at an offset distance of 200 mm from the Right plane, see Figure 9.109.

9.108

9.109

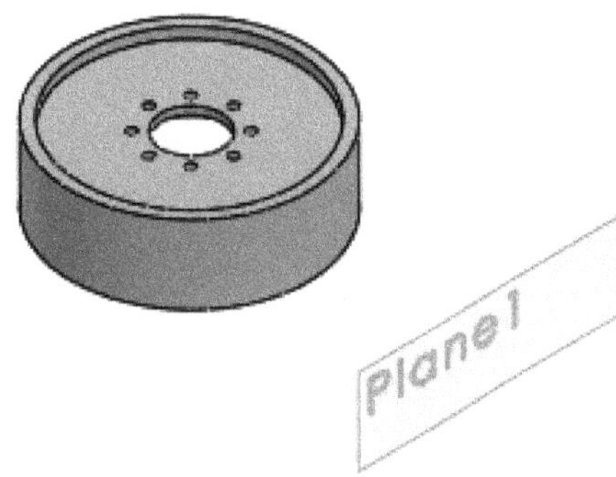

2. Invoke the Sketching environment by selecting the newly created reference plane as the sketching plane. The model gets oriented normal to the viewing direction.

3. Create a sketch of the extruded feature, see Figure 9.110. After creating the sketch, do not exit the Sketching environment.

9.110

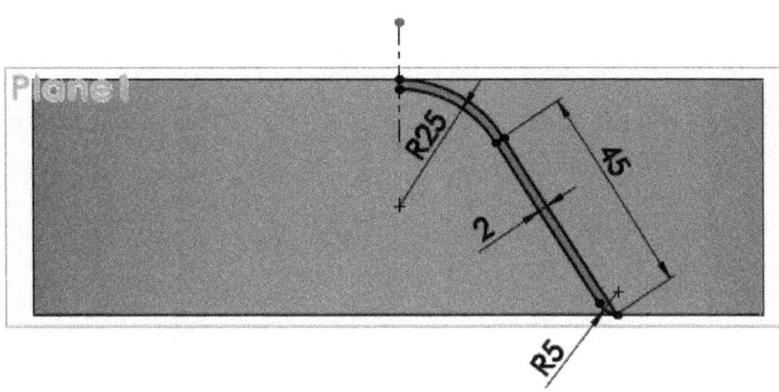

Note: In Figure 9.110, a tangent relation has been applied between the connecting tangent arcs and lines of the sketch. Also, the center point of the arc having a radius of 25 mm is coincident with the origin.

4. Click on the **Features** tab in the CommandManager and then click on the **Extruded Boss/Base** tool. The **Boss-Extrude PropertyManager** and a preview of the extruded feature appear. Next, change the orientation of the model to isometric.

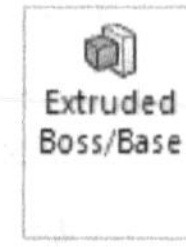

5. Invoke the **End Condition** drop-down list in the **Direction 1** rollout of the PropertyManager.

6. Select the **Up To Surface** option in the **End Condition** drop-down list. The **Face/Plane** field becomes available in the **Direction 1** rollout and is activated, by default.

7. Click on the outer circular face of the base feature. A preview of the extruded feature appears in the graphics area such that it is extruded up to the selected face, see Figure 9.111.

8. Click on the green tick-mark ✓ in the PropertyManager. The extruded feature is created, see Figure 9.112. Next, hide the reference plane.

9.111

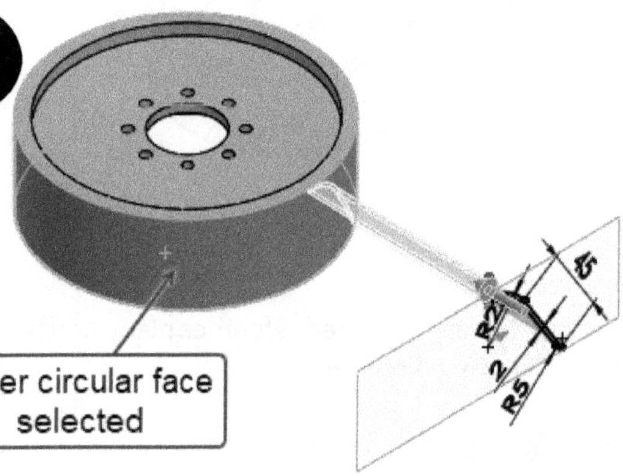

9.112

Section 8: Creating the Sixth Feature - Circular Pattern

1. Invoke the **Pattern** flyout by clicking on the arrow at the bottom of the **Linear Pattern** tool.

2. Click on the **Circular Pattern** tool in the **Pattern** flyout. The **CirPattern PropertyManager** appears.

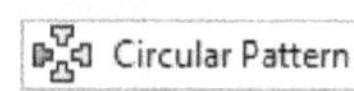

3. Select the fifth feature (previously created extruded feature) as the feature to be patterned from the graphics area.

4. Click on the **Pattern Axis** field in the **Direction 1** rollout of the PropertyManager.

5. Click on the outer circular face of the base feature in the graphics area to define the pattern axis. A preview of the circular pattern appears.

6. Ensure that the **Equal spacing** radio button is selected in the **Direction 1** rollout.

7. Ensure that **360** degrees is specified in the **Angle** field of the **Direction 1** rollout in the PropertyManager.

8. Enter **8** in the **Number of Instances** field of the **Direction 1** rollout.

9. Click on the green tick-mark ✓. A circular pattern is created, see Figure 9.113.

9.113

Section 9: Saving the Model

1. Click on the **Save** tool in the **Standard** toolbar. The **Save As** dialog box appears.

2. Browse to the Chapter 9 folder of the SOLIDWORKS folder and then save the model with the name Tutorial 2. You need to create these folders, if not created earlier.

Hands-on Test Drive 1

Create a model, as shown in Figure 9.114. The different views and dimensions are given in the same figure for your reference. All dimensions are in mm.

9.114

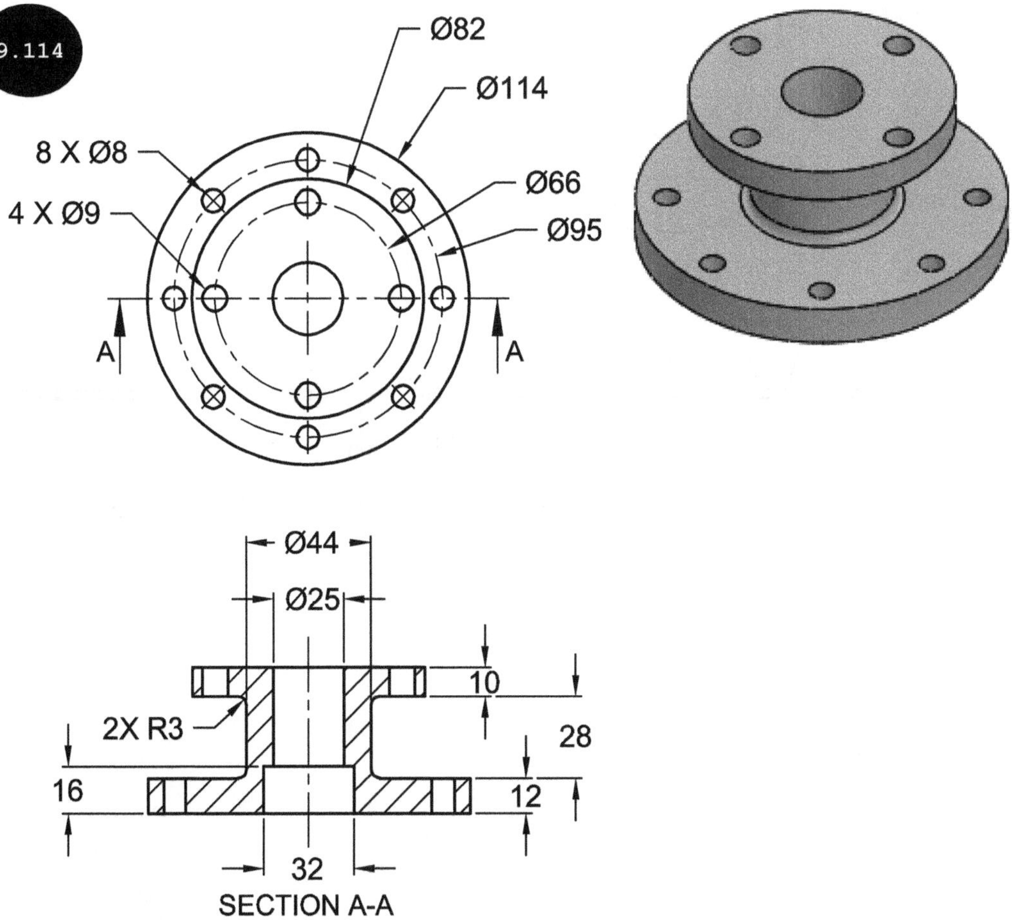

Hands-on Test Drive 2

Create a model, as shown in Figure 9.115. The different views and dimensions are given in the same figure for your reference. All dimensions are in mm.

9.115

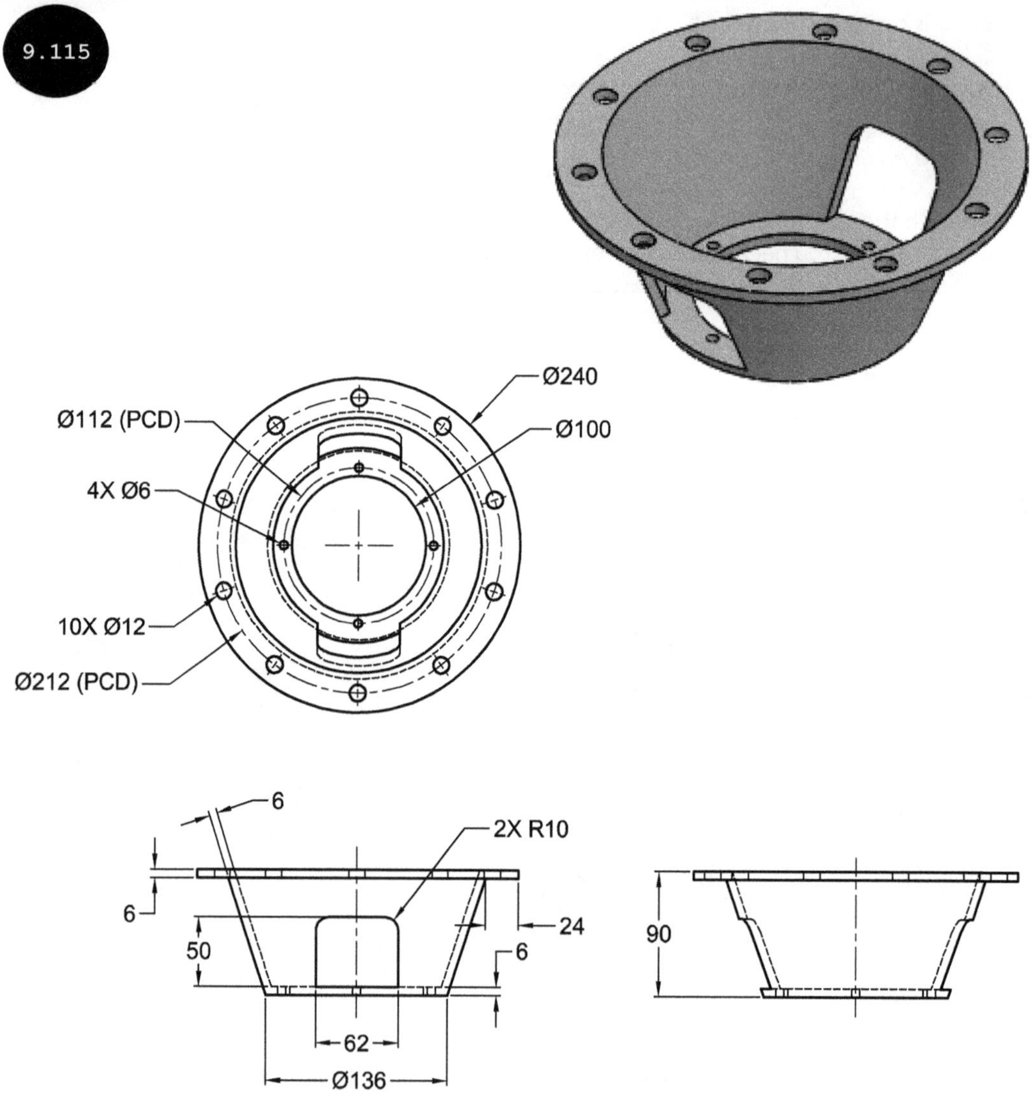

Hands-on Test Drive 3

Create a model, as shown in Figure 9.116. The different views and dimensions are given in the same figure for your reference. All dimensions are in mm.

9.116

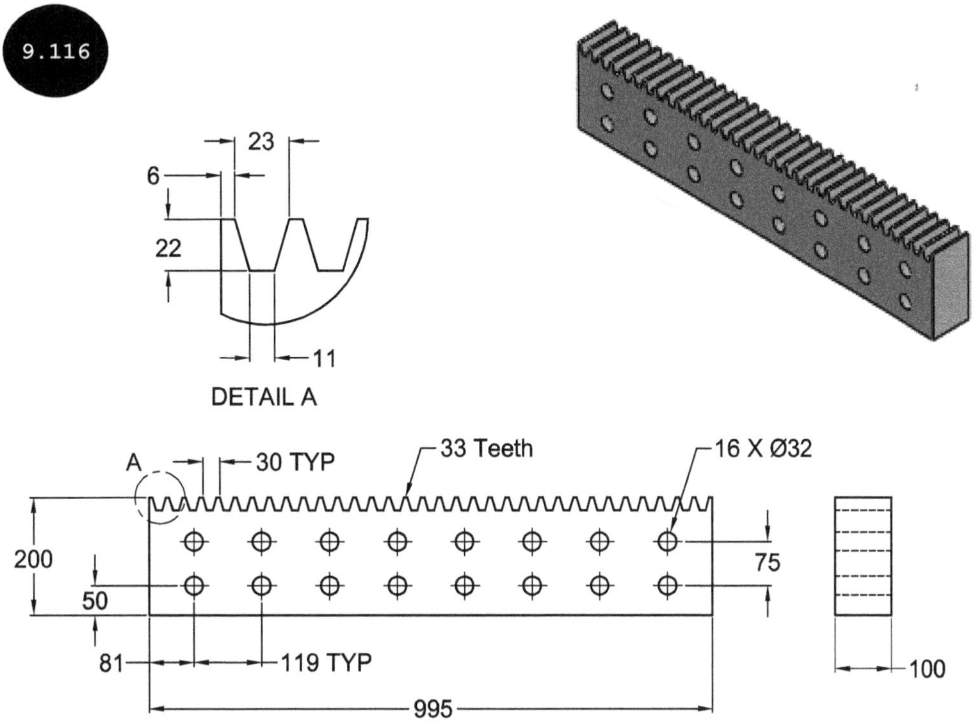

Summary

In this chapter, you explored the use of patterning and mirroring tools in SOLIDWORKS. You learned how to create various types of patterns, such as linear, circular, curve-driven, and sketch-driven patterns. Additionally, you gained an understanding of how to mirror features, faces, or bodies across selected planes, improving design efficiency and symmetry. These tools help streamline the design process, reducing manual work and ensuring consistency in your models.

Questions

Complete and verify the following sentences:

- The _________ tool is used for creating multiple instances of features, faces, or bodies in one or two linear directions.
- Creating multiple instances of features, faces, or bodies along a curve is known as a _________ pattern.
- Creating multiple instances of features, faces, or bodies, circularly around an axis results in a _________ pattern.
- The _________ tool is used for creating multiple instances of features, faces, or bodies along a curve.
- You can create a variable pattern by using the _________ tool.
- In a variable pattern, you can vary _________ and _________ of the features to be patterned.
- When the _________ check box is cleared, all the instances of the linear pattern maintain the same geometrical relations as the original or parent feature.
- The _________ pattern is created by specifying coordinate points for each pattern instance concerning a coordinate system.
- On selecting the _________ check box in the **Mirror PropertyManager**, the mirror feature is created such that only the selected seed or parent feature gets mirrored about the secondary mirroring plane.
- While creating a linear pattern, you cannot vary pattern instances concerning a path. (True/False)
- In SOLIDWORKS, you can mirror features as well as faces of a model. (True/False)

CHAPTER
10

Advanced Modeling - III

This chapter discusses the following topics:

- Working with the Hole Wizard
- Creating Advanced Holes
- Adding Cosmetic Threads
- Creating Threads
- Creating a Stud Feature
- Creating Fillets
- Creating Chamfers
- Creating Rib Features
- Creating Shell Features
- Creating Wrap Features

In this chapter, you will explore the process of creating standard and customized holes, including Counterbore, Countersink, Straight Tap, and Tapered Tap, based on standard specifications using the **Hole Wizard** and **Advanced Hole** tools. Additionally, the chapter explores advanced modeling techniques such as creating Cosmetic Threads, Threads by removing material, and features like Ribs, Shells, Wraps, Fillets, and Chamfers.

Working with the Hole Wizard

The **Hole Wizard** tool is used to create standard holes such as counterbore, countersink, and straight tap as per standard specifications. To create standard holes using the **Hole Wizard** tool, click on the **Hole Wizard** tool in the **Features CommandManager**. The **Hole Specification PropertyManager** appears, see Figure 10.1. The options in this PropertyManager are discussed next.

Type Tab

The **Hole Specification PropertyManager** has two tabs: **Type** and **Positions**. By default, the **Type** tab is activated. As a result, the options for specifying the type of hole and hole specifications are displayed in different rollouts of the PropertyManager. The options are discussed next.

10.1

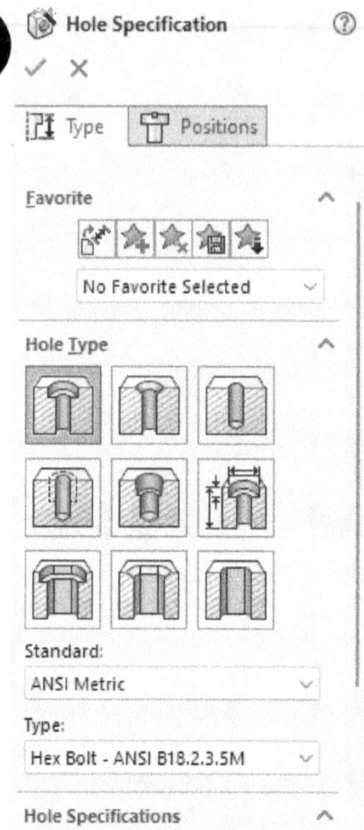

Hole Type

The **Hole Type** rollout of the PropertyManager is used to select the type of hole such as counterbore, countersink, or straight tap. Depending upon the type of hole to be created, you can click on the **Counterbore**, **Countersink**, **Hole**, **Straight Tap**, **Tapered Tap**, or **Legacy Hole** button in this rollout. Figure 10.2 shows counterbore holes and Figure 10.3 shows countersink holes created on the top face of the model.

Using this rollout, you can not only create standard holes, but also slot holes by selecting the **Counterbore Slot**, **Countersink Slot**, and **Slot** buttons. Figure 10.4 shows counterbore slots and Figure 10.5 shows countersink slots created on the top face of the model. The remaining options of this rollout are discussed next.

10.2

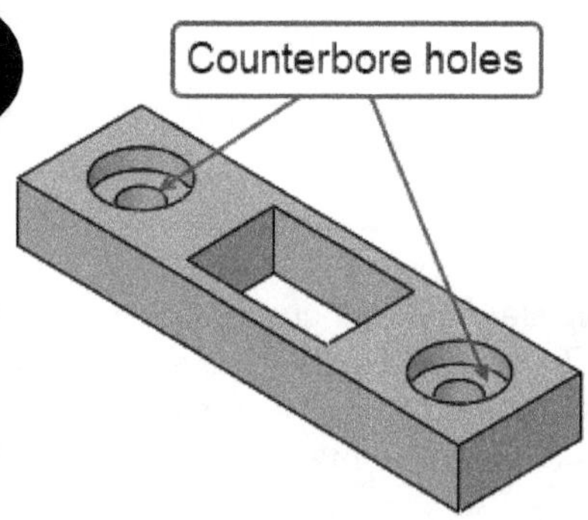

10.3

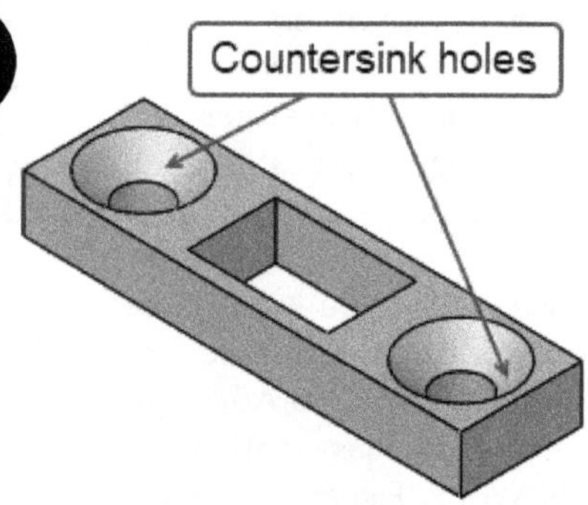

10.4

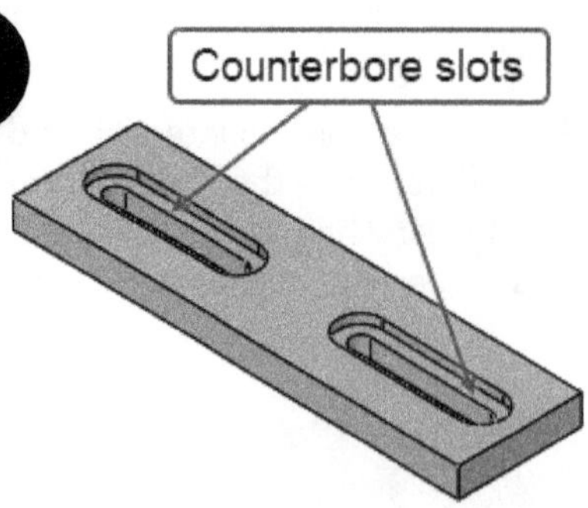

10.5

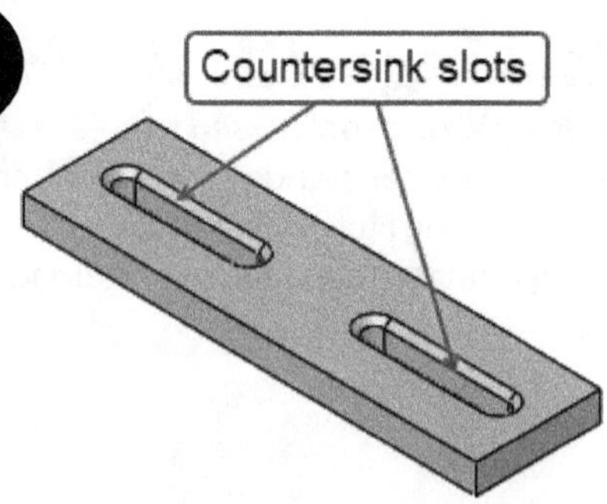

Standard

The **Standard** drop-down list is used to select the type of standard such as ANSI Metric, ANSI Inch, BSI, IS, JIS, or ISO for creating the hole, see Figure 10.6.

Type

The **Type** drop-down list is used to specify the type of fastener to be inserted into the hole. The availability of options in this drop-down list depends upon the type of hole and standard selected. Figure 10.7 shows the **Type** drop-down list when the **Counterbore** hole and the **ANSI Metric** standard are selected.

10.6

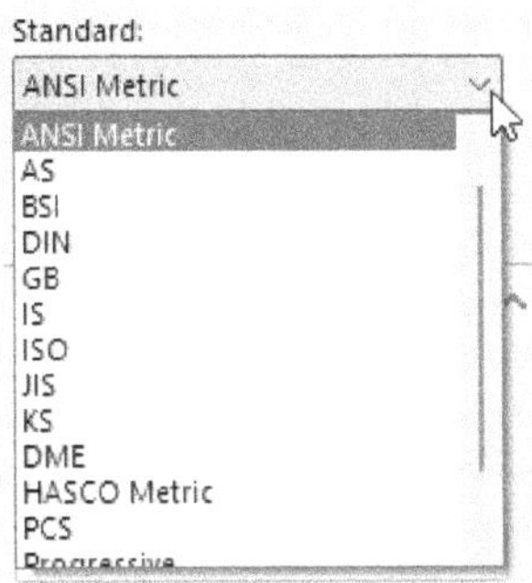

10.7

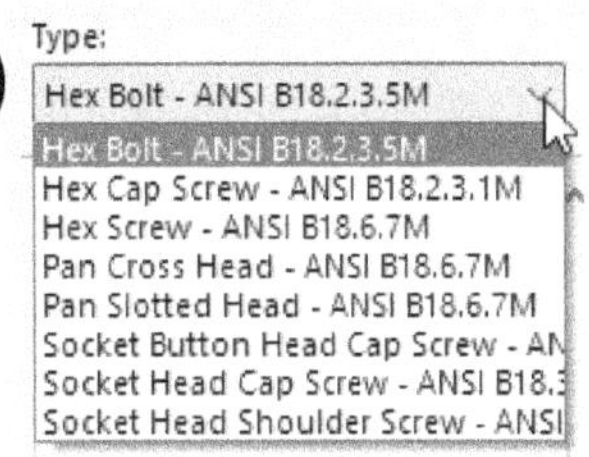

Hole Specifications

The **Hole Specifications** rollout of the PropertyManager is used to define specifications for the fastener to be inserted into a hole. The options of this rollout are discussed next.

Size

The **Size** drop-down list is used to select the size of the fastener to be inserted. The availability of options in this drop-down list depends upon the type of hole and standard selected.

Fit

The **Fit** drop-down list is used to select the type of fit between the fastener and the hole. You can specify close, normal, or loose fastener fit.

Note: The size of the hole depends upon the size of the fastener and the type of fit. In SOLIDWORKS, the size of the hole is automatically adjusted depending upon the specification of the fastener and the type of fit selected.

Show custom sizing

The **Show custom sizing** check box is used to display and customize the standard size of the hole. On selecting the **Show custom sizing** check box, the standard size of the hole as per the specified specifications appears in the respective fields of the rollout, see Figure 10.8.

10.8

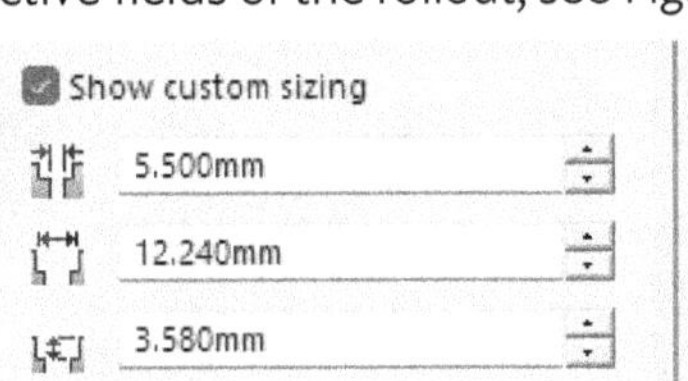

You can modify the standard specifications of the hole by entering the required values in the respective fields. Note that the background color of the fields, whose values are edited or customized, is changed to yellow color. After editing the specifications, if you want to restore the default standard specifications, click on the **Restore Default Values** button in this rollout.

End Condition

The options in the **End Condition** rollout are used to define the end condition or termination method for a hole, see Figure 10.9. Some of the options for defining the end condition of the hole are the same as those discussed earlier while creating the extruded feature. The remaining options are discussed next.

10.9

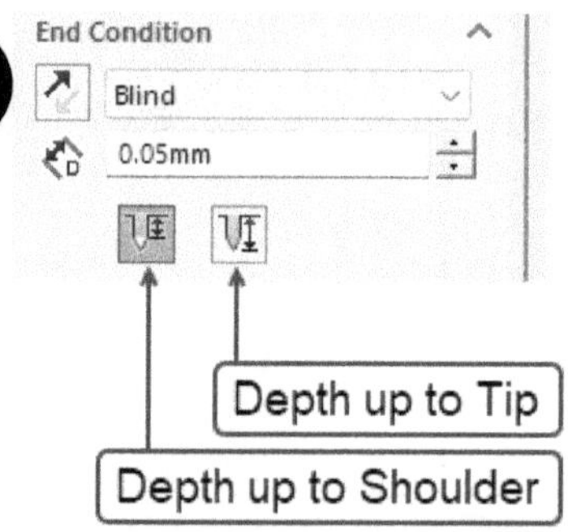

Depth up to Shoulder

On selecting the **Depth up to Shoulder** button, the specified depth of the hole is measured up to the shoulder of the hole, see Figure 10.10. Note that this button is not available if the **Through All** or **Up to Next** option is selected in the **End Condition** drop-down list of the **End Condition** rollout.

Depth up to Tip

On selecting the **Depth up to Tip** button, the specified depth of the hole is measured up to the tip of the hole, see Figure 10.11. Note that this button is not available if the **Through All** or **Up to Next** option is selected in the **End Condition** drop-down list of the **End Condition** rollout.

10.10

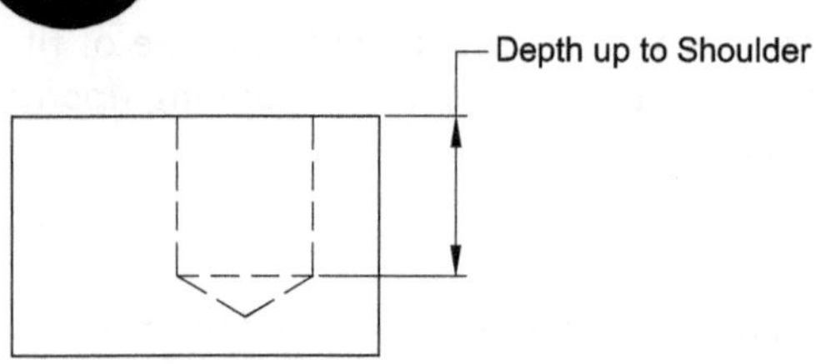

10.11

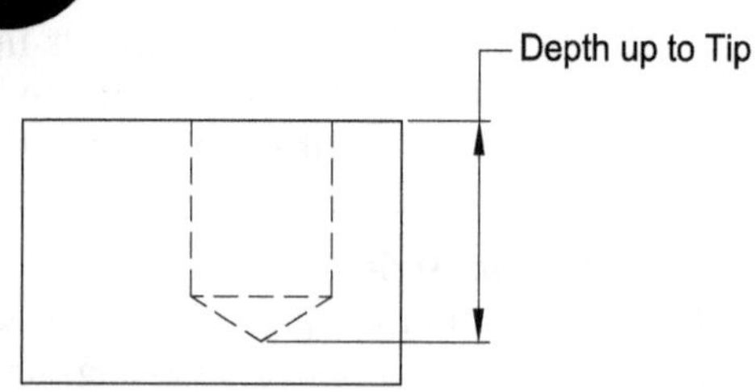

Options

The availability of the options in the **Options** rollout depends upon the type of hole selected. Figure 10.12 shows the **Options** rollout when the **Counterbore** hole type is selected. The options are discussed next.

10.12

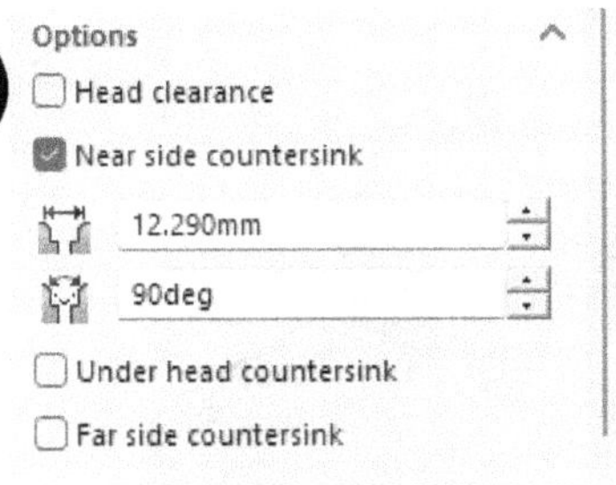

Head clearance

On selecting the **Head clearance** check box, the **Head Clearance** field appears below it. In this field, you can specify the head clearance value for the counterbore or countersink hole. In other words, the value entered in the **Head Clearance** field is used to define the clearance between the top face of the fastener head and the hole.

Near side countersink

The **Near side countersink** check box is used to create the countersink shape at the near side of the placement face of the hole, see Figure 10.13. On selecting the **Near side countersink** check box, the **Near Side Countersink Diameter** and **Near Side Countersink Angle** fields appear in the rollout. These fields are used for specifying the diameter and angle of the countersink shape to be created at the near side of the placement face of the hole. Figure 10.13 shows a counterbore hole with a countersink shape created at the near side of the placement face.

10.13

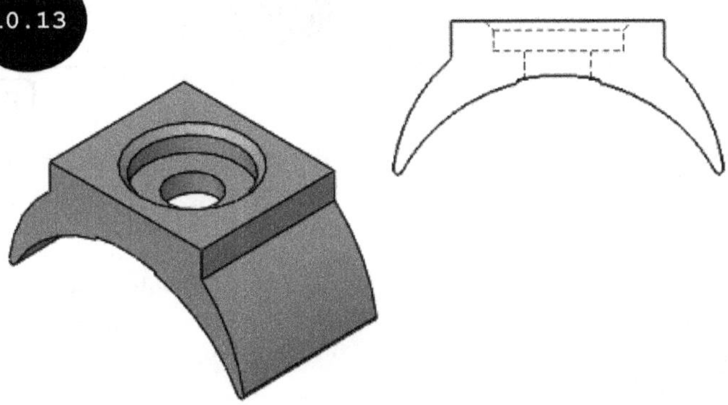

Far side countersink

The **Far side countersink** check box is used to create the countersink shape at the far side of the placement face of the hole, see Figure 10.14. On selecting the **Far side countersink** check box, the **Far Side Countersink Diameter** and **Far Side Countersink Angle** fields appear in the rollout. These fields are used for specifying the countersink diameter and angle for the countersink shape to be created at the far side of the placement face of the hole. Figure 10.14 shows a counterbore hole with a countersink shape created at the far side of the placement face.

10.14

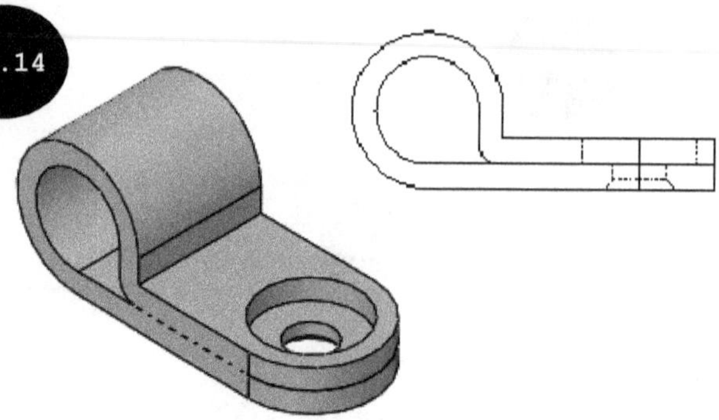

Under head countersink

The **Under head countersink** check box is used to create the countersink shape under the hole head, see Figure 10.15. On selecting the **Under head countersink** check box, the **Under Head Countersink Diameter** and **Under Head Countersink Angle** fields appear. These fields are used for specifying the countersink diameter and the angle for the countersink shape to be created under the hole head diameter. Figure 10.15 shows a counterbore hole with a countersink shape created under the head diameter.

Note that if the **Straight Tap** hole type is selected in the **HoleType** rollout, the options in the **Options** rollout appear as shown in Figure 10.16. These options are discussed next.

10.15

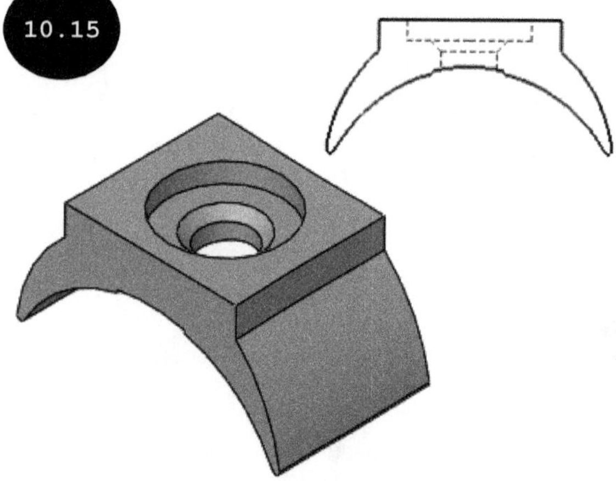

10.16

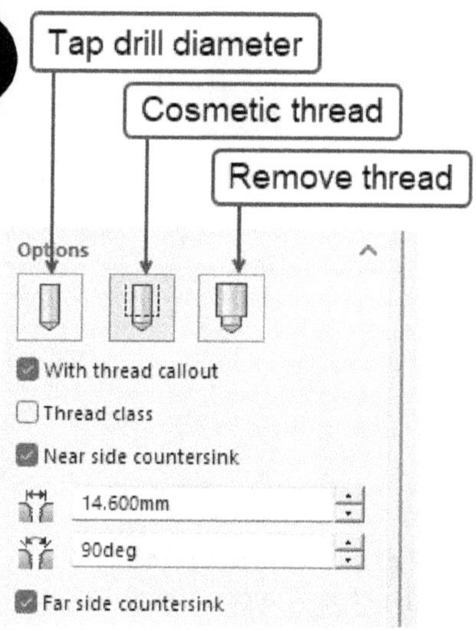

Tap drill diameter, Cosmetic thread, and Remove thread

The **Tap drill diameter** button is used to create a Straight tap hole having the same diameter as the tapped diameter of the hole with no thread representation, see Figure 10.17. The **Cosmetic thread** button is used to create a Straight tap hole having the same diameter as the tapped hole with the cosmetic representation of thread, see Figure 10.18. The **Remove thread** button is used for creating a Straight tap hole having a diameter equal to the thread diameter of the tapped hole, see Figure 10.19.

10.17

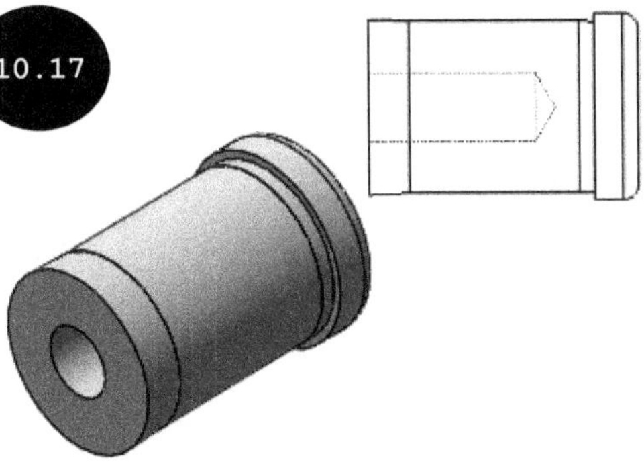

10.18

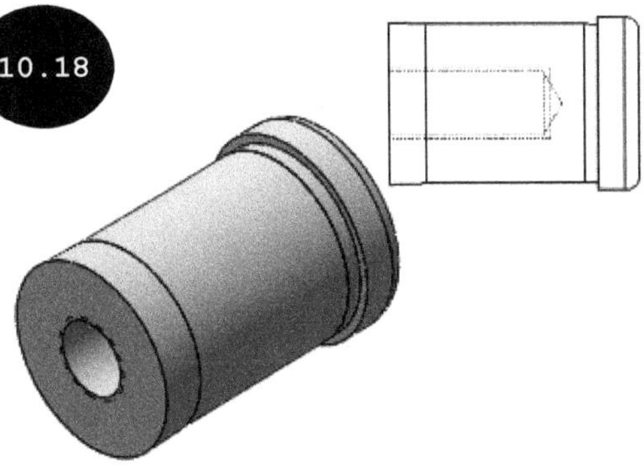

10.19

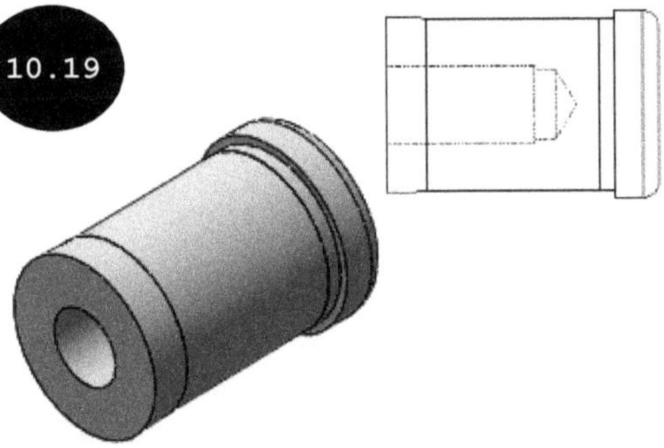

Thread class
On selecting the **Thread class** check box, the **Thread class** drop-down list becomes available in front of it. By using this drop-down list, you can select a class for the threaded or tapped holes.

Tolerance/Precision
In SOLIDWORKS, you can also specify tolerance and precision values for the hole parameters using the **Tolerance/Precision** rollout, see Figure 10.20. Note that the availability of the options in this rollout depends upon the type of hole selected. The options are discussed next.

10.20

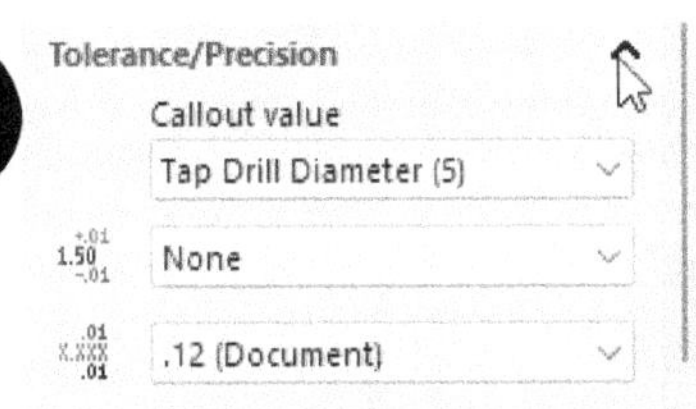

Callout value
The **Callout value** drop-down list is used to select an element of the hole such as **Thru Hole Diameter**, **CounterBore Diameter**, or **CounterBore Depth** to define the tolerance values for its parameter, see Figure 10.21. Note that the availability of the options in this drop-down list depends upon the type of hole selected. Figure 10.21 shows the **Callout value** drop-down list when the **Counterbore** hole type is selected.

Note: You can specify tolerance to the parameter of each element of the hole individually by selecting them in the **Callout value** drop-down list.

Tolerance Type
The options in the **Tolerance Type** drop-down list are used for selecting the type of tolerance to be applied to the parameter of the selected hole element. By default, the **None** option is selected in this drop-down list. As a result, no tolerance is applied. Depending upon the type of tolerance

selected, the corresponding fields are enabled below in the **Tolerance/Precision** rollout to specify tolerance values. Figure 10.22 shows the **Tolerance/Precision** rollout when the **Bilateral** option is selected in the **Tolerance Type** drop-down list.

10.21

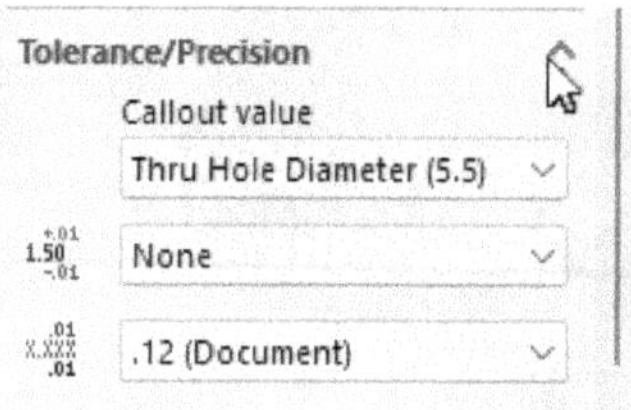

10.22

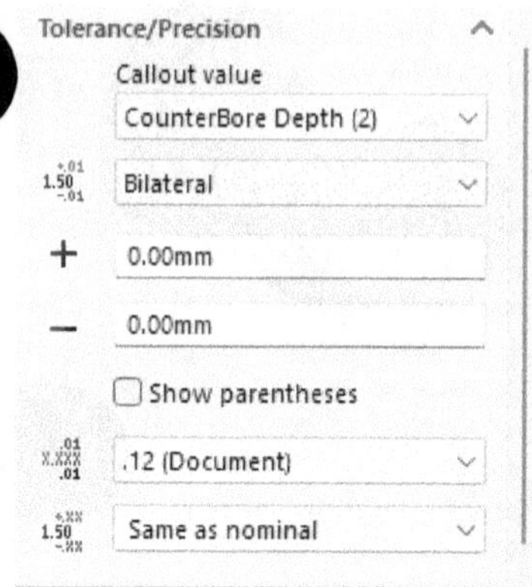

Unit Precision

The **Unit Precision** drop-down list is used to select the unit of precision or number of digits after the decimal point in a tolerance value.

Note: The tolerance values specified in this rollout will automatically propagate to the hole callouts in the drawing. Also, if you make any change in the hole callout in the Drawing environment, the same change automatically gets updated in the part and vice-versa. You will learn about creating drawings in the Drawing environment in Chapter 14.

Tolerance Precision

The **Tolerance Precision** drop-down list is used to define the number of decimal places displayed for tolerance values. It controls how precisely the upper and lower tolerance limits are displayed.

After specifying all specifications in the **Type** tab of the PropertyManager, you need to define the placement point for the hole in the model by using the **Position** tab of the PropertyManager.

Positions Tab

The **Positions** tab of the PropertyManager is used to define the position of the hole. After specifying all specifications for the hole in the **Type** tab, click on the **Positions** tab in the PropertyManager. The name of the PropertyManager changes to **Hole Position PropertyManager**, see Figure 10.23. Also, you are prompted to specify the placement face for the hole. You can select a planar face, a plane, or a curved face as the placement face of the hole.

Click on the desired face of the model to define the placement face of the hole. The placement face is set, and a preview of the hole follows the cursor as you move it over the face. Next, define the placement point for the hole by clicking the left mouse button at the desired location on the selected face. The center point of the hole is placed at the defined point. Similarly, you can specify multiple placement points to create multiple holes with the same parameters.

After defining a placement point, you can use the dimension tools available in the **Sketch CommandManager** to position the hole as needed, see Figure 10.24. You can also apply relations such as horizontal and vertical to position the hole. Once the hole's position is defined with dimensions, click the green tick-mark ✓ in the PropertyManager to create the hole.

10.23

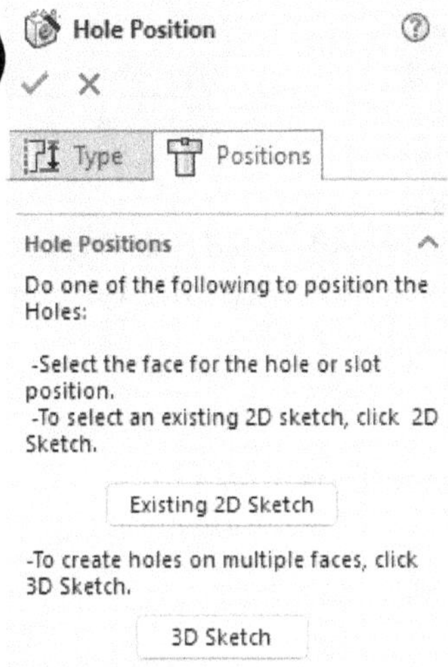

10.24

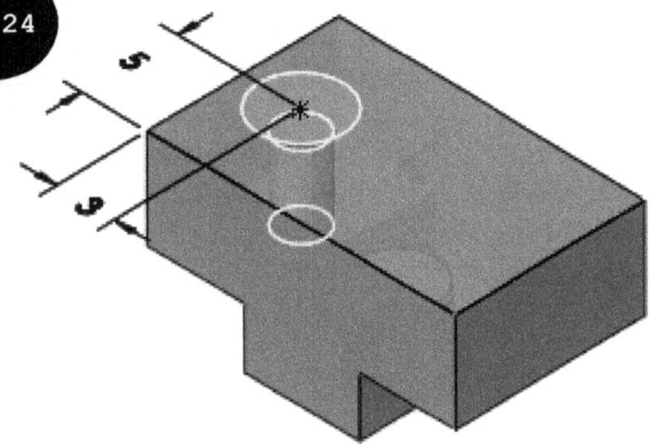

Note: On selecting the planar face as the placement face of the hole, the 2D Sketching environment gets invoked. As a result, you are limited to creating multiple holes only on the selected placement face. However, selecting a curved face as the placement face, invokes the 3D sketch environment, allowing you to create multiple holes on different faces. Additionally, you can invoke the 3D Sketching environment by clicking on the **3D Sketch** button in the PropertyManager to create holes on different faces.

In SOLIDWORKS, you can also select an existing 2D sketch to create a hole at each of its sketch points using the **Existing 2D Sketch** button of the PropertyManger. Note that when you choose an existing 2D sketch, the hole with specified parameters will be propagated to each point of the selected sketch, see Figure 10.25.

10.25

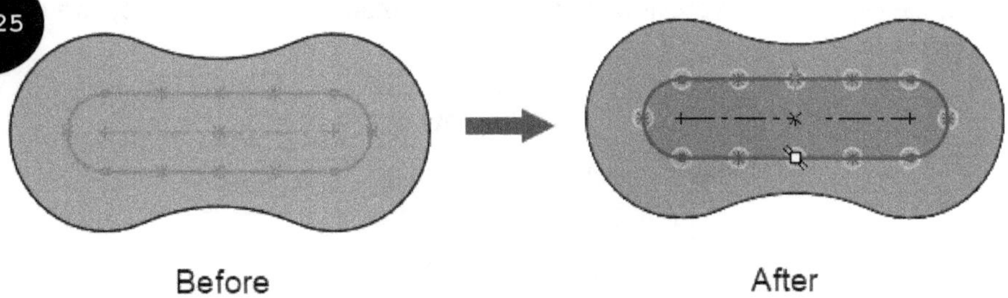

Tip: In SOLIDWORKS, the settings specified in the **Hole Specification PropertyManager** are retained and appear while editing the hole.

Creating Advanced Holes

In SOLIDWORKS, you can also create advanced holes such as manifolds and multi-stepped holes using the **Advanced Hole** tool. You can also define customized hole types with combinations of different standard holes such as counterbore, countersink, straight tap, and tapered by using this tool. This is a very powerful tool for creating complex multi-stepped holes in a single command. To invoke the **Advanced Hole** tool, click on the arrow at the bottom of the **Hole Wizard** tool. A flyout appears, see Figure 10.26. In this flyout, click on the **Advanced Hole** tool. The **Advanced Hole PropertyManager** and the **Near Side** flyout appear, see Figure 10.27. The options in the PropertyManager and the flyout are discussed next.

10.26

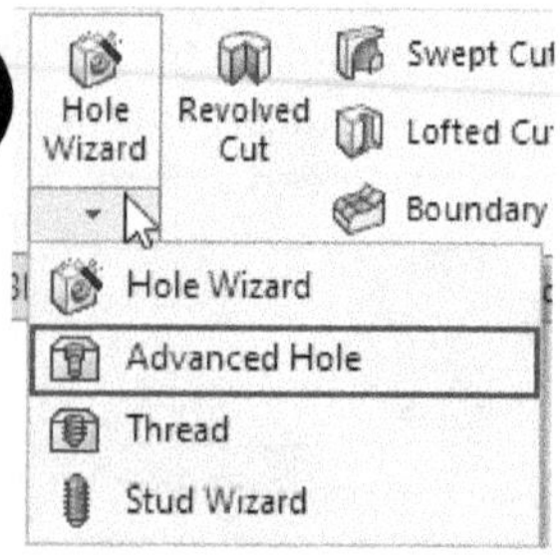

10.27

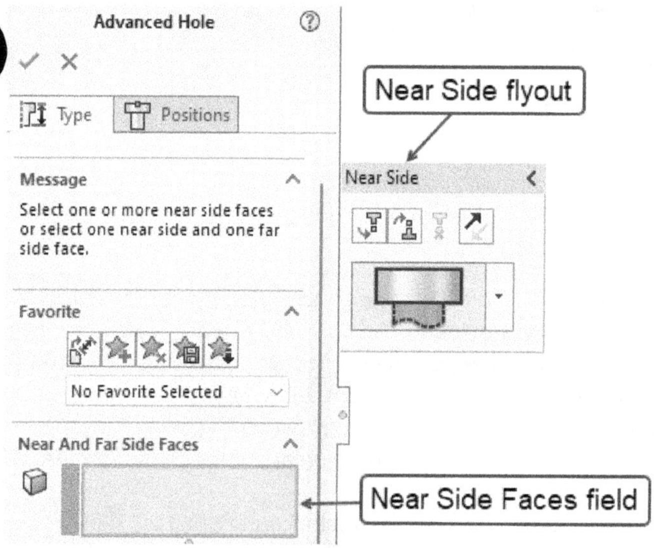

Near And Far Side Faces

The **Near And Far Side Faces** rollout of the PropertyManager is used to select the near and far side faces of a hole. By default, the **Near Side Faces** field is available in this rollout. As a result, you can select one or more faces as the near-side faces of the hole. Select a face of the model as the near-side face of the hole, see Figure 10.28. A preview of the hole with default specifications appears on the selected face, see Figure 10.28.

10.28

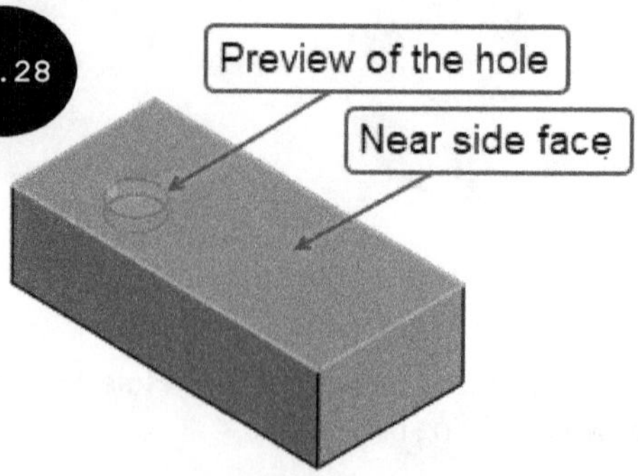

After selecting the near-side face of the hole, you can define the near-side hole elements using the **Near Side** flyout. By default, the Counterbore is selected as the first near-side element in this flyout. To open the **Near Side** flyout, click on the downward-facing arrow, see Figure 10.29. In the flyout, you can choose from the following near-side elements: **Near Side Counterbore**, **Near Side Countersink**, **Near Side Tapered Tap**, **Hole**, or **Straight Tap**.

Once you have selected the first near-side hole element, you need to define its specifications, such as type, standard, and size, using the options in the **Element Specification** rollout in the PropertyManager. These options are the same as those discussed earlier.

After defining the first near-side hole element, you can add a second near-side hole element. Click the **Insert Element Below Active Element** button in the flyout, see Figure 10.29. The default second hole element is added below the first element in the flyout (see Figure 10.30), and the preview of the hole is updated to reflect the addition of the second hole element with its default specifications. You can then define the type and specifications of the second hole element, such as Counterbore, Countersink, or Straight Tap, using the **Near Side** flyout and the **Element Specification** rollout.

10.29

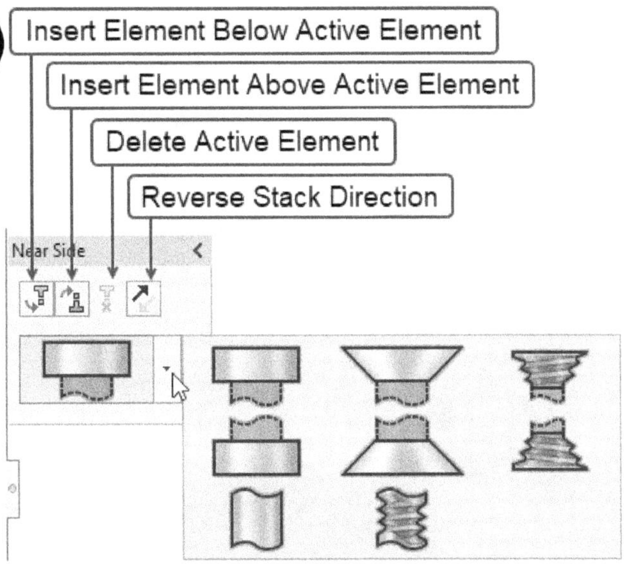

10.30

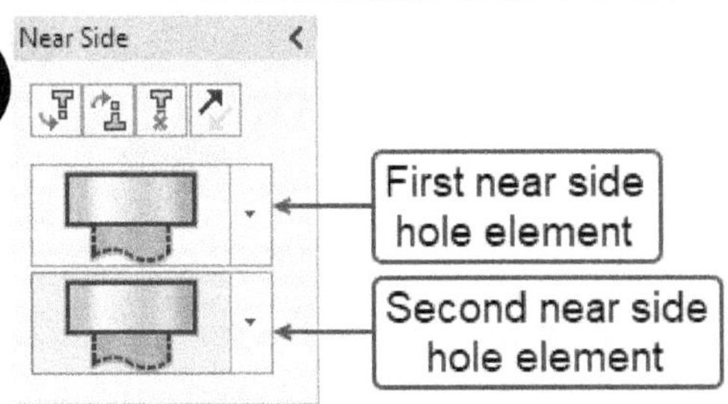

You can continue adding multiple near-side hole elements using the **Near Side** flyout. To add a hole element above the active element, click the **Insert Element Above Active Element** button in the flyout. To delete a hole element, click on it to activate it and then click the **Delete Active Element** button in the flyout. If needed, you can reverse the direction of the hole using the **Reverse Stack Direction** button in the flyout.

To define the far-side face of the hole, select the **Far Side** check box in the **Near And Far Side Faces** rollout of the PropertyManager, see Figure 10.31. The **Far Side Face** field and the **Far Side** flyout appears, see Figure 10.31. By default, the **Far Side Face** field is activated in the rollout. As a result, you can select a face of the model as the far-side face of the hole, see Figure 10.32. After selecting a far-side face, the preview of the hole is modified in the graphics area such that the default far-side hole element is added, see Figure 10.32.

10.31

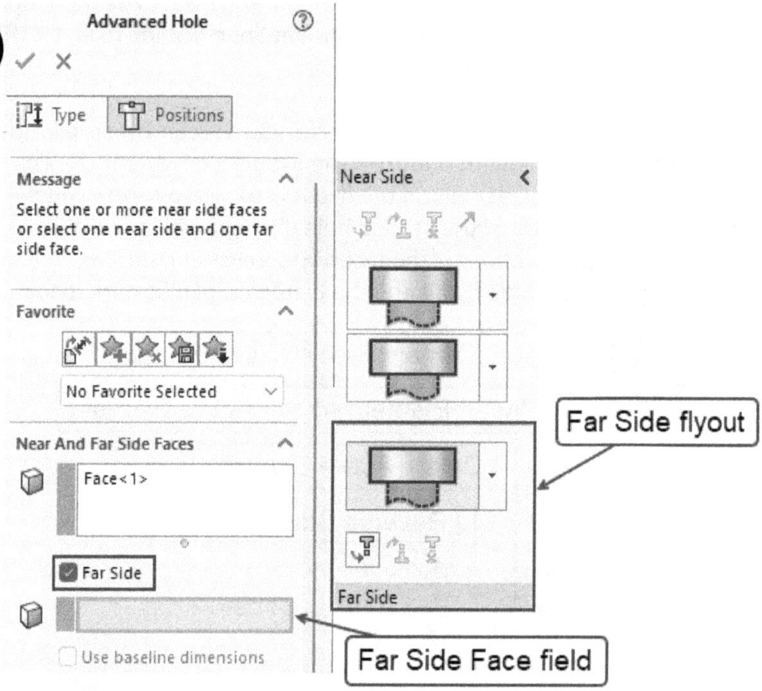

10.32

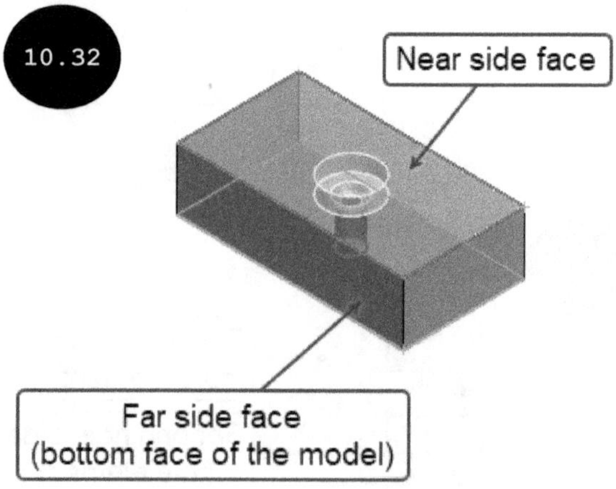

You can select a required far-side hole element by using the **Far Side** flyout. To select a far-side hole element, click on the arrow next to the far-side hole element in the **Far Side** flyout (see Figure 10.33) and then click on the **Far Side Counterbore**, **Far Side Countersink**, **Far Side Tapered Tap**, **Hole**, or **Straight Tap** button, as required.

10.33

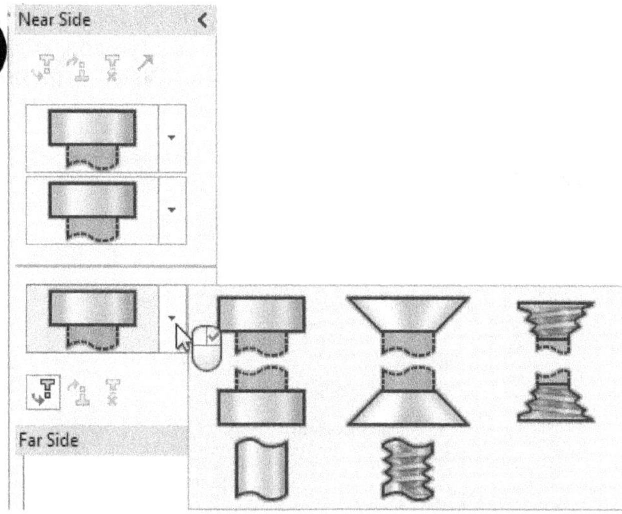

After selecting the required first far-side hole element, you need to define its specifications using the options of the **Element Specification** rollout in the PropertyManager. You can also add multiple far-side elements using the **Insert Element Below Active Element** and **Insert Element Above Active Element** buttons of the **Far Side** flyout. Figure 10.34 shows the preview of a multi-stepped hole having multiple near and far-side elements.

10.34

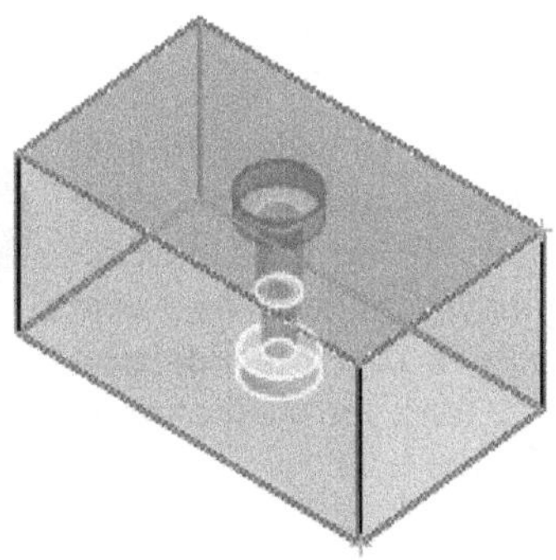

Note: The transparency of the model shown in Figure 10.34 has been changed so as to view the preview of the advanced hole clearly. To do this, right-click on the model and then click on the **Change Transparency** option in the shortcut menu that appears.

In SOLIDWORKS, you can customize the hole callout for advanced holes according to the order and variables required for the manufacturing process and apply it in the drawing. To do this, expand the **Hole Callout** rollout in the PropertyManager (see Figure 10.35) and select the **Customize Callout** radio button.

You can change the order of the callout strings using the **Move Up** and **Move Down** buttons in the rollout. These buttons are enabled when a callout string is selected for reordering in the hole callout. Additionally, you can edit the variables of a callout string by double-clicking on it. This will display the **Callout Variables** button and symbol buttons in the rollout. Click the **Callout Variables** button to open the **Callout Variables** dialog box, where you can select the required variable and click **OK**.

You can also add symbols to a callout string by clicking the respective symbol buttons in the rollout. Any changes made in the **Hole Callout** rollout of the PropertyManager will be reflected in the hole callout of the advanced hole in the Drawing environment. You will learn more about adding the hole callout in the Drawing environment in Chapter 14.

10.35

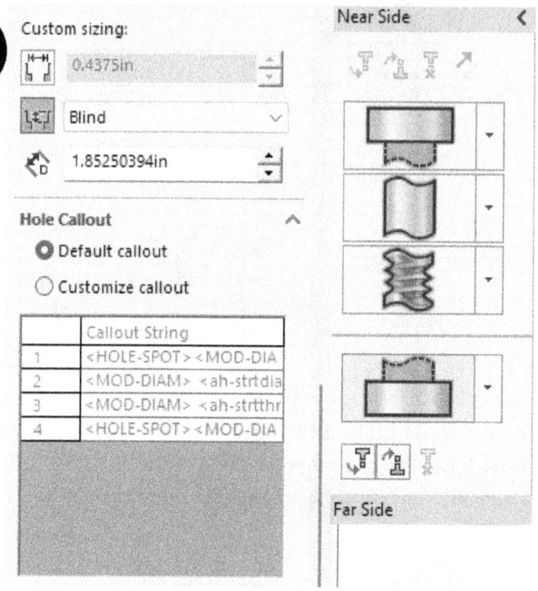

After defining the required near and far-side elements of the hole with the necessary specifications, you define the placement point of the hole. To do this, click on the **Positions** tab in the PropertyManager. The name of the PropertyManager changes to **Hole Position PropertyManager**, see Figure 10.36. Also, you are prompted to specify the placement point for the hole.

10.36

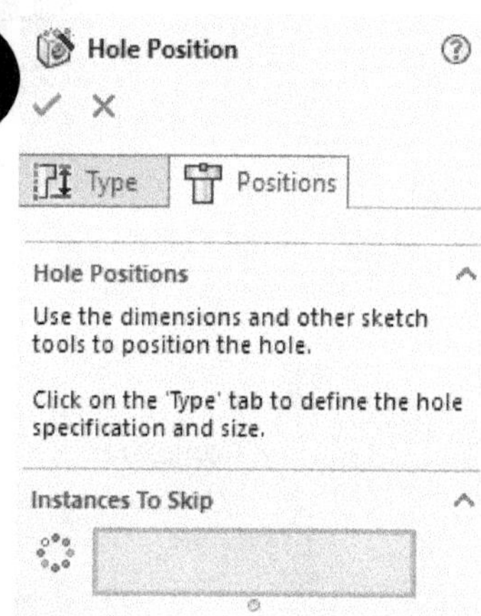

Click on the near-side face of the hole to define the placement point. The center point of the hole is placed at this location. You can create multiple instances of the hole by defining additional placement points. After specifying the placement points, you use the dimension tools available in the **Sketch CommandManager** to position the placement points as needed.

You can also skip certain instances of the hole using the **Instances To Skip** rollout in the PropertyManager. Once the placement points are defined and dimensions are applied, click the green tick-mark ✓ in the PropertyManager to create the hole.

Adding Cosmetic Threads

A cosmetic thread represents the real thread of a feature without removing the material. It is recommended to add cosmetic threads to holes, fasteners, or cylindrical features of a model because adding cosmetic threads helps reduce the complexity of the model and improves the overall performance of the system. Figure 10.37 shows a cosmetic thread added to a cylindrical feature and Figure 10.38 shows cosmetic threads added to hole/cut extruded features.

10.37

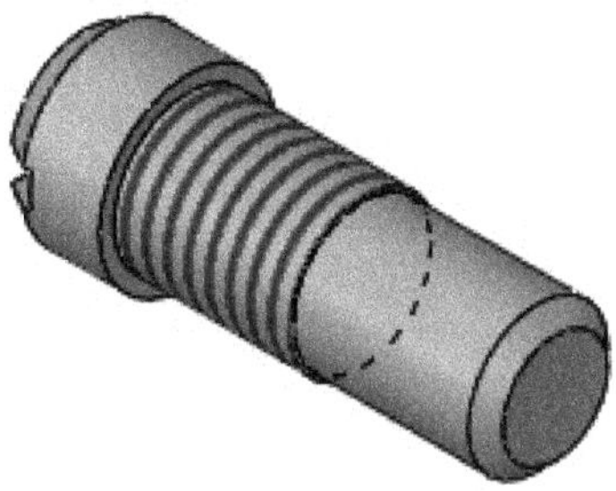

10.38

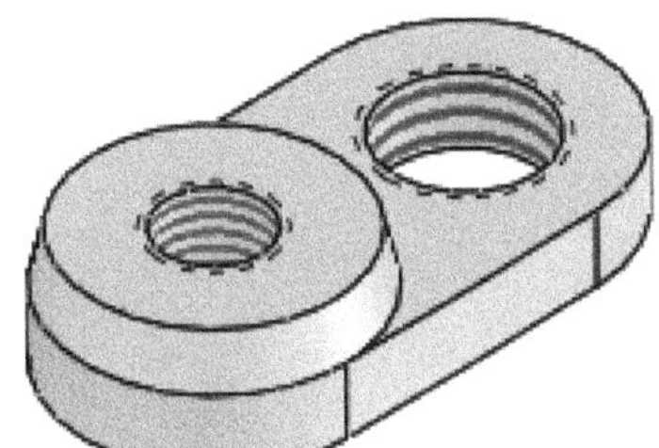

To add a cosmetic thread, click on **Insert > Annotations > Cosmetic Thread** in the SOLIDWORKS Design menus. The **Cosmetic Thread PropertyManager** appears, see Figure 10.39. The options in this PropertyManager are discussed next.

10.39

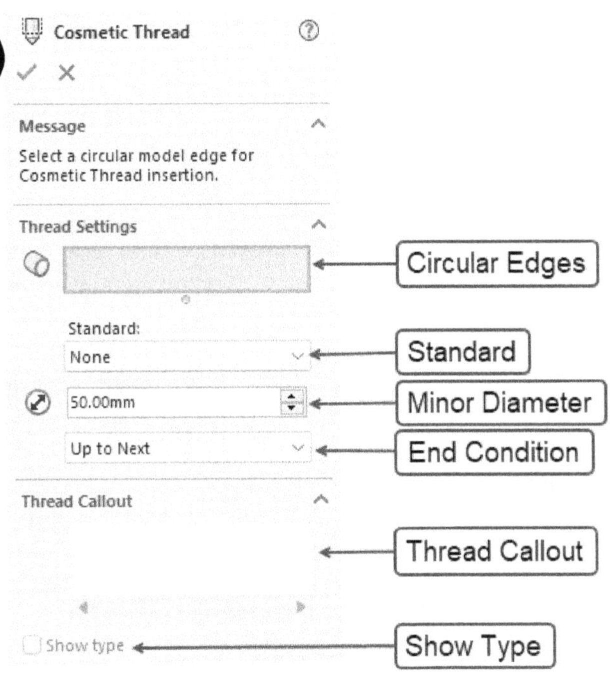

Thread Settings

The options in the **Thread Settings** rollout of the PropertyManager are used to define the thread settings and are discussed next.

Circular Edges

The **Circular Edges** field of the **Thread Settings** rollout is activated by default. As a result, you can select a circular edge of a feature for adding the cosmetic thread. Click on a circular edge of a feature. A dotted circle appears in the graphics area, which represents the minor or major diameter of the thread, see Figures 10.40 and 10.41. Also, the name of the selected edge appears in the **Circular Edges** field.

Note: On selecting the circular edge of a cylindrical feature, the dotted circle represents the minor (inner) diameter of the thread (see Figure 10.40) whereas on selecting the circular edge of a cut/hole feature, the dotted circle represents the major (outer) diameter of the thread, see Figure 10.41.

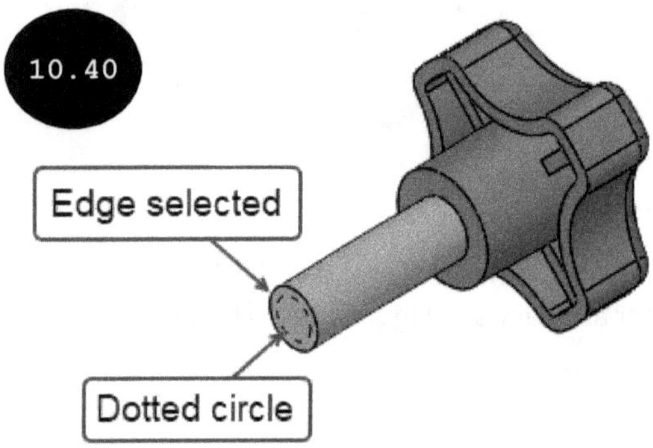

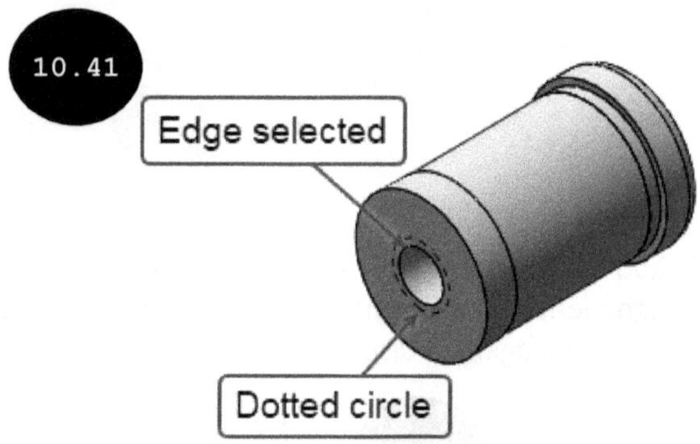

Standard

The **Standard** drop-down list is used to select the type of standard such as ANSI Inch, ANSI Metric, or ISO to be followed for creating the cosmetic thread.

Type

The **Type** drop-down list is used to select the type of thread to be added. Note that this drop-down list will not be available if the **None** option is selected in the **Standard** drop-down list.

Size

The **Size** drop-down list is used to select the standard size of the thread. Note that this drop-down list will not be available if the **None** option is selected in the **Standard** drop-down list.

Minor Diameter or Major Diameter

The **Minor Diameter** or **Major Diameter** field is used to specify the minor or major diameter of the thread, respectively. Note that this field (**Minor Diameter** or **Major Diameter**) is enabled only if the **None** option is selected in the **Standard** drop-down list. Also, the field appears, depending on the circular edge selected for applying the thread. If the circular edge of a cylindrical feature is selected, the **Minor Diameter** field appears and if the circular edge of a hole feature is selected, the **Major Diameter** field appears.

End Condition

The **End Condition** drop-down list is used to specify the end condition or termination for the cosmetic thread. Note that the circular edge that is selected for adding the cosmetic thread is the start condition of the cosmetic thread.

Thread class

When you select the **Thread class** check box in the PropertyManager, the **Thread class** drop-down list becomes available in front of it to select a thread class for the cosmetic thread.

Thread Callout

The **Thread Callout** field is used to enter text or comments for a thread, that appears in the thread callout of the drawing view. You can create drawing views in the Drawing environment of SOLIDWORKS. You will learn about creating drawing views in later chapters.

Note: The **Thread Callout** field of the **Thread Callout** rollout is activated only if the **None** option is selected in the **Standard** drop-down list. If you select a standard such as ANSI Inch or ANSI Metric then this field is not activated. However, the default standard text appears in this field, depending upon the type of standard and thread selected.

In SOLIDWORKS, you can include or exclude the display of thread type from the default standard text that appears in the **Thread Callout** field by selecting or clearing the **Show type** check box in the **Thread Callout** rollout respectively. Note that this check box is not activated if the **None** option is selected in the **Standard** drop-down list.

After specifying all parameters for adding cosmetic thread, click on the green tick-mark ✓ in the PropertyManager. The cosmetic thread is added and appears, see Figure 10.42. Also, a cosmetic thread feature is added under the node of the feature in the FeatureManager Design Tree, see Figure 10.43.

10.42

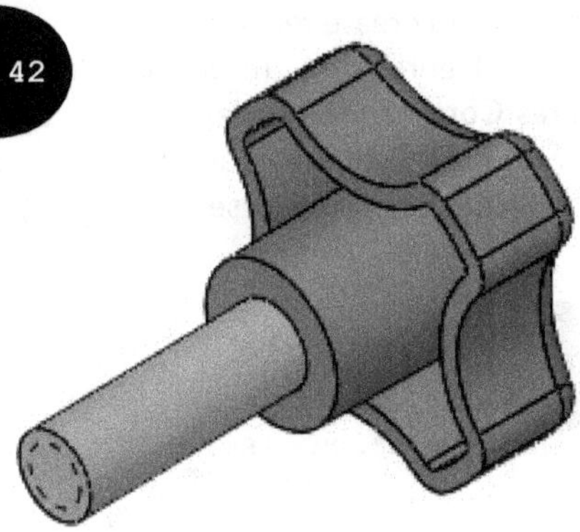

10.43

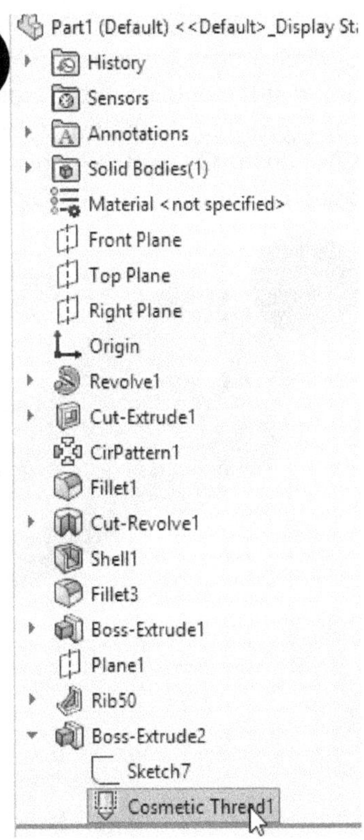

Note: In Figure 10.42, the shaded display style of the cosmetic thread is turned off. As a result, only the dotted circle representing the thread diameter appears in the graphics area. To turn on the shaded display style, right-click on the **Annotations** node in the FeatureManager Design Tree and then click on the **Details** option in the shortcut menu that appears, see Figure 10.44. The **Annotation Properties** dialog box appears. In this dialog box, select the **Shaded cosmetic threads** check box to turn on the shaded display style of the cosmetic thread. Figure 10.45 shows a cosmetic thread in the shaded display style.

10.44

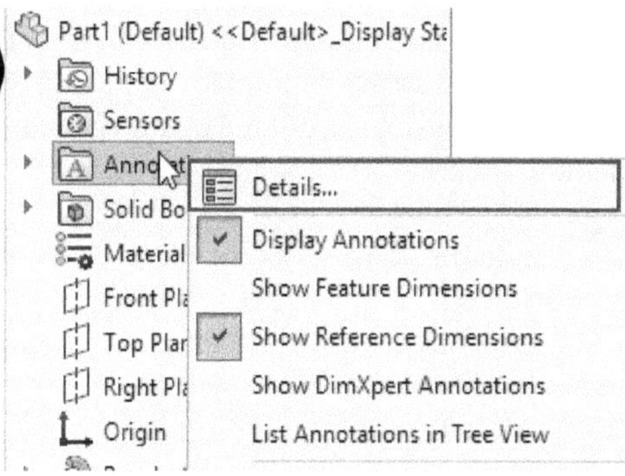

10.45

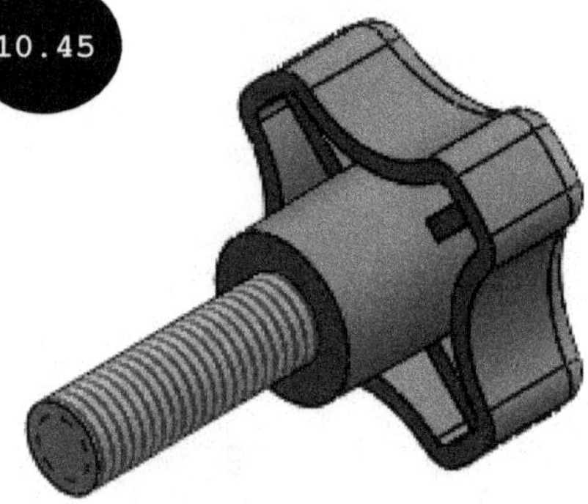

Creating Threads

In SOLIDWORKS, in addition to adding cosmetic threads, you can create real threads on cylindrical or circular features by removing material from the model, see Figure 10.46. To do this, click on the arrow at the bottom of the **Hole Wizard** tool in the **Features CommandManager**. A flyout appears, see Figure 10.47. In this flyout, click on the **Thread** tool. The **SOLIDWORKS** message window appears. Click on the **OK** button in this window. The **Thread PropertyManager** appears, see Figure 10.48. The options in this PropertyManager are discussed next.

10.46

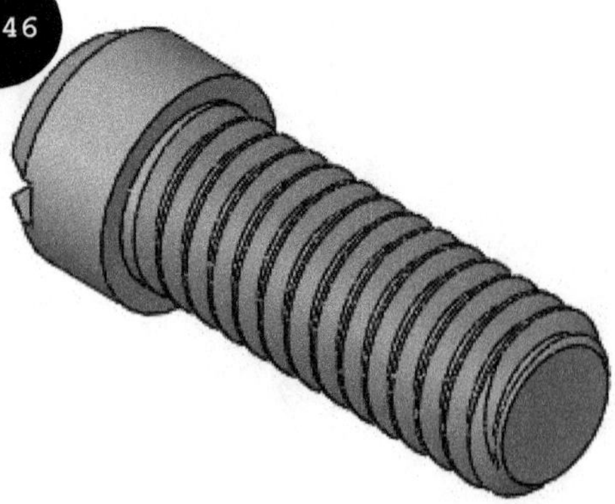

10.47

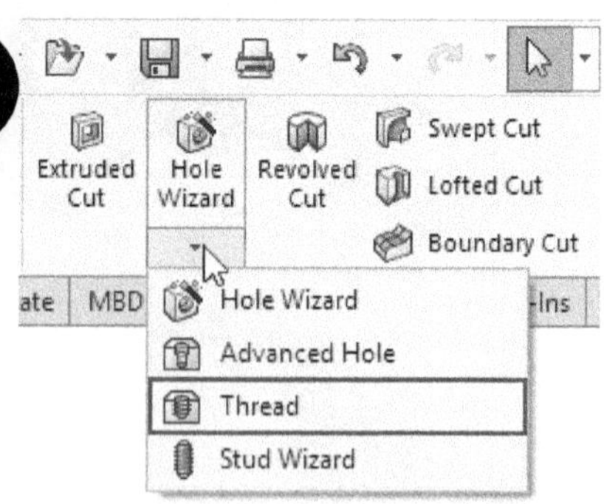

10.48

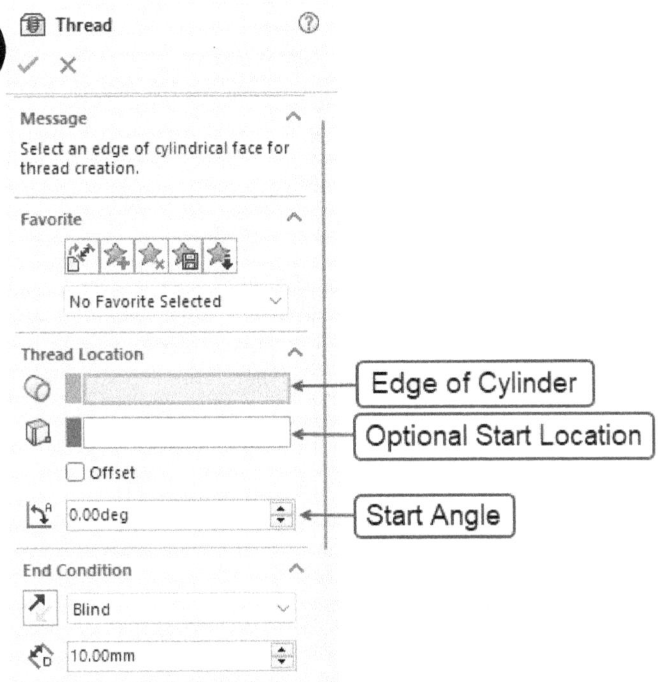

Thread Location

By default, the **Edge of Cylinder** field in the **Thread Location** rollout is activated. As a result, you can select a circular edge of a cylindrical feature or a hole feature for creating the thread. Click on a circular edge of a cylindrical feature or a hole feature. A preview of the thread appears with default parameters in the graphics area, see Figure 10.49. Note that by default, the selected circular edge is used as the start location of the thread. You can define the start location of the thread other than the selected circular edge. To do this, click on the **Optional Start Location** field in the **Thread Location** rollout and then select a vertex, an edge, a plane, or a planar face as the start location of the thread.

The **Offset** check box is used to create the thread at an offset distance from the start location, see Figure 10.50. To create the thread at an offset distance from the start location, select the **Offset** check box. The **Offset Distance** field becomes available below the check box. In this field, enter the offset distance. The **Start Angle** field of the **Thread Location** rollout is used to define the start angle for the helix of the thread. Note that the start angle must be positive.

10.49

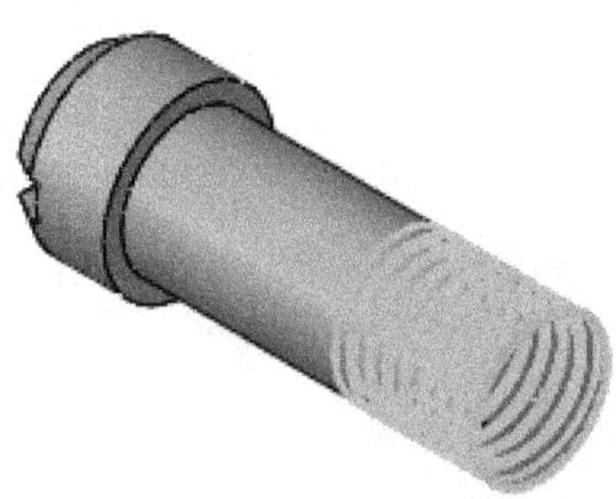

10.50

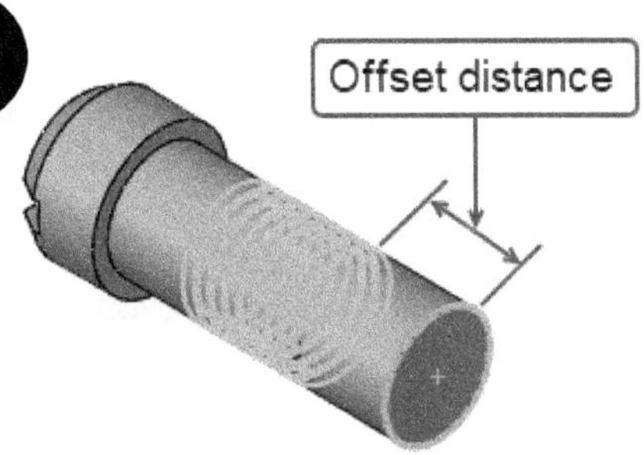

End Condition

The **End Condition** rollout of the PropertyManager is used to specify the end condition for the thread. On selecting the **Blind** option in the **End condition** drop-down list, you can enter the depth value for the thread in the **Depth** field. On selecting the **Revolutions** option in the **End Condition** drop-down list, you can specify the number of revolutions for the thread in the **Revolutions** field. On selecting the **Up To Selection** option, the **End Location** field becomes available in the rollout. As a result, you can select a vertex, an edge, a plane, or a planar face as the end condition for the thread.

The **Maintain thread length** check box is used to maintain a constant length for the thread from its starting location. Note that this check box is available only if the offset distance from the start location is defined by selecting the **Offset** check box in the **Thread Location** rollout and the **Blind** or the **Revolutions** option is selected in the **End Condition** drop-down list of the PropertyManager.

Specification

The **Specification** rollout is used to define thread specifications, such as type and size. The **Type** drop-down list allows you to select the thread type, while the **Size** drop-down list is used to choose the standard size of the thread.

The **Diameter** field of the **Specification** rollout is used to display the helix diameter of the thread, which depends on the cylindrical edge selected for creating the thread, see Figure 10.51. You can override the helix diameter of the thread using the **Override Diameter** button. On clicking the **Override Diameter** button, the **Diameter** field gets enabled. In this field, you can enter the override value for the helical diameter of the thread. Similarly, on clicking the **Override Pitch** button, the **Pitch** field gets enabled for entering the override value for the helix pitch of the thread.

10.51

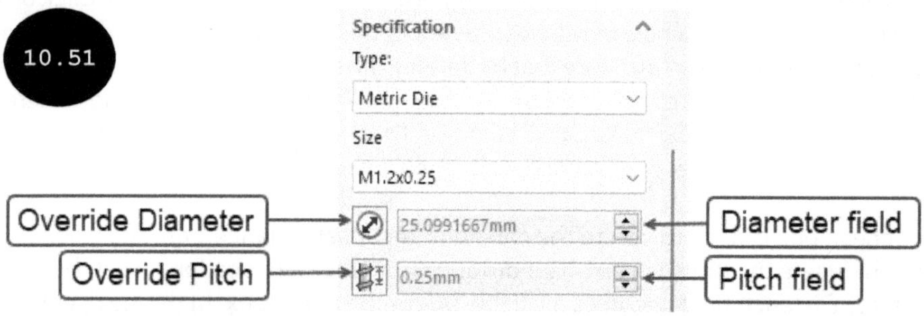

By default, the **Cut thread** radio button is selected as the thread method in the **Specification** rollout. As a result, the thread is created by removing material from the model, see Figure 10.52. On selecting the **Extrude thread** radio button, you can create a thread by adding the material in the feature, see Figure 10.53.

Note: While creating a thread on a cylindrical feature by adding material using the **Extrude thread** radio button, you need to flip the thread profile by selecting the **Mirror Profile** check box. Similarly, while creating a thread on a hole feature by removing the material using the **Cut thread** radio button, you need to flip the thread profile by selecting the **Mirror Profile** check box.

10.52

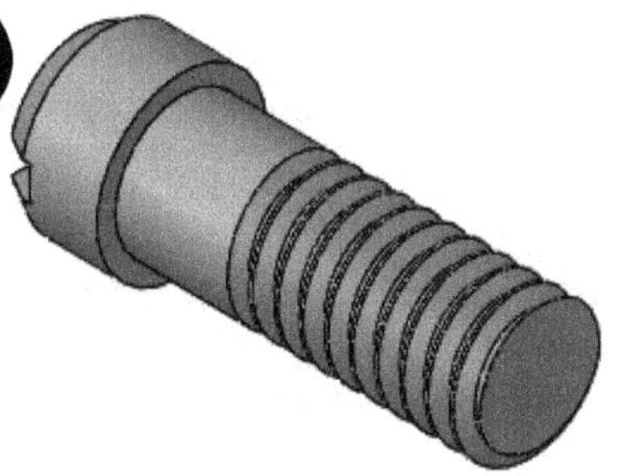

10.53

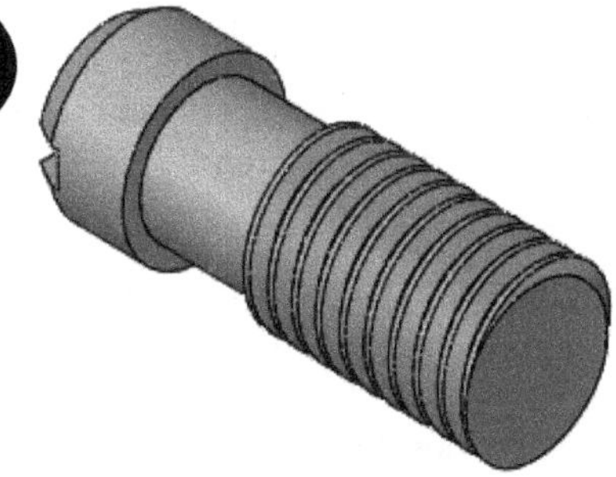

The **Mirror Profile** check box is used to flip the thread profile about its horizontal or vertical axis by using the **Mirror horizontally** or **Mirror vertically** radio button, respectively. Note that these radio buttons become available after selecting the **Mirror Profile** check box. The **Rotation Angle** field is used to specify the rotation angle for the thread helix. On clicking the **Locate Profile** button in the rollout, the profile of the thread is zoomed such that you can change the sketch points or vertices of the thread profile.

Thread Options

By default, the **Right-hand thread** radio button is selected in the **Thread Options** rollout, see Figure 10.54. As a result, the resultant thread is created as the right-hand thread (clockwise direction). On selecting the **Left-hand thread** radio button, the resultant thread is created as the left-hand thread (counter-clockwise direction).

In SOLIDWORKS, you can align the thread to the start and end faces of the feature by using the **Trim with start face** and **Trim with end face** check boxes of the **Thread Options** rollout, respectively. Figure 10.55 shows the start edge and the end face of the cylindrical feature to be selected for creating the thread by adding material using the **Extrude Thread** radio button. Figure 10.56 shows the resultant thread feature created when the **Trim with end face** check box is cleared and Figure 10.57 shows the resultant thread feature created when the **Trim with end face** check box is selected.

10.54

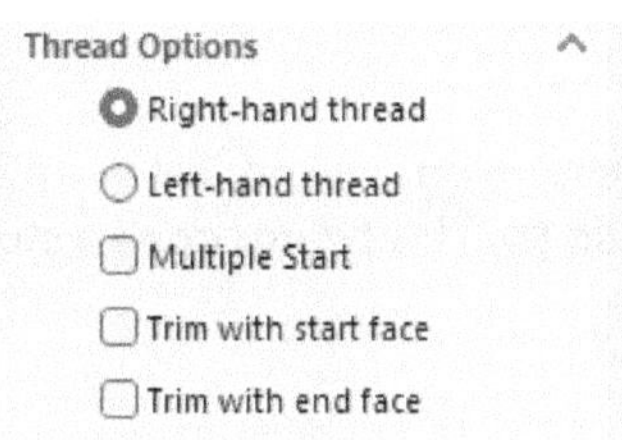

10.55

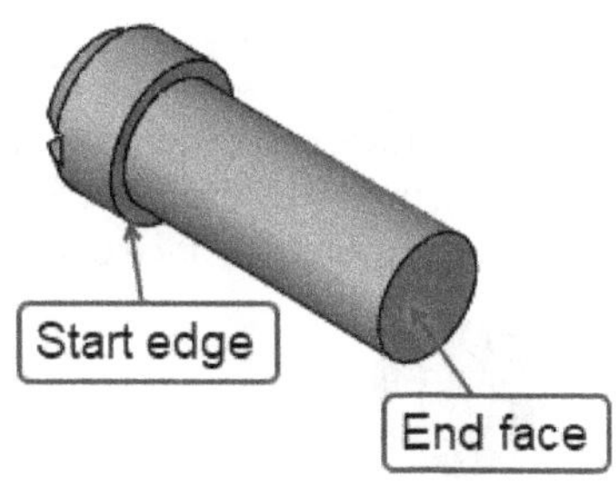

10.56

10.57

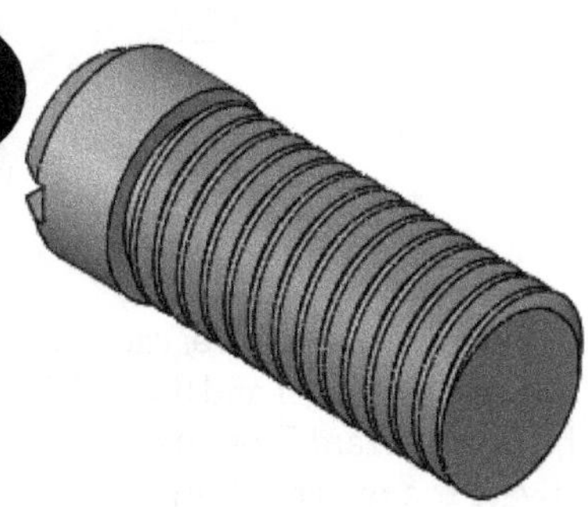

Note: To define the end face of a thread, you need to select the **Up To Selection** option in the **End Condition** drop-down list of the **End Condition** rollout and then select a face as the end face of the thread.

In SOLIDWORKS, you can also specify multiple starts for a thread by selecting the **Multiple Start** check box. On selecting this check box, the **Number of Starts** field becomes available in the rollout, which allows you to specify the number of starts for the thread. Note that the number of starts specified in this field defines the number of times the thread is created in an equally spaced circular pattern around the feature, see Figure 10.58. In this figure, the thread has been created by specifying 5 as the number of starts for the thread. Note that the pitch of the thread must allow multiple starts for the thread. If the pitch of the thread does not allow multiple starts, then self-intersection between the threads occurs which does not allow you to create a thread with multiple starts.

10.58

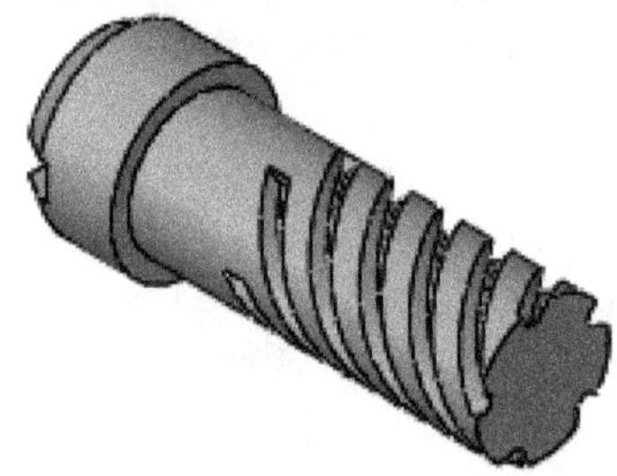

Preview Options

The options of the **Preview Options** rollout are used for specifying the type of preview to be displayed.

After specifying all the parameters for adding a thread, click on the green tick-mark ✓ in the PropertyManager. The thread is created.

Creating a Stud Feature

In SOLIDWORKS, you can create an external threaded stud feature on a cylindrical or a planar face of an existing model by using the **Stud Wizard** tool, see Figure 10.59. This figure shows a stud feature created on the cylindrical face of a model.

10.59

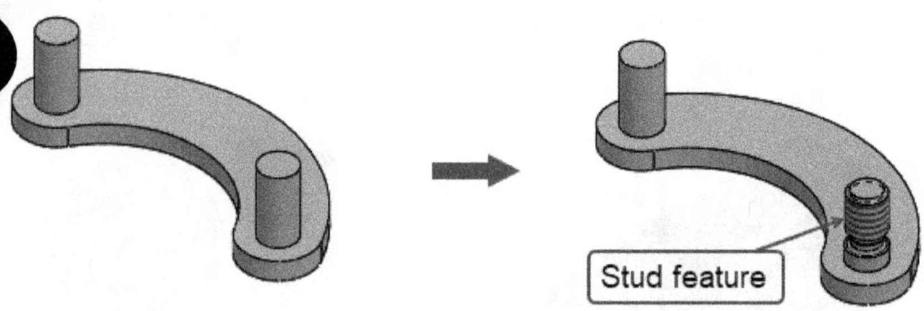

To create a stud feature, click on the arrow at the bottom of the **Hole Wizard** tool in the **Features CommandManager** and then click on the **Stud Wizard** tool in the flyout that appears, see Figure 10.60. The **Stud Wizard PropertyManager** appears, see Figure 10.61. In this PropertyManager, you need to activate the required button (**Creates Stud on a Cylindrical Body** or **Creates Stud on a Surface**) for creating a stud feature on a cylindrical or a planar face, respectively. The methods for creating stud features on cylindrical and planar faces of a model are discussed next.

10.60

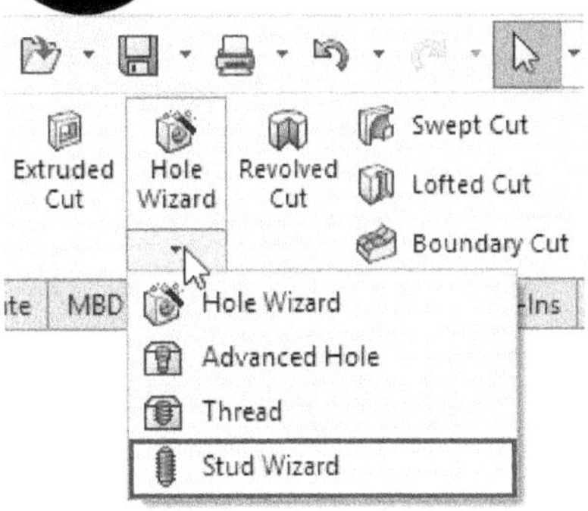

10.61

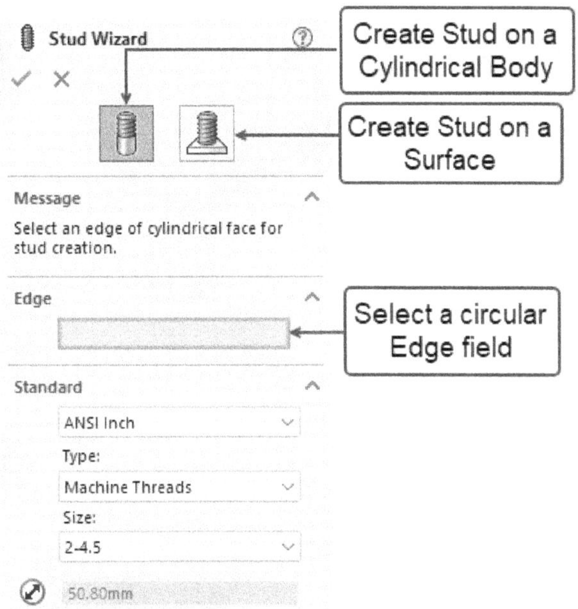

Creating a Stud Feature on a Cylindrical Face

1. Ensure that the **Creates Stud on a Cylindrical Body** button is activated in the **Stud Wizard PropertyManager** for creating a stud feature on a cylindrical face of an existing model, refer to Figure 10.61.

2. Select an edge of a cylindrical face or feature of a model in the graphics area. The edge gets selected, and its name appears in the **Select a circular Edge** field of the **Edge** rollout. Also, the preview of a threaded stud feature appears on the cylindrical feature of the selected edge with default parameters, see Figure 10.62.

3. Specify the required standard (ANSI Inch, ANSI Metric, or ISO etc.), type, and size of threads in the respective fields of the **Standard** rollout. The major diameter is calculated automatically, based on the thread size selected.

4. Specify the end condition to extend the thread of the stud feature from the selected edge of the cylindrical feature by selecting the required option in the **End Condition** drop-down list of the **Thread** rollout.

5. Select the **Thread class** check box in the **Thread** rollout of the PropertyManager and then select the required thread class in the **Thread class** drop-down list that appears, if needed.

6. If needed, you can create an undercut at the end of the threads of the stud feature by using the options in the **Undercut** rollout. To do this, select the check box in front of the **Undercut** rollout, see Figure 10.63. The options in the **Undercut** rollout get enabled with default undercut parameters based on the selected standard. Also, the preview of an undercut appears with

default specified parameters in the graphics area, see Figure 10.64. You can customize the default undercut parameters in the respective fields of the **Undercut** rollout, as required. To restore the default values in the **Undercut** rollout, click on the **Restore Default Values** button.

10.62

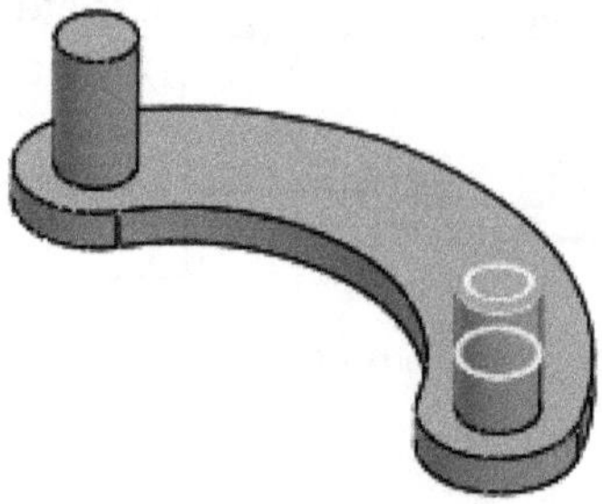

10.63

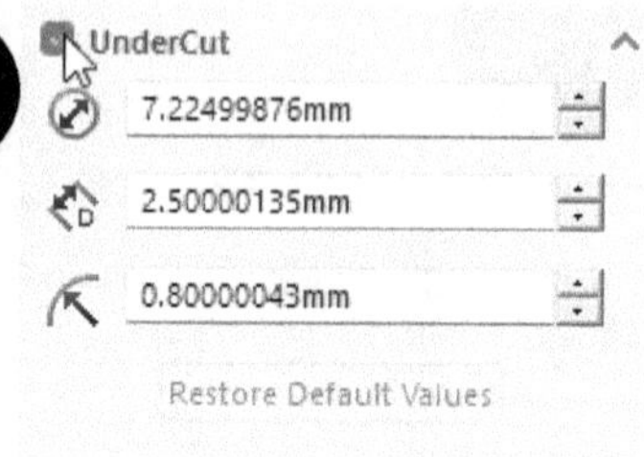

7. After defining the stud parameters, click on the green tick-mark ✓ in the PropertyManager. The stud feature is created, see Figure 10.65.

10.64

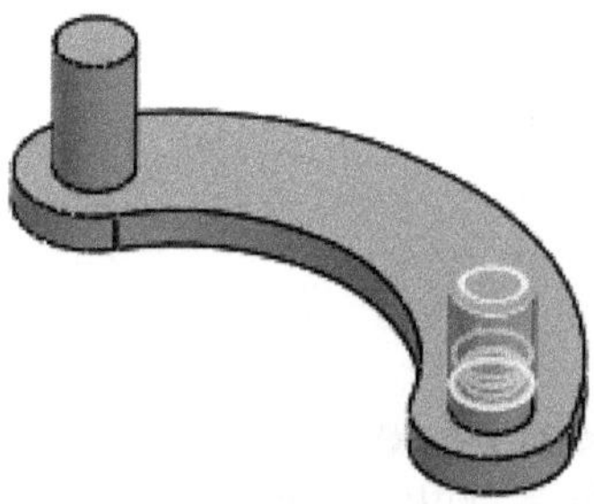

10.65

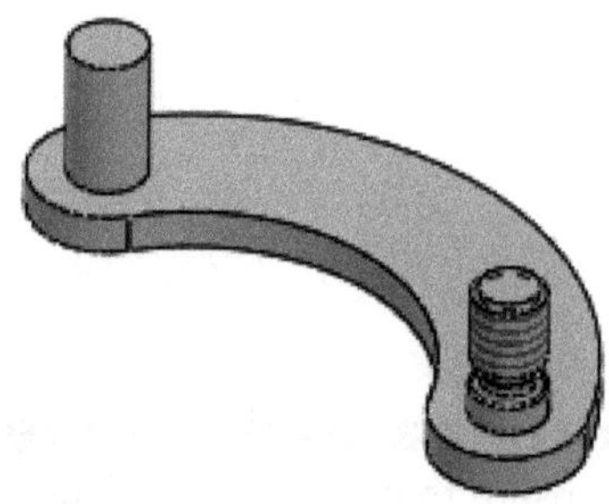

Creating a Stud Feature on a Planar Face

1. Invoke the **Stud Wizard PropertyManager** and then select the **Creates Stud on a Surface** button for creating a stud feature on a planar face of a model, refer to Figure 10.66.

2. Specify the required length and diameter of the stud shaft in the **Shaft Length** and **Shaft Diameter** fields of the **Shaft Details** rollout, respectively, see Figure 10.66.

10.66

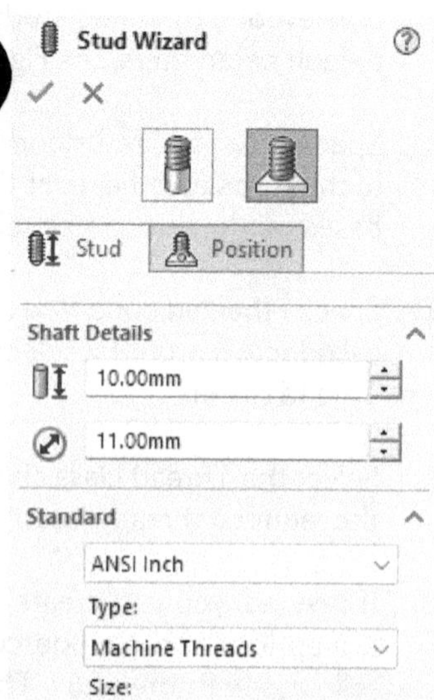

3. Specify the required standard (ANSI Inch, ANSI Metric, or, ISO, etc.), type, and size of threads in the respective fields of the **Standard** rollout.

4. Specify the end condition of the threads along the shaft length of the stud by selecting the required option in the **End Condition** drop-down list of the **Thread** rollout.

5. Select the **Thread class** check box in the **Thread** rollout of the PropertyManager and then select the required thread class in the **Thread class** drop-down list that appears, if needed.

6. If needed, create an undercut at the end of the threads of the stud feature by using the options in the **Undercut** rollout, as discussed earlier.

7. After specifying the stud parameters, click on the **Position** tab in the PropertyManager and then click on the planar face of a model as the placement face. The placement face gets selected and is oriented normal to the viewing direction. Also, the preview of a stud feature appears, which follows the cursor as you move it over the placement face.

   Now, you need to define the placement point of the stud feature.

8. Click the left mouse button on the placement face to specify the placement point of the stud feature. The center point of the stud feature is placed at the defined placement point. Next, change the orientation of the model to isometric and then click on the green tick-mark ✓ button in the PropertyManager. The stud feature is created, see Figure 10.67. In this figure, the stud feature is created on a planar face without an undercut.

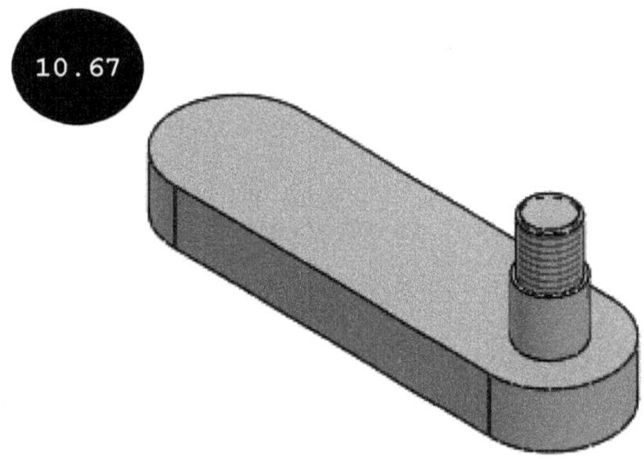

Creating Fillets

A fillet is a curved face of a constant or variable radius and is used to remove sharp edges of a model that may cause injury while handling the model. Figure 10.68 shows a model before and after creating a constant radius fillet on an edge.

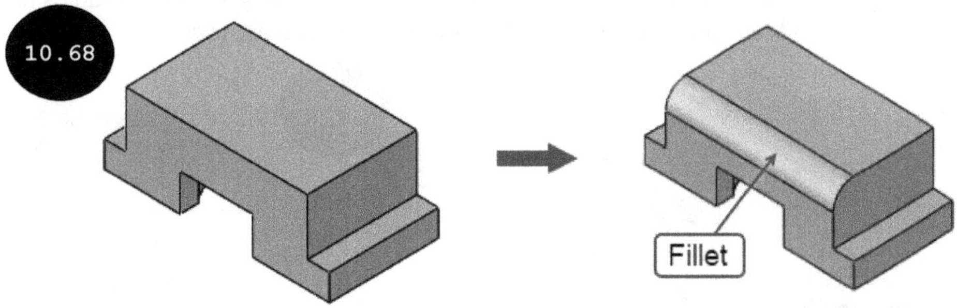

In SOLIDWORKS, you can create fillets by using two methods: Manual and FilletXpert. The Manual method is used to create fillets manually. By using this method, you can create four types of fillets: constant radius fillet, variable radius fillet, face fillet, and full round fillet. On the other hand, the FilletXpert method is used to create fillets automatically. By using this method, you can only create constant radius fillets in a model.

To create fillets by using the Manual method, click on the **Fillet** tool in the **Features CommandManager**. The **Fillet PropertyManager** appears, see Figure 10.69. If the **FilletXpert PropertyManager** appears on clicking the **Fillet** tool, then click on the **Manual** tab in the PropertyManager to invoke the **Fillet PropertyManager**. The methods for creating different types of fillets manually are discussed next.

10.69

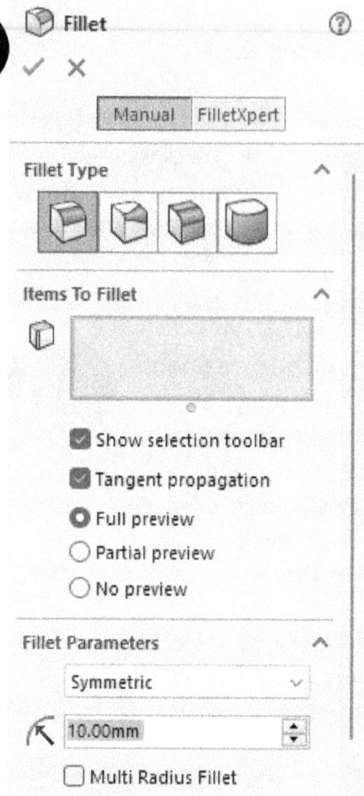

Creating a Constant Radius Fillet

A constant radius fillet is a fillet that has a constant radius throughout the selected edge, see Figure 10.70. You can create a constant radius fillet by clicking on the **Constant Size Fillet** button in the **Fillet Type** rollout of the PropertyManager, see Figure 10.71. The options for creating a constant radius fillet that appears in the PropertyManager after selecting this button are discussed next.

10.70

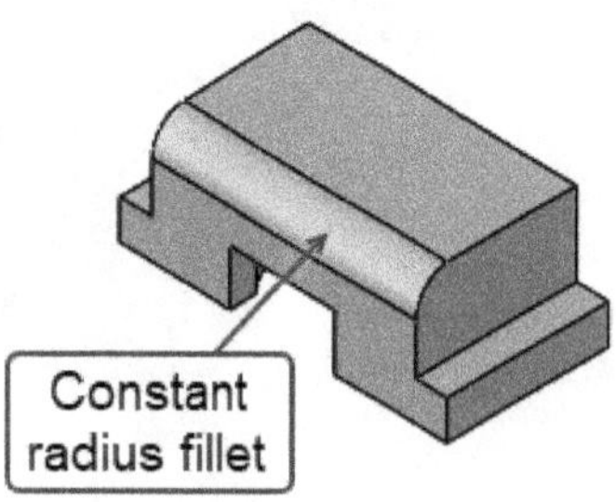

10.71

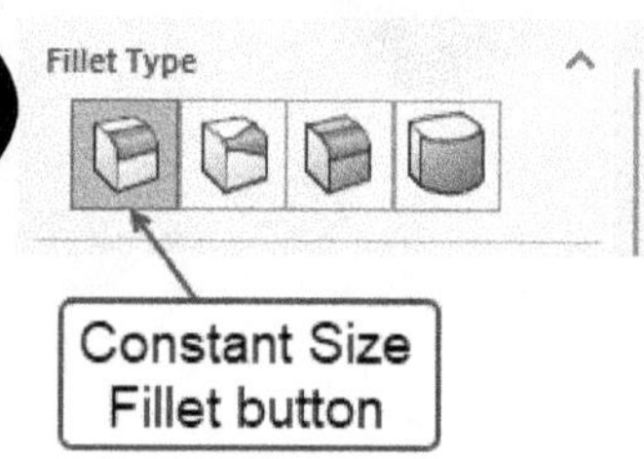

Items To Fillet

The options in the **Items To Fillet** rollout are used for selecting entities such as edges, faces, and features to create a fillet. The options are discussed next.

Edges, Faces, Features and Loops

This field of the rollout is activated by default. As a result, you can select edges, faces, features, or loops for creating a constant radius fillet. On selecting the edges, faces, features, or loops, a preview of the constant radius fillet appears in the graphics area with the default radius value.

Note: If you select a face to create a fillet, all the edges of the selected face get filleted (see Figure 10.72) and if you select a feature, all the edges of the selected feature get filleted, see Figure 10.73. Both these figures show the fillet preview.

10.72

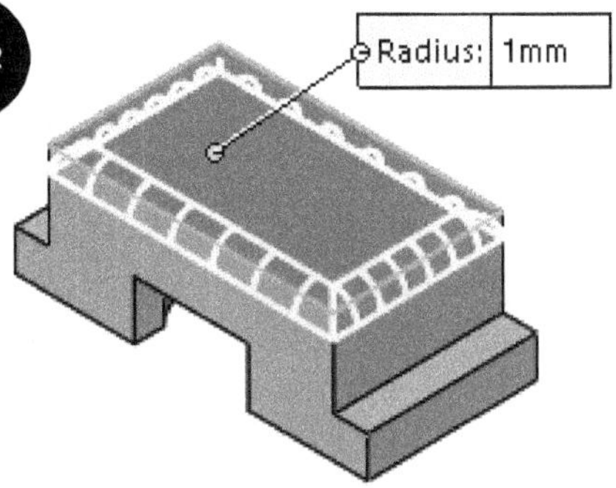

10.73

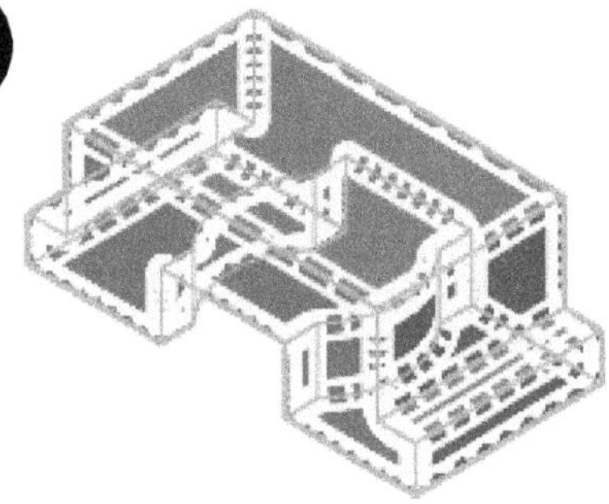

Tangent propagation

The **Tangent propagation** check box is used to apply the fillet to all edges that are tangent to the selected edge. Figure 10.74 shows an edge to be selected for applying the fillet. Figures 10.75 and 10.76 show the preview of the resultant fillet when the **Tangent propagation** check box is cleared and selected, respectively.

10.74

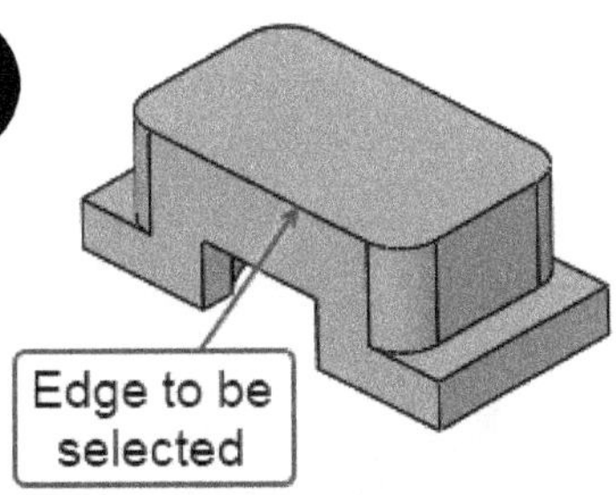

10.75

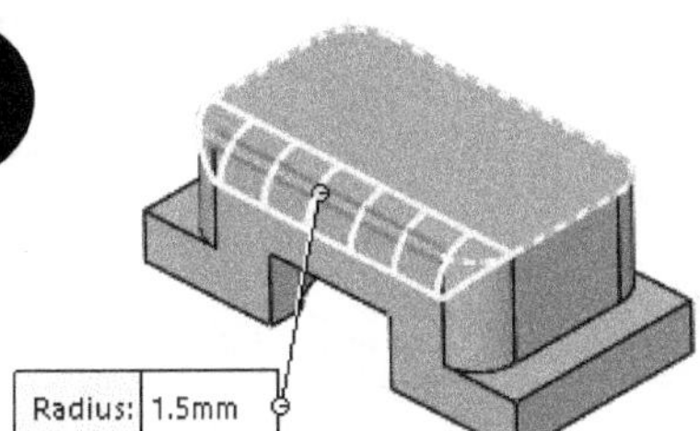

Tangent propagation check box is cleared

10.76

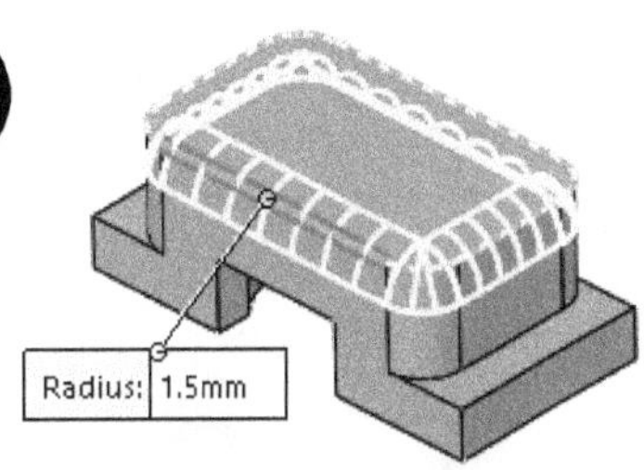

Tangent propagation check box is selected

Show selection toolbar

The **Show selection toolbar** check box of the **Items To Fillet** rollout is selected by default. As a result, the **Selection** Pop-up toolbar appears on selecting an entity for creating a fillet, see Figure 10.77. The tools of the **Selection** Pop-up toolbar help you in selecting multiple edges of the feature for creating the fillet.

10.77

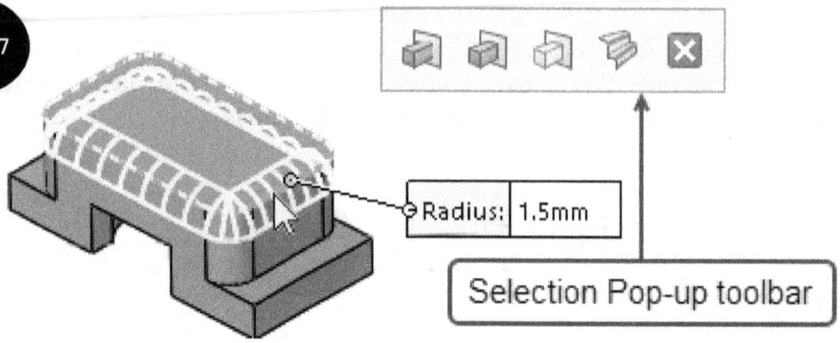

Full preview, Partial preview, and No preview

The **Full preview** radio button is used to display a full preview of the fillet, which includes the preview of all fillet edges. On selecting the **Partial preview** radio button, the partial view of the fillet appears. Note that in the case of partial preview, the preview appears only in one fillet edge. On selecting the **No preview** radio button, the display of the preview is turned off.

Fillet Parameters

The options in the **Fillet Parameters** rollout are used to specify fillet parameters, see Figure 10.78. The options are discussed next.

10.78

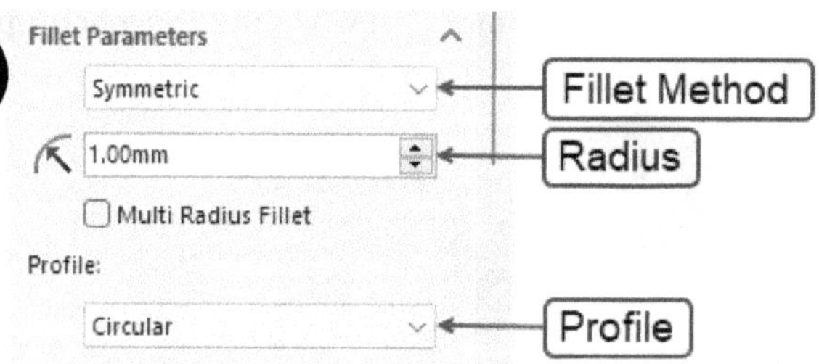

Fillet Method

The **Fillet Method** drop-down list is used to select the method for creating the fillet. By selecting the **Symmetric** option, you can create a fillet, that is symmetric on both sides of the edge selected for creating the fillet, see Figure 10.79. When this option is selected, the **Radius** field becomes available in the rollout, which is used for entering the symmetric radius of the fillet. On selecting the **Asymmetric** option, the **Distance 1** and **Distance 2** fields become available in the rollout for specifying different radii for both sides of the edge, see Figure 10.80.

10.79

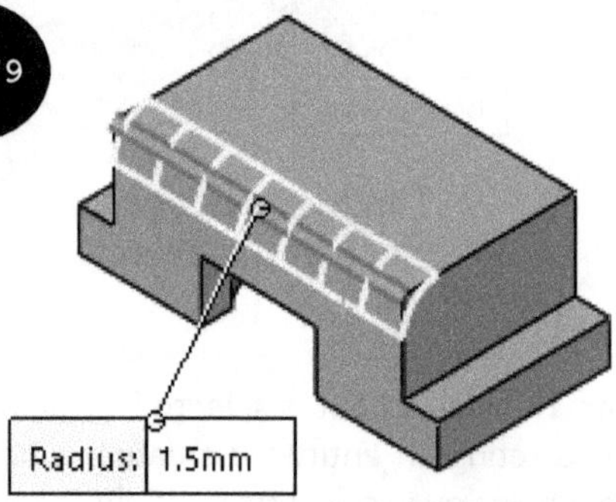

10.80

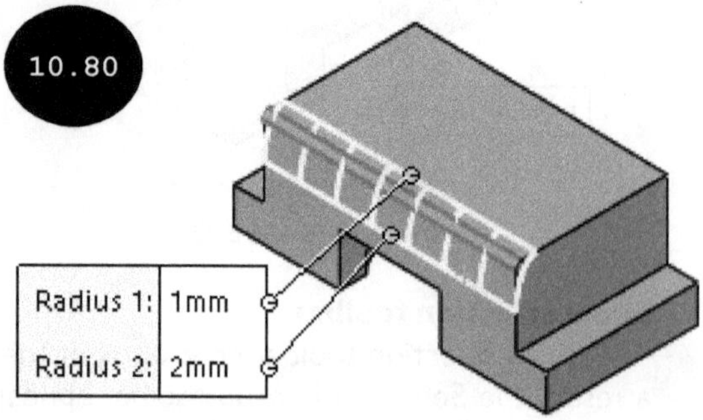

Multiple radius fillet

By selecting the **Multiple radius fillet** check box, you can assign different radius values for the selected edges. For example, if you have selected two edges for applying fillet, then on selecting this check box, you can assign different radius values or control the radius of both the edges, individually. By default, this check box is cleared. As a result, all edges selected for applying the fillet have the same radius value.

Profile

The **Profile** drop-down list is used to select the type of fillet profile, which defines the cross-sectional shape of the fillet. You can select the **Circular**, **Conic Rho**, **Conic Radius**, or **Curvature Continuous** option from this drop-down list to define the fillet profile. On selecting the **Circular** option, a fillet of circular shape is created, see Figure 10.81. If you select the **Conic Rho** option, the **Conic Rho** field becomes available below this drop-down list. In this field, you can specify the Rho value for the fillet. Note that you can define the Rho value in the range between 0 and 1, see Figures 10.82 through 10.84.

10.81

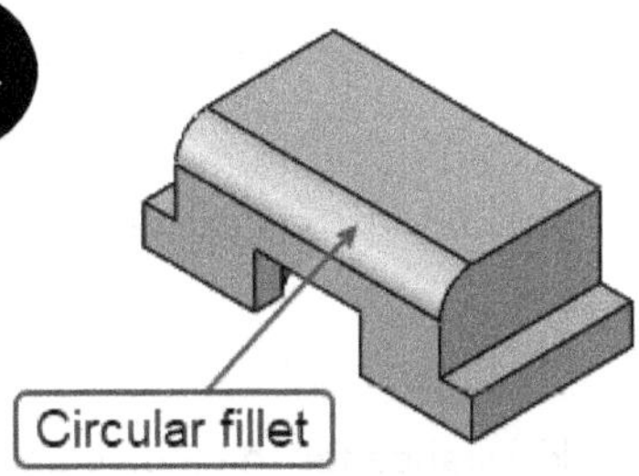

10.82

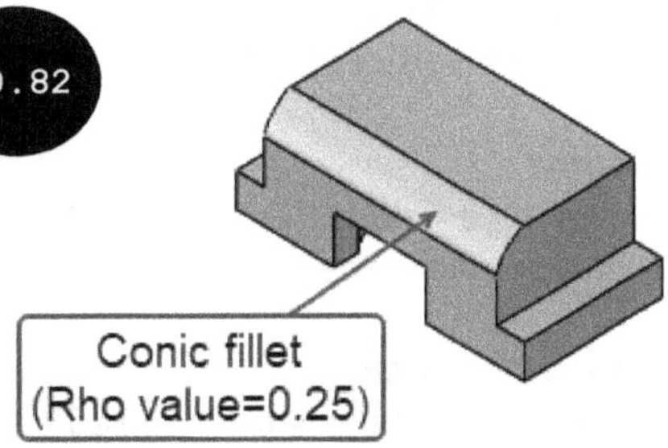

10.83

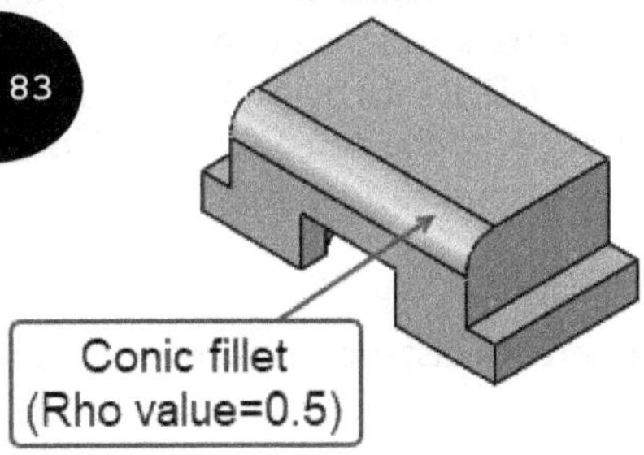

10.84

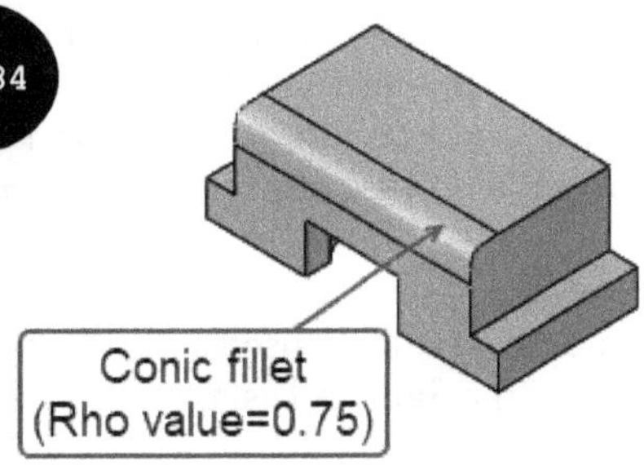

Tip: If the Rho value is less than 0.5 then the fillet profile is elliptical. If the Rho value is 0.5 then the fillet profile is parabolic. If the Rho value is greater than 0.5 then the fillet profile is hyperbolic.

By selecting the **Conic Radius** option, the **Conic Radius** field appears below the drop-down list, which is used to specify the radius of curvature at the corner of the fillet. By selecting the **Curvature Continuous** option, a fillet is created such that it maintains a smooth curvature between the adjacent faces of the edge selected for creating the fillet.

Setback Parameters

The options in the **Setback Parameters** rollout are used to define parameters for creating a setback fillet. A setback fillet is a fillet that has a smooth transition from fillet edges to a common intersecting vertex. You can create a setback fillet on three or more than three edges that intersect at a common vertex, see Figure 10.85. To create a setback fillet, expand the **Setback Parameters** rollout by clicking on the arrow that is available in its title bar, see Figure 10.86. The options in the **Setback Parameters** rollout are discussed next.

10.85

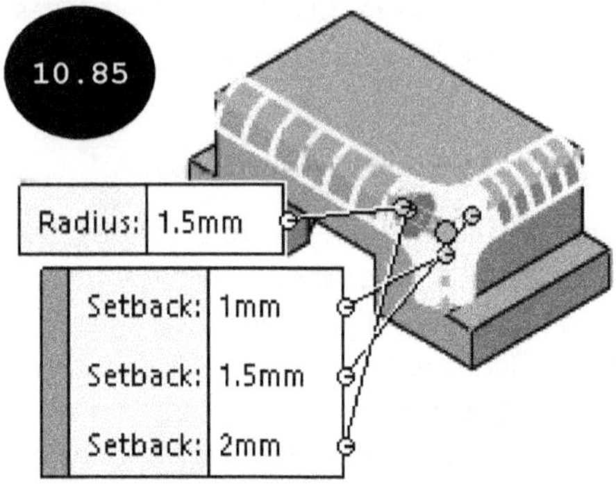

10.86

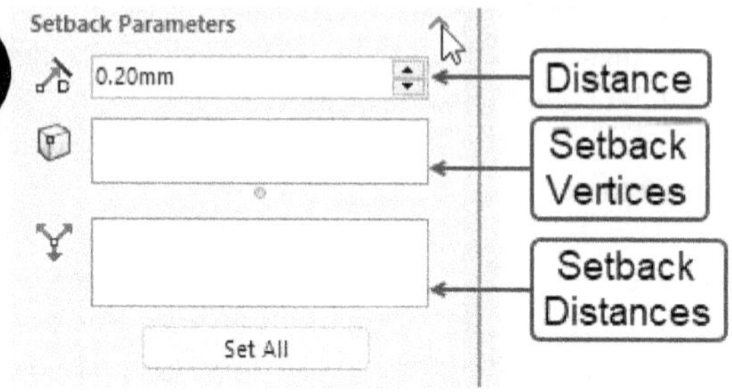

Setback Vertices

The **Setback Vertices** field is used to select a vertex where the fillet edges intersect each other.

Distance

The **Distance** field is used to specify the fillet setback distance, which is calculated from the selected setback vertex.

Setback Distances

The **Setback Distances** field is used to specify the setback distance for the individual edge of the fillet from the setback vertex. Note that as soon as you select the setback vertex, a list of corresponding edges appears in this field. To assign the setback distance to an edge, select an edge from this field and then enter the setback distance in the **Distance** field. Next, press ENTER. Similarly, you can assign the setback distance to other edges of the setback fillet. Figure 10.85 shows the preview of a setback fillet with different setback distances assigned.

Set All

The **Set All** button is used to assign the current specified setback distance to all the edges that are listed in the **Setback Distance** field.

Partial Edge Parameters

In SOLIDWORKS, you can also create a partial fillet by specifying its start and end positions along the edge of a model by using the **Partial Edge Parameters** rollout of the PropertyManager. To do this, expand the **Partial Edge Parameters** rollout by selecting the check box that is available in its title bar, see Figure 10.87. The options in the **Partial Edge Parameters** are discussed next.

10.87

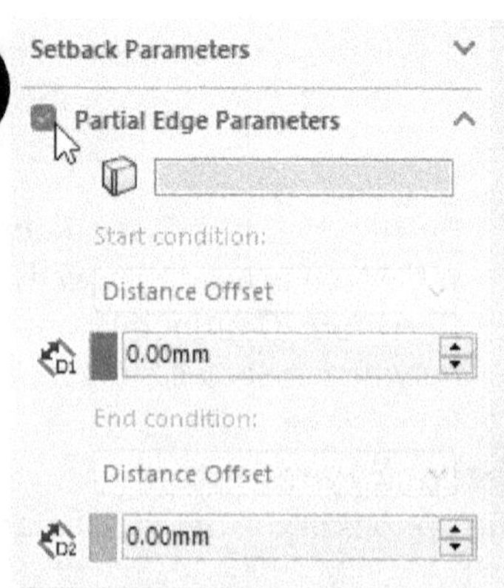

Start condition

The options in the **Start condition** drop-down list are used for defining the start condition of the partial fillet. By default, the **Distance Offset** option is selected in the **Start condition** drop-down list. As a result, you can specify the offset distance from the start point of the fillet in the **Offset distance from start point** field of the PropertyManager. Alternatively, you can also drag the start handle that appears in the graphics area to define the start position of the partial fillet along the edge, see Figure 10.88.

10.88

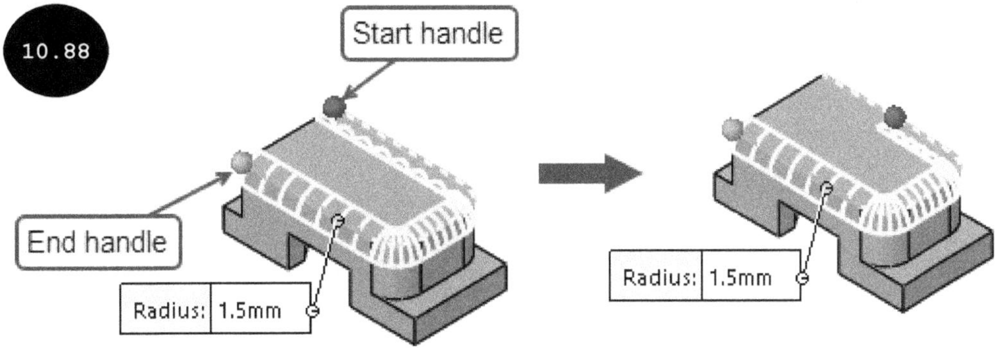

On selecting the **Percentage Offset** option in the **Start condition** drop-down list, you can define the start position of the fillet by specifying a percentage value in the **Percentage offset from start point** field that appears in the rollout. Note that the percentage value is calculated in terms of the total length of the selected edge. On selecting the **Reference Offset** option, you can select a sketch point, a reference point, or a planar face to define the start position of the fillet in the field that appears in the rollout.

End condition

The options in the **End condition** drop-down list are used for defining the end condition of the partial fillet. The options in this drop-down list are the same as discussed earlier. You can also drag the end handle that appears in the preview of the fillet to define the end condition of the fillet. Figure 10.89 shows the preview of a partial fillet by defining its start and end conditions.

Note: The **Partial Edge Parameters** rollout is only available for constant radius fillets.

Fillet Options

The **Fillet Options** rollout is shown in Figure 10.90. The options in this rollout are discussed next.

10.89

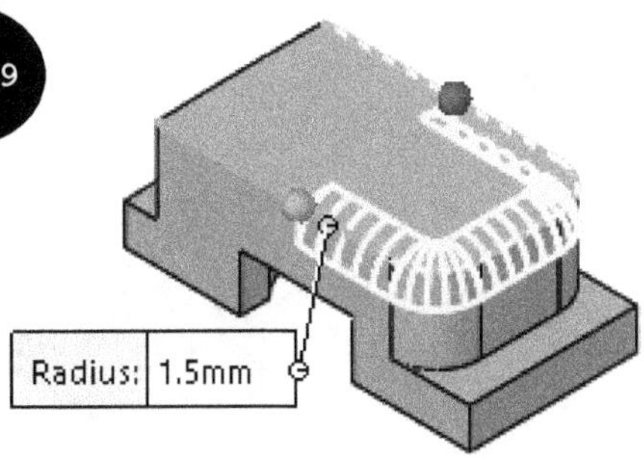

10.90

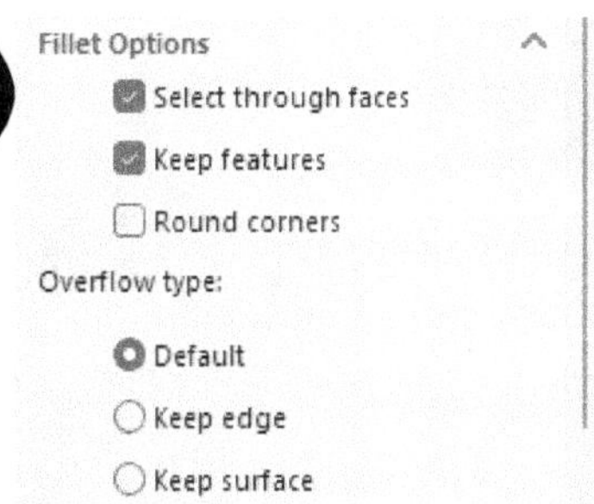

Select through faces

By selecting the **Select through faces** check box, you can select the invisible edges of the model for applying fillets, see Figure 10.91. In this figure, three edges are visible, and the fourth edge is not visible from the front. You can select the invisible edges of the model from the front when the **Select through faces** check box is selected.

10.91

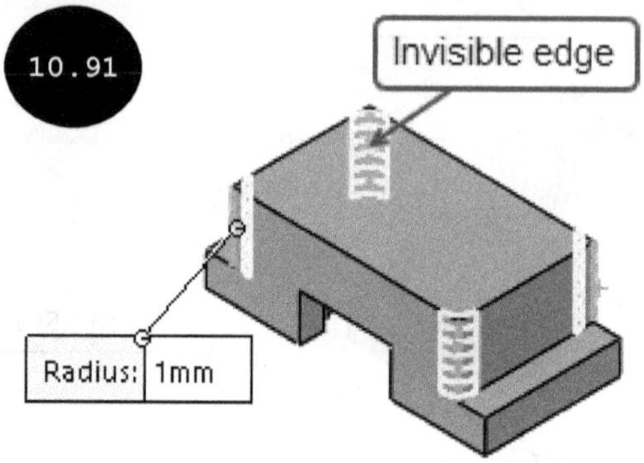

Keep features

After selecting the **Keep features** check box, if you apply a fillet of a large radius that covers the other feature (extruded boss or cut) of a model, then the covered feature remains available in the model after the fillet is created. However, if you clear this check box, then the covered feature will be removed from the model after the fillet is created. Figure 10.92 shows the preview of a fillet with a large radius, which covers a cylindrical feature of the model. Figures 10.93 and 10.94 show the resultant models after creating the fillets when the Keep features check box is selected and cleared, respectively.

10.92

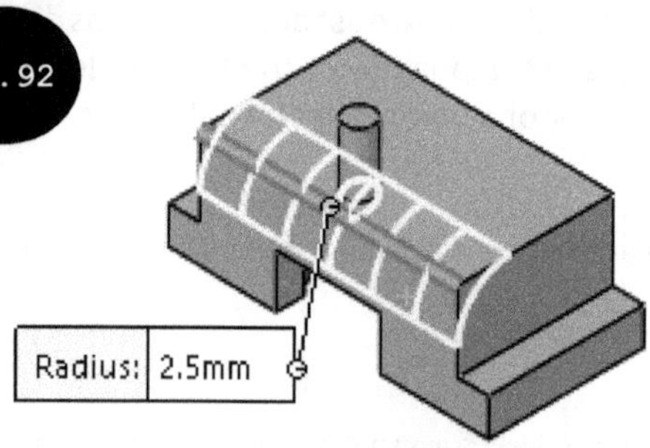

10.93

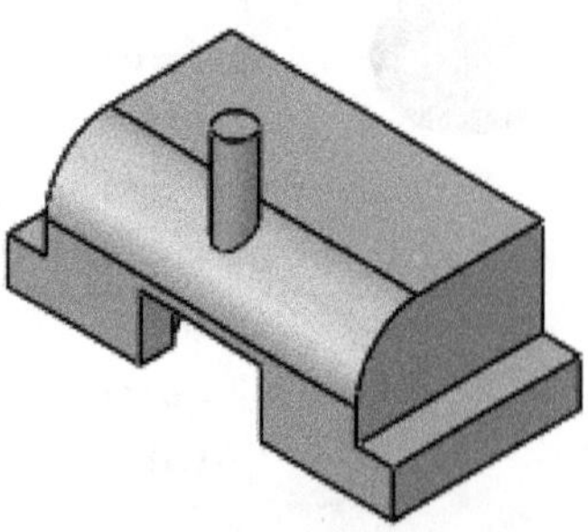

10.94

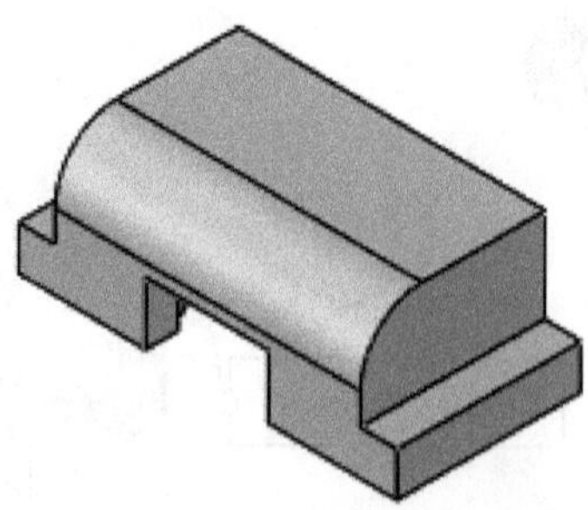

Once you have specified all the parameters for creating a fillet, click on the green tick-mark ✓ in the PropertyManager. A fillet of a specified radius is created.

Note: In SOLIDWORKS, you can repair fillets that have missing edges. For example, while creating a model, if some of the filleted edges have been removed, or are no longer available in the model, then the respective fillet feature displays an error of missing edges, see Figure 10.95. To repair a fillet that has missing edges or errors, click on it in the FeatureManager Design Tree and then click on the **Edit Feature** tool in the Pop-up toolbar that appears, see Figure 10.95. The **Fillet PropertyManager** appears with a list of all the missing edges of the fillet, see Figure 10.96. Next, right-click on the missing edge to be repaired and then click on the **Repair All Missing References** option in the shortcut menu that appears, see Figure 10.96. SOLIDWORKS attempts to reattach or repair all the missing references of the fillet. You can clear all the missing references of the fillet by using the **Clear All Missing References** option of the shortcut menu. You can also define new references for the missing edges, manually. After repairing the fillet, click on the green tick-mark button in the PropertyManager.

10.95

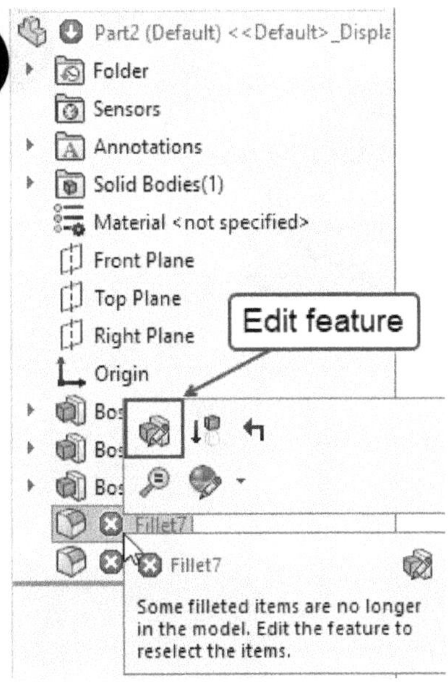

10.96

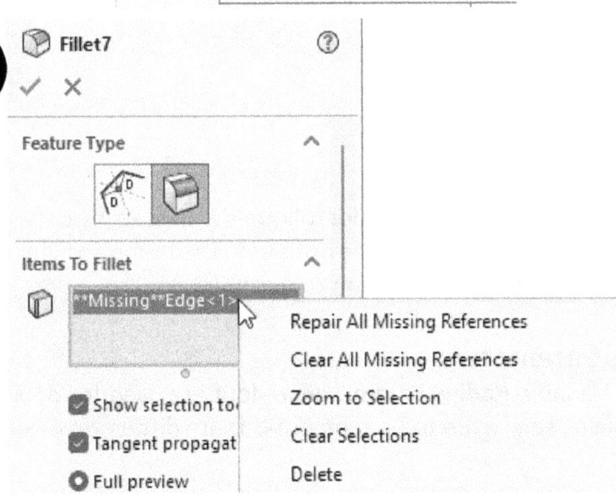

Note: In SOLIDWORKS, after creating a constant radius fillet, you can convert it into a chamfer and vice-versa. To convert a constant radius fillet into a chamfer, select the constant radius fillet in the FeatureManager Design Tree or in the graphics area. A Pop-up toolbar appears near the cursor. In this Pop-up toolbar, click on the **Edit Feature** tool. The **Fillet PropertyManager** appears. In this PropertyManager, click on the **Chamfer Type** button to convert the selected fillet into the chamfer. Next, click on the green tick-mark button.

Creating a Variable Radius Fillet

A variable radius fillet is a fillet that has variable radii along an edge, see Figure 10.97. You can create a variable radius fillet by selecting the **Variable Size Fillet** button in the **Fillet Type** rollout, see Figure 10.98. The options to create a variable radius fillet that appears in the PropertyManager after selecting the **Variable Size Fillet** button are discussed next.

10.97

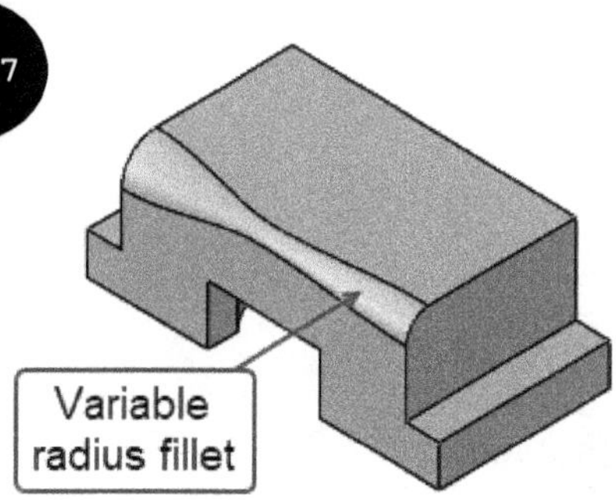

10.98

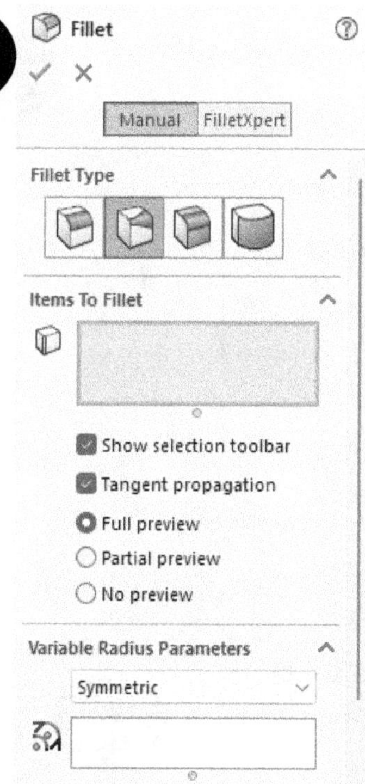

Items To Fillet

The **Edges to Fillet** field of the **Items To Fillet** rollout is activated, by default. As a result, you can select edges for creating a variable radius fillet. The options in the **Items To Fillet** rollout are the same as those discussed earlier while creating the constant radius fillet.

Variable Radius Parameters

The options in the **Variable Radius Parameters** rollout are used for defining parameters for creating the variable radius fillet, see Figure 10.99. The options are discussed next.

10.99

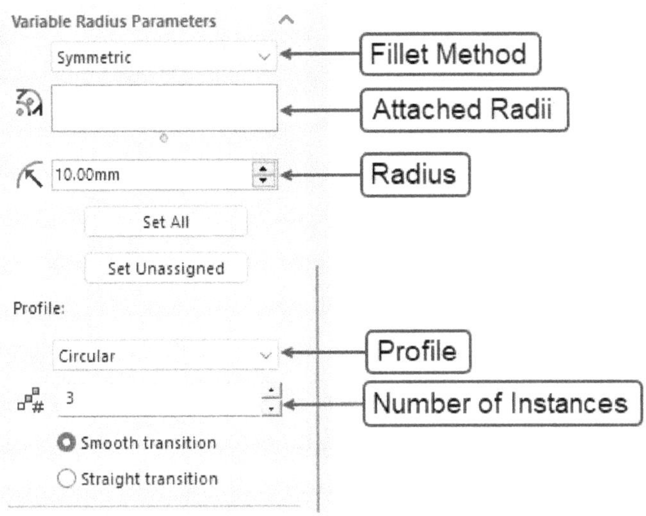

Attached Radii

The **Attached Radii** field displays a list of all vertices and control points of the selected edge or edges. Note that you can define a different radius value for each vertex and control point of the edge.

Number of Instances

The **Number of Instances** field is used to specify the number of control points to be attached along the selected edge. You can specify a different radius value for each control point. After specifying the number of control points, press ENTER. The pink dots representing control points appear along the edge selected for applying the fillet, see Figure 10.100.

10.100

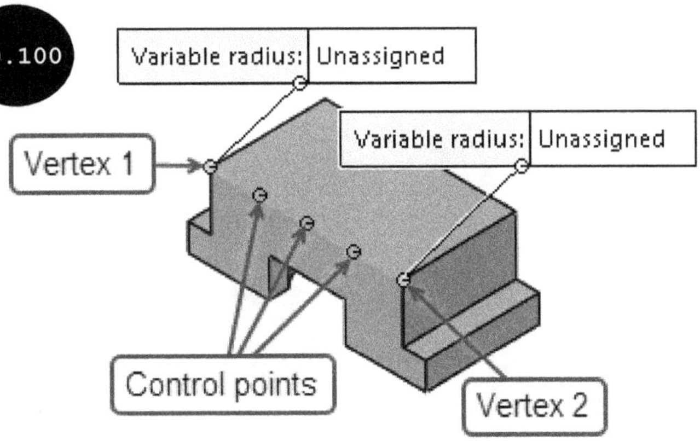

To specify a different radius value for each control point, click on the control points one by one that appear along the selected edge in the graphics area. The callouts having **R** and **P** fields appear attached to each selected control point in the graphics area, see Figure 10.101. By using the **R** field of a callout, you can specify the radius value for the control point and by using the **P** field, you can specify the location of the control point along the edge in terms of percentage value. Note that to edit the value in a callout, you need to click on its field to be edited.

10.101

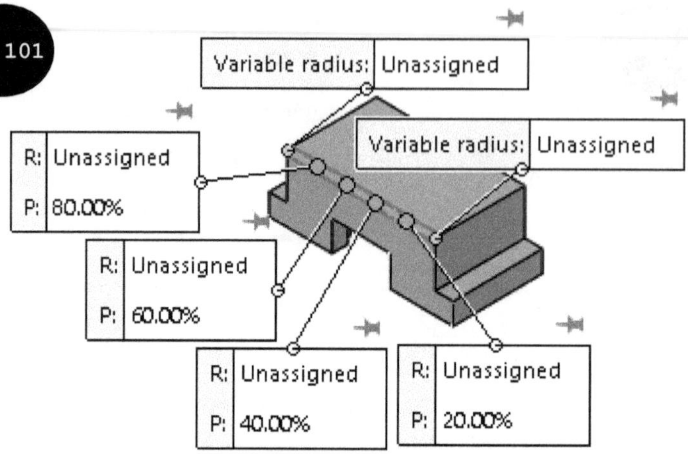

In addition to the display of callouts in the graphics area, the names of the selected control points appear in the **Attached Radii** field of the PropertyManager. You can also specify the radius value for a control point by selecting its name in the **Attached Radii** field and then entering the radius value in the **Radius** field of the PropertyManager.

Set All

The **Set All** button is used to assign the radius value that is specified in the **Radius** field to all the control points and vertices of the edge.

Set Unassigned

The **Set Unassigned** button is used to assign the specified radius value to all control points and vertices that do not have a radius value assigned.

Smooth transition

The **Smooth transition** radio button is selected by default. As a result, the variable fillet created is such that a smooth transition is carried out from one radius value to another, see Figure 10.102.

Straight transition

On selecting the **Straight transition** radio button, a linear or straight transition is carried out from one radius value to another, see Figure 10.103.

10.102

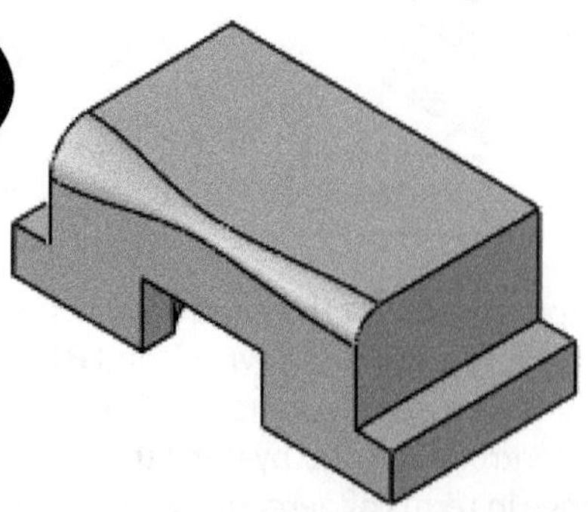

10.103

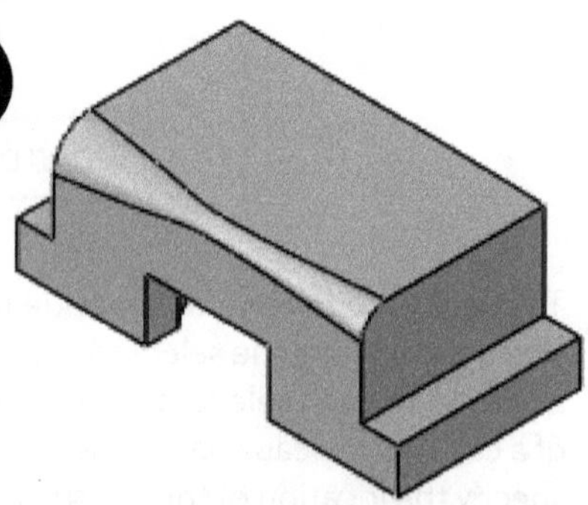

The remaining options in the PropertyManager are the same as those discussed earlier while creating the constant radius fillet.

Creating a Face Fillet

A face fillet is created between two non-adjacent or non-continuous faces of a model, see Figure 10.104.

10.104

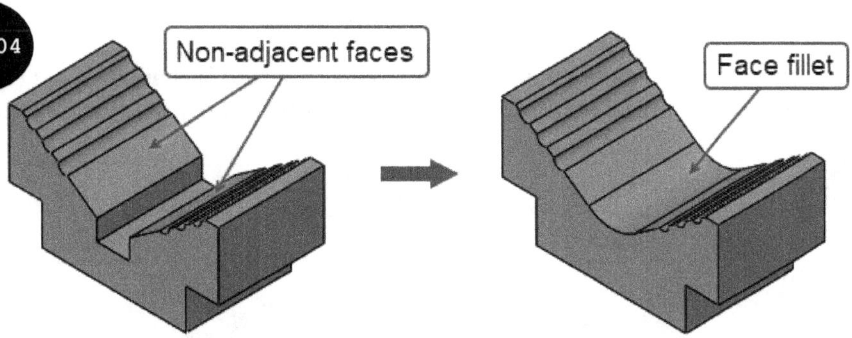

To create a face fillet, invoke the **Fillet PropertyManager** and then click on the **Face Fillet** button in the **Fillet Type** rollout of the PropertyManager, see Figure 10.105. The options for creating a face fillet are discussed next.

10.105

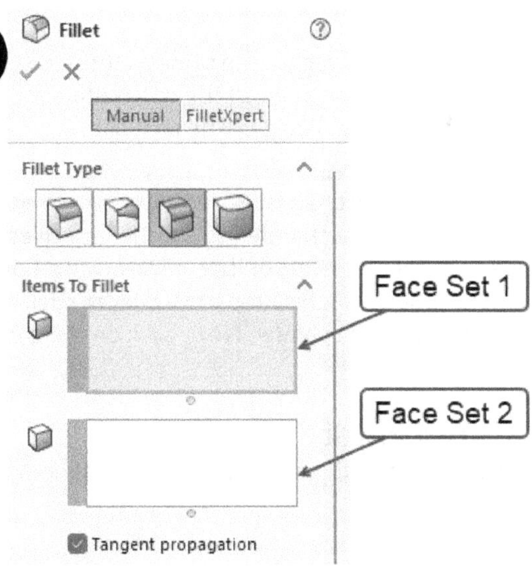

Items To Fillet

The options in the **Items To Fillet** rollout are used for selecting non-adjacent faces and are discussed next.

Face Set 1

The **Face Set 1** field is used to select the first set of non-continuous faces, see Figure 10.106.

Face Set 2

The **Face Set 2** field is used to select the second set of non-continuous faces of the model, see Figure 10.106.

Note: You need to click on the **Face Set 2** field in the **Items To Fillet** rollout to activate it for selecting the second set of non-continuous faces of the model to be filleted.

On selecting two non-continuous faces, a preview of the face fillet appears, see Figure 10.107. In case the preview of the face fillet does not appear, you need to adjust its radius value.

10.106

10.107

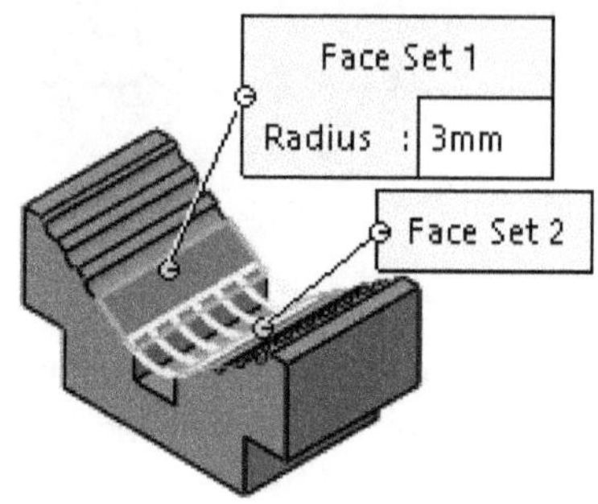

The other options in the PropertyManager are the same as those discussed earlier while creating the constant radius fillet. Once you have specified all the parameters for creating the face fillet, click on the green tick-mark in the PropertyManager. The face fillet is created.

Note: In SOLIDWORKS, after creating a face fillet, you can convert it into a chamfer and vice-versa. To convert a face fillet into a chamfer, select the face fillet in the graphics area. A Pop-up toolbar appears. In this Pop-up toolbar, click on the **Edit Feature** tool . The **Fillet PropertyManager** appears. In this PropertyManager, click on the **Chamfer Type** button to convert the fillet into the chamfer. Next, click on the green tick-mark button.

Creating a Full Round Fillet

A full round fillet is created tangent to three adjacent faces of a model, see Figure 10.108.

10.108

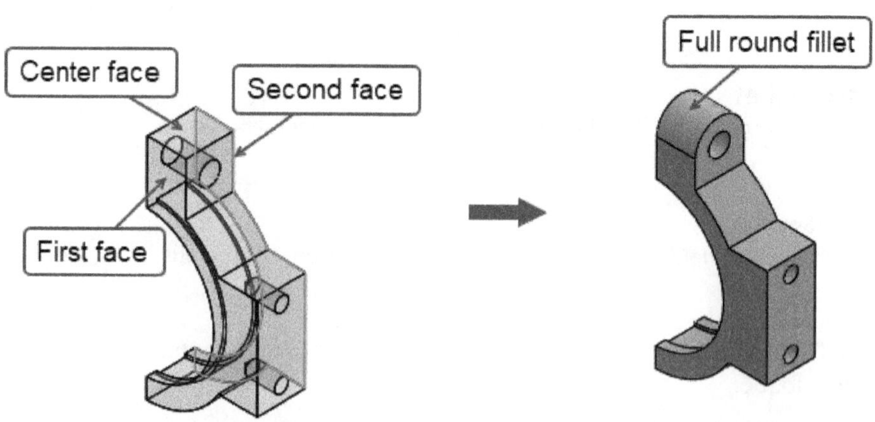

To create a full round fillet, invoke the **Fillet PropertyManager** and then click on the **Full Round Fillet** button in the **Fillet Type** rollout of the PropertyManager, see Figure 10.109. The options for creating a full round fillet are discussed next.

10.109

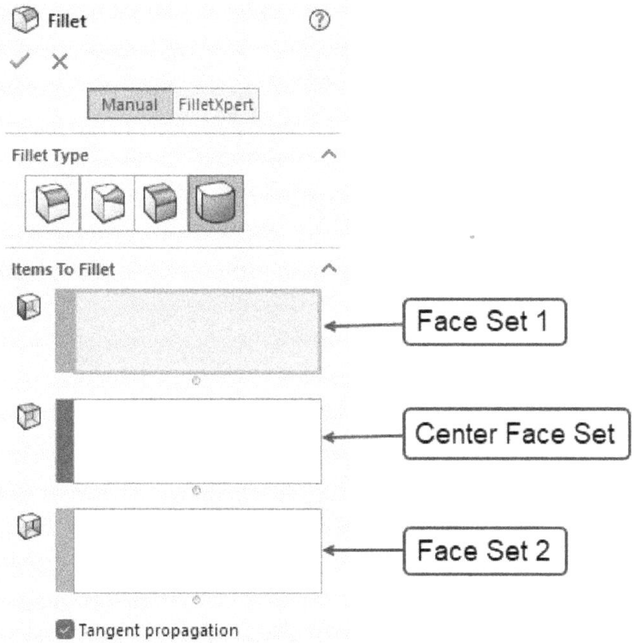

Items To Fillet

The options in the **Items To Fillet** rollout are used for selecting three adjacent faces for creating the full round fillet. The options are discussed next.

Face Set 1

The **Face Set 1** field is used to select the first or start adjacent face of the model for creating the full round fillet in the graphics area, see Figure 10.110.

Center Face Set

The **Center Face Set** field is used to select the center adjacent face of the model for creating the full round fillet, see Figure 10.110.

Face Set 2

The **Face Set 2** field is used to select the end adjacent face of the model for creating the full round fillet, see Figure 10.110.

Note: You need to click on the respective field in the **Items To Fillet** rollout to activate it for selecting the first, center, and end faces of the model to be filleted one by one.

10.110

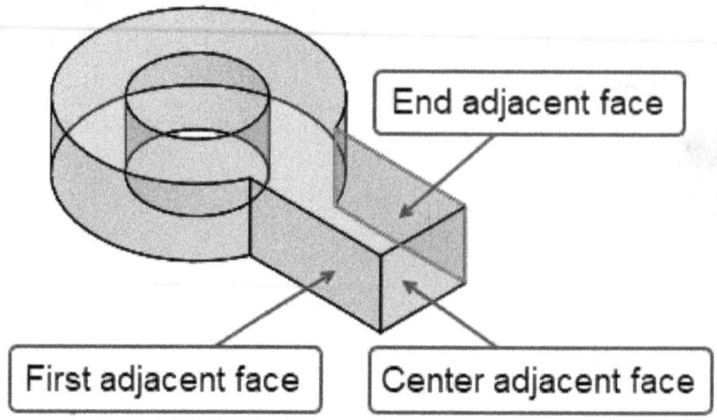

On selecting the three adjacent faces of the model, the preview of the full round fillet appears in the graphics area, see Figure 10.111.

10.111

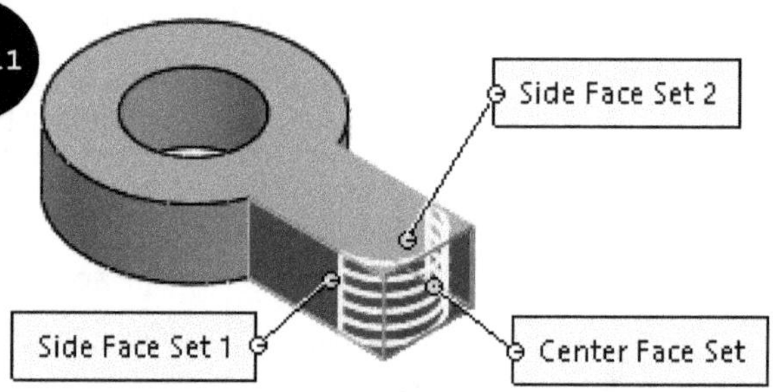

The other options in the PropertyManager are the same as those discussed earlier while creating the constant radius fillet. Once you have specified all the parameters for creating the full round fillet, click on the green tick-mark ✓ in the PropertyManager. The full round fillet is created.

Creating Chamfers

A chamfer is a bevel face that is non-perpendicular to its adjacent faces, see Figure 10.112. You can create different types of chamfers: Angle Distance chamfer, Distance Distance chamfer, Vertex chamfer, Offset Face chamfer, and Face Face chamfer by using the **Chamfer** tool.

10.112

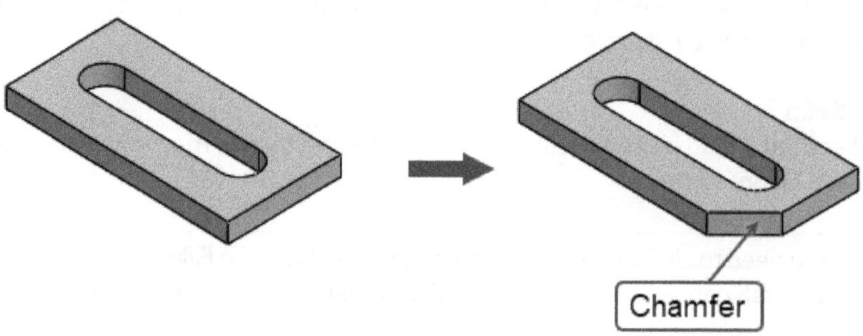

To create a chamfer, click on the arrow at the bottom of the **Fillet** tool in the CommandManager. A flyout appears, see Figure 10.113. Next, click on the **Chamfer** tool in the flyout. The **Chamfer PropertyManager** appears, see Figure 10.114. The options in this PropertyManager are discussed next.

10.113

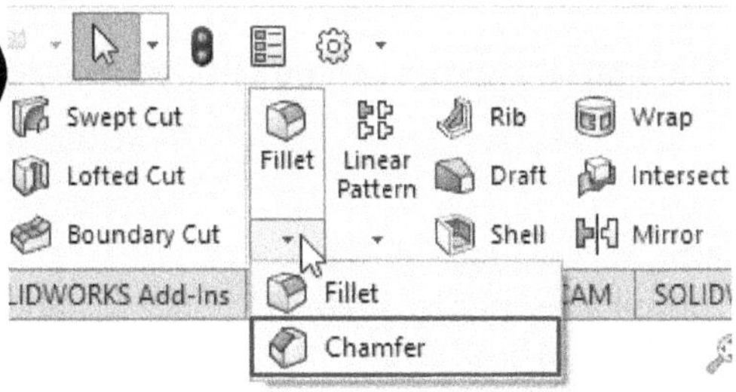

10.114

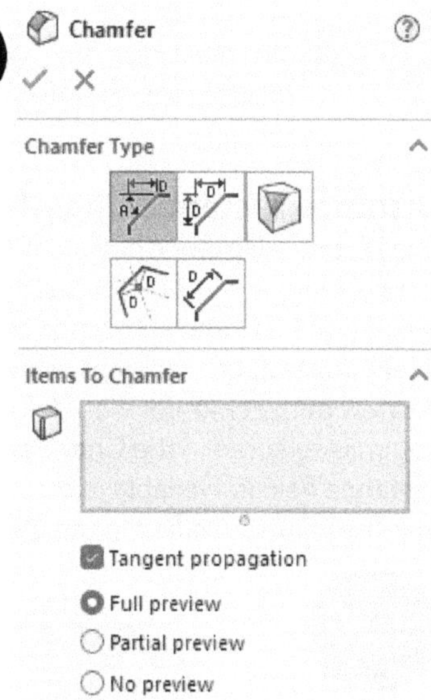

Chamfer Type

The **Chamfer Type** rollout of the PropertyManager is used to select the type of chamfer to be created by clicking on the respective button in this rollout, see Figure 10.115. The different types of chamfers are discussed next.

10.115

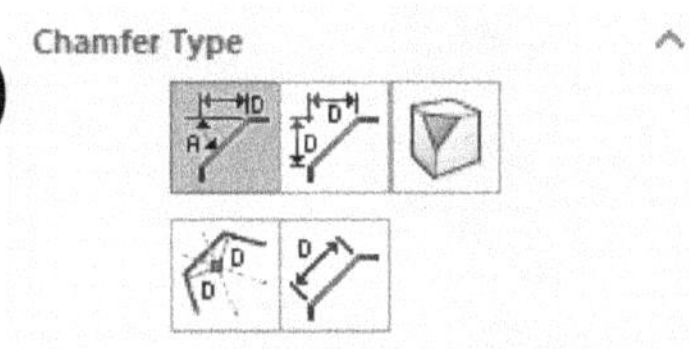

Angle Distance Chamfer 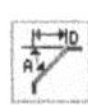

The **Angle Distance** button of the **Chamfer Type** rollout is used to create an Angle Distance chamfer by specifying its angle and distance values. To do this, click on the **Angle Distance** button and then select edges, faces, or loops as entities to create a chamfer. After selecting one or more entities, a preview of the chamfer with the default values appears, see Figure 10.116. You can specify the required angle and distance values of the chamfer by using the **Angle** and **Distance** fields of the **Chamfer Parameters** rollout, see Figure 10.117. You can also specify the distance and angle values of the chamfer by using the callout that appears in the preview of the chamfer. Note that in the preview of a chamfer, an arrow appears that points toward the direction of the distance value. You can flip the direction of the distance value by selecting the **Flip direction** check box in the **Chamfer Parameters** rollout.

10.116

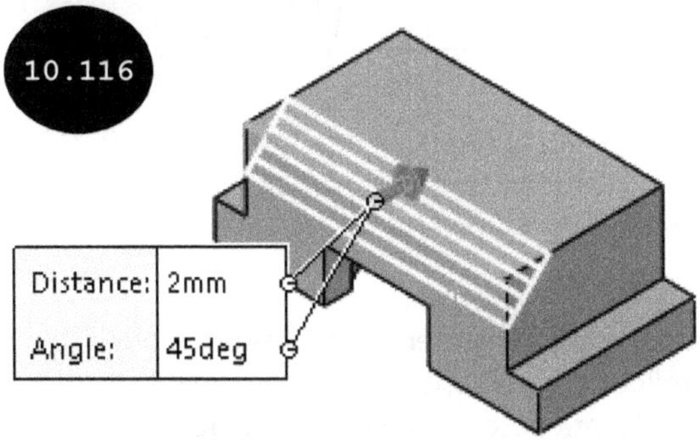

10.117

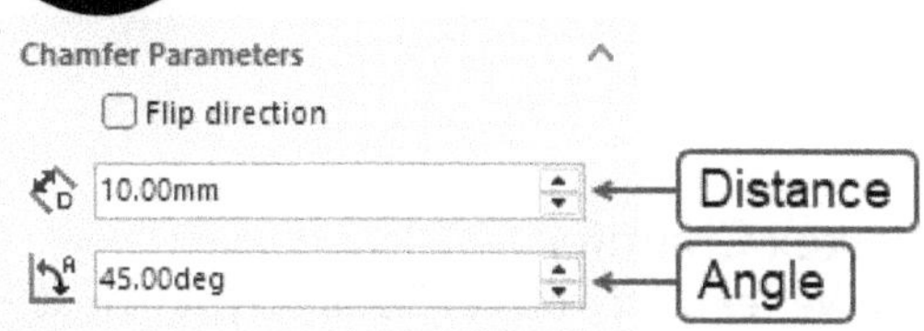

Note: On selecting a face as the entity to chamfer, all the edges of the selected face get selected to apply the chamfer.

Distance Distance Chamfer

The **Distance Distance** button of the **Chamfer Type** rollout is used to create a Distance Distance chamfer by specifying symmetric or asymmetric distance values on both sides of the chamfer edge. To do this, click on the **Distance Distance** button in the **Chamfer Type** rollout of the PropertyManager and then select edges, faces, or loops as the entities to create a chamfer. After selecting one or more entities, a preview of the chamfer with default parameters appears, see Figure 10.118. Note that if the **Symmetric** option is selected in the **Chamfer Method** drop-down list of the **Chamfer Parameters** rollout then the **Distance** field is available in the rollout, see Figure 10.119. Also, a preview of the chamfer appears such that the value specified in the **Distance** field is symmetric on both sides of the selected entity.

10.118

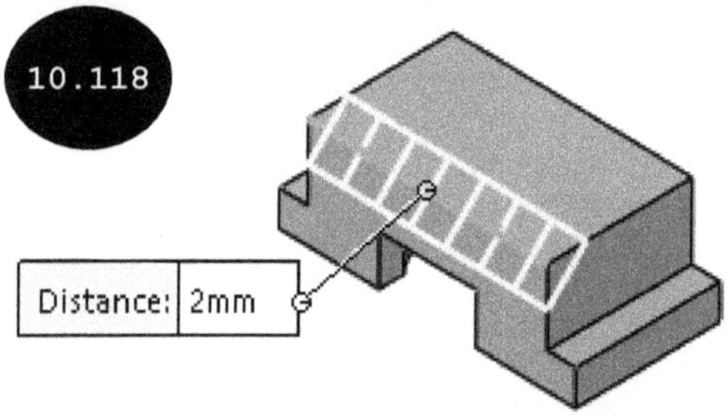

10.119

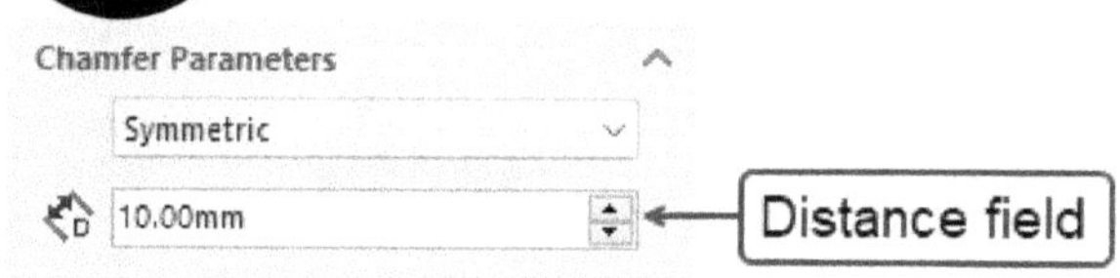

On selecting the **Asymmetric** option in the **Chamfer Method** drop-down list, the **Distance 1** and **Distance 2** fields become available in the rollout, see Figure 10.120. In these fields, you can specify different distance values on both sides of the selected entity, see Figure 10.121. You can also specify the required distance values of the chamfer by using the callout that appears in the preview of the chamfer.

10.120

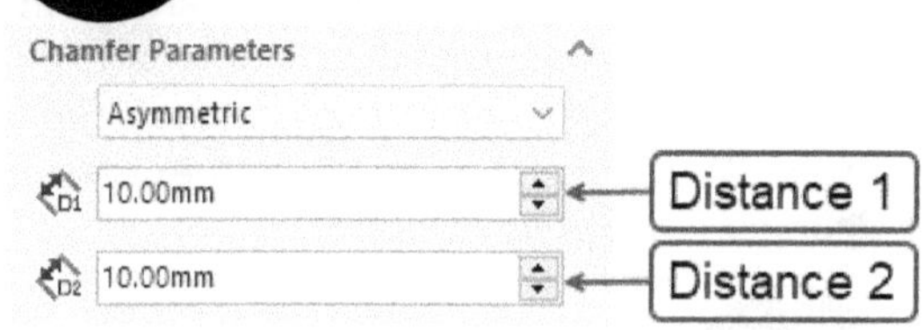

10.121

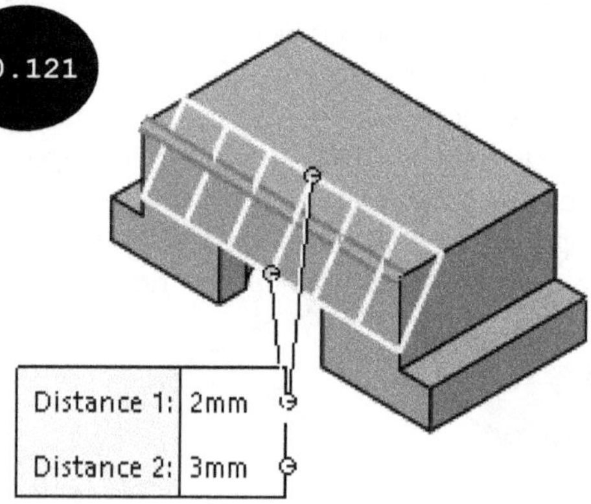

Vertex Chamfer

The **Vertex** button of the **Chamfer Type** rollout is used to create a chamfer on a vertex of a model. To do this, click on the **Vertex** button in the **Chamfer Type** rollout of the PropertyManager and then select a vertex of the model. A preview of the chamfer with default parameters appears in the graphics area, see Figure 10.122. Also, the **Distance 1**, **Distance 2**, and **Distance 3** fields appear in the **Chamfer Parameters** rollout, see Figure 10.123. These fields are used for specifying different distance values on all sides of the selected vertex. If you select the **Equal distance** check box in the rollout, only the **Distance** field becomes available and the distance specified in this field is equally applied on all sides of the vertex.

10.122

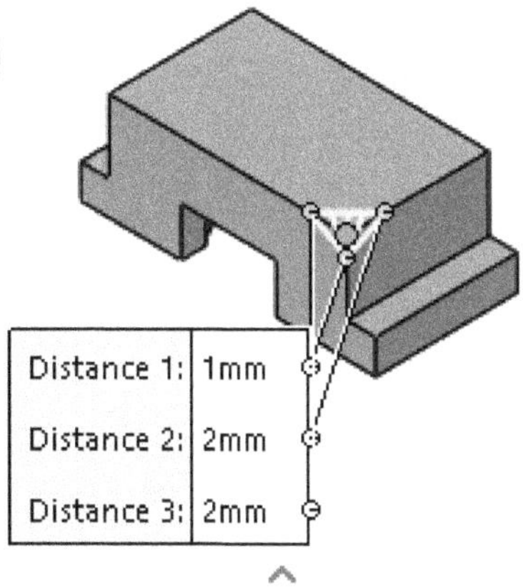

10.123

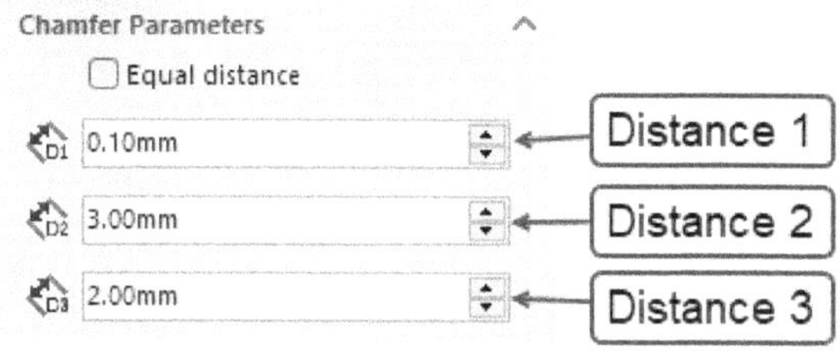

Offset Face Chamfer

The **Offset Face** button of the **Chamfer Type** rollout is used to create an offset face chamfer by specifying symmetric or asymmetric offset distance values from the adjacent faces of the chamfer edge, see Figures 10.124 and 10.125.

10.124

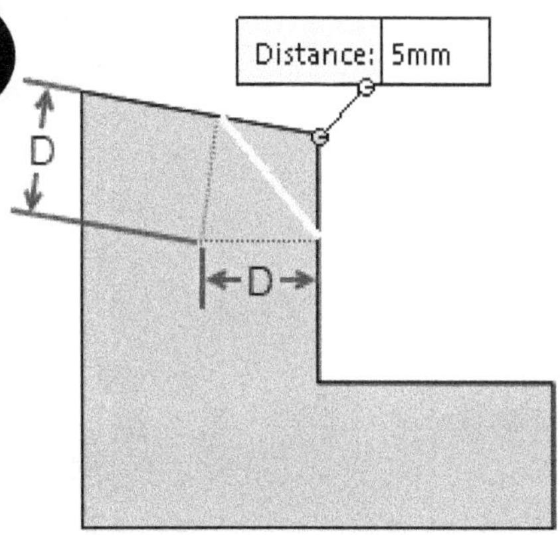

10.125

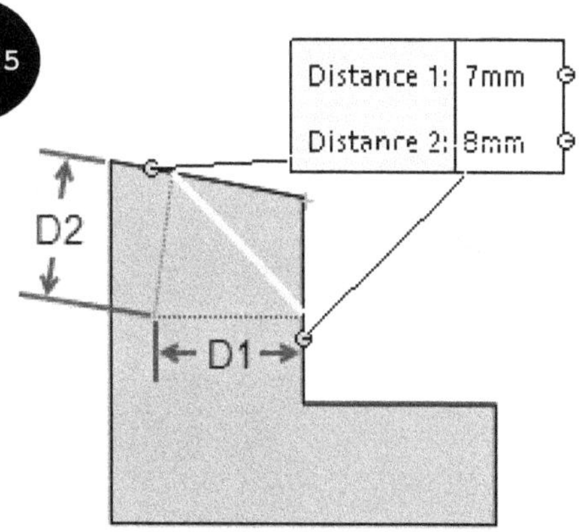

To create an offset face chamfer by specifying the offset distance values, click on the **Offset Face** button and then select one or more edges of a model. A preview of the chamfer with default offset distance values appears in the graphics area. Note that if the **Symmetric** option is selected in the **Chamfer Method** drop-down list of the **Chamfer Parameters** rollout then the **Offset Distance** field is available in the rollout. Also, the preview of the chamfer appears such that the offset distance value specified in this field is symmetric from both the adjacent faces of the chamfer edge, refer to Figure 10.124. On selecting the **Asymmetric** option in the **Chamfer Method** drop-down list, the **Offset Distance 1** and **Offset Distance 2** fields become available in the rollout. In these fields, you can specify different offset distance values from the adjacent faces of the chamfer edge, refer to Figure 10.125.

The **Multi Distance Chamfer** check box of the **Chamfer Parameters** rollout is used to create multiple offset face chamfers of different sizes. On selecting this check box, a callout attached to each selected edge of the model appears in the preview, see Figure 10.126. By using these callouts, you can specify different offset distance values for each chamfer edge. To specify an offset distance value in a callout, click on the default value specified in the callout and then specify the new offset distance value. In addition to selecting edges for creating multiple offset face chamfers of different sizes, you can also select faces, features, or loops. Note that the **Multi Distance Chamfer** check box is available in the rollout only when the **Symmetric** option is selected in the **Chamfer Method** drop-down list.

10.126

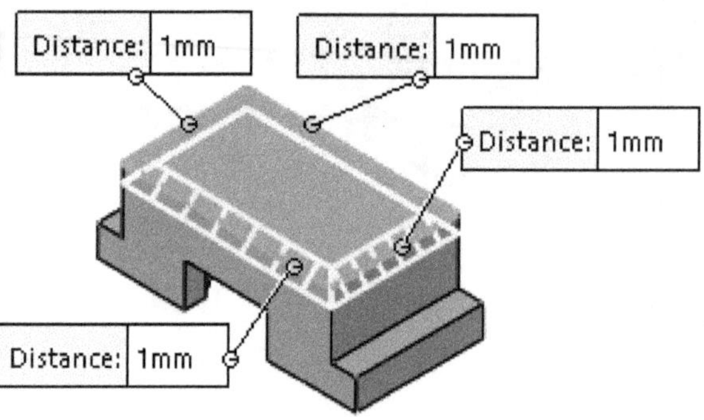

In SOLIDWORKS, you can also create a partial offset face chamfer by specifying its start and end positions along the edge of a model by using the **Partial Edge Parameters** rollout of the PropertyManager, see Figure 10.127. The method for creating a partial chamfer is the same as discussed earlier while creating a partial fillet. Note that the **Partial Edge Parameters** rollout is only available for offset face chamfers. The other options in the PropertyManager are the same as those discussed earlier. Next, click on the green tick-mark ✓ in the PropertyManager. An offset face chamfer of specified parameters is created.

10.127

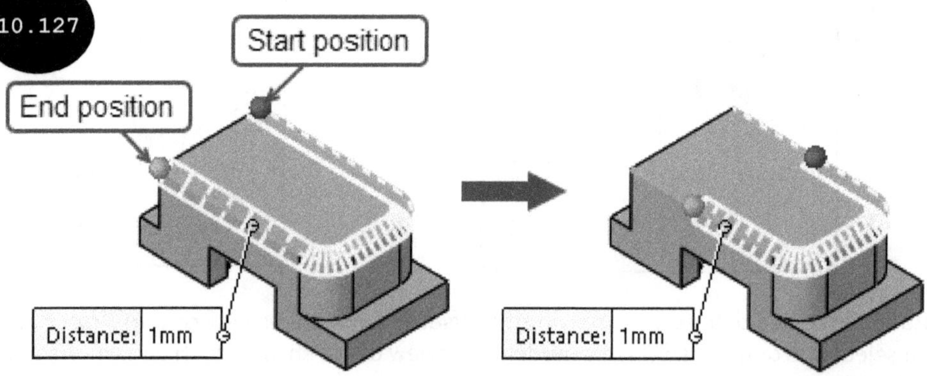

Note: The chamfer created by using the **Offset Face** button can be converted to a fillet and vice-versa. To do this, select an offset face chamfer in the FeatureManager Design Tree or in the graphics area and then right-click to display the shortcut menu. In this shortcut menu, click on the **Convert Chamfer to Fillet** option, see Figure 10.128. The offset face chamfer gets converted to a fillet. Similarly, you can convert the fillet back to the chamfer.

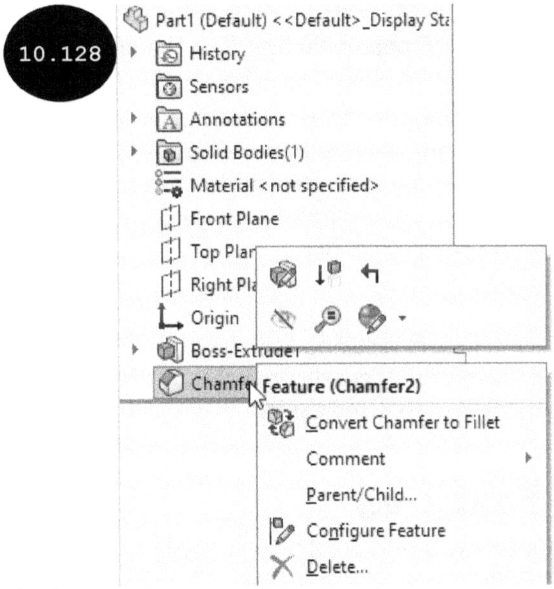

Face Face Chamfer

The **Face Face** button of the **Chamfer Type** rollout is used to create a Face Face chamfer between non-adjacent or non-continuous faces of a model. To do this, click on the **Face Face** button in the **Chamfer Type** rollout of the **Chamfer PropertyManager**. The **Face Set 1** and **Face Set 2** fields become available in the **Items To Chamfer** rollout, see Figure 10.129. The **Face Set 1** field is activated, by default. As a result, you can select the first set of non-adjacent faces. After selecting the first set of non-adjacent faces, click on the **Face Set 2** field to activate it. Next, select the second set of non-adjacent faces. A preview of the chamfer appears in the graphics area with default parameters, see Figure 10.130. In this figure, two non-adjacent faces are selected for creating the chamfer. In case, the preview of the chamfer does not appear, you need to adjust its distance value in the **Offset Distance** field of the **Chamfer Parameters** rollout.

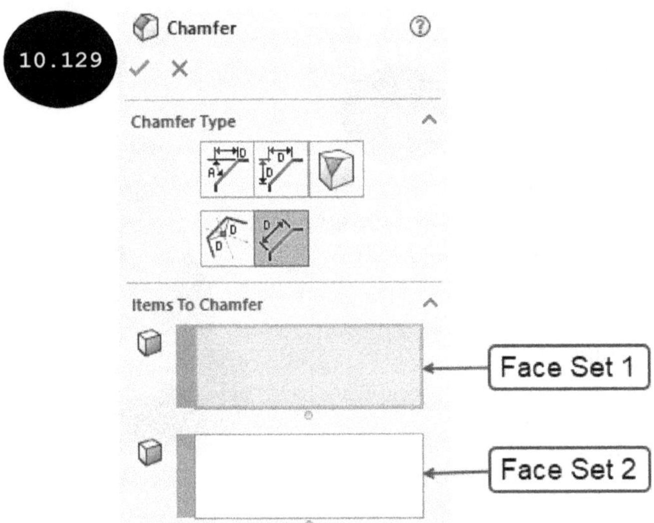

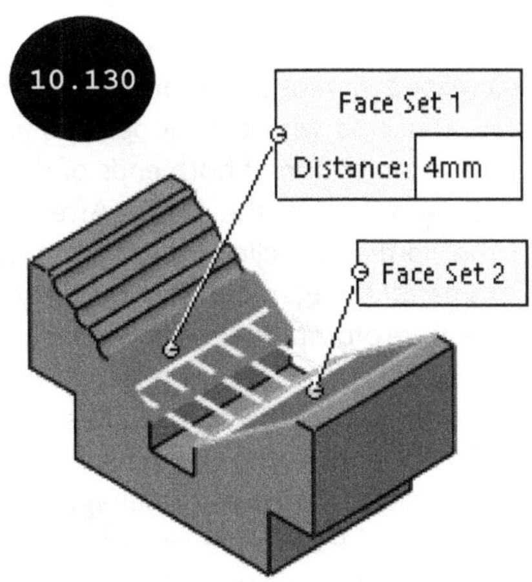

The remaining options in the PropertyManager are the same as those discussed earlier. Next, click on the green tick-mark ✓ button in the PropertyManager. The chamfer is created.

Note: The chamfer created by using the **Face Face** button can be converted to a fillet and vice-versa. To do this, select the chamfer in the FeatureManager Design Tree or in the graphics area and then right-click to display the shortcut menu. In this shortcut menu, click on the **Convert Chamfer to Fillet** option. The selected chamfer gets converted to a fillet. Similarly, you can convert the fillet back to the chamfer.

Note: In SOLIDWORKS, similar to repairing or clearing the missing edges of a fillet, you can also repair or clear all the missing edges of a chamfer that have been removed or are no longer available in the model, as discussed earlier.

Creating Rib Features

Rib features act as supporting features and are generally used for increasing the strength of a model. You can create a rib feature from an open or closed sketch by adding thickness in a specified direction. Figure 10.131 shows a model with an open sketch and the resultant rib feature created.

10.131

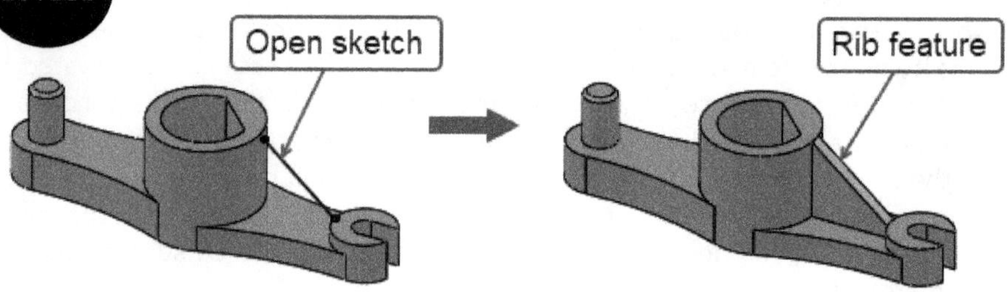

To create a rib feature, create an open sketch on a plane that intersects with the model, see Figure 10.132. Note that the projection of both ends of the sketch should lie on the geometry of the model. After creating the sketch of the rib feature, click on the **Rib** tool in the **Features CommandManager**. The **Rib PropertyManager** appears, and you are prompted to select either a sketching plane for creating the sketch of the rib feature or an existing sketch of the rib feature. If you have already created a sketch for the rib feature, then select it from the graphics area. The modified **Rib PropertyManager** appears as shown in Figure 10.133. Also, a preview of the rib feature appears in the graphics area, see Figure 10.134. The options in the PropertyManager are discussed next.

10.132

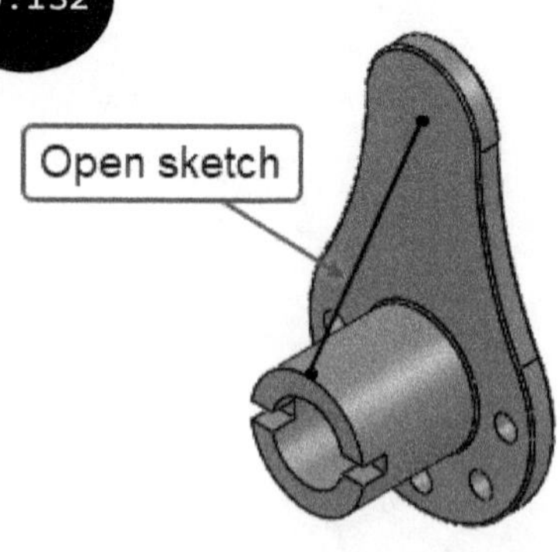

10.133

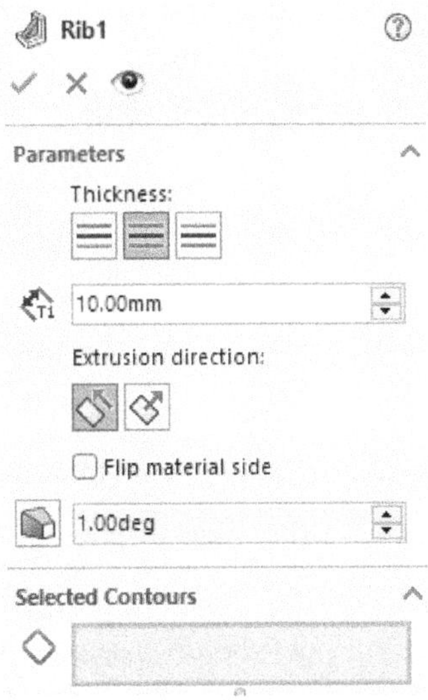

10.134

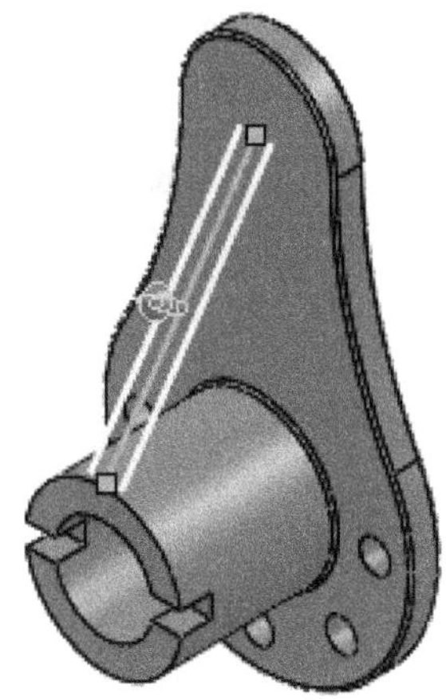

Note: You can select the sketch of the rib feature before or after invoking the **Rib** tool.

Parameters

The options in the **Parameters** rollout of the PropertyManager are used for specifying the parameters of the rib feature. The options are discussed next.

Thickness

The **Thickness** area of the **Parameters** rollout has three buttons: **First Side, Both Sides,** and **Second Side.** On selecting the **First Side** button, thickness is added to one side of the rib sketch. On selecting the **Both Sides** button, thickness is equally added to both sides of the rib sketch. On selecting the **Second Side** button, thickness is added to the second or the other side of the sketch.

Rib Thickness

The **Rib Thickness** field is used to specify the thickness value of the rib feature.

Extrusion direction

The **Extrusion direction** area has two buttons: **Parallel to Sketch** and **Normal to Sketch**. On selecting the **Parallel to Sketch** button, the rib feature is created by adding material parallel to the sketch. On selecting the **Normal to Sketch** button, the rib feature is created by adding material normal to the sketch. Figure 10.135 shows a sketch of a rib feature. Figures 10.136 and 10.137 show the resultant rib features created by selecting the **Parallel to Sketch** and **Normal to Sketch** buttons, respectively.

10.135

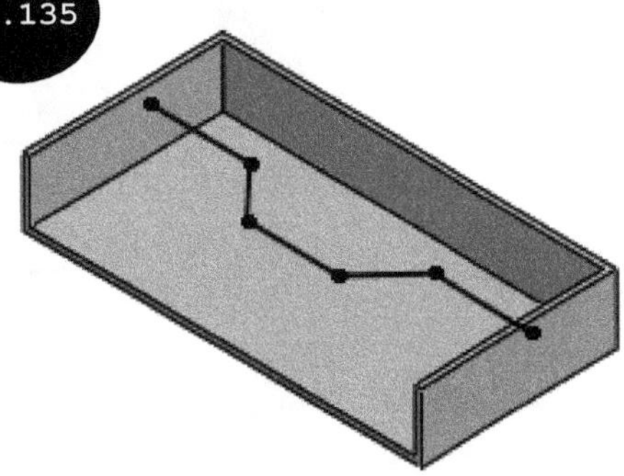

10.136

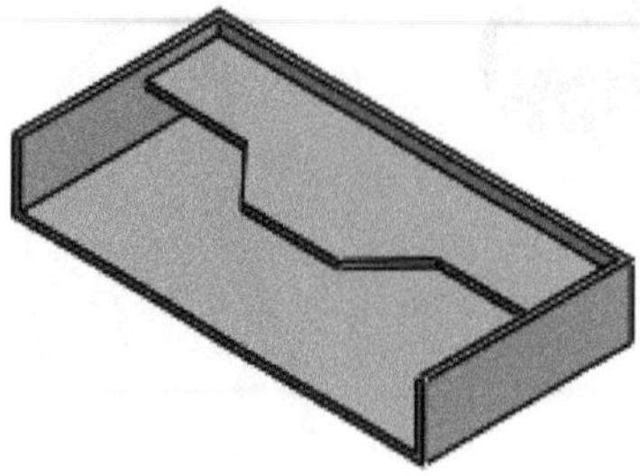

10.137

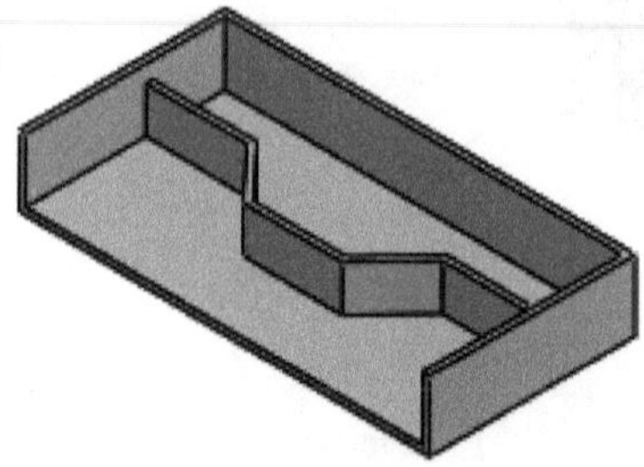

Flip material side

The **Flip material side** check box is used to flip the direction of extrusion of the rib feature.

Draft On/Off

The **Draft On/Off** button is used to add draft to the rib feature. On activating this button, the **Draft Angle** field and the **Draft outward** check box become available in the PropertyManager. Also, the **At sketch plane** and **At wall interface** radio buttons become available below the **Rib Thickness** field. By default, the **At sketch plane** radio button is selected. As a result, the specified thickness value is defined as the rib thickness at the sketching plane. On selecting the **At wall interface** radio button, the specified thickness value is defined as the rib thickness at the interface of the model. By using the **Draft Angle** field, you can specify the draft angle value of the rib feature. Note that by default, the draft angle is added inward to the sketch of the rib feature. To add the draft angle outward to the sketch, select the **Draft outward** check box.

Selected Contours

The **Selected Contours** rollout is used to select the required contour of the sketch for creating the rib feature.

After selecting the required options, click on the green tick-mark ✓ button in the PropertyManager. A rib feature is created.

Creating Shell Features

A shell feature is a thin-walled feature, that is created by making a model hollow from inside, see Figure 10.138. In this figure, the models are shown in the 'hidden line visible' display style for clarity.

10.138

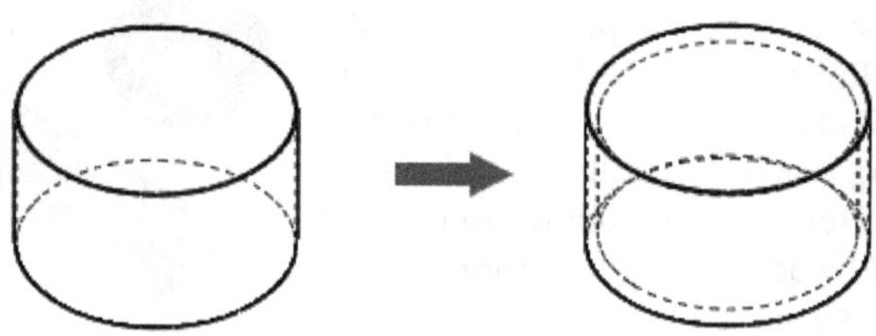

To create a shell feature, click on the **Shell** tool in the **Features CommandManager**. The **Shell PropertyManager** appears, see Figure 10.139. The options in this PropertyManager are discussed next.

10.139

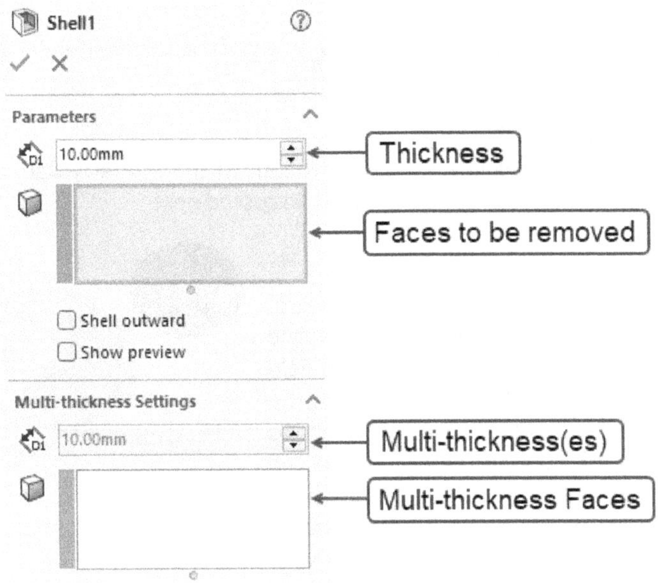

Parameters

The options in the **Parameters** rollout are used to specify parameters for creating the shell feature and the same are discussed next.

Thickness

The **Thickness** field is used to specify wall thickness for the shell feature. Note that the thickness specified in this field is applied to all walls of the feature, such that a shell feature with uniform thickness is created.

Faces to Remove

The **Faces to Remove** field is used to select faces of the model to be removed. Figure 10.140 shows the face of a model to be removed and Figure 10.141 shows the resultant model after creating the shell feature. Note that if you do not select any face to be removed then a closed hollow model is created.

10.140

10.141

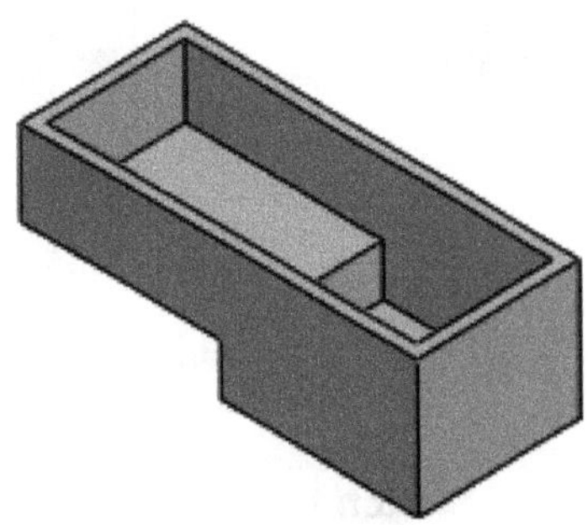

Shell outward

On selecting the **Shell outward** check box, thickness is added on the outer side of the model.

Show preview

On selecting the **Show preview** check box, a preview of the shell feature appears

Multi-thickness Settings

The options in the **Multi-thickness Settings** rollout of the PropertyManager are used for creating multi-thickness shell features. The options are discussed next.

Multi-thickness Faces

The **Multi-thickness Faces** field is used to select faces of the model on which thickness is to be applied other than the one specified in the **Thickness** field of the **Parameters** rollout. After selecting a face, the **Multi-thickness(es)** field gets enabled, which allows you to specify the thickness value for the selected face of the model. You can select multiple faces of the model and apply different thickness values to them. Figure 10.142 shows a shell model with multi-thickness walls.

10.142

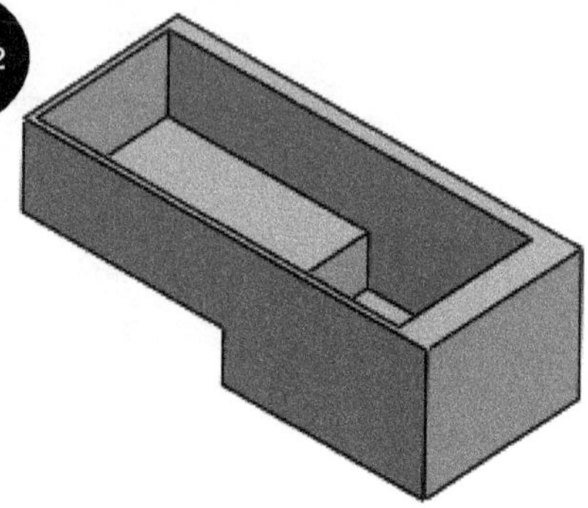

Note: The thickness value specified in the **Multi-thickness(es)** field is applied to the face currently selected in the **Multi-thickness Faces** field of the PropertyManager.

After selecting the required options, click on the green tick-mark ✓ button in the PropertyManager. A shell feature of specified parameters is created.

Creating Wrap Features

A Wrap feature is created by wrapping a sketch onto one or more faces of a model, see Figure 10.143. This figure shows a sketch to be wrapped, a face, and the resultant model after wrapping the sketch onto the face of the model.

10.143

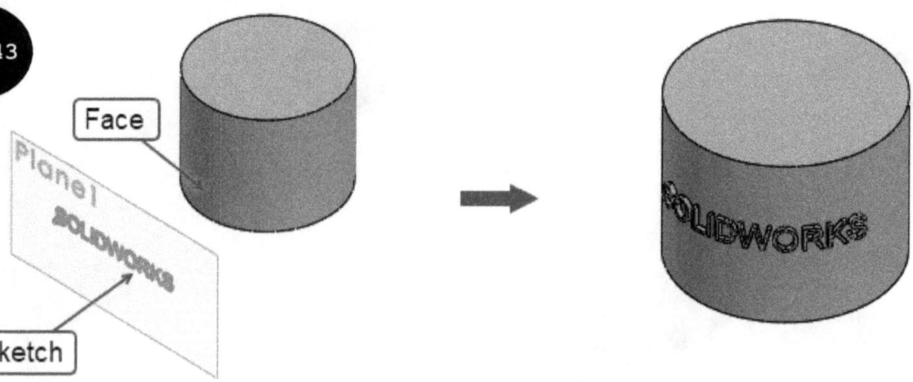

To wrap a sketch onto a face, select a sketch to be wrapped either from the FeatureManager Design Tree or from the graphics area and then click on the **Wrap** tool in the **Features CommandManager**. The **Wrap PropertyManager** appears, see Figure 10.144. The options in the PropertyManager are discussed next.

Wrap Type

The options in the **Wrap Type** rollout of the PropertyManager are used to select the type of wrap: emboss, deboss, or scribe to be created. The options are discussed next.

10.144

Emboss 

The **Emboss** button in the **Wrap Type** rollout is used to create a wrap feature by adding material on the face, refer to Figure 10.143.

Deboss 

The **Deboss** button is used to create a wrap feature by removing material from the face of the model, see Figure 10.145.

Scribe 

The **Scribe** button is used to create a wrap feature by splitting the face of the model such that an imprint of the sketch is created on the face, see Figure 10.146.

10.145

10.146

Wrap Method

The options in the **Wrap Method** rollout of the PropertyManager are used to select a wrap method: Analytical or Spline Surface for creating the wrap feature. Both are discussed next.

Analytical 

The **Analytical** button of the **Wrap Method** rollout is used to wrap a sketch completely around the cylindrical or conical face of a model. Note that by using this button, you can wrap a sketch only onto the planar or non-planar faces of cylindrical, conical, extruded, or revolved features of the model.

Spline Surface 

The **Spline Surface** button of the **Wrap Method** rollout is used to create a wrap feature by wrapping a sketch onto any face of a model. However, by using this method, you cannot wrap a sketch completely around the cylindrical or conical face of a model.

Wrap Parameters

The options in the **Wrap Parameters** rollout are used for specifying parameters for creating the wrap feature, see Figure 10.147. The options are discussed next.

10.147

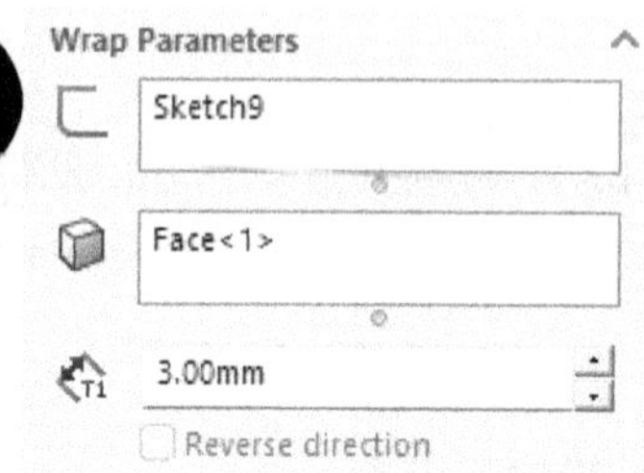

Source Sketch

The **Source Sketch** field of the PropertyManager is used to select a sketch to be wrapped. Note that if you select a sketch before invoking the **Wrap PropertyManager** then the name of the selected sketch appears in this field, which indicates that the sketch is selected.

Face for Wrap Sketch

The **Face for Wrap Sketch** field is used to select one or more faces of the model for wrapping the sketch. Note that if the **Analytical** button is selected in the **Wrap Method** rollout then you can only select planar or non-planar faces of cylindrical, conical, extruded, or revolved features of a model.

Thickness

The **Thickness** field is used to specify the thickness of the wrap feature. Note that this field becomes available only if the **Emboss** button is enabled in the **Wrap Type** rollout.

Depth

The **Depth** field is used to specify the depth of the wrap feature. Note that this field becomes available only if the **Deboss** button is enabled in the **Wrap Type** rollout.

Reverse Direction

The **Reverse Direction** check box is used to reverse the direction of projection, see Figures 10.148 and 10.149.

10.148

10.149

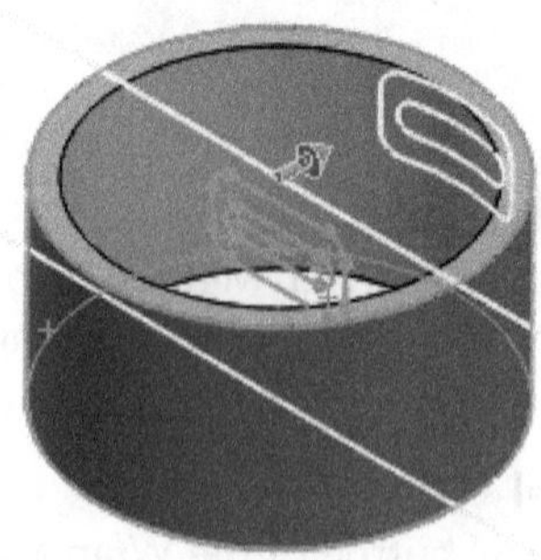

Tutorial 1

Create a model, as shown in Figure 10.150. All dimensions are in mm.

10.150

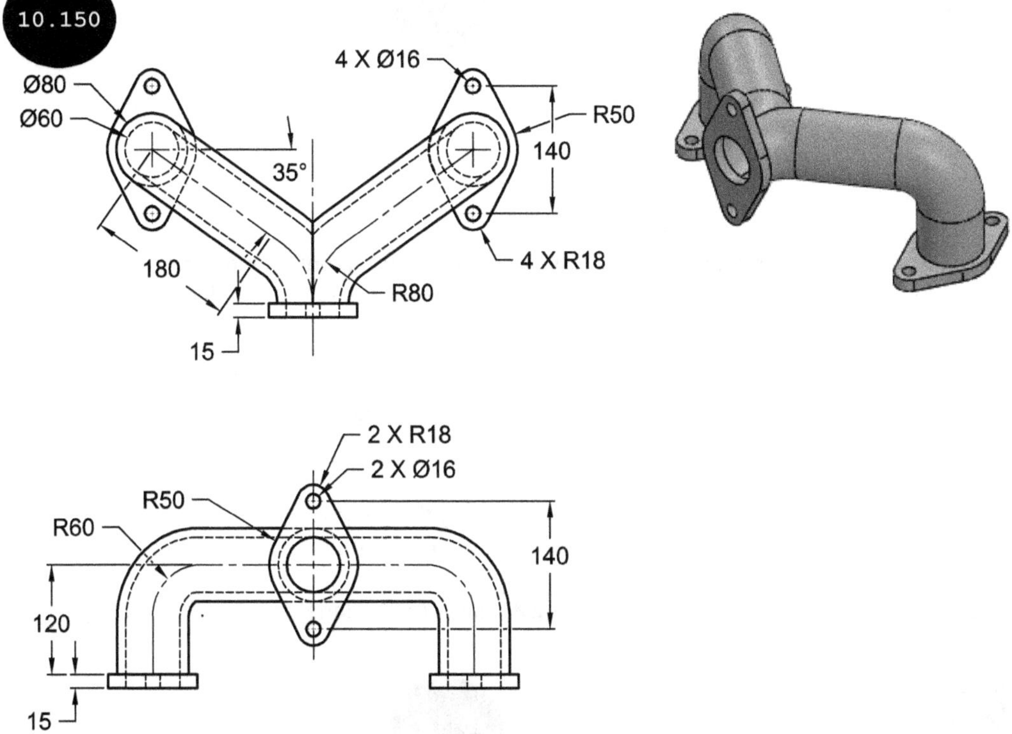

Section 1: Invoking the Part Modeling Environment

1. Start SOLIDWORKS and then invoke the Part modeling environment.

2. Ensure that the **MMGS (millimeter, gram, second)** unit system is set for the currently opened part document.

Section 2: Creating the 3D Path - Sweep Feature

The base feature of the model is a sweep feature. To create this sweep feature, you need to create a 3D sketch as the path of the sweep feature.

1. Click on the **Sketch** tab in the CommandManager to display the tools of the **Sketch CommandManager**.

2. Click on the arrow at the bottom of the **Sketch** tool in the **Sketch CommandManager**. The **Sketch** flyout appears, see Figure 10.151.

3. Click on the **3D Sketch** tool in the **Sketch** flyout. The 3D Sketching environment is invoked.

4. Click on the **Line** tool in the **Sketch CommandManager**. The **Line** tool is invoked and the display of XY appears near the cursor, see Figure 10.152. 

10.151

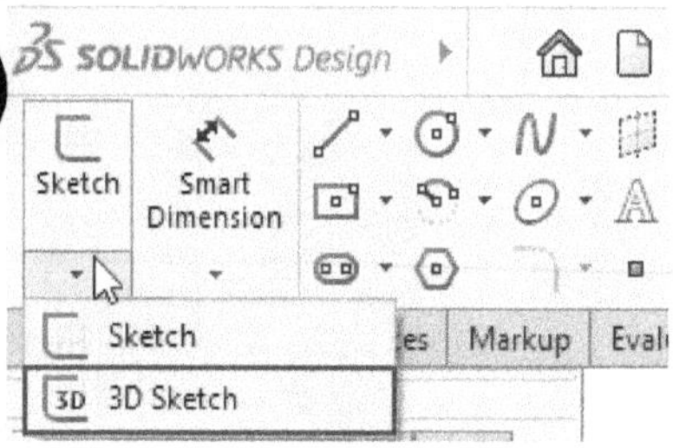

10.152

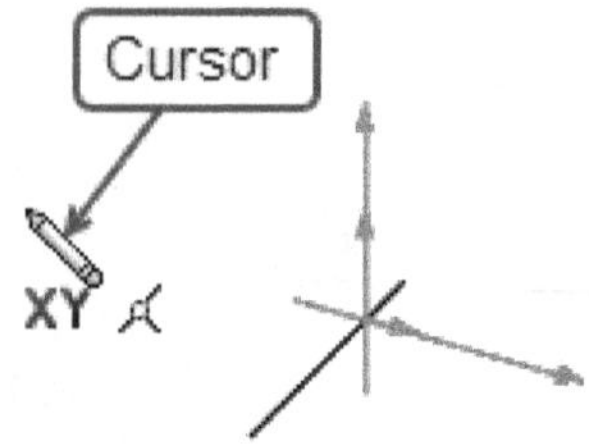

Note: The display of XY near the cursor indicates that the XY (Front) plane is the current sketching plane. You can press the TAB key to switch between the sketching planes for creating a 3D sketch.

5. Move the cursor to the origin and then click to specify the start point of the line when the cursor snaps to the origin.

6. Move the cursor vertically upward and click to specify the endpoint of the line when the length of the line appears close to 120 mm near the cursor, see Figure 10.153.

7. Press the TAB key twice to activate the ZX plane (Top plane) as the sketching plane, see Figure 10.154.

10.153

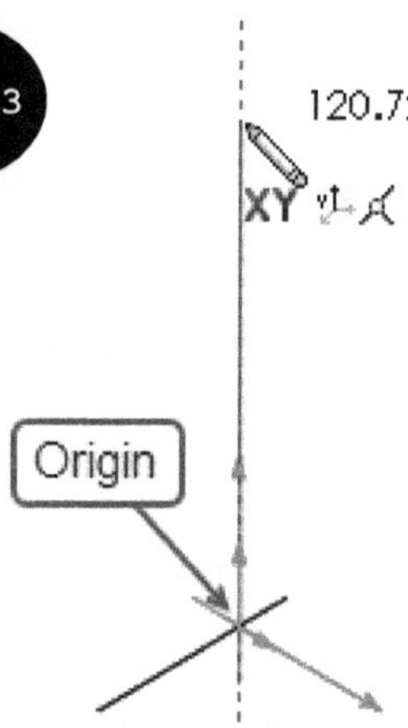

10.154

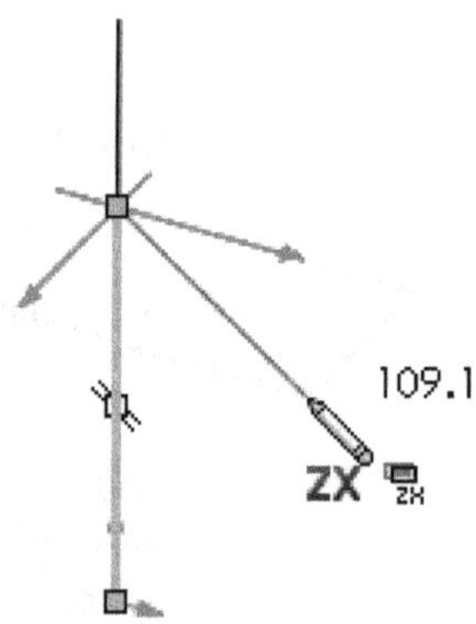

8. Move the cursor toward the right at an angle to the X axis, see Figure 10.155. Next, click to specify the endpoint of the second line when the length of the line appears close to 180 mm near the cursor, see Figure 10.155.

9. Move the cursor to a distance and then move it back to the last specified point. A dot appears at the endpoint in the graphics area, see Figure 10.156.

10.155

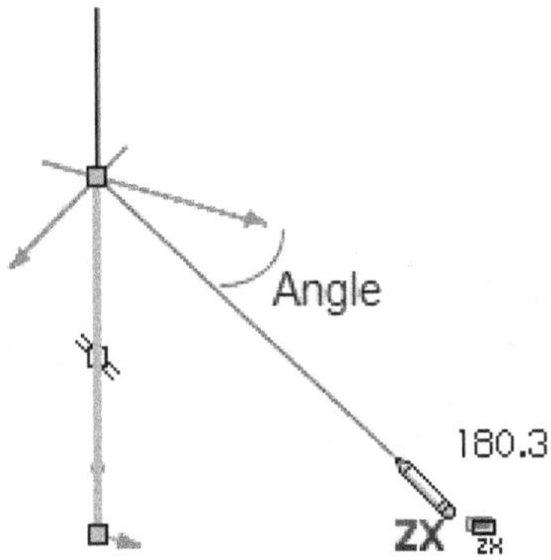

10.156

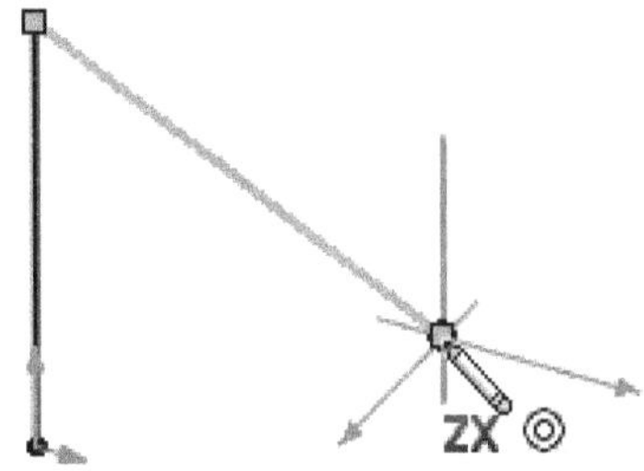

10. Move the cursor to a distance toward the right. The arc mode gets activated, and a preview of a tangent arc appears in the graphics area, see Figure 10.157.

11. Click to specify the endpoint of the arc when the radius of the arc appears close to 80 mm, see Figure 10.157.

12. Right-click in the graphics area. A shortcut menu appears. Next, click on the **Select** option in the shortcut menu to exit the **Line** tool.

13. Invoke the **Centerline** tool and then create a horizontal centerline of any length along the X-axis direction, by specifying its start point at the endpoint of the first line entity, see Figure 10.158. Next, exit the **Centerline** tool. 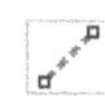

10.157

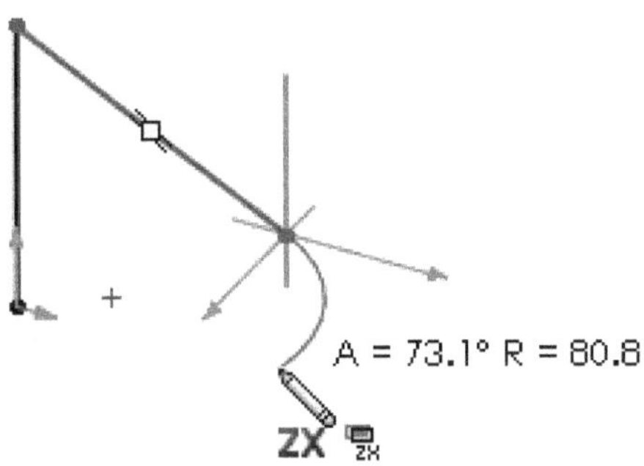

10.158

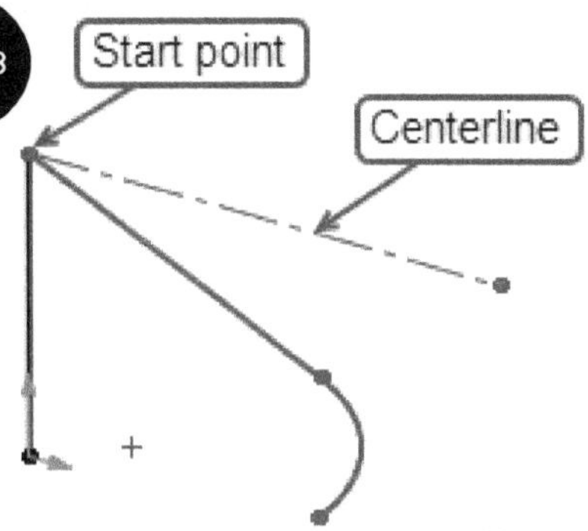

Section 3: Applying Dimensions

1. Click on the **Smart Dimension** tool and then click on the vertical line (first line entity) in the graphics area. The linear dimension is attached to the cursor.

2. Click on the graphics area to specify the placement point for the attached dimension. The **Modify** dialog box appears.

3. Enter **120** in the **Modify** dialog box and then click on the green tick-mark ✓ button. The length of the line changes to 120 mm and the dimension is applied to the line, see Figure 10.159.

4. Click on the inclined line (second line entity) in the graphics area to apply the dimension. The dimension is attached to the cursor.

5. Click in the graphics area to specify the placement point for the attached dimension. The **Modify** dialog box appears.

6. Enter **180** in the **Modify** dialog box and then click on the green tick-mark ✓ button. The length of the line changes to 180 mm and the dimension is applied to the line, see Figure 10.160.

10.159

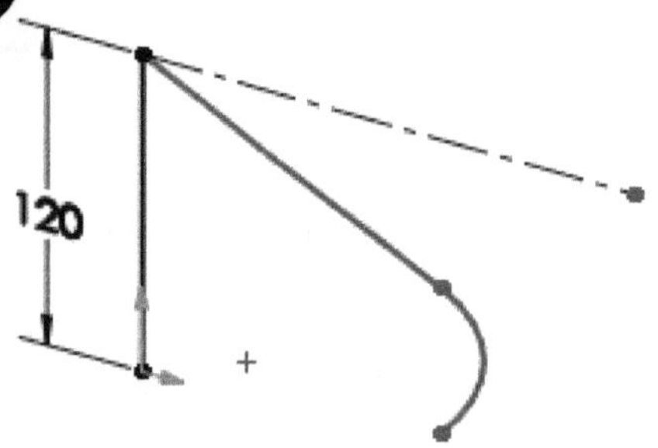

10.160

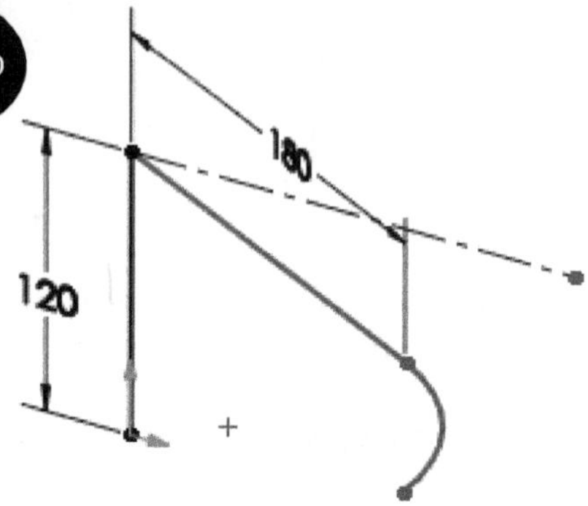

7. Click on the inclined line (second line entity) and then the horizontal centerline. An angular dimension is attached to the cursor.

8. Click in the graphics area to specify the placement point for the attached dimension. The **Modify** dialog box appears.

9. Enter **35** in the **Modify** dialog box and then click on the green tick-mark ✓. An angular dimension is applied between the inclined line entity and the centerline, see Figure 10.161.

10. Click on the arc to apply the radius dimension. The radius dimension is attached to the cursor.

11. Click in the graphics area to specify the placement point for the attached dimension. The **Modify** dialog box appears.

12. Enter **80** in the **Modify** dialog box and then click on the green tick-mark ✓. The radius of the arc changes to 80 mm and the dimension is applied to the arc, see Figure 10.162.

10.161

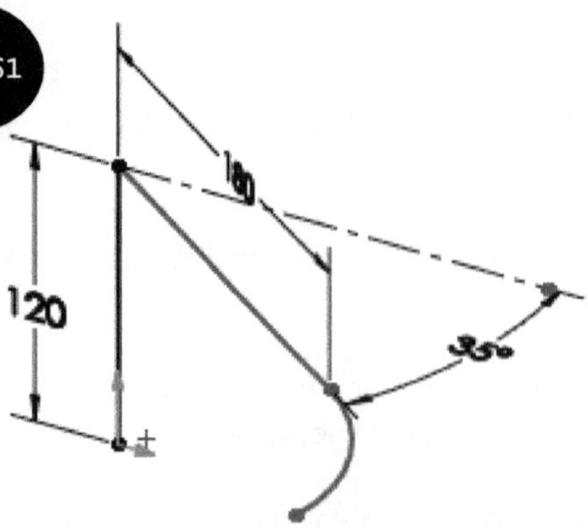

10.162

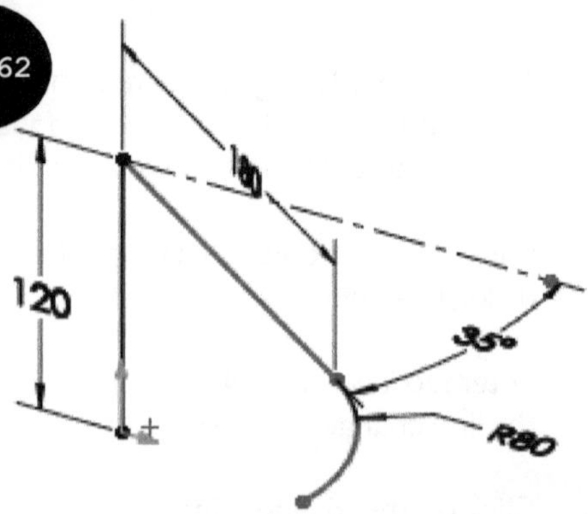

13. Change the current orientation of the sketch to the front view by clicking on the **Front** tool in the **View Orientation** flyout, see Figure 10.163. Alternatively, press CTRL + 1 to change the orientation of the sketch to the front view.

14. Click on the vertical line (first line entity) and then click on the second line entity in the graphics area. The angular dimension appears attached to the cursor.

15. Click in the graphics area to specify the placement point for the angular dimension. The **Modify** dialog box appears.

16. Enter **90** in the **Modify** dialog box and then click on the green tick-mark ✓ button. An angular dimension is applied, see Figure 10.164. Next, exit the **Smart Dimension** tool.

10.163

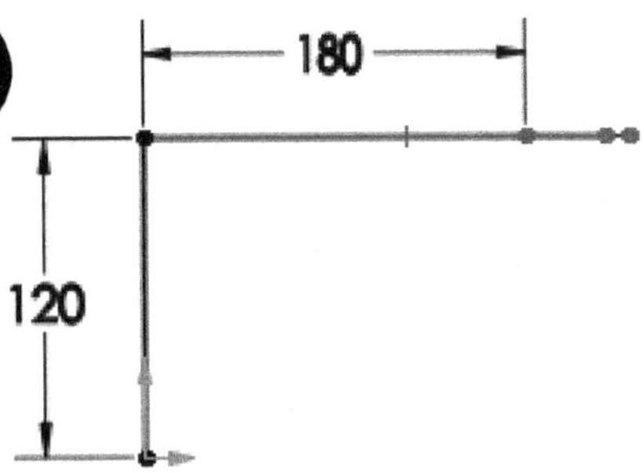

10.164

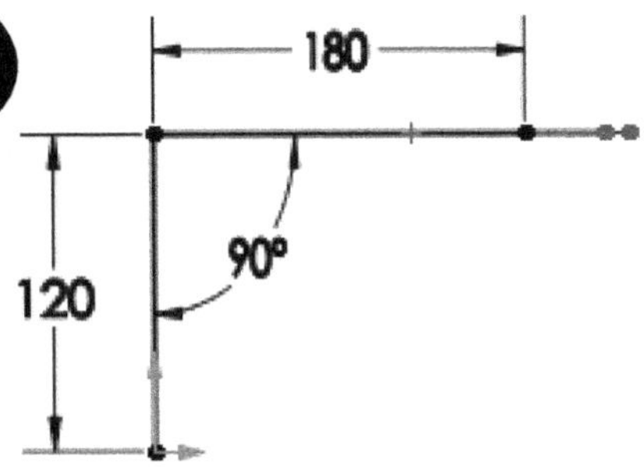

Section 4: Applying Relation

1. Press CTRL + 5 to change the current orientation of the sketch to the top view.

2. Press and hold the CTRL key and then select the center point of the arc as well as the endpoint of the arc in the graphics area, see Figure 10.165. Next, release the CTRL key. A Pop-up toolbar appears near the cursor, see Figure 10.165.

10.165

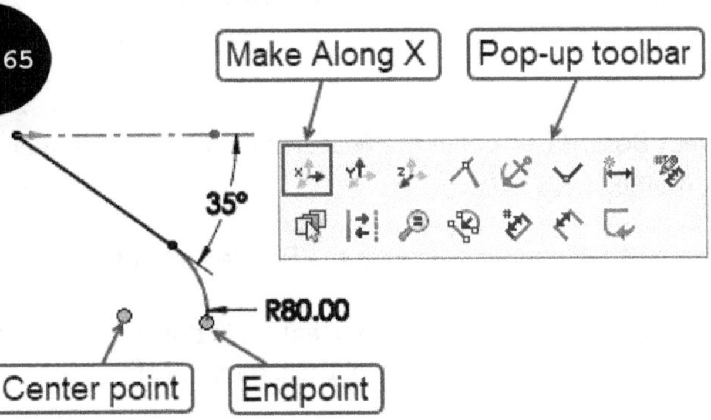

3. Click on the **Make Along X** tool in the Pop-up toolbar. The Along X relation is applied between the center point and the endpoint of the arc.

4. Similarly, apply the Along X relation to the horizontal centerline, if not applied by default.

5. Press CTRL + 7 to change the current orientation of the sketch to isometric.

Section 5: Creating Fillet

1. Click on the **Sketch Fillet** tool in the **Sketch CommandManager**. The **Sketch Fillet PropertyManager** appears.

2. Enter **60** in the **Fillet Radius** field of the **Fillet Parameters** rollout in the PropertyManager.

3. Click on the vertex of the sketch. A preview of the fillet appears, see Figure 10.166. Ensure that the **Keep constrained corners** check box is cleared.

10.166

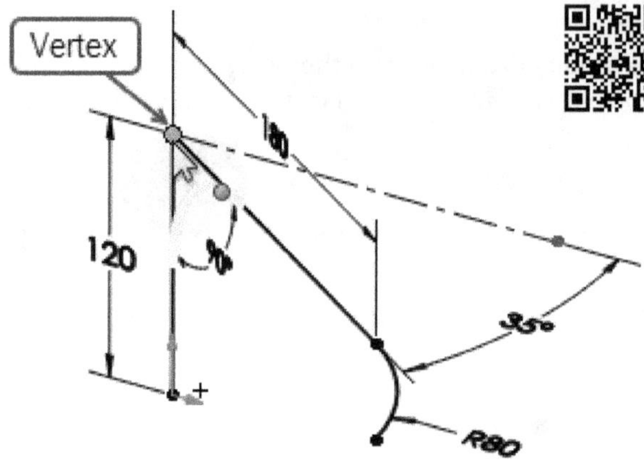

4. Click on the green tick-mark ✓ in the PropertyManager. A fillet of radius 60 mm is created on the selected vertex of the sketch. Next, exit the PropertyManager.

5. Exit the 3D Sketching environment by clicking on the **Exit Sketch** icon of the Confirmation Corner, which is available at the top right corner of the graphics area.

Section 6: Creating the Base Feature - Sweep Feature

After creating the path of the sweep feature, you need to create a sweep feature with a circular profile.

1. Click on the **Swept Boss/Base** tool in the **Features CommandManager**. The **Sweep PropertyManager** appears.

2. Click on the **Circular Profile** radio button in the **Profile and Path** rollout.

3. Select the 3D sketch as the path of the sweep feature in the graphics area. A preview of the sweep feature appears with the default diameter of the circular profile.

4. Enter **80** in the **Diameter** field of the **Profile and Path** rollout and then press ENTER. A preview of the sweep feature appears as shown in Figure 10.167.

5. Click on the green tick-mark ✓ in the PropertyManager. A sweep feature is created, see Figure 10.168.

10.167

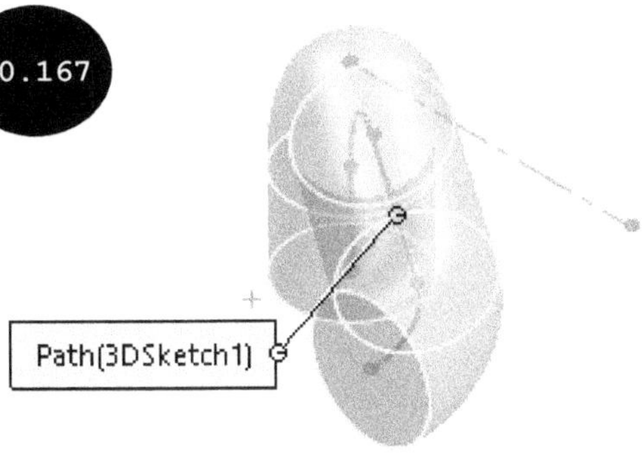

10.168

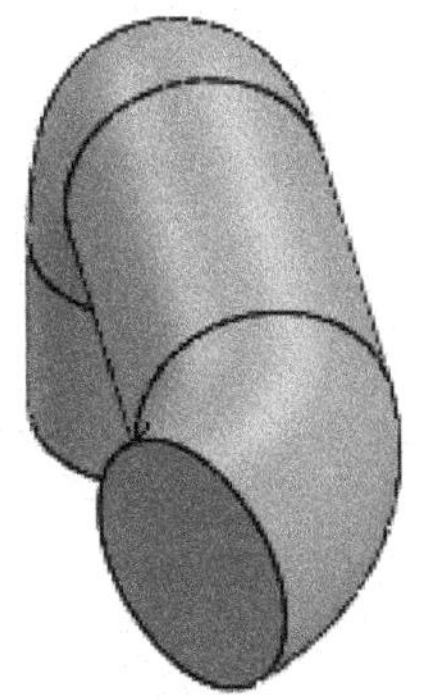

Section 7: Creating the Second Feature - Mirror Feature

The second feature of the model can be created by mirroring the first feature about a reference plane, which passes through the center of the end circular face of the first feature and is parallel to the Right plane. To create this reference plane, you need to first create a reference point at the center of the end circular face of the first feature.

1. Invoke the **Reference Geometry** flyout in the **Features CommandManager** and then click on the **Point** tool, see Figure 10.169. The **Point PropertyManager** appears.

2. Click on the end circular face of the first feature (sweep), see Figure 10.170. A preview of the reference point appears at the center of the circular face selected.

10.169

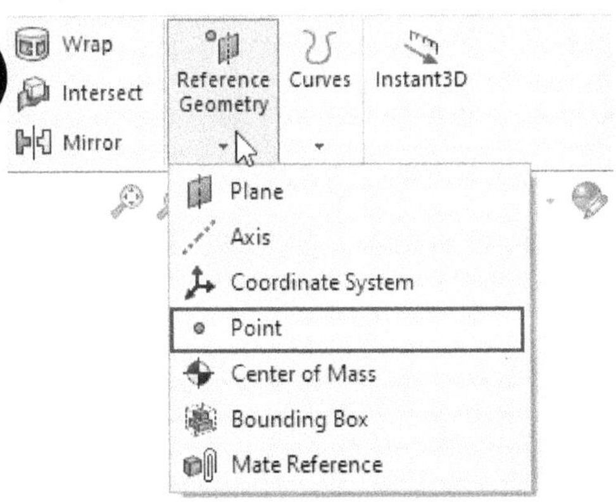

10.170

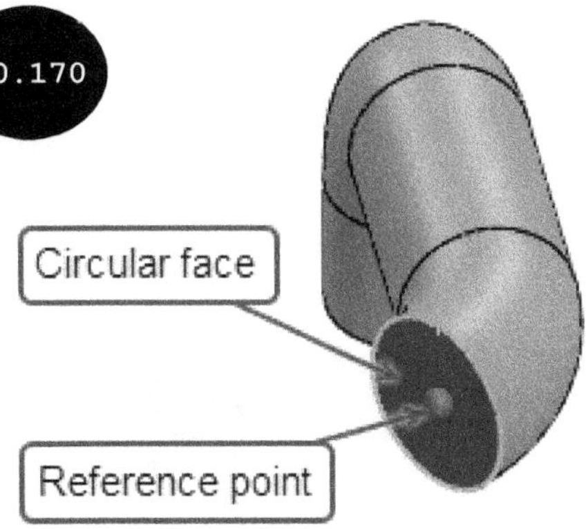

3. Click on the green tick-mark ✓ in the PropertyManager. The reference point is created.

   Now, you need to create a reference plane by using the **Plane** tool.

4. Invoke the **Reference Geometry** flyout (refer to Figure 10.169) and then click on the **Plane** tool. The **Plane PropertyManager** appears.

5. Expand the FeatureManager Design Tree, which is now available at the top left corner of the graphics area, by clicking on the arrow in front of it.

6. Click on the **Right Plane** in the FeatureManager Design Tree as the first reference. A preview of an offset reference plane appears in the graphics area.

7. Click on the reference point in the graphics area as the second reference. The preview of a reference plane, which is parallel to the Right plane and passes through the reference point appears in the graphics area, see Figure 10.171.

8. Click on the green tick-mark ✓ of the PropertyManager. The reference plane is created, see Figure 10.172.

10.171

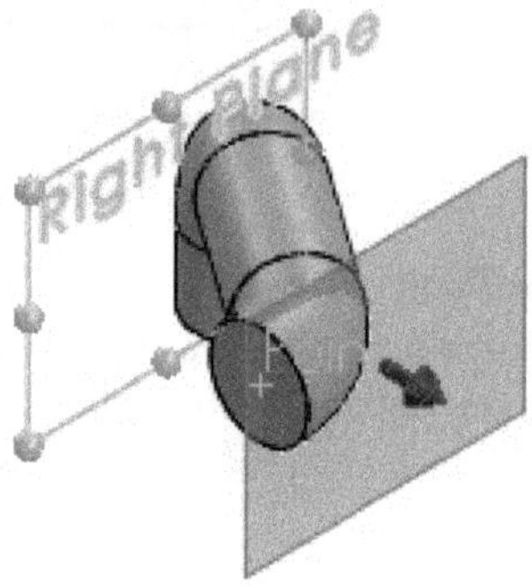

10.172

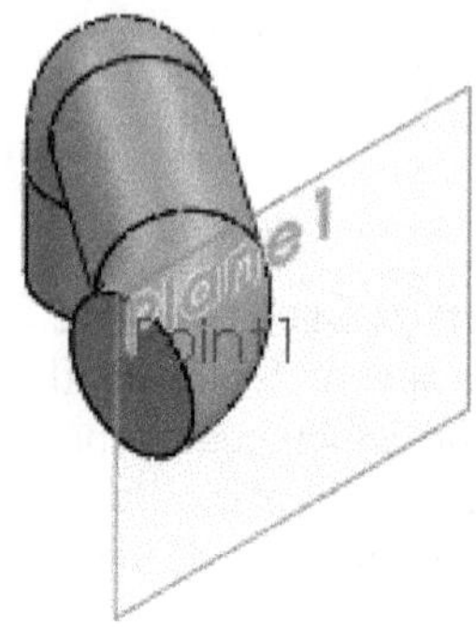

After creating the reference plane, you need to mirror the first feature (sweep) about it.

9. Click on the **Mirror** tool in the **Features CommandManager**. The **Mirror PropertyManager** appears.

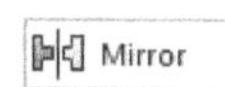

10. Click on the newly created reference plane as the mirroring plane.

11. Activate the **Features to Mirror** field and click on the base feature (sweep feature). A preview of the mirror feature appears.

12. Click on the green tick-mark ✓ in the PropertyManager. The mirror feature is created, see Figure 10.173. Next, hide the reference plane and the reference point in the graphics area.

10.173

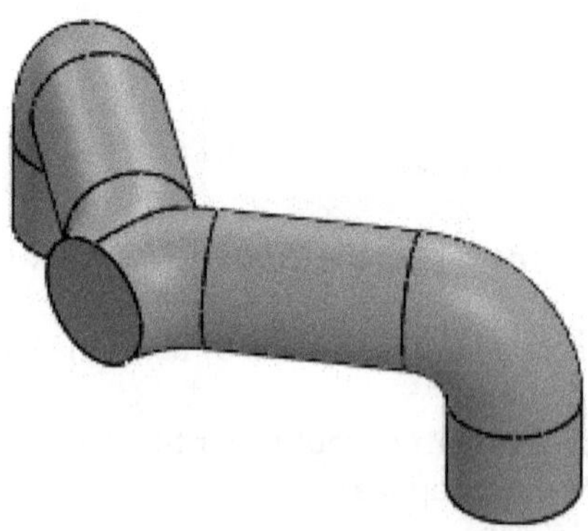

Section 8: Creating the Third Feature - Shell Feature

1. Click on the **Shell** tool in the **Features CommandManager**. The **Shell PropertyManager** appears.

2. Enter **10** in the **Thickness** field of the **Parameters** rollout in the PropertyManager.

3. Select the three end faces of the model as the faces to be removed, see Figure 10.174.

4. Click on the green tick-mark ✓ button. The shell feature is created, see Figure 10.175.

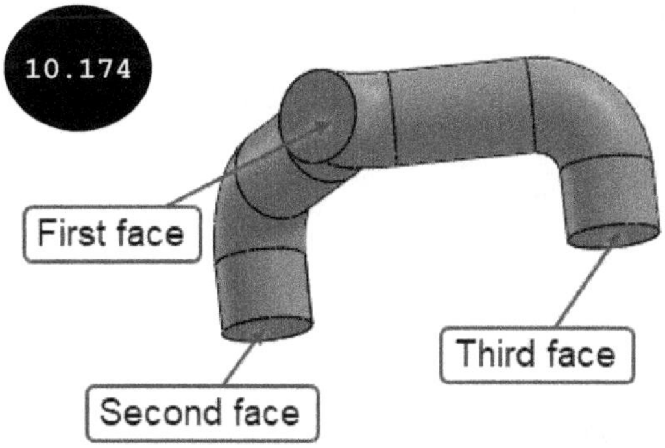

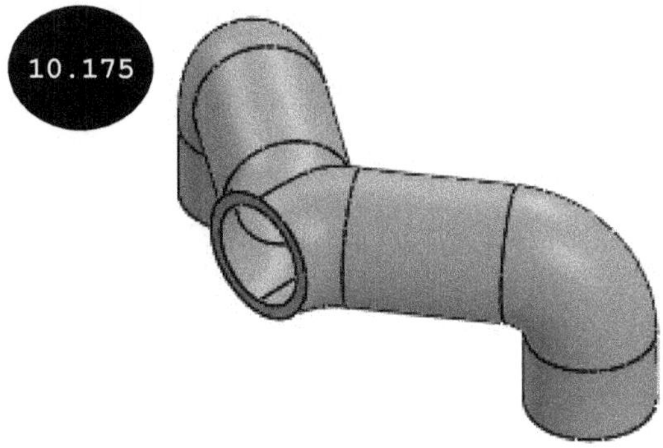

Section 9: Creating the Fourth Feature - Extruded Feature

1. Invoke the Sketching environment by selecting the Top plane as the sketching plane. The model gets oriented normal to the viewing direction.

2. Create the sketch of the fourth feature (extruded feature), see Figure 10.176. After creating the sketch, do not exit the Sketching environment.

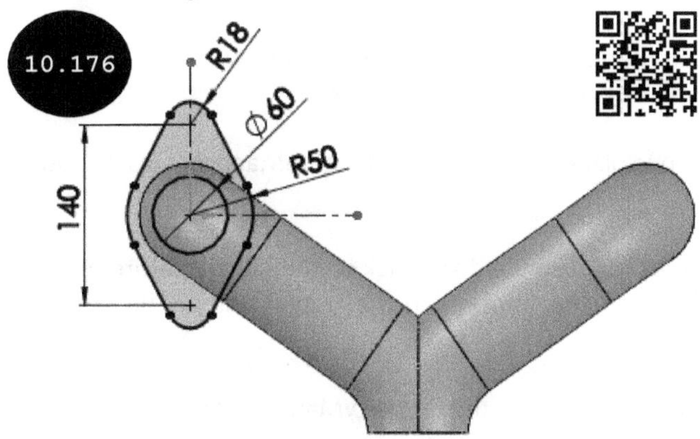

Note: The sketch of the fourth feature shown in Figure 10.176 has been fully defined by applying the required dimensions and relations. You need to apply tangent relations between each set of connected line and arc entities. You also need to apply a symmetric relation between the center points of the upper and lower arcs of the sketch concerning the horizontal centerline. Besides, you need to apply an equal relation between the upper and lower arcs.

3. Click on the **Features** tab in the CommandManager to display the tools of the **Features CommandManager**.

4. Click on the **Extruded Boss/Base** tool in the **Features CommandManager**. The **Boss-Extrude PropertyManager** and a preview of the extruded feature appear. Next, change the orientation of the model to isometric.

Extruded Boss/Base

5. Click on the **Reverse Direction** button in the **Direction 1** rollout of the PropertyManager to reverse the direction of extrusion downward.

6. Enter **15** in the **Depth** field of the **Direction 1** rollout in the PropertyManager.

7. Click on the green tick-mark ✓ of the PropertyManager. An extruded feature is created, see Figure 10.177.

10.177

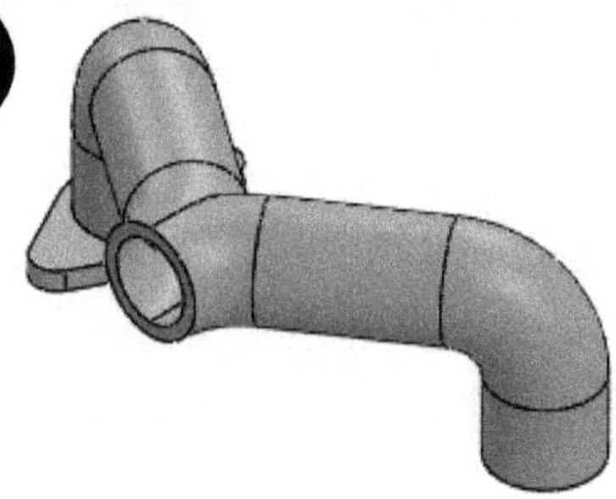

Section 10: Creating the Fifth Feature - Mirror Feature

1. Click on the **Mirror** tool in the **Features CommandManager**. The **Mirror PropertyManager** appears.

2. Expand the FeatureManager Design Tree, which is now available at the top left corner of the graphics area, by clicking on the arrow in front of it.

3. Click on the reference plane (Plane 1) in the FeatureManager Design Tree as the mirroring plane, see Figure 10.178.

4. Activate the **Features to Mirror** field and click on the fourth feature (previously created extruded feature) as the feature to be mirrored in the graphics area. The preview of the mirror feature appears, see Figure 10.178.

5. Click on the green tick-mark ✓ in the PropertyManager. The mirror feature is created.

Section 11: Creating the Sixth Feature - Extruded Feature

1. Invoke the Sketching environment by selecting the front planar face of the model as the sketching plane, see Figure 10.179. The model gets oriented normal to the viewing direction.

10.178

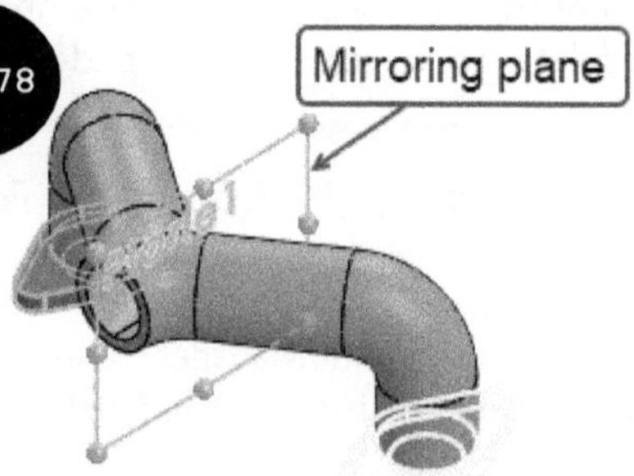

10.179

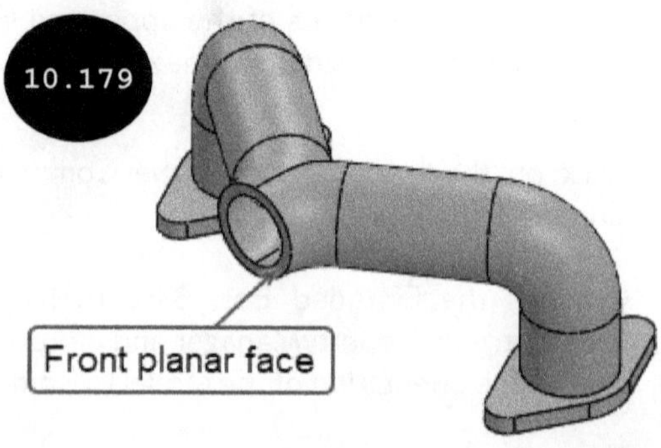

2. Create the sketch of the sixth feature (extruded feature), see Figure 10.180. After creating the sketch, do not exit the Sketching environment.

10.180

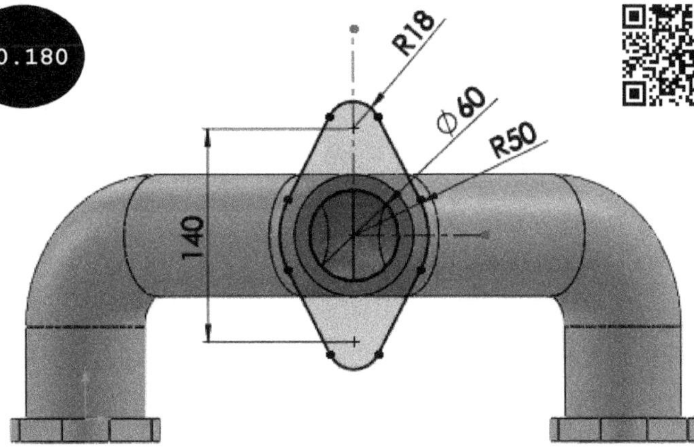

3. Click on the **Features** tab in the CommandManager to display the tools of the **Features CommandManager**.

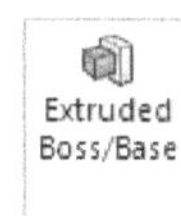

4. Click on the **Extruded Boss/Base** tool in the **Features CommandManager**. The **Boss-Extrude PropertyManager** and a preview of the extruded feature appear. Next, change the orientation of the model to isometric.

5. Enter **15** in the **Depth** field of the **Direction 1** rollout.

6. Click on the green tick-mark ✓ in the PropertyManager. An extruded feature is created, see Figure 10.181.

10.181

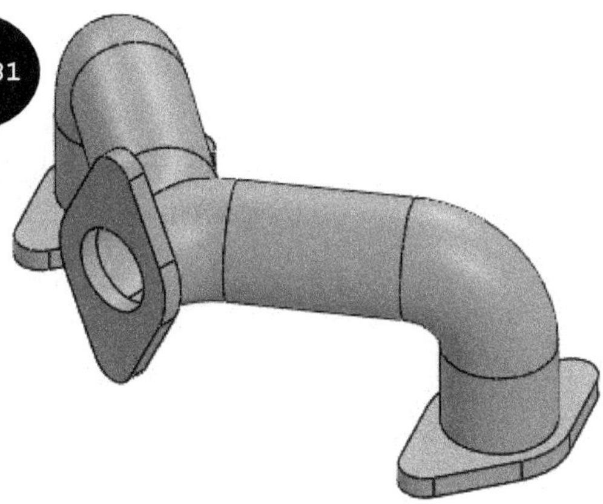

Section 12: Creating the Seventh Feature - Hole Feature

In this section, you need to create holes by using the **Hole Wizard** tool.

1. Click on the **Hole Wizard** tool in the **Features CommandManager**. The **Hole Specification PropertyManager** appears, see Figure 10.182.

2. Click on the **Hole** button in the **Hole Type** rollout of the PropertyManager.

3. Select the **ANSI Metric** option in the **Standard** drop-down list of the **Hole Type** rollout.

4. Select the **Drill sizes** option in the **Type** drop-down list.

5. Select the **ø16.0** option in the **Size** drop-down list of the **Hole Specifications** rollout.

6. Select the **Up To Next** option in the **End Condition** drop-down list.

7. Ensure that the **Near side countersink** and the **Far side countersink** check boxes are cleared in the **Options** rollout of the PropertyManager.

10.182

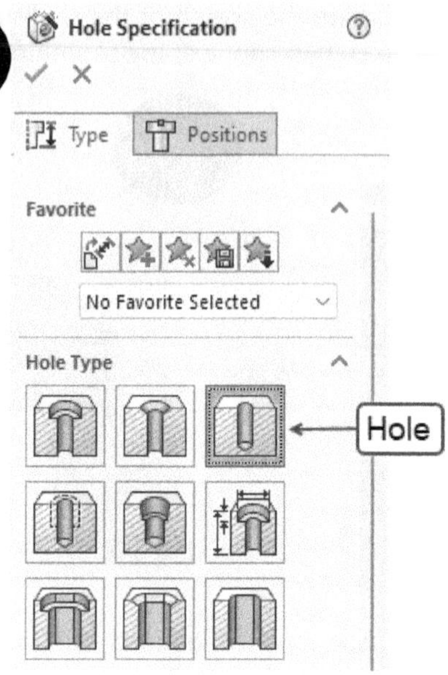

After specifying the hole type and the hole specifications, you need to define the placement of the hole.

8. Click on the **Positions** tab in the **Hole Specification PropertyManager**. The name of the PropertyManager changes to the **Hole Position PropertyManager**.

9. Move the cursor over the top planar face of the right extruded feature (see Figure 10.183) and then click on it as the placement face.

10. Move the cursor over the front semi-circular edge of the right extruded feature, see Figure 10.184. The center point of the semi-circular edge gets highlighted.

10.183

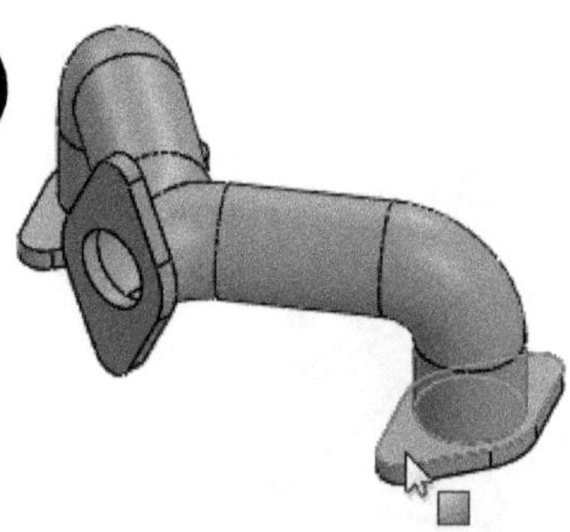

10.184

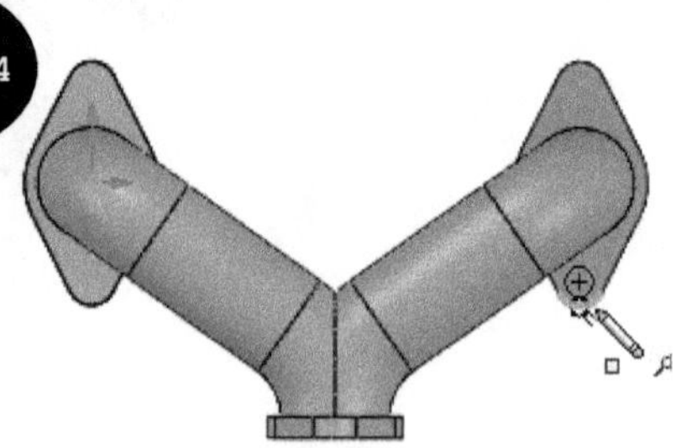

11. Move the cursor over the highlighted center point of the semi-circular edge and then click to specify the center point of the hole when the cursor snaps to it. A preview of the hole appears at the specified location in the graphics area.

12. Similarly, move the cursor over the back semi-circular edge of the right extruded feature, see Figure 10.185. The center point of the semi-circular edge gets highlighted.

13. Move the cursor over the highlighted center point of the semi-circular edge and then click to specify the center point of the hole when the cursor snaps to it. A preview of the hole appears at the specified location in the graphics area.

14. Similarly, move the cursor over the semi-circular edges of the left extruded feature and then specify the center points of the holes on its top planar face, see Figure 10.186.

10.185

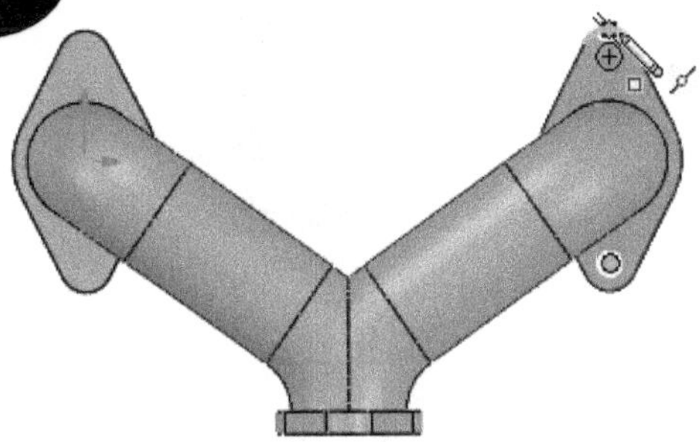

10.186

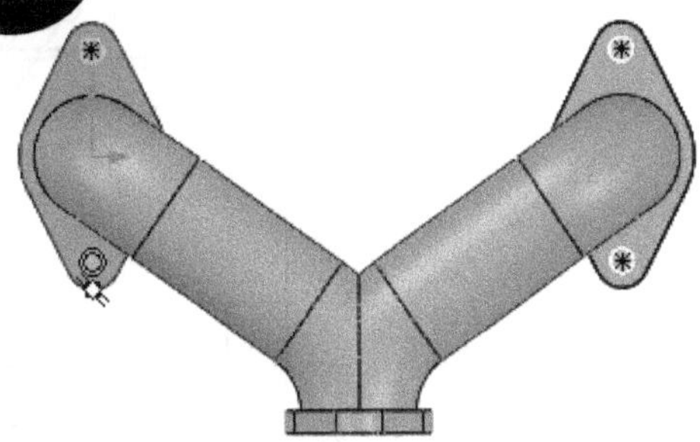

15. Click on the green tick-mark ✓ in the PropertyManager. The holes are created, see Figure 10.187. Also, the PropertyManager is closed.

16. Similarly, create holes on the front planar face of the middle extruded feature by using the **Hole Wizard** tool, see Figure 10.188.

10.187

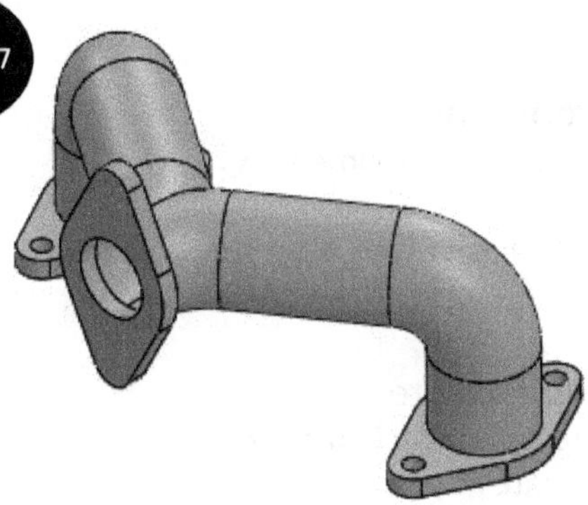

10.188

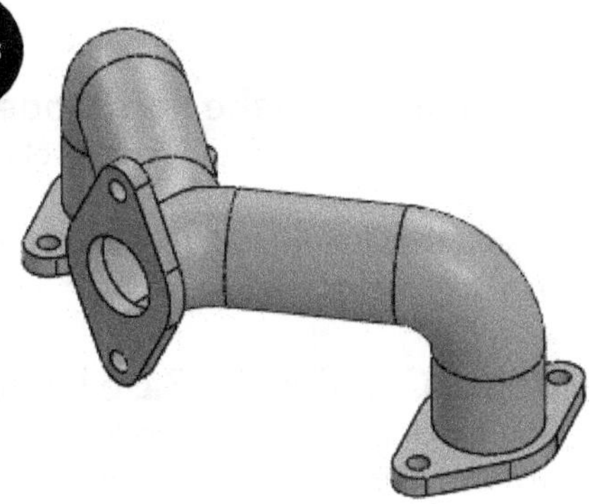

Section 13: Saving the Model

1. Click on the **Save** tool in the **Standard** toolbar. The **Save As** dialog box appears.

2. Browse to the SOLIDWORKS folder and then create a folder with the name Chapter 10.

3. Enter **Tutorial 1** in the **File name** field of the dialog box and then click on the **Save** button. The model is saved with the name Tutorial 1 in the Chapter 10 folder.

Tutorial 2

Create a model, as shown in Figure 10.189. All dimensions are in mm.

10.189

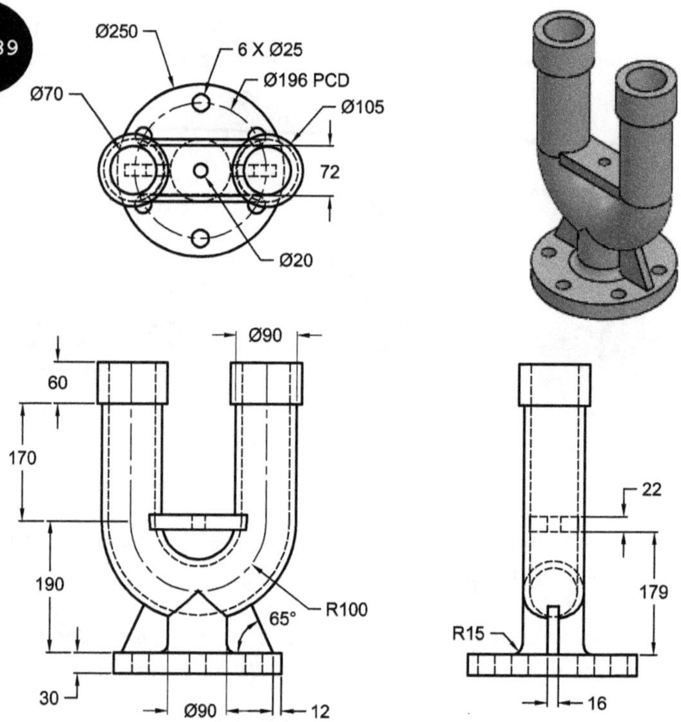

Section 1: Invoking the Part Modeling Environment

1. Start SOLIDWORKS and then invoke the Part modeling environment.

2. Ensure that the **MMGS (millimeter, gram, second)** unit system is set for the currently opened part document.

Section 2: Creating the Base Feature - Sweep Feature

The base feature of the model is a sweep feature having a circular profile. To create a sweep feature having a circular profile, you need to first create its path.

1. Invoke the Sketching environment by selecting the Front plane as the sketching plane.

2. Create the path of the sweep feature, see Figure 10.190.

Note: In Figure 10.190, the center point of the arc has coincident relation with the origin. Also, the connecting line and arc entities of the sketch have tangent relations with each other. In addition, an equal relation has been applied between the vertical lines of the sketch.

3. Exit the Sketching environment. Next, press CTRL + 7 to change the orientation of the sketch to isometric.

   After creating the path of the sweep feature, you need to create the sweep feature.

4. Click on the **Swept Boss/Base** tool in the **Features CommandManager**. The **Sweep PropertyManager** appears.

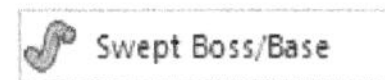

5. Click on the **Circular Profile** radio button in the **Profile and Path** rollout.

6. Select the path of the sweep feature. A preview of the sweep feature appears.

7. Enter **90** in the **Diameter** field of the **Profile and Path** rollout and then press ENTER. A preview of the sweep feature appears as shown in Figure 10.191.

10.190

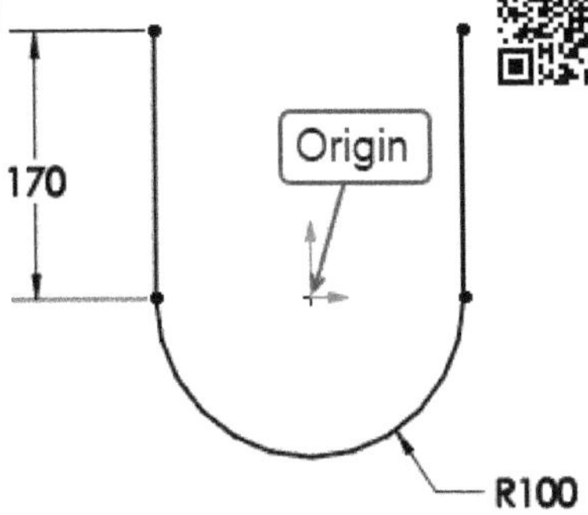

10.191

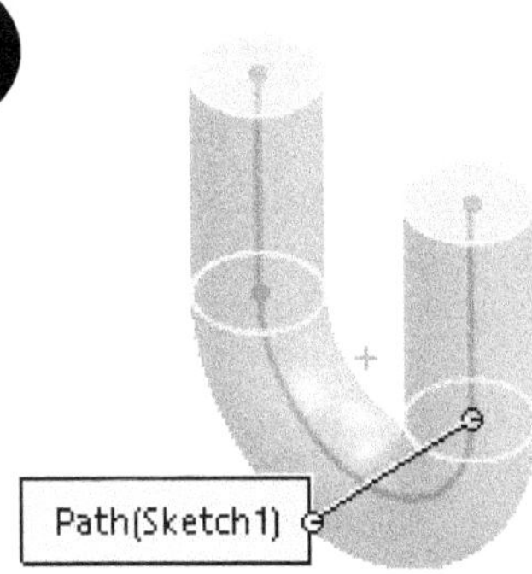

8. Expand the **Thin Feature** rollout of the PropertyManager by clicking on the check box available in its title bar, see Figure 10.192.

10.192

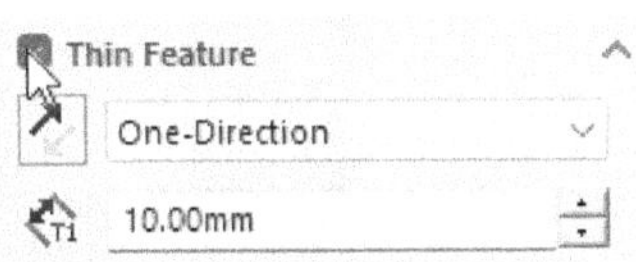

9. Enter **10** in the **Thickness** field of the **Thin Feature** rollout.

10. Click on the **Reverse Direction** button in the **Thin Feature** rollout to reverse the direction of the material inward.

11. Click on the green tick-mark ✓ in the PropertyManager. The sweep feature is created.

Section 3: Creating the Second Feature - Extruded Feature

1. Invoke the Sketching environment by selecting the top planar face of the base feature (sweep) as the sketching plane, see Figure 10.193. The model gets oriented normal to the viewing direction.

2. Create two circles as the sketch of the second feature, see Figure 10.194. After creating the sketch, do not exit the Sketching environment.

10.193

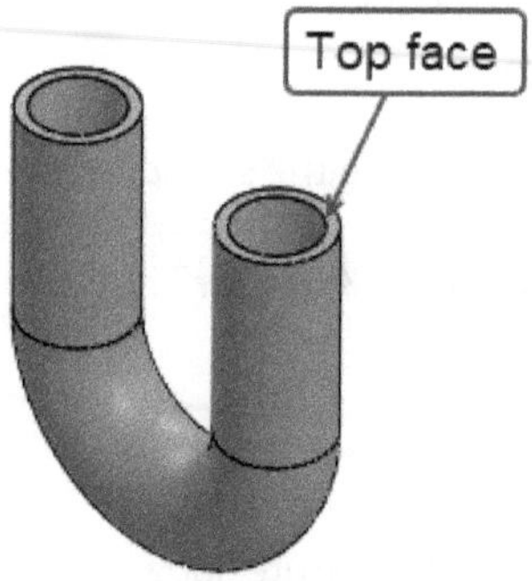

10.194

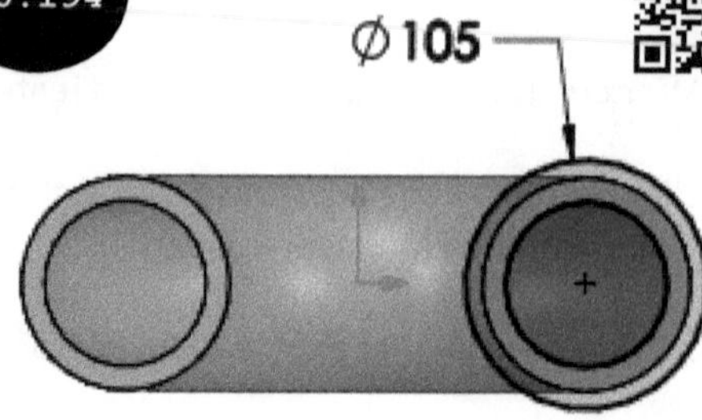

Note: The sketch of the second feature shown in the Figure 10.194 has two circles: the outer circle is of diameter 105 mm and the inner circle has a coradial relation with the inner circular edge of the sweep feature, since the inner circle of the sketch has the same diameter as the inner circular edge of the feature and shares the same center point.

3. Click on the **Features** tab in the CommandManager and click on the **Extruded Boss/Base** tool. The **Boss-Extrude PropertyManager** and a preview of the extruded feature appear. Next, change the orientation of the model to isometric.

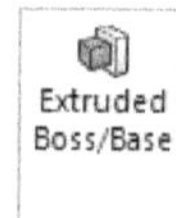

4. Enter **60** in the **Depth** field of the **Direction 1** rollout in the PropertyManager.

5. Click on the green tick-mark ✓ in the PropertyManager. The extruded feature is created, see Figure 10.195.

10.195

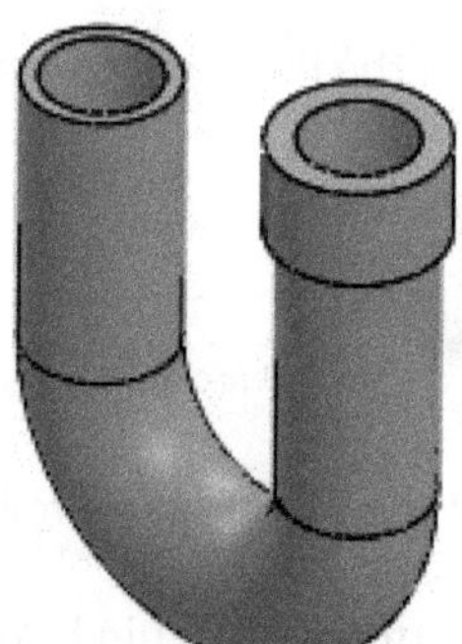

Section 4: Creating the Third Feature - Mirror Feature

Now, you can mirror the previously created extruded feature.

1. Click on the **Mirror** tool in the **Features CommandManager**. The **Mirror PropertyManager** appears.

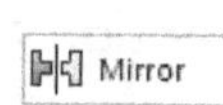

2. Expand the FeatureManager Design Tree, which is now available at the top left corner of the graphics area, and then click on the **Right Plane** as the mirroring plane.

3. Activate the **Features to Mirror** field and click on the second feature (previously created extruded feature) as the feature to be mirrored in the graphics area. The preview of the mirror feature appears in the graphics area.

4. Click on the green tick-mark ✓ in the PropertyManager. The mirror feature is created, see Figure 10.196.

10.196

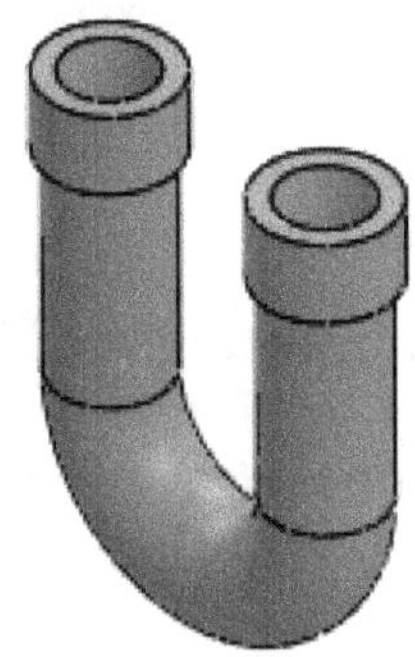

Section 5: Creating the Fourth Feature - Extruded Feature

To create the sketch of the fourth feature, you need to create a reference plane at an offset distance from the Top plane.

1. Click on the **Plane** tool in the **Reference Geometry** flyout. The **Plane PropertyManager** appears.

2. Click on the **Top Plane** in the FeatureManager Design Tree as the first reference. A preview of an offset reference plane appears.

3. Enter **190** in the **Distance** field of the **First Reference** rollout in the PropertyManager.

4. Click on the **Flip offset** check box in the rollout to reverse the direction of the plane downward.

5. Click on the green tick-mark ✓ in the PropertyManager. A reference plane is created, see Figure 10.197.

6. Invoke the Sketching environment by selecting the newly created reference plane as the sketching plane. The model gets oriented normal to the viewing direction.

7. Create a circle of diameter 90 mm as the sketch of the fourth feature, see Figure 10.198. Note that the center point of the circle is at the origin.

10.197

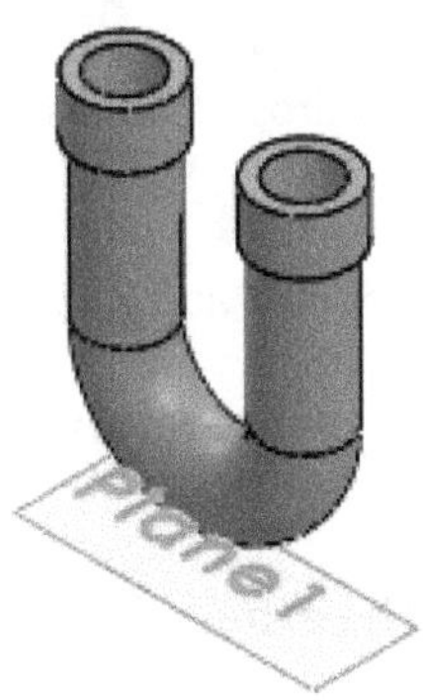

10.198

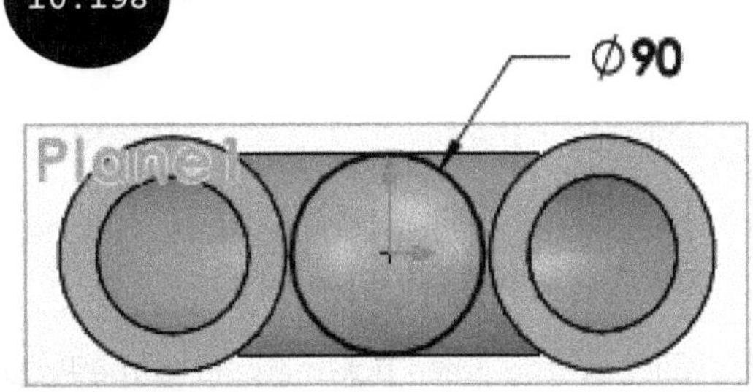

8. Click on the **Features** tab in the CommandManager and then click on the **Extruded Boss/Base** tool. The **Boss-Extrude PropertyManager** and the preview of the extruded feature appear. Next, change the orientation of the model to isometric.

9. Select the **Up To Next** option in the **End Condition** drop-down list of the **Direction 1** rollout.

10. Click on the green tick-mark ✓ in the PropertyManager. The extruded feature is created, see Figure 10.199.

Section 6: Creating the Fifth Feature - Extruded Feature

1. Click on the **Extruded Boss/Base** tool in the **Features CommandManager**. The **Extrude PropertyManager** appears. Also, you are prompted to either select a sketch to be extruded or a sketching plane.

2. Click on the reference plane (Plane 1), which is created at an offset distance of 190 mm from the Top plane as the sketching plane. The orientation of the model gets changed as normal to the viewing direction.

3. Create a circle of diameter 250 mm as the sketch of the fifth feature, see Figure 10.200.

10.199

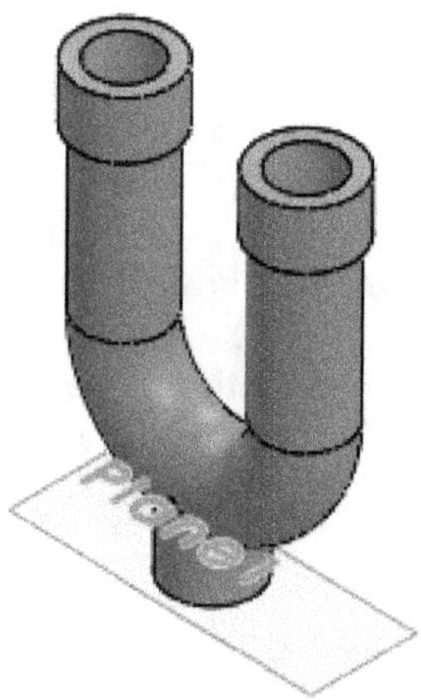

10.200

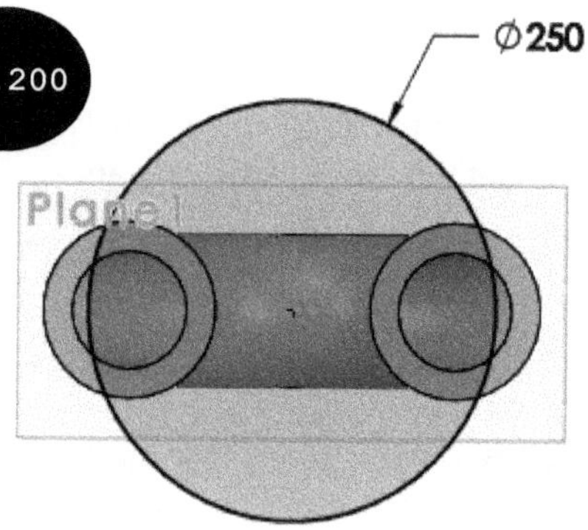

4. Click on the **Exit Sketch** tool in the **Sketch CommandManager** to exit the Sketching environment. The **Boss-Extrude PropertyManager** and a preview of the extruded feature appear. Next, change the orientation of the model to isometric.

5. Ensure that the **Blind** option is selected in the **End Condition** drop-down list of the **Direction 1** rollout.

6. Enter **30** in the **Depth** field of the **Direction 1** rollout in the PropertyManager.

7. Click on the **Reverse Direction** button in the **Direction 1** rollout of the PropertyManager to reverse the direction of extrusion downward.

8. Click on the green tick-mark ✓ in the PropertyManager. The extruded feature is created, see Figure 10.201.

9. Click on the reference plane to hide it. A Pop-up toolbar appears. In this Pop-up toolbar, click on the **Hide** tool.

Section 7: Creating the Sixth Feature - Extruded Cut Feature

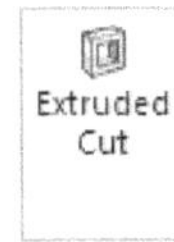

1. Click on the **Extruded Cut** tool in the **Features CommandManager**. The **Extrude PropertyManager** appears.

2. Click on the top planar face of the fifth feature (previously created extruded feature) as the sketching plane. The model gets oriented normal to the viewing direction.

3. Create a circle of diameter 25 mm as the sketch of the sixth feature, see Figure 10.202.

10.201

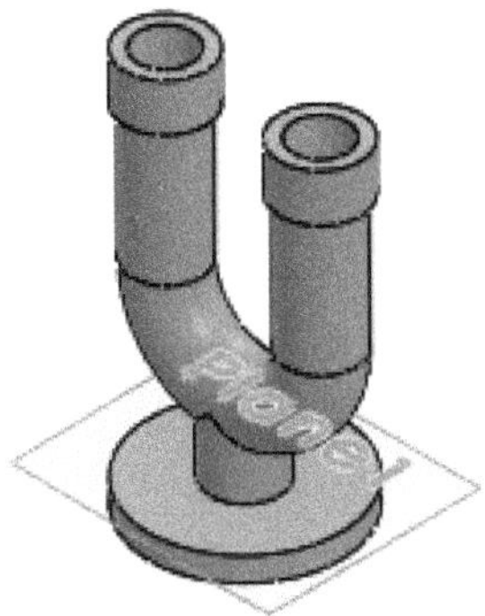

10.202

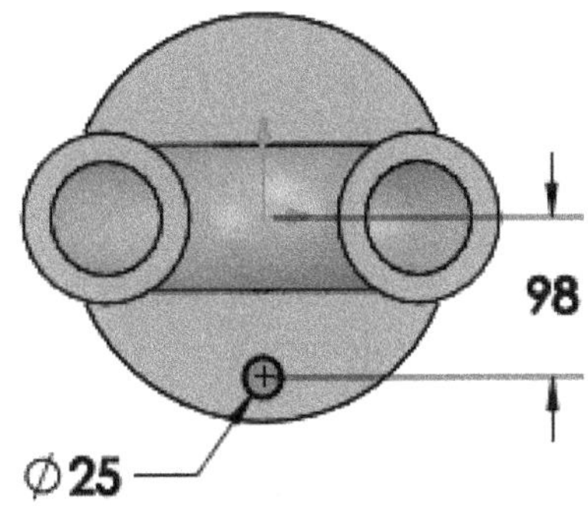

Note: In Figure 10.202, a vertical relation has been applied between the center point of the circle and the origin to make the sketch fully defined.

4. Exit the Sketching environment. The **Cut-Extrude PropertyManager** appears. Next, change the orientation of the model to isometric.

5. Select the **Through All** option in the **End Condition** drop-down list of the **Direction 1** rollout.

6. Click on the green tick-mark ✓ in the PropertyManager. The extruded cut feature is created, see Figure 10.203.

10.203

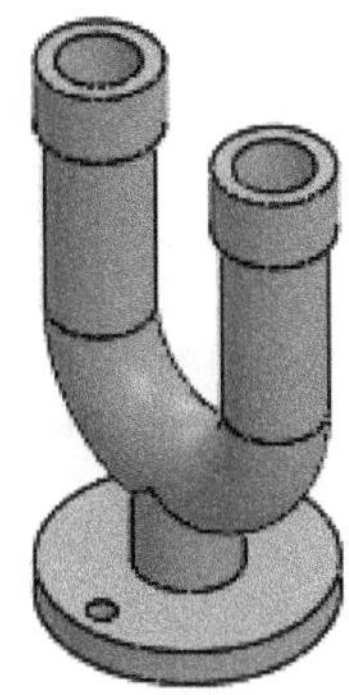

Section 8: Creating the Seventh Feature - Circular Pattern

1. Click on the arrow at the bottom of the **Linear Pattern** tool in the **Features CommandManager**. The **Pattern** flyout appears.

2. Click on the **Circular Pattern** tool. The **CirPattern PropertyManager** appears.

3. Select the sixth feature (previously created extruded cut feature) as the feature to be patterned in the FeatureManager Design Tree or the graphics area.

4. Click on the **Pattern Axis** field in the **Direction 1** rollout of the PropertyManager.

5. Click on the outer circular face of the fifth feature to define the pattern axis, see Figure 10.204. A preview of the circular pattern appears with default parameters.

10.204

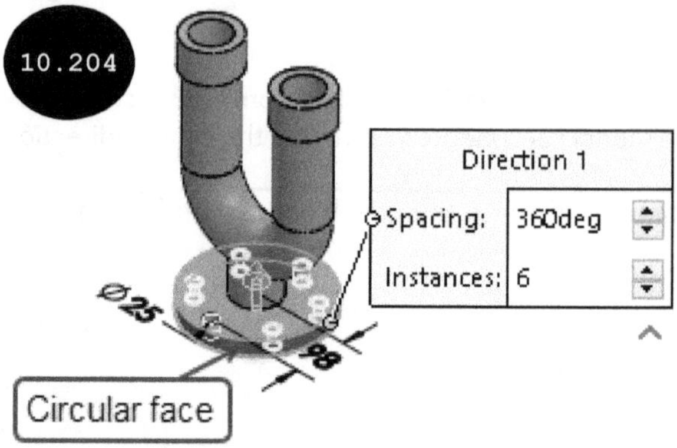

6. Ensure that the **Equal spacing** radio button is selected in the **Direction 1** rollout.

7. Ensure that the **360** degrees is specified in the **Angle** field of the **Direction 1** rollout.

8. Enter **6** in the **Number of Instances** field of the **Direction 1** rollout.

9. Click on the green tick-mark ✓ in the PropertyManager. A circular pattern is created.

Section 9: Creating the Eighth Feature - Fillet

1. Click on the **Fillet** tool. The **Fillet PropertyManager** appears.

2. Ensure that the **Constant Size Fillet** button is activated in the **Fillet Type** rollout. 

3. Click on the circular edge of the model to apply the fillet as shown in Figure 10.205.

4. Enter **15** in the **Radius** field of the **Fillet Parameters** rollout in the PropertyManager. Next, ensure that the **Symmetric** option is selected in the **Fillet Method** drop-down list.

5. Click on the green tick-mark ✓ in the PropertyManager. A fillet of radius 15 mm is created, see Figure 10.206.

10.205

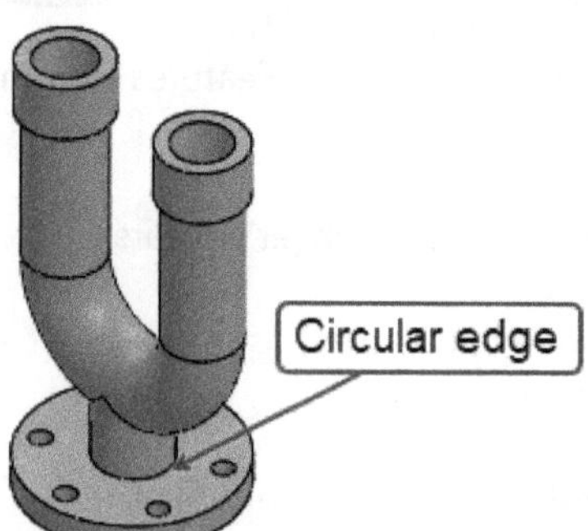

10.206

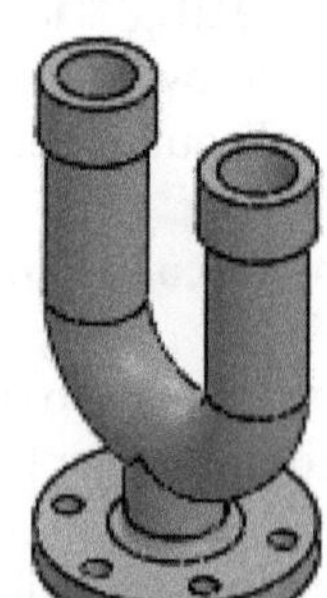

Section 10: Creating the Ninth Feature - Rib Feature

1. Click on the **Rib** tool in the **Features CommandManager**. The **Rib PropertyManager** appears.

2. Select the **Front Plane** as the sketching plane in the FeatureManager Design Tree. The model gets oriented normal to the viewing direction.

3. Create an inclined line as the sketch of the rib feature, see Figure 10.207.

4. Click on the **Exit Sketch** tool in the **Sketch CommandManager**. The **Rib PropertyManager** appears. Next, press CTRL + 7 to change the orientation of the model to isometric.

5. Ensure that the **Both Sides** button is activated in the **Parameters** rollout.

6. Enter **16** in the **Rib Thickness** field of the **Parameters** rollout.

7. Ensure that the **Parallel to Sketch** button is activated in the **Parameters** rollout.

8. Select the **Flip material side** check box to flip the direction of extrusion inward, if needed.

9. Click on the green tick-mark ✓ in the PropertyManager. The rib feature is created, see Figure 10.208.

10.207

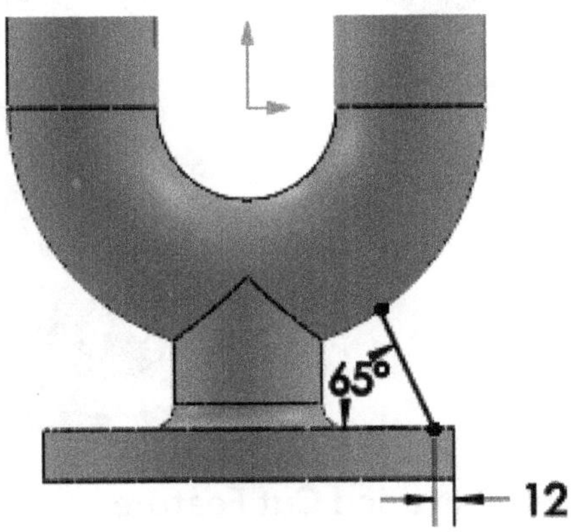

10.208

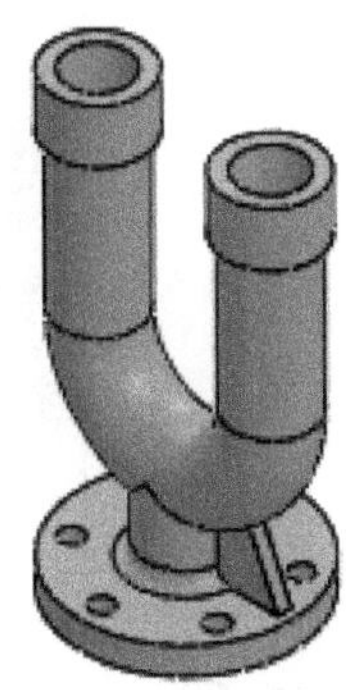

Section 11: Creating the Tenth Feature - Mirror Feature

1. Click on the **Mirror** tool. The **Mirror PropertyManager** appears.

2. Expand the FeatureManager Design Tree and then click on the **Right Plane** as the mirroring plane.

3. Activate the **Features to Mirror** field and click on the rib feature to be mirrored. A preview of the mirror feature appears.

4. Click on the green tick-mark ✓ in the PropertyManager. The mirror feature is created, see Figure 10.209.

10.209

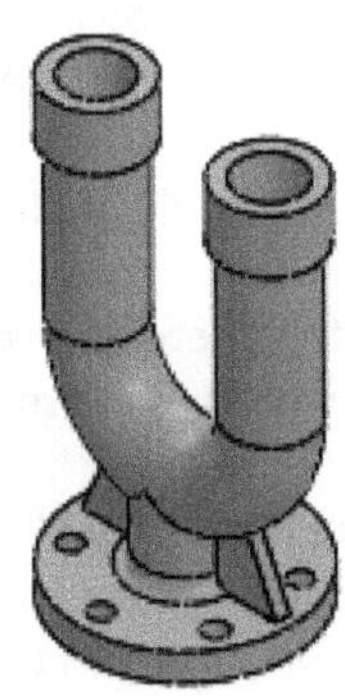

Section 12: Creating the Eleventh Feature - Extruded Feature

1. Click on the **Extruded Boss/Base** tool. The **Extrude PropertyManager** appears.
2. Expand the FeatureManager Design Tree and then click on the **Right Plane** as the sketching plane. The orientation is changed as normal to the viewing direction.
3. Create a rectangle as the sketch of the eleventh feature, see Figure 10.210.
4. Exit the Sketching environment. The **Boss-Extrude PropertyManager** and a preview of the extruded feature appear. Next, change the orientation of the model to isometric.
5. Select the **Up To Next** option in the **End Condition** drop-down list of the **Direction 1** rollout.
6. Expand the **Direction 2** rollout of the PropertyManager and then select the **Up To Next** option in the **End Condition** drop-down list of the **Direction 2** rollout.
7. Click on the green tick-mark ✓ in the PropertyManager. The extruded feature is created, see Figure 10.211.

10.210

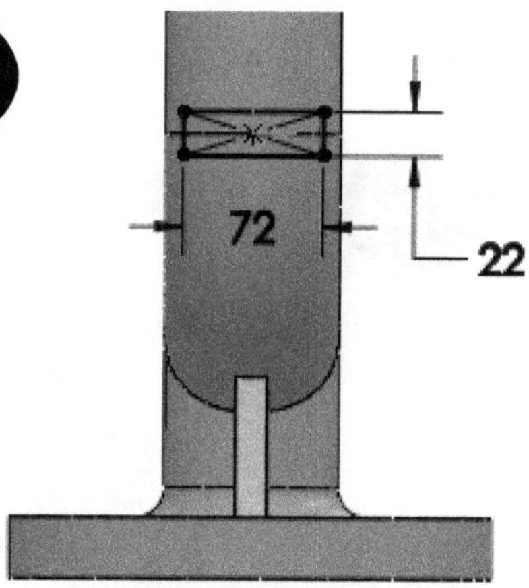

10.211

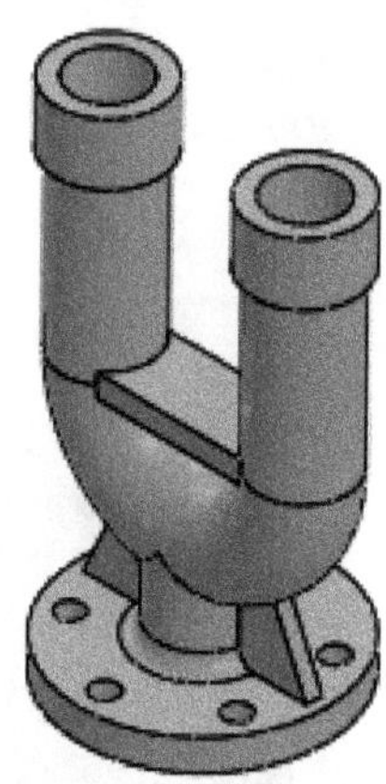

Section 13: Creating the Twelfth Feature - Extruded Cut Feature

1. Click on the **Extruded Cut** tool in the **Features CommandManager**. The **Extrude PropertyManager** appears.
2. Click on the top planar face of the eleventh feature (previously created extruded feature) as the sketching plane. The model gets oriented normal to the viewing direction.
3. Create a circle of diameter 20 mm, whose center point is at the origin, see Figure 10.212.
4. Exit the Sketching environment. The **Cut-Extrude PropertyManager** appears. Next, change the orientation of the model to isometric.
5. Select the **Up To Next** option in the **End Condition** drop-down list of the **Direction 1** rollout.
6. Click on the green tick-mark ✓ in the PropertyManager. The extruded cut feature is created, see Figure 10.213.

10.212

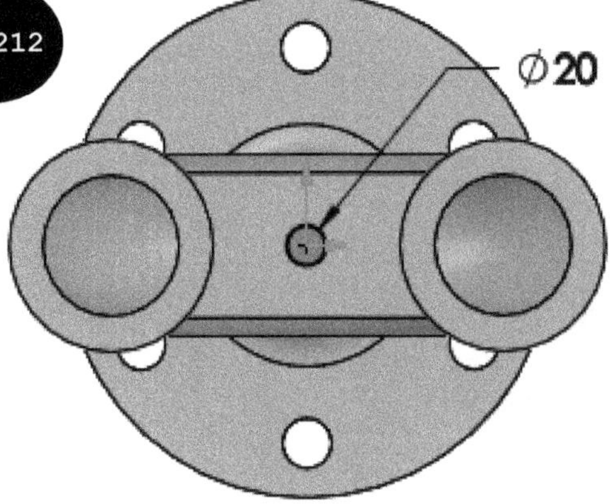

10.213

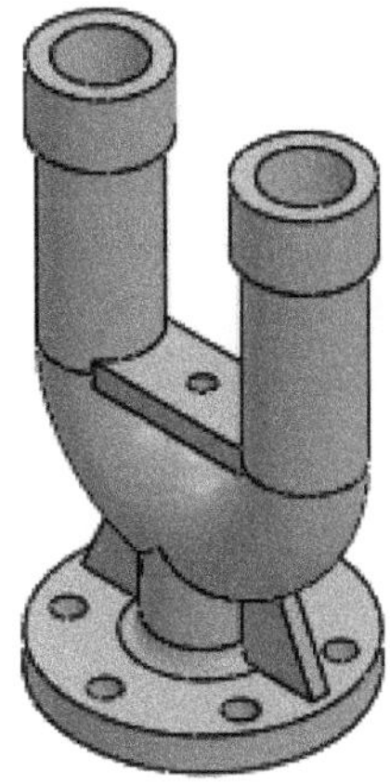

Section 14: Saving the Model

1. Click on the **Save** tool of the **Standard** toolbar. The **Save As** dialog box appears.

2. Browse to the Chapter 10 folder of the SOLIDWORKS folder and then save the model with the name Tutorial 2.

Hands-on Test Drive 1

Create a model, as shown in Figure 10.214. All dimensions are in mm.

10.214

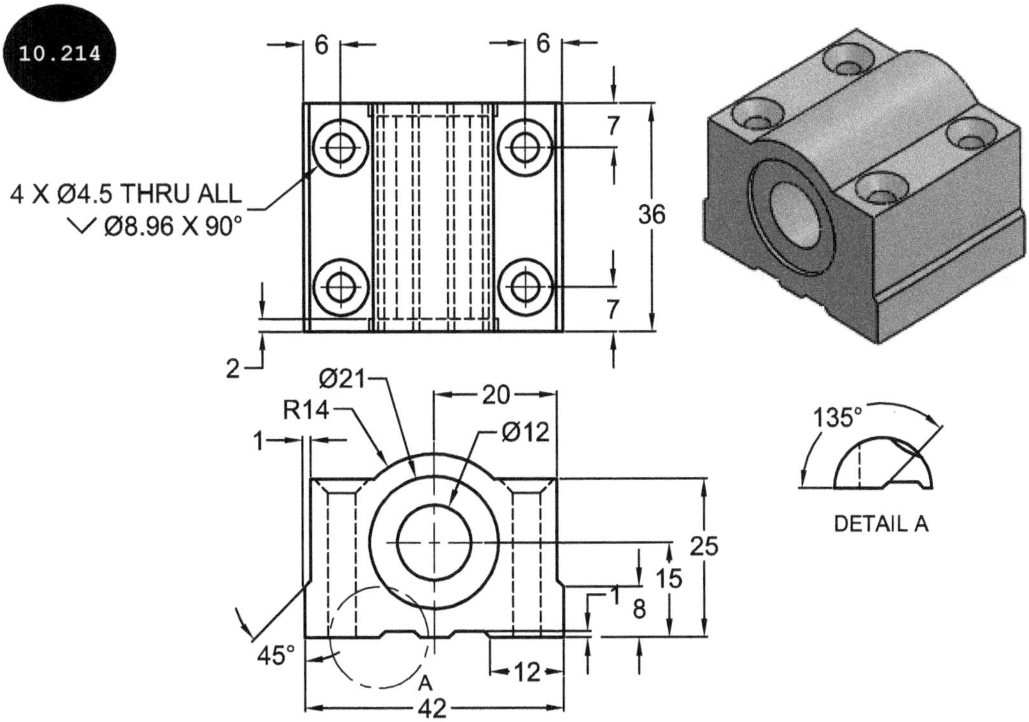

Hands-on Test Drive 2

Create a model, as shown in Figure 10.215. All dimensions are in mm.

10.215

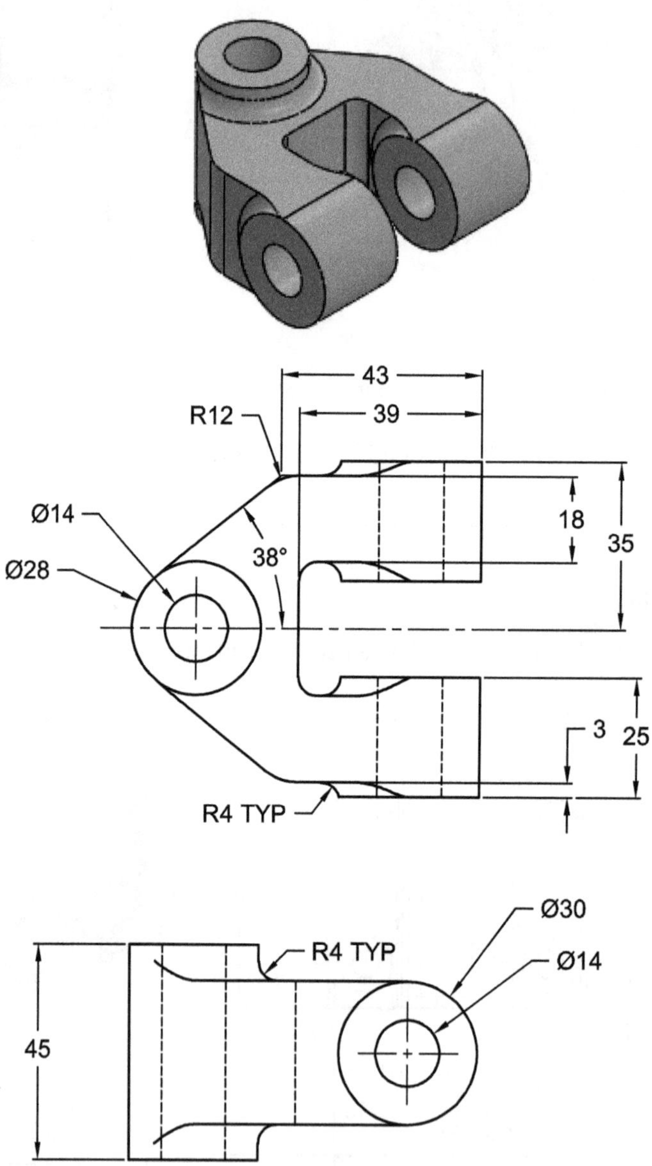

Hands-on Test Drive 3

Create a model, as shown in Figure 10.216. All dimensions are in mm.

10.216

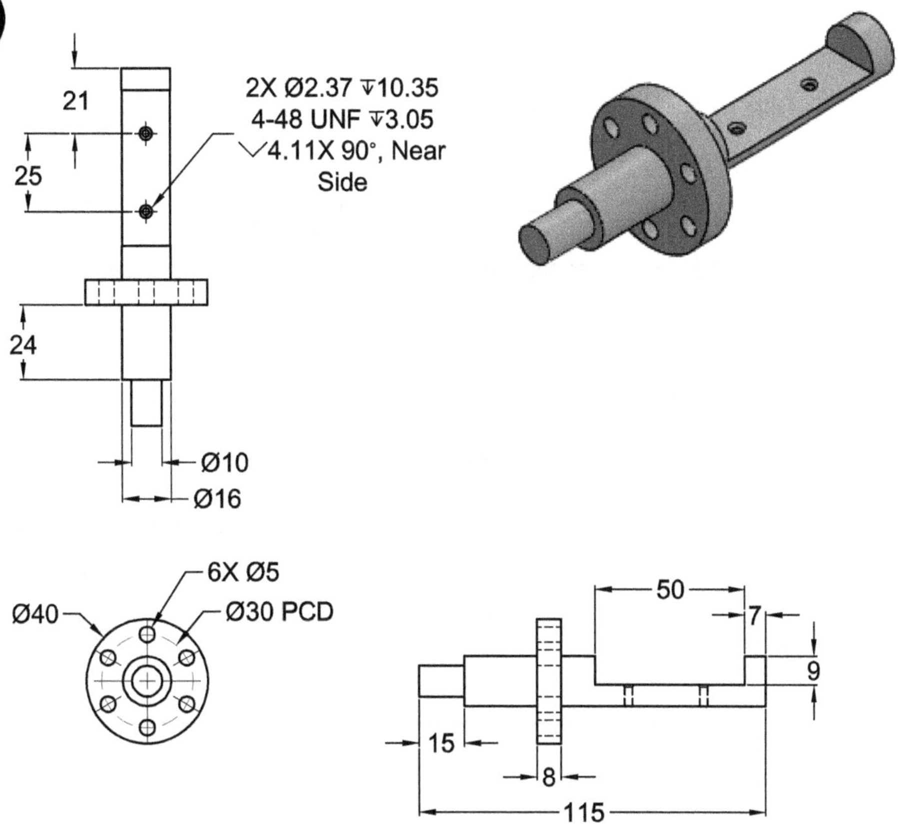

Summary

In this chapter, you learn how to create standard or customized holes such as counterbore, countersink, straight tap, tapered tap, and multi-stepped holes according to standard specifications. You also learn how to create cosmetic threads, realistic threads, stud features, constant and variable radius fillets, chamfers, rib features, shell features, and wrap features. These skills enhance your ability to design and model complex features, improving both the functionality and performance of your CAD projects.

Questions

Complete and verify the following sentences:

- The _________ tool is used to create standard holes such as counterbore and countersink.
- The _________ tool is used to add cosmetic threads to holes, fasteners, and cylindrical features.
- Using the **Fillet** tool, you can create _________, _________, _________, and _________ fillets.
- If the Rho value is less than _________ then the resultant fillet profile becomes elliptical.
- The _________ fillet is created tangent to three adjacent faces of a model.
- The _________ fillet is created between the two non-continuous faces of a model.
- You can create a rib feature by using an open or closed sketch. (True/False)
- You cannot create a rib feature with a draft angle. (True/False)
- While creating a hole by using the **Hole Wizard** tool, you cannot customize the size of the hole. (True/False)
- Using the **Hole Wizard** tool, you can create counterbore slots, countersink slots, or slot holes. (True/False)

CHAPTER

11

Working with Configurations

This chapter discusses the following topics:

- Creating Configurations by using the Manual Method
- Creating Configurations by using the Design Table
- Saving Configurations as a Separate File
- Suppressing and Unsuppressing Features

Configurations are one of the most powerful features of SOLIDWORKS, allowing you to create multiple variations of a model within a single file. This feature helps you quickly and easily manage design alternates based on different dimensions, features, materials, and more. For example, if you need to create ten hexagonal bolts with varying diameters and heights, instead of creating ten separate files, you can create one bolt model with ten different configurations.

In SOLIDWORKS, configurations can be created using two methods: the Manual method and the Design Table method. Both of these methods are discussed next.

Creating Configurations by using the Manual Method

In the Manual method, after creating the parent model in the Part modeling environment, you can create its configurations. You can create multiple configurations of a model and modify the model parameters for each configuration, as required. Consider the case of a plate as shown in Figure 11.1, in which you need to create three different designs. In the first design, you need to create four counterbore holes at each corner and one countersink hole at the center of the plate, see Figure 11.1. In the second design, you need to create only four counterbore holes at each corner, see Figure 11.2. In the third design, you need to create only one countersink hole at the center of the plate, see Figure 11.3.

11.1

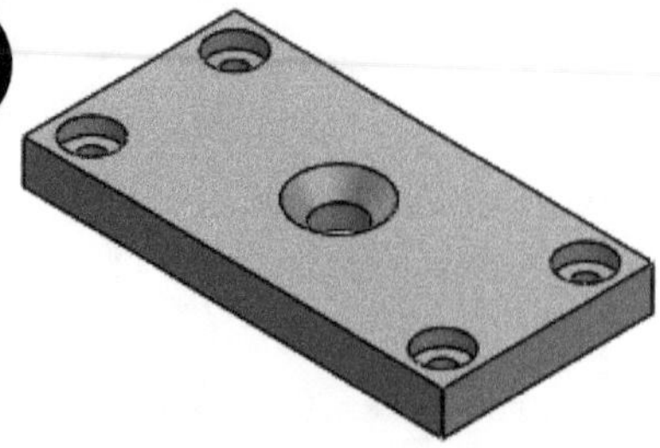

Design 1

11.2

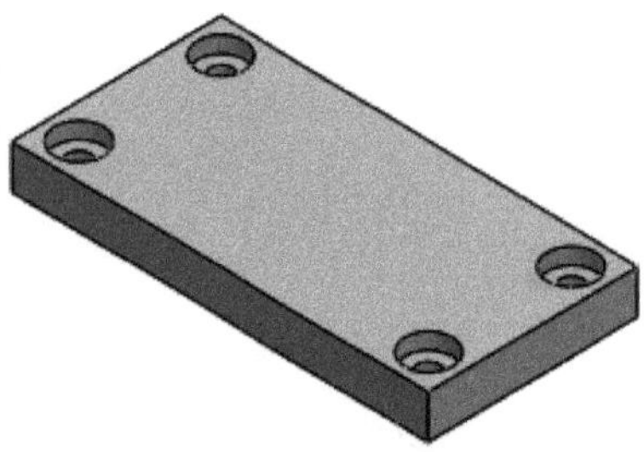

Design 2

11.3

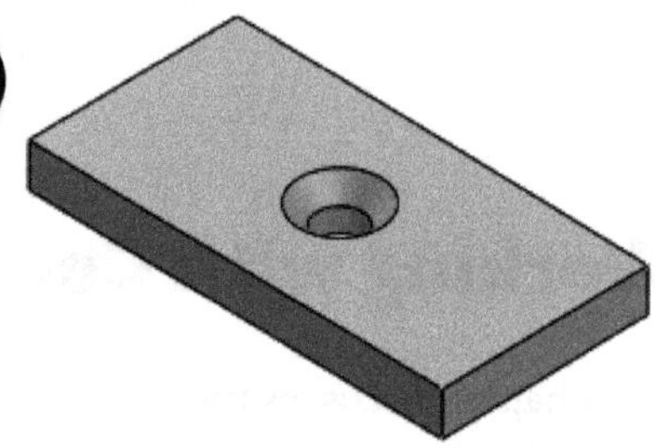

Design 3

To create multiple configurations of a model, click on the **ConfigurationManager** tab, see Figure 11.4. The ConfigurationManager appears, which displays a list of all the available configurations of the current model. By default, the Default configuration of the current model is saved and is activated, see Figure 11.4. A green tick-mark in front of a configuration indicates that it is activated. Note that the model appears in the graphics area as per its active configuration.

11.4

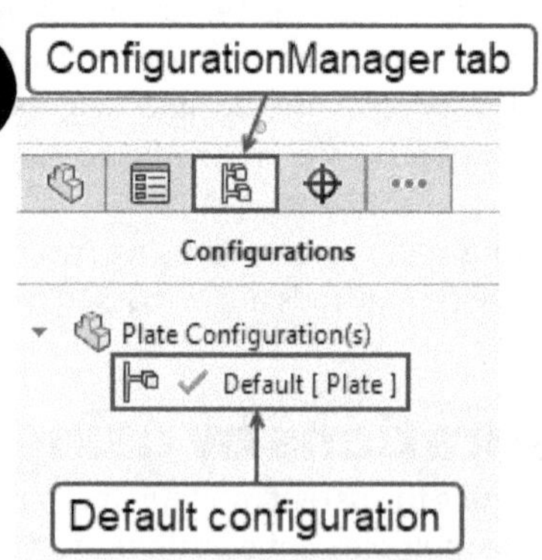

After invoking the ConfigurationManager, right-click on the name of the model. A shortcut menu appears, see Figure 11.5. In this shortcut menu, click on the **Add Configuration** option. The **Add Configuration PropertyManager** appears to the left of the graphics area, see Figure 11.6. The options in the **Add Configuration PropertyManager** are discussed next.

11.5

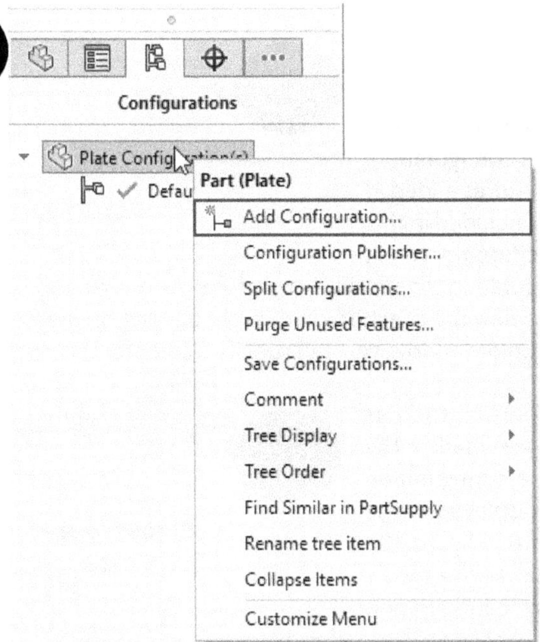

11.6

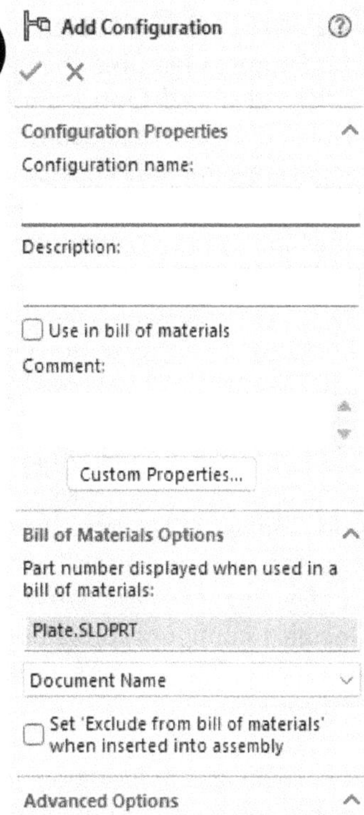

Configuration Properties

The **Configuration name** field of the **Configuration Properties** rollout in the PropertyManager is used to specify the name of the configuration. It is recommended to specify a logical name for the configuration so that you can easily identify it in later use. The **Description** field of the **Configuration Properties** rollout is used to specify a description for the configuration. On selecting the **Use in bill of materials** check box, the description specified in the **Description** field will be displayed in the BOM (Bill of Material). The **Comment** field of this rollout is used to specify comments on the configuration.

Bill of Materials Options

The **Part number displayed when used in a bill of materials** drop-down list of the **Bill of Materials Options** rollout is used to select an option to display the name of the model in the Bill of Materials (BOM) when this configuration is used in the assembly. By default, the **Document Name** option is selected in this drop-down list. As a result, the name of the model is displayed in the BOM, when this configuration is used. On selecting the **Configuration Name** option in the drop-down list, the name of the configuration specified in the **Configuration name** field of the **Configuration Properties** rollout is displayed in the BOM, when this configuration is used. On selecting the **User Specified Name** option, you can specify a new name for the configuration, to be displayed in the BOM, in the field that appears above the drop-down list in the rollout. On selecting the **Set 'Exclude from bill of materials' when inserted into assembly** check box, the model will not be included in the BOM (Bill of Material) when inserted into an assembly with this configuration.

Advanced Options

11.7

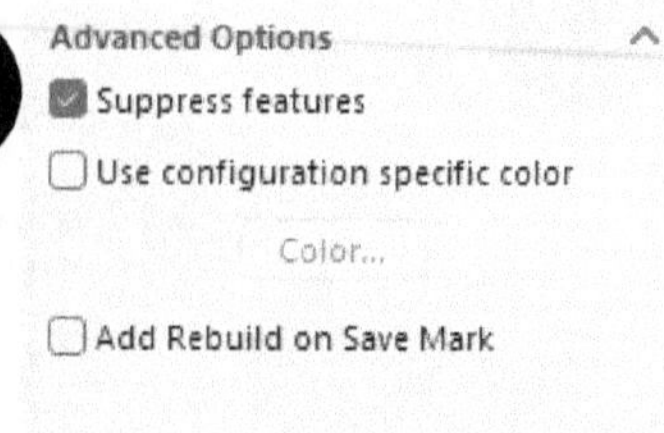

The **Suppress features** check box is selected by default in the **Advanced Options** rollout, see Figure 11.7. As a result, new features added to other configurations of the model are automatically suppressed in this configuration. If you clear this check box, then the new features added in other configurations of the model are also included in this configuration. The **Use configuration-specific color** check box is used to specify a color for this configuration. To specify a color for this configuration, select this check box. The **Color** button gets enabled below the check box in this rollout. Click on the **Color** button to display the **Color** window. By using the **Color** window, you can specify a color for this configuration.

11.8

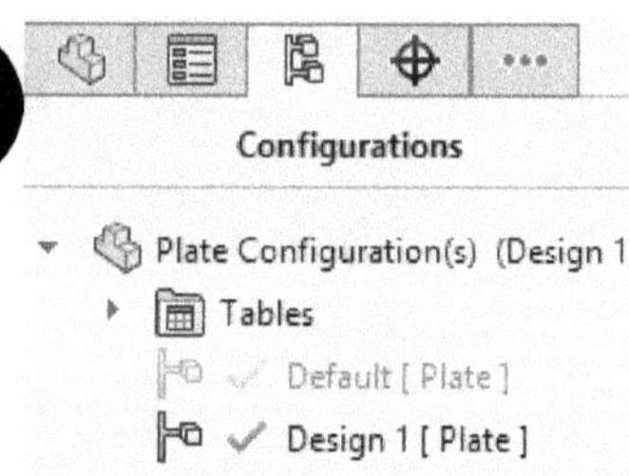

After specifying the configuration properties such as name and description, click on the green tick-mark in the **Add Configuration PropertyManager**. The configuration with specified properties is created and displayed in the ConfigurationManager, see Figure 11.8. In this figure, the **Design 1** configuration is added. Note that the newly created configuration becomes the active configuration of the model.

After creating a configuration, you can make the required modifications in the model such as suppressing or unsuppressing existing features, adding new features, and editing other properties. You will learn about suppressing and unsuppressing features later in this chapter. Note that the modifications made in the model are limited to the currently active configuration only and will not affect the default or other configurations of the model. However, if you modify feature parameters such as extruded depth and dimensions of sketches then you need to specify whether the modification is for the current active configuration only or all configurations of the model.

For example, while modifying the depth of an extruded feature, you need to select the required radio button: **This configuration**, **All configurations**, or **Specify configurations** in the **Configurations** rollout of the respective PropertyManager, see Figure 11.9. If you select the **This configuration** radio button, then the modification is made in the currently active configuration of the model only, whereas if you select the **All configuration** radio button, then the modification will be made in all configurations of the model including the default configuration. Similarly, while modifying a dimension of a sketch, you need to specify whether the modification is for the currently active configuration only or all the configurations of the model by using the **Configuration** flyout of the **Modify** dialog box, which appears while modifying a dimension, see Figure 11.10.

11.9

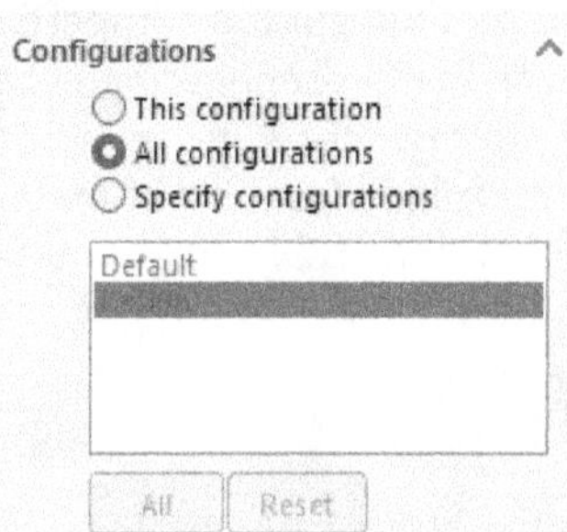

11.10

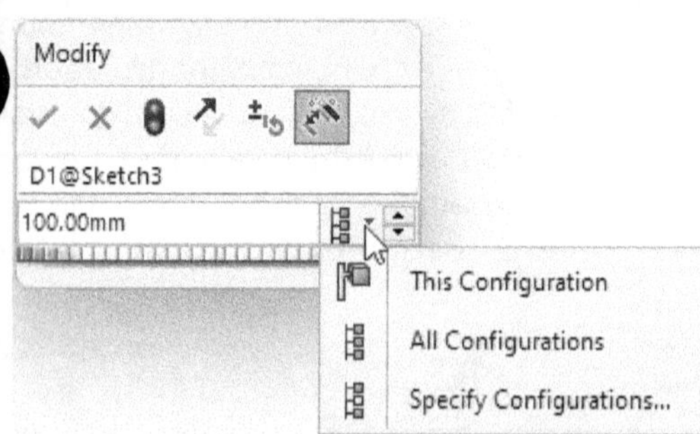

To create the second configuration of a model, right-click on the name of the model in the ConfigurationManager to display a shortcut menu, see Figure 11.11. In this shortcut menu, click on the **Add Configuration** option. The **Add Configuration PropertyManager** appears. In this PropertyManager, specify the configuration properties such as name and description, and then click on the green tick mark in the PropertyManager. A new configuration is created and its name appears in the ConfigurationManager, see Figure 11.12. In this figure, the **Design 1** and **Design 2** configurations are added. Note that the newly created configuration (**Design 2**) is the active configuration of the model. After creating the second configuration of a model, you can make the required modifications to the model. Similarly, you can create multiple configurations of a model. Figure 11.13 shows a model with three different configurations (Design 1, Design 2, and Design 3).

11.11

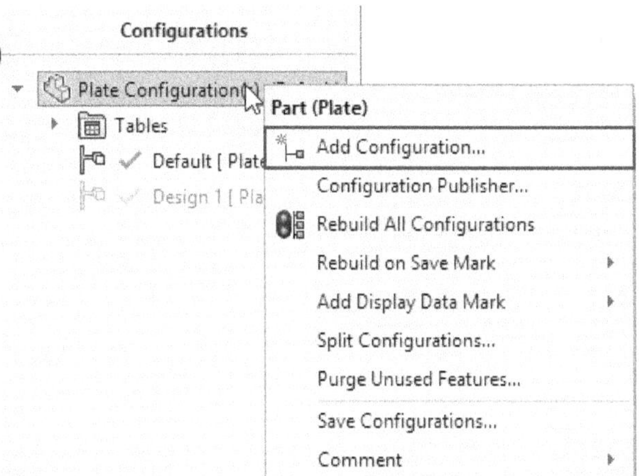

11.12

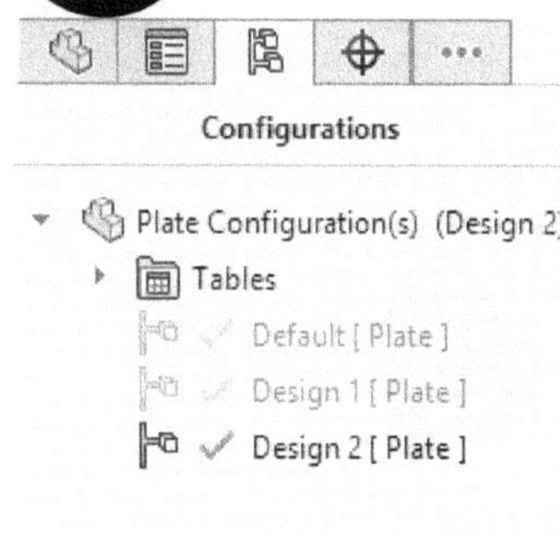

11.13

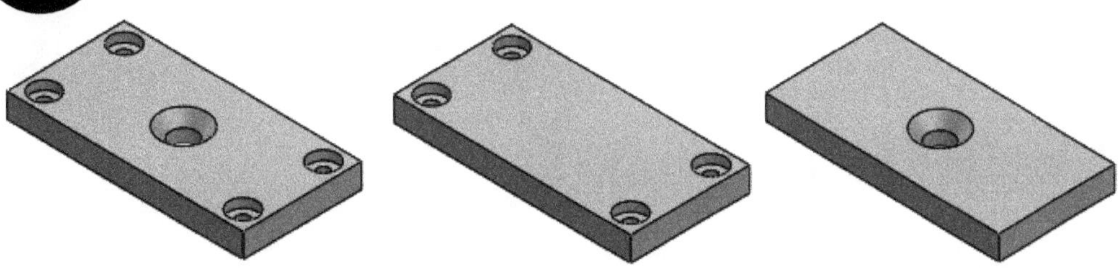

Design 1 Design 2 Design 3

Note: You can activate any existing configuration of a model by double-clicking on its name in the ConfigurationManager. Alternatively, right-click on the name of the configuration to be activated in the ConfigurationManager to display a shortcut menu and then click on the **Show Configuration** option. Once the required configuration is activated, you can make necessary modifications in the model for the active configuration.

Tip: In SOLIDWORKS, you can edit the properties of an already created configuration. To do this, right-click on the name of the configuration to be edited in the ConfigurationManager and then click on the **Properties** option in the shortcut menu that appears. The **Configuration Properties PropertyManager** appears. In this PropertyManager, you can edit the properties of the configuration, as required. Note that the options in the PropertyManager are discussed earlier, except the **Custom Properties** button. On clicking the **Custom Properties** button, the **Properties** dialog box appears in the graphics area which allows you to edit or customize the properties of a particular configuration, as required.

Creating Configurations by using the Design Table

The Design Table method is a very easy and convenient way of creating multiple configurations of a model. It provides an embedded Microsoft Excel worksheet, where you can easily create or manage multiple configurations by specifying parameters. To do this, click on the **Insert > Tables > Excel Design Table** in the SOLIDWORKS Design Menus, see Figure 11.14. The **Excel Design Table PropertyManager** appears, see Figure 11.15. The options in the PropertyManager are discussed next.

11.14

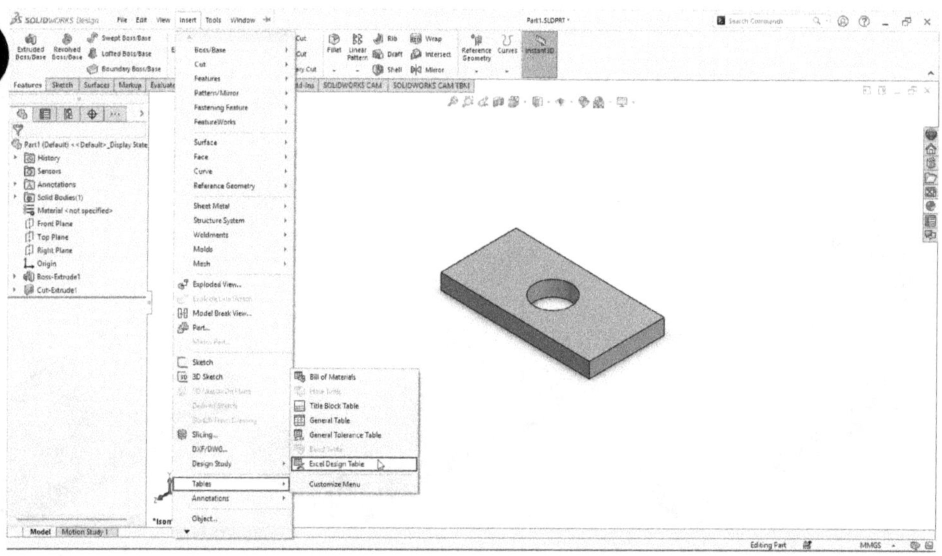

Note: To create configurations by using the Design Table, you need to ensure that Microsoft Excel is installed on your computer.

Source

By default, the **Auto-create** radio button is selected in the **Source** rollout of the **Excel Design Table PropertyManager**, see Figure 11.15. As a result, all parameters of the source model are automatically loaded into the design table.

11.15

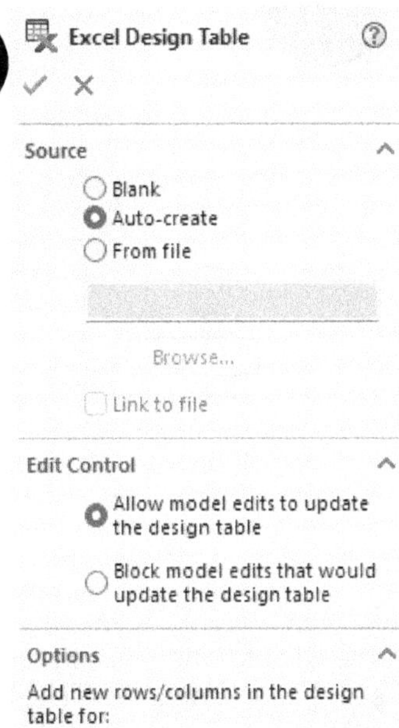

On selecting the **Blank** radio button, you are provided with a blank design table where you need to fill in the parameters for each configuration.

On selecting the **From file** radio button, you can import an existing design table or a Microsoft Excel file containing different configurations of the model with their parameters.

When you select the **From file** radio button, the **Browse** button is enabled in the rollout. Click on the **Browse** button. The **Open** dialog box appears. In this dialog box, browse to the location where the existing design table or the Microsoft Excel file is saved and then select it. Next, click on the **Open** button. The name and path of the selected design table or Microsoft Excel file appears in the field below the **From file** radio button. If you select the **Link to file** check box in the rollout then the imported Microsoft Excel file gets linked with the model. As a result, if you make any modifications in the Excel file the same modifications are reflected in the model and vice-versa.

Edit Control

The **Allow model edits to update the design table** radio button is selected in the **Edit Control** rollout, by default, see Figure 11.15. As a result, if you make any modifications to the model, the same modifications are reflected in the design table as well. On selecting the **Block model edits that would update the design table** radio button, you are not allowed to make modifications to the model, which would update the parameters of the design table.

Options

The **New parameters** check box is selected in the **Options** rollout, by default. As a result, on adding a new parameter in the model, a new column for the parameter is added automatically in the design table. If the **New configurations** check box is selected in the rollout, then on adding a new configuration in the model, a new row for the configuration is added automatically in the design table. If the **Warn when updating design table** check box is selected, then a warning message appears on updating the design table. If the **Enable cell drop-down lists (may be slower)** check box is selected, the cells of the design table contain drop-down lists for multiple entries.

In the **Excel Design Table PropertyManager**, accept the default selected options and then click on the green tick-mark in it. The process of creating the design table starts. Also, the **Dimensions** window and an embedded Microsoft Excel worksheet appear on the screen, see Figure 11.16. The **Dimensions** window displays a list of all dimensions of the model.

11.16

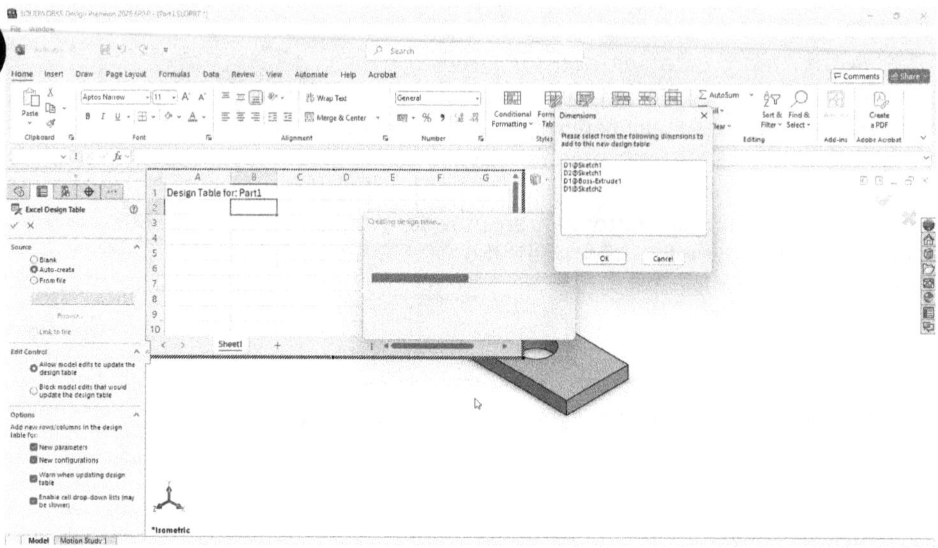

In the **Dimensions** window, select the dimensions of the model to be added to the design table by pressing and holding the CTRL key. After selecting the dimensions in the **Dimensions** window, click on the **OK** button. The design table appears as a Microsoft Excel worksheet with the Default configuration of the model, see Figure 11.17. In the design table, the names of the selected dimensions of the model are added in separate columns and the Default configuration is added in a row. Also, the dimension values of the selected dimensions are added in cells, corresponding to the dimension name column and the Default configuration row, see Figure 11.17.

11.17

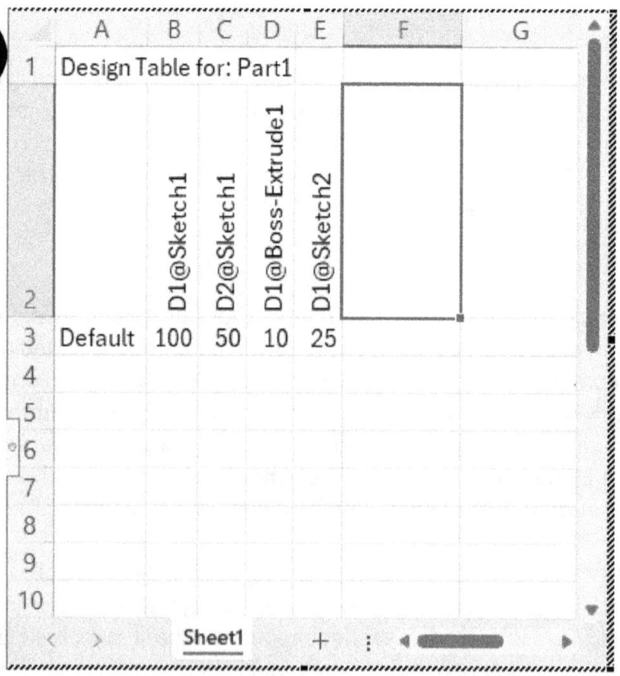

You can add multiple configurations of a model by entering their names in different rows of the table, see Figure 11.18. Note that for each configuration, you can specify different dimension values in the respective cells, see Figure 11.18. In this figure, in addition to the Default configuration, three more configurations (Plate 50X25X5, Plate 30X15X5, and Plate 200X100X10) of the model have been created with different dimension values.

11.18

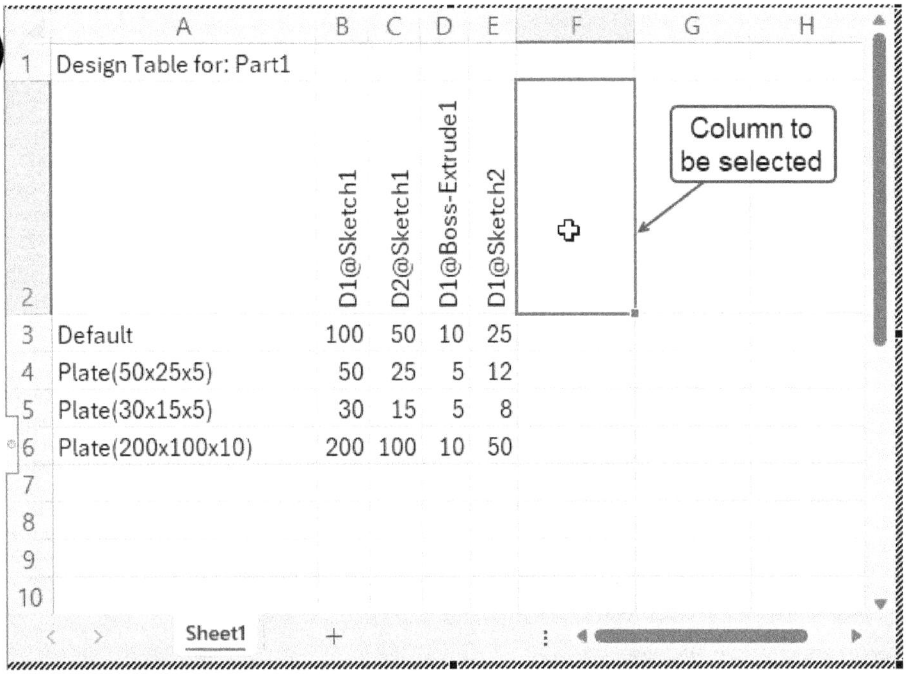

	A	B	C	D	E	F	G	H
1	Design Table for: Part1							
2		D1@Sketch1	D2@Sketch1	D1@Boss-Extrude1	D1@Sketch2			
3	Default	100	50	10	25			
4	Plate(50x25x5)	50	25	5	12			
5	Plate(30x15x5)	30	15	5	8			
6	Plate(200x100x10)	200	100	10	50			
7								
8								
9								
10								

In addition to specifying different dimension values for each configuration in the design table, you can specify the suppressed or unsuppressed state for the features of the model in each configuration.

11.19

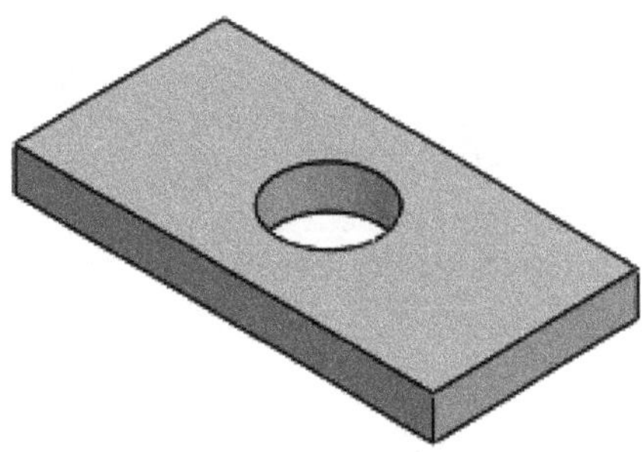

Consider a case of a plate having one circular cut feature at the center, see Figure 11.19. If you do not want the circular cut feature of the model to become a part of a configuration then you can specify its state as suppressed in the design table. To specify the suppressed or unsuppressed state of a feature in the design table, click on the column, next to the last dimension name in the design table, refer to Figure 11.18. Next, double-click on the name of the feature in the FeatureManager Design Tree. The name of the selected feature is added in the selected column of the design table, see Figure 11.20. Notice that, the unsuppressed state is specified for the Default configuration, by default. To specify a suppressed state for a feature, enter **S**, **1**, or **SUPPRESSED** in the cell corresponding to the feature and the configuration. Similarly, to specify an unsuppressed state, enter **U**, **0**, or **UNSUPPRESSED**.

11.20

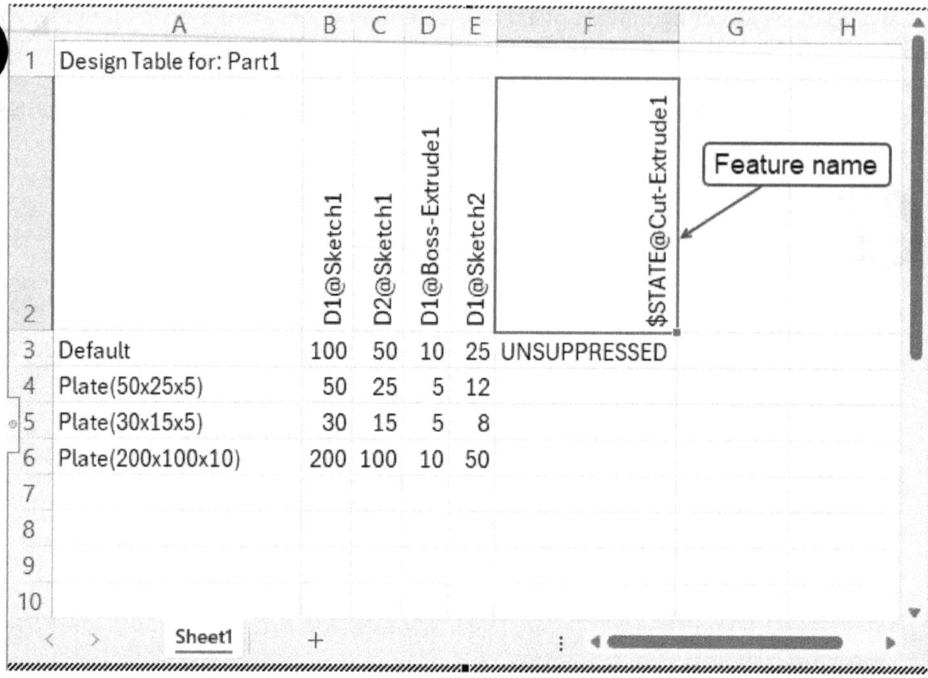

	A	B	C	D	E	F	G	H
1	Design Table for: Part1							
2		D1@Sketch1	D2@Sketch1	D1@Boss-Extrude1	D1@Sketch2	$STATE@Cut-Extrude1		
3	Default	100	50	10	25	UNSUPPRESSED		
4	Plate(50x25x5)	50	25	5	12			
5	Plate(30x15x5)	30	15	5	8			
6	Plate(200x100x10)	200	100	10	50			
7								
8								
9								
10								

After creating different configurations and specifying parameters for each configuration, click anywhere in the graphics area. The **SOLIDWORKS** message window appears which informs you that the design table is generated with the specified configurations. Click on the **OK** button in the **SOLIDWORKS** message window. The configurations are created and are listed in the ConfigurationManager, see Figure 11.21.

11.21

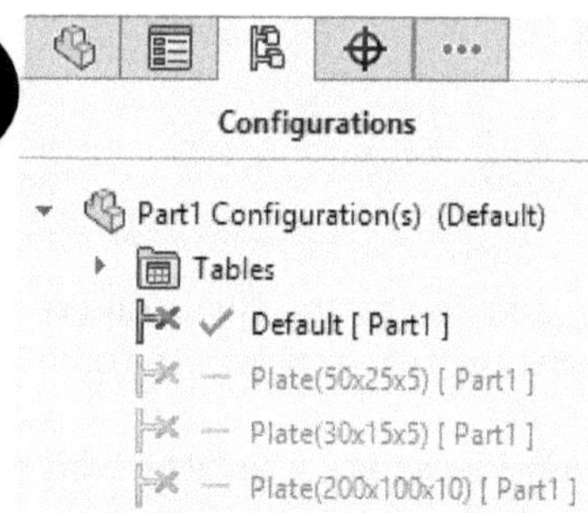

Note that in the ConfigurationManager, the Default configuration is activated. As a result, the model that appears in the graphics area is based on the parameters of the Default configuration. To activate a configuration, double-click on the name of the configuration to be activated in the ConfigurationManager. Alternatively, right-click on the name of the configuration and then click on the **Show Configuration** option in the shortcut menu that appears. The selected configuration gets activated and the model is updated in the graphics area, accordingly.

Note: After generating a design table with multiple configurations, you can further edit its parameters. To do this, expand the **Tables** node in the ConfigurationManager and then right-click on the **Excel Design Table** option in the expanded **Tables** node. A shortcut menu appears, see Figure 11.22. In this shortcut menu, click on the **Edit Table** option. The **Add Rows and Columns** window appears. Click on the **OK** button in this window. The design table appears as Microsoft Excel worksheet. Now, you can make the necessary modifications in the parameters of the existing configurations and add new configurations as well. After editing the design table, click anywhere in the graphics area.

11.22

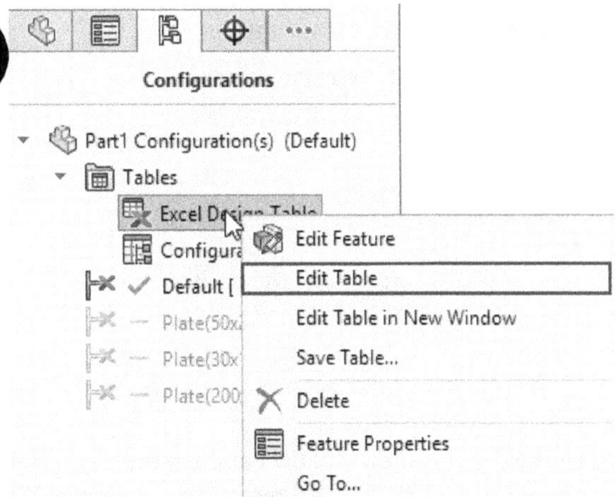

Saving Configurations as a Separate File

In SOLIDWORKS, you can save a selected configuration of a part or an assembly as a separate file. To save a configuration or multiple configurations of a part as a separate part file, right-click on a configuration of the part in the ConfigurationManager and then click on the **Save Configurations** option in the shortcut menu that appears, see Figure 11.23. The **Save Configurations as a new Part** window appears, see Figure 11.24. In this window, you can select the required configurations to be saved as a separate part file. Note that the currently active configuration of the part is selected in this window, by default and cannot be removed from the selection set. Next, click on the **Save Selected** button. The **Save As** dialog box appears. If the **SOLIDWORKS Design** message window appears, click **OK** to display the **Save As** dialog box.

11.23

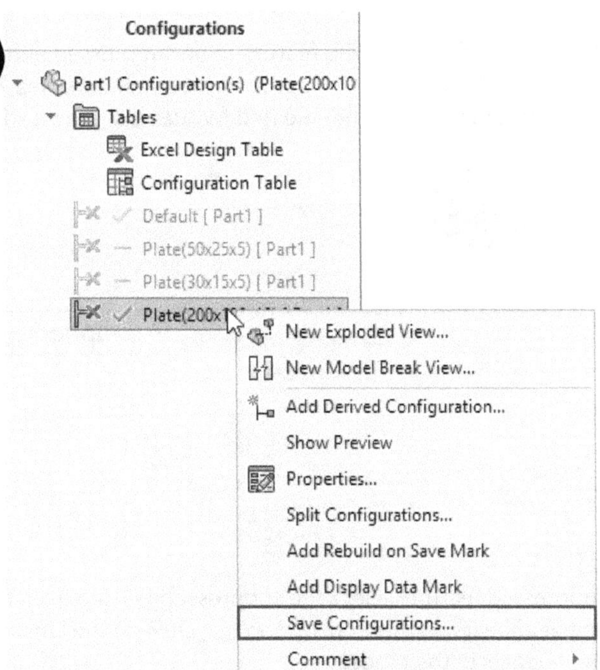

11.24

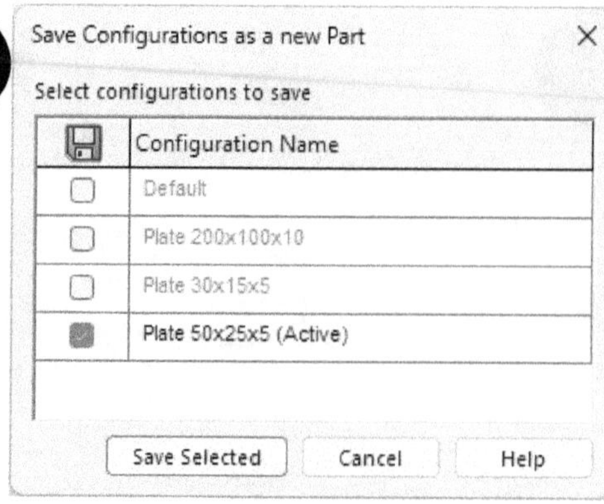

In this dialog box, browse to the required location and then enter a new name for the file in the **File name** field of the dialog box. Next, click on the **Save** button. A new part file of the specified name gets saved with the selected configurations. Similarly, you can save selected configurations of an assembly as a separate assembly file.

Suppressing and Unsuppressing Features

In SOLIDWORKS, you can suppress or unsuppress the features of a model. A suppressed feature is removed from the model and does not appear in the graphics area. Also, the name of the suppressed feature appears in gray in the FeatureManager Design Tree. Note that a suppressed feature is not deleted from the model, it is only removed such that it does not load into the RAM (random access memory) while rebuilding the model. This helps you to speed up the overall performance of the system when you are working with complex models.

To suppress a feature of a model, select the feature to be suppressed either from the graphics area or from the FeatureManager Design Tree. A Pop-up toolbar appears, see Figure 11.25. In this Pop-up toolbar, click on the **Suppress** tool. The selected feature is suppressed.

11.25

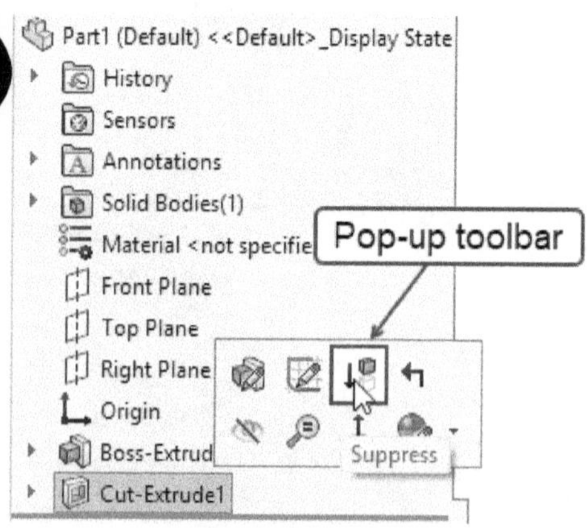

To unsuppress a suppressed feature, select the suppressed feature from the FeatureManager Design Tree. A Pop-up toolbar appears. In this Pop-up toolbar, click on the **Unsuppress** tool. The feature is unsuppressed and appears in the model.

Tutorial 1

Create a model (Weld Neck Flange), as shown in Figure 11.26. After creating the model, create its three different configurations by using the Design Table method. The details of the configurations to be created are given in the table below. All dimensions are in mm.

11.26

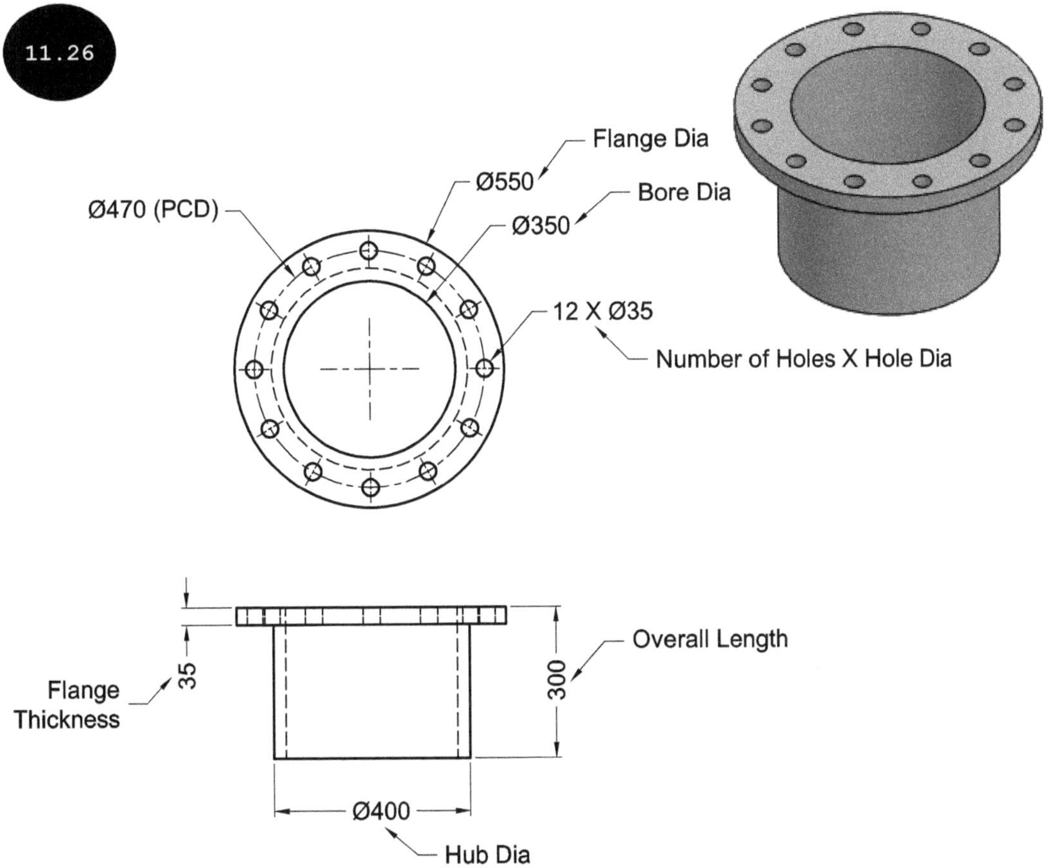

TABLE								
	Bore Dia	Hub Dia	Overall Length	Flange Dia	Flange Thickness	Hole Dia	Hole PCD	No. of Holes
350 Bore Dia	350	400	300	550	35	35	470	12
400 Bore Dia	400	450	300	600	35	35	520	16
450 Bore Dia	450	500	300	650	35	35	570	20

Section 1: Starting SOLIDWORKS

1. Start SOLIDWORKS by double-clicking on the SOLIDWORKS icon on your desktop. The startup user interface of SOLIDWORKS appears along with the **Welcome** dialog box.

Section 2: Invoking the Part Modeling Environment

1. Click on the **Part** button in the **Welcome** dialog box. The Part modeling environment is invoked. Alternatively, click on the **New** tool in the **Standard** toolbar. The **New SOLIDWORKS Document** dialog box appears. In this dialog box, ensure that the **Part** button is selected and then click on the **OK** button.

2. Ensure that the **MMGS (millimeter, gram, second)** unit system is set for the currently opened part document.

Section 3: Creating the Base Feature - Extruded Feature

1. Invoke the Sketching environment by selecting the Top plane as the sketching plane.

2. Create a circle by specifying its center point at the origin, see Figure 11.27.

3. Click on the **Smart Dimension** tool in the **Sketch CommandManager**. Next, click on the circle in the drawing area. The diameter dimension of the circle gets attached to the cursor.

4. Click to specify the placement point for the diameter dimension in the drawing area. The **Modify** dialog box appears, see Figure 11.28.

5. Enter **350** as the diameter of the circle in the **Dimension** field of the **Modify** dialog box, see Figure 11.28.

6. Enter **Bore Dia** as the name of the dimension in the **Name** field, see Figure 11.28.

11.27

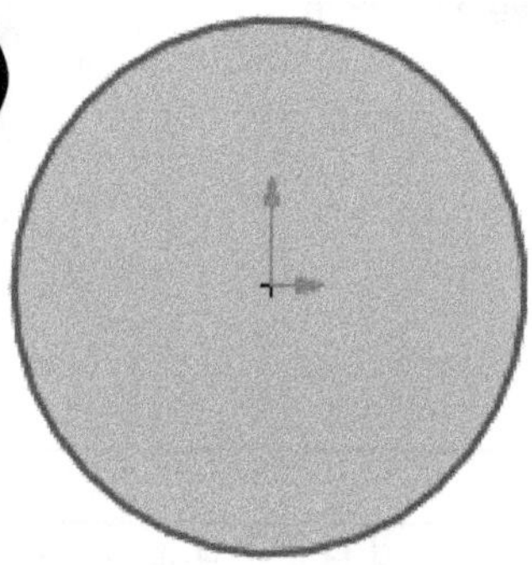

11.28

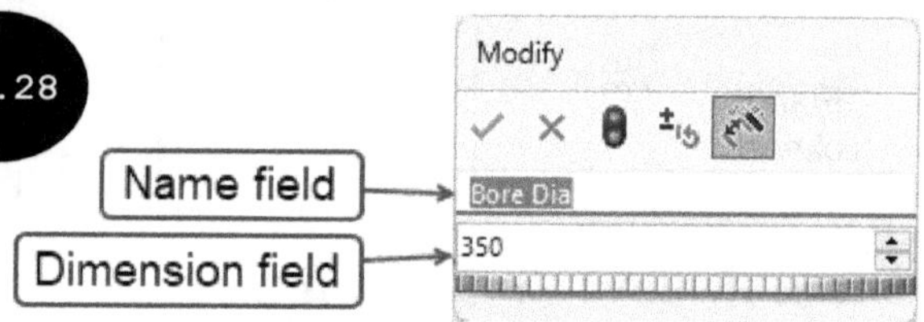

Tip: Specifying a name to each sketch dimension will help you in identifying them while specifying parameters for creating configurations in the design table.

7. Click on the green tick-mark button in the **Modify** dialog box. A diameter dimension with a specified diameter value and name is applied to the circle.

8. Similarly, create another circle and then specify its diameter value as **400 mm**, and name as **Hub Dia**, see Figure 11.29.

9. Click on the **Extruded Boss/Base** tool in the **Features CommandManager**. A preview of the extruded feature appears. Also, the **Boss-Extrude PropertyManager** appears on the left of the graphics area.

10. Enter **300** in the **Depth** field of the PropertyManager and then click on its green tick-mark. The extruded feature is created, see Figure 11.30.

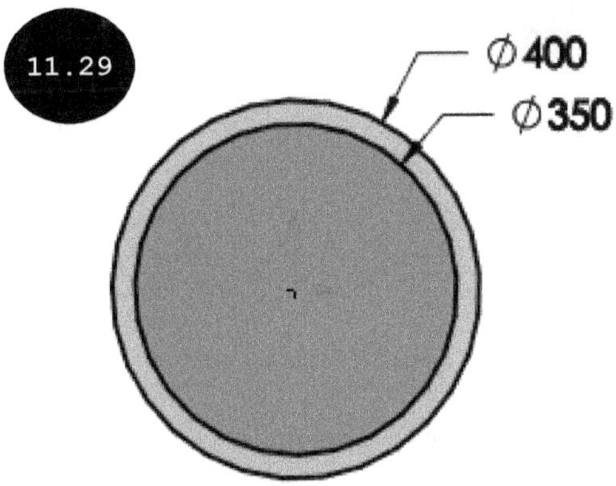

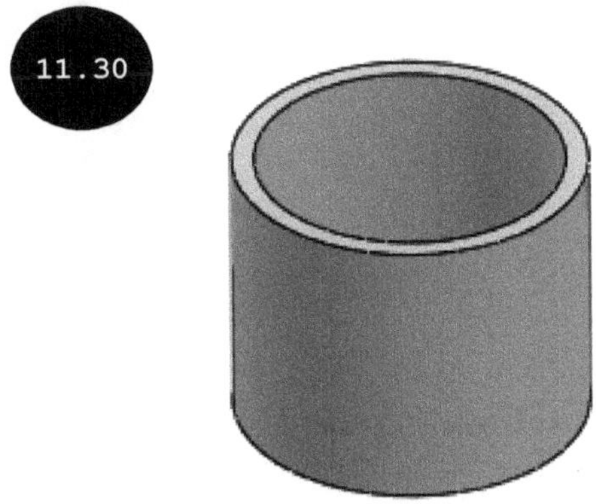

Section 4: Creating the Second Feature - Extruded Feature

1. Invoke the Sketching environment by selecting the top planar face of the base feature as the sketching plane. The model gets oriented normal to the viewing direction.

2. Create two concentric circles by specifying their center points at the origin.

3. Apply a coradial relation between one circle and the inner circular edge of the base feature.

4. Apply the diameter dimension to the second circle by specifying its diameter value as **550 mm** and name as **Flange Dia** in the **Modify** dialog box, see Figure 11.31.

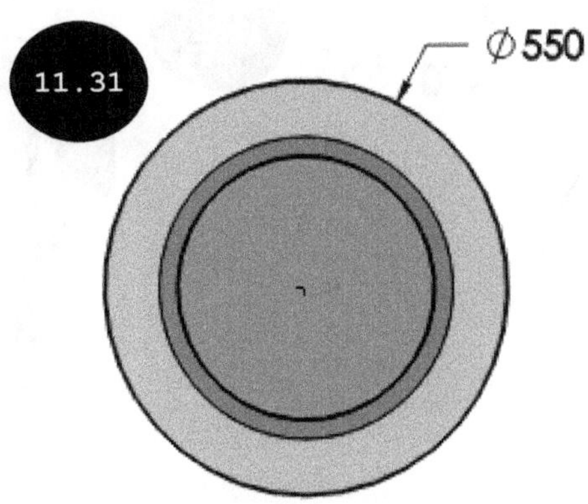

5. Click on the **Extruded Boss/Base** tool in the **Features CommandManager**. A preview of the extruded feature appears. Next, change the orientation of the model to Isometric.

6. Enter **35** in the **Depth** field of the PropertyManager and then Press ENTER.

7. Click on the **Reverse Direction** button in the **Direction 1** rollout of the PropertyManager to reverse the direction of extrusion downward. Next, click on the green tick mark in the PropertyManager. The extruded feature is created, see Figure 11.32.

11.32

Section 5: Creating the Third Feature - Cut Feature

1. Invoke the Sketching environment by selecting the top planar face of the model as the sketching plane.

2. Create the sketch of the third feature (cut feature) and then apply the required dimensions and relations, see Figure 11.33. Note that you need to specify **Hole Dia** as the name of the diameter dimension 35 mm and **PCD** as the name of the diameter dimension 470 mm.

3. Click on the **Extruded Cut** tool in the **Features CommandManager**. The **Cut-Extrude PropertyManager** appears. Next, change the orientation of the model to isometric.

4. Select the **Up to Next** option in the **End Condition** drop-down list of the **Direction 1** rollout and then click on the green tick-mark. The cut feature is created, see Figure 11.34.

11.33

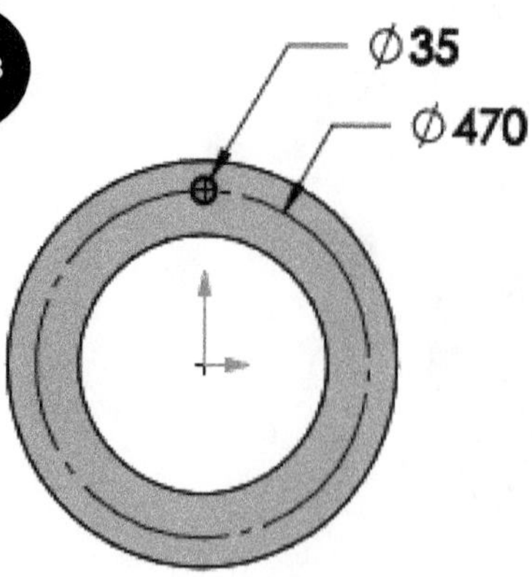

11.34

Section 6: Creating the Fourth Feature - Circular Pattern

1. Create the circular pattern of the previously created cut feature by specifying 12 as the number of instances, see Figure 11.35.

11.35

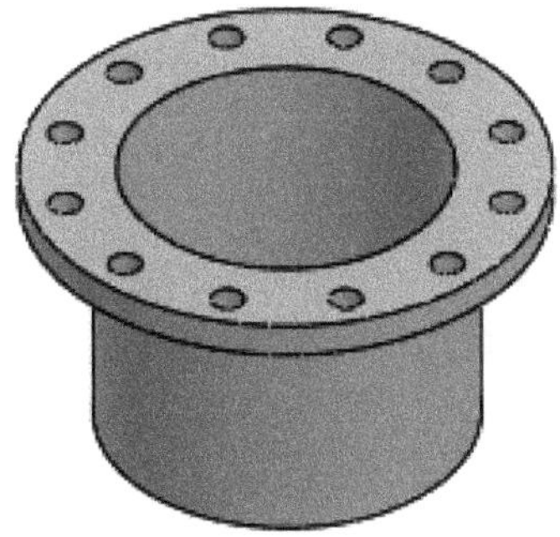

Section 7: Creating Configurations - Design Table

1. Click on the **Insert > Tables > Excel Design Table** in the SOLIDWORKS Design Menus. The **Excel Design Table PropertyManager** appears.

2. Accept the default selected options in the PropertyManager and click on the green tick mark in the PropertyManager. The process of creating the design table gets started and the **Dimensions** window appears, see Figure 11.36.

3. Press and hold the CTRL key and then select all the dimensions listed in the **Dimensions** dialog box. Next, click on the **OK** button in the dialog box. The design table appears as a Microsoft Excel worksheet with the Default configuration of the model, see Figure 11.37.

11.36

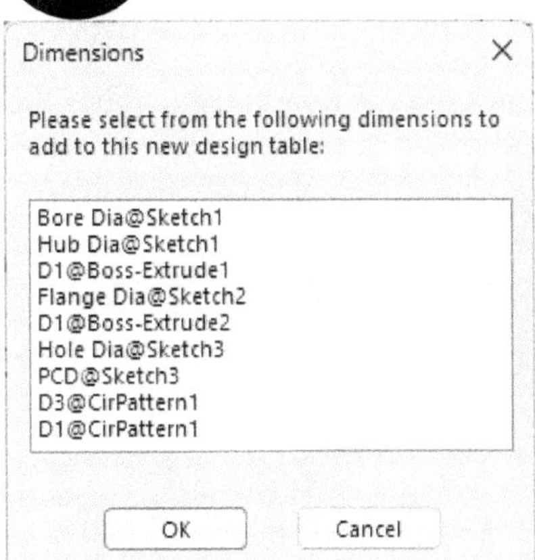

11.37

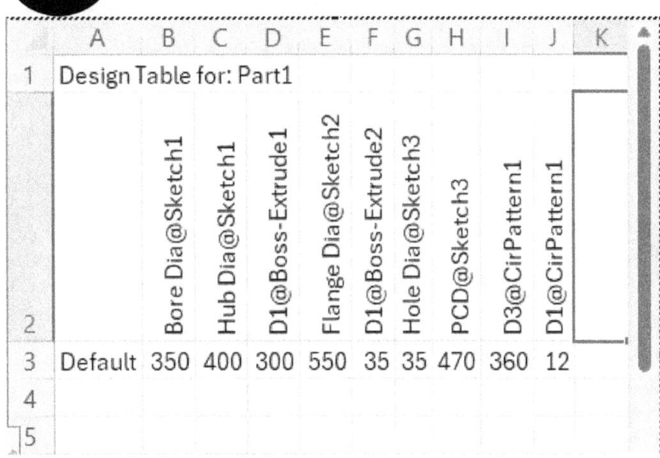

Note: You may need to expand the design table (Microsoft Excel worksheet) to make all the dimensions visible.

4. Enter three new configuration names: **350 Bore Dia**, **400 Bore Dia**, and **450 Bore Dia** below the Default configuration in the design table and then specify their parameters, see Figure 11.38. Note that working with the design table is the same as working with an Excel file.

11.38

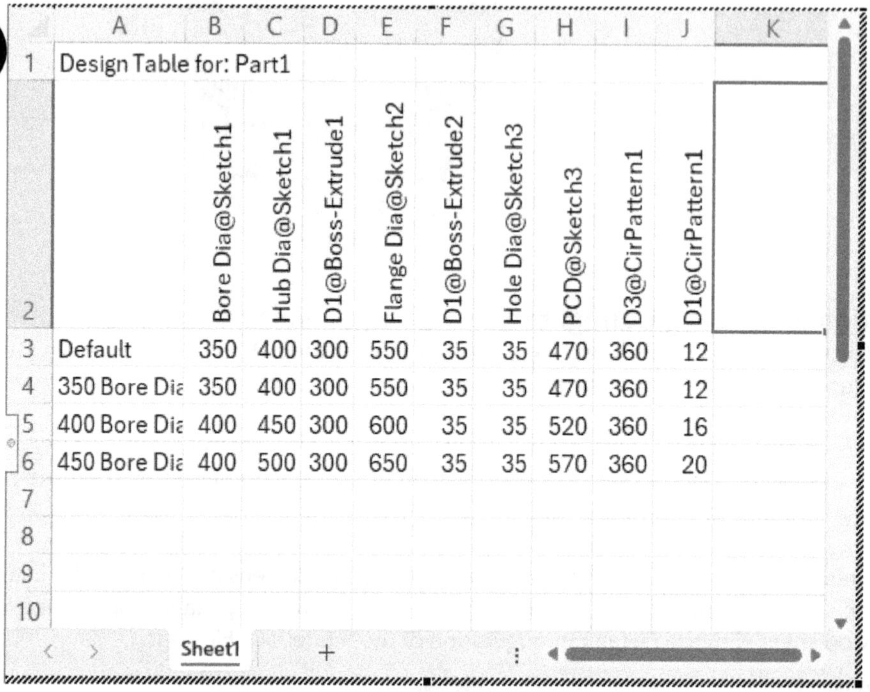

Design Table for: Part1

	Bore Dia@Sketch1	Hub Dia@Sketch1	D1@Boss-Extrude1	Flange Dia@Sketch2	D1@Boss-Extrude2	Hole Dia@Sketch3	PCD@Sketch3	D3@CirPattern1	D1@CirPattern1
Default	350	400	300	550	35	35	470	360	12
350 Bore Dia	350	400	300	550	35	35	470	360	12
400 Bore Dia	400	450	300	600	35	35	520	360	16
450 Bore Dia	400	500	300	650	35	35	570	360	20

5. After specifying parameters for each configuration in the design table, click anywhere in the graphics area. The **SOLIDWORKS** message window appears, see Figure 11.39.

6. Click on the **OK** button in the **SOLIDWORKS** message window. Three new configurations are created in addition to the Default configuration. Notice that the names of all the configurations are listed in the ConfigurationManager, see Figure 11.40. In this figure, the Default configuration is activated.

11.39

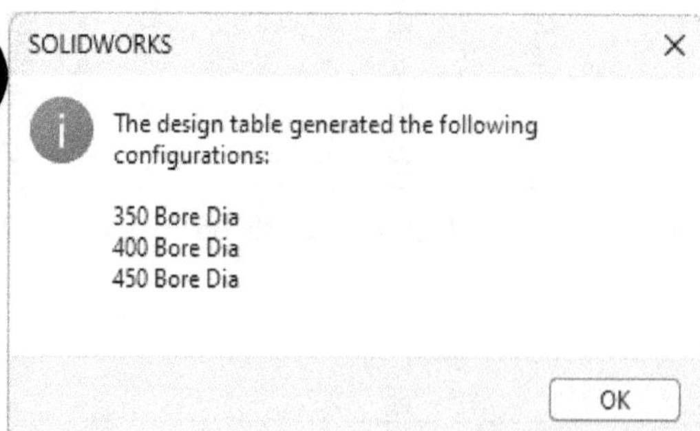

11.40

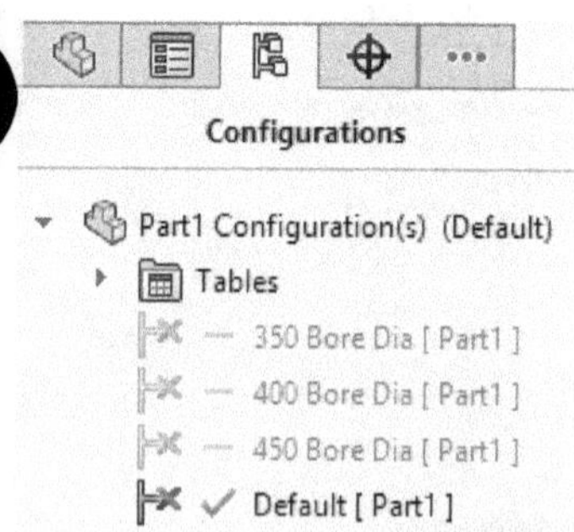

7. Double-click on the name of each configuration in the ConfigurationManager one by one to review the respective design of the model. Note that the model appears in the graphics area as per the activated configuration.

Section 8: Saving the Model

1. Click on the **Save** tool in the **Standard** toolbar. The **Save As** dialog box appears.
2. Browse to the SOLIDWORKS folder and then create a folder with the name Chapter 11.
3. Enter **Tutorial 1** in the **File name** field of the dialog box as the name of the file and then click on the **Save** button. The model is saved with the name Tutorial 1 in the Chapter 11 folder.

Hands-on Test Drive 1

Create the model shown in Figure 11.41. After creating the model, create its two configurations: **With Slot Cut** and **Without Slot Cut** by using the Manual method. All dimensions are in mm.

11.41

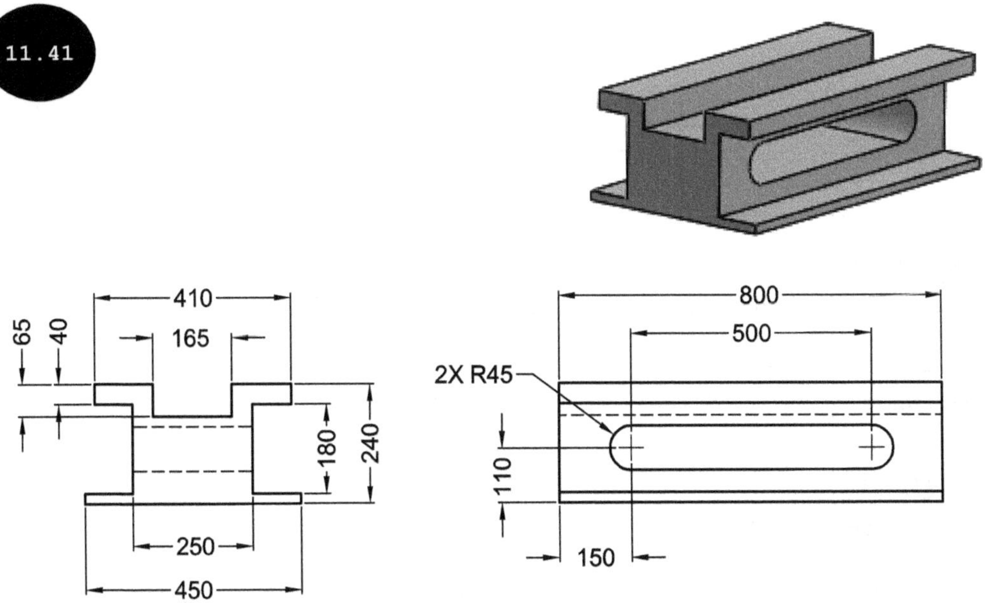

Hands-on Test Drive 2

Create the model shown in Figure 11.42. After creating the model, create its three different configurations by using the Design Table method. The details of the configurations to be created are given in the table below. All dimensions are in mm.

Table		
	Bolt Diameter	Length
20 Bolt Dia	20	100
22 Bolt Dia	22	80
26 Bolt Dia	26	120

11.42

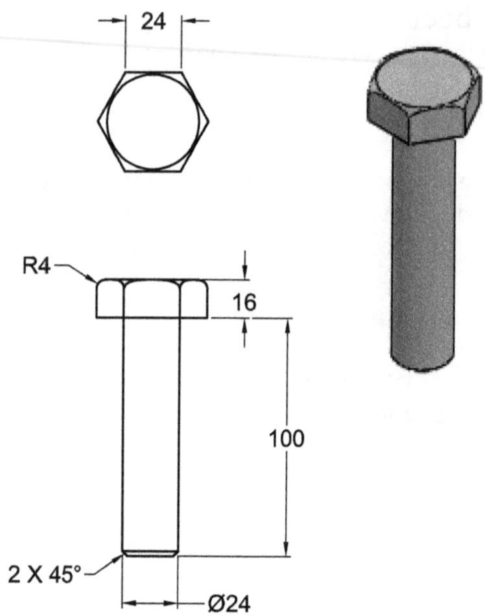

Summary

In this chapter, you learned how to create multiple configurations of a model using both the Manual and Design Table methods. You also explored how to save configurations as separate files and manage them efficiently. The chapter covered how to suppress and unsuppress features within a model, allowing you to customize and manage design variations seamlessly.

Questions

Complete and verify the following sentences:

- You can create configurations of a model by using two methods: _________ and _________.
- By default, the _________ configuration is created for a model.
- You can suppress a feature by using the _________ tool.
- The _________ option is used to save a single configuration or multiple configurations of a part as a separate part file.
- You cannot suppress features of a model by using the Design Table. (True/False)
- You cannot edit configurations once created. (True/False)
- You cannot edit a design table. (True/False).

CHAPTER

12

Working with Assemblies - I

This chapter discusses the following topics:

- Working with Bottom-up Assembly Approach
- Working with Top-down Assembly Approach
- Creating an Assembly Using Bottom-up Approach
- Working with Degrees of Freedom
- Applying Relations or Mates
- Working with Standard Mates
- Working with Advanced Mates
- Working with Mechanical Mates
- Hiding Faces while Applying a Mate
- Moving and Rotating Individual Components
- Working with SmartMates

In previous chapters, you explored fundamental and advanced methods for designing real-world mechanical components. This chapter shifts focus to the techniques involved in creating assemblies. An assembly consists of two or more individual components joined together through the application of mates. The process of applying mates will be covered in detail later in this chapter. Figure 12.1 shows an assembly where multiple components are assembled by applying the appropriate mates.

12.1

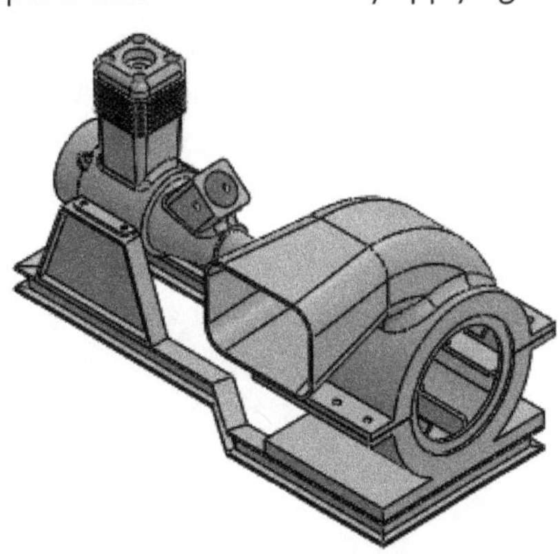

In SOLIDWORKS, assemblies can be created within the Assembly environment using two primary methods: the Bottom-up Assembly Approach and the Top-down Assembly Approach. Additionally, a hybrid method combining both approaches can be utilized to construct assemblies. The details of these approaches are discussed next.

Working with Bottom-up Assembly Approach

The Bottom-up Assembly Approach is the most commonly employed method for creating assemblies. In this approach, each component of the assembly is individually designed within the Part modeling environment and saved in a centralized location. These components are then sequentially imported into the Assembly environment, where they are positioned and connected relative to one another by applying the necessary mates.

Tip: SOLIDWORKS features bidirectional associations across all its environments. This means that any change or modification made to a component in the Part modeling environment is automatically reflected in both the Assembly and Drawing environments, and vice versa. This seamless connectivity ensures consistency throughout every stage of the design process.

Working with Top-down Assembly Approach

In the Top-down Assembly Approach, all the components of an assembly are created within the Assembly environment. It helps in creating a concept-based design, in which new components of an assembly are created by taking reference from the existing components of the assembly. You will learn about creating assemblies by using the Top-down assembly approach in Chapter 13.

Creating an Assembly Using Bottom-up Approach

After creating all components of an assembly in the Part modeling environment and saving them in a common location, you need to invoke the Assembly environment of SOLIDWORKS for assembling them. To invoke the Assembly environment, click on the **New** tool in the **Standard** toolbar or press the **CTRL + N** keys. The **New SOLIDWORKS Document** dialog box appears, see Figure 12.2. In this dialog box, click on the **Assembly** button and then click on the **OK** button. The Assembly environment is invoked with the **Begin Assembly PropertyManager** on its left. Also, the **Open** dialog box appears on the screen, see Figure 12.3.

Note that along with the **Begin Assembly PropertyManager**, the **Open** dialog box appears every time on invoking the Assembly environment. This is because, in the **Options** rollout of the **Begin Assembly PropertyManager**, the **Automatic Browse when creating a new assembly** check box is selected, by default. It is used for invoking the **Open** dialog box automatically if no components are opened in the current session of SOLIDWORKS.

By using the **Open** dialog box, you can insert a component in the Assembly environment. The methods for inserting components in the Assembly environment are discussed next.

12.2

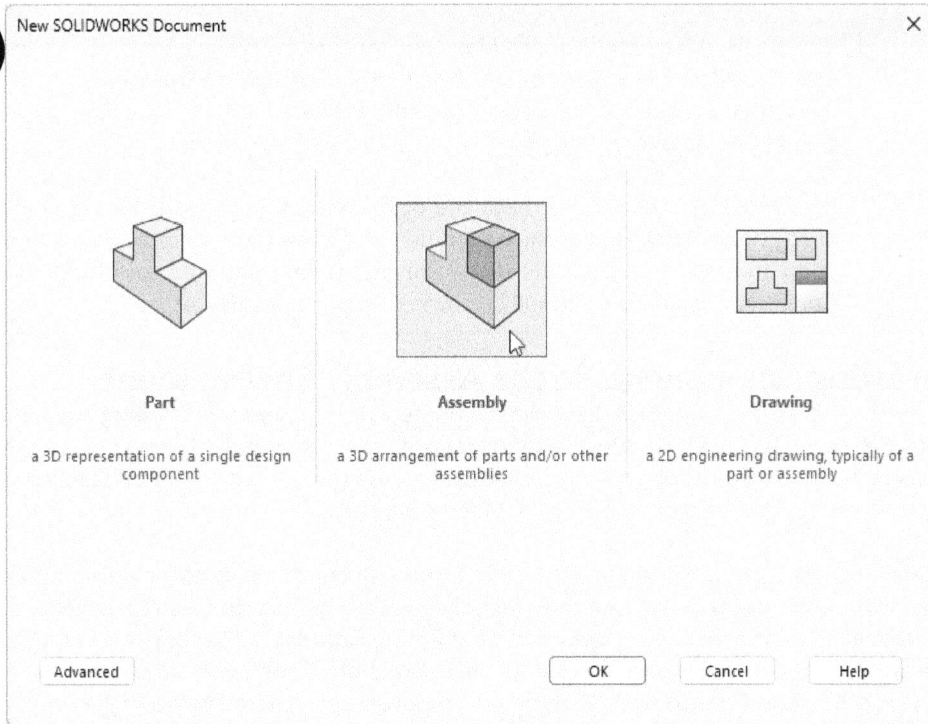

12.3

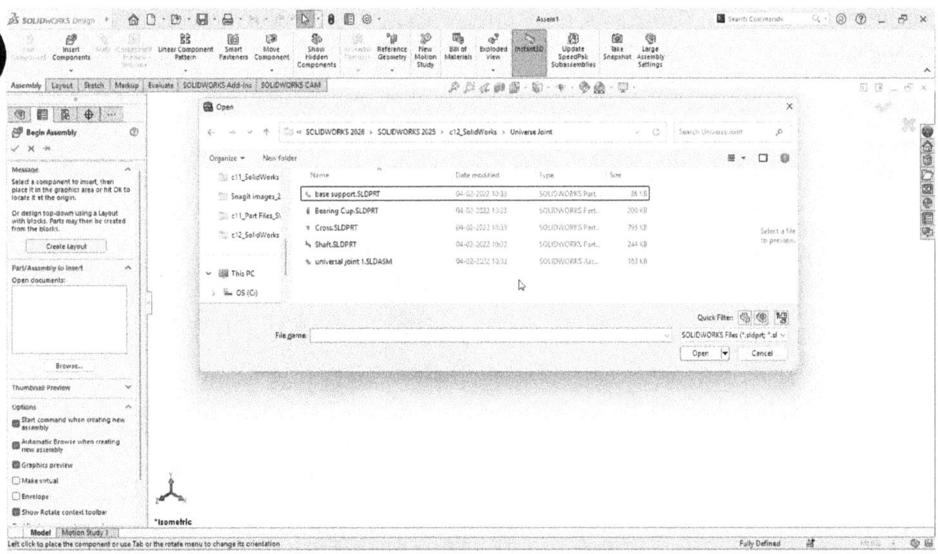

Tip: You can also invoke the Assembly environment by clicking on the **Assembly** button in the **Welcome** dialog box, which appears every time you start SOLIDWORKS.

Note: The **Begin Assembly PropertyManager** appears every time on invoking the Assembly environment for inserting components in the Assembly environment. This is because, in the **Options** rollout of the **Begin Assembly PropertyManager**, the **Start command when creating new assembly** check box is selected, by default, refer to Figure 12.3.

If you clear this check box, both the **Begin Assembly PropertyManager** and the **Open** dialog box will not appear the next time you invoke the Assembly environment. Instead, you can insert components using the **Insert Components** tool from the **Assembly CommandManager**, which will be covered later in this chapter.

Inserting Components in the Assembly Environment

As discussed, on invoking the Assembly environment, if no components are opened in the current session of SOLIDWORKS, the **Open** dialog box appears, automatically along with the **Begin Assembly PropertyManager.** If the **Open** dialog box does not appear then click on the **Browse** button in the **Begin Assembly PropertyManager** to invoke the **Open** dialog box.

In the **Open** dialog box, browse to the location where all components of the assembly are saved and then select a component to be inserted. Next, click on the **Open** button in the dialog box. The selected component gets attached to the cursor and the **Rotate Context** toolbar appears in the graphics area, see Figure 12.4. If needed, you can change the orientation of the attached component by using the tools of the **Rotate Context** toolbar. By default, **90 degrees** is entered in the **Angle** field of the **Rotate Context** toolbar. As a result, when you click on the **X**, **Y**, or **Z** tool in this toolbar; the component rotates 90 degrees about the X, Y, or Z axis, respectively. You can enter the required angle of rotation value in the **Angle** field and rotate the component about the X, Y, or Z axis by using this toolbar.

12.4

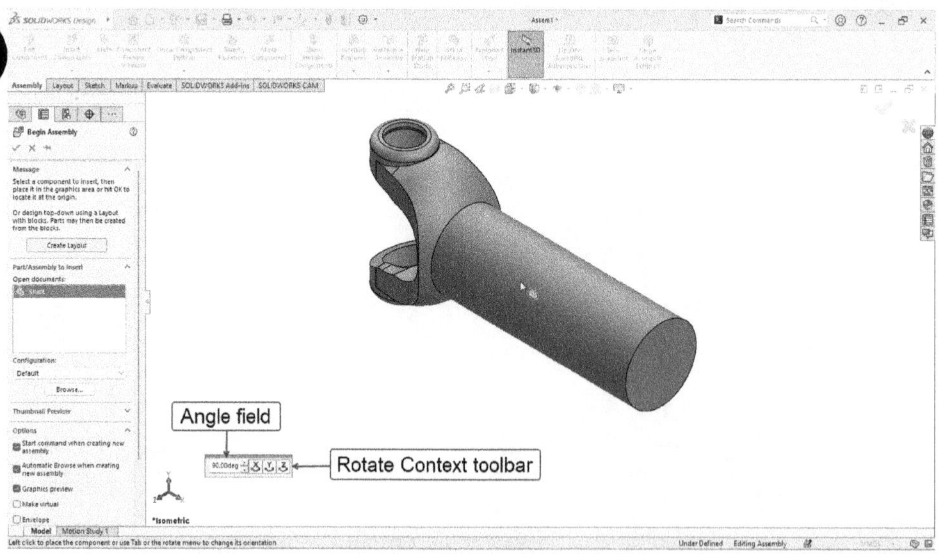

Note: By default, the **Rotate Context** toolbar appears every time you insert a component in the Assembly environment, since the **Show Rotate context toolbar** check box is selected in the **Options** rollout of the **Begin Assembly PropertyManager**.

Once the orientation of the component has been set by using the **Rotate Context** toolbar, click anywhere in the graphics area. The component moves toward the origin of the assembly and becomes a fixed component concerning the origin of the assembly. Notice that the name of the inserted component gets listed in the FeatureManager Design Tree with the '(f)' sign in front of its name, see Figure 12.5. The '(f)' sign indicates that all degrees of freedom of the component are fixed, and the component cannot move or rotate in any direction.

In SOLIDWORKS, the first component you insert in the Assembly environment becomes the fixed component automatically and does not allow any translational or rotational movement. If needed, you can change a fixed component to a floating component, which has all degrees of freedom free, allowing it to move or rotate. To do this, right-click on the name of the fixed component in the FeatureManager Design Tree and then click on the **Float** option in the shortcut menu that appears.

Additionally, once the first component is inserted, the **Begin Assembly PropertyManager** closes. To insert other components, you will need to use the **Insert Components** tool from the **Assembly CommandManager**. The method for inserting components using the **Insert Components** tool is discussed next.

Note: If any component is open in the current session of SOLIDWORKS, the **Open** dialog box will not appear automatically when invoking the Assembly environment. Instead, the names of the opened components will be listed in the **Open Documents** field of the **Begin Assembly PropertyManager**, see Figure 12.6. In this field, you can select a component to insert into the Assembly environment. Alternatively, you can click on the **Browse** button to manually open the **Open** dialog box and select additional components.

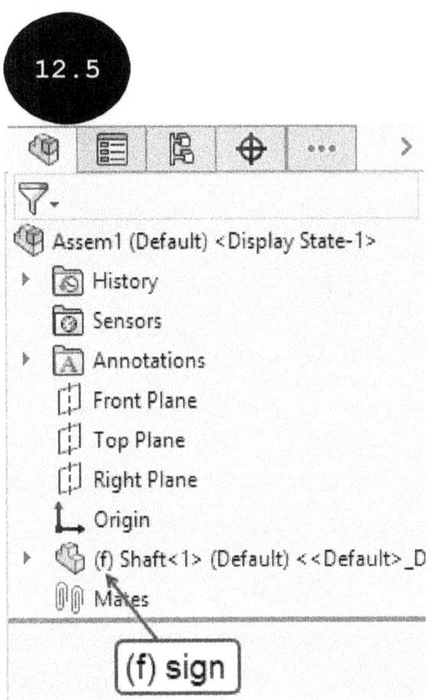

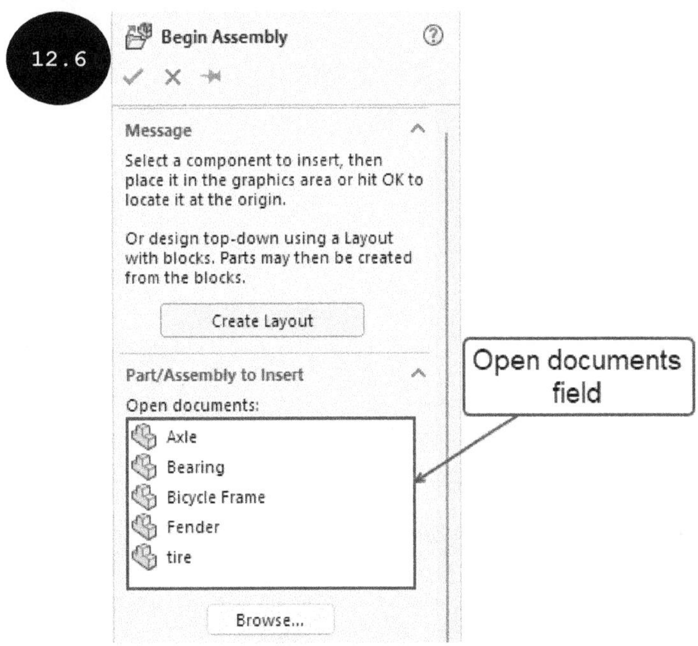

Tip: If you pin the **Begin Assembly PropertyManager** by clicking on the **Keep Visible** icon available at the upper right corner of the PropertyManager then the display of the PropertyManager will not be closed after inserting the component and you can continue inserting the components using the **Begin Assembly PropertyManager**.

Inserting Components using the Insert Components Tool

To insert a component in the Assembly environment using the **Insert Components** tool, click on the **Insert Components** tool in the **Assembly CommandManager**, see Figure 12.7. The **Insert Component PropertyManager** and the **Open** dialog box appear. Figure 12.8 shows the **Insert Component PropertyManager**.

12.7

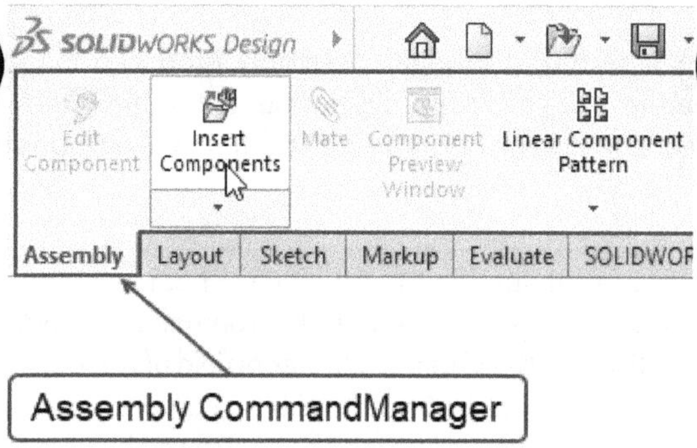

12.8

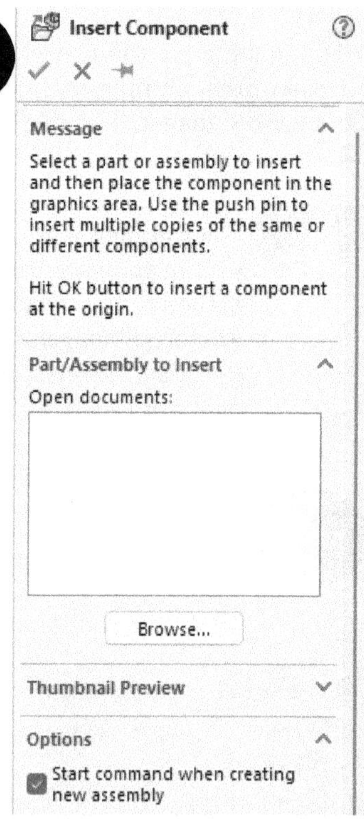

Note that in the **Insert Component PropertyManager**, the **Automatic Browse when creating new assembly** check box is selected, by default. As a result, the **Open** dialog box appears, automatically if no components are opened in the current session of SOLIDWORKS. If the **Open** dialog box does not appear, then click on the **Browse** button in the **Insert Component PropertyManager** to invoke the **Open** dialog box.

In the **Open** dialog box, browse to the location where all components of the assembly are saved and then select a component. Next, click on the **Open** button in the dialog box. The selected component is attached to the cursor. Also, the **Rotate Context** toolbar appears in the graphics area, see Figure 12.9.

12.9

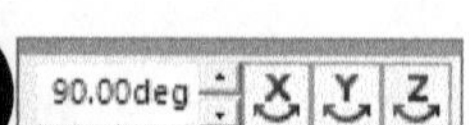

Note: The **Start command when creating new assembly** check box of the **Insert Component PropertyManager** is used for turning the display of the **Begin Assembly PropertyManager** on or off on invoking the Assembly environment.

Change the current orientation of the component using the **Rotate Context** toolbar as needed. Once the orientation is set, click the left mouse button anywhere in the graphics area to define the placement for the attached component. The component is placed in the defined location, and the PropertyManager closes.

12.10

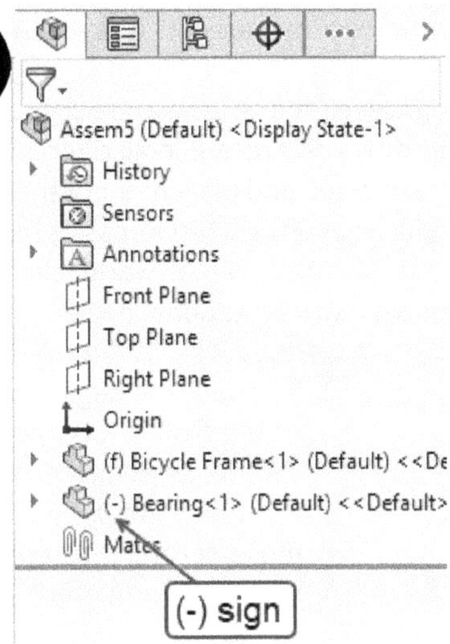

The name of the inserted component appears in the FeatureManager Design Tree with a '(-)' sign in front of its name, see Figure 12.10. The '(-)' sign indicates that all degrees of freedom of the component are not defined, meaning the component is free to move or rotate in the graphics area. To constrain it, you need to assemble the component with the existing components by applying the necessary relations or mates, which will be discussed later in this chapter..

Similarly, you can insert multiple components into the Assembly environment one by one using the **Insert Component PropertyManager**.

Tip: While defining the placement for a component in the graphics area, ensure that the component does not intersect with any existing component of the assembly.

Note: If you pin the **Insert Component PropertyManager** by clicking on the **Keep Visible** icon available at the top of the PropertyManager will not be closed after inserting the component and the second instance of the inserted component is attached to the cursor. Click in the graphics area to insert the second instance of the same component. Similarly, you can insert multiple instances of a component in the Assembly environment by clicking the left mouse button.

After inserting the second component, it is recommended that you first assemble it with the first component by applying the required mates before inserting the third or subsequent components into the Assembly environment. This ensures that the components are properly aligned and constrained before adding more parts.

However, before you can learn how to apply mates between assembly components, it's important to first understand the concept of degrees of freedom, which will be discussed next.

Working with Degrees of Freedom

A free component within the Assembly environment has six degrees of freedom: three translational and three rotational. This means that a free component in the Assembly environment can move as well as rotate along the X, Y, and Z axes. As discussed earlier, the first component inserted in the Assembly environment becomes the fixed component automatically and does not undergo any translational or rotational movement. This means that all its degrees of freedom are fixed.

However, the second and subsequent components inserted into the Assembly environment are free to move and rotate in all directions, meaning their degrees of freedom are not restricted. To control the motion and placement of these components, a designer needs to "fix" their degrees of freedom by applying mates. This process is not just about restricting the movement of components but also about maintaining their real-world relationships. For example, a shaft in an assembly is meant to rotate about its axis, so its rotational degree of freedom must remain intact to allow for rotation.

Note: To check the degrees of freedom of a component, you can use the **Move Component** tool or the **Rotate Component** tool to move or rotate the component along or about its free degrees of freedom. Alternatively, you can drag the component in the graphics area to test its movement. By doing so, you can determine which directions the component is free to move or rotate. You will learn how to move or rotate individual components in an assembly later in this chapter.

Applying Relations or Mates

In SOLIDWORKS, you can assemble components using three types of mates: Standard, Advanced, and Mechanical. All these types of mates can be applied using the **Mate** tool.

Applying Standard Mates

Standard mates such as coincident, parallel, perpendicular, concentric, and tangent are used for positioning components of an assembly by restricting or reducing the degrees of freedom of the components.

To apply a standard mate between components, click on the **Mate** tool in the **Assembly CommandManager**. The **Mate PropertyManager** appears, see Figure 12.11. In this PropertyManager, the **Standard** tab is activated, by default. As a result, all the standard mates are available in its **Mate Type** rollout, see Figure 12.11. Also, the **Entities to Mate** field is activated in the **Mate Selections** rollout of the PropertyManager, which is used for selecting entities of two different components to mate.

Select the required entities such as faces, edges, planes, or a combination of these to apply a mate. Note that the first selected component becomes transparent in the graphics area, see Figure 12.12. It helps you to easily select an entity of the second component, especially when it is not visible, or it is behind the first component in the graphics area. This is so because the **Make first selection transparent** check box is selected in the **Options** rollout of the **Mate PropertyManager**.

Notice that as soon as you select entities for applying a mate, the **Mate** Pop-up toolbar appears in the graphics area, see Figure 12.12. The availability of tools in the **Mate** Pop-up toolbar depends on the entities selected for applying the mate. Also, in the **Mate** Pop-up toolbar, the most suitable mate is applied between the selected entities by default, and a preview of the components appears after applying the most suitable mate, see Figure 12.12. In this figure, two cylindrical faces of the components are selected for applying a mate. As a result, the Concentric mate is activated by default and a preview of the selected entities appears concentric to each other. To accept the default selected mate, click on the green tick-mark ✓ in the **Mate** Pop-up toolbar. You can also apply a mate other than the mate selected by default. To do this, click on the required mate tool to be applied between the selected entities in the **Mate** Pop-up toolbar. In addition to selecting a mate from the **Mate** Pop-up toolbar, you can also choose a mate to be applied between the entities from the **Mate PropertyManager**. Different types of standard mates are discussed below:

12.11

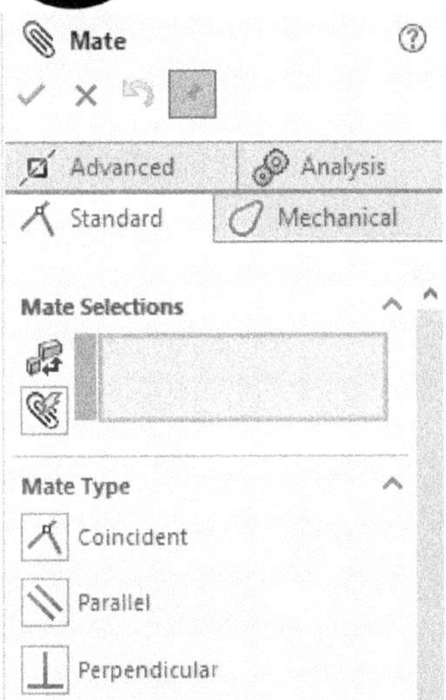

12.12

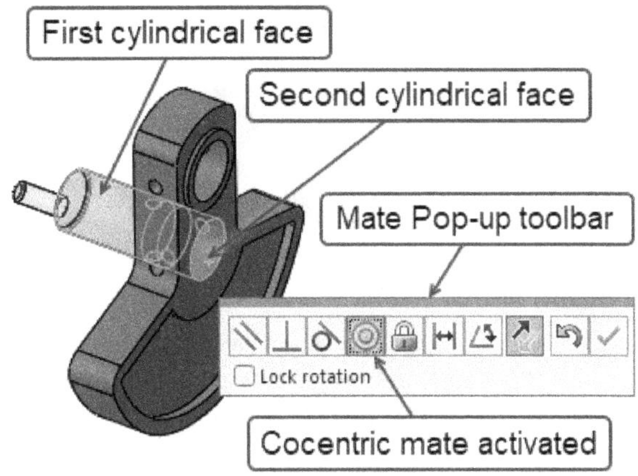

Coincident

Coincident mate is used to make the selected entities of two different components coincident with each other, see Figure 12.13. You can select faces, edges, planes, vertices, or a combination of these as entities for applying the coincident mate. On applying the coincident mate, the selected entities get aligned or share the same plane. Figure 12.13 shows two planar faces to be selected for applying the coincident mate and the resultant model after applying the coincident mate.

12.13

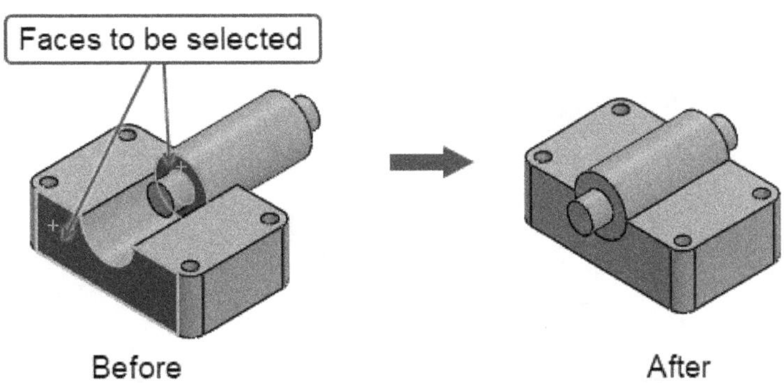

Note: If you click on the **Flip Mate Alignment** tool in the **Mate** Pop-up toolbar, the alignment of the selected entities changes from anti-aligned to aligned or vice versa, see Figure 12.14. You can also flip the alignment by using the **Aligned** and **Anti-Aligned** buttons of the **Mate alignment** area in the **Mate PropertyManager**.

12.14

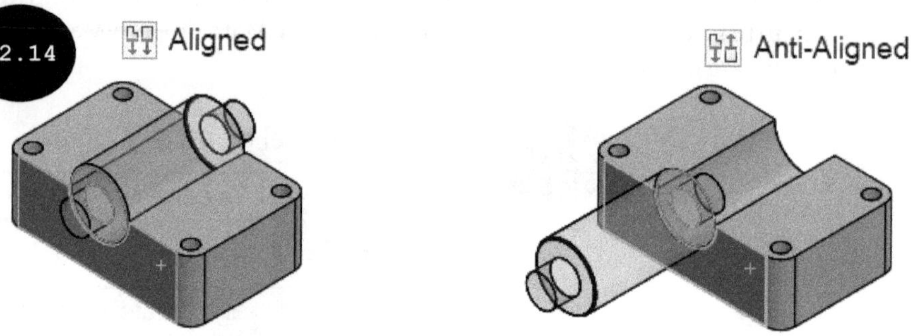

Parallel

The parallel mate is used to make the selected entities parallel to each other, see Figure 12.15. You can select planar faces, edges, planes, or a combination of these as entities for applying parallel mate. Figure 12.15 shows two planar faces and the resultant model after applying the parallel mate.

12.15

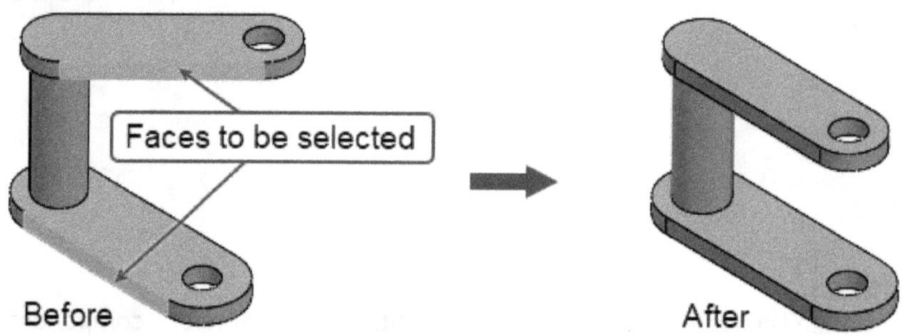

Perpendicular

The perpendicular mate is used to make the selected entities perpendicular to each other, see Figure 12.16. You can select planar faces, edges, planes, or a combination of these as entities to apply this mate. Figure 12.16 shows two planar faces and the resultant model after applying the perpendicular mate.

12.16

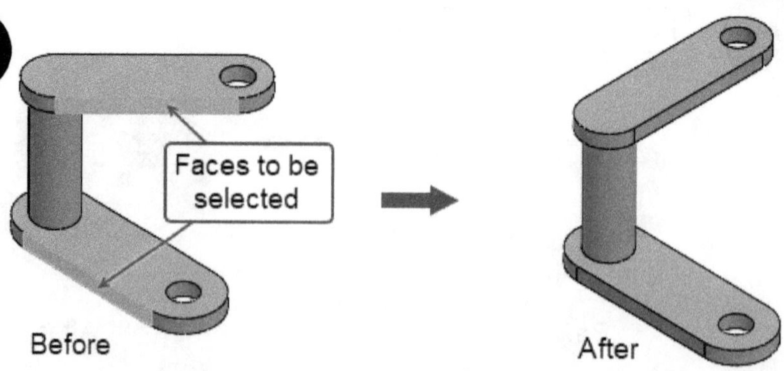

Note: In SOLIDWORKS, you can also apply a perpendicular mate between a non-analytic surface and a linear entity such as a line, an edge, an axis, or an axial entity.

Concentric

The concentric mate is used to make the selected circular entities concentric to each other, see Figure 12.17. You can apply concentric mate between two circular or semi-circular faces and edges. On applying concentric mate, both the selected circular entities share a common axis.

12.17

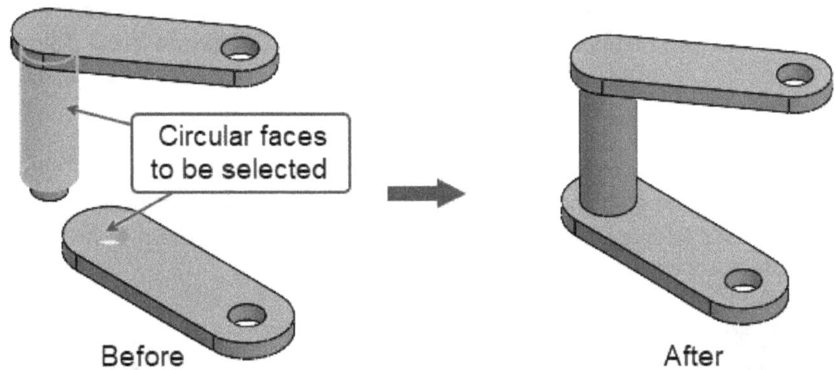

In SOLIDWORKS, you can also apply concentric mates between two pairs of misaligned holes having different center-to-center distances, see Figure 12.18. To do this, after applying the concentric mate between the first pair of holes, apply the concentric mate between the second pair of holes. The Pop-up toolbar appears, see Figure 12.18. In this Pop-up toolbar, click on the **Concentric** tool and then click on the **Misaligned** button. Next, select an alignment option (**Align Linked mate**, **Align this mate**, or **Symmetric**) in the **Misalignment** drop-down list of the PropertyManager.

12.18

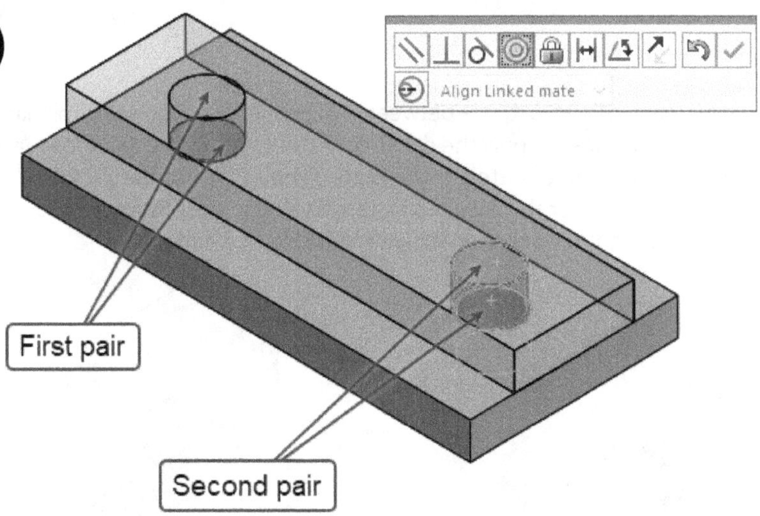

The **Align Linked mate** option is used for applying the perfect concentric mate to the first pair of holes and the misaligned concentric mate to the second pair of holes. The **Align this mate** option is used for applying the perfect concentric mate to the second pair of holes and the misaligned concentric mate to the first pair of holes. The **Symmetric** option is used for applying half misalignment to both pairs of holes.

After applying concentric mates between two pairs of misaligned holes, click on the green tick mark in the PropertyManager. Next, exit the PropertyManager. Notice that the applied concentric mates are listed separately in the **Misaligned** folder under the **Mates** folder in the FeatureManager Design Tree.

Note: You can enable or disable the creation of misalignment concentric mates. To do this, click on **Options** tool in the **Standard** toolbar. The **System Options** dialog box appears. In this dialog box, click on the **Assemblies** option and then select or clear the **Allow creation of misaligned mates** check box. Next, click on the **OK** button in the dialog box.

Tangent

The tangent mate is used to make the selected entities tangent to each other. You can select a planar face, a curved face, an edge, or a plane as the first entity and a cylindrical, conical, or spherical face as the second entity for applying the tangent mate. Figure 12.19 shows two faces for applying tangent mate and the resultant model after applying the tangent mate.

12.19

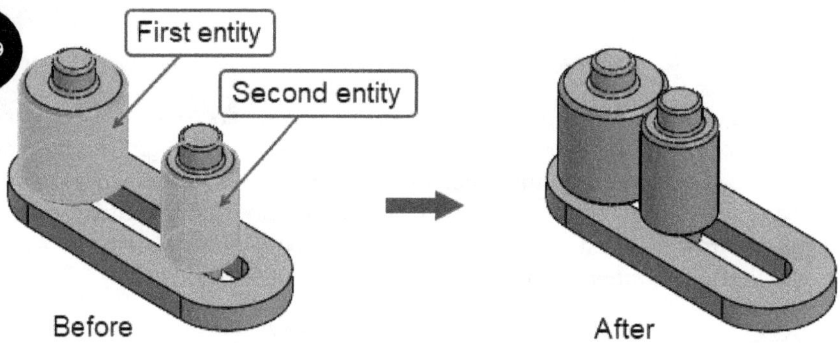

Distance

The distance mate is used to keep distance between two entities. You can select planar faces, cylindrical faces, and planes as the entities to apply the distance mate. To apply the distance mate, after selecting the entities, click on the **Distance** button in the **Mate Type** rollout of the PropertyManager or in the **Mate** Pop-up toolbar. Next, enter the required distance value in the **Distance** field. Figure 12.20 shows planar faces and the resultant model after applying the distance mate.

12.20

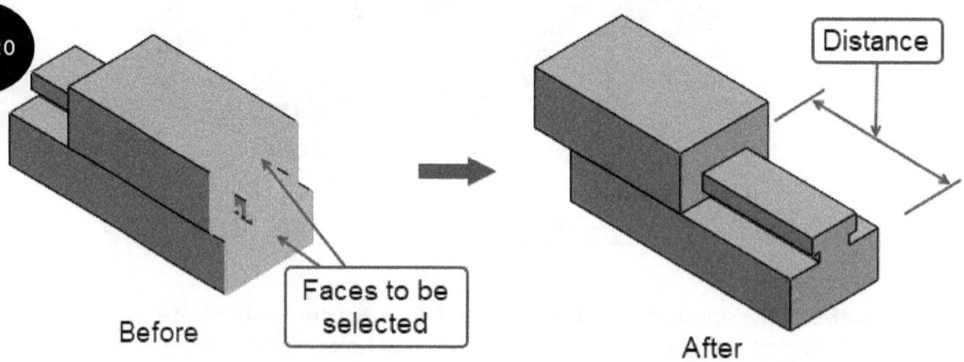

In SOLIDWORKS, when you apply the distance mate between two cylindrical faces, the **Center to Center**, **Minimum Distance**, **Maximum Distance**, and **Custom Distance** buttons become available in the **Mate Type** rollout of the PropertyManager (see Figure 12.21) and the **Mate** Pop-up toolbar. By using these buttons, you can specify the type of distance measurement between the selected cylindrical faces, refer to Figure 12.22. In this figure, the distance mate is applied by measuring the center-to-center distance between the entities.

12.21

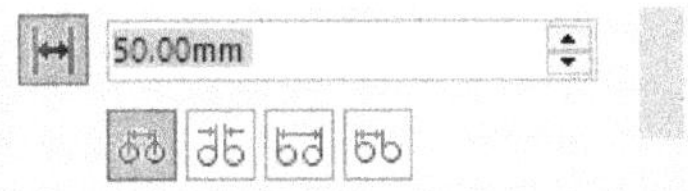

12.22

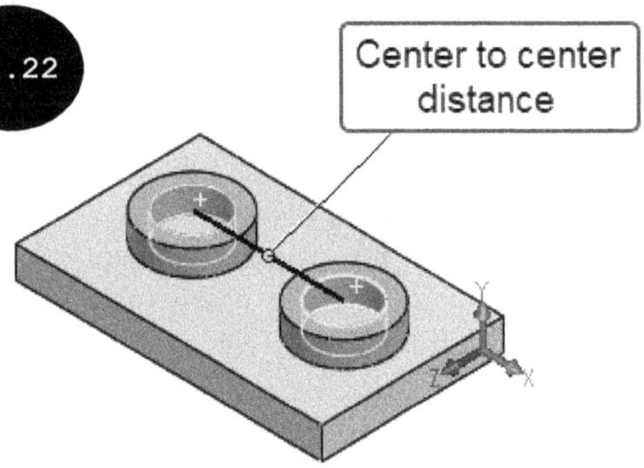

Angle

The angle mate is used to restrict entities of two components at a specified angular distance. Figure 12.23 shows the faces to be selected and the resultant model after applying the angle mate.

12.23

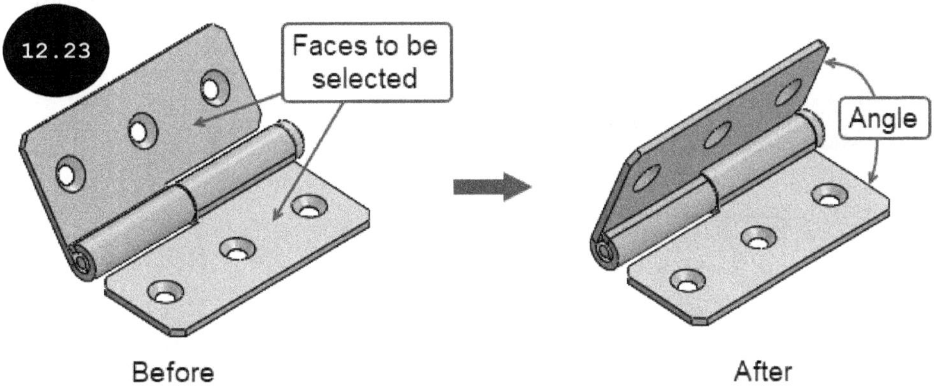

Note: In case of the coincident, parallel, distance, and angle mates, you can flip the mate alignment between the selected entities from aligned to anti-aligned or vice versa.

Lock

The lock mate is used for locking the selected entities at a desired position in the graphics area. On applying the lock mate, all degrees of freedom of the selected entities get fixed.

Applying Advanced Mates

Advanced mates are special types of mates and work one step above the standard mates for restricting or reducing degrees of freedom of components. You can apply advanced mates such as profile center, symmetric, width, path mate, and Linear/Linear coupler between components of an assembly by using the **Mate** tool.

12.24

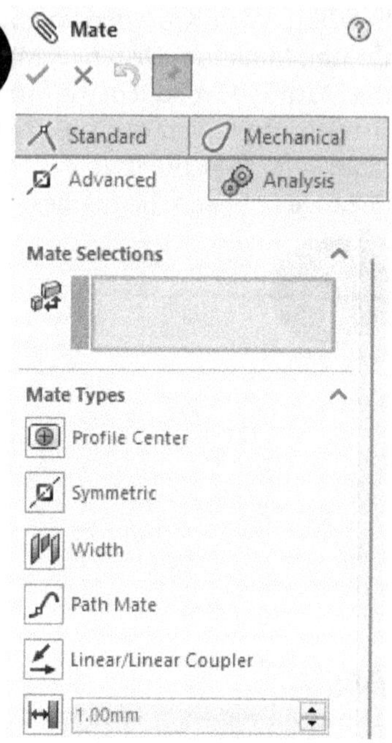

To apply an advanced mate, invoke the **Mate PropertyManager** by clicking on the **Mate** tool in the **Assembly CommandManager**. Next, click on the **Advanced** tab in the PropertyManager. All the advanced mates appear in the **Mate Types** rollout of the PropertyManager, see Figure 12.24. By activating the required button: **Profile Center**, **Symmetric**, **Width**, or **Path Mate** in the **Mate Types** rollout, you can apply the respective advanced mate between the components of an assembly. The different advanced mates are discussed next.

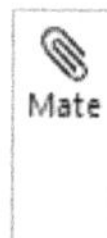

Profile Center Mate 

The profile center mate is used to center-align two rectangular profiles, two circular profiles, or a rectangular and a circular profile of different components with each other, see Figures 12.25 through 12.27.

12.25

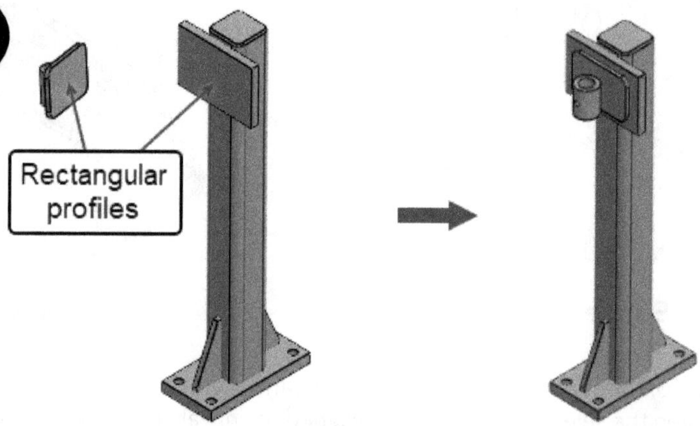

12.26

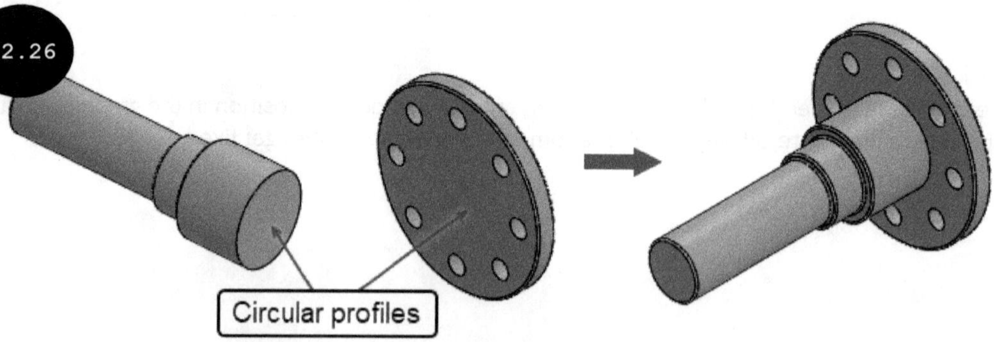

12.27

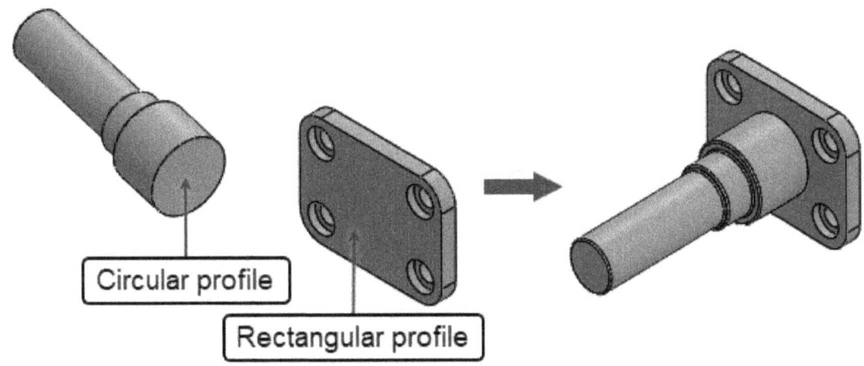

To apply the profile center mate, click on the **Profile Center** button in the **Mate Types** rollout of the **Mate PropertyManager**. The **Offset Distance** field is enabled in the rollout, see Figure 12.28. **Next,** select entities for applying the profile center mate in the graphics area. After selecting the entities, a preview appears such that the selected entities get centrally aligned to each other. You can also specify the offset distance between the selected entities/profiles by using the **Offset Distance** field of the **Mate Types** rollout. By default, 0 (zero) is entered in this field. You can enter an offset distance between the selected profiles, as required. The **Flip dimension** check box of the **Mate Types** rollout is used to flip the direction of the offset dimension between the entities. The **Lock rotation** check box is used to restrict the rotation movement of the circular profile. Note that the **Lock rotation** check box is enabled if any one of the selected entities is a circular profile.

12.28

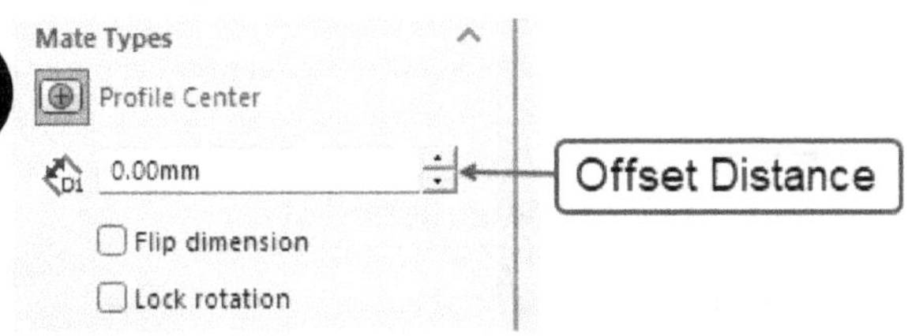

Symmetric Mate

The symmetric mate is used to make two entities of different components symmetric about a plane or a planar face. You can select two vertices, two sketch points, two edges, two axes, two sketch lines, two planes, two planar faces, and two curved faces of the same radii as the entities to be made symmetric about a plane or a planar face.

To apply the symmetric mate, click on the **Symmetric** button in the **Mate Types** rollout of the **Advanced** tab. The **Symmetry Plane** and **Entities to Mate** fields are enabled in the **Mate Selections** rollout of the PropertyManager. By default, the **Symmetry Plane** field is activated. As a result, you can select a plane or a planar face as the symmetry plane. After selecting a plane or a planar face as the symmetry plane in the graphics area, the **Entities to Mate** field gets activated, automatically. Select two entities of different components to be made symmetric about the symmetry plane in the graphics area. Next, click on the green tick-mark in the PropertyManager. The symmetric mate is applied between the entities concerning the symmetry plane. Figure 12.29 shows two planar faces as entities to be symmetric about a symmetry plane and the resultant model after applying the symmetric mate.

12.29

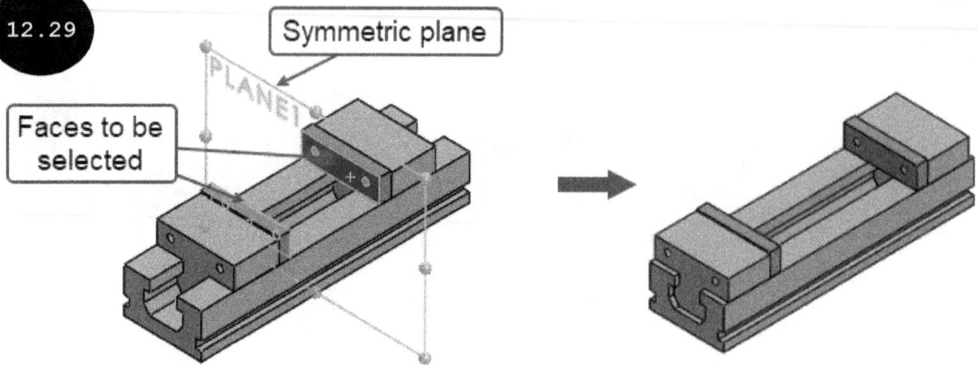

Width Mate

The width mate is used to make two planar faces, a cylindrical face, or an axis of a component centrally aligned between two planar faces of another component, see Figure 12.30. The width mate requires two pairs of selections: the first pair, referred to as width selections 1, and the second pair, referred to as width selections 2, see Figure 12.30. In this figure, two planar faces are selected as the first and second pairs of selections (width selections 1 and width selections 2), and the resultant model is shown after applying the width mate. Note that you can select two planar faces (parallel or non-parallel), a cylindrical face, or an axis as the first pair of selections (width selections 1) and two parallel or non-parallel faces as the second pair of selections (width selections 2), or vice-versa.

12.30

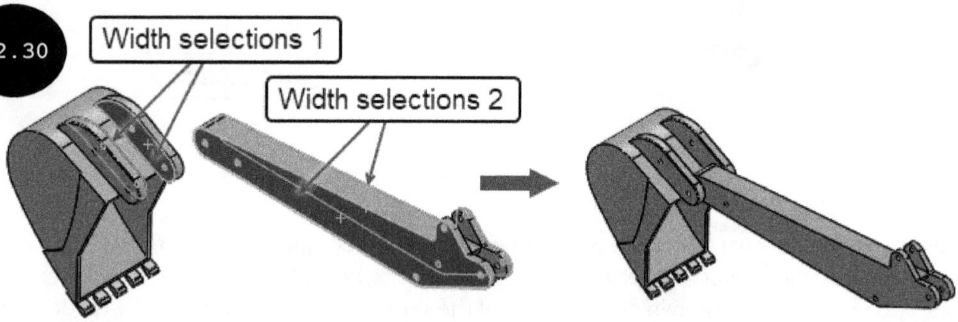

To apply the width mate, click on the **Width** button in the **Mate Types** rollout of the **Advanced** tab. The **Width selections 1** and **Width selections 2** fields are enabled in the **Mate Selections** rollout of the PropertyManager. Also, the **Constraint** drop-down list becomes available in the **Mate Types** rollout, see Figure 12.31.

12.31

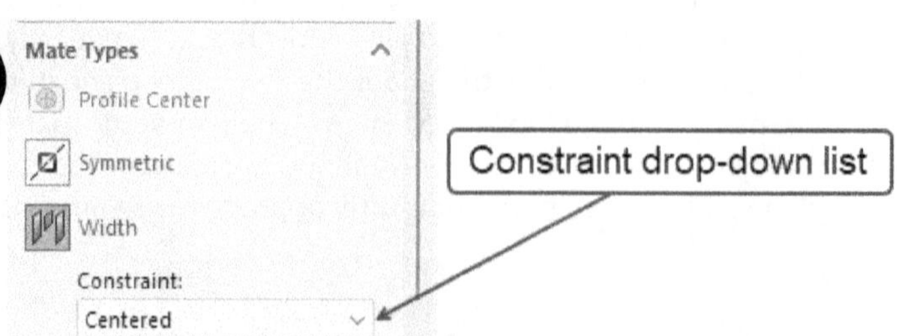

By default, the **Width selections 1** field is activated in the **Mate Selections** rollout. This allows you to select the first pair of entities such as two parallel or non-parallel faces. Upon selecting the first pair, the **Width selections 2** field gets activated, automatically. You can select two planar faces or a cylindrical face as the second pair of selections. A preview of the width mate appears such that the second pair (moveable component) is positioned centrally between the first pair of selections in the graphics area, refer to Figure 12.32. In this figure, two planar faces are selected as the first pair, while a cylindrical face is selected as the second pair of selections.

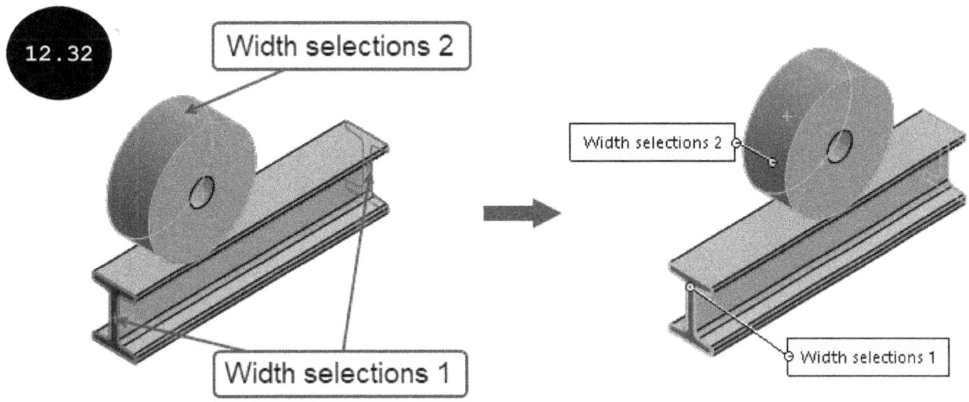

Note that the **Centered** option is selected in the **Constraint** drop-down list of the **Mate Types** rollout, by default, refer to Figure 12.31. As a result, the second pair of selections (moveable component) gets centered between the first pair of selections, or vice-versa. You can also select the **Free**, **Dimension**, or **Percent** option in the **Constraint** drop-down list, as required. On selecting the **Free** option, the moveable component can move freely within a pair of selections of the other component. On selecting the **Dimension** option, you can control the position of the moveable component by specifying a distance value in the **Distance from the End** field of the rollout. On selecting the **Percent** option, you can control the position of the moveable component by specifying a percentage value in the **Percentage of Distance from the End** field of the rollout. You can also flip the mate alignment between the selection sets by using the **Aligned** and **Anti-Aligned** buttons of the **Mate alignment** area in the **Mate PropertyManager.** After selecting the required option in the **Constraint** drop-down list, click on the green tick-mark in the PropertyManager. The width mate is applied between the selected entities.

Path Mate

The path mate constraints a point or a vertex of a component with a path such that the component can move along the defined path, see Figure 12.33.

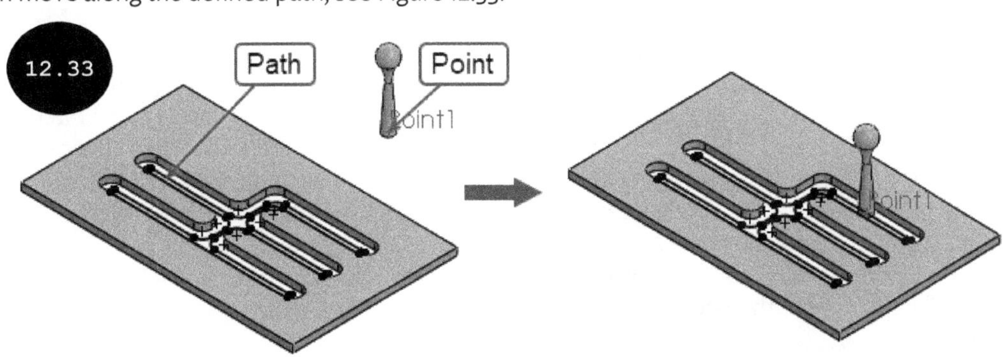

To apply the path mate, click on the **Path Mate** button in the **Mate Types** rollout of the **Advanced** tab. The **Component Vertex** and **Path Selection** fields are enabled in the **Mate Selections** rollout of the PropertyManager. By default, the **Component Vertex** field is activated. As a result, you can select a point or a vertex of a component for applying the path mate, refer to Figure 12.33. After selecting a point or a vertex, the **Path Selection** field gets activated. Select a sketch (open or closed) or an edge as the path in the graphics area. It is recommended to use the **SelectionManager** button of the **Mate Selections** rollout to select a sketch having multiple segments as a path. On clicking this button, the **Selection** Pop-up toolbar appears, see Figure 12.34. By using the **Select Closed Loop** and the **Select Open Loop** tools of this Pop-up toolbar, you can select a closed loop or an open loop sketch as the path, respectively. After selecting the path by using the **Selection** Pop-up toolbar, click on the green tick mark in the Pop-up toolbar.

12.34

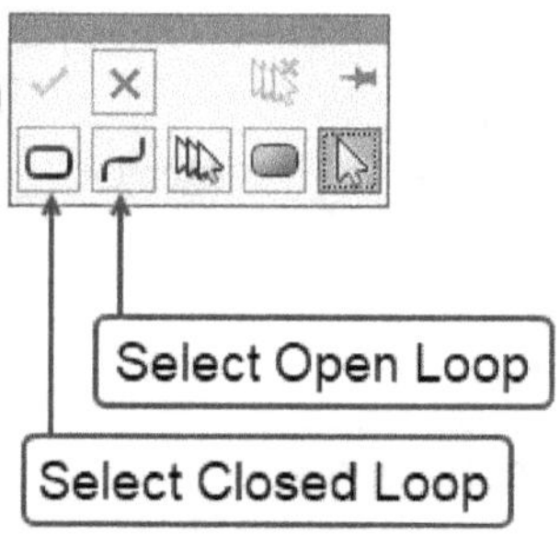

Note that the **Free** option is selected in the **Path Constraint** drop-down list in the **Mate Types** rollout, see Figure 12.35. As a result, the component moves freely along the selected path. You can also select the **Distance Along Path** or **Percent Along Path** option from the **Path Constraint** drop-down list, as required. On selecting the **Distance Along Path** option, you can control the position of the component along the path by specifying a distance value in the **Distance from the End** field of the rollout. On selecting the **Percent Along Path** option, you can control the position of the component along the path by specifying a percentage value in the **Percentage of Distance from the End** field of the rollout.

12.35

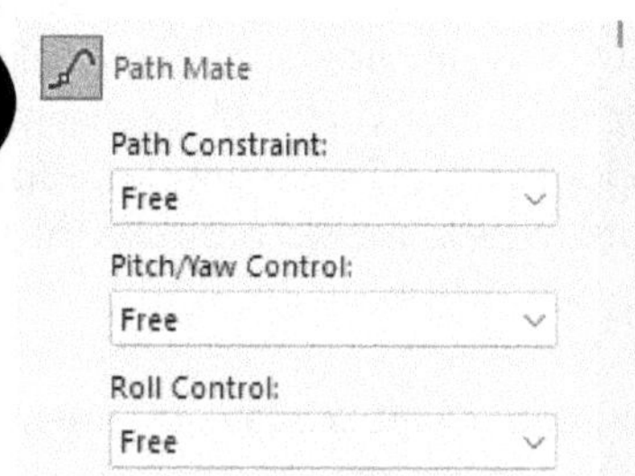

Also, in the **Pitch/Yaw Control** and **Roll Control** drop-down lists of the rollout, the **Free** option is selected, by default. As a result, the pitch, yaw, and roll of the component are not constrained and the component can move freely along the path. On selecting the **Follow Path** option in the **Pitch/Yaw Control** drop-down list, you can make an axis (X, Y, or Z) of the component tangent to the path. On selecting the **Up Vector** option in the **Roll Control** drop-down list, you can align an axis (X, Y, or Z) of the component to a vector. You can select a linear edge or a planar face as the vector by using the field that appears on selecting the **Up Vector** option. After selecting the required option in the **Path Constraint, Pitch/Yaw Control**, and **Roll Control** drop-down lists, click on the green tick-mark in the PropertyManager. The path mate is applied.

Tip: To review the movement of the component along the path after applying the path mate, select the moveable component and then drag it such that it travels along the defined path.

Note: To achieve the correct path motion, you need to define the degrees of freedom of the component to be moved such that the component can only move along the desired path.

Linear/Linear Coupler Mate

The linear/linear coupler mate is used to translate the linear motion of components concerning each other. After applying the linear/linear coupler mate between two components, when you move a component, the other component also moves accordingly, see Figure 12.36.

12.36

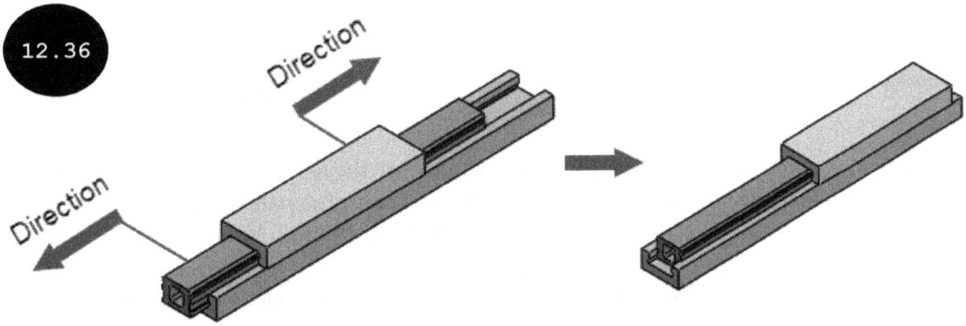

You can specify the translation ratio between the components by using the **Ratio** fields of the PropertyManager, see Figure 12.37. If the translation ratio is 1: 2 in mm unit, then on translating one component to a distance of 1 mm in a direction, the second component is translated automatically to a distance of 2 mm. You can reverse the translation direction of components by using the **Reverse** check box.

12.37

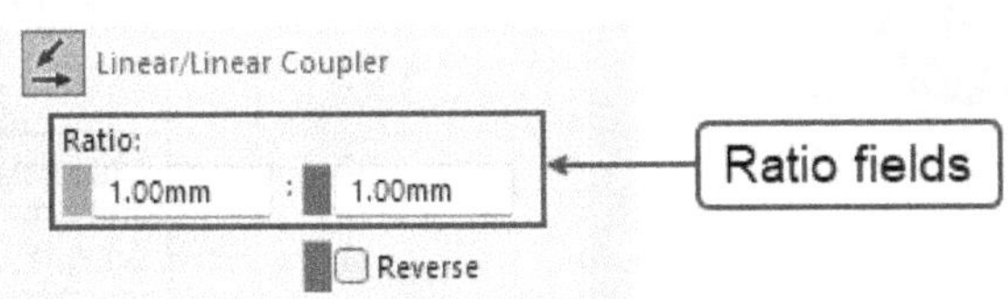

To apply the linear/linear coupler mate, click on the **Linear/Linear Coupler** button in the **Mate Types** rollout of the **Advanced** tab. Next, select the linear edges of two components one by one as the direction to move the components concerning each other. Next, specify the translation ratio in the **Ratio** fields of the PropertyManager and then click on the green tick-mark in the PropertyManager. The linear/linear coupler mate is applied.

Tip: To review the translation motion between two components after applying the linear/linear coupler mate, select a component and then drag it.

Limit Distance Mate

The limit distance mate of the **Advanced** tab is used to specify the minimum and maximum distance limit between two components. After applying this mate, the components can only move or translate within the specified distance limit, see Figure 12.38.

12.38

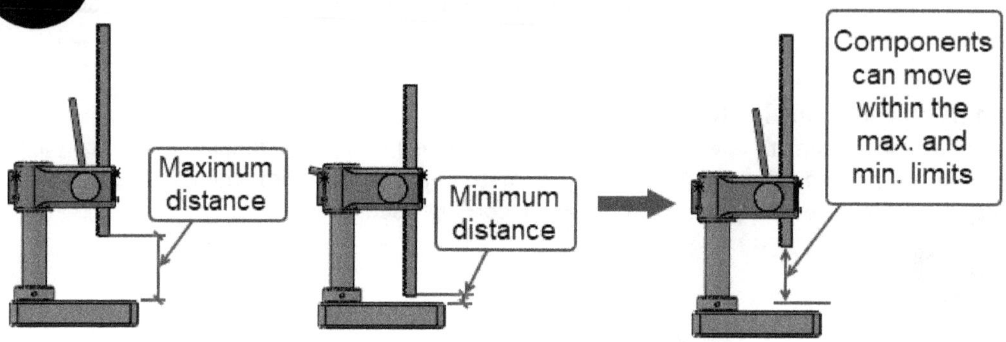

To apply the limit distance mate, click on the **Distance** button in the **Mate Types** rollout of the **Advanced** tab. The **Distance**, **Maximum Value**, and **Minimum Value** fields are enabled in the PropertyManager, see Figure 12.39. Specify the maximum distance value in the **Maximum Value** field. Next, specify the minimum distance value in the **Minimum Value** field. After specifying the maximum and minimum distance values, select two entities (faces, planes, edges, points, vertices, or a combination of these entities) of two different components and then click on the green tick-mark ✓ in the PropertyManager. The limit distance mate is applied between the selected entities of the components such that the moveable component can move within the specified maximum and minimum distance limits, refer to Figure 12.38.

12.39

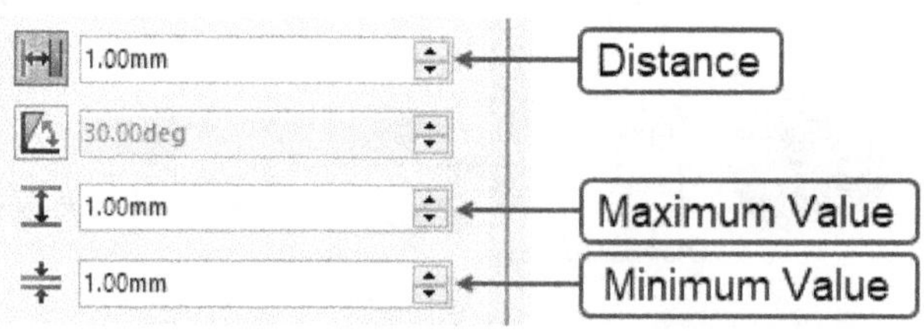

Tip: To review the distance motion between components, select the moveable component and then drag it.

Limit Angle Mate

The limit angle mate of the **Advanced** tab is used to specify the minimum and maximum angle limit between two components. After applying this mate, the components can only rotate within the specified angle limit, see Figure 12.40.

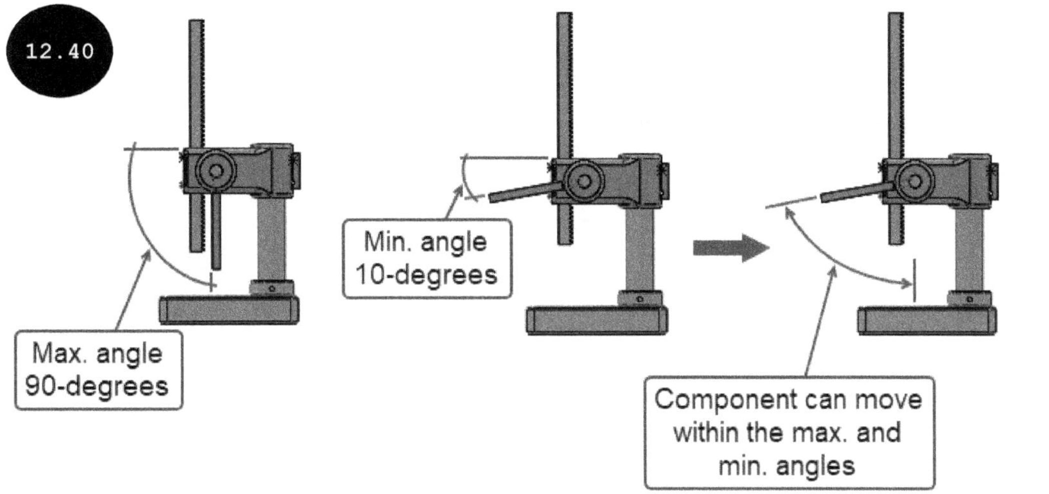

To apply the limit angle mate, click on the **Angle** button in the **Mate Types** rollout tab. The **Angle**, **Maximum Value**, and **Minimum Value** fields are enabled in the PropertyManager, see Figure 12.41. Specify the maximum angle value in the **Maximum Value** field. Next, specify the minimum angle value in the **Minimum Value** field of the rollout. After specifying the maximum and minimum angle values, select two faces of two different components and then click on the green tick-mark in the PropertyManager. The limit angle mate is applied between the selected faces of the components such that the moveable component can rotate within the specified maximum and minimum angle limits, see Figure 12.40.

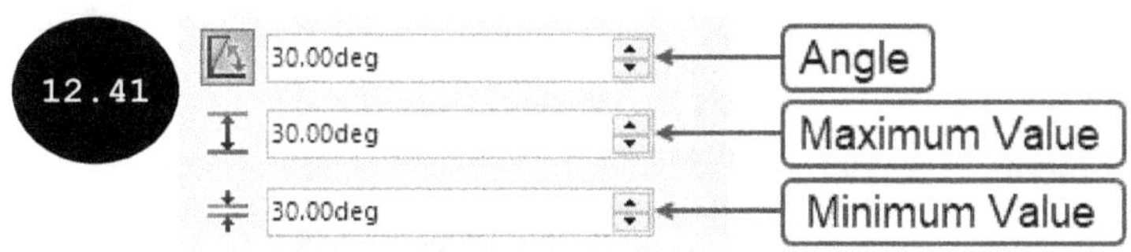

Tip: To review the angle motion between components, select the moveable component and then drag it.

Applying Mechanical Mates

Mechanical mates are used to create a mechanism between components of an assembly. You can create a cam and follower mechanism, gear mechanism, hinge mechanism, rack and pinion mechanism, screw mechanism, and universal joint mechanism between components of an assembly by using mechanical mates. Different types of mechanical mates are available in the **Mechanical** tab of the **Mate PropertyManager**.

Note: To create a mechanism between components of an assembly, it is necessary to have the required degrees of freedom of components such that the components can only be moved or rotated in the desired directions. For example, to create a gear mechanism between two components (gears), you need to first constraint the components such that they can only rotate about their axes using the standard and advanced mates.

To apply a mechanical mate, invoke the **Mate PropertyManager** and then click on the **Mechanical** tab. All the mechanical mates appear in the **Mate PropertyManager**, see Figure 12.42. Different types of mechanical mates are discussed next.

12.42

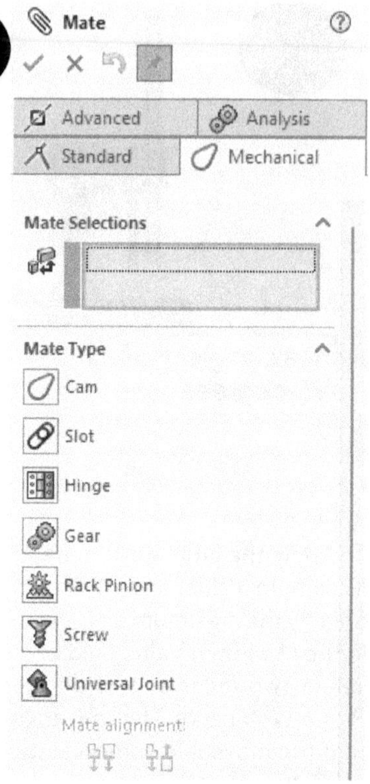

Cam Mate

The cam mate is used to create a cam and follower mechanism between two components of an assembly.

To apply the cam mate, click on the **Cam** button in the **Mate Type** rollout of the **Mechanical** tab. The **Cam Path** and **Cam Follower** fields appear in the **Mate Selections** rollout of the PropertyManager. By default, the **Cam Path** field is activated, therefore you can select a face of the cam component, which is tangent to the series of its other faces and forms a closed loop, see Figure 12.43. As soon as you select a face of the cam component, all faces that are tangent to the selected face get selected automatically and the cam component becomes transparent in the graphics area, see Figure 12.43. Also, the **Cam Follower** field gets activated in the **Mate Selections** rollout. As a result, you can select a face of the follower component.

Select a cylindrical, a semi-cylindrical, or a planar face of the follower component, see Figure 12.44. The selected face of the follower component is placed over the cam component, see Figure 12.45. Next, click on the green tick-mark ✓ in the PropertyManager. The cam mate is applied between the cam and follower components. Now, on rotating the cam component, the follower component moves up and down concerning the cam profile and forms a cam and follower mechanism.

12.43

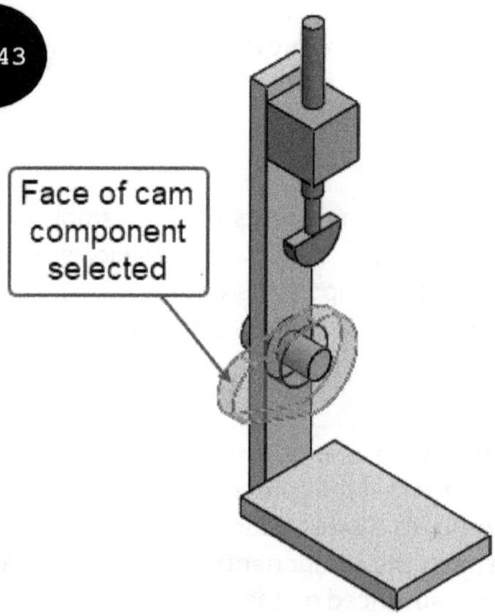

12.44

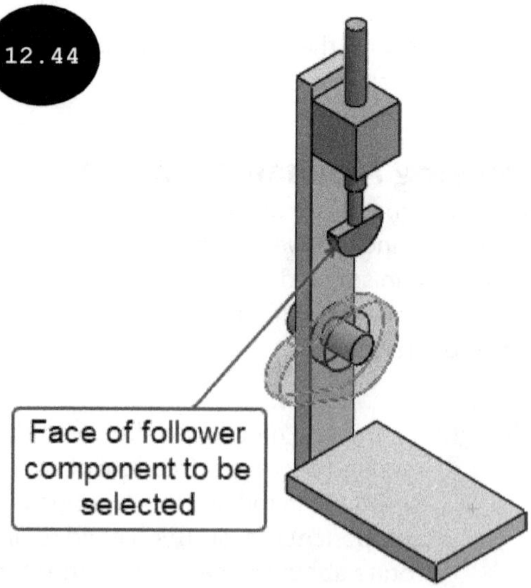

12.45

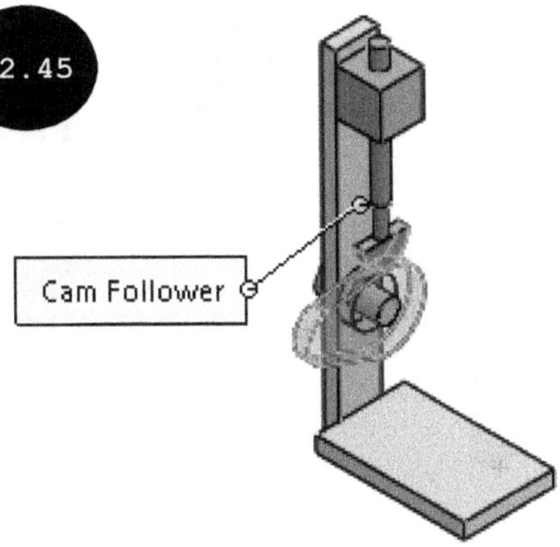

Tip: To review the cam and follower mechanism between the components, select the cam component and then drag it such that it rotates around its axis of rotation.

Note: To select faces of components for applying mates, you may need to move or rotate the assembly or its individual components. To rotate an assembly, drag the cursor by pressing and holding the middle mouse button. To pan the assembly, drag the cursor by pressing and holding the CTRL key plus middle mouse button. Alternatively, you can use the **Rotate** and **Pan** tools to rotate and pan the assembly, respectively. You will learn about moving or rotating individual components of an assembly later in this chapter.

Slot Mate

The slot mate is used to drive a bolt, a pin, or a cylindrical feature of a component along the slot feature of another component in an assembly, see Figure 12.46. You can also apply the slot mate mechanism between two slots of the components.

12.46

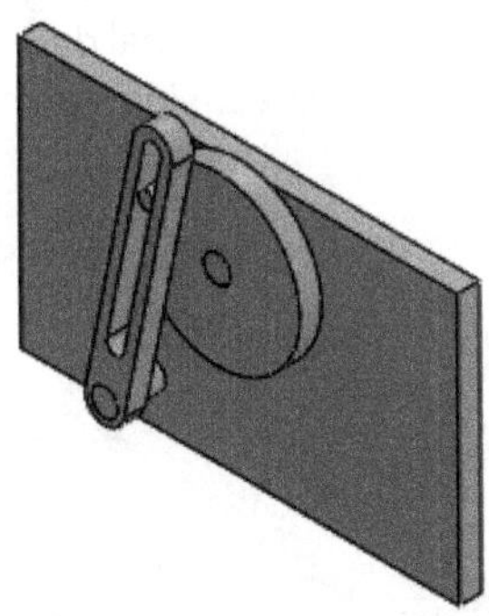

To apply the slot mate, click on the **Slot** button in the **Mate Type** rollout of the **Mechanical** tab. Next, select a face of the slot feature of a component, see Figure 12.47. All the remaining tangent faces of the slot feature get selected automatically, and the component becomes transparent in the graphics area, see Figure 12.47. Next, select a cylindrical face of another component (a bolt, a pin, or a cylindrical feature), see Figure 12.47. The cylindrical face is placed between the slot, see Figure 12.48. Next, click on the green tick-mark in the PropertyManager. The slot mate is applied between the components and now you can review the slot mechanism by dragging the components.

12.47

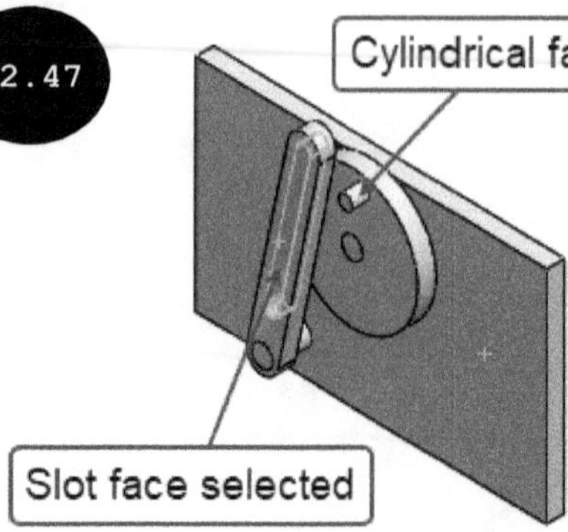

12.48

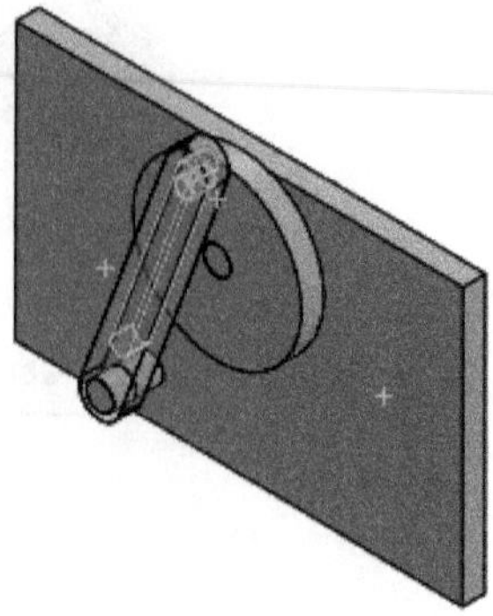

Note: When you click on the **Slot** button, the **Constraint** drop-down list and **Lock rotation** check box appear in the rollout, see Figure 12.49. By default, the **Free** option is selected in this drop-down list. As a result, the component having the bolt, pin, or cylindrical feature can move freely within the slot feature of the other component. You can also constraint the movement of the component and define its position by selecting the **Center in Slot**, **Distance Along Slot**, or **Percent Along Slot** option of the **Constraint** drop-down list, as required. Moreover, you can lock the rotation of the component by selecting the **Lock rotation** check box in the PropertyManager.

12.49

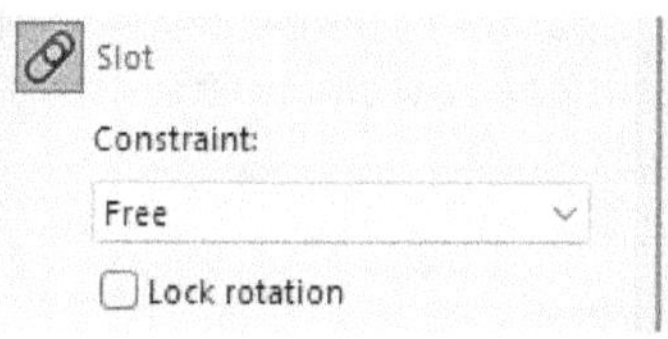

Hinge Mate

The hinge mate is used to create a hinge mechanism between two components by fixing all degrees of freedom of the components except the rotational degree of freedom, see Figure 12.50. You can also limit the rotational degree of freedom by specifying the minimum and maximum angles of rotation.

12.50

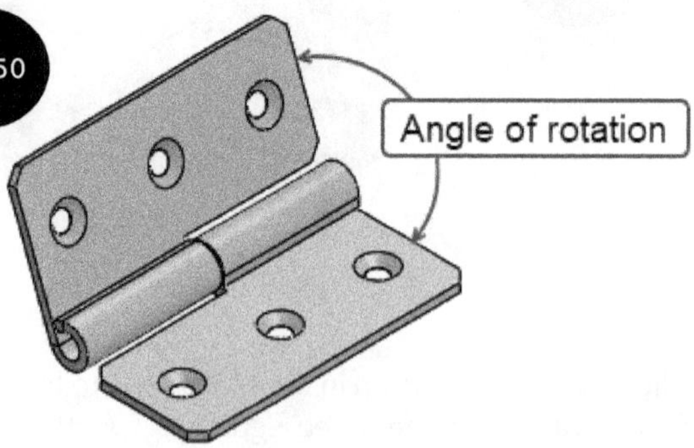

To apply the hinge mate, click on the **Hinge** button; the **Concentric Selections** and **Coincident Selections** fields get enabled in the **Mate Selections** rollout of the PropertyManager. Select two circular faces or circular edges of two different components to be concentric with each other, see Figure 12.51. Next, select two planar faces of the components to be coincident with each other, see Figure 12.52. The concentric and coincident mates are applied between the selected faces of the components, see

Figure 12.53. Next, click on the green tick-mark ✓ in the PropertyManager. The hinge mate is applied and now you can review the hinge mechanism by dragging the components.

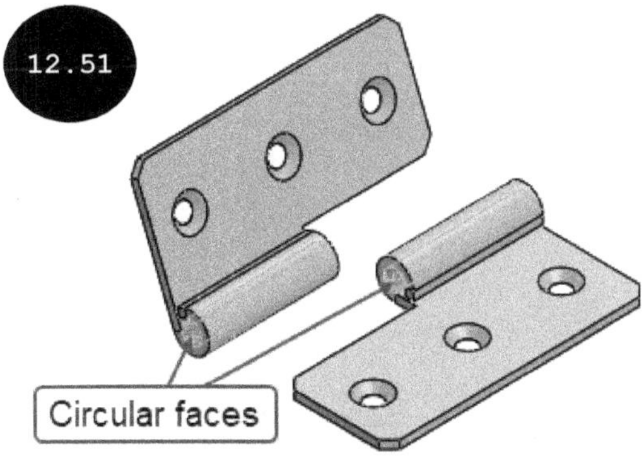

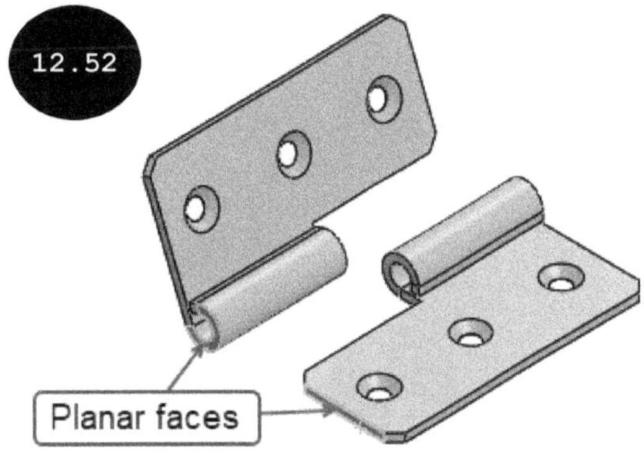

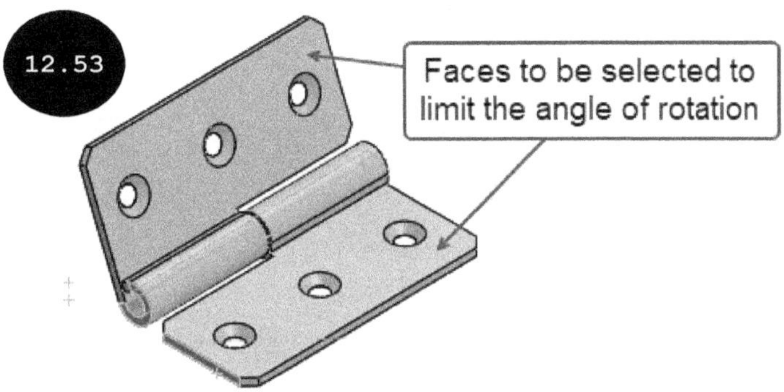

Note: By default, the angle of rotation for the hinge mechanism is 360 degrees. To limit the angle of rotation for the hinge mechanism, click on the **Specify angle limits** check box in the **Mate Selections** rollout of the PropertyManager. The **Angle Selections**, **Angle**, **Maximum Value**, and **Minimum Value** fields get enabled in the rollout. By default, the **Angle Selections** field is activated. As a result, you can select faces of the components to limit the angle of rotation between them. Select two planar faces of components, refer to Figure 12.53. Next, specify the maximum and minimum angle values in the **Maximum Value** and **Minimum Value** fields, respectively and then click on the green tick-mark ✓ in the PropertyManager.

Gear Mate

The gear mate is used to create a gear mechanism between components such that the components can rotate relative to each other, see Figure 12.54.

To apply the gear mate, click on the **Gear** button in the **Mate Type** rollout of the **Mechanical** tab. Next, select a circular face of a gear teeth of the first gear component and the second gear component one by one, see Figure 12.55. On selecting the circular faces of the gear components, the axes of rotation of the gears are defined automatically. You can select circular faces, conical faces, axes, or linear edges of the gear components to define the axes of rotation. Next, specify the gear ratio in the **Ratio** fields of the **Mate Type** rollout. Notice that based on the relative size of the faces selected for defining the axis of rotation, the gear ratio is automatically calculated. You can also reverse the direction of rotations of the gears by selecting the **Reverse** check box. After defining the gear ratio, click on the green tick-mark ✓ in the PropertyManager. The gear mate is applied and now you can review the gear mechanism by dragging the gears.

12.55

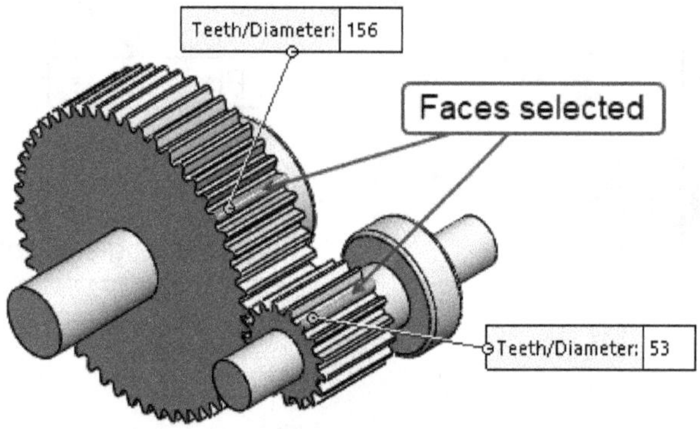

Rack Pinion Mate

The rack pinion mate is used to translate the linear motion of one component to the rotational motion of another component and vice versa. This mate creates the rack and pinion mechanism (see Figure 12.56) where the linear motion of the rack component creates rotatory motion in the pinion component and vice versa.

12.56

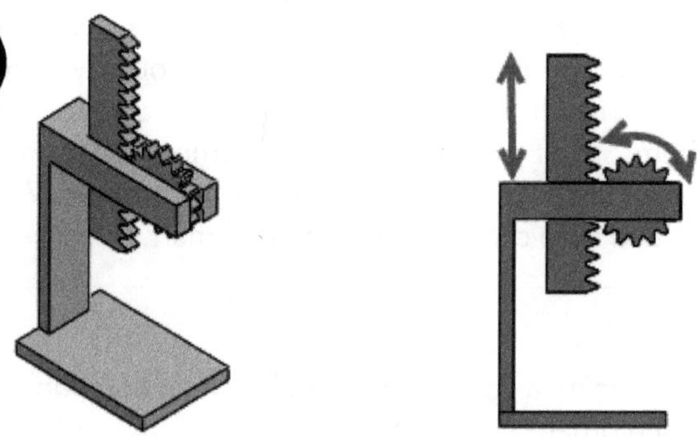

To apply the rack pinion mate, click on the **Rack Pinion** button; the **Rack** and **Pinion/Gear** fields get enabled in the **Mate Selections** rollout of the PropertyManager. Select a linear edge of the rack component, which defines the direction of movement of the rack component, see Figure 12.57. After selecting a linear edge of the rack component, the **Pinion/Gear** field gets activated. Select a circular face of the pinion/gear component, which defines the axis of rotation of the pinion component, see Figure 12.57. Note that for each full rotation of the pinion/gear component, the rack component translates a distance equal to π (pi) multiplied by the pinion diameter. You can specify either the diameter of the pinion or the distance traveled by the rack component per revolution by selecting the **Pinion pitch diameter** or the **Rack travel/revolution** radio button, respectively. Next, click on the green tick-mark ✓ in the PropertyManager. The rack pinion mate is applied between the components and now you can review the rack and pinion mechanism by dragging the components.

12.57

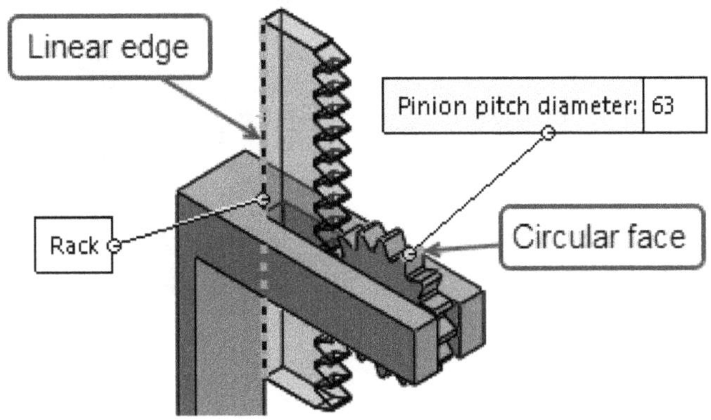

Screw Mate

The screw mate applies the pitch relationship between the rotation of one component and the translation of the other component such that it forms a screw mechanism, see Figure 12.58. On applying the screw mate, the translational motion of one component causes rotational motion in the other component based on the specified pitch relationship. You can specify the pitch relationship between two components either by defining the number of revolutions of one component concerning the per millimeter translation of another component or by defining the distance traveled by one component concerning a revolution of the other component.

12.58

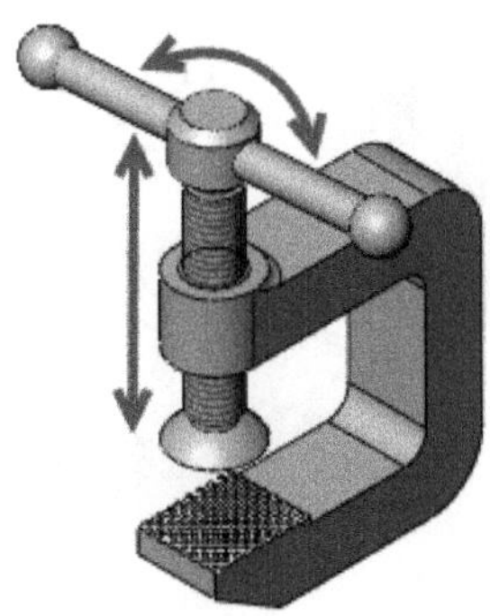

To apply the screw mate, click on the **Screw** button in the **Mate Type** rollout of the **Mechanical** tab. Next, select a circular face of the first component and then select a circular face of the second component to define their axes of rotation, see Figure 12.59. On selecting the circular faces of both the components, an arrow appears in the graphics area which indicates the direction of revolution, see Figure 12.59. You can reverse the direction of revolution by using the **Reverse** check box of the **Mate Type** rollout. By default, the **Revolutions/mm** radio button is selected in the **Mate Type** rollout, see Figure 12.60. As a result, you can specify the number of revolutions of one component with respect to the per-millimeter translation of the other component in the **Revolutions/Distance** field. If you select the **Distance/revolution** radio button, then you can specify the distance traveled by one component concerning a revolution of the other component in the **Revolutions/Distance** field. Next, click on the green tick-mark ✓ in the PropertyManager. The screw mate is applied between the components and now you can review the screw mechanism by dragging the components.

12.59

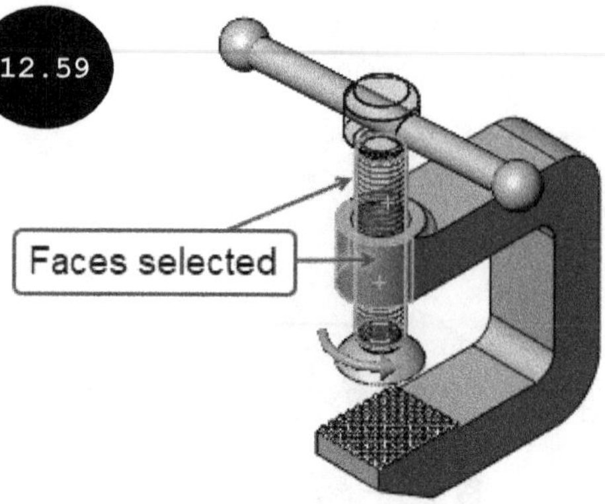

12.60

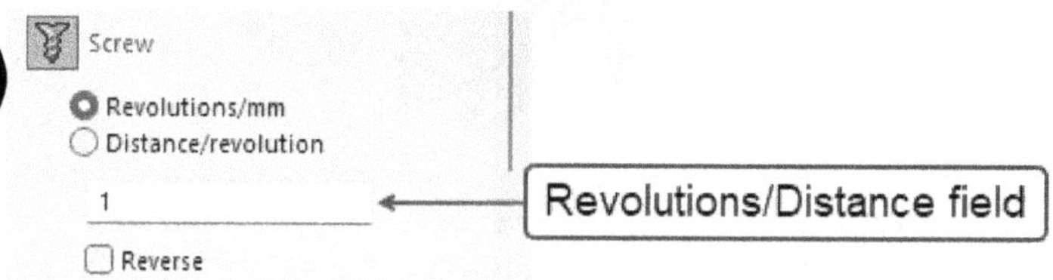

Universal Joint

The universal joint mate is used to translate the rotational movement of one component to the rotational movement of another component about their axes of rotations, see Figure 12.61.

12.61

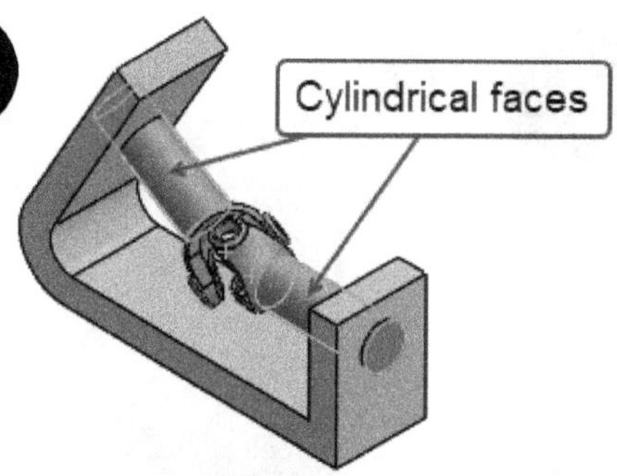

To apply the universal joint mate, click on the **Universal Joint** button in the **Mate Type** rollout of the **Mechanical** tab. Next, select two cylindrical faces of different components one by one, see Figure 12.61. After selecting the cylindrical faces, click on the green tick-mark in the PropertyManager. The universal joint mate is applied. You can review the joint mechanism by dragging the components.

Hiding Faces while Applying a Mate

In SOLIDWORKS, while applying a mate, you can temporarily hide a face to select an obscured face of the assembly by pressing the ALT key. To do this, click on the **Mate** tool and then hover the cursor over the face to be hidden, and then press the ALT key. The face is temporarily hidden and the obscured face becomes visible. You can temporarily hide multiple faces by pressing the ALT key. To show the temporarily hidden face, hover the cursor over the face and then press the SHIFT + ALT keys. You can also show the hidden faces in a semi-transparent state by pressing the CTRL + SHIFT + ALT keys.

Tip: After selecting a face to apply a mate, the temporarily hidden faces become visible, automatically. You can also press the ESC key to restore the visibility of all the temporarily hidden faces.

Moving and Rotating Individual Components

In SOLIDWORKS, you can move and rotate individual components of an assembly about their free degrees of freedom by using the **Move Component** and **Rotate Component** tools of the **Assembly CommandManager** respectively, see Figure 12.62. Both tools are discussed next.

12.62

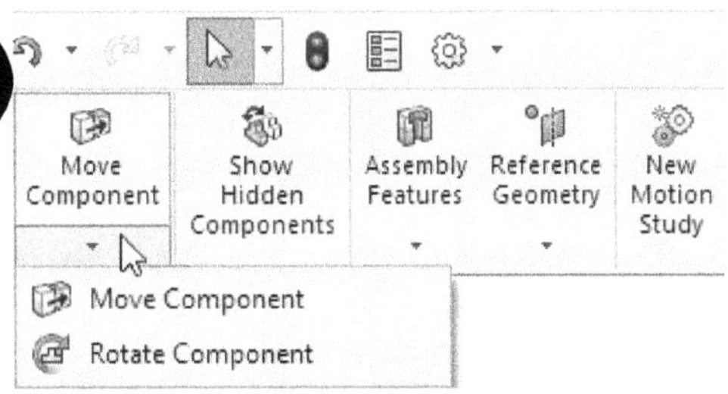

Moving a Component by using the Move Component Tool

In SOLIDWORKS, you can move individual components of an assembly along their free degrees of freedom by using the **Move Component** tool. To do this, click on the **Move Component** tool in the **Assembly CommandManager**. The **Move Component PropertyManager** appears, see Figure 12.63. By default, the **Free Drag** option is selected in the **Move** drop-down list of the **Move** rollout. As a result, you can move the component freely along its free degrees of freedom. Select the component to be moved and then drag the cursor by pressing and holding the left mouse button. The selected component starts moving along with the cursor. To stop the movement of the component, release the left mouse button. The other options in the **Move** drop-down list are **Along Assembly XYZ**, **Along Entity**, **By Delta XYZ**, and **To XYZ Position**, see Figure 12.64. All these options are discussed next.

12.63

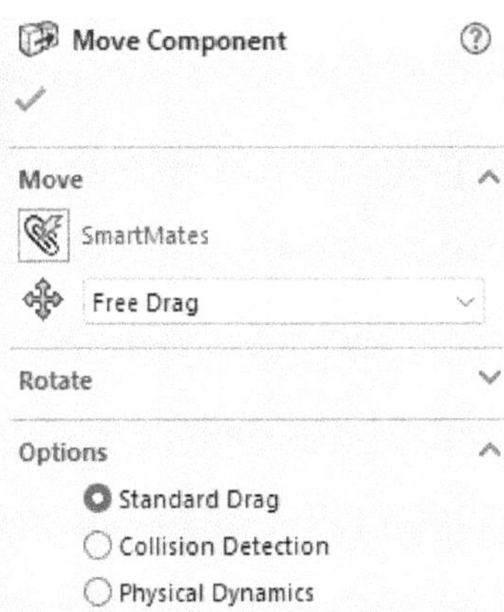

12.64

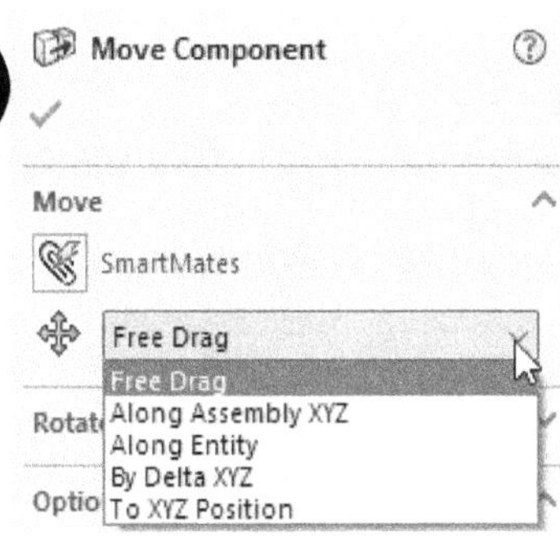

Note: A component cannot move along its fixed or restricted degrees of freedom. For example, if the translational degree of freedom along the X axis of the component is fixed by applying mates then you cannot move the component along the X axis.

Along Assembly XYZ

On selecting the **Along Assembly XYZ** option, you can move a component along the X, Y, or Z axis of the assembly coordinate system.

Along Entity

On selecting the **Along Entity** option, the **Selected item** field appears in the **Move** rollout, see Figure 12.65. This field is used for selecting an entity as the direction along which the selected component has to be moved. You can select a linear edge, a sketch line, or an axis as the entity to define the direction along which the component has to be moved. After selecting the entity, select the component to be moved and then drag the cursor. The selected component starts moving in the direction of the entity selected.

By Delta XYZ

On selecting the **By Delta XYZ** option, the **Delta X**, **Delta Y**, and **Delta Z** fields appear, see Figure 12.66. In these fields, you can specify the X, Y, and Z distance values for moving the component concerning the current location of the component. After specifying the X, Y, and Z distance values in the respective fields, select the component to be moved and then click on the **Apply** button. The selected component moves concerning the specified distance values.

12.65

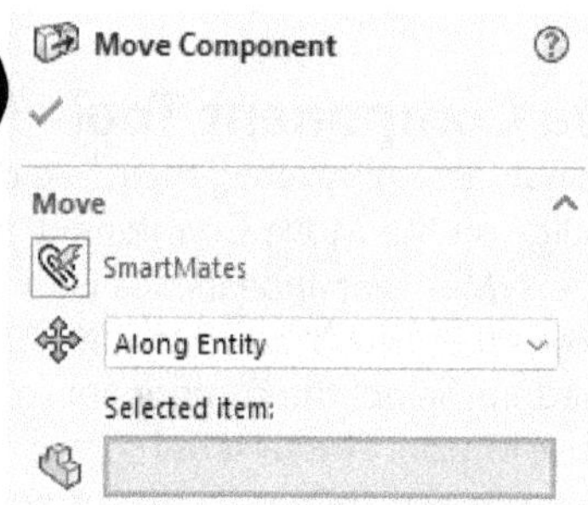

12.66

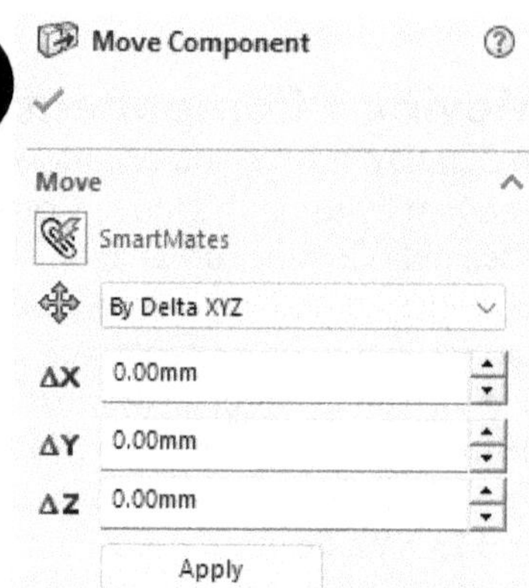

To XYZ Position

On selecting the **To XYZ Position** option, the **X Coordinate**, **Y Coordinate**, and **Z Coordinate** fields get enabled in the **Move** rollout of the PropertyManager, see Figure 12.67. These fields are used for specifying the X, Y, and Z coordinate values of the location where you want to move the selected component. After specifying the coordinate values, click on the **Apply** button. The origin of the selected component is moved to the specified coordinate. Note that if you select a vertex or a point of the component to move then after clicking on the **Apply** button, the selected vertex or point of the component is moved to the specified coordinate location.

12.67

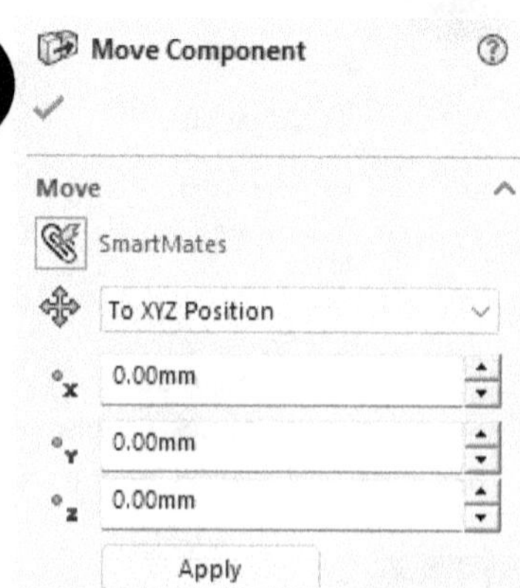

Note that, by default, the movement of a component is not prevented from any interference or collision occurring with other components of the assembly. This means that the component moves continuously even if any other component comes across its way, since the **Standard Drag** radio button is selected in the **Options** rollout of the **Move Component PropertyManager**, see Figure 12.68. By selecting the **Collision Detection** or **Physical Dynamics** radio button, you can detect collisions or analyze the motion between components of an assembly. The methods for detecting a collision and analyzing motion between components by using the **Collision Detection** and **Physical Dynamics** radio buttons are discussed next.

12.68

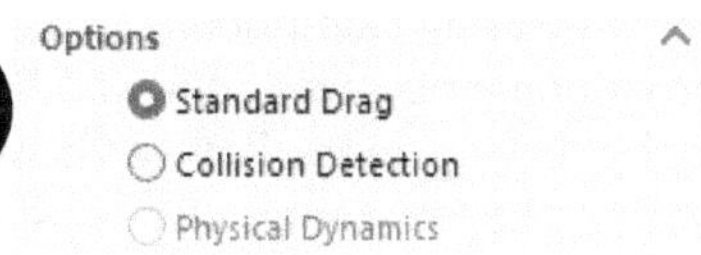

Detecting Collision between Components

You can detect a collision between components of an assembly while moving a component by using the **Collision Detection** radio button. To do this, select the **Collision Detection** radio button in the **Options** rollout of the PropertyManager. The **All components** and **These components** radio buttons as well as the **Stop at collision** and **Dragged part only** check boxes appear in the **Options** rollout of the PropertyManager, see Figure 12.69.

By default, the **All components** radio button is selected. As a result, a collision is detected when the moveable component collides with any component of the assembly. Note that as soon as a collision is detected between the components, the components get highlighted in the graphics area, see Figure 12.70. If the **Stop at collision** check box is selected in the rollout then the movement of the component is stopped as soon as it collides with the other component of the assembly.

12.69

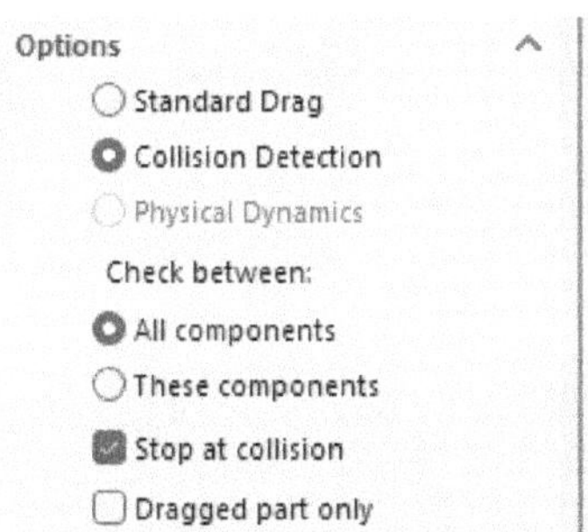

12.70

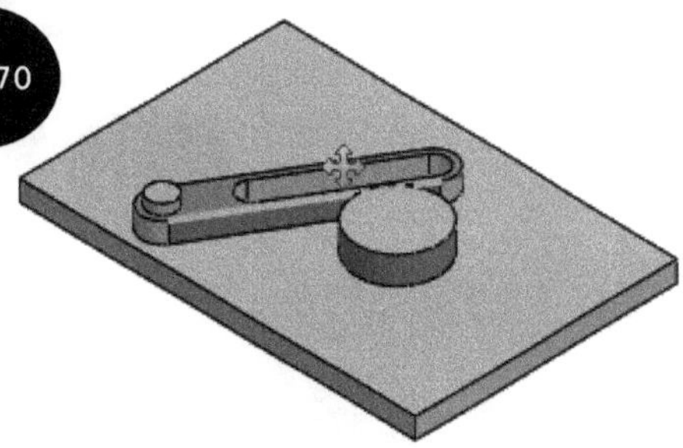

On selecting the **These components** radio button, the **Components for Collision Check** field appears in the PropertyManager. This field is used for selecting components for the detection of collision. After selecting the components, click on the **Resume Drag** button and then drag the component to be moved. Note that the collision is detected only when the component being moved touches any of the selected components of the assembly. Note that the components that are not listed in the **Components for Collision Check** field are ignored by the moveable component.

When the **Dragged part only** check box is selected in the **Options** rollout, collision is checked only for the component that is selected to be moved. If this check box is cleared then the collision is checked even for the components that move along with the moveable component because of the mates with the moveable component.

Detecting Collision and Analyzing Motion between Components

Similar to the **Collision Detection** radio button, the **Physical Dynamics** radio button is also used for detecting a collision, with the only difference being that it forces the components to move along with the moveable component when a collision is detected between them. Note that components can only move or rotate within their free degrees of freedom.

Note: In addition to moving individual components and detecting collision, you can also rotate components by using the **Rotate Component PropertyManager**. You can invoke the **Rotate Component PropertyManager** by expanding the **Rotate** rollout of the **Move Component PropertyManager** or by clicking on the **Rotate Component** tool in the CommandManager. The method for rotating a component is discussed next.

Rotating a Component by using the Rotate Component Tool

Similar to moving individual components, you can rotate individual components of an assembly about their free degrees of freedom by using the **Rotate Component** tool. To do this, click on the **Rotate Component** tool in the **Assembly CommandManager**, see Figure 12.71. The **Rotate Component PropertyManager** appears, see Figure 12.72.

12.71

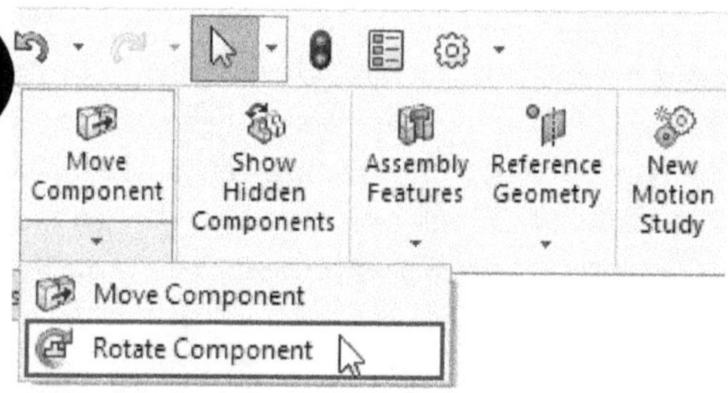

12.72

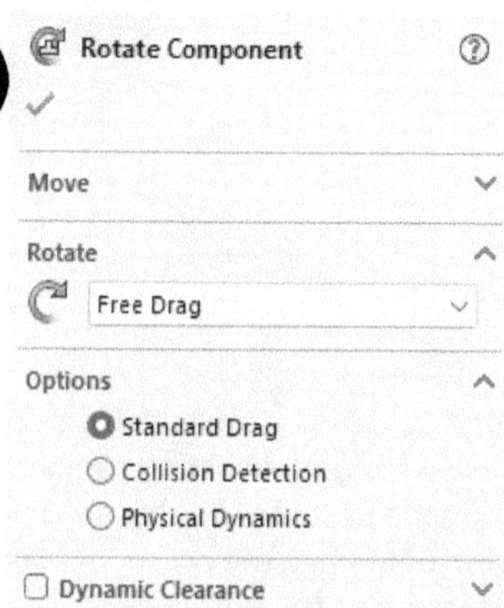

By default, the **Free Drag** option is selected in the **Rotate** drop-down list of the **Rotate** rollout in the PropertyManager. As a result, you can rotate a component freely about an axis by dragging the component. Select the component to be rotated in the graphics area and then drag the cursor about its free degrees of freedom by pressing and holding the left mouse button. The selected component starts rotating about the axis of rotation. Once you have rotated the component, release the left mouse button. All the options in the **Rotate Component PropertyManager** are the same as those discussed earlier while moving the component by using the **Move Component PropertyManager**.

Working with SmartMates

SmartMates is a smart method for applying standard mates such as coincident, parallel, and perpendicular between the components of an assembly. By using this method, the design process becomes faster and, more efficient. The SmartMates method for applying mates can be invoked by clicking on the **SmartMates** button in the **Move Component PropertyManager**. Note that as soon as you click on the **SmartMates** button, the **SmartMates PropertyManager** appears, see Figure 12.73. As discussed, you can invoke the **Move Component PropertyManager** by clicking on the **Move Components** tool in the **Assembly CommandManager**.

12.73

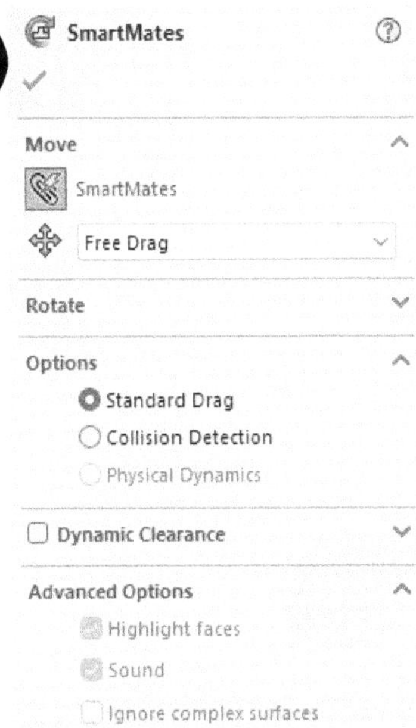

Once the **SmartMates PropertyManager** has been invoked, double-click on an entity of the component for applying a mate. The selected entity is highlighted, and the component becomes transparent in the graphics area, see Figure 12.74. Next, click on an entity of another component of the assembly for applying the mate. The **Mate** Pop-up toolbar appears with the most suitable mate activated in it. Also, a preview appears such that the most suitable mate is applied between the selected entities of the components, see Figure 12.75. You can apply a mate by clicking the respective tool in the Pop-up toolbar. Next, click on the green tick-mark ✓ in the toolbar. The selected mate is applied between the entities of the components.

12.74

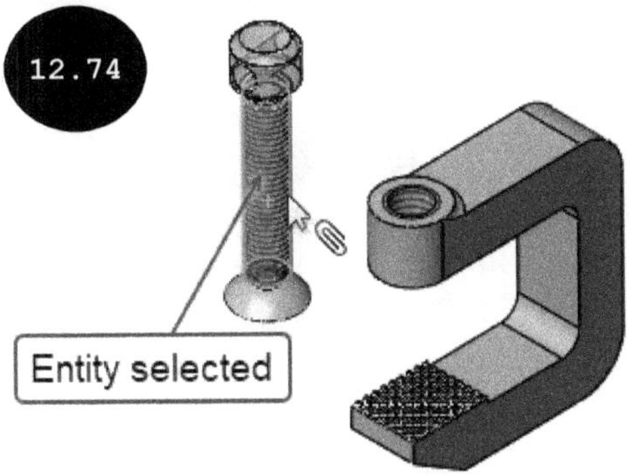

12.75

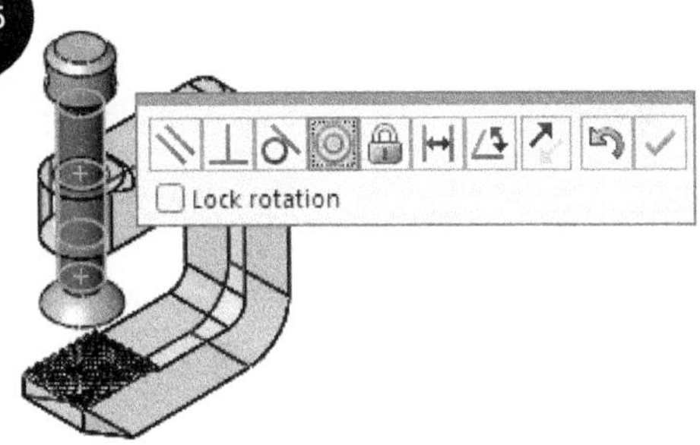

Note: You can also press the ALT key and then drag a component toward another component for applying a standard mate without invoking the **SmartMates PropertyManager**.

Tutorial 1

Create the assembly shown in Figure 12.76. Different views and dimensions of individual components of the assembly are shown in Figures 12.77 through 12.81. All dimensions are in mm.

12.76

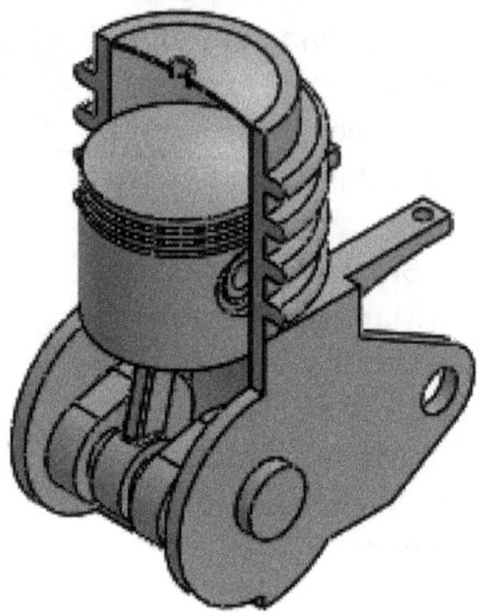

12.77

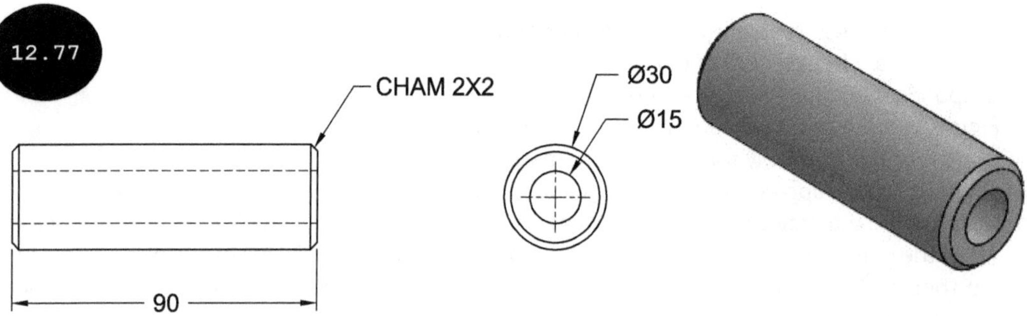

Piston Pin

12.78

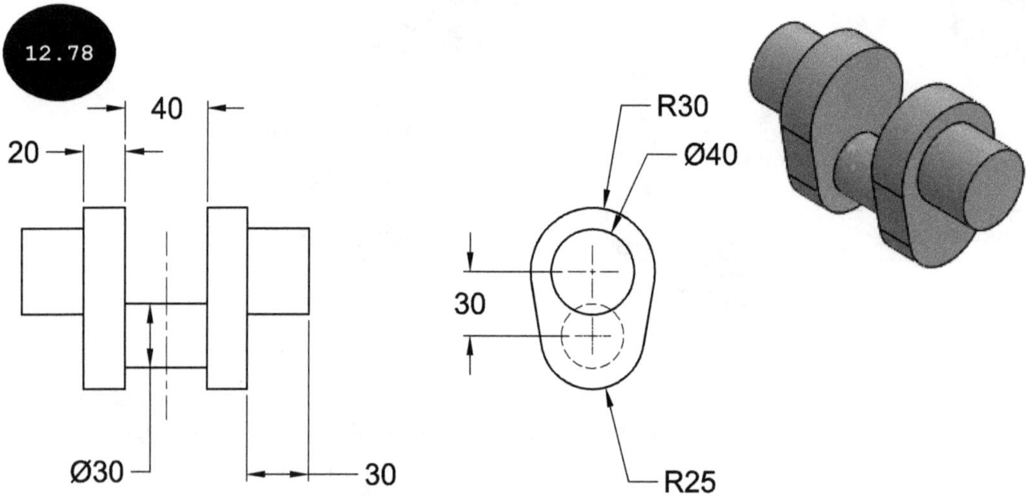

Crank Shaft

12.79

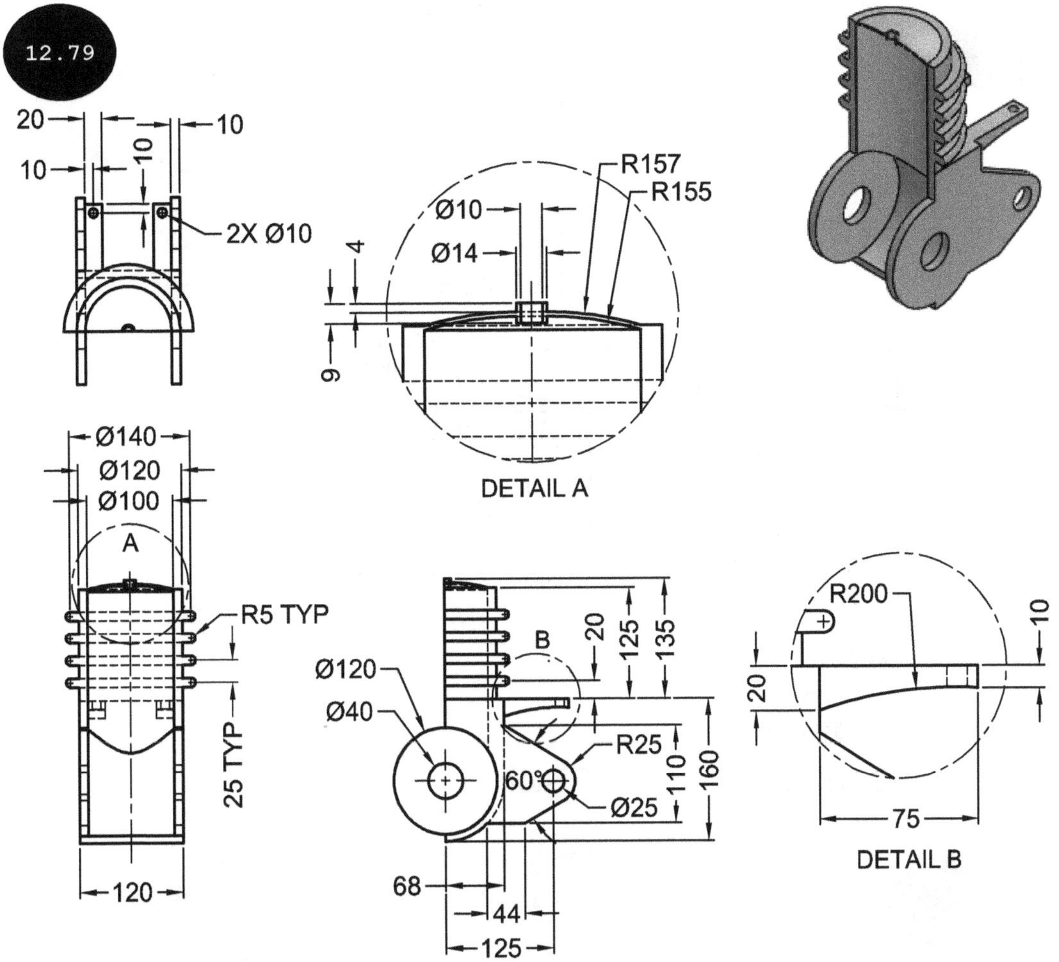

Crank Case

12.80

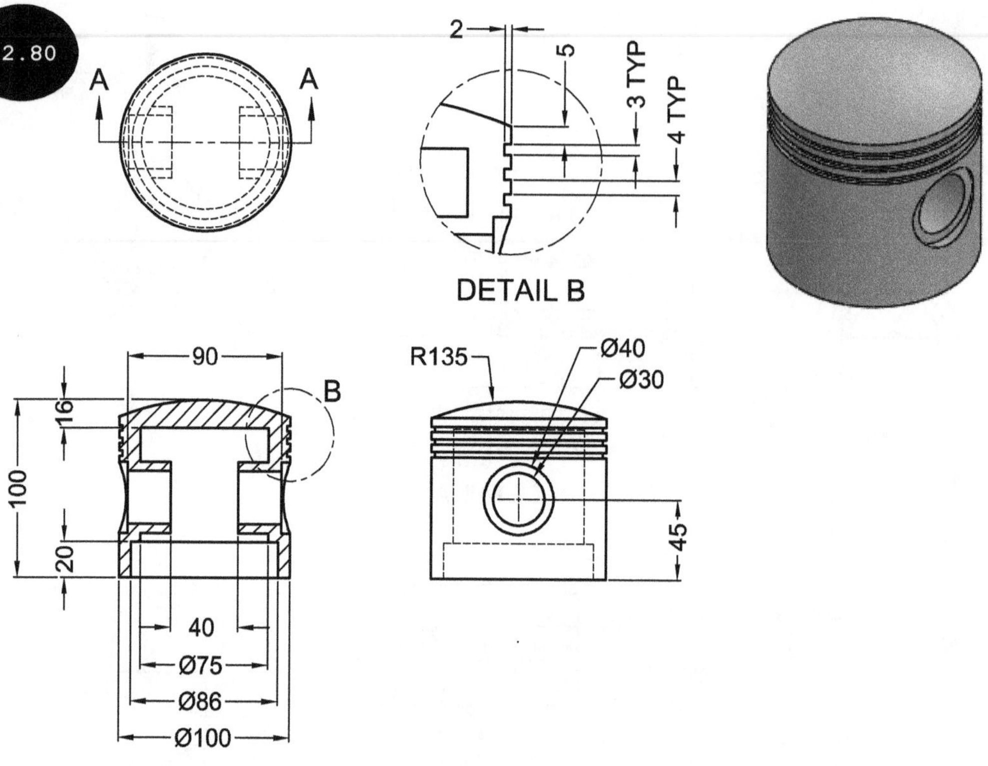

Piston

12.81

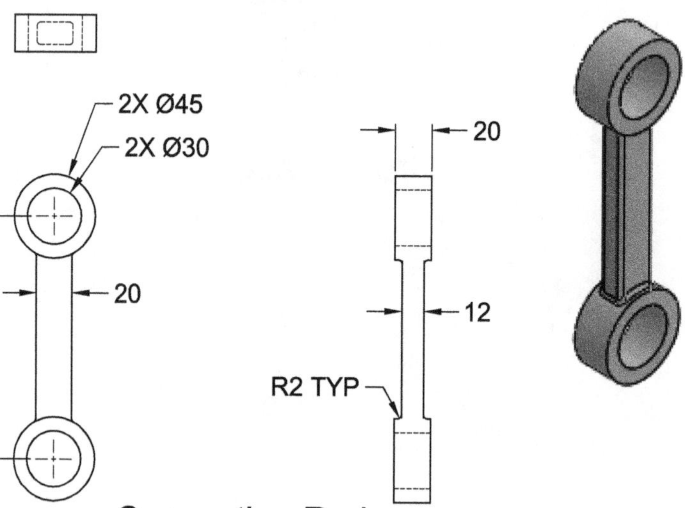

Connecting Rod

Section 1: Starting SOLIDWORKS and Creating Assembly Components

In this section, you will create all the components of the assembly in the Part modeling environment one by one.

1. Start SOLIDWORKS by double-clicking on the SOLIDWORKS icon on your desktop.

2. Create all components of the assembly one by one in the Part modeling environment. Refer to Figures 12.77 through 12.81 for the dimensions of each component. After creating the components, save them in the Tutorial 1 folder of the Chapter 12 folder. You need to create these folders in the SOLIDWORKS folder.

Note: You can also download all the components of the assembly by logging in to your account on CADArtifex website (***cadartifex.com/login***). If you are a new user, you need to first sign up on the website (***cadartifex.com/register***) to access the online resources.

Section 2: Invoking the Assembly Environment

After creating all the components, you need to assemble them in the Assembly environment.

1. Click on the **New** tool in the **Standard** toolbar. The **New SOLIDWORKS Document** dialog box appears.

2. Click on the **Assembly** button and then click on the **OK** button in the dialog box. The Assembly environment is invoked, and the **Open** dialog box appears along with the **Begin Assembly PropertyManager**, see Figure 12.82.

12.82

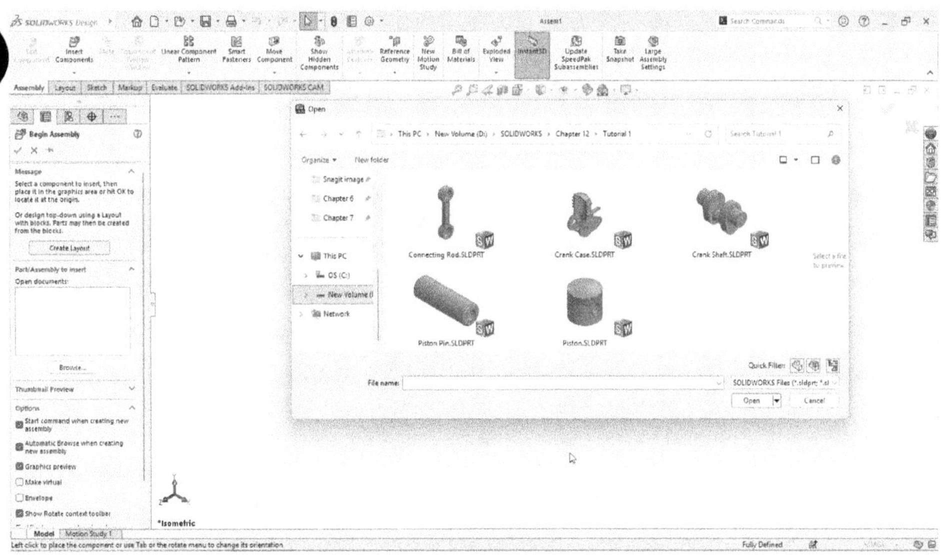

Note: On invoking the Assembly environment, the **Open** dialog box appears, automatically along with the **Begin Assembly PropertyManager**, if none of the components are opened in the current session of SOLIDWORKS. If the **Open** dialog box does not appear, then click on the **Browse** button in the **Begin Assembly PropertyManager** to open it.

Section 3: Inserting the First Component

1. Browse to the location where all the components of the assembly are saved (*\SOLIDWORKS\Chapter 12\Tutorial 1*) by using the **Open** dialog box.

2. Select the **Crank Case** component and then click on the **Open** button in the dialog box. The selected component is attached to the cursor, see Figure 12.83. Also, the **Rotate Context** toolbar appears in the graphics area.

12.83

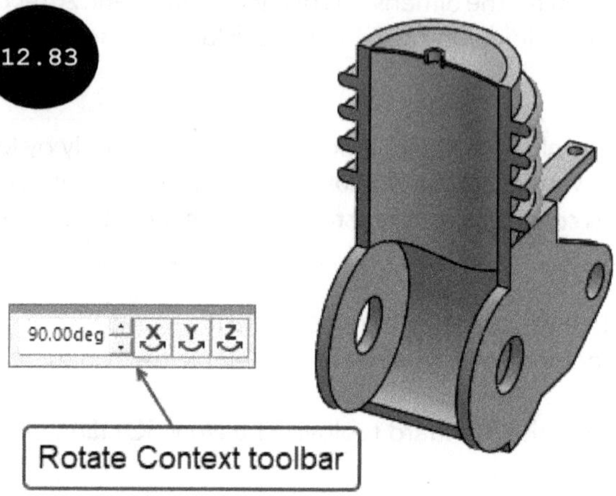

3. Click anywhere in the graphics area, the attached component moves toward the origin of the assembly and becomes the fixed component.

Section 4: Inserting the Second Component

1. Click on the **Insert Components** tool in the **Assembly CommandManager**. The **Open** dialog box appears, automatically along with the **Insert Component PropertyManager**.

Note: The **Open** dialog box appears only if none of the components are opened in the current session of SOLIDWORKS. If the **Open** dialog box does not appear automatically, then click on the **Browse** button in the **Insert Component PropertyManager** to open the **Open** dialog box.

2. Browse to the location where all the components of the assembly are saved and then select the **Crank Shaft** component. Next, click on the **Open** button in the dialog box. The selected component is attached to the cursor, see Figure 12.84.

3. Click anywhere in the graphics area to specify the placement point for the second component (**Crank Shaft**). The component (**Crank Shaft**) is placed in the specified location, see Figure 12.85. Ensure that you specify the placement point such that the inserted component does not intersect the first component of the assembly.

12.84

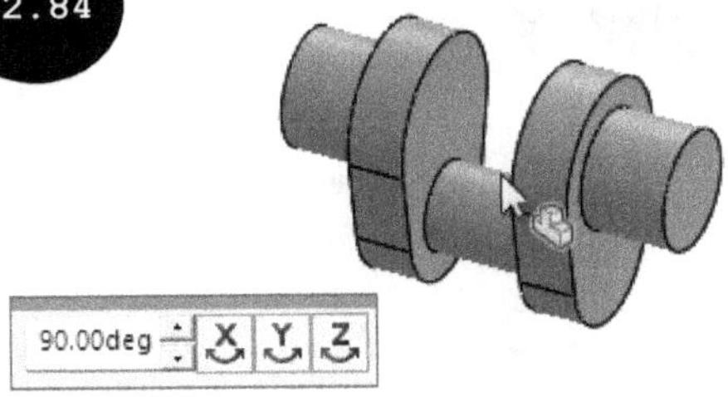

12.85

Note: By default, all degrees of freedom of the second component are free, which means that the second component is free to translate and rotate along and about its axes. You need to apply the required mates to fix its required degrees of freedom with respect to the first component of the assembly.

Section 5: Assembling the Second Component

Before you insert the third component in the Assembly environment, it is recommended to first assemble the second component with the first component of the assembly.

1. Click on the **Mate** tool in the **Assembly CommandManager**. The **Mate PropertyManager** appears.

Mate

2. Select the circular face of the second component (**Crank Shaft**) as the first entity to apply a mate, see Figure 12.86. The circular face gets selected, and the component (**Crank Shaft**) becomes transparent in the graphics area, see Figure 12.87.

12.86

12.87

3. Select the circular face of the first component (**Crank Case**) as the second entity to apply the mate, see Figure 12.88. A Pop-up toolbar appears with the **Concentric** tool activated in it, by default. Also, the selected faces of the components become concentric to each other, see Figure 12.89.

12.88

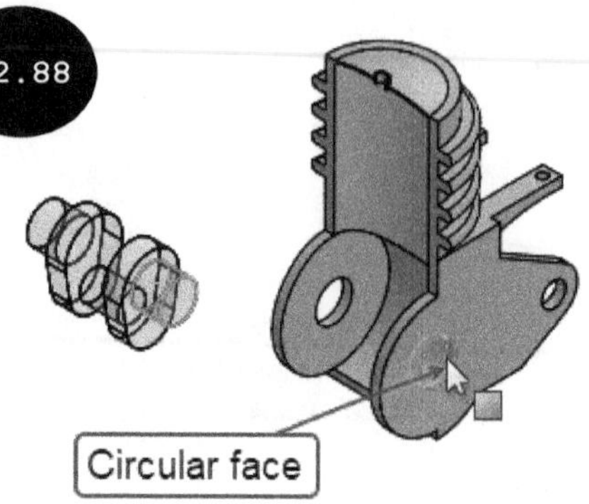

12.89

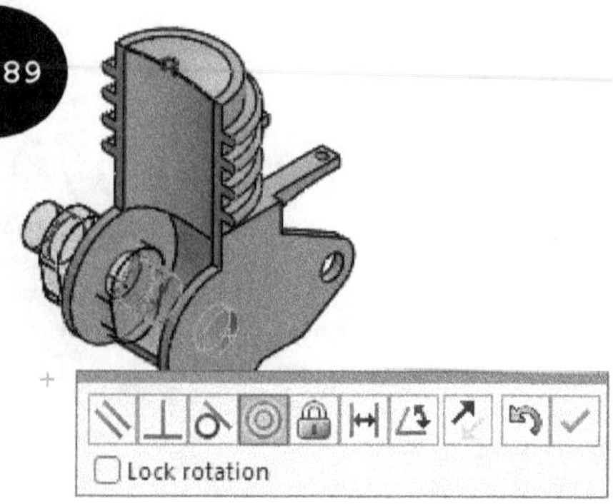

4. Click on the green tick-mark button in the Pop-up toolbar. The concentric mate is applied between the selected faces of the components.

Note: After applying the concentric mate, the degrees of freedom of the **Crank Shaft** component get fixed except one translational and one rotational degree of freedom. This means that the **Crank Shaft** component can only translate and rotate along the x-axis.

Now, you need to fix the translational degree of freedom of the **Crank Shaft** component.

5. Expand the FeatureManager Design Tree, which is now available in the top left corner of the graphics area, by clicking on the arrow in front of it.

6. Expand the **Crank Shaft** node in the FeatureManager Design Tree and then select its **Right Plane** as the first entity to apply the mate. The Right Plane gets selected, and the component (**Crank Shaft**) becomes transparent in the graphics area, see Figure 12.90.

7. Expand the **Crank Case** node in the FeatureManager Design Tree and then select its **Right Plane** as the second entity to apply the mate. A Pop-up toolbar appears with the **Coincident** tool activated in it, by default. Accordingly, the selected planes of the components become coincident with each other, see Figure 12.91.

12.90

12.91

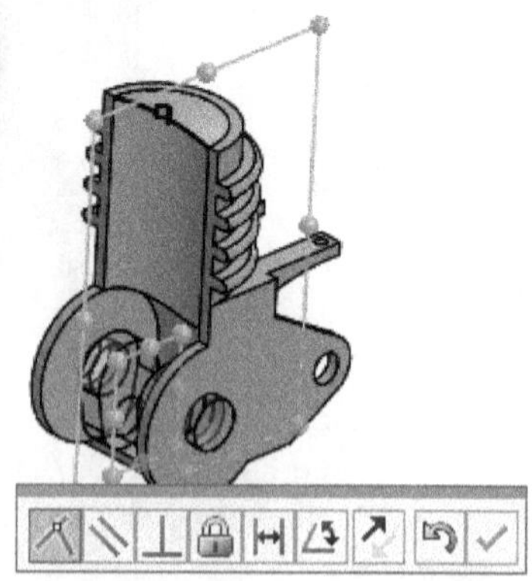

8. Click on the green tick-mark button in the Pop-up toolbar. The coincident mate is applied between the selected planes of the components. Next, exit the **Mate PropertyManager** by clicking on its green tick-mark.

Note: After applying the concentric and coincident mates, the second component (**Crank Shaft**) cannot translate in any direction. However, it can rotate about its axis. This is because the rotational degree of freedom of the component has not been restricted.

Section 6: Inserting the Third Component

1. Click on the **Insert Components** tool in the **Assembly CommandManager**. The **Open** dialog box appears along with the **Insert Component PropertyManager**. If the **Open** dialog box does not appear automatically, then click on the **Browse** button in the **Insert Component PropertyManager** to open the **Open** dialog box.

2. Select the third component (**Connecting Rod**) and then click on the **Open** button in the dialog box. The third component (**Connecting Rod**) is attached to the cursor, see Figure 12.92.

12.92

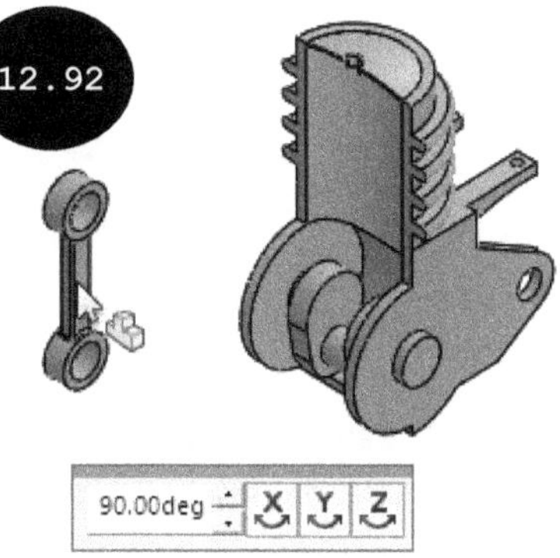

3. Click anywhere in the graphics area to specify the placement point for the third component (**Connecting Rod**). The component is placed in the specified location. Ensure that you specify the placement point such that the inserted component does not intersect with the other components of the assembly.

Section 7: Assembling the Third Component

1. Click on the **Mate** tool in the **Assembly CommandManager**. The **Mate PropertyManager** appears.

2. Select the circular face of the third component (**Connecting Rod**) as the first entity to apply the mate, see Figure 12.93. The circular face gets selected, and the component becomes transparent in the graphics area.

12.93

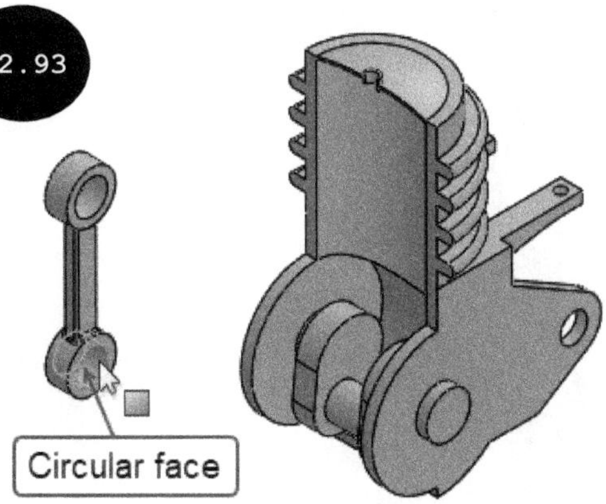

3. Select the circular face of the second component (**Crank Shaft**) as the second entity to apply the mate, see Figure 12.94. A Pop-up toolbar appears with the **Concentric** tool activated in it, by default. Accordingly, the selected faces of the components become concentric to each other, see Figure 12.95.

12.94

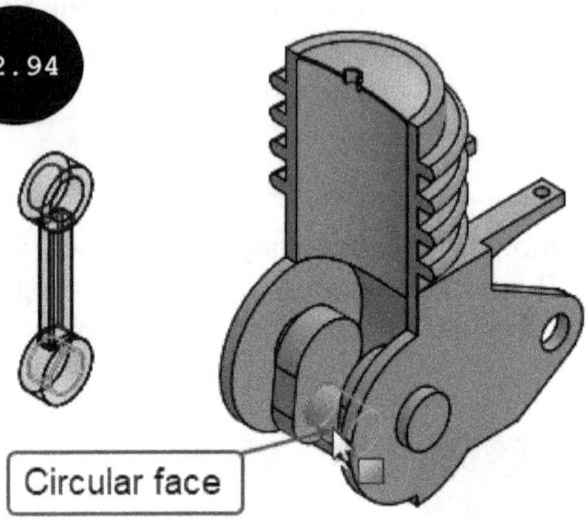

12.95

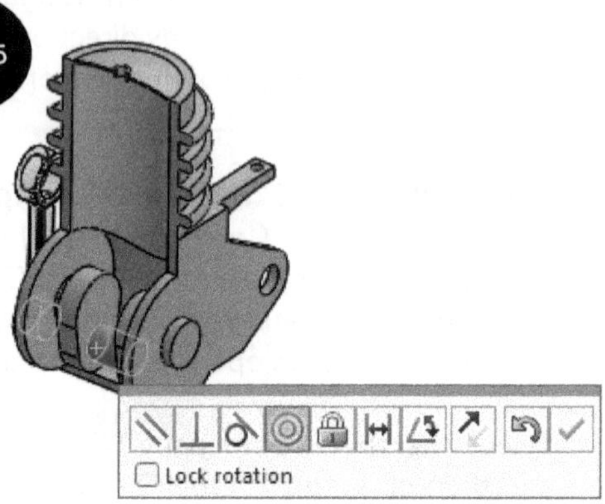

4. Click on the green tick-mark button in the Pop-up toolbar. The concentric mate is applied between the selected faces of the components.

   Now, you need to fix the translational degree of freedom of the **Connecting Rod** component.

5. Expand the FeatureManager Design Tree, which is now available in the top left corner of the graphics area, by clicking on the arrow in front of it.

6. Expand the **Connecting Rod** node in the FeatureManager Design Tree and then select its **Right Plane** as the first entity to apply the mate. The Right Plane gets selected, and the component (**Connecting Rod**) becomes transparent in the graphics area, see Figure 12.96.

   Now, you need to select an entity of the other component for applying the mate.

7. Expand the **Crank Shaft** node in the FeatureManager Design Tree and then select its **Right Plane** as the second entity to apply the mate. A Pop-up toolbar appears with the **Coincident** tool activated in it, by default. Accordingly, the selected planes of the components become coincident with each other, see Figure 12.97.

12.96

12.97

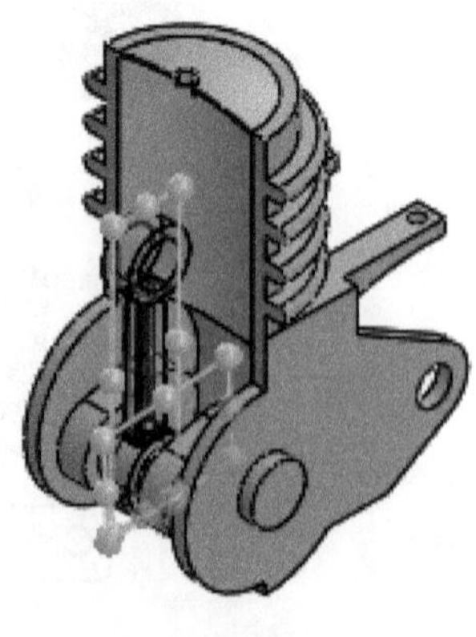

8. Click on the green tick-mark button in the Pop-up toolbar. The coincident mate is applied between the selected faces of the components. Next, exit the **Mate PropertyManager**.

Note: After applying the concentric and coincident mates, all degrees of freedom of the **Connecting Rod** component get fixed with respect to the **Crank Shaft** component except one rotational degree of freedom.

Section 8: Inserting and Assembling the Fourth Component

1. Insert the fourth component (**Piston Pin**) of the assembly by using the **Insert Component** tool of the **Assembly CommandManager**, see Figure 12.98.

   Now, you need to assemble the **Piston Pin** component.

2. Click on the **Mate** tool in the **Assembly CommandManager**. The **Mate PropertyManager** appears.

3. Select the outer circular face of the fourth component (**Piston Pin**) as the first entity to apply the mate, see Figure 12.99. The circular face gets selected, and the component becomes transparent in the graphics area.

12.98

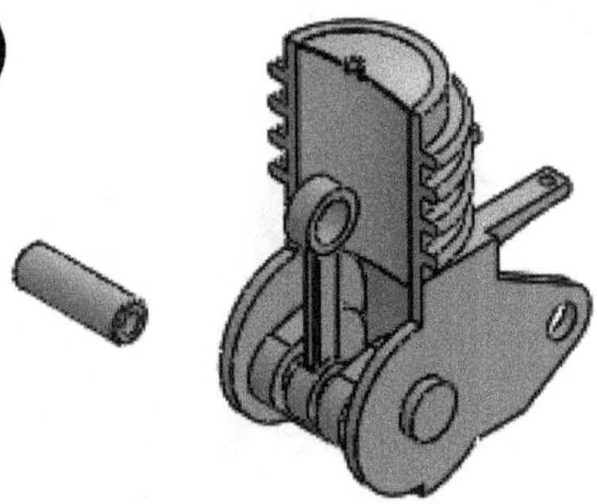

12.99

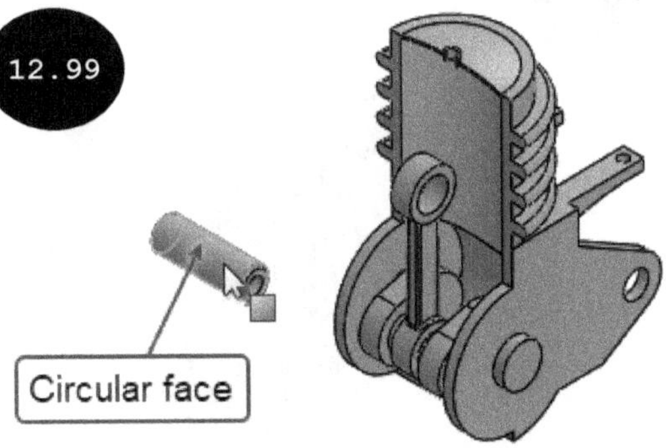

4. Select the upper inner circular face of the third component (**Connecting Rod**) as the second entity to apply the mate, see Figure 12.100. A Pop-up toolbar appears with the **Concentric** tool activated in it. Accordingly, the selected faces of the components become concentric to each other, see Figure 12.101.

12.100

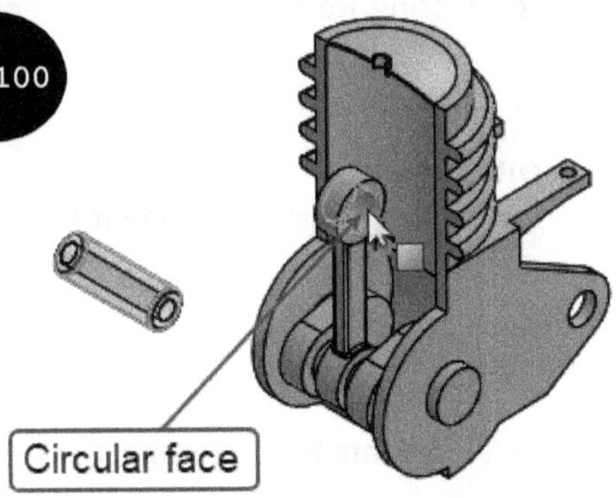

12.101

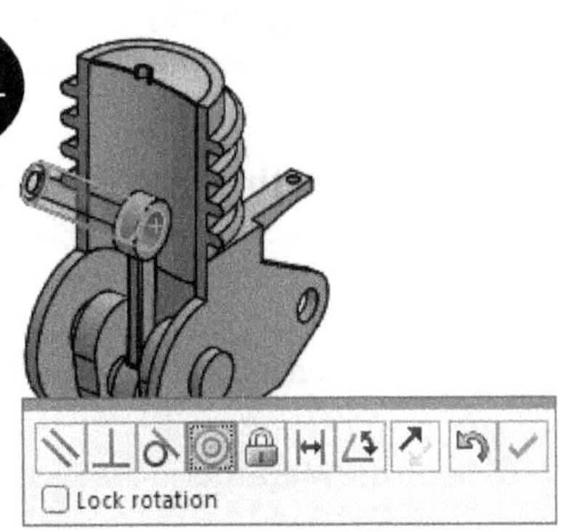

5. Click on the green tick-mark ✓ in the Pop-up toolbar. The concentric mate is applied between the selected faces of the components.

   Now, you need to fix the translational degree of freedom of the **Piston Pin** component.

6. Expand the FeatureManager Design Tree, which is now available in the top left corner of the graphics area, by clicking on the arrow in front of it.

7. Expand the **Connecting Rod** node in the FeatureManager Design Tree and then select its **Right Plane** as the first entity to apply the mate. The Right Plane gets selected, and the component (**Connecting Rod**) becomes transparent in the graphics area, see Figure 12.102.

   Now, you need to select an entity of the other component for applying the mate.

8. Expand the **Piston Pin** node in the FeatureManager Design Tree and then select its **Right Plane** as the second entity to apply the mate. A Pop-up toolbar appears with the **Coincident** tool activated in it, by default. Accordingly, the selected planes of the components become coincident with each other, see Figure 12.103.

12.102

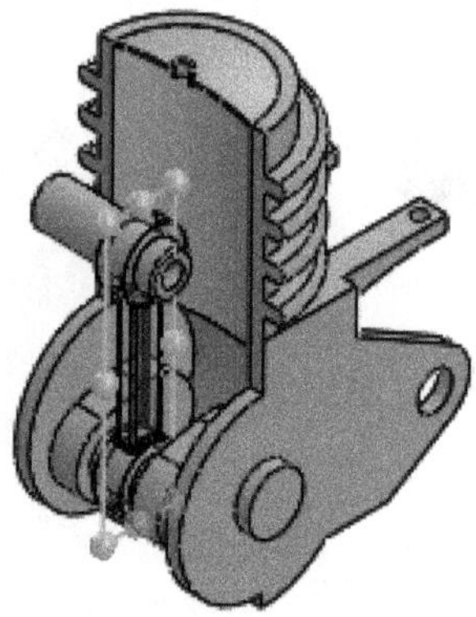

12.103

9. Click on the green tick-mark button in the Pop-up toolbar. The coincident mate is applied between the selected planes of the components. Next, exit the **Mate PropertyManager**.

Note: After applying the concentric and coincident mates, all degrees of freedom of the **Piston Pin** component get fixed with respect to the **Connecting Rod** component except one rotational degree of freedom.

Section 9: Inserting and Assembling the Fifth Component

1. Insert the fifth component (**Piston**) of the assembly by using the **Insert Component** tool of the **Assembly CommandManager**, see Figure 12.104.

   Now, you need to assemble the **Piston** component.

2. Click on the **Mate** tool in the **Assembly CommandManager**. The **Mate PropertyManager** appears.

3. Select the circular face of the hole of the fifth component (**Piston**) as the first entity to apply the mate, see Figure 12.105. The circular face gets selected, and the component becomes transparent in the graphics area.

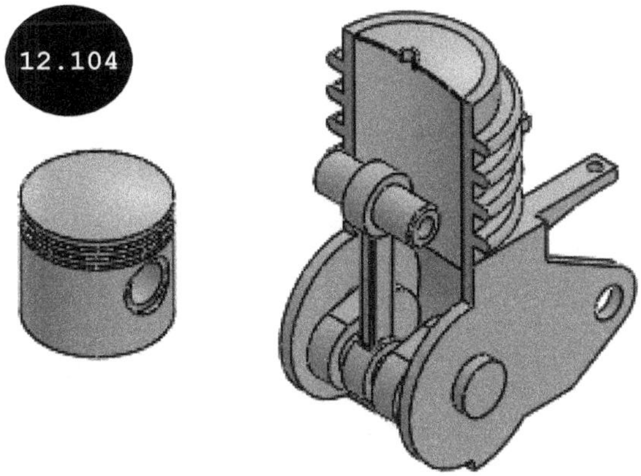
12.104

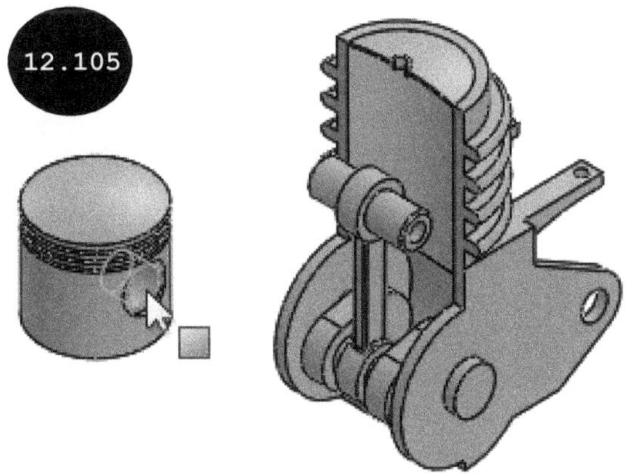
12.105

4. Select the outer circular face of the fourth component (**Piston Pin**) as the second entity to apply the mate, see Figure 12.106. A Pop-up toolbar appears with the **Concentric** tool activated in it. Accordingly, the selected faces of the components become concentric to each other, see Figure 12.107.

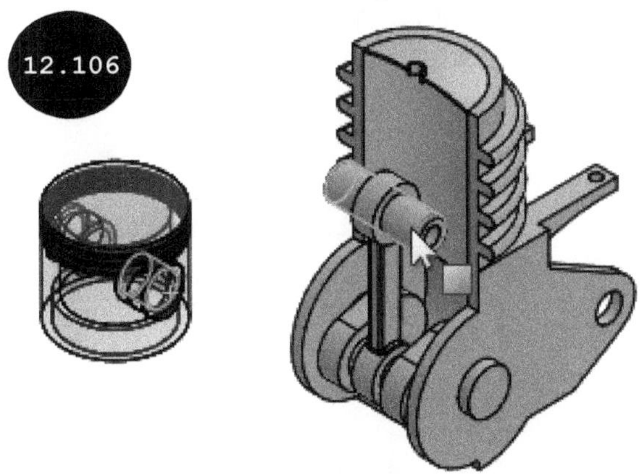
12.106

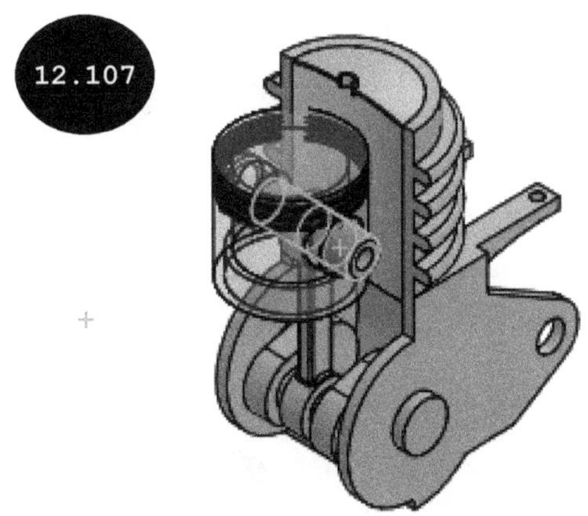
12.107

5. Click on the green tick-mark ✓ in the Pop-up toolbar. The concentric mate is applied between the selected faces of the components.

   Now, you need to fix the translational degree of freedom of the **Piston** component concerning the **Connecting Rod** component.

6. Select the planar face of the fifth component (**Piston**) as the first entity to apply the mate, see Figure 12.108. The planar face gets selected, and the fifth component (**Piston**) becomes transparent in the graphics area.

12.108

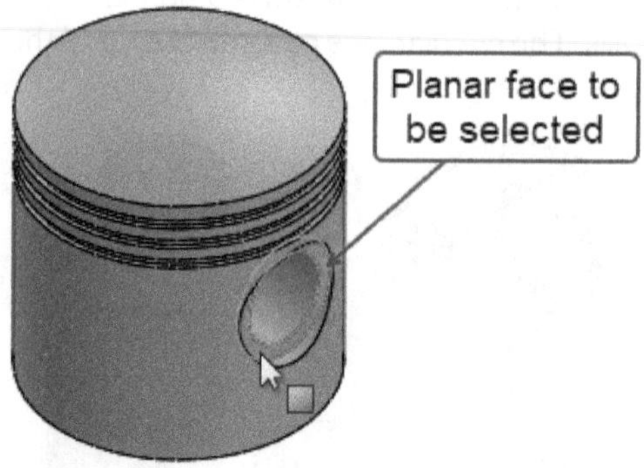

7. Select the end planar face of the fourth component (**Piston Pin**) as the second entity, see Figure 12.109. A Pop-up toolbar appears with the **Coincident** tool activated in it. Also, the selected faces of the components become coincident with each other, see Figure 12.110.

12.109

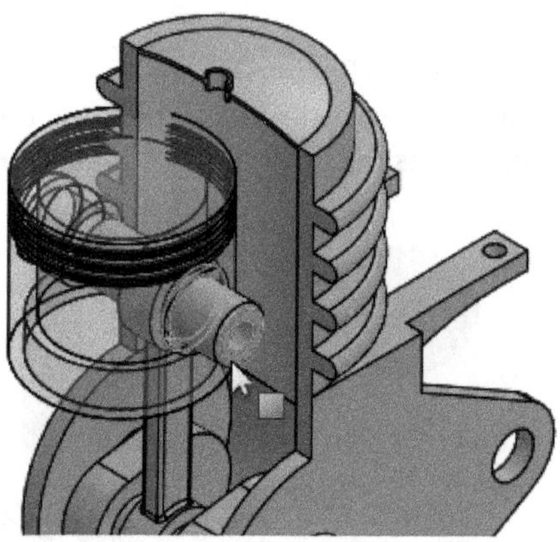

12.110

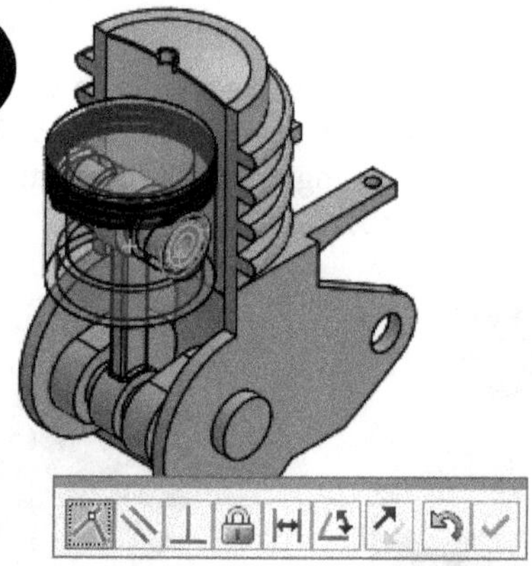

8. Click on the green tick-mark button in the Pop-up toolbar. The coincident mate is applied between the selected faces of the components, see Figure 12.111. Note that the **Mate PropertyManager** remains invoked.

12.111

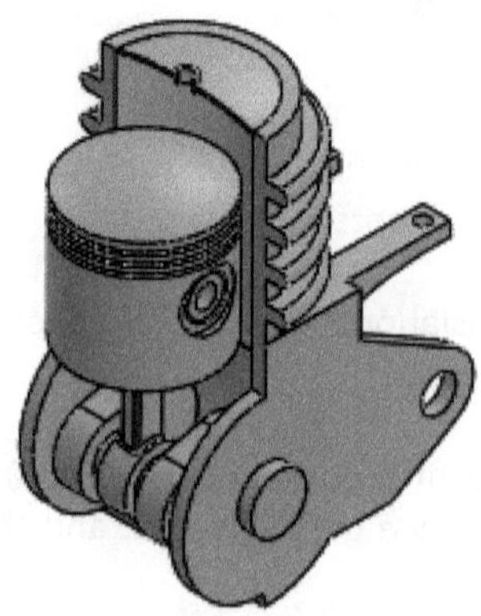

Now, you need to fix the rotational degree of freedom of the **Piston** such that it can only slide up and down when the **Crank Shaft** rotates about its axis, which is connected to the *Piston* through the **Connecting Rod**.

9. Select the outer circular face of the fifth component (**Piston**) as the first entity, see Figure 12.112.

12.112

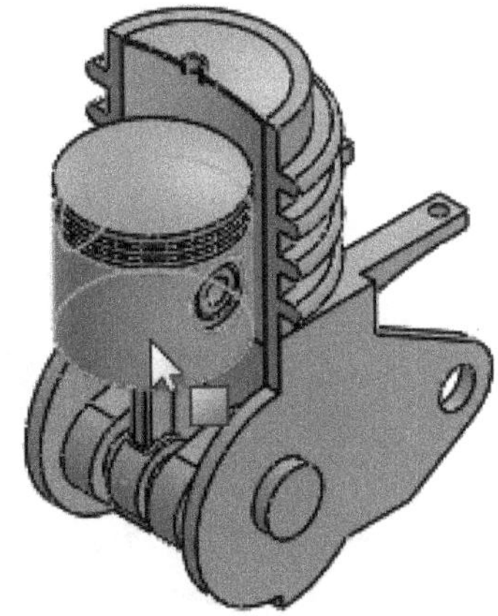

10. Select the inner circular face of the first component (**Crank Case**) as the second entity to apply the mate, see Figure 12.113. A Pop-up toolbar appears with the **Concentric** tool activated in it. Also, the selected faces of the components become concentric to each other, see Figure 12.114.

12.113

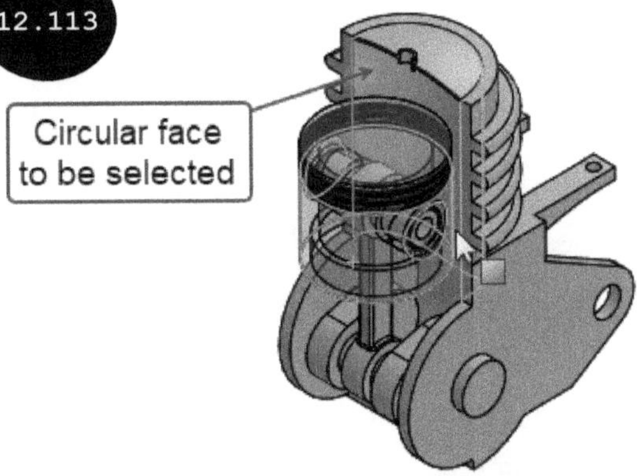

12.114

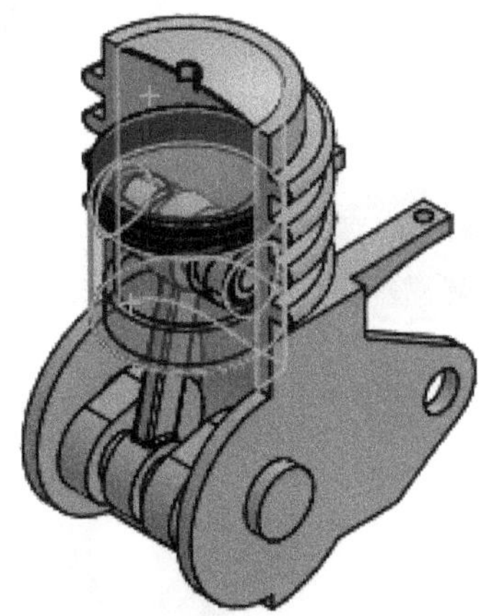

11. Click on the green tick-mark ✓ in the Pop-up toolbar. The concentric mate is applied between the selected faces of the components. Next, exit the **Mate PropertyManager**.

Tip: After creating the assembly, you can review its motion. To do this, drag the **Crank Shaft** component of the assembly by pressing and holding the left mouse button.

Section 10: Saving the Assembly

1. Click on the **Save** tool of the **Standard** toolbar. The **Save As** dialog box appears.

2. Browse to the Tutorial 1 folder of the Chapter 12 folder and then save the assembly with the name Tutorial 1.

Tutorial 2

Create the assembly, as shown in Figure 12.115. An exploded view of the assembly is shown in Figure 12.116 for your reference only. Different views and dimensions of individual components of the assembly are shown in Figures 12.117 through 12.125. All dimensions are in mm.

12.115

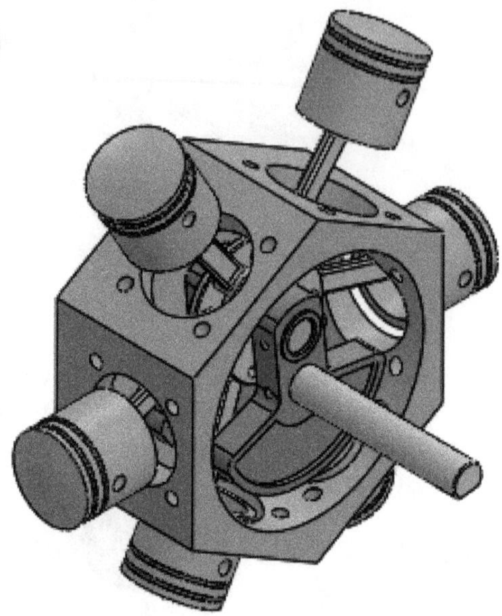

12.116

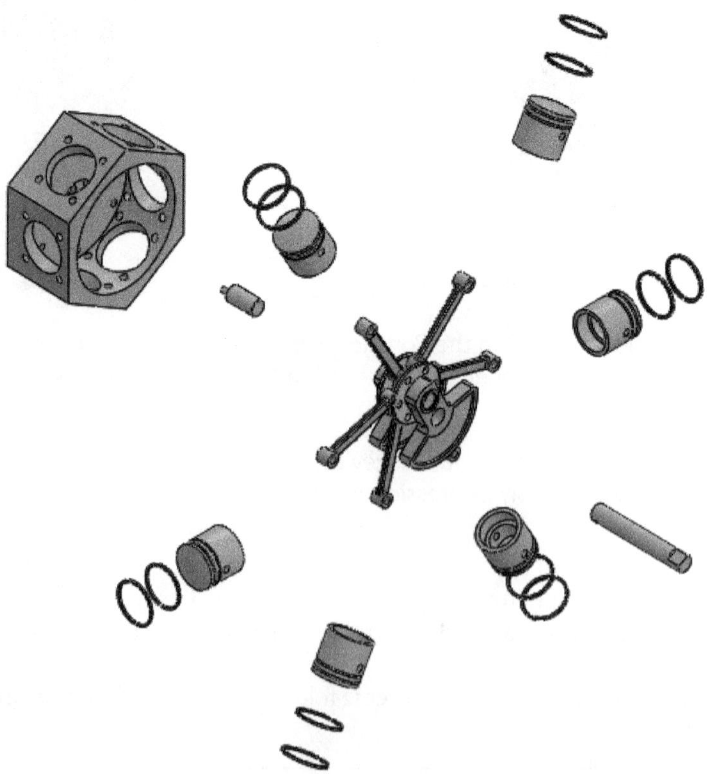

12.117

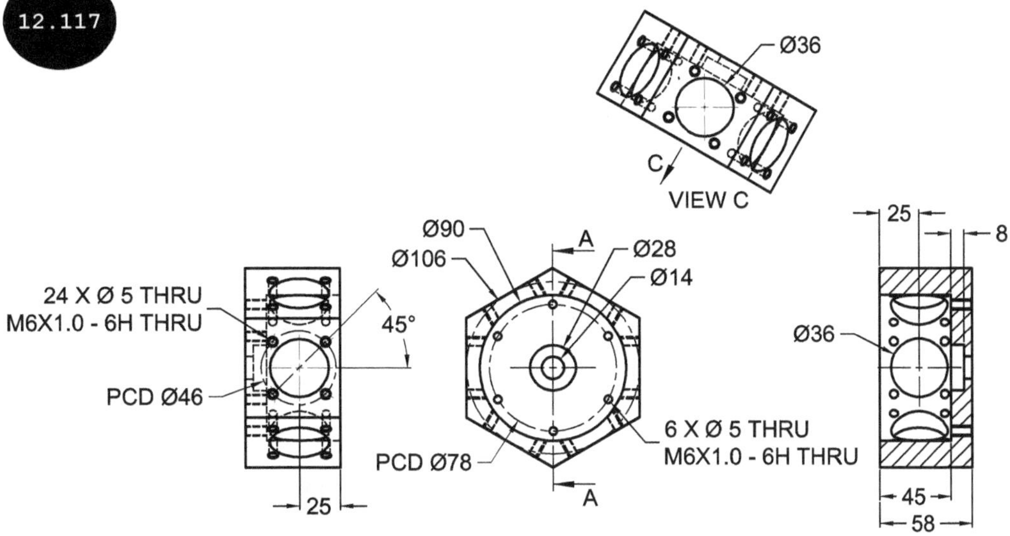

Crank Case

SECTION A-A

12.118

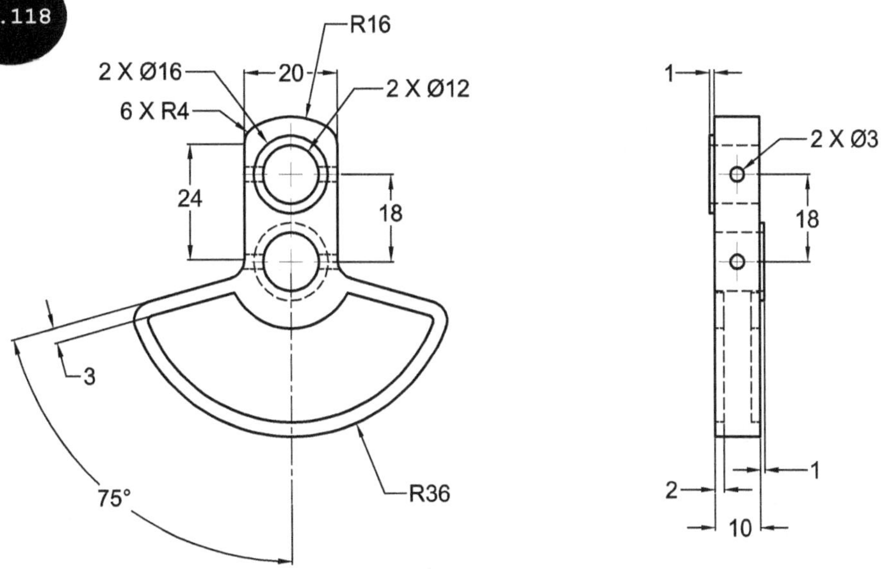

Crankshaft Counterweight

12.119

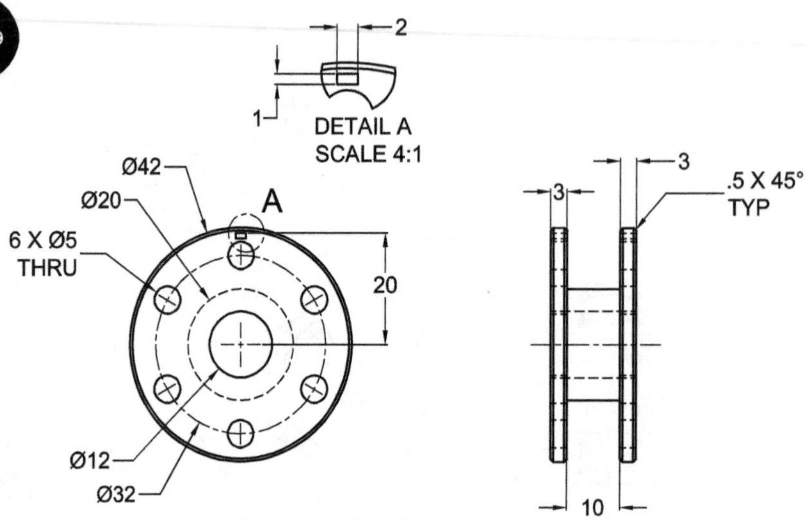

Connecting Rod Hub

12.120

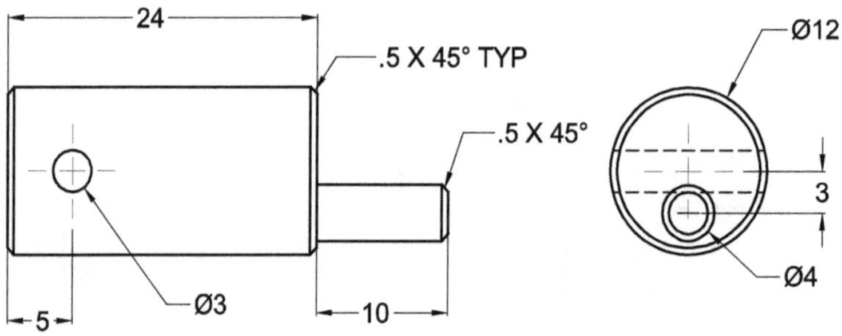

Crankshaft Valve Crank

12.121

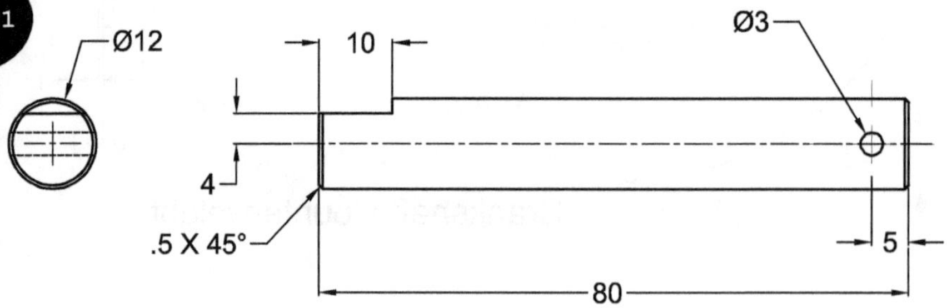

Crankshaft

12.122

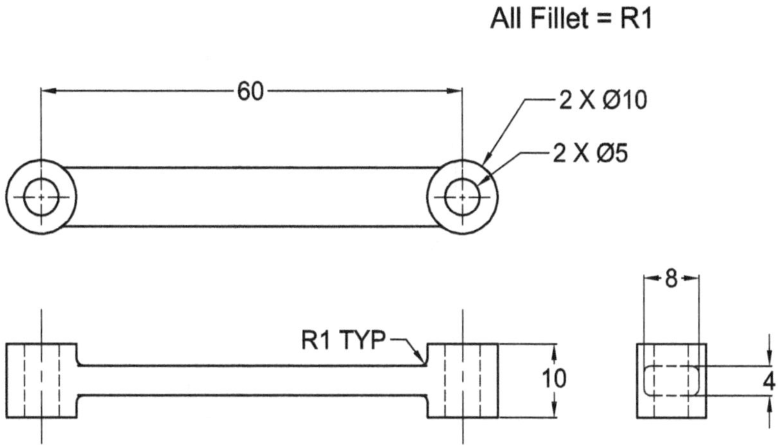

Connecting Rod

12.123

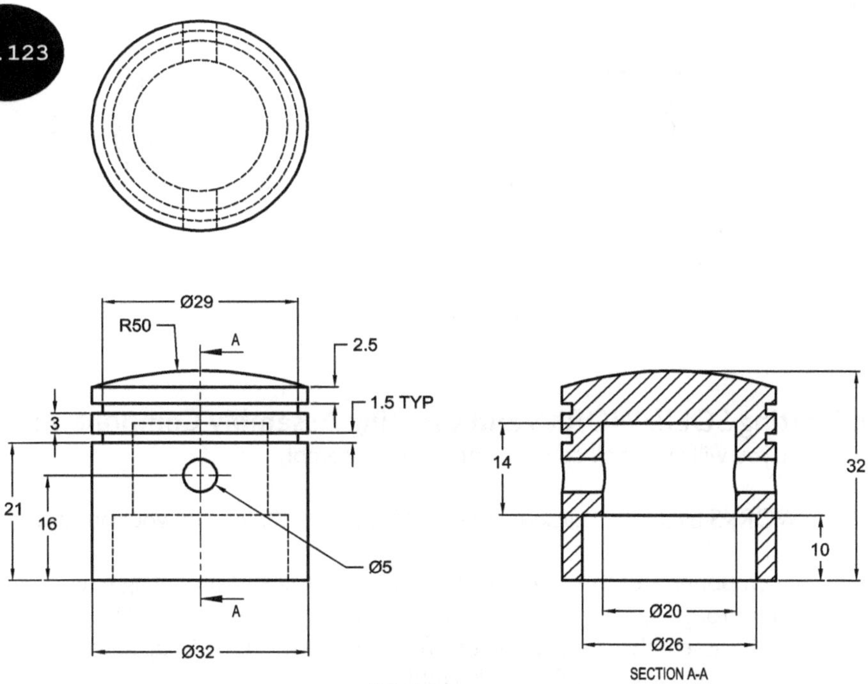

Piston

12.124

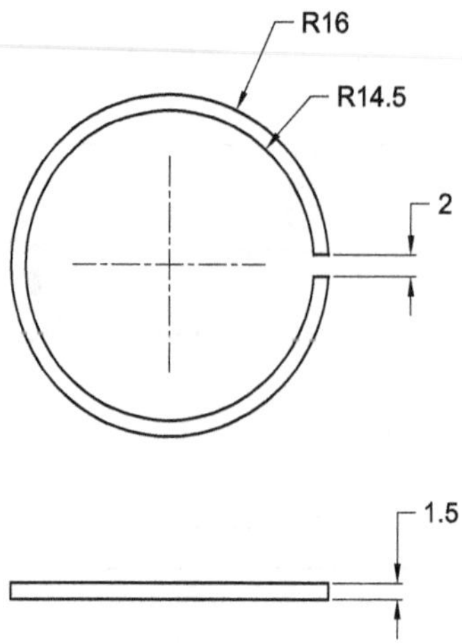

Piston Ring

12.125

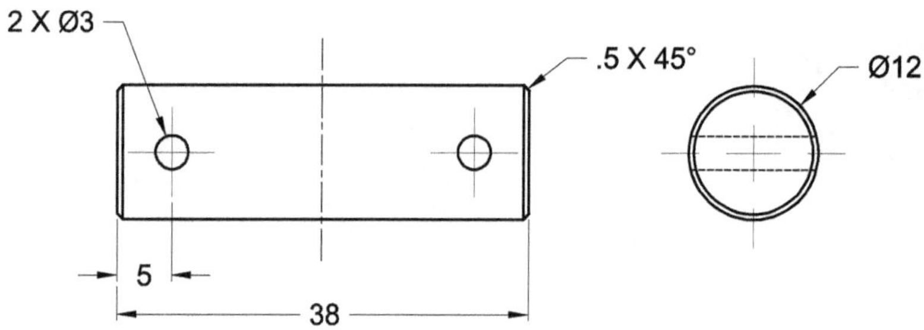

Crankshaft Pin

Section 1: Starting SOLIDWORKS and Creating Assembly Components

In this section, you will create all components of the assembly.

1. Start SOLIDWORKS by double-clicking on the SOLIDWORKS icon on your desktop.

2. Create all the components of the assembly one by one in the Part modeling environment. Refer to Figures 12.117 through 12.125 for the dimensions of each component. After creating all the components of the assembly, save them in the Tutorial 2 folder of the Chapter 12 folder. You need to create these folders in the SOLIDWORKS folder.

Note: You can also download all the components of the assembly by logging in to your account on CADArtifex website (***cadartifex.com/login***). If you are a new user, you need to first sign up on the website (***cadartifex.com/register***) to access the online resources.

Section 2: Invoking the Assembly Environment

1. Click on the **New** tool in the **Standard** toolbar. The **New SOLIDWORKS Document** dialog box appears.

2. Double-click on the **Assembly** button in the dialog box. The Assembly environment is invoked, and the **Open** dialog box appears along with the **Begin Assembly PropertyManager**, see Figure 12.126.

12.126

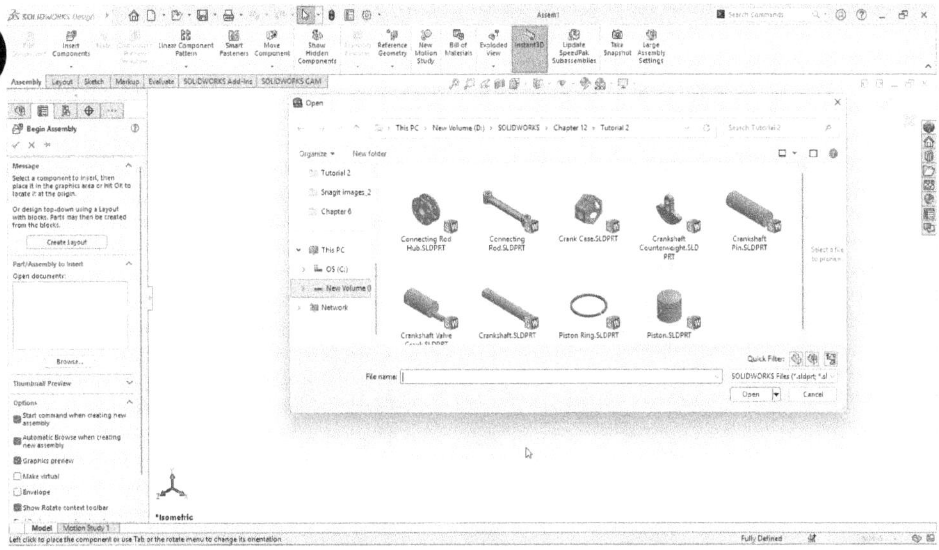

Note: On invoking the Assembly environment, the **Open** dialog box appears, automatically along with the **Begin Assembly PropertyManager**, if none of the components are opened in the current session of SOLIDWORKS. If the **Open** dialog box does not appear, then click on the **Browse** button in the **Begin Assembly PropertyManager** to open it.

Section 3: Creating the Piston Sub-Assembly

In this section, you will create the Piston sub-assembly.

1. Browse to the Tutorial 2 folder of the Chapter 12 folder in the **Open** dialog box, where all the components of the assembly have been saved.

2. Select the first component (**Piston**) and then click on the **Open** button in the dialog box. The first component (**Piston**) is attached to the cursor. Also, the **Rotate Context** toolbar appears in the graphics area.

3. Click anywhere in the graphics area. The first component (**Piston**) moves toward the origin of the assembly and becomes the fixed component automatically, see Figure 12.127.

12.127

Now, you need to insert the second component of the Piston sub-assembly.

4. Click on the **Insert Components** tool in the **Assembly CommandManager**. The **Open** dialog box appears along with the **Insert Component PropertyManager**. If the **Open** dialog box does not appear automatically, then click on the **Browse** button in the **Insert Component PropertyManager** to open the **Open** dialog box.

5. Browse to the location where all components of the assembly have been saved and then select the second component (**Piston Ring**). Next, click on the **Open** button in the dialog box. The second component (**Piston Ring**) gets attached to the cursor.

6. Click anywhere in the graphics area to specify the placement point of the second component (**Piston Ring**). The component (**Piston Ring**) is placed in the graphics area, see Figure 12.128. Ensure that you specify the placement point such that the component does not intersect with the first component of the assembly.

12.128

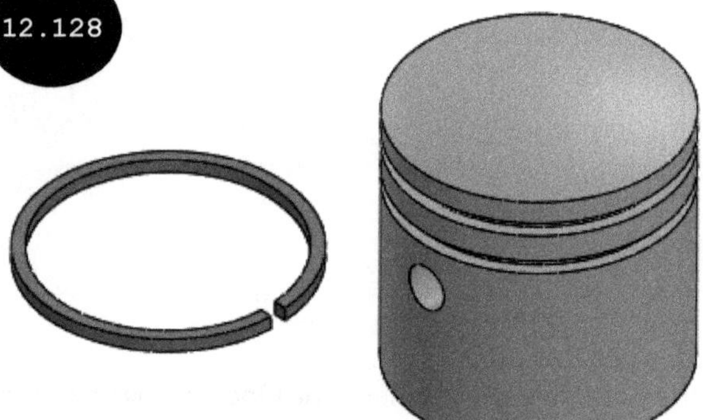

Note: By default, all degrees of freedom of the second component are free, which means that the second component is free to translate and rotate along and about its axis. You need to apply the mates to fix its required degrees of freedom with respect to the first component of the assembly.

Now, you need to assemble the second component (**Piston Ring**) with the first component (**Piston**) by applying the required mates between them.

7. Click on the **Mate** tool in the **Assembly CommandManager**. The **Mate PropertyManager** appears.

8. Select the bottom planar face of the second component (**Piston Ring**) as the first entity to apply the mate, see Figure 12.129. The bottom face of the component (**Piston Ring**) is selected, and the component becomes transparent in the graphics area. Note that to select the bottom face of the second component (**Piston Ring**), you need to rotate the assembly. After selecting the face, you can change the orientation of the assembly back to isometric.

Tip: To select the bottom face of the second component (**Piston Ring**) for applying the mate, you can also hover the cursor over the top planar face of the second component (**Piston Ring**) and then press the ALT key to hide it temporarily and then select its bottom planar face.

9. Select the planar face of the first component (**Piston**) (see Figure 12.130) as the second entity to apply the mate. A Pop-up toolbar appears with the **Coincident** tool activated in it, by default. Accordingly, the selected faces of the components become coincident with each other.

12.129

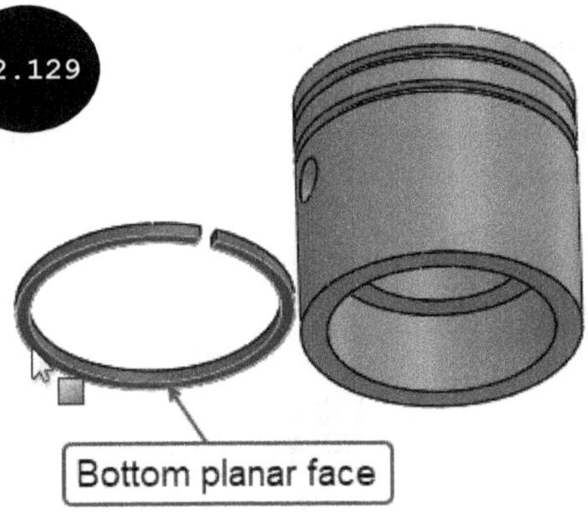

12.130

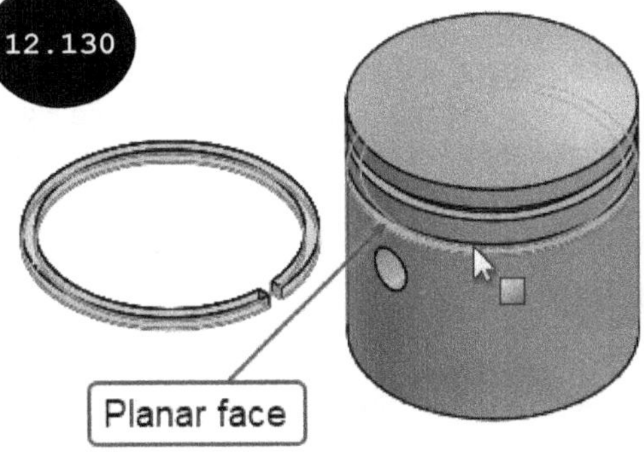

10. Click on the green tick-mark ✓ in the Pop-up toolbar. The coincident mate is applied between the selected faces of the components.

11. Select the inner circular face of the second component (**Piston Ring**) as the first entity to apply the mate, see Figure 12.131.

12. Select the outer cylindrical face of the first component (**Piston**) as the second entity to apply the mate, see Figure 12.132. A Pop-up toolbar appears with the **Concentric** tool activated in it. Accordingly, the selected faces of the components become concentric to each other.

12.131

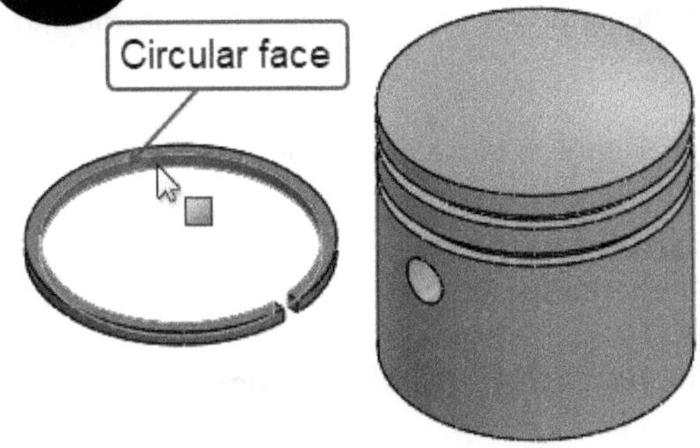

12.132

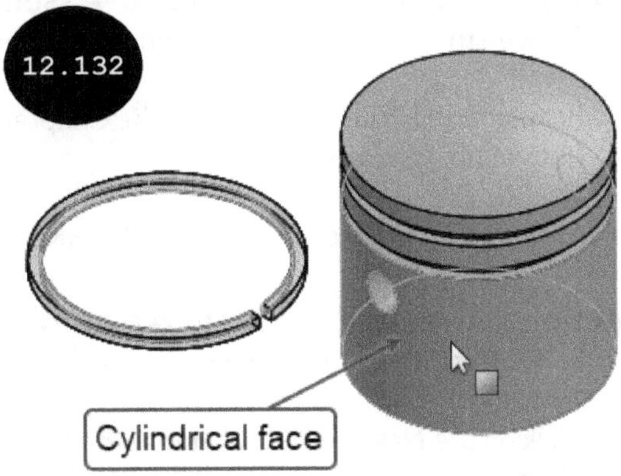

13. Click on the green tick-mark ✓ in the Pop-up toolbar. The concentric mate is applied between the selected faces of the components. Next, exit the **Mate PropertyManager**.

Now, you need to insert the second instance of the **Piston Ring** component.

14. Move the cursor over the name of the second component (**Piston Ring**) in the FeatureManager Design Tree and then press and hold the left mouse button and the CTRL key. Next, drag the cursor toward the graphics area. The second instance of the **Piston Ring** component appears attached to the cursor in the graphics area, see Figure 12.133.

15. Release the left mouse button and then the CTRL key. The second instance of the **Piston Ring** component is inserted in the Assembly environment.

16. Invoke the **Mate PropertyManager** and then assemble the second instance of the **Piston Ring** component with the first component (**Piston**) by applying the coincident and concentric mates between them, as discussed earlier, see Figure 12.134. After assembling the second instance of the **Piston Ring** component, exit the **Mate PropertyManager**.

12.133

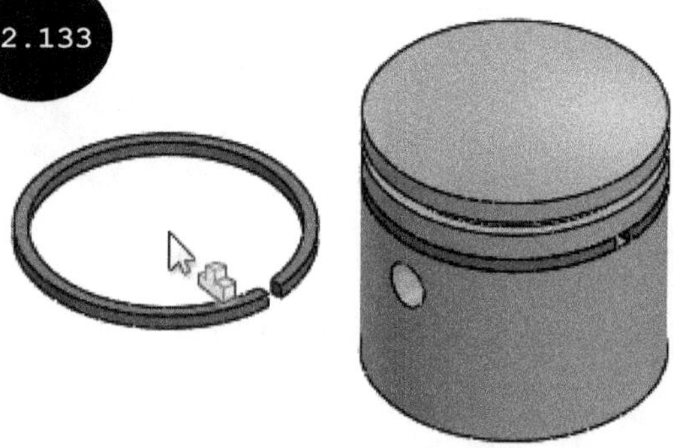

12.134

Note: You can also insert the second instance of a component by using the **Insert Components** tool of the **Assembly CommandManager**.

Section 4: Saving the Piston Sub-Assembly

1. Click on the **Save** tool in the **Standard** toolbar. The **Save As** dialog box appears.

2. Browse to the Tutorial 2 folder of the Chapter 12 folder and then save the assembly with the name Piston Sub-Assembly.

3. Click on **File > Close** in the SOLIDWORKS Design Menus to close the Piston Sub-Assembly.

Section 5: Creating the Main Assembly - Radial Engine

In this section, you need to create the main assembly (**Radial Engine**).

1. Click on the **New** tool in the **Standard** toolbar. The **New SOLIDWORKS Document** dialog box appears.

2. Double-click on the **Assembly** button in the dialog box. The Assembly environment is invoked, and the **Open** dialog box appears along with the **Begin Assembly PropertyManager**. If the **Open**

dialog box does not appear automatically, then click on the **Browse** button in the **Begin Assembly PropertyManager** to open the **Open** dialog box.

3. Select the first component (**Crank Case**) of the main assembly (**Radial Engine**) and then click on the **Open** button in the dialog box. The first component (**Crank Case**) gets attached to the cursor. Also, the **Rotate Context** toolbar appears in the graphics area.

12.135

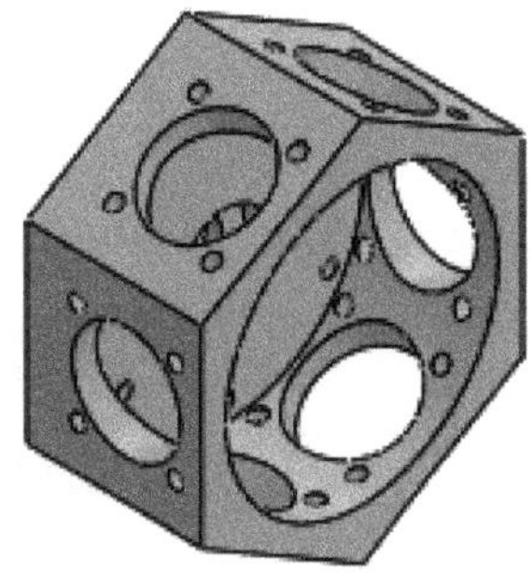

4. Click anywhere in the graphics area. The first component (**Crank Case**) moves toward the origin of the assembly and becomes the fixed component, see Figure 12.135.

Section 6: Inserting and Assembling the Second Component

Now, you need to insert the second component (**Crankshaft Valve Crank**) of the main assembly (**Radial Engine**) in the Assembly environment.

1. Click on the **Insert Components** tool in the **Assembly CommandManager**. The **Open** dialog box appears along with the **Insert Component PropertyManager**. If the **Open** dialog box does not appear automatically, then click on the **Browse** button in the PropertyManager to open the **Open** dialog box.

2. Select the second component (**Crankshaft Valve Crank**) and then click on the **Open** button. The second component (**Crankshaft Valve Crank**) gets attached to the cursor, see Figure 12.136. Also, the **Rotate Context** toolbar appears in the graphics area.

3. Enter **180** in the **Angle** field in the **Rotate Context** toolbar and then click on the **Y** tool in the **Rotate Context** toolbar. The orientation of the component is changed similar to the one shown in Figure 12.137.

12.136

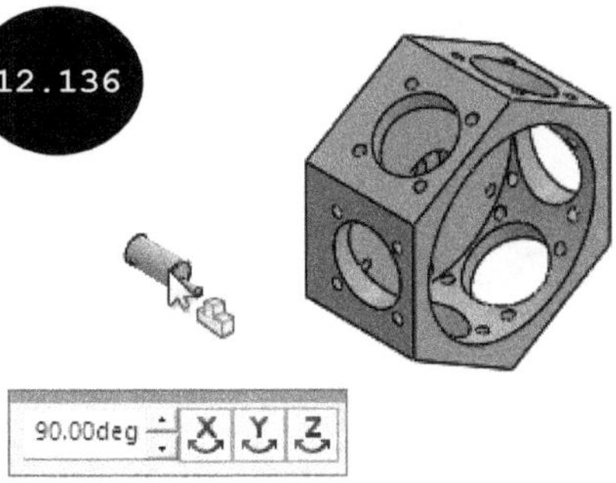

12.137

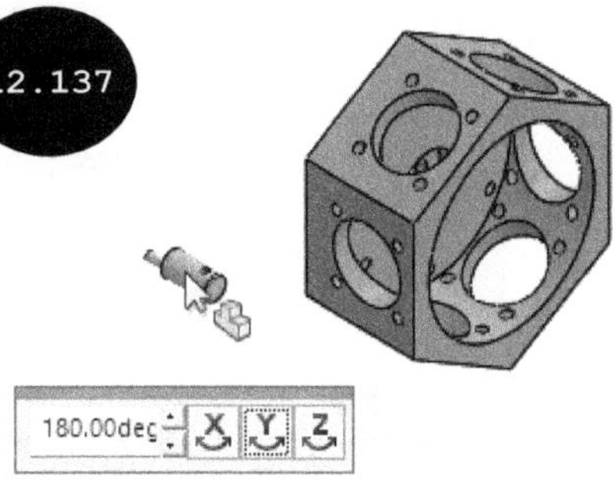

4. Click anywhere in the graphics area. The second component (**Crankshaft Valve Crank**) is placed in the specified location.

Now, you need to assemble the second component (**Crankshaft Valve Crank**) with the first component of the assembly.

5. Invoke the **Mate PropertyManager**. Next, select the circular face of the second component (**Crankshaft Valve Crank**) and the circular face of the hole of the first component (**Crank Case**), (see Figure 12.138) to apply the concentric mate. A Pop-up toolbar appears with the **Concentric** tool activated in it. Note that to select the faces of the components, you need to rotate the assembly such that the faces can be viewed.

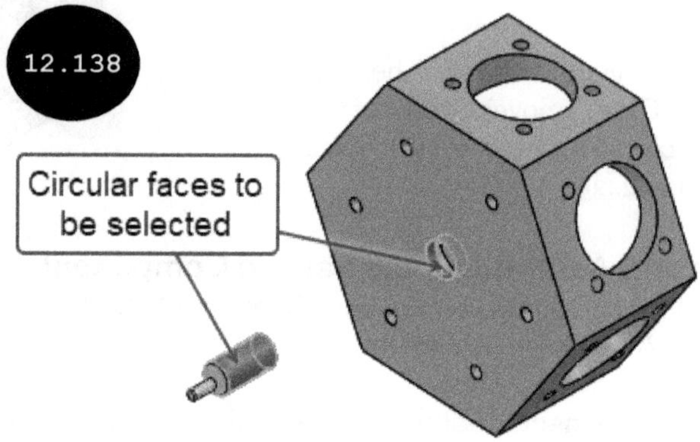

6. Click on the green tick-mark ✓ in the Pop-up toolbar. The concentric mate is applied between the selected faces of the components.

7. Select the planar face of the second component (**Crankshaft Valve Crank**) and the planar face of the first component (**Crank Case**), see Figure 12.139. A Pop-up toolbar appears with the **Coincident** tool activated in it.

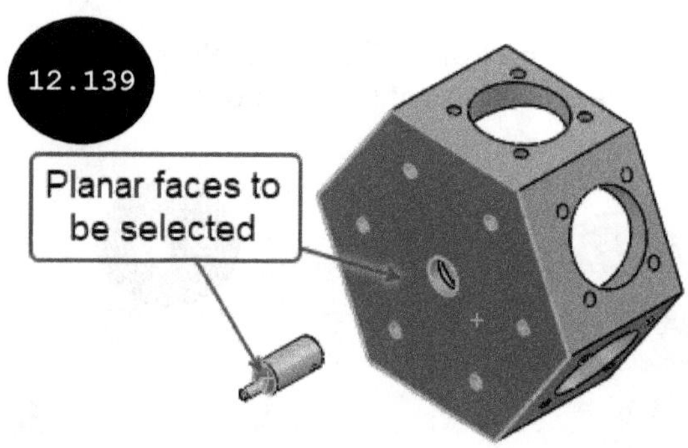

8. Click on the green tick-mark ✓ in the Pop-up toolbar. The coincident mate is applied between the selected faces of the components.

9. Exit the **Mate PropertyManager** and then change the orientation of the assembly to isometric.

Section 7: Inserting and Assembling the Third Component

1. Insert the third component (**Crankshaft Counterweight**) in the Assembly environment by using the **Insert Components** tool, see Figure 12.140.

2. Hide the first component (**Crank Case**) so that you can easily select the faces of the other components for applying mates, see Figure 12.141. To hide the first component (**Crank Case**), click on it in the graphics area. A Pop-up toolbar appears. In this Pop-up toolbar, click on the **Hide Components** tool .

12.140

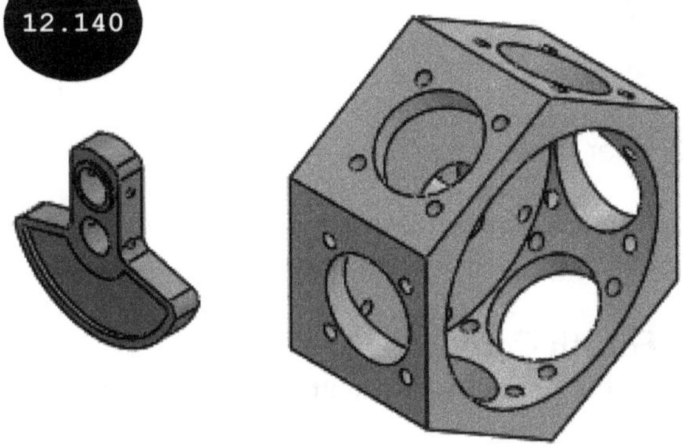

12.141

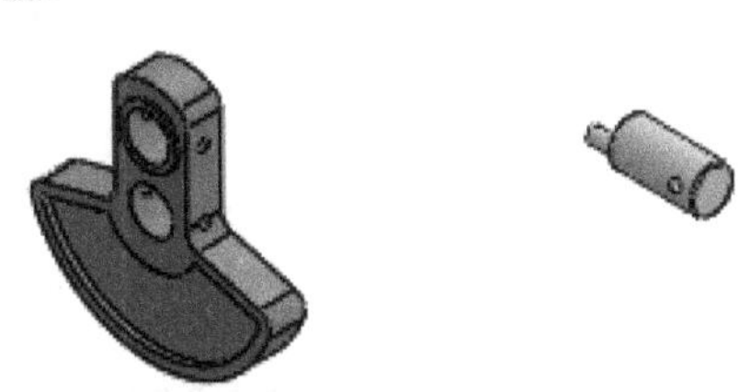

Now, you need to assemble the third component (**Crankshaft Counterweight**).

3. Invoke the **Mate PropertyManager** and then select the outer circular face of the second component (**Crankshaft Valve Crank**) and the inner circular face of the third component (**Crankshaft Counterweight**) as the entities to apply the mate, see Figure 12.142. A Pop-up toolbar appears with the **Concentric** tool activated in it, by default. Accordingly, the selected faces of the components become concentric to each other in the graphics area, see Figure 12.143.

4. Click on the **Flip Mate Alignment** tool in the Pop-up toolbar, if the alignment of the third component (**Crankshaft Counterweight**) does not appear similar to the one shown in Figure 12.143.

12.142

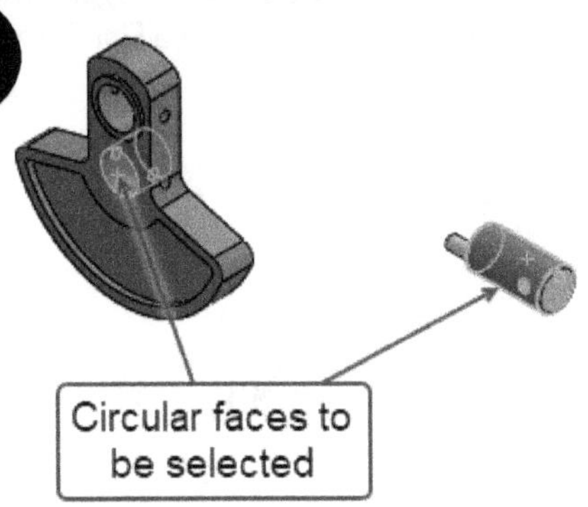

12.143

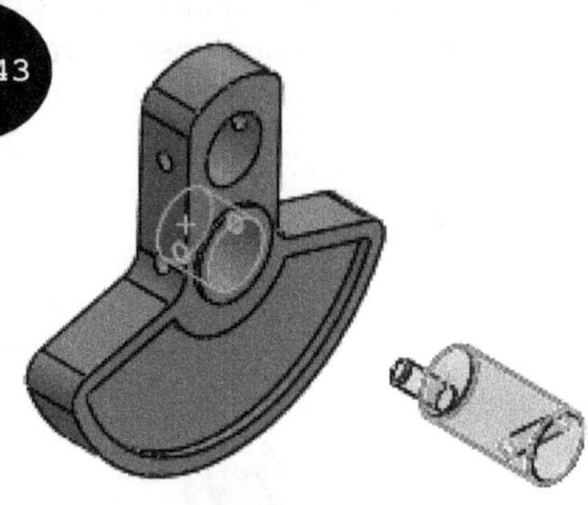

5. Click on the green tick-mark ✓ in the Pop-up toolbar. The concentric mate is applied between the selected faces of the components.

6. Select the circular face of the hole of the third component (**Crankshaft Counterweight**) and the circular face of the hole of the second component (**Crankshaft Valve Crank**), see Figure 12.144. A Pop-up toolbar appears with the **Concentric** tool activated in it.

12.144

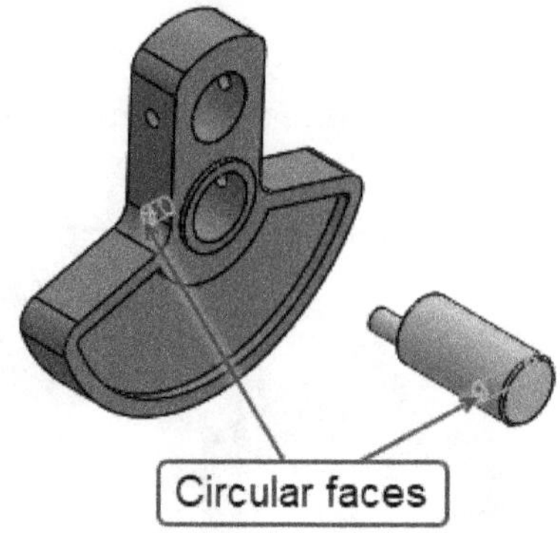

7. Click on the green tick-mark ✓ in the Pop-up toolbar. The concentric mate is applied between the selected faces of the components, see Figure 12.145. Next, exit the **Mate PropertyManager**.

Section 8: Inserting and Assembling the Fourth Component

1. Insert the fourth component (**Crankshaft Pin**) in the Assembly environment by using the **Insert Components** tool, see Figure 12.146.

12.145

12.146

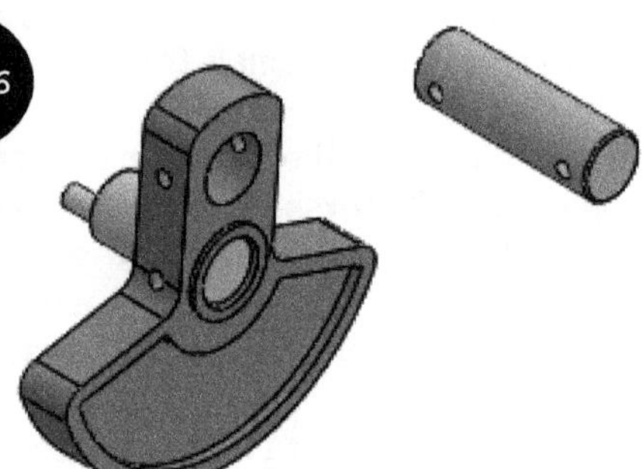

2. Select the inner circular face of the third component (**Crankshaft Counterweight**) and the circular face of the fourth component (**Crankshaft Pin**) by pressing the CTRL key, see Figure 12.147. Next, release the CTRL key. A Pop-up toolbar appears, see Figure 12.147.

12.147

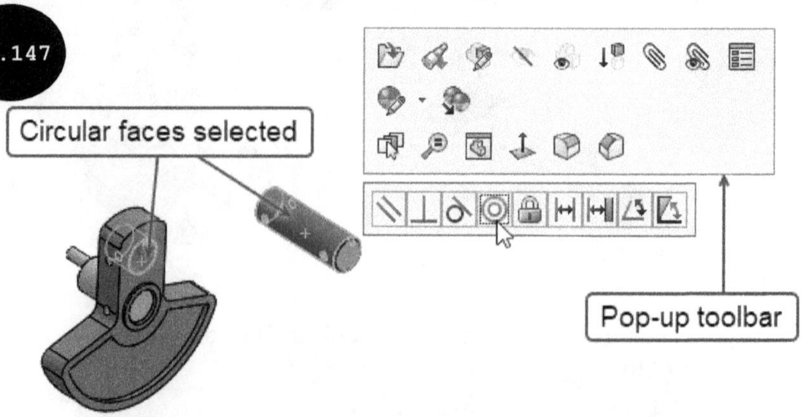

3. Click on the **Concentric** tool in the Pop-up toolbar, see Figure 12.147. The selected faces of the components become concentric to each other.

4. Similarly, select the circular face of the hole of the third component (**Crankshaft Counterweight**) and the circular face of the hole of the fourth component (**Crankshaft Pin**) by pressing the CTRL key, see Figure 12.148. Next, release the CTRL key. A Pop-up toolbar appears.

12.148

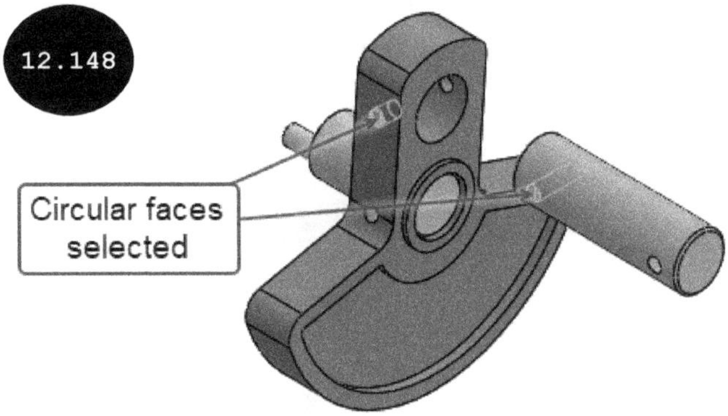

Tip: You can press the ALT key to temporarily hide faces of the assembly components to select an obscured face of a component to apply a mate.

Besides, you may need to move components to select their faces for applying mates. To move a component, press and hold the left mouse button over the component to be moved and then drag the cursor.

5. Click on the **Concentric** tool in the Pop-up toolbar. The selected faces of the components become concentric to each other.

Section 9: Inserting and Assembling the Fifth Component

1. Insert the fifth component (**Crankshaft Counterweight**) in the Assembly environment by using the **Insert Components** tool, see Figure 12.149.

2. Invoke the **Mate PropertyManager** and then assemble the fifth component (**Crankshaft Counterweight**) with the fourth component (**Crankshaft Pin**) by applying two concentric mates, see Figure 12.150. After applying the mates, exit the **Mate PropertyManager**.

12.149

12.150

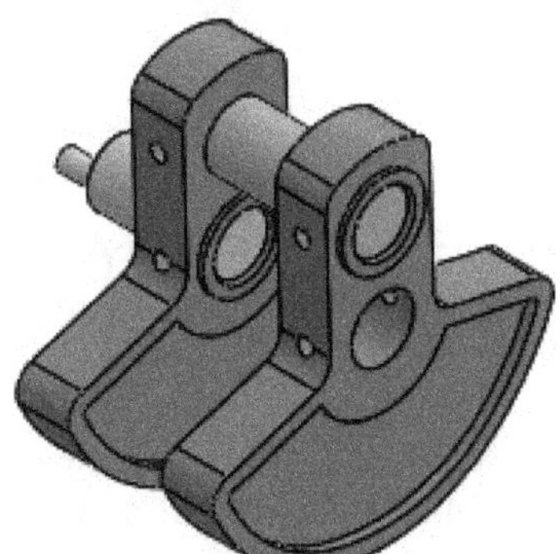

Section 10: Inserting and Assembling the Sixth Component

1. Insert the sixth component (**Crankshaft**) in the Assembly environment, see Figure 12.151. You need to change the orientation of the component (**Crankshaft**) similar to the one shown in Figure 12.151 by using the **Rotate Context** toolbar.

2. Invoke the **Mate PropertyManager**. Next, select the circular face of the sixth component (**Crankshaft**) and the inner circular face of the bottom hole of the fifth component (**Crankshaft Counterweight**) as the entities to apply the mate, see Figure 12.152. A Pop-up toolbar appears with the **Concentric** tool activated in it and the selected faces of the components become concentric to each other, see Figure 12.152.

12.151

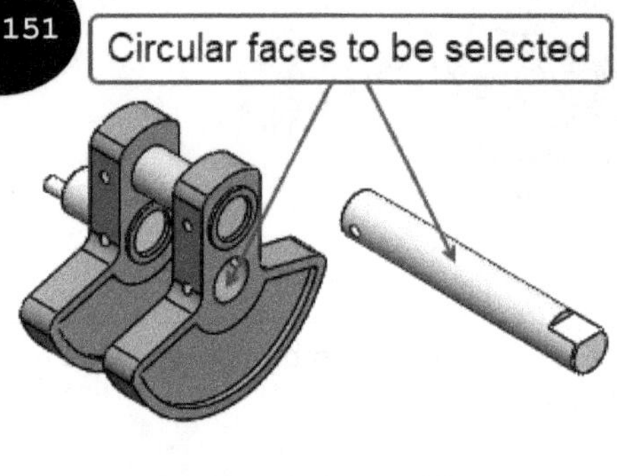

12.152

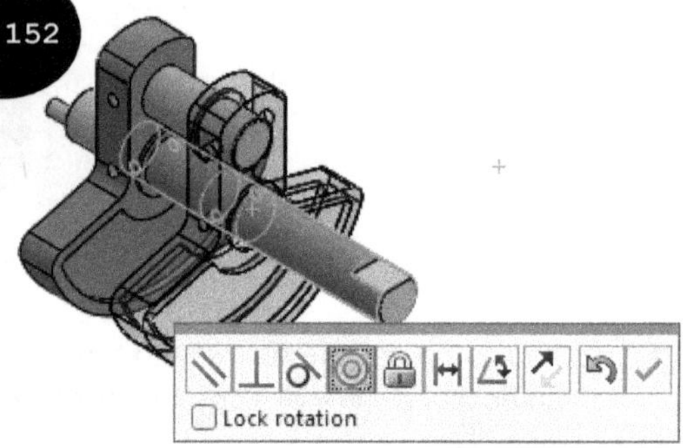

3. Click on the green tick-mark ✓ in the Pop-up toolbar. The concentric mate is applied between the selected faces of the components.

4. Similarly, apply the concentric mate between the circular face of the hole of the fifth component (**Crankshaft Counterweight**) and the circular face of the hole of the sixth component (**Crankshaft**), see Figure 12.153. After applying the mate, exit the **Mate PropertyManager**.

12.153

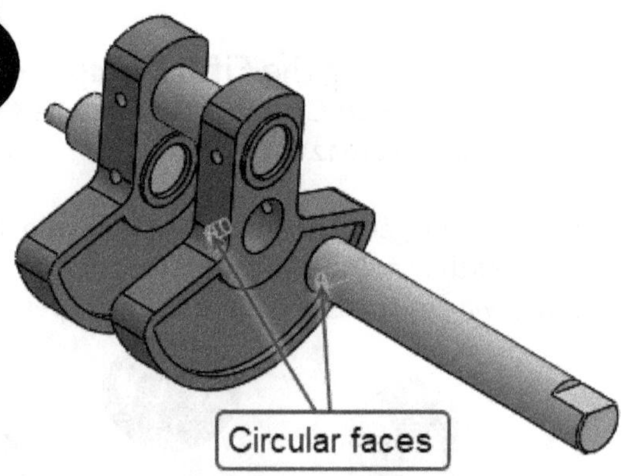

Section 11: Inserting and Assembling the Seventh Component

1. Insert the seventh component (**Connecting Rod Hub**) in the Assembly environment by using the **Insert Components** tool, see Figure 12.154.

2. Invoke the **Mate PropertyManager**. Next, select the inner circular face of the seventh component (**Connecting Rod Hub**) and the circular face of the fourth component (**Crankshaft Pin**), see Figure 12.155. A Pop-up toolbar appears with the **Concentric** tool activated in it.

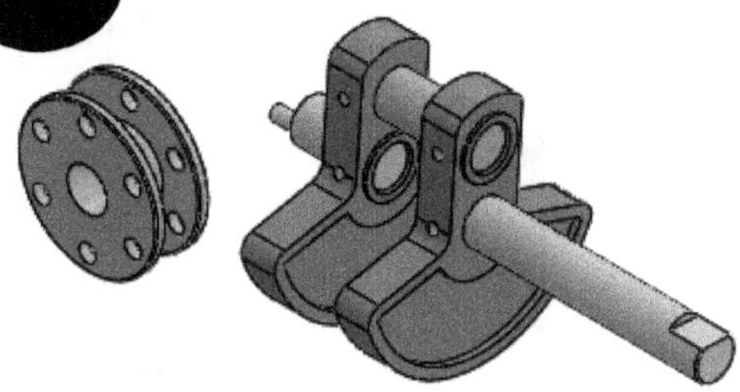
12.154

12.155

3. Click on the green tick-mark ✓ in the Pop-up toolbar. The concentric mate is applied between the selected faces of the components.

4. Select the back planar face of the seventh component (**Connecting Rod Hub**) and the front planar face of the third component (**Crankshaft Counterweight**) as the entities to apply the mate, see Figure 12.156. A Pop-up toolbar appears with the **Coincident** tool activated in it.

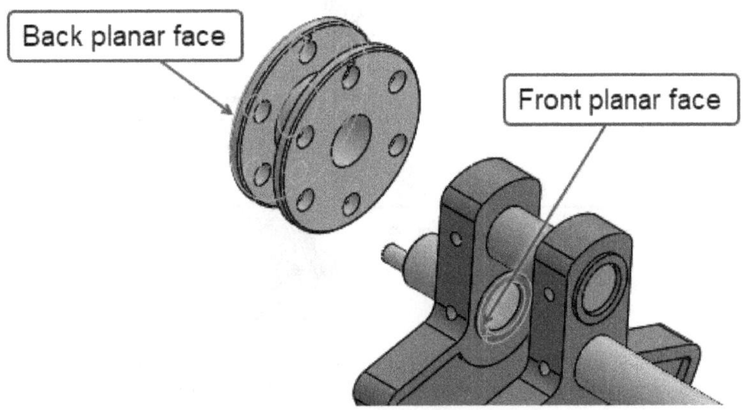

12.156

5. Click on the green tick-mark ✓ in the Pop-up toolbar. The coincident mate is applied between the selected faces of the components. Next, exit the **Mate PropertyManager**.

Section 12: Inserting and Assembling the Eighth Component

1. Insert the eighth component (**Connecting Rod**) in the Assembly environment, see Figure 12.157. Note that you need to change the orientation of the eighth component (**Connecting Rod**) similar to the one shown in Figure 12.157 by using the **Rotate Context** toolbar.

2. Invoke the **Mate PropertyManager**. Next, select the circular face of the bottom hole of the eighth component (**Connecting Rod**) and the circular face of a hole of the seventh component (**Connecting Rod Hub**) as the entities to apply the mate, see Figure 12.158. The Pop-up toolbar appears with the **Concentric** tool activated in it.

12.157

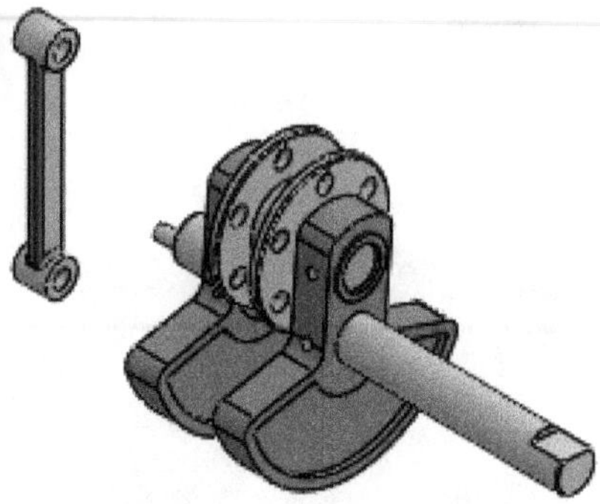

12.158

3. Click on the green tick-mark ✓ in the Pop-up toolbar. The concentric mate is applied between the selected faces of the components.

4. Select the back planar face of the eighth component (**Connecting Rod**) and the inner planar face of the seventh component (**Connecting Rod Hub**), see Figure 12.159. A Pop-up toolbar appears with the **Coincident** tool activated in it.

12.159

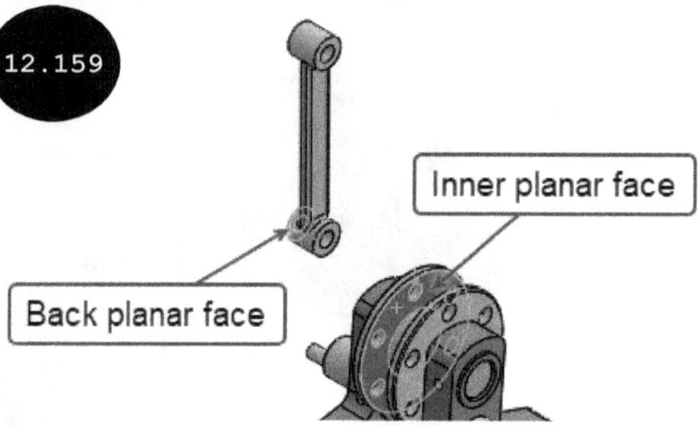

5. Click on the green tick-mark ✓ in the Pop-up toolbar. The coincident mate is applied between the selected faces of the components, see Figure 12.160. Next, exit the PropertyManager.

Section 13: Inserting and Assembling the Remaining Connecting Rods

1. Insert and assemble five more instances of the **Connecting Rod** component with the remaining holes of the seventh component (**Connecting Rod Hub**) as discussed earlier, see Figure 12.161.

12.160

12.161

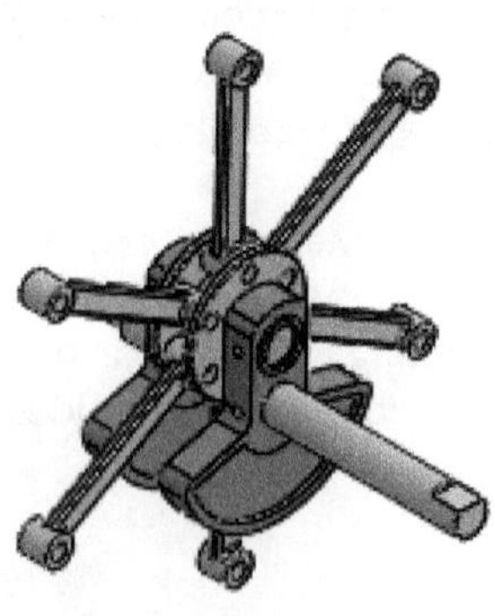

Note: To arrange the **Connecting Rod** components similar to the one shown in Figure 12.161, you need to fix the seventh component (**Connecting Rod Hub**). To do this, right-click on the seventh component (**Connecting Rod Hub**) in the graphics area. A shortcut menu appears. Next, click on the **Fix** option in the shortcut menu. Once the seventh component (**Connecting Rod Hub**) has been fixed, you can arrange the **Connecting Rod** components one by one by dragging them. After arranging the **Connecting Rod** components, you need to make the seventh component (**Connecting Rod Hub**) a floating component again. To do this, right-click on the seventh component (**Connecting Rod Hub**) in the graphics area and then click on the **Float** option in the shortcut menu that appears.

Section 14: Inserting and Assembling Piston Sub-Assembly

1. Insert the **Piston Sub-Assembly** in the Assembly environment by using the **Insert Components** tool, see Figure 12.162.

12.162

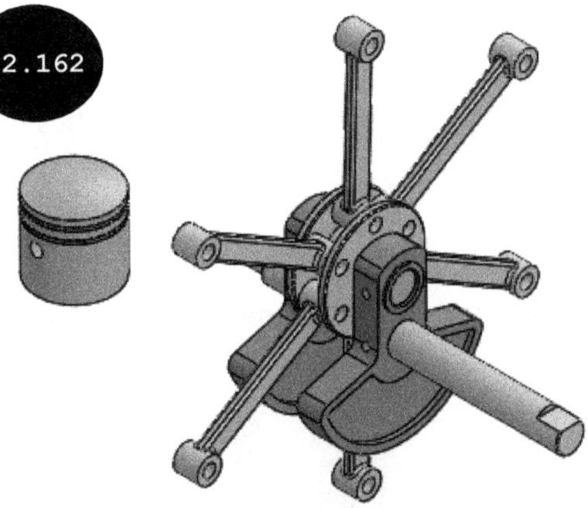

Tip: When you insert a sub-assembly in the Assembly environment, the sub-assembly becomes rigid and acts as a single component in the Assembly environment. You can change a rigid sub-assembly to a flexible sub-assembly, whose all components are free to move individually in their free degrees of freedom. To do this, click on a rigid sub-assembly in the FeatureManager Design Tree. A Pop-up toolbar appears. In this Pop-up toolbar, click on the **Component Properties** tool. The **Component Properties** dialog box appears. In this dialog box, select the **Flexible** radio button in the **Solve as** area of the dialog box. Next, click the **OK** button.

2. Invoke the **Mate PropertyManager**. Next, select the inner circular face of the hole of the **Piston Sub-Assembly** and the inner circular face of the upper hole of a **Connecting Rod** component as the entities to apply the mate, see Figure 12.163. A Pop-up toolbar appears with the **Concentric** tool activated in it.

12.163

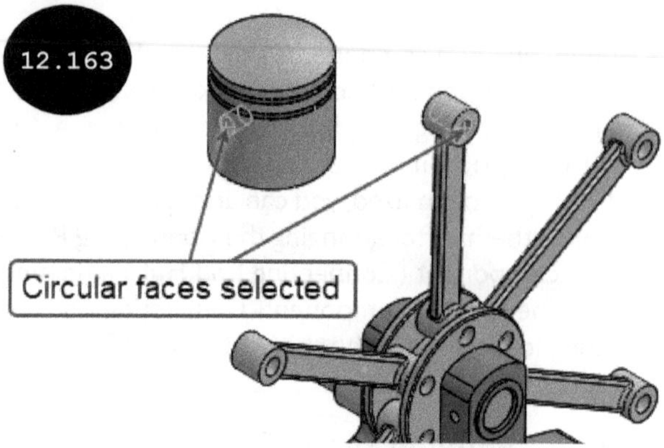

3. Click on the green tick-mark ✓ in the Pop-up toolbar. The concentric mate is applied between the selected faces of the components.

4. Click on the **Advanced** tab in the **Mate PropertyManager** for applying an advanced mate. Next, click on the **Width** button in the **Mate Types** rollout. The **Width selections 1** and the **Width selections 2** fields are enabled in the **Mate Selections** rollout of the PropertyManager.

5. Select the front and back planar faces of the **Connecting Rod** component as the width selections 1, see Figure 12.164. Next, select the outer circular face of the **Piston Sub-Assembly** as the width selections 2, see Figure 12.164. The axis of the circular face of the **Piston Sub-Assembly** is centered to the planar faces of the **Connecting Rod** component in the graphics area.

12.164

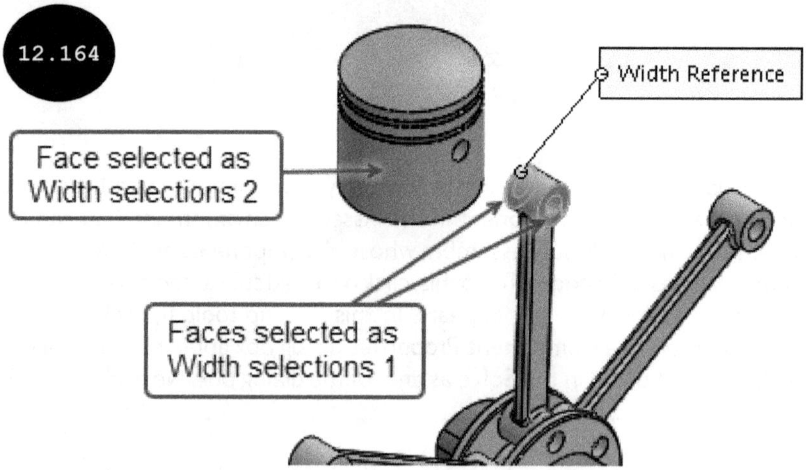

6. Click on the green tick-mark ✓ in the PropertyManager. The width mate is applied between the selected faces of the components. Next, exit the **Mate PropertyManager**.

Section 15: Inserting and Assembling the Remaining Piston Sub-Assemblies

1. Insert and assemble five more instances of the **Piston Sub-Assembly** with the remaining **Connecting Rod** components as discussed earlier, see Figure 12.165.

2. Turn on the visibility of the first component (**Crank Case**), see Figure 12.166. To turn on the visibility or display of the first component (**Crank Case**) in the graphics area, click on its name (**Crank Case**) in the FeatureManager Design Tree. A Pop-up toolbar appears. Next, click on the **Show Components** tool in the Pop-up toolbar.

12.165

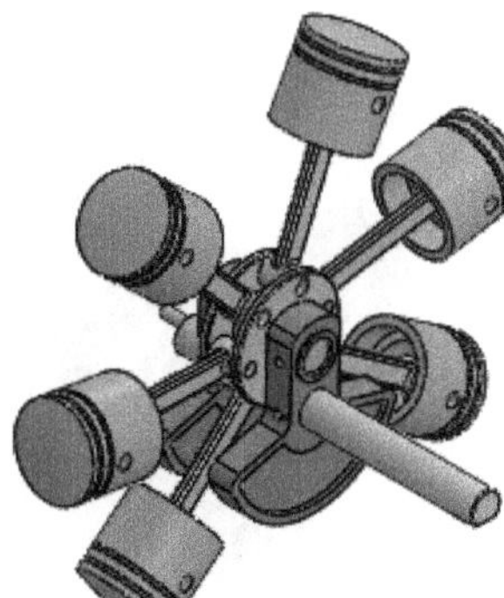

12.166

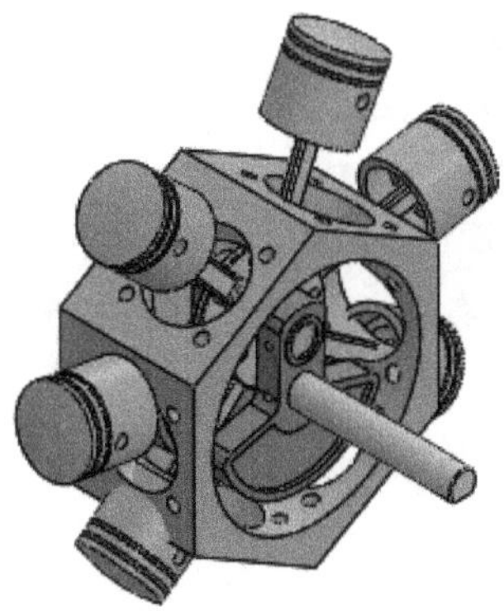

Now, you need to apply the concentric mate between each **Piston Sub-Assembly** and the first component (**Crank Case**).

3. Invoke the **Mate PropertyManager**. Next, select the outer circular face of a **Piston Sub Assembly** and the inner circular face of the respective hole of the first component (**Crank Case**), see Figure 12.167. A Pop-up toolbar appears with the **Concentric** tool activated in it.

4. Click on the green tick-mark in the Pop-up toolbar. The concentric mate is applied between the selected faces of the components.

5. Similarly, apply the concentric mate between the remaining instances of the **Piston Sub-Assembly** and the respective holes of the first component (**Crank Case**), see Figure 12.168.

12.167

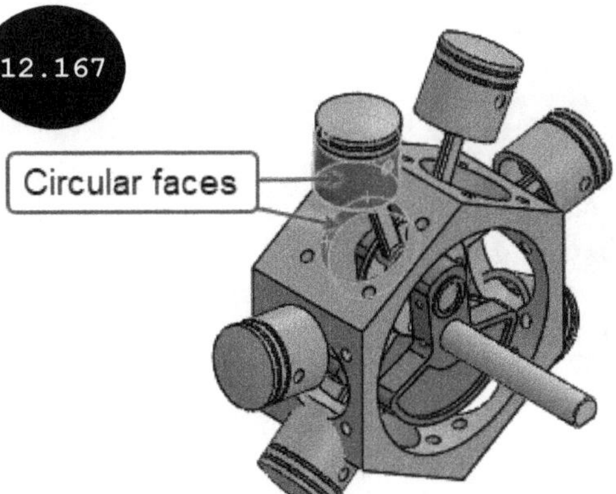

12.168

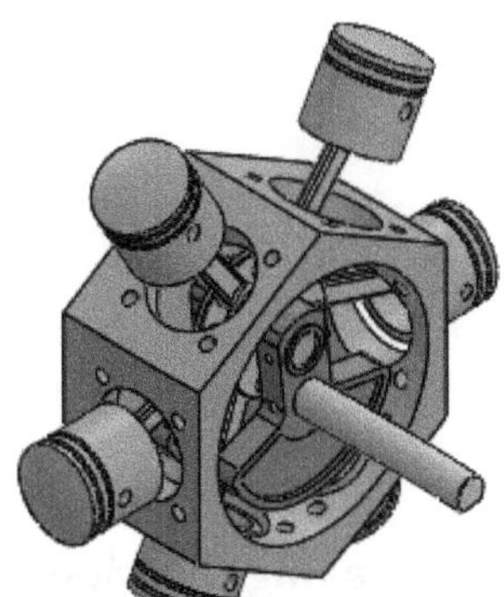

Now, you need to apply the parallel mate between a face of the rectangular cut in the seventh component (**Connecting Rod Hub**) and an outer planar face of the first component (**Crank Case**).

6. Click on the **Parallel** button in the **Mate PropertyManager**. Next, select a planar face of a small rectangular cut in the seventh component (**Connecting Rod Hub**), (see Figure 12.169) and then select the parallel outer planar face of the first component (**Crank Case**), see Figure 12.170. A Pop-up toolbar appears with the **Parallel** tool activated in it.

12.169

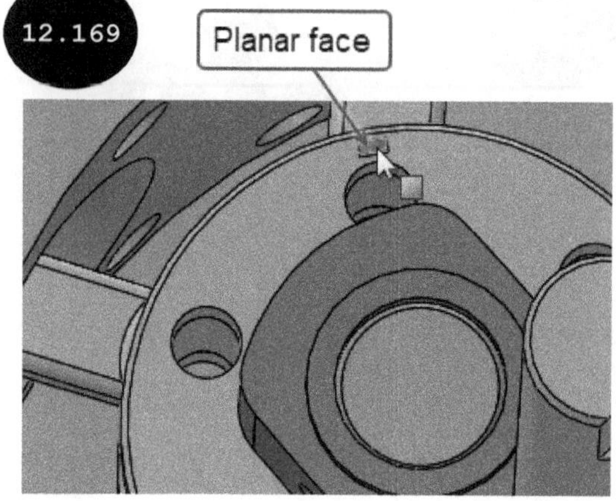

12.170

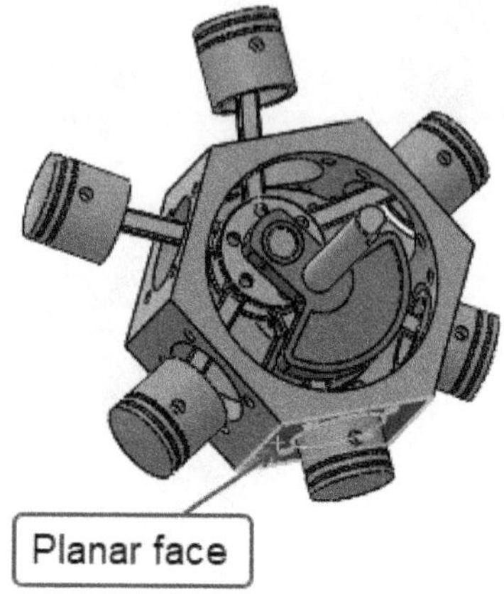

7. Click on the green tick-mark ✓ in the Pop-up toolbar. The parallel mate is applied between the selected faces of the components. Next, exit the **Mate PropertyManager**. Figure 12.171 shows the final assembly after assembling all its components.

Tip: You can review the motion of the assembly. To do this, drag the **Crankshaft** component of the assembly by pressing and holding the left mouse button.

12.171

Section 16: Saving the Model

1. Click on the **Save** tool in the **Standard** toolbar. The **Save As** dialog box appears.

2. Browse to the Tutorial 2 folder of the Chapter 12 folder and then save the assembly with the name Tutorial 2.

Hands-on Test Drive 1

Create the assembly, shown in Figure 12.172. An exploded view of the assembly is shown in Figure 12.173 for your reference only. Different views and dimensions of individual components of the assembly are shown in Figures 12.174 through 12.181. You can also download all components of the assembly by logging on to the CADArtifex website (www.cadartifex.com). All dimensions are in mm.

12.172

ITEM NO.	PART NUMBER	DESCRIPTION	QTY.
1	BASE		1
2	FIXED JAW		1
3	SLIDING JAW		1
4	JAW PLATE		1
5	JAW SCREW		1
6	HANDLE BAR		1
7	NUT		2
8	VICE NUT		1

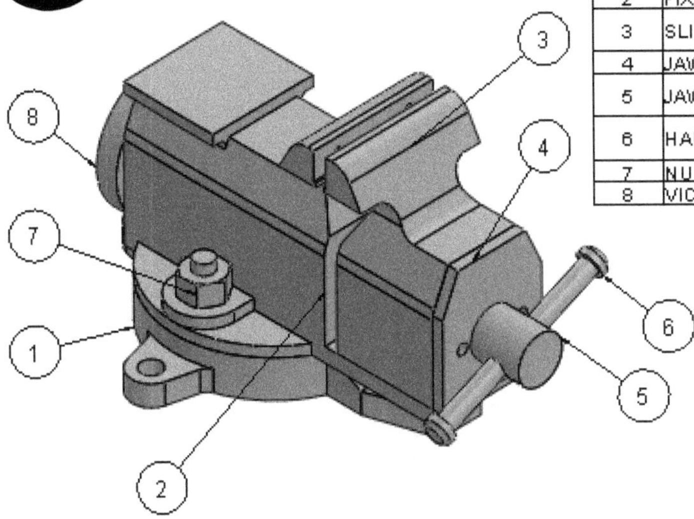

12.173

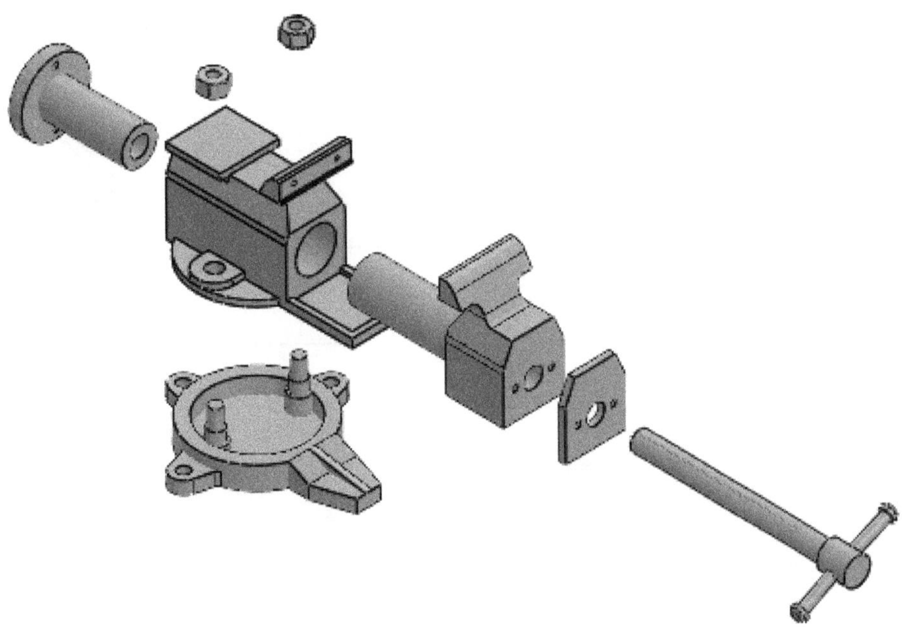

12.174

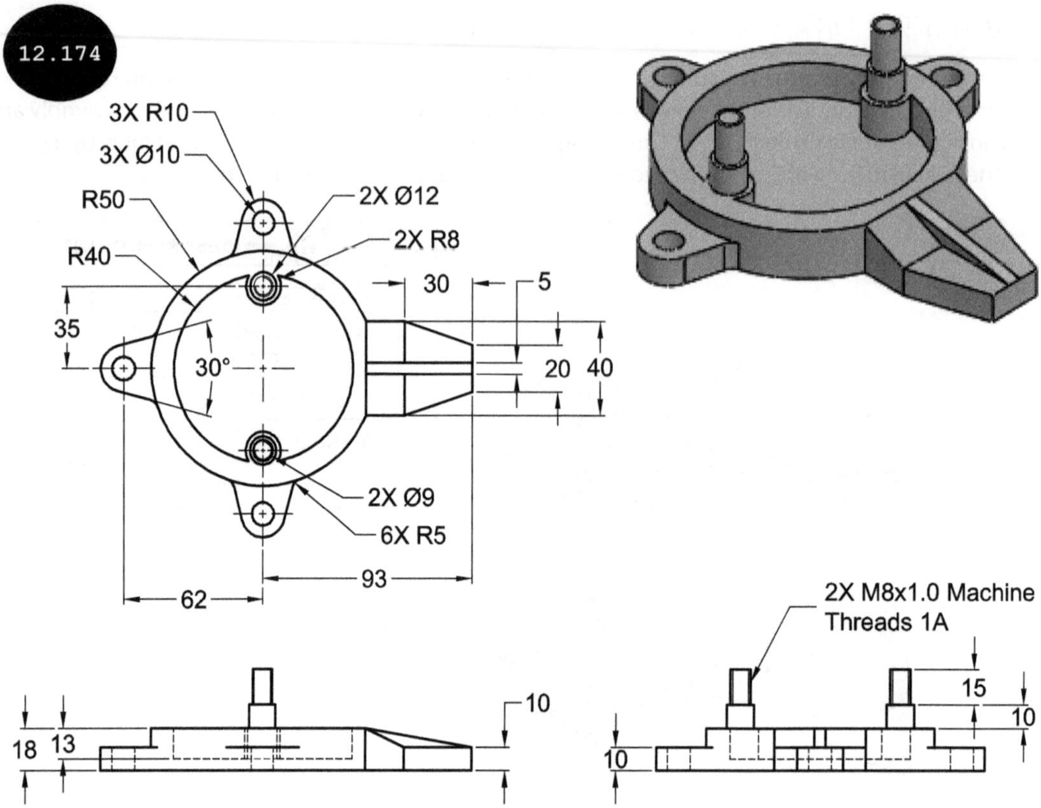

Base

12.175

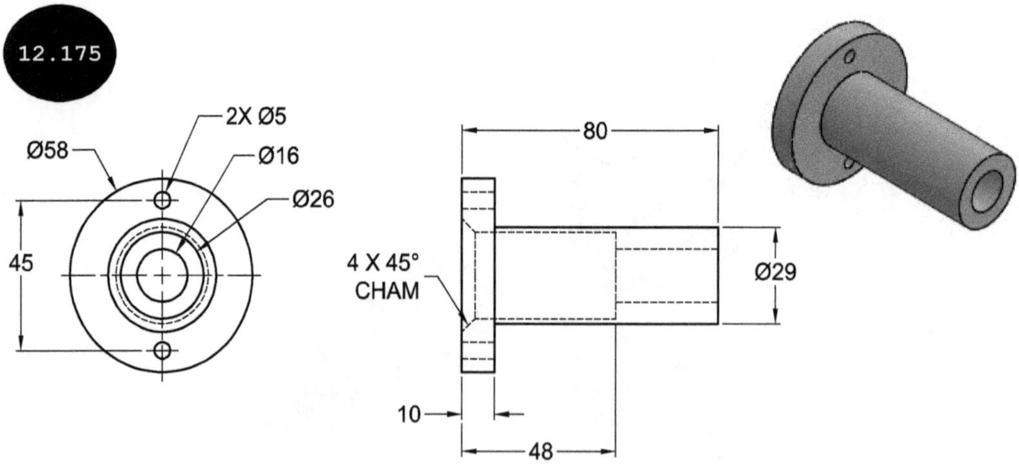

Vice Nut

12.176

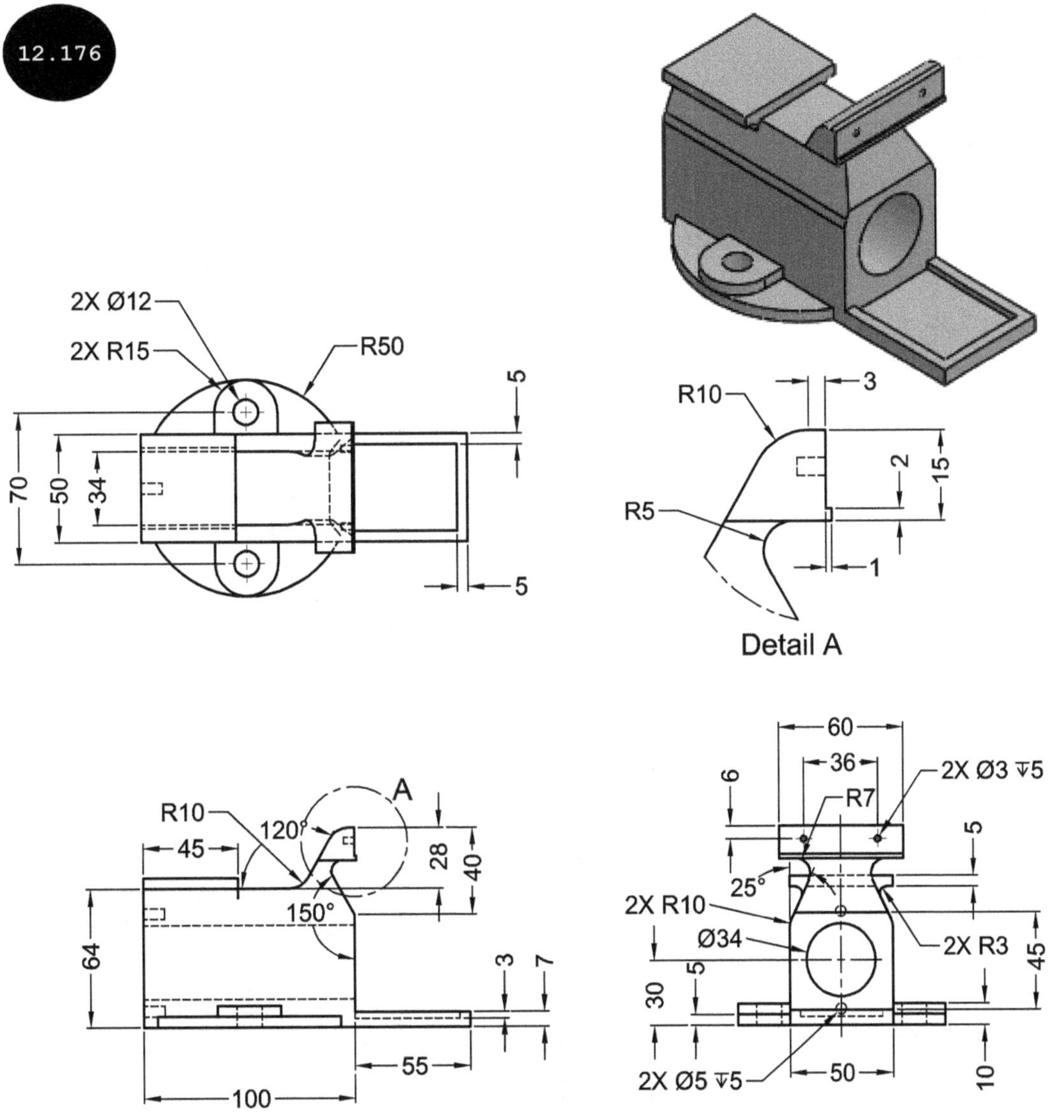

Fixed Jaw

12.177

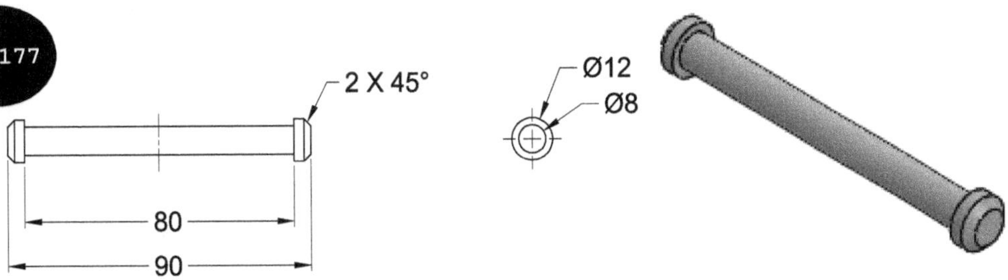

Handle Bar

12.178

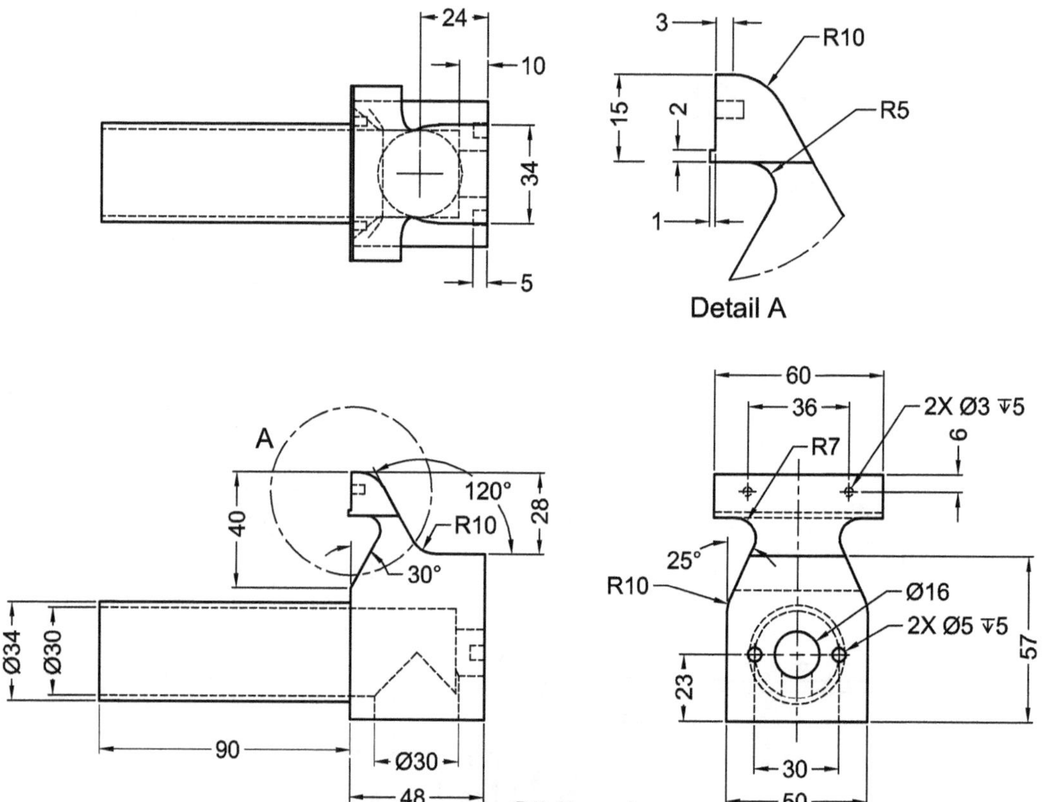

Sliding Jaw

12.179

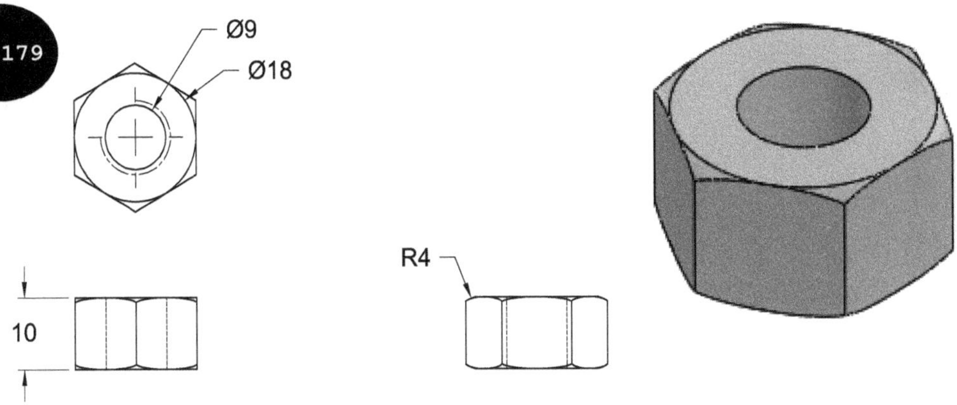

Nut

12.180

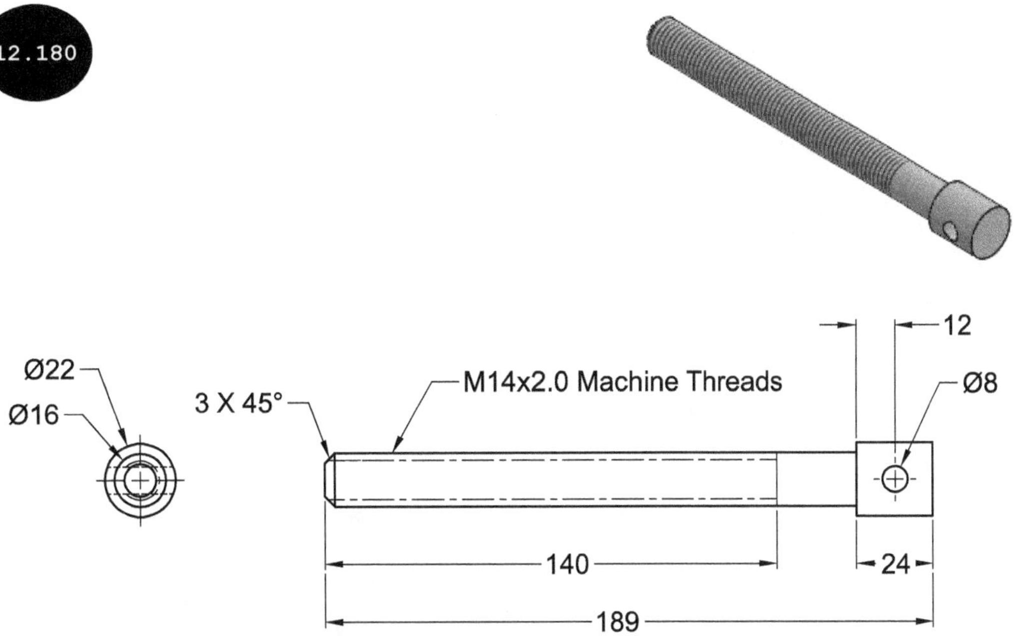

Jaw Screw

12.181

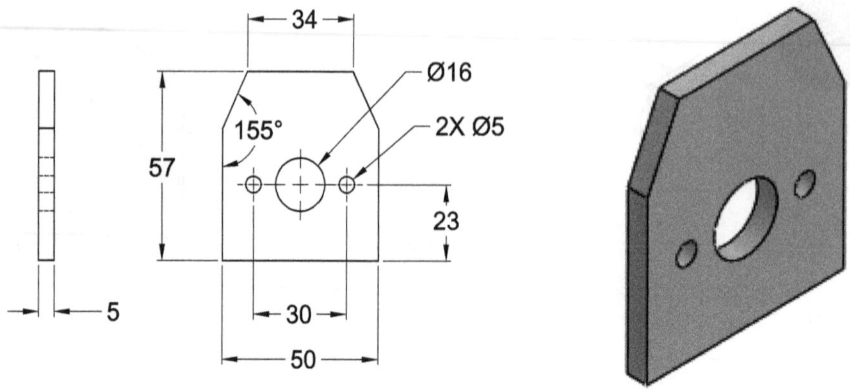

Jaw Plate

Hands-on Test Drive 2

Create an assembly, as shown in Figure 12.182. The exploded view of the assembly is shown in Figure 12.183 for your reference only. Different views and dimensions of individual components of the assembly are shown in Figures 12.184 through 12.193. You can also download all components of the assembly by logging on to the CADArtifex website (www.cadartifex.com). All dimensions are in mm.

12.182

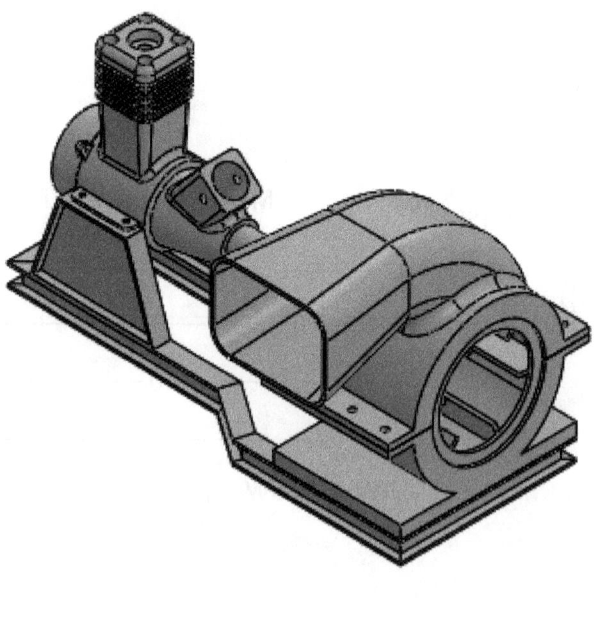

12.183

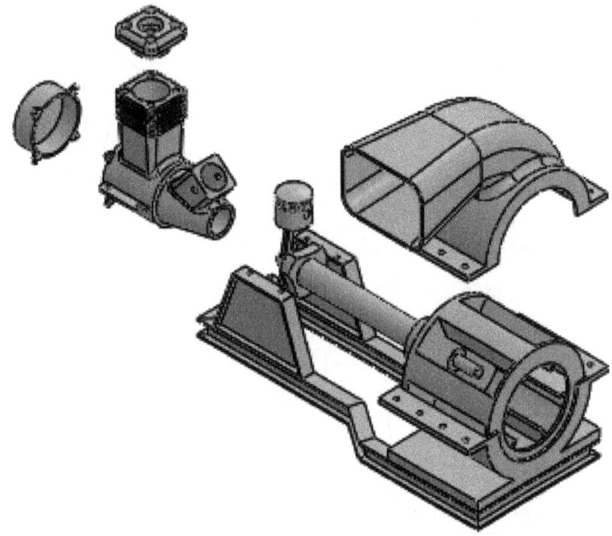

12.184

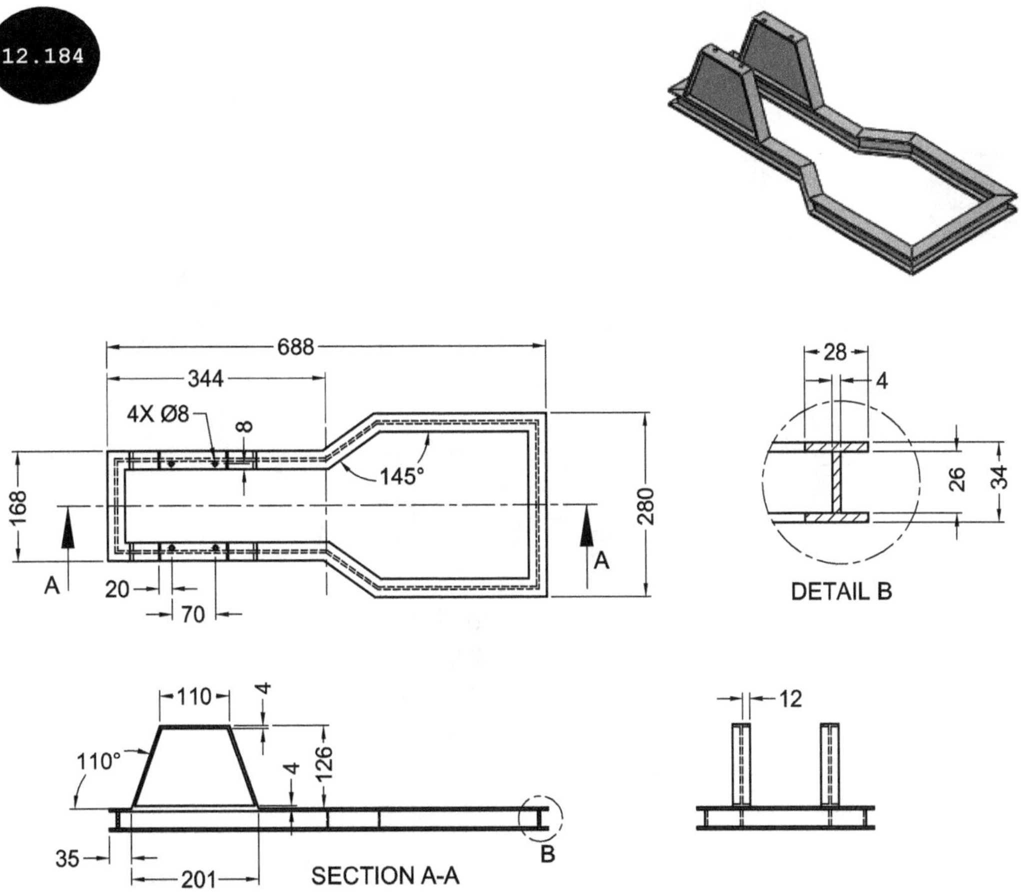

Base Frame

12.185

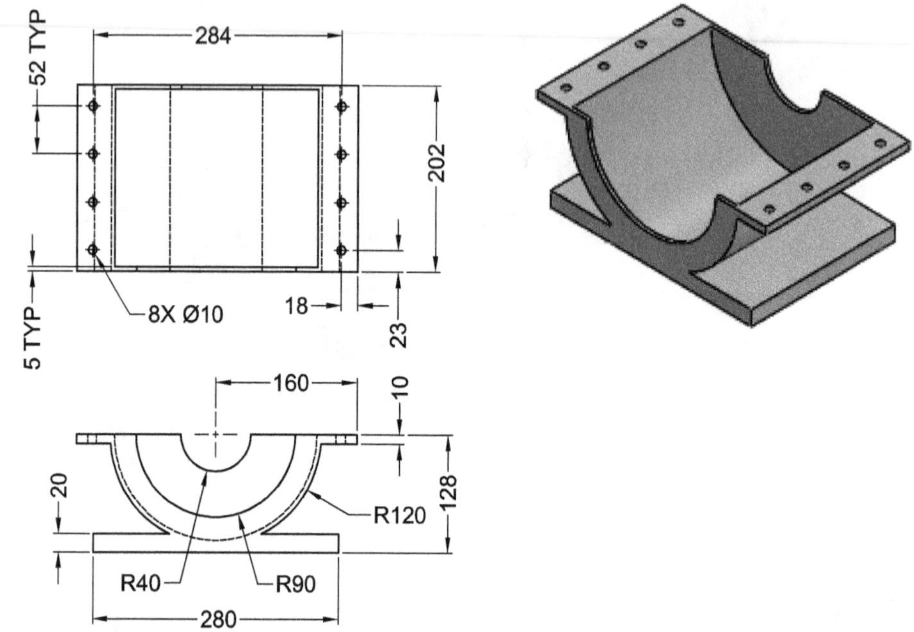

Lower Housing

12.186

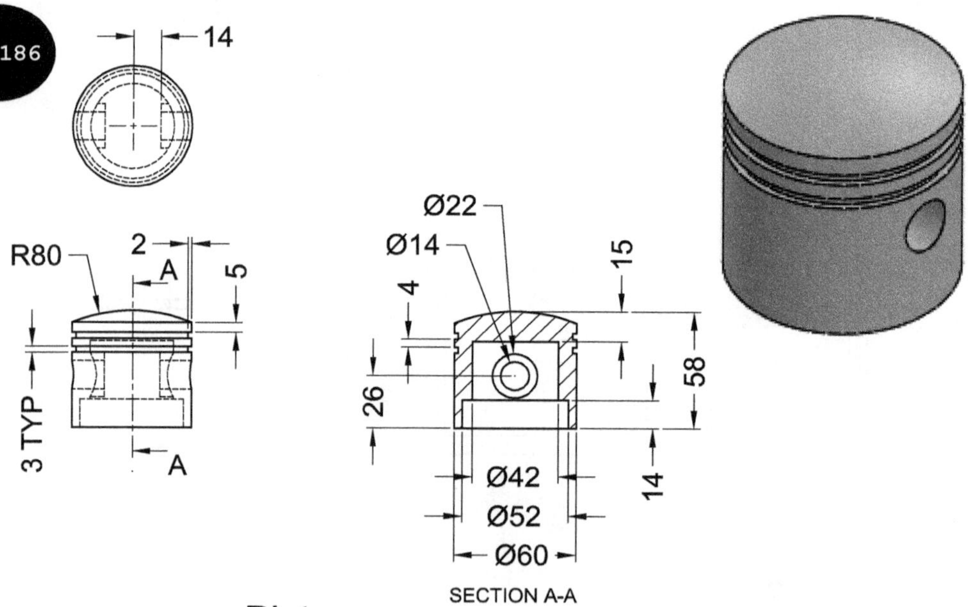

Piston

12.187

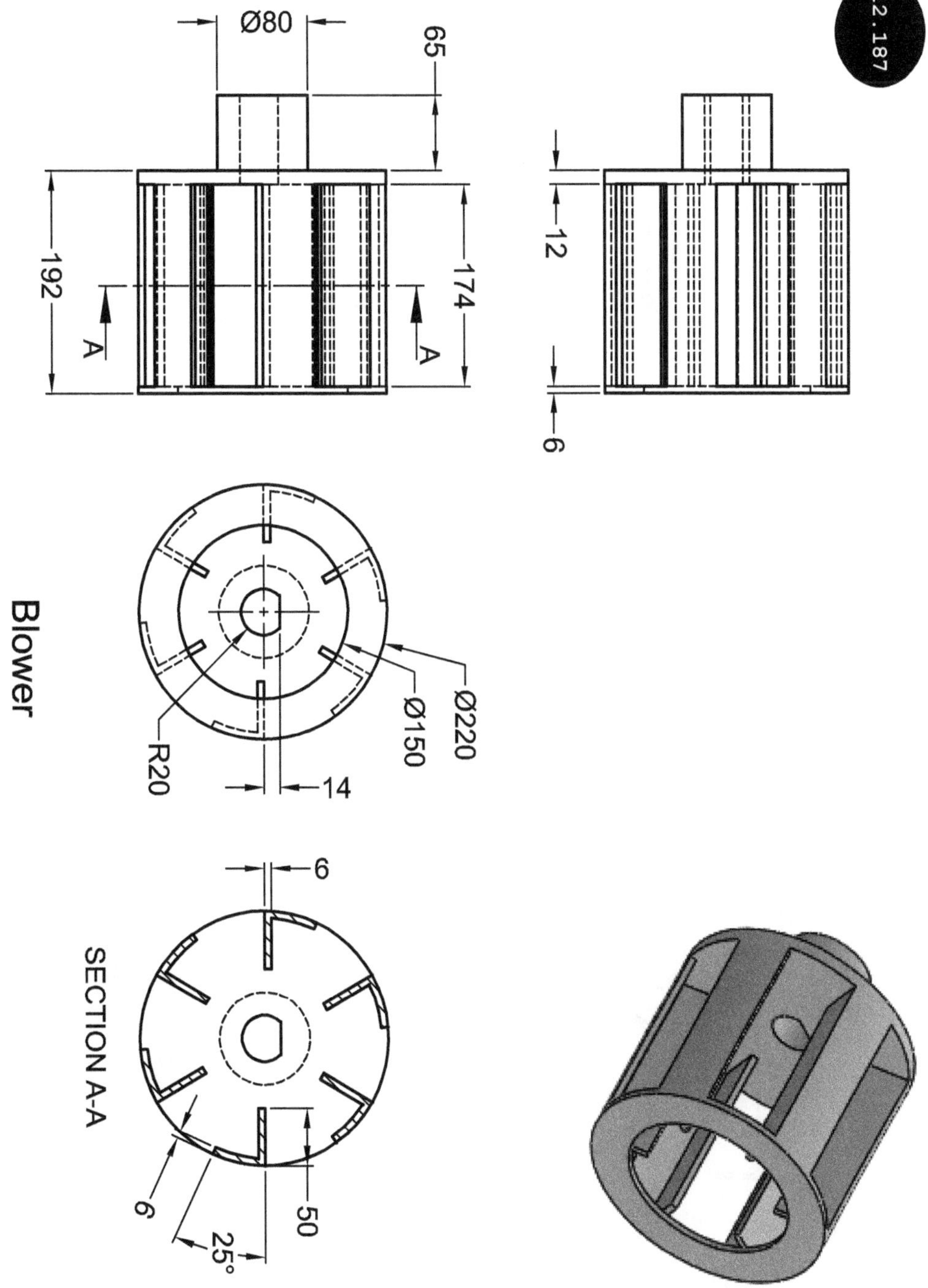
Ø80
65
192
174
A
A
12
6
Blower
Ø220
Ø150
R20
14
6
SECTION A-A
6
50
25°

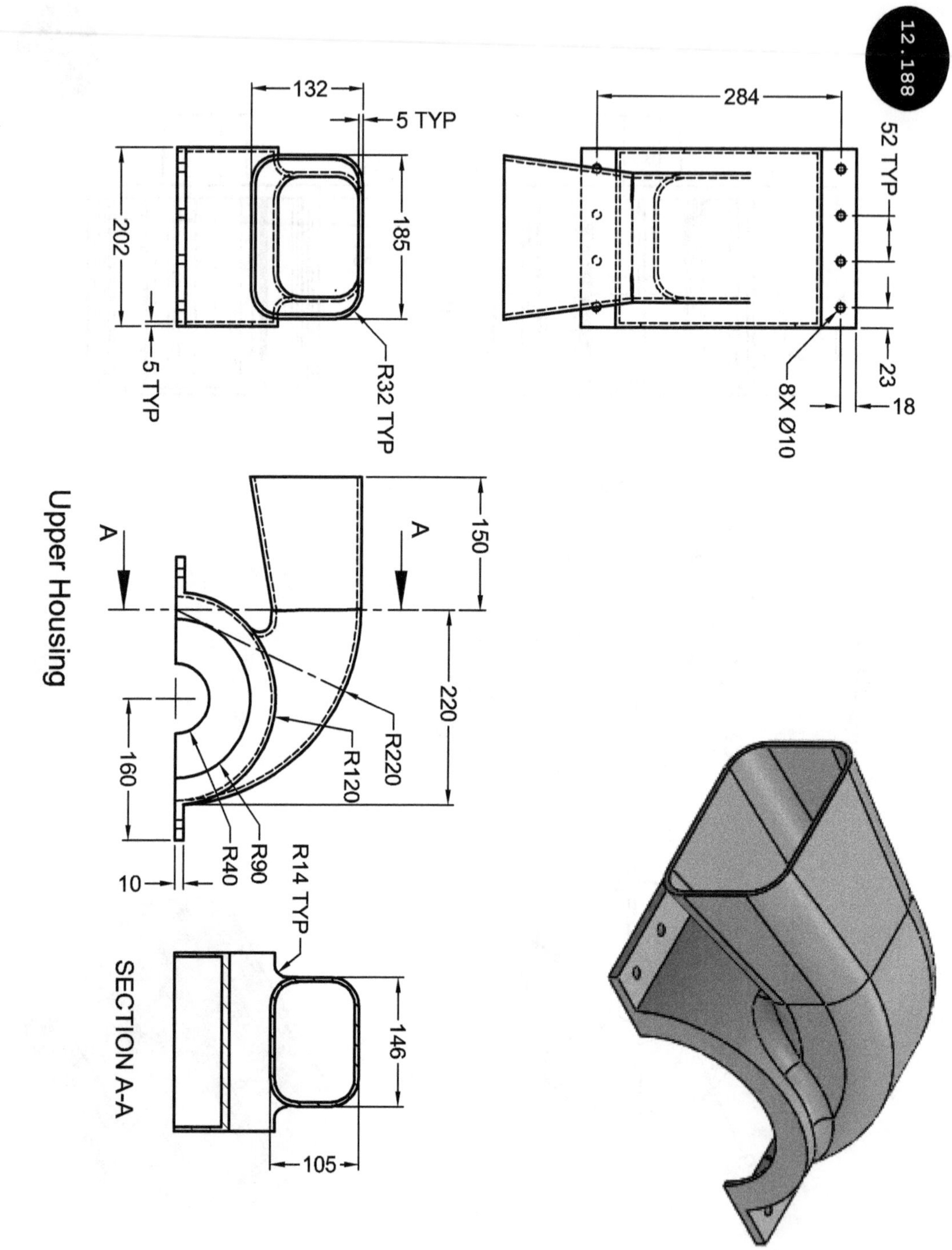
12.188
132
5 TYP
202
185
5 TYP
R32 TYP
284
52 TYP
23
18
8X Ø10
150
A
A
220
R220
R120
160
R90
R40
R14 TYP
10
146
105
Upper Housing
SECTION A-A

12.189

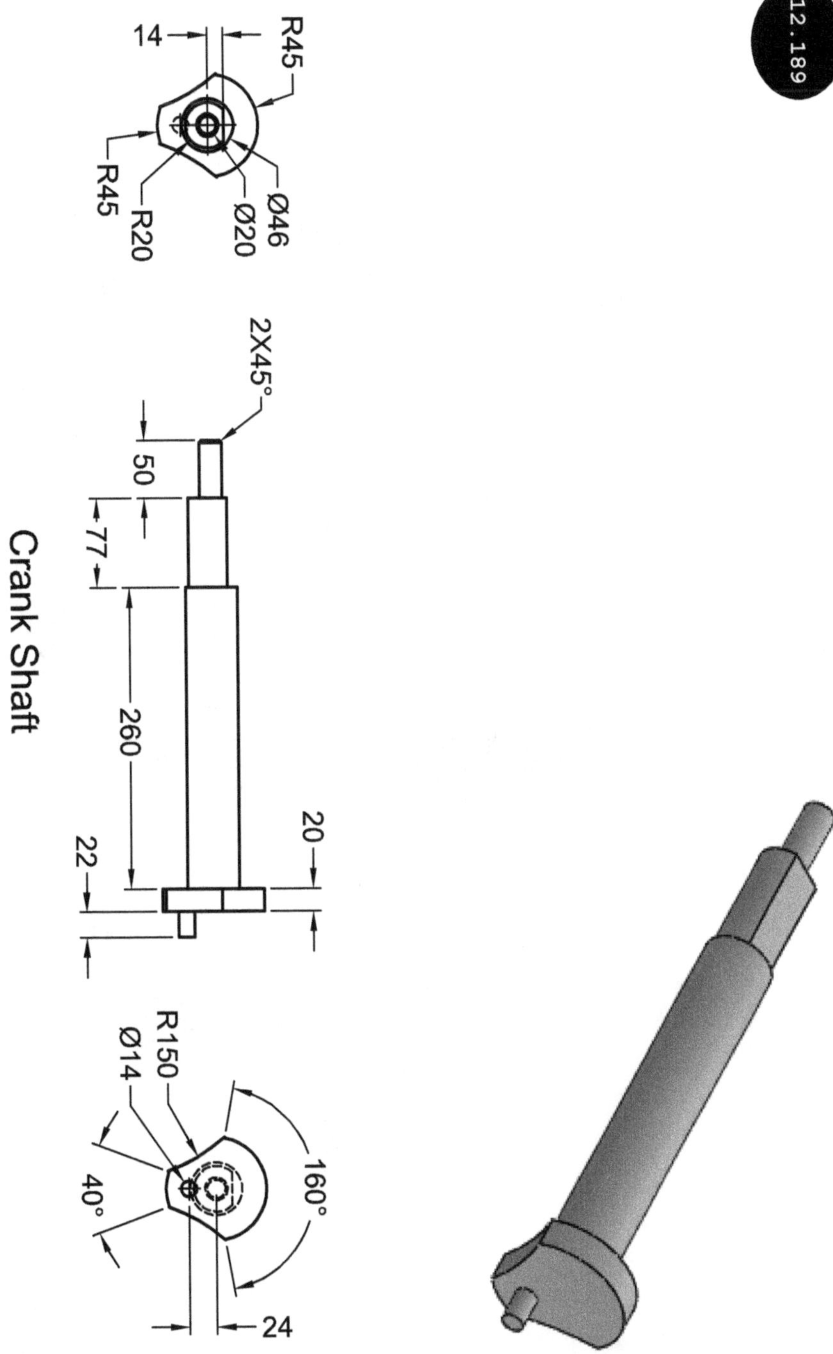
14
R45
R45
R20
Ø20
Ø46
2X45°
50
77
260
20
22
Crank Shaft
R150
Ø14
40°
160°
24

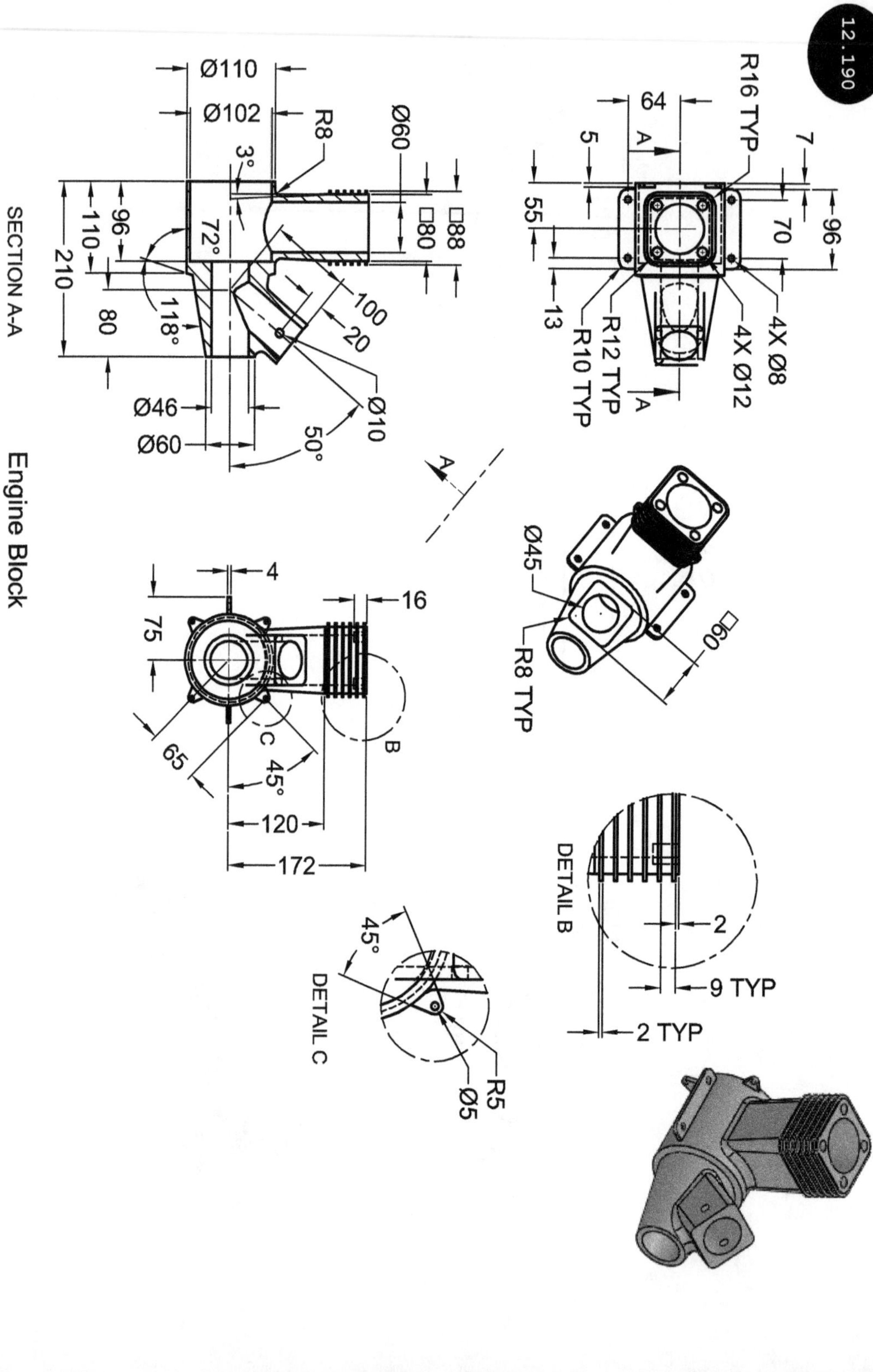

Engine Block

12.191

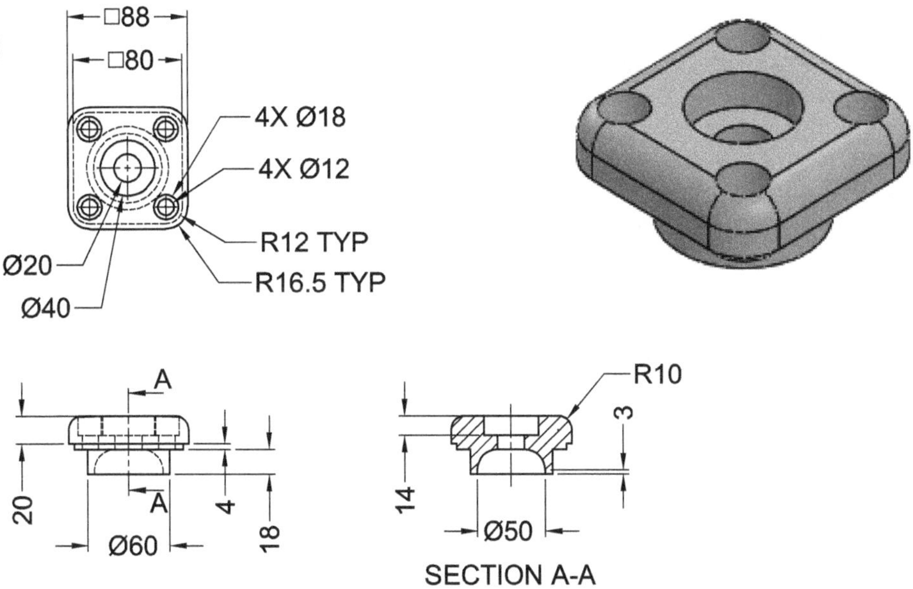

Engine Head

12.192

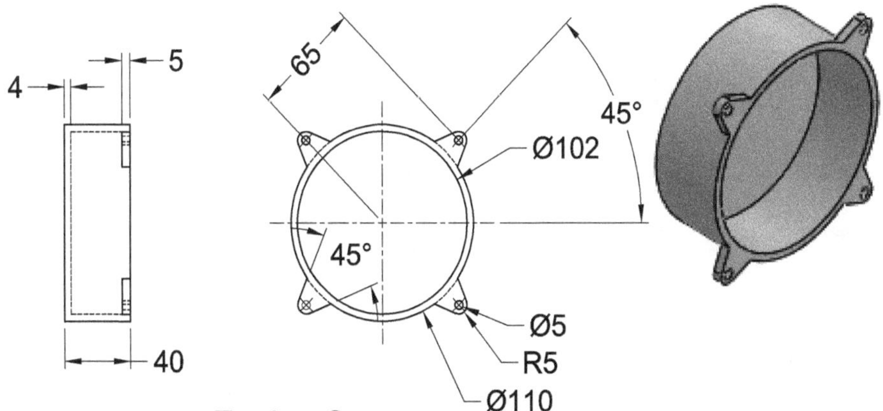

Engine Cover

12.193

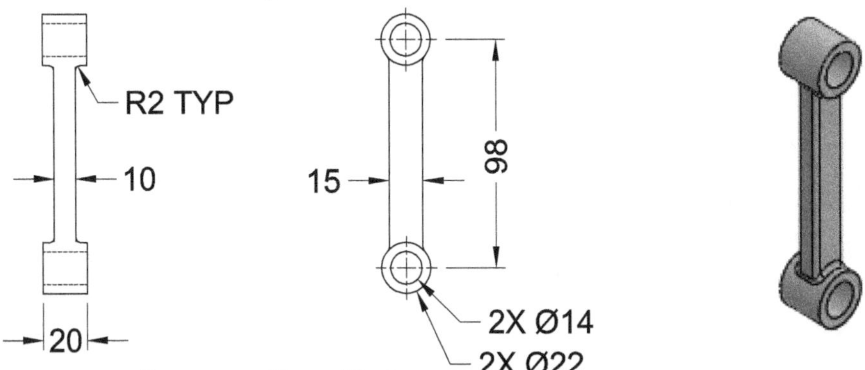

Connecting Rob

Summary

In this chapter, you learned how to create assemblies using the bottom-up assembly approach. The chapter covered the use of standard, advanced, and mechanical mates to position components in relation to each other. You also explored methods for moving and rotating components within the Assembly environment, detecting collisions between parts, and applying mates using the SmartMates method. By mastering these techniques, you are now prepared to efficiently assemble and manage components in SOLIDWORKS.

Questions

Complete and verify the following sentences:

- In SOLIDWORKS, you can create assemblies by using the ________ and ________ approaches.
- If you make any change in a component in the Part modeling environment, the same change is automatically reflected in the assembly environment and vice-versa. This is because of the ________ property of SOLIDWORKS.
- The ________ toolbar allows you to change the orientation of a component before defining its placement point in the Assembly environment.
- A free component within the Assembly environment has ________ degrees of freedom.
- The ________ mate is used for center aligning two rectangular profiles, two circular profiles, or a rectangular profile and a circular profile with each other.
- The ________ mate allows two components to rotate relative to each other and form a gear mechanism.
- The ________ mate is used for translating linear motion into rotational motion from one component to another and vice versa.
- The ________ mate allows a component to move along a defined path.
- You can move the individual components of an assembly along its degrees of freedom. (True/False)
- You can apply the mechanical mates by using the SmartMates method. (True/False)
- In SOLIDWORKS, you can detect collisions between the components of an assembly. (True/False)

CHAPTER

13

Working with Assemblies - II

This chapter discusses the following topics:

- Creating an Assembly by using the Top-down Approach
- Creating Flexible Components
- Editing Assembly Components
- Editing Mates
- Patterning Assembly Components
- Mirroring Components of an Assembly
- Creating Assembly Features
- Suppressing or Unsuppressing Components
- Inserting Parts having Multiple Configurations
- Creating and Dissolving Sub-Assemblies
- Publishing Envelopes
- Creating an Exploded View
- Collapsing an Exploded View
- Animating an Exploded View
- Editing an Exploded View
- Adding Explode Lines
- Detecting Interference in an Assembly
- Creating Bill of Material (BOM) of an Assembly

In the previous chapter, you learned about creating assemblies using the Bottom-up Assembly Approach, the different types of mates, and how to move or rotate individual components of an assembly.

In this chapter, you will learn about creating assemblies using the Top-down Assembly Approach, editing assembly components, patterning and mirroring components within the assembly, creating assembly features, and working with exploded views of assemblies, among other topics.

Creating an Assembly by using the Top-down Approach

In the Top-down Assembly Approach, all components of an assembly are created within the Assembly environment itself. By using this approach, you can create a concept-based design, where new components of an assembly can be created by taking reference from the existing components and maintaining relationships between them. The method for creating an assembly by using the Top-down Assembly Approach is discussed below:

1. Invoke the Assembly environment by using the **New** tool of the **Standard** toolbar, see Figure 13.1. Note that the **Open** dialog box appears along with the **Begin Assembly PropertyManager** in the startup user interface of the Assembly environment, by default.

13.1

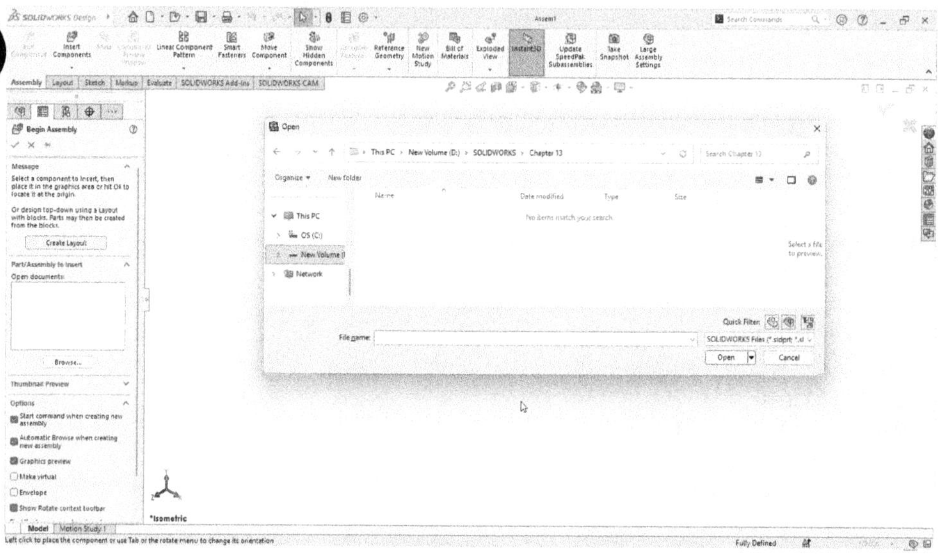

2. Close the **Open** dialog box by clicking on the **Cancel** button and then close the **Begin Assembly PropertyManager** by clicking on the red cross-mark [×] available at its top. The reason behind closing the **Open** dialog box and the PropertyManager is to create components in the Assembly environment itself instead of importing them.

3. Click on the arrow at the bottom of the **Insert Components** tool in the **Assembly CommandManager**. A flyout appears, see Figure 13.2.

13.2

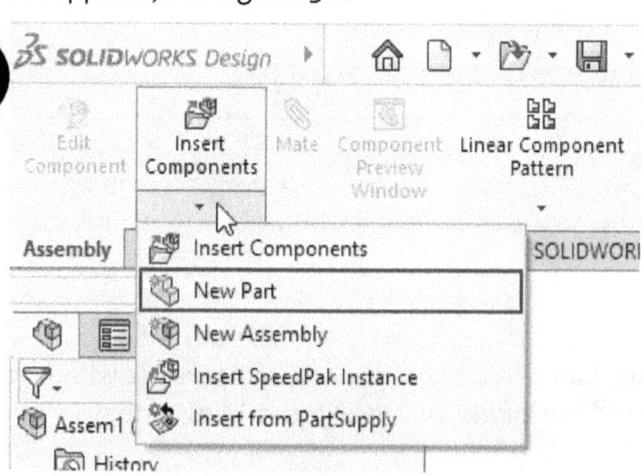

4. Click on the **New Part** tool in the flyout. A new empty part is inserted in the Assembly environment and its default name appears in the FeatureManager Design Tree, see Figure 13.3. Also, a green colored tick-mark appears attached to the cursor in the graphics area.

13.3

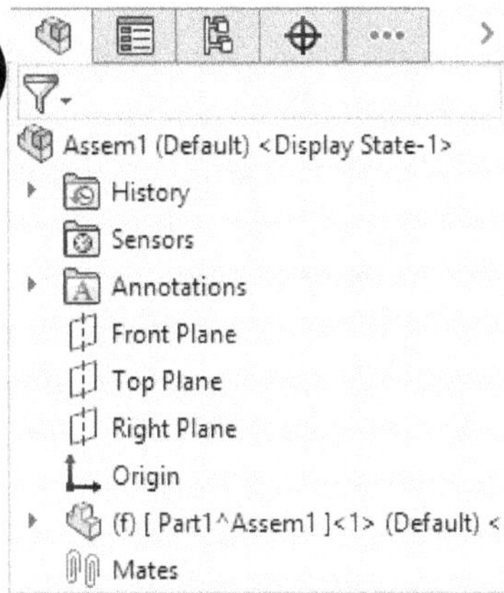

5. Click on a plane in the FeatureManager Design Tree as the sketching plane for creating the sketch of the base feature of the inserted part. The Sketching environment is invoked within the Assembly environment for creating the base feature of the part, see Figure 13.4.

13.4

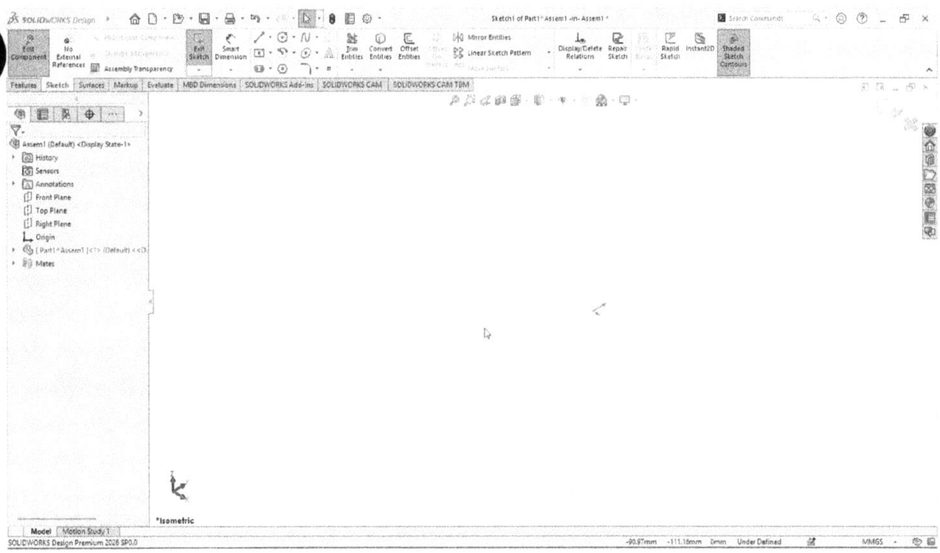

Note: If you can click anywhere in the graphics area to define the position of the part instead of selecting a plane. Then, the position of the part gets defined such that the origin of the part becomes coincident to the origin of the assembly. However, the Sketching environment for creating the base feature does not get invoked, automatically. In this case, to invoke the Sketching environment, click on the name of the part in the FeatureManager Design Tree and then click on the **Edit Component** tool in the **Assembly CommandManager**. Next, click on the **Sketch** tool in the **Sketch CommandManager** and then select a plane or a planar face as the sketching plane for creating the sketch of the base feature.

6. Press CTRL + 8 to change the orientation of the model as normal to the viewing direction. Alternatively, click on the **Normal To** tool in the **View Orientation** flyout, see Figure 13.5.

13.5

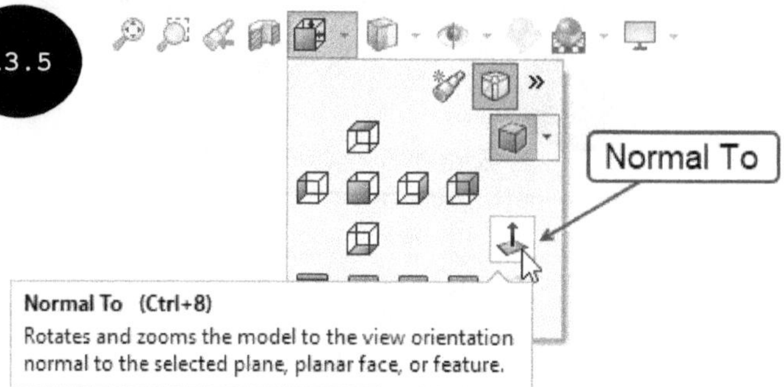

7. Draw the sketch of the base feature by using the sketching tools, refer to Figure 13.6.

   After creating the sketch, you need to convert it into a solid feature by using solid modeling tools.

8. Click on the **Features** tab in the CommandManager. The tools of the **Features CommandManager** appear. Now, by using tools such as **Extruded Boss/Base** or **Revolved Boss/Base**, you can convert the sketch into a solid feature, refer to Figure 13.7. In this figure, the sketch is extruded to a depth of 15 mm by using the **Extruded Boss/Base** tool.

13.6

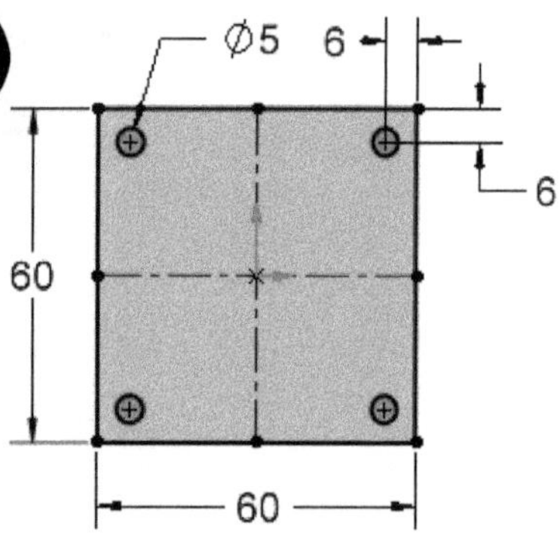

13.7

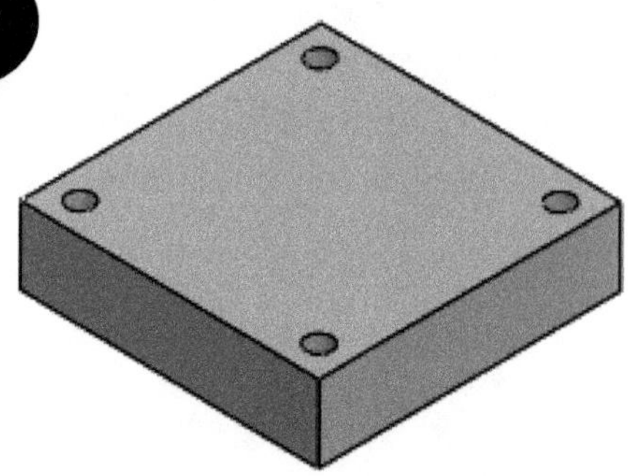

You need to create the second feature of the component.

9. Invoke the Sketching environment again by selecting a planar face or a plane as the sketching plane for creating the second feature of the component.

10. Create the sketch of the second feature, refer to Figure 13.8, and then convert it into a feature by using the solid modeling tools of the **Features CommandManager**, refer to Figure 13.9. In Figure 13.9, the sketch is extruded to a depth of 75 mm by using the **Extruded Boss/Base** tool. Similarly, you can create the remaining features of the part one by one.

13.8

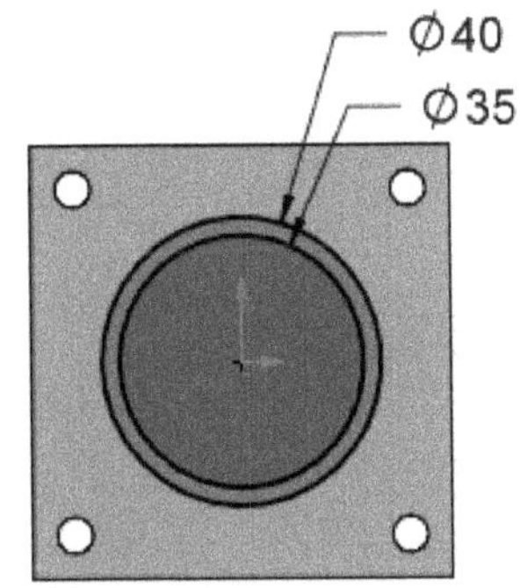

13.9

11. After creating all the features of the component, click on the **Edit Component** tool in the **Features CommandManager**. The first component is created, and the Assembly environment is invoked.

Note: By default, the components created in the Assembly environment are fixed components and their degrees of freedom are restricted. This is because the Inplace mate is applied automatically between the plane of the component and the plane of the assembly. You can convert a fixed component into a floating component by deleting the Inplace mate. To delete the Inplace mate, expand the **Mates** node in the FeatureManager Design Tree and then select the InPlace mate to be deleted. Next, press the DELETE key.

If you have defined the placement of a component in the Assembly environment by clicking in the graphics area instead of selecting a plane, then the component becomes fixed in the Assembly environment without applying the Inplace mate. In such cases, to convert a fixed component into a floating component, select the component in the FeatureManager Design Tree and then right-click to display a shortcut menu. Next, click on the **Float** option in the shortcut menu.

After creating the first component, you can create the second component of the assembly.

12. Click on the arrow at the bottom of the **Insert Components** tool, see Figure 13.10. Next, click on the **New Part** tool in the flyout that appears. A new empty part is inserted in the Assembly environment and its default name appears in the FeatureManager Design Tree.

13.10

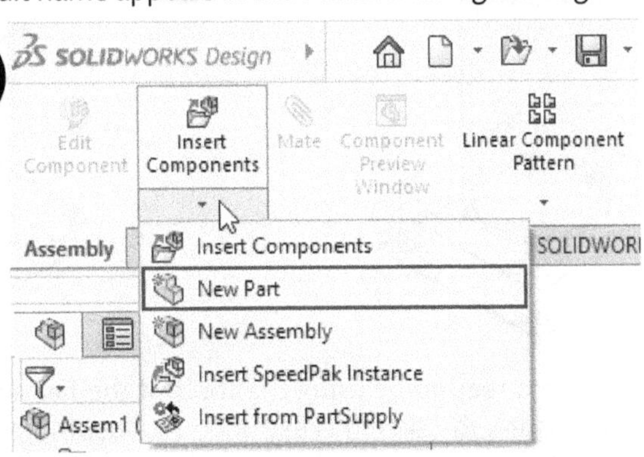

13. Click anywhere in the graphics area. The position of the part gets defined such that the origin of the part becomes coincident with the origin of the assembly.

14. Click on the name of the newly inserted component in the FeatureManager Design Tree. A Pop-up toolbar appears, see Figure 13.11.

13.11

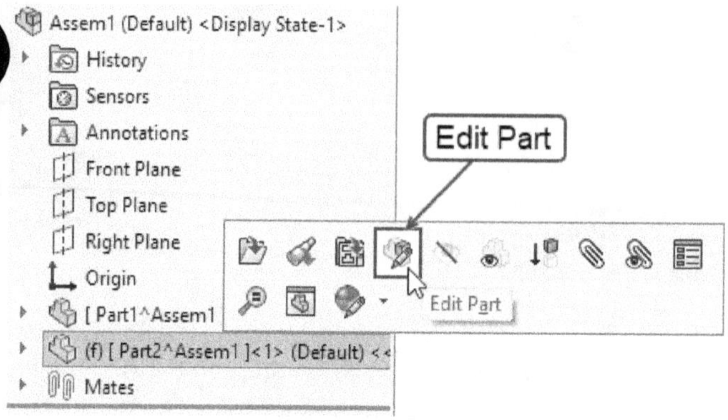

15. Click on the **Edit Part** tool in the Pop-up toolbar, see Figure 13.11. The Part modeling environment is invoked within the Assembly environment for creating the features of the second component. Also, the first component becomes transparent so that you can easily create the second component and take reference from the first component while creating it, refer to Figure 13.12.

16. Invoke the Sketching environment for creating the base feature of the second component by selecting a plane or a planar face of the first component as the sketching plane.

Note: While creating a component, if you take reference of a plane or a planar face of another component, then the selected reference acts as external reference for the component being created.

17. Create a sketch of the base feature of the second component by taking reference from the first component, refer to Figure 13.13. In this figure, a rectangle and four circles have been created by projecting the edges of the first component onto the sketching plane.

13.12

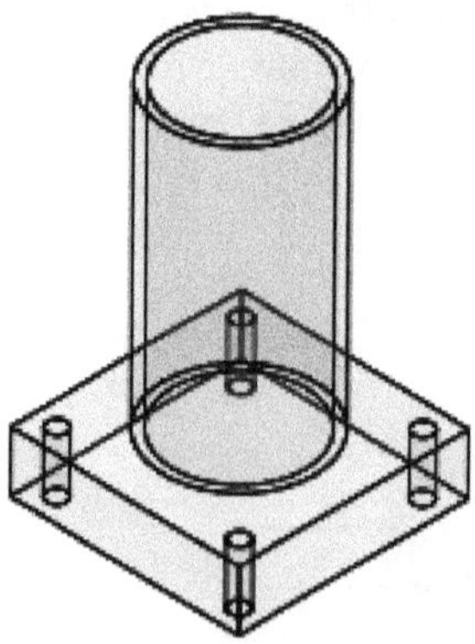

13.13

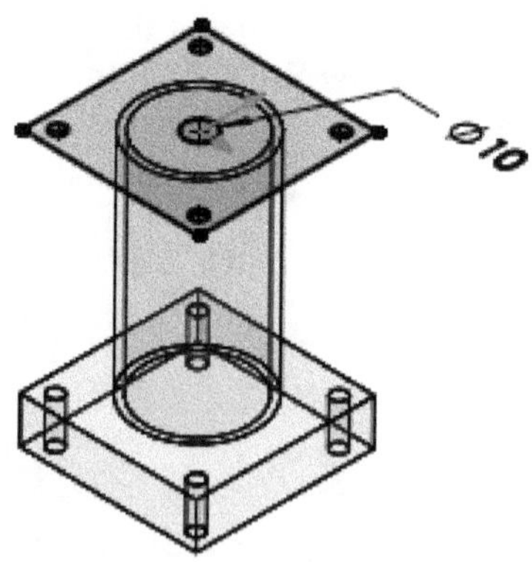

18. Convert the sketch into a feature by using the tools of the **Features CommandManager**, refer to Figure 13.14. In this figure, the sketch is extruded to a depth of 15 mm by using the **Extruded Boss/Base** tool. Similarly, you can create the remaining features of the second component.

13.14

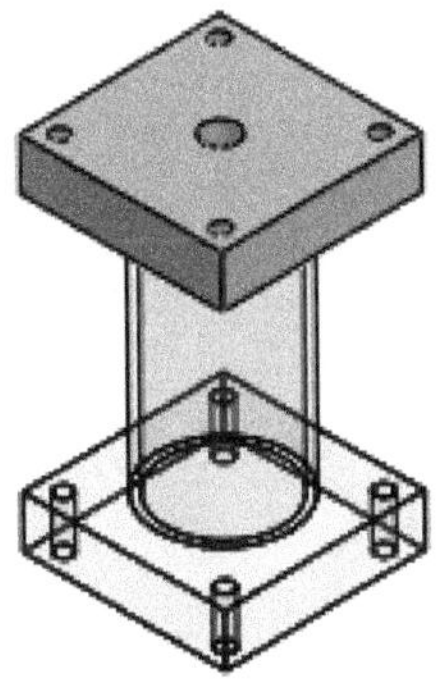

19. After creating all the features of the second component, click on the **Edit Component** tool in the **Features CommandManager**. The second component is created, and the Assembly environment is invoked. Also, all components of the assembly appear in the shaded display style, refer to Figure 13.15.

20. Similarly, create the remaining components of the assembly one after another. Figure 13.16 shows an assembly in which all components are created one by one in the Assembly environment by using the Top-down Assembly Approach.

13.15

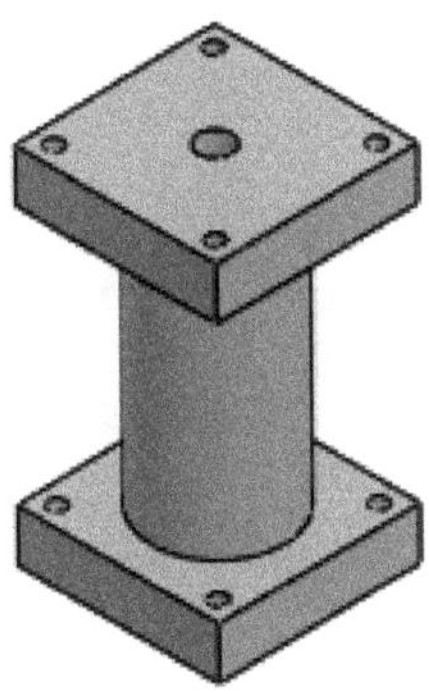

13.16

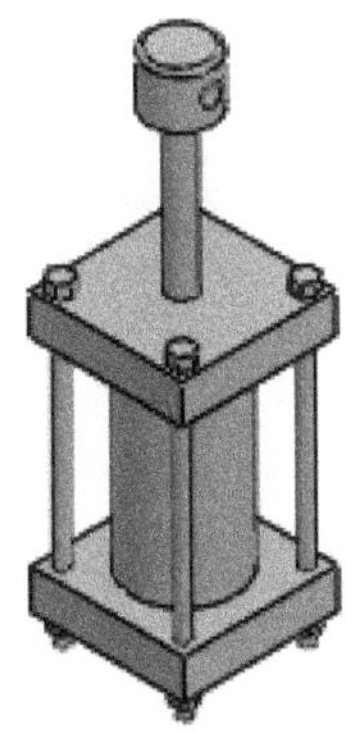

Note: As discussed, the components created by using the Top-down Assembly Approach become fixed in the Assembly environment. You can make these components floating components by deleting their respective Inplace mates or by selecting the **Float** option in the shortcut menu that appears on right-clicking on the component. A floating component can translate and rotate in all directions, which means all its degrees of freedom are free. You can restrict the required degrees of freedom of a floating component and assemble it with the other components of the assembly by applying the required mates. The method for applying mates between the components is the same as discussed in the previous chapter.

After creating all the components of the assembly, you can save the assembly file and its components externally or internally in the assembly file.

21. Click on the **Save** button in the **Standard** toolbar. The **Save Modified Documents** dialog box appears, see Figure 13.17.

13.17

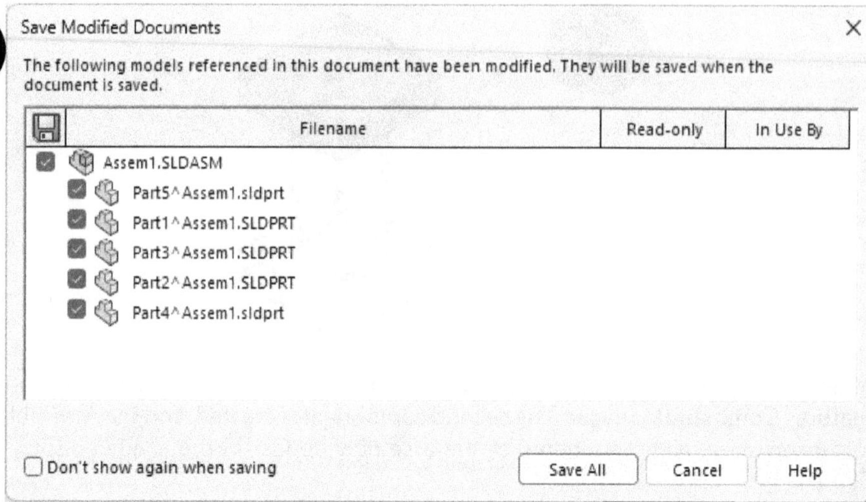

22. Click on the **Save All** button in the dialog box. The **Save As** dialog box appears. Next, browse to the location where you want to save the assembly.

23. Enter the name of the assembly in the **File name** field of the dialog box and then click on the **Save** button. Another **Save As** dialog box appears, see Figure 13.18.

13.18

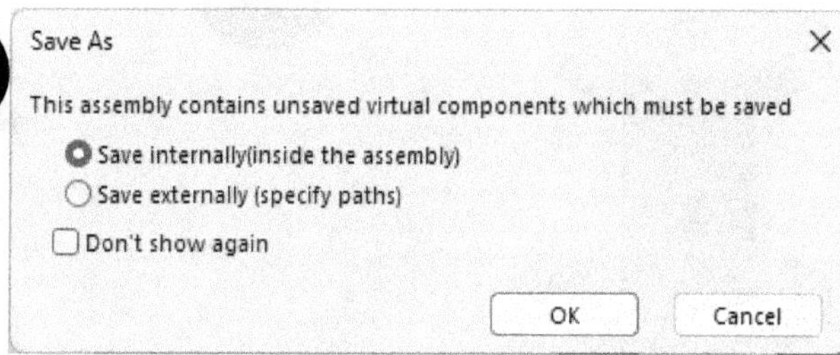

By default, the **Save internally (inside the assembly)** radio button is selected in the **Save As** dialog box, see Figure 13.18. As a result, all the components of the assembly will be saved internally in the assembly file. On selecting the **Save externally (specify paths)** radio button, all the components of the assembly will be saved externally as individual components in the same folder, where the assembly file is saved.

24. Select the **Save externally (specify paths)** radio button and then click on the **OK** button. All the components of the assembly and the assembly file are saved in the specified folder, individually.

Creating Flexible Components

In SOLIDWORKS, you can make a part flexible using the **Make Part Flexible** tool. The **Make Part Flexible** tool is used when you have inserted a component of an assembly into another assembly and it gives an error of out-of-context references. In such cases, you can use the **Make Part Flexible** tool for re-attaching or defining the out-of-context references of the inserted component with the components of the new assembly.

To make a component flexible, click on a component of an assembly in the FeatureManager Design Tree and then click on the **Make Part Flexible** tool in the Pop-up toolbar that appears, see Figure 13.19. The **Activate Flexible Component PropertyManager** appears with a list of all external references of the selected component, see Figure 13.20. Note that the **Make Part Flexible** tool is available in the Pop-up toolbar only when the selected component is created by taking references from other components of an assembly file.

13.19

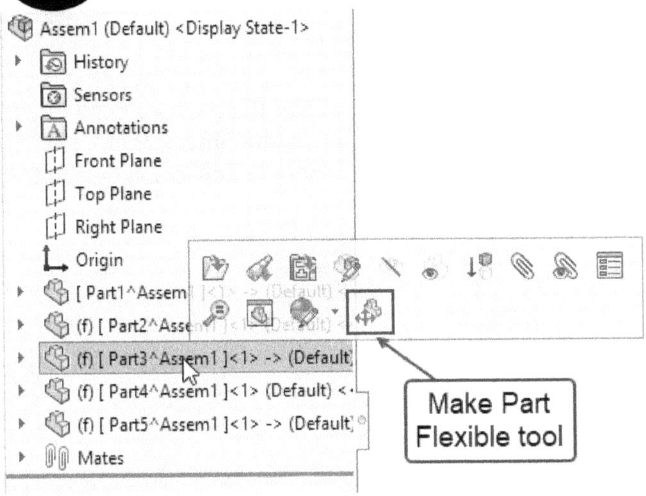

13.20

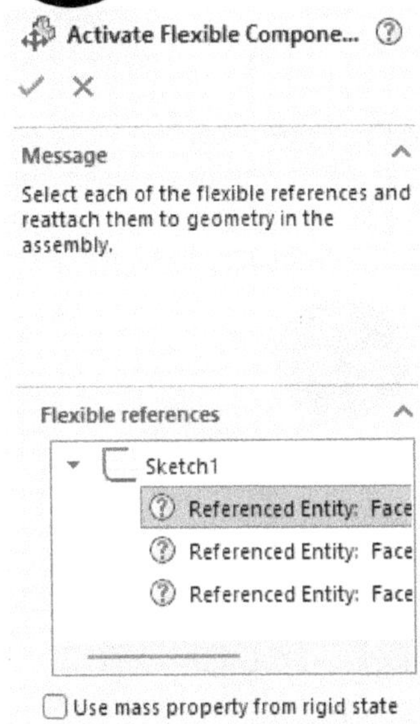

Once the **Activate Flexible Component PropertyManager** is invoked, you can select an external reference in the PropertyManager and then re-attach or define its new reference with the geometry of an assembly component. A green tick-mark appears in front of the selected reference in the PropertyManager indicating that a new reference is defined correctly. Similarly, you can define new references for each of the external references one by one. Next, exit the PropertyManager. The external references of the component have been re-defined, and the component becomes a flexible component. Now, if the position of any of the redefined references of the flexible component changes, the flexible component adjusts itself accordingly.

Tip: To change the state of a component from flexible to rigid, click on the flexible component in the FeatureManager Design Tree and click on the **Make Part Rigid** tool in the Pop-up toolbar that appears.

Editing Assembly Components

In the process of creating an assembly, you may need to edit its components depending on the changes in the design, revisions, or so on. SOLIDWORKS allows you to edit each component of an assembly within the Assembly environment as well as in the Part modeling environment. Different methods for editing assembly components are discussed next.

Editing Assembly Components within the Assembly Environment

To edit a component of an assembly within the Assembly environment, select it either from the graphics area or from the FeatureManager Design Tree. A Pop-up toolbar appears, see Figure 13.21.

13.21

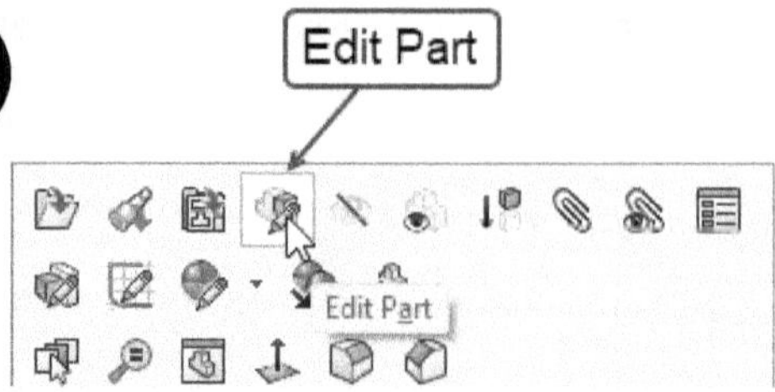

In this Pop-up toolbar, click on the **Edit Part** tool. The editing mode to edit the selected component is invoked within the Assembly environment itself, see Figure 13.22. Also, the other components of the assembly become transparent, and the name of the selected component appears in blue in the FeatureManager Design Tree, see Figure 13.22.

13.22

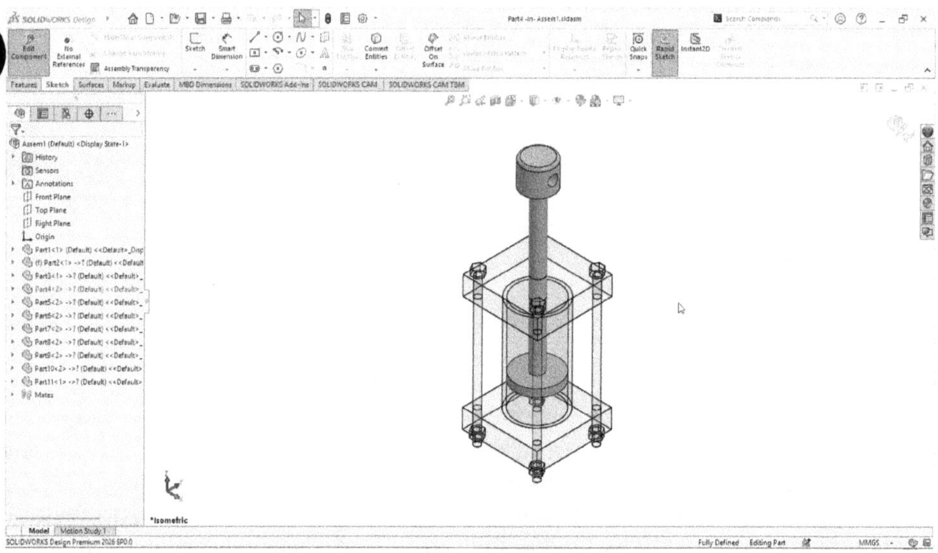

Expand the node of the component being edited in the FeatureManager Design Tree to list all its features, see Figure 13.23. Next, select the feature to be edited in the expanded node of the FeatureManager Design Tree. A Pop-up toolbar appears, see Figure 13.23. Next, click on the **Edit Feature** tool in the Pop-up toolbar to edit the feature parameters such as extrusion depth and end condition. If you want to edit the sketch of the feature then click on the **Edit Sketch** tool in the Pop-up toolbar, see Figure 13.23. Depending upon the tool selected (**Edit Feature** or **Edit Sketch**), the respective environment gets invoked for editing the selected feature or sketch of the component. In addition to editing the existing feature of a component, you can also create new features of the component by using the tools of the **Features CommandManager**. Once all the required editing operations have been performed on the component, click on the **Edit Component** tool in the **Features CommandManager** to exit the editing mode and switch back to the Assembly environment. Alternatively, to exit the editing mode, click on the Confirmation corner, which is available in the upper right corner of the graphics area.

13.23

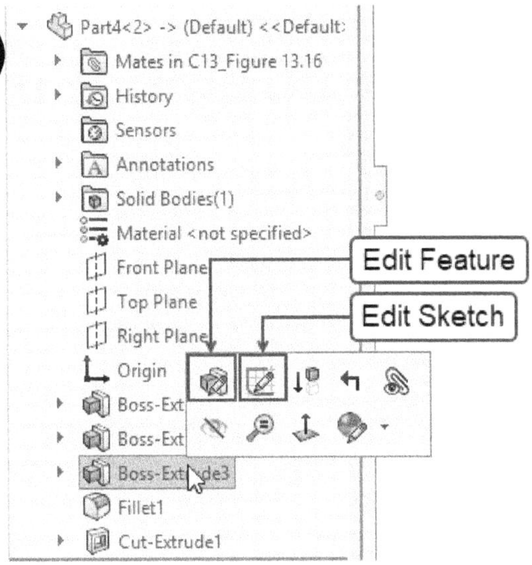

Editing Assembly Components in the Part Modeling Environment

In addition to editing the components of an assembly in the Assembly environment, you can open a component of an assembly in the Part modeling environment and then perform the editing operations. To do this, click on the component to be edited either in the FeatureManager Design Tree or in the graphics area. A Pop-up toolbar appears, see Figure 13.24. Next, click on the **Open Part** tool in the Pop-up toolbar, see Figure 13.24. The selected component is opened in the Part modeling environment. Now, you can edit the component by editing its features and sketches.

13.24

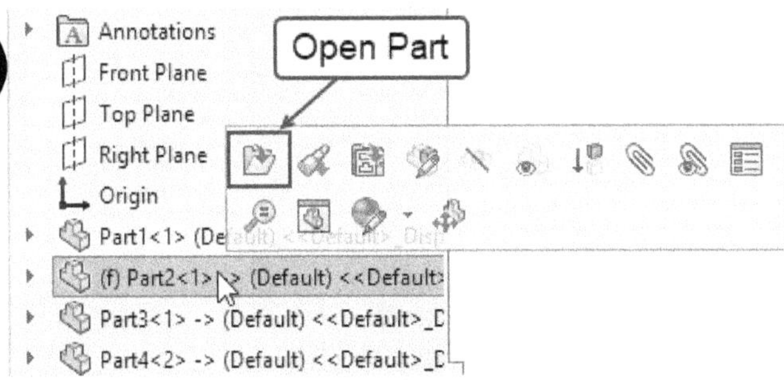

To edit a feature, click on the feature to be edited in the FeatureManager Design Tree and then click on the **Edit Feature** tool in the Pop-up toolbar that appears. To edit the sketch of a feature, click on the **Edit Sketch** tool in the Pop-up toolbar. Depending upon the tool selected (**Edit Feature** or **Edit Sketch**), the respective environment gets invoked, which allows you to edit the selected feature. You can also create new features in the component by using the tools of the **Features CommandManager**.

Once you have edited the component by using the tools of the Part modeling environment, click on the **Save** tool in the **Standard** toolbar to save the modified component. Next, click on **Window** > ***name of the assembly*** in the SOLIDWORKS Design Menus to switch to the Assembly environment. The **SOLIDWORKS** message window appears. Click on the **Yes** button in this window. The process of updating the assembly starts and once the assembly has been updated, the updated assembly with the modified component appears in the Assembly environment. The modifications made in the component are also reflected in the Assembly environment.

Note: SOLIDWORKS has bi-directional associative properties, which means that the modifications made in a component in any environment are also reflected in other environments of SOLIDWORKS.

Editing Mates

In SOLIDWORKS, you can edit existing mates of an assembly, which are applied between the components. To edit existing mates, expand the **Mates** node available at the bottom of the FeatureManager Design Tree, see Figure 13.25. The **Mates** node consists of a list of all mates that are applied between components of an assembly. Next, click on the mate to be edited in the expanded **Mates** node of the FeatureManager Design Tree. A Pop-up toolbar appears, see Figure 13.26. Also, the entities between which the selected mate is applied are highlighted in the graphics area. Next, click on the **Edit Feature** tool in the Pop-up toolbar, see Figure 13.26. The PropertyManager appears depending on the type of mate selected. By using the options of the PropertyManager, you can select new entities for the mate, change the type of mate, type of mate alignment, and so on. Once the editing has been done, click on the green tick-mark ✓ in the PropertyManager to accept the changes and to exit the PropertyManager.

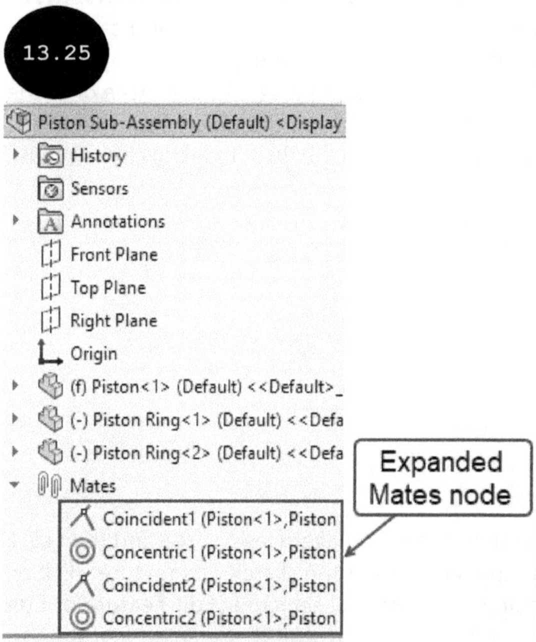

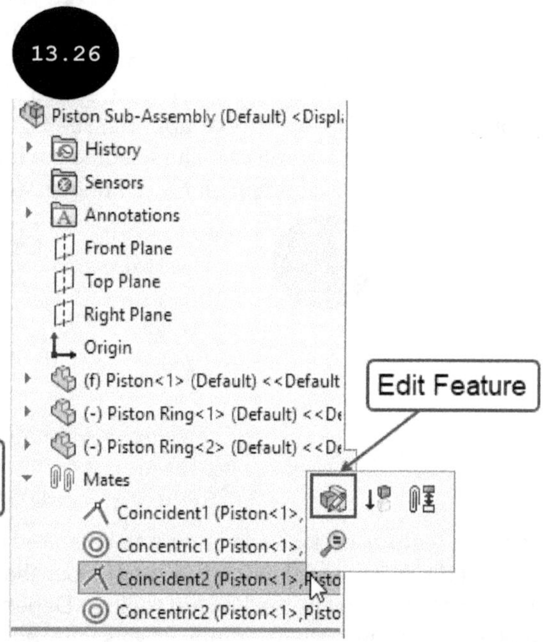

Patterning Assembly Components

Similar to patterning a feature of a component in the Part modeling environment, you can also pattern one or more components of an assembly in the Assembly environment, see Figure 13.27. In this figure, two components of the assembly are patterned to create its other instances.

13.27

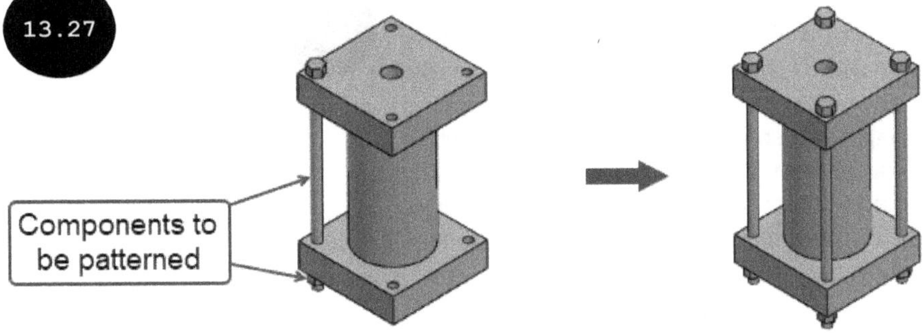

In the Assembly environment, you can create different types of patterns such as linear component patterns, circular component patterns, sketch driven component patterns, curve driven component patterns, pattern driven component patterns, and chain component patterns, by using the respective tools available in the **Pattern** flyout of the **Assembly CommandManager**, see Figure 13.28. The methods for creating a linear component pattern, circular component pattern, sketch driven component pattern, and curve driven component pattern are the same as discussed earlier while creating patterns in the Part modeling environment. The only difference is that in the Part modeling environment, you pattern features to create multiple instances, however, in the Assembly environment, you pattern components to create multiple instances. The methods for creating some of the pattern types are discussed next.

13.28

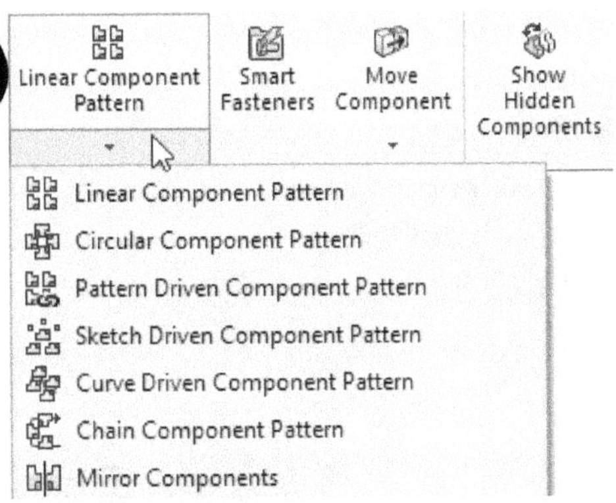

Creating a Linear Component Pattern

A linear component pattern is created by patterning a component or components in an assembly, linearly in one or two linear directions, refer to Figure 13.27. Besides, you can also create a linear component pattern by rotating the pattern instances of a component along the pattern direction, see Figure 13.29.

13.29

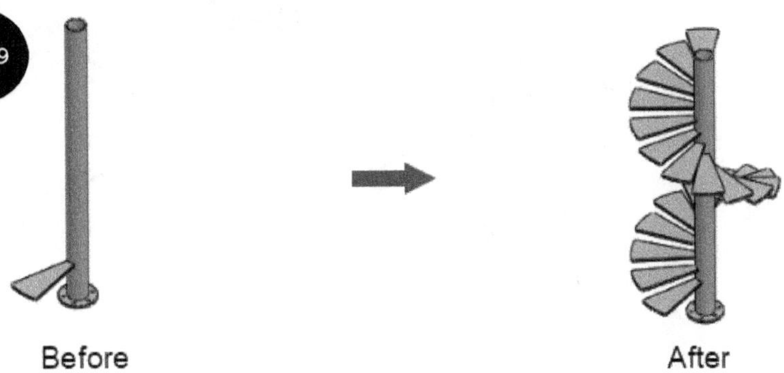

To create a linear component pattern, click on the **Linear Component Pattern** tool in the **Assembly CommandManager**. The **Linear Pattern PropertyManager** appears, see Figure 13.30. The options in this PropertyManager are same as discussed earlier while creating a linear pattern of features in the Part modeling environment except for the **Rotate instances** check box. This check box is used for rotating the pattern instances along the pattern direction.

13.30

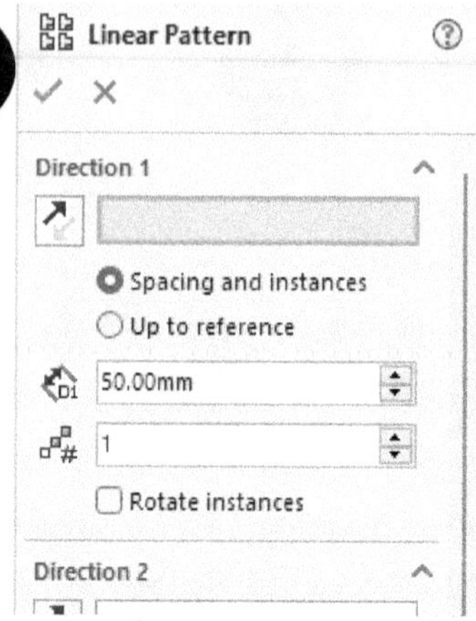

To rotate the pattern instances along the pattern direction, select the **Rotate instances** check box in the **Direction 1** rollout of the PropertyManager. The **Axis of Rotation** field, **Angle** field, and **Fixed axis of rotation** check box appear in the rollout, see Figure 13.31. The **Axis of Rotation** field is used for defining the axis of rotation for the pattern instances. You can select an axis, a line, or an edge as the axis of rotation. The **Angle** field is used for specifying the angular increment value for each pattern instance. On selecting the **Fixed axis of rotation** check box, the pattern instances rotate around a common axis that is selected in the **Axis of Rotation** field of the PropertyManager, see Figure 13.32. When the **Fixed axis of rotation** check box is cleared, each pattern instance rotates around its respective axis of rotation along direction 1, see Figure 13.33.

13.31

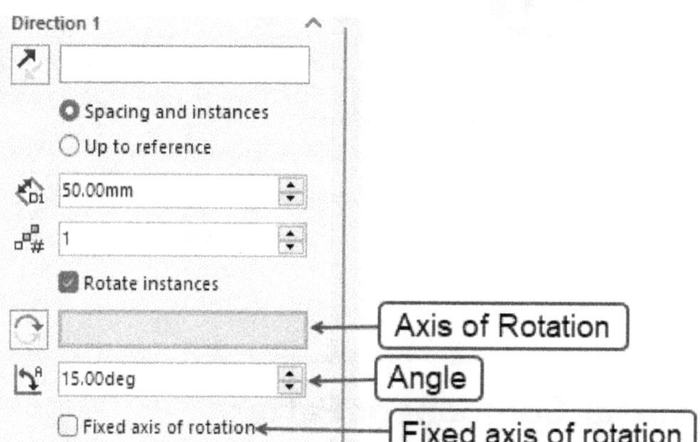

13.32

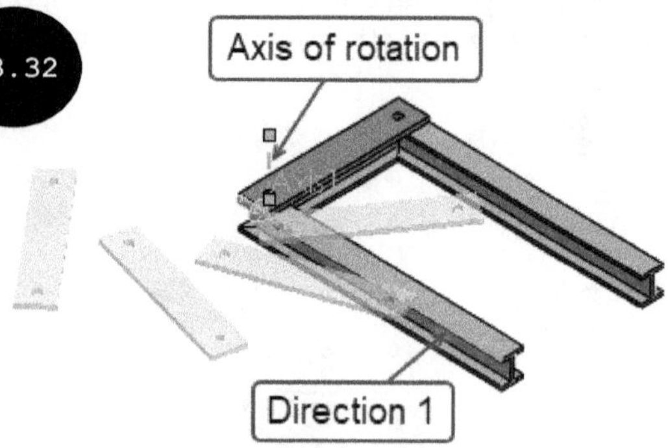

13.33

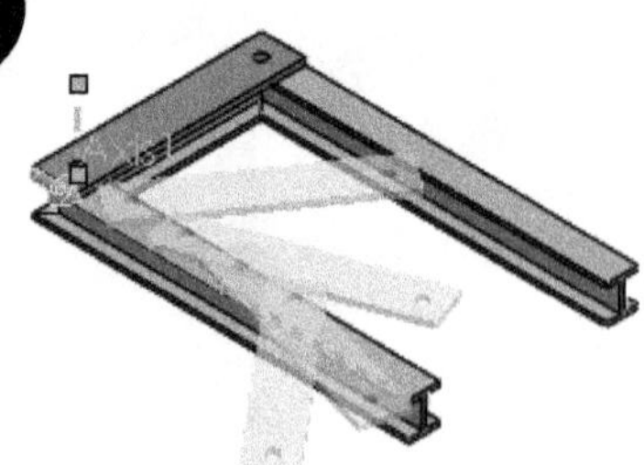

On selecting the **Align to seed** check box, each pattern instance is aligned to match the alignment of the parent component. Note that this check box is available only when the **Fixed axis of rotation** check box is selected in the PropertyManager. Figure 13.34 shows the preview of a linear component pattern with rotating pattern instances along the axis of rotation when the **Align to seed** check box is cleared. Figure 13.35 shows the preview of a linear component pattern when the **Align to seed** check box is selected.

13.34

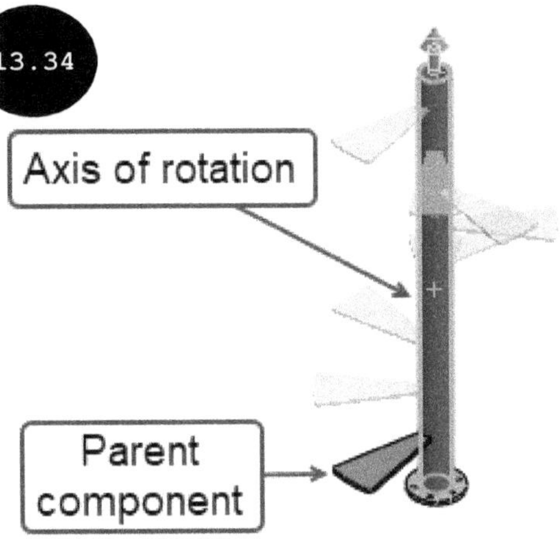

13.35

You can also define the alignment type for the pattern instances by using the **Bounding box center** and the **Component origin** radio buttons. Note that these radio buttons become available when the **Align to seed** check box is selected. Figure 13.35 shows the alignment of pattern instances when the **Bounding box center** radio button is selected, and Figure 13.36 shows the alignment of pattern instances when the **Component origin** radio button is selected.

13.36

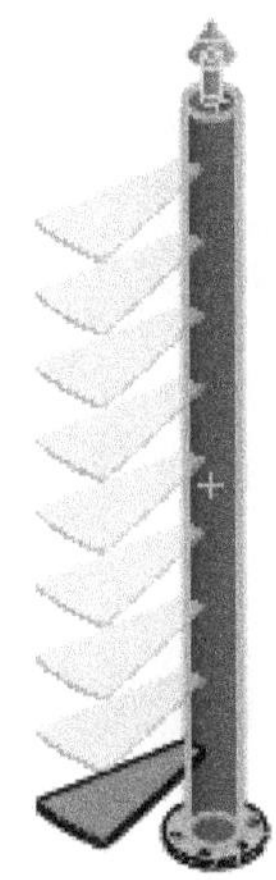

In SOLIDWORKS, you can also vary the linear spacing for individual instances, without disturbing other instances of the pattern. To do this, click in the **Modified instances** field of the **Instances to Override** rollout in the PropertyManager. The pink dots are displayed at the center of all pattern instances in the graphics area, see Figure 13.37. Move the cursor over the pink dot of a pattern instance to be modified and then click the left mouse button when the appearance of the cursor changes to a hand cursor. A callout gets attached to the selected instance with **Dir 1 distance from seed** and **Dir 1 offset from nominal** fields, see Figure 13.37. The **Dir 1 distance from seed** field displays the current distance of the selected instance from the parent instance while the **Dir 1 offset from nominal** field displays the current distance of the selected instance from its current position. You can specify the required distance value in these fields. The position of the selected instance gets changed, as specified.

13.37

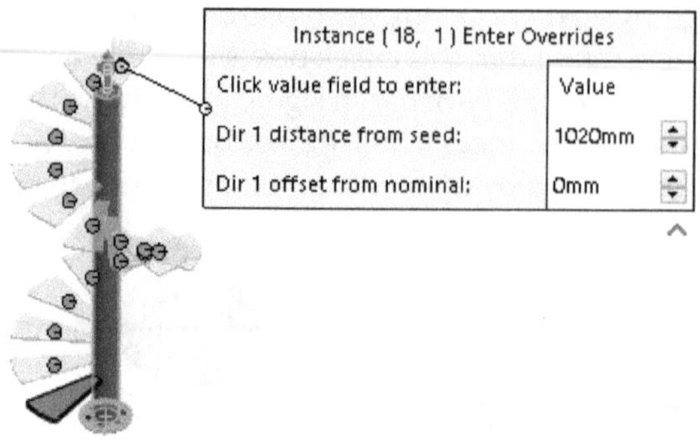

In SOLIDWORKS, while patterning a component having multiple configurations, you can ensure that all pattern instances use the same configuration as that of the parent component by selecting the **Synchronize configuration of patterned components to seed** check box in the **Options** rollout in the PropertyManager. It blocks any variations in the resultant pattern such that the option to change the configuration of a pattern instance gets disabled.

Note: In SOLIDWORKS, if the assembly file has multiple configurations, you can select the **This Configuration**, **All Configurations**, or **Specify Configurations** option for selected skipped instances to skip them from the current configuration, all configurations, or selected configurations, respectively in the **Skipped instances** area of the **Instances to Override** rollout, see Figure 13.38. These options are available for linear component pattern, circular component pattern, pattern driven component pattern, sketch driven component pattern, and curve driven component pattern.

13.38

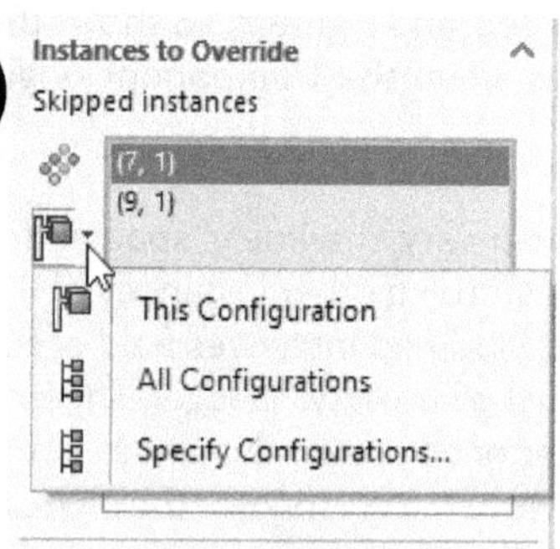

The remaining options of the PropertyManager are the same as discussed earlier in the Part modeling environment. After specifying the parameters for creating the linear component pattern, click on the green tick-mark in PropertyManager.

Creating a Circular Component Pattern

A circular component pattern is created by patterning one or more components of an assembly, circularly around an axis, see Figure 13.39. In the Assembly environment, you can create a circular component pattern by using the **Circular Component Pattern** tool. The method for creating a circular component pattern is the same as discussed earlier while creating a circular pattern in the Part modeling environment.

13.39

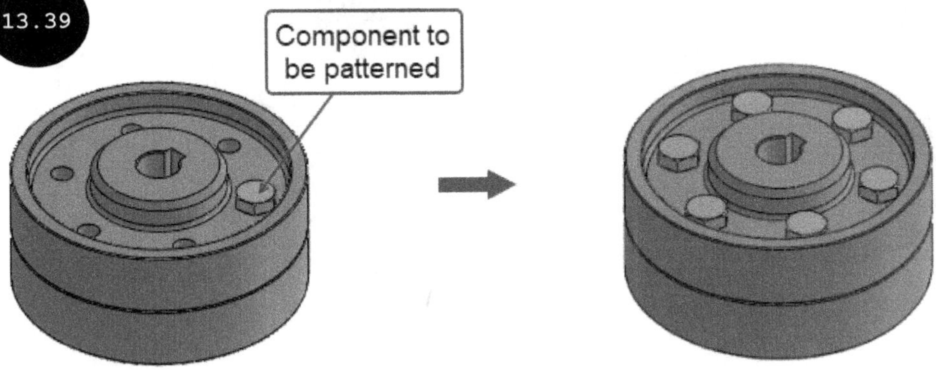

In SOLIDWORKS, you can also vary the angle spacing for individual instances, without disturbing other instances of the pattern. To do this, click in the **Modified instances** field of the **Instances to Override** rollout in the PropertyManager. The pink dots are displayed at the center of all pattern instances in the graphics area. Move the cursor over the pink dot of a pattern instance to be modified and then click the left mouse button when the appearance of the cursor changes to a hand cursor. A callout gets attached to the selected instance with **Angle from seed** and **Offset from nominal** fields, see Figure 13.40. The **Angle from seed** field displays the angle value of the selected instance from the parent instance while the **Offset from nominal** field displays the angle value of the selected instance from its current position. You can specify the required angle value in these fields. The position of the selected instance gets changed, as specified. Note that all other options in the PropertyManager are the same as discussed earlier.

13.40

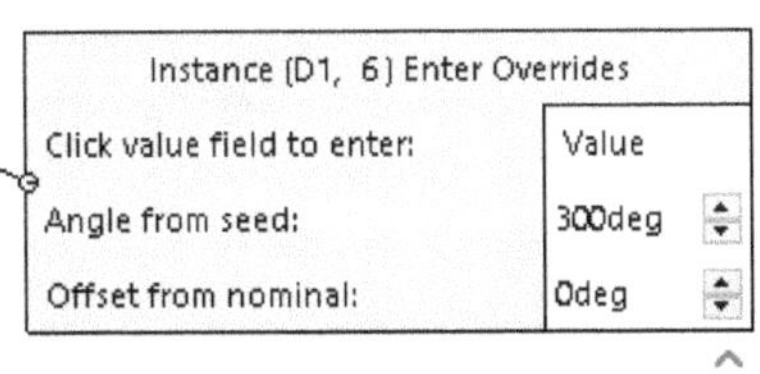

Creating a Pattern Driven Component Pattern

A pattern driven component pattern is created by patterning a component in an assembly concerning a pattern feature of another component. In this type of pattern, the component to be patterned is driven by a pattern feature of another component. Consider the case of an assembly shown in Figure 13.41, which has two components: Component 1 and Component 2. In this assembly, Component 2 is to be patterned concerning the circular pattern feature of Component 1. Figure 13.42 shows the resultant assembly, in which a pattern driven component pattern is created by patterning Component 2 concerning the circular pattern feature of Component 1. Note that on modifying the number of instances of the pattern feature of Component 1, the number of instances of the pattern driven component pattern is also modified, automatically. This is because the instances of the pattern driven component pattern are driven by the instances of the pattern feature.

13.41

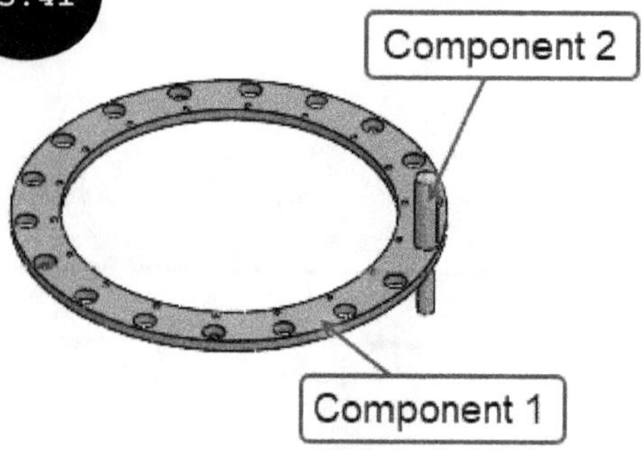

13.42

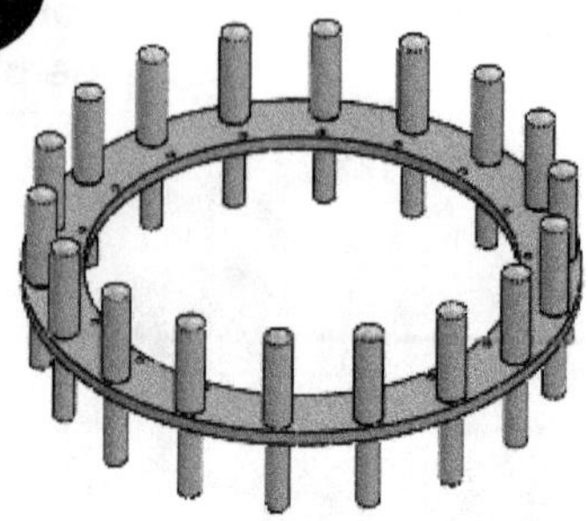

To create a pattern driven component pattern, click on the arrow at the bottom of the **Linear Component Pattern** tool in the **Assembly CommandManager** and then click on the **Pattern Driven Component Pattern** tool in the **Pattern** flyout that appears. The **Pattern Driven PropertyManager** appears, see Figure 13.43. The options of the PropertyManager are discussed next.

13.43

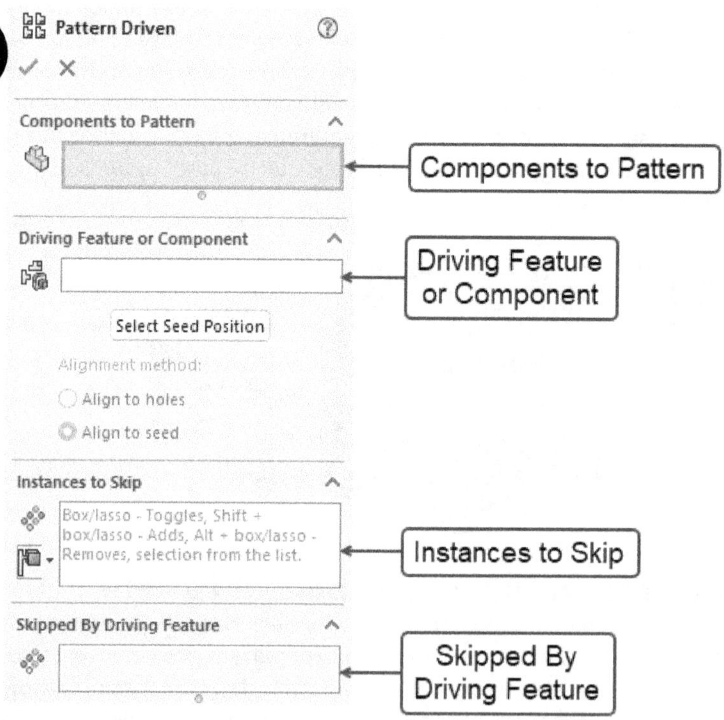

Components to Pattern

The **Components to Pattern** field is used for selecting components to be patterned. By default, this field is activated. As a result, you can select components to be patterned either from the graphics area or from the FeatureManager Design Tree.

Driving feature or component

The **Driving feature or component** field is used for selecting an instance of a pattern feature of a component as the driving feature, see Figure 13.44. To select a pattern instance (driving feature), click on this field in the PropertyManager and then select a pattern instance of a pattern. After selecting the component to be patterned and a pattern instance (driving feature), a preview of the pattern driven component pattern appears in the graphics area, see Figure 13.45.

Note: By default, the position of the seed/parent instance of a pattern is taken as the position of the component being patterned. You can change the default position of the seed pattern instance by using the **Select Seed Position** button of the **Driving Feature or Component** rollout. On clicking the **Select Seed Position** button, a blue dot appears in the preview of each pattern instance in the graphics area. You can click on the blue dot of the pattern instance to select it as the seed feature of the pattern.

13.44

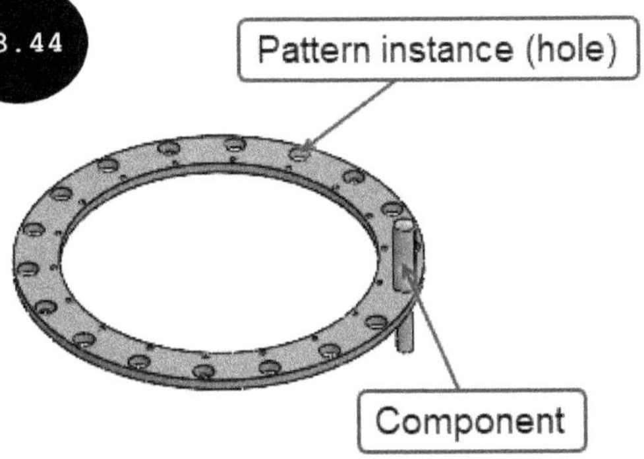

13.45

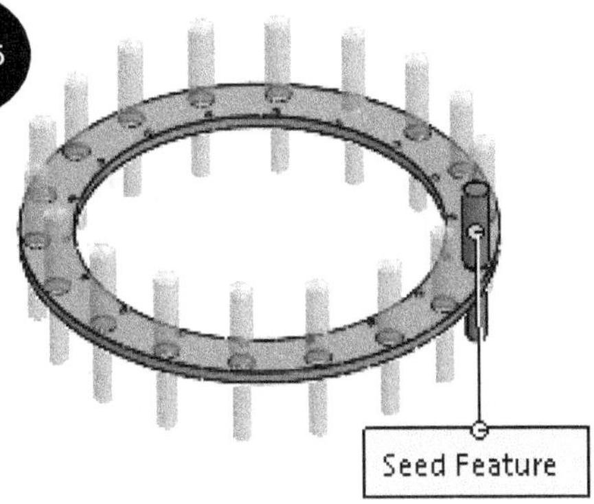

The **Alignment method** area becomes available in the PropertyManager if a hole feature is created using the **Hole Wizard** or **Advanced Hole** tool and is selected as a driving feature for creating the pattern, see Figures 13.46 and 13.47. In the **Alignment method** area, the **Align to holes** radio button is selected, by default. As a result, all the pattern instances get aligned parallel to the respective hole axes, see Figure 13.48. On selecting the **Align to seed** radio button, all the pattern instances get aligned as per the alignment of the seed component, see Figure 13.49.

13.46

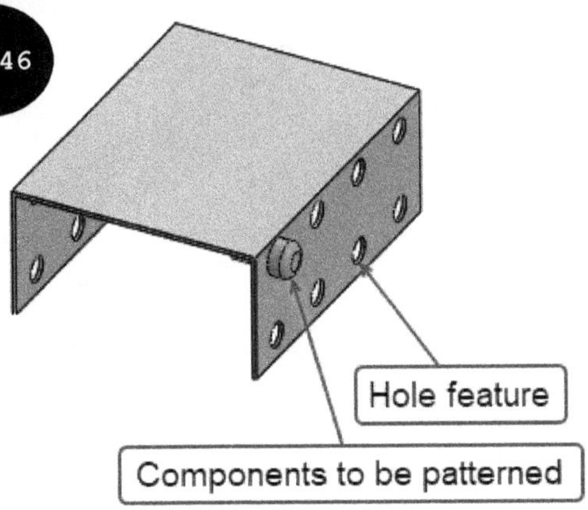

13.47

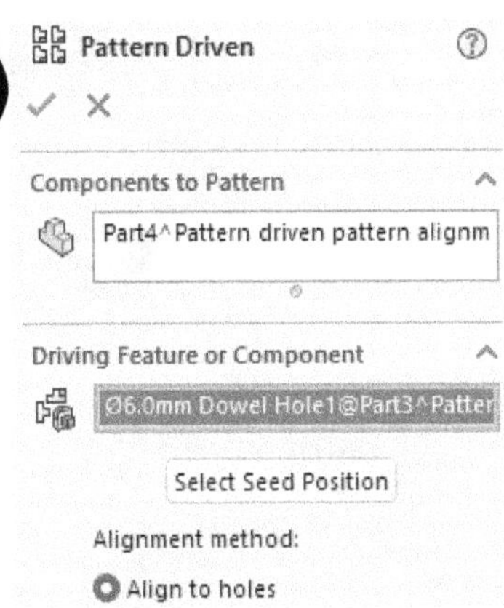

13.48

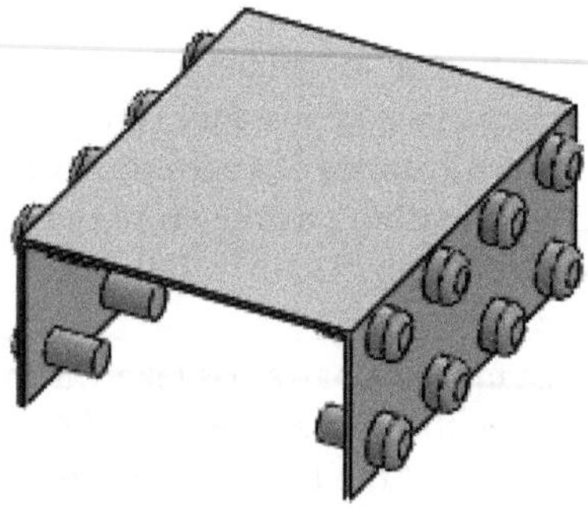

13.49

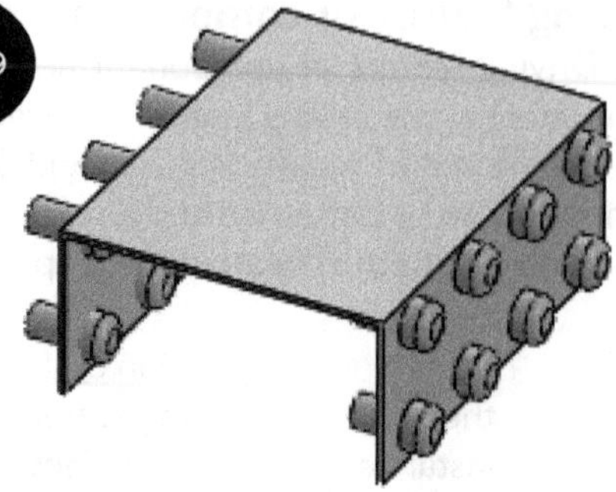

Instances to Skip

The **Instances to Skip** field is used for skipping pattern instances of the pattern. To skip pattern instances, click on the **Instances to Skip** field in the rollout. A pink dot appears on each pattern instance in the graphics area, see Figure 13.50. Move the cursor over the instance to be skipped and then click on it.

13.50

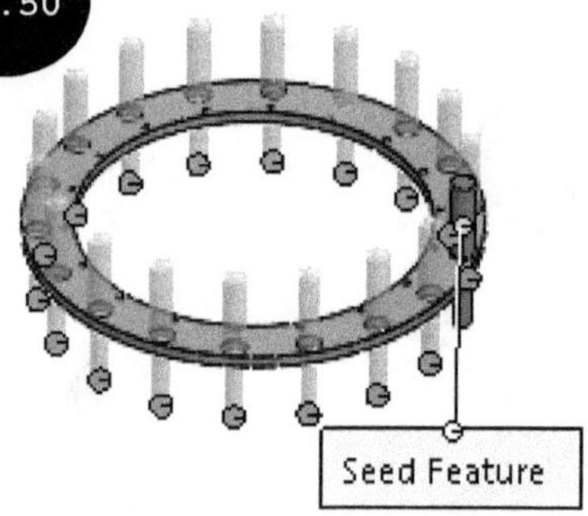

Skipped By Driving Feature

The **Skipped By Driving Feature** field is used for displaying the list of pattern instances, which are skipped in the pattern feature (driving) of the component.

After selecting the components to be patterned and a pattern instance, click on the green tick-mark ✓ in the PropertyManager. The pattern driven component pattern is created.

Creating a Chain Component Pattern

A chain component pattern is created by patterning a component along an open or a closed path to simulate the chain drive or cable carrier mechanism dynamically in an assembly, see Figure 13.51. In SOLIDWORKS, you can create a chain component pattern by using the **Chain Component Pattern** tool.

13.51

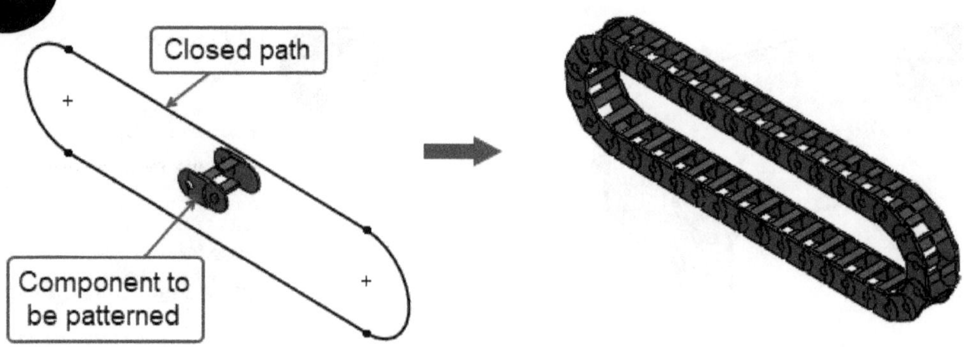

In a chain component pattern, the component drives along an open or closed path such that you can simulate its motion dynamically by dragging the pattern instances. To create a chain component pattern, invoke the **Pattern** flyout (see Figure 13.52) and then click on the **Chain Component Pattern** tool. The **Chain Pattern PropertyManager** appears, see Figure 13.53.

13.52

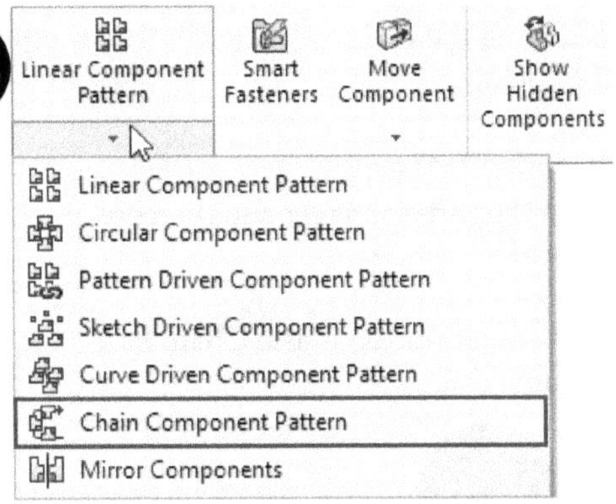

13.53

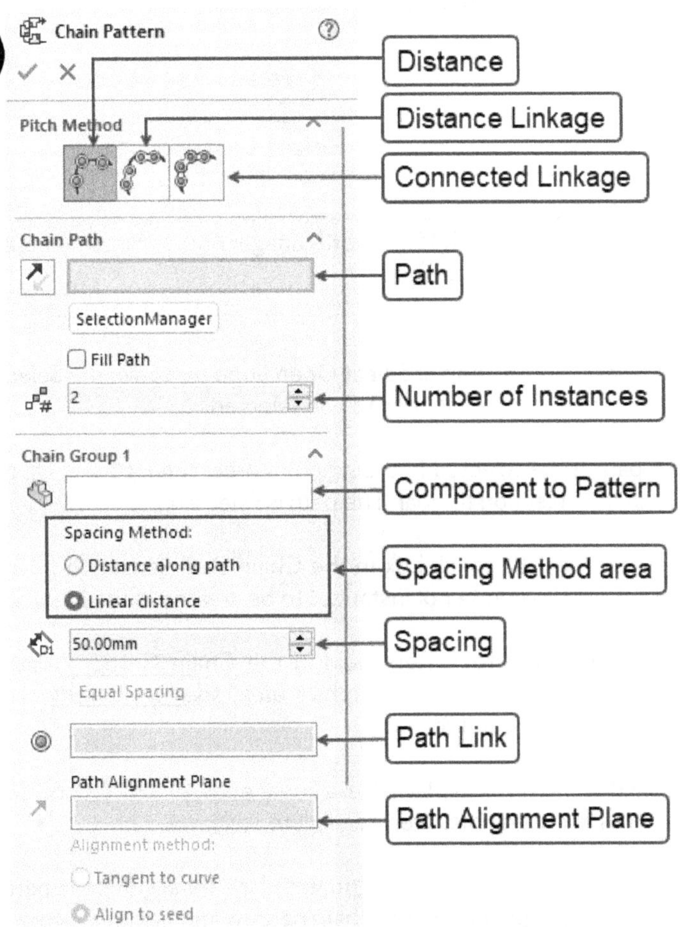

The **Chain Pattern PropertyManager** is used for creating three types of chain patterns: Distance, Distance Linkage, and Connected Linkage. The Distance chain pattern is used for patterning a component along a path with a single link among the pattern instances. The Distance Linkage chain pattern is used for patterning a component along a path with two non-connected links among the pattern instances. The Connected Linkage chain pattern is used for patterning a component along a path with connected links among the pattern instances. The methods for creating different types of chain patterns are discussed below:

Creating a Distance Chain Pattern

1. Invoke the **Chain Pattern PropertyManager** and then ensure that the **Distance** button is selected in its **Pitch Method** rollout.

2. Click on the **SelectionManager** button in the **Chain Path** rollout to select a path. The **Selection** toolbar appears, see Figure 13.54.

13.54

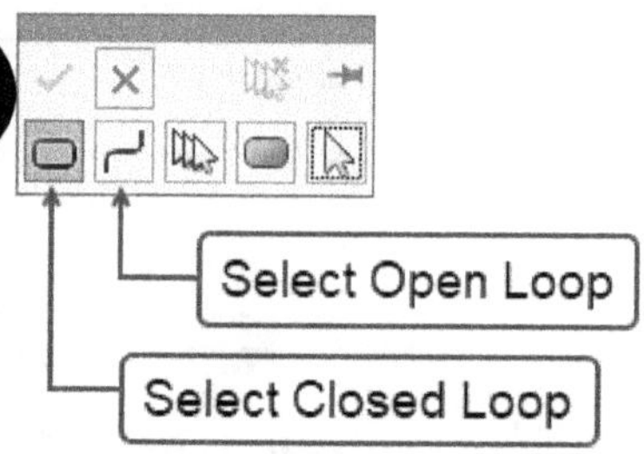

Tip: It is recommended to use the **SelectionManager** button for selecting an open or closed sketch as a path having multiple segments.

3. Click on the **Select Closed Loop** or **Select Open Loop** button in the **Selection** toolbar, depending upon the type of path (closed or open) to be selected.

4. Click on the path to be selected in the graphics area, see Figure 13.55. Next, click on the green tick-mark ✓ in the **Selection** toolbar. The path is selected.

5. Either select the **Fill Path** check box in the **Chain Path** rollout to fill in the path with pattern instances or specify the number of instances to be created in the **Number of Instances** field.

6. Click on the **Component to Pattern** field in the **Chain Group 1** rollout and then select the component to be patterned in the graphics area, see Figure 13.55. The **Path Link** field gets activated in the **Chain Group 1** rollout.

7. Click on a cylindrical face, a circular edge, a linear edge, or a reference axis as the link among the pattern instances in the graphics area, see Figure 13.55.

8. Select a plane or a planar face as the alignment plane for aligning the pattern instances along the path, see Figure 13.55. A preview of the chain pattern appears, see Figure 13.56.

13.55

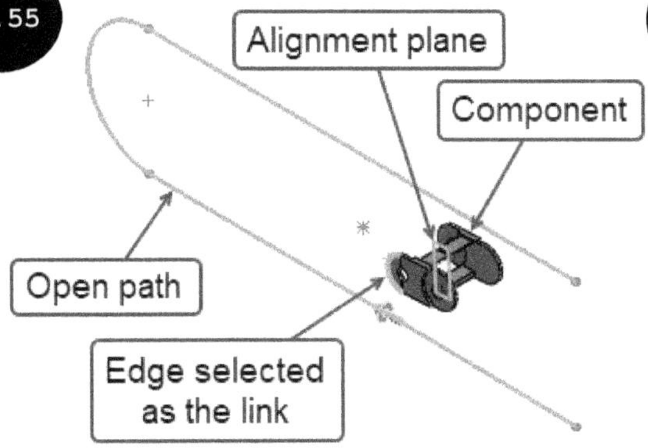

13.56

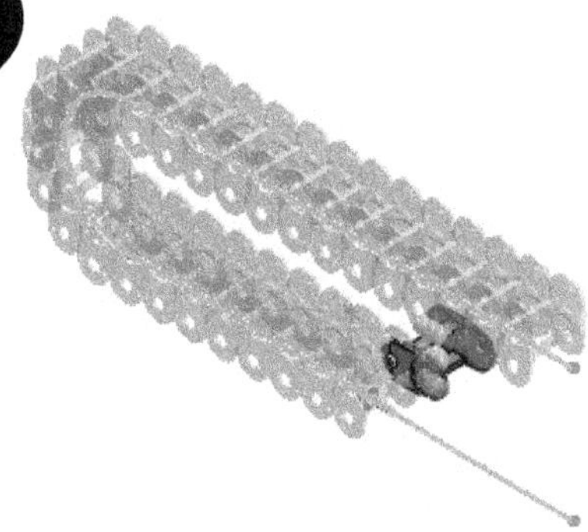

9. Select the required radio button (**Distance along path** or **Linear distance**) in the **Spacing Method** area for defining the spacing between the pattern instances, refer to Figure 13.53.

Note: On selecting the **Distance along path** radio button, the spacing is measured along the path. On selecting the **Linear distance** radio button, the spacing is measured as a linear distance.

10. Specify the spacing between the pattern instances in the **Spacing** field depending upon the radio button selected in the **Spacing Method** area.

11. Click on the green tick-mark ✓ in the PropertyManager. The chain component pattern is created, see Figure 13.57.

13.57

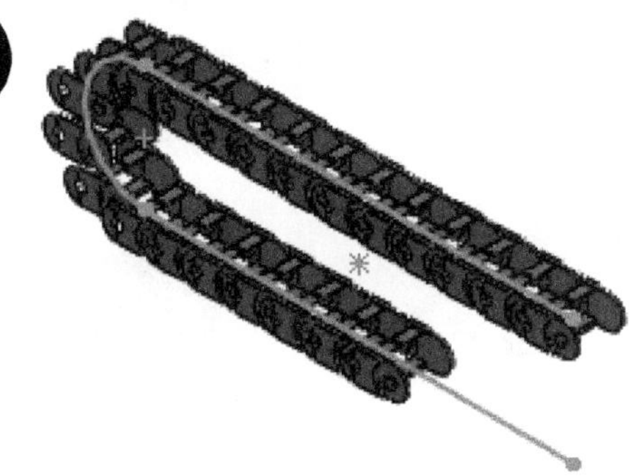

Creating a Distance Linkage Chain Pattern

1. Invoke the **Chain Pattern PropertyManager** as discussed earlier, and then click on the **Distance Linkage** button in the **Pitch Method** rollout to create a distance linkage chain pattern.

2. Select an open or closed sketch as a path by using the **SelectionManager** button of the **Chain Path** rollout, as discussed earlier.

3. Either specify the number of pattern instances to be created along the path in the **Number of Instances** field or select the **Fill Path** check box to fill in the path with pattern instances.

4. Click on the **Component to Pattern** field in the **Chain Group 1** rollout and then select the component to be patterned in the graphics area, see Figure 13.58. The **Path Link 1** field gets activated in the **Chain Group 1** rollout.

5. Click on a cylindrical face, a circular edge, a linear edge, or a reference axis as the link 1 among the pattern instances in the graphics area, see Figure 13.58.

6. Click on a cylindrical face, a circular edge, a linear edge, or a reference axis as the link 2 among the pattern instances, see Figure 13.58.

7. Click on a plane or a planar face as the alignment plane, see Figure 13.58. A preview of the pattern appears, see Figure 13.59.

13.58

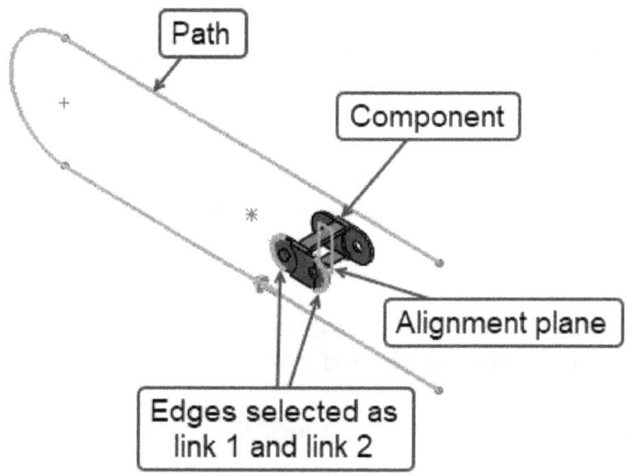

8. Select the required radio button (**Distance along path** or **Linear distance**) in the **Spacing Method** area and then specify the spacing between the pattern instances in the **Spacing** field accordingly.

9. Click on the green tick-mark ✓ in the PropertyManager. The distance linkage chain pattern is created, see Figure 13.60.

13.59

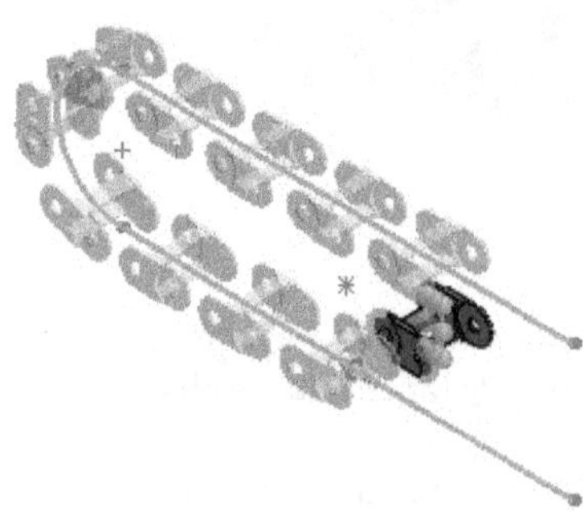

13.60

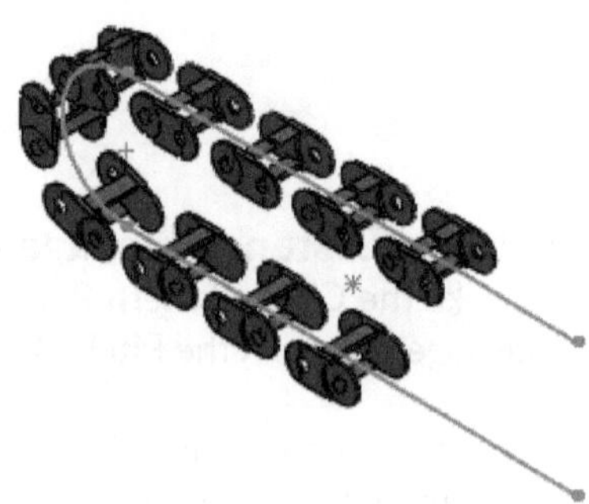

Note: In the **Options** rollout of the **Chain Pattern PropertyManager**, the **Dynamic** radio button is selected by default, see Figure 13.61. As a result, you can drag any pattern instance to move the chain. On selecting the **Static** radio button, you can move the chain only by dragging the parent or seed component of the pattern. The **Static** radio button helps in improving the overall performance of the system for large assemblies.

13.61

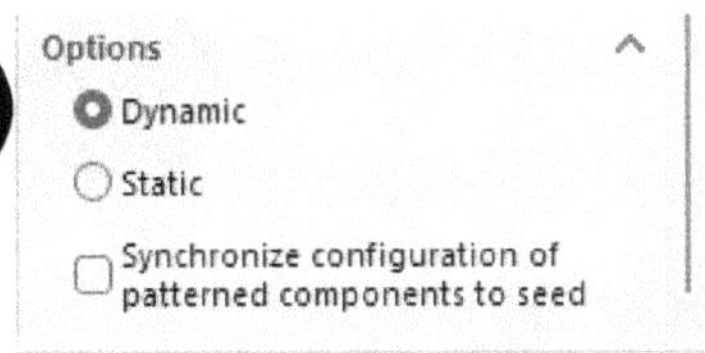

Creating a Connected Linkage Chain Pattern

1. Invoke the **Chain Pattern PropertyManager** and then click on the **Connected Linkage** button in the **Pitch Method** rollout to create a connected linkage chain pattern.

2. Select an open or a closed sketch as a path by using the **SelectionManager** button of the **Chain Path** rollout, as discussed earlier, see Figure 13.62.

3. Either specify the number of pattern instances to be created along the path in the **Number of Instances** field or select the **Fill Path** check box to fill in the path with pattern instances.

4. Click on the **Component to Pattern** field in the **Chain Group 1** rollout and then select the component to be patterned in the graphics area, see Figure 13.62. The **Path Link 1** field gets activated in the **Chain Group 1** rollout.

5. Click on a cylindrical face, a circular edge, a linear edge, or a reference axis as the link 1 between the pattern instances in the graphics area, see Figure 13.62.

6. Click on a cylindrical face, a circular edge, a linear edge, or a reference axis as the link 2 between the pattern instances, see Figure 13.62.

13.62

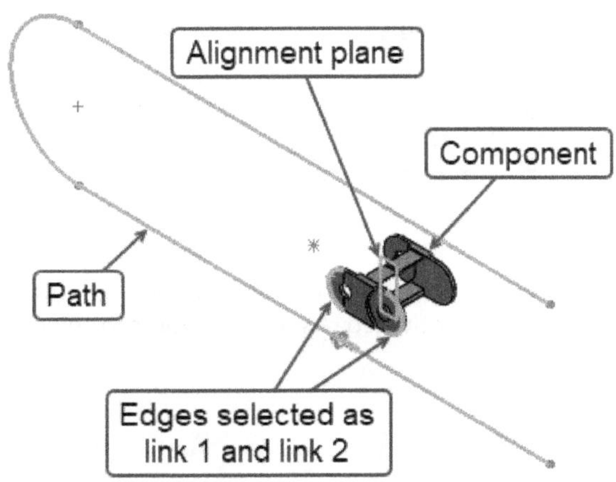

7. Click on a plane or a planar face as the alignment plane, see Figure 13.62. A preview of the pattern appears, see Figure 13.63. If the pattern preview does not appear in the graphics area, you need to reverse the direction of the pattern by clicking on the arrow that appears along the path in the graphics area.

8. Click on the green tick-mark ✓ of the PropertyManager. The connected linkage chain pattern is created, see Figure 13.64.

13.63

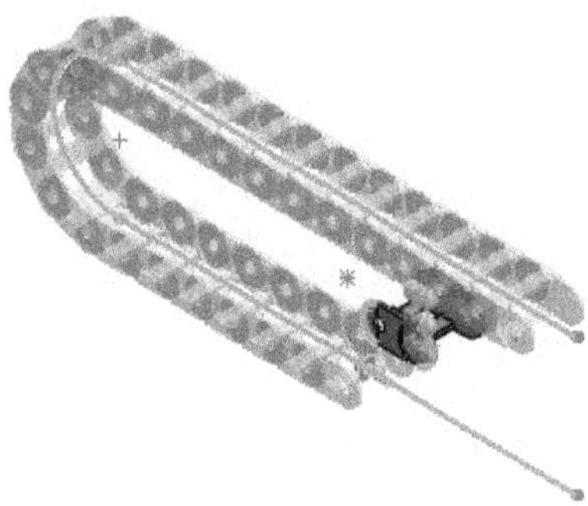

13.64

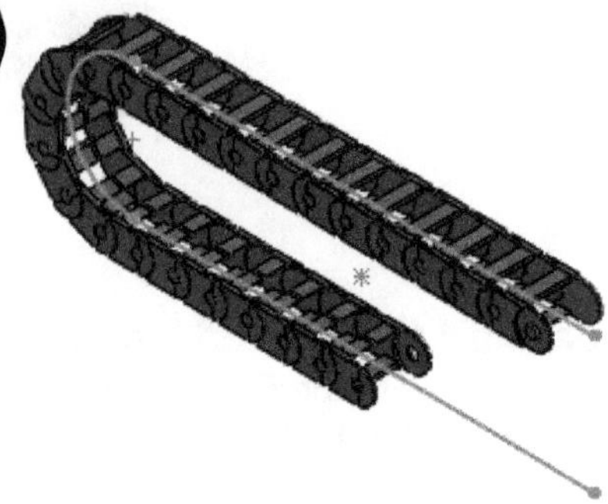

Mirroring Components of an Assembly

Similar to mirroring features in the Part modeling environment, you can also mirror components in the Assembly environment by using the **Mirror Components** tool of the **Pattern** flyout, see Figure 13.65.

To mirror components of an assembly, invoke the **Pattern** flyout and then click on the **Mirror Components** tool, see Figure 13.65. The **Mirror Components PropertyManager** appears, see Figure 13.66. The options of the PropertyManager are discussed next.

13.65

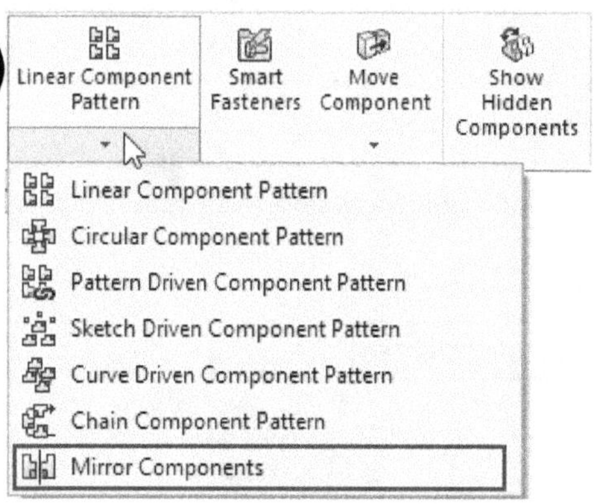

13.66

Mirror plane

The **Mirror plane** field is used for selecting a mirroring plane to mirror the selected components of an assembly. By default, this field is activated. As a result, you can select a plane or a planar face as the mirroring plane, see Figure 13.67.

Components to Mirror

The **Components to Mirror** field is used for selecting components to be mirrored about the mirroring plane. This field gets activated as soon as you select the mirroring plane. Select one or more components to be mirrored, see Figure 13.67.

After selecting the mirroring plane and the component to be mirrored, click on the green tick-mark ✓ in the PropertyManager. The selected component is mirrored about the mirroring plane, see Figure 13.68.

13.67

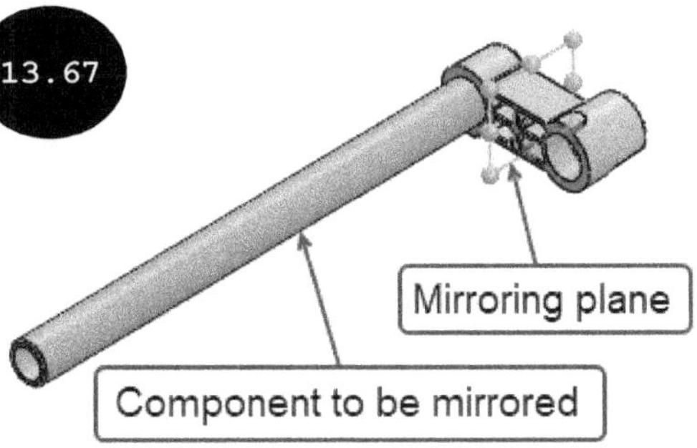

13.68

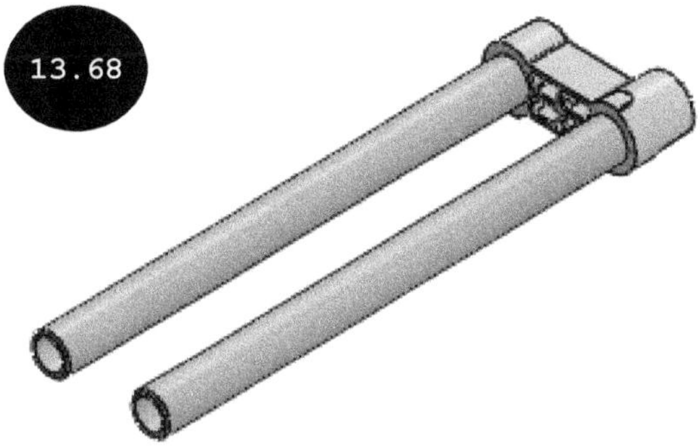

Note: You can also change the orientation of the mirrored component. To change the orientation of the mirrored component, click on the **Next** button in the **Mirror Components PropertyManager** to display the **Step 2: Set Orientation** page of the PropertyManager. Select the required radio button (**Center of bounding box, Center of mass**, or **Component origin**) as the mirror type. Next, choose an orientation for the mirrored component by selecting the required button in the **Orient Components** rollout.

If you have selected a flexible sub-assembly as the component to be mirrored, then you can synchronize the movement of the components of the mirrored sub-assembly with respect to the movement of the parent sub-assembly (flexible) by selecting the **Synchronize movement of flexible subassembly components** check box of the PropertyManager. After selecting this check box, if you move the components of the flexible sub-assembly (parent), the respective components of the mirrored sub-assembly also move respectively and vice versa. Note that this check box is enabled only if the selected sub-assembly to be mirrored is a flexible sub-assembly. When the **Create opposite hand version** button is activated in the **Orient Components** rollout of the PropertyManager, you can click on the **Next** button in the **Mirror Components PropertyManager** to display the **Step 3: Opposite Hand** page of the PropertyManager. The options in the **Step 3: Opposite Hand** page of the PropertyManager are used for defining whether to create the mirrored component as a new derived configuration in the existing file or create a new file. You can also display the **Step 4: Import Features** page of the PropertyManager by again clicking on the **Next** button in the **Mirror Components PropertyManager**. The options in the **Step 4: Import Features** page are used for defining the properties to be imported or transferred from the parent component to the mirrored component. You can also include custom properties in the mirrored component by selecting the **Custom properties** check box in the **Step 4: Import Features** page of the PropertyManager. Also, on selecting the **Break link to original part** check box in the **Step 4: Import Features** page, the changes made in the parent component will not be reflected in the mirrored component.

Creating Assembly Features

In a manufacturing unit or a shop floor, after assembling all components of an assembly, several cut operations may be carried out in the components to give a final touch-up and align the components perfectly with each other. For this, SOLIDWORKS has tools to create cut features in the Assembly environment. Cut features created in the Assembly environment are known as assembly features and do not affect the original geometry of the components. For example, if you create an assembly feature (cut feature) on a component of an assembly in the Assembly environment; the assembly feature created will exist only in the assembly and if you open the same component in the Part modeling environment, you will not find the existence of the assembly feature. This means that the assembly features exist in the assembly only and will not affect the original geometry of the component.

In SOLIDWORKS, you can create assembly features such as holes, extruded cuts, revolved cuts, swept cuts, and fillets. The tools for creating assembly features are provided in the **Assembly Features** flyout, see Figure 13.69. The method for creating assembly features is the same as creating features in the Part modeling environment. For example, to create an extruded cut feature, click on the **Extruded Cut** tool in the **Assembly Features** flyout. The **Extrude PropertyManager** appears. Select a plane or a planar face as the sketching plane. The Sketching environment is invoked. Create the sketch of the extruded cut feature and then exit the Sketching environment. As soon as you exit the Sketching environment, a preview of the cut feature appears in the graphics area. Specify the required parameters for the extrusion in the PropertyManager and then click on the green tick mark. The extruded cut feature is created in the Assembly environment.

13.69

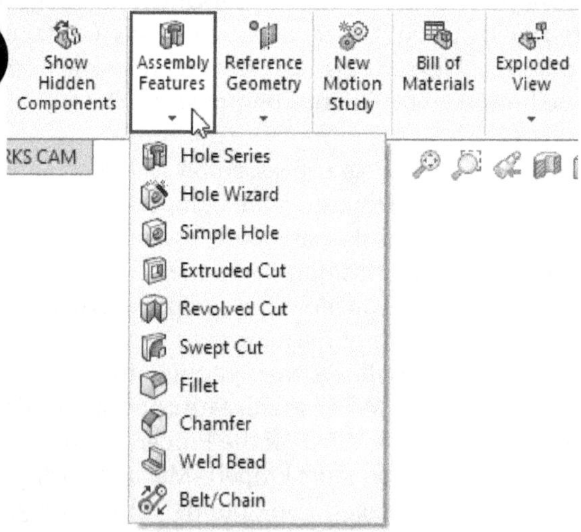

Note: You can also invoke the tools for creating the assembly features by clicking on **Insert > Assembly Feature** in the SOLIDWORKS Design Menus. In addition to creating the assembly features (cut features), you can mirror the assembly features about a mirroring plane by using the **Mirror** tool of the **Assembly Features** flyout. You can also create a linear pattern, circular pattern, table driven pattern, sketch driven pattern, and so on of the assembly features by using the respective tools available in the **Assembly Features** flyout. The tools for creating mirror and pattern features become available in the **Assembly Features** flyout only after creating an assembly feature in the Assembly environment.

Suppressing or Unsuppressing Components

In SOLIDWORKS, you can suppress or unsuppress components of an assembly. A suppressed component is removed from the assembly and does not appear in the graphics area. Also, the name of the suppressed component appears in gray in the FeatureManager Design Tree. Note that the suppressed component is not deleted from the assembly, it is only removed such that it is not loaded into the RAM (random access memory) while rebuilding the assembly. It helps you to speed up the overall performance of the system when you are working with larger assemblies.

To suppress a component of an assembly, select the component to be suppressed either from the graphics area or from the FeatureManager Design Tree. A Pop-up toolbar appears, see Figure 13.70. In this Pop-up toolbar, click on the **Suppress** tool. The selected component is suppressed.

13.70

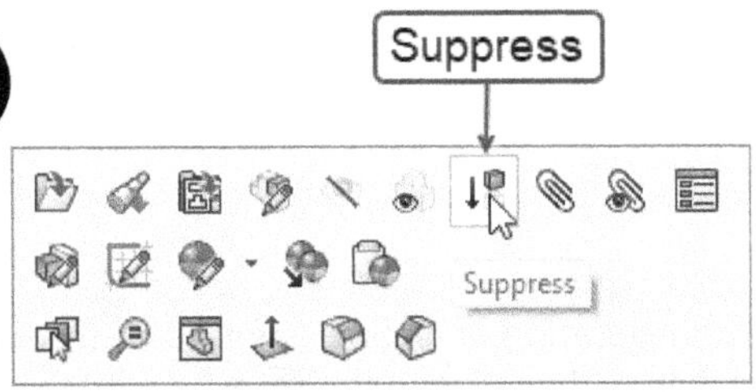

To unsuppress a suppressed component, select the suppressed component from the FeatureManager Design Tree. A Pop-up toolbar appears. Next, click on the **Unsuppress** tool in the Pop-up toolbar. The component is now unsuppressed and appears in the assembly.

Inserting Parts having Multiple Configurations

In SOLIDWORKS, you can choose a configuration of a component to be inserted in the Assembly environment. To choose the configuration of a component while inserting it in the Assembly environment, click on the **Insert Components** tool in the **Assembly CommandManager**. The **Open** dialog box appears automatically along with the **Insert Component PropertyManager**. Note that if the **Open** dialog box does not appear then click on the **Browse** button in the **Part/Assembly to Insert** rollout of the PropertyManager to open the **Open** dialog box. In the **Open** dialog box, browse to the location where the component to be inserted has been saved. Next, select the component that has multiple configurations and then invoke the **Configuration** drop-down list in the **Open** dialog box, see Figure 13.71. Now, select the required configuration of the component from this drop-down list that is to be inserted in the Assembly environment. Next, click on the **Open** button in the dialog box. The selected configuration of the component is attached to the cursor. Now, click on the graphics area to specify the position of the component.

Note: In SOLIDWORKS, you can create multiple configurations of a component in the Part modeling environment. For example, if a bolt of same geometry has to be used in an assembly several times with a different diameter, then you can create a single bolt with multiple configurations having different diameters. The different methods for creating multiple configurations are discussed in Chapter 11.

13.71

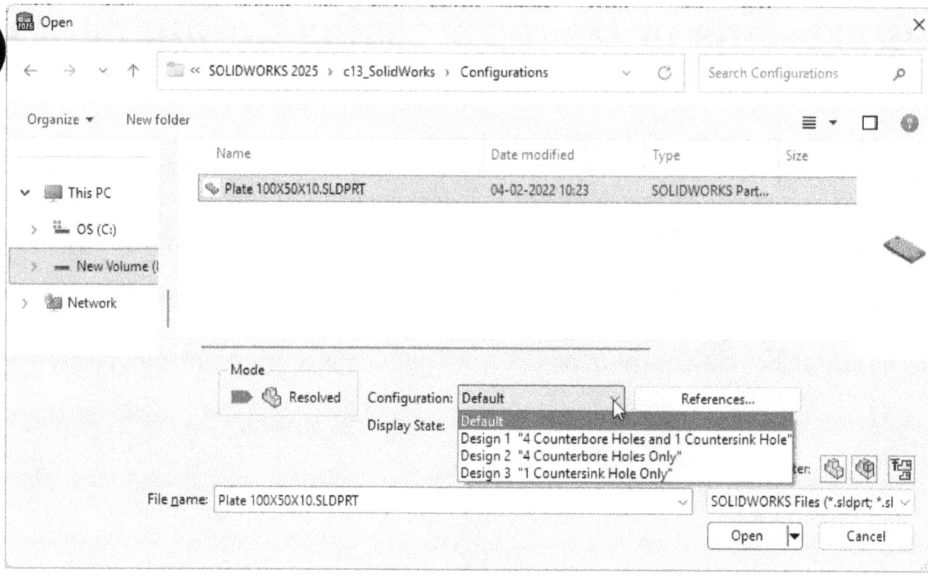

You can also choose the configuration of a component to be inserted in the Assembly environment by using the **Configuration** drop-down list of the **Insert Component PropertyManager** or the **Begin Assembly PropertyManager**. Additionally, you can change the configuration of a component even after inserting it in the Assembly environment. To change the configuration of an already inserted component, click on the component whose configuration has to be changed. A Pop-up toolbar appears with the **Configuration** drop-down list, see Figure 13.72. Next, invoke the **Configuration** drop-down list by clicking on the arrow and then select the required configuration of the component. Next, click on the green-tick mark that appears in front of the drop-down list to confirm the selection of the configuration. The configuration of the component changes to the selected configuration in the Assembly environment.

13.72

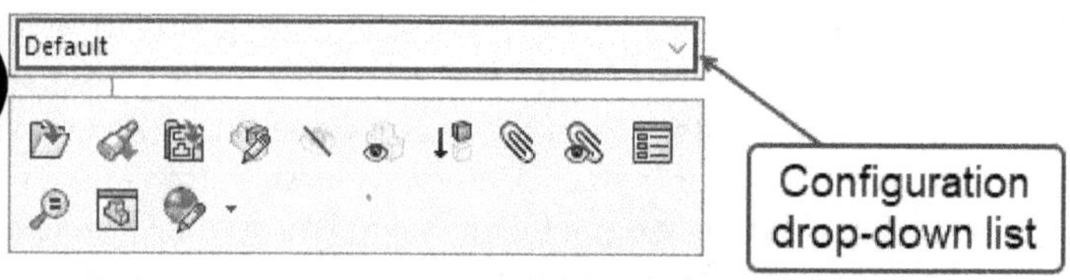

Creating and Dissolving Sub-Assemblies

SOLIDWORKS allows you to create sub-assemblies from the components of an assembly within the Assembly environment. To create a sub-assembly, select components to be included in the sub-assembly from the FeatureManager Design Tree by pressing the CTRL key and then right-clicking. A shortcut menu appears. In this shortcut menu, click on the **Form New Subassembly** option, see Figure 13.73. After selecting this option, a sub-assembly is created with a default name and the selected components become a part of the sub-assembly. In case, the **Assembly Structure Editing** window appears after selecting the **Form New Subassembly** option, click on the **Move** button. You can also include patterned and mirrored components in the sub-assembly. To rename the sub-assembly, select the sub-assembly in the FeatureManager Design Tree and then right-click. Next, click on the **Rename Assembly** option in the shortcut menu that appears. The name of the sub-assembly appears in an edit field. Now, you can enter a new name for the sub-assembly.

13.73

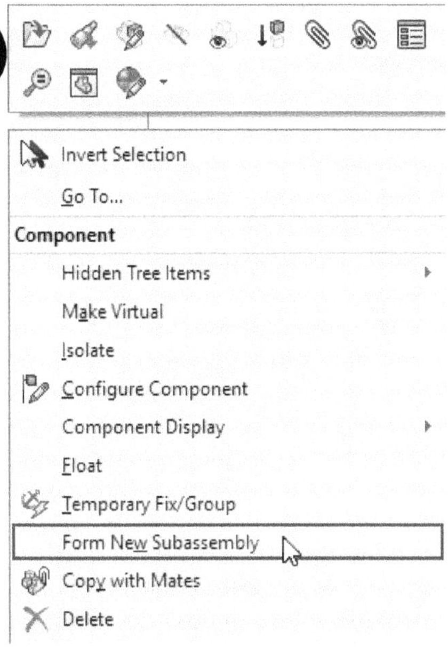

You can also dissolve the created sub-assembly in the Assembly environment. To dissolve a sub-assembly, select the sub-assembly to be dissolved in the FeatureManager Design Tree and then right-click to display a shortcut menu. Next, click on the **Dissolve Subassembly** option in the shortcut menu. The selected sub-assembly is dissolved and its components become the individual components of the main assembly.

Publishing Envelopes

In SOLIDWORKS, you can include components from a top-level assembly (main assembly) as envelopes in a sub-assembly by using the **Envelope Publisher** tool. It helps to work in the sub-assembly with the included enveloped components, together in isolation from the main assembly. Figure 13.74 shows a component of an assembly to be included as an envelope in a sub-assembly. Figure 13.75 shows a resultant sub-assembly and the enveloped component in isolation from the top-level assembly. It helps to work easily and collaboratively in large assemblies.

13.74

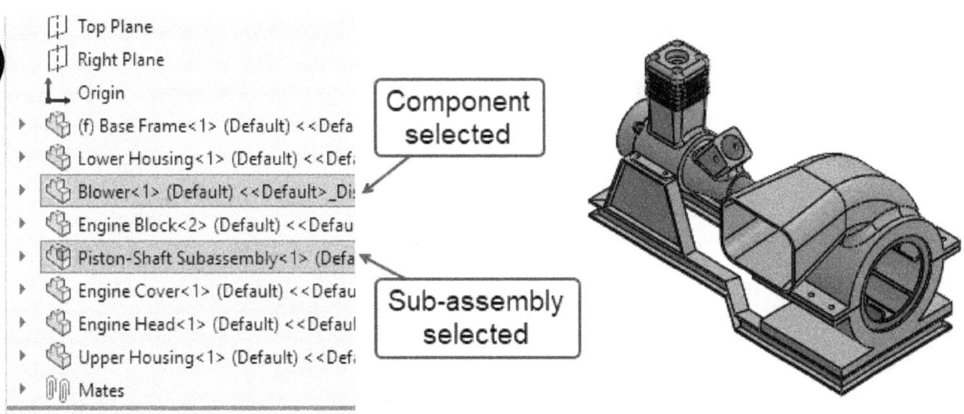

13.75

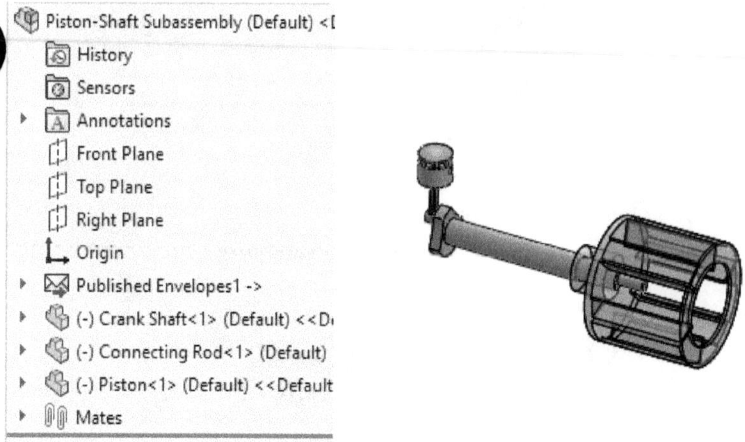

To include components of a top level assembly as envelopes in a sub-assembly, click on **Tools > Envelope Publisher** in the SOLIDWORKS Design Menus. The **Envelope Publisher PropertyManager** appears and you are prompted to select components to be published as envelopes in a destination sub-assembly, see Figure 13.76. Note that the **Envelope Publisher** tool is available only when the main assembly contains a sub-assembly. The options in the PropertyManager are discussed next.

13.76

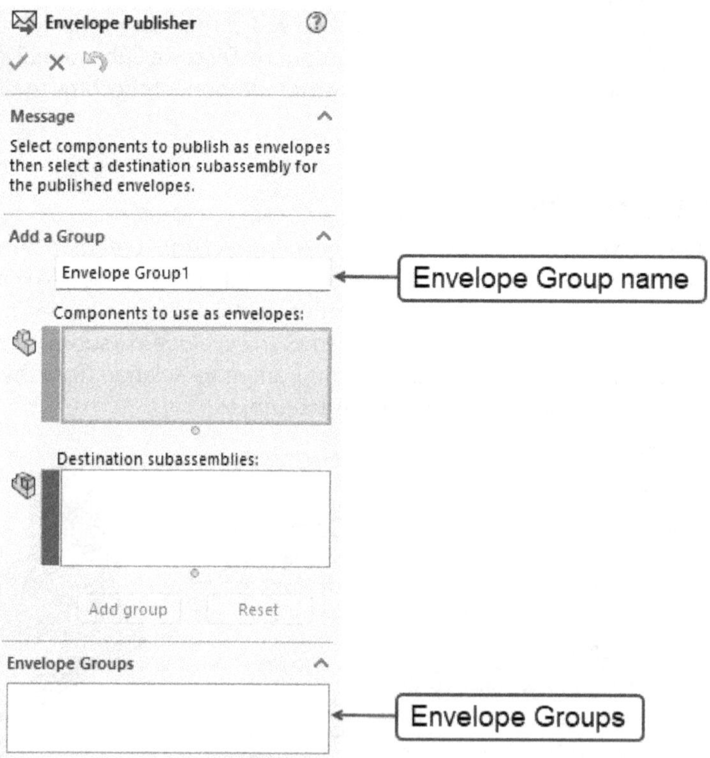

Note: If the **Envelope Publisher** tool is not available in the **Tools** menu of the SOLIDWORKS Design Menus, then click on the **Options** tool in the **Standard** toolbar. Next, click on the **External References** option in the **System Options** tab of the dialog box that appears. Next, ensure that the **Allow creation of references external to the model** check box is selected in the **Assemblies** area of the right panel in the dialog box. Also, ensure that the **Any component** radio button is selected as the **Reference component type** and the **Top level assembly** radio button is selected as the **In the context of** in the **Assemblies** area of the dialog box.

Envelope Group name

The **Envelope Group name** field of the **Add a Group** rollout displays a default name for the envelope group being created. You can use the default name or edit it, as required.

Components to use as envelopes

By default, the **Components to use as envelopes** field is activated in the PropertyManager. As a result, you can select the components of a top-level assembly to be published as envelopes in a destination sub-assembly. You can select components one by one either in the graphics area or in the FeatureManager Design Tree.

Destination subassemblies

The **Destination subassemblies** field is used for selecting a sub-assembly as a destination for the enveloped components that are selected in the **Components to use as envelopes** field of the PropertyManager. It is recommended to select a destination sub-assembly from the FeatureManager Design Tree.

After selecting the enveloped components and a destination sub-assembly, click on the **Add group** button in the PropertyManager. The envelope group gets created and its name appears in the **Envelope Groups** field of the PropertyManager. Similarly, you can create multiple envelope groups. Next, click on the green tick-mark in the PropertyManager. The selected components get published as envelopes in the selected destination sub-assembly and the **Published Envelopes** folder gets added under the sub-assembly folder in the FeatureManager Design Tree, see Figure 13.77. Now, when you open the sub-assembly by using the **Open Subassembly** or **Open Subassembly in Position** tool of the Pop-up toolbar that appears when you click on the sub-assembly in the FeatureManager Design Tree, the sub-assembly gets opened in a new window with its envelope components as an external reference. Now, you can work with the sub-assembly and the included enveloped components together, in isolation from the main assembly.

13.77

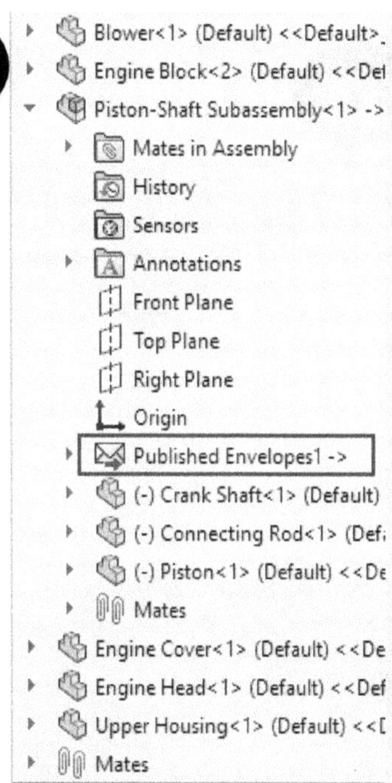

Creating an Exploded View

Creating an exploded view of an assembly is important from the presentation point of view. It helps you easily identify the position of each component of an assembly and in making technical documentation. It also helps technical and non-technical clients easily understand the inner components of an assembly. Figure 13.78 shows an assembly and Figure 13.79 shows its exploded view.

13.78

13.79

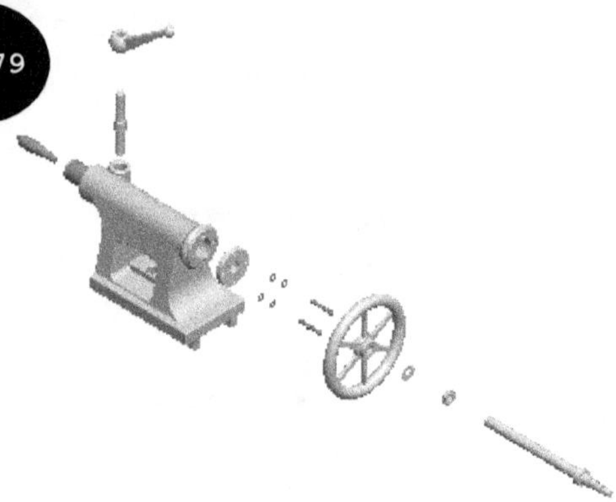

To create an exploded view of an assembly, click on the **Exploded View** tool in the **Assembly CommandManager**, see Figure 13.80. The **Explode PropertyManager** appears, see Figure 13.81. The options in the **Add a Step** rollout of the PropertyManager are used for creating two types of explode steps: Regular and Radial by activating the respective button (**Regular step** or **Radial step**) in this rollout. By activating the **Regular step** button, you can explode the components of an assembly by translating and rotating them along and about an axis and create a regular exploded step, see Figure 13.82. By activating the **Radial step** button, you can explode the components of an assembly by aligning them radially or cylindrically about an axis and create a radial step, see Figure 13.83. The methods for creating both these types of exploded steps are discussed next.

13.80

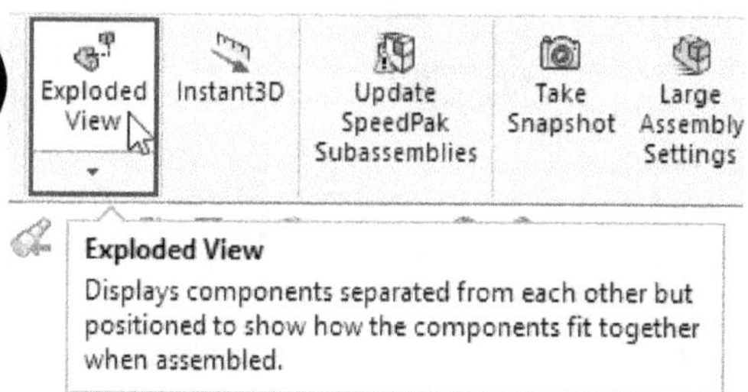

13.81

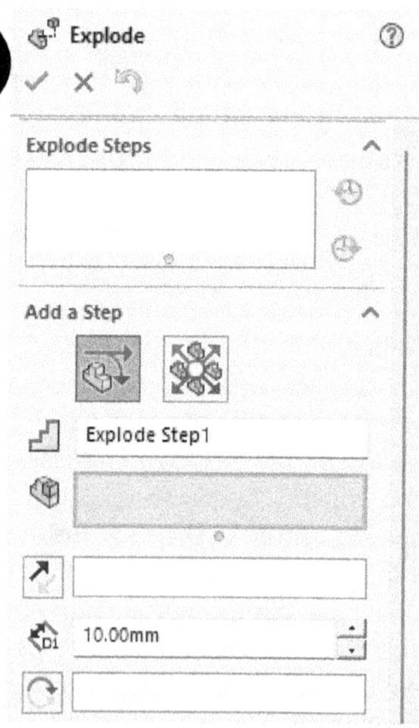

13.82

13.83

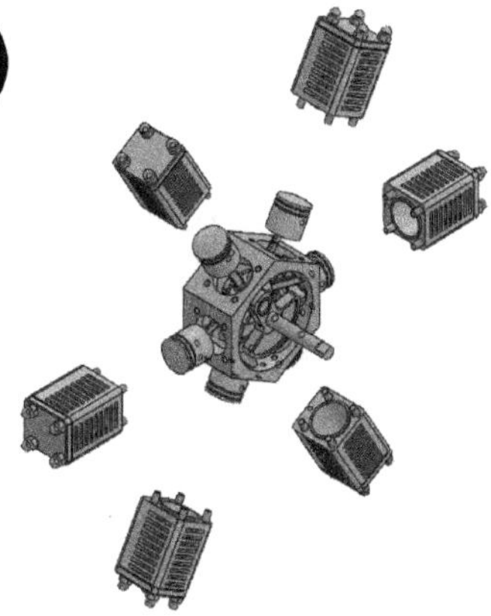

Creating a Regular Exploded Step

1. Ensure that the **Regular step** button is activated in the **Add a Step** rollout for creating a regular exploded step, see Figure 13.84.

13.84

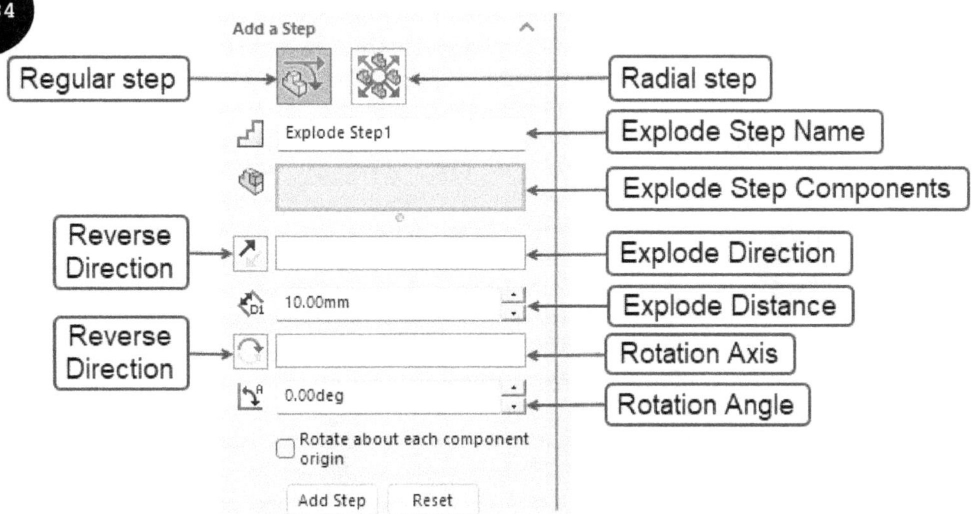

2. Specify a new name for the exploded step to be created or accept the default specified name in the **Explode Step Name** field of the PropertyManager.

3. Select one or more components to be exploded in the graphics area or the FeatureManager Design Tree one by one by clicking the left mouse button. The names of the selected components appear in the **Explode Step Components** field of the PropertyManager. Also, three rotation handles and three translation handles appear in the graphics area, see Figure 13.85.

4. Drag a translation handle or a rotation handle that appears in the graphics area by pressing and holding the left mouse button. Once the desired location has been achieved, release the left mouse button and then click on the **Done** button in the **Add a step** rollout of the PropertyManager. The first regular step is created in the graphics area, see Figure 13.86. Also, its name is listed in the **Explode Steps** rollout of the PropertyManager.

13.85

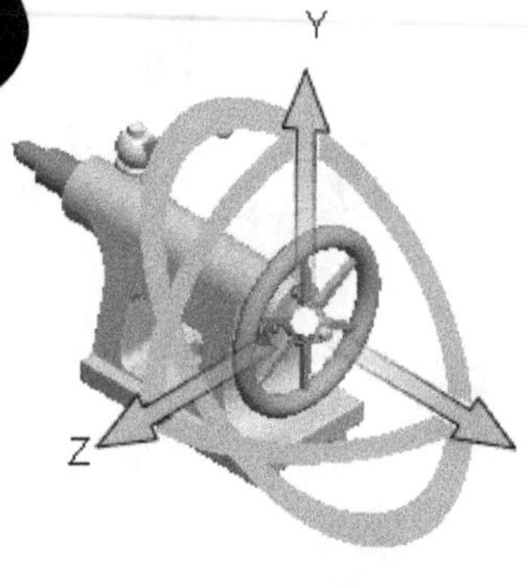

13.86

Note: Instead of dragging a translation or a rotation handle for creating an exploded step, enter the translation distance or the rotational angle value in the **Explode Distance** or **Rotation Angle** field of the PropertyManager, respectively, see Figure 13.87. Next, click on the **Add Step** button in the **Add a step** rollout of the PropertyManager. Note that the display of exploded direction depends upon the translation or rotational handle selected in the **Explode Direction** or **Rotation Axis** field of the PropertyManager, respectively. You can select the required translation or the rotation handle in the graphics area by clicking the left mouse button. Note that if you translate the components by dragging a translation or a rotational handle, then the translation distance or rotational angle values get updated automatically in these fields.

13.87

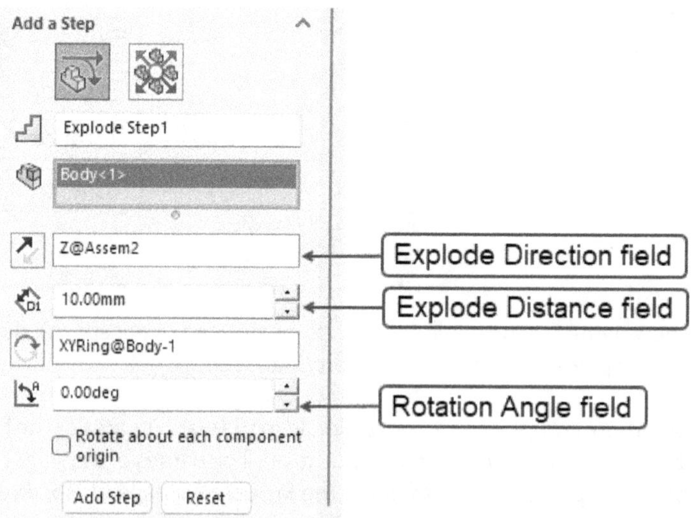

5. Similarly, create other exploded steps for the assembly one by one, see Figure 13.88. The names of all the exploded steps appear in the **Explode Steps** rollout, see Figure 13.89.

13.88

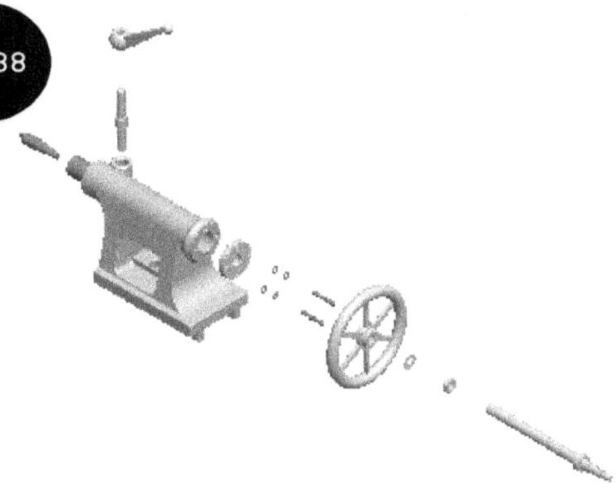

13.89

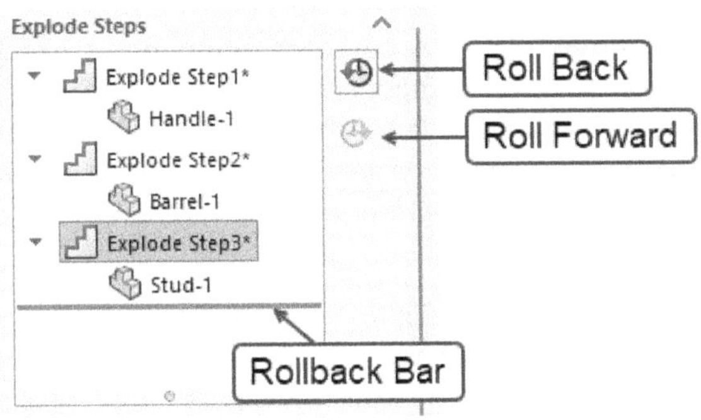

Note: The **Explode Steps** rollout displays a list of all exploded steps created for an exploded assembly, see Figure 13.89. To create an exploded assembly, you may need to create multiple exploded steps (regular and radial steps). In each exploded step, one or more than one component can be exploded. You can also roll back or roll forward through the exploded steps to display the results of each exploded step by using the **Roll Back** and **Roll Forward** buttons of the **Explode Steps** rollout, respectively. You can also drag the **Rollback Bar** that appears at the end of the last exploded step in the **Explode Steps** rollout to roll back through the explode steps.

You can also reset the specified settings of the **Add a step** rollout in the PropertyManager to the default state by clicking on the **Reset** button.

Tip: To delete an explode step, right-click on it in the **Explode Steps** rollout and then click on the **Delete** option in the shortcut menu that appears. You can also suppress or unsuppress an explode step. To do this, right-click on an explode step in the **Explode Steps** rollout and then click on the **Suppress** or **Unsuppress** option in the shortcut menu that appears, respectively.

6. Select the required option in the **Options** rollout of the PropertyManager for controlling the creation of the exploded view, if needed. Figure 13.90 shows the **Options** rollout when the **Regular step** button is selected in the **Add a Step** rollout. Some of the options are discussed below:

13.90

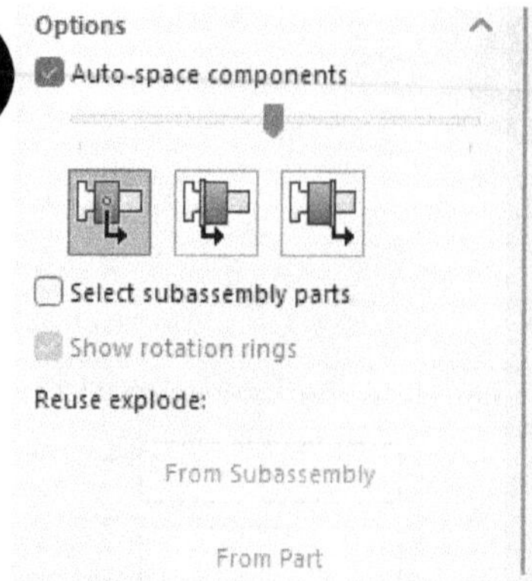

Auto-space components: The **Auto-space components** check box is used for translating or rotating a set of selected components with equal spacing automatically, on exploding the components along or about the selected direction. Note that the equal spacing value for exploding a set of selected components with equal spacing can be increased or decreased by using the **Spacing** slider that appears below this check box.

Note: You can change the order of auto-spacing of the selected components by selecting the required button (**Bounding box center, Bounding box rear,** or **Bounding box front**) available below the **Spacing** slider. You can also change the order of explosion by dragging the arrows that appear on individual exploded components in the graphics area.

Spacing: The **Spacing** slider is used to adjust the spacing between a set of selected components to explode them, equally.

Show rotation rings: By default, the **Show rotation rings** check box is selected. As a result, the rotation handles/rings appear in the graphics area after selecting the components to be exploded. If you clear this check box, the display of rotation handles/rings is disabled.

Select subassembly parts: By selecting the **Select subassembly parts** check box, you can select individual components of a sub-assembly for explosion.

From Subassembly and From Part: The **From Subassembly** and **From Part** buttons are used for exploding components by using the previously defined explode steps for a sub-assembly or a multibody part, respectively. Note that the **From Subassembly** button is enabled when a sub-assembly has an exploded view and the **From Part** button is enabled when a multibody part has an exploded view.

7. After creating all the exploded steps, click on the green tick-mark ✓ button in the PropertyManager. The exploded view of the assembly is created.

Creating a Radial Exploded Step

As discussed earlier, the radial step is created by exploding a set of components of an assembly radially or cylindrically about an axis. The method for creating a radial exploded step is discussed below:

13.91

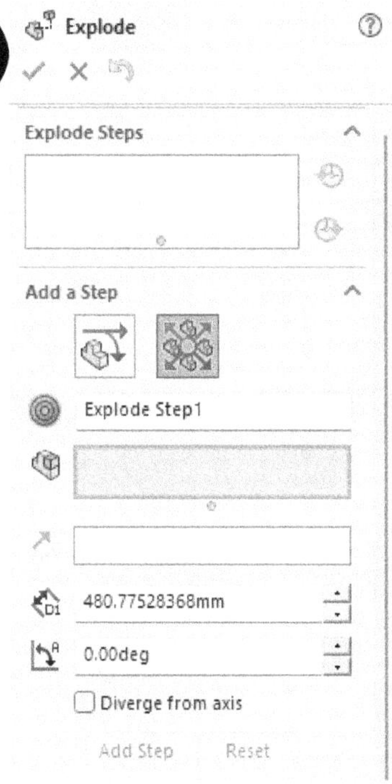

1. Invoke the **Explode PropertyManager** and then click on the **Radial step** button in the **Add a Step** rollout to create a radial exploded step. The options for creating a radial step appear in the rollout, see Figure 13.91. Most of the options in this rollout are the same as discussed earlier.

2. Specify a name for the exploded step to be created or accept the default specified name in the **Explode Step Name** field of the PropertyManager.

3. Select a set of components to be exploded as the first explode radial step. The names of the selected components appear in the **Explode Step Components** field of the PropertyManager. Also, one rotation handle and one translation handle appear in the graphics area, see Figure 13.92. In this figure, the six-piston components are selected for exploding them radially.

13.92

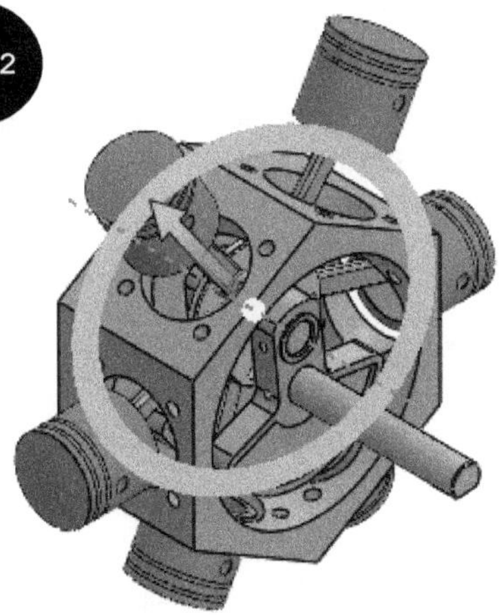

4. Drag the translation handle or the rotation handle that appears in the graphics area by pressing and holding the left mouse button. Once the desired location has been achieved, release the left mouse button and then click on the **Done** button in the **Add a step** rollout of the PropertyManager. The first radial step is created in the graphics area, see Figure 13.93. Also, its name is added to the **Explode Steps** rollout of the PropertyManager. Alternatively, enter the translation distance or rotation angle value in the respective fields of the rollout and then click on the **Add Step** button.

13.93

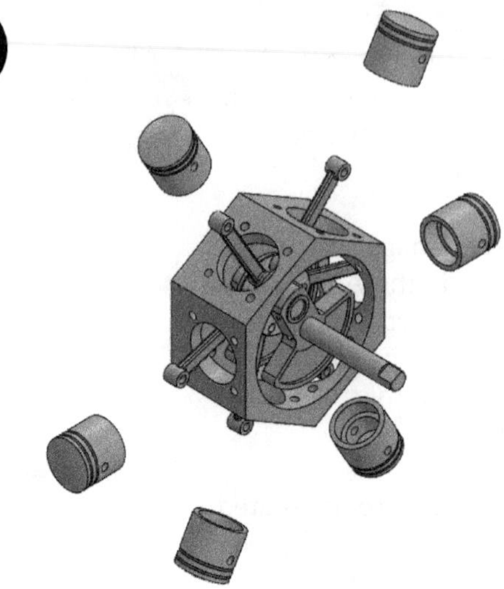

5. Similarly, create the other explode steps for the assembly.

6. After creating all the explode steps, click on the green tick-mark ✓ in the PropertyManager. The exploded view of the assembly is created.

Note: You can create the exploded view of an assembly with a combination of the regular and radial explode steps.

Collapsing an Exploded View

After creating an exploded view of an assembly, you can restore the components of the assembly to their original positions by collapsing the exploded view. To collapse the exploded view of an assembly, select the name of the assembly in the FeatureManager Design Tree and then right-click. A shortcut menu appears, see Figure 13.94. In this shortcut menu, click on the **Collapse** option.

13.94

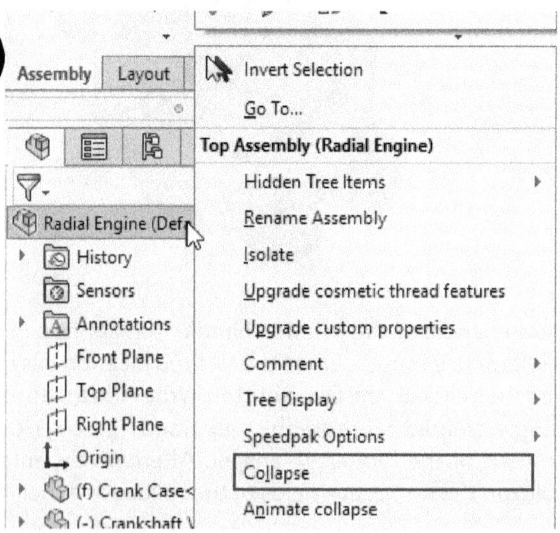

After the collapsed view of an assembly has been displayed, you can display the exploded view again. To display the exploded view of the assembly again, right-click on the name of the assembly in the FeatureManager Design Tree and then click on the **Explode** option in the shortcut menu that appears. The exploded view of the assembly is displayed.

Animating an Exploded View

After creating an exploded view of an assembly, you can animate the components of the assembly to display its collapsed and exploded states. To do this, right-click on the name of the assembly in the FeatureManager Design Tree and then click on the **Animate collapse** or **Animate explode** option in the shortcut menu that appears. The components start animating and the **Animation Controller** toolbar appears, see Figure 13.95. By using the **Animation Controller** toolbar, you can control the animation of the components. You can also record the animation and save it as a *.avi*, *.bmp*, or *.tga* file.

13.95

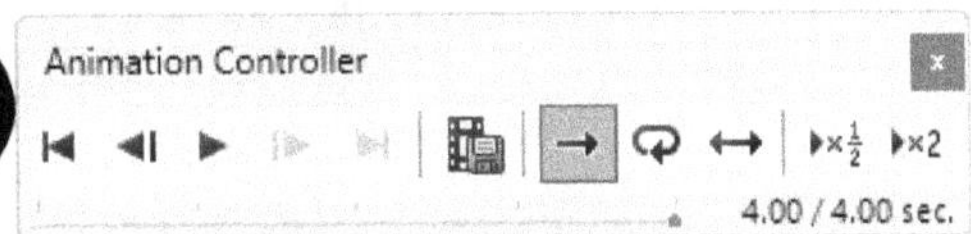

Note: The availability of the **Animate collapse** or **Animate explode** option in the shortcut menu depends upon the current state of the assembly. If the assembly appears in its exploded state in the graphics area, the **Animate collapse** option appears in the shortcut menu. If the assembly appears in its collapsed state, the **Animate explode** option is available in the shortcut menu.

Editing an Exploded View

You can edit an existing exploded view of an assembly to make necessary changes in its explode steps and to create new explode steps. To edit an exploded view of an assembly, invoke the ConfigurationManager by clicking on the **ConfigurationManager** tab, see Figure 13.96. The ConfigurationManager displays a list of all configurations of the assembly. Figure 13.96 shows the default configuration of the assembly (**Default** [*name of the assembly*]). Expand the configuration of the assembly by clicking on the arrow that appears in front of it, see Figure 13.97.

13.96

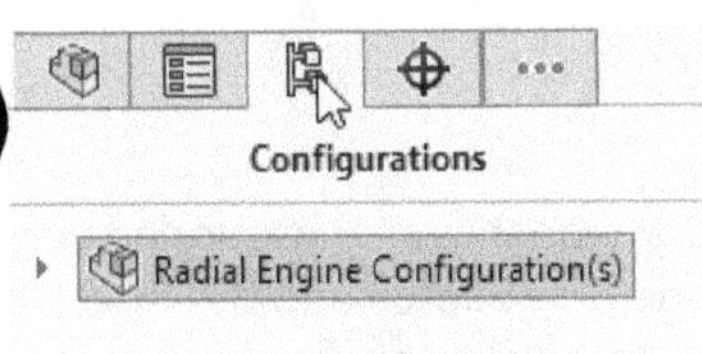

13.97

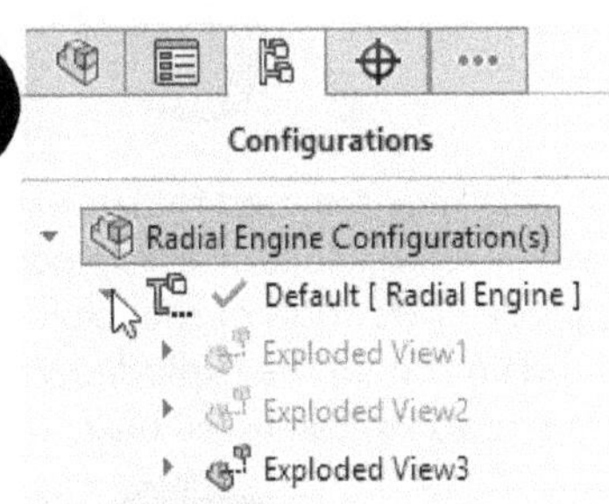

Figure 13.97 shows two exploded views: **Exploded View1** and **Exploded View2**, created for the assembly, out of which the **Exploded View1** is activated by default. You can activate the required exploded view by double-clicking on its name. To edit an exploded view, select the exploded view to be edited and then right-click to display a shortcut menu, see Figure 13.98. Next, click on the **Edit Feature** option in the shortcut menu. The **Exploded View PropertyManager** appears. Now, by using the options of this PropertyManager, you can edit the exploded view, as required.

13.98

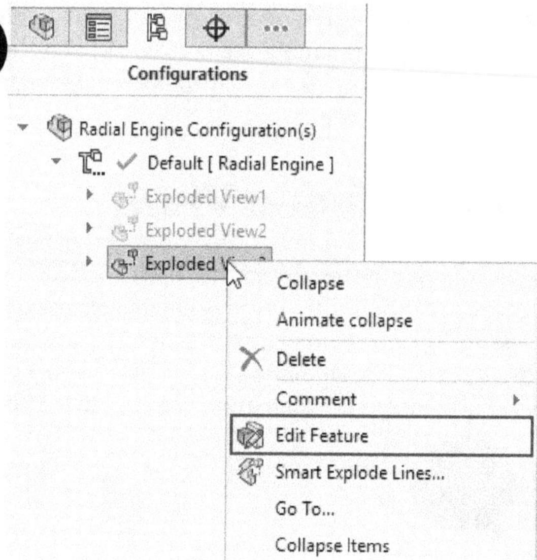

Adding Explode Lines

After creating an exploded view of an assembly, you can add explode lines in it. Figure 13.99 shows an assembly and Figure 13.100 shows an exploded view of the assembly with explode lines.

13.99

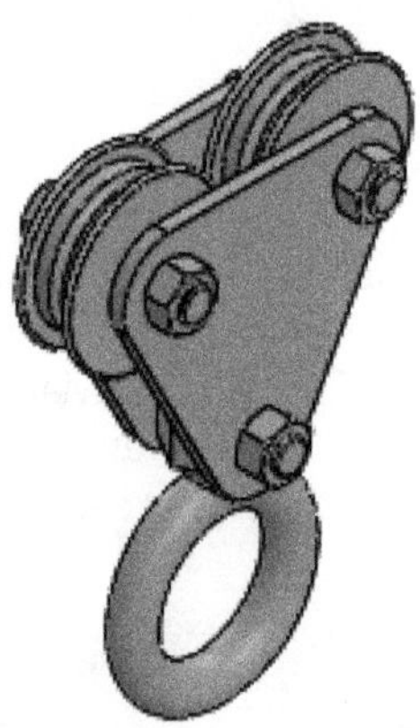

13.100

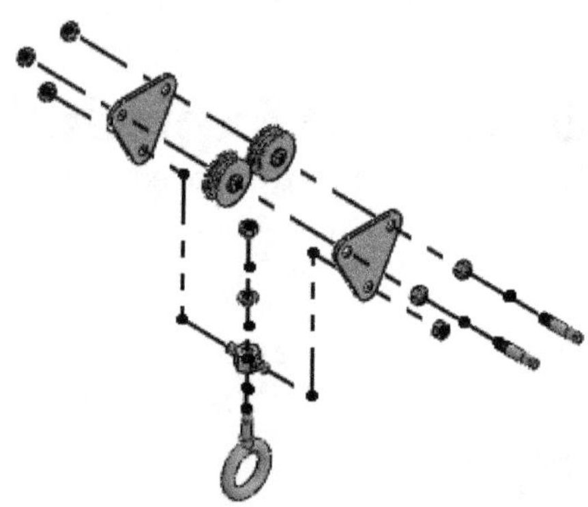

Explode lines are used for showing relationships between components in an exploded view. You can create explode lines in an exploded view by using the **Explode Line Sketch** and the **Insert/Edit Smart Explode Lines** tools of the **Explode** flyout, see Figure 13.101. To invoke this flyout, click on the arrow at the bottom of the **Exploded View** tool in the **Assembly CommandManager**, see Figure 13.101. Both these tools are discussed next.

13.101

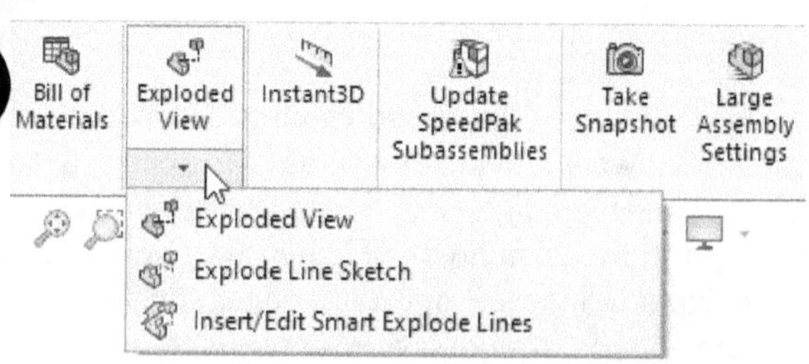

Creating Explode lines by using Explode Line Sketch

The **Explode Line Sketch** tool is used for creating the explode lines manually by selecting the faces or edges of the components in an exploded view. The steps for creating the explode lines by using this tool are discussed below:

1. Invoke the **Explode** flyout, (refer to Figure 13.101), and then click on the **Explode Line Sketch** tool. The **Route Line PropertyManager** appears, see Figure 13.102.

13.102

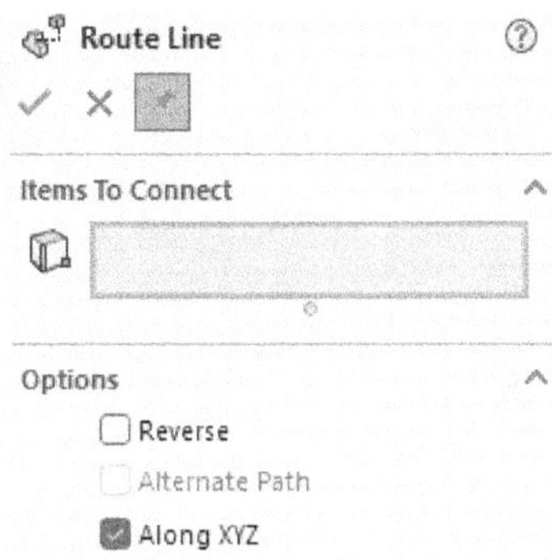

2. Select faces, circular edges, straight edges, or planar faces of the components having the same assembly line, one after another to connect them with a single route line.

3. Select the **Reverse** check box to reverse the direction of the route line, if needed. Also, you can select the **Alternate Path** check box to view the alternate route option between the selected components.

4. Click on the green tick-mark ✓ in the PropertyManager. A route line is created among the selected components, which represents the assembly line of the components.

5. Similarly, create route lines for the remaining sets of components having the same assembly line.

6. After creating all the explode lines, click on the green tick-mark in the PropertyManager.

Creating Explode lines by using Insert/Edit Smart Explode Lines

The **Insert/Edit Smart Explode Lines** tool is used for creating the explode lines automatically in an exploded view. The steps for creating the explode lines by using this tool are discussed next.

1. Click on the **Insert/Edit Smart Explode Lines** tool in the **Explode** flyout of the **Assembly CommandManager**. The **Smart Explode Lines PropertyManager** appears, see Figure 13.103. Also, the preview of the explode lines appears automatically in the graphics area, see Figure 13.104. By default, all the exploded components of the assembly are selected in the **Components** rollout of the PropertyManager and the respective explode lines appear in the graphics area.

2. Click on the green-tick mark in the PropertyManager. The explode lines are created.

13.103

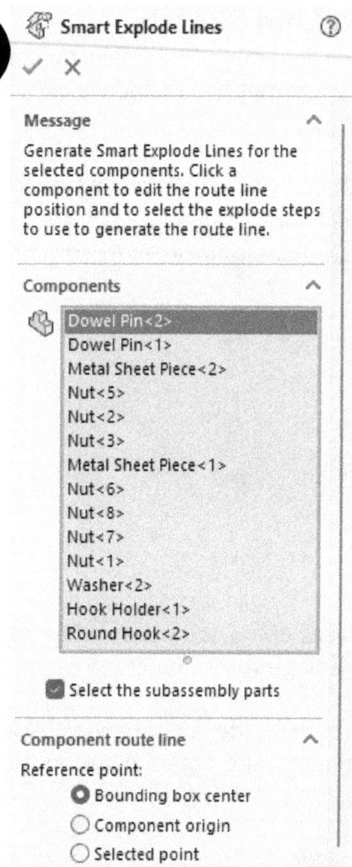

13.104

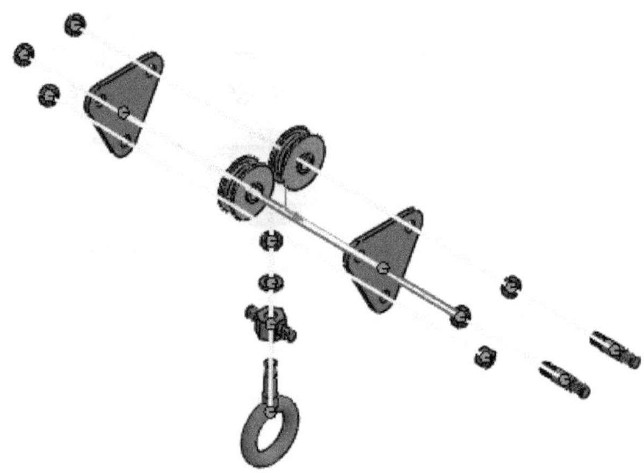

Note: The options in the **Component route line** rollout are used for locating the route line of the component which is selected in the **Components** rollout of the PropertyManager. By default, the **Bounding box center** radio button is selected in the **Component route line** rollout. As a result, the explode line gets located relative to the bounding box center of the selected component. On selecting the **Component origin** radio button, the explode line gets located relative to the origin of the selected component. On selecting the **Selected point** radio button, you can select a point, a vertex, a sketch arc, an edge arc, a sketch line, or an edge line as the point to locate the explode line of the selected component relative to it. On selecting the **Select the subassembly parts** check box in the **Components** rollout, the selection of the individual components of a sub-assembly is enabled.

Tip: To edit the explode lines created by using the **Insert/Edit Smart Explode Lines** tool, click on the **ConfigurationManager** tab and then expand the active configuration. Next, right-click on the **Exploded View** option and then click on the **Edit Smart Explode Lines** tool in the shortcut menu that appears. Now, you can edit the settings of the explode lines in the **Smart Explode Lines PropertyManager** that appears. Next, click on the green tick-mark.

Detecting Interference in an Assembly

In complex assemblies, sometimes it becomes difficult to visually point out interference between components. The **Interference Detection** tool helps in determining any interference between the components of an assembly. To detect interference, click on the **Interference Detection** tool in the **Evaluate CommandManager**, see Figure 13.105. The **Interference Detection PropertyManager** appears, see Figure 13.106. The options in this PropertyManager are discussed next.

13.105

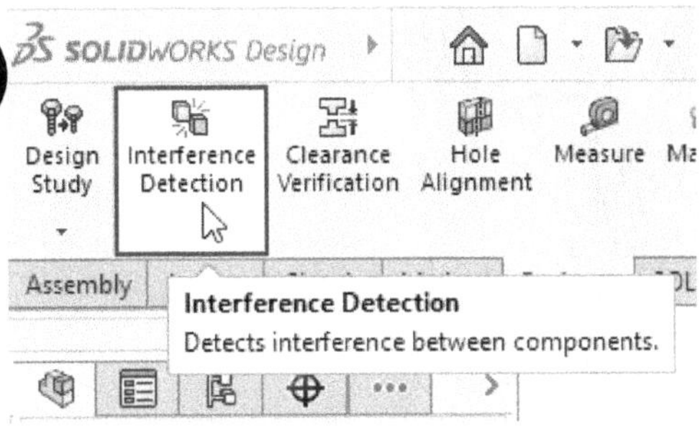

13.106

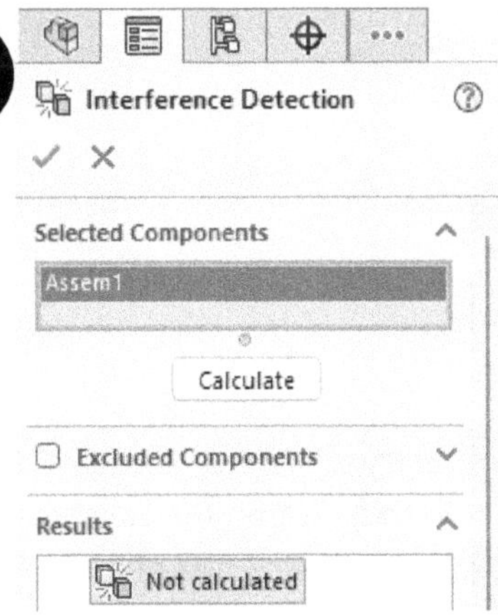

Selected Components

The name of the assembly appears in the **Selected Components** field, by default. Hence, you can calculate interference between all the components of the assembly. You can also check interference between required components instead of the entire assembly. To do this, you first need to clear the current selection set by right-clicking on the **Selected Components** field and then clicking on the **Clear Selections** option in the shortcut menu that appears, see Figure 13.107. Next, select the required components in the graphics area or the FeatureManager Design Tree. The names of the selected components appear in the **Selected Components** field. Next, click on the **Calculate** button. The interference results get calculated between the selected components and are displayed in the **Results** field of the PropertyManager.

13.107

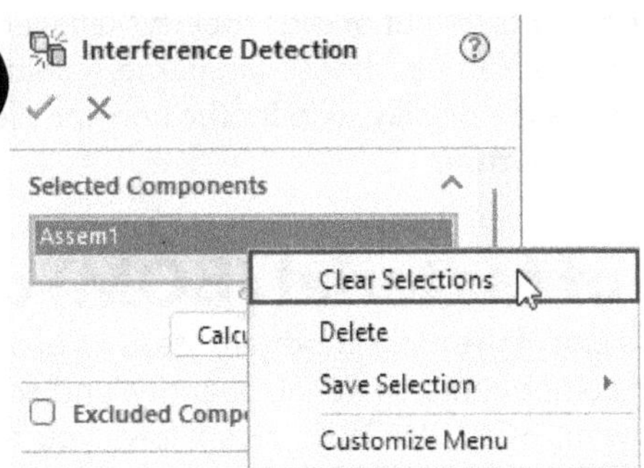

Results

The **Results** field displays a list of all interferences that are determined between the selected components. On selecting an interference from the list, the selected interference gets highlighted in red in the graphics area, see Figure 13.108. You can also ignore the selected interference using the **Ignore** button such that it is no longer considered as an interference. On right-clicking an interference, you can choose to sort interferences according to size, ignore an interference, ignore certain interferences below a value, or isolate them in the graphics area to properly review them. Note that the **Results** field displays a list of interferences if the **Component view** check box is cleared. On selecting this check box, the **Results** field displays a list of all the components causing interference.

13.108

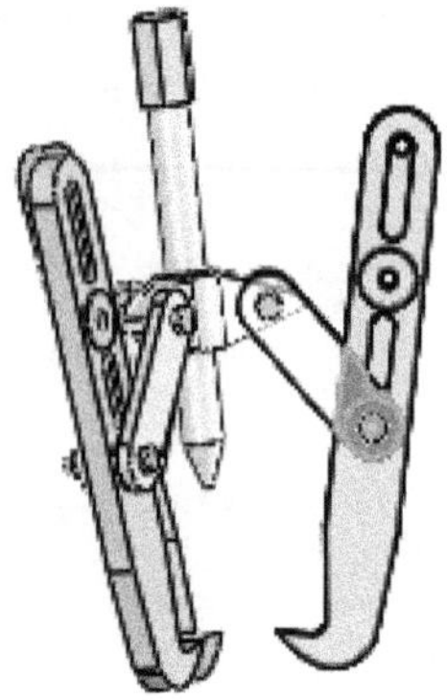

In SOLIDWORKS, you can export results for interference detection to a Microsoft Excel spreadsheet. To do this, click on the **Save Results** button in the **Results** rollout. The **Save As** dialog box appears. Next, browse to the location where you want to export the results and then click on the **Save** button.

Excluded Components

The **Excluded Components** rollout of the PropertyManager is used for excluding components from interference calculation. To activate this rollout, select the check box in front of it.

Options

The options in the **Options** rollout of the PropertyManager are used to define whether to treat coincidence as interference, show ignored interferences, treat sub-assemblies as components, make interfering parts transparent, and so on by using the respective check boxes.

Non-interfering Components

The **Non-interfering Components** rollout of the PropertyManager is used to select a display style for the non-interfering components. You can choose wireframe, hidden, transparent, or the currently used display style of the assembly as the display style for the non-interfering components of the assembly by selecting the required radio button.

Creating Bill of Material (BOM) of an Assembly

A Bill of Material (BOM) is one of the most important features of any drawing. It contains information related to the number of components, material, quantity, and so on. In addition to creating Bill of Material (BOM) in a drawing, SOLIDWORKS also allows you to create a BOM in the Assembly environment. You will learn about creating a Bill of Material (BOM) in a drawing later in Chapter 14. To create BOM in the Assembly environment, click on the **Bill of Materials** tool in the **Assembly CommandManager**. The **Bill of Materials PropertyManager** appears, see Figure 13.109. Accept the default parameters specified in the PropertyManager for creating the BOM and click on the green tick-mark ✓. The Bill of Material (BOM) gets attached to the cursor. Now, click on the graphics area to specify the location of the BOM. The BOM is placed in the specified location, see Figure 13.110.

13.109

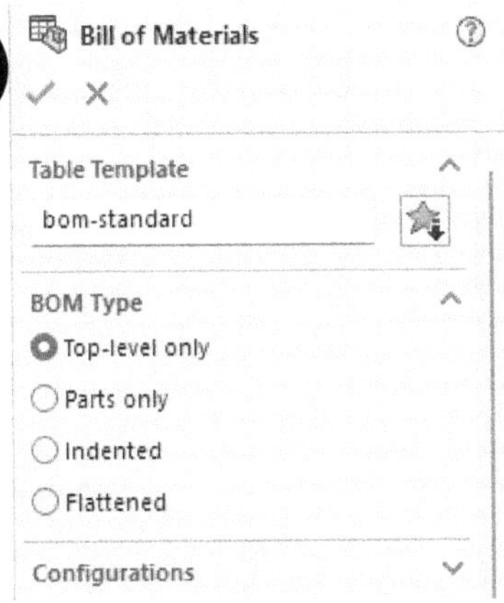

13.110

ITEM NO.	PART NUMBER	DESCRIPTION	QTY.
1	Metal Sheet Piece		2
2	Dowel Pin		2
3	Pulley		2
4	Hook Holder		1
5	Round Hook		1
6	Nut		7
7	Washer		1

Tutorial 1

Create an assembly, as shown in Figure 13.111 by using the Top-down Assembly approach. Different views and dimensions of each assembly component are shown in Figures 13.112 through 13.114. All dimensions are in mm.

13.111

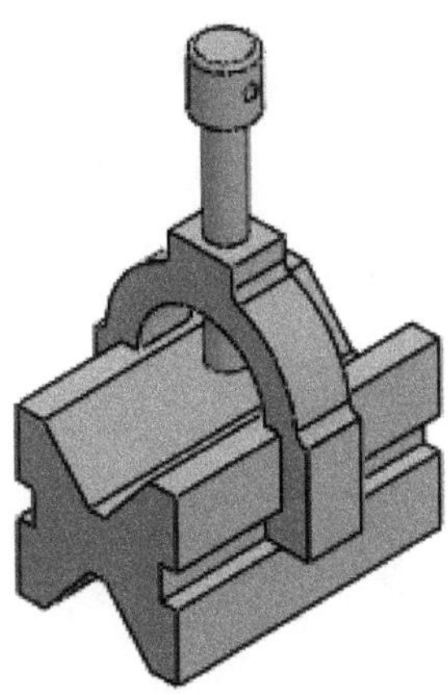

13.112

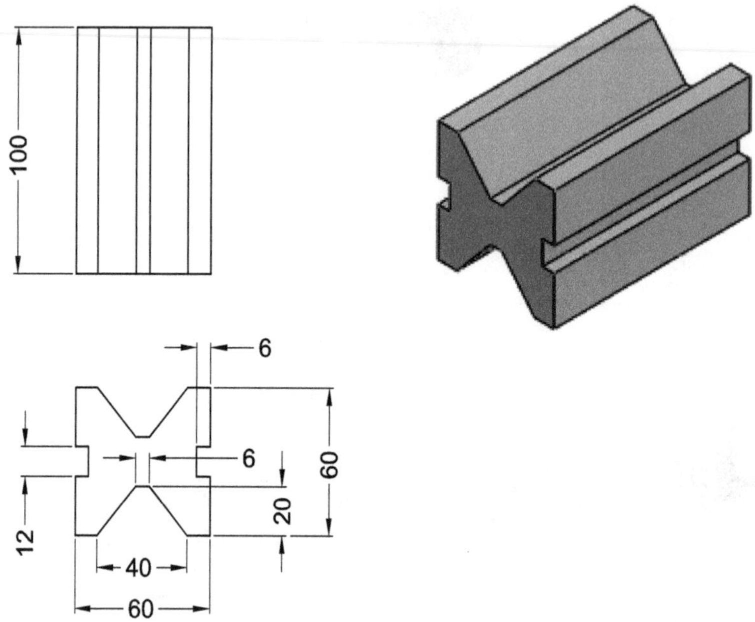

V-Block Body

13.113

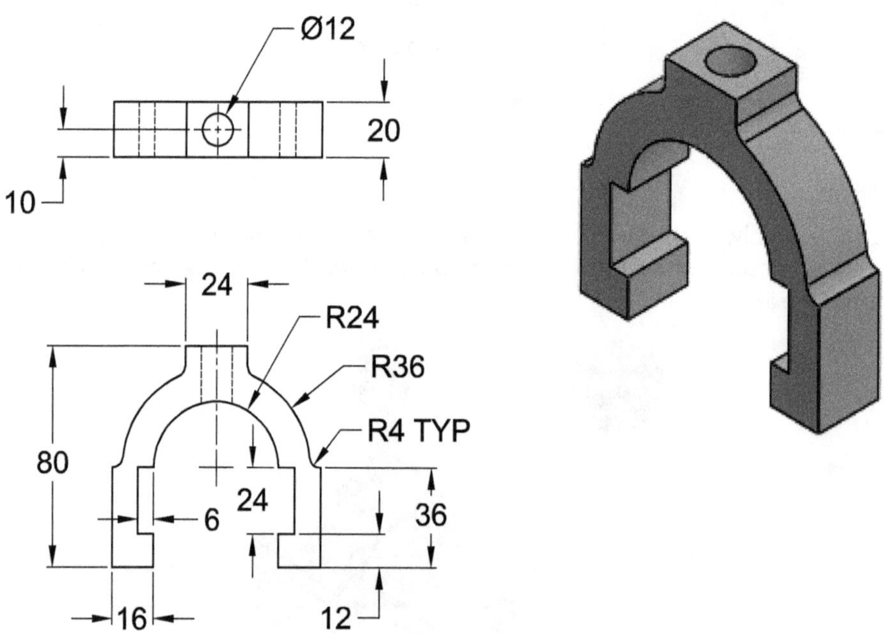

U-Clamp

13.114

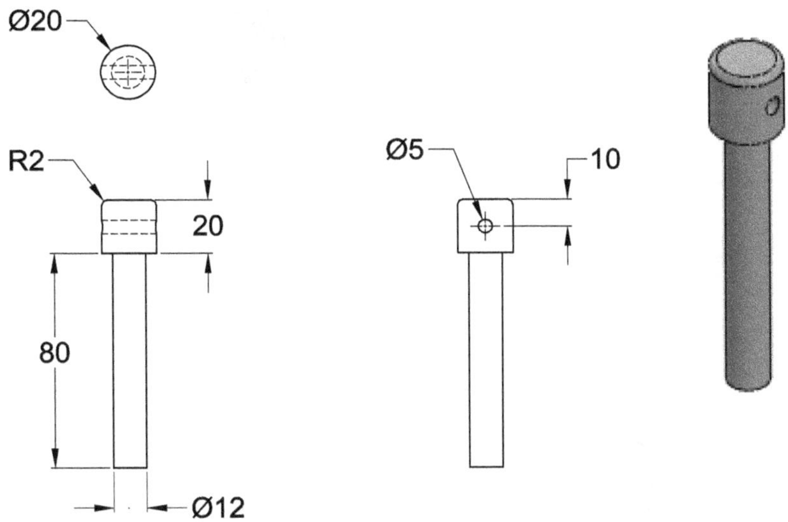

Fastener

Section 1: Starting SOLIDWORKS

1. Start SOLIDWORKS by double-clicking on the SOLIDWORKS icon on your desktop. The startup user interface of SOLIDWORKS appears along with the **Welcome** dialog box.

Note: If SOLIDWORKS is already open and the **Welcome** dialog box does not appear on the screen, then you can invoke the **Welcome** dialog box by clicking on the **Welcome to SOLIDWORKS** tool in the **Standard** toolbar.

Section 2: Invoking the Assembly Environment

1. Click on the **Assembly** button in the **Welcome** dialog box. The assembly environment is invoked with the display of the **Open** dialog box along with the **Begin Assembly PropertyManager**, by default.

Section 3: Creating the First Component

1. Close the **Open** dialog box by clicking on the **Cancel** button and then close the **Begin Assembly PropertyManager** by clicking on the red cross mark available at its top. This is because, in this tutorial, you need to create all components of the assembly within the Assembly environment itself.

2. Click on the arrow at the bottom of the **Insert Components** tool. A flyout appears, see Figure 13.115.

3. Click on the **New Part** tool in the flyout. A new empty part is added in the Assembly environment and appears in the FeatureManager Design Tree with its default name, see Figure 13.116. Also, a green color tick-mark appears attached to the cursor in the graphics area and you are prompted to define the placement for the newly added component in the graphics area.

13.115

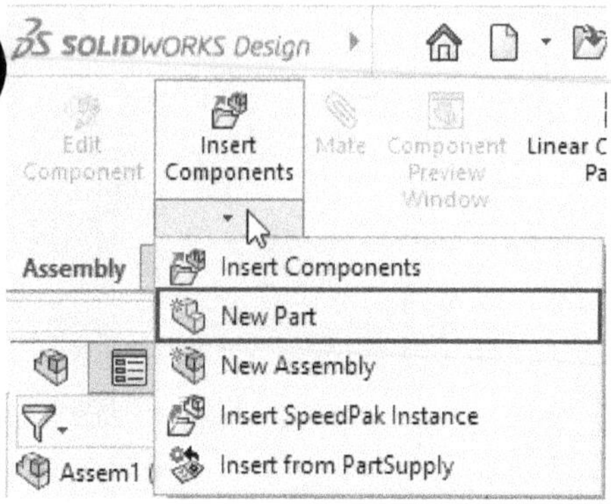

13.116

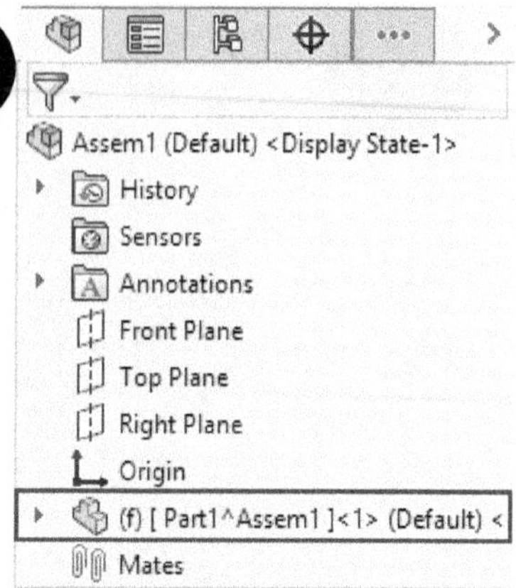

4. Click anywhere in the graphics area to define the position of the first component. The position of the component gets defined such that its origin becomes coincident with the origin of the assembly. Also, the inserted component becomes a fixed component, by default.

   Now, you can change the default name of the newly added component.

5. Right-click on the default name of the component (**Part1**) in the FeatureManager Design Tree and then click on the **Rename Part** option in the shortcut menu that appears, see Figure 13.117. The default name of the component appears in an edit field.

13.117

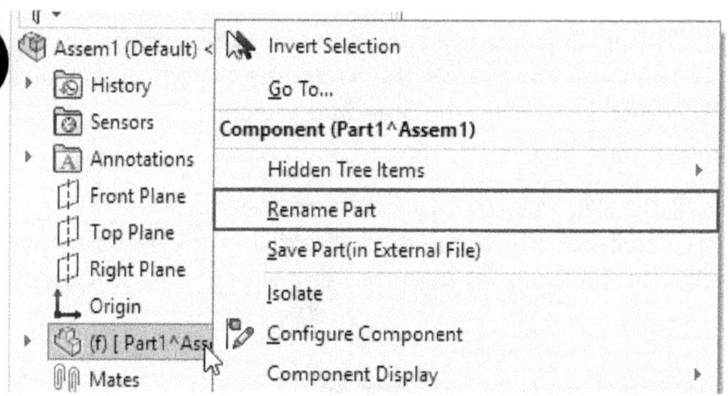

6. Enter **V-Block Body** in the edit field as the new name of the component and then click anywhere in the graphics area. The name of the component gets changed, as specified.

   Now, you need to add features of the newly added empty component.

7. Click on the newly added component in the FeatureManager Design Tree. A Pop-up toolbar appears, see Figure 13.118.

8. Click on the **Edit Part** tool in the Pop-up toolbar, see Figure 13.118. The Part modeling environment is invoked within the Assembly environment.

13.118

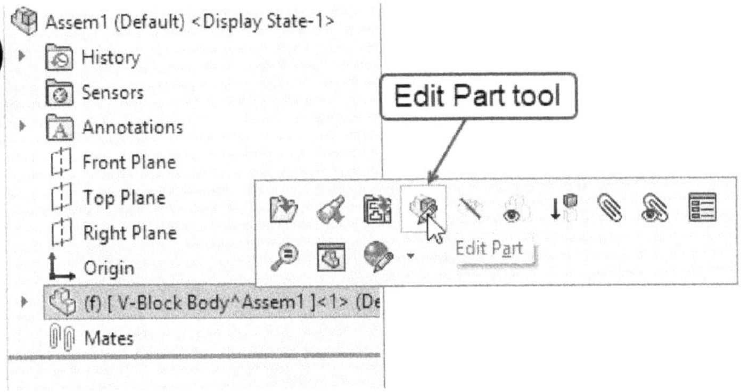

9. Click on the **Features** tab in the CommandManager to display the tools of the **Features CommandManager**.

10. Click on the **Extruded Boss/Base** tool in the **Features CommandManager**. The **Extrude PropertyManager** appears.

11. Expand the FeatureManager Design Tree, which is now available at the top left corner of the graphics area, and then expand the **V-Block Body** node in it, which appears in blue, see Figure 13.119.

12. Click on the **Front Plane** available under the expanded **V-Block Body** node in the FeatureManager Design Tree as the sketching plane, see Figure 13.119. The Sketching environment is invoked and the model gets oriented normal to the viewing direction.

13.119

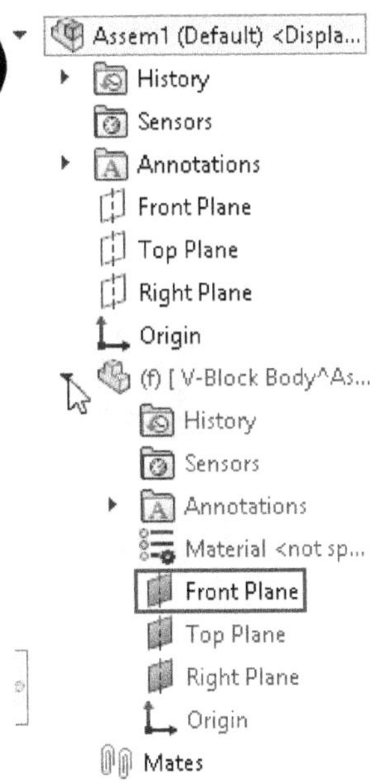

13. Create the sketch of the base feature of the component by using the sketching tools, see Figure 13.120. You need to apply all the required relations and dimensions to make the sketch fully defined.

13.120

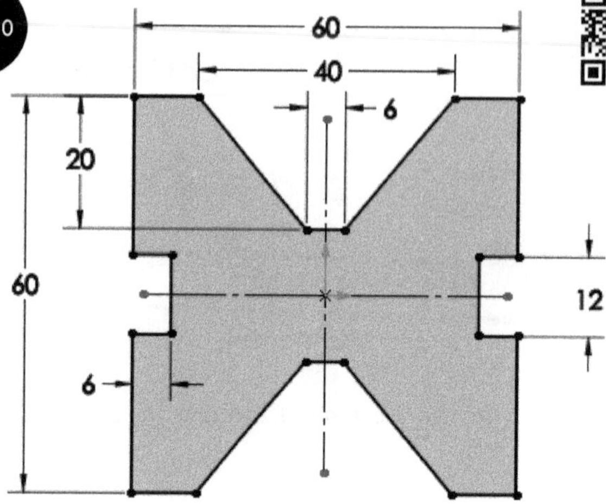

14. After creating the sketch of the base feature, click on the **Exit Sketch** tool in the **Sketch CommandManager** to exit the Sketching environment. The **Boss-Extrude PropertyManager** and a preview of the extruded feature appear.

15. Change the orientation of the model to isometric.

16. Invoke the **End Condition** drop-down list of the **Direction 1** rollout in the **Boss-Extrude PropertyManager** and then click on the **Mid Plane** option in it.

17. Enter **100** in the **Depth** field of the **Direction 1** rollout of the PropertyManager.

18. Click on the green tick-mark ✓ in the PropertyManager. The extruded feature is created, see Figure 13.121.

13.121

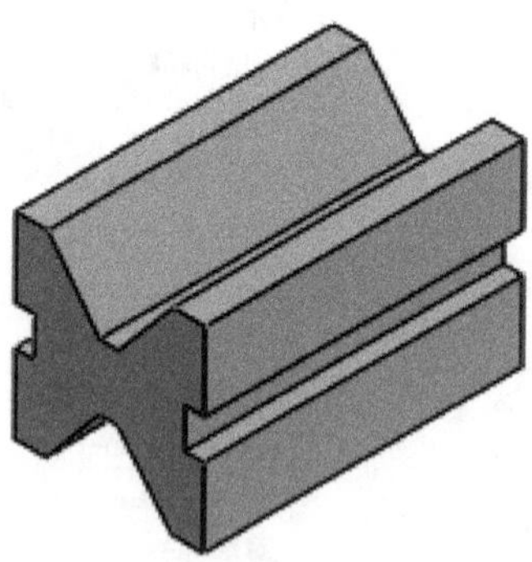

Tip: You can create multiple features of a component one after another. The methods for creating multiple features of a component is same as discussed earlier while creating a part in the Part modeling environment.

19. Click on the **Edit Component** tool in the CommandManager to exit the Part modeling environment and switch to the Assembly environment. The first component (**V-Block Body**) is created.

Section 4: Creating the Second Component

1. Click on the arrow at the bottom of the **Insert Components** tool. A flyout appears, see Figure 13.122.

2. Click on the **New Part** tool in the flyout. A new empty part is added in the Assembly environment and appears in the FeatureManager Design Tree with its default name.

3. Click anywhere in the graphics area to define the position of the second component concerning the origin of the assembly.

   Now, you can change the default name of the newly added component.

13.122

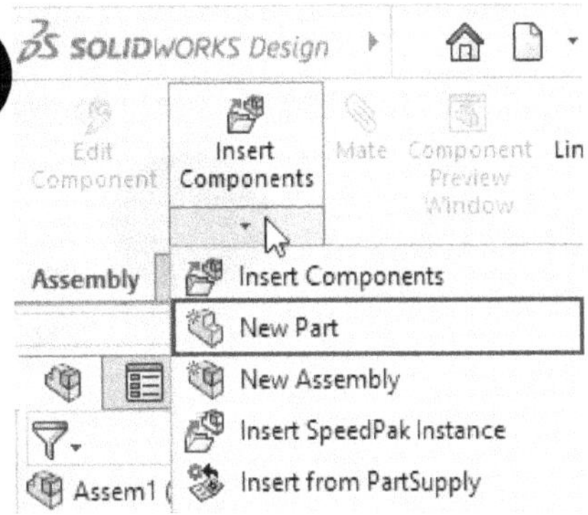

4. Click on the name of the newly added component (**Part2**) in the FeatureManager Design Tree and then click again after a pause. The name of the component appears in an edit field.

5. Enter **U-Clamp** in the edit field as the new name of the component and then click anywhere in the graphics area. The name of the component gets changed, as specified.

   Now, you can create the features of the **U-Clamp** component.

6. Click on the name of the newly added component (**U-Clamp**) in the FeatureManager Design Tree and then click on the **Edit Part** tool in the Pop-up toolbar that appears, see Figure 13.123. The Part modeling environment is invoked, and the first component of the assembly becomes transparent in the graphics area.

13.123

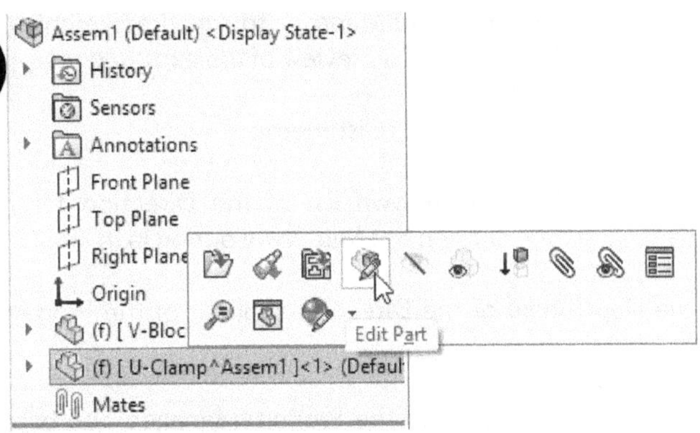

7. Click on the **Features** tab in the CommandManager to display the tools of the **Features CommandManager**.

8. Click on the **Extruded Boss/Base** tool in the **Features CommandManager**. The **Extrude PropertyManager** appears.

9. Expand the FeatureManager Design Tree, which is now at the top left corner of the graphics area. Next, expand the **U-Clamp** node of the FeatureManager Design Tree, which appears in blue.

10. Click on the **Front Plane** in the expanded **U-Clamp** node as the sketching plane. The Sketching environment is invoked and the model gets oriented normal to the viewing direction.

11. Create the sketch of the first feature of the **U-Clamp** component, see Figure 13.124.

13.124

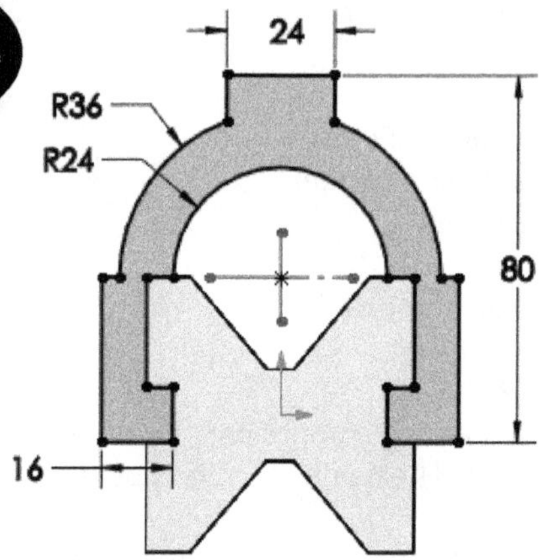

Note: To create the sketch of the base feature of the second component as shown in Figure 13.124, you can take the reference of the edges of the first component. You can project edges of the first component as sketch entities on to the current sketching plane by using the **Convert Entities** tool.

12. After creating the sketch of the base feature of the second component, click on the **Exit Sketch** tool in the **Sketch CommandManager** to exit the Sketching environment. The **Boss-Extrude PropertyManager** and a preview of the extruded feature appear.

13. Change the orientation of the model to isometric.

14. Invoke the **End Condition** drop-down list of the **Direction 1** rollout in the **Boss-Extrude PropertyManager** and then click on the **Mid Plane** option in it.

15. Enter **20** in the **Depth** field of the **Direction 1** rollout of the PropertyManager and then press ENTER.

16. Click on the green tick-mark ✓ in the PropertyManager. The base feature of the **U-Clamp** component is created, see Figure 13.125.

13.125

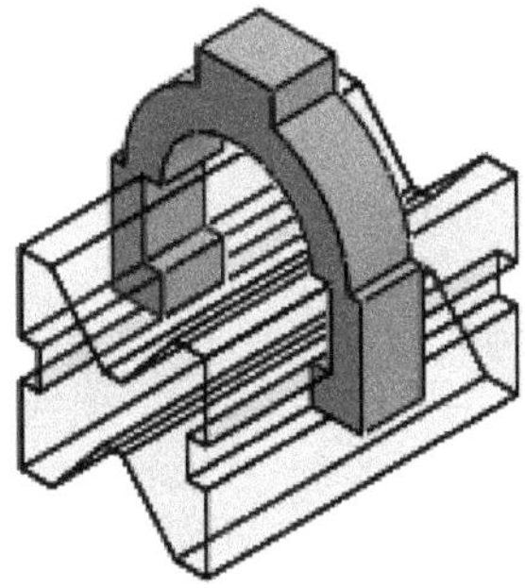

Now, you need to create the second feature of the **U-Clamp** component.

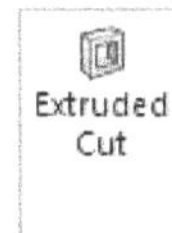

17. Click on the **Extruded Cut** tool in the **Features CommandManager** and then click on the top planar face of the previously created feature (base feature) of the **U-Clamp** component as the sketching plane. The model gets oriented normal to the viewing direction.

18. Create a circle of diameter 12 mm as the sketch of the second feature, see Figure 13.126.

19. After creating the sketch of the second feature, click on the **Exit Sketch** tool in the **Sketch CommandManager** to exit the Sketching environment. The **Cut-Extrude PropertyManager** and a preview of the cut feature appear.

20. Change the orientation of the model to isometric.

21. Invoke the **End Condition** drop-down list and then click on the **Through All** option in it.

22. Click on the green tick-mark ✓ in the PropertyManager. The second feature of the **U-Clamp** component is created, see Figure 13.127.

13.126

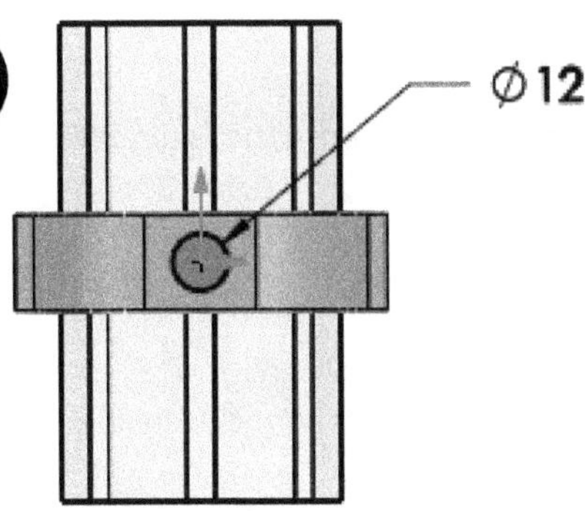

13.127

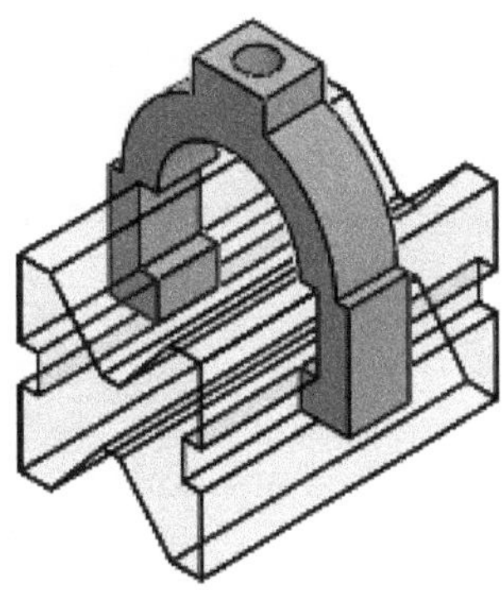

Now, you need to create the third feature of the **U-Clamp** component.

23. Click on the **Fillet** tool in the **Features CommandManager**. The **Fillet PropertyManager** appears.

24. Ensure that the **Constant Size Fillet** button is selected in the **Fillet Type** rollout for creating a fillet of constant radius.

25. Enter **4** in the **Radius** field of the **Fillet Parameters** rollout in the PropertyManager.

26. Click on the required edges (4 edges) of the **U-Clamp** component one by one as the edges to create the fillet. The preview of the fillet appears, see Figure 13.128.

27. Click on the green tick-mark ✓ in the PropertyManager. The third feature of the **U-Clamp** component is created.

28. After creating all features of the **U-Clamp** component, click on the **Edit Component** tool in the CommandManager to exit the Part modeling environment and switch to the Assembly environment. Figure 13.129 shows the assembly after creating its two components.

13.128

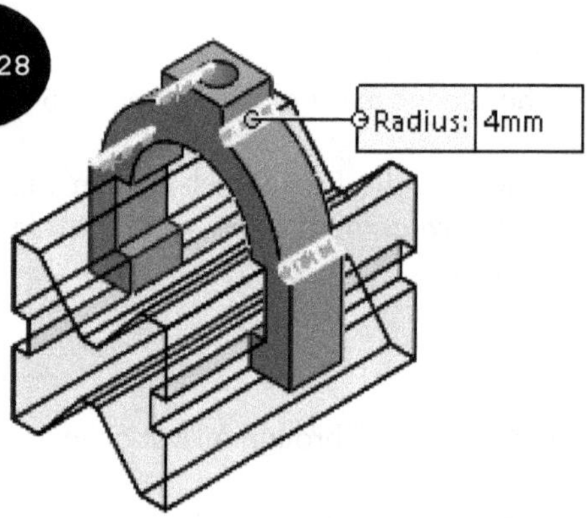

13.129

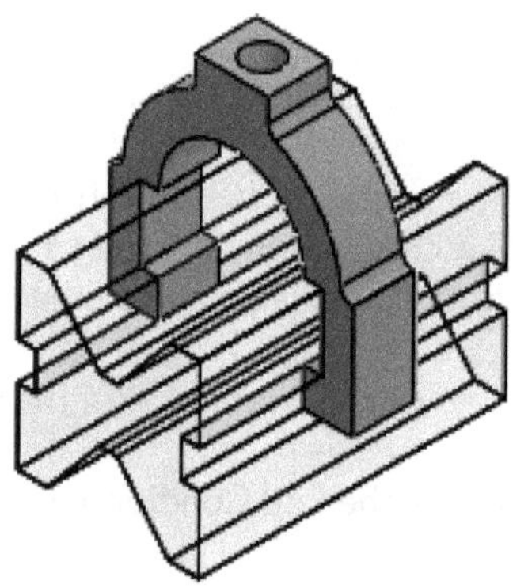

Section 5: Creating the Third Component

1. Click on the arrow at the bottom of the **Insert Components** tool. A flyout appears.

2. Click on the **New Part** tool in the flyout. A new empty part is added in the assembly and its default name gets added in the FeatureManager Design Tree.

3. Click anywhere in the graphics area to define the position of the third component.

4. Click on the name of the newly added component in the FeatureManager Design Tree and then click again on it after a pause. The default name of the component appears in an edit field.

5. Enter **Fastener** in the edit field as the new name of the component and then click anywhere in the graphics area. The name of the component gets changed, as specified.

   Now, you need to add features to the component.

6. Click on the name of the component (**Fastener**) in the FeatureManager Design Tree and then click on the **Edit Part** tool in the Pop-up toolbar that appears, see Figure 13.130. The Part modeling

environment is invoked, and the other components of the assembly become transparent in the graphics area, refer to Figure 13.131.

13.130

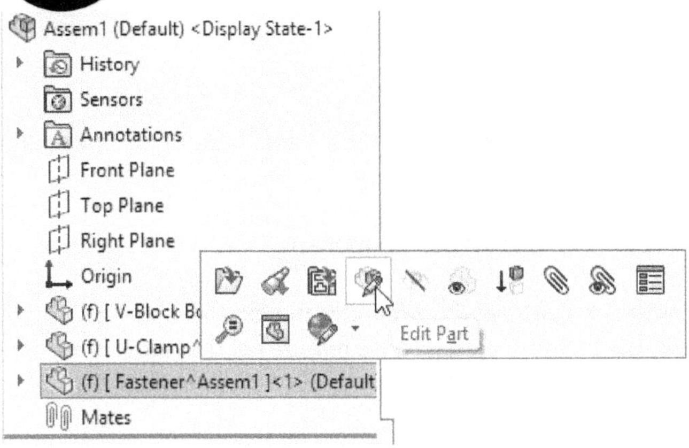

13.131

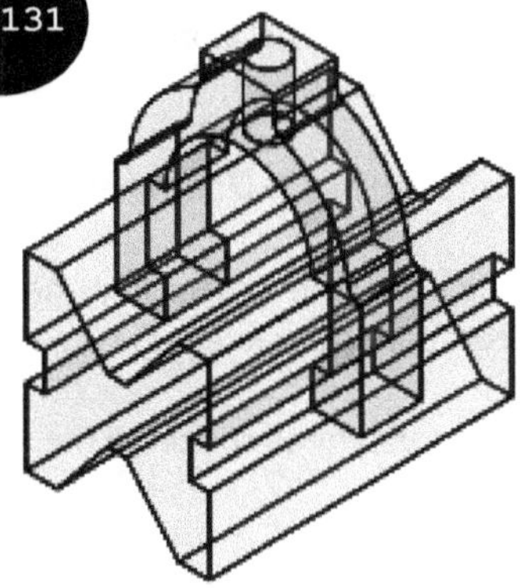

7. Click on the **Extruded Boss/Base** tool in the Features CommandManager. The **Extrude PropertyManager** appears and you are prompted to select a plane for creating the sketch.

8. Click on the top planar face of the **U-Clamp** component as the sketching plane for creating the sketch of the base feature of the third component (**Fastener**), see Figure 13.132. The Sketching environment is invoked, and the selected planar face becomes the sketching plane.

9. Create a circle of diameter 12 mm as the sketch of the base feature, see Figure 13.133.

13.132

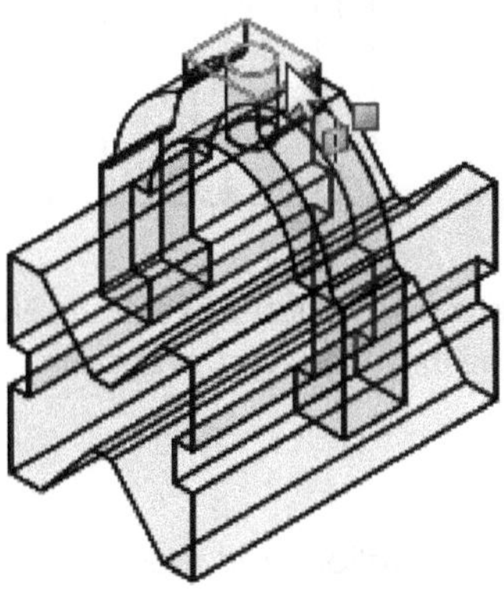

13.133

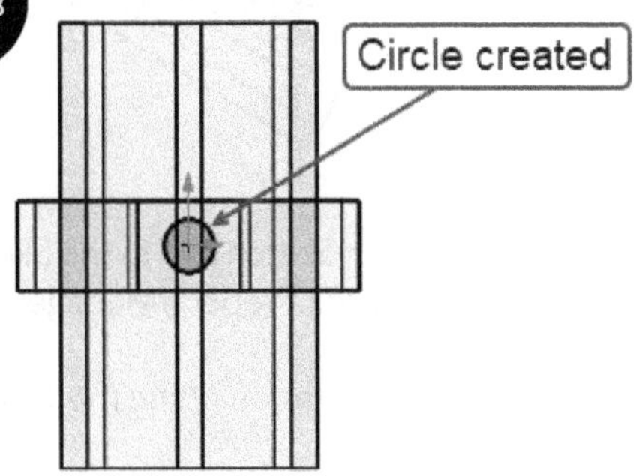

Note: To create a circle of diameter 12 mm as shown in Figure 13.133, you can take the reference of the circular edge of the second component and apply the coradial relation between them. Alternatively, you can use the **Convert Entities** tool to project the circular edge of the second component for creating a circle of diameter 12 mm.

10. After creating the sketch, click on the **Exit Sketch** tool in the **Sketch CommandManager** to exit the Sketching environment. The **Boss-Extrude PropertyManager** and a preview of the extrude feature appear. Next, change the view orientation to isometric.

11. Invoke the **End Condition** drop-down list of the **Direction 1** rollout and then click on the **Mid Plane** option in it.

12. Enter **80** in the **Depth** field of the **Direction 1** rollout.

13. Click on the green tick-mark ✓ in the PropertyManager. The base feature of the third component (**Fastener**) is created, see Figure 13.134.

    Now, you need to create the second feature of the **Fastener** component.

14. Click on the **Extruded Boss/Base** tool in the **Features CommandManager** and then click on the top planar face of the previously created feature (base feature) of the third component as the sketching plane. The model gets oriented normal to the viewing direction.

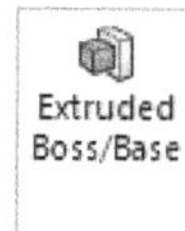

15. Create a circle of diameter 20 mm as the sketch of the second feature, see Figure 13.135.

13.134

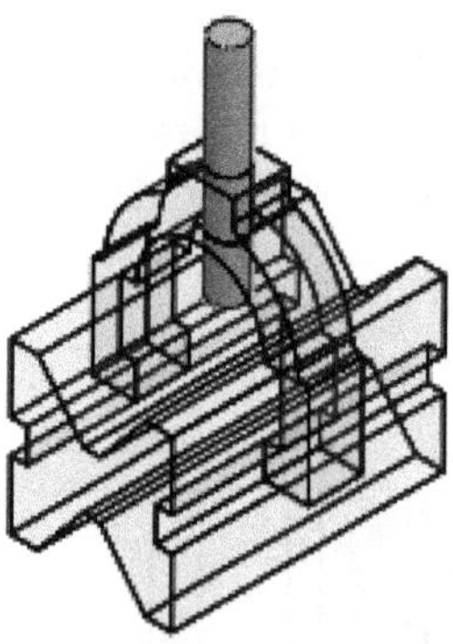

13.135

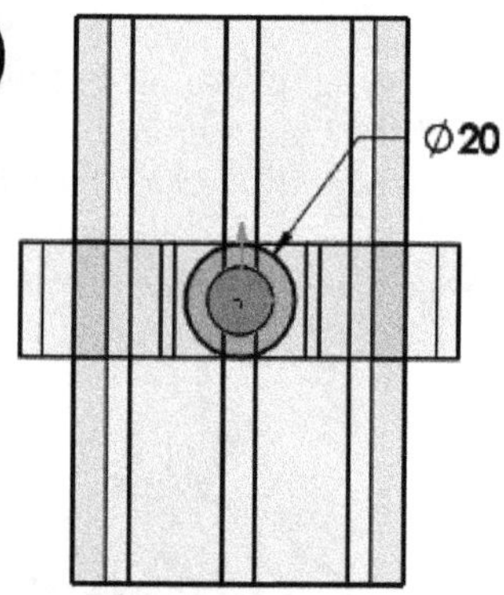

16. Click on the **Exit Sketch** tool in the **Sketch CommandManager** to exit the Sketching environment. The **Boss-Extrude PropertyManager** and a preview of the extruded feature appear.

17. Change the orientation of the model to isometric.

18. Invoke the **End Condition** drop-down list of the **Direction 1** rollout and then click on the **Blind** option in it.

19. Enter **20** in the **Depth** field of the **Direction 1** rollout in the PropertyManager.

20. Click on the green tick-mark ✓ in the PropertyManager. The second feature of the **Fastener** component is created, see Figure 13.136.

13.136

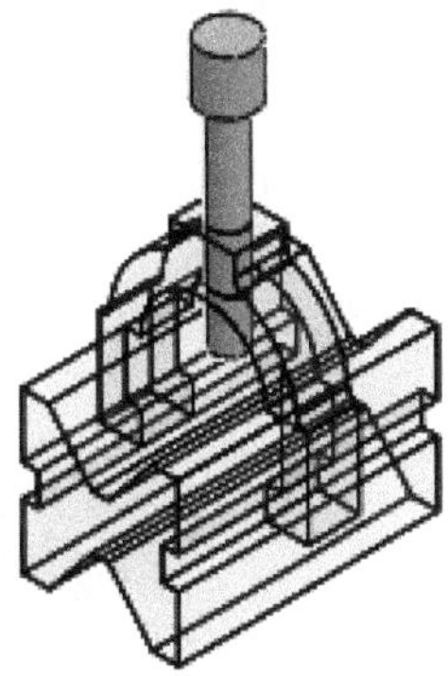

Now, you need to create the third feature of the **Fastener** component.

21. Click on the **Extruded Cut** tool in the **Features CommandManager.** The **Extrude PropertyManager** appears.

22. Expand the FeatureManager Design Tree, which is now at the top left corner of the graphics area. Next, expand the **Fastener** node, which appears in blue in the FeatureManager Design Tree.

23. Click on the **Right Plane** in the **Fastener** node of the FeatureManager Design Tree as the sketching plane. The Sketching environment is invoked. The orientation of the model gets changed as normal to the viewing direction.

24. Create a circle of diameter 5 mm as the sketch of the third feature, see Figure 13.137.

13.137

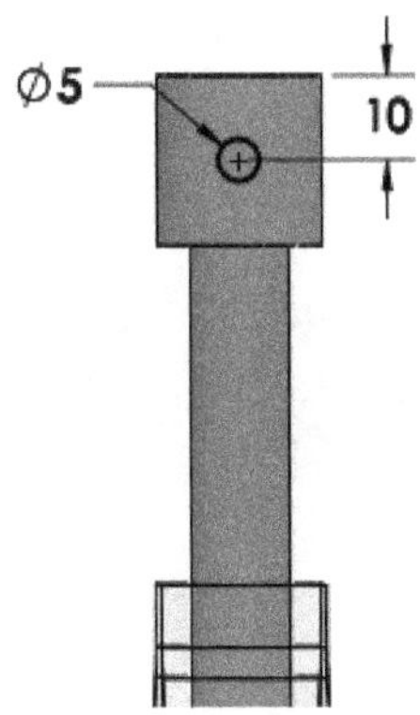

25. Click on the **Exit Sketch** tool in the **Sketch CommandManager** to exit the Sketching environment. The **Cut-Extrude PropertyManager** and a preview of the cut feature appear. Next, change the orientation of the model to isometric.

26. Invoke the **End Condition** drop-down list of the **Direction 1** rollout and then click on the **Through All - Both** option in it.

27. Click on the green tick-mark ✓ in the PropertyManager. The third feature of the third component is created, see Figure 13.138.

    Now, you need to create the fourth feature of the third component (**Fastener**).

28. Create a fillet of radius 2 mm on the top circular edge of the third component (**Fastener**) by using the **Fillet** tool, see Figure 13.139.

13.138

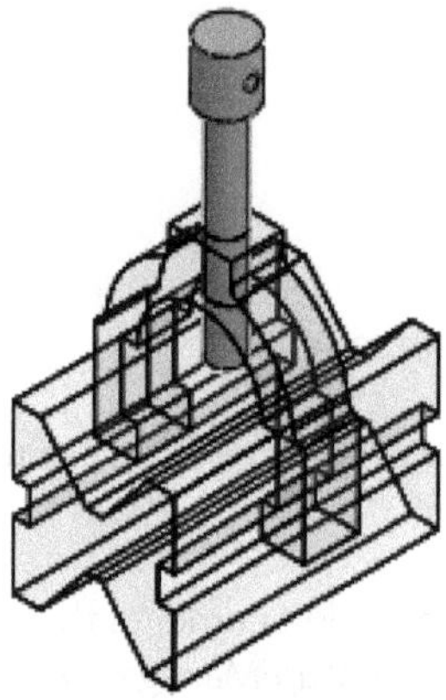

13.139

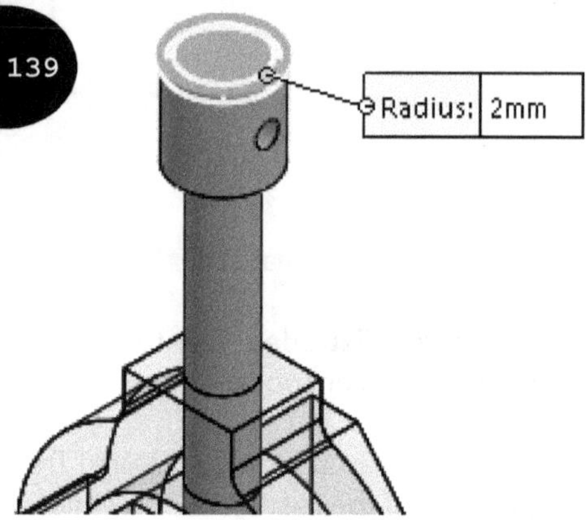

29. After creating all the features of the third component, click on the **Edit Component** tool in the CommandManager to exit the Part modeling environment and switch back to the Assembly environment. Figure 13.140 shows the final assembly after creating all the components.

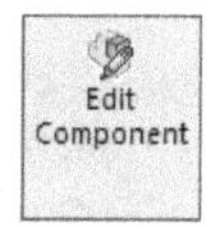

13.140

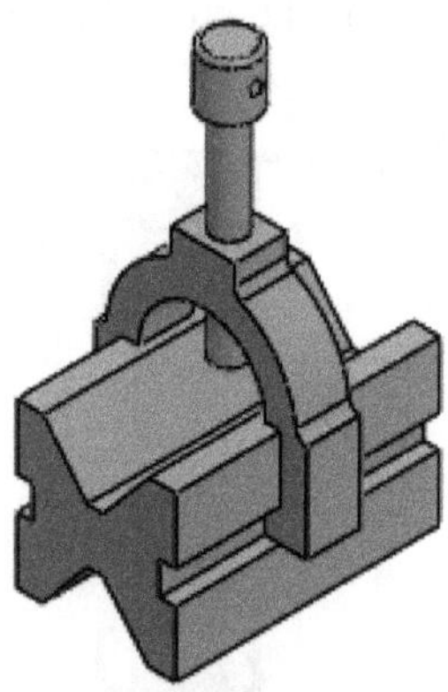

Note: By default, the components created by using the Top-down approach become fixed components in the Assembly environment and applying mates between the components is not required. However, you can make the components float and then apply required mates between the components of the assembly.

Section 6: Saving Assembly and its Component

1. Click on the **Save** button. The **Save Modified Documents** dialog box appears.

2. Click on the **Save All** button in the dialog box. The **Save As** dialog box appears. Browse to the Tutorial folder of the Chapter 13 folder to save the assembly file. You need to create these folders in the SOLIDWORKS folder.

3. Enter **Tutorial 1** in the **File name** field of the dialog box as the name of the assembly and then click on the **Save** button in the dialog box. Another **Save As** dialog box appears, see Figure 13.141.

13.141

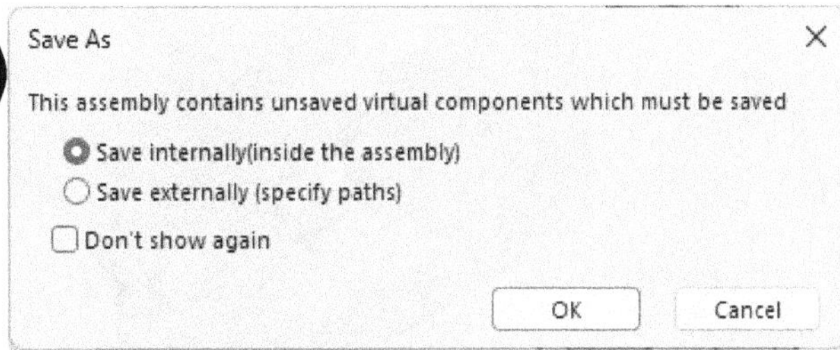

4. Select the **Save externally (specify paths)** radio button and then click on the **OK** button in the dialog box. All the components and the assembly file are saved in the specified location, individually.

Hands-on Test Drive 1

Open the assembly created in Tutorial 2 of Chapter 12, (see Figure 13.142) and then create its exploded view similar to the one shown in Figure 13.143. You also need to create explode lines in the exploded view of the assembly. You can assign an arbitrary value to the spacing between the exploded components of the assembly.

13.142

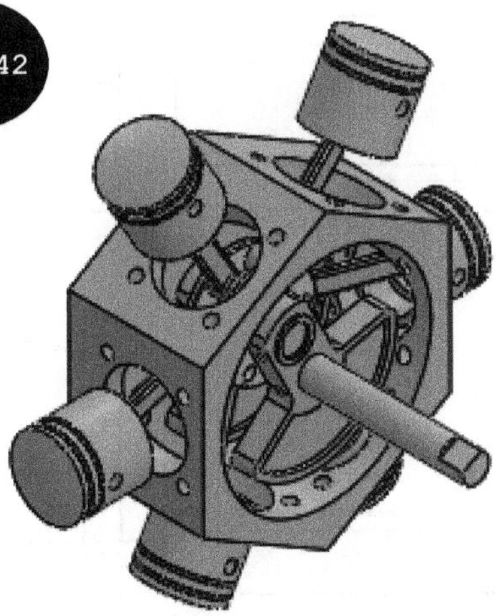

13.143

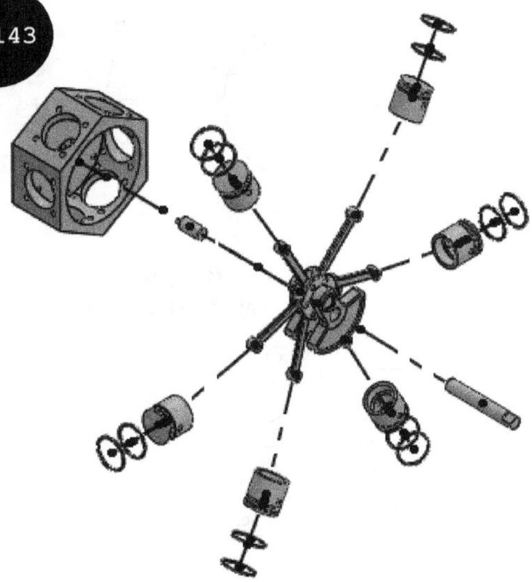

Hands-on Test Drive 2

Create an assembly, as shown in Figure 13.144 by using the Top-down approach. Different views and dimensions of the individual components of the assembly are shown in Figures 13.145 through 13.150. All dimensions are in mm.

13.144

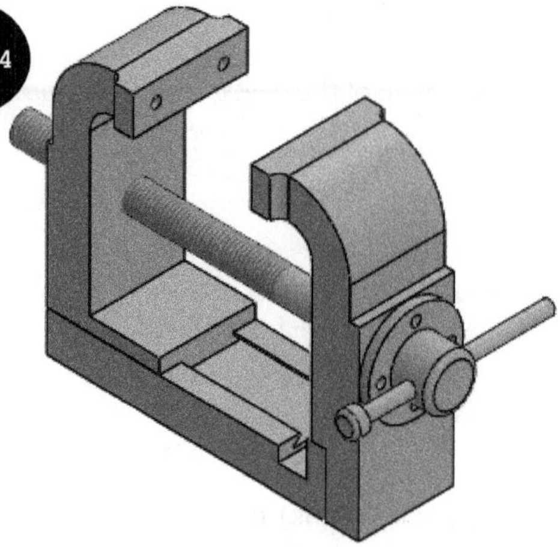

13.145

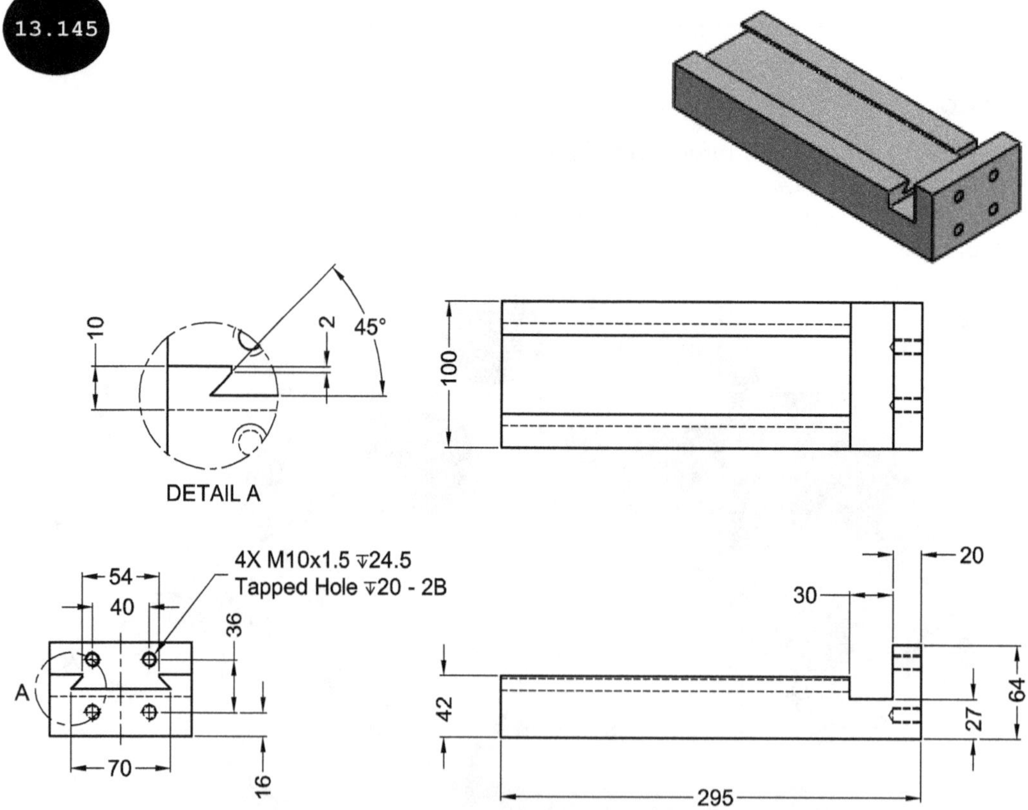

Base

13.146

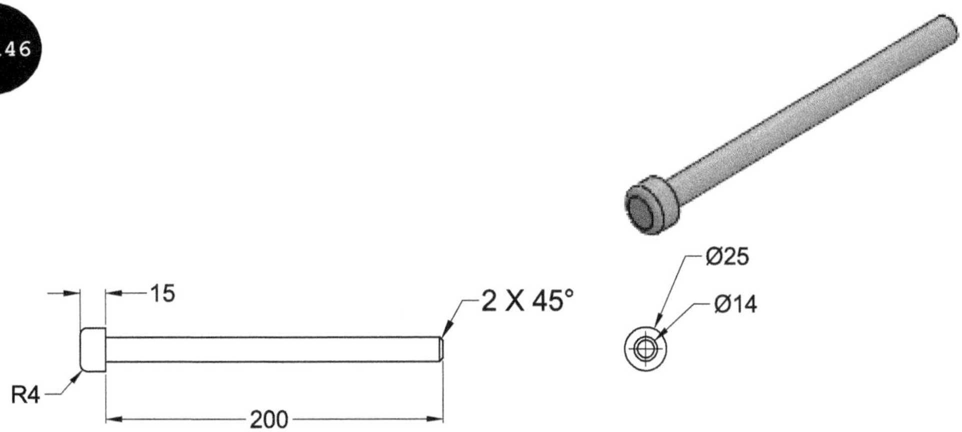

Screw Bar

13.147

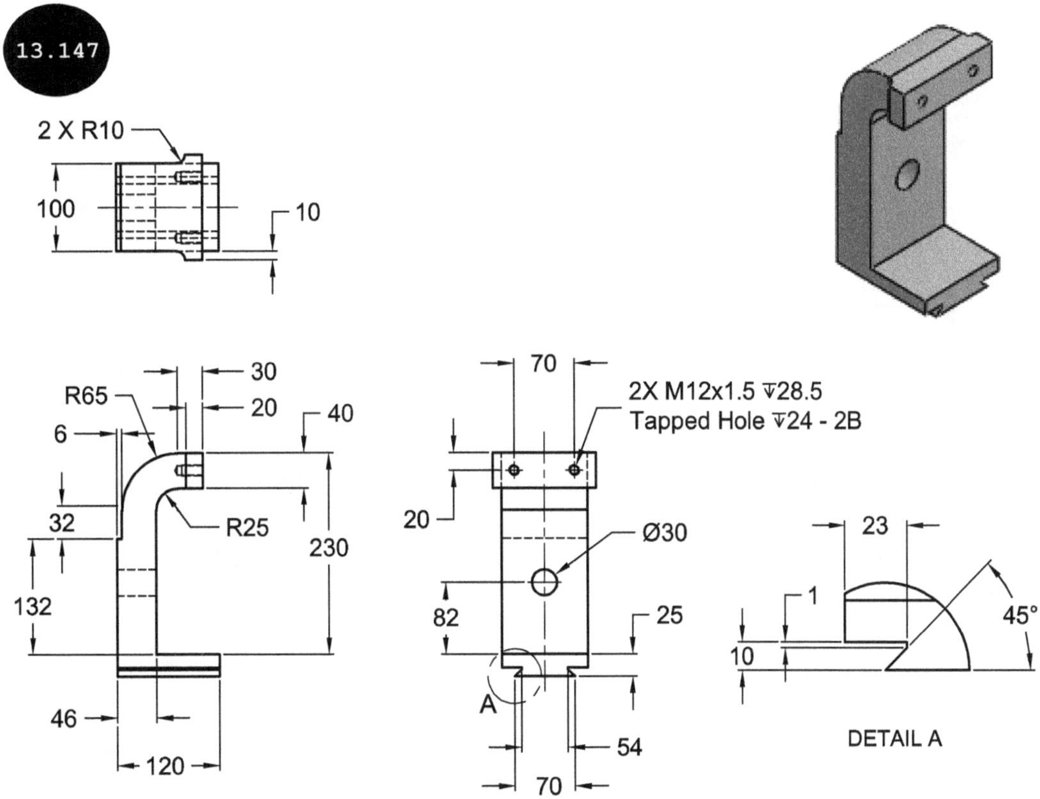

Moving Jaw

13.148

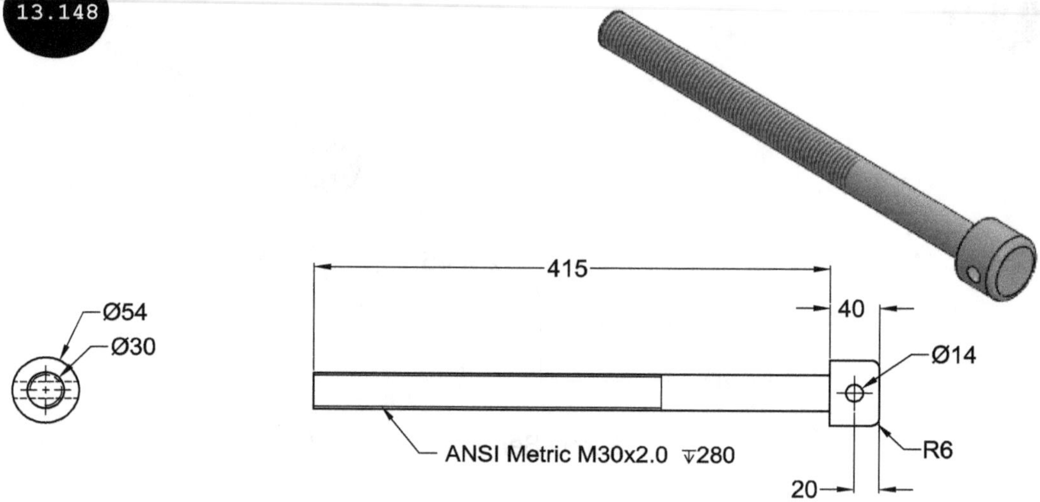

Jaw Screw

13.149

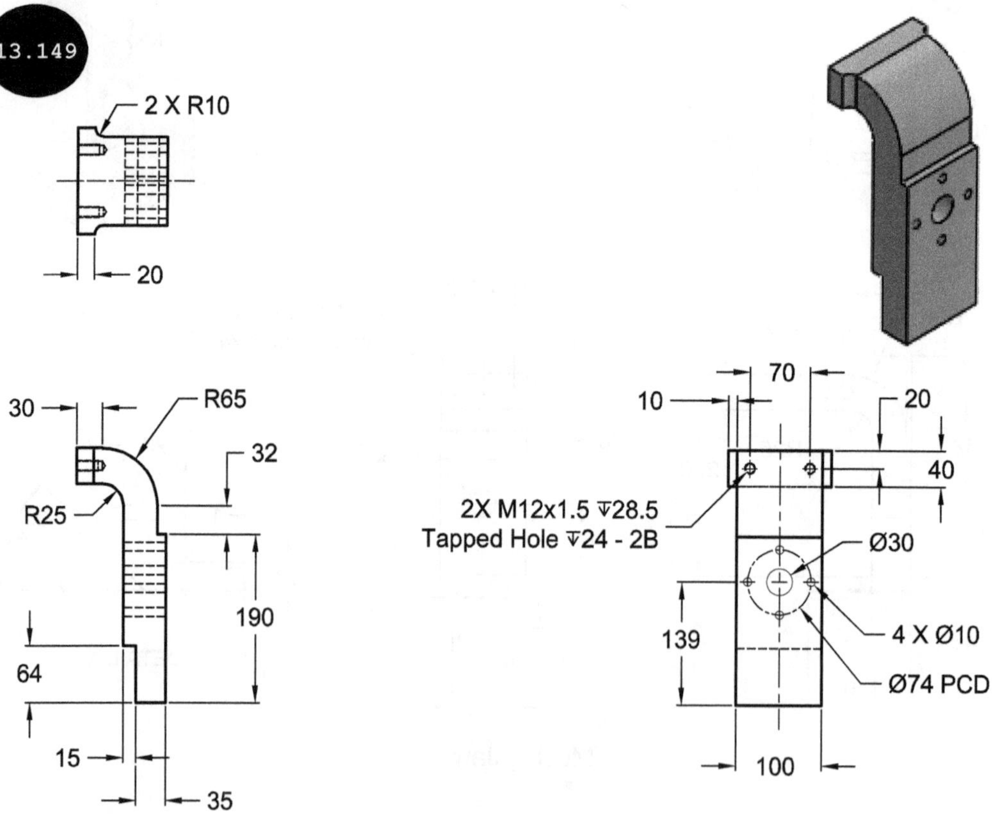

Fixed Jaw

13.150

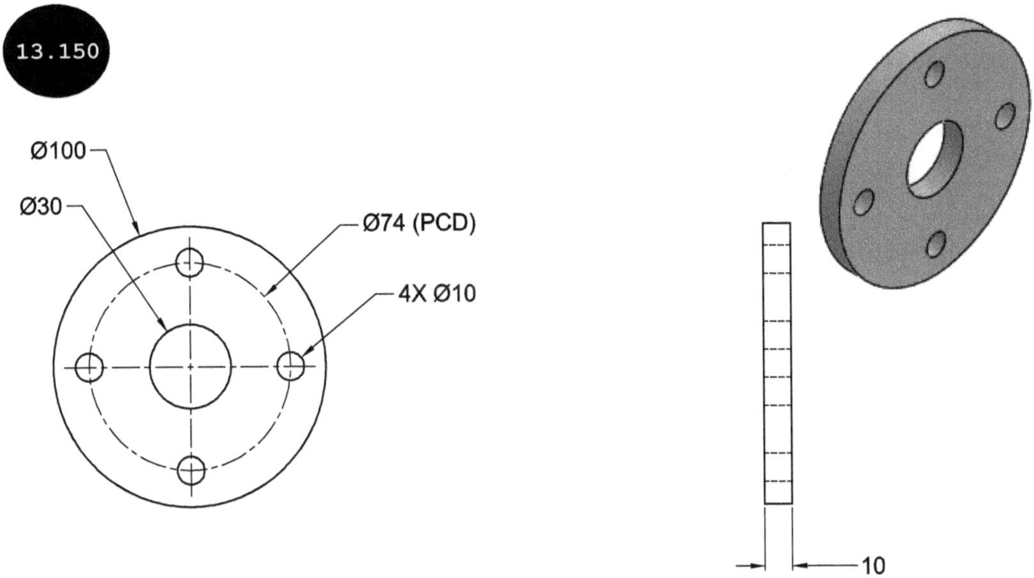

Washer

Summary

In this chapter, you learned about the Top-down Assembly Approach for creating assemblies. You explored how to edit components within both the Assembly and Part modeling environments. The chapter also covered editing mates between assembly components and creating various types of component patterns, such as Linear, Pattern Driven, and Chain Component Patterns.

Additionally, you gained an understanding of mirroring components, creating assembly features, and managing the suppression or unsuppression of components. The chapter also demonstrated how to insert components with multiple configurations, create and dissolve sub-assemblies, and check for interferences between components.

Furthermore, the chapter demonstrated how to create, edit, and animate exploded views of assemblies, add explode lines, and generate the Bill of Materials (BOM). By mastering these techniques, you are now equipped to streamline your assembly design process and create organized, detailed models ready for further analysis or production.

Questions

Complete and verify the following sentences:

- In the _________ approach, you can create all the components of an assembly in the Assembly environment.
- In the _________ pattern, the pattern components are driven by the pattern instances of the other components of an assembly.
- The _________ pattern allows you to dynamically simulate a chain drive or a cable carrier in an assembly.
- In SOLIDWORKS, you can create three types of chain patterns: _________, _________, and _________.
- The _________ tool is used for creating an exploded view of an assembly.
- In SOLIDWORKS, you can create _________ and _________ types of exploded views.
- The _________ tool is used for creating explode lines in an exploded view.
- You can edit the components of an assembly within the Assembly environment. (True/False)
- In SOLIDWORKS, you can create cut features in the Assembly environment. (True/False)
- In SOLIDWORKS, you cannot create sub-assemblies from the components of an assembly. (True/False)

CHAPTER

14

Working with Drawings

This chapter discusses the following topics:

- Invoking the Drawing Environment
- Creating the Base View of a Model
- Invoking Drawing Environment from the Part or the Assembly Environment
- Creating a Model View
- Creating Projected Views
- Creating 3 Standard Views
- Working with the Angle of Projection
- Defining the Angle of Projection
- Editing the Sheet Format
- Creating other Drawing Views
- Creating a Section View
- Creating an Auxiliary View
- Creating a Detail View
- Creating a Removed Section View
- Creating a Broken-out Section View
- Creating a Break View
- Creating a Crop View
- Creating an Alternate Position View
- Applying Dimensions
- Modifying the Driving Dimension
- Modifying Dimension Properties
- Controlling the Default Dimension/Arrow Style
- Adding Notes
- Adding a Surface Finish Symbol
- Adding a Weld Symbol
- Adding a Hole Callout
- Adding Center Marks
- Adding Centerlines
- Creating the Bill of Material (BOM)
- Adding Balloons
- Detailing Mode

After creating parts and assemblies, the next step is to generate 2D drawings. These technical drawings serve as the primary means of communication, conveying detailed information about the end product to be manufactured. 2D drawings are not just visual representations; they act as a language used by engineers to express ideas and provide crucial details about engineered products. Through these drawings, a designer can effectively communicate the specifications of components to the engineers on the shop floor.

The accuracy of these drawings is critical; any errors or missing information can result in faulty production. Therefore, the role of the designer in producing precise and error-free drawings is crucial. To support this, SOLIDWORKS offers a dedicated environment known as the Drawing environment, designed to facilitate the generation of reliable, error-free 2D drawings for production.

There are several ways to access the Drawing environment. You can open it by clicking the **Drawing** button in the **Welcome** dialog box. Alternatively, you can use the **Make Drawing from Part/Assembly** tool, which is available in both the Part and Assembly environments. These methods for accessing the Drawing environment are discussed in the next sections.

Invoking the Drawing Environment

To invoke the Drawing environment, click on the **New** tool in the **Standard** toolbar. The **New SOLIDWORKS Document** dialog box appears, see Figure 14.1. Next, click on the **Drawing** button in this dialog box and then click on the **OK** button. The **Sheet Format/Size** dialog box appears, see Figure 14.2. The options in this dialog box are used for selecting the sheet size/format to be used for creating drawings. You can also invoke the **Sheet Format/Size** dialog box by clicking on the **Drawing** button in the **Welcome** dialog box. The options in the **Sheet Format/Size** dialog box are discussed next.

14.1

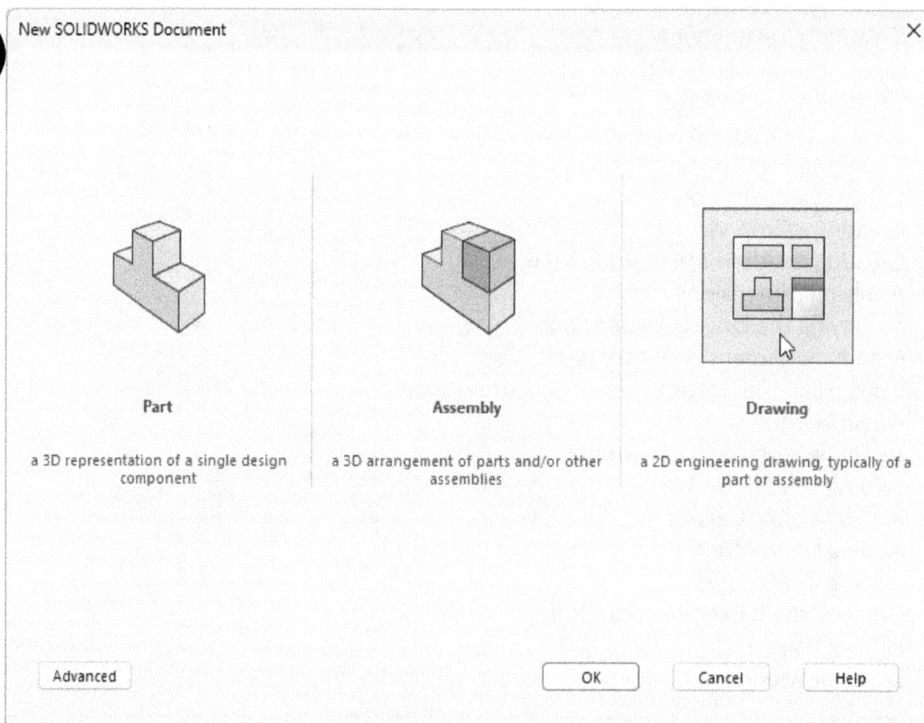

14.2

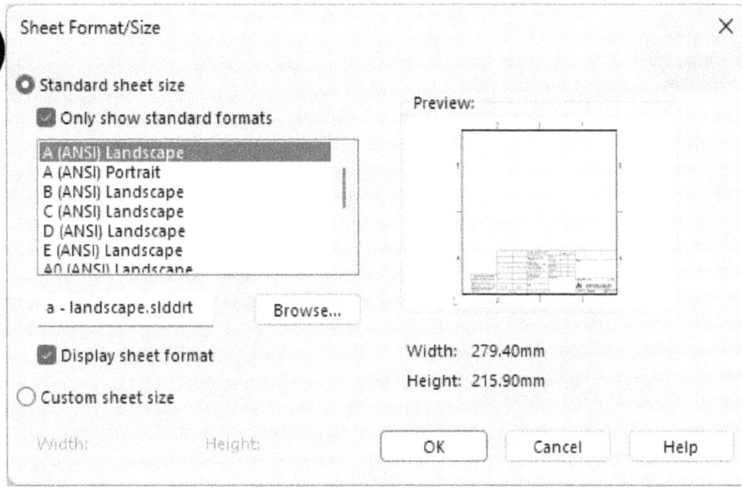

Standard sheet size

By default, the **Standard sheet size** radio button is selected in the **Sheet Format/Size** dialog box. As a result, a list of standard sheet sizes appears in the **Selection** area of the dialog box, see Figure 14.2. You can select a required standard sheet size in this area for creating drawing views. Note that if the **Only show standard formats** check box is selected in the dialog box, then a list of standard sheet sizes appears as per the current drawing standard only. If this check box is cleared, all the standard sheet sizes are listed in this area.

Display sheet format

By default, the **Display sheet format** check box is selected in the dialog box. As a result, a drawing sheet will be displayed with the default standard sheet format. You can also select a sheet format other than the default one by clicking on the **Browse** button in the dialog box. When you click on the **Browse** button, the **Open** dialog box appears. In this dialog box, select the required sheet format and then click on the **Open** button. A preview of the sheet format appears in the **Preview** area of the dialog box. If you clear the **Display sheet format** check box, a blank drawing sheet will be displayed for creating drawings. Note that the **Display sheet format** check box is enabled only if the **Standard sheet size** radio button is selected in the dialog box.

Custom sheet size

On selecting the **Custom sheet size** radio button in the dialog box, the **Width** and **Height** fields are enabled and the other options in the dialog box are disabled, see Figure 14.3. In the **Width** and **Height** fields, you can specify the custom width and height values for the drawing sheet.

14.3

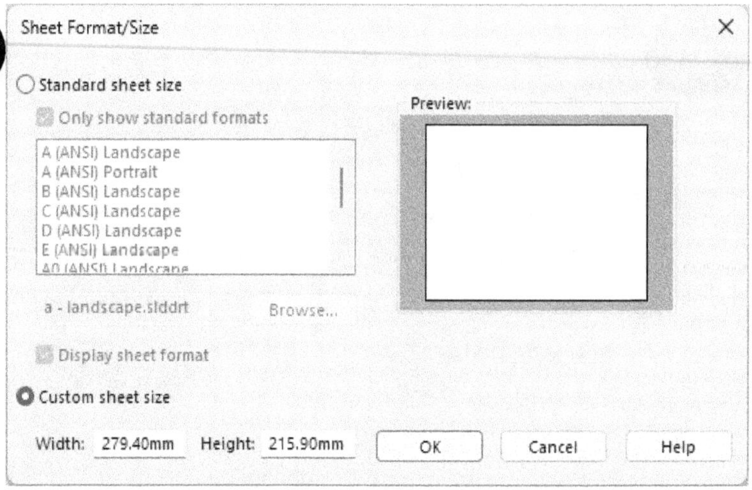

After selecting the required sheet size by using the options of the **Sheet Format/Size** dialog box, click on the **OK** button. The Drawing environment is invoked with a drawing sheet of a specified size/format. Also, the **Model View PropertyManager** appears on its left, see Figure 14.4.

14.4

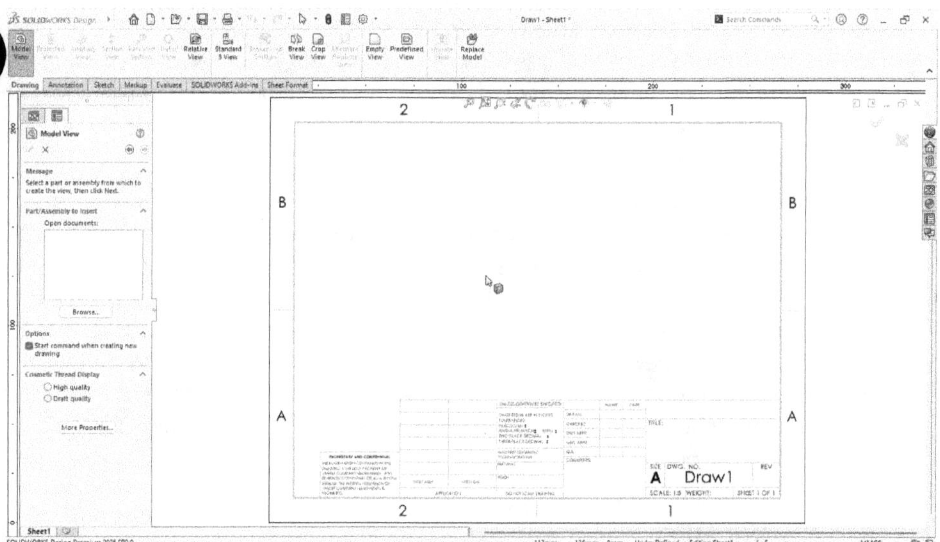

The options of the **Model View PropertyManager** are used for creating the base/model view of a component or an assembly. The method for creating the base/model view of a component or an assembly by using this PropertyManager is discussed next.

Note: The **Model View PropertyManager** appears each time on invoking the Drawing environment. This is because, in the **Options** rollout of the **Model View PropertyManager**, the **Start command when creating new drawing** check box is selected by default, see Figure 14.4. If you clear this check box, the **Model View PropertyManager** will not appear the next time you invoke the Drawing environment. In such a case, you can invoke the **Model View PropertyManager** by clicking on the **Model View** tool.

Creating the Base View of a Model

To create the base view of a model, click on the **Browse** button in the **Part/Assembly to Insert** the rollout of the **Model View PropertyManager**. The **Open** dialog box appears. In this dialog box, browse to the location where the model, whose drawing view is to be created has been saved, and then select it. Next, click on the **Open** button in the dialog box. A rectangular box representing, the base view of the model is attached to the cursor, see Figure 14.5. Also, the options of the PropertyManager are modified. The options are discussed next.

14.5

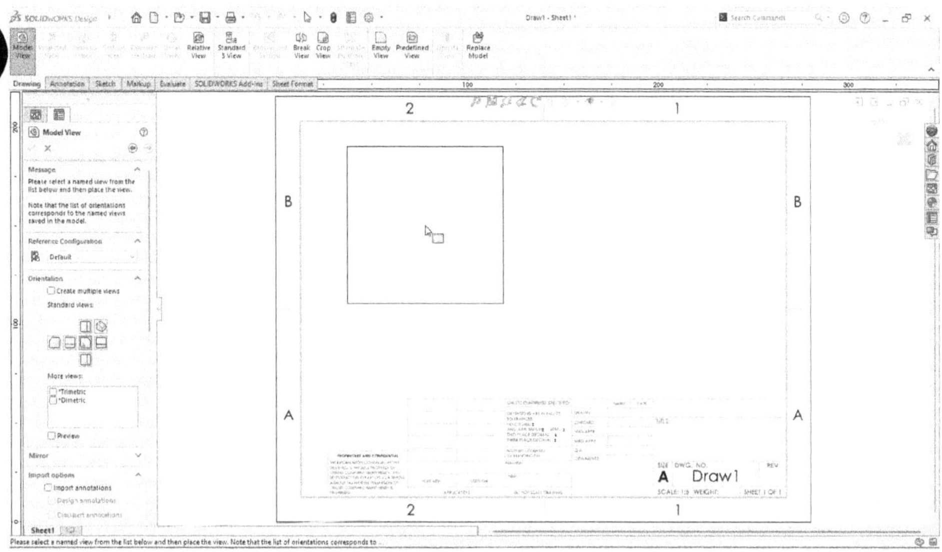

Tip: You can also select a component or an assembly, for which drawing views are to be created from the **Open documents** field of the **Part/Assembly to Insert** rollout in the PropertyManager. Note that the models that are opened in the current session of SOLIDWORKS are displayed in the **Open documents** field of the PropertyManager. To select a model from the **Open documents** field, double-click on the name of the model in this field.

Reference Configuration

The drop-down list in the **Reference Configuration** rollout of the PropertyManager contains a list of all the configurations of the selected model. You can select the required configuration of the model for creating its drawing views. Note that if the selected model does not have any configuration created, then only the **Default** option is available in this drop-down list, see Figure 14.6.

Orientation

The options in the **Standard views** area of the **Orientation** rollout are used for selecting a standard view of the model to be created. By default, the **Front** button is activated in the **Standard views** area, see Figure 14.6. You can click on the required button in this area to create the respective front, top, right, left, back, bottom, or isometric drawing view.

You can also create dimetric or trimetric drawing views of the model by selecting the respective check box in the **More views** field of the rollout, see Figure 14.6.

By default, the **Preview** check box of the **Orientation** rollout is cleared, see Figure 14.6. As a result, an empty rectangular box appears attached to the cursor, which represents the selected view of the model. On selecting this check box, a preview of the selected standard view appears in the rectangular box. You can also create multiple drawing views of the selected component or the assembly by selecting the **Create multiple views** check box of this rollout, see Figure 14.6.

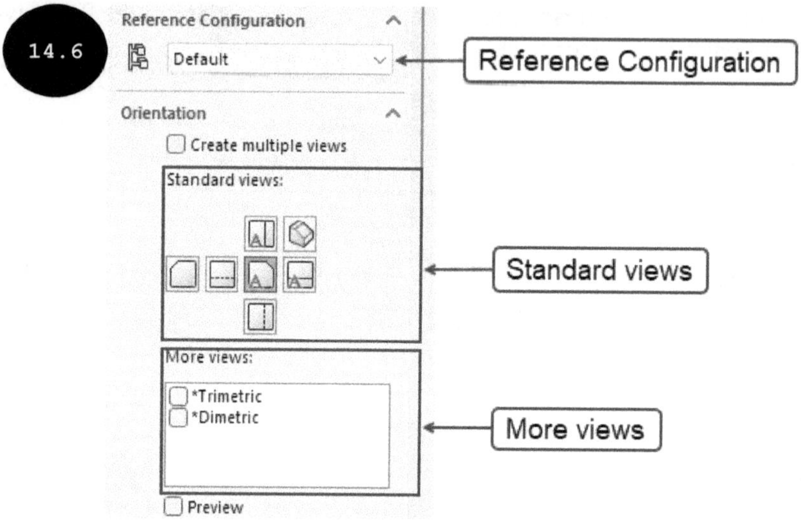

Import Options

The options in the **Import options** rollout are used for importing annotations of the model into the drawing view, see Figure 14.7. On selecting the **Import annotations** check box, the **Design annotations**, **DimXpert annotations**, **Include items from hidden features**, and **3D view annotations** check boxes are enabled in the rollout. Depending upon the check boxes selected in this rollout, the annotations of the model are imported into the drawing view. Note that the **DimXpert annotations** check box is enabled only if the model contains any dimxpert annotations.

Options

By default, the **Auto-start projected view** check box is selected in the **Options** rollout, see Figure 14.7. As a result, soon after creating the base/model view, the **Projected View PropertyManager** appears automatically. Also, a projected view of the model is attached to the cursor. The **Projected View PropertyManager** is used to create the projected views of the model. You will learn more about projected views later in this chapter.

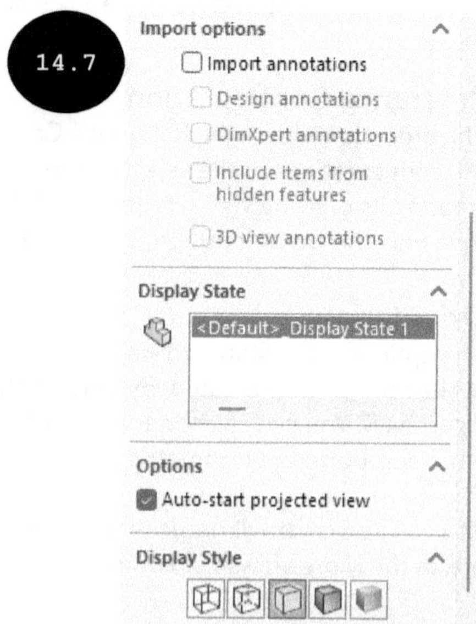

Display Style

The options in the **Display Style** rollout are used for selecting the type of display for the drawing view, see Figure 14.7. On selecting the **Wireframe** button, all the visible and hidden edges of the model appear as continuous lines in the drawing view, see Figure 14.8 (a). If you select the

Hidden Lines Visible button, the visible edges appear as continuous lines and the hidden edges appear as dotted lines in the drawing view, see Figure 14.8 (b). On selecting the **Hidden Lines Removed** button, only the visible edges of the model appear in the drawing view as continuous lines, see Figure 14.8 (c). On selecting the **Shaded With Edges** button, the drawing view is displayed in the shaded display style with the appearance of visible edges, see Figure 14.8 (d). If you select the **Shaded** button, the drawing view is displayed in the shaded model with the visible and hidden edges turned off, see Figure 14.8 (e).

14.8

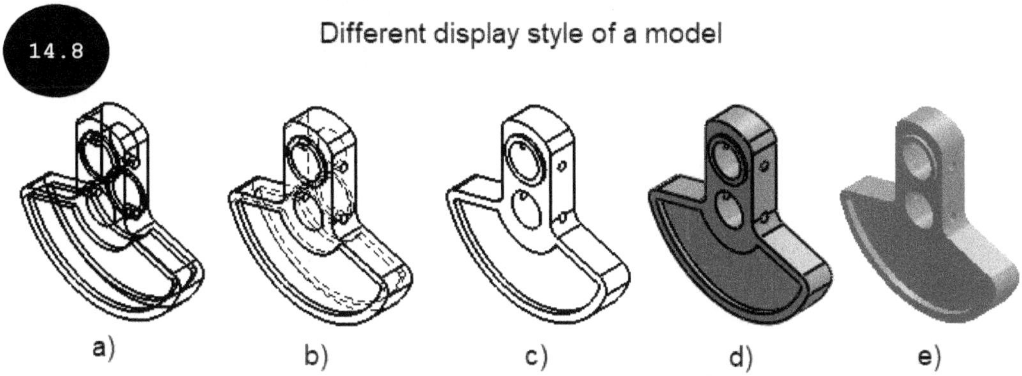

Mirror

The **Mirror** rollout of the PropertyManager is used to create a horizontal or vertical mirror view of the model relative to the selected standard view. To create the horizontal or vertical mirror view of the model, expand the **Mirror** rollout of the PropertyManager and then select the **Mirror view** check box, see Figure 14.9. Next, select the **Horizontal** or **Vertical** radio button to create the respective mirror view of the model relative to the selected standard view.

14.9

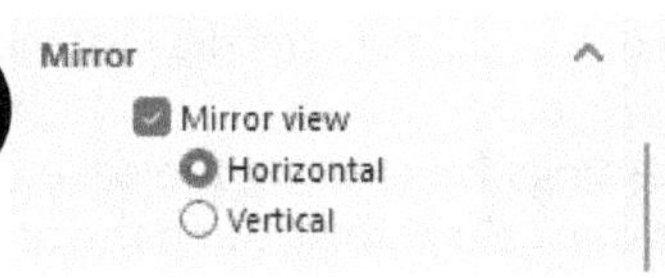

Scale

By default, the **Use sheet scale** radio button is selected in the **Scale** rollout, see Figure 14.10. As a result, the scale of the drawing view is the same as the scale of the drawing sheet. On selecting the **Use custom scale** radio button, the **Scale** field gets enabled. You can enter the required scale value in this field or choose a pre-defined scale value from the drop-down list which can be accessed by clicking on the down arrow available in this field.

14.10

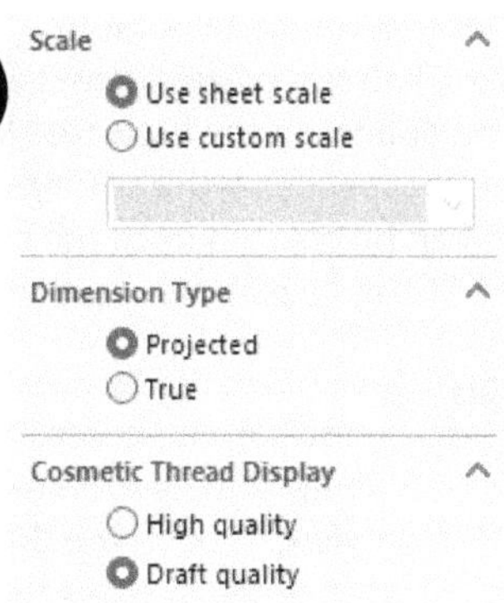

Dimension Type

The **Dimension Type** rollout is used to specify the type of dimensions: True or Projected, for the drawing view. The Projected dimensions appear as 2D dimensions in a drawing view. They are mainly used in orthogonal views such as front, top, and right, see Figure 14.11. The True dimensions appear as accurate model dimensions in isometric, dimetric, and trimetric drawing views, see Figure 14.12.

14.11

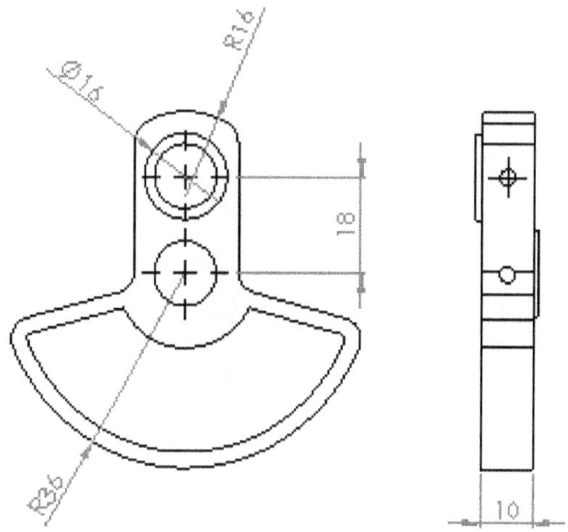

14.12

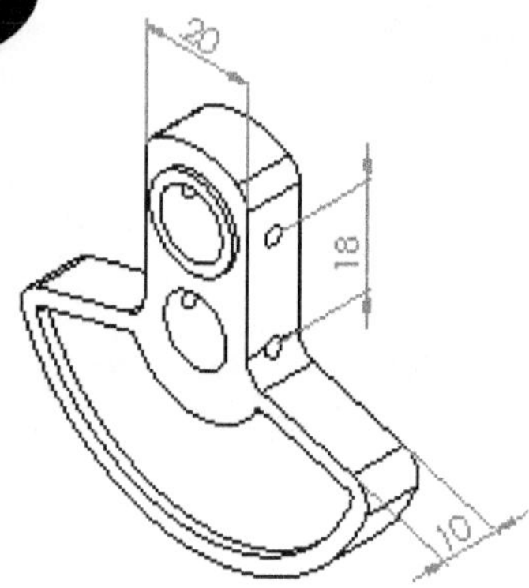

Cosmetic Thread Display

The **High quality** and **Draft quality** radio buttons of the **Cosmetic Thread Display** rollout are used for controlling the display of cosmetic threads in the drawing view. On selecting the **High quality** radio button, the cosmetic threads appear in precise line fonts. On selecting the **Draft quality** radio button, the cosmetic threads appear with less detail in the drawing views.

After specifying the required settings for creating the base view such as type of view, display style, and scale factor, click on the drawing sheet to position the drawing view. The drawing view is created and placed in the specified position on the drawing sheet. Also, the **Projected View PropertyManager** appears automatically. Notice that on moving the cursor, a projected view appears attached to the cursor. You can create projection views by specifying the placement points in the drawing sheet. Most of the options of the **Projected View PropertyManager** are the same as those discussed earlier and are used for specifying the settings for the projected views. Figure 14.13 shows different projected views that can be created from the base view. Once you have created the required projected views, press the ESC key to exit the creation of projection views.

Note: You can also control or modify the settings such as display style and scale factor for a drawing view that has been already placed in the drawing sheet. To modify the settings of a drawing view, click on the drawing view in the drawing sheet. The **Drawing View PropertyManager** appears. By using the options of this PropertyManager, you can control the settings of the selected drawing view. All options of this PropertyManager are same as those discussed earlier.

14.13

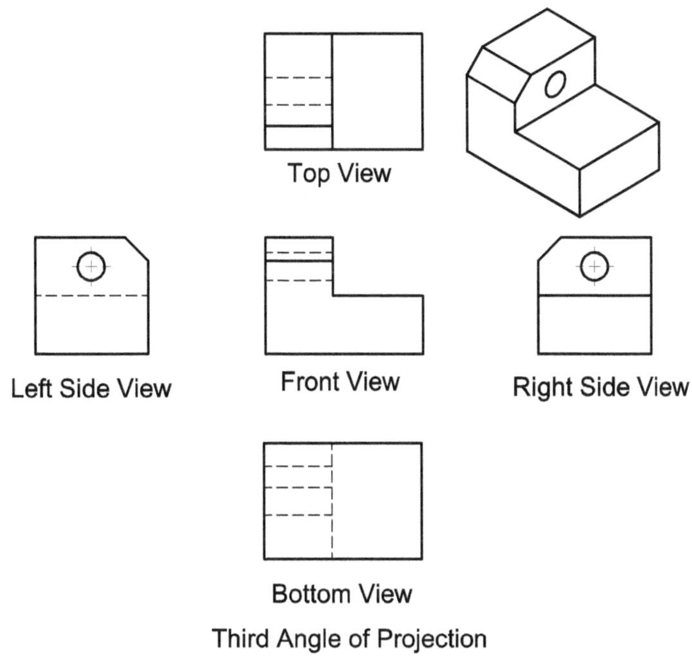

Invoking Drawing Environment from the Part or the Assembly Environment

Similar to invoking the Drawing environment using the **New** tool and creating different drawing views of a model, you can also invoke the Drawing environment from the Part modeling environment or the Assembly environment. If you are in the Part modeling environment or the Assembly environment, you can directly invoke the Drawing environment from there and start creating drawing views of a model that is currently available in the respective environment. To invoke the Drawing environment from the Part modeling environment or the Assembly environment, click on the down arrow available next to the **New** tool in the **Standard** toolbar. A flyout appears, see Figure 14.14.

14.14

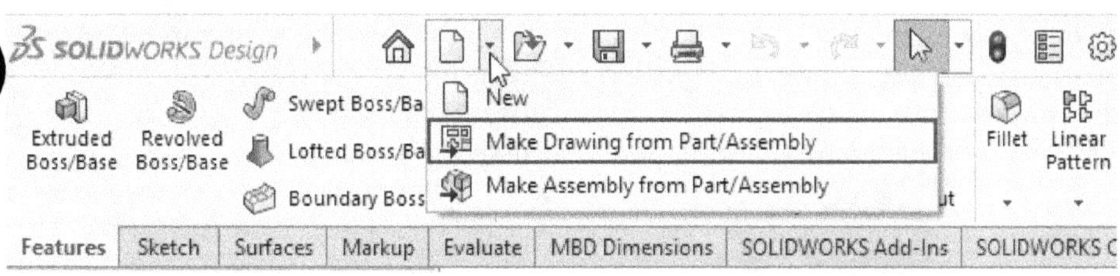

Click on the **Make Drawing from Part/Assembly** tool in this flyout. The **Sheet Format/Size** dialog box appears. The options in this dialog box are used for specifying the required format/size of the drawing sheet and are the same as those discussed earlier. After defining the format/size of the drawing sheet, click on the **OK** button. The Drawing environment is invoked with the display of the **View Palette Task Pane** to the right of the drawing sheet, see Figure 14.15.

14.15

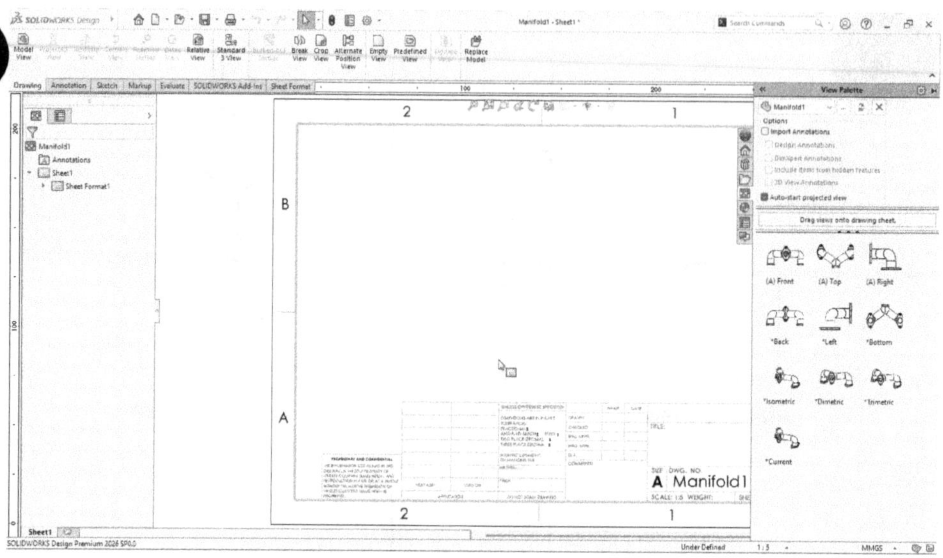

Note that the bottom half area of the **View Palette Task Pane** displays drawing views of the model that were opened in the Part modeling environment or the Assembly environment. By using this task pane, you can drag and drop the required drawing view of the model onto the drawing sheet. The first placed view in the drawing sheet is known as a model, base, or parent view. As soon as you place the model/base view in the drawing sheet, the **Projected View PropertyManager** appears to the left of the drawing sheet. This is because the **Auto-start projected view** check box is selected in the upper half of the **View Palette Task Pane**, see Figure 14.15. Now, on moving the cursor in the drawing sheet, a projected view appears and attaches with the cursor, automatically. You can click on the drawing sheet to specify the position of the projected view. You can create multiple projected views one after another by clicking the left mouse button. Once you have created the required projected views, press the ESC key to exit the creation of projection views.

Creating a Model View

A model view is an independent view of a model. It is also known as the base, first, or parent view. You can create a model view of a model using the **Model View PropertyManager** and the **View Palette Task Pane**, which appears automatically on invoking the Drawing environment, as discussed earlier. Besides, you can also invoke the **Model View PropertyManager** by clicking on the **Model View** tool in the Drawing CommandManager for creating the model/base view of a model, see Figure 14.16. The method for creating a model or base view is discussed below:

14.16

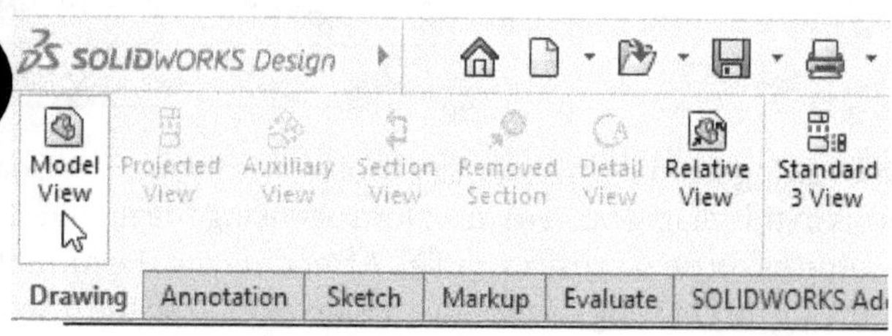

1. Invoke the **Model View PropertyManager** by clicking on the **Model View** tool, if not invoked by default.

2. Click on the **Browse** button in the **Part/Assembly to Insert** rollout of the PropertyManager.

Tip: If the component or the assembly whose drawing view is to be created appears in the **Open documents** field of the **Part/Assembly to Insert** rollout in the PropertyManager, then you can directly select it from this field by double-clicking on it for creating its model view. The **Open documents** field displays a list of models, which are opened in the current session of SOLIDWORKS.

3. Select a part or an assembly, whose drawing views are to be created and then click on the **Open** button in the dialog box. A rectangular box appears attached to the cursor, which represents the model/base view of the selected part or assembly.

4. Specify the required settings such as standard view, display style, and scale factor for the drawing view by using the options in the PropertyManager.

5. Click on the drawing sheet to specify the position for the model/base view in the drawing sheet. The model view is created. Also, the **Projected View PropertyManager** appears. By using the **Projected View PropertyManager**, you can create the projected views of the model.

6. After creating the required views, press the ESC key to exit the creation of drawing views.

Creating Projected Views

Projected views are orthogonal views of an object, which are created by viewing an object from its different projection sides such as top, front, and side. Figure 14.17 and Figure 14.18 show different projected views of an object.

14.17

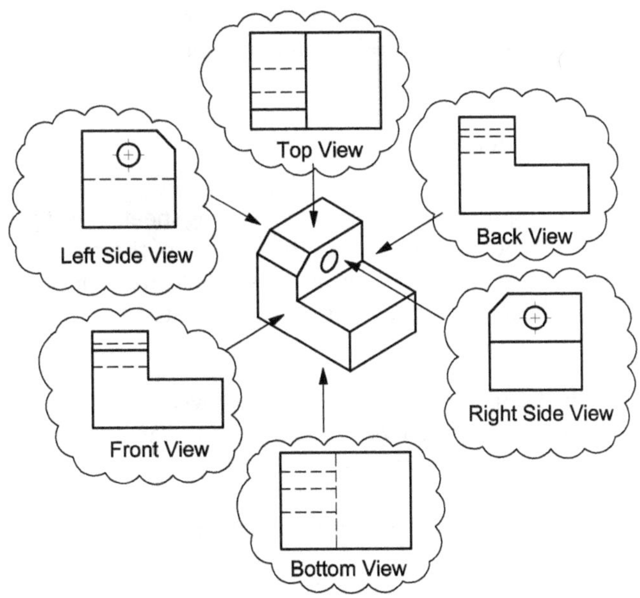

Projected Views

14.18

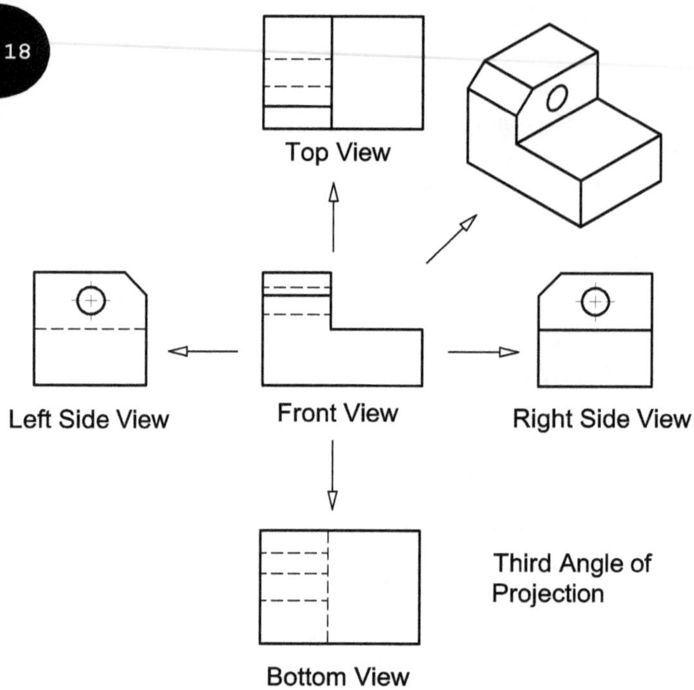

You can create projected views using the **Projected View PropertyManager**. As discussed earlier, the **Projected View PropertyManager** is invoked automatically as soon as you create the model/base view of a model by using the **Model View PropertyManager**. You can also invoke this PropertyManager by clicking on the **Projected View** tool in the **Drawing CommandManager** or in the Pop-up toolbar that appears when you click on a view in the drawing area. The options in the **Projected View PropertyManager** are the same as those discussed earlier and are used for creating the projected views of a selected model/base view. The method for creating a projected view is discussed below:

1. After invoking the **Projected View PropertyManager**, select a view in the drawing sheet as the parent view whose projected views are to be created.

Note: If only one drawing view is available in the drawing sheet, then it gets automatically selected for creating its projected views. Also, the preview of the projected view is attached to the cursor. However, if two or more views are available in the drawing sheet, then you need to select a view whose projected views are to be created.

2. Move the cursor to the required location in the drawing sheet and then click to specify the placement point for the projected view attached. You can continue creating other projected views by clicking the left mouse button on the drawing sheet.

3. Once you have created the projected views, press the ESC key.

Creating 3 Standard Views

In addition to creating drawing views using the **Model View PropertyManager** and the **Projected View PropertyManager**, you can create three standard orthogonal views: front, top, and side using the **Standard 3 View** tool of the **Drawing CommandManager**. On clicking this tool, the **Standard 3 View PropertyManager** appears. If the part or assembly, whose drawing views are to be created is displayed in the **Open documents** field of the PropertyManager then double-click on it. The three standard views are created automatically in the drawing sheet, see Figure 14.19. If the model is not displayed in the **Open documents** field, then click on the **Browse** button. The **Open** dialog box appears. In this dialog box, browse to a location where the required part or assembly has been saved and then select it. Next, click on the **Open** button in the dialog box.

14.19

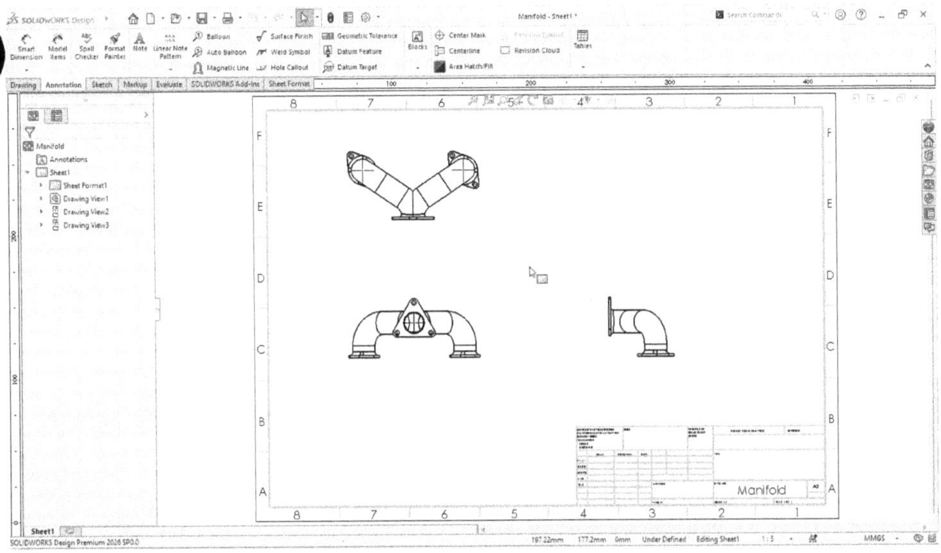

Note: The creation of standard views depend upon the angle of projection defined for the drawing sheet. You can define the first angle of projection or the third angle of projection for creating the standard drawing views. The concept of angle of projection and the procedure to define the angle of projection for a drawing sheet are discussed next.

Working with the Angle of Projection

Engineering drawings follow two types of angles of projection: the first angle of projection and the third angle of projection. In the first angle of projection, the object is assumed to be kept in the first quadrant and the viewer views the object from the direction as shown in Figure 14.20. As the object has been kept in the first quadrant, its projections of views are on the respective planes as shown in Figure 14.20. Now on unfolding the planes of projections, the front view appears on the upper side and the top view appears on the bottom side. Also, the right-side view appears on the left and the left-side view appears on the right side of the front view, see Figure 14.21. Similarly, in the third angle of projection, the object is assumed to be kept in the third quadrant, see Figure 14.20. In this angle of projection, the projection of the front view appears on the bottom and the projection of the top view appears on the top side of the drawing. Also, the right-side view appears on the right and the left-side view appears on the left of the front view, see Figure 14.22.

14.20

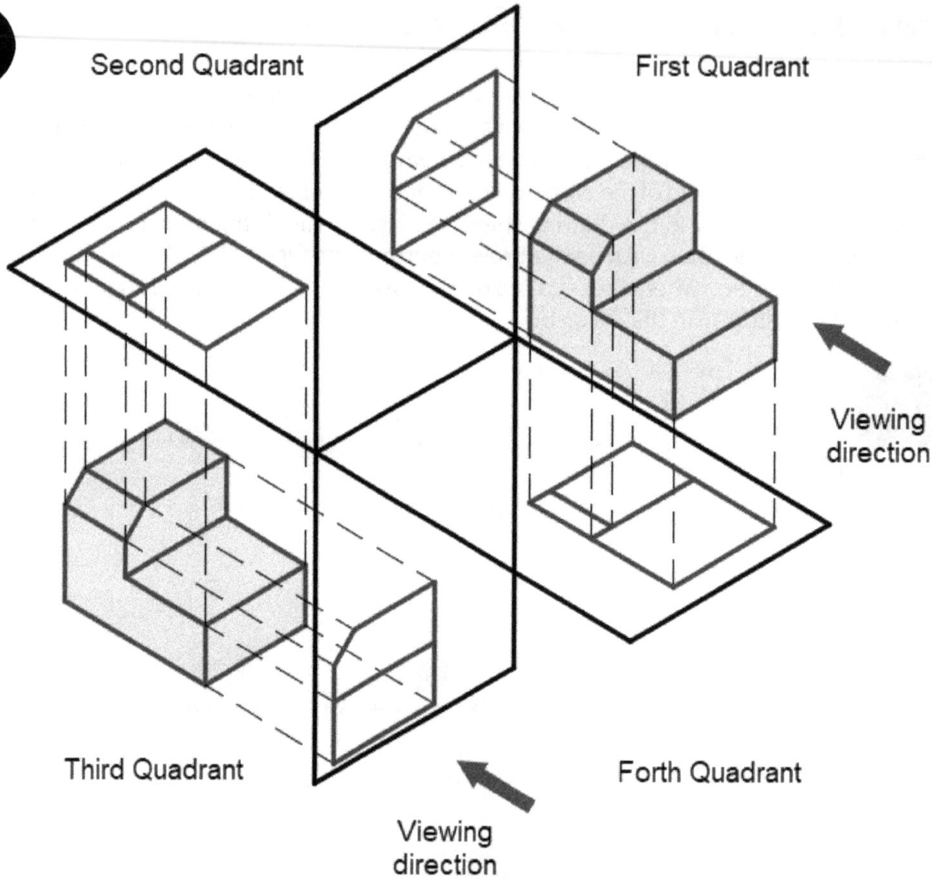

14.21

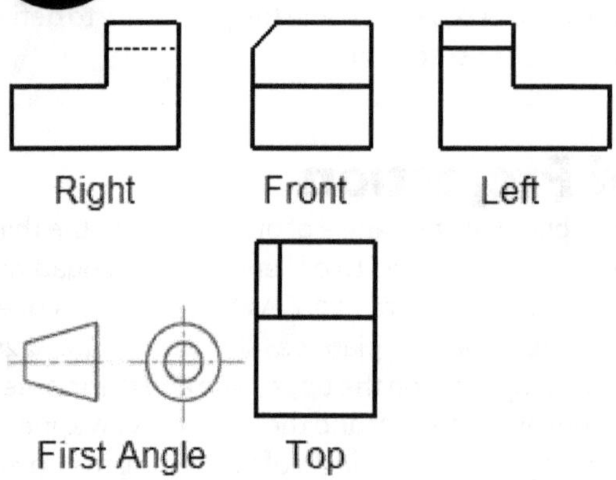

14.22

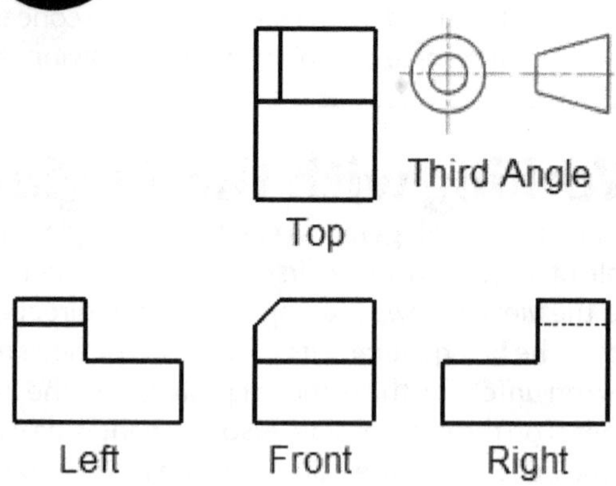

Defining the Angle of Projection

In SOLIDWORKS, to define the required angle of projection for creating drawing views, select the **Sheet** node in the FeatureManager Design Tree and then right-click. A shortcut menu appears, see Figure 14.23. Next, click on the **Properties** option in the shortcut menu. The **Sheet Properties** dialog box appears, see Figure 14.24. In this dialog box, you can select the type of projection to be followed for creating drawing views by selecting the respective radio button in the **Type of projection** area of the dialog box. Next, click on the **Apply Changes** button to accept the change and exit the dialog box.

14.23

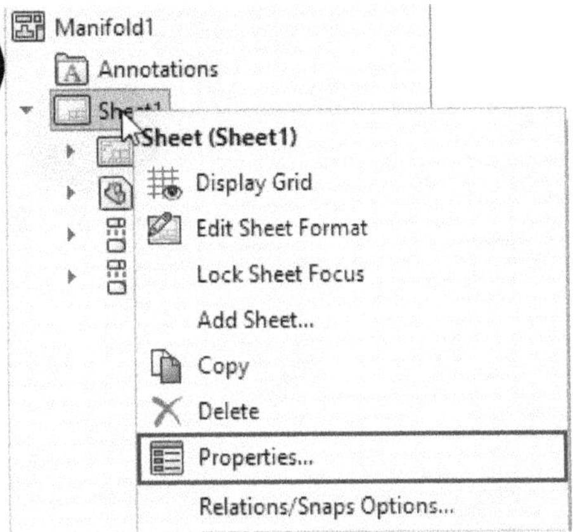

14.24

Tip: In the **Sheet Properties** dialog box, you can also define the scale of the drawing sheet using the **Scale** fields, refer to Figure 14.24. Alternatively, you can also define the sheet scale by selecting a pre-defined scale value in the **Scale** drop-down list available at the bottom right of the Status Bar, see Figure 14.25. In SOLIDWORKS, on selecting the **User Defined** option in the **Scale** drop-down list, you can also define a custom scale for the drawing sheet. When you select this option, the **User Defined Sheet Scale** dialog box appears, see Figure 14.26. In the dialog box, enter the required sheet scale in x:x format and then click on the **OK** button.

14.25

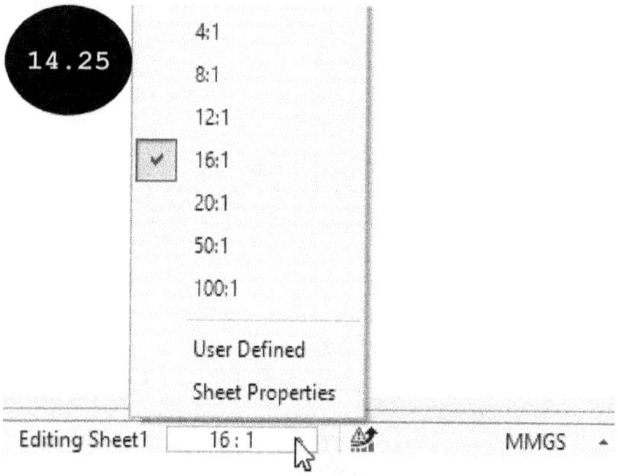

14.26

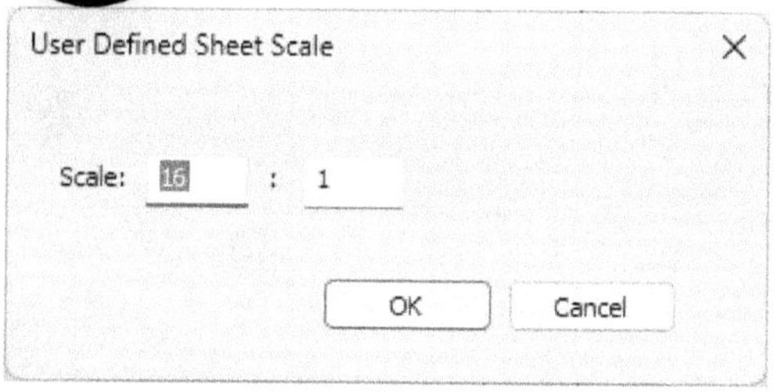

Editing the Sheet Format

While invoking the Drawing environment, you can select the required sheet size and sheet format. Note that the sheet format contains a title block, which has drawing information such as project name, drawn by, checked by, approved by, date, sheet number, and so on. You can create or edit the sheet format such that it matches the standard format of your company. To edit the sheet format of a sheet, select the **Sheet** node in the FeatureManager Design Tree and then right-click to display a shortcut menu, refer to Figure 14.23. Next, click on the **Edit Sheet Format** option in the shortcut menu. The editing mode for editing sheet format is invoked, see Figure 14.27.

Now, you can edit or modify the existing text and lines of the title block. Also, you can add new lines and text in the title block by using the sketching tools of the **Sketch CommandManager**. To delete existing lines and text, select the lines and text of the title block to be deleted and then press the DELETE key. To edit the existing text, double-click on the text to be edited. The editing mode is invoked such that the text appears in the edit field. Now, you can write new text in the edit field. Once you have edited the sheet format, click on the Confirmation corner in the upper right corner of the drawing area to exit the editing mode and switch back to the drawing sheet.

Tip: In SOLIDWORKS, you can also add surface finish and geometric tolerance annotations on the sheet format by using the respective tools available in the **Annotation CommandManager**. The method for adding surface finish annotations on the sheet format is same as adding them on a face of a model which is discussed later in this chapter with the only difference that the annotations on the sheet format do not include leaders.

14.27

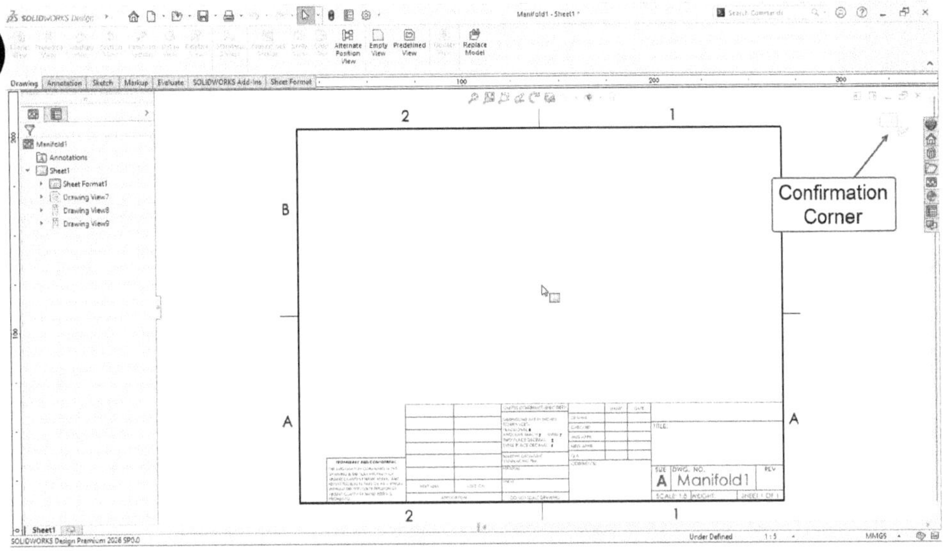

After modifying the sheet format or creating a new sheet format, as per the requirement, you can also save it for future use in other drawings. To save the sheet format, click on **File > Save Sheet Format** in the SOLIDWORKS Design Menus. The **Save Sheet Format** dialog box appears. In this dialog box, specify the name and location for the sheet format and then click on the **Save** button.

Creating other Drawing Views

In SOLIDWORKS, in addition to creating orthogonal views such as the front, top, and right of an object, you can also create the following types of drawing views:

- Section View
- Aligned Section View
- Auxiliary View
- Detail View
- Removed Section View
- Broken View
- Crop View
- Alternate Position View
- Broken-out Section View

Creating a Section View

A section view is created by cutting an object using an imaginary cutting plane or a section line and then viewing the object from the direction normal to the cutting plane. Figure 14.28 shows a section view created by cutting an object using a cutting plane. A section view is used to illustrate the internal features of the object clearly. It also reduces the number of hidden-detail lines, facilitates the dimensioning of internal features, shows cross-section, and so on. In SOLIDWORKS, you can create a full section view and a half section view by using the **Section View** tool of the **Drawing CommandManager**.

14.28

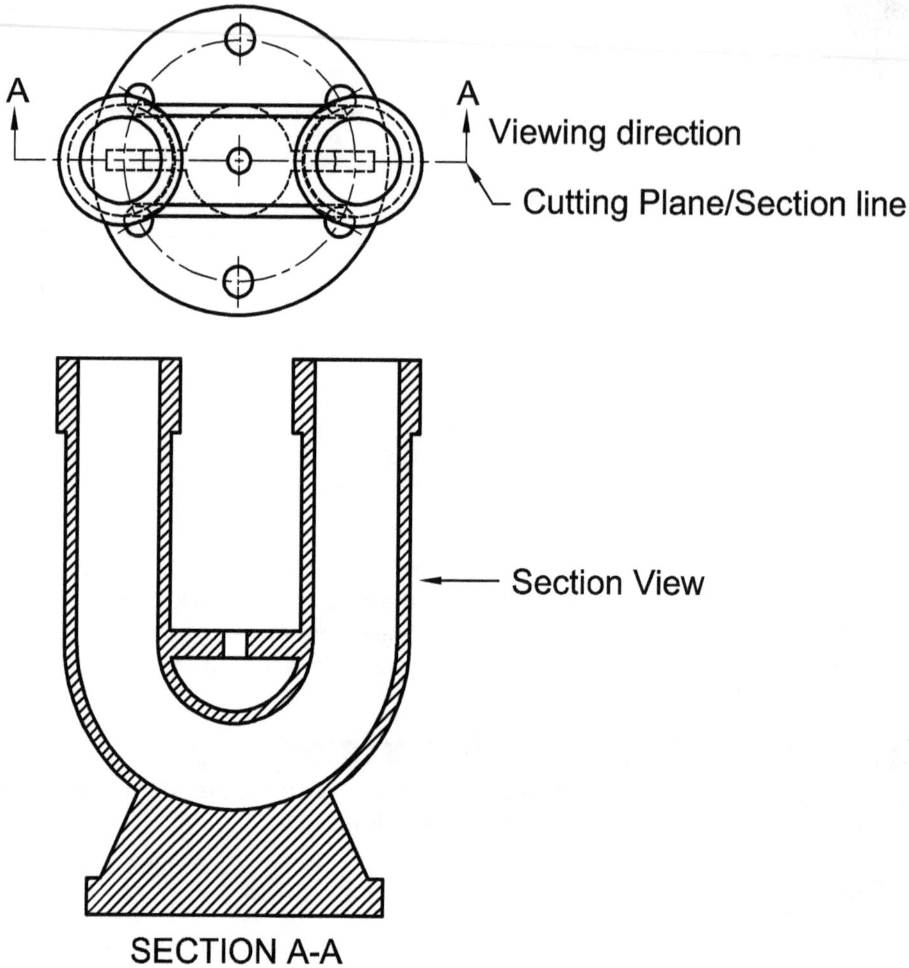

Creating a Full Section View

Full section views are the most widely used section views in engineering drawings. In a full section view, an object is assumed to be cut through all its length by an imaginary cutting plane or a section line, refer to Figure 14.28. In SOLIDWORKS, you can create four types of full section views: horizontal, vertical, auxiliary, and aligned, using the **Section View** tool.

To create a full section view, click on the **Section View** tool in the **Drawing CommandManager**. The **Section View Assist PropertyManager** appears, see Figure 14.29.

Note: In the **Section View Assist PropertyManager**, two tabs are available on its top: **Section** and **Half Section**, out of which the **Section** tab is activated by default. As a result, the options to create a full section view appear in the PropertyManager. On activating the **Half Section** tab, the options to create a half section view appear. You can learn about creating half section views later in this chapter.

The **Cutting Line** rollout of the PropertyManager is used to select the type of cutting line for creating the respective full section view. You can create a vertical section view, horizontal section view, auxiliary section view, and aligned section view by using the respective buttons of the **Cutting Line** rollout. Different types of full section views are discussed next.

14.29

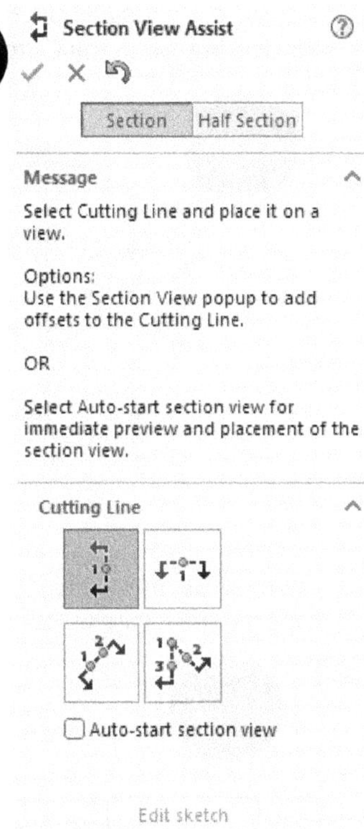

Creating a Horizontal/Vertical Section View

To create a horizontal section view, click on the **Horizontal** button in the **Cutting Line** rollout of the PropertyManager. A horizontal cutting line attached to the cursor appears. Next, select the **Auto-start section view** check box in the **Cutting Line** rollout. Now, move the cursor toward an existing drawing view and then click to specify the placement point for the horizontal cutting line. A preview of the horizontal section view appears attached to the cursor. Also, the **Section View PropertyManager** appears with additional options. Note that the direction of the arrows of the cutting section line represents the viewing direction. You can reverse the viewing direction by clicking on the **Flip Direction** button in the PropertyManager.

In SOLIDWORKS, you can emphasize the outlines of the cutting faces such that they appear thicker than the object lines in the section view by selecting the **Emphasize outline** check box in the **Section View** rollout of the PropertyManager. Also, if needed, you can scale the hatch pattern of the section view by selecting the **Scale hatch pattern** check box of the **Section View** rollout in the PropertyManager. Next, click to specify the placement point for the horizontal section view at the required location on the drawing sheet. The horizontal section view is created, refer to Figure 14.28.

Note: If the **Auto-start section view** check box in the **Cutting Line** rollout is cleared, the **Section View** Pop-up toolbar appears soon after defining the placement point for the section line in a drawing view, see Figure 14.30. By using the tools of this Pop-up toolbar, you can modify or edit the section line, as required. Once you have edited or modified the section line, click on the green tick-mark in the Pop-up toolbar. The preview of the section view appears attached to the cursor based on the modified section line. Now, you can specify the placement point for the section view in the drawing sheet.

14.30

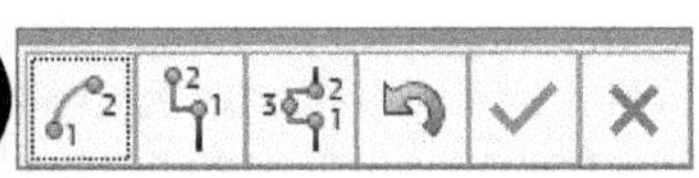

Similar to creating a horizontal section view, you can create a vertical section view by using the **Vertical** button of the **Cutting Line** rollout. Figure 14.31 shows a vertical section view created.

14.31

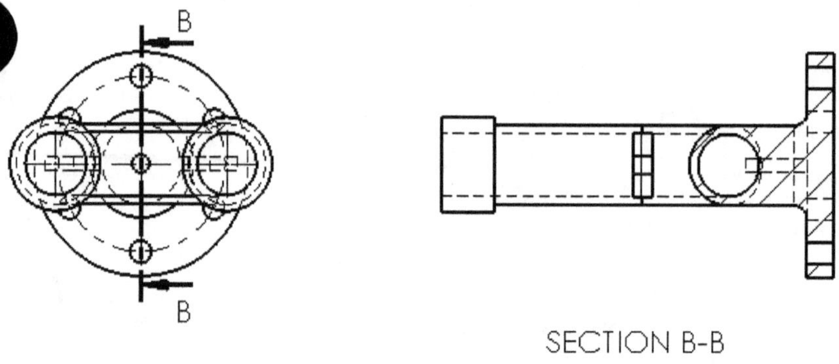

Note that if you are creating a section view of an assembly or a component having rib features, then soon after specifying the placement point for the section line, the **Section View** dialog box appears, see Figure 14.32.

14.32

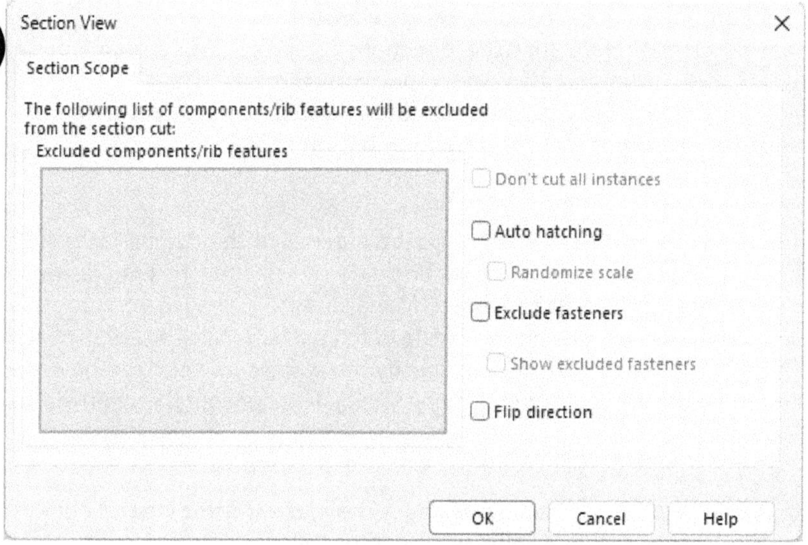

Note: The availability of the options in the **Section View** dialog box depends upon whether you are creating a section view of an assembly or a component having rib features. Figure 14.32 shows the **Section View** dialog box, which appears on creating the section view of an assembly.

By default, the **Excluded components/rib features** field is activated in the **Section View** dialog box. As a result, you can select components like fasteners and features like ribs to be excluded from the section cut. On selecting the **Auto hatching** check box, the alternate crosshatch patterns will be created between components of an assembly in the section view. In SOLIDWORKS, you can also randomize the hatch scale for the components having the same material in the section view by selecting the **Randomize scale** check box. If this check box is cleared, the section view will be created by keeping the hatch scale identical for all the hatches of the components having the same material. Once you have selected the components/features to be excluded, click on the **OK** button in the dialog box. A preview of the section view appears attached to the cursor, without cutting the selected components or features. Next, click to specify the placement point for placing the section view in the drawing sheet.

Tip: You can set the line font for the emphasized outlines of the cutting faces in the section view. To do this, click on the **Options** tool in the **Standard** toolbar to invoke the **System Options** dialog box. Next, click on the **Document Properties** tab in the dialog box and then click on the **Line Font** option. Next, select the **Emphasized Section Outline** option in the **Type of edge** area of the dialog box and then set the font/style for the emphasized outlines using the options that appear in the dialog box.

Creating an Auxiliary Section View

An auxiliary section view is created by cutting an object using a sight line that is not parallel to any of the principal projection planes: frontal, horizontal, or profile, and then viewing the object from the direction normal to the sight line, see Figure 14.33.

14.33

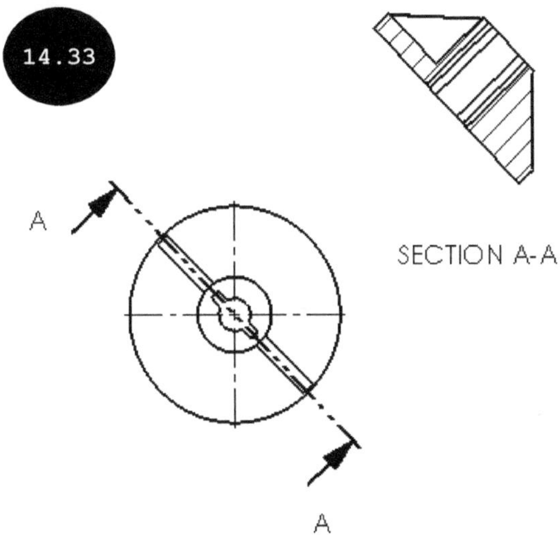

To create an auxiliary section view, click on the **Section View** tool to invoke the **Section View Assist PropertyManager**. Next, click on the **Auxiliary** button in the **Cutting Line** rollout. A section line is attached to the cursor. Move the cursor to an existing drawing view. Next, click to specify the center point of the section line and a placement point to define the angle of the section line. A preview of the auxiliary section view is attached to the cursor. If the **Section View** Pop-up toolbar appears soon after specifying the placement point then click on its green tick-mark to display the preview of the auxiliary section view. You can reverse the default viewing direction by clicking on the **Flip Direction** button in the PropertyManager. Next, click to specify the placement point for the auxiliary section view at the required location in the drawing sheet. The auxiliary section view is created, see Figure 14.33.

Creating an Aligned Section View

An aligned section view is created by cutting an object using the cutting section line, which comprises of two non-parallel lines, and then straightening the cross-section by revolving it around the center point of the section line, see Figure 14.34. The method for creating an aligned section view is discussed below:

1. Invoke the **Section View Assist PropertyManager** by clicking on the **Section View** tool.

2. Click on the **Aligned** button in the **Cutting Line** rollout. A cutting section line, which comprises two non-parallel lines gets attached to the cursor.

3. Move the cursor toward an existing drawing view as the parent view for creating the aligned section view.

4. Click to specify the center point for the cutting section line, see Figure 14.34.

5. Move the cursor to a distance and then click to specify the position for the first cutting line, see Figure 14.34.

6. Move the cursor to a distance and then click to specify the position for the second cutting line, see Figure 14.34. A preview of the aligned section view gets attached to the cursor.

7. Move the cursor to the required location and then click to specify the placement point for the aligned section view in the drawing sheet, see Figure 14.34.

8. Press ESC to exit.

14.34

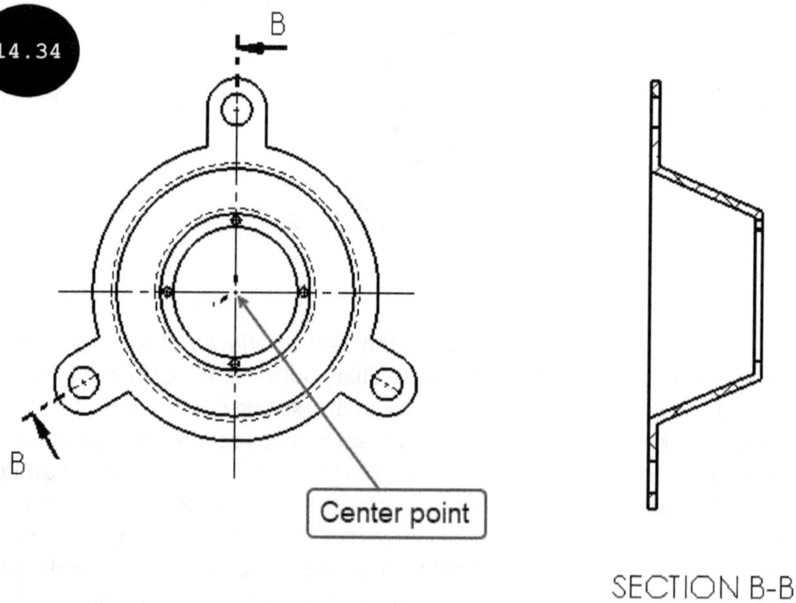

Creating a Half Section View

A half section view is created by cutting an object using an imaginary cutting plane or section line that passes halfway through the object, see Figure 14.35. In SOLIDWORKS, you can create a half section view by using the **Section View** tool. The method for creating a half section view is discussed below:

14.35

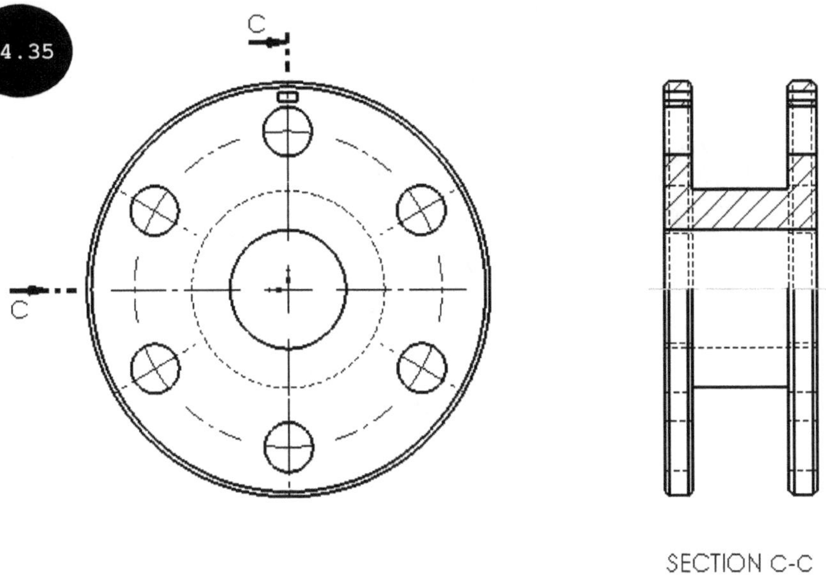

1. Click on the **Section View** tool. The **Section View Assist PropertyManager** appears.

2. Click on the **Half Section** tab available at the top of the PropertyManager, see Figure 14.36. The options for creating pre-defined shapes of half section views appear in the PropertyManager.

3. Click on the required button in the **Half Section** rollout of the PropertyManager. The respective half section cutting line gets attached to the cursor.

4. Move the cursor over an existing view in the drawing sheet and then click to specify the placement point for the half section cutting line at the required location. A preview of the half section view gets attached to the cursor.

5. If you want to flip the viewing direction, click on the **Flip Direction** button in the **Cutting Line** rollout of the PropertyManager, or else skip this step.

14.36

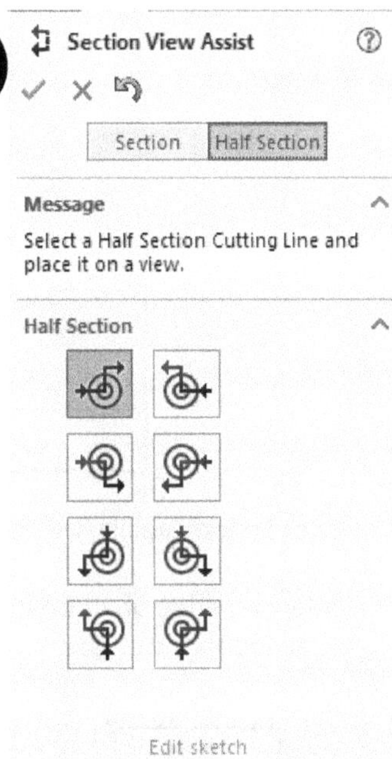

6. Click to specify the position for the half section view at the required location in the drawing sheet. The half section view is created. Next, press the ESC key.

Creating an Auxiliary View

An auxiliary view is a projected view, which is created by projecting the edges of an object normal to the edge of an existing drawing view, see Figure 14.37. You can create an auxiliary view by using the **Auxiliary View** tool in the **Drawing CommandManager**. The method for creating an auxiliary view is discussed below:

14.37

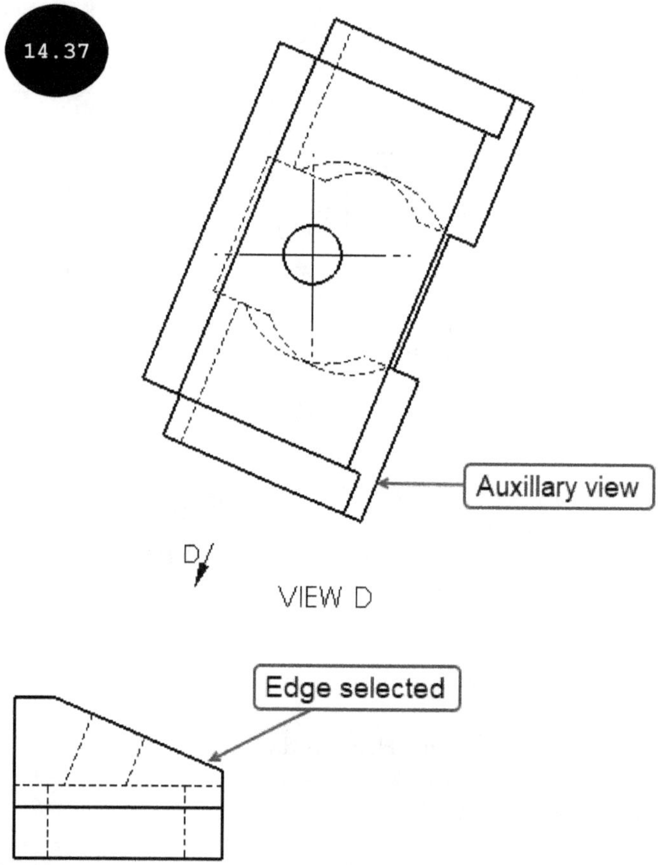

1. Click on the **Auxiliary View** tool in the **Drawing CommandManager**.
2. Select an edge of an existing drawing view, see Figure 14.37. A preview of the auxiliary view gets attached to the cursor.
3. Click to specify the position of the auxiliary view in the drawing sheet, see Figure 14.37.
4. Press ESC to exit.

Creating a Detail View

A detail view is used to show a portion of an existing drawing view in an enlarged scale, see Figure 14.38. You can define the portion of an existing drawing view to be enlarged by creating a circle or a closed sketch. You can create a detailed view of a portion of an existing view using the **Detail View** tool. The method for creating a detailed view is discussed below:

14.38

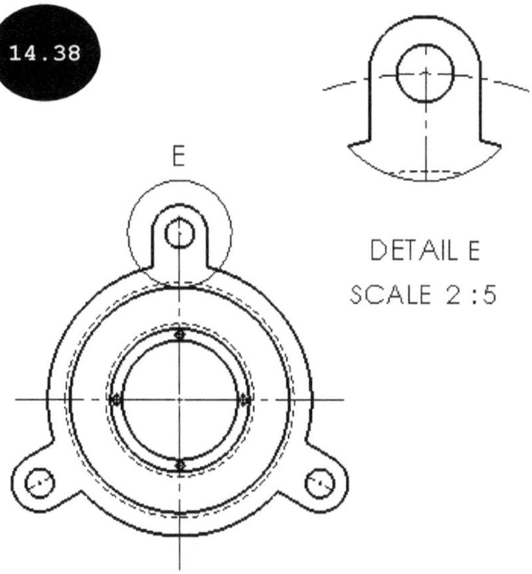

1. Click on the **Detail View** tool in the **Drawing CommandManager**. The **Detail View PropertyManager** appears. Also, you are prompted to draw a circle to define the portion of an existing drawing view to be enlarged.

2. Draw a circle around the portion of an existing view to be enlarged. If the **SOLIDWORKS** message window appears, click on the **OK** button to continue creating an enlarged view. An enlarged view of the portion of the existing view gets attached to the cursor. Also, the **Detail View PropertyManager** appears with additional options.

3. You can increase or decrease the default scale factor for the attached detail view by using the options of the **Scale** rollout in the PropertyManager, as required.

Note: In SOLIDWORKS, you can display the detail view with a full outline around it by selecting the **Full outline** check box in the **Detail View** rollout of the PropertyManager, see Figure 14.39. Also, you can display the detail view without any outline by selecting the **No outline** check box in the **Detail View** rollout of the PropertyManager, see Figure 14.39. Moreover, you can also display the detail view with a jagged outline by selecting the **Jagged outline** check box in the **Detail View** rollout, see Figure 14.39.

14.39

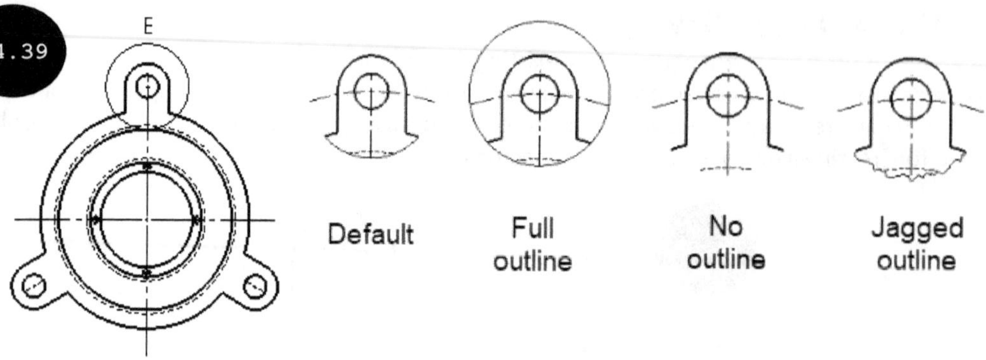

4. After specifying the required settings for the detail view, move the cursor to the required location in the drawing sheet and then click to specify the placement point in the drawing sheet. A detailed view is created.

5. Press the ESC key to exit.

Note: In addition to defining the portion of a view to be enlarged by drawing a circle, you can also use a closed sketch, which defines the portion of a view to be enlarged. To do this, before invoking the **Detail View** tool, first select an existing view and then draw a closed sketch by using the sketching tools of the **Sketch CommandManager**. Once the closed sketch is drawn, select it and then click on the **Detail View** tool. Figure 14.40 shows a detail view created by a closed sketch, which is drawn by using the **Spline** tool.

14.40

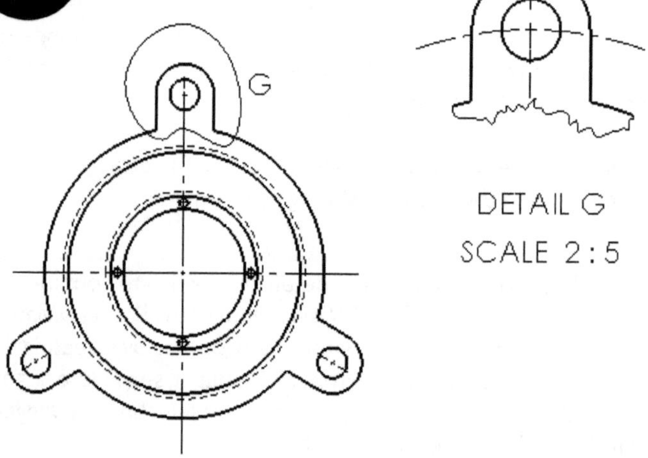

Creating a Removed Section View

A removed section view is used to show a cross-sectional slice of an object at a specified location, see Figure 14.41. In this figure, the two cross-sectional slices of an object are shown at different locations. The method for creating a removed section view is discussed below:

14.41

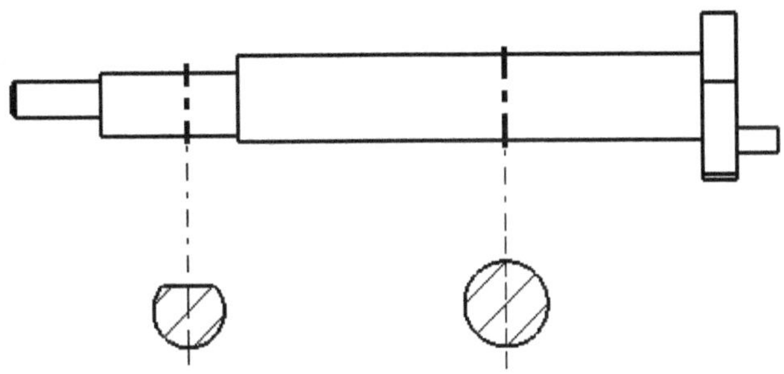

1. Click on the **Removed Section** tool in the **Drawing CommandManager**. The **Removed Section PropertyManager** appears.

2. Select two opposite or partially opposite edges of a drawing view one by one between which an object is to be sectioned, see Figure 14.42. A cutting line appears attached to the cursor. Also, the names of the selected edges appear in the **Edge** and **Opposed Edge** fields of the PropertyManager, respectively.

3. Ensure that the **Automatic** radio button is selected in the **Cutting Line Placement** rollout of the PropertyManager to define the position of the cutting line automatically between the selected edges.

Note: On selecting the **Manual** radio button, you need to manually define the position of the cutting line between the selected edges by specifying two points.

4. Click to specify the placement point for the cutting line in the drawing view. A preview of the removed section view (slice) appears attached to the cursor, see Figure 14.42.

14.42

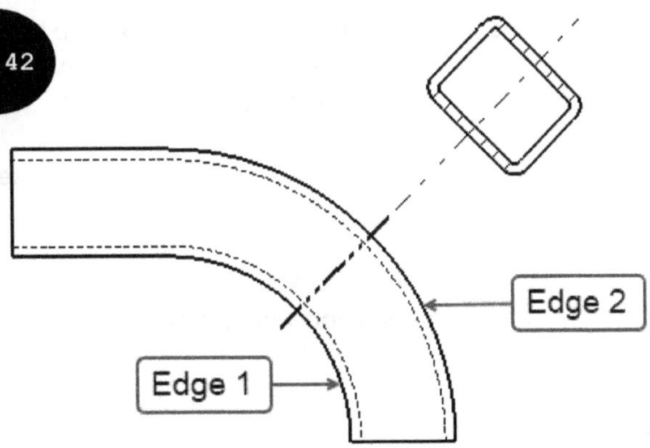

5. Click to specify the placement point for the removed section view in the drawing sheet. The removed section view is created.

Creating a Broken-out Section View

A broken-out section view is created by removing the portion of an existing view up to a specified depth to view the inner details of an object, see Figure 14.43. You can define the portion of an existing view to be removed by drawing a closed sketch. The method for creating a broken section view is discussed below:

14.43

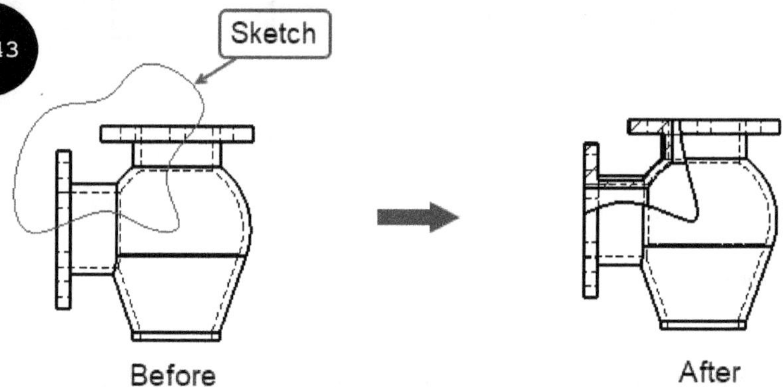

1. Click on the **Broken-out Section** tool in the **Drawing CommandManager**. The **Spline** tool is invoked to create a closed sketch for defining the portion to be removed.

2. Move the cursor over the existing drawing view whose portion is to be removed up to a specified depth.

3. Draw a closed profile around the portion of the existing drawing view to be removed. As soon as you draw a closed profile, the **Broken-out Section PropertyManager** appears.

Note: In SOLIDWORKS, you can also create broken-out section view on a section view, a detail view, and an alternate position view. You will learn about creating an alternate position view later in this chapter.

4. Enter the depth value in the **Depth** field of the PropertyManager up to which the material is to be removed. Alternatively, you can select an edge or an axis of the view to define the depth by using the **Depth Reference** field of the PropertyManager.

5. Select the **Preview** check box to display the preview of the broken-out section view in the drawing sheet.

6. Click on the green tick-mark ✓ in the PropertyManager to accept the defined settings and to exit the PropertyManager. The broken-out section view is created, refer to Figure 14.43.

Creating a Break View

A break view is created by breaking an existing view using a pair of break lines such that the portion existing between the breaking lines is removed, see Figure 14.44. A break view is used to display a large, scaled view on a small-scale sheet by removing a portion of the view that has the same cross-section, see Figure 14.44. The method for creating a break view is discussed below:

14.44

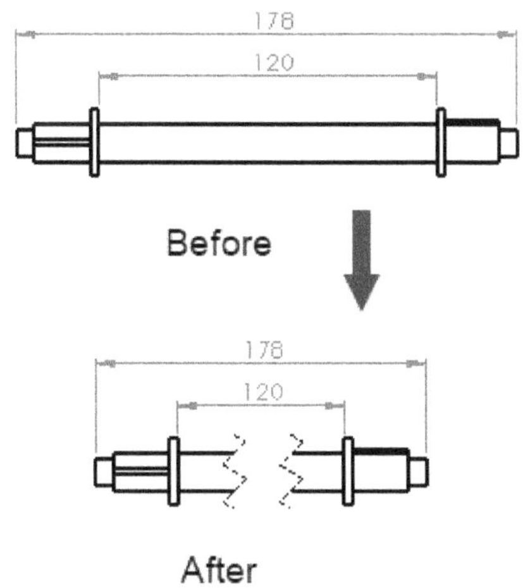

Note: The dimension applied to a break view represents its actual dimension, see Figure 14.44. It is evident from this figure that even on breaking the view, the dimension value associated with it remains the same. You will learn more about applying dimensions later in this chapter.

1. Click on the **Break View** tool. The **Break View PropertyManager** appears.

2. Move the cursor over an existing drawing view to be broken and then click on it. The first vertical or horizontal break line is attached to the cursor.

Note: The display of break line (vertical or horizontal) depends upon whether the **Add vertical break line** or the **Add horizontal break line** button is activated in the PropertyManager. If the **Add vertical break line** button is activated, a vertical break line appears and if the **Add horizontal break line** button is selected, a horizontal break line appears.

3. Ensure that the required button: **Add vertical break line** or **Add horizontal break line** is activated in the **Break View PropertyManager**.

4. Specify the placement point for the first break line by clicking the left mouse button on the required location of the drawing view. The second break line gets attached to the cursor.

5. Specify the placement point for the second break line in the view. The view is broken and the portion inside the break lines is removed, refer to Figure 14.44.

Note: You can also control the gap between the break lines by using the **Gap size** field of the PropertyManager. You can also select a required style or type for break lines by selecting the required button in the **Break line style** area of the PropertyManager. In SOLIDWORKS, you can also use the jagged break lines for breaking the view by selecting the **Jagged Cut** button in the **Break line style** area of the PropertyManager.

In SOLIDWORKS, you can also clip the sketch block in the break view by selecting the **Break sketch blocks** check box of the PropertyManager. If this check box is cleared, the sketch block will not be clipped in the break view. The method for creating sketch blocks are not covered in this textbook.

6. Click on the green tick-mark in the PropertyManager to confirm the creation of a break view and to exit the PropertyManager.

Creating a Crop View

A crop view is created by cropping an existing view by using a closed sketch in such a way that only the portion that is lying inside the closed sketch is retained in the view, see Figure 14.45. You can create a crop view using the **Crop View** tool. Note that to create a crop view, first, you need to create a closed sketch by using the sketching tools of the **Sketch CommandManager**. The method for creating a crop view is discussed below:

14.45

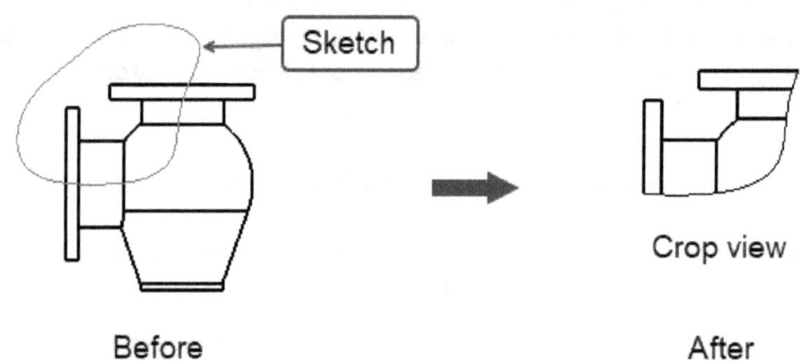

1. Select the view to be cropped.
2. Draw a closed sketch around the portion of the view to be cropped, refer to Figure 14.45.
3. Ensure that the sketch created is selected.
4. Click on the **Crop View** tool. The crop view is created by retaining only the portion that lies inside the closed sketch. Next, press the ESC key.

Note: In SOLIDWORKS, after creating a crop view, you can display it with no outline or with a jagged outline. To do this, select the crop view in the drawing sheet. The **Drawing View PropertyManager** appears. In this PropertyManager, expand the **Crop View** rollout and then select the required check box: **No outline** or **Jagged outline**.

Creating an Alternate Position View

In SOLIDWORKS, you can show or create an alternate position of an assembly in a drawing view using the **Alternate Position View** tool, see Figure 14.46. You can also create multiple positions of an assembly in a drawing view by using this tool. The method for creating an alternate position view is discussed below:

14.46

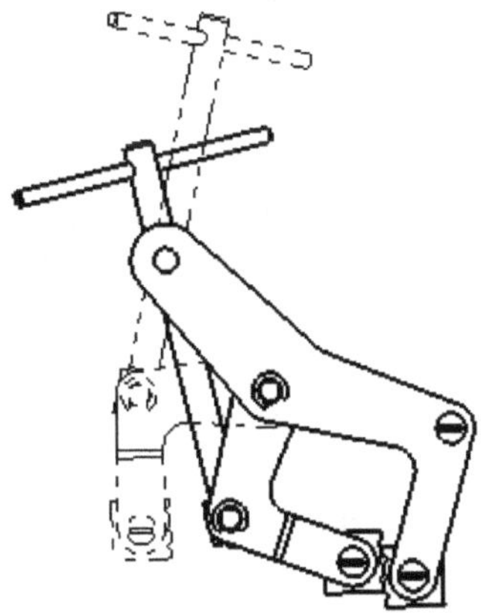

1. Click on the **Alternate Position View** tool in the **Drawing CommandManager**. The **Alternate Position PropertyManager** appears.

2. Select a drawing view of an assembly. The **Alternate Position PropertyManager** is modified.

Note: In the **Configuration** rollout of the PropertyManager, the **New configuration** radio button is selected by default. As a result, you can create a new alternative position for the assembly. Also, a default name for the alternate position appears in the **New Configuration Name** field. You can accept the default name or enter a new name in this field. The **Existing configuration** radio button is used to select the existing configuration of an assembly as the alternative view.

3. Ensure that the **New configuration** radio button is selected in the **Configuration** rollout.

4. Accept the default settings and then click on the green tick-mark in the PropertyManager. The Assembly environment is invoked with the display of the **Move Component PropertyManager** to the left of the graphics area.

Note: In the **Move Component PropertyManager**, the **Free Drag** option is selected by default. As a result, you can freely drag the components of the assembly to the desired position.

5. Drag to rotate or move the components of the assembly whose alternate position is to be created, to the desired position.

6. Once the desired position of the assembly components has been achieved, click on the green tick-mark in the **Move Component PropertyManager**. The Drawing environment is invoked again, and the alternate position of the assembly components is created in the drawing view, refer to Figure 14.46. Note that the alternate position of the components is displayed in dotted lines.

Applying Dimensions

After creating various drawing views of a part or an assembly, you need to apply dimensions to them. In SOLIDWORKS, you can apply two types of dimensions: reference dimensions and driving dimensions. Reference dimensions are applied manually using the dimension tools such as **Smart Dimension**, **Horizontal Dimension**, and **Vertical Dimension** whereas driving dimensions are generated automatically by retrieving the model dimensions. You can apply driving dimensions using the **Model Items** tool of the **Annotation CommandManager**. The methods for applying both types of dimensions are discussed next.

Applying Reference Dimensions

You can apply reference dimensions using the dimension tools such as **Smart Dimension**, **Horizontal Dimension**, and **Vertical Dimension** available in the **Dimension** flyout of the **Annotation CommandManager**, see Figure 14.47.

14.47

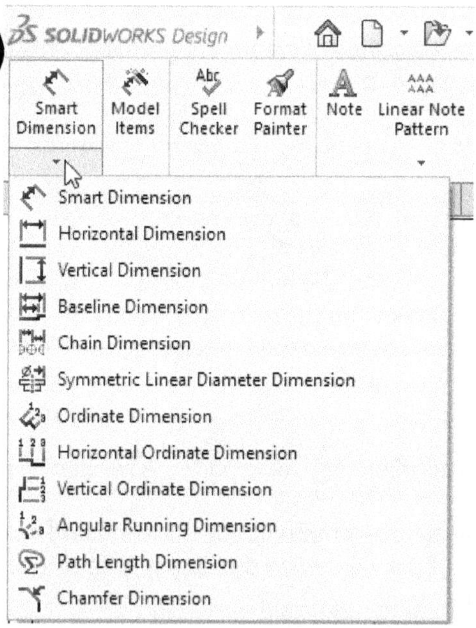

Applying reference dimension is the manual method of applying dimensions to drawing views and is the same as discussed in the Sketching environment while dimensioning sketch entities. For example, to apply a dimension to a linear edge in a view, click on the **Smart Dimension** tool and then select the edge. The dimension value of the selected edge is attached to the cursor. Next, place the dimension to the required location in the drawing sheet.

Applying Driving Dimensions

Driving dimensions are applied automatically in drawing views by retrieving the model dimensions, which are applied in the sketches and features of the model. Note that on modifying a driving dimension, the respective sketch or feature of the model is also modified and vice-versa.

To apply driving dimensions, click on the **Model Items** tool in the **Annotation CommandManager**. The **Model Items PropertyManager** appears, see Figure 14.48. By using the options in the PropertyManager, you can retrieve dimensions, symbols, annotations, and other elements of the model in the drawing views. Some of the options of this PropertyManager are discussed next.

Source/Destination

The options in the **Source/Destination** rollout of the PropertyManager are used for selecting features or the entire model as the source and destination for retrieving and applying dimensions, symbols, and annotations. By default, the **Selected feature** option is selected in the **Source** drop-down list. As a result, you can select a feature of the model in a drawing view as the source and destination for retrieving and applying dimensions, respectively. As soon as you select a feature in a drawing view, the dimensions of the selected feature are retrieved and applied to the drawing views. In Figure 14.49, the driving dimensions are applied to a hole feature by selecting it as the source and destination feature in the drawing view.

14.48

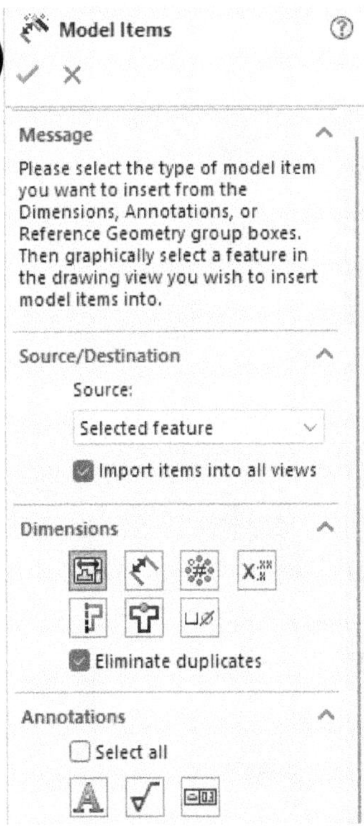

14.49

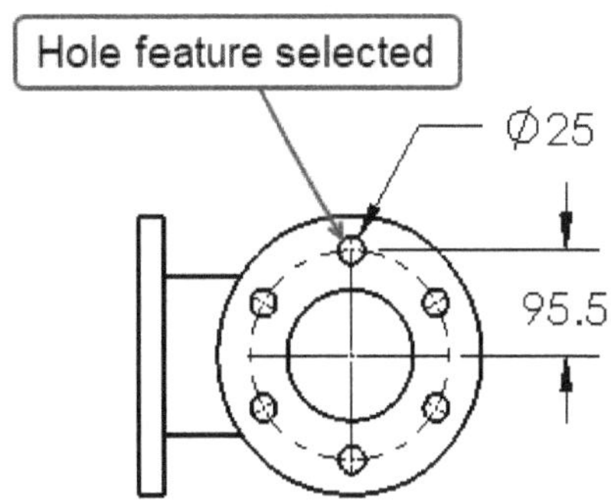

On selecting the **Entire model** option in the **Source** drop-down list, all dimensions, symbols, and annotations, which are applied in the model get retrieved and are applied in the drawing views. By default, the **Import items into all views** check box is selected in the **Source/Destination** rollout. As a result, items such as dimensions and annotations are applied to all views present in the drawing sheet.

Dimensions

The buttons in the **Dimensions** rollout of the PropertyManager are used for selecting the type of dimensions to be retrieved from the model and to be applied to the drawing views. On selecting the **Eliminate duplicates** check box in this rollout, duplicate dimensions in the drawing views will not be applied.

Annotations

The buttons in the **Annotations** rollout are used for selecting the type of annotations to be retrieved from the model and applied to the drawing views. You can click on the buttons to activate them to retrieve respective annotations in the drawing views. If you select the **Select all** check box, all the buttons of this rollout get activated, automatically.

Reference Geometry

The buttons in the **Reference Geometry** rollout are used for selecting the type of reference geometries such as planes, axes, and origin to be retrieved from the model and applied to the drawing views.

After selecting the required options in the **Model Items PropertyManager**, click on the green tick-mark in the PropertyManager. The respective dimensions, annotations, and reference geometries are retrieved and applied in the drawing views, see Figure 14.50.

14.50

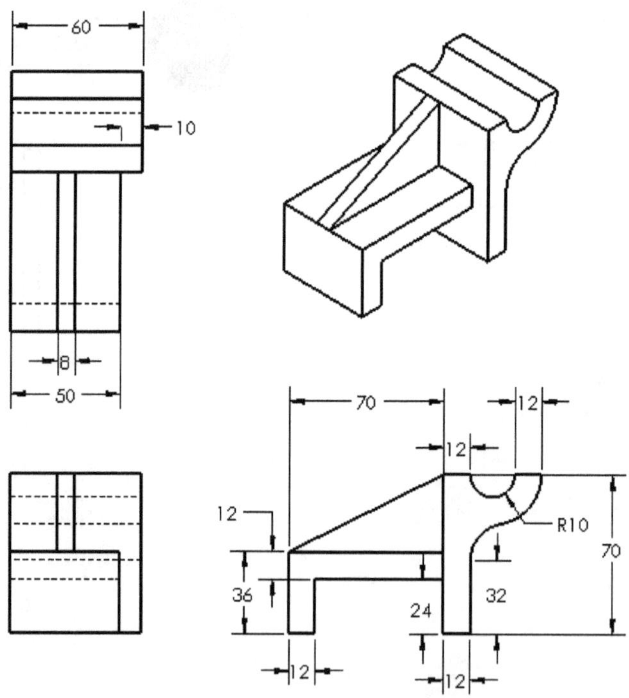

Note: Sometimes the driving dimensions applied in the drawing views neither appear in the required positions, nor do they maintain uniform spacing in the drawing. You can drag the dimensions and place them in the required positions for maintaining proper spacing between them.

Modifying the Driving Dimension

On modifying a driving dimension in the Drawing environment, the same modification is reflected in the model as well. To modify a driving dimension, double-click on it in the drawing view. The **Modify** dialog box appears, see Figure 14.51. Enter the new dimension value in this dialog box and then click on the green tick mark. The respective dimension and the feature of the model are modified accordingly.

14.51

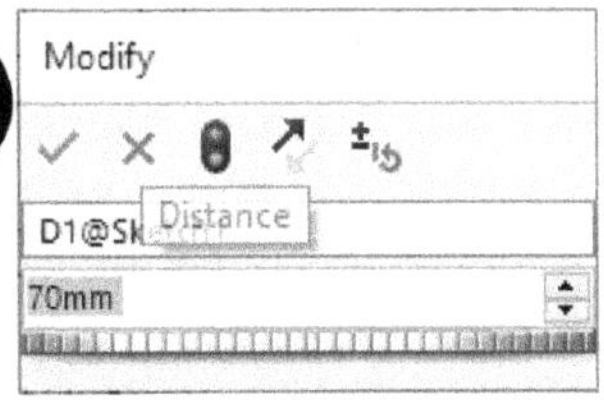

Modifying Dimension Properties

In SOLIDWORKS, when you apply a dimension, it is applied with default properties. You can modify default dimension properties such as dimension style, tolerance, precision, and so on using the **Dimension PropertyManager** that appears when a dimension is selected in the drawing sheet. To modify the properties of a dimension, select it in the drawing sheet. The **Dimension PropertyManager** appears, see Figure 14.52. The options in the **Dimension PropertyManager** are discussed next.

14.52

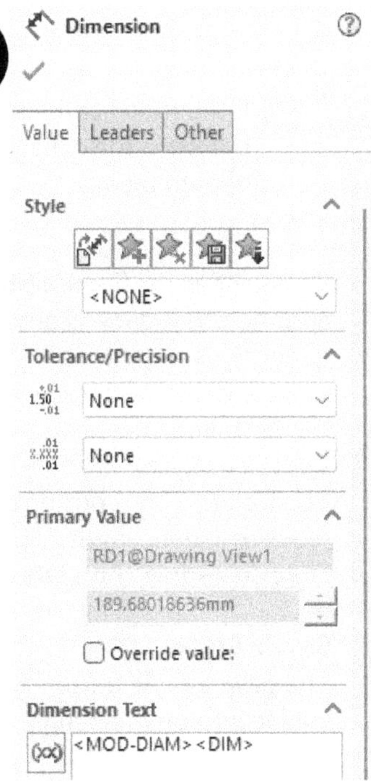

Value Tab

By default, the **Value** tab is activated in the **Dimension PropertyManager**. The options of this tab are used for modifying the properties related to the dimension value. The options are discussed next.

Style

The **Style** rollout of the **Value** tab is used to restore default attributes such as dimension height, fonts, and arrow type. You can also add a new style, update an existing style, delete a style, save a style, and load an existing style in the current document using the options of this rollout. The options of this rollout are discussed next.

Apply the default attributes to selected dimensions

This button of the **Style** rollout is used to apply the default dimension attributes such as dimension height, font, and arrow type to the selected dimension. If you have modified dimension attributes, then on clicking this button, the dimension attributes will be restored to the default.

Add or Update a Style

This button is used to add a new dimension style or updating the existing dimension style. To add a new dimension style, specify different attributes such as dimension height, font, and arrow type, that you want in the new dimension style and click on the **Add or Update a Style** button. The **Add** or Update a Style dialog box appears, see Figure 14.53. Enter the name of the style to be added in the **Enter a new name or choose an existing name** field of this dialog box and then click the **OK** button. The new style is added and set as the current style for the document. Also, its name appears in the **Set a current Style** drop-down list of the **Style** rollout. You will learn more about specifying dimension attributes later in this section.

14.53

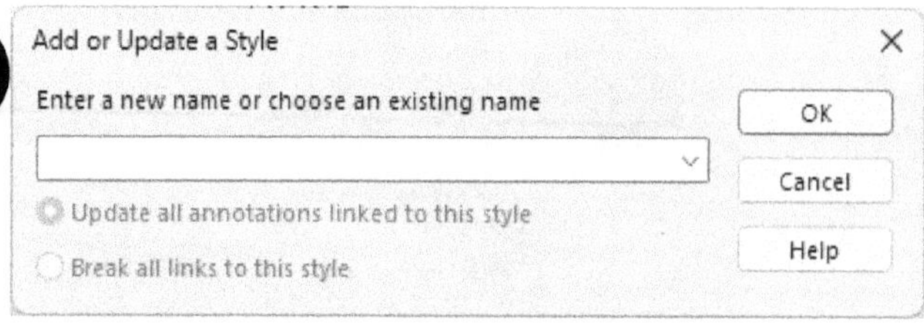

To update the existing dimension style, specify the required dimension attributes and click on the **Add or Update a Style** button of the **Style** rollout to display the **Add or Update a Style** dialog box. In this dialog box, click on the arrow on the right of the **Enter a new name or choose an existing name** field and then select a dimension style to be updated in the drop-down list that appears. The **Update all annotations linked to this style** and **Break all links to this style** radio buttons are enabled in this dialog box. By default, the **Update all annotations linked to this style** radio button is selected. As a result, the modifications made in the attributes of the selected style reflect in all dimensions that are associated with it.

Note: If the modifications are not reflected in all dimensions of the style after choosing the **OK** button in the dialog box, then you need to click on the dimensions in the drawing sheet to update them.

On selecting the **Break all links to this style** radio button, the link between the selected dimension and the other dimensions assigned to the same style will be broken. In other words, the other dimensions associated with the selected dimension style will no longer be associated with it and modifications will only be reflected in the selected dimension.

Delete a Style

The **Delete a Style** button of the **Style** rollout is used to delete an existing style, which is no longer required in the current document. To delete an existing style, select the style from the **Set a current Style** drop-down list of the **Style** rollout and then click on the **Delete a Style** button.

Save a Style

The **Save a Style** button is used to save a style as an external file so that the same style can be loaded into other documents as well. To save a style, select the style from the **Set a current Style** drop-down list and then click on the **Save a Style** button. The **Save As** window appears. Browse the location where the style is to be saved and then click on the **Save** button. The selected style is saved in the specified location with the *.sldstl* file extension.

Load Style

The **Load Style** button is used to load the existing saved style in the current document. To load a style, click on the **Load Style** button. The **Open** window appears. Browse to a location where the style has been saved and then select it. Next, click on the **Open** button in the dialog box. The selected style is loaded in the current document and set as the current style.

Set a current Style

The **Set a current Style** drop-down list displays a list of all the styles that are added to the current document. By default, the **None** option is selected in this drop-down list. As a result, the default dimension style is used. You can select any dimension style from this drop-down list as the current dimension style for the document.

Tolerance/Precision

The options in the **Tolerance/Precision** rollout are used for specifying the tolerance and precision values for the selected dimension style. The options in this rollout are discussed next.

Tolerance Type

The **Tolerance Type** drop-down list is used to select the type of tolerance for the selected dimension style and dimension value. By default, the **None** option is selected in this drop-down list. As a result, no tolerance has been applied. Depending upon the type of tolerance selected in this drop-down list, the corresponding fields are enabled below this drop-down list in the **Tolerance/Precision** rollout to specify tolerance values. Figure 14.54 shows a dimension with a symmetric tolerance value of 0.05 mm applied.

14.54

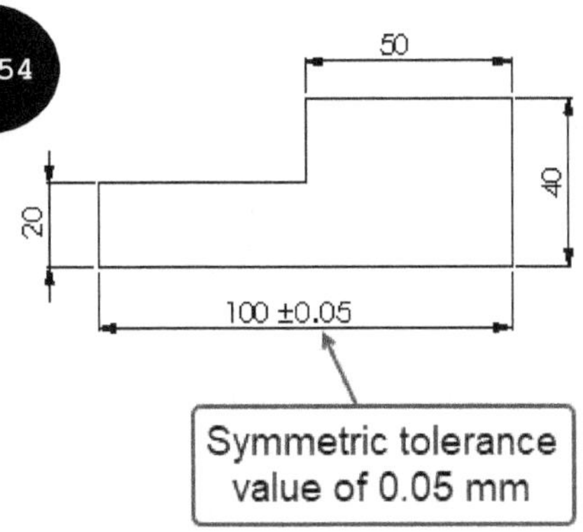

Unit Precision

The **Unit Precision** drop-down list is used to select the unit of precision or number of digits after the decimal point in the dimension value.

Tolerance Precision

The **Tolerance Precision** drop-down list is used to select the precision or number of digits after the decimal point in the tolerance value.

Tolerance modifier

The options in the **Tolerance modifier** rollout are used for adding geometric symbols and text to the selected dimension and its tolerance limits, see Figure 14.55. Note that this rollout is not available if the **None** or **Basic** tolerance type is selected in the **Tolerance Type** drop-down list of the **Tolerance/Precision** rollout. The options in the **Tolerance modifier** rollout are discussed next.

General

On selecting the **General** radio button in the **Tolerance modifier** rollout, you can add symbols and text to the entire dimension, see Figure 14.55.

14.55

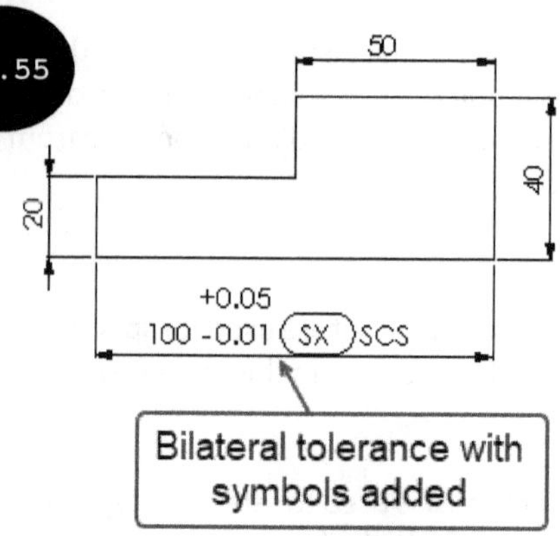

14.56

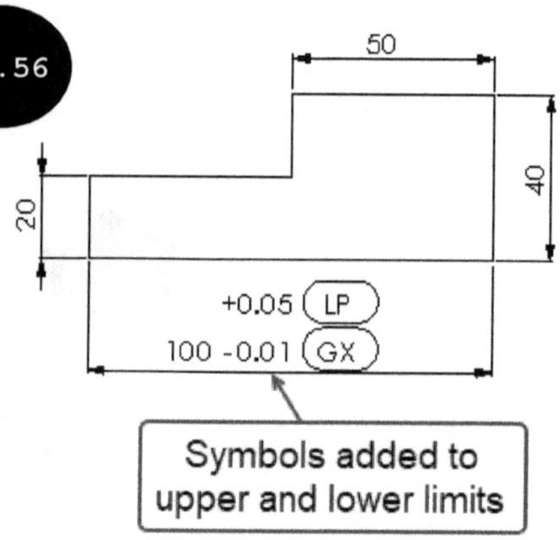

Specified limits

On selecting the **Specified limits** radio button, you can add symbols and text to the upper and lower tolerance limits of the dimension, see Figure 14.56. Note that the **Specified limits** radio button is enabled only when the **Bilateral, Limit, Fit, Fit with tolerance,** or **Fit (tolerance only)** option is selected in the **Tolerance Type** drop-down list of the **Tolerance/Precision** rollout.

Primary Value

The **Primary Value** rollout is used to control the information of the primary dimension value. The primary dimension value is the original dimension value of entities. The options in this rollout are discussed next.

Name

The Name field of the **Primary Value** rollout is used to display the name of the dimension selected. By default, the default names are assigned to the dimensions. You can enter a new name for the selected dimension in this field. Note that the name entered in this field is automatically followed by a suffix such as *@Sketch1* depending upon the dimension.

Dimension value

The **Dimension Value** field of the **Primary Value** rollout is used to modify the dimension value of the selected dimension. You can enter a new dimension value in this field. The value entered in this field drives the entity.

Note: The **Name** and **Dimension value** fields of the **Primary Value** rollout are enabled only when the selected dimension is a driving dimension that is applied using the **Model Items** tool of the **Annotation CommandManager**.

Override value

On selecting the **Override value** check box in the **Primary Value** rollout, you can override the original dimension value by entering a new dimension value in the **Primary** field that appears below this check box. Note that the override dimension value is not the actual dimension of the entity.

Dimension Text

The **Dimension Text** rollout is used to add text and geometric symbols for the selected dimension style and dimension text. The options in this rollout are discussed next.

Add Parenthesis

The **Add Parenthesis** button of the **Dimension Text** rollout is used to display dimension as a driven or reference dimension with parentheses, see Figure 14.57 (a).

Inspection Dimension

The **Inspection Dimension** button is used to display dimensions with inspection, see Figure 14.57 (b).

Center Dimension

The **Center Dimension** button is used to display dimension text at the center of the extension lines of the dimension. Note that when you drag dimension text, the text snaps to the center of the extension line, see Figure 14.57 (c).

Offset Text

The **Offset Text** button is used to display dimension text at an offset distance from the dimension line by using a leader, see Figure 14.57 (d).

14.57

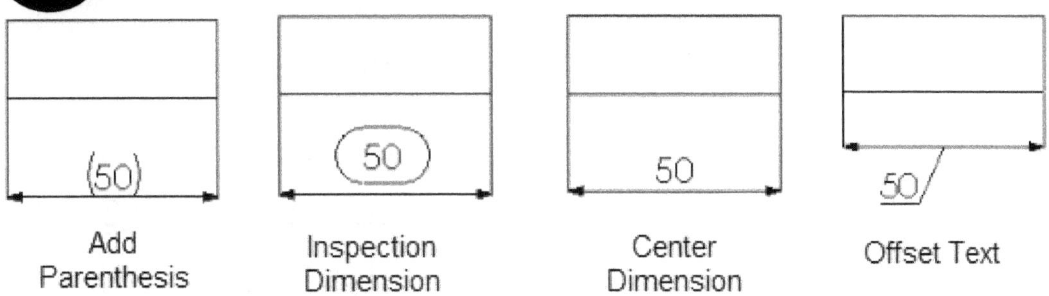

(a) (b) (c) (d)

Text Field

The **Text** field displays <DIM>, where **DIM** represents the dimension value. You can add text, prefixes, and suffixes before or after <DIM> in the field. Figure 14.58 shows a dimension value after adding 'L -' in front of <DIM> in the **Text** field.

14.58

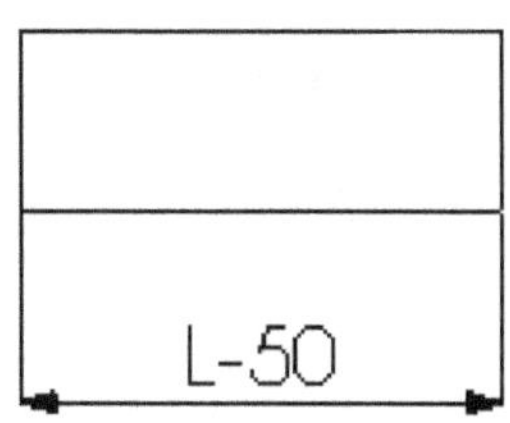

Note: If you delete <DIM> from the **Text** field, the dimension value will also be deleted or removed from the drawing area. Also, the **Add Value** button gets enabled in the **Dimension Text** rollout. On choosing the **Add Value** button, the dimension value gets restored in the drawing area. Also, <DIM> is displayed again in the **Text** field.

Left Justify/Center Justify/Right Justify

The **Left Justify, Center Justify,** and **Right Justify** buttons are used for defining the dimension text justifications to left, center, and right, respectively.

Symbols

The **Symbols** area of the rollout is used to add different types of symbols to the selected dimensions, see Figure 14.59. To add a symbol, click to place the cursor where you want to insert or add a symbol in the **Text** field and then click on the respective symbol button. The selected symbol is added in the field as well as displayed in the drawing area. On clicking the **More Symbols** button in this area, a flyout appears with the display of additional symbols. You can click the required symbol to be added to the dimension. If you click on the **More Symbols** option in this flyout, the **Symbol Library** dialog box appears, see Figure 14.60.

14.59

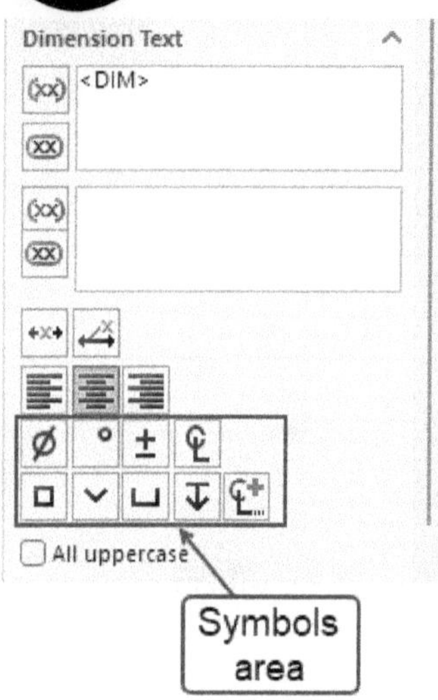

14.60

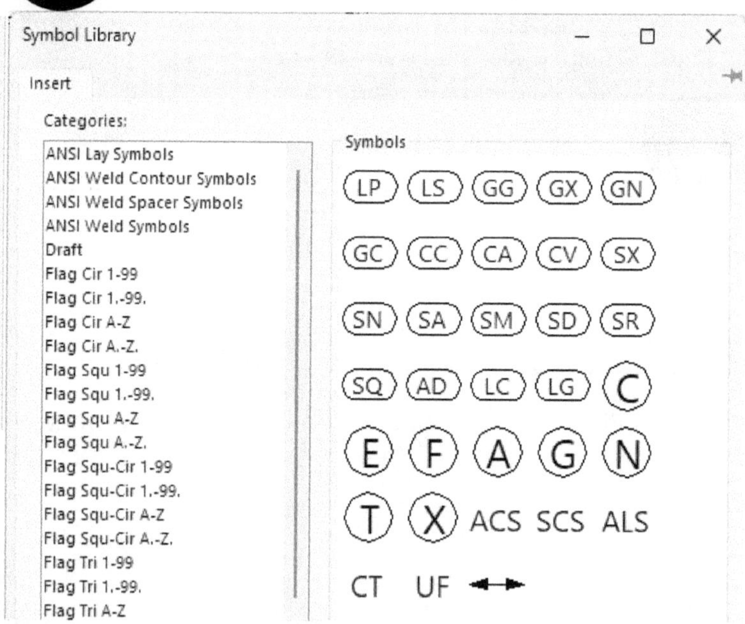

All uppercase

In SOLIDWORKS, you can choose to display all dimension text in uppercase by selecting the **All uppercase** check box in the **Dimension Text** rollout.

Dual Dimension

The **Dual Dimension** rollout is used to display dual or alternative dimension measurements for entities. By default, this rollout is collapsed. As a result, the dimension values of entities are displayed only in the current document's unit system. To display dimensions in dual dimension unit, enable the **Dual Dimension** rollout by selecting the check box in its title bar. The options of the **Dual Dimension** rollout are enabled. Also, the default dual dimension unit along with the current document unit are displayed in the selected dimension, see Figure 14.61. You can specify a precision value and tolerance as required for the dual dimension using the **Unit Precision** and **Tolerance Precision** drop-down lists of the expanded **Dual Dimension** rollout.

14.61

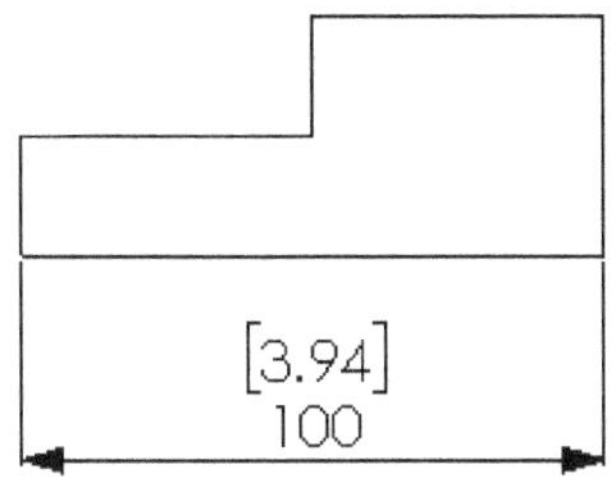

Note: You can also specify a required unit system for dual dimensions using the **Document Properties - Units** dialog box. To do this, click on the **Options** tool in the **Standard** toolbar. The **System Options - General** dialog box appears. In this dialog box, click on the **Document Properties** tab and then select the **Units** option. The **Document Properties - Units** dialog box appears. Next, specify the dual dimension unit in the field corresponding to the **Unit** column and **Dual Dimension Length** field in the dialog box.

Leaders Tab

The options in the **Leaders** tab of the **Dimension PropertyManager** are used for controlling the properties of the dimension leader. Figure 14.62 shows the PropertyManager with the **Leaders** tab activated. The options in this tab are discussed next.

14.62

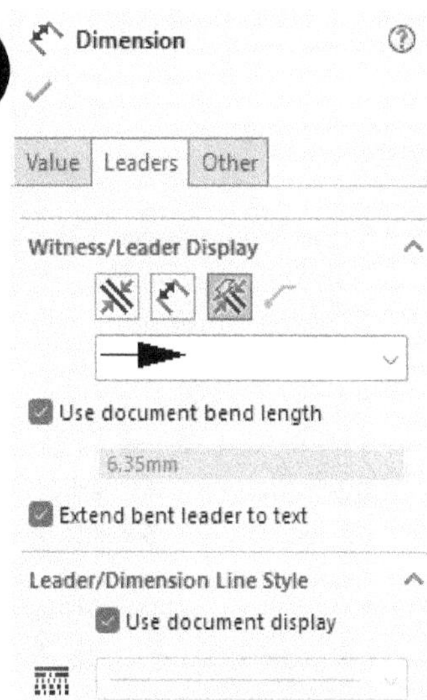

Witness/Leader Display

The **Witness/Leader Display** rollout is used to specify parameters for dimension arrows. The options in this rollout are discussed next.

Outside

The **Outside** button is used to place dimension arrows outside the extension lines of the dimension, see Figure 14.63 (a).

Inside

The **Inside** button is used to place dimension arrows inside the extension lines of the dimension, see Figure 14.63 (b).

14.63

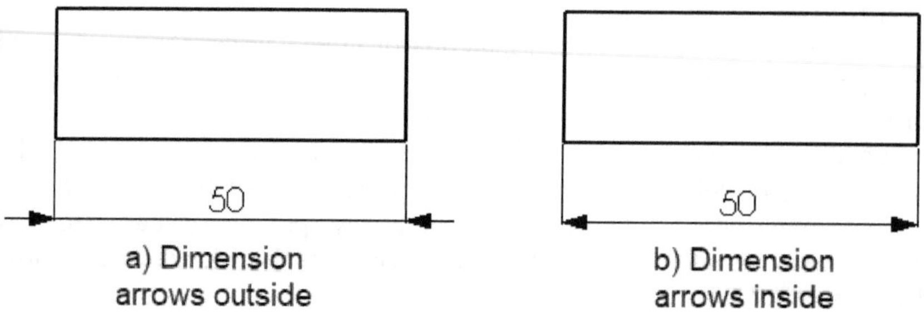

Smart 

By default, the **Smart** button is activated in this rollout. As a result, the placement of the arrows is either inside or outside the extension lines depending on the availability of space between the extension lines of dimensions. For example, if the space available between the extension lines of a dimension is not adequate to place arrows inside, then the arrows are automatically placed outside the extension lines.

Directed Leader 

The **Directed Leader** button is used to change the orientation of a leader at an angle concerning the surface on which it is applied in the Part modeling environment, see Figure 14.64. Note that this button is enabled only when the selected leader is applied on a cylindrical surface by using the tools available in the **MBD Dimensions CommandManager**.

14.64

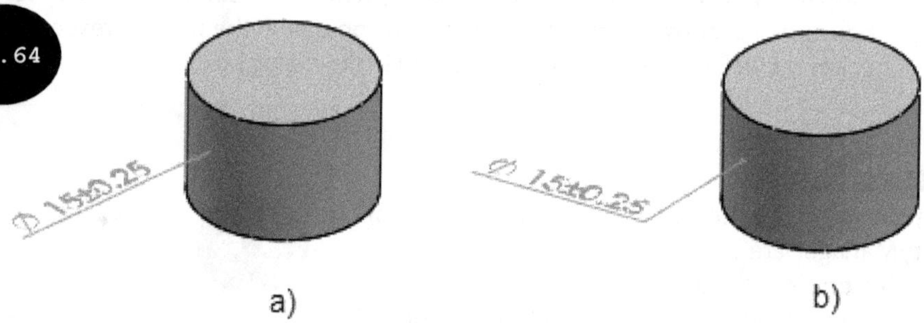

Style Drop-down List 

The **Style** drop-down list of the rollout is used to select the type of arrow style to be used for the selected dimension.

Radius 

The **Radius** button is used to convert a diameter dimension to a radius dimension. Note that this button is enabled only if the selected dimension is either a diameter dimension or a radius dimension. On selecting the **Radius** button, the selected diameter dimension changes to the radius dimension. Also, three buttons: **Foreshorten**, **Solid Leader**, and **Open Leader** are enabled below this button in the rollout, see Figure 14.65. By using these buttons, you can specify the type of leader for the radius dimension, see Figure 14.66.

Tip: You can also convert a diameter dimension to a radius dimension by clicking on the **Display as Radius** tool in the context toolbar that appears on selecting a diameter dimension.

14.65

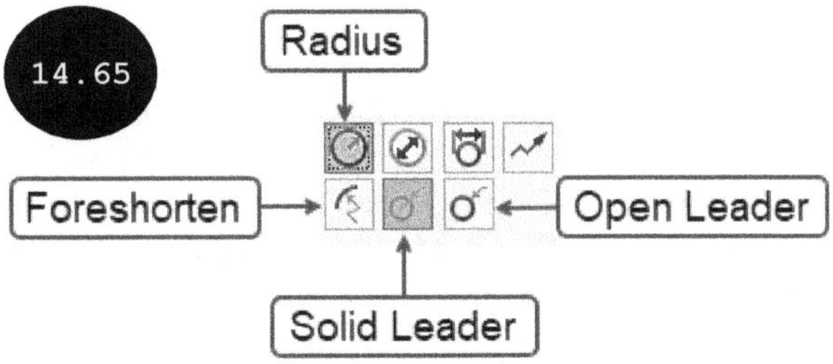

14.66

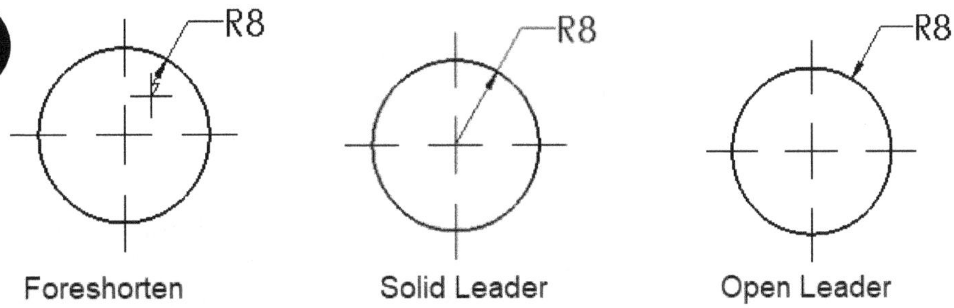

Diameter

The **Diameter** button is used to convert a radius dimension to a diameter dimension. Note that this button is enabled only if the selected dimension is either a diameter dimension or a radius dimension. On selecting the **Diameter** button, the selected radius dimension changes to the diameter dimension. Also, four buttons: **Two Arrows / Solid Leader**, **Two Arrows / Open Leader**, **One Arrow / Solid Leader**, and **One Arrow / Open Leader** appear below the **Diameter** button, see Figure 14.67. These buttons are used for specifying the type of leader, see Figure 14.68.

14.67

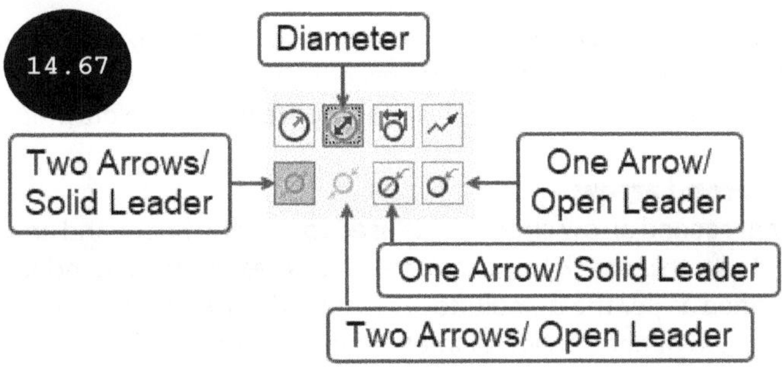

14.68

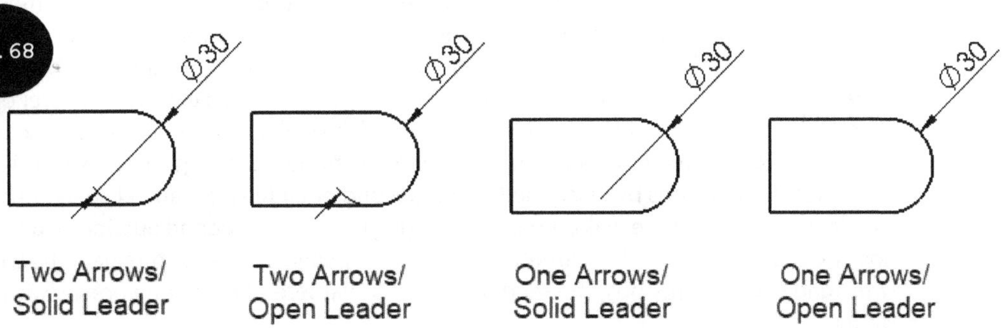

Note: The **Two Arrows / Solid Leader** and **Two Arrows / Open Leader** buttons are enabled only when the **Use document second arrow** check box is cleared in the rollout. Besides, the availability of the buttons in the rollout depends upon the type of drafting standard selected in the **Document Properties - Drafting Standard** dialog box. To set the drafting standard, click on the **Options** tool in the **Standard** toolbar and then click on the **Document Properties** tab in the **System Options - General** dialog box that appears. Next, select the required drafting standard in the **Overall drafting standard** drop-down list of the dialog box.

Tip: You can also convert a radius dimension to a diameter dimension by clicking on the **Display as Diameter** tool in the context toolbar that appears on selecting a radius dimension.

Linear

The **Linear** button is used to display the radius or diameter dimension as a linear diameter dimension. On selecting the **Linear** button, the selected radius or diameter dimension changes to the linear diameter dimension in the drawing. Also, two buttons: **Perpendicular To Axis** and **Parallel To Axis** get enabled. By using these buttons you can define whether the linear diameter dimension is perpendicular or parallel to the axis of the object.

Tip: You can also convert a radius or diameter dimension to a linear diameter dimension by clicking on the **Display as Linear** tool in the context toolbar that appears on selecting a radius or diameter dimension.

Multi-jog Leader

The **Multi-jog Leader** button is used to display the radius, diameter, chamfer dimension, or a hole callout with a multi-jog leader. On selecting this button, the selected radius, diameter, chamfer dimension, or hole callout is displayed with a multi-jog leader in the drawing.

Use document second arrow

The **Use document second arrow** check box is used to specify the second arrow style for diameter dimension. By default, this check box is selected. As a result, the second arrow of the diameter dimension is specified as per the default document settings. Note that this check box is available only when the selected dimension is a diameter dimension or a radius dimension.

Note: To specify the default document settings for the second arrow of the diameter dimension, click on the **Options** tool in the **Standard** toolbar. The **System Options - General** dialog box appears. Next, click on the **Document Properties** tab and then expand the **Dimensions** node by clicking on the plus (+) sign available in front of it. Next, select the **Diameter** option from the expanded **Dimensions** node. The name of the dialog box is changed to **Document Properties - Diameter**. Now, you can specify the document settings for the second arrow of diameter dimensions by using the **Display second outside arrow** and **Display with solid leader** check boxes of the dialog box. On selecting the **Display second outside arrow** check box, the second arrow of the diameter dimension appears outside. If you select the **Display with solid leader** check box, the second arrow for diameter dimension appears with solid leader.

Use document bend length

The **Use document bend length** check box is used to specify the dimension leader length after the bend. If this check box is selected, then the default bend length, which is specified in the **Document Properties - Dimensions** dialog box is used for dimensions. However, if you clear this check box, you can specify the bend length for the selected dimension leader in the field available below this check box.

Note: To specify the default bend settings for leaders, click on the **Options** tool in the **Standard** toolbar. The **System Options - General** dialog box appears. In this dialog box, click on the **Document Properties** tab and then select the **Dimensions** node. The options related to dimension styles appear to the right of the dialog box. Also, the name of the dialog box changes to **Document Properties - Dimensions**. In this dialog box, specify the default bend length for dimension leaders in the **Leader length** field of the **Bent leaders** area.

Leader/Dimension Line Style

The options in the **Leader/Dimension Line Style** rollout are used for specifying style and thickness properties for the dimension leader. By default, the **Use document display** check box is selected in this rollout. As a result, the default properties of the leader style specified in the **Document Properties** dialog box are used. When you clear this check box, the **Leader Style** and **Leader Thickness** drop-down lists get enabled in this rollout. By using these drop-down lists, you can specify the style and the thickness for the selected dimension leader.

You can also specify the default leader style and thickness for angle dimensions, arc length, chamfer, hole, linear, ordinate, and radius dimensions. To specify the default leader style and thickness for angle dimension, click on the **Options** tool in the **Standard** toolbar. The **System Options - General** dialog box appears. In this dialog box, click on the **Document Properties** tab and then expand the **Dimensions** node by clicking on the plus (+) sign available in front of it. Next, select the **Angle** option in the expanded **Dimensions** node. The name of the dialog box changes to **Document Properties - Angle**. In this dialog box, you can specify the default leader style and thickness for angular dimensions by using the **Leader Style** and **Leader Thickness** drop-down lists of the **Leader/Dimension line style** area. Similarly, you can specify the default leader style and thickness for arc length, chamfer, hole, linear, ordinate, and radius dimensions.

Custom Text Position

The options of the **Custom Text Position** rollout are used for customizing the position of the dimension text concerning the dimension leader. By default, this rollout is collapsed. As a result, the dimension text and leader are placed as per the default settings. Expand the **Custom Text Position** rollout by selecting the check box available in front of its title bar. If you click on the **Solid Leader, Aligned Text** button in the expanded rollout, the selected dimension will have the solid dimension leader with aligned dimension text, see Figure 14.69. On clicking the **Broken Leader, Horizontal Text** button, the selected dimension will have the broken dimension leader with horizontal dimension text, see Figure 14.69. On the other hand, if you click on the **Broken Leader, Aligned Text** button, the selected dimension will have the broken dimension leader with aligned dimension text, see Figure 14.69.

14.69

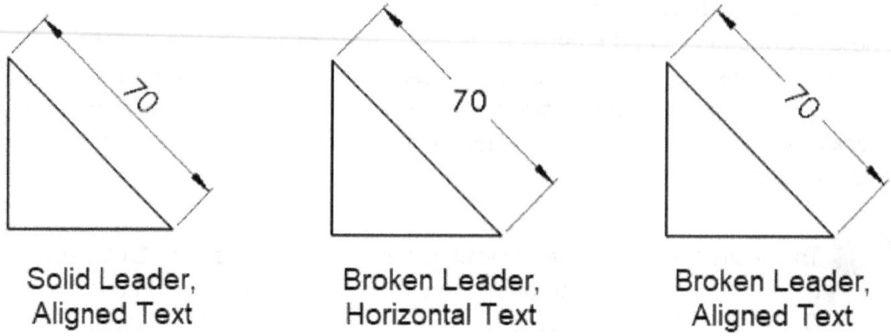

Other Tab

The options in the **Other** tab of the **Dimension PropertyManager** are discussed next.

14.70

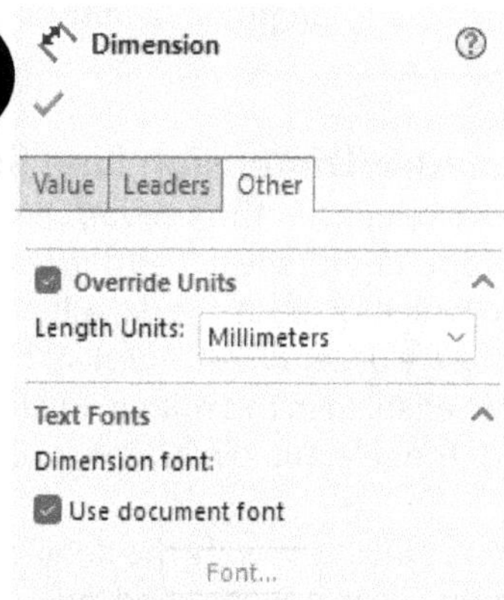

Override Units

The **Override Units** rollout is used to override the default unit specified in the **Document Properties - Units** dialog box. To do this, expand the **Override Units** rollout by selecting the check box in front of its title bar, see Figure 14.70. Next, select the unit type as the override unit for the selected dimension in the **Length Units** drop-down list of the rollout.

Note: The availability of other options in the **Override Units** rollout depends upon the type of unit selected in the **Length Units** drop-down list. For example, if **Inches** is selected in the **Length Units** drop-down list, then the **Decimal** and **Fractions** radio buttons become available in the **Override Units** rollout of the PropertyManager. You can select the required radio button in the rollout to display the override unit either in decimal or fractions.

Text Fonts

The **Text Fonts** rollout is used to specify the font for the selected dimension. By default, the **Use document font** check box is selected in the rollout. As a result, the default dimension font is used for all dimensions. However, if you clear the **Use document font** check box, then the **Font** button gets enabled below this check box. Click on the **Font** button. The **Choose Font** dialog box appears, see Figure 14.71. By using this dialog box, you can specify the required font, font style, and dimension text height for the selected dimension.

14.71

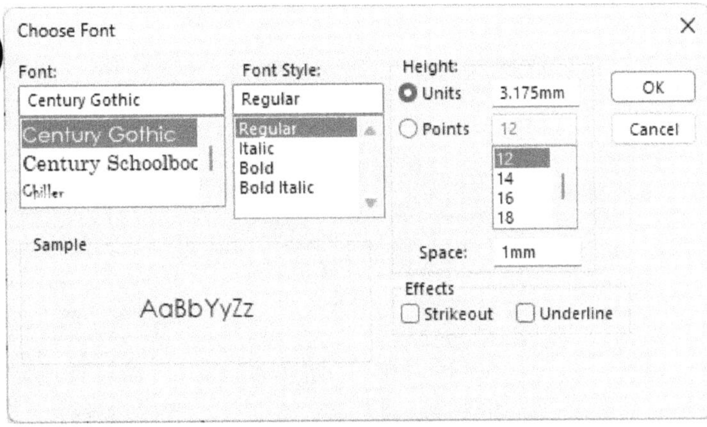

To specify the default dimension font for dimensions, click on the **Options** tool in the **Standard** toolbar. The **System Options - General** dialog box appears. In this dialog box, click on the **Document Properties** tab and then select the **Dimensions** option. Next, click on the **Font** button in the **Text** area of the dialog box. The **Choose Font** dialog box appears. Now, you can specify the default font, font style, and text height for dimensions using this dialog box. Once the default dimension font for dimensions has been set, click on the **OK** button in the dialog box.

Options

The **Options** rollout is provided with the **Read only** and **Driven** check boxes. On selecting the **Read only** check box, the selected dimension becomes read only and cannot be modified. Similarly, on selecting the **Driven** check box, the selected dimension becomes a driven or reference dimension which cannot drive the entity.

Note: Similarly, you can modify the properties of dimensions in the Sketching environment by using the **Dimension PropertyManager**. The options for modifying dimension properties of a dimension in the Sketching environment are same as discussed above.

Controlling the Default Dimension/Arrow Style

In SOLIDWORKS, you can control dimension and arrow styles such as dimension font, dimension height, and arrow height using the options in the **Document Properties - Dimensions** dialog box. To invoke this dialog box, click on the **Options** tool in the **Standard** toolbar. The **System Options - General** dialog box appears. Next, click on the **Document Properties** tab in the dialog box and then click on the **Dimensions** option. The name of the dialog box changes to **Document Properties - Dimensions**, see Figure 14.72. In this dialog box, click on the **Font** button in the **Text** area. The **Choose Font** dialog box appears. By using this dialog box, you can specify the required font, style, and height for dimension text. Next, click on the **OK** button in the **Choose Font** dialog box.

You can also control the dimension arrow height by using the options in the **Arrows** area of the **Document Properties - Dimensions** dialog box, see Figure 14.72. After specifying the settings for the dimension and arrow styles, click on the **OK** button.

14.72

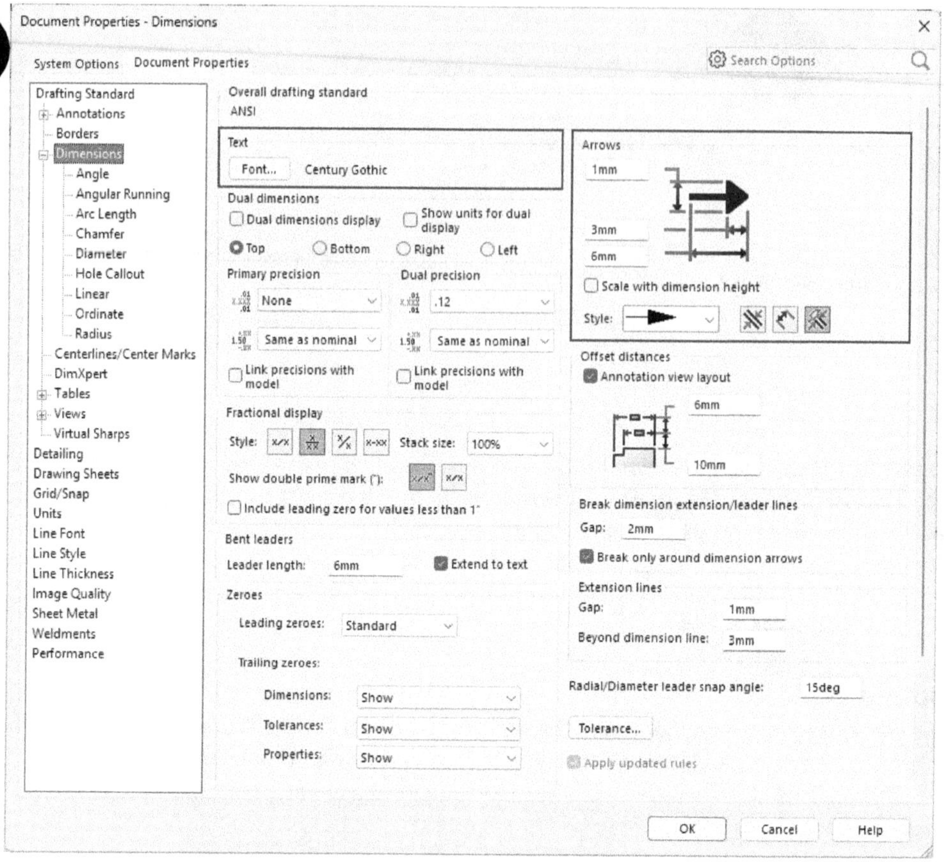

Adding Notes

In SOLIDWORKS, you can add notes on a drawing sheet using the **Note** tool. Generally, adding notes in drawings is used for conveying or providing additional information that is not available in the drawing views.

To add a note, click on the **Note** tool in the **Annotation CommandManager**. The **Note PropertyManager** appears, see Figure 14.73. Also, a rectangular box gets attached to the cursor. Now, specify the required settings such as text style, text format, type of leader, and leader style for the note by using the options in the PropertyManager. Next, move the cursor over an entity of a drawing view to add the note. A preview of the note with the leader attached to the entity of the drawing view appears. Next, click on the entity to add the note. The leader arrow is attached to the selected entity. Now, move the cursor to the required location and then click to place the note. An edit box and the **Formatting**

14.73

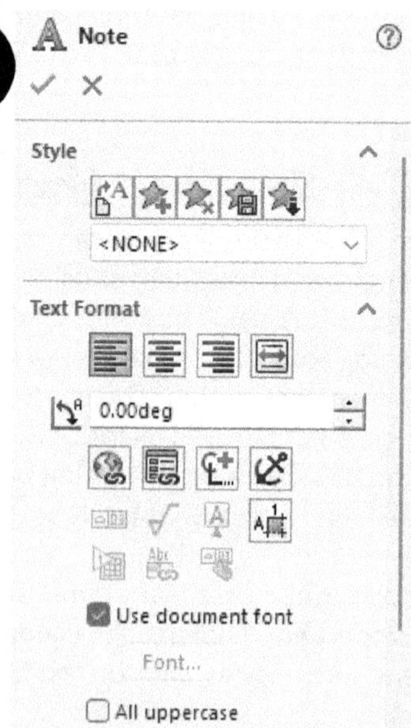

toolbar appear. Now, you can type text in the edit box. You can use the **Formatting** toolbar to control the formatting of the text such as font, style, height, and alignment. Next, click anywhere on the drawing sheet. The note is added to the selected entity, see Figure 14.74. You can also add a note anywhere in the drawing sheet without selecting any entity.

14.74

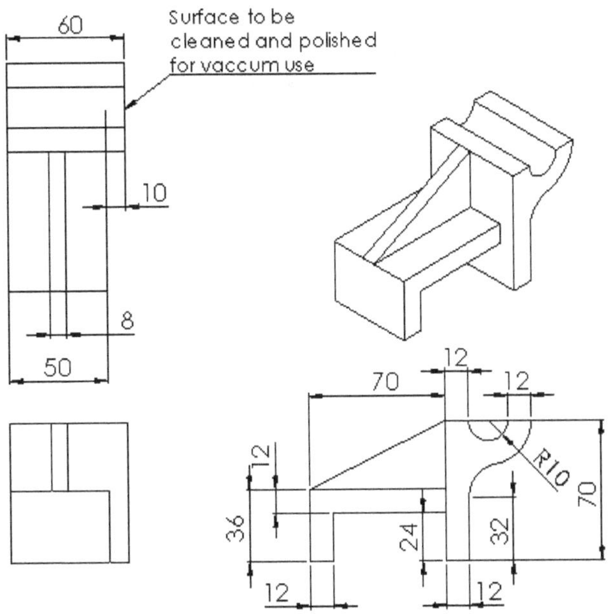

Adding a Surface Finish Symbol

In SOLIDWORKS, you can add a surface finish symbol to specify the surface texture/finish for the face of a model. A surface finish symbol has three components: surface roughness, waviness, and lay, see Figure 14.75. Specifications for the surface finish given in a surface finish symbol are used to machine the respective surface of the object. You can add a surface finish symbol to an edge of a surface in a drawing view using the **Surface Finish** tool.

14.75

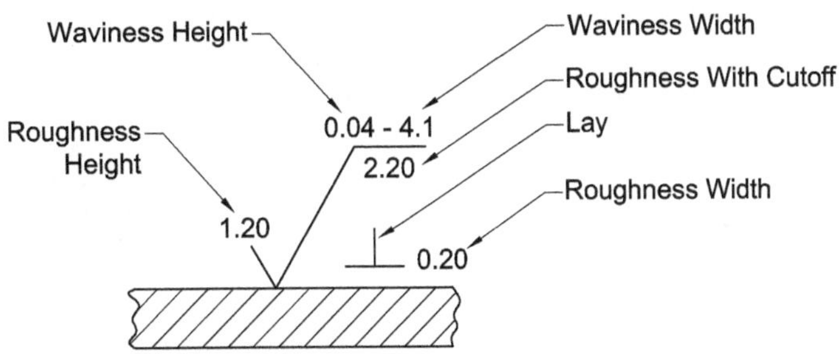

To add a surface finish symbol, click on the **Surface Finish** tool in the **Annotation CommandManager**. The **Surface Finish PropertyManager** appears, see Figure 14.76. Also, the default selected surface finish symbol gets attached to the cursor. Select the required type of surface finish symbol to be added from the **Symbol** rollout of the PropertyManager. Next, in the **Symbol Layout** rollout, specify the required specification for the surface finish (roughness, waviness, and lay) in the respective fields.

If needed, you can rotate the surface finish symbol at an angle by using the options in the **Angle** rollout of the PropertyManager. By using the options of the **Leader** rollout, you can select the type of leader to be attached to the surface finish symbol. Once you have specified the surface finish specification, move the cursor over the required edge in the drawing view and then click on it when it gets highlighted. The surface finish symbol is applied and attached to the selected edge, see Figure 14.77.

14.76

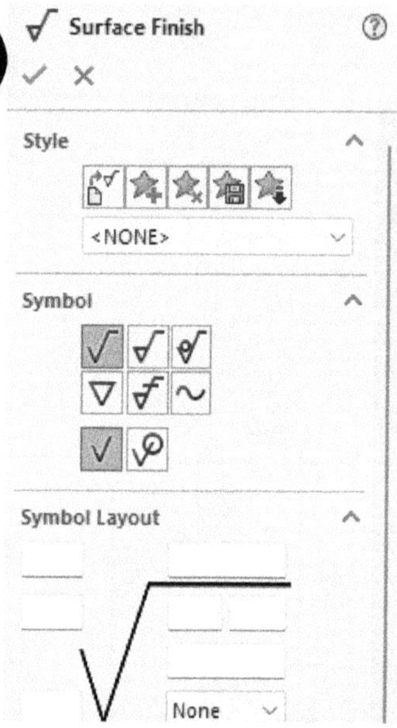

14.77

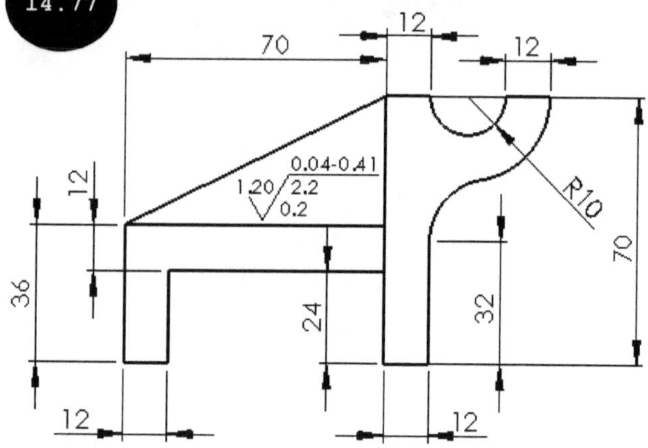

Adding a Weld Symbol

A weld symbol is added in a drawing view to represent the welding specification used while welding two parts. To add a weld symbol, click on an edge of a model in the drawing view, and then click on the **Weld Symbol** tool in the **Annotation CommandManager**. The **Properties** dialog box appears, see Figure 14.78. Also, the **Weld Symbol PropertyManager** appears to the left of the drawing sheet. By using the **Properties** dialog box, you can specify the welding properties to be included in the weld symbol. Note that the availability of options in the **Properties** dialog box depends upon the type of drafting standard selected in the **Document Properties - Drafting Standard** dialog box. Once you have specified the welding properties, click on the **OK** button in the dialog box. The weld symbol is added to the selected edge of the model, see Figure 14.79.

14.78

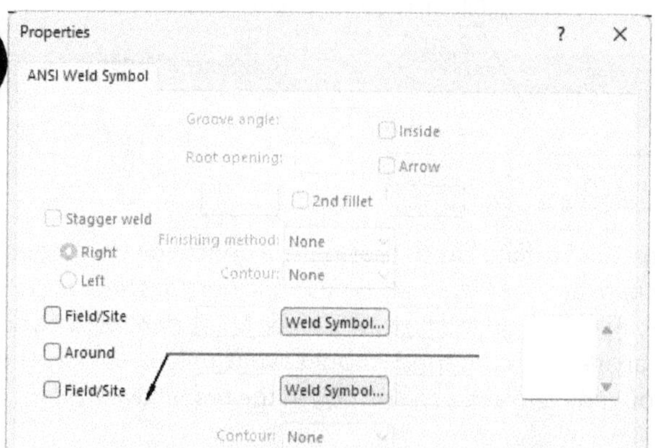

14.79

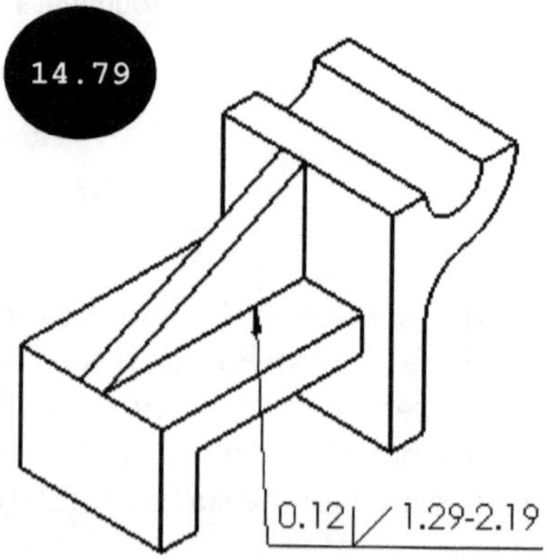

Tip: To invoke the **Document Properties - Drafting Standard** dialog box for specifying the drafting standard, click on the **Options** button in the **Standard** toolbar. The **System Options - General** dialog box appears. In this dialog box, click on the **Document Properties** tab. The **Document Properties - Drafting Standard** dialog box appears. Now, select the required type of drafting standard to be followed in the drawing by using the **Overall drafting standard** drop-down list of the dialog box. Next, close the dialog box.

Adding a Hole Callout

In SOLIDWORKS, you can add a hole callout to a hole in a drawing view. A hole callout contains hole specifications such as diameter and type of hole, see Figure 14.80. Note that on modifying the hole parameters of a model in the Part modeling environment, the respective hole callout gets updated accordingly in the Drawing environment.

14.80

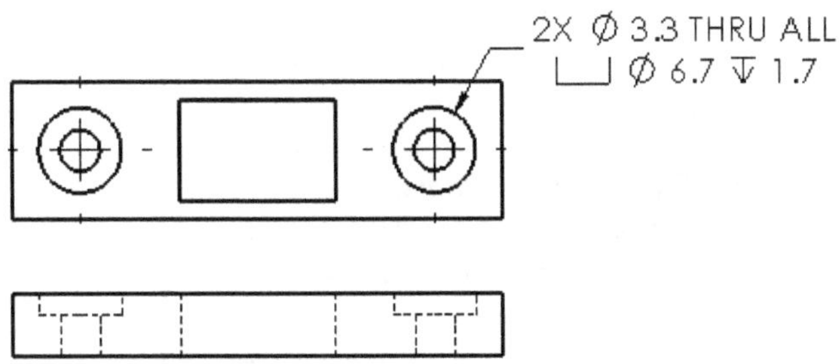

To add a hole callout to a hole in a drawing view, click on the **Hole Callout** tool in the **Annotation CommandManager**. The symbol of the hole callout gets attached to the cursor. Move the cursor over the hole for adding the hole callout in a drawing view and then click the left mouse button on the hole when it gets highlighted. A preview of the hole callout gets attached to the cursor. Now, move the cursor to the required location and then click to specify the placement point for the hole callout, see Figure 14.80. Note that a hole callout also includes the mirrored holes in the count.

Note: In SOLIDWORKS, you can also add hole callouts to cross-sectioned holes in section views, broken-out section views, and detail views. To do this, click on the **Hole Callout** tool in the **Annotation CommandManager**. The symbol of the hole callout gets attached to the cursor. Move the cursor over an edge (side edge) of a hole cross-section in a section view, broken-out section view, or detailed view and then click the left mouse button when the hole edge gets highlighted. A preview of a hole callout gets attached to the cursor. Now, move the cursor to the required location and then click to specify the placement point for the hole callout. Note that to select the top or the bottom hole edge for adding a hole callout, you need to press SHIFT key.

In SOLIDWORKS, you can also add hole callouts to the advanced holes which are created using the **Advanced Hole** tool in the Part modeling environment. You can also reverse the callout order of the advanced hole when you place it on the far side of the face by selecting the **Reverse callout order** check box of the **Dimension PropertyManager**, which appears to the left of the drawing sheet. Besides, you can add additional text, above or below the hole callout by using the **Text Above** and **Text Below** fields of the PropertyManager.

Adding Center Marks

14.81

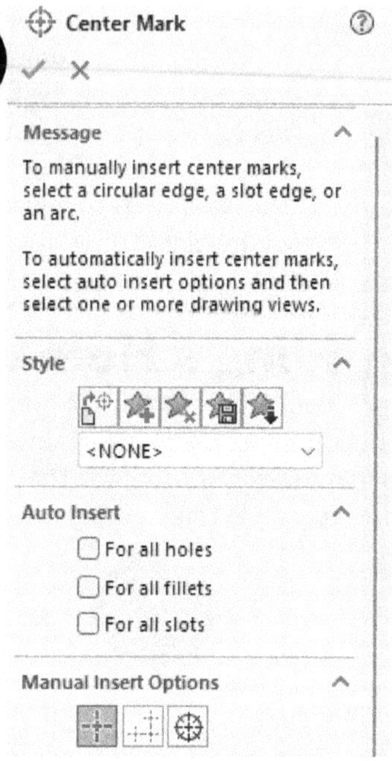

Center marks are used as references for dimensioning circular edges, slot edges, or circular sketch entities in drawing views. To add center marks, click on the **Center Mark** tool in the **Annotation CommandManager**. The **Center Mark PropertyManager** appears, see Figure 14.81. By using this PropertyManager, you can add center marks automatically as well as manually.

To add center marks automatically to all holes, fillets, slots, or all of them in a drawing view, select the respective check boxes such as **For all holes** and **For all fillets** in the **Auto Insert** rollout of the PropertyManager. Next, select a drawing view for adding center marks. The center marks are added automatically in the drawing view, depending upon the check boxes selected. In the automatic method of adding center marks, you can further control the connection among the center marks by using the check boxes: **Connection lines**, **Circular lines**, **Radial lines**, and **Base center mark** in the **Options** area of the **Auto Insert** rollout, see Figures 14.82 through 14.85. Note that the **Options** area appears after selecting a check box in the **Auto Insert** rollout, see Figure 14.86.

14.82

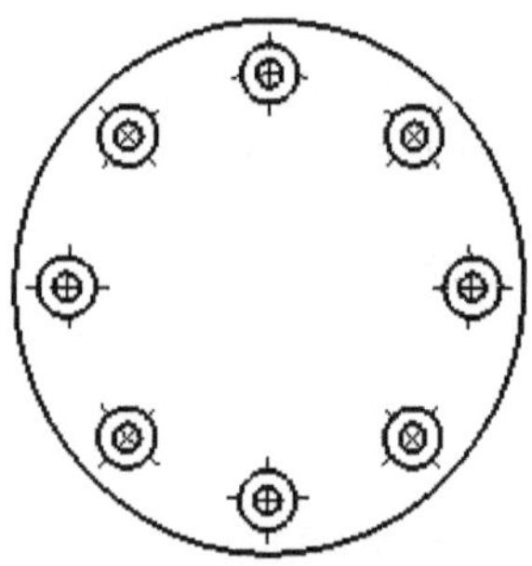

Center mark with connection lines

14.83

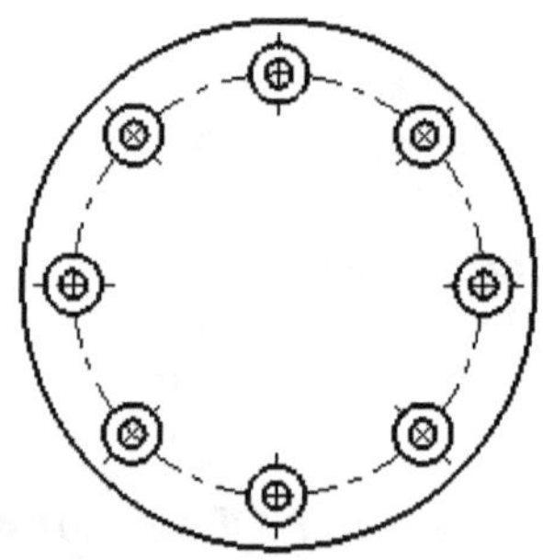

Center mark with circular lines

14.84

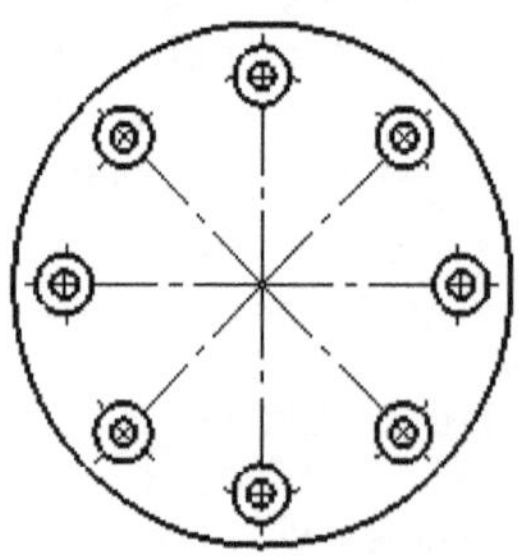

Center mark with radial lines

14.85

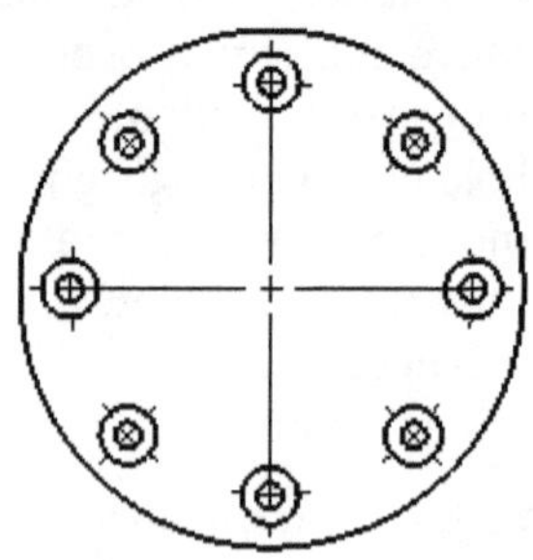

Center mark with base center mark

To add center marks manually, invoke the **Center Mark PropertyManager** and then move the cursor over a circular edge, a slot edge, or a circular sketch entity in a drawing view. Next, click on the entity when it gets highlighted. The center mark is added. Similarly, you can add center marks to the other entities of drawing views manually. In the manual method of adding center marks, you can select the type of center marks to be added by activating the respective button in the **Manual Insert Options** rollout of the PropertyManager, see Figure 14.87.

14.86

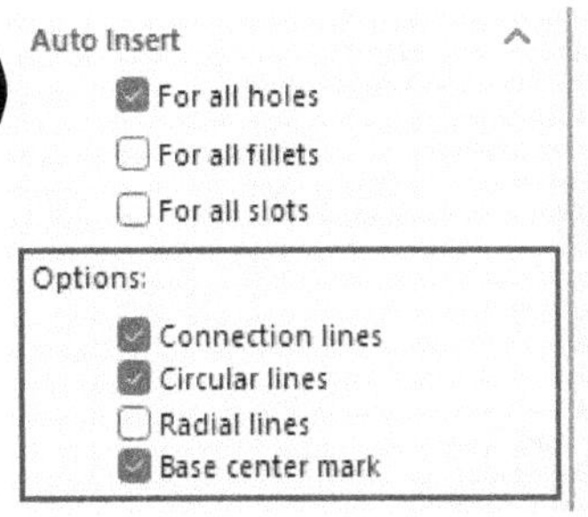

14.87

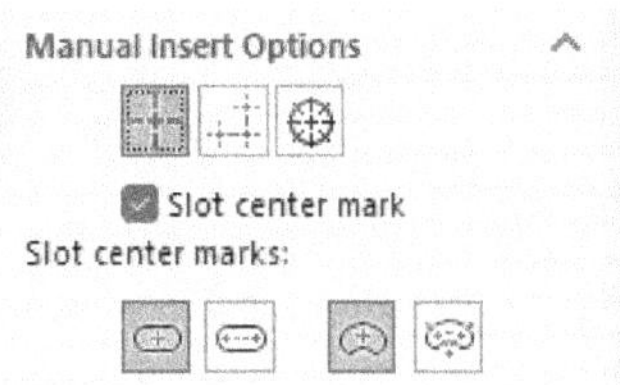

Once you have added center marks either by manual or automatic method, click on the green tick-mark ✓ in the PropertyManager.

Adding Centerlines

Centerlines are used as references for dimensioning circular cut features and hole features in drawing views, see Figure 14.88. In SOLIDWORKS, you can add a centerline between two linear edges that represent the edges of a circular cut or hole feature in a drawing view using the **Centerline** tool, see Figure 14.88.

To add a centerline, click on the **Centerline** tool in the **Annotation CommandManager**. The **Centerline PropertyManager** appears. Next, select two linear edges one by one by clicking the left mouse button. The centerline is added at the center of the two selected edges, see Figure 14.88. You can also select two sketch segments, or a single cylindrical, conical, toroidal, or swept feature for adding a centerline.

14.88

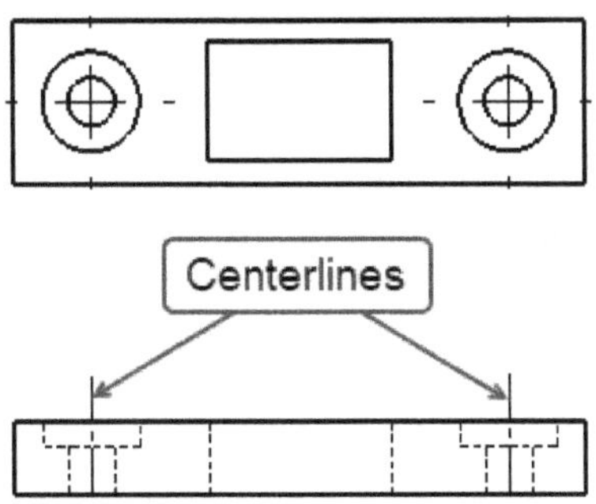

Creating the Bill of Material (BOM)

After creating all the required drawing views of an assembly in the Drawing environment, you need to create the Bill of Material. The Bill of Material (BOM) contains all the required information such as the number of parts used in an assembly, part number, quantity of each part, and material. Since the Bill of Material (BOM) contains all the information, it serves as a primary source of communication between the manufacturer and the vendors as well as the suppliers.

To create the Bill of Material (BOM), click on the down arrow below the **Tables** tool in the **Annotation CommandManager**. A flyout appears, see Figure 14.89. In this flyout, click on the **Bill of Materials** tool. The **Bill of Materials PropertyManager** appears. Next, click on a drawing view of the assembly whose Bill of Material has to be created. The **Bill of Materials PropertyManager** gets modified and appears, as shown in Figure 14.90. The options of this PropertyManager are used to set the parameters for creating the Bill of Material. Some of the options of this PropertyManager are discussed next.

Tip: If a drawing view of an assembly is selected before invoking the **Bill of Materials** tool, then the modified **Bill of Material PropertyManager** appears directly as shown in Figure 14.90.

14.89

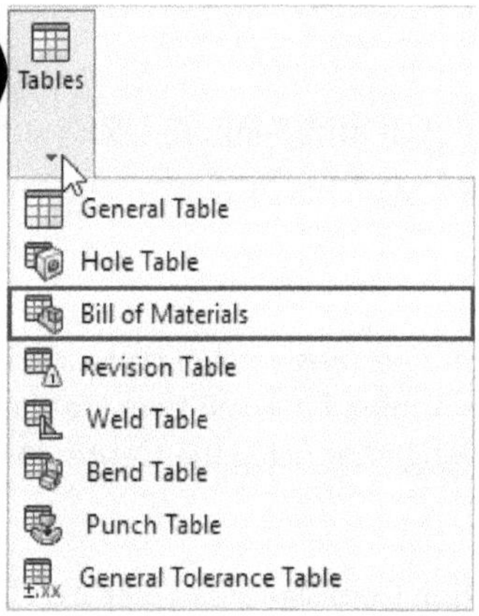

14.90

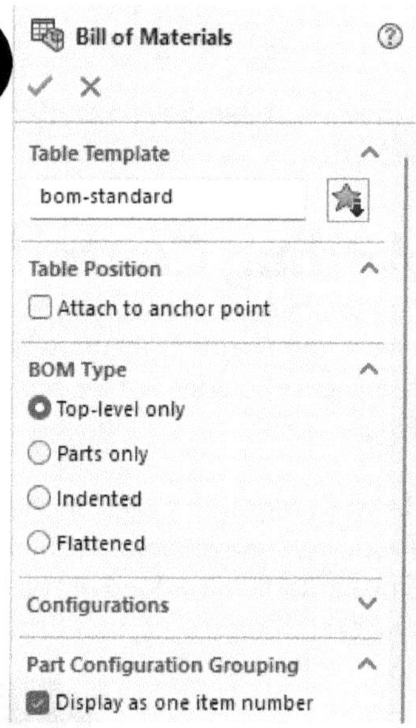

Table Template

The **Table Template** rollout is used to specify a template for the Bill of Material (BOM). By default, **bom-standard** template is selected in this rollout. You can select a template other than the default one by clicking on the **Open table template for Bill of Materials** button of this rollout. As soon as you click on this button, the **Open** dialog box appears such that all the template files are displayed in it. You can select a required template in this dialog box and then click on the **Open** button.

Table Position

The **Table Position** rollout is used to specify the position of the BOM table in the drawing sheet. By default, the **Attach to anchor point** check box is cleared in this rollout. As a result, on clicking the green tick-mark in the PropertyManager, the BOM gets attached to the cursor and you need to define its position in the drawing sheet by specifying the placement point. However, on selecting the **Attach to anchor point** check box, the BOM is placed directly in the drawing sheet such that the top left corner of the BOM is attached to the anchor point of the drawing sheet.

Note: You can define the position of the anchor point in the drawing sheet, as required. To do this, select the **Sheet** node in the FeatureManager Design Tree and then right-click to display a shortcut menu. Next, click on the **Edit Sheet Format** option in the shortcut menu. The editing mode for defining the anchor point location is invoked, see Figure 14.91. Now, click on an existing vertex or a point of the drawing sheet (see Figure 14.91) and then right-click to display a shortcut menu. In this shortcut menu, select **Set as Anchor > Bill of Materials**, see Figure 14.92. The selected vertex/point is defined as the anchor point for the BOM. In addition to selecting an existing vertex or a point, you can create a new sketch point using the **Point** tool of the **Sketch CommandManager** and then define it as the anchor point. After defining the anchor point, click on the Confirmation corner available at the upper right corner of the drawing sheet.

14.91

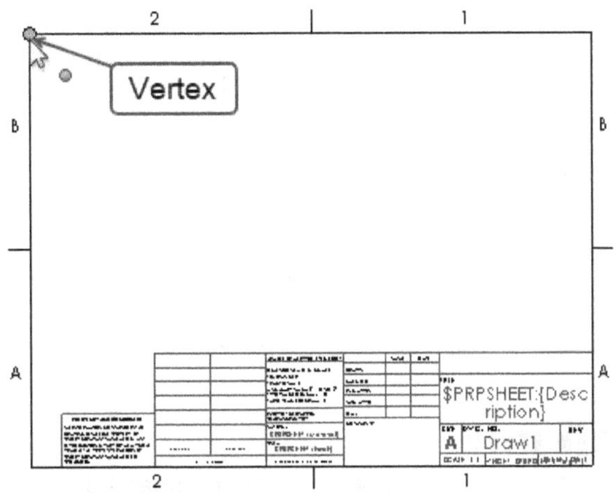

14.92

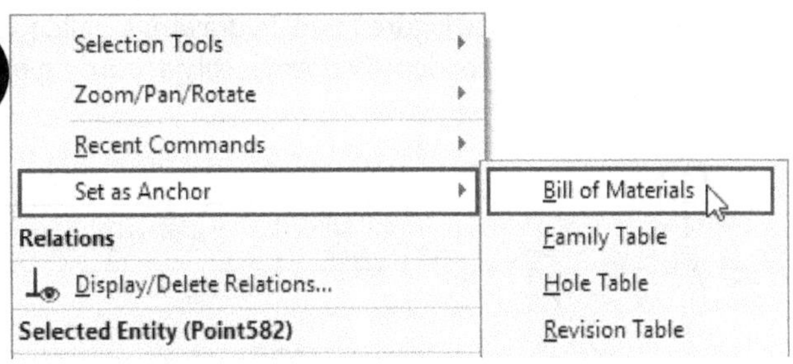

Item Numbers

The **Start at** field of the **Item Numbers** rollout in the PropertyManager is used to specify the start number for the count of components, see Figure 14.93. By default, **1** is entered in this field. As a result, the counting of components starts from number **1** in the BOM. In the **Increment** field, you can specify the incremental value for the count of components. Note that on selecting the **Do not change item numbers** button of this rollout, the assigned components count/numbers are locked.

14.93

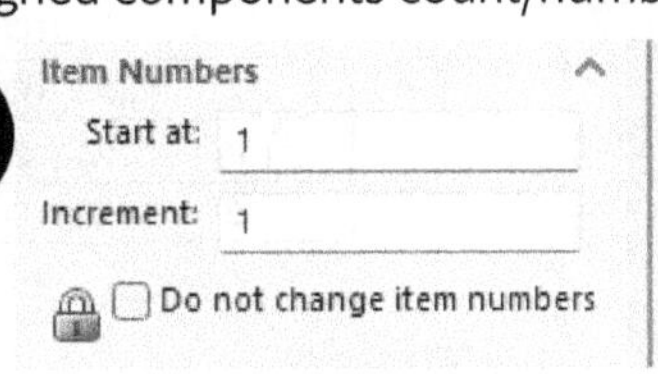

Border

The options of the **Border** rollout of the PropertyManager are used to define the thickness of the Bill of Material (BOM) border, see Figure 14.94.

14.94

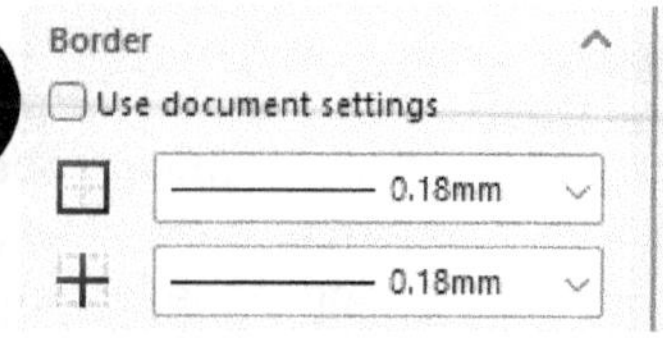

Accept the default parameters specified in the PropertyManager and then click on the green tick-mark ✓ in the PropertyManager. The Bill of Material (BOM) gets attached to the cursor. Next, click on the drawing sheet to specify the position of the Bill of Material (BOM). The Bill of Material (BOM) is placed at the specified position in the drawing sheet, see Figure 14.95.

14.95

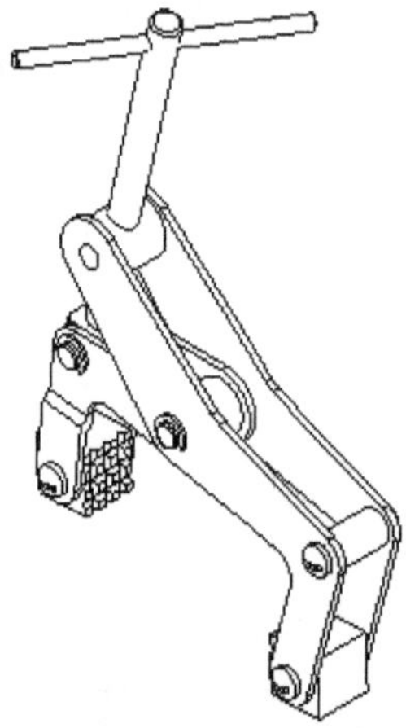

ITEM NO.	PART NUMBER	DESCRIPTION	QTY.
1	Clamp Base		2
2	Clamp Spacer		1
3	Clamp foot		2
4	Clamp Left Elbow		1
5	Clamp Right Elbow		1
6	Clamp Tee		1
7	Clamp Rod		1
8	Clamp Hinge		1
9	Clamp Support		1
10	Clamp Lever		1
11	Clamp Screw		6
12	Clamp Waser		4

Adding Balloons

A Balloon is attached to a component with a leader line and displays the respective part number assigned in the Bill of Material (BOM), see Figure 14.96. In drawings, balloons are generally added to the individual components of an assembly to identify them easily according to the part number assigned in the Bill of Materials (BOM).

14.96

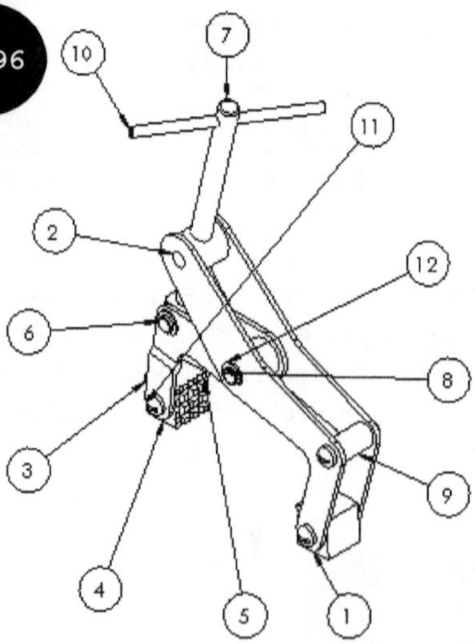

ITEM NO.	PART NUMBER	DESCRIPTION	QTY.
1	Clamp Base		2
2	Clamp Spacer		1
3	Clamp foot		2
4	Clamp Left Elbow		1
5	Clamp Right Elbow		1
6	Clamp Tee		1
7	Clamp Rod		1
8	Clamp Hinge		1
9	Clamp Support		1
10	Clamp Lever		1
11	Clamp Screw		6
12	Clamp Waser		4

In SOLIDWORKS, you can add balloons to the components of an assembly by using two methods: Automatic and Manual. In the Automatic method, balloons are added automatically to all the components of an assembly concerning the part number assigned in the BOM whereas, in the Manual method, you need to add balloons manually to the components of an assembly one by one. Both these methods of adding balloons are discussed next.

Adding Balloons Automatically

To add balloons automatically to the components of an assembly, click on the **Auto Balloon** tool in the **Annotation CommandManager**. The **Auto Balloon PropertyManager** appears, see Figure 14.97. The options of this PropertyManager are used for setting parameters for balloons. Some of these options are discussed next.

14.97

Balloon Layout

The **Balloon Layout** rollout is used to define the type of layout for balloons. The options of this rollout are discussed next.

Pattern type

The buttons in the **Pattern type** area of the **Balloon Layout** rollout are used for selecting the required type of layouts (Square, Circular, Top, Bottom, Left, or Right) for arranging balloons in the sheet.

Ignore multiple instances

By default, the **Ignore multiple instances** check box is selected in the **Balloon Layout** rollout. As a result, the duplicates are avoided by not adding balloons to all the instances of a component.

Insert magnetic line(s)

By default, the **Insert magnetic line(s)** check box is selected in the rollout. As a result, magnetic lines are inserted along with balloons such that balloons are aligned with each other. Note that this check box is not enabled if the **Layout Balloons to Circular** button is selected in the **Pattern type** area of the rollout.

Leader attachment

By default, the **Edges** radio button is selected in the **Leader attachment** area of the rollout. As a result, the leader lines of balloons are attached to the edges of the components. On selecting the **Faces** radio button, balloons are attached to the faces of components through leader lines.

Balloon Settings

The **Balloon Settings** rollout is used to define the settings for balloons such as balloon style, balloon size, and balloon text. The options of this rollout are discussed next.

Style

The **Style** drop-down list in the **Balloon Settings** rollout is used to select the required type of style for the border of balloons. By default, the **Circular** option is selected in this drop-down list. As a result, balloons appear with circular borders, refer to Figure 14.96. You can select a style such as triangle, hexagon, and diamond in this drop-down list. Note that on selecting the **None** option, balloons appear without borders, see Figure 14.98. If you select the **Circular Split Line** option, the border of balloons appears such that the circles are split into two areas, see Figure 14.99. By default, its upper area displays part number information and the lower area displays information about the quantity of component.

Size

The **Size** drop-down list of the **Balloon Settings** rollout is used to select a pre-defined size for balloons. In addition to selecting a pre-defined size, you can also select the **User Defined** option in this drop-down list and specify the value for the required size of balloons in the **User defined** field of the rollout.

Balloon text

The **Balloon text** drop-down list is used to select a required text to be displayed in the balloons. By default, the **Item Number** option is selected. As a result, balloons appear with part numbers.

Lower text

The **Lower text** drop-down list is used to select a required text to be displayed in the lower area of the balloons. Note that this drop-down list is available only if the **Circular Split Line** option is selected in the **Style** drop-down list. By default, the **Quantity** option is selected in the **Lower text** drop-down list. As a result, the lower area of balloons displays the quantity information, refer to Figure 14.99.

14.98

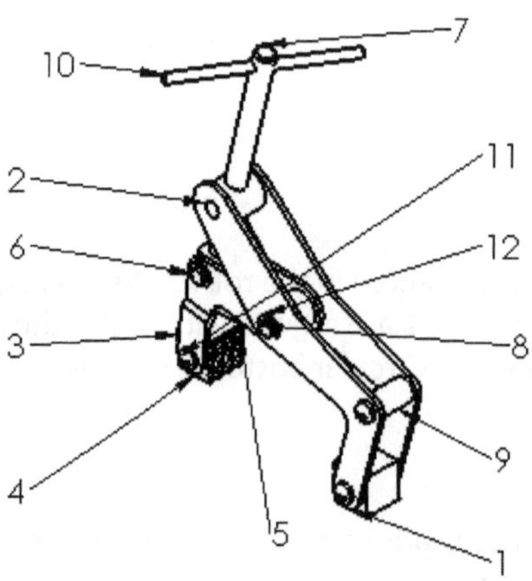

14.99

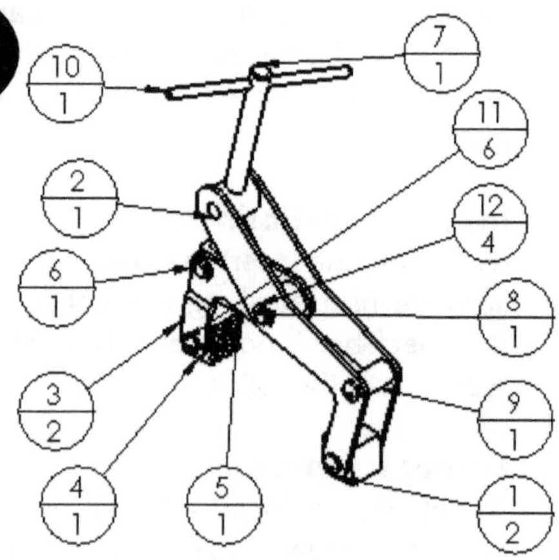

After specifying the required parameters for balloons, click on the green tick-mark ✓ in the PropertyManager. The balloons are attached to the components of the assembly in the drawing view.

Adding Balloons Manually

To add balloons manually to the components of an assembly, click on the **Balloon** tool in the **Annotation CommandManager**. The **Balloon PropertyManager** appears, see Figure 14.100. The options in this PropertyManager are the same as those discussed earlier. By using this PropertyManager, you can add balloons to the components of an assembly one by one by selecting them in the drawing view. As soon as you click on a component in the drawing view, the leader line of the balloon gets attached to the component. Next, move the cursor to the required location and then click to specify the location for the balloon in the drawing sheet. Similarly, you can add balloons to all the components of the assembly one by one. Once you have added balloons to all the components, click on the green tick-mark ✓ in the PropertyManager.

14.100

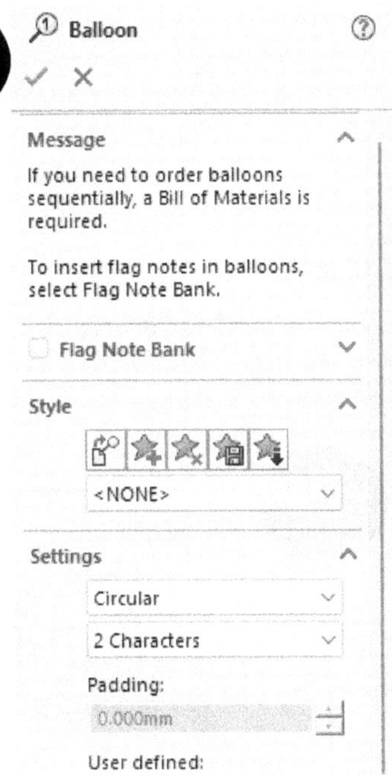

Detailing Mode

In SOLIDWORKS, you can open large drawings or drawings containing a large number of sheets or configurations, quickly using the detailing mode. This is useful in case you need to do minor editing to a large drawing. When you open a drawing in detailing mode, the model data is not loaded. Hence, only a limited number of features can be accessed. The following actions are permissible in detailing mode:

- Adding annotations such as notes, symbols, balloons, hole callouts, magnetic lines, and surface finish symbols
- Creating and modifying break, crop, and detail views
- Print and Save As
- Creating sketch entities
- Adding and editing dimensions that do not require model information such as linear dimensions, radial dimensions, and diameter dimensions

Features such as creating new drawing views, centerlines, center marks, hatching, adding and editing dimensions, or annotations that require model information such as hole callouts, cosmetic threads, and so on are not available when you open a drawing in detailing mode.

To open a drawing in detailing mode, click on the **Open** tool available in the **Standard** toolbar as well as in the **File** menu of the SOLIDWORKS Design Menus. The **Open** dialog box appears. In this dialog box, select the **SOLIDWORKS Drawing (*.drw;*.slddrw)** file extension in the **File Type** drop-down list. Browse to the location where the SOLIDWORKS document is saved and then click on the document to be opened. Select the **Detailing** option in the **Mode** area of the dialog box and click on the **Open** button. The selected document gets opened in detailing mode. Now, you can make the required changes and then save the file.

Note that the detailing mode symbol appears with the file name in the FeatureManager Design Tree when the drawing is opened in detailing mode. Also, [Detailing] appears along with the file name in the top bar. To shift from detailing mode to resolved mode, click on the **Resolve Drawing** tool available on the top left corner of the CommandManager.

Tutorial 1

Open the model created in Tutorial 2 of Chapter 7 and then create different drawing views: front, top, side, isometric, section, and detail, as shown in Figure 14.101 in the **A3 (ANSI) Landscape** sheet size. You also need to apply driving dimensions to the front, top, and right side drawing views of the model.

14.101

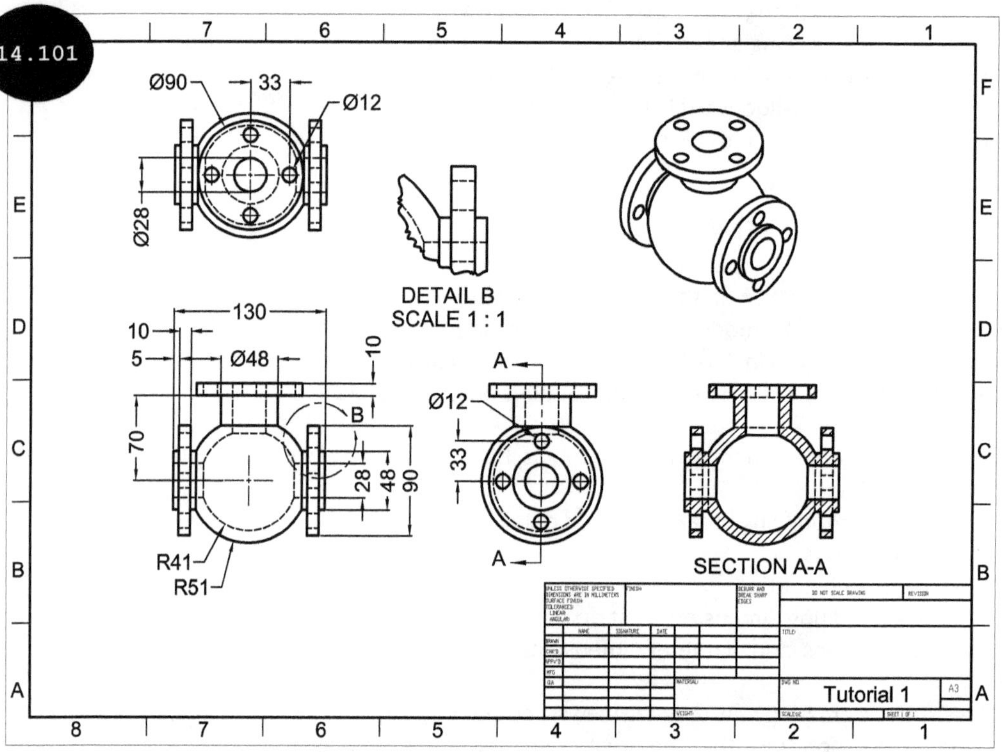

Section 1: Starting SOLIDWORKS

1. Double-click on the **SOLIDWORKS** icon on your desktop to start SOLIDWORKS.

Section 2: Opening and Saving Model Created in Tutorial 2 of Chapter 7

1. Open the model created in Tutorial 2 of Chapter 7 by using the **Open** button of the **Standard** toolbar, see Figure 14.102.

14.102

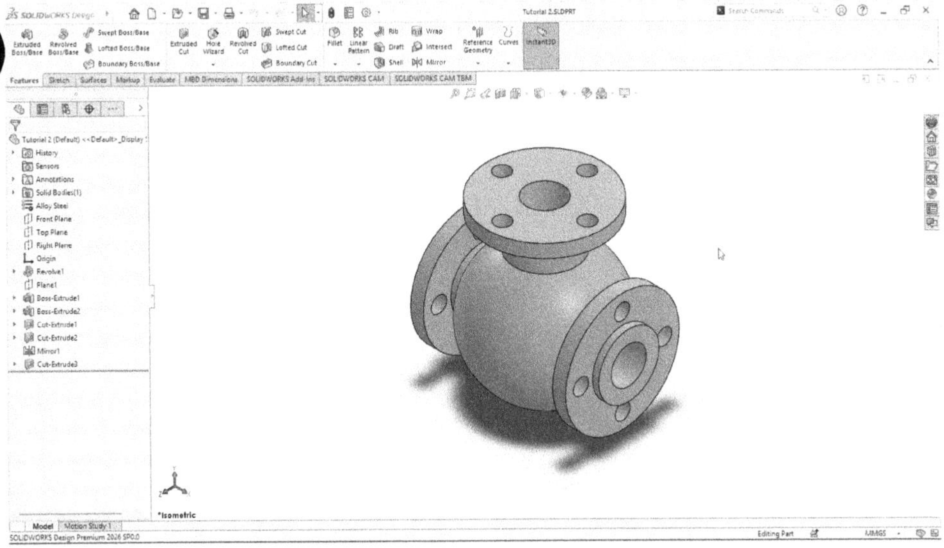

2. Click on **File > Save As** in the SOLIDWORKS Design Menus and then save the model with the name Tutorial 1 inside the Tutorial folder of the Chapter 14 folder. Note that you need to create these folders inside the SOLIDWORKS folder.

Section 3: Invoking Drawing Environment

1. Click on the arrow next to the **New** tool in the **Standard** toolbar. A flyout appears, see Figure 14.103.

14.103

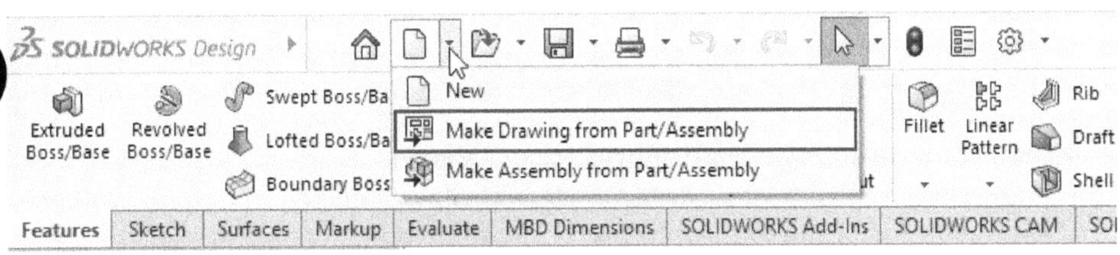

2. Click on the **Make Drawing from Part/Assembly** tool in the flyout. The **Sheet Format/Size** dialog box appears, see Figure 14.104.

14.104

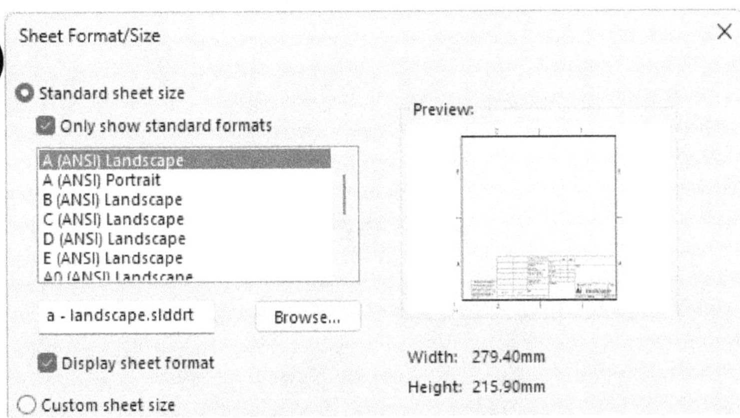

3. Ensure that the **Standard sheet size** radio button is selected in this dialog box, see Figure 14.104.

4. Select the **A3 (ANSI) Landscape** sheet size in the **Selection** area of the dialog box. If the **A3 (ANSI) Landscape** sheet size is not available in the **Selection** area of the dialog box, then you need to clear the **Only show standard formats** check box of the dialog box.

5. Ensure that the **Display sheet format** check box is selected in the dialog box.

6. Click on the **OK** button in the dialog box. The Drawing environment is invoked with the display of the **View Palette Task Pane** on the right of the drawing sheet, see Figure 14.105.

14.105

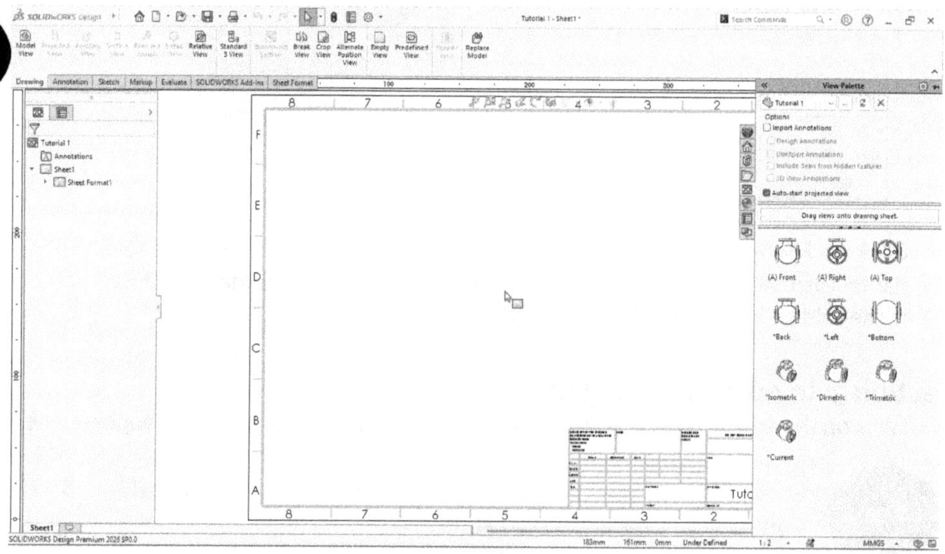

Section 4: Creating Front, Top, and Right Views

1. Drag and drop the front view of the model on the lower left corner of the drawing sheet from the **View Palette Task Pane** by pressing and holding the left mouse button, see Figure 14.106.

14.106

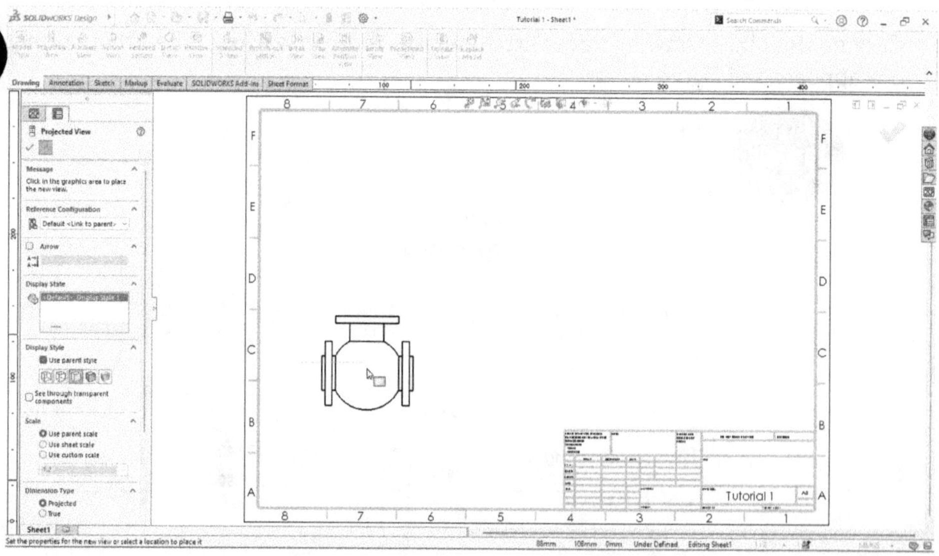

2. Move the cursor vertically upward. The projected view (top view) is attached to the cursor.

3. Click on the drawing sheet to specify the position for the top view, see Figure 14.107.

14.107

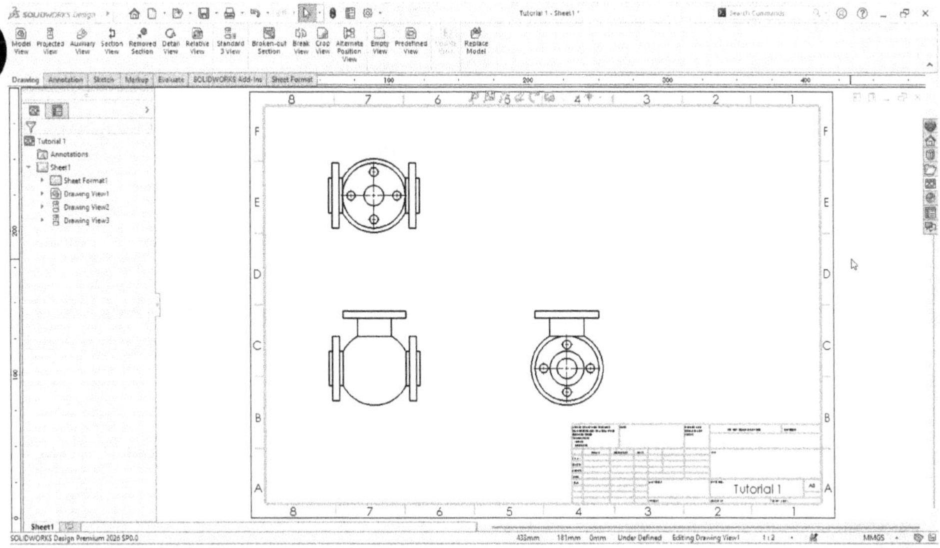

4. Move the cursor horizontally toward the right. The projected view (right-side view) of the model is attached to the cursor.

5. Click on the drawing sheet to specify the position for the right-side view of the model, see Figure 14.107. Next, click on the green tick-mark ✓ in the PropertyManager or press ESC. The front, top, and right side views of the model are created.

Section 5: Creating the Vertical Section View

1. Click on the **Section View** tool in the **Drawing CommandManager**. The **Section View Assist PropertyManager** appears, see Figure 14.108.

2. Click on the **Vertical** button in the **Cutting Line** rollout of the PropertyManager to activate it. Note that on activating the **Vertical** button, the vertical section line appears attached to the cursor.

3. Move the cursor over the right side view of the model in the drawing sheet.

4. Click to specify the placement point for the vertical section line when the cursor snaps to the center point of the right-side view of the model, see Figure 14.109. A preview of the section view appears attached to the cursor. If the **Section View** toolbar appears, click on the green tick-mark ✓ in the **Section View** toolbar.

14.108

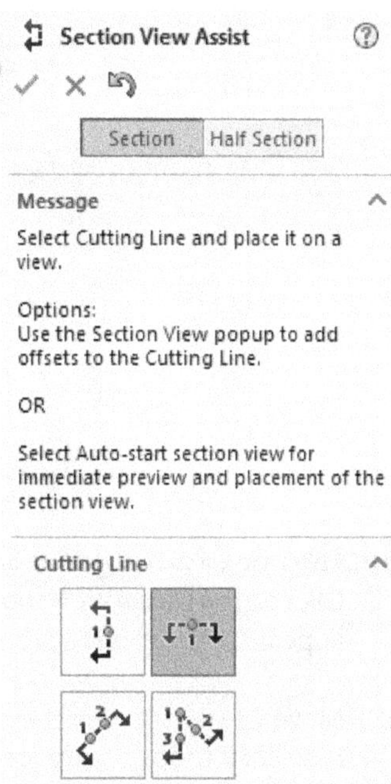

14.109

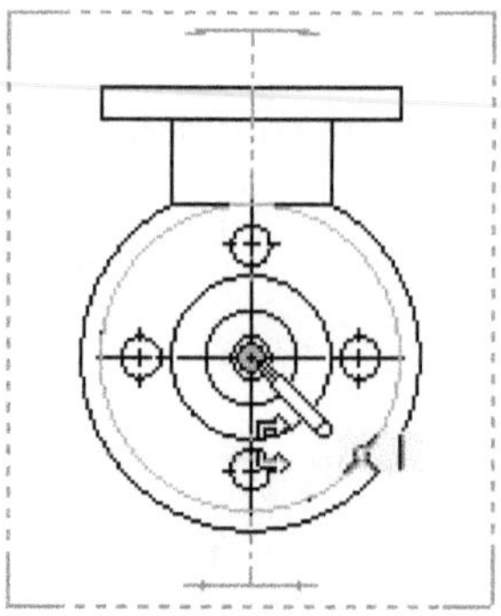

Tip: The **Section View** toolbar appears, if the **Auto-start section view** check box is cleared in the PropertyManager. By using the tools of the **Section View** toolbar, you can modify or edit the section line, as required.

5. Move the cursor horizontally toward the right and then click on the drawing sheet to specify the placement point for the section view, see Figure 14.110.

14.110

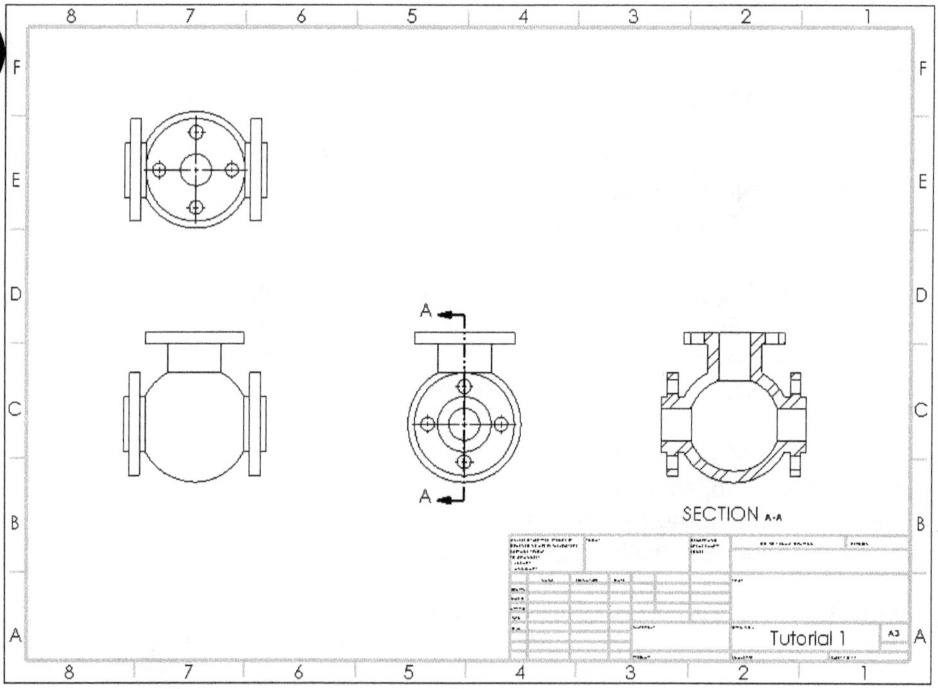

Section 6: Creating the Detail View

1. Click on the **Detail View** tool in the **Drawing CommandManager**. The **Detail View PropertyManager** appears. Also, you are prompted to specify the center point of the circle.

2. Move the cursor over the right vertical edge of the model in the front view (see Figure 14.111) and then click to specify the center point of the circle.

3. Move the cursor to a distance and then click to define the radius of the circle, see Figure 14.112. If the **SOLIDWORKS** message window appears, click on the **OK** button to continue creating a detailed view. The preview of the detail view gets attached to the cursor.

14.111

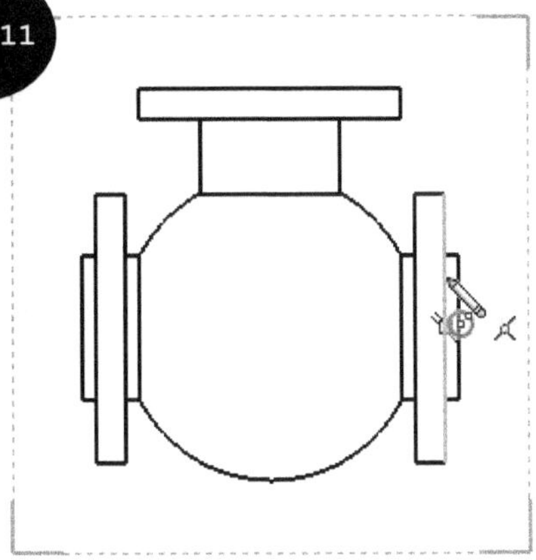

14.112

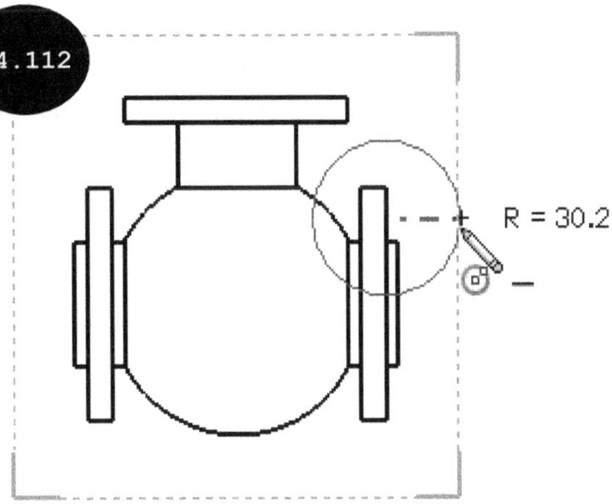

4. Ensure that the **Jagged outline** check box is selected in the **Detail View** rollout of the PropertyManager.

5. Click on the drawing sheet to define the placement point for the detail view, see Figure 14.113. The detailed view is placed on the drawing sheet in the defined position.

14.113

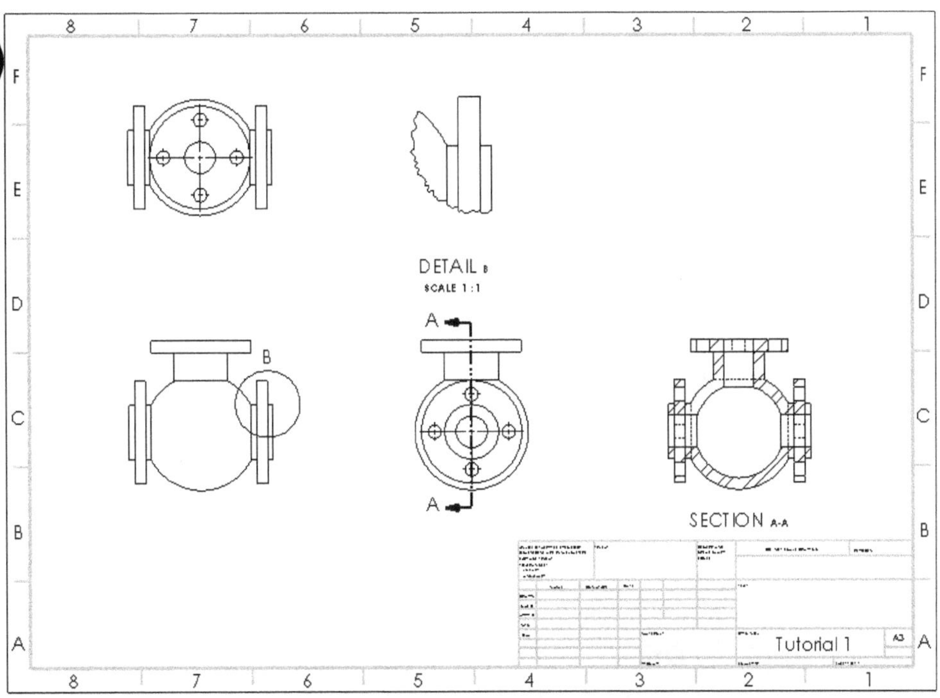

Section 7: Creating the Isometric View

1. Click on the **Model View** tool in the **Drawing CommandManager**. The **Model View PropertyManager** appears.

2. Double-click on the **Tutorial 1** model in the **Open documents** area of the **Part/Assembly to Insert** rollout in the PropertyManager. A rectangular box representing the model view gets attached to the cursor. Also, the options of the PropertyManager get modified.

3. Click on the **Isometric** button in the **Standard views** area of the **Orientation** rollout to create an isometric view of the model. 

4. Move the cursor toward the upper right corner of the drawing sheet and then click to specify the placement point for the isometric view, see Figure 14.114. Next, click anywhere on the drawing sheet.

Section 8: Changing the Display Styles

1. Click on the front view of the model in the drawing sheet. The **Drawing View PropertyManager** appears.

2. Click on the **Hidden Lines Visible** button in the **Display Style** rollout of the PropertyManager to display the hidden lines of the model in the drawing views, see Figure 14.114. 

14.114

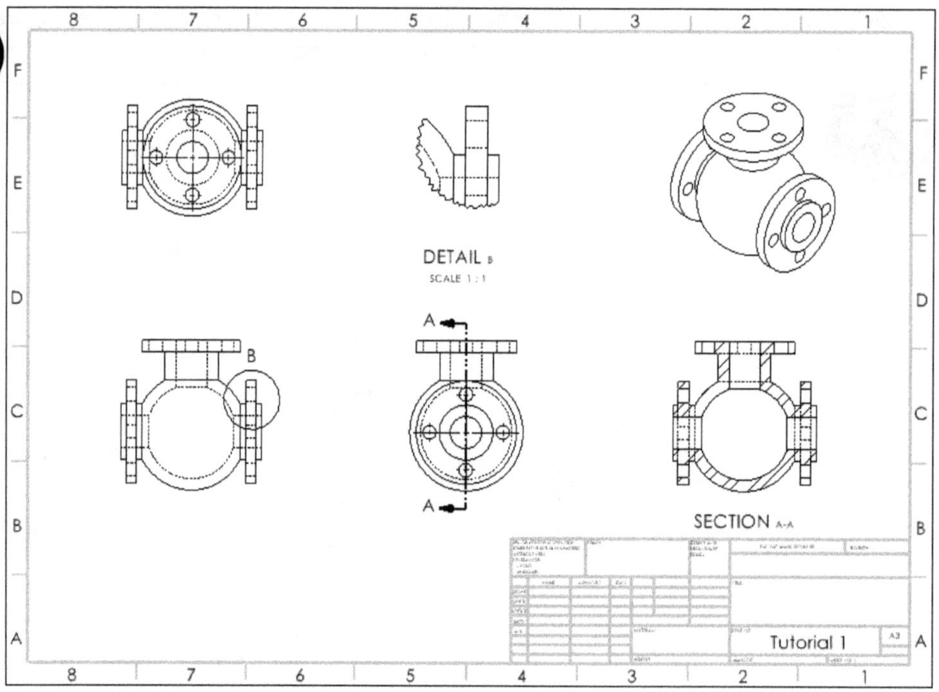

Section 9: Applying Driving Dimensions

1. Click on the **Annotation** tab in the CommandManager. The tools of the **Annotation CommandManager** are displayed.

2. Click on the **Model Items** tool in the **Annotation CommandManager**. The **Model Items PropertyManager** appears.

3. Ensure that the **Entire model** option is selected in the **Source** drop-down list, see Figure 14.115.

14.115

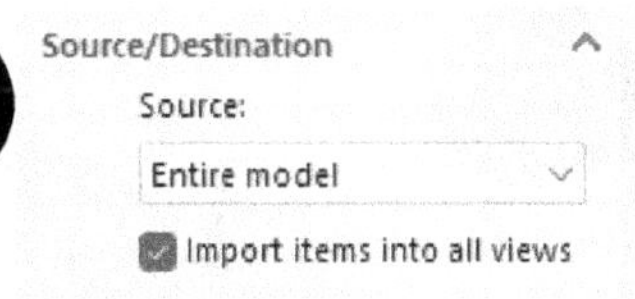

4. Clear the **Import items into all views** check box in the **Source/Destination** rollout. The **Destination view(s)** field appears in the rollout.

5. Click on the front, top, and right side views of the model one by one in the drawing sheet as the views to import driving dimensions.

6. Click on the green tick-mark in the PropertyManager. The driving dimensions are applied to the selected drawing views, refer to Figure 14.116. Note that the applied dimensions are not placed in the proper locations nor do they maintain uniform spacing. You will learn about arranging driving dimensions in the next section of this tutorial.

Tip: Instead of applying driving dimensions, you can apply reference dimensions to the drawing views by using the dimensions tools. The methods for applying a reference dimension are same as applying dimensions to the sketch entities in the Sketching environment.

Section 10: Arranging Driving Dimensions

1. Select all driving dimensions by dragging the cursor over the front, top, and right side views after pressing and holding the left mouse button, see Figure 14.116. Next, release the left mouse button, the **Dimension Palette Rollover** button appears in the drawing sheet.

14.116

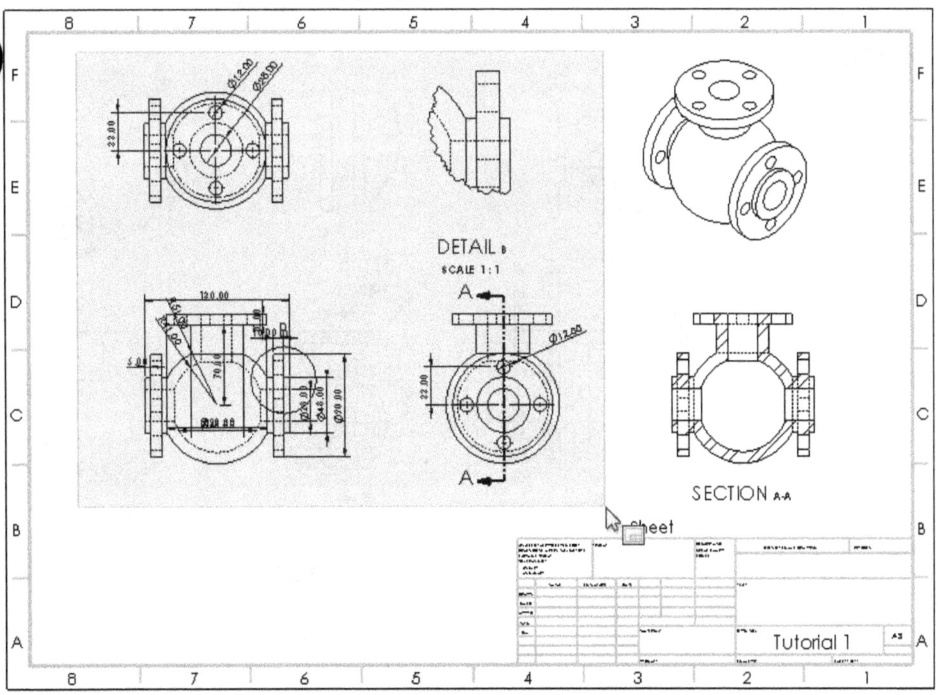

2. Move the cursor over the **Dimension Palette Rollover** button in the drawing sheet. The **Dimension Palette** appears, see Figure 14.117.

14.117

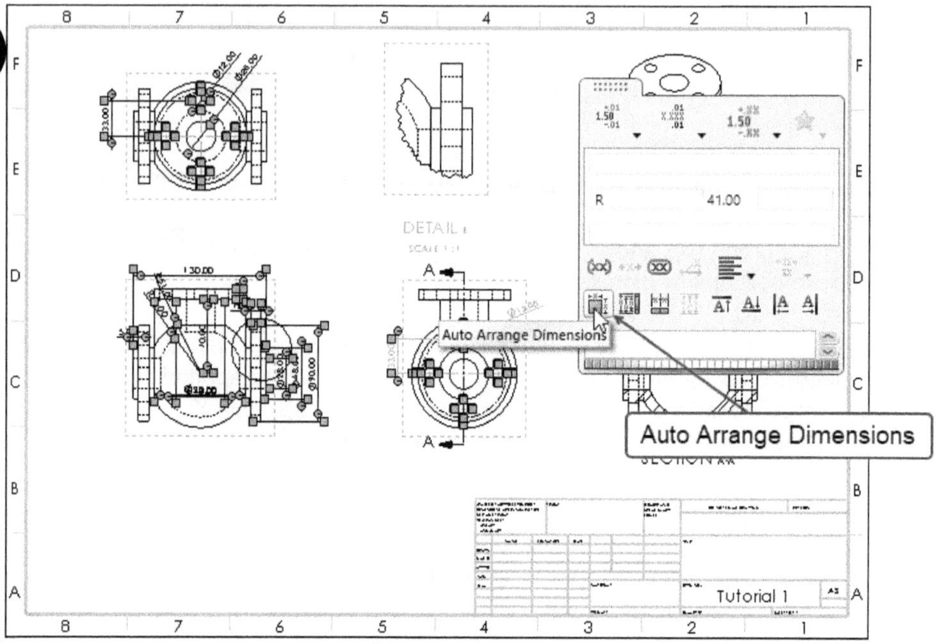

3. Click on the **Auto Arrange Dimensions** button in the **Dimension Palette**, see Figure 14.117. All the dimensions are arranged automatically in the drawing sheet, refer to Figure 14.118. You can further drag individual dimensions and place them in the required location, see Figure 14.118. Next, click anywhere on the drawing sheet.

14.118

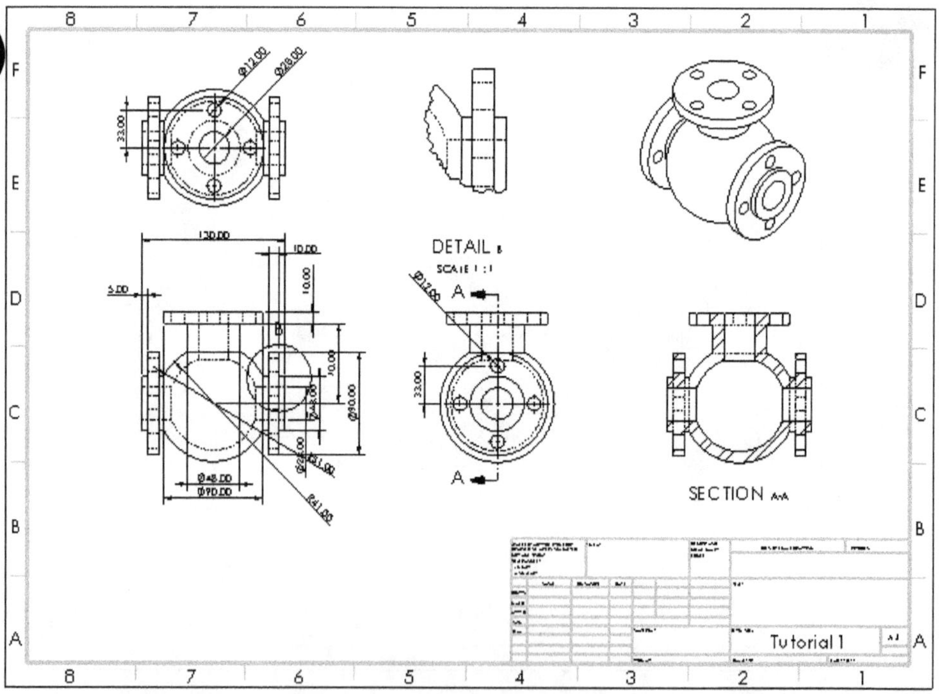

Note: You can also control dimension parameters such as dimension font, dimension height, and arrow height. To do this, click on the **Options** tool in the **Standard** toolbar. The **System Options - General** dialog box appears. Next, click on the **Document Properties** tab in the dialog box and then click on the **Dimensions** option. Next, click on the **Font** button in the **Text** area of the dialog box. The **Choose Font** dialog box appears. By using this dialog box, you can specify the required font, style, and height for dimensions text. Next, click on the **OK** button in the **Choose Font** dialog box. You can also control the dimension arrow height by using the options in the **Arrows** area of the **Document Properties - Dimensions** dialog box.

Section 11: Saving the Model

Now, you need to save the drawing.

1. Click on the **Save** tool in the **Standard** toolbar. The **Save As** dialog box appears.

2. Browse to the Tutorial folder of Chapter 14 folder and then save the drawing with the name Tutorial 1.

Hands-on Test Drive 1

Open the assembly created in Hands-on Test Drive 1 of Chapter 12 and then create different drawing views as shown in Figure 14.119. Also, you need to add balloons in the isometric view of the assembly and create the Bill of Material (BOM). In addition to creating different views and BOM, you need to create an alternate position view of the assembly in the front view, see Figure 14.119.

14.119

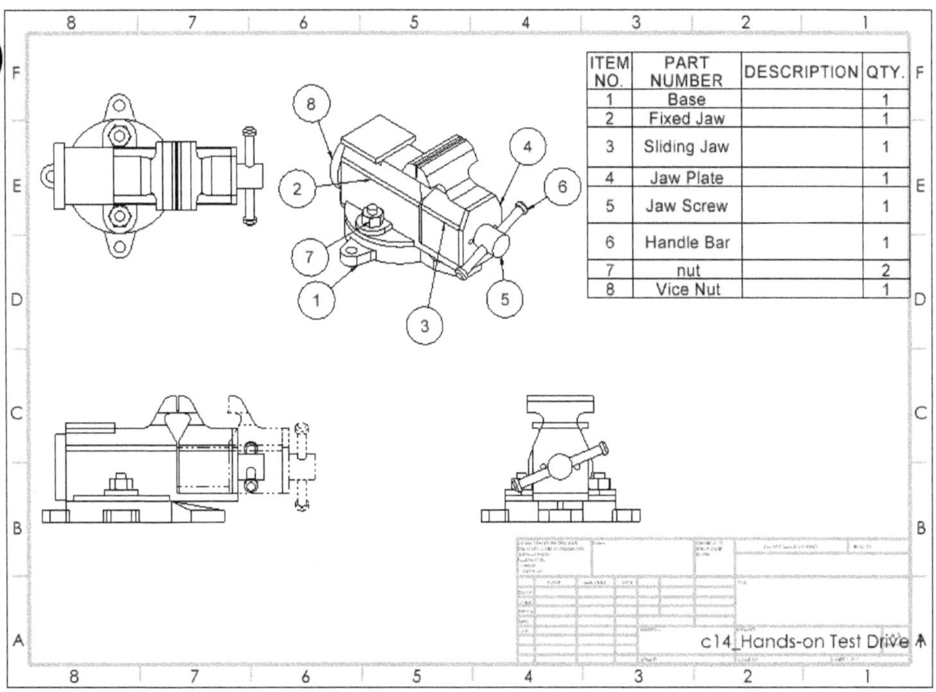

Summary

In this chapter, you learned to create 2D drawings from parts and assemblies in the Drawing environment. Key topics included generating various drawing views, such as model/base views, projected views, section views, auxiliary views, and detail views. You also explored defining and editing the angle of projection and sheet formats. Additionally, the chapter covered applying dimensions, adding notes, surface finish symbols, weld symbols, hole callouts, and incorporating center marks, centerlines, Bill of Materials (BOM), and balloons. Finally, opening drawings in detailing mode was explained. These skills will help you create comprehensive and precise technical drawings for effective communication in design and manufacturing.

Questions

Complete and verify the following sentences:

- By using the _________ environment of SOLIDWORKS, you can generate error-free 2D drawings of a component or an assembly.
- The _________ PropertyManager is invoked automatically on invoking the Drawing environment.
- A _________ view is an independent first drawing view.
- The **Standard 3 View** tool is used to create three standard orthogonal views: _________, _________, and _________.
- Engineering drawings follow the _________ and the _________ angles of projections.
- A _________ view is created by cutting an object with an imaginary cutting plane and viewing the object from a direction normal to the cutting plane.
- A _________ view is created to show the portion of an existing view at an enlarged scale.
- A _________ view is created by removing the portion of an existing view up to a specified depth to view its inner details.
- In SOLIDWORKS, you can apply the _________ and _________ dimensions in a view.
- A surface finish symbol has three components: _________, _________, and _________.
- On modifying reference dimensions in a drawing view, respective modifications are also reflected in a model. (True/False)
- In SOLIDWORKS, you can select standard or custom sheet size for creating drawing views. (True/False)

INDEX

INDEX

D

G

H

I

J

K

L

M

P

Q

R

S

T

U

V

W

Z

Other Publications by CADArtifex

Some of the other Publications by CADArtifex are given below:

AutoCAD Textbooks

AutoCAD 2026: A Power Guide for Beginners and Intermediate Users
AutoCAD 2025: A Power Guide for Beginners and Intermediate Users
AutoCAD 2024: A Power Guide for Beginners and Intermediate Users
and more

AutoCAD For Architectural Design Textbooks

AutoCAD 2023 for Architectural Design: A Power Guide for Beginners and Intermediate Users
AutoCAD 2022 for Architectural Design: A Power Guide for Beginners and Intermediate Users
and more

Autodesk Fusion 360 Textbooks

Autodesk Fusion 360: A Power Guide for Beginners and Intermediate Users (8th Edition)
Autodesk Fusion 360: A Power Guide for Beginners and Intermediate Users (7th Edition)
Autodesk Fusion 360: A Power Guide for Beginners and Intermediate Users (6th Edition)
and more

Autodesk Fusion 360 Surface and T-Spline Textbooks

Autodesk Fusion 360 Surface Design and Sculpting with T-Spline Surfaces (8th Edition)
Autodesk Fusion 360 Surface Design and Sculpting with T-Spline Surfaces (7th Edition)
and more

Autodesk Inventor Textbooks

Autodesk Inventor 2026: A Power Guide for Beginners and Intermediate Users
Autodesk Inventor 2025: A Power Guide for Beginners and Intermediate Users
Autodesk Inventor 2024: A Power Guide for Beginners and Intermediate Users
and more

FreeCAD Textbooks

FreeCAD 1.0: A Power Guide for Beginners and Intermediate Users
FreeCAD 0.21: A Power Guide for Beginners and Intermediate Users
and more

Onshape Textbooks

Onshape 2025: A Power Guide for Beginners and Intermediate Users
and more

PTC Creo Parametric Textbooks

Creo Parametric 12.0: A Power Guide for Beginners and Intermediate Users
Creo Parametric 11.0: A Power Guide for Beginners and Intermediate Users
and more

SOLIDWORKS Textbooks

SOLIDWORKS 2026: A Power Guide for Beginners and Intermediate User
SOLIDWORKS 2025: A Power Guide for Beginners and Intermediate User
SOLIDWORKS 2024: A Power Guide for Beginners and Intermediate User
and more

SOLIDWORKS Sheet Metal and Surface Design Textbooks

SOLIDWORKS Sheet Metal and Surface Design 2026 for Beginners and Intermediate Users
SOLIDWORKS Sheet Metal and Surface Design 2025 for Beginners and Intermediate Users
and more

SOLIDWORKS Simulation Textbooks

SOLIDWORKS Simulation 2026: A Power Guide for Beginners and Intermediate User
SOLIDWORKS Simulation 2025: A Power Guide for Beginners and Intermediate User
SOLIDWORKS Simulation 2024: A Power Guide for Beginners and Intermediate User
and more

Exercises Books

100 AutoCAD Exercises - Learn by Practicing (2 Edition)
Autodesk Inventor Exercises - Learn by Practicing
Autodesk Fusion 360 Exercises Learn by Practicing (2023-24)
SOLIDWORKS Exercises - Learn by Practicing (3 Edition)

Video Courses by CADArtifex

CADArtifex offers a range of video courses designed to support students, educators, and professionals in developing practical CAD skills through structured, project-based learning. Available video courses include:

- SOLIDWORKS for Beginners and Intermediate Users
- Learn SOLIDWORKS Sheet Metal: From Concept to Creation
- SOLIDWORKS Mechanical Design & Assemblies Masterclass
- Complete Fusion 360 All-in-One Course for Beginners (2025)
- Fusion 360 Surface Design & T-Spline Sculpting
- Complete FreeCAD for Beginners – No Experience Needed
- Complete Onshape for Beginners: Project-Based Approach
- Master Autodesk Inventor: From Basics to Advanced
- Mastering AutoCAD 2D & 3D for Beginners

For full course details and access, visit: ***cadartifex.com***

---

www.ingramcontent.com/pod-product-compliance
Lightning Source LLC
Chambersburg PA
CBHW061149240926
51846CB00006B/959
9789394074941